ABC primer
academy/college broadside
account-book label
accounts, domestic
accounts, institutional
acquaintance card
admission ticket
advertisement
advertising booklet
advertising envelope
advertising fan
advertising novelty
advertising ring (embossed)
aerial leaflet
agency certificate
agricultural/horticultural
show card
air-raid papers
air-sickness bag
air-transport label
album card
album frontispiece
almanac
amateur journal
ambrotype label
American Civil War papers
American seaman's
certificate
amusement sheet
anamorphic image
anonymous letter
appointment card
AQ letter sheet
armed forces papers
army printing
arrangement of carriages
diagram
artisan's bill/receipt
artwork for reproduction
assignat
at home' card
attendance record, school
auditorium seating plan
badge
baggage sticker
ballad
ballot paper
band/banderole
bandbox
bando
banknote
banknote', promotional
banknote, specimen
banknote-duty stamp
baptismal papers
bastardy papers
battledore
beer label
beer mat
bellman's verses
benefit ticket
bill of lading
bill of mortality
billhead
binder's ticket
birth certificate
biscuit/cracker label
blasphemy
blotting paper
boardgame
bond, personal
book label
book token
book-donor label
bookmark
bookmatch
bookplate
book-prize label
bookseller's label
braille
broadside/broadsheet
broom label
bumper sticker
burial club papers
burial in woollen affidavit
burial papers
burial-right deed
by-law/ordinance
cachet, postal
calendar
calendar of prisoners
call-back handbill
cameo card

campaign souvenir
can label
candle label
card of thanks
carmen figuratum
carrier bag
carrier's address
carte-de-visite
carte pneumatique
catalogue
cavallino
census papers
certificate
change of proprietor card
change packet
change pin-paper
changeable gentlemen/ladies
card
chapbook
charity election card
charity petition
charity sermon hymn sheet
charity subscription list
charity ticket
charm/curse
charter party
cheese label
chemist's label
cheque/check
child lost/found form
children's advertising booklet
chimney-sweep certificate
chop paper
Christmas card
Christmas charity seal
chromo
church brief
cigar band/box label
cigarette card
cigarette pack
cigarette paper
'Cinderella' stamp
city ordinance broadside
classroom label
club flyer
coach ticket
coachmen's instructions
coal-seller's ticket
coin disc/sticker
colouring book/sheet
comic
commonplace book
compliments slip
compound-plate printing
compulsive note
copy-book
cotton bag
cover, postal
crate label
credit/cash card
crest/monogram
Cuban wrapper
Currier & Ives
cut-out toy
cutwork
cypher label
dance programme
dance token
dart flight
death certificate
deck plan
decorated paper
degree certificate/diploma
dental papers
deposit label
dice-duty wrapper
dietary tables
directions for use
directories
disinfected mail
display card
distraint, papers of
doctor's bill
donation list
donor card
draft
drawing book
driving licence
dust wrapper
eccentric advertising
election papers
electro-medical papers
electrotype

e-mail
embossing/lace paper
embroidery pattern
enclosure badge
engraved label
envelope
envelope, illustrated
envelope, stationer's
equivoque
erratum slip
evidence, notes of
execution broadside
facsimile
farthing novelette
fax
feather letter
fez label
film wallet
fire reward certificate
fireman's discharge
certificate
fireman's membership
certificate
firework/firecracker label
fish tally
flagday emblem
flap picture
Fleet marriage certificate
flicker book
fly-paper
fly-wagon bill
folk recipe
football programme
'foreign' English
forgery
form
form of prayer
Fraktur
free frank
frost-fair papers
fruit/vegetable sticker
fruit wrapper
funeralia
furniture label
game record
game-law papers
gaol papers
garment label
gift coupon
give-aways
gold-miners' papers, Australian
greetings card
greetings telegram
Gretna Green marriage certificate
guest list
hackney papers
hand-knitting pattern
handwritten ephemera
harlequinade ('turn-up')
hat-duty stamp
hidden-name card
hold-to-light
holiday card
hornbook
hospital recommendation
document
hostel admission ticket
hotel/tour coupon
hotel papers
house journal
household regulations
housekeeping accounts
hymn number card
ice papers
illuminated address
imagerie populaire
imprint, printer's
imprint, publisher's
improvised currency
indenture
indulgence
inn tally
inset, magazine
inventory
invitation
iridescent printing
itinerary
jigsaw puzzle
joke ephemera
jumping jack
jury papers
keepsake
keepsake, novelty

king's evil certificate
kite bag
label
labour account
lavatory paper
leaflet
lecture ticket
letter seal
letterhead
licence
Liebig card
lighthouse-dues papers
linen-button card
linen-button label
lobby card
Lord's prayer
lottery papers
lunacy papers
magazine sample sheet
manual alphabet card
marriage certificate
marrowbone announcement
match-tax stamp
medicine-show papers
menu
milk-bottle closure
miniature newspaper
miniature text
mock money
moral-lesson picture
motto, shop window
Mulready caricature
Mulready envelope
myriorama
neck paper
needle packet
needle-box print
news bill
newspaper
notice to quit
nuisance papers
oath
opticians' papers
packaging
panorama, entertainment
panorama, newspaper
give-aways
paper bag
paper clothing
paper doll
paper napkin
paper pattern
paper-cut
paper-duty label
papyrus
parking ticket
parliamentary envelope
pass/permit
passport
pastiche, printer's
peal card
peep-show
pen-box label
penman's flourish
pennant
perfume card
perfume label
perfume-duty label
petition
pew papers
pharmaceutical package
phenakistoscope disc
photographic ephemera
photo-lithographic view
phrenological chart
physician's directions
physiognomical chart
pillbox label
pin paper
pin synopsis card
pin-box label
place card
place mat
plague papers
plaster package
playing card
playing card, secondary uses
playing-card duty
playing-card wrapper
pledge card
pocket mirror, advertising
point-of-sale display
poison-gas papers

poor-law papers

post-horse duty ticket
pratique, papers of
prescription
prescription paper/envelope
press book, film
pressed flowers
price list
price tag/ticket
printed handkerchief
printing, 'primitive'
procession programme
proclamation
prospectus, publisher's
public apology
public notice
punctuality card
puzzle
quack advertising
QSL card
race bill
rag book
rail ticket
railway carriage panel
railway luggage label
railway travelling chart
rainbow printing
ration papers
razor-blade wrapper
ream wrapper/label
rebus
receipt
recipe, folk
record, advertising
record cover
relief printing for the blind
religious card
removal card
reward of merit
reward papers
ribbon, lapel
riddle book
ring-gauge card
riot act
roll of honour
round robin
rules and regulations
sabbath papers
sailing notice/card
sale catalogue
sale notice
sales-tax token/receipt
satirical print
scholar's letter
school/college bill
school list
school prospectus
school report
school return
schoolboy's piece
scrap
scrapbook/album
seating plan, table
secondary uses of
ephemera
security printing
seed packet
Seidlitz-powder label
sentiment card
servant's award
servant's 'character' reference
servant's registry papers
servant's timetable
Shaker papers
share certificate
sheet-music cover
shelf strip
shipping
ship's newspaper
shoe pattern
shoemaker's label
showcard
showcard, stock
signal code, navy

silhouette

stationery, decorative
stencil
stereotype
sticker
stock block
stock poster
street literature
street view
stud card/notice
sugar leaf
summons
tag label
tall-tale postcard
tax abstract
tax stamp
taxation papers
telegram/telegram form
telephone card
telephone directory
temperance papers
testimonial
textile label
thaumatrope
theatre programme
theatre ticket
thread paper
ticket
timetable
tinsel print
tithe papers
title-page
tobacco paper
toll/ferry rate-list
toll/turnpike ticket
touring map
toy book
toy theatre
trade advertiser
trade card
trade label
trade list
trade rhyme
trade union membership
certificate
tramping card
transfer lithography
transparency
transportation papers (penal)
travellers' guide
trompe-l'oeil announcement
Tyburn ticket
typographica
unemployed appeal
union label
university mail
unstamped newspaper/
periodical
vaccination papers
valentine
vice card
view card
violin label
visiting card
visiting craftsmen's papers
visitors' register
wafer
warrant
watchpaper
watermark
waybill
weight card
will
window bill, shop
window card, domestic
wine label
winkle bag
wood-engraving
writing paper, illustrated
writing tablet
xerography
'zine
zöetrope strip/disc

THE ENCYCLOPEDIA OF EPHEMERA

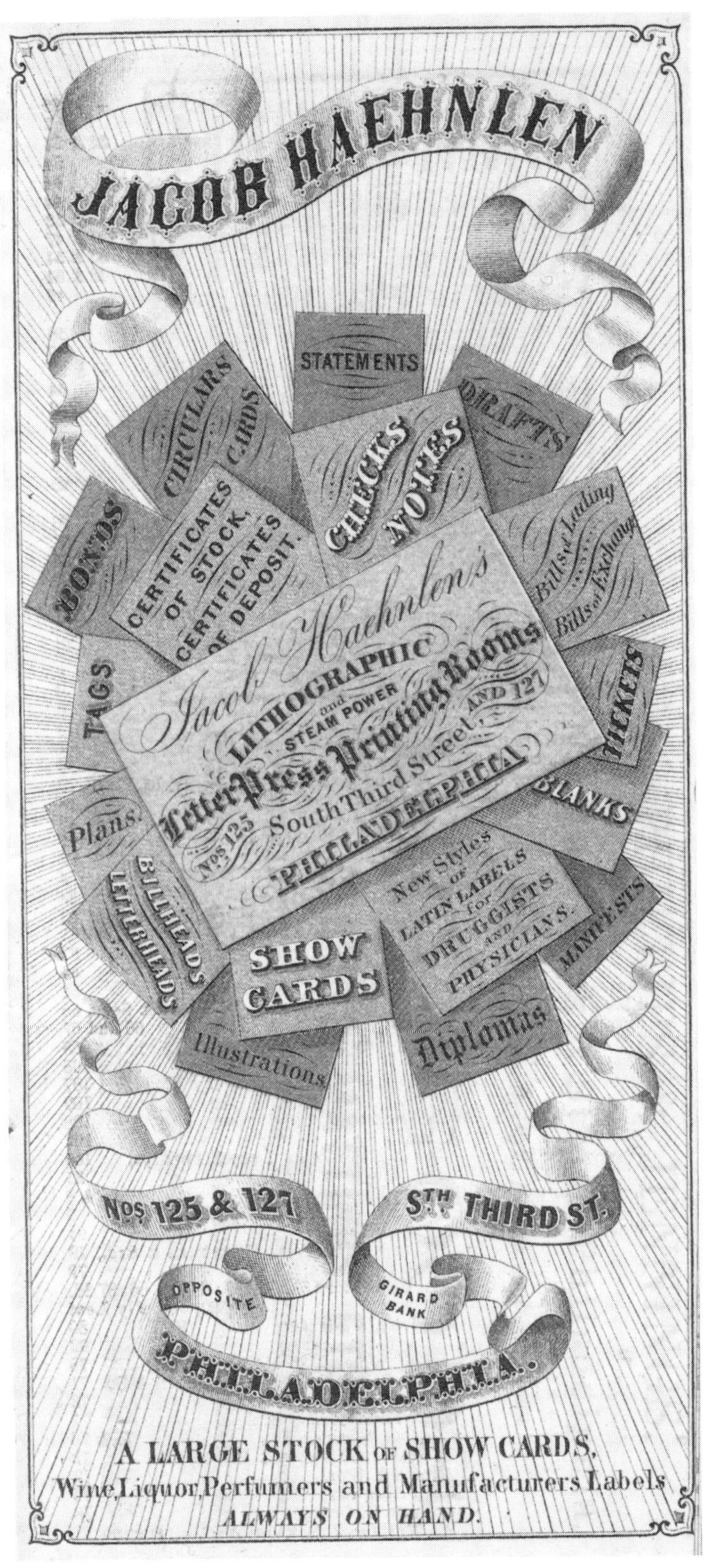

Advertisement showing the range of printed ephemera undertaken by the lithographic and letterpress printer Jacob Haehnlen in Philadelphia. From *Butler's Southern Trade Directory and Merchants Memorandum Book* (Philadelphia, 1859). Lithographed in two colours. 150 × 68 mm (6 × 2⅝ in)
The Library Company of Philadelphia

THE ENCYCLOPEDIA OF EPHEMERA

A Guide to the Fragmentary Documents of Everyday Life for the Collector, Curator, and Historian

MAURICE RICKARDS

Edited and completed by
Michael Twyman
with the assistance of
Sally de Beaumont and Amoret Tanner

ROUTLEDGE
New York

Published in the United States of America in 2000 by
Routledge
29 West 35th Street
New York, NY 10001

Published in Great Britain in 2000 by
The British Library
96 Euston Road
London NW1 2DB

Designed and typeset in the Department of Typography & Graphic Communication, The University of Reading, apart from the half title, title page, and jacket, which were designed in the publisher's office, New York

Library of Congress Cataloging-in-Publication Data

Rickards, Maurice, 1919.
The encyclopedia of ephemera / Maurice Rickards.
p.cm.
Includes bibliographical references and index.
ISBN 0-415-92648-3
1. Printed ephemera-Dictionaries. 2.Printed ephemera-Collectors and collecting. 1. Title.

NC1280 R52 2000
769.5'03-dc21

00-062569

Printed in Great Britain by St Edmundsbury Press, Bury St Edmunds

The decorated letters at the head of each section are mainly from an issue of Wood & Sharwoods's *Specimen Book of Types* of the early 1840s. C, O, T & U are from the guard book referred to in the caption to plate 1. J, K, M, P, Q, V, X–Z were designed by the following students of the Department of Typography & Graphic Communication of The University of Reading: Davina Chung, Pauline Lock, Kelly Mason, Sallie Morris, Elizabeth Powell, Glynn Seeds

Editor's introduction

This encyclopedia is essentially the work of Maurice Rickards, whose death in 1998 after a long illness prevented him from seeing it through to completion. It has been added to, revised, checked, and made ready for publication by a team of enthusiasts whose specific contributions are referred to below. Their participation in this exercise is both an acknowledgement of the author's pioneering work to promote the serious study of ephemera and a measure of the value of this particular text.

Ephemera is the plural form of the Greek word *ephemeron* (*epi* = on, about, round; *hemera* = day). Literally, it refers to something that lasts through the day, which is the case with some winged insects. The word *ephemeris* has long been used in titles of Greek newspapers and *ephemerides* to describe a category of document (calendar, diary, etc.). Among several definitions of ephemera that Maurice Rickards proposed, the one that has gained widest currency is the 'minor transient documents of everyday life' (M. Rickards, *Collecting Printed Ephemera*, Oxford, Phaidon/Christie's, 1988, p.7). It is appropriate to refer to it here, though its shortcomings were as obvious to him as they are to others; for example, not every item of ephemera can be regarded as minor or even transient. What can be said of this definition is that it has stood the test of time better than any other. Collectively, however, the entries in this encyclopedia define ephemera even more effectively, since they include manuscript and printed matter, records of the past and present (both humble and prestigious), items designed to be thrown away (bus tickets) and to be kept (cigarette cards), and documents of considerable importance (at least to the individual concerned) through to the most trivial. Such variety – the very lifeblood of literate societies – can hardly be encapsulated in a few words.

This encyclopedia is intended for anyone who sees ephemera as providing a link with the past, and for collectors of ephemera who take a broader view of the field than their own particular specialism. Collectors of, for example, bookmarks, Christmas cards, football programmes, lottery bills, railway tickets, and what are called 'Cinderella' stamps may find little in these entries that is new to them, though the encyclopedia as a whole should help them to see their own special interests in a different light. For those primarily concerned with documents as records of social or business history, or with the conventions of written language, graphic design, and printing, it reveals much of interest and opens up many areas that call for further study. Understandably, most of the entries relate to English-language ephemera (both American and English), though work in other languages is discussed where appropriate (particularly French, German, and Italian).

Maurice Rickards began to conceive the idea of a dictionary or encyclopedia of ephemera – for a long while he was uncertain which word to use – in the early 1970s. From then on until around 1991, when he suffered the first of a series of debilitating strokes, it was the main focus of his research. In his final years, while he was Hon. Senior Research Fellow at the Centre for Ephemera Studies at Reading, I was able to discuss with him the form the encyclopedia might take and to show him first proofs of all the text that had at that time been transcribed from his draft entries. Since then over forty additional entries have been written and many more worked up from his drafts.

There is reason to believe that Maurice Rickards may have come to realize that the scope of any encyclopedia of the kind he envisaged made it virtually impossible to complete. After all, there is almost no end to the entries that might have been included. The pressing need to publish what had already been written forced the issue, and it has been easier for others to step in and decide what should be included and what should not than it would have been for its author. In expanding the number of entries beyond those written by Maurice Rickards, consideration has been given to categories of ephemera that have emerged since the 1980s, when the framework for the encyclopedia was established. In addition, a few essential entries that he had not begun to tackle have also been written. All the same, this encyclopedia has to be seen as exemplary in the sense that it illuminates its field by example, much as the Rickards Collection of ephemera (now housed at the Centre for Ephemera Studies at the University of Reading) is exemplary.

Topics of interest to many readers are certain to have been omitted. Some categories of ephemera, such as those revealing man's inhumanity to man in times of repression and war, were perhaps too painful to write about, and those relating to protest and propaganda – which Maurice Rickards discussed elsewhere – too varied and diffuse. Less consequentially, it could be asked why broom labels are covered, but garden spade and fork labels are not; or why fruit wrappers find a place, whereas the equally collectable sugar wrapper does not. The only riposte to any such criticisms is to point to the first editions of one-man encyclopedias in other fields.

At some stage in the future it is hoped that this encyclopedia will be expanded in scope, though it would be unrealistic to expect any one person to undertake such a task. As it stands, it represents a significant personal achievement and, inevitably, reflects the experiences, interests, and views of its author. Underpinning the entire work is his view that ephemera can bring the past to life more vividly and often with greater particularity than many other forms of documentation. Both his selection of entries and the issues he chose to highlight within them testify to his belief that most historians have undervalued the importance of ephemera as source material. It may not be too fanciful to see a parallel here with the activities of Syriac of Ancona, Felice Feliciano, Bartolomaeus Fontius and others who eagerly sought out and transcribed ancient inscriptions in the 15th century. Though they knew about antiquity from the texts of classical authors, inscriptions spoke to them with a particular directness, much as ephemera can to us.

Another important aspect of ephemera – developed in many entries of the encyclopedia – is the fascination they hold for the collector, either for their content, their appearance, or both. There is, of course, a link between the use of ephemera as evidential material by historians and the interests of collectors, though this is not made explicit in the text. Collectors provide a useful service in preserving items and, thereafter, making them available for historians to study. This raises a matter which is developed in the encyclopedia only by example: the need for ephemera to be catalogued and studied with something of the rigour applied to other kinds of documents, such as books, music, maps, prints, and archival material.

I am credited with having edited this volume and must therefore take ultimate responsibility for the errors that, almost inevitably, have escaped detection. It should be stressed, however, that this publication would not have seen the light of day but for the unstinting efforts of a whole team of people. Behind the entire exercise stands Elizabeth Greig, Maurice Rickards's partner during the gestation period of the encyclopedia and the person closest to his thinking about it. She managed to coax contributions from him in troubled times and acted as his scribe and general factotum. It fell to her and Johanna Harrison to decipher his neat but, to everyone else, almost illegible handwritten drafts, and to the latter to undertake the unenviable task of keyboarding the first draft of the text. This draft was then given a provisional typographic styling by Bryony Newhouse at Reading in the hope that the author would have an opportunity to read most of his text and, perhaps, add to it. Sadly these hopes were not realized, and at his death no precise arrangement for publication had been made.

With the British Library's acceptance of the book for publication late in 1998 work began afresh. All the entries were edited in the light of the better overall view that had been gained of the text. This involved some updating, the identification of gaps, and the writing or commissioning of new entries. Initials follow those entries that were not written by Maurice Rickards; they relate to the names of those listed separately below (p.x) who kindly offered their services in the spirit of cooperation that has characterized the publication of this work. The revising and editing of the text involved changes that went far beyond those I would normally ask a keyboard operator to make, and very special thanks are owed to Jennie Welsh of the Department of Typography & Graphic Communication of the University of Reading for her tenacity, interpretative skills, and good humour when dealing with such difficult proofs.

The checking of material has, likewise, been an exercise of teamwork and has principally fallen on staff of the Centre for Ephemera Studies and those associated with it. Sally de Beaumont, a good friend of the Centre, took on the truly formidable task of checking factual information, including names of people, companies, dates, and much else. This has involved everything that could reasonably be checked, though the names of ordinary people referred to in quoted matter defy such treatment (short of recourse to, for example, parish records). The scale of this exercise and the research skills and knowledge of ephemera required to undertake it call for special recognition.

In tandem with this exercise several people worked through the book systematically, undertaking specific tasks. Amoret Tanner gave it the benefit of her remarkable fund of knowledge about ephemera, checked place names for accuracy and consistency, and helped with the finding and selection of illustrations; Diana Mackarill read it for sense with more of a generalist's eye and focused on grammatical and orthographic accuracy; Graham Hudson devised a convention for imperial/metric conversion, which he applied throughout; Michael Perkin checked most of the bibliographical references. Chris Stray, who kindly agreed to check references to Latin and Greek, went far beyond his brief and read the whole text, spotting errors and making many useful suggestions; Peter Jones applied his considerable knowledge of postal history to help sort out entries relating to this complex field. Without these contributions my task of editing and seeing the book through to production would have been much more arduous and my inadequacies more evident. In addition, I have appreciated the skills and interest of staff in the Department of Typography & Graphic Communication at Reading in the later stages of the work, in particular Andy Cross, who scanned and edited the illustrations, and Jennie Welsh who coped with the subtleties of two-column page make-up. I should also like to thank Jill Ford for completing the index so ably within a very tight schedule.

There is reason to believe that the author's original drafts are accurate on names (though they may not always be legible) and that they can also be trusted in terms of material quoted from items of ephemera that can no longer be traced. Nevertheless, capitalization and other typographic aspects of quoted matter may not always have been transcribed exactly, and for this reason and for the sake of clarity period practices in typographic style, such as initial word and all-word captitalization, have sometimes been ignored.

Finally, in the process of ensuring that this encylopedia is as useful and accurate as can reasonably be expected (bearing in mind its range and that it is a reconstruction from an author's drafts), the following Trustees of the Foundation for Ephemera Studies have been kind enough to read part or all of the final proofs: Ralph Hyde, Peter Jackson, Nicholas Oppenheim, and Patrick Hickman-Robertson.

More generally, I should like to thank Elizabeth Greig, Diana Mackarill, and Amoret Tanner for their continuing support and encouragement at the Centre for Ephemera Studies while this publication has been in preparation, and Martin Andrews, my deputy at the Centre, for his enthusiastic involvement with all its activities, including this publication.

The Centre for Ephemera Studies offers its thanks to the Research Endowment Trust Fund of the University of Reading for generous financial support in the early stages of the preparation of this text for publication and to the Foundation for Ephemera Studies for covering the cost of the indexing. The Department of Typography & Graphic Communication at the University of Reading, through Sue Walker (Head of Department) and Mick Stocks (Head of its Print Unit), has given generous support of a practical kind, as has David Way of the British Library's Publishing Office. The confidence shown by all those who have supported this project has been a real encouragement to everyone who has worked to provide what I hope is a fitting memorial to Maurice Rickards.

Michael Twyman
Centre for Ephemera Studies
Department of Typography & Graphic Communication
The University of Reading
Spring 2000

Additional acknowledgements

The original text included (after some entries) acknowledgements to 'informants' – that is, people or institutions who provided the author with information on specific topics or, perhaps, simply answered his queries. In some cases the same people were referred to under 'references' and 'sources'. Since some of these people cannot be traced and a few may no longer be alive, their contributions are acknowledged here by listing them in alphabetical order with the headword of the entry or entries they helped with in parentheses: Alistair Allen (Album frontispiece; Scrap); Robin Amlôt (Can label); John Armstone (Postal-strike label); Roger Atkinson (Post-horse duty stamp); J. B. Attenbarrow (Seed packet); Yasha Beresiner (Banknote; Improvised currency; Playing card, secondary uses); J. H. Chandler (Hat-duty stamp); Ken Claxton (Cheese label); Pierre Couperie (Comic); Grover Criswell (Banknote); Andrew Cunningham (Beer label); Trefor David (Railway luggage label); Lee Dennis (Boardgame); Pe[t]er Emmens (Cigarette paper); Gordon Fairchild (Rail ticket); Michael Farr (Rail ticket); John Frost (Newspaper); the late Denis Gifford (Comic); David Godfrey (Newspaper); Trevor Harris (Cheese label); William Helfand (Chemist's label; Electro-medical papers; Quack advertising); Peggy Hickman (Silhouette); Maurice Horn (Comic); Insurance Company of North America (Card of thanks); Peter Jackson (Drawing book); Ralph Jackson (Charm/curse); Doris Jones (Chemist's label); Lindon Jones (Degree certificate/diploma); Mark Kander (Bumper sticker); John Kobal (Lobby card); Diana Korzenik (Drawing book); Brian North Lee (Book label; Bookplate; Book-prize label); Desmond Lewis (Chemist's label); Brian Love (Boardgame; Flagday emblem); Leslie G. Matthews (Chemist's label); Bernard Middleton (Bookseller's label); Trevor May (Hackney papers); Giorgio Migliavacca (Bando); Colin Narbeth (Banknote; Banknote, 'promotional'); Norfolk Museums Service (Braille); Office of Population Censuses and Surveys, London (Death certificate); Robert Opie (Record advertising); Graham Page (Rail ticket); Tom Pattie (Papyrus); Pharmaceutical Society of Great Britain; Barry Pliskin (Record advertising; Record cover); the late Philip Poole (Pen-box label); Marcus Samuel (Cypher label; Hat-duty stamp; Post-horse duty label); Allan Sands (Dental papers); Freeman Sayer (Flicker book); Kenneth Schultz (Deck plan); Leslie Shepard (Chapbook); Peter Stockham (Battledore; Chapbook); Hugh Street (Game record); Ben Swanson (Dental papers); Amoret Tanner (Seed packets); United States Office of Education, Washington DC (Degree certificate/diploma); United States Public Health Services, Washington DC (Death certificate); the late David Van Der Plank (Cheese label); Denis Vandervelde (Bando; Disinfected mail;

Pratique, papers of); the late E. C. Wharton-Tigar (Cigarette card); the late Martin Willcocks (Cachet, postal; Cover, postal).

Those who contributed new entries (or, in one or two cases, substantially revised ones) are indicated beneath the relevant entry, or sub-entry, as follows:

AA A J Allnutt (Licence)
MA Martin Andrews (Electrotype; Stereotype; Wood-engraving)
SB Sarah du Boscq de Beaumont (Telephone card)
JB John Berry (Playing card; Playing card duty; Playing-card wrapper)
DC David Cheshire (Club flyer)
DSC Diana Cook (Sports papers: Rowing)
HG Honor Godfrey (Sports papers: Tennis)
HRJG H R J Grant (Sports papers: Golf)
EG Elizabeth Greig (Shipping)
RH Ralph Hyde (Panorama, entertainment; Panorama, newspaper give-aways)
PJ Peter Jackson (Burial in woollen affidavit; Directories; Fleet marriage certificate; Gretna Green marriage certificate; Sports papers: Boxing; Vice card)
FL Fred Lake (Sports papers: archery)
TN Tim Nicholson (Touring map)
PS Peter Standley (Bookmark)
AT Amoret Tanner (Wine label)
TT Teal Triggs ('Zine)
MT Michael Twyman (Advertisement; Certificate; E-mail; Fax; Form; Greetings card; Label; Opticians' papers; Parking ticket; Secondary uses of ephemera; Security printing; Sheet-music cover; Sports papers: general and cricket; Ticket; Transfer lithography; Xerography)
SW Stephen Werner (Passport)
JW John Wilson (Photographic ephemera)

For advice on specific points the editor would like to thank Mohamad Agha, Colin Banks, Zyg Baránski, Chris Burke, Ian Burn, Helen Burns, Beverley Cole (National Railway Museum, York), Andrew Cook, Amanda Fergusson (Hallmark Cards UK), John Ford, John Foster (British Parking Association), Ian Fraser, Brian Gegg, Debbie Heatlie (Institute of Ophthalmology), Michal Itzhaki, David Knott, Luigi Majno, H. C. Marshall, Hugo Dunn-Meynell, John Miles, Stephen Miller, Dennis Morris, James Mosley, Ian Mumford, Marjorie Norcross, Ewald Osers, Calvin P. Otto, Vickram Sembi, Margaret M. Smith, Geoff Sparke (Advantage Ticketing), Glenys Williams (Lord's), Conte Alvise Zorzi.

Most of the illustrations have been scanned from items in the Rickards Collection of the Centre for Ephemera Studies at the University of Reading. Some come from other collections and are listed here with their page number (where more than one illustration appears on a page letters have been added following the normal sequence of reading): Sarah du Boscq de Beaumont (65a, 72c, 89c, 90a, 153a&b, 193a, 304b, pls 3, 10); Diana Cook (308); Department of Typography & Graphic Communication, The University of Reading (212, 301, pls 1, 8); Peter Jackson (65c, 187, 199b, 305, 306a, pl.7); Peter Jones (18, 107, 207b, 208); Library Company of Philadelphia (frontispiece); M.C.C. Museum (306b); Calvin P. Otto (pls 13a, 13b); Reading University Library (54, 286, pls 2b, 6); Rural History Centre, The University of Reading (pl. 2a); Steve Screed (364); Amoret Tanner (1, 14, 19b, 35, 51c, 72b, 76b, 89b, 92, 99, 112, 113, 119, 134, 142, 144b&c, 176, 197, 230, 234, 237, 254, 258, 267a, 287, 317b, 345, pls 4, 9a); Michael Twyman (7b, 8, 110, 114, 121, 126, 137, 151, 178, 209, 216, 219, 221, 226, 268, 285b, 292, 294a&b, 326, 338, 342, 354, pl. 12); Jennie Welsh (158); Stephen Werner (227).

colour plates between letters R and S

Notes

(—) = a space left in a printed document for manuscript insertion

(with text) = a manuscript insertion in a printed document

[ ] = editorial comment

cross references to other entries are shown in SMALL CAPITALS

dimensions in text and captions give height before width

addresses of institutions referred to after entries are provided on pp. 367–68

British money before decimalization in 1971

1 pound (shown as £1, £1 0s 0d, £1. 0*s*. 0*d*.) = 20 shillings

1 guinea (shown as 1gn, 1g., £1 1s 0d, £1. 1*s*. 0*d*.) = 21 shillings

1 shilling (shown as 1s, 1*s*., 1s 0d, 1*s*. 0*d*., 1sh., 1/–) = 12 pence

1 penny (shown as 1d, 1*d*., 1^{D}) = 2 halfpennies or 4 farthings

1 halfpenny (shown as ½d, ½*d*.) = 2 farthings

1 farthing (shown as ¼d, ¼*d*., far., f.)

£1 7s 6½d = one pound seven shillings and sixpence halfpenny

£1 11s 6d = one and a half guineas

5/6 = five shillings and sixpence

2/6 = two shillings and sixpence (half a crown)

ABC primer
academy/college broadside
account-book label
accounts, domestic
accounts, institutional
acquaintance card
admission ticket
advertisement
advertising booklet
advertising envelope
advertising fan
advertising novelty
advertising ring (embossed)
aerial leaflet
agency certificate
agricultural/horticultural show card
air-raid papers
air-sickness bag
air-transport label
album card
album frontispiece
almanac
amateur journal
ambrotype label
American Civil War papers
American seaman's certificate
amusement sheet
anamorphic image
anonymous letter
appointment card
AQ letter sheet
armed forces papers
army printing
arrangement of carriages diagram
artisan's bill/receipt
artwork for reproduction
assignat
'at home' card
attendance record, school
auditorium seating plan

ABC primer

The term 'ABC' (rendered also as 'abece', 'apecy', 'apsie', 'absie', etc.) refers generally to an elementary spelling book for children. Also used in the period 1500 to 1800 were the terms 'abecedary', 'absedarie', and others derived from 'abecedarium'. ('Abecedarian', used to refer to a pupil learning the alphabet, was current in America until the early part of the 19th century.)

The word 'primer' (pronounced 'primmer' in 16th-century England and present-day America) was applied originally to a booklet containing not only spelling instruction but prayers and orders of service in church. The booklet, principally designed for children acting as servers at Mass, was printed in the black-letter (Old English) of the time. It began with the setting out of the alphabet and continued with key sentences pronounced by the priest at various stages of the service. With its dual reference (to religious as well as to secular instruction) the primer extended the principal of the hornbook and BATTLEDORE.

The two concepts, the ABC and the 'primer', at some periods tended to merge; at others to separate. The term 'ABC primer' presents a late 19th-century view of their close identity. With the passage of time the religious element became much diminished, though the word primer continued in use.

Among the earliest of surviving ABC primers is an undated booklet of sixteen pages 'Imprynted at Londó in Paules Chyrche yarde at the sygne of the maydens heed by thomas Petyt'. The work is presented 'both in Latyn and in Englyshe', setting out the alphabet, vowels, and vowel-consonant conjunctions; and adding the Pater Noster, the Hail Mary, the Creed, the Lord's Prayer, Grace before Meals, the Commandments, 'and other devoute prayers' in both languages. The booklet, published sometime between 1536 and 1554 (probably in 1538), is preserved in the Library of Emmanuel College, Cambridge. The work contains, incidentally, a crucial misprint: the first line of the text describes the booklet as a 'BAC'.

The Petyt primer was one among numerous versions, some 'authorized', many modified to the religious views of the publisher concerned. Also recorded are an ABC produced in London by William Powell (c.1547); another, also in London, by John Day (c.1553); and another published in Dublin in English and Irish for the Stationers' Company in 1631.

In the late 18th and early 19th centuries illustrated alphabets took the place of the black-letter ABC. In these pictorial charts, mnemonic images matched each letter. At a later stage whole words were similarly treated. The charts were of various sizes and formats, but most were intended for use with small groups of children at school or at home. Illustrations are of an engaging naïvety, often printed from blocks or plates that were out-dated even at the time of publication.

The pictorial alphabet, printed as a composite sheet or as separate letters, played the same central role as the ABC primer and the battledore of earlier times. Like the ABC primer, it appeared in various media, including woodcut, wood- and steel-engraving, lithography; and in colour by means of hand-colouring, stencilling, woodblock printing, chromolithography, and, later, photomechanical processes.

A Present for a Good Child.
THE CHRISTIAN ALPHABET,
Or, Parents' and Children's Guide and Instructor.

ABC primer, printed by J. Catnach, London, early 19th century. Letterpress. 380 × 253 mm (14⅞ × 10 in)

The underlying concept was the use of simple pictures to reinforce the phonic impact of initial letters. As with the ABC primer, the idea migrated from the classroom to the nursery and the hearth. It became recognized as an 'improving' toy. It underwent a further change of role when it became a matter for attention in its own right. The alphabet became a peg on which to hang a succession of related subjects (A is for Ambulance; B is for Bandage; C is for Crutch; D is for Doctor, etc.). It also appeared in anthropomorphic form, in which human figures were presented as letterforms; a similar principle was applied to fanciful landscapes and architectural constructions.

It may be noted that the pictorial alphabet and other forms of spelling aids are English-language based. 'Spelling' as a subject (and its corollary the 'spelling bee') was scarcely necessary in the phonetic context of the majority of other languages.

Academy/college broadside

In America in the mid 19th century it was customary to announce the resumption of schools and academies at the new term by means of a locally posted broadside. A printed notice, measuring some 250 × 200 mm (9⅞ × 7⅞ in) to 500 × 350 mm (19¾ × 13¾ in) set out the date of recommencement, the names of academic staff and their subjects, terms of tuition, and other details. The notice bore an official appearance, consistent with the sobriety of the subject matter, but there was clearly an intention to catch the eye with an attractive display, in most cases by means of a decorative border.

Public posting of schools' announcements was rare in Britain, surviving examples usually take the form of small prospectus folders distributed through the mail or by hand (*see* SCHOOL PROSPECTUS).

Evening classes were also advertised by broadside: James W. Angier, principal of the newly-established night school 'For the Benefit of the Laboring Classes' in the public hall at Darby, Delaware County, Pennsylvania, offers studies in 'Arithmetic, Geography, Grammar, Reading, Writing and Spelling. Tuition – One Dollar per month, payable in advance…'.

REFERENCE William Frost Mobley, *American Nineteenth-Century Historical and Advertising Broadsides*… (catalogue 1, Wilbraham, Mass.: The Author, 1980)

COLLECTION American Antiquarian Society, Worcester, Mass.

Account-book label

The term is used to apply to labels not only in account books but in ledgers, journals, notebooks, copybooks, day books, stock books, and other volumes ruled for handwritten entry. Like the miniature label used by binders and early stationers, the account-book label first appears in the mid 18th century. It is initially a small engraved item, as unobtrusive, and often as elegant, as its binders' and stationers' counterparts. Like them, its style is commonly an echo of the TRADE CARD.

The account-book label grew rapidly in size and visual impact however; and as the industry developed it moved from a role of discreet identification to publicity. In the 1890s, re-order numbers began to appear. Sizes of up to 150 × 120 mm (5⅞ × 4¾ in) are not uncommon and in some cases, as with files and binders, the label may reach 200 × 120 mm (7⅞ × 4¾ in) and carry up to two hundred words of promotional copy.

Diagonally cropped corners are often found, and some specimens (c.1860–70) have quarter-round cut-out corners. Brightly coloured papers, notably yellow, blue, and green, are also common.

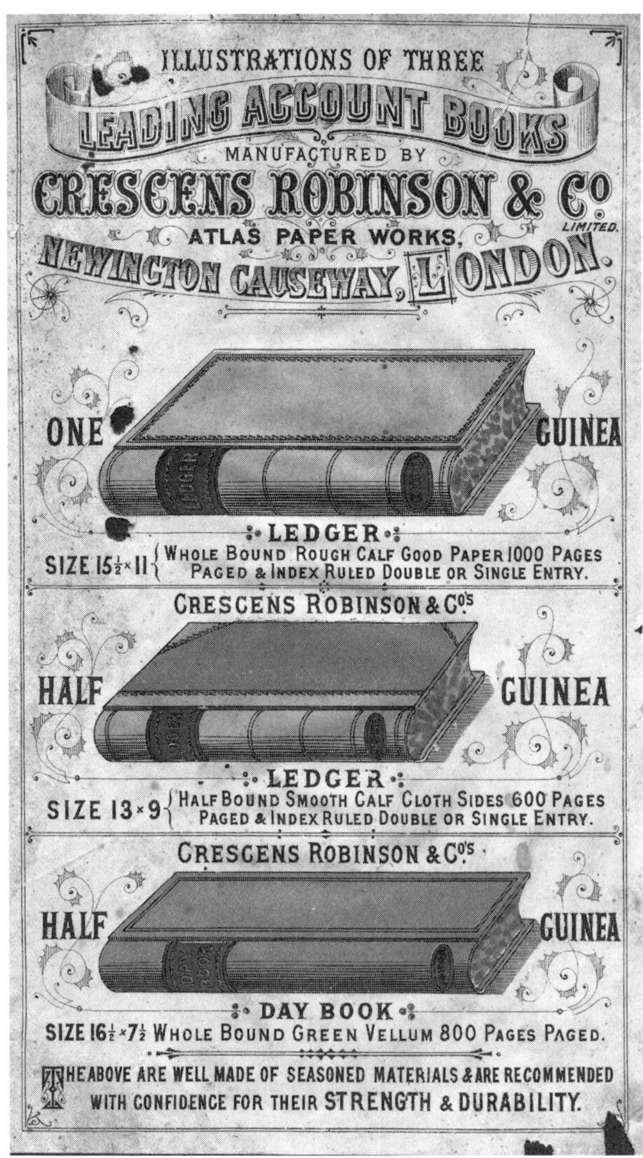

Account-book label of Crescens Robinson & Co. Ltd, London, late 19th century. Lithographed in five colours. 203 × 120 mm (8 × 4¾ in)

Accounts, domestic

Handwritten records of income and expenditure are a fruitful source of social-history detail. As with their printed counterparts (institutional and public-service accounts), they may reveal not only prices, commodities, quantities, etc., but sidelights on contemporary modes and conditions. Such entries as 'Mourning buckles: 3/6' and 'Ten days asses milk: 15/–' (London 1789) convey more than simple accountancy.

Confined largely to personal and household records, manuscript accounts are not as common as might be thought. External compulsions in the keeping of accounts in earlier times were relatively few. In the absence of such forces as income tax and Companies' Acts, ordinary citizens were satisfied with visible stocks of goods and treasures to show them how they were doing. Even among the wealthy, the money chest itself was often the only barometer of the owner's affairs.

The keeping of manuscript accounts was confined largely to two classes: those who saw the account as a form of personal journal, and those entrusted with stewardship – of monies, estates, etc. – in the name of a supervising authority.

Prominent in the first category is the farmer or smallholder, whose accounts record the buying, breeding, and selling of cattle and the seasonal work of sowing and reaping. Many of these, more properly viewed as family archives than ephemera, were maintained over decades – sometimes even over generations. Typical is a record kept by a Welsh farmer in the 1830s. This carries such entries as 'Paid for Oatmeal for Pultice for the lame Cow: 1/-; to molecatcher for half a year: 7/-; to W. Smallwood for 3 birch beasoms at 6d each: 1/6; for eight quarts of Ale for Christmas day: 4/-; to Jno Evans for killing large fat Pig: 2/-; to Edward Williams Cow doctor: £1'. Accounts occasionally appear as spasmodic entries in COMMONPLACE BOOKS or on single sheets of paper. These may chronicle the expenses of a week or a day or two, apparently without relevance to accompanying recipes, provender, etc. Others may list items bought at a sale or goods sold to friends or neighbours.

Institutional manuscript accounts may include records kept by churchwardens, overseers of the poor, selectmen, etc., and sometimes by those in charge of schools, workhouses, hospitals and similar bodies.

Manuscript accounts are not necessarily presented as a listing with columns of figures and a totalled bottom line. In the accounts of the selectmen of Brighton, Boston, Massachusetts in the early 1800s, details of costs of boarding out appear in journal form:

> 1808: Sussanah Oldham age 61 at Boston no Expense at Present
> Mary Hanker age 75 Bording at Mr Stone 50 Framingham at 44 dollars 50 per year Cloathing including
> Caleb Coolidge agd 56 Bording at Doc[r] Ball at 3 dollars per week… to the 4 of January 1808 and 5 dollars Per week to the 17 of February 1808. From that date he went to Live with his Son Henry Coolidge at Westminster for one year at one dollar Per week the Town to be at the Expenc of Doctring and Cloathing.

Among the earliest of manuscript parish accounts in Britain are those of the churchwardens of Saffron Walden. Dated 1478, these record such outgoings as 'mendynge of a boke in seyntmary chapel'; 'to tomas semer ys wyfe for a sorplys for the Payrshe pryste'; and 'to John frenshe for mendyng of the iiij the belle klapyr'.

Archaisms, both of spelling and handwriting, may make such accounts 'difficult' to read. Numerals derive from the Roman usage of the Norman Conquest (though in fact practice varies over the course of the years and between one writer and another). In the period of the account cited above the lower-case letter *i* is used for *I* (1) and *v* for *V* (5); *l* = *L* (50); *c* = *C* (100); *x* = *X* (10). The *i-longa* or *j* is used to indicate *I* (1) on its own or finally. Thus, in the item quoted above, the bell clapper in question was the fourth: *iiij* = *IIII*. (The form *iv* = *IV* did not appear in handwriting until later.)

The letters *s* and *d* are used for shilling (*solidus*) and penny (*denarius*). Thus: for example *jd* = one penny; *ijd* = two pence; *iijd* = threepence; *iiijd* = fourpence; *vs xd* = five shillings and ten pence; *ijs vijd* = two shillings and seven pence.

Each item in the listing of the period commonly carries the abbreviation *It* for *Item* (Latin: likewise, also).

REFERENCES J. J. Bagley, *Historical Interpretation*, vol. II (London: Penguin, 1971); F. G. Emmison, *Archives and Local History* (London: Methuen, 1966); Hilda E. P. Grieve, *Examples of English Handwriting 1150–1750* (Chelmsford: Essex Education Committee, 1954); L. C. Hector, *The Handwriting of English Documents* (London: Arnold, 1958)

Accounts, institutional

As with the handwritten account, the printed annual account may reveal more than the simple facts of profit and loss. Among its listed items, as well as in its record of quantities and prices, the account may often carry pointers to the social climate of its time.

Printed annual accounts first began to appear in the late 18th century with the rise of organized charities, whose public appeals relied largely on an annual declaration of achievement. Charities were followed shortly by local authority institutions. Local poor-law 'unions', hundreds, and county councils, published accounts of their stewardship. The balance sheets of schools, workhouses, lunatic asylums, prisons, hospitals, infirmaries, dispensaries and institutions for the blind, deaf and handicapped, as well as general local services, brought the detail of their management to a wider public than at any time before.

In the middle of the 19th century (in both Britain and the United States) it became legally binding on all public companies in those countries to publish formally edited accounts, and by the end of the 19th century there were few classes of institution exempt from the requirement.

As indications of the incidental intelligence to be found in early accounts we may note the following:

WORKHOUSE LIVERPOOL 1820		
Credits:	Sunday girls making bonnets and knitting stockings value	£23.12. 0
	Profited by picking oakum	407.11. 5
	Urine collected in the House	149. 6. 9
Stock:	Wood bowls, noggins, trenchers ladles etc	1.10. 0
	1¾ cases soft soap	2. 5. 6
	24 men's coffins, 12 women's ditto, 72 Boys' and Girls' ditto; 27 infants' ditto	68. 8. 6
COUNTY OF SOUTHAMPTON 1828		
	Burial of dead bodies cast on shore	17. 5. 4
	Conveyance of Scotch and Irish paupers	155. 2. 9
NEW-ENGLAND INSTITUTION FOR THE EDUCATION OF THE BLIND 1839		
	Old matresses made over 74	
	New pew cushions made 1161 ft	
GALWAY PRISON 1841		
	24 spoons, cleansing hospital privy, postage and brushes	0. 13.10
	24 chamber pots for prison	1. 1. 2
	oil for treadmill	0. 2. 0
HUNDRED OF SALFORD, COUNTY OF LANCASTER NEW BAILEY PRISON 1844		
	Taskmaster's salary	25. 0. 0
	Thomas Barton for straw	9.15. 0
	T Satterthwaite for clog soles	9.13. 6
	John Colton for hair cutting &c	1.14. 6
YORK PLACE RAGGED SCHOOLS LONDON 1867		
	giving boys outfits to various places as pages &c; sending boys to sea	23. 9. 6
WHITECHAPEL UNION LONDON 1884		
	quantity of oakum picked by vagrants 336 lb	

Acquaintance card

A novelty variant of the American calling card of the 1870s and 1880s, the acquaintance card was used by the less formal male in approaches to the less formal female. Given also as an 'escort card' or 'invitation card', the device commonly carried a brief message and a simple illustration.

A typical specimen, headed with a quotation from Hamlet 'Gaze on this picture then on that', shows to the left a cockerel and to the right a donkey. The message, headed 'Escort Card', reads: 'Fair Lady: may I become the proud bird who shall accompany you to your leafy bower, or must I suffer the misery of seeing you borne away in triumph by that individual whose chromotintype appears at the right'.

The cards were also available as assignation notes, with space for name, time, and place to be filled in by hand, and in hieroglyphic and other cryptic forms ('May I.C.U. Home?').

Examples are also found of similar cards for the use of ladies. 'Leap Year Compliments' cards invoked the feminine right of proposal on 29 February, and for everyday use in normal years there were cards of introduction with space for overprinting.

Acquaintance card. American. Relief printed. 37 × 74 mm (1⁷⁄₁₆ × 2⁷⁄₈ in)

One surviving example reads: 'I am Mabel Dearborn; who the —— are you?' (The dash is rendered as a figure of a devil.)

Novelty-card printers produced acquaintance cards in large quantities. A typical source was L. Hathaway of Washington Street, Boston, who offered twenty-eight different styles in one package for ten cents (1000 cards for $1.35).

Flirtatious and fun, the acquaintance card brought levity to what otherwise might have seemed a more formal proposal. A common means of introduction, it was never taken too seriously. Often kept as a token of subsequent friendship, many have survived in scrapbooks and collections of VISITING CARDS. No contemporary counterpart of the acquaintance card existed in Britain, although non-pictorial, crudely printed cards bearing similar messages had a brief vogue in England in the 1910s.

Admission ticket

Admission tickets are normally defined as those bearing the word 'Admit', followed by a number ('two, three', etc.) or a space, or a name or names.

The admission ticket is to be distinguished from the invitation card, which it may sometimes resemble. (For cataloguing purposes the term 'invitation' is normally confined to items actually bearing the word in one of its forms.) Ambiguous cases are not uncommon however, and collections of ephemera may often include items of one category among items of the other.

In some cases the distinction is made clear by the sender. Certain invitations declare in a footnote: 'This card will not admit'. Here the invitation presents a first stage. The second stage – despatch of a ticket of admission – follows only after acceptance.

The admission ticket is also normally distinguished from a ticket received at the time of entry as a receipt for payment. It is essentially a document of advance engagement.

Admission tickets relate to a vast range of events. Included in any typical listing will be ceremonial occasions such as coronations; royal wedding, jubilee, and funeral processions; royal visits and garden parties; launches, inaugurations, and openings; social functions such as weddings, banquets, dinners, suppers, teas, dances, picnics, etc.; as well as concerts, lectures, firework displays, wakes, cockfights, and entrance to exhibitions, zoos, galleries, state apartments, parks, gardens, and other places of interest and entertainment.

Engraved tickets from London in the 18th and early 19th centuries established a style distinctly their own. Printed in a single colour (commonly black) and measuring as much as 200 × 250 mm (7⁷⁄₈ × 9⁷⁄₈ in) these images were substantial works of art. They were produced in many cases by artists of distinction, often as gestures of goodwill on the part of the artist rather than as professional commissions.

The style was elaborate, those for concerts and similar functions featuring groups of muses, musical instruments, cherubs, and other classical set-piece elements.

Some designs, commissioned for permanent use by societies and learned bodies, carried space for handwritten insertions of time and date, but in many cases these details appear as part of the printed engraving, successively updated on the plate for each occasion. It is recorded by Tuer in *Bartolozzi and his Works* (London, 1881) that Cipriani's 1775 design for a Mansion House Ball ticket, engraved by Bartolozzi, remained in use for over twenty years.

Tickets of this kind came to be known as 'Bartolozzi tickets', and were much sought after in their time – more particularly as their rarity was increased by destructive door-keepers. They have remained collectors' items ever since. Among distinguished connoisseurs have been Horace Walpole and Sarah Banks, whose collection is housed in the British Museum. Bartolozzi himself was also a collector of the engraved ticket (his own and those of others); he formed a special collection for his patron Richard Dalton, librarian to the then Prince of Wales, the future George III.

Another category of admission ticket is the British 'Royal Occasion' ticket, an item of special significance, and generally of some ceremonial splendour. Typical in this field are tickets for attendance at coronations. Among the earliest of these is the ticket of admission to Westminster Abbey for the crowning of George III and Charlotte Sophia in 1761. Engraved by George Bickham, the ticket consists substantially of a representation of the scene in the Abbey (with angels and allegorical females also in attendance), the whole bearing the foot-line 'Coronation ticket Westminster Abbey Sept 22 1761'. Head and foot margins carry seating location details and authorizing signatures. The illustration, which is only barely competent, measures 200 × 230 mm (7⁷⁄₈ × 9 in).

The ticket for the coronation of William IV and Queen Adelaide (8 September 1831) is by contrast much restrained. On a card measuring 193 × 268 mm (7⁵⁄₈ × 10½ in) it presents the title of the ceremony, 'The Coronation of Their Most Sacred Majesties', with the crown and joint cyphers as a centre-piece above the legend 'Admit into Westminster Abbey'. Queen Victoria's coronation ticket is a similar presentation, somewhat smaller, 170 × 230 mm (6¾ × 9 in). It also carries the reference to 'Sacred Majesty'.

By far the most impressive of coronation ticket operations was that for George IV (19 July 1821). The main ticket, measuring 236 × 262 mm (9¼ × 10¼ in) presents a virtuoso example of Congreve's COMPOUND-PLATE PRINTING within a blind-embossed border by Dobbs. There are two versions of the ticket, one admitting to Westminster Hall, the other to the Abbey. Marked respectively 'Hall' and 'Abbey' in oval cut-outs to the left of the central motif, the tickets also differ in colour treatment (black, red, and blue for the Hall; black and blue for the Abbey) as well as in the design of the embossed border. Used specimens bear a manuscript numeral in the right-hand oval, the name of the holder in the lower left margin, and authorizing signatures and wax seal to the right. Centrally at the foot appears the die-stamped seal of the Earl Marshal of England. (Examples are also found in which the lower margin has been trimmed off to provide an even all-round margin in framing. These of course are incomplete.) A number of plate-maker's proofs are also to be found. These, of extreme rarity, show modifications in the design of the printing plates prior to final commissioning. Printed on unembossed paper and without the broad lower margin, they present the royal cypher and coat of arms against a patterned background instead of the white slab which appears in the final version. The ovals to the left and right are similarly patterned. It would appear from these 'states' that the original versions were felt to lack legibility. Other tickets for the George IV coronation gave admission to the vaultings within the Abbey and to seats in nearby buildings to view the external procession. 'Pass tickets' were also supplied, allowing the holder to move in and out of a given area and from one location to another. Small 'Pass and Re-pass' tickets, 75 × 105 mm (3 × 4⅛ in), were also issued prior to the event to personnel working on arrangements for the ceremony. It may be that the splendour and profusion of tickets for the George IV coronation derived at least in part from the promotional zeal of Congreve and Dobbs, both of whose companies were keen to have their productions seen in places of influence. (Certainly Congreve, though his compound-plate printing process had originated as an anti-counterfeit measure, must have seen this royal occasion as setting the seal on his status as a potential contractor to the Government.)

Other coronations brought noticeably less extravagance in the matter of admission tickets. The William IV ticket, already noted, was in fact a re-drawing of the George IV Centre House Procession ticket, and the Queen Victoria version is clearly a re-working of her predecessor's ticket.

Of a different order of extravagance were the admission cards produced for the Corporation of London in the period from c.1820 to 1900. These, of an average size of 260 × 320 mm (10¼ × 12½ in), appeared in connection with civic and state occasions, royal visits, banquets, openings, etc. As with coronation tickets, they had high prestige value and were produced in distinctly competitive spirit by leading London printers. The printing process was largely chromolithography, using in many cases ten or a dozen colours, often with additional gold and silver. Colour embossing was occasionally used (as in De La Rue's three-colour 'porcelain' card for the state visit of the King of Sardinia

Admission ticket for a 'music meeting' in Worcester (UK) in the early nineteenth century. Relief printed from wood blocks and type. 64 × 95 mm (2½ × 3¾ in)

to the Guildhall on 4 December 1855), and heavy blind embossing was also sometimes used as a decorative frame enclosing the text of the announcement (Queen Victoria's dinner with the Corporation on Lord Mayor's Day, 9 November 1837, provides an excellent example of such work by Dobbs). A novelty in the latter part of the century was the occasional use of Woodbury-type photographs, which were individually mounted in panels and form part of the overall chromolithographed design. Printers' imprints on Corporation of London tickets include Collingridge, Maclure, Macdonald & Macgregor, Sly, Field & Tuer, Sherborn, Jackson, De La Rue, Kell, Letts, Waterlow, Turner, Collins, Terry, Standidge, Grant, Dobbs, and Blades, East & Blades. The last-named firm produced an average of one Guildhall ticket per year in the period 1873 to 1899, a quantity far in excess of any other printer.

The large-scale ticket of the great occasion must be seen as an exception. For most ordinary purposes the admission ticket is barely larger than a playing card. Notwithstanding its modest size, however, it may still convey a sense of occasion. Elegance of layout and typography, the use of crests, seals, embossing, and other devices may often effectively suggest what the larger item asserts. In this category may be found carriage admission tickets for Windsor Castle, Royal Academy Lecture Tickets, and tickets for readers at the British Museum.

Less elegant, but no less effective, are the small admission tickets popular in American church communities in the late 19th century for picnics, tea parties, suppers, outings, and other functions. Often printed on brightly coloured card, these may bear no more than a word or two: 'Picnic: Wells Street: June 25 1893', 'Lebanon Springs: Singing School: Admit Miss Clemmie Ball', 'One supper', 'Entertainment', etc.

Admission tickets vary widely in size. In one collection the smallest specimen (for the Ashby-de-la-Zouch Bazaar, 1843) measures 35 × 57 mm (1⅜ × 2¼ in), while the largest (for the Royal Luncheon at the coronation of George V and Queen Mary in 1911) measures 380 × 570 mm (14⅞ × 22½ in).

See also BENEFIT TICKET; HOSTEL ADMISSION TICKET; LECTURE TICKET; THEATRE TICKET

REFERENCE Victoria Moger, *The Favour of Your Company* (London: The Museum of London, 1980)

Advertisement

The word was originally applied to a written or printed document that brought something to the notice of the public

(French, *avertir*: to warn, inform). Advertisements have a long history and examples survive from Roman times, painted on the walls of buildings in Pompeii or set in mosaic on the pavements of Ostia, the seaport of ancient Rome. There is reason to believe that wherever goods or services were on offer, advertisements would have been produced.

One lasting kind of advertisement is the paid insertion in a newspaper, magazine or specialist publication, either in the form of an undisplayed entry set more or less as text, or, later, displayed to occupy a portion of the page or the whole page (occasionally a spread). Advertisements of the first category, later known as 'small ads' in Britain and 'wants-ads' in America, date from the late 17th century in Britain and the early years of the 18th century in America and are normally charged according to the depth of the space they occupy. Advertisements of the second kind are charged according to their size and location in the publication and are designed to attract attention through their overall concept, copy writing, typography, illustration, and photography.

Many advertisements take the form of separate written or printed documents, either for fixed display (usually on a vertical surface, such as a wall or tree) or to be distributed by hand. The first category includes the POSTER, PUBLIC NOTICE, and WINDOW BILL; the second the flyer, leaflet, and handbill. In the 20th century advertisements were created to take advantage of most of the new technologies and media, beginning with the flashing electric-light advertisement and closing with the world wide web (www). In the second half of the century commercial television opened the way for some of the most inventive and witty advertisements of the period, often using pioneering approaches and techniques with the help of generous budgets.

Advertising, though derived from the same linguistic root as advertisement, is interpreted more broadly. Its products include items that might not always be called advertisements, such as ADVERTISING ENVELOPE; ADVERTISING FAN; ADVERTISING NOVELTY; ADVERTISING RING; CIGARETTE CARD; CLUB FLYER; CIGAR BAND/BOX LABEL; 'CINDERELLA' STAMP; ECCENTRIC ADVERTISING; LEAFLET; STUD CARD/NOTICE; TRADE CARD. With the growth of trade and industry in the 19th century, advertising grew with remarkable speed particularly in America and Europe. This led to the beginnings of the advertising manager, advertising agency and, later, the establishment of one of the most influential and widespread commercial activities in the world.

The original, low-key form of advertisement, which simply informed the public of a product or service, has been transformed into a vehicle through which advertising specialists with a range of skills, and armed with data from market surveys, use every legitimate (sometimes illegitimate) trick in the book to attract and persuade. [MT]

See also QUACK ADVERTISING; TRADE ADVERTISER

REFERENCES An adept, *Publicity. An Essay on Advertising* (London, 1878); Henry Sampson, *A History of Advertising* (London: Chatto and Windus, 1874); William Smith, *Advertising. How? When? Where?* (London: Routledge, Warne & Routledge, 1863); E. S. Turner, *The Shocking History of Advertising!* (rev. edn, Harmondsworth: Penguin, 1965).

Advertising booklet

The word 'booklet' first appeared in the late 1850s, although the miniature paper book, the CHAPBOOK, was a common feature of life in the 17th and 18th centuries, and by the 18th century the tract had also appeared in booklet form.

The advertising booklet, given free of charge, was a forerunner of the 20th-century advertising brochure. It came into general use in the 1850s and 1860s, at first as a flimsy eight-page or sixteen-page miniature, later in larger format, with thin board covers and coloured wrappers. The booklet was often presented in the guise of a household guide, offering recipes, remedies, child-care hints, etc., with more or less explicit references to the advertisement's products.

Advertising envelope

The advent in 1840 of the MULREADY ENVELOPE brought a wave of interest in the concept of the envelope as such and in the illustrated envelope as a novelty. Not least of the ideas that stemmed from it was the advertising envelope.

This began with the use of Mulready lettersheets by advertisers, the reverse of the sheets being over-printed with announcements for individual companies or for an assortment of different firms. Some twenty-five publishers took up the idea of the 'collective' sheet, acting as agents for fee-paying advertisers and distributing the sheets to the public at less than their postal face value. Typical examples were *Hallett's Postage Advertiser, Smith's Envelope Advertiser,* and *The New Envelope Select Advertiser*, each carrying a dozen or so advertisements.

Sixty or seventy individual companies used Mulreadys for whole-sheet advertisements, and some tax and revenue offices used them for notices, reminders, etc.

The 'envelope advertisement' idea survived sporadically throughout the rest of the century. When the Stamp Office introduced the practice of stamping stationers' own paper in pre-payment of postage, the advertising-envelope specialists were able to offer their clients advertising space on ready-stamped sheets for sale to the public (as with the Mulreadys) at much reduced rates.

In the 1880s the International Envelope Co., London, offered a stamped envelope sheet, wholly covered with advertising on its inner surface, at five shillings per gross. The Anglo-Colonial Letter Co., Liverpool, provided a stamped letter sheet with blank writing space surrounded by advertisements, at nine pence per dozen.

In America in the 1860s and 1870s the principle of the envelope advertiser was applied to the backs of made-up envelopes (in spite of the technical difficulties of printing on an uneven surface and controlling a loose flap). Sometimes as many as twenty-four small panels, each advertising a different firm, covered the whole of the back of an envelope no larger than 85 × 140 mm ($3\frac{3}{8} \times 5\frac{1}{2}$ in). In the American version, however, the envelope was sold unstamped, but at a virtually give-away price.

Envelope advertising was developed into a major publicity medium in America. The 1850s and 1860s had seen the introduction of the 'corner card', a pictorial motif derived from trade card and billhead use, applied to the left-hand portion of the front of the envelope. The corner card initially appeared as a single-colour cameo embossing, often depicting the premises or product of the advertiser with identifying text incorporated within a shaped or squared-up panel. Later, the advertising element spread to cover a major portion of the front of the envelope, leaving only nominal space for the address and stamp. In Britain the trend was much less widespread and, on the whole, less robust.

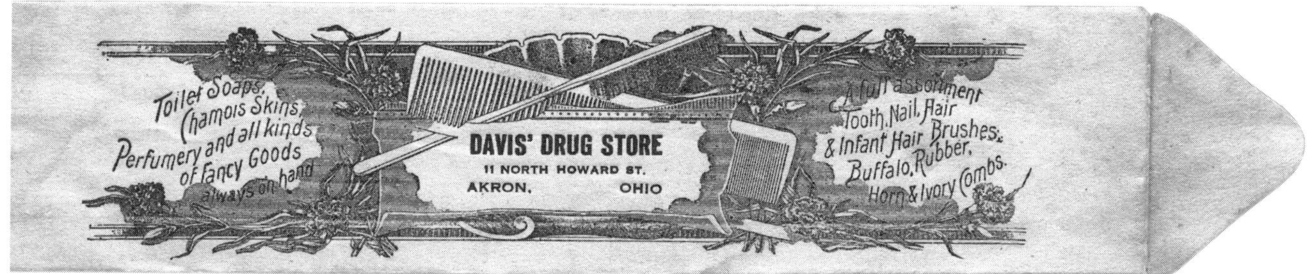

Advertising envelope of Davis's drug store, Akron, Ohio, early 20th century. Lithographed and overprinted letterpress with the name of the firm. 52 × 260 mm with flap (2 × 10¼ in)

The advertising-envelope principle was also extended in some countries to pre-paid postcards and lettercards. These, duly overprinted with advertising, were sold at less than the cost of card and postage combined. In France around 1900 an advertising lettercard bearing a 15-centime stamp was available for only 5 centimes.

REFERENCES Lou W. McCulloch, *Paper Americana* (San Diego: A. S. Barnes, 1980); Frank Staff, *The Picture Postcard and its origins*, 2nd edn (London: Lutterworth, 1979); Uberto Tosco, *Postage Stamps: Modern History in the Mail* (London: Orbis, 1972)

COLLECTIONS John Johnson Collection, Bodleian Library, Oxford; National Postal Museum, London

Advertising fan

Advertising and commemorative fans had their heyday in the period 1880 to 1910. Their use on the margins of the publicity and promotional scene continued well into the 20th century. Distinctions between commemorative, propaganda, and advertising functions, sometimes present in one fan simultaneously, are hard to draw. The general category may be distinguished by its role as a GIVE-AWAY rather than as an article for sale.

Structurally, fans are of two basic types, the screen fan and the folding fan. Both have been widely used as give-aways. The screen fan consists of a rigid panel attached to a light-weight stick or handle. (Included in this category is the 'cockade' fan, in which a pleated panel unfolds to form a rigid disc, the handle being formed at the point of completion.)

The classic folding fan consists of a semicircular pleated 'mount', or leaf, supported on sticks or blades which are held together at the lower end by a rivet. The outermost sticks are known as 'guards'. Advertising matter may appear not only on the mount but on the sticks and guards.

The rigid screen fan, simplest to produce, was a major publicity medium in pre-airconditioning America. Consisting of little more than a shaped trade card on a stick, the advertising fan carried messages from a vast range of shopkeepers and manufacturers, as well as theatres, circuses, and other entertainments.

As with the conventional trade card, chromolithographed stock designs were available for overprinting with the advertiser's message, resulting often in the same design being used for widely disparate businesses. In one example a design showing flowers and bluebirds on the front is backed by a detailed price list for the services of a dentist. Elsewhere the same design is used by a corset-maker.

Specially produced designs were made for buyers in quantity. Big hotels, restaurants, department stores, and rail and steamship companies were among major users. Political parties used them extensively at presidential elections.

The rigid advertising fan flourished at periods of commercial expansion in warmer climates. Specimens survive from Spain and Portugal; from Hong Kong, Singapore, Cairo, Panama, Bombay, and Calcutta; from Japan, Jamaica, Algeria, and Tenerife. In America, the rigid advertising fan was still widely in use in the 1920s. Specimens from this period include fans put out not only by ordinary commercial enterprises but, in one case at least, a funeral parlour.

The use of the folding fan for souvenir, commemorative, and advertising purposes dates back to the late 18th century. Among the earliest is an example commemorating the trial of Warren Hastings. The trial occupied more than seven years and 145 sittings; the fan, which showed a keyed illustration of the court arrangements, was produced in September 1788. Also published in 1788 was a fan showing the disposition of seating at the King's Theatre, London. This showed the pit as blank, but boxes, galleries, etc., bore the names of their distinguished occupants.

The great international exhibitions of the 19th century were marked by commemorative fans, many of them featuring the event itself on one side and commercial advertising on the other. Typical of these are examples from the 1867 Paris Exhibition and the Philadelphia Centennial in 1876.

The theatre (in whose summer interiors the fan was specially welcome) was a prominent user. Gala openings and first nights were specially commemorated. The opening of the Richard Wagner Theatre in Bayreuth in 1876 was honoured with a specially designed fan, as was the opening of the Bijou Theatre, Boston, in 1883. In Paris in 1880 appeared the *Éventail Journal Programme*, a daily journal of theatre, concert, and racing programmes which was supported by panels of commercial advertising on fans, updated each day, in cafés, bars, and theatres.

By the turn of the century the folding advertising fan had become a firmly established medium. Restaurants, night-clubs, hotels, and major stores distributed them freely to guests and hundreds of thousands of a new, cheaper version (smaller and

Advertising fan for Sorin & Co.'s Cognac, 1930s. Lithographed in six colours and manufactured by E. Chambrelent & Co., Évantailliste, Paris. Radius 190 mm (7½ in)

with only half the former complement of sticks) were given away by makers of aperitifs, chocolates, and other products. It survived as a give-away into the 1930s. Typical examples advertise Suchard chocolate, the Grand Magasin du Louvre, and the Paris Exhibition (1937). There was a further short lease of life in the 1950s and early 1960s. One 'royal' specimen celebrates, on the front, the coronation of Queen Elizabeth II (1953), and on the back the Hong Kong restaurant, Shaftesbury Avenue, London. A number of airlines, notably BOAC (British Overseas Airways Corporation), Air France, and JAL (Japan Air Lines), provided travellers with folding fans, among many other promotional extras, in the 1940s and 1950s. Among commercial manufacturers of folding fans in America have been the Massachusetts firm of Edmund Hunt & Co. and their successors the Allen Fan Company.

SOCIETY The Fan Circle

COLLECTION The Fan Museum, London

Advertising novelty [plate 13b]

Parallel with the development of the TRADE CARD and LEAFLET, there appeared in the first half of the 19th century a new and distinctive form of advertisement – the eye-catching oddity. An early item was the mock currency note: in 1832 Henry Brett, London supplier of wines and spirits, distributed an engraved paper in which he promised 'to supply the Bearer with pure Patent Brandy, Patent Hollands and every other genuine Article in the Wine and Spirit Trade at fair and reasonable prices or forfeit one thousand pounds...'. In paper, printing, and layout, the item resembled a £1000 note. In similar vein La Maison des Deux Nègres, rue Neuve, Brussels, in the 1870s informed gentlemen that 'pour cinquante francs la Maison ... offre un magnifique costume complet'. Here again a handsomely drawn design simulates a bank note, but in this case the bearer is actually promised a discount of two per cent.

Simulated currency was widely distributed, either by hand or by scattering in the street. In the late 1890s, the Mellin's Food Co. produced advertising 'coins' – cardboard discs whose face bore a convincing silver die-stamped rendering of the Queen, complete with numismatic inscription. The reverse bore the legend 'for infants and invalids: Mellin's Food'. 'Mock' items appeared in great variety. They included share certificates, bills of exchange, railway tickets, telegrams, postage stamps, and other such ephemera. In the 1840s a popular item was the 'summons': 'By virtue of a Warrant under the hand and Seal of W Williams, one of Her Majesty's Hair Cutters for the City of London, you are required to appear before him, personally, at your most convenient opportunity... Hereof fail not at the peril of a Bald Head...'.

Advertisement for Pears' Soap, late 19th century. Chromolithographed. 103 × 107mm (4 × 4¼in)

Less common were items printed on unusual substances. Here the appeal lay in the curiosity value or attractiveness of the material in question: D. Miller, 'Turner and Toyman' of Lowndes Street, London, printed his trade list on pale blue 'lace' paper – a presentation so attractive that few could throw it away. A. Valentine & Co., corner of Broadway and 18th Street, New York, printed a spring show invitation on wood foil. Lilly, Addinsell and Co., cork-hat manufacturers of Liverpool, printed their advertising leaflet on paper-thin cork. Japanese paper also appeared: John Moses and Co. of Newcastle-upon-Tyne added a footnote to their Spring 1881 announcement: 'Don't destroy this!!! It is printed on a Japanese handkerchief, expressly imported. It is a curiosity!!!' Other materials for advertising novelties include leather, celluloid, linen, metal foil, and parchment.

In another novelty area advertisers attached samples of net and other materials to leaflets and magazine insets. Ackermann's magazine *The Repository of Arts, Literature, Commerce, Manufactures, Fashions and Politics* (1809–29) was a well-known vehicle for this gambit, but manufacturers themselves also produced leaflets, either for inclusion in magazines or as separate items, bearing actual specimens of their products. A further well-explored area was the 'transparency' – the leaflet in which an advertising message is transformed by images revealed when the paper is held to the light. The hold-to-light effect had its origins in the early 19th-century 'protean views'. In these, translucent landscapes were enlivened by volcanic eruptions, fires, illuminations, and other effects (*see* TRANSPARENCY). The principle was also widely used in turn-of-the-century novelty postcards.

Other transformation or 'metamorphic' items featured folds, flaps, and lattice interlay. Lattice novelties showed a change of image at the movement of a projecting tab, one picture appearing on one set of slats, a second on the other. This too was derived from an earlier novelty, popular at the turn of the 19th century in animated political lampoons.

Folds and flaps were less complicated, offering image change at the touch of a finger. The device had a major vogue in America in the 1880s and 1890s. Chromolithographed folding cards showed split images of indigestion sufferers before and after Seltzer aperients, white beards rejuvenated by Buckingham's dye, and bathing beauties revealed *en deshabillé* in Rockaway beach huts.

The field of the advertising novelty owes much to Lothar Meggendorfer, the Munich illustrator of the period. Meggendorfer produced a varied range of 'mechanical' children's books using tabs, flaps, levers, three-part pictures, lattice interlay, and every form of cut-out, animation, and transformation, some of them derived from turn-of-the-century novelties, others of his own devising. Many of his constructions were adapted directly to advertising. Closely related to the Meggendorfer genre were

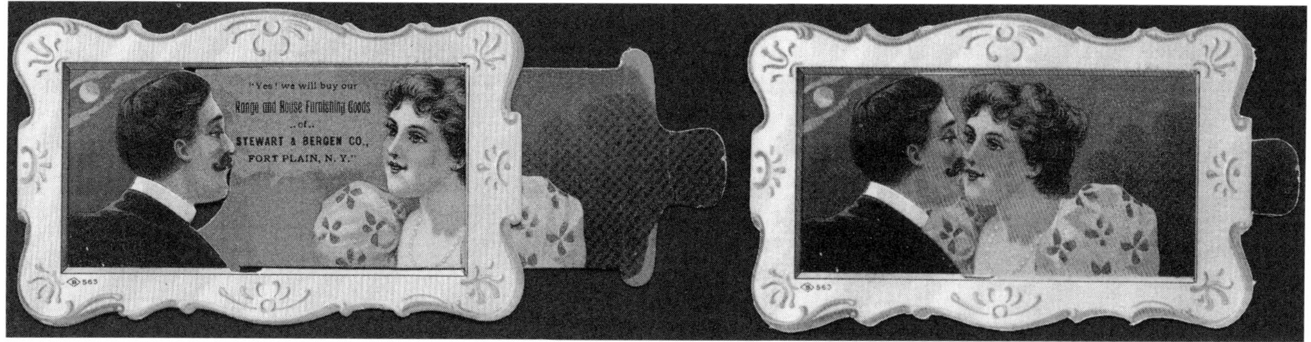

Advertising novelty of Stewart & Bergen Co., house furnishers, of Fort Plain, New York, late 19th century. Chromolithographed. 73 × 165 mm when open (2⅞ × 6½in)

sets of cut-out stand-up dolls put out by such firms as Au Bon Marché in Paris, and Barbour Brothers, and the Pearson Co. in New York. Au Bon Marché also produced a wide range of cut-out novelty folders in which the cover served as a partially cut-out exterior to an interior view revealed on opening.

Puzzles, games, and optical illusions provided a further focus of attention for prospective customers and their children, as did 'magic' items – pictures developed from a blank sheet by heating, messages traced out in smouldering saltpetre, and 'mystery' painting books, in which colours appeared by application of plain water. No opportunity was missed for the provision of off-beat items – particularly those for which an extended life might be expected. Obvious choices were the ALMANAC, BOOKMARK, CALENDAR, and TIMETABLE.

No less desirable were musical albums (miniature music booklets), tape measures (in linen or card) and, especially in pre-airconditioning America, the paper fan. As with promotional premium schemes and competitions, by the end of the 19th century few stones in the field of advertising novelty had been left unturned.

See also ADVERTISING FAN; BEER MAT; BLOTTING PAPER; BOOKMATCH; CAMPAIGN SOUVENIR; CARTE-DE-VISITE; CHILDREN'S ADVERTISING BOOKLET; COIN DISC/STICKER; ECCENTRIC ADVERTISING; GIVE-AWAYS; HOLD-TO-LIGHT; MOCK MONEY; PERFUME CARD; POCKET MIRROR, ADVERTISING; PUZZLE; RECORD, ADVERTISING

Advertising ring (embossed)

The term is applied to the 'name collar' appearing as an addition to the official embossed stamp on British stationery in the period 1857 to 1888. The collar, which was also embossed, bore the name of the company mailing the item concerned.

Though referred to as an advertising ring, it is probable that the idea originated as a security measure. Pilfering of postage stamps by employees had become a significant problem, and a number of firms, having experimented with various methods of identifying their own stocks of stamps, accepted the facility of 'extra embossing'. The advertising aspect of the scheme may have been seen merely as an incidental bonus.

The work of embossing the postage stamp image was carried out at Somerset House where, in addition to stamping postal stationery for the normal output of the post office, the Inland Revenue also stamped paper and card for use as envelopes, wrappers, and postcards of private concerns. Such items were delivered to Somerset House for stamping, and then collected for cutting, folding, gumming, etc., as finished products.

The first firms to avail themselves of the 'collar' facility were Stevens & Norton, Lincoln's Inn; Smith Elder & Co., East India agents; J. F. Pawson; Saunders Otley & Co.; the *British Workman* magazine; W. H. Smith & Son; *Home News* magazine; Grindlay & Co.; and Samuel Allsopp & Sons. In each case collar and stamp were printed in one operation from a combined die, the collar thus appearing in the same colour as the stamp.

At a later stage it was arranged that private firms could add the embossing of the collar themselves, relieving Somerset House of an increasing burden. In this second phase, which continued until 1893, efforts to match the colour of the new embossing to that of the stamp were rarely successful, and many firms solved the problem by using a completely different colour. An additional problem was register; many examples are seen to be badly centred on the stamp.

Embossed advertising ring of W. H. Smith & Son, London, 1885, printed in brown. Diameter 38 mm (1½in)

Specimens of privately embossed collars survive from some thirty different firms, among them George Farmiloe & Sons; W. & T. Avery; Alldays & Onions Ltd; W. H. Smith & Son, and Parkins & Gotto. First to use the private embossing facility was Stafford Smith & Smith of Bath in 1863, quickly followed in the same year by Collier & Co. of Plymouth, Frank E. Millar of Dalston, London, and George Prior of Fenchurch Street, London.

REFERENCES John Chandler and H. Dagnall, *The Newspaper and Almanac Stamps of Great Britain and Ireland* (Saffron Walden: Great Britain Philatelic Publications, 1981); Alan Huggins, *British Postal Stationery* (London: Great Britain Philatelic Society, 1971)

COLLECTION National Postal Museum, London

Aerial leaflet

Leaflets dropped from the air, in peace as well as in war, have for the most part carried hard-line messages of persuasion or propaganda. Among early examples, however, are those dropped by enthusiasts as souvenirs of ballooning success. In this category are the leaflets of the American pioneer Charles Ferson Durant in the early 1830s, and of Salomon Andrews in 1866.

Charles Durant, fired by the example of French aeronaut Eugene Robertson, made a number of ascents from Castle Garden, New York. On the first and second occasion he distributed handbills on the ground before going up, but on his third flight on 24 August 1831 distribution was 'From his Car in the Air'. The leaflet bore a poetic celebration entitled 'The Aeronaut's Address'. The style was reminiscent of the CARRIER'S ADDRESS, though it contained no appeal for money. In another ascent two years later, this time in the presence of Andrew Jackson, the President of the United States, Durant released another leaflet, 'Mercury's Proudest Message, or Durant's Valedictory', an effusion in similar vein. Specimens of the Durant leaflets, together with other documents relating to his exploits, were prepared by the aeronaut himself. At his death, two volumes of ballooning ephemera were presented by his family to the New York Public Library.

The Salomon Andrews leaflet, distributed from the car of his airship *Aereon* some thirty years later, survives in a single example. It bears a woodcut illustration of the craft and the words 'From the car of Andrews' flying-ship; a souvenir of her trial trip'. There is no evidence that the leaflet was released from the car while aloft: the words 'from the car' may well have referred to hand distribution while still on the ground.

War propaganda leaflets were first dropped from the air in May 1807, when Admiral Thomas Cochrane conducted a 'leaflet raid' on the coast of France. The leaflets, 'printed proclamations addressed to the French people', were tied in bundles and carried on the strings of kites flown from a ship in the Channel. Slow-burning fuses released the leaflets by stages and the wind carried them over enemy territory.

The first recorded balloon-drop in war took place in September 1870, during the siege of Paris, when printed propaganda material was scattered by balloonists as they soared out of the capital over the besieging Germans. These items included a bilingual proclamation signed by Bonvalet, mayor of the third arrondissement, and Victor Hugo's address *Aux Allemands*.

Aerial propaganda was first dropped from planes in the Italo-Turkish war of 1911–12 when leaflets printed by the Italians offered a reward to every enemy soldier who surrendered. In the same year French pilots dropped 'greetings leaflets' over Morocco, enjoining recipients to godly neighbourliness with their French friends.

Use of aerial leaflets in World War I began tentatively but later developed into a significant weapon of psychological warfare. In August 1914 a German monoplane piloted by Lieutenant Hiddessen dropped messages to Parisians calling on them to surrender, and leaflets improvised from message pads accompanied bombs dropped on Nancy in September during the attack on the Grand Couronne.

Britain's entry into the field was led by a purely personal enterprise of Major General Sir Ernest Swinton, who persuaded the Royal Flying Corps to deliver over the German trenches some 25,000 copies of a propaganda leaflet printed at his own expense. A second such operation was frustrated by the War Office, but by the early months of 1915 the idea had been adopted officially and pilots began to drop government leaflets in considerable number.

After German threats to kill captured pilots whose planes carried 'inflammatory' leaflets, the British resorted to balloon drops. British releases by unmanned balloons over the German lines in August 1918 totalled 100,000 per day. By October of the same year the monthly total was over 5 million. At one stage the German government offered money rewards for enemy leaflets handed in: thirty pfennigs for a copy of a leaflet already in official hands; three marks for an unrecorded 'new issue'. In all, during the period of the war British balloons dropped over 26 million printed papers behind enemy lines.

Aerial propaganda leaflets appeared in some strength in the Spanish Civil War (1936–39), both sides using planes, shells, and rockets for delivery, and in December 1938 Germany dropped leaflets by airship over the Sudentenland in the Czech Republic. World War II, in which the civilian was often as directly involved as the soldier, brought war leaflets aimed at those at home. Leaflets were dropped by the Germans in the attack on Warsaw in the first days of September 1939, and later there were drops over Poland by the Russians. Britain carried out numerous leaflet raids in the same period, scattering some 12 million leaflets over towns in north-west Germany.

The theme of warnings to civilians was taken up later in the war when Britain's bombing of German industrial targets was intensified. In September 1943 the British warned civilians in German industrial areas: 'It is our firm resolve to destroy the industries of the German war machine and we have the means to carry out this resolve. We will drive home our attack until all war production in Germany has ceased .... Only the unconditional surrender of the Hitler government can put an end to this process. So long as this unconditional surrender remains unachieved German industrial towns remain a theatre of war...'. The leaflet pointed out that a battlefield is no place for women and children and that employees in the war industries must be considered as soldiers in an army doomed to inescapable destruction: 'Soldiers in such a case may, without loss of honour, give up the fight. Whoever disregards this warning must take upon himself responsibility for the consequences...'.

In similar vein the Supreme Commander of the Allied Expeditionary forces warned the populace on the invasion of Europe in 1945 to take to the countryside: 'The vital target near you will be attacked incessantly.... Leave the danger zone, with your family, without delay *for several days*.... Leave immediately. You have not a moment to lose!'

To the soldier the pressure came in the form of a 'safe conduct': 'The German soldier who carries this safe conduct is using it as a sign of his genuine wish to give himself up. He is to be disarmed, to be well looked after, to receive food and medical attention as required, and is to be removed from the danger zone as soon as possible.' This legend, in English and German, overprinted on the insignia of the US and British governments, carried on the reverse an outline of the rights of a prisoner of war as laid down in the Geneva Convention. 'Passes' of this kind – more specifically invitations to surrender – were used in many theatres of war.

Less subtle were suggestions that shirkers behind the lines

were safe while heroes died at the front; that the heroes' leaders were cynically irresponsible; that privileged minorities at home were cashing in on shortages, evading rationing, seducing soldiers' wives and girlfriends.

Other gambits were instructions on how to simulate illness so as to be sent out of the war zone ('Better a few days' illness than be dead all your life'); atrocity pictures showing victims of 'saturation-bombing' raids; and comparison pictures showing, on one side of a leaflet, manufacturers' cartons of war medals and on the other endless vistas of military graves.

'Newspapers by air' formed a major item in the repertoire. By the war's end Britain was producing and air-dropping two daily newspapers, each with a circulation of over a million, and fourteen magazines in colour in addition to a daily output of 3 to 4 million two-colour leaflets. The US Office of Information's *Sternenbanner* [Stars and Stripes], also published from London, was at one time described as 'the German newspaper with the world's largest circulation – 4 million'.

Among a wide range of 'novelty' items, which included gifts to people in occupied countries (cigarettes, matches, soap, pencils, packets of tea and coffee, etc.) much use was made of the concept of the 'falling leaf' effect in which more or less realistic facsimiles of natural leaves, each bearing a message, are scattered. It is believed that the falling leaf, with its overtones of death and decline, has primordial psychological responses; its use as an air-dropped symbol of inevitability has been widespread.

Classic examples were the Germans' cut-out 'plane-tree leaves' printed in autumn colours and scattered over French troops in 1939. Their message, in French, was headed with the word 'Autumn'; it carried an image of a French-helmeted skull. The text read: 'The leaves fall. We fall as they do, the leaves die because God wills it. But we die because the English will it. Next spring, no-one will recall either the dead leaves or the fallen soldiers. Life will pass over our graves ...'. In 1941 the British scattered facsimile oak-leaves over Germany: 'In Russia, fallen leaves cover fallen soldiers ... and snow covers the leaves that cover the fallen soldiers'. In 1943, in response to the non-arrival of invasion forces after Churchill's promise of a second front 'before the leaves fall', Germany scattered autumn leaves in France: 'I have fallen, Oh Churchill. Where are you? Where are your soldiers?'

In 1956 real magnolia leaves, suitably conserved and over-printed with anti-communist slogans, were released on the wind by Formosan planes over the coast of China.

The aerial leaflet, with its many variants, has grown from an enterprising novelty in the 19th century to a major weapon of war. The Monroe 'leaflet bomb', America's specially developed air-delivery device, is said to have dropped nearly 500 million leaflets on Europe in World War II, and Britain's parachute device dropped some 80 million leaflets in the D-day and post-invasion period alone. American leaflet raids on Vietnam used an estimated '48 million billion' items.

Air-delivery of leaflets has commonly employed aircraft – balloon, airship, and plane – but leaflets have also been scattered by rocket, mortar shell, and rifle grenade. Small rockets and mortars were used by both sides in the Spanish Civil War, and Germany's V1 rockets carried leaflets as well as high explosives. The Germans fired single 'postcards' in rifle grenades in the 1944 fighting in France. The cards, directed to American soldiers, contained allegedly genuine personal messages from US prisoners of war advising friends still fighting to give up. Propaganda leaflets have also been dropped in wartime by aircraft over their own territory. In World War II patriotic fund-raising campaigns such as 'Salute the Soldier Week' and 'Wings for Victory' were reinforced by leaflets dropped over Britain by the RAF.

See also AIR-RAID PAPERS; CIVIL-DEFENCE PAPERS; FORGERY

REFERENCES *The Falling Leaf, Aerial Dropped Propaganda 1914–1968*, introduction by Reginald Aukland (Oxford: Museum of Modern Art, 1978); Max Kronstein, *Pioneer Airpost Flights of the World, 1830–1935* (Washington, DC: American Air-mail Society, 1978); James MacKay, *Airmails 1870–1970* (London: Batsford, 1971)

Agency certificate

The appointment of retail agents for the sale of branded products was marked in the mid 19th century in America by the use of manufacturers' certificates for display in shop premises. The certificates, chiefly of foolscap format, were printed forms in which details of the retailer's name, place of business, and date of appointment were entered by hand. The reverse commonly bore details of the arrangement between the manufacturer and retailer.

Chief among the considerations cited was the understanding that the retailer would sell the product as received from the manufacturer, leaving packaging, seals, containers, etc., unopened and contents intact. The arrangement was a novelty at the time, as previously it had been the general practice to sell unbranded products in quantity as required, wrapping papers – where these were considered necessary – being provided by the shopkeeper.

The new system, which was largely to replace handling, weighing, and packaging by the vendor, placed the onus of quality and quantity control on the manufacturer, whose name and reputation assumed increasing importance. Public display of the certificate (which also included a clause prohibiting the retailer from dealing in competitive products) conferred on the product, the supplier, and the retailer an air of distinction and promised the customer a product of consistently high quality. The certificate normally carried a decorative border and sometimes a woodcut illustration showing the manufacturer's premises. Also commonly featured was the manufacturer's signature, which often appeared on the package as well.

COLLECTIONS American Antiquarian Society, Worcester, Mass.; New York Historical Society

Agricultural/horticultural show card

Bestowal of certificates, diplomas, and other awards at county shows and fairs became general in the 19th century. The shows, derived from the traditional local fair and country market, were progressively formalized as regional annual events, in Britain sponsored by agricultural societies as part of an effort to combat the rural drift to the towns. The awards served to complement those of the 'Labourers' and Servants' Friends Societies', which rewarded the loyalty and industry of the worker and tenant, usually at about Christmas time (*see* SERVANT'S AWARD). Agricultural society prizes were given both in Britain and America for outstanding examples of farm produce and performance. Prizes were silver cups, purses, and certificates or diplomas. Entries were accepted in a wide range of categories. Typical awards are recorded on surviving certificates:

1845 Ploughman John Butcher awarded 2 pounds

(Arundel & Bramber Agricultural Association)

1871 'Best display of Fruit in County' Col. Thomas G. Kingsley Franklin: Diploma (New London County Agricultural Society Connecticut)

1876 'Six apples' E. Elton: First Prize Certificate (Andover Horticultural Society)

1903 'Butter, not less than three lbs in weight, made in dairies where no cow or heifer in milk or any Channel Island or Norman breed is kept' Mrs E. Gillett, Ashford, Castle Cary Commended Certificate (Frome District Agricultural Society)

Awards were not always confined to matters purely agricultural. In the New Hampshire Agricultural Society's show of 1853 some hundreds of categories included family needlework, millinery, blacksmithing, cooper's work, boots, shoes, and leatherware, farm buildings, harnesses, furniture, and paper, printing, and binding.

As with servants' awards, certificates appeared in many formats; they were printed lithographically or by letterpress and were often embellished by die stamping. They were commonly displayed at the show against the exhibits they referred to. Many were punched or eyeletted for hanging and many of the major awards were subsequently framed.

Agricultural shows also generated a minor industry in the manufacture of prize rosettes and neck cards for cattle, as well as a wide range of badges for committee members, judges, stewards, and other personnel.

COLLECTION Rural History Centre, The University of Reading

POSSIBLE AIR-CRAFT RAID OVER MAIDSTONE.

CAUTION.

IN the event of a Zeppelin or Aeroplane Raid, Maidstone must be immediately placed in total darkness.

Three Bombs will be fired from the Police Station at short intervals when the danger is imminent, and if at night the Electric Light supply will be cut off.

Inhabitants must immediately, if the raid is at night, take steps to turn out all gas and render their premises absolutely dark when viewed from outside, and should remove themselves to the basements and cellars wherever possible, and keep there till the raid is over.

Three more Bombs will be again fired when all danger from the raid is over.

Town Hall,
28th January, 1915.

W. H. MARTIN,
Mayor.

Vivian & Baker, General Printers, King Street, Maidstone.

First World War air-raid leaflet. Letterpress, printed by Vivian & Baker, Maidstone, January 1915. 280 × 216 mm (11 × 8½ in)

Air-raid papers

Civilian defence against air attack has been concerned primarily with five areas of activity: blackout; shelter and evacuation; casualty rescue and treatment; fire-fighting; and maintenance of essential services.

In World War I virtually the whole precautionary effort was focused on concealing the presence of targets by extinguishing lights. In Britain the matter was dealt with by various provisions of the 'Defence of the Realm' regulations, making the showing of light after sunset an offence in law. Posters, notices, and leaflets announcing lighting regulations appeared in Britain's major cities in the winter of 1914. They quoted the relevant portions of the Act requiring extinction of 'all sky signs and illuminated lettering ... lights along the waterfront', and 'the aggregation of flares in street markets', as well as reduction of lighting in trams and omnibuses to the minimum 'sufficient to enable fares to be collected'. The use of powerful lamps on motor and other vehicles was prohibited.

In the matter of shelter, formal provisions were minimal. Official advice was to take cover. No special provision was made for dealing with the air-raid casualties and for firefighting; public services were assumed to continue as in peacetime.

The ephemera of civil defence in World War I is thus limited. Apart from posters relating to blackout, relatively little survives. Air raids are referred to in theatre programmes: 'Arrangements have been made for warning of a threatened air raid to be communicated by the Military Authorities to this Theatre'...; a poster for the Stoll Picture Theatre asserts that in its stalls tearooms 1000 people may be accommodated under a three-foot flint-concrete roof ('one foot is considered bomb-proof... a veritable Gibraltar of safety...'). Remaining ephemera consists largely of a few printed notices ('During an air raid persons may take shelter in this building at their own risk') and numerous postcards showing Zeppelins in searchlights.

The threat of Zeppelin raids brought a wave of additional blackout announcements. The mayor of Maidstone published a printed notice in January 1915, warning that in the event of an air raid 'Maidstone must be immediately placed in total darkness', and to that end, 'the Electric Light supply will be cut off'. Hotels, restaurants, and other public places displayed their own warnings about unscreened lights, indicating that visitors themselves would be responsible for observing precautions and would be liable for any penalty imposed.

Lighting regulations in World War II were more stringent and more rigidly enforced. The national exercise of 9/10 August 1939, on the eve of the war, is embodied in leaflets put out by local authorities under a Home Office order and full instructions for the blacking-out of domestic premises appeared in 'Public Information Leaflet No 2', one of a series of air-raid precaution folders distributed by the Post Office.

World War II provision of air-raid shelters, public and domestic, was also a major concern. Distribution and installation of 'Anderson' (garden) shelters and later 'Morrison' (interior) shelters is recorded in numerous local authority leaflets and folders, giving details of their availability and advice on siting and assembly. Among many items relating to public air-raid shelters are posters urging their use and a wide variety of double-sided notices for display in public places, one side reading 'Air raid warning in operation', the other 'All clear'. One printed poster put out by the City of Westminster in October 1940 reflects something of the conditions of the time: 'Vaults have stood the test: the heavy bombing which has taken place recently in this area has proved the value of the vaults under the pavements as air raid shelters. Residents who are not making use of this excellent protection are strongly advised to do so in the interests of their own safety. Whenever houses have been damaged, look at the basements and then look at the vault'.

Other civil-defence ephemera recall the work of rescue, first-aid, ambulance, and hospital services. Posters announce rest-centre care and accommodation in school halls, community centres, and other buildings prior to rehousing. Evacuation of children was another major operation, also marked by printed advice. Families in safer areas were urged to play a part in taking in children, expectant mothers, the old and infirm ('caring for evacuees is a national service'), and townspeople were in turn pressed to send their children to the country: 'Let them go: give them a chance of greater safety and health'.

Widespread fire-bomb raids were met by the National Fire Service and by voluntary (later compulsory) civilian fire-watch duty. Posters, leaflets, handbooks, and large numbers of administrative forms, duty-rosters, and incident report sheets convey a record of nationwide effort.

Disruption of essential services – water, food supplies, gas, electricity, public transport, broadcasting, etc. – brought further printed paper to the record. Typical is a leaflet from London's Water Authority, September 1941: 'A supply of pure drinking water, sufficient to tide over a short emergency of, say, two or three days, should be kept ready for use if the supply to your premises is cut off by enemy action.... Should the enemy use mustard gas it might be present in water as oily globules which sink to the bottom. If this is seen the water should not be used for any purpose and the A.R.P. [Air Raid Precautions] authorities should be informed'. As with virtually every aspect of World War II, air-raid precautions generated an enormous volume of printed matter, some of it secret, most of it distributed to every family in the country.

See also AERIAL LEAFLET

REFERENCES Raynes Minns, *Bombers and Mash: The Domestic Front 1939–45* (London: Virago, 1980); Maurice Rickards and Michael Moody, *The First World War: Ephemera, Mementoes & Documents* (London, Jupiter, 1975)

COLLECTION Imperial War Museum, London

Air-sickness bag

Sickness bags, still a feature of commercial flying, are a poignant reminder of the pioneering days of the industry.

Early airline flights were subject to the turbulence of conditions below 10,000 feet, which was for a decade or so the maximum airliner flying height. This, coupled with non-pressurized passenger cabins and inadequate air conditioning, led to much air-sickness. The air-sickness bag was thus an operational necessity. The first bags were of plain moisture-proof brown paper, unlined, unprinted with designation or company identification, and had no method of closure. With the advent of pressurization and high-altitude flight, turbulence was reduced and bags were rarely used. Their quality was much improved, linings and fold-over closures were added, and front and back surfaces were used for promotional logos and other matter as well as for a discreet mention of the bag's purpose.

In the 1970s and 1980s bags were in some cases provided to airlines free of charge in exchange for the right to use them for publicity or promotional purposes. In one example, carried by Eastern Airlines in the early 1980s, the bag was used to despatch a roll of film to a laboratory for processing at special-offer rates. A cheque or money-order was enclosed with the film together with the customer's address, and the bag was secured by folding tags, addressed and stamped for mailing.

As with other airline promotional material (sugar sachets, napkins, etc.), air-sickness bags are often taken away as souvenirs – sometimes as containers for the smaller ephemera – and may sometimes be found in collections.

See also PAPER BAG

Air-transport label

This expression is used to refer to baggage labels, for air freight as well as for passenger baggage. It is also taken to cover tie-on tags and other forms of baggage-handling destination markers. In some cases it extends to promotional correspondence labels and lapel stickers.

Labels, stickers, and tags for airline baggage are seen primarily as publicity media. Early specimens echo the practice of the shipping lines, providing space for the passenger's name, destination, and date and place of departure. The shipping tradition is seen in a mid 1920s Imperial Airways label bearing the legend 'Wanted on voyage'. But the design treatment commonly favours the poster rather than the classic luggage label.

Airline labels began to appear in the early 1920s. Among the first recorded examples are, in Britain, the London-to-Paris stickers provided by Handley Page Transport, and in America those of the Curtiss Flying Service and the Robertson Aircraft Corporation. The earliest Australian examples include those of Western Australian Airways (1921) and the Queensland and Northern Territory Aerial Services Ltd (1922) (later Qantas).

Labels of the 1920s record a worldwide proliferation of companies, large and small. Many of these were short-lived, soon to be incorporated in larger groupings. One famous name among these was Daimler – 'Daimler Airway' – briefly operating in 1922 between London and Paris (later London and Amsterdam), and internally. The company, with Instone Airlines, Handley-Page, and British Marine Air Navigation was absorbed into a new company, Imperial Airways, in 1924. Of the Daimler label only a single copy appears to have survived.

The process of successive amalgamation and re-grouping continued after World War II. By the 1970s and 1980s the use of the publicity label was much reduced, the problem of baggage identification and routeing having become predominant.

Labels appear in a wide variety of shapes and sizes, printed commonly in two or three colours, at first (c.1924–50) on gummed paper, later as 'instant' press-on stickers.

Those from the pre-World War II period include specimens from the following companies: ABA (Sweden); Aer Lingus (Eire); Aeroflot (Poland); Aeroput (Yugoslavia); Air Union (France); Alpar Berne (Switzerland); American Airlines; Ansett Airways (Australia); ABA (Sweden); BOAC/British Overseas Airways Corporation; Chicago & Southern Airlines (US); Ceskoslovenské Státní Aerolinie (Czechoslovakia); CIDNA (France); Deutsche Luft Hansa (Germany); DDL/Det Danske Luftfartselskab (Denmark); Eastern Airlines (US); Imperial Airways (UK); Inter-Island Airways (Hawaii); KLM/Koninklijke Luchvaart Maatschappij (Holland); LAI/Lines Aeree Italiane (Italy); LOT/Polska Linja Lotnicza; MISR/Egyptian Airlines; New England Airways (Australia); Northwest Airlines (US); Pennsylvania Central Airlines; Qantas Empire Airways (Australia); SCADTA/ Sociedad Colombo-Alemania de Transportes Aereos; SHCA/ Société Hellenique de Communications Aériennes (Greece);

South African Airways; TWA/Transcontinental & Western Air Inc. (US); Union Airways (New Zealand).

Post-World War II labels include specimens from AA/Air Algérie; Aeroflot (USSR); Aeronaves de Mexico; Air Atlas Maroc; Air France; Alaska Airlines; Alitalia (Italy); Allegheny (US); Austrian Airlines; BAL/Bahamas Airways; BEA/ British European Airways; BIA/Brazilian International Airways; BOAC/British Overseas Airways Corporation; BWIA/British West Indian Airways; Canadian Pacific; Capital Airlines (US); Compañía Cubana de Avación (Cuba); Continental Airways (US); Cyprus Airways; Eagle Airways (Bermuda); El Al/Israel Airlines; Ethiopian Airlines; Finnair (Finland); Laker Airways (UK); Lufthansa (German Federal Republic); Mohawk (US); National Airlines (US); Pan-Am/Pan American World Airways (US); Piedmont Airlines (US); Scandinavian Airlines System; SABENA/Société Anonyme Belge d'Exploitation de la Navigation Aérienne (Belgium); TWA/Trans-World Airlines (US); United Air Lines (US); VARIG/Viaçâo Area Riograndense (Brazil); West Coast Airlines (US).

The air freight label, because of its restricted visibility, is commonly less promotional in its design, often confining itself to a nominal company identification and featuring factual handling details, dates, destinations, etc. Some bear only a single word or phrase: 'Personnel' or 'Live animals'. An early Imperial Airways label announces 'Passenger's luggage unaccompanied'.

A full listing of the world's label-issuing airlines past and present would run to many hundreds. In Britain alone the list numbers about 140. A provisional world estimate by the Aeronautica and Air Label Collectors Club in the mid 1980s exceeded 10,000. A complete catalogue of individual labels, with their modifications, variants, and updates, would be virtually impossible.

REFERENCES Martin & Aten, *Air Label Catalog* (Illinois: AALCC, reprint, 1977); *Airmail Magazine,* December 1943, January, March 1944, (Newport, Monmouthshire: Phillips); Donald W. Thomas, *Air Transport Label Catalog,* vols I–V, plus addenda (St. Elgin, Illinois: AALCC, 1975–85)

SOCIETY Aeronautica and Air Label Collectors Club

Album card

The 19th-century craze for scrapbooks led to an increasingly acquisitive search for suitable material for inclusion in their pages. With terms of reference that had never been wholly clear, the scrap collector viewed almost any oddment as eligible. A miscellany of press cuttings, engravings, mottoes, and verses was progressively leavened in the second half of the century by the all-dominating chromolithographed SCRAP. Additional ingredients from the 1870s to the 1890s were colour advertisements, at first cut from their context, and latterly, as commerce grasped the opportunity, the whole field of the chromolithographed TRADE CARD.

Also seizing the opportunity, the chromolithography industry itself (represented in the main by American firms such as J. H. Bufford, Kimmel and Forster, Major and Knapp, and L. Prang and Co.) printed 'album cards'.

These were sold in packaged sets of ten or a dozen. The cards showed birds, flowers, landscapes, mottoes, friendship verses, puzzles, etc., and were specifically designed for scrapbook use. They measured some 70 × 115 mm (2¾ × 4½ in), and were so popular that the Prang company offered albums to go with them – the 100-card size at $3.00, the 1000-card size at $18.00. The company also offered to supply albums ready filled.

See also CHROMO; SCRAPBOOK/ALBUM

REFERENCES Alistair Allen and Joan Haverstadt, *The History of Printed Scraps* (London: New Cavendish, 1983); Peter C. Marzio, *The Democratic Art: Chromolithography, 1840–1900* (Boston, Mass.: David R. Godine, 1979)

COLLECTION Bella C. Landauer Collection, New York Historical Society

Album frontispiece

Scrapbook fever in the 19th century led to the manufacture not only of the SCRAP and SCRAPBOOK/ALBUM but of decorative printed pages, often referred to as 'frontispieces', but widely used as title-pages for scrap albums. The term 'frontispiece' properly applies to a pictorial left-hand page facing a title-page, but the 'album frontispiece' was inserted more often than not on the right. True title-pages were also available. As with frontispieces, they were supplied as part of complete albums or available as separate sheets for insertion in existing albums.

The pictorial theme of the frontispiece was commonly the acquisition of scraps, often with a central figure, a tramp or a beggar girl, appealing to the reader for contributions in kind. Alternatively, the figure was shown scavenging for scraps of paper and stowing them in bag or basket. The tone of the illustrations, clearly conceived as self-mockery, was of romantic poverty. The message of the picture was often reinforced in words, either as an improvised notice appearing as part of the illustration or as a separate caption. Typical of these were 'I only want a few more', 'Scraps thankfully received', 'A thing of shreds and patches', and 'Pray give a trifle'. Some captions appeared to suggest a level of flirtation: 'Kind Sir, do bestow your charity!'; 'I hope you'll pay for peeping'.

Illustrations, as well as caption themes, were freely pirated.

SCRAPS
"A Snapper-up of unconsider'd Trifles."
Winter's Tale

Album frontispiece drawn by Edward Hull and published by Rowe & Walters, December 1824. Hand-coloured lithograph. Image with letters 192 × 135 mm (7⅝ × 5¼ in)

Reproduction was largely by colour lithography, though black and white versions were also available for hand colouring.

Printers and publishers were centred in London. They included many of the leading names in the 'fancy stationery' business, among them the following: R. Ackermann; Thomas Bird; W. Cooke; J. Dickinson; Engelmann, Graf, Coindet; S. & J. Fuller; O. Hodgson; C. Hullmandel; H. Lacey; J. McCormick; Edward Orme; E. Purcell; W. H. Rock; Rowe & Walters; J. Royle; William Spooner; Charles Tilt; and J. Tregear. The De La Rue Company, major manufacturers of the albums themselves, also published frontispieces, as well as true title-pages. Marcus Ward published frontispieces in Belfast, and in America a prominent imprint was that of A. Brett of Philadelphia.

REFERENCE Alistair Allen and Joan Hoverstadt, *The History of Printed Scraps* (London: Cavendish, 1983)

COLLECTION Madame Tussaud's, London

Almanac

The term 'almanac' commonly refers to an annual publication (book, pamphlet, or single sheet) containing a whole year's calendar details, astronomical data, and general information. With its roots in the ancient ecclesiastical calendar, and its stress on seasons, holidays, fairs, feast days, and saints' days, the popular almanac early acquired the role of prognosticator. It accurately forecast the rising and setting of sun and moon and the behaviour of the tides, predicted eclipses and other heavenly happenings, and it was soon forecasting much else. (We may note an alternative word for almanac – *ephemerides* – which indicates its concern with the *daily* changing positions of the stars.)

Almanacs first appeared in manuscript, but with the advent of printing they rapidly became a familiar feature in Europe in the 15th and 16th centuries. They were at first devised to cover lengthy periods (up to fifty years). The first single-year versions appeared only in the 16th century. The first printed almanac, *Pro Pluribus Annis* (Latin: For a number of years) was published in Vienna in 1457. Almanacs appeared in Nuremberg, Tübingen, Liège, Lille, Lyon, and Paris. Their wide circulation and popular influence was in some quarters viewed with alarm; in France in 1579 Henry III issued an edict forbidding the inclusion of political forecasts in almanacs.

The first almanac to make a major impact in Britain was the *Vox Stellarum* (Voice of the stars), published under the patronage of the Stationers' Company in 1697. (The Stationers, together with the universities of Oxford and Cambridge, enjoyed the exclusive right to publish almanacs in Britain. The monopoly was abolished in 1775.) *The Vox Stellarum* appeared under the editorship of one 'Francis Moore, Physician', a name which has continued to appear on subsequent issues, pirated or otherwise, into the 1980s. Britain's celebrated *Old Moore's Almanac*, published by Foulsham Ltd, claims direct descent from the original.

The first American almanac, *Almanack Calculated for New England*, was published in 1639 by William Pierce in Cambridge. Later titles include *The American Almanac and Repository of Useful Knowledge* (1828–61), and *The Old Farmer's Almanac*, founded by Robert Bradley Thomas in 1792 and still in publication from Dublin, New Hampshire under the 'Yankee' imprint. Best-known of American almanacs was Benjamin Franklin's *Poor Richard's Almanac* (1732–57). The wit and wisdom of Franklin's almanac became part of America's folk heritage.

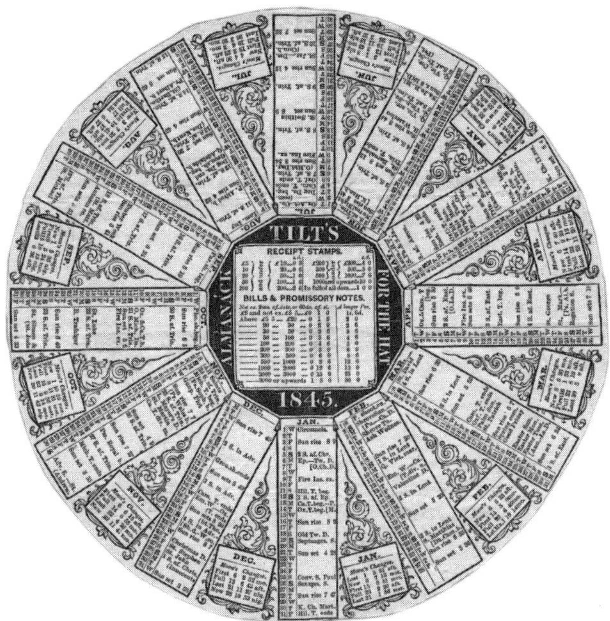

Tilt's 'Almanack for the hat', 1845. Letterpress, printed in blue. Diameter 180 mm (7⅛ in)

The British almanac duty, first imposed in 1711, dealt a heavy blow to the almanac trade, forcing the selling price to as much as two shillings and threepence by 1817. As with the newspaper duty, payment of almanac tax was recorded by means of a stamp printed directly on the paper of the almanac itself. Predictably, many hundreds of thousands of illegal unstamped versions appeared. In America, though tax plates were prepared for its imposition, the duty was never brought into effect. Together with the other provisions of the Stamp Act it was rejected at the Boston Tea Party (1773) and by the Declaration of Independence which followed. The duty was repealed in Britain in 1834.

Almanacs have appeared as single sheets and as booklets, but the more conveniently portable booklet has predominated, for centuries forming part of the stock-in-trade of the pedlar. Editorial formula and general layout have remained substantially unchanged, only the addition of a flourishing advertising section distinguished the almanac of the middle of the 18th century from that of its beginning.

Almanacs proliferated: by the 1850s and 1860s in both Britain and America the almanac had become the one universally received item of printed literature, the much-thumbed standby of cabin and cottage fireside. By now purveying medical information, general-knowledge snippets, jokes, anecdotes, cookery and gardening notes, household hints, postal information, and short stories, the almanac had become a major publishing operation and an important advertising medium.

Almanacs were published by printers, stationers, and local newspapers. With advertising space paid for by local traders, publishers could afford to distribute them free of charge.

From the 1850s to the 1870s the sheet almanac, published by commercial firms as promotional wallcharts, also had a wide vogue. One firm, White & Co. of the Borough, London, described its sheet as being 'issued gratis with the view to give respectable and increased publicity to their tea establishment'.

Less timid, particularly in America, were manufacturers of popular cures and tonics. As well as advertising in existing almanacs, in the 1840s they began printing and distributing their own, liberally interspersing household hints and anecdotes with information about their products. By the end of the century some companies were printing and distributing between 10 and 15 million copies a year. To cater for immigrant needs, many appeared in foreign languages. Ayer's almanac was printed in over twenty separate language editions.

In the United States, as in Britain, conservatism has been the keynote of the almanac. Continuing American features, virtually unchanged for generations, are listings of dates of State Court sittings; title-page mention of the number of the year of the Independence of the United States; early nineteenth-century seasonal woodcuts; and diagrams, dating back through *Vox Stellarum* to the 17th century, showing 'The Anatomy of Man's Body, as said to be governed by the twelve constellations'.

One feature, common to most American book almanacs but absent in the British, is a loop of string or wire in the top left-hand corner for hanging them up. Latter-day versions have a punched hole.

The spelling of the word 'almanac' has been less than consistent. It appears with a final 'ck' as a general rule in Britain from the mid 1600s to the end of the 19th century (though Boswell has it with a 'c' in the 1770s, and it appears with that spelling spasmodically throughout the period). The 'ck' began to disappear in the 1870s. In America the change to 'c' began in the 1780s, though here again usage was inconsistent. *The Maine Farmers' Almanac* of 1829 is at odds with *The Farmer's Almanack* of the same year, and the 1890s version of the latter title appears with a 'c' on the cover and 'ck' on its title page.

See also CALENDAR

REFERENCES Eustace F. Bosanquet, *English Printed Almanacks and Prognostications: A Bibliographical History to the Year 1600* (London: Bibliographical Society, 1917); John H. Chandler and H. Dagnell, *The Newspaper & Almanac Stamps of Great Britain & Ireland* (Saffron Walden: Great Britain Philatelic Publications, 1981)

COLLECTION American Antiquarian Society, Worcester, Mass.; Guildhall Library, London; Library of Congress, Washington, DC; Stationers' Company, Stationers' Hall, London;

Amateur journal

The designation 'amateur journal' is imprecise. It is commonly taken to refer to publications produced by teenage enthusiasts, generally for free distribution, often executed in manuscript, and in most cases in a very limited production run – even, sometimes, in only a single copy for passing from hand to hand.

The term is also applied to journals of a more ambitious kind, professionally printed (and possibly sold to the public), but devised, written, and edited by amateurs. In the second half of the 20th century, with the advent of popular reprographics, the concept of the *Samizdat* emerged. Here the minority-lobby publication, the protest sheet, and the 'underground' journal received general recognition. Also included under the heading 'amateur journal' are school magazines and kindred publications. (The house magazine, produced by commercial companies for their employees or customers, is not normally included.) For the most part, particularly in America, the term relates specifically to teenage publishing, often to a teenage readership.

The teenage journal had its greatest vogue in America in the period 1870 to 1900, when large numbers of titles appeared, some of them lasting a few years, others disappearing after only a few issues.

There had been a number of earlier American examples in the 18th century. Among these were a single-sheet school magazine, edited and handwritten by George Foster and Caspar Wistar at the Philadelphia Latin School in 1774, and the *Gentleman's Magazine* published later by 'Robinson' at the same school. Six further titles (together with a renewed effort in the 1880s) brought the school's total of handwritten publications to nine.

Further amateur journals appeared in America in the first years of the nineteenth century. The earliest recorded titles are 13-year-old John Howard Payne's *Thespian Mirror* (1805), and *The Spectator* (1820), devised and produced by another teenager, 16-year-old Nathaniel Hawthorne. In 1840 appeared *The Lowell Offering*, devised, edited, and written by the mill girls of the town of Lowell, Massachusetts: 'A Repository of Original Articles, Written exclusively by females Actively employed in the Mills'. According to Charles Dickens in his *American Notes* (1842), this printed journal 'will compare advantageously with a great many English Annuals'.

In the period 1852 to 1860 appeared Britain's *Strines Journal*, 'A Monthly Magazine of Literature, Science and Art', edited, written, and illustrated wholly by two young employees of the Strines Printing Co., Cheshire. Each issue of the journal was produced as a single hand-executed copy. It appeared monthly until 1856, and afterwards quarterly until 1860. Co-authors were John Gregory and Joel Wainwright. Their news stories (and Gregory's illustrations) covered events ranging from Christmas Festival Suppers to the Fall of Sebastopol.

In 1862 America saw the world's first newspaper to be printed on a train, also an amateur journal. Thomas Alva Edison, then a 15-year-old railway newsboy, bought a quantity of printers' type and a small press which he installed on his line. From this mobile office he produced and sold his *Grand Trunk Herald*, a journal for passengers and station loungers.

America's vogue for the printed amateur journal began in 1867 with the introduction of a 'home' printing press, specifically designed for use by teenagers. Amateur publications appeared in thousands across the country, in some areas preceding the commercial press.

Among Europe's best-known amateur journal in the early twentieth century was the *Wipers Times* [i.e. from Ypres], a magazine printed by British soldiers in the battle areas of World War I. This satirical journal, which used a miscellany of battered type and stock blocks, appeared irregularly and in limited runs. Amateur journals have also appeared in prisoner-of-war camps, in siege situations, and in civil prisons and criminal lunatic asylums.

See also PRINTING, 'PRIMITIVE'; 'ZINE

REFERENCE Almon Horton, *The Hobby of Amateur Journalism* (Manchester: The Author, 1955); Truman J. Spencer, *The History of Amateur Journalism* (New York: The Fossils Inc, 1947)

COLLECTIONS American Antiquarian Society, Worcester, Mass.; Imperial War Museum, London; New York Public Library

SOCIETY United American Amateur Press Association

Ambrotype label

An early form of photographic image, the ambrotype (1854–60), appeared as a positive image on glass as opposed to Daguerre's silver-plated copper. Though it was superseded in the photographic advances of the 1860s and 1870s, the process remained popular as a 'poor man's' likeness over a long period.

In America, where it had a special vogue, the ambrotype was sold in a metal case 50 × 60 mm (2 × 2⅜ in) resembling that of a

O. R. WILKINSON'S
PHOTOGRAPHIC
—AND—
Ambrotype Rooms,
MEDFORD, MASS.
Ambrotypes, Melainotypes, and Photographs, plain or colored, in all the various styles of the art. Paintings, Engravings, and Photographs, framed in any style desired, at the lowest prices.

Label for the Ambrotype rooms, Medford, Mass. Letterpress. 50 × 63 (2 × 2½in)

daguerreotype. At the back of the frame was inserted a printed card carrying the photographer's name, address, and promotional text. A number of the cards – some still in their original frames – have survived.

Unlike the later CARTE-DE-VISITE, whose text was commonly lithographed, ambrotype labels were printed in metal type by local jobbing printers; their layout and typographic treatment was as unpretentious as their wording. As with the carte-de-visite, however, the text reflects the technological and social background of the time:

> ...Children's likenesses inserted in lockets, breast pins or bracelets at very low prices...
>
> ...Boston Daguerreotype company... portraits 25 cents and upwards. 600 executed daily by the double camera – two at a pop...
>
> ...J White and Co's 25 cent daguerreotypes... this establishment has the best arranged light in the State. Up one flight of stairs only...
>
> ...Ambrotypes!... pictures taken as well in cloudy as in fair weather.
>
> ...Ambrotypes of sick or deceased persons taken at their residence...

American Civil War papers

The ephemera of the American Civil War may be divided into three areas. In the first are the military and operational papers of the armies in the field – orders, signals, passes, discharges, etc. In the second are items of public appeal and information – broadsides, proclamations, etc. In the third is a mass of peripheral material put out by private enterprise, including patriotic stationery, mementoes, sheet music, playing cards, and other war-theme novelties.

Military and operational. A full listing of categories in this area is impossible. The paperwork of warfare, even in the 1860s, was already extending widely into the civil and industrial section; the field includes not only the papers of military administration but of materials requisition and control; production of weapons, munitions, uniforms, and equipment; food and medical supplies; railway working; butler's operations; and countless other areas of service and support.

Most commonly found are part-printed documents of central discipline – oaths of allegiance, officer's warrants and commissions, discharge certificates, etc. – personal relics of those whose names they bear. Also not uncommon is the military pass, filled in with the bearer's name, and allowing access to special areas. The pass was in widespread use, not only for guards and pickets but for barrack visitors and front-line news reporters (*see* PASS/PERMIT).

Printed camp regulations are also found, referring to specific military establishments and their personnel. One such listing for Camp Defiance at Cairo, Illinois, is in the collection of the Chicago Historical Society. Among other regulations it stipulates: 'After 8pm, no loud singing, no cheering or firing arms... nor any firing or cheering on the Sabbath'.

Medical items include field-hospital admission and discharge chits, patients' property check-lists, and surgeons' pharmaceutical bottle and box labels. Cartridge and powder labels are also found. Among miscellaneous Civil War papers are items at the fringe of the military and operational area. The Rickards Collection has a quartermaster's stores receipt for February 1864; it records a delivery to Quartermaster Captain George B. Cadwallader, Nashville, Tennessee, of forty-six mules and twenty-two horses. In a column headed 'Condition when delivered' appears the word 'unserviceable'.

Public appeal and information. The course of the Civil War was marked by the appearance on both sides of posters, most of them calling for support, some celebrating successes, rumoured or confirmed. Others, in the form of ordinances or proclamations, announced measures of control and punishment. Many of these have since been reproduced as historical mementoes; they feature widely as illustrations in historical surveys and are among the most familiar of Civil War images.

Typical are those bearing such headlines as 'Our country calls; rally to her support!' (New York, 1861); 'Freemen of Tennessee! To arms!' (Tennessee, 1861); 'Men of Virginia: to the rescue!' (Staunton, Virginia, 1861); 'War meeting! On to the rescue!! Kingsville!' (Ohio, 1862); 'By His Excellency... a proclamation: citizens of Connecticut: you are again called upon to rally to the support of our government...' (New Haven, Connecticut, 1862); 'Mulligan's Brigade! Last chance to avoid the draft... $402 bounty!' (Chicago, 1863); 'The enemy is approaching!: defence of the State!' (Philadelphia, Pennsylvania, 1863); 'Freedom to slaves! Whereas the County of Frederick is included in the territory designated by the proclamation of the President in which the slaves should become free ... I therefore, hereby notify ... of my intention to maintain and enforce the same ... R. H. Milroy, Brig. Gen'l Commanding' (Winchester, Virginia, 1863); '2000 army horses wanted!' (Madison, Wisconsin, 1865); 'Surrender of Gen Lee!: the year of jubilee has come! Let all the people rejoice!' (Appomattox, 1865).

Also of significance are posters for the presidential campaign of 1864, at which Lincoln was re-elected.

Among the last of the posters of the Civil War period are the reward notices put out on Lincoln's assassination, barely a fortnight before the war's end. These too have been widely reproduced and are part of America's corpus of national memorabilia.

Other war-related items are 'extra' bills put out by Southern newspapers in 1860 announcing withdrawal from the Union ('The Union is dissolved!') and a proclamation published by the Governor of Virginia in November 1859 before the execution of the anti-slavery campaigner John Brown. This was designed to prevent demonstrations at the execution: '... from now until after Friday next [2 December, the day of the execution] ... strangers found within the County of Jefferson and counties adjacent, having no known and proper business here, and who cannot give a satisfactory account of themselves, will be at once arrested'.

Private and commercial. The Civil War was fought by an industrialized Union and a more or less agricultural Confederacy. In the matter of productivity the advantage lay from the start with the Union, and it is not surprising that both in range and quantity surviving Civil War ephemera favours the North. The Southern states were hard-pressed for essential war supplies, and even the printing of Confederate banknotes, share certificates, and postage stamps presented problems. (Two Confederate postage-stamp issues were in fact printed in London by De La Rue – one of these being intercepted by the North's blockade and ultimately pulped.)

Best-known of the memorabilia of the Civil War is the 'patriotic envelope', a craze which swept the country on both sides of the battle-front. Printed commonly in two or three colours, the envelopes carried pictorial decorations showing battle scenes, war celebrities, flags, etc. 'Patriotic' lettersheets also appeared, either as individual items or as matching pieces to go with envelopes. Foremost in the field were printers Charles Magnus of New York and John L. Magee of Philadelphia, but the concept was exploited by innumerable printers both in letterpress and lithography.

In the South, because of shortages, printed envelopes gave way to home-made concoctions of wallpaper, wrapping paper, maps, military orders, and ledger paper. 'Turned covers' also appeared, used envelopes being turned inside out for re-use.

A further prolific field of Civil War ephemera is sheet music. Here again, both sides made use of the medium, commonly with rousing martial airs and anthems. Typical titles are 'General Burnside's Grand March' (J. Church Jr, Cincinnati); 'Our National Confederate Anthem: God Save the South' (C. T. de Coëniél, Richmond, Virginia), and 'Dixie for the Union' (Firth, Pond & Co, New York). Also popular were illustrated ballad sheets, designed for inclusion in soldiers' mail. Many hundreds of different patriotic subjects appeared, most of them produced as sidelines by the printers of patriotic stationery.

Civil War ballad sheets were also published in their own right as part of the prolific output of the 'fancy job printers' of the period c.1840 to 1890. These single-sheet productions had first appeared as popular 'poems' in the 18th century, notably as celebrations of the defeat of the British. They extended their

American Civil War pictorial envelope. Letterpress, printed in red and blue. 77 × 138 mm (3 × 5½ in)

coverage to current events in general and, as in Britain, to scandal and satire. In the Civil War period the tone was patriotic and sentimental. Typical titles are: 'The Soldier's Farewell to Home' and 'Songs For The Crisis – The Conflict, The Prospect'. Prominent among publishers were Thomas M. Scroggy of Philadelphia, and Richard Thayer of Boston. The sheets were commonly some 240 × 150 mm (9½ × 6 in).

Scholars' REWARD OF MERIT cards, already well established as educational incentives, were also produced in patriotic guise. Battle scenes replaced the formerly peaceable images, though decorative frames remained as tradition required.

PLAYING CARDS too appeared as propaganda on both sides (the British firm of Goodall produced a Confederate pack in 1862). Popular prints also lent their weight to the conflict. James Queen, one of America's greatest chromolithographers, produced some of his most accomplished work in the Civil War period. His set-piece 'The Volunteers in Defence of the Government Against Usurpation' (1861) is a classic of the genre.

The period saw a popularization of numerous forms of ephemera, and in virtually each case the Civil War imposed its mark. Among a wide range of minor novelties are such items as bookmarks, 'hidden-name' calling cards, and valentines. Also bearing witness to the war are stereographs, ambrotypes, and ferrotypes ('tintype').

REFERENCES Andrea Dinoto (ed.), 'Civil War Equipment', *Encyclopedia of Collectibles* (Alexandria, VA: Time Life, 1978); Lester S. Levy, *Picture the Songs: Lithographs from the Sheet Music of nineteenth-century America* (Baltimore and London: Johns Hopkins UP, 1976); Francis A. Lord, *Civil War Collector's Encyclopedia* (Secaucus, NJ: Castle Books, 1977); Peter C. Marzio, *The Democratic Art: Chromolithography 1840–1900* (Boston, Mass.: David R. Godine, 1979); Lou W. McCulloch, *Paper Americana* (San Diego: A. S. Barnes, 1980); William Frost Mobley, *American Nineteenth-Century Historical and Advertising Broadsides ...* (catalogue 1, Wilbraham, Mass.: The Author, 1980)

American seaman's certificate

Britain's laws for the forcible recruitment of men for the armed forces ('impressment'), together with her assumption of the right to stop and search neutral shipping in time of war, brought Britain and America into serious conflict after the American Revolution, during the Napoleonic Wars, and on occasion during the American Civil War.

In the period 1790 to 1815 some 20,000 British seamen deserted to American ships. When challenged by British boarding parties they claimed to be American, but were nevertheless seized, together with numbers of genuine American seamen. It was estimated that of 10,000 men forcibly removed from American ships by the British between 1790 and 1815 only about 1000 were actually British subjects. Wholesale 'impressment' from American vessels led the United States authorities to provide their seamen with certificates, signed and sealed by the Collector (or Customs Inspector) of the seaman's port of departure.

Wording of the part-printed certificate was specified in 'An Act for the Protection and Relief of American Seamen' (1792). The text remained unchanged for decades. A typical example, measuring 170 × 205 mm (6¾ × 8 in), dated 5 December 1796, reads: 'United States of America: I (Dudley A Byng) Collector of the District of Newburyport, do hereby certify That (Seth Woodbury) an American Seaman, aged (twenty two) years, or thereabouts, of the height of (five) feet (five) inches (and one half, having a dark complexion freckled, fair short hair and

E PLURIBUS UNUM

I, JAMES S. WHITNEY, Collector of the District of Boston and Charlestown, do hereby certify that David Hollingsworth an American Seaman, aged Nineteen years, or thereabouts, of the height Five feet, six 1/2 inches, dark complexion, brown hair, hazel eyes, born in Woodstock in the State of Connecticut has this day produced to me proof in the manner directed by the Act, entitled "An Act for the relief and protection of American Seamen," and pursuant to the said Act, I do hereby certify that the said D. H. Hollingworth is a Citizen of the United States of America.

In Witness Whereof, I have hereunto set my Hand and Seal of Office, this 2d day of July in the year of our Lord, 1860.

James S. Whitney Collector.

American seaman's certificate, Boston and Charlestown, 1860. Letterpress with manuscript and embossed stamp. 265 × 198 mm (10½ × 7⅞ in)

haizle coloured eyes) has this day produced to me proof in the manner dircted in the act… and … I do hereby certify, that the said (Seth Woodbury) is a citizen of the United States of America…. in witness whereof, I have hereunto set my hand and seal …' and so on.

The certificates, often referred to as 'protections', were largely ignored by the British who claimed, not without truth, that they were freely bought, sold, and borrowed by American seamen.

Amusement sheet

Among home entertainments in the mid 19th century was the children's broadside, a single printed sheet bearing puzzles, games and other pastimes for family use. Notable among these was a sheet headed 'Nuts to crack', a publication put out by Robert Macdonald of Clerkenwell, London, subtitled 'Enigmatical Repository – containing near 200 hieroglyphics, enigmas, conundrums, curious puzzles, and other ingenious devices'.

The Macdonald sheet, measuring 505 × 355 mm (20 × 14 in), was illustrated with some fifty or sixty woodcuts. Sold for one penny, it appeared in a series of twenty-four different issues – without, however, disclosing answers to problems. These were available in 'The Nutcrackers', a companion series from the same publisher, which reprinted questions and provided their answers on the same sheet, also at one penny per sheet. In competition with Macdonald's sheet (if not in direct imitation of it) was Thomas Goode's 'American Nuts and Crackers', also issued as a series at one penny per sheet, somewhat larger than the Macdonald version at 570 × 450 mm (22½ × 17¾ in). This bore the subtitle 'Containing nearly 200 Conundrums, Enigmas, Puzzles &c &c with the answers'. Answers appeared at the foot of the sheet under the heading 'Nut Crackers'.

Also put out by Goode was an outsize sheet of 'Winter Evening Amusements'. This print, measuring 870 × 560 mm (34¼ × 22 in), presented similar material in a broadside twice as large as the others. It is not known whether it ran to more than a single issue. A surviving specimen in the John Johnson Collection bears neither series number nor selling price.

See also PUZZLE

COLLECTION John Johnson Collection, Bodleian Library, Oxford

Anamorphic image

The production of distorted images, restored to intelligibility by oblique viewing or by other optical means, was popular at various periods in the 18th and 19th centuries. The trick is an old one, and appears as a conceit in a number of paintings of the 15th and 16th centuries. Best known is the example in Hans Holbein's 'The Ambassadors' (1533), in which an elongated streak in the lower portion of a double portrait appears, on oblique inspection, as a skull.

Anamorphic pictures (Greek, *anamorphosis*: transformation), also known as 'metamorphoes' or 'polyoptic pictures', emerged in Europe in printed form in the 19th century. In one example a series of twelve humorous hand-coloured engravings appear at first sight as semicircular smears. Their mystery is solved by the use of a vertical reflecting cylinder placed at the centre point of their circumference to correct their distortion.

Semicircular prints were popular, sometimes disguising satirical, dissident, or pornographic subjects. Distortions also appeared as simple elongations, though their subjects were on the whole fairly readily discernible. An example measuring 572 × 216 mm (22½ × 8½ in) published by Richard Bankes in London and entitled 'The Horizontorium' carries a hand-coloured engraving showing a landscape with castle – clearly visible even without oblique viewing. Less readily distinguishable is a 'George and Dragon' set-piece published by R. H. Laurie, also in London, in 1821. Here the viewer is informed that the scene has been 'drawn in opticks' and there are directions to 'place the letter A [in the instruction] close to the eye and look on it as you fire a piece at a mark'.

The anamorphic image had a further minor vogue in printed ephemera at the end of the 19th century, when it was used as a novelty in the presentation of advertising messages and in puzzle cards. Here the letters of the legend were so attenuated as to be illegible by direct vision. Oblique viewing revealed the message. The trick was further complicated by multiple 'cross-writing', which required successive views from separate viewpoints.

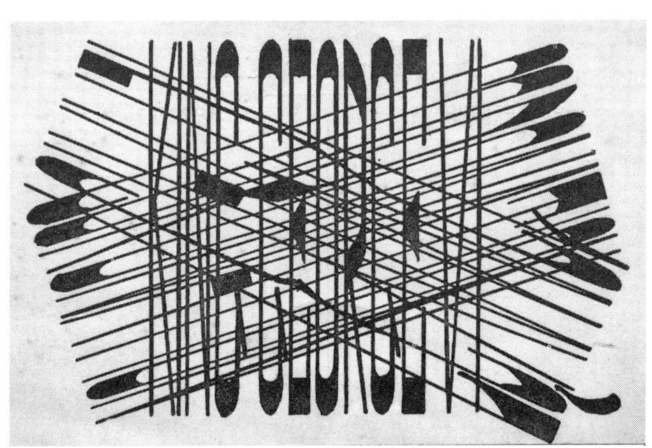

Anamorphic card, which reads 'King George VI', 'Coronation', '12 May 1937'. Relief printed. 89 × 139 mm (3½ × 5½ in)

REFERENCE *The Magic Mirror or Wonderful Transformations* (New York: McLoughlin Brothers, nd; re-published New York: Dover, 1979)

COLLECTION Museum of the City of New York

Anonymous letter

The anonymous letter may be concerned with blackmail, physical threats, obscenity, or disclosures of private information for the public good. Documents in these categories rarely survive. Of the few that do, the 'public good' type are the most common. Examples may occasionally be found as apparently unrelated items among miscellaneous papers, sometimes filed with long-discarded records. (Their retention in these cases suggests that not all such letters are destroyed out of hand, and that recipients' responses, in annotations or appended memoranda, sometimes indicate positive action.)

Working conditions in the 19th century were a common subject of 'public good' letters. Commissioners of sewers, inspectors of factories, and medical officers of health were frequent recipients of notes, often from outside observers, or from workers themselves. Increasingly stringent legislation, both for industry and everyday business, brought growing numbers of infractions – and consequently 'disclosures'. Local authorities, professional bodies, trade associations, church leaders, as well as newspapers and magazines, received a steady trickle of letters signed 'Pro bono publico', 'A hater of injustice', 'Ratepayer', etc. A typical example, addressed to 'The Vestry of St Saviour's' (July 1889), complains that dairymen are being unfairly undersold by itinerant milk-sellers who 'cry their rubbish about the streets unfettered by the rules of hygiene imposed on honest dairymen, and taking the bread out of the mouths of struggling ratepayers'. In a markedly different vein is a letter of 1911 to the Royal Pharmaceutical Society signed 'Pharmacist'. It draws attention to a chemist's shop in Hanley, Staffordshire, where two unqualified people, whom the letter names, 'are selling poisons freely'. The anonymous informant concludes: 'Ought it not to be stopped?'

Apart from its well-recognized role as 'poison pen' mischief-maker, the anonymous letter has played a significant part in many areas of social and political history. Britain's 'Captain Swing', pseudonymous – and possibly mythical – writer of threatening letters in the rick-burning disturbances of the 1830s, is among the best known signatories. Less celebrated is the equally elusive 'General Ludd' or 'Ned Ludd', whose threatening letters similarly preceded machine-breaking and unrest in the Luddite period thirty years earlier. Some observers believed 'Ludd' and 'Swing' to be the same person, others that neither character really existed; certainly a multiplicity of literary styles and handwriting point to more than a single author.

A number of 'Ludd' and 'Swing' letters are to be found among Home Office papers and the archives of the Public Record Office, but it is by no means certain that there are not others awaiting discovery elsewhere. Though normally undated and bearing no sender's address, they show a variety of hands, with signatures in differing styles. However, their provenance and context are readily recognizable. A typical 'Swing' letter reads:

> This is to inform you what you have to undergo. Gentlemen if providing you dont pull down your NESHENES and rise the poor mens wages the married men give tow and six pence a day ... the singel tow shillings. Or we will burn down your barns and you in them this is the last notis.

In another context altogether is a slip of paper bearing a cyclostyled typewritten message, circulated in Paris early in the German occupation of World War II. It reads, 'Urgent and for reproduction. Jews of all nationalities, you are threatened from March 23 with arrest and deportation'. It is signed, 'The Socialist Party'.

The anonymous letter or note is certainly no less valid an item of social-history record than other categories of ephemera. It may be expected to attract increasing attention as a productive field of study.

REFERENCE E. Royston Pike, *Human documents of the Victorian Golden Age (1850–1875)* (London: Allen & Unwin, 1967)

Appointment card

Still in use by dentists and others in the late 20th century, the appointment card emerged in the early 19th century as a modified trade or business card, engaging the persons concerned to a date and time as entered by hand in spaces provided. The card was often decoratively engraved, showing premises, stock in trade, or heraldic devices, but by the end of the century it had become a purely typographic item.

See also DENTAL PAPERS

AQ letter sheet

The AQ sheet relates to a tax imposed by the Collegio alle Acque of the Republic of Venice in 1595, and confirmed and extended by laws of 26 June 1604 and 12 November 1608. It bears the winged lion of St Mark and the letters AQ (Italian, *acque* – in early Italian *aque:* waters), and measures some 200 × 300 mm (7⅞ × 11⅞ in). The letters AQ were also inscribed on stones that defined the limits of Venetian waters. The tax was levied to finance work on local rivers, and took the form of a surcharge of 4 soldi on the cost of posting a letter by the official service of the Republic. The sheet also bore a declaration of the statute under which the system operated, specifying the classes of correspondence it covered. Failure to observe the statute incurred a penalty of 100 ducats. The statute remained in force until the end of 1797. The sheets provide an early example of printed sequential numbering, individual digits being changed by hand between each impression.

REFERENCE David Lidman, *Treasury of Stamps* (New York: Abrams, 1976)

Armed forces papers

In peace or war, the paperwork generated by the military is multifarious. A fully comprehensive survey cannot be attempted, but the mass may be reviewed in more or less generalized functional divisions. These relate to: (1) Raising troops; (2) Orders, messages, signals, etc.; (3) Supplies, transportation, etc.; (4) Health, medical, etc.; (5) Training and proficiency; (6) Returns and records; (7) Crime and punishment; (8) Communication with civilian population; (9) Provision of pensions etc.; (10) Service etiquette and ceremonial. Among the many categories embraced by these divisions, the part-printed FORM is prominent.

(1) Raising troops. The raising of men for military service has been effected by means ranging from bland invitation to physical abduction. The method has varied according to the pressure of events, and the tides of economic, political, and military change have left a complex pattern of recruiting history.

The pattern is reflected in a wide range of ephemera. Orders, proclamations, posters, certificates, and other papers reflect every shade of imperative. One item, open-ended in its implications, is a printed order from the Court of St James's in January 1778. It authorized the recipient, 'Our Right Trusty and Right Well-Beloved Cousin, Kenneth, Earl of Seaforth', to raise men for a Highland Regiment of Foot 'By beat of drum or otherwise'. The expression 'beat of drum' referred to the classic use of a drummer to attract attention to the public persuasions of the recruiting officer (*see* PROCLAMATION). The words 'or otherwise' may be taken to admit of wide interpretation.

Less draconian in tone, from October 1915, is a printed facsimile letter from the 17th Earl of Derby, Britain's Director General of Recruiting, addressing the nation's unlisted men: 'The parliamentary recruiting committee ... are organising a great recruiting campaign to induce men who can be spared to come forward voluntarily for service in the army.... Will you not be one of those who respond to your country's call?'

In November 1917 an Order of Induction into Military service of the United States concluded its instructions as to place and date of induction with direct simplicity: 'From and after the day and hour just named you will be a soldier in the military service of the United States'.

Among the earliest forms of recruitment was impressment. This was a system of 'man-catching', in which groups of servicemen – 'press gangs' – were charged with the task of trapping and forcibly delivering civilians for enlistment in the Army or Navy. The method was widely used, both in Britain and in France and Germany, for centuries. Cromwell's New Model Army was raised largely by impressment, and Britain's impressment of seamen, both British and American, from American ships in the early years of the 19th century was one of the causes of the War of 1812 (*see* AMERICAN SEAMAN'S CERTIFICATE). The principle of forcible enlistment had also been used by the Americans in the War of Independence (1775) and again during the tension with Britain in 1807.

The term 'impressment' was also used to apply to forcible acquisition of vehicles and other property, and requisition of premises for lodging, etc. (The word 'billet', in the sense of soldiers' lodging, derives from the Anglo-Norman *billette*, a short document, the paper or ticket presented to the householder as a military order.)

Impressment ephemera are not common. Chief among surviving items are orders for impressment ('Impress warrants'); 'Press tickets', carried by press-gang members as authorization; proclamations announcing terms of reward for successful impressments: 'Three Pounds for every Able Seaman ... fit to serve on board Our Ships' (London, 1805); certificates of 'Discovery', attesting details of 'Name or Names and Number and Quality of Seaman procured' (London, 1805); and documents of exemption carried by those classes of men – certain apprentices, fishermen, and others – legally protected from impressment.

Closely allied to the concept of impressment is the drawing up of lists of communities, individuals, or vehicles committed to service of the military in time of need. Thus, for example, in 1797 a handwritten foolscap document from Pitnacree, Scotland: 'We the Proprietor and Tennants of Pitnacree make offer to Government (free of any Expense) of our Carts and Horses, that is one Double Cart and Driver... in case of invasion to Convey Troops with their arms and Baggage Twenty miles through our district when ever required so to do ...'.

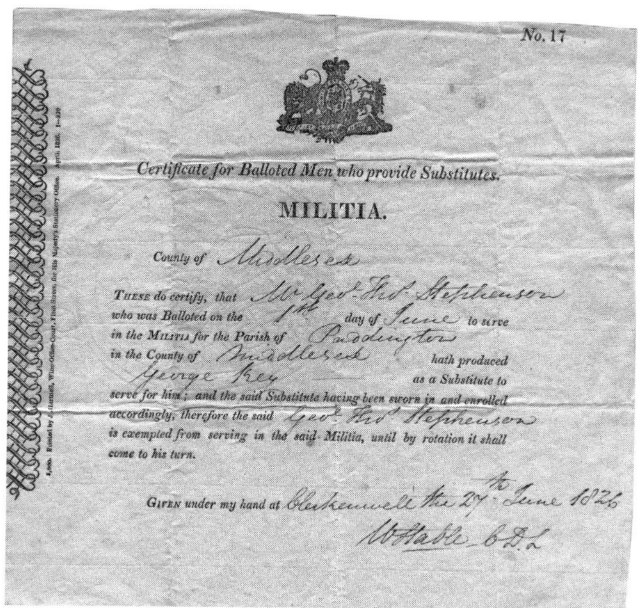
No. 17

Certificate for Balloted Men who provide Substitutes.

MILITIA.

County of Middlesex

These do certify, that Mr Geo. Thos. Stephenson *who was Balloted on the* 1st *day of* June *to serve in the Militia for the Parish of* Paddington *in the County of* Middlesex *hath produced* George Key *as a Substitute to serve for him; and the said Substitute having been sworn in and enrolled accordingly, therefore the said* Geo. Thos. Stephenson *is exempted from serving in the said Militia, until by rotation it shall come to his turn.*

Given under my hand at Clerkenwell the 27th June 1826

Militia certificate for balloted men who provide substitutes. Signed at Clerkenwell, London, June 1826. Letterpress and manuscript. 183 × 207 mm (7¼ × 8⅛ in)

From the same period, an undertaking from the Pitlochry area offers the armed services of sixty citizens for the defence of the country, 'the condition of our offer being that we are only to serve within the district of the Deputy Lieutenant where we reside, on the Shire of Perth, Except in the case of actual Invasion, or the actual appearance of an Enemy on the coast, in which event to serve within the limits of the Military District to which we belong...'.

A further form of limited commitment was service in the Militia. The term 'Militia', defined variously from one period to another, commonly refers to forces enlisted for local defence for short terms of service. Though a paid force, the Militia is seen, in general terms, as a non-professional body, supporting – but distinct from – the regular army. Historically, service in the Militia has been compulsory, often by ballot (though exemption has been available by substitution on payment of a 'penalty'). The system may be said to be the forerunner of conscription.

Surviving ephemera of the Militia reflects the profusion of documentation it engendered and the impact of the system on ordinary lives in the 18th and 19th centuries. Papers include proclamations, orders, returns, oaths, warrants of arrest for non-compliance, certificates of exemption, substitution or penalty payments, orders of maintenance for Militia men's or substitutes' dependants, and a wide range of ancillary forms and manuscript notes and declarations.

The printed form is dominant. One such item (c.1829) provides space for the recruit's oath of identity and fitness: '... I have no rupture, nor ever was troubled with fits, and am nowise disabled by lameness, or otherwise, but have the perfect use of my limbs'; and for a passport-style description: 'Height; Complexion; Hair; Eyes; Pitted with Small Pox ...'. Others of the same period convey the news of the recipient's fate: 'I do hereby give you ... notice, that you are chosen by Ballot to serve in the Militia of the County'. There are also forms recording the enrolment of substitutes, and payment of money in lieu of service: 'Received ... the Sum of Fifteen Pounds Sterling, as a Penalty for not Serving, in consideration of which he is relieved from any future Ballot'. Among items less commonly found is a form directed to 'The Parochial Schoolmaster' (Scotland, c.1831) on which a record is required of his services in the distribution of Militia documents to householders. The schoolmaster's visits are to be recorded and details are to be shown of hours employed and miles travelled. Also to be recorded are name listing ('Two Copies') and attendance at Meetings of Lords Lieutenants, through whose office the Militia Service was administered.

Parallel with the Militia concept – and at times even in competition with it – has been the 'Volunteer' system. In Britain the idea originated in the middle of the 18th century as an adapted form of the Militia, allowing voluntary enlistment of Militia men as opposed to compulsory service by ballot. The Militia and Volunteers became two distinct organizational concepts, though at some periods there was a blurring of definition. There was also at times a whole or partial transfer of services, together with arms and equipment, from one body to another. A hundred years later, in the Volunteer Act of 1863, the terms of volunteer service were changed to permit call-out in the event of expected invasion instead of, as formerly, on the sighting of the enemy at the coast.

Volunteer ephemera, like that of the Militia, reflect not only minutiae of organization and control, but the occasions of mustering and deployment. A printed notice put out by the committee of the Shilland Volunteers, Chesterfield, conveys the mood of defiance elicited by the threat of French invasion. Dated 18 August 1803, the announcement resolves that 'the names of the Loyal Shilland Volunteers who have enrolled themselves to stand forward in defence of their King and Country, at this important and dangerous crisis, be engrossed on vellum ... framed and glazed ... and put up in the Church!' In similarly excited vein, the notice continues with the intimation that names of female subscribers to a war fund will likewise be displayed 'so that these patriotic examples may be transmitted not only to the rising generation but to ... posterity!'

The volunteer spirit is also seen in other contexts. A printed appeal in the Anglo-American War of 1812–14 calls on Kentuckians in the fight against the British. The signatory, Isaac Shelby, the State's first Governor, declares (31 July 1813): 'I have appointed the 31st Day of August next, at Newport, for a general rendezvous of Kentucky Volunteers. I will meet you there in person. I will lead you to the field of battle, and share with you the dangers and honors of the campaign ... now is the time to act; and by one decisive blow, put an end to the contest...'.

In both the United States and Great Britain, military history provides numerous other examples of 'support' bodies called into being to provide or augment forces in times of special need. Among these, in the United States, have been the Organized Reserve Corps and the National Guard (formerly the Militia), and in Britain the Territorial Army (formerly the Territorial Force) and the Home Guard (originally Local Defence Volunteers). Of these bodies, as of Britain's Special Constabulary, the 'Second Police Reserve', The Volunteer Defence Corps, and other such forces, ephemera provide a kaleidoscopic corpus of evidence. Notable among the mass of material, and casting an unusual light on the subject of the Special Constabulary, is a broadside issued by the Registrar of the Royal Hospital, Chelsea, 29 November 1830. Printed in black on a sheet measuring 720 × 480mm (28⅜ × 19in), the message is addressed to 'Out-Pensioners and Registered Men' of the hospital, giving notice that they are 'required and commanded, whenever they may be called upon ... to render their Services as Special constables ... for the purpose of aiding in the preservation of the Public Peace wherever they may be required'.

Compulsion has played a major part in the raising of troops, both in impressment and in conscription, but it must be said that the 'volunteer' appeal has also been much to the fore. The first recruiting posters began to appear in the 18th century, mostly as single-colour typeset broadsides, but in Europe pictorial designs are also found – some, even at that early date – in colour. Among the earliest is an illustrated appeal for recruits to the Duke of Orleans' Regiment of Dragoons. A footline expresses a convention that was to become universally recognized: 'Those who bring good men will be rewarded'. ('Bringing money' or, more formally, 'a small pecuniary reward' was being paid to recruitment agencies by the British Army into the 1930s.)

The recruiting broadside resorted early to colourful copywriting. Typical of the genre in 1776 was Sir William Howe's call for recruits to his First Battalion of the Pennsylvania Loyalists:

> All intrepid Able-Bodied Heroes, Who are willing to serve His Majesty King George the Third in Defence of their Country, Laws and Constitution, against the arbitrary Usurpations of a tyrannical Congress, have now not only an opportunity of manifesting their Spirit, by assisting in reducing to obedience their too-long deluded Countrymen, but also of acquiring the polite Accomplishments of a Soldier, by serving only two Years, or during the present Rebellion in America. Such spirited Fellows, who are willing to engage, will be rewarded at the End of the War, besides their laurels, with 50 Acres of Land, where every gallant Hero may retire and enjoy his Bottle and Lass. Each Volunteer will receive, as a Bounty, Five Dollars, besides Arms, Cloathing and Accoutrements, and every other requisite proper to accommodate a Gentleman Soldier....

In the following century the concept of recruitment for individual actions and expeditions gave way to generalized recruiting campaigns by the services themselves. By the time of World War I the matter had in Britain been put in the hands of a 'Parliamentary Recruiting Committee' and in America a 'Division of Pictorial Publicity' (*see* POSTER).

Britain's Parliamentary Recruitment Committee was responsible not only for poster production but a range of recruiting booklets and folders. In an eight-page booklet from World War I the 'Committee of the Rural League' appeals to 'the Manhood of our Rural Districts':

> The People of our Countryside, – Labourers, Farmers and Squires – are the backbone of the Nation, and now is the time to show it. Already they have given generously of Men and Money. More of both is required. Lord Kitchener wants the Men; and to whom should he look with more confidence than to our sons of the soil? They have never yet failed in the Hour of their country's need; they will not do so now!

In Britain, where even in recent times the custom prevailed of sealing a bargain with a symbolic payment of a coin, acceptance of 'the King's Shilling' was commonly viewed as a binding commitment. But since 1694 the British soldier had been required to be attested on enlistment before a civil authority (though army officers may also in practice attest). The document of attestation was regarded as the confirmation of a bargain initiated by the taking of the shilling. In World War I the term 'attestation' was also applied, prior to the introduction of conscription, to a 'halfway' form of commitment in which the man pledged himself to service in the event of his being required.

Recruitment by persuasion came to an end in World War I with the introduction of conscription, in Britain in January 1916, and in America (by 'Selective Service') in May 1917. The change brought a massive increase in control, a bureaucracy of which a large body of ephemera is evidence.

Documentary control of enlistment and discharge is a continuing feature of military history, and relevant papers survive in some numbers. Even in earliest times the engaging of service was seen as a matter in which evidence of agreement, however one-sided, was imperative.

In the documentation of military service, whether voluntary or compulsory, there are three basic sectors: papers relating to call-up (US, 'draft'), Certificates of Exemption, and Evidence of Formal Discharge.

In the first sector, typically, is the 1918 'Order of Induction into Military service of the United States', already noted, and a 'Notice Paper' (Britain, 1917): 'You are hereby warned that you will be required to join for service with the Colours on (May 29th).... You should therefore present yourself at (Recruiting Office, Epsom) on the above date not later than (8 am) o'clock, bringing this paper with you'.

Documents of exemption include medical certificates, apprentice's certificates of protection from impressment, certificates of alternative service (agriculture, forestry, social relief, etc.), and evidence of diplomatic immunity.

Key documents in military organization are officers' warrants and commissions. These may be traced to the formation of armies in earlier times, when selected individuals were commanded and empowered by the sovereign to raise regiments for local or regional operations. Commissions may also originate with the Lord Lieutenant or 'Principal Justice of the Peace' (*Custos Rotulorum:* Keeper of the Rolls) of a county; in the United States Civil War commissions were issued in the name of State Governors. (The wording of certain such documents resembles that of the British prototype so closely as to suggest its source.)

In Britain, the officer's commission was originally inscribed wholly by a calligraphic hand and signed personally by the Monarch. At a later period it was engraved, with blanks for insertion of details. By the Officer's Commission Act of 1862, however, Queen Victoria was relieved of the task, her signature appearing as an engraved facsimile. The Act did not preclude her signing personally; the signature on post-1862 commissions may, in special cases, be in her own hand.

Other documents of appointment were less gracious. A part-printed foolscap form (1897) enshrines the navy's desires in the matter of Mr George Hickey: 'the Lords Commissioners of the Admiralty hereby appoint you (chief carpenter) of Her Majesty's Ship (*Majestic*) and direct you to repair on board that Ship at (Portsmouth). Your appointment is to take effect from (20 December 1897). You are to acknowledge receipt of this appointment forthwith, addressing your letter to the (Captain of *HMS Majestic*) taking care to furnish your address. By command of their Lordships, (Euan MacGregor, W M Turner).

In Britain, until the 1870s, it was possible to buy commissions in the army. The system stemmed from early times, when those who raised regiments for the Monarch were paid according to the number of men they could muster. The raising of men thus became a form of business enterprise, the commanding officer acquiring, in addition to social standing, profit derived from 'economies' in provision of food and other supplies.

A part-printed document issued from the Horse Guards on 21 January 1867 enshrined the system in its last stages: Directed to Mr A. M. Harrington, it reads:

> Sir, I am directed by the Field Marshall Commander in Chief to request that you will immediately lodge the sum of £450 in the hands of Messrs Cox & Co., Craigs Court, SW, when His Royal Highness will have much pleasure in submitting your name to Her Majesty for the purchase of (an Ensigncy) in the (Rifle Brigade)... I have the honor to be, Sir, Your obedient Servant (W F Forster)

Discharge could also be purchased. A part-printed letter from the Admiralty Office dated 22 December 1810 assures Sir George Clayton of Camberwell that his application has succeeded:

> (Sir) In reply to your Letter of (18 Instant) I am commanded by my Lords Commissioners of the Admiralty to acquaint you, that directions have been given for the discharge of (Samuel Hopkins) on the Payment of Fifty Guineas to the Paymaster of Royal Marines, towards raising two Recruits to serve in his room. (I am Sir, Your very humble servant John Farrow).

Papers associated with discharge are commonly no less detailed than those of induction. In many cases they bear a report of the holder's conduct as well as description and duration of service. Naval discharge certificates at some periods also bore reference to prize money. Prize money was often a substantial supplement to a sailor's pay, being a portion of the value of ships and cargoes captured in action. The 'certificate of service', as it was called, thus became the sailor's proof of right when appointment of prizes had been completed. Rather than wait for completion, many sold their certificates to others who cashed them in due course; the practice gave rise to the printing on the back of the certificate a warning in red: 'Persons purchasing this paper subject themselves to prosecution'.

Certificates commonly bore the reason for the holder's discharge: 'Having been invalided ... for gun Shot Wound Right Shoulder' (Royal Marine Artillery, Portsmouth, December 1879); 'Having paid the sum of £30 by Order of the Master General of the Ordnances' (Royal Artillery, Leith Fort, December 1846); 'His term of service having expired' (Sixth Regiment of Massachusetts Infantry Volunteers, Readville, October 1864).

To enhance durability, many early certificates were printed on parchment. Some are even entitled 'Parchment Certificate'. Many were designed to allow the 'character' space at the foot to be cut off if, as the footnote says, 'the general conduct of a soldier... has been such as to give him no claim to have anything said in his favour'. This was to give no opportunity 'for any addition to be made after the Certificate is given to the Man'. The footnote adds, however, that 'when a Soldier is *discharged* on account of *disgraceful conduct*, that will appear in the body of the Certificate'. The back of the certificate commonly carries

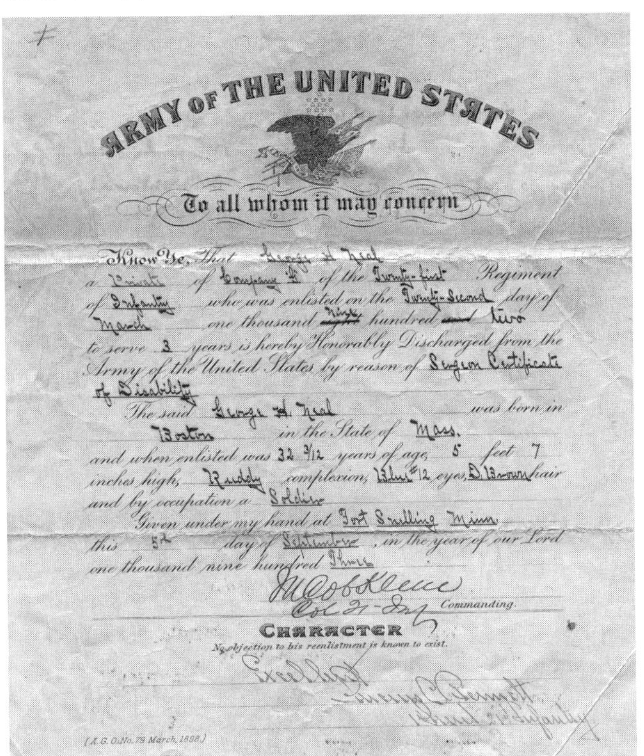

ARMY OF THE UNITED STATES

To all whom it may concern

Know Ye, That George H. Neal a Private of Company H of the Twenty-first Regiment of Infantry who was enlisted on the Twenty-Second day of March one thousand Nine hundred two to serve 3 years is hereby Honorably Discharged from the Army of the United States by reason of Surgeon Certificate of Disability

The said George H. Neal was born in Boston in the State of Mass. and when enlisted was 32 3/12 years of age, 5 feet 7 inches high, Ruddy complexion, Blue eyes, D. Brown hair and by occupation a Soldier

Given under my hand at Fort Snelling Minn. this 5th day of September, in the year of our Lord one thousand nine hundred Three

Col 21 Inf Commanding.

CHARACTER

No objection to his reenlistment is known to exist.

Excellent

(A. G. O. No. 79 March, 1898.)

United States Army discharge certificate, 1903. Printed intaglio on imitation parchment, with manuscript. 278 × 228 mm (11 × 9 in)

additional details of the holder, but we may note one case, 'Army form B2079, Certificate of Discharge no. PS 8498' (August 1915), in which the reverse sets out rates of reward payable to 'recruiting agents': quoting the 'Recruitment Regulations' (1912), it states that 'any man, whether Soldier or Civilian, who brings a recruit to a Recruiter, or to a Military Barrack, is a Recruiting Agent, and it is not necessary that he should have been formally appointed as such'. There follows a rate list, viz: '5*s* to 2*s* 6*d* Regular Army; 1*s* 6*d* Special Reserve'.

Among numerous other items associated with discharge, commonly found are cards of application issued to departing members of the Royal Air Force ('The general officer commanding Royal Air Force ... hopes that the experiences gained ... will be of material benefit to you in your future career') and decorative certificates designed for framing that record war service.

(2) Orders, messages, signals, etc. Military instructions may be divided between standing orders, covering general practice, and orders issued as occasion requires. Both sections are wide-ranging in subject matter. Standing orders may relate to matters as disparate as shoeing horses (King's Regulations 1912, paragraphs 1254–55) and artillery salutes to ambassadors (ibid, paragraphs 1810, 1812). Standing orders may also be modified or augmented. A printed 'memorandum' from the Admiralty of 21 October 1874 states:

> The Board of Ordnance having represented that the Gun and Carronade Carriages of several of his majesty's Ships which have been returned into Store, have had a Coating of Coal Tar applied to them while on board instead of Paint, which is detrimental to the carriages, as they cannot be scraped sufficiently clean to allow of the subsequent application of Paint with good effect, the Lords Commissioners of the Admiralty are pleased to direct that the practice above mentioned be entirely discontinued....

Best-known of the British Army's message and signals system of World War I is 'Army Form C2121', extensively used in the trench warfare of the Western Front. Pencil-written messages on the telegraph-style form convey the spirit of the conflict: 'A bombardment of the enemy's trenches will be carried out tonight....The 1st Northumberland Fusiliers on our left will send out tonight strong offensive patrols to gain contact with the enemy.... Should the enemy be found *not* holding the line ... it will be occupied by the 1st Northumberland Fusiliers and patrols pushed on to gain contact...'.

The Armistice, 11 November 1918, is itself enshrined on a 'messages and signals' form:

> Urgent operation priority: Hostilities will cease at 11.00 hrs today Nov 11 Troops will stand by fast on line reached at that hour which will be reported to Advanced Army by wire. Defensive precautions will be maintained. There will be no intercourse of any description with the enemy until receipt of instructions from Army HQ. Further instructions follow.

A notable feature of military history is the series of printed orders issued by the Honourable Artillery Company, London's volunteer body. Said to be the oldest regiment in the world, the company originated in 1537 as a guild of archers and handgunmen; it has an offshoot in America, the Ancient and Honourable Artillery Company of Boston, Massachusetts, the oldest military formation in the New World.

Printed orders of the Honourable Artillery Company cover both the long term and the immediate: 'Ordered (August 1800) that the General Field-Day be discontinued in the Artillery-Ground until further orders; but that Private Drives be held every Wednesday Evening at the Armory-House, at Five o'Clock precisely'; 'Ordered (6 November 1795) that the Members do assemble in the Artillery Ground on Monday, the 9th day of November instant, at Nine o'Clock in the Forenoon precisely completely armed and accoutred, and with two spare flints.' (The Honourable Artillery Company's commitment was not only to the sovereign against foreign enemies but in defence of 'public tranquillity'. The last-mentioned order reflects the unrest of the period, referring to 'well grounded Apprehensions' that 'Attempts may be made on that Day [9 November] to disturb the public Tranquillity'.

(3) Supplies, transportation, etc. The provisioning and movement of large bodies of fighting men has always demanded as much attention as battle efficiency. In fine detail, as well as in breadth of scale, documentation of supply and movement conveys a compelling image. Commodities and services of every kind are called for. Some are supplied from base; others are found 'off the country', acquired by purchase or persuasion from friendly natives; yet others by force.

Reflecting the field of 'base' supplies are such items as stores accounts; estimates of sums required for recruitment and clothing; applications requesting provision or replacement of horses or vehicles; and railway travel warrants. In the field of requisition are notices warning that goods, vehicles, services, etc., may be taken without warning; receipts given to the owners of requisitioned materials; and tickets of command instructing householders to accept soldier-lodgers until further notice.

Typical of items relating to orthodox supply are a quartermaster's declaration of receipt of ordnance stores: '510 muskets with bayonets and scabbards complete; 33 sergeants spears; 21 drummers swords; 20 drums and sticks; and 16 drum cases'

(Pocklington, 1809); a warrant authorizing payment of £9 7*s* 3*d* for 'extra allowance for horse medicines' (Hanover, 1814); and a receipted application for renewal of an officer's silk tie, originally issued in 1865 (Paris, May 1866).

In the requisition category are a British army broadside enjoining prompt payment of 'country people' for transportation, provisions, military stores, etc. (New York, 1769) ; a proclamation from the 'New-York Commitee-Chamber' (29 May 1775) recommending fellow citizens not to dispose of certain goods ('striped and plain blankets... barrel'd beef... tin plates etc.') as the Provincial Congress may decide to detain them 'for our own use'. Also in this category is a part-printed slip requiring the citizen recipient to furnish lodging, fire, salt, light, and bed to two soldiers for one night (France, 16 December 1799).

Not uncommon among early papers of supply are requests for replacement or reimbursement. A typical manuscript statement, undated, shows a 'list of sundries lost by Major Chrystie belonging to himself and the Company Stores of the Light Infy Compy, 42nd R A Regt, lost on the Continent':

A Compys Cloathing Chist	1.12.0
An Army chist	2. 5.0
A Light Infy Horn Chist	15.0
A new Cloathing Chist burnt at [...] by order of Lt Gen Harcort	1.10.0
60 pairs shoes @ 5/7 per pair	16.15.0
7 Regimentle Coats @ 5/8 each	1.19.0
A Box with 100lbs Soap @ 9 per 16	3.15.0
5 flannel Shirts @ 2/6 each	12.6
9 check Shirts @ 3/5 each	1.10.9
48 white Shirts @ 5/7 each	13. 8.0
32 pairs contract shoes @ 5/7 ea	8.18.8
A Box of Soals heels thread and Wax valued at	18.6
Two Boxes Containing sundries valued at	10. 0.0
	£64. 7.5

In another hand, in the space below the application, appears a list of 'articles allowed', with revised valuations:

1 Army Chest	1.14.8
60 pairs Shoes @ 5/–	15. 0.0
5 flannel shirts 2/6	12.6
48 shirts 3/9	9. 0.0
32 pairs shoes 5/–	8. 0.0
A Box of Seals, Heels, Thread & Wax	18.6
	£35. 5.8

Also the subject of documentation are enquiries into the condition and serviceability of supplies. For these, as with most service matters, printed forms may be filled in as occasion demands. An order from Vice-Admiral Sir James Saumarez, dated 18 August 1810, required 'the Master and Purser of His Majesty's Ship *Plantagenet* to repair on board the sloop *Fury* to survey and report on the condition of a quantity of Men's Flannel Drawers and Waistcoats, and also Boys Blue Jackets, Trowsers, and Hats, which are much eaten by the Mice, and thereby rendered unfit to Issue'.

(4) Health, medical, etc. Within this sector comes a wide range of documentation covering, among other things, first aid; field hospital, ambulance, and base hospital administration; control of infection and epidemic; and provision of such ancillary services as dentistry. As in other sectors, items from the 18th and 19th centuries are often the ones most striking in the image they convey of their time. In the 1730s, for example, the rules of the British Navy ('Regulations and Instructions Relating to His Majesty's Service at Sea') include sections on 'The Surgeon', 'Hospital Ships', and 'The Physician'. The surgeon is required, 'in an engagement... to keep himself in the Hold, where a Platform is to be prepared for the Reception of the wounded Men; and himself, and his Mates and Assistants, are to be ready and have every thing at Hand, for stopping their Blood, and dressing their Wounds...'. The hospital ship is to have 'the Gun Deck entirely set apart for the Reception of Sick Men, which shall be flush, without any Cabbins or Bulkheads, except a Deal or Canvas one (to Roll up) for separating such as have malignant Distempers, from the rest...'. The physician is to visit 'the ships of the squadron or division he belongs to, as often as the Circumstances of the Sick and Hurt Men in them shall make it needful, taking the Surgeon of the Ship with him in his Visitation, and prescribing to him the Remedies to be applied for their Cure...'.

No small matter at various periods was the control of epidemics by quarantine (*see* PLAGUE PAPERS). It is clear, however, that the stringent quarantine regulations were not always observed. A letter from the office of the Lords of the Privy Council in June 1810 requires the authorities at the coast ('at Exmouth or Sidmouth, or at some Port... between Plymouth and Portsmouth') to allow a group of distinguished passengers to land without hindrance: 'It will be extremely desirable on account of the state of the Marchioness of Bute's health, that she should be immediately liberated from the strain of quaran-

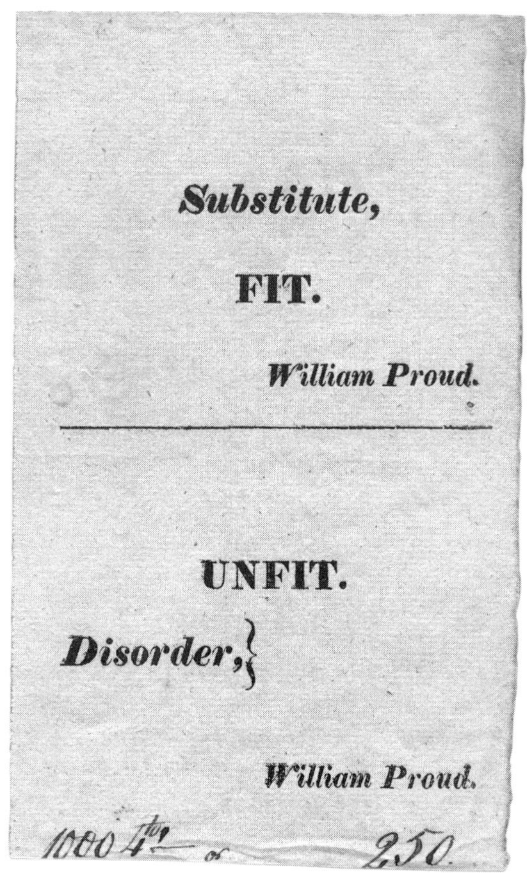

Substitute,

FIT.

William Proud.

UNFIT.

Disorder,

William Proud.

Statement of fitness, or otherwise, of a substitute for the Militia. Early 19th century. Letterpress. 162 × 100 mm (6⅜ × 4 in)

tine...'; the Marquis and Marchioness and their children, together with two friends, 'their suites, servants, trunks and baggage' should be brought ashore immediately 'provided the crew... shall be found to be free of any malignant or infectious disorder'.

In another context altogether is a printed Admiralty memorandum of 15 September 1835, in which captains, commanders, commanding officers, surgeons, and pursers are informed:

> The Lords Commissioners of the Admiralty having noticed the numerous claims in the Accounts of the Pursers of His Majesty's Ships for extra issues of Spirits under the authority of the respective Commanding Officers; I am commanded by their Lordships to state, that such issues will never be allowed unless in cases of extraordinary and unavoidable exposure or fatigue, and even then the recommendation of the Surgeon, and his statement of the necessity thereof should accompany the usual Certificate....

A major aspect of health in the forces is the threat of venereal disease, and the subject has generated its own portion of printed ephemera. The matter is approached with varying degrees of candour: in 1914 Field-Marshall Kitchener touched on the problem in a 'confidential' leaflet distributed to troops on their way to France:

> Your duty cannot be done unless your health is sound. So keep constantly on your guard against any excesses. In this new experience you may find temptations both in wine and women. You must entirely resist both temptations, and, while treating all women with perfect courtesy, you should avoid any intimacy. Do your duty bravely. Fear God. Honour the King....

The subject is dealt with more specifically in later items, often controversially, with much public discussion of the morality of the 'prophylactic packets' supplied to troops and official recognition of medically inspected brothels.

(5) Training and proficiency. Development of specialized training bodies ('schools of instruction', 'schools of musketry', etc.) was a feature of 19th-century military history, and the certificate of proficiency distinguished not only the successful student but, more importantly, the qualified instructor. Technological advance brought wholly new disciplines within the ambit of the forces, and by the early years of the 20th century it had become necessary to train in such subjects as 'practical chemistry', 'military bicycles, care of', 'military electric lighting', 'practical treatment of sewage', 'telegraphy and telephony', and 'mechanical transport'. In each of these fields and others the certificate of proficiency formed part of the training structure. In some cases the certificate was given as evidence of full proficiency; in others it merely recorded completion of a specific course.

Among the earliest of certificates conferring operational status were those issued to surgeons or their 'mates' in His Majesty's Service in the first years of the 19th century. An example dated July 1815 is signed by seven examiners and the master and governors of the Royal College of Surgeons, and directed to the Right Honourable the Secretary at War: 'We have Examined Mr (Peter Naverty) and find him qualified to serve as Surgeon('s mate) to any (hospital) in His Majesty's Service'. (The title 'Surgeon's Mate', much resented by the holders, was at about this time changed by the Admiralty to 'Surgeon's Assistant', and pay was raised from six shillings and sixpence to ten shillings a day. It was to be almost half a century before the assistant surgeon left his cockpit hammock for a so-called 'cabin', a canvas compartment outside the gunroom on the lower deck. He was to become a commissioned officer only in 1866.)

(6) Returns and records. Historically, as the scale and scope of military operations expanded, the need for improved record-keeping, stock control, and accountancy became more pressing. The matter is epitomized in the fighting ship at sea, where shore control is remote, personnel and stores numerous, and the daily situation subject to radical change. By the beginning of the 19th century the work of the captain's clerk and purser had become extensive, and there was scarcely a transaction on board for which paperwork of some kind was not provided. Forms proliferated – not only as part-printed blanks for filling by hand, but as set textual models of letters, orders, certificates, affidavits, etc., for adapted use as occasion required (*see* FORM).

The Seaman's New Vade-Mecum (1811) published for the use of naval clerks, prints specimens of 125 forms, tables, vouchers, accounts, returns, lists, etc., and some 250 model letters, orders and other more or less standard communications. Forms carry titles from 'List of killed and wounded' to 'account-current of water purchased'. One form provides for 'an account of paper, tickets, certificates &c', and another, 'account of paper received', enumerates sheets and quires of blank paper. Model letters include 'from captain to admiral, requesting survey on decayed provisions', 'Surgeon's letter to captain for extra supply of wine to the sick', and 'letter in behalf of French prisoners, to be liberated on being non-combatants'. (It is to be noted that in both naval and military listings of men, entries are found bearing annotations. These are: D (Discharged); DS (Discharged Sick); DD (Discharged Dead); DSQ (Discharged, Sick Quarters); R (Run, i.e. deserted); CP (Civil Power, i.e. handed over to).

Reports of numbers and quantities (known for their role as answers to demands for information as 'returns') are frequent. They may cover not only men and animals but weapons, vehicles, accoutrement, clothing, food supplies, tobacco, musical instruments, carpenters' supplies, or any other form of naval or military supply. They are called for from armies in the field, from men-of-war in action, from volunteer and Militia regiments, prison ships, training schools, and hospitals, and they may relate to the incidence of anything from impressment to venereal disease, trials by court martial to vaccination, desertion to dysentery. Orders may also be made for surveys of the condition and serviceability of supplies. For these too, printed forms may be filled in as occasion requires.

(7) Crime and punishment. Punishment of offenders in the early days of the armed forces is known to have been extremely severe. Private Waterfield's diary account of his army service (1842–57) records 150 lashes for a man who threw a can of coffee at a sergeant, and Lloyd (1968) cites the 18th-century case of Admiral Boscowen, whose men rioted for lack of shore leave. Three were hanged, one was sentenced to 100 lashes, two to 400, three to 300, and four to 500. Such punishments were not formally laid down. Naval regulations of the time stipulate a maximum of 12 lashes ('according to the ancient practice of the sea'), beyond which the ship's Commander may not go without application to the Commander in Chief. But in practice, as the log books and other documents show, the regulation was largely ignored.

Well-known as the facts may be, it must be said that early ephemera of crime and punishment in the forces are scanty. Among the earliest surviving items are handwritten copies of the Articles of War, a listing of military law as it affected the service man. Such notices were posted up as the writ of final authority.

Originating in the military 'Statutes, Ordnances and Customs' of Richard II (1385), Articles of War have taken various forms. Their function was to place in a military context offences which in civilian life would have been mere breaches of contract. Defection, desertion, and disobedience of almost any kind were punishable by death. Conditions were slow to ameliorate; even in the Navy's Articles of War of 1749 capital offences included 'Not preparing for fight', 'Not pursuing enemy', 'Cowardice or other neglect', 'Buggery or sodomy'; and the punishment of death 'or such other punishment as the offence, by a court martial shall be judged to deserve' was laid down for lesser crimes, among them 'not acquainting superior officers with any letter or message sent from an enemy'. In this 'option' category the army's Articles of War included disobeying any lawful command or striking a superior officer. Non-capital, but high on the list in the Army's Articles was the crime of using 'traiterous or disrespectful Words against the Sacred Person of His Majesty, His Royal Highness the Prince of Wales, or any of the Royal Family'. Officers were cashiered; non-commissioned officers and soldiers were to be dealt with as a court-martial saw fit.

Articles of War were suspended in Britain by provisions in the Army Act and Air Force Act. In America they were embodied in the annual Army Regulations and the Naval Discipline act.

Early copies of the Royal Navy's Articles, handwritten by the Captain's Clerk on three or four foolscap sheets, form a notable feature of the ephemera record of the military law of the 18th and early 19th centuries. Towards the end of the 18th century other items began to appear, among them papers relating to prisoners, courts-martial, and desertion. High rates of desertion, largely the product of appalling conditions of service, are a major concern in this period. In May 1775, from the city of New York, a proclamation by staunch loyalist James De Lancey called on Justices of the Peace to 'cause strict enquiry' for deserters from His Majesty's Forces and reminded the public at large of the penalty of five pounds for harbouring or helping them. In February 1779 Sir Henry Clinton K.B., also from New York, appealed to deserters to return to their duty. Knowing that they would return but for the fear of punishment, he offered a free pardon: 'to every deserter of whatever rank or denomination, who shall voluntarily surrender himself… before the first day of May next'. (The offer is the more remarkable for its recognition that the men in question have not only deserted but are 'known to be serving with the Enemy'.)

Desertion remained a problem well into the 20th century, as successive issues of the *Police Gazette* or *Hue and Cry* proclaim. A whole-page War Office announcement of 31 December 1836 lists details of seventy-five offenders. On 4 September 1866 a similar whole-page listing appears with an offer of a twenty shilling reward for apprehension. In this case the list names ninety men, all from Her Majesty's Service in Ireland.

The institution of the court-martial provides its measure of paperwork throughout the period, but by the 1860s Naval Courts Martial, still steeped in the harsh precedents of the past, were felt to be in need of examination. From the Admiralty in December 1866 comes a foolscap document headed 'Confidential: Severity of Court Martial Sentences':

> My Lords…. Have no desire to interfere… with the independent and responsible duties of Members of Courts Martial, but they are of the opinion… that the severity of very many of the Sentences… must tend more to harden the Prisoners than to improve their character, and must act prejudicially on the service itself….

(8) Communications with civilian population. Military communications addressed to the general public have classically taken the form of proclamations, generally printed, though also sometimes handwritten and, in certain circumstances, spoken (*see* PROCLAMATION). The printed document was commonly posted in public areas in occupied territory; in areas within enemy territory the message may have been delivered by AERIAL LEAFLET.

The military proclamation may refer to a wide range of subject matter. At its simplest it serves initially to assert the authority of the signatory and by extension to validate further pronouncements. At a later stage it may announce curfews, the taking or killing of hostages, punishment of individuals or whole communities, requisitioning of supplies and services, impending bombardment of civilian areas, forcible evacuation of towns, and punitive transportation of populations.

War proclamations are by definition charged with the drama of the moment; presented in sequence they may provide a telling record of the progress of a campaign. In Britain in the early months of 1916 there appeared such a record, entitled *Scraps of Paper: German Proclamations in Belgium and France.* It was published by Hodder & Stoughton, in the form of a thirty-eight-page booklet reproducing placards and proclamations signed by Generals Von Emmich, von Bulow, Fasbender, Knoerzer, Von Moltke, Von Bissing, Von Der Golz, and others over a twenty-month period. In the series, subject matter moves from expressions of regret to the Belgian people for the enforced crossing of their frontier (4 August 1914), to a warning with a very different tone (22 August 1914) to the public at large for their 'treacherous attack on German troops'. Subsequent placards deal with forcible requisition (Lunéville, 29 August 1914), the taking of hostages against possible disorder (Rheims, 12 September 1914), and executions of civilians harbouring enemy personnel (Lille, 22 September 1915). The series also includes the announcement at Brussels (12 October 1915) of the execution of a group of civilians convicted of treason, among them Edith Cavell. (We may note that this is not the only example of proclamations being used as propaganda by opponents. 'Butler's Proclamation' issued in the American Civil War as an order to Union soldiers to treat contemptuous Southern women as 'women of the town', was reprinted as 'an outrageous insult' in the Confederacy. Other cases have occurred in more recent times.)

English-language proclamations in World War II include those posted by the German Military Government during the occupation of the Channel Islands and those issued (in English and German) by Dwight D. Eisenhower on the landings in Europe by the Armed Expeditionary Force.

(9) Provision of pensions etc. Pension papers form another major area of documentation. In Britain, prior to the setting up of the Chelsea Hospital (1682) and the Royal Hospital for Seamen at Greenwich (1694), arrangements for the care of old and disabled servicemen were sketchy. Till that time, as Lloyd (1968) reports, the Chatham Chest was the only source of grants and pensions for navy men. The Chest established a 'going rate' of compensation – £6 13*s* 4*d* for loss of an eye or leg; £4 0*s* 0*d* for a hand.

Pension 'tickets' of the 19th century, often printed on parchment or linen, show a fully organized approach to the matter. Pension rates, if not munificent, are noticeably higher. In one linen-printed example from the 1880s the holder, a 28-year-old bombardier in the Royal Marine Artillery, is recorded as having served in the navy for 9 years and 120 days and as suffering from 'Disability'. His entitlement was £24 7*s* 0*d* a year for life.

Also shown in the papers of pensions and grants is an increasing awareness of the plight of dependants. Among early signs (c.1800) are forms providing for parish allowances to be made for 'the Subsistence of the Families of Militia-men serving in the Militia'. An Admiralty form (1830s) is designed to respond to requests for help from the 'Compassionate Fund'. A surviving example indicates, however, a policy of careful stewardship: 'Admiralty, (20th February 1837): (Madam) My Lords Commissioners of the Admiralty having had under their consideration the claim to relief from the Compassionate Fund which you have preferred on behalf of the Orphan Child of the late (Lieutenant Robert Thomas Reid), I am commanded by their Lordships to acquaint you that (they regret the limited sum placed at their disposal does not admit of their making this child any allowance from the Fund in question…)'. The form, addressed to Mrs Reid of Coburg Cottage, Chudleigh, is signed by John Munrow, 'Your very humble servant'.

Relations with next of kin have ranged from manifest sincerity to irreducible formality. A personal letter to the Vicar at Quidenham, Norfolk, is datelined Mauritius, 19 July 1850, and signed by Major General William Sutherland: 'Sir: I have the honor to acknowledge the receipt of your letter of the 1st May last, and regret to acquaint you, that Private James Sayer of the 5th Fusiliers died at Port Louis on the 2nd of March last of Dysentry. I have the honor to be, Sir, your most obedient servant…'.

(10) Service etiquette and ceremonial. Social and ceremonial order in the services may be seen as a logical extension of the discipline of the drill- and parade-ground. Its codified observances cover a wide spectrum, ranging from trumpet and bugle sounds ('Commence Firing', 'Pursue', etc.) to the drills observed by escorts of honour and funeral parties.

The majority of observances are covered in standard manuals and books of rules and regulations. Many combine matters of etiquette and military prudence. In the *Royal Navy's Regulations and Instructions Relating to His Majesty's Service at Sea* (1731) appear provisions for succession of command:

> In the Absence of the Captain… the Eldest Lieutenant shall have Charge of the Ship…. If there be no Lieutenant, the Master shall command, after him the Second Master; but if, by Loss in Battle, or other Accident, all these Officers shall be wanting, the Command shall devolve in Succession upon the Boatswain, Gunner, Carpenter.

Again, in the matter of the 'wearing' of colours at the mast'-head:

> If any Officer, wearing a Flag or broad Pendant (pennant), shall happen to be slain in Fight with the Enemy, the said Flag… shall nevertheless continue flying, and not be taken in whilst the Enemy is in Sight; but the Admiral, who commands in Chief… to whose Squadron… he belonged, shall immediately be acquainted with it… and the next commanding Officer is to be forthwith informed of it who shall immediately repair on board the Ship of the deceased Commander… leaving his own Flag or broad Pendant flying in his own Ship.

Regulations were often drawn up to cover particular areas, occasions, or contingencies. A manuscript 'running order', dated September 1842, sets out the 'Proposed form to be observed at the Investiture of His Excellency Lt General Sir Hugh Gough with the Insignia of Knight Grand Cross of the Bath' on board the ship *Cornwallis*. The arrangements are noted on two sides of a foolscap sheet, describing the order of procession as the participants 'issue at 10 o'clock from Larboard door of the cabin… two by two', setting out in detail the order of speakers, salutes, prayers, etc., and finishing with the procession of participants back to the cabin they came from.

Another special-occasion item records instructions issued to naval officers at the time of the surrender of the German fleet to the British in November 1918. Headed 'Memorandum: Relations with Germans', the printed document points out that although British naval personnel were shortly to be brought into personal contact with officers and men of the German Navy, the declaration of an armistice did not mean the end of a state of war; relations with the Germans were to be of a strictly formal character: 'No international compliments are to be paid and all conversation is forbidden… if it is necessary to provide food for German Officers and Men they are not to be entertained, but it should be served to them in a place specially set apart. If it is necessary to accept food from the Germans a request is to be made that it is to be similarly served'.

In a printed instruction to British troops in Egypt in June 1939 Army Headquarters sets out a detailed list of 'Notes on Social Observance'. These cover the formality of 'calling' and the leaving of cards; dress to be worn at receptions, levées, etc.; the signing of visitors' books at the Abdin Palace (the King's Book, the Queen's Book, the Queen's Harem Book) and requirements as to attendance at functions ('invitations received from The Palace should be regarded as in the nature of a Command, and as such require no reply.')

Other aspects of etiquette and ceremony reflected in military ephemera include precedence, use of titles, saluting, handing of standards and colours, religious services, guards of honour, and messroom courtesies and conventions.

(11) Enlistment, etc., papers. The raising of armed forces is normally attended by much paperwork. A large proportion of this, too detailed and multifarious to come within the ambit of the ordinary ephemerist, relates to matters of internal organization. Much of it, however, is directed to areas in the public domain. In documents of persuasion, coercion, or conscription the military encounters the civilian, bending his will to that of the state.

The field may be divided between voluntary service and conscription. In the first may be counted recruiting posters, volunteer Militia forms, applications to buy commissions, and documents of 'readiness to fight in the event of actual invasion'. In the second are such items as mobilization proclamations, registration and attestation papers, and call-up documents.

INFANTERIE.
REGIMENT d'Anjou
CONGÉ MILITAIRE.
NOUS soussignez, certifions à tous ceux qu'il appartiendra, avoir donné Congé
au nommé dit
de la Compagnie de au Regiment
d'Anjou natif de en la
Province de jurisdiction de
âgé de ans, de la taille de
Fait à le jour du mois de Decembre
mil sept cens trente
Approuvé par Nous
Certifié par Nous

Notice of military leave from the Anjou Infantry Regiment, France, 1736. Printed in relief from woodcuts and type. The seal removed. 216 × 280 mm (8$\frac{1}{2}$ × 11in)

Under both headings may come oaths of allegiance, medical certificates, identity papers, as well as papers of discharge, demobilization, or desertion. A mixed collection of such documents might include the following items:

Handwritten paper, 140 × 200 mm (5$\frac{1}{2}$ × 7$\frac{7}{8}$in). Company Orders, Yonkers, 18 June 1807: 'Pursuant to Regimental Orders you are Commanded to warn all the Able Bodyed men from the age of Eighteen to forty five years, within your Beat to appear at the house of Jacob Lyntson Monday 22 Instant at 2 O'Clock in the Afternoon Compleat in arms as the Law Directs – Samuel Lyon Capt. NB Where you do not see them personally Leave a written Notis'.

Handwritten paper, 160 × 200 mm (6$\frac{1}{4}$ × 7$\frac{7}{8}$in). County of Brecon to the Constable of Cray in the Parish of Devynnock: These are in His Majesty's name to order you forthwith to bring George Morgan Taylor before us being two of His Majesty's Justices of the Peace for the sd County to shew cause why He should not pay the penalty of forty pounds which He has forfeited for refusing to March with the Militia of the sd County in pursuance of His Majesty's order for that purpose – hereof fail not at your peril. given under our hand and seal this 27th day of February 1760 – E Williams, John Williams.'

Proclamation, 280 × 187 mm (11 × 7$\frac{3}{8}$in): 'By His Excellency Sir Henry Clinton, K.B. General and Commander in Chief of all His Majesty's forces, within the Colonies laying on the Atlantic Ocean, from Nova-Scotia to West-Florida, inclusive &c, &c, &c. Proclamation: Whereas there are several deserters from His Majesty's troops, as well as from the Foreign Troops under my command, who are known to be serving with the enemy, and who, from a just reflection upon the infamy of bearing arms against their sovereign and their country, would return to their duty, did not the fear of punishment to deter them: I do hereby proclaim a free pardon to every deserter of whatever rank or denomination, who shall voluntarily surrender himself to any of His Majesty's troops before the first day of May next. Given under my hand at headquarters in New York, the 23rd day of February 1779. H Clinton. By His Excellency's command John Smith, Sec'ry'.

Printed four-page folder, 137 × 110 mm (5$\frac{3}{8}$ × 4$\frac{3}{8}$in), November 1915: Parliamentary recruiting committee: Directions for canvassers:

1 You should canvass for His Majesty's forces, whether regular, new army, special reserve or territorials, or the Royal Navy.

2 You will be provided with a card which will give you the authority to call upon recruitable men.

3 The cards that you receive contain names of men who, according to the National Register, can be spared to enlist.

4 Make a point of calling repeatedly until you actually see the man himself. You must not be put off by assurances or statements by other people. Make a special report if ultimately you fail to see him.

5 Put before him plainly and politely the need of the Country. Do not bully or threaten....

9 Note all removals and try to ascertain from neighbours or others the new address....

16 Canvassers must endeavour to get all the men they possibly can for the infantry. It is infantry that is required to maintain the Armies in the Field, and the issue of the War largely depends on this Arm. They should be told that their services are equally useful, whether they join the regular, new, special reserve, or territorial force.

REFERENCES Donald F. Featherstone, *All for A Shilling a Day* (London: Jarrolds, 1966); W. F. Fulham, *Recruit's Handy Book* (Annapolis: The Naval Institute, 1913); Anselm John Griffiths, *Observations on Some Points of Seamanship* (Cheltenham: J. J. Hadley, 1824); *King's Regulations and Orders for the Army* (London: HMSO, 1912); Michael Lewis, *The Navy in Transition* (London: Hodder & Stoughton, 1965); Robert Liddel, *The Seaman's New Vade-Mecum* (London: Steel, 1811); Christopher Lloyd, *The British Seaman* (London: Collins, 1968); John Masefield, *Sea Life in Nelson's Time* (London: Methuen, 1905); James A. Moss, *Manual of Military Training* (US) (Menaha, Wis.: Banta, 1917); *Instructions Relating to His Majesty's Service at Sea* (London, 1731); Maurice Rickards, *Posters of the First World War* (London: Evelyn, Adams & Mackay, 1968); Maurice Rickards, *The Public Notice* (Newton Abbot: David & Charles, 1973); Maurice Rickards and Michael Moody, *The First World War: Ephemera, Mementoes, Documents* (London: Jupiter, 1975); [Alfred H. Stradling], *Customs of the Service* (RAF) (Aldershot: Gate & Polden, 1941); Robert Waterfield, *The Memoirs of Private Waterfield* (London: Cassell, 1968)

COLLECTION Imperial War Museum, London

Army printing

In World Wars I and II, armies in the field used their own on-the-spot printing services for the provision of a large range of special needs. Though much printed matter was produced for the military under contract by commercial printers at home, battle-area material was printed, often in considerable quantity, under direct military control on Army presses by soldiers.

The term 'Army printing' is generally applied specifically to this on-the-spot material – orders, circulars, leaflets, and booklets – as opposed to items produced for the Army at home. In some cases, however, a later edition of an initial on-the-spot printing may also have been produced on presses at home.

The concept of in-the-field printing in modern warfare may be said to have originated in July 1915 when the British Expeditionary Force established a 'Base Stationery Unit' at Le Havre. The unit formed the basis of Army Printing and Stationery Services, (APSS) commanded by Captain (later Colonel) S. G. Partridge, (and re-formed in World War II with Second Lieutenant (later Major) Edward Budd as its chief executive).

The APSS of World War I were based at first on Le Havre ('Press B') and, additionally, in January 1916 on Boulogne ('Press A'). (Index letters were derived from the Army's listing of French channel ports.) A further printing unit was set up in Italy in 1917.

The function of APSS was later in the war extended to manufacture and supply of rubber stamps, salvage of waste paper, typewriter repair, and other duties, but its main work was in printing and distributing manuals, regulations, and orders. In addition to a wide range of general printing, APSS produced field service postcards, telephone books, and translations of captured German documents.

Handbooks covered subjects from horse-management to booby traps. Runs varied widely: some secret publications were produced only in tens; others (many printed in Britain and distributed by APSS) appeared in tens of thousands. Not all of the output of presses A and B were short-run items however. *Cooking in the Field*, printed by Press A, ran to a total of 55,000 copies. *Standing Orders for Defence against Gas*, also printed by Press A, totalled 108,000. *Gas Warfare: Monthly Summary of Information*, printed by Press A between July 1917 and October 1918, appeared in runs of between 4300 and 10,000. These booklets contained information of varying degrees of secrecy. The majority bore the words 'For official use only' and many carried a warning against communicating the content to the press 'or any person not holding an official position in His Majesty's Service'. Some also carried a further note: 'Not to be taken into action or front line trenches'.

Between 400 and 500 titles appeared, though the record is incomplete. Of some, as for example *Defensive Measures Against Gas Attacks*, apparently issued to Indian troops in Urdu in 1917, no copy is known to survive.

Publications of APSS bear the code letters CDS (Central Distribution Section) and later SS (Stationery Services). Many of the SS series were printed by Press A; a number bore the imprint 'Printed in France by Army Printing and Stationery Services' and some also carry the identification 'Press A'. The SS coding may not be taken to indicate printing in France. Some twenty commercial printers – among them William Clowes & Sons; Darling & Son; Eyre & Spottiswoode; Harrison & Sons; Hazell, Watson & Viney; and Mackie & Co. – also printed SS titles. Their imprints may appear in full or, more commonly, as initials. Publication dates and quantities are also shown.

A number of manuals in the SS series were reprinted, by Press A or Press B, or by commercial printers. Some were also reprinted by the US Army and issued as War Department publications. Thus SS 126, *The Training and Employment of Bombers*, produced as a revised edition in September 1916, appeared in 1917 as US War Department document 581.

In World War II the production of handbooks was largely in the hands of commerical printers (many of the World War I names or initials appear again in imprints) and printing in the field was concerned less with long-term supplies than with immediate needs from day to day.

Edward Budd, Officer Commanding no. 1 GHQ Printing Press based at Arras, 1939, lists among his first assignments general routine orders, military secretaries' lists, and classified training manuals, but before long the press was producing leaflets for distribution to refugees as they steamed northwards. Also required at short notice were large printed red arrows on white paper for signing the roads to the ports. These Budd improvised by pulling up the cork linoleum of the printshop and cutting arrow-shapes, each a metre long, using them as printing blocks. His team produced 1000 copies of the arrows and 50,000 leaflets overnight. Later in the war, after the surrender of Italy, and with the setting up of the Psychological Warfare Branch, there came into being one of the largest army printing organizations ever known. With Budd in charge, four separate printing plants in Italy began to turn out huge quantities of printed matter. These included propaganda leaflets, sabotage instructions, surrender passes, newsletters, and newspapers. Much of the material (including a faked version of a German forces' newspaper) was distributed by air-drop over battle areas and behind enemy lines.

Toward the end of the war in Europe the plants were producing six million leaflets and four newspapers every day. This output was in addition to a standing quota of administrative forms – over a thousand variations in eight languages – and provision, as in World War I, of a large range of official rubber stamps.

American on-the-spot printing in World War II was carried out largely in mobile field units, but production of psychological warfare material was the responsibility of an Anglo-American organization formed in 1942 as a Joint Production Unit. The staff of the unit worked interchangeably on British or American material. Much of the distribution of the unit's output was done by a squadron of American B29s.

See AERIAL LEAFLET; FORM; NEWSPAPER

REFERENCES Peter T. Scott, 'The Army Printing & Stationery Services, 1914–1918', *Antiquarian Book Monthly Review* (March, 1979); Edward Budd, *A Printer Goes to War* (London: H. Baker, 1975)

COLLECTION Imperial War Museum, London

SOCIETY Western Front Association (World War I)

Arrangement of carriages diagram

Diagrams showing the composition of trains came into use in Britain in the 1860s, principally in connection with royal journeys. The railway company concerned printed a more or less elaborate representation of the train in question showing the sequence of carriages and the identity of their passengers.

Thus, typically, for a journey from Windsor to Holyhead, (2 and 3 April 1900), the sequence reads: 'Engine; Guard; For Men Servants; Dressers and Ladies' Maids; The Countess of Antrim, Hon Harriet Phipps; Princess Christian of Schleswig-Holstein; Queen's Dressers; HER MAJESTY and Princess Henry of Battenburg; Personal Servants; Sir Fleetwood Edwards; Sir Arthur Bigge; Lt-Col Hon W. Carington; Capt Ponsonby; Sir James Reid; Indian Attendants; For Pages and Upper Servants; Directors; Guard'. The twelve-carriage train is represented pictorially, with London and North Western livery correctly rendered in colour and engine steam grey against a blue sky.

Arrangement of carriages diagrams were printed as cards, commonly of the order of 150 × 300 mm (6 × 11⅞ in), ostensibly for the use only of passengers and personnel on the journey, but it must be supposed that extra copies were printed as promotional souvenirs for wider distribution. The diagram was often designed and produced with the elegance associated with palace menus and concert programmes. Decorative borders and floral motifs, as well as the royal coat-of-arms, conveyed the importance of the occasion.

The idea was also applied, generally in a single colour, to continental tourist literature. In the early 1900s diagrams appeared showing the composition of long-distance trains. These indi-

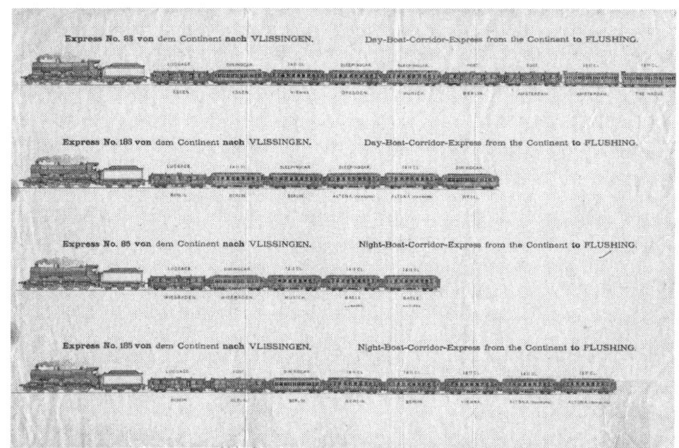

Arrangement of carriages diagram for a German rail company. Letterpress. 206 x 332mm (8⅛ × 13 in)

cated 'Dining car', 'Sleeping car', 'Post', 'Luggage', etc., with appropriate pictograms, as well as indications of destination for specific carriages where trains divided *en route.* The diagrams were made up from separate printing blocks, arranged by the printer as required. (This principle was a continuation of the earlier use of such units in decorative headings for general railway announcements.)

Carriage-arrangement diagrams continue in use in railway working today, though their application is largely confined to internal administration.

REFERENCE Elizabeth Longford, *Louisa Lady in Waiting* (London: Jonathan Cape, 1979)

COLLECTION National Railway Museum, York

Artisan's bill/receipt

The handwritten business papers of artisans, casual workers, and minor tradesmen, are valued as records of everyday transactions of ordinary people. In subject matter, terminology, and orthography, as well as in the matter of price levels, they provide information not always obtainable elsewhere.

Many are barely legible and were laboriously, and perhaps reluctantly, penned to satisfy customer's accounting records. Nevertheless, they repay deciphering.

The following, mostly made out to unspecified churchwardens, are typical:

Received, May 19 1784 of Mr Handy. Four Shilling and six pence for Greace for the bells. The mark of X Jas. Hodges

Aprill 1 1780 To Mending a Ensine: 0.5.0. Used 9½ of Bunting att 5 per yd: 0.3.11½ : 0.8.11½ Received by Mr George Young

Messrs Pernell & Bradshaw, Churchwardens: October 22 1774 : To Thomas Hodgkins : For Paving Work Done in The Church Yard 35 yds at 8 Pence per Yard : £1.3.4. Mr Pernell Sir, Please to Pay This Bill you oblige your Humble Servant Thomas Bradshaw.

Received the Contents of the Above Bill for the Use of my Master Thos Hodgkins : Willm. Popjoy.

Mr Harrison : Churchwarden : To D. Bucquet : To Half Years Winding £5.0.0. July 10 To a new Pandlum Spring 1.1.0 : Aug 10th Two Men and My Self 3 quarters of Day fixing Hands and Rodwork 0.18.0 : Aug 30th To Mending the Rodwork of the Striking Part and new Copper Wyer 0.15.6 : Octr 6 To Easing the Pulleys and get it going 0.5.6 : £8.0.0.

Feby 5 1814 : Recd of Mr Moody Three Shillings & Eight Pence pd to Jackson the Beadle for Beer allowed men in Clearing Snow from St Geo Church : S Powell.

Secular examples are no less evocative:

1811 April 4 : Mrs Howard to E Gummer : Making 3 shirts at 4/- : 12s

Received: Eliza Gummer

Painting done for Mr Gordon in 1771 by Wm Butler: March 2nd to writeing the name on the street door £0.2.0 : March 18th to painting two large new casks done 4 times in oyl, each a deep green colour 0.8.0. £0.10.0 : Feby 11th 1772 : Recd the contents in full of all demands, William Butler.

The George : Ratcliff Hiwaye : 1800 April 10: To wine 1.1.0: to punch 0.15.0. To mixt lickers 0.3.6 : to Backow 0.0.6 : to paper 0.0.3 : to bread & chees 0.3.0 : The butles 0.2.0 : to beear 0.2.1 : survents 0.1.8 [Total] £2.18.11.

Headquarters Dept Virginia: In the Field : July 8th/64: I certify that I have this day sold to Gilman F. Jones One sound horse and Equipments for which I have received my pay in full : W. S. Webb.

Requests for payment of outstanding bills form a related category:

January 31 1881 : Paynes Cottage, Spizal Road, Windsor, Berks : Sir: I would feel much obliged if you would forward the little account for the Alm Houses Chimney Sweeping as I have a little account to make up & would be much obliged if you would forward it: Yours: E. Davis.

May 4 1824 : Elizabeth Buckingham: Melmerby, Ripon, Yorkshire: My Lord: I hope you will pardon the liberty I take in writing to you but Having An Account Against your Lordship when you Wass at Harrow School which I Consider hath Quite Slipt your Memory Or you did not no where I Lived since I Left Harrow the Acct is £8.16.2 which if your Lordship would have the goodness to remit

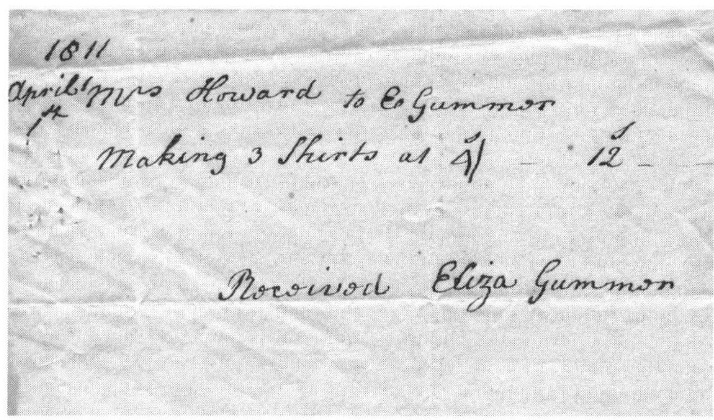
1811
April 4 Mrs Howard to E Gummer
Making 3 Shirts at 4/ — 12 —
Received Eliza Gummer

Eliza Gummor, bill for shirt-making, 1811. Manuscript. 112 × 186 mm (4⅜ × 7¼ in)

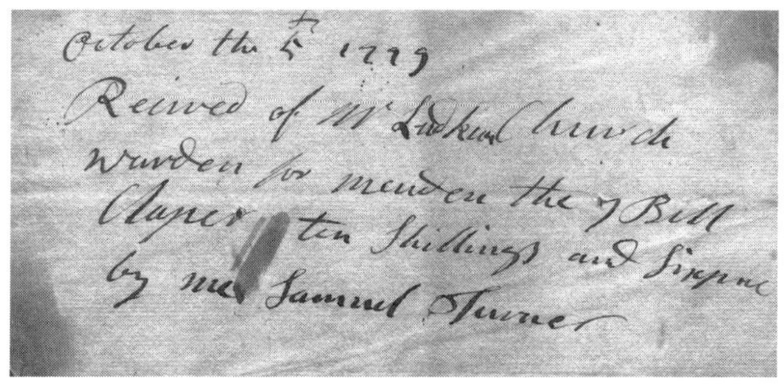
October the 5 1779
Reeived of Mr Lodkin Church
warden for menden the Bell
Claper ten Shillings and Sixpene
by me Samuel Turner

Samuel Turner, receipt for mending a bell clapper, 1799(?). Manuscript. 97 x 210 mm (3⅞ x 8¼ in)

to Me would be of great Service to Me In the Station of Life I am now. In by so doing you will greatly Assist : Your Lordship's Most Humble & Obedient Servt: Eliz' Buckingham.

Many of these items show signs of the effort they have involved. A significant number, signed with a cross, have clearly enlisted another hand – sometimes, it may be thought, the customer's. Receipts are often found with the word 'settled' rather than 'received', and the phrase 'in full of all demands' is common. This would appear to be a relic of an earlier form of wording, 'in full discharge of all demands', though no example of this is recorded.

Artwork for reproduction

Artists' advertising drawings and designs, prepared as originals from which reproductions are made, have always tended to be short-lived. Seen for the most part as a purely transitional stage in the production process, their function is discharged on completion of the plates, blocks, etc., from which the actual printing is done. When printing is finished, original artwork becomes one stage further removed from the end product and is often discarded, damaged, or even destroyed.

Such items of early artwork as do survive (by accident, neglect or, occasionally, by archival care) are rare. Their scarcity value is enhanced by the light they throw on early advertising and graphic design production methods – not least by their disclosure of retouching and 'fudging' techniques and the evidence they provide of studio craftsmen's skills and diligence. No detailed analysis of the material is possible, but the specialist may note the advent of the airbrush in the late 19th century. Its capacity to 'beautify' advertising illustrations and retouch photographs intended for reproduction led to all kinds of visual manipulation in the photomechanical age. Still largely an unexamined field, original artwork must be viewed as a potentially valuable area of ephemera studies.

Detail of artwork in sepia wash and pencil, with a similar detail of a wood-engraving made from it. Late 19th century. Each 90 × 34 mm (3½ × 1 5/16in)

Assignat

The assignat, representing confiscated crown and church lands assigned to the bearer by the revolutionary French Government, was devised as a substitute for metal currency in the financial emergency of the period 1789 to 1796.

Assignat for 50 sols. French, late 18th century. Printed from a stereotype relief block engraved by Gateaux, and blind stamped. Image 72 × 84 mm (2⅞ × 3¼in)

In a first issue to the value of 400 million livres in 1790, the assignat appeared as a form of 'bearer bond', offering interest at a rate of five per cent and entitling the holder to purchase land acquired by the State from its former owners, to be exchanged for goods and services by other potential land buyers. Notes thus finally exchanged for land would be returned to the State and destroyed. The scheme failed. The interest rate was reduced to three per cent later in 1790, and a second issue, to the value of 800 million livres, was declared legal tender and carried no interest at all. Initially it was resolved to avoid inflation by limiting the number of notes in circulation; nevertheless, successive issues appeared, reducing the exchange value of the 100-livre assignat to 20 livres in metal.

By this time there had emerged a two-tier system, in which goods were priced in both forms of currency – paper and coin. People paid their taxes in paper and sold goods for coin. Toward the end of the period, with no Treasury funds available, the Government was reduced to a galloping production of assignats, printing the next day's requirements the night before. By 1796 the total of assignats in circulation reached the value of 45,500 million livres, making them virtually worthless.

The inflationary process had been hastened by contributions from neighbouring countries, among them Britain, whose agents had injected large numbers of counterfeits into the system to swell the tide of disaster.

An attempt to save the situation by the issue of *mandats territoriaux* (effectively assignats in another form) also failed. These, after six months, were redeemed at about one-seventieth of their face value in metal currency. Finally, the Government repudiated all paper currency, replacing it with coin, and ruining many thousands of people in the process.

The assignat survives in considerable quantity. Printed in black on white paper, it appears in a variety of styles and formats. Sizes range, according to face value, from 60 × 100 mm (2⅜ × 4 in) to 115 × 200 mm (4½ × 7⅞ in), and the currency is found in units of, for example, 25, 50, 100,125, 300, 10,000 livres.

Lower value notes are rough-cut from multiple sheets (which may also be found intact). Higher values are printed on a single watermarked sheet, deckle-edged. Highest values (e.g. 10,000 livres) show an irregular cut, indenturewise, at the left-hand margin, indicating separation from a counterfoil. The notes bear blind-embossed stamps depicting symbols and slogans of the revolution, and later issues carry the legend 'La loi punit de mort le contrefacteur; la nation recompense le denonciateur'. (The law punishes the forger with death; the nation rewards the informer.)

The *mandat territorial*, also printed in black on white paper, was in use for a short period only, and is thus less common.

See also FORGERY; SECURITY PRINTING; STEREOTYPE

REFERENCES Yasha Beresiner, *A Collector's Guide to Paper Money* (New York: Stein & Day, 1977; London: Andre Deutsch, 1977); Kenneth Lake, *Discovering Banknotes* (Aylesbury: Shire Publications, 1972)

'At home' card

The 'at home' was a British upper middle-class institution which flourished in the period 1860 to 1914. 'At homes' took place regularly on a set day, allowing a lady's friends to call more or less informally in the knowledge that the hostess would not only be present but pleased to receive and entertain.

To make known her 'day' (which might occasionally vary), the lady left an intimation with her friends, a card bearing the discreet printed legend 'at home', with, for example, 'Thursdays' or 'First Friday' added by hand in the top left-hand corner. (The card had originally been a normal calling card, similarly inscribed.) Additionally, specific dates might be added as an aid to the recipient. Cards were also sometimes sent by post in appropriate miniature envelopes, though opinions differed as to the courtesy of this practice. The expression 'at home' was also used to refer to a single specific occasion, either in the afternoon or evening, less formal than a major gathering, but nevertheless requiring invitations and RSVP acknowledgements. Here the printed card carried the whole announcement with, perhaps, a penned addition, for example 'To meet the Duke and Duchess of Blankshire'.

'At home' cards, for the most part somewhat austere, became at one period guardedly decorative. Lace paper and other conceits appeared, the printed words 'at home' remaining nevertheless discreetly small. They were widely available as a standard stationer's item until World War I. They remained in use – though often with such printed addenda as 'Bridge', 'Tennis', 'Cocktails', or 'Dancing' – in the inter-war period. They survived informally into the 1990s, often as a substitute for a fully-fledged party invitation. They normally bear the simple legend 'at home', and dotted lines for the insertion of details.

It may be conjectured that the expression 'at home' arose not, so to speak, in its own right, but in contradistinction to 'not at home', the universally accepted phrase used by servants to indicate that her mistress, though present, was not receiving. We may note that the 'at home' card is generally recognized, today as in the past, as an intimation from a lady. Its use by gentlemen is rare, though 'at homes' held by British male diplomats provide an exception. Here the home in question may be an embassy or, in some cases, the House of Lords.

Attendance record, school

Records of school attendances have two purposes: they provide a ready check on those who are late or absent; and they provide funding bodies with a basis for funding an institution and its staff.

Records were originally kept informally, and in many British schools, even up to the end of the 19th century, attendances were marked up in chalk on an 'Attendance board'. The record covered one week, each day being divided between morning and afternoon, and the figures relating to specific classes or to the school as a whole. Also available were 'Attendance banners'. Fringed in silk, the satin banner bore the legend: 'This class made the highest attendance this week'.

Numerous devices were used to keep figures high. These ranged from inducements such as reward cards, medallions, and tickets for outings, etc., to threats by school attendance committees and 'kid catchers', their appointed officers.

Use of the printed attendance register became mandatory in Britain with the introduction of compulsory education in 1870 and it was adopted by Sunday Schools and private schools at about the same time. Registers were also used for 'evening continuation' classes, art schools, colleges, etc.

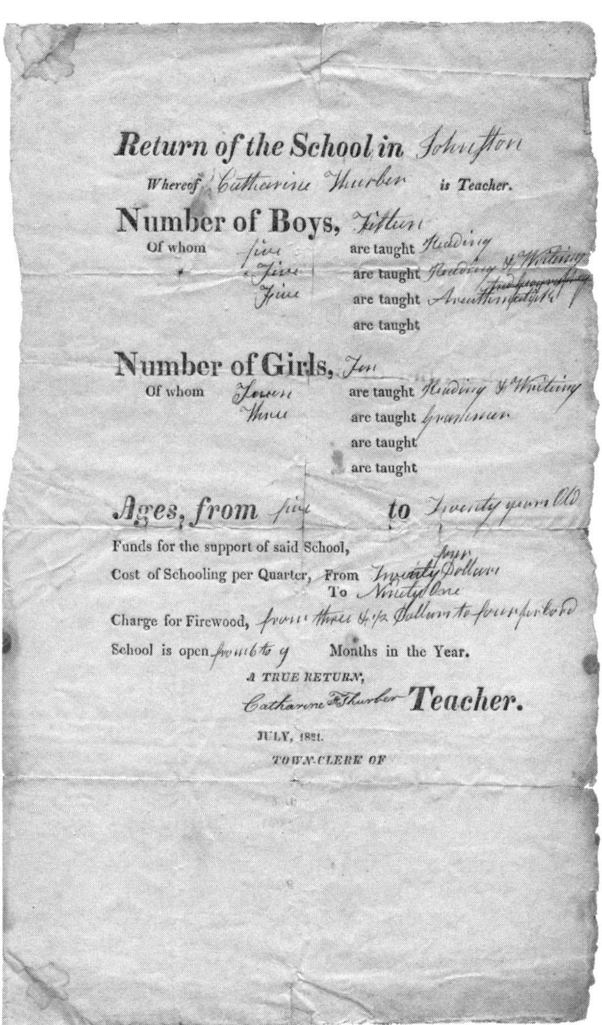

Return of the School in Johnston

Whereof Catharine Thurber is Teacher.

Number of Boys, Fifteen

Of whom five are taught Reading

five are taught Reading & Writing

five are taught Arithmetic

are taught

Number of Girls, Ten

Of whom Seven are taught Reading & Writing

Three are taught Grammar

are taught

are taught

Ages, from five ***to*** Twenty years old

Funds for the support of said School,

Cost of Schooling per Quarter, From Twenty four Dollars

To Ninety one

Charge for Firewood, from three & 1/2 Dollars to four per cord

School is open from 6 to 9 Months in the Year.

A TRUE RETURN,

Catharine F. Thurber **Teacher.**

JULY, 1821.

TOWN-CLERK OF

Attendance return for a school in Johnston (US), July 1821. Letterpress. 350 × 215 mm (13¾ × 8½ in)

Registers provided for varying numbers of names and attendances over periods from one term to a year. 'Summary registers', extending over three or five years, are also found. Some registers also provided space for recording payment of fees, marks awarded, and levels of conduct. Also to be found in Sunday School registers are provisions for scholars' addresses and ages, parents' occupation and 'Cause of Leaving', or 'Remarks'.

See also REWARD OF MERIT

REFERENCES Stuart Maclure, *One Hundred Years of London Education, 1870–1970* (London: Allen Lane, 1970); Stuart Maclure, *A History of Education in London 1870–1990* (London: Allen Lane/Penguin Press, 1990)

Auditorium seating plan

Auditorium seating must have been controlled to some degree even in ancient Roman times, though apart from metal tokens (which may have been used as tickets) there is little evidence of the methods used. Seating plans, used by management to allocate seats and by the public to choose them, emerged much later.

In the 17th century, plans confined themselves to unnumbered blocks of viewing areas. With or without numbers the systems had little actual discipline, members of the audience stepping from one area to another at will.

Seating plans are a feature of presentations today, numbered seating being shown on plans at the box office, with availability cancelled as the positions are disposed of.

In modern times seats may be booked by number on the telephone using credit cards in lieu of cash. In the early 1990s London theatres, of which there were some thirty or forty, collaborated in the production of a monthly compendium of seating plans for sale from box offices and newsagents.

Plans were also published in promotional material, appearing sometimes as separate fliers and often on ticket envelopes.

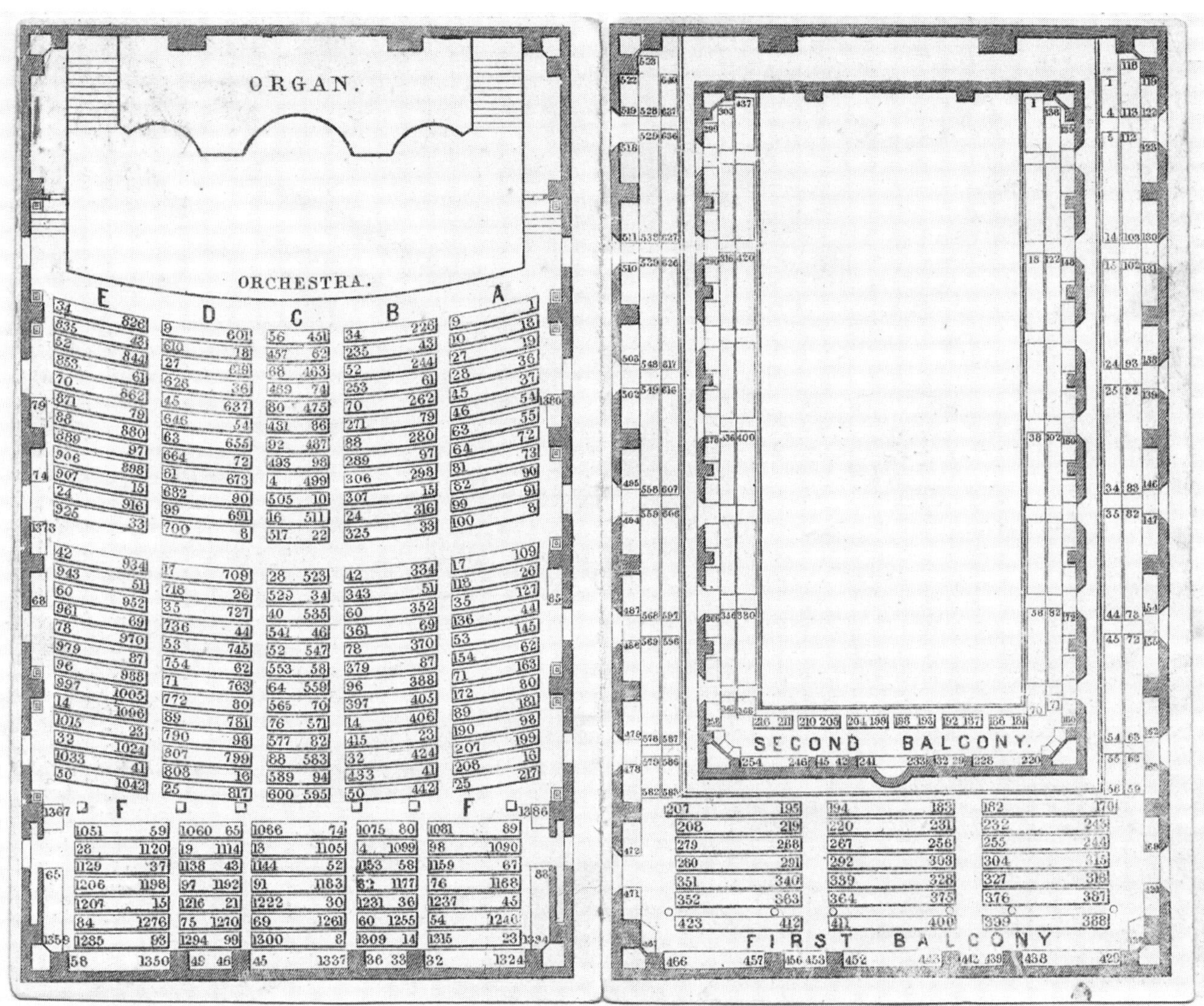

Auditorium seating plan for Boston Music Hall, 1863. Lithographed on pale blue glazed card. 120 × 147 mm (4¾ × 5¾ in)

Back of the book stamp *See* 'CINDERELLA' STAMP

Badge

A badge is a distinguishing emblem, worn as a mark of status, allegiance or obligation. It has its origins in medieval heraldry, when it was a mark borne by knights and their followers and also appeared on their family furnishing, horse regalia, and heraldic banners.

The badge was also used as a distinguishing mark, the wearing of which was obligatory. By the fourth Lateran Council in 1215 it was laid down that Jews were compelled to wear a circular piece of cloth on their coats. The practice was followed in other countries, including England. In German-occupied Europe in the 1930s and 1940s the Star of David was similarly used.

The badge has been imposed at various periods in history. It is recorded (Plymouth Colonial Record, 1639) that in 17th-century America 'The Bench doth therefore censure the said Mary (an adulteress) to be whipt ... and to wear a badge upon her left sleeve.' The badge in her case was a large capital 'A'. The wearing of badges was made compulsory for beggars in Elizabethan England, the wearers becoming known as 'badge men'. In the 19th century workhouse paupers, working in public, were compelled to wear a large letter 'P' sewn to the seat of their pants. The principle was applied in certain British prisons in the 1990s; inmates with a history of escape attempts were obliged to wear a capital 'E' on their jackets.

The badge as a mark of allegiance re-emerged in the latter part of the 19th century. In some contexts it acquired the status of a valued pass or permit. The rise of trade unionism and the closed shop brought the badge (by then an enamelled metal lapel motif) to near-magical levels. Wearing the badge was rigidly insisted on by the unions. At a later stage, when employers forbade union membership – and the wearing of badges – workers took to wearing the badge on the underside of the lapel, the brass retaining button becoming the only visible sign of membership.

Dock workers' dues were payable quarterly, and to ensure that the member was fully paid up the colour of the badge was changed quarterly to allow detection of backsliders. The badge had thus become a major feature of the employment scene.

The tensions generated by the union badge are illustrated by ephemera of the period. A National Union of Dock Labourers' circular states that 'the wearing of the badge is not only an essential duty to yourselves and your fellow workmen ... it is a badge of nobility ... at present the only sign a working man can show that he wishes to better his own condition'. The NUDL rulebook states (1901): 'Each member shall be supplied with a badge. He shall when seeking employment prominently exhibit his badge and on demand of any member ... produce it for inspection'. A printed dock notice (undated) declares that 'Men wearing union badges will be immediately dismissed'.

Badges in Britain at this time were largely die-stamped in brass, with enamelling, on a low-relief surface. The process had been introduced by the Fattorini family who had by the beginning of the 20th century dominated the market.

The new century also saw the appearance of the pin-back button. These buttons made their first appearance in their present form in America in the mid 1890s. They had found popularity initially as collectable items given with chewing gum and cigarettes as a variation on the cigarette-card theme. Their use as party badges in the 1896 McKinley and Bryan presidential campaign established them as an accepted mark of appreciation (Republican sympathies were expressed in some seven or eight hundred different buttons and badges – many more than in most subsequent campaigns). The word 'button' in the designation is accounted for by the fact that the item was derived from the ordinary clothes button. Leading button manufacturers in the United States were the patentees (1896). These were the Whitehead & Hoag Co., the St Louis Button Co., The Parisian Novelty Co., The American Art Works Inc., and Bastian Brothers.

In Britain the badges appeared in the early 1900s as souvenirs of the Boer War and of royal and other occasions, but did not reach general acceptance until the 1920s and 1930s when their use was largely confined to children. They were used in simple colour ranges in schools for team identification and pupil 'dis-

Boer-War badges, printed in colour on metal, c.1900. Diameter 35mm (1⅜in)

tinctions', and were also available with legends such as 'Prefect', 'Monitor', etc. They were adopted as membership badges by a wide range of commercially-sponsored children's clubs, the emblem and the name of the club appearing commonly in two colours on a plain ground.

Printing was originally done on paper, which was given a celluloid covering. With the advent of offset lithography direct on metal, productivity was much increased, though the printed surface was more vulnerable. For short runs today the protective surface is normally acetate. Longer runs are still produced on metal by lithography.

In America the pin button proliferated, mostly as a campaign badge, but in the 1930s as a medium of general propaganda – notably protest. Sizes, which formerly had averaged 25 mm (1 in) in diameter, increased noticeably, even up to 75 mm (3 in). They began to carry lengthy slogans, occasionally extending to fifteen or twenty words. A similar trend in political campaign buttons continued to flourish. The influence of the advertising agency was seen in their design. Prior to the late 1950s and early 1960s, style had changed little since the McKinley era; the J.F. Kennedy campaign brought a distinct design change.

On both sides of the Atlantic the button cult extended, moving in the 1970s from an exclusive propaganda role to quirky self-indulgence. 'Fun buttons' expressed wit, irreverence, and occasional insanity, though organized dissidence remained a key application.

See also ENCLOSURE BADGE

REFERENCES Ken Sequin, *The Graphic Art of the Enamel Badge* (London: Thames and Hudson, 1999); Frank R. Setchfield, *The Official Badge Collector's Guide from the 1890's to the 1980's* (Harlow: Longman, 1986)

Baggage sticker

Baggage stickers were first issued by shipping companies to passengers as an aid to identification and dockside handling, to distinguish between items wanted in cabins and those to be stowed in baggage holds, and to indicate destinations.

The stickers (which were at first not gummed, but required pasting) carried space for the passenger's name, sailing date, cabin number, and destination, a large capital initial corresponding to the first letter of the passenger's name, and the company's name, logo, and house colours. The words 'Not wanted on voyage' or 'Cabin' appeared either on the sticker itself or on a separate item.

The stickers were at first simply informative, but their value to the companies as free advertising was soon recognized, and logos and house colours began to predominate. A convention was thus established in which the customer readily concurred: the passenger advertised his affluence and the company advertised itself. With only minor changes in degree and accent the formula survived into the jet age.

The hotel industry adopted the pictorial sticker towards the end of the 19th century. Specimens survive showing horse-and-carriage street scenes, and the coming of the motor car is recorded in the designs of the early 1900s. Air travel too makes a tentative debut: Palace Hotel, San Francisco, c.1908, shows the roof of the building apparently in use as an airport. The new century also brought references to such amenities as 'Eau courante' and 'Eau chaude et froide'. The Hotel Central, Innsbruck, offers 'Elektrisches Licht' and others have 'Ascenseur', 'Garage', and 'Telefon'.

The hotel sticker came to be accepted for what it was – a portable mini-poster. By the 1920s and 1930s it had adopted a recognizably poster style. In Europe particularly, where tourism was a growing industry, label printers commissioned designs that echoed the work of the up-and-coming poster specialists. A distinctive hotel-label idiom emerged.

Not surprisingly, printers prominent in the field are found to hail from tourist centres; best-known, and much admired, are the labels of the S. A. Richter & Co. of Naples, Giaccone Salucci of Florence, Barabino & Graeve of Genova, Modiano of Trieste, and Molteni of Milan. The Richter Co. was a major influence; its clients included not only hotels in Italy but, among others, The Winter Palace at Luxor, The Savoy Palace, Alexandria, and The Hotel de la Paix, Singapore. In America the developing hotel industry brought its own profusion of labels, many of them in the 1940s and 1950s bearing such inducements as 'Radio in every room' (Hotel Times Square, New York), 'Albany's only "garage-in" hotel' (The Wellington, Albany), and 'Television' (Hotel Olympic, San Francisco).

Much-travelled guests acquired stickers to the point of ostentation. Hotel baggage was also embellished with resort labels. These, bearing only the name and symbol of town or area, were produced by municipal and regional tourist offices and were distributed to participating hotels to add to their own offerings. Baggage became over-labelled.

Gummed labels came into general use in the early 1930s, 'non-curl' gum appearing later in the decade. The STICKER was used by airways too, whose logos were also seen at first as status symbols. By the 1950s application of the stickers to baggage had been speeded by instant adhesive, but as passenger flights became commonplace the use of stickers in this status role diminished (*see* AIR-TRANSPORT LABEL).

In the general travel field, too, an increasingly sophisticated public began to view the sticker as vaguely juvenile. Production of stickers, which had become in the 1960s a minor industry, dropped. Some hotels however continued to use them and in the 1980s and 1990s there were some signs of a revival. Many of the world's leading hotels re-introduced them, some of them reportedly distributing fifty or sixty thousand stickers a year. At least two major hotels, Clark's Amer Hotel in Jaipur, India, and the King George Hotel in Athens, were still using paste-applied stickers in the early 1980s.

Bale label *See* TEXTILE LABEL

Ballad

The popular ballad, sentimental, satirical, or scandalous, has its roots in the oral tradition of folk-song. It was undoubtedly recorded in manuscript form well before the 15th century, but with the advent of printing it became a universally recognized medium of popular expression. The earliest printed ballads in Britain are said to have been produced by Wynkyn de Worde in about 1495, but the earliest surviving example is Thomas Skelton's ballad on Flodden Field (1513). Ballad printers were numerous in the 15th and 16th centuries. In the period to 1600 over 150 printers were in business, and ballad broadsheets were among the commonest printed items of the time. During the years 1557 to 1709, when ballads were required to be registered at Stationers' Hall, some 3000 titles were listed, and Samuel Pepys's collection, which incorporates that of John Selden, contains over 1600 specimens. Among Britain's earliest ballad publishers were John Clarke, Francis Coles, W. Gilbertson,

E. Millet, J. Millet, William Onley, Thomas Passinger, William Thackeray, Thomas Vere, John Wright, and M. Wright. These names feature in a succession of publishing partnerships and associations throughout the latter part of the 17th century. Also prominent, as single operators, were Charles Bates, Joseph Blare, Charles Brown, Joshua Conyers, J. Crowch, John Deacon, A. Milbourn, and Thomas Norris. Prominent in the 18th century were William Dicey, John Cluer, and Richard Marshall.

Early ballad sheets were printed in black-letter (also known as 'Old English') and were presented very largely without decoration or illustration. Later a two-column layout became common, presenting two ballads side by side, each headed by a separate woodcut illustration and displayed title. Single-column ballads were also sold, the 'double' sheet being cut in two to produce 'ballad slips'. In the Victorian era multiple ballad sheets were compiled, sometimes comprising fifty or a hundred separate ballads in a continuous sheet. These 'long songs' were sold virtually by the yard, the seller displaying them as streamers hanging from a hand-held stave.

Street-selling of ballads and other popular prints was widespread. Displays of 'long songs' were also strung from twine by 'pinners up' on walls and railings, often showing one or two thousand ballads, with an admixture of BROADSIDES/BROADSHEETS, ALMANACS, CHAPBOOKS, and SATIRICAL PRINTS. (Outdoor displays of this kind were a feature of cities elsewhere. Contemporary prints show 'pinners up' in major towns in France, Germany, and Italy.)

The heart of the Victorian ballad trade in Britain was the Seven Dials area of London, centred at the junction of today's Monmouth Street, Mercer Street, Earlham Street, and Short's Gardens (at that time, respectively, Great and Little Andrew's Streets, Great and Little White Lion Streets, Great and Little Earl Streets, and Queen Street). Here, among the seediest of second-hand dealers and gin shops, there flourished for over half a century a 'neighbourhood' of street-literature production. Of a wide range of popular printing – 'catch-pennies', 'cocks', execution broadsides, etc. – the ballad sheet was for long a best-seller.

Chief among Seven Dials practitioners were John Pitts, James Catnach, and William Fortey. Together with their associates, competitors, and successors (among them Jacob Bird, Thomas Birt, Duncan Campbell, Henry Disley, George Farrell, E. Hodges, Thomas Major, James Paul, and Anne Ryle), these firms generated the bulk of London's street literature.

John Pitts must be seen as the leading figure among the 'Diallists', setting up his business in Great Andrew Street in 1802. He began as a publisher only, but shortly installed his own printing press, remaining the undisputed doyen of the London ballad trade until the advent of 'Jemmy' Catnach in 1813.

The Catnach establishment was an ever-open port of call, both for street vendors and for ballad versifiers whose efforts, if accepted, might be committed to type on the spot and set up in a battered assortment of old type, headed by woodcut blocks. These title-pieces were sometimes a century out of date, and in most cases unrelated to the subject matter of the ballad. In one example, 'The Mariner's Compass' put out by John Pitts, the title-piece is a single decorative initial D – printed upside down. Payment of authors, a continuing source of contention, was nominal – often, it is reported, in the form of a pint or two of beer. Material proffered in the evening might be on sale in the streets on the following morning, and possibly be reprinted by pirate competitors the next day.

A great many other printers in the London area also produced ballads. Unlike most of the Seven Dials men, these were for the most part jobbing printers for whom the occasional ballad was incidental to general work. Among recorded imprints are those of D. H. Carpue, J. Clarke, Thomas, Edward and Charles Evans, J. Fairburn, George Higham, J. Lucksway, John Marks, D. W. Murcott, Charles Pigott, J. V. Quick, T. Rockliffe, Taylor, W. H. Tickle, Smith, H. Such, T. Such, Walton, and J. Wilson.

Elsewhere in the country printers followed the London lead, pirating Seven Dials material and adapting it to local application, as well as producing their own original material. Provincial imprints include the following: John Elliott (Barnsley), Simms & McIntire (Belfast), Theophilus Bloomer (Birmingham), William Harris (Birmingham), William Jackson (Birmingham), King (Birmingham), William Wrightson (Birmingham), C. Phillips (Brighton), W. & H. Byles (Bradford), Spencer (Bradford), W. Smith (Chester), John Aston (Coventry), Stephen Knapp (Coventry), Walker (Durham), W. Parker (Gosport), J. Lister (Halifax), W. Midgley (Halifax), John Procter (Hartlepool), Weir (Horncastle), J. Beaumont (Leeds), W. Smith (Lincoln), William McCall (Liverpool), William John Bebbington (Manchester), Cadman (Manchester), G. Jacques (Manchester), T. Pearson (Manchester), John Swindells (Manchester), T. Allen (Newcastle), T. Dodds (Newcastle), Douglas & Kent (Newcastle), William & Thomas Fordyce (Newcastle), John Marshall (Newcastle), W. Stewart (Newcastle), Henson (Northampton), Henry Jones (Oxford), Oxlade (Portsea), John Harkness (Preston), Joseph Ford (Sheffield), W. Ford (Sheffield), J. Garnet (Sheffield), King (Sheffield), J. France (Shrewsbury), E. Jackson (Stockport), Corvan (Sunderland), J.B. Hodge (Sunderland), James Kendrew (York).

The printed ballad was also an American institution. The most prominent imprints were those of Andrews of New York, Richard Thayer of Boston, and – perhaps best-known – Thomas M. Scroggy of Philadelphia. The American ballad tended generally to the sentimental and declamatory rather than the satirical, though here too the common touch was dominant. British broadsides were popular in America, and many thousands were imported. To most purchasers their origin was neither apparent nor questioned.

In Britain the ballad also appeared as an aid to workers in industrial disputes. Miners on strike or locked out sold specially-written ballad sheets in the streets to raise money and to state their case, and the 'ballad appeal' was widely sold by the unemployed, not only in the 19th century, but well into the 1930s. The ballad sheet was sometimes used as a vehicle for publicity for the stationers who sold them. In the 1850s 'Mr Green' at his music stall near the City Road, London, and at his shop in Featherstone Street, offered, in a footnote to his ballad sheets, 'an extensive collection of old and new songs, harp and violin strings & fancy stationery'. In addition, he used all four margins for an extended enumeration of his stock-in-trade (which also included fancy walking sticks and toys). Mr Green's ballads, printed for him by T. King of Birmingham, cover a wide range of interests; one specimen, entitled 'You don't know what you can do till you try', extols the virtues of tenacity; another, 'Brixton Tread Mill', weighs up the pros and cons of Brixton

Prison with its 'merry click-clack' and Pentonville, with its regime of enforced silence.

See also BELLMAN'S VERSES; EXECUTION BROADSIDE

REFERENCES Charles Hindley, *Curiosities of Street Literature*, 2 vol. reprint (London: Neuburg, 1966); Louis James, *Print and the People*, rev. edn (Harmondsworth: Peregrine, 1978); Victor E. Neuburg, *Popular Literature* (Harmondsworth: Penguin, 1977); Roy Palmer, *A Ballad History of England* (London: Batsford, 1979); Leslie Shepard, *The Broadside Ballad: A Study in Origins and Meaning* (London: Jenkins, 1962); Martha Vicinus, *Broadsides of the Industrial North* (Newcastle-upon-Tyne: Graham, 1975); Philip Ward, *Cambridge Street Literature* (Cambridge: Oleander, 1978); *John Pitts, Ballad Printer of Seven Dials* (London: Private Libraries Association, 1969); Leslie Shepard, *The History of Street Literature* (Newton Abbott: David & Charles, 1973)

COLLECTIONS Bodleian Library, Oxford; British Library, London; Harvard College Library, Cambridge, Mass.; Pepys Library, Magdalene College, Cambridge

Ballot paper

The word 'ballot' refers either to the drawing of lots (beans, straws, balls, papers, etc.) or to the deposition of such tokens by way of vote. The term 'ballot paper' normally refers to papers used in voting. These are commonly printed, providing a choice of spaces for the user to mark.

The concept of the secret vote, in which preference is expressed without external influence, is long established. Strict adherence to the principle has been patchy, however. South Australia was the first state to introduce a secret ballot, in 1856. In Britain, the parliamentary and municipal ballot was not made secret by law until 1872. The first American States to introduce the Australian system were Kentucky and Massachusetts in 1888. At about this time systems of varying degrees of secrecy began to be adopted in other countries. The use of ballot papers, as opposed to other tokens, did not become general until the latter quarter of the century. The expression 'ballot paper' is first recorded in England in 1865 (*Cornhill Magazine*, vol. XI, p. 115: 'The ballot-papers of the electors were collected in a bucket'). In America, paper or cards were used before that date. The *Annals of Congress* (I Sess., 168, 1803) record that 'As the Constitution stands, each Elector is to write the names of two persons on a piece of paper called a ballot'.

Ballot papers are normally destroyed after use, and surviving examples are thus scarce; those that have escaped destruction relate in the main to elections at institutional rather than governmental level. These indicate a broad range of electoral practice. One example, clearly far from secret, is preserved in the St Bride Printing Library, London. This refers to a ballot of the 'Compositors of London', who are asked to vote on a proposal that they become a branch of the 'National Typographic Association'. The paper, entitled 'Balloting Paper', measures 140 × 222 mm (5½ × 8¾ in) and carries boxes marked 'For' and 'Against'; the voter had to sign his name in either of the spaces provided.

A more significant, though ambiguous, survival is a 105 × 87 mm (4⅛ × 3⅜ in) paper bearing the printed title 'Bulletin de vote'. It carries a small printer's imprint, 'Napoleon Chaix', and the single word 'Oui', centred between two horizontal rules. The specimen is mounted on a card, apparently contemporaneous, bearing the handwritten caption in English 'Paris 10th December 1848'. The paper is a memento of the election of Louis Napoleon as president of France. Voting procedure is not indicated; it is not clear therefore whether the paper was withheld by the voter in favour of a 'Non' paper which failed or was retrieved from the ballot box after the count. Creases in the paper show that before mounting it has been kept for a period folded into a small compass.

In America the democratic process began in New England with open 'voice vote' at public meetings, but the Massachusetts Bay Colony introduced paper ballots in 1634. In these, however, votes could be traced to the voters. Later, ballot papers or 'tickets' were issued by political parties. These bore whole lists of single-party candidates to be signed on the back by the voter, who dropped the signed paper into the box at the polls. The papers were often of distinctive colours, and clearly revealed the voter's choice at the time of the poll.

After the 1880s the American voter was provided in some states with an official 'multi-ticket' list showing candidates in their respective party columns. The voter showed his choice with a cross, either at the head of the column (indicating a block vote for all candidates in the same party) or against individual names, regardless of party. In many states, party identification is now forbidden, the elector having only an alphabetical list to choose from. Party designations were prohibited in Britain until the election of 1979, when they appeared on voting papers for the first time.

In the mid 1980s the ballot paper looked likely to be superseded by other methods. 'Voting machines' have been in use in America in a number of states for many years (Thomas Edison's first patent, taken out in 1868, was for a 'vote recorder'), and the first practical voting machine was introduced in Lockport, New York, in 1892. By the 1980s it was estimated that some eighty-five per cent of US electors cast their votes on machines.

See also ELECTION PAPERS

REFERENCE Klapthor, Collins, Mayo, Sawyer, *We the People* (Washington, DC: Smithsonian Institution Press, 1975)

Band/banderole

'Band' and 'banderole' are more or less synonymous, both terms referring to paper strips encircling a product or package. 'Band' is more commonly applied to a label somewhat broader in relation to its length, as in those used for shoe-laces and hanks of thread. 'Banderole' is applied to the longer and narrower label used, typically, for packets of stationery and as an outer retaining strip for boxes of pens.

Both forms are normally decorative, and generally bear a trade description, with or without the maker's name. In some products, notably such items as gloves, stockings, and linen, the band was a dominant visual element, sometimes elaborately gold- or silver-embossed and often bearing multi-coloured chromolithographed images – portraits, landscapes, etc. – having no relation to the product itself, but enhancing its apparent status.

The narrower banderole appeared not only as a device for retaining box lids, but as a final touch of authenticity and integrity. Introduced at a period when industrial counterfeiting was rife, and when many product labels sought to mimic the anti-forgery devices of currency notes, the banderole too adopted the geometric patterns and complexities associated with security. The notion of security was reinforced by the use of the government tax band as a closure for pillboxes. The design of these bands was based on the anti-counterfeit principles of COMPOUND-PLATE PRINTING and their prestigious intricacy was widely echoed. Chemists tended to adopt the convention for their own (untaxed) preparations, using the band

Banderoles for unknown products. *Above:* chromolithographed; *below:* printed letterpress in blue. Both approx. 65 × 375 mm (2½ × 14¾ in)

for sealing powder packets and wrapped medicine bottles as well as for pillboxes.

See also PILLBOX LABEL; TAX STAMP

Bandbox

The word derives from the 17th-century 'bandel, cuffs and ruffs' which the box was originally designed to contain.

First mention of the bandbox occurs in Britain in 1631 in Thomas Powell, *Tom of All Trades* (p. 173) and in America (Probate Records of Essex County, Mass. 1, 4) in 1636. It is in America, however, that the bandbox has its spiritual home, being widely adopted by settlers as a home-made domestic container for use by households often on the move. It was revived in both countries in the 19th century as a receptacle for bonnets, goffered and pleated linen, and other fragile items, and was used as a carry-all by coach travellers as well as for domestic storage. In America the covering of the box was a popular field for decorative expression.

The box was made of card or thin chipboard (scaleboard, or 'scabbard') similar to that later used in matchbox production. Covering was of hand-painted or printed decorated paper. (The production of bandboxes was for a period an adjunct to that of wallpaper, and in many specimens the wallpaper design element is clearly seen). The box was also lined with paper, commonly undecorated. The components of the box and its lid were effectively held together by the paper covering, both inside and out, though glue and stitching were also used to unite the overlaps, the base to the sides, and the top of the lid to its rim. The box commonly measured some 265 × 400 mm (10½ × 15¾ in), with a height of about 300 mm (11⅞ in). It was generally ovoid in shape.

In America, covering papers developed a design style of their own, often featuring American buildings of the period (1830s to 1850s), early railway motifs and landscapes, and purely decorative abstract patterns. Many bandboxes were home-made, though they were also bought from itinerant vendors and, later, from shops.

The bandbox had much in common with the so-called 'Shaker box', the home storage container devised by the Shakers, 18th-century immigrants to America from England and a sectarian offshoot of Britain's Quakers. Shaker boxes, made of thin maple, were undecorated and designed for durability rather than display (though their utilitarian simplicity also expresses the aesthetic of the Shaker theology).

The Shaker box, and to a lesser extent the decorated bandbox, may be said to have provided the pattern on which the ubiquitous pillbox, forerunner of commercial packaging, was formed. The bandbox survived in both countries – and spread elsewhere – in the form of the hatbox, generally finished in plain white paper for men's hatters and brightly coloured for milliners. These were made by home-workers in backstreets at the end of the 19th century. By the 1920s they were standard items of the industrialized boxmaker.

See also PILLBOX LABEL

REFERENCES *Bandboxes and Shopping Bags in the Collection of the Cooper-Hewitt Museum* (Washington, DC: Smithsonian Institution, 1978); Lilian Baker Carlisle, *Hat Boxes and Bandboxes at Shelburne Museum* (Shelburne, Vermont: Shelburne Museum, 1960); Nina Fletcher Little, *Neat and Tidy: Boxes and their Contents used in Early American Households* (New York: E.P. Dutton, 1980)

COLLECTIONS Metropolitan Museum of Art, New York; Cooper-Hewitt National Design Museum, Smithsonian Institution (New York); American Museum, Claverton Manor, Bath

Bando

The Italian word 'bando', signifying 'proclamation', is commonly used in a prohibitory sense in connection with early health-control edicts forbidding movement of people, animals, or goods in times of plague or other epidemic, chiefly in Italy.

The word first appears in English, together with the related noun 'bandit' (Italian, *bandito:* proclaimed or outlawed), in the last years of the 16th century. Specifically, the health-control bando was a printed BROADSIDE/BROADSHEET (also sometimes known as a *notificazione* or *editto*) placing certain areas 'out of bounds' to travellers. The notice enumerated towns, villages, and locations falling within the ban, stipulating the period of quarantine required for movements out of the areas in question, and listing penalties for infraction. The term 'bando' is also used to refer to notices announcing the relaxing of such controls. The language of the bando is commonly Italian, but examples are also found in other languages of the Mediterranean.

See also PRATIQUE, PAPERS OF

REFERENCES Carlo Cipolla, *Public Health and the Medical Profession in the Renaissance* (Cambridge: Cambridge University Press, 1973); Carlo Ravasini, *Documenti Sanitari* (Torino: Minerva Medica, 1958)

Banknote

Paper currency needs to inspire confidence, to be difficult to counterfeit, and to have such distinctive characteristics of paper and image that any variant is recognizable, even to the least expert eye. These requirements have led to the formulation of a design idiom and a production technique known broadly as SECURITY PRINTING. They have also led to the preservation of a jealously-guarded body of expertise dating from the 18th and 19th centuries. Its techniques, though geared to the mass-production needs of today, are founded in skills that have now almost everywhere else disappeared.

Banknote printing relies heavily on the principle of metal engraving, in which an image is incised in the surface of a copper or steel plate. The incised image, executed in reverse to allow for its appearance the right way round when printed, is composed of a multiplicity of lines, dots, and other marks. These incisions may be perceived as separate lines, or they may be too fine to be distinguished individually at a casual glance, collectively conveying an impression of smooth tonal variation. The surface of the plate is inked, and then wiped clean; ink remains in the incisions and is transferred to paper when it is brought into contact with it under pressure.

The complexity of the banknote design is enhanced by multiple printing in superimposed colours, by gradation and change of colour within the image of individual plates (*see* RAINBOW PRINTING), and by the use of mechanically generated patterns. The combined effect of these measures is to produce an image beyond the capacity of camera or human skill to imitate. Finally the printed image, through the special nature of its ink and the pressure with which it is applied to the paper, appears not as a flat mark but as a relief impression, discernible to the touch.

Additional deterrents to the forger are serial numbering; watermarks, fluorescing and magnetic inks; and threads, strips, or other features built into the paper during its manufacture. A further deterrent, present throughout the history of paper currency, has been the threat of punishment – at some periods, even of death.

Two major developments in security printing took place in the 19th century. The American Jacob Perkins devised a method for hardening soft engraving metals, so that they would stand up to printing runs of 30,000 rather than the formerly accepted maximum of 5000. In addition he devised the technique of 'transferring' the incised image from one plate to another, thereby producing multiple facsimile plates. After hardening, each of these multiple plates was capable of runs six times longer than that of the single original. Perkins's innovation had a security advantage too. Previously, long runs had required a succession of hand-engraved plates, none of which precisely matched the other, thus making forgeries harder to detect. Now it was possible to produce virtually unlimited copies of an exactly uniform image.

The other major development came also from an American, Asa Spencer. Spencer invented 'guillochage', the production of intricate geometric patterns by machine. With Spencer's patterning and Perkins's transfer system, it became possible to compose complex security designs and print them rapidly. Both principles remain in use today.

In Britain, banknotes emerged in the late 17th century as simple handwritten notes addressed to individuals by name, promising to repay a specified sum deposited by the addressee with the bank. The note was actually evidence of credit, and it was used as such in transactions with third parties. The note would be passed from hand to hand in the manner of a modern printed note. At a later stage the note was part-printed, with spaces for insertion of details. To allow for transfer from one holder to another, the words 'or Bearer' were printed after the name space. Soon afterwards handwritten wording showed only the date of issue of the note against the original deposit, and the signature of the bank's cashier.

A proliferation of banks in the early part of the 19th century brought a mass of different banknotes. By 1810 Britain had well over 700 'country banks', each issuing its own locally engraved notes. Designs were on the whole elementary and became easy subjects for the forger.

In spite of the imposition of the death penalty, counterfeiting was widespread. In the year 1817, there were 28,412 forgeries reported, probably only a small proportion of those actually in circulation. In the period between 1797 and 1829 Britain sentenced 618 people to death for forging banknotes. It was this state of affairs that led George Cruikshank in 1819 to issue his famous 'skit' note, a bitter commentary on what he saw as a combination of inadequacy and brutality (*see* FORGERY). His dual advocacy of the abolition of the death penalty for forgery and the introduction of less easily forged notes played no small part in initiating Britain's anti-counterfeit drive and the researches of Perkins, Spencer, and others (*see* COMPOUND-PLATE PRINTING).

The financial crisis of 1825–26 saw the collapse of sixty banks in England and Wales. Bankruptcies were widespread, and large numbers of bankruptcy notes have survived to tell the tale. These bear cancellation marks, mutilations, and other signs of collapse, with overstampings showing the amount paid in the pound.

In America, an early issue of notes was engraved and printed clandestinely in Boston, Massachusetts, with the British still present and the area virtually under siege. Paul Revere, silversmith, engraver – and shortly national hero – manufactured £100,000 worth of notes in a secret plant, constructing his own improvised press for the job. He afterwards completed two more orders for notes, with a face value totalling £120,000. Notes in this later consignment bear the image of a minute man with a sword in one hand. An inscription reads: 'Issued in Defence of American Liberty'. The notes became famous as 'Sword hand money'.

As with Britain, America was also to see a proliferation of private banks. By 1837 they numbered 788, but in that year came a financial crisis. The collapse of many British banks (and the consequent withdrawal of gold from the United States by British investors) contributed to the failure of American banks. From this period date large numbers of American 'broken bank' notes.

Later, however, there was again an increase in the number of American banks. By 1860 the United States had 1562 banks, each with its own note issue and, it is said, a total of 30,000 varieties of notes. As earlier in Britain, forged notes were common.

By the mid 19th century the banknote industry had begun to be concentrated in a number of major firms. In America such names as Danforth, Perkins & Co.; Danforth, Vail & Hufly; Bald Cousland & Co.; Toppan Carpenter & Co.; Jocelyn, Draper, Welsh & Co.; John E. Gavit; Rawdon, Wright, Hatch & Edson; and Wellstood, Hay & Whiting had emerged. They were to be formed in 1858 into The American Bank Note Co. Later the company was joined by a number of other leading security printers, among them the National Bank Note Co.; the Continental Bank Note Co.; Bradbury Wilkinson & Co. (of Britain); and the Canadian Bank Note Co. Ltd.

The 20th-century banknote has maintained many of the devices and conventions of its forebears, partly as a matter of design tradition and partly in the continuing interests of the security needs that first engendered them. The skills of the engraver, increasingly rare in the world outside the security printing field, are themselves a measure of defence against imitation. In addition, specialization in different fields – lettering, borders, portraits, figures, etc. – means that no single engraver could ever expect to handle the whole of a banknote design on his or her own. This division of skills, each at its highest pitch of perfection, poses a multiple obstacle to the forger.

The prominent use of the portrait, monarch or national leader, also provides a contribution to security. While changes in details of borders, numerals, and decoration might escape casual notice, the human eye is quick to spot changes in portrait features. It is in this field too that the forger most often fails.

Among the more or less standard ingredients of banknote design, the portrait is followed in popularity by the typical national scene, representations of national products, flora and fauna, and well-known public buildings. These elements, drawn from material supplied by the client state or from the printing company's own library, are incorporated in an original hand-executed design for approval. It is from this artwork that the required engravings are afterwards made.

In earlier times pictorial ingredients were often lifted from popular paintings or other sources. Edwin Landseer's well-known 'Monarch of the Glen' was a favoured image, much used by the American Bank Note Co. in the 1860s, and by the British American Bank Note Co. in the early 1900s. It appeared, as did many such images, on notes for a wide variety of different companies. At least twelve of Landseer's paintings served as models for engravings, not only for banknotes but for cheques, stock certificates, and other fiscal documents. Today's designs, however, are invariably derived from materials exclusive to the client.

The banknote is studied and collected under a variety of headings. These include, as well as nation of origin, the work of specific printers; 'specimen' notes; serial-number oddities; misprints and errors; bisected notes (in currency adjustment or for safety in transmission); overprinted and overstamped notes; broken-bank notes; 'skit' notes (*see* MOCK MONEY); notes sharing common design ingredients; engravers' and printers' proofs; original banknote artwork; and emergency or provisional issues.

See also 'BANKNOTE', PROMOTIONAL; BANKNOTE, SPECIMEN; FORGERY; PLAYING CARD, SECONDARY USES

REFERENCES Gunnar Andersen, *Banknotes: Principles and Aesthetics in Security Graphics* (Copenhagen: Danmarks Nationalbank, 1975); Yasha Beresiner, *A Collector's Guide to Paper Money* (New York: Stein & Day, 1977; London: Andre Deutsch, 1977); Yasha Beresiner, *The Story of Paper Money* (New York: Arco Publishing, 1973); Grover C. Criswell, *Confederate and Southern States Currency*, 2nd rev. edn (Citra, Florida: Criswell, 1976); R. M. Fitzmaurice, *British Banks and Banking* (Truro: Barton, 1975); William H. Griffiths, *The Story of the American Bank Note Company* (New York: American Bank Note Co., 1959); A. D. Mackenzie, *The Bank of England Note* (Cambridge: Cambridge University Press, 1953); Chuck O'Donnell, *The Standard Handbook of Modern United States Paper Money*, 6th edn (New York: Harry J. Forman, 1977); Fred Schwan, *The Paper Money of the E. A. Wright Bank Note Company* (Portage, Ohio: BNR Press, 1978)

COLLECTIONS Bank of England Museum, London; Smithsonian Institution, Washington, DC; Western Reserve Historical Society, History Library, Cleveland, Ohio

SOCIETIES International Bank Note Society (US); Society of Paper Money Collectors Inc.; World Banknote Collector's Club

'Banknote', promotional

Quotation marks in this title convey the fact that the item in question is not – nor does it purport to be – a real BANKNOTE. The term is applied to 'no value' specimens designed and printed by banknote manufacturers as examples of their work.

These promotional specimens display the full range of engraving and printing expertise. Because their design is not constrained by a client's stipulations, they show an unusual range of graphic treatment, and the artists and craftsmen concerned take full advantage of the opportunity to show off their skills.

As Douglas (1980) points out, their 'notes' are not to be confused with speculative designs produced with specific banks in mind as 'try-ons'. Nor may they be described as 'unadopted designs', which term implies a commission by the bank in question. Nor are they 'essays' – trial drawings of commissioned work. In the majority of cases the designs incorporate the printing company's name and address, sometimes with additional promotional copy: 'We will be pleased to prepare designs and submit estimates for all classes of Monetary Documents, such as Bank Notes, Postage and Revenue Stamps, Bonds, Share Certificates, Letters of Credit, Drafts, Cheques, etc.' (Bradbury Wilkinson).

'Notes' have occasionally been printed from actual plates of current issues, but these bear an overprint – as for example: 'Waterlow & Sons Ltd. Specimen Note. Of No Value'. They may also be printed in colours different from the official issue. These too must be seen as promotional items – not, as sometimes claimed, commissioned 'specimens' or 'colour trials'.

The promotional note has been a feature of the security printing business in many countries. In Britain their use dates from at least the 1890s. Bradbury Wilkinson & Co. Ltd and Waterlow & Sons Ltd have been the principal producers.

See also BANKNOTE, SPECIMEN

REFERENCE James Douglas, *Promotional Banknotes* (St Albans: Transatlantic Authors Ltd, 1980)

Banknote, specimen

As new note issues appear it is the practice to circulate examples to banks and other institutions as a matter of advance information and reference. These notes are identical in every respect to those in the actual issue, except for an obviously fictitious numbering (for example '000000') and an obliterating cancellation. This usually takes the form of the word 'Specimen' ('Campione', 'Muster', etc.) or such variants as 'Muestra sin valor', 'Ungyldig', 'Annullée', etc. The cancellation may be printed or perforated.

The notes are, of course, invalid as currency; but in some cases their scarcity may give them a high value to the collector. As a general rule a few hundred examples are distributed to the issuing bank. These, though rare, are in the lower order of scarcity. In another category are those from banks which actually sell specimens; most in demand, for obvious reasons, are notes from banks known to release specimens to private individuals. 'Specimen' notes may also be used by banknote printers as promotional items.

See also BANKNOTE; 'BANKNOTE', PROMOTIONAL

REFERENCES Gunnar Andersen, *Banknotes: Principles and Aesthetics in Security Graphics* (Copenhagen: Danmarks Nationalbank, 1975); Yasha Beresiner, *A Collector's Guide to Paper Money* (New York: Stein & Day, 1977; London: Andre Deutsch, 1977)

Banknote-duty stamp

Except for issues of the Bank of England and those of some of the leading Scottish banks, banknotes of the British Isles in the period 1783 to 1921 were subject to duty. The exempt banks paid an annual sum in place of the duty. Payment of the duty was indicated by the addition of an official stamp, applied to each note individually at Somerset House, London. As with a wide range of Stamp Office duty stamps, the stamps in question were not separate entities, affixed to the notes with glue, but impressions conveyed directly to the surface by embossing or printing, or a combination of both. The system had been in use in Britain since 1694, when it was applied to a duty on vellum, parchment, and paper in legal instruments.

The banknote duty stamp is to be found only on notes of the many 'country banks' (most of which had failed by 1830).

Prior to 1821, the duty was denoted by means of a stamp embossed in colourless relief on the face of the banknote. After that date the stamp was printed on the back of the note, the stamp taking the form of a two-colour compound-plate printed design produced by Sir William Congreve's 'anti counterfeit' method (*see* COMPOUND-PLATE PRINTING). Of the compound-plate printed stamps, two also bore central motifs in blind relief. The £1 value showed St George and the dragon and the £5 value showed the head of George IV. Each of the designs appeared with minor changes of plate and die in the period 1821–30, and in a considerable number of 'varieties'.

The Congreve process was cumbersome and slow. Delays through mechanical breakdowns brought complaints from bankers, some of whom on occasion were so short of notes that they requested and paid for higher-denomination stampings of the earlier (colourless non-compound) kind. The system proved inadequate not only because of production and handling problems but because the compound-plate printing effect did not afford the degree of security expected. In addition, the blind-embossing tended to flatten and disappear as the notes became worn, and the 'relief' effect was counterfeited as readily as the rest of the stamp and note itself.

The Congreve stamp was abandoned for English banknotes in 1828, when duties were again denoted by colourless embossing on the front of the note as before. Scottish banks continued to use the Congreve stamps until 1845. As payment by composition became more widespread, use of stamps of any kind disappeared.

REFERENCE Marcus Samuel, 'The stamp duties on British and Irish bank notes, 1783–1891', *Essay Proof-Journal*, nos. 83–90, 1964–66

Baptismal papers

Ceremonial immersion or sprinkling with water was widely practised in antiquity as a form of religious initiation and was universal among Christians from the inception of the Church. At first the rite was administered to adults, but by the 6th century it had become general for children and was specifically associated with the ceremony of naming. Among Baptists the rite is of total immersion of the adult as an indication of conversion.

Certificate

Of Baptism administered with water, in the Name of the Father, and of the Son, and of the Holy Ghost.

This is to certify that Elizabeth daughter of Joseph and Hannah Goldthorp of Greenwall in the Parish of Glossop in the County of Derby was born December 8th 1845 and baptized March 8th 1846 By Ambrose Kirkland

Minister of the Gospel.

Given under my hand, this 28th day of May 1846.

Certificate of baptism, Glossop, Derbyshire, 28 May 1846. Letterpress. 124 × 200 mm (4⅞ × 8⅝ in)

In Britain, records of Anglican baptism are kept in parish registers together with those of births, marriages, and deaths. As with registers, certificates are transcripts of entries in the church record. In many cases evidence of birth and baptism is combined in one document.

Most certificates of baptism appear as printed forms filled in by hand, but are also found as wholly handwritten papers. Wholly handwritten records are also found as notes on odd slips of paper; most of these are not certificates, but memoranda from which the officiating minister would later enter details in the register. For long the baptismal certificate served not only as a record of formal admission into the Church but often as evidence of age (on enlistment, marriage, etc.). It was issued either at the time of the ceremony or at later dates on special application. It commonly bears the signature of the vicar, sometimes of a curate or locum. In some cases the certificate records baptism by a layman in an emergency.

Printed baptismal certificates of the 18th and 19th centuries were variously worded. They ranged from the general, in which details were entered on a Register-Keeper's form: 'truly extracted from the Register of the Parish', to the specific: 'Certificate of Baptism, administered with water, in the Name of the Father, and of the Son, and of the Holy Ghost ...'. The forms measure some 120 × 200 mm (4¾ × 7⅞ in). Later forms adopt the landscape columnar format introduced for the birth and marriage certificates of the General Register Office and still in use today.

In Britain, because of the risk of the use of registers as aids in persecution, most records for nonconformist congregations prior to the 1640s and 1650s are rare. As a general rule they were simply not kept; nonconformist baptismal certificates of the period are similarly rare.

In the second half of the 18th century nonconformists sought parity with Anglicans in legal recognition of their certificates of birth and baptism. Nonconformist records were by this time kept openly. Though church leaders had formerly resisted government scrutiny, now they pressed for acknowledgement of their records as documents admissible in law. The year 1742 saw the inception of an 'unofficial' record, a 'General Register of the Births of the Children of Protestant Dissenters of the three Denominations' (Presbyterians, Independents, and Baptists). This voluntary register, of baptisms as well as births, was based at Dr Williams's Library in Red Cross Street, London. It gave thousands of nonconformists a quasi-legal status. In 1783, when Stamp Duty was imposed on certificates, nonconformist ministers took out licences and duly stamped their birth and baptism certificates, paying the required fee. The move was advocated as a further step toward official recognition.

By the time the register closed in 1837 the Library had registered a total of 48,975 names. Numerous specimens of 'Dr Williams's certificates' survive. Their printed wording was changed from time to time during their 195 years' run to take account of new legislation and administrative methods. Parchment gave way to paper in 1826. Baptisms are indicated by the presence of a capital 'D' in the top right-hand corner.

With the advent of the General Register Office in 1836, births, marriages, and deaths were henceforth to be registered by the State. Marriage could be solemnized in church or at Registrars' Offices. Baptism became a matter for the churches alone, and their own certificates (as with confirmation and marriage) continue to be issued today.

In Germany, baptism certificates were often viewed not merely as formal records but as decorative mementoes. The FRAKTUR, later brought by immigrants to America, featured births and marriages as well as baptisms. The *Taufscheine* (baptism certificate) became a component of the later American *Family Register*, which later also gained some currency in Britain.

In the Catholic Church the record of baptism appears, together with details of confirmation, marriage, ordination, etc., in the original records of the church of the subject's birthplace. Baptism is seen not as an isolated event but as part of the continuum of the subject's religious life, and the baptismal certificate commonly provides space for details of confirmation. Similarly, baptismal details also appear on the marriage certificate.

See also BIRTH CERTIFICATE; CURRIER & IVES; DEATH CERTIFICATE; MARRIAGE CERTIFICATE

REFERENCE D. J. Steel, *Sources for Nonconformist Genealogy and Family History* (London: Phillimore/Society of Genealogists, 1973)

Bastardy papers

Papers relating to illegitimacy, both in the matter of statistics and individual detail, are of uncertain evidential value. Historically, methods of report and compilation have varied greatly, and even in the 20th century practices may differ as between one country or state and another. In America, for example, while most states require illegitimacy figures, many do not. In most countries evasion of the record has always been widespread, with or without the cooperation of the social and family circle. It may generally be assumed that official figures, where published, are low rather than high.

In Britain, the incidence of illegitimacy and its social and economic repercussions, are reflected in an extensive range of early legal forms, each designed to meet a specific contingency. They are to be found, duly filled in with their respective details, in considerable numbers among miscellaneous papers of the 18th and 19th centuries. It must be said that their chief concern, as expressed in their wording, appears economic rather than moral. Warrants for the detention of the alleged father refer to the sworn declaration of the mother-to-be and to the fact that 'the said Child is likely to be born a Bastard, and to be chargeable to the parish'. Many of these forms are in fact framed specifically as applications by Overseers of the Poor to Justices of the Peace, seeking protection, or redress, in the matter of charges on the parish.

The forms, of which there had been sixteen different types in

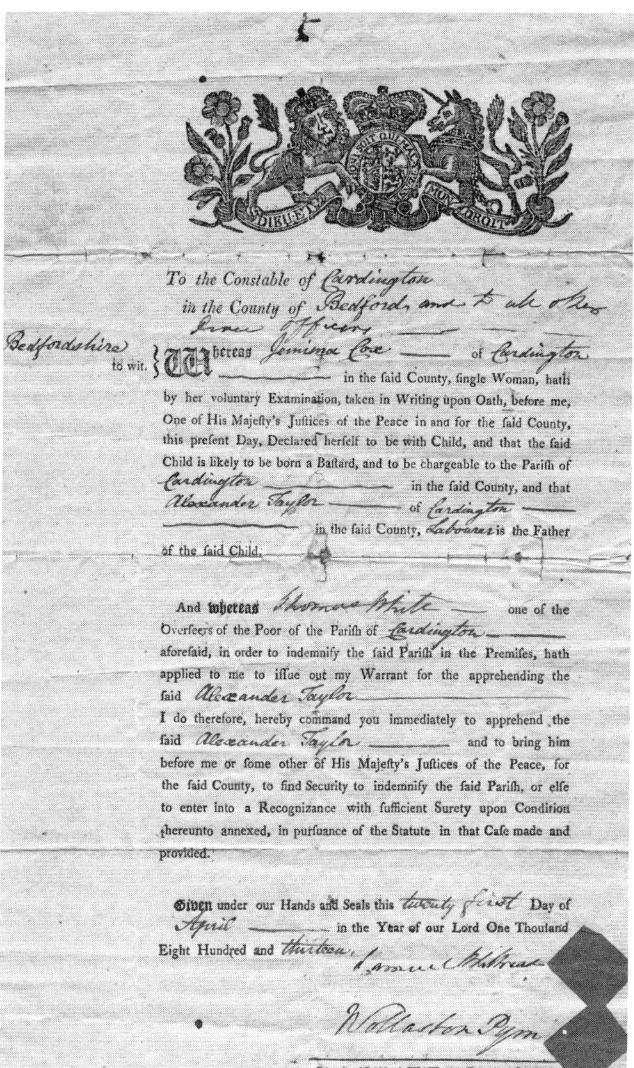

DIEU ET MON DROIT

To the Constable of Cardington
in the County of Bedford, and to all other Peace Officers

Bedfordshire to wit. } Whereas Jemima Cox of Cardington in the ſaid County, ſingle Woman, hath by her voluntary Examination, taken in Writing upon Oath, before me, One of His Majeſty's Juſtices of the Peace in and for the ſaid County, this preſent Day, Declared herſelf to be with Child, and that the ſaid Child is likely to be born a Baſtard, and to be chargeable to the Pariſh of Cardington in the ſaid County, and that Alexander Taylor of Cardington in the ſaid County, Labourer is the Father of the ſaid Child.

And whereas Thomas White one of the Overſeers of the Poor of the Pariſh of Cardington aforeſaid, in order to indemnify the ſaid Pariſh in the Premiſes, hath applied to me to iſſue out my Warrant for the apprehending the ſaid Alexander Taylor

I do therefore, hereby command you immediately to apprehend the ſaid Alexander Taylor and to bring him before me or ſome other of His Majeſty's Juſtices of the Peace, for the ſaid County, to find Security to indemnify the ſaid Pariſh, or elſe to enter into a Recognizance with ſufficient Surety upon Condition thereunto annexed, in purſuance of the Statute in that Caſe made and provided.

Given under our Hands and Seals this twenty first Day of April in the Year of our Lord One Thouſand Eight Hundred and thirteen.

Wollaston Pym

Baſtards, 7. Printed and Sold by J. SHAW, 137, Fetter-lane, London.

Form declaring a child likely to be born a bastard, with a warrant for the apprehension of the alleged father, Cardington, Bedfordshire, 21 April 1813. Letterpress and manuscript. 340 × 205mm (13⅜ × 8⅛in)

the 1760s, extended in the 1840s to twenty-four. They reveal a relentless pursuit of the putative father, with provision for every stratagem in his attempted escape. The 1840s series includes warrants of arrest; of distraint on goods and chattels for payment of parish charges; of attachment of wages for the same; and of arrest for imprisonment of the employer in failure of distraint. Among other papers of bastardy are convicted fathers' petitions from prison, pleading inability to pay, and assize-calendar charges of concealment of birth or 'having feloniously and wilfully murdered a new-born female child'.

See also BIRTH CERTIFICATE; FORM

REFERENCES Joseph Shaw, *Parish Law*, 19th edn (London, 1763); Bere (Commissioner) and Thomas Chitty, *Burn's Justice of the Peace and Parish Officer*, 29th edn, 6 vol. (London: Sweet, 1845); William Addington, *An Abridgement of Penal Statutes*, 2nd edn (London: T. Whieldon, 1783)

Battledore

The name 'battledore' was used at first as a secondary term for the HORNBOOK, a handled wooden panel bearing a schoolchild's alphabet, and faced with a sheet of transparent horn. The word is thought to be cognate with 'bat' and 'beat' (Spanish, *batidero*: beater) and its use in this sense is attributed to its unofficial function in playground ball games. However, the bat-shaped hornbook or battledore was slowly superseded in the

18th century by a folding card, also showing the alphabet and often including illustrations, verses, and other educational material. The card was also for a period described as a 'horn-book', though neither term was strictly appropriate to the handle-less card. William Hone, in a note cited by Tuer (1896) reports one such card in 1830 as bearing the printed title *The Horn-Book or Battledore,* a designation which he decries, 'for it is neither in shape or substance what it is called'.

It was with the cardboard item that the term 'battledore' became chiefly associated, notwithstanding its unsuitability for use in ball games. So close did the association become during the hundred years or so of its currency that the word was in turn transferred to the alphabet booklets of the Victorian era. Tuer records a six-page booklet in the British Museum dated 1835, entitled *The Battledore, or First Book for Children.* The introduction of the cardboard battledore is attributed to Benjamin Collins of Salisbury, who claimed to have invented it in 1746 and, in the period 1770–80, to have printed and sold over a hundred thousand of them.

The battledore was folded icon-wise to present three vertical panels on which were printed alphabets, one- and two-syllable word lists, numerals, and sometimes elementary stories and captioned woodcuts. The average size of the folded card was 135 × 70 mm (5¼ × 2¾ in). A consistent feature of the battledore is its relatively narrow left-hand panel; while the centre and right-hand panels are of equal width, the left-hand unit is hardly more than a flap, cut at top and foot at forty-five degrees in the manner of a wallet. In some instances the flap is less than a third of the width of the main panels, though it is always used as a printing area, even if only for the maker's imprint.

The inner printed face of the battledore was commonly coated with varnish, the outside being covered in patterned Dutch paper. Later the Dutch paper and varnish were omitted, the card printed on both surfaces, and the price reduced from twopence to one penny. Later the price came down to a half-penny (though toward the end of its run, in the first half of the 19th century, the general price was restored to one penny). Battledores were commonly published and sold by printers, who produced them in multiples of sixteen to a single sheet, afterwards cutting them into separate units. They were sold by stationers and by chapbook vendors who bought them whole-sale.

The battledore became such a universally recognized item of stationery that stock alphabet woodcuts, showing familiar items with their capital initials, were used by printers, to be composed into battledore panels as desired. Among major printers and publishers of battledores were the Rushers, father and son, whose establishment at Banbury was famous for its juvenilia and chapbook productions. Other names were Davison of Alnwick; Thomas Richardson (Derby); Leighton and Wright (Nottingham); G. R. Barber (Eastwood); Toller (Kettering); James Kendrew (York); Fordyce (Newcastle); Stark and Mozely (Gainsborough); G. Nall (Bakewell); Whitehorne (Penryn); W. Humphreys (Carnarvon [Caernarfon]); Spurrell (Carmarthen); and Newbery, Innes, and Catnach (London).

Battledore, early 19th century. Letterpress with wood-engravings, printed by J. Appleton, Stockton. 135 × 207 mm (5¼ × 8⅛ in)

In the early 1840s a series of six battledores appeared over the imprint of Chapman & Hall under the title *Gaffer Goodman's Picture Horn-Books.* These 'Instructions cards', as the publishers called them, were designed to be presented to the child one at a time, 'each having all the allurements of a new plaything'. The series was among the last of the British battledores. By the early 1850s they had given way to the child's reader or *Reading Made Easy.* (This also was to contribute a schoolroom term; throughout the British Isles it was known as a 'reader-me-daisy'.)

The battledore appeared in America, though its currency was narrower, and the term was often applied to more elaborate learning aids. Wilbur Macey Stone, the American collector, quoted by Beulah Folmsbee (1971), describes *The Uncle's Present,* printed by Jacob Johnson of Philadelphia (1810): 'Four leaves, all engraved, English Street Cries'. Also recorded is a six-page booklet, by Jacob Johnson. This carried the alphabet on the cover wrapper and presented six letters per page, each with its pictorial mnemonic. Here the title is *The Uncle's Present – A New Battledore.*

REFERENCES Andrew W. Tuer, *History of the Horn-Book* (London, 1896; reprint Amsterdam: Emmering, 1971); Beulah Folmsbee, *A Little History of the Horn-Book* (Boston: The Horn Book Inc., 1971)

Beer label

Marketed at first in barrels, and later largely in unmarked bottles, beer was virtually unbranded until the mid 1830s. At about that time brewers and bottlers began identifying themselves and their product by an impression stamped into the wax of the seal covering the cork. Later, it is thought, the seal was replaced by a metal foil cap, which was similarly impressed. Low survival rates of bottles, closures, and labels alike make verification difficult.

Printed paper beer labels appeared in the early 1840s. Such labels, pasted on the side of the bottle, were generally circular, sometimes square or diamond-shaped, rarely measured more than some 60 or 70 mm (2⅜ × 2¾ in), and were printed in a single colour on white paper. The small circular label was afterwards replaced by a larger oval label, but the smaller roundel remained in use among local breweries in some areas into the 1930s. Bottling was carried out at first by individual beer shops and pubs, but in the 1860s and 1870s agents and exporters, as well as brewers themselves, took over.

Earliest labels bear the names not only of brewers – Bass & Co. (Burton-upon-Trent); Thomas Salt & Co. (Burton-upon-Trent); Scholfield (Ashton-under-Lyne); Young & Stephen (Dudley) – but of bottlers, agents, and exporters. Surviving examples bear such names as Roberts & Son (London); Robert B. Byass (London); J. W. Bridges (London); and J. Goldart (Norwich). The majority of these relate to pale ale, a brew specially suited for export and generally styled 'East India Pale Ale' (or, as geography required, 'West India Ale').

'Senate' beer label of Chr. Heurich Brewing Co., Washington, DC., early 20th century. Lithographed in three colours. 82 × 116 mm (3¼ × 4½in)

The introduction of the screw-top in 1879 led to the use of the stopper label, a paper strip covering the closure as a guard against unauthorized opening. This label acquired added significance with the passing of the Intoxicating Liquors (Sale to Children) Act, 1901, which made it illegal to serve unsealed beer to under-age messengers, then widely used by parents on errands. The label commonly bore the legend 'See that this label is unbroken', and in some cases cited the Act.

The stopper label began to disappear with the introduction of the crown cork in 1892 (though it continued in use in some areas until the 1950s). As the stopper label was phased out, the side label became the focus of attention. The larger oval label came into widespread use, and there was a general consolidation of trade marks, brand names, and label designs, with frequent prosecutions under the Trade Marks Acts of the 1870s and 1880s. Forgery of labels was rife. A collection of some 2000 counterfeits and close imitations is in the archives of the Bass company at Burton-upon-Trent. Close imitations continued to appear in some countries in the latter part of the 20th century. The ubiquitous oval was followed over the years by a wide range of shapes and sizes, but the advent of automatic labelling brought a preference for the straight-edged label (at least one straight edge being essential for handling by machine). A number of companies compromised by printing ovals and other shapes on a dark rectangular background, thus preserving a visual link with tradition.

Public-relations enterprise induced many of the brewery companies of the 20th century to produce so-called 'commemorative' brews on special occasions. This has led to a corresponding increase in the number of published labels; though the number of individual companies has fallen (in Britain from 6000 in 1900 to fewer than 150 in the 1980s), the number of different brews continues to be high.

Britain's pattern of brewery mergers, take-overs, and closures is reflected throughout the world, and a major field of label research and study is among the thousands of obsolete names, some of them long defunct, some still remembered. In the late 1970s, countering the generally downward trend in the total of individual breweries, a number of new local companies were started. These, seeking to 'de-industrialize' the product and its public image, brewed their own formula and contributed new names and labels. Numerous minor variants also began to appear in Britain in the 1960s with the introduction of legislation requiring details of content, ingredients, metric measure, and dating to be included on the label.

REFERENCES Keith Osborne and Brian Pipe, *The International Book of Beer Labels, Mats & Coasters* (London: Hamlyn, 1979; New Jersey: Chartwell, 1979)

COLLECTIONS Bass Ltd, Burton-upon-Trent; Keith Osborne, c/o Labologists Society, Farnborough, Hants

SOCIETIES Adelaide Labology Group, South Australia; Brewery History Society (UK); East Coast Breweriana Collector Society; Labolog Club (Czech Republic); Labologists Society (UK)

Beer mat

Known also as 'drip mat' or 'coaster', 20th-century beer mats originated as disposable versions of the porcelain or metal mug and bottle stand used domestically to protect table surfaces. (The word 'coaster' derives from the silver decanter tray, originally on wheels, which 'coasted' the table, making a circuit from one diner to the other.)

The first wood-pulp mat was produced in Germany and patented by Robert Sputh of Dresden in 1892. By the 1920s the device had been adopted in a number of countries in Europe, America, and Australasia, its value as an advertising medium far outweighing its utility as a protector of pub tables and bar counters. Early mats were thick, often rough in texture or embossed. Later specimens are thinner, smoother, and in general more colourful. A variety of materials have been used; they include – as well as wood pulp – cork, rubber, leather, felt, linen, plastic, linoleum, aluminium, paper, card, and paper-encapsulated wood pulp.

Among the first British mats were those produced by Watney, Combe, Reid & Co. Ltd for Watney's Pale Ale and Reid's Stout in the 1930s. Worthington & Co. Ltd, Bass, and Ratcliffe & Gretton Ltd also produced mats in the pre-1939 period, notably a series of eight featuring British pubs.

Beer-mat collecting had its origins in the souvenirs pocketed by 1930s tourists. Visitors to Germany, where the beer mat was firmly established, were specially attracted to them, sometimes using them as greetings cards and addressing, stamping, and posting them from cafés without either a wrapper or an envelope. At least one such souvenir, now in a private collection, was thus addressed from the airship the Graf Zeppelin. Postal use was later to become a standard promotional ploy, and brewery companies produced mats that were designed specifically as greetings cards, complete with space for message, address, and stamp.

Mats were at first cut and printed individually, but multiple production soon demanded sheets of six at a time, later seventy-two at a time.

Output has grown enormously. The publicity impact of the mat has been exploited not only by the drinks industry itself but by a multitude of other advertisers. Among many 'non-brewery' users have been tobacco companies, newspapers, employment agencies, dry-cleaners, museums, country clubs, hotels, and agricultural shows. The beer mat has also been used in election propaganda, for road safety campaigns, and by anti-pollution and other lobbyists.

Much ingenuity has been devoted to the development of the mat as a 'collectable', some advertisers issuing sets of mats and, in a number of cases, mats which together compose a larger visual unit. Sets first began to appear in 1957, when McMullen's issued a twelve-item mat under the title 'Collector's Series of Vintage Cars'. Series issues may appear as numbered sets or simply as extended 'themes', running indefinitely. A Frankfurt company, Binding Brew, has been issuing a series of cartoon mats since the 1950s. Some 300 subjects have appeared. Novelty issues have included interlocking 'jigsaw' mats; 'giant' mats for counters and trays; shaped mats representing animals, maps, barrels, etc.; and riddles and puzzles. At least one mat has appeared, suitably notched, in the guise of a wool-winding spool. As with beer labels, which may celebrate special occasions (and their corresponding special brewings), beer-mat issues are often commemorative. Such occasions have included the 1951 Festival of Britain, the Coronation of 1953, the Empire and Commonwealth Games of 1958, and the Brussels 'Expo 58'.

Apart from those issued for special occasions and commemorations, beer mats commonly show little or no indication of date or issue, and most manufacturers and issuing companies have neglected to keep records. A notable exception is the Imperial Tobacco Co., which has allocated code numbers to every item of its advertising since 1905. The company's beer mats, promoting cigarettes and tobaccos, carry four- and five-figure numbers preceded by the initials ITC. A dated list of these, covering the period 1930–73, appears in Osborne and Pipe (1979).

Advertising beer mats are prohibited by law by some authorities. There are thus no recent specimens from Canada or from a number of states in America, notably California, Indiana, Kentucky, Michigan, Ohio, Oregon, Utah, and Virginia. Mats from companies in these areas may however be found in places outside the jurisdiction of their respective courts.

REFERENCE Kenneth Osborne and Brian Pipe, *The International Book of Beer Labels, Mats & Coasters* (London: Hamlyn, 1979; New Jersey: Chartwell, 1979)

SOCIETIES American Breweriana Association (Coaster Corner); British Beermat Collectors' Society; The Canadian Brewerianist; Gambrinus Club van Belgie; German Breweriana Collector Society; Guinness Collectors Club; Internationaler Brauereikultur-Verband; New South Wales Coaster Collectors Club Inc

Bellman's verses

The greetings sheets known as 'bellman's verses' were a feature of London's Christmas season for some two hundred years, and were common in many provincial towns too. Printed to order by local jobbing printers, the sheets purported to convey the good wishes of the parish night-watchman or bellman to the individual householder. They were left at houses free of charge, with intimations that a suitable token of remembrance would be appreciated. They form part of the large body of 'call-back' literature, in which handbills, envelopes, and other items announced the impending return of the caller for alms, orders, wastepaper, etc. (*see* CALL-BACK HANDBILL).

Bellman's verse sheets carried a score or so of doggerel verses, allegedly composed by the bellman himself, commonly with a border of woodcut biblical scenes and a title picture showing the bellman at his nightly watch and ward in the streets. The sheets varied in size. At the height of their currency in the first half of the 19th century they commonly measured some 550 × 450 mm (21⅝ × 17¾in), though earlier specimens are less than half that size.

The sheets first appear in the 17th century. Dr Chambers, in his *Edinburgh Journal*, cites an example in the Luttrell Collection of broadsides in the British Museum dated 1683–84. It bears the title 'A copy of verses presented by Isaac Ragg, Bellman, to his Masters and Mistresses of Holbourne Division, in the Parish of St Giles-in-the-Fields'. Below the title picture are verses – all of them, says Chambers, 'very proper and very insufferable'. He quotes the prologue:

Time, Master, calls your bellman to his task
To see your doors and windows are all fast
And that no villany or foul crime be done
To you or yours in absence of the sun.
If any base lurker I do meet,
In private alley or in open street,
You shall have warning by my timely call,
And so God bless you and give rest to all.

Chambers also reports an earlier specimen (unlocated) in which one Thomas Law in 1666 greets 'his masters of St Giles Cripplegate, within the Freedom'. This specimen is reported as without illustration, and it would appear that the convention of the decorative woodcut was introduced as an 18th-century addition, reaching its final flowering in the period 1800 to 1850. The verse sheets disclose a variety of titles among the supplicants. The single word 'beadle' appears, but there is also 'Beadle and Bellman', 'Beadle, Bellman & Cryer', 'Beadle, Constable, Bellman and Engine Keeper', and 'Beadle, Constable and Summoning Officer for Coroner's Inquests'. Also featured, in a sheet from 1782 for the Parish of Christ Church, Middlesex, is James Rogers, 'Steeple-Keeper and Ringer of the Six and Eight o'Clock Bell'.

Upper part of a broadside of bellman's verses, Camberwell, London, 1831. Letterpress with wood-engraving. 175 × 235 mm (6⅞ × 9¼in)

Sheets from the mid 19th century show signs of standardization, not simply by imitation but by common sources. A number of printers specialized in bellman's verses, and one firm, Reynell & Weight, of Little Pulteney Street, served bellmen all over London. In some cases the same sheet appeared in different parishes simultaneously, only the district and name and address of the bellman being changed. Reynell & Weight (later C. & W. Reynell) claimed over a hundred years of bellman's verses 'originally and continuously printed at this establishment since the year 1735'.

The verses themselves were separately titled 'To my Masters', 'To my Mistresses', 'On Christmas Day', 'On the King', etc., and expressed little more than obsequiousness and sentimentality. There were however occasional ventures into moralizing ('On Idleness and Drunkenness'), and mentions of the personalities and events of the year: 'Memory of the Late Queen' (1822), 'Garibaldi' (1861), and 'The Prince of Wales in America' (1861).

Authorship of the verses is problematic: Norwich had a corporation poet who 'composed' for the bellman for twenty years. Their quality ranges from (in the main) hopeless doggerel, to occasional common competence. It is said, apparently on little evidence, that impoverished *literati* were sometimes induced to contribute. Among these were Charles Lamb and Leigh Hunt (from prison).

REFERENCE D. R. Mackarill, 'A history of Bellman's verses', *Journal of the Printing Historical Society*, no. 26, 1997, pp. 14–32.

Benefit ticket

A 'benefit' performance (of a play or other spectacle) devoted its proceeds wholly or partly to named recipients, commonly members of the company concerned. Tickets for such performances, specially printed for the purpose and bearing the name of the beneficiary, were sold by the nominees themselves, who also sometimes promoted the benefit performance at their own expense with advertising in newspapers and handbills.

The first recorded benefit performance was for Mrs Barry in January 1687. The idea, which started as a mark of royal appreciation, became a theatrical institution. Individual actors' receipts under the sharing system of the early stock companies were generally so low that many relied on their allotted benefit nights for survival.

Benefits were arranged not only for performers but for general theatre personnel – even occasionally scene painters and stage carpenters. Dramatists were also allowed benefits. The favour was also sometimes granted to families of deceased actors and to outside charities. The system was generally disliked by players, not only for the fact that it was an unsatisfactory substitute for a formal wages structure but for its often invidious and humiliating failure to draw support for individuals. The benefit nevertheless persisted as an institution, in London until the end of the 1890s and in the provinces until the early years of the 20th century. In America it began to die out in the 1860s and 1870s.

Early benefit tickets were often elaborately engraved in the manner of invitation cards, and for notable occasions they were designed by distinguished artists. In this field, as in many others, forgery was not uncommon, and the tickets were often provided with seals, blind embossing, numbering, signatures, and other security devices.

Later benefit tickets are generally about the size of a playing card, commonly landscape in format, and may be engraved or printed by letterpress with type and wood or metal decorations. In the majority of cases the tickets omit reference to the title of the play, printing only the name of the theatre and the beneficiary. The main legend is usually in the form 'Mrs Siddons's Night' (or 'Mrs Siddons's Benefit'), the date appearing sometimes in type, more often in manuscript. It was not unusual for a player to be allocated more than one benefit during a season, and tickets from the same print run could therefore be used, suitably dated by hand, for a number of occasions.

There is some evidence to indicate that among the 'peripheral' recipients of benefits were the printers on whom theatres relied, not only for the production of playbills but of the benefit tickets themselves. Local printers' files in some cases suggest a reciprocal arrangement, the printer providing tickets (and possibly other items) against the proceeds of one or more benefit nights. In one case, that of G. R. Gitton, printer of Bridgnorth, Shropshire, a number of surviving benefit tickets for the Bridgnorth Theatre bear the legend 'J Gittos's Night' and 'John Gittos's Ticket Night'. The name might be a pseudonym.

REFERENCES Judith Milhous, *The London Stage 1660–1800* (Carbondale: Southern Illinois University Press, 1960); Victoria Moger, *The Favour of Your Company* (London: Museum of London, 1980)

COLLECTION Museum of London; Victoria & Albert Museum, London

Bill of lading

The term commonly refers to a statement of goods loaded for transportation in a sea-going vessel, though it may also be used in air- and land-freightage. The document, which is not a contract in itself, but which implies the presence of a contract, itemizes the goods to be carried and names the carrier and the places between which the journey is to be made. In effect it is a RECEIPT by which the carrier takes responsibility for the goods listed and their safe delivery at their specified destination. The document (and hence the goods) may be bought and sold any number of times while the goods are on board.

Like the CHARTER PARTY, the bill of lading is among the earliest of marine documents. It is first recorded in *Hakluyt's Principall Navigations* (1599) as 'bills of lading' and appears in *Capt. Smith's Seaman's Grammar* (1627) as 'bills of loading'.

In terminology and general layout the bill of lading remained virtually unchanged for centuries and its terms were more or less universally adopted by the world's maritime traders. Typically, in its earliest form, it appears as a printed blank, landscape in format, often bearing an engraved illustration or large decorative initial, and having a broad left-hand margin. Spaces are left in the body of the text for insertion of details. The document commonly opens with the words 'Shipped in good order and well conditioned', the opening word generally being stressed typographically or by decorative embellishment. In many examples of the first half of the 19th century the heading is strengthened by a marginal illustration, sometimes of a dockside scene, more often of a ship at sea.

The wording in early versions makes frequent reference to God, often concluding with a prayer for safe arrival. A typical example made out in Middletown, Connecticut, in 1745 reads:

> Shipped in good Order and well Conditioned, by (Thos. Elmer and ye Rest of the owners of the Sloop Susannah) In and upon the good (Sloop) Called, The (Susannah) whereof is Master [under God] for this present Voyage (Stephen Williams) and now Riding at Anchor in the (harbour at Middletown) and (by God's Grace) Bound for (Barbadoes). To say, (ten horses, three thousand and two hundred of Lumber on the proper acct and Risque of the Shippers and goes Consigned to Mr Thomas Elemer) Being Marked and Numbered as in the Margent, and are to be Delivered in the like good Order and well Conditioned, at the aforesaid Port of (Barbadoes) [the Danger of the Seas only Excepted] unto (Sd Thos. Elmer) or to (his) Assigns, he or they paying Freight for the said (—) with Primage and Average accustomed.'.

'Primage and Average accustomed' refers to normal additional charges payable on freightage: primage was an *ex gratia* payment to the ship's master; average covered port charges, pilotage fees, etc.

After reciting further details the document concludes:

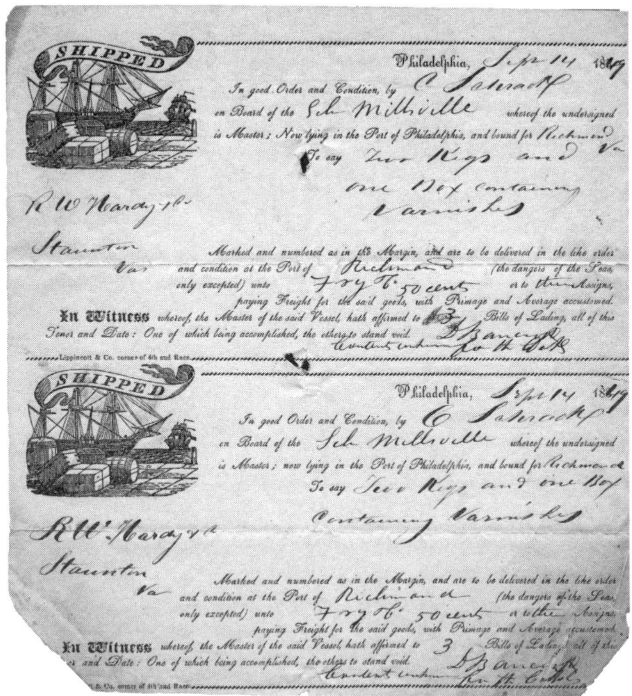

SHIPPED

Philadelphia, Sept 14 1849

In good Order and Condition, by
on Board of the whereof the undersigned
is Master; Now lying in the Port of Philadelphia, and bound for
To say

Marked and numbered as in the Margin, and are to be delivered in the like order
and condition at the Port of (the dangers of the Seas,
only excepted) unto 50 cents or to their Assigns,
paying Freight for the said goods, with Primage and Average accustomed.
In Witness whereof, the Master of the said Vessel, hath affirmed to 3 Bills of Lading, all of this
Tenor and Date: One of which being accomplished, the others to stand void.

Lippincott & Co. corner of 4th and Race.

SHIPPED

Philadelphia, Sept 14 1849

In good Order and Condition, by
on Board of the whereof the undersigned
is Master; now lying in the Port of Philadelphia, and bound for
To say

Marked and numbered as in the Margin, and are to be delivered in the like order
and condition at the Port of (the dangers of the Seas,
only excepted) unto 50 cents or to their Assigns,
paying Freight for the said goods, with Primage and Average accustomed.
In Witness whereof, the Master of the said Vessel, hath affirmed to 3 Bills of Lading, all of this
Tenor and Date: One of which being accomplished, the others to stand void.

Bills of lading, Philadelphia, 1830, with manuscript additions 14 September 1849. Letterpress, with stereotyped wood-engravings, printed two-up. 211 × 197 mm (8¼ × 7¾ in)

And so GOD send the good (Sloop) to her desired Port in safety, AMEN. Dated in (Middletown July 2d 1745. Stephen Williams).

The use of the margin for bale and barrel identifying marks became a more or less standard convention, and reflects a similar usage in naval reports for explanatory diagrams of engagements at sea.

With the passage of time, wording became less pious (though the final prayer, as noted in the example cited, remained in use in some cases into the 1890s). References to the hazards of the seas were greatly extended. In the 19th century they included 'Act of God, the Queen's Enemies, Pirates, Thieves, Robbers, Restraint of Princes, Rulers, and People; Damage by Vermin, Sweating, Leakage or otherwise, Jettison, Barratry, and Collision, Fire on Board … all Accidents, Loss, and Damage, whatsoever, from Machinery, Boilers, and Steam…'. An additional note disclaimed responsibility for inadequate packing.

Foreign-language examples, though differing in detail, present the same general tenor and appearance, sailing 'sous la garde de Dieu' and promising 'sauf les périls et fortunes de la mer' to deliver the goods 'marqué et numéroté comme en marge'.

It has commonly been the practice to make out bills of lading in sets of three, the first being retained by the consignor, the second accompanying the goods with the carrier, and the third (where practicable) being sent to the consignee by way of advice. The forms generally indicate that three copies have been made out 'the one of which, being accomplished, the other two to stand void'. The bills were often printed in sets on a single sheet, and specimens survive where two adjacent forms, identically completed by hand, remain undivided, the third having been despatched with the goods and 'accomplished'.

Many 19th-century examples bear illustrations of schooners (later steamships) as decoration at the head of the left-hand margin. These, STOCK BLOCKS and engraving motifs, convey a laggardly account of the changing image of the shipping of the period. Typically, an 1895 example, entered at London 'for the good ship called the Harwich' and bound for 'the Solant, near Fowey', bears an illustration of an 1830s square-rigger. With similarly slow response to change, early copper and wood engravings were successively reproduced on bills of lading by modern printing methods, unchanged from their original renderings.

Traditionalism, not only in illustration but wording, layout, and format has remained a feature of the bill of lading into the 20th century. Lewis (1962) shows an example still in use in the 1950s, in which virtually every feature of the 19th-century treatment appears, including phraseology ('Shipped in good order and well conditioned … upon the good ship …'), neo-copperplate script, and 1830s square-rigger.

REFERENCE John Lewis, *Printed Ephemera* (Ipswich: W. S. Cowell, 1962)

Bill of mortality

Earliest references to bills of mortality occur in England and Wales early in the 16th century, when records began to be kept 'of the number of such persons as be declared of the common sickness'. Weekly lists, at first handwritten, and later printed, were kept sporadically until the Births and Deaths Registration Act of 1836, when they were replaced by the official returns of the Registrar General.

Introduced in an effort to quantify outbreaks of disease, the bills appeared more or less regularly in plague years and irregularly, or not at all, in plague-free periods. In the worst times they were published weekly, with separate annual summaries.

Methods of compilation were rough and ready; layout and format varied, and not until 1728, when the ages of the dead were included, did the lists acquire any true statistical value. Figures were commonly analysed in three columns: burials; of the plague; christenings. Further analysis showed geographical distribution. The year's totals for London and its nine 'out-parishes' in 1665 were: burials 97,306; of the plague 68,596; christenings 9967.

The lists were untrustworthy in their plague figures. Relatives of the dead sought to conceal plague deaths so as to avoid quarantine regulations. They often bribed the official 'searchers' (the elderly women whose task was to report on deaths and their causes) to make false entries in returns. Medical ignorance further confused the picture, the searchers sometimes filing in good faith such diagnoses as 'greefe', 'aged', 'starved at nurse', 'suddenly', 'plannet struck', 'frighted'. In spite of their obvious inadequacy, bills of mortality were the sole source of statistical information on the course of the disease, and the authorities sought to eliminate conjecture and rumour by limiting the right to publish to a single printer. Pre-publishing the bills (by disclosure prior to submission to the required authority) was severely punished.

By virtue of their 'barometer' effect the bills were in great demand; at some periods they were sold in the streets for a penny or two and were avidly read for intimations of relief. They may be considered as among the earliest form of popular STREET LITERATURE.

The expression 'bill of mortality' was later applied to the districts within which the bills were rendered. The bill for London for the year 1832 (Guildhall Library) is thus entitled 'A General Bill of the Christenings and Burials within the City of London and Bills of Mortality'. By this time diagnosis had become more specific: the list of causes of death runs to 56 and includes

A Table shewing how many died weekly, as well of all Diseases, as of the Plague, in the Years 1592, 1603, 1625, 1630, 1636; and this present Year 1665.

Buried of all Diseases in the Year 1592.	Total	Pla.
March 17	230	3
March 24	351	31
March 31	219	29
April 7	307	27
April 14	203	33
April 21	290	37
April 28	310	41
May 5	350	29
May 12	339	38
May 19	300	42
May 26	450	58
June 2	410	62
June 9	441	81
June 16	399	99
June 23	401	108
June 30	850	118
July 7	1440	927
July 14	1510	893
July 21	1491	258
July 28	1507	85[illegible]
August 4	1502	33
August 11	1550	797
August 18	1532	651
August 25	1508	449
September 1	1490	507
September 8	1210	563
September 15	621	451
September 22	629	349
September 29	450	330
October 6	408	327
October 13	422	323
October 20	330	308
October 27	320	302
November 3	310	301
November 10	309	209
November 17	301	107
November 24	321	93
December 1	349	94
December 8	331	86
December 15	329	71
December 22	386	39
The Total of all that have been buried is 25886		
Whereof of the Plague 11503		

Buried of all Diseases in the Year 1603.	Total	Plag.
March 17	108	3
24	60	2
31	78	6
April 7	66	4
14	79	4
21	98	8
28	109	10
May 5	90	11
12	112	18
19	122	22
26	122	32
June 2	114	30
9	131	43
16	144	59
23	182	72
30	267	158
July 7	445	263
14	612	424
The Out-Parishes this Week were joyn'd with the City.		
July 21	1186	917
28	1728	1396
August 4	2256	1922
11	2077	1745
18	3054	2713
25	2853	2539
September 1	3385	3035
8	3078	2724
15	3129	2818
22	2456	2195
29	1961	1732
October 6	1831	1641
13	1312	1149
20	766	642
27	625	508
November 3	737	594
10	545	442
17	384	251
24	198	105
December 1	223	102
8	163	55
15	200	96
22	168	74
The Total of all is 37294		
whereof of the Plag. 30561		

Buried of all Diseases in the Year 1625.	Total	Plag.
March 17	262	4
24	226	8
31	243	11
April 7	239	10
14	256	24
21	230	25
28	305	26
May 5	292	30
12	232	45
19	379	71
26	401	78
June 2	395	69
9	434	91
16	510	161
23	640	239
30	942	390
July 7	1222	593
14	1781	1004
21	2850	1819
28	3583	2471
August 4	4517	3659
11	4855	4115
18	5205	4463
25	4841	4218
September 1	3897	3344
8	3157	2550
15	2148	1672
22	1994	1551
29	[illegible]	[illegible]
October 6	833	538
13	815	511
20	651	331
27	375	134
November 3	357	89
10	319	92
17	274	48
24	231	27
December 1	190	15
8	181	15
15	168	6
22	157	1
The Total of all is 51578		
Whereof of the Plague 35403		

Buried of all Diseases in the Year 1630.	Tot.	Pl.
June 24	205	19
July 1	209	25
8	217	43
15	250	50
22	229	40
29	279	77
August 5	250	56
12	246	65
19	269	54
26	270	67
September 2	230	66
9	259	63
16	264	68
23	274	57
30	269	56
October 7	236	66
14	261	73
21	248	60
28	214	34
November 4	242	29
11	215	29
18	200	18
25	226	7
December 2	221	20
9	198	19
16	212	5
Buried in the 97 Parishes within the Walls 2656		
Whereof of the Plague 190		
Buried in the 16 Parishes without the Walls 4813		
Whereof of the Pl. 603		
Buried in the 9 Out-Parishes in *Middlesex* and *Surrey*, and at the *Pest-house* 3045		
Whereof of the Pl. 524		
Buried in *Westminster* 566		
Whereof of the Pl. 31		
The Total of all the Burials this time 10545		
Whereof of the Pl. 1317		

Buried of all Diseases in the Year 1636.	Total	Pla.
April 7	119	2
14	205	4
This Week these Parishes were added: S. Marg. Westminster, Lambeth Parish, S. Mary Newington, Redriff Parish, S. Mary Islington, Stepney and Hackney Parishes.		
April 21	285	14
28	259	17
May 5	251	10
12	308	55
19	299	35
26	330	62
June 2	339	77
9	345	87
16	381	103
23	304	79
30	352	104
July 7	215	81
14	372	104
21	365	12[illegible]
28	423	151
August 4	491	206
11	538	283
18	638	321
25	787	429
September 1	1011	638
8	[illegible]	[illegible]
15	1306	865
22	1229	775
29	1403	928
October 6	1405	921
13	1302	792
20	1002	555
27	900	458
November 3	1300	838
10	1104	715
17	950	573
24	857	476
December 1	614	321
8	459	167
15	385	85
The Total of the Burials this year is 23359		
Whereof of the Pl. 10400		

Buried of all Diseases in the Year 166[illegible].	Total	Plag.
December 27	291	
January 3	349	
10	394	
17	415	
24	474	
31	409	
February 7	393	
14	461	1
21	393	
28	396	
March 7	441	
14	433	
21	365	
28	353	
April 4	344	
11	382	
18	344	
25	390	2
May 2	388	
9	347	9
16	353	3
23	385	14
30	399	17
June 6	405	43
13	558	112
20	611	[illegible]
27	684	26[illegible]
July 4	1006	47[illegible]
11	1268	727
18	1761	1089
25	2785	1843
August 1	3014	2010
8	4030	2817
15	5319	3880
22	5568	4237
29	7496	6102
September 5	8252	6988
12	7690	6544
19	8297	7165
26	6460	5533
October 3	5720	4929
10	5068	4327
17	3219	2665
24	1806	1421
31	1388	1031
November 7	1787	1414
14	1359	1050
21	905	652
28	544	333
December 5	428	210
12	442	243
19	525	281
The Total of the Burials this year is 973[illegible]6		
Whereof of the Pl. 68596		

Bill of mortality, London, 1665. Letterpress. 275 × 245 mm (10¾ × 9⅝ in)

'dropsy on the brain' (858), 'inflammation' (2555), 'mortification' (262), 'venereal' (5), and 'worms' (6). In addition to the high figure for 'inflammation' there are 'convulsions' (2075), 'cholera' (3200), and 'consumption' (4499). In the same bill appears a separate listing for casualties ('drowned', 'found dead', etc.). The list also records that in the year 1832 sixty-five people died 'by Visitation of God'.

Early bills of mortality were commonly approximately foolscap quarto, 250 × 200 mm (9⅞ × 7⅞ in), though 'plague bills' – questionnaire-forms filled in by hand – were printed four at a time on a single sheet. In their later form ('A General Bill of the Christenings and Burials …') they measured approximately 450 × 280 mm (17¾ × 11 in).

See also BURIAL PAPERS; PLAGUE PAPERS; PRATIQUE, PAPERS OF

REFERENCES Daniel Defoe, *A Journal of the Plague Year* (London, 1722); F. P. Wilson, *The Plague in Shakespeare's London* (Oxford: Clarendon Press, 1927; Oxford Paperback, 1963); 'A List of Works in Guildhall Library relating to the Plague in London, together with the Bills of Mortality 1532–1858', *The Guildhall Miscellany*, vol. 2, no. 7 (September, 1965)

COLLECTIONS Guildhall Library, London; Bodleian Library, Oxford; Houghton Library, Harvard University, Cambridge, Mass.

Billhead

The printed billhead evolved in the 18th century from the tradesman's all-purpose name-and-address slip known as the TRADE CARD. It was to evolve in turn into the commercial LETTERHEAD of the 20th century.

Like trade cards, early billheads were printed from hand-engraved copper plates, and the impression of the outer edges of the plate may generally be seen as a rectangular 'dish' effect on the surface of the headed part of the paper. The heading appeared on paper of varying vertical dimensions, thus allowing room on the lower part of the sheet for a single handwritten entry or for an extensive list.

Average billhead width was some 200 mm (7⅞ in), but depth varied from about 105 mm (4⅛ in) to 330 mm (13 in) or more. Narrower, and sometimes even longer, formats were favoured by some tradesmen, notably grocers, haberdashers, and innkeepers. In some cases bills covered very long periods – even occasionally a year or so at a time – and some shopkeepers are known to have lengthened the document accordingly, pasting papers together to form a long continuous strip. One such extended bill, submitted by Moore & Son, a Rochester, Kent (UK), butcher in August 1880, covers a period of eight months and extends to 1.3 metres (51¼ in) in length.

Rulings for item and cash columns appeared only rarely in the 18th and early 19th century. Introduced at first as an integral part of the engraved heading design, these were later printed in a separate operation (commonly in red or blue) on the accountancy ruling machines of the mid 19th century.

Headings commonly occupied the whole of the width of the printing paper, but smaller plates were also employed. These, measuring some 70 × 100 mm (2¾ × 4 in), were placed centrally on the paper or to one side, adjacent space being used for insertion of a date and the customer's name.

As with the trade card, the text of the heading was often embellished with an illustration. This might show the shopkeeper's sign (formerly displayed on a swinging board outside the shop), a royal-appointment coat of arms or, later, pictures of the products on sale. Until the introduction of street numbering in London in the 1760s, addresses appear (also as in the trade card) as generalized locations: 'Over against the West End of the New Exchange in the Strand'; 'The Cross Keys in Leadenhall Street near ye East India House'.

As an economy measure many traders used their billhead plates for trade cards and for entries in local trade directories. Some also used them for product labels. Typical of these were shoemakers, whose decorative insignia may appear on the billhead as a roundel or oval, to be cut out and pasted into the heel of the product. Watchmakers too might often use a decorative roundel on a billhead and trade card, the same engraving also being used for the WATCHPAPER. Saddlers' trade cards, if not their billheads, also often do duty as product labels.

Billheads, from their inception, and in some cases until the middle of the 20th century, commonly bore the expression 'Bought of' (or 'Bot' or 'Bt. of'). The expression 'Dr. to' ('Debtor to') is also often found. Both continued vestigially into the 1950s and 1960s. A further billhead convention is provision of a dateline at the top right hand of the layout, naming the town of the transaction and allowing space for insertion of the date. This practice derives from the early BANKNOTE and CHEQUE/CHECK form. It is retained as a conscious archaism by a few old-established firms (who also, in general, preserve their image from the18th or 19th centuries), but the custom at large fell into disuse in the early 1920s.

General billhead style remained basically unchanged for 150 years. The main distinguishing feature between early and later specimens is the post-1760 London street numbers, sometimes added to existing plates, sometimes incorporated into new designs.

Handwritten entries in bills provide much information on contemporary products, services, and prices, as well as occasional social sidelights in the form of annotations and salesman-like assurances of future attention. Some bills, long overdue, bear requests for early payment. Many are signed by the tradesman or his representative under the legend 'Received the Contents' or 'Settled' or 'Received in full of all demands'. (This last appears to be a time-worn echo of 'Received in full discharge of all demands'.)

In the latter part of the 19th century the four-page folder appears, a billhead allowing page three for correspondence and transmission of the document, suitably folded and sealed, through the post.

Early accountancy and filing methods required endorsement of documents with brief details of their content. Many surviving billheads bear these notes, the paper having been folded to a narrow format for taping in bundles. It was thus possible in locating a paper to look through files without untying bundles or unfolding each item. A less demanding system was the bill-spike, which left its characteristic impression on many early bills in the form of a central hole. (We may observe that the formal method of folding, endorsing and tying survives widely in the legal world. Large numbers of law documents – briefs, contracts, etc. – were still presented in this way in the latter part of the 20th century.)

Until the general introduction of wood-pulp paper in the 1860s and 1870s, billheads were printed for the most part on good quality handmade rag paper, often watermarked. The transition to wood pulp is clearly apparent, the paper being noticeably more brittle, thinner, and subject to discoloration. Coloured papers, notably blue, pale green, and pink, were introduced in the 1880s, and printing was generally in black.

The advent of lithography as a commercial printing method made the production of billheads cheaper and quicker. The lithographic method allowed the image from a copperplate engraving to be transferred to stone, singly or in multiples, with greatly increased productivity (*see* TRANSFER LITHOGRAPHY). Billheads printed by this method bear all the 'copperplate' characteristics of flourish and curlicue, but of course they show no sign of the 'dishing' produced by the pressure of a plate.

Parallel with the development of copperplate engraving and lithography, letterpress printing provided an economical medium for billheads of more modest calibre. The letterpress method may generally be identified by the 'relief' effect, in which a raised impression of the type matter is conveyed to the back of the paper through sheer pressure. The effect is characteristic of most early letterpress printing, which was done on dampened paper, thus producing an actual indentation in the surface.

Early 19th-century billheads are not generally illustrated, though the better class jobbing printer did provide wood or metal 'stock' blocks depicting trades, themes, and armorial or decorative motifs.

Toward the end of the 19th century lithographic billheads acquired a new and distinctive style, closely related to that developed by designers and engravers of security documents, bonds, share certificates, and paper currency. Chief features of the style are heavily three-dimensional lettering with a vigorous rendering of tonal gradation and shadow effects. A characteristic treatment involved the use of a vignetted 'cloud-work' background against which lettering appeared in lighter tone, with heavy shadowing to hold outlines where these overlapped on to plain paper. A wealth of heavy scroll- and strap-work, also rendered in three dimensions, filled in the interstices of the design.

The style, for which at the time no specific name emerged, is thought to have been inspired by the chiaroscuro effects of gas lighting, and has subsequently received the designation 'gaslight style'. The engravers and designers of the time, regarding the style as the accepted norm, had neither name for it nor a need to name it. The style had a universal vogue, appearing in printed matter from the New World to Imperial Russia. It was used for labels, packaging, and display sign-writing, but it was in business stationery and security printing that it chiefly flourished. As with other business styles, conservatism was to result in the survival of isolated examples of the treatment long after the general fashion had changed.

The 1880s also brought another design fashion, the 'art style' or 'artistic printing', which ran for a period parallel with the 'gaslight style'. Stemming from the advent of the newly introduced American jobbing platen, and the new levels of precision that it offered, it allowed the letterpress printer opportunities hitherto offered only by the free hand of lithography. Working now in two or more colours, and using a plethora of fancy types and borders, the art-style printer began to produce ornamentation of great complexity. The era is epitomized in the pages of the *Printers' International Specimen Exchange*, an annual volume of expertise produced in London by printers for printers between 1880 and 1898. Most of its contributed items, though they undoubtedly reflect the trends of the period, were not in fact genuine commissions. Its pages provided a show-case for exercises specially prepared for the purpose. Items from the *Exchange* are often mistaken for run-of-the-press productions; they may generally be recognized by their conformity to the page size of the *Exchange*, 290 × 215 mm (11⅜ × 8½ in), and by the extra-high-quality stock on which they are printed. They may also show an extravagance of treatment beyond the reasonable budgetary reach of the 'clients' they feature.

A further billhead style, emerging in the 1890s and also displayed in the *Exchange* in its later years, was known as the 'Leicester Free Style'. In this style, which was popularized by the de Montfort Press, Leicester, the essential symmetry of conventional letterpress printing (and even of the revolutionary 'art style') was abandoned. Headings, sub-titles, decorative vignettes, and fancy-work were now thrown ruthlessly off-centre – a gambit that relieved the jobbing printer of some of the rigours of the 'art style' symmetry while retaining its revolutionary flavour.

The illustrated billhead provides much evidence for the social, commercial, and industrial historian. Goods and equipment, transportation methods, commercial and industrial architecture are profusely depicted. There may be reservations, however, in acceptance of some of this evidence. As Hudson (1977) has pointed out, the customary over-statement of the 19th-century advertiser appears at an early stage, principally in the rendering of scale in shops and factory premises. Typical are engravings in which, to render the building more imposing than it really is, passers-by and street vehicles are shown at approximately half size. In factory premises the number of chimney stacks may be overstated, as also the flow of delivery vans from the main gates. Other evidence, equally suspect, though nonetheless informative, may be provided by successive billheads from the same company, in which premises are enlarged

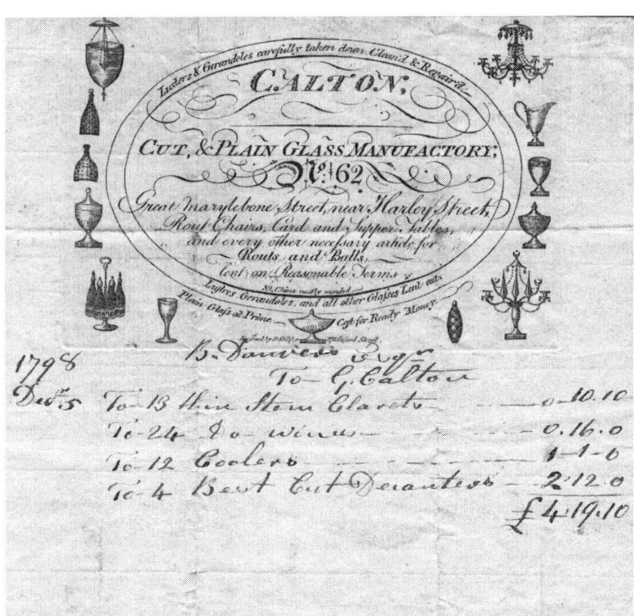

Billhead of Calton, cut and plain glass manufacturers, Marylebone Street, London, 1798. Copper-engraved heading with manuscript. 147 × 153 mm (5¾ × 6 in)

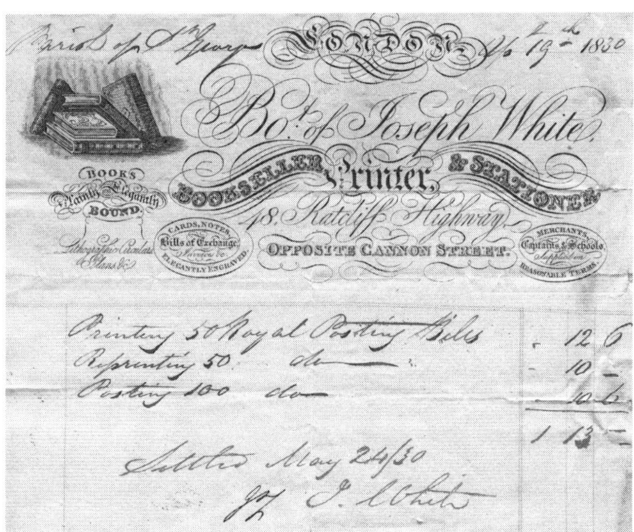

Billhead of Joseph White, bookseller, printer, and stationer, Cannon Street, London, 1830. Copper-engraved heading with manuscript. 162 × 205 mm (6⅜ × 8⅛ in)

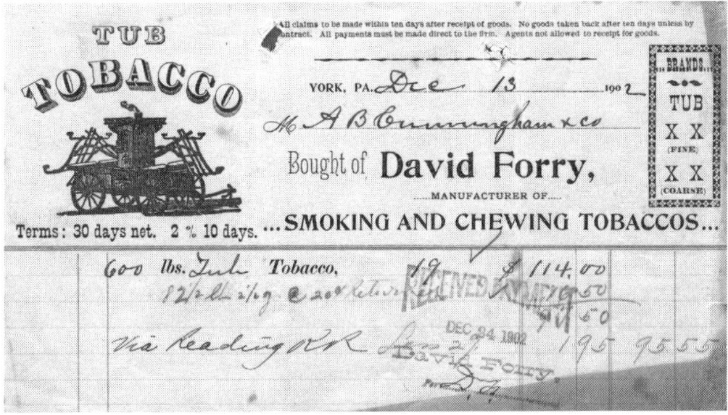

Billhead of David Forry, tobacco dealer, York, Pennsylvania, 1902. Letterpress, printed in two colours on ruled paper, with manuscript. 120 × 218 mm (4¾ × 8⅝ in)

or 'modernized' over an extended period, with illustrations adapted accordingly.

Information of a more reliable kind derives from a study of sub-headings, slogans, and terms of business. The following is a selection:

Search & Spencer: Who lights gentlemen's Lamps by ye wick or quarter (London, 1768)

William Churton: Great variety of curious Welch flannels, patent fleecy hosiery etc. (London, 1815)

T. Palmer: Bells hung on the most approved principles (York, 1830)

Jeremiah Evans [Stove manufacturer]: Prompt payment and no abatement (London, 1834)

J. H. Tuck: Balls and routs supplied with flowers (London, 1836)

Charles Woodward: Goods neatly turned and repaired (Shrewsbury, 1838)

Barnard & Bishop: Patentees of the self-rolling mangle (Norwich, 1860)

Holliday & Lewis: In consequence of the very small profit marked on all goods no credit can be given (Birmingham 1864)

Josiah Chesterman: Gas fitter and brass manufacturer; gas apparatus for singeing horses (London, 1865)

G. Brunt: Draper, grocer and tea dealer; Funerals furnished (Biggleswade, 1865)

J. Charles: Fish and barrelled oysters sent to all parts of the country (London, 1867)

John George: Chemists and druggists, genuine patent medicines, fish sauces and pickles (Wigton, 1881)

Col. William Beals [Flag, etc, contractor]: The only exclusive public decorator in New England (Boston, 1891)

Frye, Phipps & Co. [Hardware dealers]: Business founded 1816: Connected by telephone (Boston, 1896)

John Merch: Publicans' can manufacturers; No hawkers employed (London, 1897)

Manhattan Horse Manure Co.: Gatherers, dealers and shippers of manure (New York, 1912)

The evolution of the American billhead presents, except for its later start, a close parallel to that of the British version. The earliest American specimens commonly found date from the first decades of the 19th century. The '18th-century-engraving' phase, where it is present, is confined largely to the New England area and is represented only by a few rare examples. Generally speaking, design styles, format, and typographic treatment are noticeably similar to those of Britain. Most marked is the enthusiastic adoption of the late 19th-century 'gaslight' style, popularized, it may appear, through the impact of the European immigrant engravers whose design influence may also have been responsible for its vogue in Britain.

The 'art-style' too had its vogue in America, as did a version of the Leicester Free Style, though it is uncertain that in either case the trend was consciously imported. In matters of detail there are also similarities. The expressions 'Bought of', 'Dr to', etc., and the use of the town name and date line are present in American billheads throughout the period of their currency in Britain, and they also disappear at about the same time (1900–20). A single distinguishing feature may be said to be in the editorial 'tone' of the billheads. Whereas the British approach is clearly influenced by a sense of the deference required of the tradesman to his patron, the American view is distinctly less obsequious: 'Any articles in this invoice which you do not receive we are temporarily out of… but will send as soon as possible unless the order is countermanded by you' (Miner, Beal & Co. Boston, 1895); 'If terms as stated in this bill are not correct or if prices are not as bought, notify at once or settle by this invoice' (Saville Somes & Co. Boston, 1896).

See also COVER, POSTAL (PRE-STREET-NUMBERING); DOCTOR'S BILL; INN TALLY; LETTERHEAD; SCHOOL/COLLEGE BILL; TRADE CARD

REFERENCES Graham Hudson, 'Printed Ephemera and Design History', *Art Libraries Journal*, vol. 6, no. 1, (1981); Graham Hudson, 'Printed Ephemera and the Industrial Historian', *Industrial Archeology*, vol. 12, no. 4, (1977); John Lewis, *Printed Ephemera* (Ipswich: W. & S. Cowell. 1962); Michael Twyman, *Printing 1770–1970* (London: Eyre & Spottiswoode, 1970; reprinted The British Library, 1998)

COLLECTION John Johnson Collection, Bodleian Library, Oxford

Binder's ticket

Known also as binder's labels, binder's tickets serve as a form of signature to the work of bookbinders. Designedly inconspicuous, these small printed labels are rarely more than a few square centimetres in size, and in some cases measure as little as 5 or 10 mm (3/16 or 3/8 in) in either dimension. They are normally found pasted at the top left-hand corner of the verso of the flyleaf of a book, sometimes in the same position on the front pastedown. They are also found at the top right-hand corner of the recto of the flyleaf. In rare cases they appear in lower corners. Their unobtrusiveness is underlined by the fact that they have on occasions been inadvertently obscured by re-endpapering in the course of renovation.

They carry briefest details of the binder's name and address and were printed, often on colour-tinted paper, by copperplate or lithography. Toward the end of the 19th century, and in the first few decades of the 20th, they were also letterpress printed.

They are for the most part rectangular, though many appear as discs, ovals, octagons, or shields. Their general appearance reflects an idiom widely adopted for the BOOKSELLER'S LABEL and by the book and allied trades, including library proprietors, stationers, printers, and engravers.

The binder's ticket was in fact one of a number of different kinds of binder's signature. The earliest of these took the form of initials incorporated in the metal of the rolls used to impress the decorative bands on the leather of the cover or spine. In another method an un-inked ('blind') impression of the binder's name was impressed into the pastedown of the front cover or on the verso of the flyleaf. In this form the signature is often so small and sometimes so perfunctorily stamped that it may be said to be visible only to those who look for it. This form is first seen during the second decade of the 19th century. In another method, introduced at about the same period, the stamping die was inked, producing a clearly legible impression.

The binder's signature is also found as a discreet addendum to the elaborate blind embossing of cases of the period 1820 to 1875. Here again the name is scarcely discernible, being secreted in the interstices of the design in the manner of Dobbs, Wood, Mansell and others in the paper embossings of the same period. The embossed book case, produced from a mechanical die-stamping, appeared in cloth as well as leather. In a further method, equally inconspicuous, the binder's name appears in almost microscopic letters as part of the gold tooling on the lower turn-in of the front cover.

In early publishing, books were commonly produced as unbound sheets, initially in paper wrappers, later (1800–20) in 'publisher's boards', a rough temporary binding bearing only a

Binders' tickets of E. Paul, Southampton; Hunt & Sons, Birmingham; Davison, London. All smaller than 20 × 15 mm (¾ × ⅝ in)

paper spine label. The purchaser, acquiring a book from a bookseller, had the book bound in a style of his own choice, either by his own binder or by the bookseller's. The binding thus figures as a separately acknowledged element of the production. At a later stage, when publishers began producing the complete volume ready-bound, it nevertheless remained the custom for the binder to register his part in the production with a paper-label signature. The binder's ticket thus continues to appear toward the latter part of the 19th century, some time after the introduction of industrialized commercial binding.

The earliest known ticket appears to be that of John Browne of London, and dates from around 1610 (Mitchell, 1953). This appears to have been unusual and the next earliest tickets to have survived date from the 18th century. Munby (1953) cites tickets of Thomas Edlin, a London binder, dating from the 1720s, of Ettles & Young of Elgin on an Edinburgh schoolbook of 1788, and of a Wigan binder, Lyon, on a book printed in Warrington in 1787.

Binder's tickets begin to appear in greater numbers in the 1830s. Among surviving examples are those of the well-known binder Francis Westley, whose first ticket appears in a copy of the annual *The Keepsake*, 1828. The Westley ticket continues to appear in a series of no fewer than nine variants of company style and address until the 1900s, when the firm became Trickett, Westleys & Co. (Westley's signature had appeared as both blind and inked impressions as described above, more than a decade before the appearance of his first paper ticket.)

One other form of binder's signature, relatively rare, is printed or stencilled directly on the pastedown of the front endpaper. Here the whole of the pastedown may be said to constitute the label, though the legend itself may occupy only a small portion of the area. This form of signature, not uncommon in the 1830s, is first seen in the work of the London binders Remnant, John Bird, and A. & T. Camp.

Though binder's tickets are often found as separate items (sometimes still affixed to surviving covers of vanished books), they are generally considered to be better left in the volumes of their origin. In cases where labelled and unlabelled bindings possess similar characteristics, the presence of a binder's ticket in the one may confirm the workmanship of the other.

The early 19th-century binder's label reflects a scattered pattern of geographical distribution. Whereas the binder was later to be found in the major centres, at an earlier period the presence of private libraries in smaller towns (and even in villages) provided work for local binders. Munby cites, from his own collection, examples of tickets from such places as Alresford, Babcary, Helston, Llanerchymedd, Shepton Mallet, and South Molton.

Use of binder's tickets is a predominantly British practice, though examples are found in Europe and North America, where the stationer's, bookseller's, and printer's label also appear. The Roland Knaster Collection of Bookbinder's, Bookseller's and Stationer's Labels, housed in the Guildhall Library, includes binders' tickets from Allahabad, Cairo, Calcutta, Geneva, Hamburg, Hobart, Hong Kong, Leipzig, Melbourne, New York, Stuttgart, and Sydney. The collection of booksellers' labels in the American Antiquarian Society, numbering some 1700 'loose' items, includes a large number of binders' tickets. It is thought that this number might be doubled if those still affixed in books were included in the figure.

REFERENCES Douglas Ball, *Victorian publishers' bindings* (London: The Library Association, 1985); Donald Fraser, 'Binders' Tickets and Other Marks on Signed Publishers' Bindings' (London: unpublished monograph, 1984); Bernard Middleton, *History of English Craft Bookbinding Technique*, 4th edn (New Castle, DE: Oak Knoll; London: The British Library, 1996); William Smith Mitchell, 'Bookbinders' Tickets', *Durham University Journal* (December 1953), pp. 1–4; A. N. L. Munby, 'Collecting English Signed Bindings', *The Book Collector* (Autumn 1953)

COLLECTIONS Guildhall Library, London; American Antiquarian Society, Worcester, Mass.

Birth certificate

Formal records of births, marriages, and deaths became legally compulsory in Britain in 1530, when clergy were required to keep a weekly record of christenings, weddings, and burials. Similar provisions began in the American Colonies in 1632, when the record was required to be declared manually, and in 1630 a Massachusetts Bay law called for government registration of births, marriages, and deaths, rather than leaving the record to church registers of baptism, marriages, and burials.

By the first years of the 19th century in much of Europe and parts of America, formal registration had become general, though it was not until toward the middle of the century that fully centralized records were instituted.

Early British certificates took a number of forms. In many cases they consisted of a small handwritten paper signed by the medical attendant. An example reads: 'Dundee 29th [December] 1821. I do hereby certify that I delivered Mrs Downs of a Boy on the 11th Dec 1821. Peter Mudie, Surgeon'. Stillbirths were not generally required to be recorded (in Britain not formally until 1927), though doctors' handwritten declarations of stillbirths are also found: 'I certify that Mrs Barry Bennett was this day delivered of a female child which was virtually stillborn. D M Steedman LRCPE Stonehouse, March 27/[18]96'. More formal certificates, part-printed and provided by the church concerned, testified to baptism only, simply transcribing entries from the parish register. In other cases church evidence of baptism was given on a certificate which also recorded the date of birth (*see* BAPTISMAL PAPERS).

In other cases a handwritten paper signed by the vicar certified that the holder had been born on a given date 'as appears by the Register of Births and Baptisms'.

In America, among the Swiss and German immigrants in Pennsylvania (known as 'Pennsylvania Dutch') family events were recorded in a document called a FRAKTUR, a decorative certificate designed for display in the house. Part-printed, wholly printed, or hand-drawn, the Fraktur provided a general family record, showing births, marriages, and deaths. Other forms of Fraktur announced births and baptisms, others births alone. The Fraktur birth announcement is a direct forerunner of the formal certificate of modern times. An example, decorated with a surround of biblical images, reads: 'Peter Baker and wife Anamari was born a daughter to the world on the 14th Day of Novemr 1797. And Received the Name Sarah. Halleluia'.

For the majority of people in most Christian societies, the concepts of birth and baptism were virtually synonymous (baptism generally following very shortly after birth). The introduction, as in Britain in 1836–37, of general registration of birth created some public confusion. The General Register Office published a leaflet explaining at some length the value of establishing exact birth dates, not only for 'the wealthier classes... for proof of pedigree' but for 'the Children of the poorer classes' in gaining admittance to apprenticeships, schools, charities, etc. 'It is right to explain,' concludes the leaflet, in pointing to the difference between Church Registers of Baptisms and the keeping of the New Registration of Births, 'that the one is not a substitute for the other, but that they are entirely different, the new Register being... only of Births, the Church Register... only of Baptisms; That Registry of Birth does not warrant neglect of the sacred rite of Baptism, nor is the fact that the child has been baptized a sufficient reason for neglecting to register the Birth; That the church Register is ... a legal record of Baptisms, but not of Births...'. The explanation finishes by pointing out that it has been decided by judges in courts of law 'That an entry of a birth made by a Clergyman in the Register of Baptisms is not evidence of the time or place of birth'.

It will be seen that the term 'birth certificate', though there are many from earlier periods which may carry such titles as 'Record of birth and baptism', may rightly be applied only to the document issued under the registration laws. The legally prescribed birth certificate remains, as in former times, an attested copy of an entry in a register, today administered by the Registrar General in England and Wales, and in Scotland by an officer with the same title. The form of the birth certificate has been adapted, since its inception in 1837, to accommodate a number of changes in the registration laws. Chief among these is the introduction of a modified certificate, under the Birth Certificate (Shortened Form) Regulations (1968) which provide for non-disclosure of illegitimacy.

See also DEATH CERTIFICATE

Biscuit/cracker label [plate 2b]

Emerging in the early 19th century from its status as a cottage industry product, the biscuit (US: cracker) was at first sold loose, unidentified by maker's name or other mark of origin.

First steps in industrialisation came with the move to brand naming (moulded into the biscuit itself) and packing in orderly arrangement in protective tins. This was soon followed by the use of makers' labelling on the tins.

In Britain, the biscuit tin became a more or less standard-size container. It formed a prominent feature of grocers' shops where it was used as a display/dispenser unit in front of the counter. In a later development the tops of the tins were glazed, allowing display of the actual product.

The mid 1920s saw the extension of the biscuit market to the sale of single chocolate biscuits. These products, wrapped in foil and banded with a paper label, appeared under a wide variety of titles, the same wafer appearing, for example, in one locality as the 'Holiday' wafer, and elsewhere as the 'Royal Scot'. Pictorial designs were altered accordingly. As with the majority of popular products, no opportunity was lost in exploiting names and events in the news.

In Britain, which had led the way in biscuit manufacture, there was little aspiration to elegant design, whereas in France, where the industry had been enthusiastically taken up by the firm of Lefèvre-Utile, no less an artist than Alphonse Mucha was called in. A number of his label designs (for example

Six biscuit labels of Huntley & Palmers, Reading (UK), from a sheet of eighty, c. 1880. Lithographed in two colours. Diameter of each label 53 mm (2⅛in)

'Gaufrettes Vanille' and 'Gaufrettes Pralinées') rate among the best.

Lefèvre-Utile's prestige in Europe was matched by the world reputation of Britain's numerous biscuit firms, namely Huntley & Palmers; Peek Frean; Macfarlane Lang; McVitie & Price; Meredith & Drew; McCall & Stephen; George Kemp; Amery; and Jacob.

REFERENCES Graziella Buccellati (ed.) *Biscuits: A Pictorial Story of a Sweet Tradition* (Milan: Franco Maria Ricci, 1982); T.A.B. Corley, *Quaker enterprise in biscuits: Huntley and Palmers of Reading, 1822–1972* (London: Hutchinson, 1972); Robert Opie, *The Art of the Label* (London: Simon & Schuster, 1987)

COLLECTIONS Museum of Advertising and Packaging, Gloucester; Reading University Library

Blasphemy

Bad language and swearing and cursing were held in the same official disgust as absence from Sunday worship (*see* SABBATH PAPERS). By a Statute of George II it was laid down that offenders would be fined according to a sliding scale: 'every day labourer: one shilling; Every other person under the degree of a gentleman: two shillings'.

Second offences incurred a double penalty. The law held that 'all blasphemies against God as denying his being or provenance ... or profane scoffing at the Holy Scriptures or exposing any part of them to contempt or ridicule ... seditious words, in derogation of the established religion are indictable as tending to a breach of the peace'. Documents to this effect survive in printed quotations from law books of the period. It is reported that Christopher Wren printed and posted a warning to labourers on St Paul's Cathedral. The notice reads: 'Whereas among labourers and others, that ungodly custom of swearing is so frequently heard to the dishonour of GOD and contempt of his authority; and to the end that such impiety may be utterly banished from these works, which are intended for the service of GOD and the honour of Religion, it is ordered that profane swearing shall be a sufficient crime to dismiss any labourer that comes to the call; and the Clerk of the Works upon a sufficient proof shall dismiss him immediately'.

In America, in the so-called 'Blue Laws' of Connecticut, prohibitions were also rigorous, and there was a similar link between sabbath breaking, blasphemy, and drinking. The Blue Laws were later held up to ridicule and published in mock seriousness by waggish commentators, but there is little doubt that they were based on reality and directly linked with England's statutes.

The term Blue Laws is said to derive from their being printed on blue paper. The term was extended to apply to other stringent laws in other states, including the witchcraft code enforced in New England.

Blotting paper

This was first used in Britain in the 15th century. It is first referred to in print in 1519 by William Horman in his *Vulgaria:* 'Blottynge papyr serveth to drye weete wryttynge, lest there be made blottis or blurris'. Thomas Fuller, in his *Worthies of England* (1562) mentions 'charta bibula [drinking paper] sucking up the ink with the sponginess thereof'.

Early blotting paper was grey and coarse. Fragments are found (as are traces of the sand or 'pounce' which it replaced) between the leaves of accounts and other documents where they have remained since they were last used. Blotting paper came into widespread general use in the 19th century. It was made from the same high-quality rag as other papers of the time, differing only in that it was unsized. (Size was added to the normal paper mix to reduce absorbency, thus easing the passage of the pen in writing.) Its characteristic pink colour was due to the use of turkey red cotton rags, which resisted bleaching and were thus unsuitable for other purposes. Queen Victoria is said to have used a thin red blotting paper, each piece carefully destroyed after use. Benjamin Disraeli used a thick black blotting paper, specially made to prevent decipherment. A wide range of colours later became available, though white, buff, and green were favoured in royal households and government departments. Daily provision of fresh blotting paper was (and often remains) a feature of writing rooms. The advertising blotter came into use in the latter part of the 19th century. Its absorbency made it suitable only for the simplest line-block printing, but a specially treated surface was later developed which allowed a finer image without interfering with absorbency. Known as 'advertising blotting', this paper was still however unable to accept the four-colour half-tone printing then being developed. It also had the disadvantage of the earlier form: its use on the printed side rendered the advertising message illegible. Many such blotters bear the instruction 'Use only on other side'.

An innovation at the turn of the century was the blind-embossed blotter, which presented the advertising message as an unprinted relief on the front of the paper. This idea, which does not appear to have found favour, is embodied in a specimen put out by its inventors, Cattell & Co. of Finsbury Circus, London, in 1895.

The calendar and the blotter (separately or in combination) became by far the most widely used ADVERTISING NOVELTIES of the period, and the introduction of blotting paper with a suitably coated printing surface in the early 1900s brought about a huge proliferation of the advertising blotter, often available in monthly calendar-bearing 'issues'. Such blotters, carrying colourful half-tone illustrations on a glossy surface, were available with or without a calendar overprint for use as blanks to which the advertiser's name could be added. They were also designed, for large-quantity orders, to the requirements of the individual advertiser.

The advertising blotter, effectively a desk-top trade card and year-round promotion piece, remained in general use until the advent of the ballpoint pen, which in the period 1945 to 1960 progressively replaced the steel nib and liquid inks.

Smith Bro's special blotter, Poughkeepsie, New York. Lithographed. Early 20th century. 102 × 240 mm (4 × 9½ in)

In its heyday, blotting paper was a universal commercial and domestic requisite. It appeared in a wide variety of forms: as interleaving in household and business diaries; as 'blotting books' with or without hard bindings; as desk blotting pads in leather-cornered holders; and in various hand-held devices.

In America, the use of the word 'blotter' in the present sense dates only from about the middle of the 19th century. Prior to that date, as also in Britain, the word was used to refer to a rough scribbling book or record book, most commonly in America the police-station daybook.

In the mid 1980s sales of blotting paper were very much reduced, though manufacture continued of the desk blotter, for use in banks, hotels, and boardrooms, and of the multi-leaved signature book for office use.

Boardgame

'Table' games, at first doubtless played on the ground with sand and pebbles, have been played since before the dawn of history. They are generally thought to have been played specifically for gambling.

The commercially-produced children's boardgame appeared in the mid 18th century. In Britain its advent may be said to have been marked by the appearance in 1759 of John Jefferys's 'Journey Through Europe, or The Play of Geography', a linen-mounted folding map game, hand-coloured, and sold in a slip-case in the manner of a conventional map. The game provided players with a seventy-seven stop trip through Europe, with a brief detour to Archangel, Siberia, and Moscow.

Earlier printed boardgames had appeared in Europe. Among these are the 'Game of Goose' (*Il Gioco dell'Oca*) introduced by Francesco de' Medici, Grand Duke of Tuscany, in the 1560s, and sent as a present to the rather dour Philip II of Spain, and Pierre du Val's 'Le Jeu du Monde', published in France in 1645. These titles, forerunners of countless variants to appear in the 18th and 19th centuries, epitomize the two distinct approaches to the boardgame: on the one hand that of entertainment, on the other, of education. The 'Royall & Most Pleasant Game of the Goose' was to become an international favourite, played in one form or another for over 300 years – specifically and wholly for fun. Pierre du Val's game, though cast in the form of a pastime, was frankly instructional.

The games were played by the movement of counters in sequence, the number and nature of the moves being governed by throw of dice or, more commonly, use of a numbered spinning top called a 'tetotum' or 'teetotum'. The name derives from an earlier, gambling, version of the top, featuring initial letters instead of numbers. The most significant of these was 'T' (Latin, *totum*: indicating 'take all').

Many boardgames featured a spiral track, in which play

began at the perimeter and finished at the centre. ('The Goose' used this principle.) Other systems are based on the 'racetrack' layout (for every form of locomotion from horse to aircraft), variations on the chequerboard theme (for example, 'Snakes and Ladders'), zig-zags, and multi-choice paths to elude opponents' interception.

In Britain, it was more or less by accident that the approach was for many years educational. Printers of maps found that the geographical boardgame presented a profitable new field, and that with only a minimum of adaptation the product could be presented as a novel teaching aid. It was the same logic that led to the 19th-century JIGSAW PUZZLE; here too the first in the field were map publishers with their 'New Dissected Maps' divided county by county. It was to be some twenty years before the boardgame began to move into the field of entertainment, and the 'improving' game continued dominant for a century. Typical titles were 'The New Game of Human Life', John Wallis & E. Newbery (1790); 'Walker's Tour Through England & Wales', William Darton (1809); 'Wallis's New Game of Universal History & Chronology' (1814); 'New Game of Virtue Rewarded and Vice Punished', William Darton (1818); 'Cottage of Content or Right Roads and Wrong Ways', William Spooner (1848). The element of entertainment increased with the notion of topicality. The middle years of the century saw such titles as 'Wallis's New Railway Game' (1835); 'Game of the Great Exhibition', Spooner (1851); 'Russia Versus Turkey', James Reeves (c.1855); and 'The Siege of Paris', produced by an unnamed publisher in 1871. The trend to topicality, as well as the mounting popularity of the 'entertainment' games (Ludo, Halma, Snakes and Ladders, etc.), continued into the 20th century. The makers of boardgames responded quickly to each new matter of public interest, adapting the product to such themes as steeplechasing, aerial adventure, scouting, mountain-climbing, sport, warfare, etc.

In America, the boardgame was at first an importation from Europe. F. & R. Lockwood of New York were in 1823 offering a selection of the 'Travellers' Tours', the latest novelty from London; but in 1843 the firm of W. & S. B. Ives, of Salem, Massachusetts, offered its own version of the British game 'The Mansion of Happiness', and in 1844 'The Game of Pope or Pagan, or the Siege of the Stronghold of Satan by the Christian Army'. The same firm published 'The National Game of the American Eagle' (1844), and William Chancey Langdon of New Orleans put out 'The Game of American Story and Glory'.

The 1850s saw the advent of the McLoughlin Brothers, a name that dominated the American children's game, toy, and book field until the acquisition of the company by Milton Bradley in 1920. Typical McLoughlin boardgames are 'The Game of the District Messenger Boy' (1886), 'The Game of the Telegraph Boy' (1888), and 'The Game of the Man in the Moon' (1901). In 1883 the boardgame business was joined by Parker Brothers of Salem, Massachusetts, who in 1886 issued yet another version of 'The Mansion of Happiness'; this was followed by a long series of titles, many of them of an 'improving' tone ('Famous Men', 'Christian Endeavour', etc.), and in 1935 by 'Monopoly'.

In Britain the period from the 1890s to the 1930s was dominated by the Chad Valley Company, originating in Birmingham in the 1860s, and by J. W. Spear. Notable names in the history of the boardgame include, in addition to those already noted, the following: in Britain, John Harris (1830s), David Ogilvy (1830s), Grant & Griffith (1840s), John Betts (1850s), A. N. Myers & Co. (1860s); in America, Selchow & Righter (1860s), George A. Childs (1890s).

REFERENCES *Catalogue of McLoughlin Brothers*, 1886 (facsimile) (Siegel Box 75 Wyncote PA 19095); *Parker Brothers. 93 Years of Fun, 1883–1973: the History of Parker Brothers* (Salem, Mass.: Parker, 1973); *Encyclopedia of Collectibles* (Alexandria, VA: Time-Life, 1978); Linda Hannas, *The Jigsaw Book* (London: Hutchinson, 1981; New York: Dial Press, 1981); Constance Eileen King, *Encyclopedia of Toys* (London: Hale, 1978); Brian Love, *Play the Game* (London: Michael Joseph/Ebury Press, 1978); James Shea and Charles Mercer, *It's All in the Game* (New York: Putnam, 1960)

COLLECTIONS Museum of the City of New York; Bethnal Green Museum of Childhood, London; Waddesdon Manor, Aylesbury, Buckinghamshire

Bond, personal

A bond is a signed undertaking to perform (or to refrain from performing) a specified act on pain of a penalty if the condition or conditions of the undertaking are not met. The undertaking may also apply to the conduct of a third party, whose behaviour the signatory thus underwrites.

The bond was an instrument much used in the 19th century in America in cases of undischarged debt as a preliminary to the process of distraint. Effectively, it gave the debtor a specific period within which to pay, with or without interest, at the same time holding him responsible until settlement of the debt by attachment of his property or, failing that, by imprisonment. Acknowledged and signed before a Justice of the Peace, the terms of the bond had the force of law.

The printed form commonly bore the opening phrase 'Know all men by these presents' and committed the signatory on failure to pay by a given date, to surrender of 'my goods and chattels, lands and tenements,' or alternatively 'my body' (for imprisonment).

In another formulation, where the debtor had already been imprisoned for non-satisfaction, it was possible for him and others to enter into a bond whereby he remained in prison until his colleagues outside had paid the debt on his behalf: 'The condition of the ... obligation is such that if the above-bounden (—) now a prisoner in the (—) goal ... shall from the Time of the execution of this Bond, continue a true prisoner, in the Custody of the goaler, and within the Limits of the said Goal, until he shall be lawfully discharged, without committing any Manner of Escape: then the above written Obligation shall be null; otherwise it shall remain in full Force and Virtue ...'.

Release of bond prisoners, effected by payment of the debt, was marked by delivery to the goaler of a signed paper testifying to its discharge.

See also GAOL PAPERS

Book jacket *See* DUST WRAPPER

Book label

Though loosely applied to a wide range of labels designed to be pasted in books, the term 'book label' is commonly taken to refer to the owner's name label, generally printed letterpress, sometimes handwritten, an item distinct from the more elaborate, often heraldic, BOOKPLATE.

The bookplate, it may be said, is essentially the work of an artist, often an engraver, presenting the owner's name in a unified decorative context specific to that name alone. Typically, the bookplate incorporates the owner's coat of arms or images conveying his or her interests, activities, and associations.

The book label, on the other hand, though also sometimes appearing as an engraving, is commonly the work of a jobbing printer, who uses stock borders and devices as a frame for the setting of his customer's name in type. The same frame may well appear as a setting for other names, regardless of the identity or interests of the owner. Historically, whereas the bookplate has tended to serve those entitled to bear arms, and hence stresses the heraldic, the more modest book label is generally identified with the untitled and the learned. Both items, the personal book label and the bookplate, may be said to have their ultimate origins in handwritten inscriptions on flyleaves or pasted slips, and decorative hand-executed labels continued to appear in special volumes throughout the 18th and 19th centuries.

The printed personal book label has an additional precursor in the book stamp, an identification impressed from type by hand, generally on the title page. Lee (1976) records the earliest of these as appearing in a volume entitled *A briefe discourse against the outwarde apparell and Ministring garmentes of the Popishe church* (1566) in the University Library, Cambridge. This bears the legend 'James Harttun, his booke' and the date 1567.

The book label itself may be said to have its inception in Cambridge University. In the latter part of the 16th century it became the custom to record gifts of books by inserting labels of acknowledgement in the volumes concerned. The practice had the effect of not only flattering the donors and encouraging others, but of spreading the notion of the book label as such. Among early examples is that of Gilbert ('Gilbertus') Wightman, vicar of Claxby, Lincolnshire. His label, dated 1587, appears in a copy of Wotton's *De Differentiis Animalium Libri Decem* (Paris, 1552) in Cambridge University Library.

Apart from the influence of the book-gift label, already noted, an additional stimulus to the adoption of the personal book label was the popularity of the printer's KEEPSAKE. This was a printed slip bearing a recipient's name set in type, presented as a souvenir of a visit or other event. Set up and printed in the presence of the recipient, the keepsake had a characteristic charm of its own. In its simplicity (and often in its rough-and-ready workmanship) it conveyed the informality of a personal occasion. It was inevitable that it should eventually be put to practical use, and before long the words 'His Book' began to appear below the printed name.

As its early associations indicate, the book label is essentially a 'short-run' printed item. Whereas the owner of an extensive library could afford to commission engraved bookplates by the hundred, the book-label customer might call for only dozens. In some cases book labels were printed in twos and threes, and even on occasions as a single copy for a specific volume. Thus it is that the book label long retained its air of modest spontaneity; thus too its tendency to appear with different names in unchanged borders, successive printers' apprentices inserting names of newcomers as required.

The majority of book labels make do with the statement of the owner's name alone, but from earlier periods there are such phrases as 'This book belongs to...' or (particularly in 17th-century Scotland) 'This book appertaineth to...'. The 17th century also provides a record of the formerly current 'oweth' for 'owneth' ('Elias Ashmole oweth this booke. 1635').

Book label of S. E. Leith. Letterpress. 50 × 65 mm (2 × 2½ in)

Labels may also reflect something of the personality of the owner and the scale of the library. Occasionally there is a hint of borrowings damaged or returned. The label of Stephen Fellows, *c.*1840, is an example of the much-quoted appeal: 'If thou art borrow'd by a friend Right welcome shall he be To read, to study Not to lend *But to return to me*'. The request is rounded off with a further thought: 'Read slowly, pronounce perfectly, pause frequently, think seriously, keep cleanly, return duly, with corners of the leaves not turned down'. It is clear that the larger the library the more hazardous were its lendings. As a security measure, some labels quote press, shelf, and volume numbers. Others adopt an imperious tone: 'This book belongs to Sir G. Thomas's Library, Dale Park, Sussex. If mislaid, to be instantly returned, when found'.

Personal book labels, unlike bookplates and institutional library labels, are often found bearing a printed date, sometimes a printer's imprint. This underlines the view that the personal book label appeared not as a long-run production from a printing house, but as an item produced on a specific occasion for a special volume or volumes, sometimes perhaps as a gesture from a local printer personally known to the owner.

As already noted, the personal book label appears initially as a predominantly typeset item ('conjured up,' as Brian North Lee has it, 'from an assortment of printers' devices and decorations'), though engraved labels are also found in the earlier period. From 1780 to 1830, however, the engraved label dominates. The earlier Jacobean and Chippendale styles give way to the swags, garlands, and urns of the Georgian era, and it is clear that the label is acquiring a new sense of stateliness and poise. It tended to deteriorate in quality in the 19th century, but in the 1890s a revival of interest in quality printing of the book label centred on William Morris's Kelmscott Press. This trend continued in the 20th century.

The book label survives among bibliophiles, its design greatly influenced by the calligraphy and lettercutting of Eric Gill, David Kindersley, Reynolds Stone, and Leo Wyatt. Many contemporary labels are engraved on wood, some in metal.

The cult of the book label has flourished not only at specific periods but in geographic areas. 18th-century East Anglia yields a notably high number of specimens, many of them printed with their date and place of origin. There is little doubt that this concentration in a restricted area at a specific period is due to the effects of neighbourly emulation. The effect is seen, in fact, as far away as New England, where Henry Dunster, first President of Harvard College, introduced the idea from his native England in the 1640s.

Henry Dunster's own labels, dated at Cambridge (UK) in 1629, 1633, and 1634, were clearly printed in England before his arrival in America in 1640. The label dated 1642 of Stephen Day (or Daye), the first American printer, then employed by Dunster at Harvard, is a strong contender for the first American label. Lee contests this, thinking it to be English. If so, the title of first American in the field appears to lie with John Cotton, also of Cambridge, who produced a label dated 1674. As with its localized adoption in England, the book label spread from one New England academic to another, slowly to be taken up by bibliophiles throughout the country.

It is to be noted, in the matter of book labels from the 19th and 20th centuries in general, that the printed words, 'From the library of' appearing above a name, may be misleading. The phrase generally refers to books disposed of by auction after the owner's death, and the label itself would thus not have been seen by the person named.

See also BINDER'S TICKET; BOOK-DONOR LABEL; BOOKSELLER'S LABEL; STATIONER'S LABEL

REFERENCES Brian North Lee, *Early Printed Book Labels* (Pinner: Private Libraries Association and the Bookplate Society; Newton Abbot: David & Charles, 1976); R. W. G. Vail, 'Seventeenth-Century American Book Labels', *The American Book Collector* (Metuchen, New Jersey, September / October, 1933)

COLLECTIONS American Antiquarian Society, Worcester, Mass.; British Library, London; Franks and Viner Collection, Massachusetts Historical Society, Boston

SOCIETY The Bookplate Society, London

Book token

Originally conceived in 1926 by Harold Raymond of Chatto & Windus, the book token was launched in Britain by the National Book Council on 14 November 1932. It was at first viewed by the Council as a useful project on which to employ potentially redundant staff.

The scheme initially met with coolness from the book trade, but with W. H. Smith Ltd as a founder member and the backing of the Booksellers' Association of Great Britain and Ireland, it steadily gained ground and in the first six years increased turnover ten fold. The book token became firmly established in World War II, when it provided the answer to the gift problem for separated friends and relatives. In 1943 the scheme was formed into a limited company (Book Tokens Ltd) owned by the Booksellers' Association. The Book Token organization had an annual turnover of around twenty million pounds at the close of the 20th century and produced well over a million cards a year. There have been some 300–400 different card designs and in the mid 1980s new designs averaged some sixteen per year. In 1997, the organization's 65th year, a new card format was introduced with an integral bookmark, with the new cards available in twenty-four designs.

Pictures reproduced on the cards have featured original commissions from such artists as Sir Muirhead Bone, Roland Hilder, and Norman Thelwell, and existing works by Ernest Shepard, Russell Flint, and H. M. Bateman. Early cards included a tipped-in book plate (featuring the picture on the cover of the card itself), and to promote the sale of tokens extensive use was made of the BOOKMARK.

The perforated stamps used in conjunction with the cards were produced until 1965 by Waterlow & Sons, later by Harrison's. The first designs remained unchanged until 1947; there have been four changes of design, each generally appearing in five different denominations.

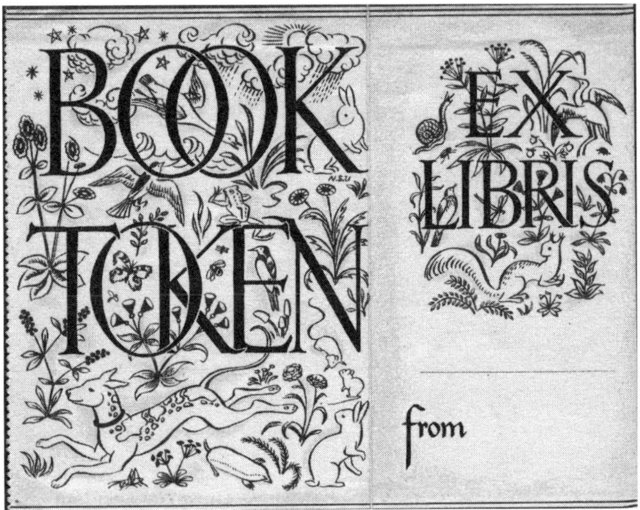

Book token designed by Nora Unwin in the mid 20th century. Lithographed in three colours. 128 × 153 mm (5 × 6 in)

No complete collection of book-token ephemera is known to exist, either of cards or stamps. There is no authoritative listing of cards issued, and the company's archive is thought to contain less than half the full published series. The stamps, by virtue of official disposal after use, are extremely rare.

Book token schemes also operate in Australia, Germany, Holland, Japan, South Africa, Switzerland and New Zealand. In the United States the special structure of the book trade has not favoured development of the idea.

COLLECTIONS Book Tokens Ltd, Minster House, 272–274 Vauxhall Bridge Road, London SW1V 1BA

Book-donor label

Books donated to libraries are often identified by a printed slip of acknowledgement, sometimes affixed to the pastedown, sometimes tipped in at the title-page. The slip may be referred to as a 'book-donor label' or as an 'ex-dono label' (sometimes simply as an 'ex-dono').

The label may be part-printed, allowing the name of the donor to be inserted by hand, or it may be wholly printed, giving as well as the donor's name details of his or her status and the nature of the gift. The label may also cite a number of other volumes included in the gift, and may additionally record an endowment or other bequest.

The practice originated in the older British universities, when academic libraries competed for a relatively small supply of books, and donors by this means enjoyed a measure of immortality. At first the gift was recorded as a handwritten inscription, but printed acknowledgement developed in the latter part of the 16th century. It was pasted in as a separate slip, or printed or hand-impressed directly on the title page, or printed on a blank sheet and inserted during binding as a single leaf preceding the title-page. In some cases the printing was carried out by the printer of the book, who himself may have been the donor. A number of such gifts were made to King's College, Cambridge by John and Richard Day, in the later 1500s, and Aberdeen University Library has a volume containing a printed inscription: 'The Gift of J Bill (His Majesties Printer) to the New College of Aberdene. 1624'. In general the practice was to use Latin for the inscriptions ('Dedit huic Collegio Rich. Dayus eiusdem Socius, An. Dom. 1575': Given to this College by Richard Day, a Member of it, 1575). Donor labels continued to appear in Latin in Cambridge college libraries until the 20th century.

The book-donor label also appeared widely in the period of expansion of the privately founded library in the 18th and 19th centuries. Books donated to various institutional libraries may be found to contain quite large donor labels, measuring, typically, 150 × 90 mm (6 × 3½ in), and showing not only the name of the donor but detailed terms of the bequest and, in the manner of the classic bookplate, a coat of arms. The donor label remains a feature of many privately maintained libraries.

REFERENCES Brian North Lee, 'Book-label, Bookplate – Ephemera?', *The Ephemerist* (March, 1984); Brian North Lee, *Early Printed Book Labels* (Pinner: Private Libraries Association and the Bookplate Society; Newton Abbott: David & Charles, 1976)

Bookmark

The device used for keeping the reader's place in a book was known in the Middle Ages as a 'register' and in the early 19th century as a 'marker'. The advent of the printed bookmark in the 1870s necessitated a printed title and on Victorian bookmarks both 'Bookmark' and 'Bookmarker' (with or without hyphens) were used indiscriminately with the former the most common. Both terms continue in use today.

As early as the 15th century for monastic, courtly, and ceremonial life three types of registers were in use. Narrow, protruding strips of parchment or vellum would be attached to certain leaves of the manuscript or book (few were paginated or had tables of contents); a narrow band of silk ribbon or cord would be fastened to the volume for use between any of the leaves, which might then be embroidered or otherwise embellished; or a loose marker, which might take several forms, would be used which could be moved from volume to volume. An interesting early bookmark in monastic use enabled the reader to indicate both the page and the column reached by use of a revolving disc graduated from I to IIII, attached to a ribbon (revolving the disc denoted the column). An example in Hereford Cathedral Library dates from about 1200.

In the 18th and early 19th centuries better-quality books were frequently provided with narrow ribbons as part of the binding, the upper end being stitched or glued to the inside of the headband. Bibles, prayer books, diaries, and some reference books are still so equipped.

From about 1840 perforated board ('Bristol' board) which could be embroidered with coloured thread, cut to a rectangular shape and attached to a ribbon, began to be used as a bookmark. The commercial potential of these home-made bookmarks was realized by such manufacturers as Dobbs, Mansell, Windsor, and Wood, who marketed pieces of card first with decorated edges then with pierced and embossed borders and vignettes. In some cases the design to be embroidered was printed in colour on the card. Embroidered with religious texts, mottoes, or other legends (e.g. commemorative), these Victorian craft bookmarks were given to relatives, friends, and sweethearts or retained for personal use. They were also sometimes embellished with chromolithographic prints, photographs, or scraps as pictorial centre-pieces.

The 1860s saw the advent of woven silk bookmarks (many by Thomas Stevens of Coventry, later renowned for Stevengraphs). These came in a variety of designs (religious, greetings, or commemorative) which could be given as gifts, a tradition which continues to the present day. From about 1890 silk ribbon bookmarks printed with religious texts or mottoes were available, and during the early 20th century printed silk was used as a mourning bookmark.

In the 1870s bookmarks printed on card bearing religious themes could be purchased from such manufacturers as Rimmels and Campbell & Tudhope. Towards the end of the 1870s the bookmark moved into the hands of advertisers, becoming thenceforward almost exclusively their province for some seventy years. The era of the free, give-away ephemeral bookmark had dawned.

Bookmarks of the late 19th and early 20th centuries from Britain, the Netherlands, and America. All chromolithographed. The largest (in area) measures 192 × 70 mm (7⅝ × 2¾ in)

Early advertising bookmarks reflected the artistic and advertising styles of the day, as they have continued to do since. Many carried chromolithographed pictures and designs, although less extensively in Britain than in America and on the continent. In America the chromolithographed bookmark, like the chromolithographed TRADE CARD, was made available in a range of decorative designs for overprinting by the advertiser. Continental chromolithographic bookmarks, though rarer than trade cards, reached a high degree of printing excellence, some designs requiring a dozen or more colour workings.

Attempts have been made at various stages to add to the bookmark's usefulness. It has served as a calendar (a feature of the earliest advertising bookmarks), timetable, puzzle, picture card, measure, metric conversion table, greetings card, an insurance-premium payment schedule and, in more rigid materials (celluloid, tortoise-shell, wood and some metals) as a paper cutter. They have also been made in silver for more lasting use.

A limited number have aspired to aesthetic appeal, carrying art-nouveau and art-deco designs. A series of twelve for The Scottish Widows' Fund issued in 1910–12 with Walter Crane designs is notable; less successful is the company's series of reproductions of oil paintings. The appeal of the bookmark is also heightened in some examples by die-cutting to create a shape relevant to the product advertised. Examples include toothpaste tubes, petrol pumps, fountain pens and nibs, bottles, medals, fish, and more recently a computer key-board with attached 'mouse' indicating the thought which still goes into the design of these items. Some designs, in silk and in card, were registered, an early example being a small, plain embossed bookmark 'Registered 28 June 1851'.

The range of advertisers who have used bookmarks to promote their business or product, in some cases over many years, is vast. Among the more prolific have been: insurance companies; publishers, libraries, and the book trade (not unexpectedly); suppliers of household commodities and shops; the transport industry (road, rail, sea, and air); the pharmaceutical industry; charities; hospitals and health and safety organizations; magazine and newspaper publishers; the cinema, radio and television; advertising agencies (composite bookmarks featuring several advertisers); greetings card manufacturers (including 'Book Post Cards'); and Government (e.g. war time propaganda, savings committees, metrication etc.). Today local authorities distribute several million bookmarks annually through their libraries and other outlets. At the other extreme are, for example, bookmarks issued by local operatic societies, magicians, and restaurants.

The idea of the bookmark has never wholly lost its links with improvisation, however, and a wide range of paper oddments may be found in books of all periods. Some of these may have a V-shaped cut close to one end, allowing a flap to be tucked over the head of the page required. Early playing cards and visiting cards are sometimes found to have been cut in this way. The cut is also a feature of numerous advertising bookmarks of the 19th, and to a lesser extent the 20th, century.

In the second half of the 20th century the purely commercial use of bookmarks declined but was more than compensated for by their use for greetings and gifts, as tourist souvenirs, or as publicity material and propaganda for non-profit-making enterprises. [PS]

See also CHROMO; SECONDARY USES OF EPHEMERA

REFERENCES The Bookmark Society, *Newsletter*, 1989–; A. W. Coysh, *Collecting Bookmarkers* (Newton Abbot: David & Charles, 1974); Frank Hamel, 'The History and Development of the Bookmarker', *Book-lover's Magazine*, vol. 6, part 4, Otto Schultze & Co., Edinburgh, 1906

COLLECTIONS John Johnson Collection, Bodleian Library, Oxford; Abraham Jonker, c/o 'De Verzamelaar' Stadhoudersstraat 55, Arnhem, Holland; Peter Standley, c/o The Ephemera Society

SOCIETIES Bookmark Society, c/o Centre for Ephemera Studies, The University of Reading

Bookmatch

The bookmatch is called by a variety of names. In Britain it is known either as a 'bookmatch' or a 'match booklet'. In America it is a 'match folder' or 'matchbook cover'. By collectors in both countries it is described as a 'match cover' – often printed as one word: 'matchcover'.

The basic concept, in which each match is torn from partial attachment to its neighbour, derives from an early form of the phosphorus match, the 'fusee' (French, *fusée:* rocket). The fusee was patented in London in 1828 by Samuel Jones, and was devised as a slow-burning match for use outdoors. When ignited, it smouldered with a spluttering 'wind-proof' flame. Its stalk or 'stem' was made of a thick, coarse cardboard impregnated with nitre; the head was a red phosphoric compound. Unlike the ordinary match, or 'friction light' (1826), which was an individual wooden splint, the fusee formed part of a strip of card cut transversely, but not completely, into twelve sections. The divided edge of the card was dipped into the 'inflaming composition' and allowed to dry. Individual units could be detached and used as required. The same principle was applied to strips of thin wooden 'chip', the resultant product being described as 'comb' matches. Some sixty years later, with the addition of a folded cardboard tuck-in cover, matches of either kind became 'book' matches.

The phosphoric compound used for the striking heads of matches at the time was liable to ignition by accident, however, and it was not until the last years of the century that the phosphorus component was transferred to a separate striking surface. The bookmatch thus became a safe proposition, the special striking surface being incorporated in the booklet, initially inside the cover, later on the outside.

The bookmatch was patented by Joshua Pusey, a patent lawyer, in Lima, Pennsylvania, in 1892. He sold the patent outright to the Diamond Match Co. (later the Diamond Match Corporation) of Barberton, Ohio, in 1896. The idea was at first slow to gain ground, but it was shortly to become hugely popular, more particularly as an advertising give-away. The first crudely printed example of its use in this way, promoting a New York presentation of the small-town 'Mendelssohn Opera Company', appeared in 1898. Several hundred copies were produced, complete with numerous spelling and typographic errors. A single example, believed to be the only survivor, is held in the Diamond Match Corporation's own collection. The Diamond Co.'s first big order was for ten million booklets from the Pabst Brewing Co. of Milwaukee. It is said that this was the order which really started the bookmatch industry.

Bookmatches appeared in Britain in 1899, manufactured by the (British) Diamond Match Co. Manufacture continued on an increasing scale when the company was acquired by Bryant & May in 1901.

On both sides of the Atlantic bookmatches were at first seen as being primarily for outdoor and 'non-domestic' use. Their popularity grew with the spread of smoking in public, and it became the practice to put a separate booklet at the place of the individual diner at banquets and in hotels and restaurants. Booklets were also provided, sometimes together with a single cigarette, in railway luncheon baskets. (One such specimen, put out by the Great Eastern Railway Co., and listed in Bryant & May's museum catalogue (1926) is described as containing a cigarette.)

In America, as in Britain, the match folder became closely identified with hotels and restaurants, and it is in these fields that its role as an advertising GIVE-AWAY has grown from the start. Early specimens from the Diamond Match Co. promote such names as the Hotel Hurth, Portsmouth, Ohio ('Rates $3.00 and up'); the Bernard Hotel, Chicago ('$2 Single; $3.50 Double; No Ups'); and the Eola Hotel, Natchez, Mississippi ('125 Fireproof Rooms; Every Room with Ceiling Fan and Circulating Ice Water'). Other advertisers include rail companies, shipping lines, country clubs, and insurance companies.

In America in recent years match folders have appeared bearing State Governors' names and insignia and, in the United States Senate Restaurant, the embossed insignia of the United States of America. Promotional bookmatches are also used in America in political campaigning, and it is said that every President since the elder Taft has had special issues made for free distribution.

The bookmatch has also been used in psychological warfare, 'propaganda issues' being air-dropped behind enemy lines (*see* AERIAL LEAFLET).

The booklet normally contains ten or twenty paper or splint matches. Other standard sizes contain fifteen or thirty matches or twenty or forty matches. Extra-long booklets measuring up to around 305 mm (approximately 12 in) have also appeared, and specimens measuring 460 mm (18⅛ in) are reported. Exceptionally, booklets measuring as little as 13 mm (½ in) are found.

Advertising variants are found with matches printed and shaped to portray bottles etc., and with advertising messages covering the whole of the face of the matches, printed as an unbroken design across their combined surface. Outsize versions of this type have also appeared, the closed folder measuring some 110 × 85 mm (4⅜ × 3⅜ in).

In America, as in Britain, the bookmatch also appears marginally in a non-advertising context as a commercial product for general sale. During the 1930s, and in a revival in the 1950s, commercial issues appeared in America as collector-sets. These featured baseball players and other sportsmen; movie, radio, and musical stars; cities, states, landmarks, etc.; and a range of miscellaneous subjects.

A novelty variant of the bookmatch was introduced in Britain in the 1930s. Marketed under the name of 'Pullmatch', this provided ten or twenty paper matches, each housed in an individual channel in a corrugated card folder. The matches lit automatically when pulled out. They were also available in ashtray stands for table use. A similar principle was used by the Diamond Match Co., New York, in the 'Pullquick', a folder containing ten wooden matches, which were also ignited by withdrawal.

Both systems were foreshadowed by a German or Austrian invention (British Patent no. 161972, 1921), in which the matches were to be ignited by placing the head between two surfaces of a fold in the booklet, drawing it out sharply. This idea may in turn be traced to the provision in the earliest lucifer boxes (c.1829) of a piece of folded sandpaper for pinching the head of the match and withdrawing it to light it.

Accidental ignition of bookmatches – for long the bugbear of the match industry in general – remains a hazard with bookmatches even after the introduction of the 'safety match' (which ignited only on the striking strip provided). Sparks from the igniting match would sometimes fire the rest of the matches, and the instruction 'close cover before striking' appeared early in the 1920s. Later practice was to place the striking strip on the back of the folder.

The popularity of the match folder in America is attributed by some (as with that of the paper cigarette pack) to its being less solid and angular than the shell-and-slide version. Carried often in shirt pockets, both items have fewer uncomfortable corners. America is not the only country where the bookmatch predominates, however. In many European countries the shell-and-slide matchbox is in decline; in Germany it is virtually unknown.

REFERENCES J. R. Burdick, *The American Card Catalog* (East Stroudsburg, PA: Burdick, 1960); Joan Rendell, *The Match, The Box and the Label* (Newton Abbot: David and Charles, 1983); H. Thomas Steele, Jim Heimann, Rod Dyer, *Close cover before striking* (New York: Abbeville Press, 1987)

COLLECTION Burdick Collection, Metropolitan Museum of Art, New York

SOCIETIES America Matchcover Collecting Club; British Matchbox Label and Booklet Society; Pacific Northwest Matchcover Collector's Club; Rathkamp Matchcover Society; Trans Canada Matchcover Club

Bookplate

As its name suggests, the bookplate is classically printed from an engraved metal plate, although in the course of time it has been produced by a variety of processes including, notably, WOOD-ENGRAVING. It commonly bears a decorative or pictorial motif expressive of the book's owner. The device may show armorial bearings or any other specifically relevant mark of ownership. Non-armorial designs may convey the owner's special interests and activities through still-life arrangements, landscapes, etc. Sometimes a pictorial rendering of the name appears in REBUS form. In most cases, armorial or otherwise, the owner's name is engraved on the plate integrally with the design.

Often the words *ex libris* (Latin: from the books [of]) appear on the bookplate. The expression, introduced in France in the 17th century, is widely used as a substitute for 'bookplate', and additionally covers any mark of ownership in books. The term is thus applied to the ordinary BOOK-DONOR LABEL and the BOOK LABEL. It is also used as a plural noun: 'these ex libris'; and as an adjective: 'ex libris labels'. The term also appears as a generalized noun: 'research in the field of ex libris'. A similar though less extensive development occurs in the case of the book-donor label, sometimes referred to, from its classic use of the phrase *ex dono,* as an 'ex dono label'.

There has been much discussion as to the admissibility of bookplates as ephemera, and it is indeed arguable that any form of ex libris label is too permanent an item to come within the designation. It may also be argued that the bookplate, like the ordinary book label, is often to be found as a loose item on its own, part of the general mass of paper bygones. As Brian North Lee observes (*The Ephemerist*, no. 44, March 1984), 'Quite a number of bookplates seem so transient as scarcely to have survived at all. Though noted in the literature of some eighty years ago, collectors still search in vain for original prints of them'.

The bookplate takes its origins from handpainted marks of ownership in manuscript books. The first recorded examples of these appear in Germany in the 15th century, and the first printed examples are also German. Albrecht Dürer engraved at least six bookplates in the period 1503 to 1516, and other plates ascribed to Hans Holbein and Lucas Cranach survive from about the same period.

The bookplate appears in France (for de la Tour-Blanche) in 1529; in England (for Thomas Wolsey b. 1515); in Holland (for Anna van der Aa) 1597; and in Italy as an unnamed armorial plate in 1622. Among notable American bookplates are those of Paul Revere, believed to have been engraved by himself (c.1775), and George Washington, engraved at about the same time, probably in England.

In Britain, bookplate design tended at first to follow that of France, but the 18th century saw a reflection (as in other fields) of the work of architects, furniture makers, and other designers. There are thus bookplates in the style of Chippendale (who himself engraved a number of examples), Adam, Hepplewhite, Sheraton, and Wedgwood.

Bookplates may be seen to fall not only into design categories but a number of basic genres. Chief among these are the armorial, the library interior, the book-pile (a quasi-architectural construction composed of books), the portrait, and the landscape.

The 20th century saw a revival of interest in the bookplate, with a number of distinguished artists contributing designs in individual, non-traditional styles in a variety of media. The revival was also reflected in the proliferation of societies of bookplate collectors. By the end of the century there were societies in some twenty countries, including Japan and the USSR.

Closely related to the bookplate is the BOOK-PRIZE LABEL, a convention established in the early 18th century, widely revived in the latter part of the 19th century, and still not extinct. The prize label appeared at first as a decoratively presented engraving. Wording was commonly in Latin and spaces allowed insertion of details of the recipient's name and achievements. Late Victorian labels appeared often as highly coloured chromolithographed productions, sometimes with gold and silver embellishment, in a style reminiscent of the scholar's proficiency certificate. The device was widely adopted by the Sunday-school movement.

The bookplate was occasionally used as a promotional GIVE-AWAY. One firm, Globe-Wernicke, bookcase manufacturers of Cincinnati, provided sets of three-colour bookplate blanks for its potential customers in the 1920s. The BOOK TOKEN, launched in 1932, also entered the bookplate field, providing a detachable portion for use by the recipient as a memento of the gift.

REFERENCES Clifford N.Carver, *Bookplates of Well-Known Americans* (Princeton, NJ, 1911); Brian North Lee, *British Bookplates: A Pictorial History* (Newton Abbot: David & Charles, 1979);

COLLECTIONS American Antiquarian Society, Worcester, Mass.; Franks Collection, British Museum, London

SOCIETIES American Society of Bookplate Collectors and Designers; The Bookplate Society, London

Book-prize label

The awarding of books as school prizes dates from the latter part of the 17th century and labels recording such awards are found from the early 18th century onwards. They were particularly favoured and ambitious in Ireland where they were awarded for success in studies and examinations from the 1730s. Such labels, engraved with decorative swags, laurels, and cherubs are inscribed in Latin with spaces for the insertion of the name of the recipient, date, and subject. A typical example measures 152 × 84 mm (6 × 3¼ in). The convention was taken up by religious institutions and continued into the 19th century, when it was adopted by schools and colleges generally.

Major institutions used their own specially-printed labels; others used general-purpose labels from educational suppliers' standing stocks. Toward the middle of the 19th century the prize label had become an elaborately printed item in the style of the stock diploma or certificate, produced in the main by the chromolithography specialists. The convention remains current in present-day prize-giving, particularly in Sunday Schools, with modified conventions of 19th-century chromolithographed designs and a liberal use of gold.

Bookseller's label

Like the BINDER'S TICKET which it resembles, the bookseller's label is commonly found pasted on the upper left-hand corner of the front pastedown of the book or in the corresponding position on the recto of the flyleaf. Widely used in the 19th century, and not wholly extinct among quality booksellers in the 20th century, the bookseller's label is in effect a miniature trade card. It is generally printed in black on a thin colour-tinted paper (latterly often in gold or silver on a solid colour) and in a variety of shapes (rectangular, ovoid, shield-shaped, etc.).

The 19th-century bookseller's label generally bore the briefest of details, sometimes only the surname of the bookseller and the town name. Early labels are copperplate engravings, later examples are lithographed. Toward the end of the century, many were printed from type or blocks, and more recently photolithography has been used. In most methods, printing is from a multiple plate or setting, thus allowing production of a number of identical images at one impression. Until the latter part of the 19th century, division into separate units was by scissors, sometimes by the booksellers themselves from multi-image sheets supplied uncut by the printer. The bookseller's label differs from the binder's ticket only in that it is an item added to a product by a retailer rather than being inserted by a craftsman as an individual 'signature'.

The bookseller's label may thus have been placed in the book at any time after its publication, often, in the case of second-hand books, many years after. Additionally, unlike the majority of binders' tickets, which generally relate only to binding, the bookseller's label may advertise other goods or services – typically stationery, printing, engraving, die-sinking and stamping, publishing, as well as the services of reading rooms, news agencies, and circulating libraries. Roland Knaster's manuscript introduction to his collection of booksellers' labels in the Guildhall Library, London, lists 176 different combinations, including, as additional designations, apple sellers, cutlers, curio finders, drawing teachers, monogram designers, natural history agents, parasol dealers, passport agents, retail fishing tackle manufacturers, toymen, and wholesale fowling jacket manufacturers.

As with the binder's ticket, use of the bookseller's label is predominantly an English-language practice, much in evidence in Britain and also found to a considerable extent in America.

Booksellers' labels of Reeve, Leamington; Pawson & Brailsford, Sheffield; H. & C. Treacher, Brighton. All smaller than 13 × 22mm (½ × ⅞in)

Elsewhere it appears in smaller numbers, though examples are reported from a wide variety of sources. These include the following: Amiens, Amsterdam, Antwerp, Barcelona, Berlin, Boulogne, Bordeaux, Bremen, Breslau, Brussels, Budapest, Cadiz, Cairo, Cambrai, Capri, Frankfurt, Hannover, Johannesburg, Livorno, Mannheim, Milan, Montreal, Munich, Paris, Pretoria, Quebec, Rotterdam, Rouen, St Petersburg, Tournai, Torino, and Venice.

The 19th-century bookseller's label has its origins in the much larger bookseller's label in use in the 18th century. Some of these early labels are indistinguishable from the ordinary TRADE CARD; they measure up to 180 × 115 mm (7⅛ × 4½ in) and were printed, it may be assumed, from trade-card plates. Unlike its unobtrusive successor, the large label often occupied a dominant position on the front or back pastedown, filling virtually the whole of the space available (*see* STATIONER'S LABEL). The minuscule format introduced in the 1820s was apparently encouraged by the example of the binder's ticket, possibly the least obtrusive of any label, before or since.

COLLECTION Roland Knaster Collection, Guildhall Library, London

Braille

Efforts at devising tactile reading systems for the blind are recorded in the 16th and 17th centuries, but it was not until the 18th century that Valentin Haüy developed the idea of embossing paper with large-size ordinary characters. He was the first to apply the principle to the production of books for the blind.

In 1821 Haüy's school in Paris, the Institution Nationale des Jeunes Aveugles, received a visit from Charles Barbier, an ex-army officer, who told Haüy about his own invention for 'night-writing' on active service. The system used dots punched in paper with a steel pointer and a metal frame as a guide. The matter came to nothing, however, although similar ideas were being mooted by Zeune in Berlin and Johann Wilhelm Klein in Vienna.

Inspired by the work of Haüy, an Edinburgh printer – James Gall – produced his own relief system. This also used a modified form of orthodox type. In 1827 he published his *A First Book for Teaching the Art of Reading to the Blind*. A number of other modifications emerged in the course of the next few years and by mid-century the New England Asylum for the Blind in Boston, later known as the Perkins Institution and Massachusetts School for the Blind, had formulated the system later to become known as Boston Line Letter. This incorporated features from a number of European systems. However, it proved no easier to read than previous type-based systems, and other methods using short lines, curves, half circles, dots, and other signs.

In 1847 Dr William Moon, of Brighton, devised a nine-character system of lines, half-circles, etc., each character's function changing according to which way up it was printed. Two of the twenty-six alphabet characters are recognizably derived from orthodox capital letters. Other characters were added to express contractions, whole-word signs, and punctuation. The system was at first printed from shaped copper characters fixed on sheet metal plates, but in the early 1920s a form of printing type was developed. The system was more successful than any of its forerunners, especially among older people whose touch was not sensitive enough for finer reading, and has survived in everyday use by such people.

It was the contribution of Louis Braille (first published in a pamphlet in 1829 and improved in a more compact version in 1834) that brought the biggest step forward. He was himself blind – the first of the innovators to work from personal knowledge of the problem – and became a student, and later a teacher, at Haüy's school. His studies brought him to an appraisal of Barbier's 'night-writing' dots. By the time he was sixteen, in 1825, his own six-dot 'domino' concept had been formulated. It was more than a quarter of a century later, two years after his death in 1852, that his system was formally adopted. Only in 1932 was a standard form agreed upon internationally for English-speaking users.

Mass production of braille publications was by the use of whole-page stereotyped plates, texts being punched into stiff paper to produce relief impressions on the reading side. In the 1960s the solid-dot principle was introduced. In this, solid dots of plastic are heat-sealed onto the surface of a thin paper. The method reduces bulk by some forty-five per cent, and the dots are virtually indestructible.

Ephemera in modern braille exist in considerable quantity. Commonly available are such items as domestic container labels, instruction sheets, card games and boardgames, jigsaw puzzles, maps, and greetings cards, as well as an extensive range of periodicals.

Early embossed ephemera for the blind survive in the form of specimen sheets put out by advocates of various systems and, more rarely, embossed communications to or from the blind. Also found are teaching aids, maps, diagrams, portrait profiles, and religious items. The Moon Society, deeply imbued with its founder's Christian principles, put out a vast quantity of devotional material. At the turn of the century its publication list, including chapters from the Bible, psalms, and general religious works, both in English and foreign languages, ran to some 350 items. The Lord's Prayer and other small sections of scripture, were available in 400 languages and dialects.

A typical survival from the era of the type-based systems is a specimen included with the *Seventh Annual Report* (1839) of the New England Institution for the Education of the Blind, Boston. This shows a paragraph of improving text and an example of a relief-printed map, in this case of the Nantucket Island area. These items, executed in type-based characters, are of course legible to the sighted reader, and it is clear that they served to arouse the interest and sympathy of potential benefactors.

Legible to the sighted – as potential customers – is a listing of charges made by the workrooms of the Perkins Institution for the Blind in the 1890s in Boston. This sets out costs of mattress and pillow renovation by the blind of the institution and adds 'We sell brass and iron beds'. The paper forms a publicity broadside, complete with address and telephone number.

A variant of the type-based principle is embodied in a foolscap sheet (c.1860) bearing a message in characters pin-pricked from the other side of the paper. In this system each character is composed of a number of spikes set in a square wooden peg, placed together in reverse order on the reverse side of the paper. The pegs are pressed into the surface, the spikes piercing holes that can afterwards be read by touch. In the example cited, a passage of religious verse carries the footline 'Hannah Miles from Emily Taylor'.

Certain aids for the blind are custom-made for the individual. An exhibit in the Norwich Castle Museum shows plans of the building published at the time of its conversion from a prison in the 1880s for the benefit of John Gurney, the museum's leading initiator, who had become blind. The main features of the layout are outlined in sand.

REFERENCES Elizabeth M. Harris, *In Touch: Printing and Writing for the Blind in the Nineteenth Century* (Washington, DC: Smithsonian Institution Press, 1981); *Reading By Touch* (London: Royal National Institute for the Blind, 1972); *Seventh Annual Report* (Boston: New-England Institution for the Education of the Blind, 1839); Henry J. Wagg, *A Chronological Survey of Work for the Blind* (London: Pitman & Sons, 1932)

Broadside/broadsheet

The words 'broadside' and 'broadsheet' are by many regarded as synonymous ('A large printed sheet of paper'); but specialist opinion favours 'broadside' for a single-sided sheet and 'broadsheet' where both sides are printed.

Historically the broadside is first to appear, emerging in the 16th century as a bill for posting in the market place as confirmation of the public crier's spoken announcement. Here, clearly, the context logically allows printing on one side only. The broadsheet, printed on both sides, is identified with the printing of such items as the CHAPBOOK, in which a single *sheet* is folded to compose a sixteen- or thirty-two-page booklet, and later with the extra-large newspapers of the 1830s and 1840s (so-called by contrast with their old-style small-format competitors). The term 'broadsheet' later extends to refer to the two-sided advertising folder, which unfolds to disclose a single overall image on each side.

The broadside is a single-sided printed sheet of virtually any size, ranging from a PROCLAMATION measuring 1000 × 500 mm (39½ × 19¾ in) to a handbill of 200 × 150 mm (7⅞ × 6 in). Subject matter is also widely disparate. The broadside may be a theatre bill, a royal proclamation, or a public apology. It must be said that the term is so generalized as to be almost meaningless. Its imprecision must be ascribed to the wide range of situations that called for the printed word in the era before the popular newspaper. The broadside appeared as formal pronouncement in matters of law and order; as a purveyor of warning in emergency; as an instrument of protest, political controversy, and personal dispute; as a medium of entertainment and irreverence in the form of ballad, verse, and satire; and as commercial advertising. It was in fact the universal medium of expression at every level, augmented only – for the more literate – by the pamphlet.

Of the huge variety of surviving broadsides we may note a few titles by way of example: 'The Names of the Streets, Lanes and Alleys Within the Town of Boston, New England' (1708); '[An Act] For the Encouragement of Piety and Virtue, and for the Preventing and Punishing of Vice, Profaneness and Immorality' (Dublin, 1837); 'By the King, a Proclamation Restraining the Abusive Venting of Tobacco' (London, 1633); 'A List of a Few Cures Performed by Mr and Mrs de Loutherbourg, of Hammersmith Terrace, Without Medicine' (London, 1789); 'The Great Lock-out of Miners at Barnsley. New Song: The South Yorkshire Miners Shall Never Despair' (Barnsley, c.1835); execution broadside: 'The Agonies of a Soul Departing out of Time into Eternity' (Cambridge, Massachusetts, 1757); 'North Eastern Railway : Discontinuance of Trains : Funeral of Her Late Majesty Queen Victoria' (York, 1901); 'A Declaration [of Independence] by the Representatives of the United States of America in General Congress Assembled' (Boston, July 1776).

See also ACADEMY/COLLEGE BROADSIDE; BELLMAN'S VERSES; CITY ORDINANCE BROADSIDE; EXECUTION BROADSIDE

REFERENCES *Calamities, Wonders and Topics of the Town, 1603–1902: A List of Items in the Guildhall Library* (London: Guildhall, 1968); Goldsmith's Library of Economic Literature, *Catalogue of the Collection of Broadsides in the University Library* (London: University of London Press, 1930); Charles Hindley, *Curiosities of Street Literature* (London: Reeves and Turner, 1871; reprinted The Broadsheet King, 1966); *The J E Hodgkin Collections: Catalogue of the Trade Cards, Bookplates, Broadsides, etc* (London: Sotheby, Wilkinson & Hodge, 27, 28 April 1914); Louis James, *Print and the People 1819–1851* (London: Allen Lane, 1976); Robert Lemon, *Catalogue of a Collection of Printed Broadsides in the possession of the Society of Antiquaries of London* (London: Society of Antiquaries, 1866); James L. Lindsey-Crawford, *Catalogue of English Broadsides 1505–1897* (printed for the author, 1898; reprinted Burt Franklin, NY, 1968); Maurice Rickards, *The Public Notice* (Newton Abbot: David & Charles, 1973); *Some Early Massachusetts Broadsides* (Boston: Massachusetts Historical Society, 1964); Martha Vicinus, *Broadsides of the Industrial North* (Newcastle-upon-Tyne: Graham, 1975)

COLLECTIONS Guildhall Library, London; John Johnson Collection, Bodleian Library, Oxford; St Bride Printing Library, London; Society of Antiquaries, London; Massachusetts Historical Society, Boston

Broom label

The broom label flourished in the United States in the period 1890 to 1910. In common with many other products of a newly emerging mass-production economy, brooms were often provided with stock colour labels overprinted with the name of the individual manufacturer or supplier. Designs featured a central pictorial element and generally bore a panel above and below to carry a brand name and other details.

The three- or four-colour label measured 120 × 90 mm (4¾ × 3½ in) and was pasted on the handle, enwrapping it fully. Major visual elements were confined to a narrow vertical area, which allowed recognition from a single frontal viewpoint.

Many designs featured an aproned figure using a broom. Others were merely decorative, presenting pictures of locomotives, steamboats, and other images of currently popular appeal.

American broom labels of the first half of the 20th century. *Left:* lithographed in four colours, 152 × 90 mm (6 × 3½ in); *above:* lithographed in two colours, 128 × 89 mm (5 × 3½ in)

Bumper sticker

The practice of applying printed messages to cars originated in America from the use in World War II of self-adhesive paper or plastic labels to identify and explain the functioning of military equipment. The first civilian examples were produced at the Gill Studios, Kansas, in 1945. Early slogans include 'Vote for…', 'Come to…', 'Buy…'.

The bumper sticker may be seen as providing an element of individual self-expression in an increasingly depersonalized society. It is said to offer the otherwise anonymous driver a measure of distinction – as philosopher, wit, or lobbyist. The wording of one sticker, popular in the early 1980s, may be symptomatic: 'The majority of us belong to some minority group'.

Bumper stickers have proliferated in America since the 1960s, reaching the proportions of a minor industry. The work of slogan-writers, design studios, and printers was brought together in specialist groupings. They produced not only a large number of 'stock' lines, but provided stickers to order for advertising campaigns, pressure groups, political parties, and private individuals. Some advertisers employed latter-day fly-posters to tour parking areas, applying stickers gratuitously (a practice which brought paragraphs in the motoring press on methods of removal). An early British precursor of this practice was the application of advertising stickers to carriages in the 1850s to advertise the play 'The Dead Heart' (W. Smith, *Advertise. How? When? Where?* London 1863, pp. 69–70).

In Britain, bumpers remained largely blank. Instead, the car sticker took the form of a rear-window sticker applied from the inside, using gum-tipped paper for topical announcements (carnival dates etc.) and self-adhesive plastic for the more durable legend. As in America, topics have a strong bias to minority groupings, sexual prowess, and irreverent wit.

COLLECTION University of Texas Library

Bumper sticker in support of the American presidential candidate Eldridge Cleaver, Hempstead, New York, 1968. Lithographed in red and black. 93 × 375 mm (3⅝ × 14¾ in)

Burial club papers

The burial club was one among a number of mutual-aid institutions set up as a result of British working-class initiatives in the early 19th century. In the absence of government insurance schemes, the societies provided subscribers with a measure of financial security, paying specific sums in the event of sickness or death. The societies, which were generally local rather than national, were closely linked to the concept of the medieval guild, the ancient 'order' (of Mechanics, Druids, Oddfellows, Foresters, etc.), the friendly society, and the trade union. Later there emerged the major benefit societies (Hearts of Oak Benefit Society, The National Deposit Friendly Society, etc.). Numbers declined progressively following the introduction of National Social Security after World War II.

The burial club assured the contributor full payment of funeral and burial expenses regardless of how long he or she had contributed. Those joining the club in youth paid less than older recruits, and payment scales varied according to the class of funeral and burial desired. Payments were commonly of the order of a halfpenny a week. The contributor's card (the 'burial card') was regularly marked by the society's agent, in many cases on a door-to-door visit, sometimes on his own premises – often a public house. The card, commonly measuring some 100 × 140 mm (4 × 5½ in), carried dated 'boxes' for filling in during the operative period (one to four years) and brief explanations of terms of membership. In a typical example the Royal Liver Friendly Society notes that 'All applications for funerals made before twelve o'clock will be paid the same day if under £10; if above £10 within one week after all is found correct…'.

Burial club card, Hollingworth, of the early 20th century. Letterpress. 113 × 152 mm (4½ × 6 in)

The principal was also applied to the use of a communal hearse, members having the right to its use for half the price chargeable to non-members (Easter-Strath [Strath Avon], W. Lothian 1795): other schemes offered sickness pay after three years' membership and entitlement to a 'decent funeral… so far as the said subscription will admit of' (Shrawley, Hereford, 1789).

REFERENCE Maurice Rickards, *The Public Notice* (Newton Abbot: David & Charles, 1973)

Burial in woollen affidavit

In 1667 (18, 19, Charles II, c.4), in an attempt to rescue the declining woollen industry, an Act came into force which decreed that all corpses had to be buried in shrouds made of wool rather than linen or any other material. The Act was

Willm Bethell Maketh Oath that the Body of Ann Stone of the Parish of St Sepulchre London which was buried at Edgware in y County of Middx was not wrapped in any thing but what was made of Sheepswool only July 22: 1764

Jurat coram me
Tho: Richards Min

Burial in woollen affidavit relating to the parish of St Sepulchre, London, 22 July 1764. Intaglio printed. 117 × 157 mm (4⅝ × 6¼ in)

largely ignored and had to be strengthened in 1678 by another Act (Charles II, c. 30) which imposed a fine of £5 on defaulters, half of which went to the relief of the poor of the parish. Although it was a highly unpopular Act, it remained on the statute books until 1815. The Act instructed that the curate of every parish keep a register of all burials, together with an affidavit taken by a justice of the peace 'or such like chief officer' swearing that the corpse was buried in wool.

Some of these affidavits were handwritten, but most were blank forms provided by local jobbing printers. The wording varied but always included the necessary elements: '(—) of the Parish of (—) maketh Oath, that the Body of (—) late of the Parish of (—) which was Buried at (—) was not wrapt in, or put into any Suit, Sheet or Coffin, but what was made of Sheepswool only'. The forms were frequently decorated with illustrations of skulls, skeletons, coffins, and shrouded corpses – in wool of course. [PJ]

REFERENCES D.G.C. Allan, 'Burials in Woollen 1667–1814', *Wool Knowledge*, Spring 1955; Julian Litten, *The English Way of Death: The Common Funeral since 1450* (London: Robert Hale, 1991)

Burial papers

Attempts at recording burials (as well as births and marriages) were made as early as 1538, when Henry VIII issued an instruction to clergy to record every wedding, christening, and burial week by week in a register kept specially for the purpose. With varying degrees of efficiency the system remained operative for centuries, but centralized records were not established until the setting up of the General Register Office (Births, Deaths & Marriages) in 1837 (6, 7, Wm IV, c. 86). This required *inter alia* that no burial take place without delivery of a certificate from the registrar showing formal registration of death. This, the Certificate of Registry of Death, is distinct from the Medical Certificate of Cause of Death (*see* DEATH CERTIFICATE), a supporting document signed by a qualified physician. The 'cause-of-death' element in this declaration, long advocated by Jeremy Bentham and Sir Edwin Chadwick as an aid in public health studies, was to prove vital in the struggle against cholera.

In the 19th and 20th centuries regulations governing disposal of the dead became progressively more detailed and comprehensive. Analysis of papers relating to the subject is complicated, not only by this proliferation but by division of approach as between the ecclesiastical and the temporal and by generalized differences of denomination, period, and place. Additional complication resides in the multiplicity of facets that the subject shows. These include such matters as death by contagious or communicable disease; still-birth burials; excavation of burial grounds; violation of graves; re-interment; disposal of unidentified bodies; preservation of bodies pending enquiries; transportation of bodies; cremation; burial at sea; exhumations; rights of custodianship of bodies; exclusion of dissenters, the unbaptized, the excommunicated, and suicides; and measures to avoid burial alive (this last a major concern in Britain in the 1830s and 1840s).

Among the many health problems of 19th-century Britain was the mounting risk of epidemic through burial in towns. Church buildings and churchyards, traditional repositories of the dead, had by the 1830s become so grossly overcrowded as to pose a serious threat to public health. In London there appeared a number of notorious private-enterprise cemeteries. George Walker's *Gatherings from Graveyards* (1839) and Mrs Basil

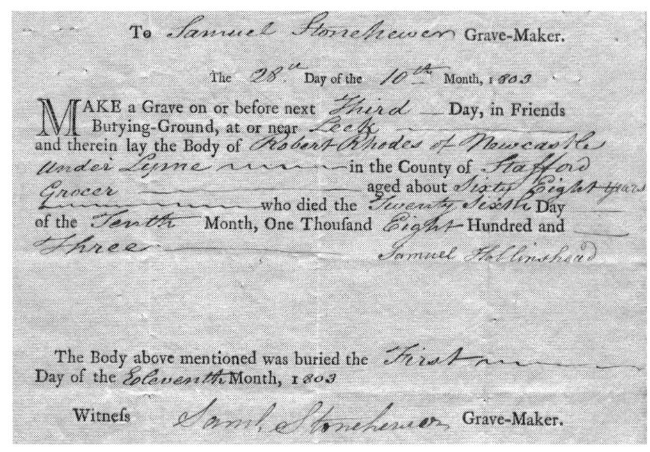

To Samuel Stonehewer Grave-Maker.

The 28th Day of the 10th Month, 1803

MAKE a Grave on or before next Third Day, in Friends Burying-Ground, at or near Leek and therein lay the Body of Robert Rhodes of Newcastle under Lyme in the County of Stafford Grocer aged about Sixty Eight years who died the Twenty Sixth Day of the Tenth Month, One Thousand Eight Hundred and Three

Samuel Hollinshead

The Body above mentioned was buried the First Day of the Eleventh Month, 1803

Witness Saml. Stonehewer Grave-Maker.

Grave-maker's form, 1803. Letterpress and manuscript. Printed by William Phillips, Lombard Street, London. 156 × 203 mm (6¼ × 8 in)

Holmes's *London Burial Grounds* (1896) describe these ventures as infinitely more horrifying than the evils they professed to relieve.

The position was no less precarious in rural areas, where levels of churchyards were seen to rise as layer succeeded layer, coffins sometimes barely covered by the earth. Notable among the ephemera of the rural church, at this period and after, are notices of churchyard extensions and regulations governing depth and proximity of graves, exclusion of non-parishioners, etc.

In the towns, as the ephemera of the period confirm, major commercial enterprise moved in. By the 1840s Londoners were receiving prospectuses of no fewer than seven spacious cemeteries, organized and maintained on efficient and hygienic lines by big limited companies. These cemeteries, at Kensal Green (1832), Norwood (1837), Highgate (1839), Nunhead (1840), Abney Park (1840), Brompton (1840), and Tower Hamlets (1841), were to become respected symbols of the Victorian view of death. In another burst of activity, in the 1850s, a further twenty-one cemeteries were opened. By the end of the century London cemeteries unattached to church or chapel numbered nearly one hundred.

Publication of Chadwick's horrific report, *On the Results of a Special Inquiry into the Practice of Interment in Towns* (1843), brought the scandal of overcrowded burial grounds finally into the open, and legislation followed. The Cemeteries Clauses Act of 1847, and a series of Burial Acts (1852, 1853, 1855, and 1857) laid down the basis for more rigid controls. Burial in towns was entirely prohibited and local vestries were empowered to form Burial Boards and to establish their own cemeteries as a non-profit public service. The latter part of the century saw tighter control of such matters as death certificates, mortuary procedures, registration of still-births, and due despatch in burial.

The ephemera of the cemetery are concerned at first with gravediggers' and sextons' fees, and burial certificates (records of entries in parish registers), but increasingly stringent legislation and the advent of the cemetery companies and burial boards brings a big increase in such papers.

Most commonly found, in addition to death and burial certificates, are receipts and scale-of-charges papers, and certificates from burial boards and cemetery companies. These relate to purchase of the right to burial in a specified plot; costs of digging and turfing graves; erecting and moving monuments, head- and foot-stones, railings, kerbs, etc.

General promotional material is also found, outlining the virtues and facilities offered by the new establishments of the 1830s and 1840s ('The South Metropolitan Cemetery, Norwood, Surrey; Most eligibly situated for the convenience of the inhabitants of the metropolis… sufficiently removed to insure seclusion, and near enough to be accessible to all ranks…'). Such material, appearing as separate items or incorporated with scale-of-charges folders, is based on the statutory provisions of the Burial Act (1852) and may in some cases be extended by the company concerned to forty or fifty numbered articles.

Forms and other papers used in cemetery administration are less readily found, although by the turn of the century these had greatly increased in number. A handbook published in 1907 shows that each individual interment might involve, in addition to entries in grave plans and burial registers, thirteen separate forms, notices, receipts, etc.

A further group of forms and other ephemera appeared with the advent of statutorily controlled cremation in 1902. Here the impossibility of post-interment enquiry brought the need for even more stringent controls. Statutory requirements as to construction and conduct of crematoria, the rendering of doctors' and coroners' certificates etc., account for a notable increase in the paper record.

The range of ephemera relating to interment is extensive. Among the less predictable items we may note the following:

Metropolitan Borough of Lewisham, Public Mortuary regulations 1929, broadsheet, 685 × 420 mm (27 × 16½ in). A listing of twenty rules, based substantially on the Public Health (London) Act (1891), deals not only with physical details but standards of conduct: 'A body brought to the mortuary… shall be conveyed… in a hearse or otherwise in a decent and proper manner… no public procession or large assemblage of persons shall be allowed inside the gates…. The mortuary keeper… shall be responsible for the keeping of due order decency and decorum at all times and also see that all persons having occasion to visit the mortuary conduct themselves… with decency and propriety'.

The disposal of ashes after cremation; a four-page folder, 125 × 190 mm (4⅞ × 7½ in), published by the London Cremation Company, c.1905, in respect of their establishments at Woking and Golders Green. It describes disposal options: retention in a container in the home; burial in private grounds; scattering on the earth or at sea; deposit in an 'urn-niche' garden; deposit around or beneath a memorial tree ('The ashes before they leave the crematorium are always reduced to fine particles so that they cannot be recognised as human remains…'). After reviewing various methods of disposal the folder recommends tree or shrub dedication: 'In the place of many acres now being given over yearly to the undisturbed Rest of the Dead, the land would be preserved for the enjoyment of the Living for whom it was intended…'.

Coroner's disbursements, four-page folding card, 115 × 75 mm (4½ × 3 in), published by the County of Southampton, 1899. It lists allowances to be made for services rendered to the coroner (sums to be reimbursed to coroner's office against receipted invoices): 'For finding a Dead Body, drowned or otherwise exposed, watching the same and giving notice to the nearest police constable… 5*s* 0*d*.'; 'For Removing any such Body so found… and keeping it until the inquest: 2*s* 6*d*.'; 'For Inquest Room, when hired, per day: 2*s* 6*d*…'.

Public notice, single-sided paper, 260 × 210 mm (10¼ × 8¼ in), published by unnamed local authority, c.1900: 'Notice! No Burial of a Stillborn Child will be allowed on the certificate of a mid-wife unless supplemented by one from a Medical Man. Every Stillborn Child, or Child for which no Service is required, shall be placed in a separate Coffin or Box (except in cases where the Child is placed in the same Coffin as the Mother), and every such coffin or box shall have affixed on its lid the name of the Undertaker, with the date on which it is delivered at the cemetery. By order'.

See also BILL OF MORTALITY; BURIAL CLUB PAPERS; BURIAL IN WOOLLEN AFFIDAVIT; BURIAL-RIGHT DEED; FUNERALIA

REFERENCES Edwin Austin, *Burial Grounds and Cemeteries* (London: Butterworth/Shaw, 1907); Sir Edwin Chadwick, *A Supplementary Report on the Results of a Special Enquiry into the Practice of Interment in Towns* (London: HMSO, 1843); Hugh Meller, *London Cemeteries: an Illustrated Guide and Gazeteer* (Amersham: Avebury Publishing Co., 1981)

Burial-right deed

Known strictly as a 'Deed of conveyance', this document confers on the person it names the right to burial in a numbered grave space in a specific cemetery 'in perpetuity' (or, in some versions, 'for ever').

Deeds were generally printed on parchment, numbered and counterfoiled. Local burial board deeds measured some 200 × 160 mm (7⅞ × 6¼ in) and bore a more or less standard form of wording, quoting the Act or Acts under which the transaction was made. They sometimes also carried an indication of the number of interments the grave would accommodate (depths of 7 feet, 9 feet, 11 feet, and 13 feet taking respectively two, three, four, or five coffins). A form in the margin of the deed allowed entry of details of dates, names, and register numbers of interments as they occurred.

Deeds from major private cemeteries were generally larger – up to 240 × 300 mm (9½ × 11⅞ in) – and were often illustrated with an engraved vignette of the cemetery and cast in a style reminiscent of a company share certificate. All such deeds, though granting perpetual rights, nevertheless allowed the board or company an escape clause: burial board terms were 'subject to the regulations now in force, or which may hereafter be issued with regard to interments in the said cemetery by Her Majesty's Secretary of State, or by the said Burial Board, or any

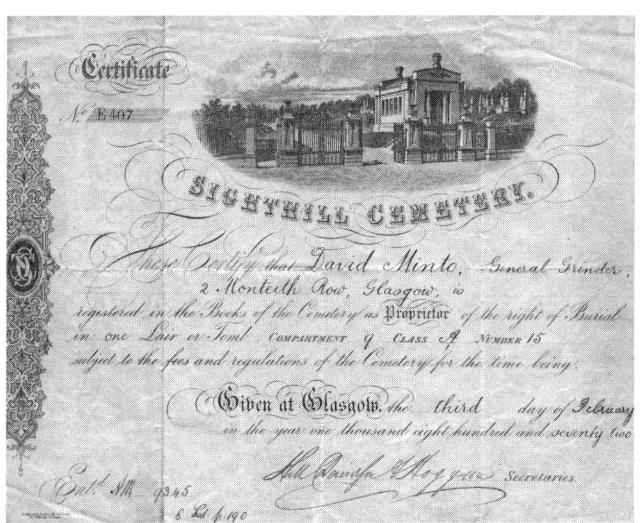

Certificate

No E 407

SIGHTHILL CEMETERY.

These Certify that David Minto, General Grinder, 2 Monteith Row, Glasgow, is registered in the Books of the Cemetery as Proprietor of the right of Burial in one Lair or Tomb Compartment 9 Class A Number 15 subject to the fees and regulations of the Cemetery for the time being.

Given at Glasgow the third day of February in the year one thousand eight hundred and seventy two

Secretaries.

Burial-right deed, Sighthill Cemetery, Glasgow, 3 February 1872. Intaglio and manuscript. Designed and engraved on steel by Gilmour & Dean. 235 × 298 mm (9¼ × 11¾ in)

other competent authority'. Private cemetery arrangements were 'subject to the fees and regulations of the cemetery for the time being'.

REFERENCE Edwin Austin, *Burial Grounds and Cemeteries* (London: Butterworth/Shaw, 1907)

By-law/ordinance

Known variously as 'Rules', 'Orders', 'Regulations', etc., local enactments were published by councils, manorial lordships, provosts, magistrates, baillies etc. in pursuit of their rights of governance, real or assumed. Whereas state law is seen as controlling the conduct of affairs at large, by-laws are the expression of authority within specific local limits. They are thus concerned with the minutiae of public behaviour: 'laying down ashes, foul water and other filth' are among the offences dealt with.

Virtually all such regulations are the product of practical experience. Each prohibition commemorates an act of human mischief; the ordinance archive reveals a sorry chronicle. A couple of extracts set the tone:

Manors of South and North Lofthouse, Yorkshire, 1789: 'If any person shall without leave from the constable … lodge or harbour any Vagabond, Wandering Rogues or beggars … he, she, or they, shall for every such offence forfeit the sum of six shillings and eightpence'; 'If any Persons shall suffer any of his Swine to go unringed in or upon any of the streets … he, she, or they, shall … forfeit … Three Shillings and Fourpence'.

Edinburgh, 1737: 'The Peace and good Government of this city has been frequently disturbed and insulted, and many pernicious and fatal Consequences have ensued to the Citizens and Inhabitants thereof, by the most insolent and illegal Practices of throwing Stones, Mud and other Garbage, at the proper Officers of the Law, City-guard and Common executioner, when in the exercise of their Duty and Office at lawful and public Executions of Criminals …'.

See also RULES AND REGULATIONS

Cachet, postal

The word *cachet* (French: seal) appears in English for the first time in the 17th century, in the sense of stamp, mark, or special sign: 'She had appointed, instead of his hand, a Cachet to be used in the signing of Letters' (Spottiswood, *History of the Church of Scotland* (1677)). Use of the word in postal history is relatively recent and, strictly speaking, refers to a printed, embossed, or handstamped legend or device applied privately on a postal cover as an indication of a special circumstance. Other postal marks are normally referred to by the postal historian as handstamps. The term cachet does not apply to ordinary cancellation marks or town marks.

The cachet may be said to have its origins in the manuscript addenda inserted by correspondents on the outside of their letters in former times. These invoked God's aid in guarding the message and its bearer and urged the messenger himself to special effort. A common device was the sign of a cross. The initials QDC (Latin, *Quem Deus Conservat:* Whom God Preserve) are also found. To the messenger the inscription was 'Per postas, cito, cito et fidelis' (By post, swiftly, swiftly and faithfully), or 'Cito, cito, cito, citissime, volantissime' (Swiftly, swiftly, swiftly, most swiftly, fly!). In some cases the words were reinforced by representations of a gallows, the fate awaiting the unfaithful messenger. The expression 'post haste' entered the English language, and was much used in the addressing of letters. In the Public Record Office is a letter from Edward Doddington to the Lords of the Privy Council warning of the sighting of the Spanish Armada. Doddington adds to the address: 'hast post hast ffor lyffe hast; hast post hast ffor lyffe'.

The term is also used here to cover the printed, embossed, or handstamped cachet, normally applied by a postal authority. Such cachets may be said to fall into two categories: those concerned with day-to-day annotation of ordinary postal administration, and those concerned with special arrangements.

The postal cachet emerges as an instructional mark ('More to pay', 'To be delivered by 10 o'clock') and as an indicator of special circumstance ('Put in after 7 o'clock at night', 'Too late for morning post'). The emergency cachet relates to a wide range of contingencies, including war, civil unrest, earthquake, epidemic, robbery, wrecks, and crashes.

Typical war cachets are, from World War I: 'Undelivered through capitulation at Kut' and 'Part of a mail captured by Germans and delayed'; and from World War II: 'Delayed by enemy action' and 'Detained in France during German occupation'. Similar cachets appeared in the Boer War: 'Recovered from mails looted by the enemy'. The American Civil War produced its own cachets: 'Cannot be forwarded', 'Southern letter unpaid', 'No service', and 'Return to sender'.

Cachets from the 1920s in Ireland include examples used by the postal authorities: 'Recovered from raided mail' and 'Salved from fire GPO Dublin'; and by the Irish Republican Army: 'Censored by IRA'. Numerous manuscript notes are also recorded: 'Found open, recovered from raided mails', 'Passed by censor IRA', and 'Opened by censor IRA'.

Other manuscript notes are found on American covers after mail raids. An example from Salt Lake City in 1868 reads: 'This was opened by the robbers in the coach robbery August 25/68: 265 miles east of S.L.C'. Another in Texas in 1921 reads: 'This mail was recovered from stolen pouch'. The earliest of such manuscript notes date from 1745 and appear on letters addressed to Alexander Hamilton, Solicitor of London. They bear the endorsement: 'Opened by the rebels' [the followers of Bonnie Prince Charlie]. Manuscript notes are also found among mail salvaged from the waters of the Tay after the disaster in 1879, as well as on letters damaged on less serious occasions. Among examples of these are: 'Recovered from flooded box'; 'Postage paid' (Herne Bay, 1953); 'Found in mail box, wet' (Paducah, Kentucky, 1942); 'Stamp found eaten off by snails' (Looe, Cornwall, 1946); 'Caution: damaged by rodents' (Argentina, 1945); and 'Destruction by tomtits' (Exeter, 1957). Manuscript notes may occasionally record problems within the post office itself. A cover posted in Cavriago, Italy, in 1865 has been cancelled by pen and bears the manuscript explanation 'Rotto l'annullatore' (obliterator broken).

Among handstamped cachets are 'Ship letter' (*see* COVER, POSTAL) and 'To be delivered free' (*see* FREE FRANK). Less common are the cachets used during the period of the newspaper tax stamp: 'Newspaper regulations not complied with', 'Stamp not visible', 'Contains an enclosure', etc. Also relatively rare are 'advertising' letters, items uncalled for and listed unclaimed in a newspaper before being returned to the sender. These carry, in addition to their normal handstamped date marks and obliterations, the single handstamped word 'Advertising'.

Rare cachets are those relating to earthquakes. When postage stamp supplies were disrupted in Quetta in 1935 mail from the area was accepted free of charge, and covers exist bearing the handwritten cachet 'Quetta Earth Quake. Postage Free'.

See also DISINFECTED MAIL; FEATHER LETTER; POSTAL HISTORY

REFERENCES Arthur Blair, *The World of Stamps and Stamp Collecting* (London, New York: Hamlyn, 1972); John H. Chandler, *The Newspaper & Almanack Stamps of Great Britain and Ireland* (Saffron Walden: Great Britain Philatelic Publications, 1981); E. A. Hopkins, *A History of Wreck Covers Originating at Sea, on Land and in the Air*, 3rd edn (London: Robson Lowe, 1970); R. M. Willcocks, *England's Postal History to 1840, with notes on Scotland, Wales and Ireland* (London: Willcocks, 1975)

Calendar

The word 'calendar', in the sense of a printed indicator of days, has for centuries run parallel with 'almanac' – earlier 'almanack' (*see* ALMANAC). The first English-language example, translated from the French and published by Richard Pynson in 1497, was described as an 'almanack' but actually entitled *The Kalendar of Shepardes*. The ambiguity continues well into the 19th century: Manning and Trumbull's thirty-two-page *Town and Country Almanack* for 1821, printed in Worcester, Massachusetts, carries the subtitle 'Complete Farmer's Calendar'. Eugene Rimmel's calendar card, showing January to June on one side, July to December on the other, and published in London in 1851, is entitled *Perfumed Almanack*. An avowed hybrid, and a novelty in its own right, is *The Scottish Hat Almanac*, published in Edinburgh in 1837. This circular-format calendar is designed for retention in the crown of the user's top hat. Substantially it presents a simple calendar, though it also adds information on costs of stamps for bills, promissory notes, and receipts. The term 'calendar', as now applied, refers to the basis and essentials of chronology, ignoring the annotations, ancillaries, and predictions of the almanac.

Advertising calendar of J. Ponthenier, Vichy, France, 1914. Chromolithographed on card and embossed. 412 × 312mm (16¼ × 12¼in)

Among the calendar's functions, apart from dividing time into convenient and agreed intervals, was the listing of days of religious observance, feasts, holidays, saints' days, anniversaries, etc. Many printed calendars present each month as a vertical listing, each day duly annotated. This construction remained in general use until the latter part of the 19th century (and continued until at least the 1980s in a few almanacs, and vestigially in business diaries and 'year planners').

A rectangular layout, in which each month appears roughly as a square, came into general use in the 1870s, though in some cases days appeared at the head of the display and in others in a column on the left. The arrangement has remained optional, though late 20th-century practice tended to favour the latter form.

The relative compactness of the rectangular format allowed the calendar to be produced as a small single-sided card, as a folding double-spread, or as a miniature twelve-page booklet. The booklet version, commonly stitched at its upper edge, became a virtually standard item and was produced in millions. This development in turn generated another minor industry, the production of 'calendar backs', offering a vast range of decorative wall cards, strutted cut-outs, and other novelties as mounts for the booklets.

Also popular at this time, and used in the same way as the booklet, was the 'daily tear-off', a pad giving one leaf per day throughout the year, together with aphorisms or quotations, the number of days past and to come, and holidays and other festivals.

Year-long visibility made the calendar a natural choice for the advertiser, whose message – discreet or otherwise – had been present in one form or another on almanacs and calendars since the middle of the 19th century. By the 1880s and 1890s the major chromolithographic printing houses, already producing large full-colour pictures for general sale and as advertising give-aways, were also offering pictures for calendar overprinting. The advent of the paste-on booklet brought the advertising calendar into homes and offices by mass mailing. The success of the medium led to the development of the multi-page glossy hanging calendar, commonly carrying a single four-colour picture and one printed table per month. Spiral- or comb-binding production techniques allowed a full turn of the page; this obviated removal of outdated sheets, and led to calendars with twelve single or six double-sided sheets plus cover and backing.

In the 1960s and 1970s the advertising calendar became the focus of much promotion and public relations attention. Calendars became larger and more lavish. In many cases pictorial content, already risqué, became candidly erotic. Some calendars, notably those of the Pirelli Company, acquired a high second-hand value as collectors' items.

In its miniature form the calendar has appeared as an adjunct to every conceivable ADVERTISING NOVELTY, notably those relating to the desk. BOOKMARKS, paper-knives, pens, pencils, blotters, rulers, notebooks, and other such items, a large proportion of which are produced as GIVE-AWAYS, have carried a calendar as an added incentive to retention. Other items of ephemera with calendars include trade cards and fans from the middle of the 19th century and postcards and greetings cards from the end of the century.

Calendar of prisoners

The word 'calendar' in this context is used in the sense of a list or register (Latin, *calendarium*: account book), recording the names of prisoners awaiting trial at assize.

The publishing of the 'Calendar of prisoners' was designed primarily to prevent clandestine imprisonment and additionally to acquaint visiting judges of the workload awaiting them at assize. The list enumerated prisoners in each of the gaols in the area concerned, giving names, ages, and charges. Entries appeared in order of the date of commitment and in descending order of seriousness of the charge (murder, manslaughter, rape, bigamy, forgery, issuing of threatening letters, etc.), the cases normally being heard and decisions listed in the same order.

Calendars of prisoners also appeared as part-printed ledgers; they combined printed details of charges etc., with columns for post-trial insertion in manuscript of details of previous offences and sentences and the trial judgement. Such ledgers may contain up to twenty-four pages, depending on the number of cases listed, with column-ruled interleaves for previous-offence details. The ledgers may be found as a bound volume, recording trials at assizes on a particular circuit throughout a given year.

The ledger-type calendar also carries information on the prisoner's education. A column headed 'Instruction' or 'Degree of education' allows insertion of indications: 'N. signifies neither Read nor Write; R. Read; Imp. Read and Write imperfectly; W. Both well; Sup. superior Education'. Each ledger also bears a printed declaration by a surgeon certifying that the 'Prisoners on trial ... are free from infectious disease, and in a fit state to take their trials ...'. Where a prisoner is not deemed by the surgeon to be fit, his or her name is given and the case is recorded as being remanded to the next assize.

The calendar of prisoners remained in use in various forms until the abolition of the assizes in the early 1970s.

Call-back handbill

The rag, bone, and bottle dealer of the early 19th century announced his presence in the neighbourhood by slipping leaflets under front doors. The leaflet listed the sort of article required and advised that the caller would return for the leaflet – and any available waste material – in due course. The method allowed a lengthy recital of the dealer's needs, at the same time giving the householder time to consider possible offerings. It was also an economical form of publicity, the same leaflet serving for an indefinite number of calls.

The handbill was generally devised and composed by the dealer himself. The style (and often the spelling) is readily recognizable: 'W. Taylor (Spitalfields, 1841) begs leave to inform the inhabitants of this place, that he has just arrived; now his

A Calendar of the PRISONERS

Confined in his Majesty's Gaols at Durham, Newcastle, and Morpeth, for Trial at the Spring Assizes, February, 1831, before the Honourable SIR JOSEPH LITTLEDALF, KNIGHT, and the Honourable SIR JAMES PARKE, KNIGHT, Justices of the King, assigned to hold Pleas before the King himself.

DURHAM GAOL.

Thomas Clark, aged 19, charged with the wilful murder of Mary Ann Westhorpe, at Pittington.

Alexander Grant, 35, charged with having, at South Shields, intermarried with Mary Forrest, his lawful wife being then alive.

George Ferry, 25, charged with stealing at Morton Blue House, nineteen sovereigns and a half sovereign.

Antonio Salvio, 14, and John Smith, 13, severally charged with having at Woodenburn, feloniously stolen six silver spoons, two blankets, and various articles of wearing apparel.

Thomas Welsh, 20, charged with having at Houghton le-Spring assaulted Jane Ward, and carnally known her against her will.

Mary Rawling, 32, and John Rawling, 47, severally charged with having at Hartlepool, entered the shop of John Coverdale, and stolen therefrom two pistols, certain monies, and promissory notes.

Detained, severally charged with having at Trimdon, entered the shop of Valentine Allison, and stolen therefrom five pairs of shoes, his property, and one pair of boots, the property of William Scurr.

James Trotter, 21, charged with stealing at Tweed-

George Marwood, aged 13, charged with having stolen a cheese.

John Close, aged 22, charged with stealing three ropes, at Bishop Wearmouth.

NEWCASTLE GAOL.

Walter Drummond, aged 40, charged with having feloniously stolen a silver watch, value five pounds.

William Naters, 50, and Thomas Naters, 27 charged with having feloniously stolen three promissory notes, of five pounds each.

Mary Anderson, 20, charged with feloniously stealing one silver watch, value 10s.

Alexander Ducher, 16, charged with having feloniously stolen 1 boat's fender, 1 sprit-sail and a quantity of rope.

Alexander Hall, 31, and Robert Miller, 29, charged with having feloniously stolen 32 yards of rope, value 15s 1 iron chain, value 3s. and 120 yards of rope, value £2.

James Macglinchy, 26, G. Riley, 47, W. Wilson, 19, and W. Murphy, 28, charged with feloniously stealing 12st. of lead, value 20s. and the said William Murphy, with receiving five stone thereof, knowing the same to have been stolen.

Calendar of prisoners at Durham, Newcastle, and Morpeth gaols (UK) for trial in February 1831. Letterpress, printed by Douglas, Newcastle-upon-Tyne. Upper half of a sheet 377 × 255 mm (14¾ × 10 in)

— SPECIAL NOTICE. —
Dear Sir (or Madam),
We are buying the following Articles at the Highest Prices. Motor Cars & Cycles, in any condition. Metals of all kinds, Scrap Iron, Rags, Cast off clothing of every description, Bedsteads & Bedding, Musical Instruments Pianos Organs &c.
WE BUY ANYTHING AND EVERYTHING
Will call with Motor Same Day. Please Return Card.
HUTCHISON BROS., 114, 116, 118, Causewayend.
GARAGE:—44, CANAL ROAD, ABERDEEN.

Call-back card, Hutchison Bros, Aberdeen, early 20th century. Letterpress on peach coloured card. 76 × 115 mm (3 × 4½ in)

DRY BONES WANTED
We are still having an excellent demand for DRY BONES and can pay very high prices. If you have anything in this line, either carloads or less, please let us hear from you.
Hyde Park, Vt., Dec. 1, 1915. Carroll S. Page

Call-back card, Hyde Park, Vermont, 1915. Letterpress. 84 × 158 mm (3¼ × 6¼ in)

[sic] your time, ready money and the best price given for all kinds of Rags, white, Coloured or wollen …'.

The call-back method was used not only by waste dealers but also by those soliciting Christmas boxes. Street sweepers, lamplighters, dustmen, postmen, and others left handbills, their appeals often warning the householder to beware of interlopers who might masquerade as the rightful recipients. To avoid the risk of such impersonation, the reader was urged to give only to callers who could show a card or token bearing a facsimile of an image as printed on the leaflet. Alternatively, some other means of identification was specified. The inhabitants of Cornhill and Walbrook in the 1830s are advised 'We (the dustmen) have authorised our Partner Bill Bishop to receive what Gifts you may please to bestow in behalf of us all and to prove to you he is the right Man, he will produce his licence for slaughtering horses, which Business he formerly carried on'.

Call-back handbills were also used in appeals by the unemployed. One London example, headed 'Cotton Spinners from Manchester', seeks support 'until the Lord assists us with some employment', advising that 'the person who will call for this bill will bring a sample of the very best reels of cotton for sale'.

The call-back method continues into the 21st century. Scrap merchants and second-hand and antique dealers leave similar cards and leaflets; charity organizations leave empty gift envelopes, and in some parts of the world the 'Christmas Card' from the local postman carries an unmistakable implication, as does the Australian greetings card from 'your Garbagologist'.

See also BELLMAN'S VERSES; CARRIER'S ADDRESS; UNEMPLOYED APPEAL; VISITING CRAFTSMEN'S PAPERS

Calling card *See* ACQUAINTANCE CARD; VISITING CARD

Cameo card

The word 'cameo' was originally applied to a stone having two or more layers of different colours, the upper layer being carved in relief as a figure or portrait. The effect, in brooches, pendants, etc., is typically a white or cream head on a coloured ground. In printing the term came to be applied to any colourless embossing on a colour ground, commonly the white embossed profile on die-stamped postal stationery.

It was commonly used in the second quarter of the 19th century in Britain, especially for work which required some visual distinction. Many such designs printed by the firm of Whiting are based on the style of stucco decoration made popular by Robert Adam in the previous century. The process also had a wide showing on American trade cards in the 1850s and early 1860s.The Philadelphia firm of die sinkers A. & G. McClement (later McClement Brothers), was a leading exponent of the genre, adapting the established idiom of the notarial and institutional seal to commercial use. The dies made for the trade cards were also used extensively on billheads and commercial envelopes. It is from its position on the top left-hand corner of the envelope that the device also came to be known as a 'corner card'.

The typical cameo card bears a white central illustration with lettering above and below, the whole bordered with a white rule. Ground colour is usually blue, but shades of green, violet, pink, etc. also appear. The overall shape is commonly rectangular, often landscape, sometimes upright. Corner cuts are common, and ovals and other shapes are also found. Image size is of the order of 60 × 90 mm (2 3/8 × 3½ in).

The cameo card was widely used by American business firms, notably in such fields as furnishing and hardware. Notable users were hotels and restaurants, as well as livery stables, carriage makers, and harness, saddle, and bridle makers. In the latter part of the cameo-card period McClement Brothers produced a form of 'blank' cameo card for overprinting. Such cards, bearing a central embossed shield or other motif, were decorated in the border areas with white embossed images depicting trades – provision merchant, watchmaker, jeweller, etc. – the central panel carrying the tradesman's name and address in letterpress. Other die sinkers in the field were John Spittall,Thomas B. Calvert, and Jacob and Charles E. Maas, all of Philadelphia, and William Murphy of New York.

The embossed corner card gave way in the later 1860s and 1870s to the cheaper process of lithography, but some of the

Cameo card for Patterson's Bazaar, Pittsburgh, Pennsylvania, mid 19th century. Embossed and printed in blue by A. & G. McClement, Philadelphia. 50 × 81 mm (2 × 3⅛ in)

cameo dies remained in use as letterpress blocks (without embossing) for long afterwards.

REFERENCES Thomas Beckman, 'American Diesinkers and their Cameo Stamps, 1850–1880', *Maine Antique Digest*, May 1999; Richard Friz, 'The Truly Ephemeral World of Cameo Cards', *Ephemera News*, special issue 1984, Ephsoc US

Campaign souvenir

In America the term commonly refers to items relating to presidential elections, though souvenirs of other campaigns, including local politics, are not wholly excluded.

The earliest American campaign material dates from the late 1820s, but the campaigns of 1840 (William Henry Harrison/Martin van Buren) and 1896 and 1900 (William McKinley/William Bryan) are specially notable for the quantity and variety of their output. The Harrison campaign of 1840 may be said to have launched the concept of the classic American campaign, complete with parades, banners, posters, slogans, songs, and souvenirs.

By the early years of the 20th century there were few items of ADVERTISING NOVELTY that had not been put to campaign service. Some were brought into being specifically as campaign items. Among these may be counted lapel 'silks' (printed ribbons, often attached with metal badges), pin-back buttons (later to be adopted by lobbyists at large), and paper lanterns (used in torchlight parades). Other slogan-bearing items are umbrellas, walking sticks, bandanas, ties, kerchiefs, straw hats ('skimmers'), skullcaps ('beanies'), and paper collars.

Campaign material may be divided into three categories: badges and 'medallions' (including 'tintype' portraits); flags, banners, kerchiefs, etc. (often described as 'political cloth'); and paper. In a separate, peripheral, category are such items as procession torches, crockery, trays, and car licence-plate attachments. Paper campaign souvenirs include – as well as the paper lanterns and paper collars already noted – paper hats, postcards, stickers, almanacs, posters, leaflets, pictorial envelopes, mock currency, sheet music and song books ('songsters'), campaign newspapers, and campaign-orientated commercial advertising cards.

Output of campaign souvenirs diminished in the latter part of the 20th century, partly because of the impact of television and also because of spending limits imposed by the Federal Election Campaign Act of 1971.

The popularity of the campaign souvenir as a collector's item led, particularly in the field of the pin button, to widespread fraudulent reproduction, an abuse which prompted the passing of the United States Hobby Protection Act (1973). The law requires that imitation 'political items' be permanently marked with the date of manufacture, and that imitation 'coins and other numismatic items' be marked 'copy'. It appears likely that most, if not all of the material here referred to may be subject to the requirements of the Act.

See also BADGE; BUMPER STICKER; ELECTION PAPERS; PIN BUTTON; PRINTED HANDKERCHIEF; RIBBON, LAPEL

REFERENCES Herbert Collins, *Threads of History: Americana Recorded on Cloth 1775 to the Present* (Washington, DC: Smithsonian Institution, 1979); Edmund Sullivan, *Collecting Political Americana* (Hanover, VA.: Christopher, 1991)

COLLECTIONS Cornell University Archives; De Witt College of Political Americana, Hartford University; Smithsonian Institution, Washington, DC

Can label

Earliest labels were rudimentary, often consisting of a mere paper of identification showing the maker's name. An 1780s example from Fribourg & Treyer, the London tobacconists, appears on a metal snuff container (thought to be the earliest known metal box used in commercial packaging). The engraved paper label enwraps one half of the container and bears the company's name and address and designation ('Tobacconists ... Importers of Foreign Snuffs and ... High Dry'd Irish Snuff'). The label is designed in the manner of a trade card or billhead, and may well have been printed from a trade-card plate. There is no specific description of the contents of the container.

Can label for 'Anne Arundel Pride' tomatoes, Maryland. Chromolithographed by Simpson & Doeller Co., early 20th century. 107 × 283 mm (4¼ × 11⅛ in)

The food-canning industry derived from the early work of Nicholas Appert in bottling. It may be said to have started with Bryan Donkin, who in the 1820s successfully developed the tinned iron container. Some of the cans of Donkin's successor, John Gamble & Co., bore embossed lettering on a soldered metal strip: 'Carrots & Gravey' (1824) (*see* Davis, 1967; pl. 157); others carried a contents-cum-directions printed paper label. Another example reads: 'Roasted veal. Directions. Cut round on the top near to the outer edge with a chisel and hammer. The contents may be eaten cold, or gradually heated with the gravy ...'. It should be borne in mind that these instructions were designed, like the product itself, for use on Arctic and other expeditions rather than in the home.

In spite of an increasingly widening domestic demand for canned food, the container appears to have remained only nominally labelled until the 1860s, when the American canning industry introduced the pictorial coloured label. Among earliest known examples is a can found in a house in Salem, Indiana. The label, produced for the proprietors, Reckhow & Larne of Cedar Street, New York, bears a decorative panel with the words 'Fresh Tomatoes' and a picture of the product on a table dish. An adjacent panel carries the firm's name and address, and directions for use of the product: 'This valuable article is prepared ready for the table and fit for use with the exception of a little seasoning as suits the taste. If to be used warm, the case must be put into hot water fifteen minutes before opening ...'. This can is notable not only for its colour label but for a coat of sky-blue paint covering the whole of its exterior metal.

It was in the 1860s that the lightweight steel can first appeared (and with it the 'bull's head' can-opener) and the labelled can took its place as a point-of-sale eye-catcher, often in pyramid displays in shop windows. By the 1870s the American canning industry had expanded enormously, and can-label printing had grown correspondingly. Packing and labelling plants (typically that of Libby, McNeill & Libby in Chicago) became mechanized and label design and production reached high levels of excellence. Chromolithography in numerous workings, sometimes embellished with embossing and workings in silver and gold, was used to produce labels which in a number of cases vied with those of the now ubiquitous CIGAR BAND/BOX LABEL. The chromolithographed can label disappeared, however, with the development of the four-colour half-tone process in the 20th century. Today's can label, still heavily reliant on colour illustration – now largely photographic – continues for the most part to use such methods.

In Britain, canned foods have been available since their introduction by Bryan Donkin in the second decade of the 19th century (the Duke of Kent wrote Donkin a letter of appreciation of his 'patent beef' in June 1813). Tinned meat formed part of the diet of the poor from the 1870s, but it was the introduction in Britain of baked beans by the American H. J. Heinz in 1901, and the opening of the company's factory in Harlesden in 1928, that marked the beginnings of the industry in the United Kingdom.

As with many other kinds of ephemera, the paper can label has few chances of survival unless specifically collected at the time of use. The vast majority of early examples are found as unused items in platemakers', printers', or manufacturers' specimen files. One range of can labels has been recorded for posterity in a well-known work of art by Andy Warhol: in 1962 he produced his '200 Campbell's soup cans' based on the familiar red and white labels of Campbell's Soup Co. that were originally designed in-house in 1898.

REFERENCES Hyla Clark, *The Tin Can Book* (New York: New American Library, 1977); Alec Davis, *Package and Print* (London: Faber & Faber, 1967); Robert Opie, *The Art of the Label* (London: Simon & Schuster, 1987)

Candle label [plate 15a & b]

The candle era, which dates back at least to Roman times, continued well into the period of industrialization of the 19th century. With the introduction of gas lighting in the earlier part of the century the role of the candle began to diminish, but it remained, together with its contemporary the oil lamp, for long an essential feature of everyday life.

The candle was in use in the early part of the century in virtually every public building: in the Houses of Parliament, royal palaces, courts of law, hospitals, and prisons, as well as in factories, mills, workshops, and offices. It was a familiar feature of coach travel, railways, and shipping. The Eddystone Lighthouse was lit by candles – twenty-four at a time – until 1807.

Until the last years of the 19th century the candle was an accepted adjunct to the music stand, the piano and the lecturer's lectern, and the nursery. The bedside food warmer and the illuminated watch-holder were still in widespread use in the years before World War I. Its multiple uses are recorded in a wide range of 19th and early 20th century ephemera: commercial stationery, advertising, packaging; and its labels reflect an ever-expanding world market. The candelabra and chandeliers of the aristocracy were later matched by mass-production 'fairy lights' ('as used by Her Majesty the Queen') and 'Burglars' Horrors' (in patent fireproof plaster cases); improved smokeless wicks, odourless burning, and a conical fluted base to fit any socket size, brought the product close to perfection.

In 1987 Price's Patent Candle Co. approached the Ephemera Society concerning their file collection of thousands of early candle labels dating from the 1850s. An arrangement was made to sort, mount, and box two sets of the Company's early labels, one selection to be held by Price's for reference and the other to be incorporated into a collection now housed at the Centre for Ephemera Studies at The University of Reading. These pictorial and mainly chromolithographed labels provide an insight into the social and technological history of the second half of the 19th century: they refer to such products as double-wick Railway signal candles, Short-burning candles for servants' bedrooms, Miners' candles, Yachtsmen's candles, Carriage candles, and Ballroom candles.

Label for 'Radiant Carriage Candles' manufactured by J. L. Thomas & Co. Ltd, Exeter and Bristol, late 19th century. Lithographed in a single colour. 92 × 138mm (3⅝ × 5½in)

Card of thanks

The card of thanks, a specifically 19th-century American convention, conveyed a public expression of indebtedness, commonly from a fire engine company to an outside agency for services rendered at a fire.

The 'card' utilized a pre-printed decorative chromolithographed certificate, approximately 255 × 200 mm (10 × 7⅞in), bearing a blank title space and central main panel. The certificate, copiously equipped with illustrations of classic statuary, garlands, and Chippendale decor, conveyed no specific theme; it could therefore be put to a wide range of ceremonial uses. The card of thanks was a typical application. One such example (14 September 1863) records the thanks of the Fairmount Steam Fire Engine Co., Philadelphia, to a military-aid refreshment committee 'For the bounteous supply of Refreshments and the kindness manifested towards the Company whilst at the fire which occurred at the US Navy Yard on the morning of the 13th inst.'. The message is printed by letterpress in the blank spaces of its chromolithographed base.

Public expressions of thanks after fires appeared in Britain too; but these were printed broadsides rather than filled-in certificates, and were posted up by the proprietors of the property concerned. In these cases thanks were commonly extended to the fire fighters and to friends and neighbours at large for additional help.

Carmen figuratum

Carmen figuratum (Latin, *carmen*: song, poem, incantation; *figura*: shape, form) is a typographic arrangement conveying in outline the theme or subject matter of its content. For example, the words of a prayer might be contained within the cruciform shape, or a VALENTINE message be disposed to make the shape of a heart. The shaped verse appears on devotional items, such as cards, prayer-book bookmarks and keepsake cards.

The device stems from the use in ancient Roman and medieval times of letters disposed in arcane arrangements for the purposes of magic. Whatever the content, the trick of their construction lay in the precisely planned disposition of the text to fill out the shape, the last character of the legend coinciding exactly with the final portion of the design.

REFERENCE Massin, *La Lettre et l'Image* (Paris: Gallimard, 1973)

Carrier bag

Known in America as a shopping bag, the carrier bag has its origins in the shopkeeper's PAPER BAG, made by hand in the 1840s, and by machine for the first time in the early 1850s.

A major improvement in the ordinary paper bag was the so-called 'satchel bag', constructed so as to stand on a base when full. Elisha Smith Robinson, founder of E. S. & A. Robinson of Bristol, acquired the patent for the bag in America in 1873 and began machine bag-making in Britain on a large scale.

The Robinson bag, used for flour, sugar, tea, coffee, etc., and forerunner of the earliest American grocery bag and the disposal bag, required only enlargement and the addition of handles to become the carrier bag novelty of the 1920s. String handles were later replaced by reinforced paper strips and other materials, and improved flexigraphic printing (from rubber blocks) allowed the shopkeeper's name and trade mark to appear in two or three colours on both sides of the bag.

As with the ordinary paper bag, printing could be carried out from standard decorative blocks, with the trader's name and address, or from blocks specially designed for the purpose. The carrier bag of the early 1930s, made commonly of tough brown paper, and generally associated with the local butcher, grocer, and greengrocer, was upgraded to a minor status symbol in the mid 1930s. Used by bigger stores, and designed as part of an overall house-style, the carrier assumed the role of a portable poster; it became a symbol of success on the one hand for the store, and of affluence on the part of the customer. As Oliver (1978) points out, the bag replaced the outward sign of yesterday's prestigious home delivery: 'Carrying the smart bag has become the contemporary equivalent ... of the smart delivery van conspicuously parked in front of the house'.

In the closing decades of the 20th century, with paper giving way to plastic, and the whole bag conceived as a designer item, a comparatively new publicity medium evolved. Designs range from the blatantly promotional to the intriguingly discreet, from the serious to the hilarious. The carrier bag now appears in virtually any size and may be designed to carry goods as disparate as a small bottle, a roll of wallpaper, or a suit of clothes.

The bag is also available as a 'straight' commercial project in its own right, sometimes presenting the decoration of advertising graphics of times past.

REFERENCES Cooper-Hewitt Museum, *Bandboxes and Shopping Bags* (Washington: Smithsonian Institution's National Museum of Design, 1978); Bernard Darwin, *Robinsons of Bristol 1844–1944* (Bristol: E. S. & A. Robinson, 1945); Michael Turner and David Vaisey (ed.), *Art for Commerce* (London: Scolar Press, 1973)

COLLECTIONS Cooper-Hewitt National Museum of Design, Smithsonian Institution (New York); Design Museum, London

Carrier's address

The word 'carrier' has since the 17th century been applied to any person or agency regularly engaged in transportation of goods or passengers between specific places. In America, the word was applied in particular to the mail-man (UK: 'postman') and to the newspaper delivery man. In Britain, 'letter carrier' or 'carrier' was used as an optional alternative to 'postman', and the word 'newsman' applied to the newspaper delivery man.

In common with numbers of other such year-round servants, it was the custom at Christmas and the New Year for newsmen and postmen to deliver a printed greeting to their addressees, reminding them of the rigours of house-to-house delivery. In America the document commonly bore the heading 'Carrier's Address'; in Britain, 'The Newsman's Address to his Customers' or, for postmen, 'The Letter Carrier's Respectful Compliments of the season'. Invariably in doggerel verse, and embellished with decorative borders and occasionally a woodcut illustration, the single-sided sheet measured anything from 450 × 300 mm (17¾ × 11⅞ in) to 300 × 200 mm (11⅞ × 7⅞ in).

The American newsman's 'Carrier's Address' was generally produced for him by the printing office of the newspaper he delivered, the paper declaring its interest through the wording of the title, a typical heading is: 'Carrier's Address to the patrons of the *Morning Express* January 1st 1858'. Other carriers, as with Britain's newsmen, saw to their own printing.

The American carrier's address, though generally naming the newspaper concerned, is often nonetheless difficult to identify geographically; as with the example cited, the title of the journal *Northern Star, Courier, Herald*, etc. may offer no clue as to locations.

See also BELLMAN'S VERSES; CALL-BACK HANDBILL

Carte porcelaine *See* IRIDESCENT PRINTING

Carte-de-visite

The photographic carte-de-visite, so-called from its resemblance in size to the visiting card, was introduced by the Paris photographer André-Adolphe-Eugène Disdéri in 1854. It remained fashionable until the end of the century and had not altogether disappeared at the outbreak of World War I. The dimensions of the mounted photographs, 100 × 60 mm (4 × 2⅜ in), became a world standard (as did the basic designation) and within a few years albums designed to take the cards were to be found in front parlours in many countries. The visiting card format was in fact derived from Disdéri's use of a four-lensed camera which produced eight images on one plate. The pictures could be taken individually, or a number of them exposed simultaneously. The essential factor was economy. A print taken from a single glass negative at one operation could be cut into eight separate pictures and mounted as individual studies.

Disdéri's success dated from his securing Napoleon III as a sitter. A cheap novelty became a fashionable necessity and within a short time the fad had caught on everywhere. The format was followed in 1866 by the more generous 'cabinet' size, 165 × 104 mm (6½ × 4⅛ in), and in 1870 by the intermediate 'Victoria', 125 × 90 mm (4⅞ × 3½ in). Numerous other sizes appeared later.

Carte-de-visite photographs differ from other photographs only by their mounts which, at whatever size, conformed to a broadly similar specification. Many bore the photographer's name in the margin at the foot of the picture, with the same information in extended form on the back. At first the carte-de-visite was cut by the photographer from plain card, but by the early 1860s pre-cut mounts were being mass-produced – many of them by the firm of Marion of Paris and London – with rounded corners, bevelled and gilt edges, and elegantly designed backs. A later refinement was a printed cover paper, pasted to the upper edge of the back and folded over the front. The paper covers commonly bore additional mention of the photographer, though some are found with 'collectable' images, free of advertising.

The mounts to the photographs became progressively more elegantly presented as time went on. The basic card became thicker, and front and back surface finishes smoother and more

Window-mounted carte-de-visite with surround printed lithographically in gold. 103 × 69mm (4 × 2¾in)

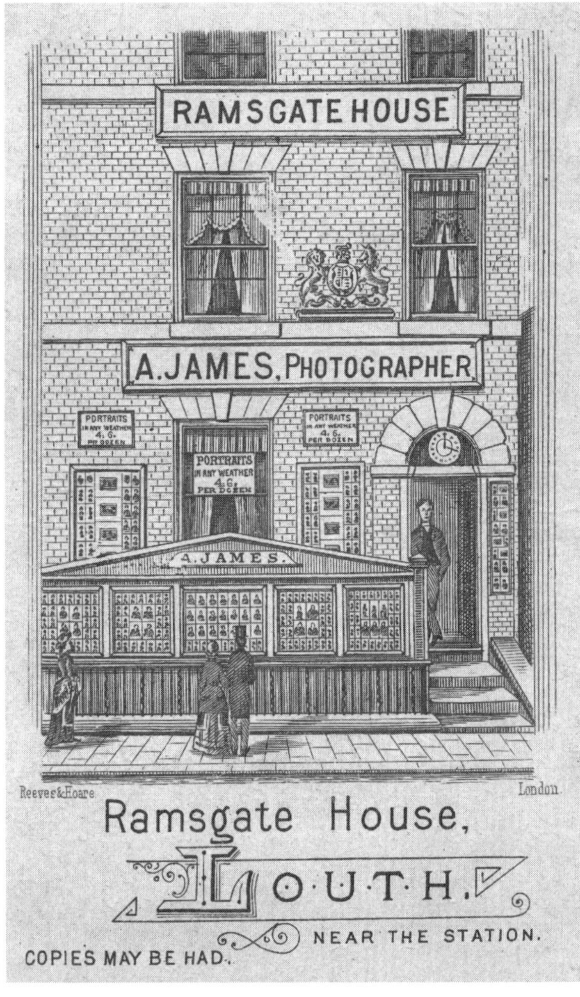

Carte-de-visite (back of mount) of A. James, photographer, Louth. Lithographed by Reeves & Hoare. Late 19th century. 104 × 63mm (4⅛ × 2½in)

variously tinted. 'Enamelled' card was widely used. Lined borders were gold. Silver and colour blocking appeared on the cover front margins. In 1864 Messrs Window & Bridge introduced the Diamond Cameo Portrait, the photograph appearing as an oval or group of four ovals impressed from behind to form a raised panel. In a variant of it, the portrait oval was cut out and mounted within an oval frame.

The backs of the mounts became increasingly important. Whereas some early examples carry the photographer's name as a rubber stamp, stencil, or stuck-on label, later specimens are of considerable elegance. The printers, publishers, and distributors of the cards took time to feed photographers with a succession of new styles, and the backs reflect increasing awareness not only of design trends but of competitive publicity.

The verso may be seen as a direct descendant of the TRADE CARD. It addresses the lower-middle class in terms appropriate to the gentry, and offers distinction on the cheap. Disdéri's success with the Emperor is reflected in Britain in innumerable 'Royal Appointments'. Among others were W. & D. Downey of London, and Hills & Saunders of Eton, both of whom advertised themselves as photographers 'By Appointment to Her Majesty' (Downey also to the imperial and royal families of Europe); G. Henshall of Hanley cites 'HRH The Prince of Wales, HRH The Princess of Wales and the Prince of Prussia', and T. H. Hall of Matlock Bath mentions 'The Emperor and Empress of Brazil' and 'The Japanese'.

Other matters dealt with among the images of easels, palettes, cherubs, and drapery – symbols of aristocracies – related to the new technology. As artificial lighting released the camera from reliance on the skylight this point was stressed: 'Taken after dark', 'No clamps – instantaneous exposure', 'Portraits taken in any weather'. The role of the stored negative, and its possible enlargement, was pointed out: 'Copies of this picture can always be had', 'Life-size enlargements, finished in oils, crayons or watercolours …'.

The photo-mount industry was based very largely in Europe, and was dominated, as already noted, by the Marion Company. Less prominent were J. H. Nacivet of Paris and two German companies, Trapp & Münch and T. H. Prumm, both of Berlin. In America, seventy per cent of the market was in the hands of a single firm, A. M. Collins & Son of Philadelphia; its range, as Darrah reports, extended to 300 kinds of carte-de-visite mounts between 1872 and 1882.

The carte-de-visite appeared not only as a personal memento but in collectable series (celebrities, views, etc.), and Mathew B. Brady achieved lasting fame in America with his 'Scenes and Incidents of the War' series, a record of the fighting in the Civil War. The carte-de-visite also appeared as an ADVERTISING NOVELTY. Typical British examples, produced by the Woodburytype process, show music-hall star Jenny Lind with a backing of promotional text for 'Taunus', the royal table water, and comedian Edward Terry backed by Miss E. Rutherford of Old Ford, London, 'Shirt, Collar and Cuff Ironer'.

Also described as a carte-de-visite is the mounted ferrotype or tintype, a metal-based 'no-negative' image popular in the carte-de-visite period. The picture was developed directly by the wet collodion process on a thin iron sheet, enamelled black. The metal (often still wet) was slipped into a 'window' of carte-de-visite size, the photographer's publicity appearing – if at all – on the back of the mount. In this form the tintype was described as a 'gem', the practitioner as a 'gem photographer'. Tintypes mounted in this way may also be found displayed in the carte-de-visite slots of contemporary photograph albums.

See also AMBROTYPE LABEL; PHOTOGRAPHIC EPHEMERA

REFERENCE W. C. Darrah, *Carte de Visite in Nineteenth Century Photography* (Gettysburg PA: Darrah); Audrey Linkman, *The Victorians: Photographic Portraits* (Tarris Parke Books, 1993)

Carte pneumatique

The term was applied to correspondence cards used in the pneumatic-tube postal system installed in Paris in the latter part of the 19th century. The mail was inserted in tubular containers and propelled by compressed air and vacuum suction through underground tubes to selected post offices on a city-wide circuit. Final delivery was by express messenger.

The printed cards appeared as single-sheet cards or 'double' (i.e. folded, so that they could be torn along perforations on receipt.) The service, introduced in 1866, may be seen as a forerunner of the public telegram service; in fact the cards bore a printed pre-payment stamp featuring the word 'Telegraphe'. Similar stationery was used in Germany (1867) and Austria (1873). Italy introduced a pneumatic system in 1913, issuing postage stamps ('Posta pneumatica') instead of stationery. Cards printed in Czech and German were reported from Praha [Prague] at the turn of the century, but there is no evidence of a service actually starting up there.

Pneumatic systems were introduced for postal handling in several countries, and the principle was in widespread in-house use in commerce.

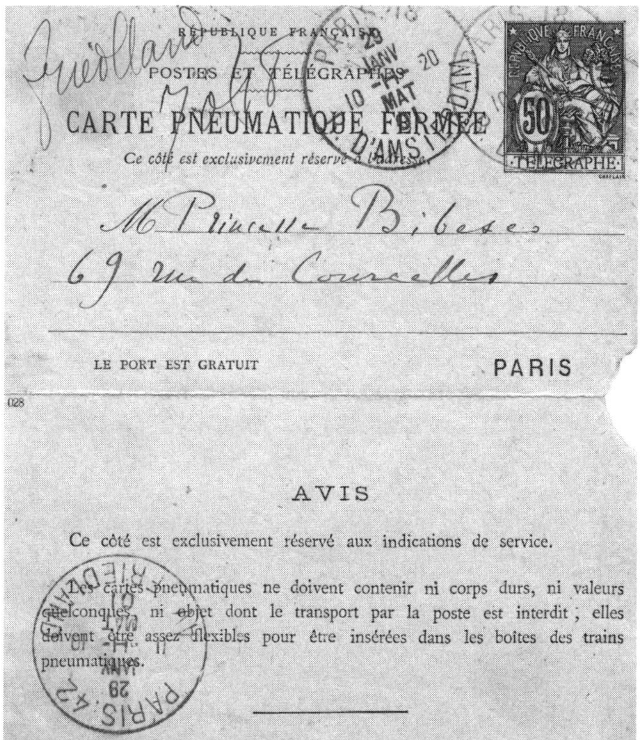

Carte pneumatique, Paris to Amsterdam, 29 January 1901. Letterpress and manuscript. 133 × 112 mm (5¼ × 4⅜in)

See also POSTAL HISTORY

REFERENCES James A. Mackay, *The Guinness Book of Stamps Facts and Feats*, rev. edn (New York: Canopy, 1992); Carl H. Scheele, *A Short History of the Mail Service* (Washington: Smithsonian Institution Press, 1970)

Catalogue

In its earliest form the catalogue consisted of a listing of a tradesman's goods as an addition to the bare statement of his name and address on a TRADE CARD or BILLHEAD. Such listings (without price markings) appear widely in the 18th century, often embellished with a loosely related assortment of illustrations. In the late 18th and early 19th centuries appeared the formalized shop list or TRADE LIST, though this, a letterpress production, normally bore no illustration, and likewise carried no price marking. The printed PRICE LIST, precursor of the catalogue proper, emerged with the rise of an industrial economy in the 1840s and 1850s.

Printers themselves were among the first to exploit the medium of the trade list and the catalogue. With a wide range of products and services (sometimes including the supply of such disparate items as theatre tickets, newspapers, perfumes, and pharmaceuticals) the local printer had not only the facility but the need for a product listing.

Among notable names in this field are the Diceys, father, son, and grandson, for whose business in the latter half of the 18th century at least two extensive catalogues appeared. One of these, published in 1764 when Cluer Dicey, the son, was in partnership with Richard Marshall, runs to 104 pages. Neuburg (1977) cites this and others as examples of their period.

Also widely current in the 18th century was the illustrated catalogue or 'pattern book' of the manufacturer of metal knobs, handles, fittings, and other decorative hardware. Produced for the travelling merchant as a substitute for an actual sample pack, they were compiled from sheets of engravings, selected by the traveller himself as likely sellers in his sales area. In a typical brassfounder's example, reprinted in 1973 by Rupert Gentle of Pewsey, Wiltshire, there are twenty-seven sheets, measuring 305 × 200 mm (12 × 7⅞in), showing a range of thirty-nine candlesticks, seven 'tea bells', and nine hanging bells. The manufacturer's item numbers are engraved with the illustrations; the merchant's prices are added in ink. The original of this reprint was found in Philadelphia. It may well have been taken there in 1800, but the style of the engravings suggests that it was produced at a rather earlier date. It is known that pattern books of this kind had been produced in Britain from the 1760s and, it is thought, on the continent of Europe from the 1740s.

The full-scale illustrated catalogue, itself an example of industrialized production, appeared widely in the 1860s and 1870s, in the wake of the 1851 Great Exhibition, and subsequent international exhibitions. Among the first in the field in Britain and France were manufacturers of hardware, whose ever-expanding range of products required detailed presentation to the shopkeepers on whom they relied for mass-market sales. Not far behind were makers of building materials, plumbing and sanitary ware, domestic bell systems, door and window furniture, kitchen ranges, etc. Distributed to their contractor customers and generally updated annually in the latter part of the century, these catalogues became a recognized part of the industrialized trading scene.

In America, mass-market distribution was beset by problems of distance, as well as multiplicity of product. The mail-order concept, in which selling was done by text and illustration, began in earnest in the 1860s and 1870s. By the 1880s 'mail order papers' – magazine-type publications of 16, 32, or 48 pages – claimed circulations of upwards of 200,000. Typical were: the *Semi-annual Illustrated Catalogue* of E. G. Rideout and Co., New York, 32 pages, 255 × 210 mm (10 × 8¼ in); *Novelties and Notions* of A. Coulter and Co., Chicago, 48 pages, 145 × 225 mm (5¾ × 8⅞ in); and *New Inventions* of M. Young, New York, 16 pages, 400 × 270 mm (15¾ × 10⅝ in). Such publications took their place in the isolated farmhouse with the Bible and the ALMANAC as the basic literary fare of the late 19th-century rural American.

By the turn of the century these 'magazines' had been largely replaced by the major publications of Sears, Roebuck and Montgomery Ward. Founded respectively in 1866 and 1872, these companies initially concentrated on small lightweight items of the kind listed in the mail-magazines, but the introduction of the US parcel post in 1913 allowed an increase (maximum 4 pounds in weight per parcel) in the weight of the goods offered. The catalogues also expanded. In 1915 the Sears, Roebuck catalogue numbered 1600 pages; its merchandise ranged from toupees to tombstones. By 1940 the catalogue was appearing twice-yearly in print runs of seven million copies each.

Others notable on the American mail-order scene were the clothing catalogues of the National Cloak and Suit Co., first published in 1888, and Bellas Hess and Co., who merged in 1926 to form National Bellas Hess. The National Bellas Hess catalogue had a circulation of three million.

In a faint echo of the American scene, Britain's Littlewoods and Kays catalogues claimed large circulations. As with the American catalogues, they present a graphic conspectus of the changing social scene. Both text and illustrations reflect the tastes and aspirations of a grass-roots readership. Classics of their kind in Britain are the catalogues of Gamages, the Army and Navy Stores, and the Civil Service Supply Association. Directed at a distinctly middle-class readership, and catering, as with the American catalogues, largely for out-of-town customers, these catalogues also chronicle social history. Their value as a record is underlined by the fact that one of them (the Army and Navy catalogue for 1907) was reprinted in its entirety in 1969. Selections from the Sears, Roebuck catalogue were republished in 1940 and again in 1976.

REFERENCES Alison Adburgham (introduction to reprint), *Yesterday's Shopping: Army and Navy Stores Catalogue 1907* (Newton Abbot: David & Charles, 1969); *The Country Gentlemen's Catalogue... 1894* (reprint) (London: Garnstone, 1969); David L. Cohn, *The Good Old Days: A History of American Morals and Manners as seen through the Sears, Roebuck Catalogs* (New York: Simon & Schuster, 1940); Rupert Gentle, *Brass Candlesticks* (facsimile of catalogue, Chilton Designs, 1973); Victor E. Neuburg, *Popular Literature: a History and Guide* (Harmondsworth: Penguin, 1977); Keith Wheeler, *The Townsmen*, rev. edn (Alexandria, VA: Time-Life, 1978)

COLLECTIONS Manchester Metropolitan University Library; Reading University Library

Cavallino

The term *cavallino* (Italian: little horse) derives from the image of a cherub on a horse, used by the Sardinian Government on taxed letter paper issued from November 1818. The image, contained in a circular, oval, or oblong border, was printed or embossed on the letter paper, appearing at the lower left-hand corner of the front of the letter when it was folded for transmission. The *cavallini* (plural) were produced in three denominations: 15, 25, and 50 centesimi.

Cavallini sheets, issued in 1819, were watermarked with the insignia of the cross and eagle of Savoy and the legend 'Direzione Generale delle Regie Poste: Corrispondenza autorizzata in corso particolare per Pedoni ed altre occasioni'.

Census papers

Early censuses were confined largely to single towns or localized regions, and methods of enumeration varied widely. The first major attempts at counting inhabitants were made in Canada between 1665 and 1754, and enumerations were carried out in the latter part of the 18th century in various European states and in a number of American colonies. The first full-scale census took place in the United States in 1790, and there has been a census in America at ten-year intervals ever since. In Britain, where the idea had been mooted in 1753 but rejected as a potentially oppressive weapon of the state in taxation and conscription, it was adopted in 1800. Britain's first census was held in 1801 and, as in America, there has been an enumeration every ten years from that time forward (an exception in Britain was 1941, in World War II).

In addition to the economic and administrative problems of counting populations, there has been a continuing difficulty in setting and maintaining consistency of method and content. In the earlier experimental stages it was found that some questions failed to elicit meaningful answers, and that questions which might have been usefully asked had been omitted. Successive examples of census forms provide, therefore, a developmental study of demographic technique. They reflect at the same time the widening spectrum of official enquiry into the citizen's private affairs.

In Britain, early census forms were designed to be filled in by overseers of the poor, the clergy, and others appointed as enumerators. In 1841, forms were delivered direct to householders for the individual to fill in. Final returns were then completed on separate forms by the enumerator, who transferred answers on householders' forms to his own.

In 1851 the scope of the enquiry was greatly extended. Questions covered relationship to the head of the household, marital status, exact age (as opposed to quinquennial or decennial age groups), and whether persons were blind or deaf and dumb. Also included in the census were persons on ships (at sea or in harbour). There has been a progressive extension of scope subsequently, but this has not necessarily been consistent. Questions included in one census may be omitted from the next (as in 1841, when enquiry as to 'family occupation' was dropped). In America, a census category dropped in the 1870 enumeration was 'slaves', and in 1940 the category 'gainfully occupied' was changed so as to show whether those not 'gainfully occupied' were 'out of work' or merely not part of the normal labour force.

In Britain the essential chronology of the form is as follows:

1801 Form to be filled in by overseers of the poor or by local clergy; no names or other details required
1821 Form requires entry of decennial age (i.e. ten-year groups), though still no names
1841 Names and places of birth
1851 Questions as to marital status and relationship to 'head of household'
1901 Question as to how many rooms people had
1911 (First census processed by machine) 'Fertility' questions asked
1921 Questions as to dependent children and orphans

1951 Household amenities (baths, lavatories, etc.) to be reported
1979 Ethnic questions proposed, but dropped
1991 Ethnic questions included

A census requires two distinct operations. The first is compilation and distribution of the questionnaire and subsequent collection of completed forms. The second is consolidation and analysis of results, with final publication in the form of a report. Reports are normally readily available in libraries, but few questionnaires survive – filled-in or otherwise. This is partly because few papers are retained by the individual (there normally being a penalty for failure to complete and return the form) and partly because of the requirement of confidentiality; in Britain all census forms are destroyed after the transfer of details (excluding names and addresses) to (now) electronic records.

Census-taking is clearly a major operation, and the printing and distribution of the forms themselves requires great effort. For the census of 1841 the printer of the foolscap double-sided form, 'Joseph Hartnell, Fleet Street, London', recorded a printing run of 3,600,000. For the 1991 British census almost 29 million forms were printed (for England 23,529,000; for Northern Ireland 700,000; for Scotland 3,100,000; for Wales 1,602,000).

In Britain, responsibility for the taking of censuses was at first in the hands of overseers of the poor, but from 1841 it was undertaken by the General Register Office (inaugurated in 1837); in 1970 the work of the General Register Office was combined with that of the Government Social Survey Department, the two bodies being fused in the Office of Population Censuses and Surveys, in whose archives (as well as those at the Public Record Office) much relevant material is stored.

In America, censuses are administered through individual states by the US Census Bureau, based at Suitland, Maryland. America's first census (1790) was taken by US federal marshals to meet the requirement of Article 1 Section 2 of the Constitution, which provides that representation in the Congress shall be in proportion to population. The principle continues to operate, as it also does in most individual State legislatures, where representation, as well as in many cases the number of judges and other officials, is in proportion to population.

In addition to a general population census, America also takes a number of regular censuses in specialized fields: agriculture (every five years); irrigation and drainage (every ten years); governments (every five years); manufacturers, mineral industries, business, and transportation (every five years); and religious bodies (every ten years).

American census-form details, as in Britain, are confidential. In the 1960s and 1970s the forms were microfilmed and also physically stored on shelves at the Bureau's building at Jeffersonville, Indiana. In the 1980s recording methods were changed to eliminate the forms themselves, details being transferred to electronic storage.

As with many other classes of administrative ephemera, it appears likely that electronic documentation will ultimately eliminate the paper census form altogether.

REFERENCES *Census Reports of Great Britain 1801–1931* (London: HMSO, 1951); *Population and Health Statistics in England and Wales* (London: Office of Population Censuses and Surveys, 1980)

COLLECTIONS Office for National Statistics, London; US Census Bureau, Suitland, MD

Certificate [plate 14]

Certificate is the generic term given to documents that certify (Latin, *certus*: certain; *facere*: to make) a fact or sets of facts. Some certificates provide evidence of achievement, as, for example, a DEGREE CERTIFICATE or a REWARD OF MERIT. Others have legal authority, such as a BIRTH CERTIFICATE, DEATH CERTIFICATE, MARRIAGE CERTIFICATE, a certificate registering a ship, or a document produced in one court that gives notice of its proceedings to another. A category of certificate that provides authority to do something is often called a LICENCE (Latin, *licentia*: leave to do what one pleases), which, under certain circumstances, might be referred to as a PASS/PERMIT or PASSPORT.

The physical form of a certificate ranges from a utilitarian handwritten, typed, or simple printed document to an elaborately designed and colour-printed SHARE CERTIFICATE or TRADE UNION MEMBERSHIP CERTIFICATE. Most certificates require specific information to be completed individually. Until the early years of the 20th century this was nearly always done by hand. This practice continues, often in the form of calligraphy that is out of keeping with the design of the certificate as a whole. Increasingly, and particularly after the introduction of desk-top computers in the 1980s, such details are added by machines. Many certificates are signed on behalf of the authorizing body, and may also bear its seal or other device.

Some certificates, particularly those that relate to academic or professional qualifications are designed to impress, and even to grace the recipients' walls. Such certificates often incorporate graphic features – including flourished copperplate lettering and black-letter types – that have long since disappeared from other sorts of documents. A graphic characteristic of some certificates is the coloured pictorial or decorative border, often chromolithographed, and commonly found on reward of merit and trade union membership certificates. It so happens that the amount of elaboration a certificate displays is frequently in inverse relation to its importance.

Modernist typography of the twentieth century, with its concern for asymmetrical arrangement and tendency towards simplicity, found difficulty meeting the requirements of the prestigious-looking certificate. This kind of certificate has therefore remained one of the most traditional categories of ephemera. [MT]

See also AGENCY CERTIFICATE; AMERICAN SEAMAN'S CERTIFICATE; ARMED FORCES PAPERS; BAPTISMAL PAPERS; BURIAL-RIGHT DEED; CHIMNEY-SWEEP CERTIFICATE; DEGREE CERTIFICATE; DRIVING LICENCE; FIRE REWARD CERTIFICATE; FIREMAN'S DISCHARGE CERTIFICATE; FLEET MARRIAGE CERTIFICATE; GOLD-MINERS' PAPERS, AUSTRALIAN; GRETNA GREEN MARRIAGE CERTIFICATE; KING'S EVIL CERTIFICATE; LIGHTHOUSE-DUES PAPERS; LOTTERY PAPERS; PASSPORT; VACCINATION PAPERS

Change of proprietor card

In the late 18th century and throughout the 19th century it was not uncommon for change of business ownership to be announced by a card or paper bearing thanks for past custom from the departing proprietor and greetings from the new. The convention generally presented the note as a two-part message, sometimes on one side of a card, sometimes on facing pages of a folded sheet.

The convention survived briefly into the 20th century. In World War I, with many thousands of one-man businesses

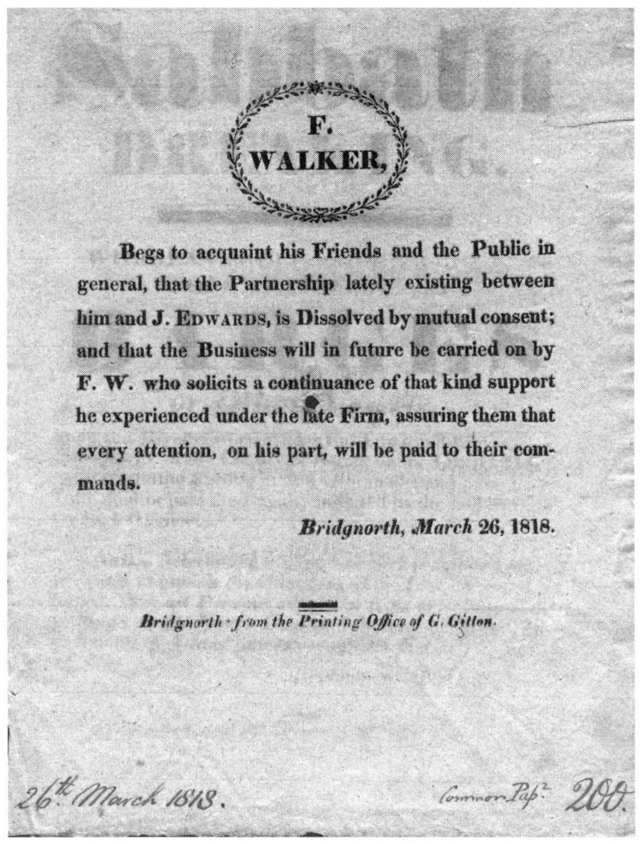
F. WALKER,

Begs to acquaint his Friends and the Public in general, that the Partnership lately existing between him and J. EDWARDS, is Dissolved by mutual consent; and that the Business will in future be carried on by F. W. who solicits a continuance of that kind support he experienced under the late Firm, assuring them that every attention, on his part, will be paid to their commands.

Bridgnorth, March 26, 1818.

Bridgnorth : from the Printing Office of G. Gitton.

26th March 1818. Common Pap.r 200.

Change of proprietor notice, Bridgnorth, 1818. Letterpress, printed by G. Gitton, Bridgnorth, with manuscript note that 200 copies were printed. 250 × 197mm (9⅞ × 7¾in)

handed over to new proprietors as former owners joined the army, the change of owner card was a familiar item. A typical specimen combines a two-part message on a single folded sheet. The folder, opening to 180 × 230mm (7⅛ × 9in), bears on the left a farewell and on the right a salutation:

[left page]

High Street, Broadstairs: Dear Sir or Madam,

Owing to being called up, I have been compelled to let or close my business, and I have pleasure to inform you I have disposed of the same to the well-known Butchers Messrs. Dale & Son, of Margate, who will, I feel confident, supply the very best English Meat at lowest possible prices, as markets will allow; and I trust you will give them the same support as you have bestowed on me for many years. Again thanking you for all past favours. I remain, Yours Obediently

Ed Britton

[right page]

6 Market Place, 270 Northdown Road, 4 Tivoli Road, 103 Canterbury Road, Margate

Dear Sir or Madam

We beg to inform you that owing to Mr Britton, Butcher, being called up, he is compelled to let his business or close down and we respectfully beg to inform you that we have acquired the Business, and trust, by supplying the very best English meat, with strict supervision, we may still retain the confidence and support which you have bestowed on him for a number of years. We remain, Yours Obediently

M Dale & Son

Change packet

Among the refinements of middle-class Victorian shopping was the giving of change not directly from hand to hand but in paper packets. Chambers's *Edinburgh Journal*, in a review of London shops and shopping (15 October 1853), makes passing note of the custom. A customer seeking to buy a pair of kid gloves 'is met at the door by a master of the ceremonies, who escorts him to the precise spot where what he seeks awaits him .... He walks over rich carpets, in which his feet sink as though upon a meadow-sward; and he may contemplate his portrait at full length in half-a-dozen mirrors, while that pair of gentlemen's kids at *2s* 10½*d* is being swaddled in tissue-paper, and that remnant of change in the vulgar metal of which coal-scuttles are made ... is being decently interred in a sort of vellum sarcophagus ere it is presented to his acceptance'.

The envelope, known as a 'change packet', measured some 60mm (2⅜in) square and was printed with the legend 'The change, with thanks', often in a decorative roundel or other device. Printing was generally in a single colour; sometimes the design appeared as a white, embossed image on a coloured background.

The packets were supplied to the shopkeeper either as a stock design in which there was no trade message, or printed specially to order with name, address, and designation presented as a form of miniature trade card. Additionally, the shopkeeper might be supplied with the packets at much reduced rates, if not free of charge, by the new breed of national advertisers who used the printing space on the packet for their own message. Typical of these were Huntley & Palmers, biscuit manufacturers, whose change packets were widely used. Their Royal

Change packet issued by Huntley & Palmers, Reading (UK), late 19th century. 83 × 54mm (3¼ × 2⅛in)

Appointment design appears in two packet sizes and a variety of colours.

Stock packets supplied by printers and stationers are also found with topical references, as for example one specimen commemorating the International Exhibition of 1862. Wording also provided some variation; a number of specimens bear, in addition to an expression of thanks, the words 'The favour of your recommendation is respectfully solicited'.

See also CHANGE PIN-PAPER

Change pin-paper

In the latter part of the 19th century and until after World War II, pre-decimal currency allowed reduction of 'round figure' sums by one farthing (a quarter of a penny) thus producing the psychologically more attractive figure of, for example, nineteen shillings, eleven pence three-farthings (19*s* 11¾*d*), instead of the full twenty shillings (£1.00). The practice was specially prevalent among drapers and haberdashers, for whom the expressions 'nineteen and eleven-three', 'one and eleven-three', and so on, were recognized shopkeeper's terms.

The customer received the farthing change either in the form of the coin itself, or as a small quantity of pins. The pins were dispensed as strips torn from a standard pin-paper or in a folder-wallet bearing the legend 'Farthing change with thanks' or 'Your change with thanks'. The folder-wallet generally contained forty-two pins on a folded paper, the paper being pasted or stapled to the wallet. The outer face of the wallet bore a decorative three-colour design, sometimes incorporating a

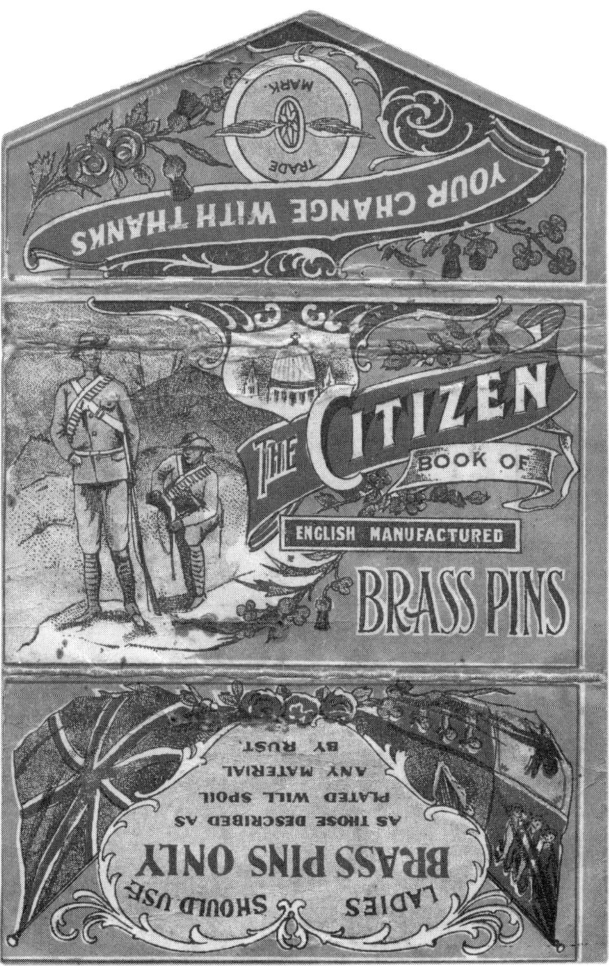

Change pin-paper, 'The citizen book of English manufactured brass pins', c. 1900. Lithographed in three colours. 138 × 90 mm (5½ × 3½in)

calendar and postal information. Many are found overprinted with the name and address of the shopkeeper. A typical pack measures some 60 × 95 mm (2⅜ × 3¾in) folded.

As Adburgham (1964) points out, the customer made a loss on the deal. From prices listed in a trade catalogue of haberdashers' wholesalers I. & R. Morley, it is clear that shopkeepers were making a profit on the pins of twopence per gross in 1883 and sixpence per gross by 1908. Adburgham also records a substitute for the change pin-paper, the 'farthing novelette'. These tiny publications cost the shopkeeper the same as the pin-paper, but were not greatly in demand. They were regarded as unsuitable for a middle-class clientele.

Printed pin-papers, bearing extensive advertising copy and some forty or fifty pins, were later given away as promotion items by dyers, cleaners, and other traders with a housewife clientele.

See also CHANGE PACKET; FARTHING NOVELETTE; GIVE-AWAYS

REFERENCE Alison Adburgham, *Shops and Shopping, 1800–1914* (London: Allen and Unwin, 1964)

Changeable landscape *See* MYRIORAMA

Changeable gentlemen/ladies card

Followed rapidly by 'Changeable Ladies' (1819), the Changeable Gentleman' novelty was introduced by Rudolph Ackermann in London in 1818. It consisted of a set of caricature-profile cards, 90 × 64 mm (3½ × 2½in), in which each picture is horizontally cut into three divisions corresponding, roughly, to hair, forehead, and eyes in the top portion; nose and ear in the narrower middle part; and mouth, chin, and neck in the lower part. The divisions allow productions of an infinite variety of faces. The cards are presented in wooden slide-top boxes, 105 × 74 × 32 mm (4⅛ × 2⅞ × 1¼in), each having wooden dividers to separate upper, middle, and lower sections.

COLLECTION Victoria & Albert Museum, London

Chapbook

The chapbook takes its name from the itinerant 'Chapman' or street vendor, who included it as part of his stock-in-trade of buttons, laces, pins, ribbons, and other oddments in Britain and America from the 17th to early 19th centuries. Like most of his stock, the chapbook was sold for a penny. For many thousands of newly or partly literate readers it represented a first serious step in the world of literature; prior to its advent popular reading had been confined to single-sheet broadsides.

Primitively printed, often from worn-out type and irrelevant second-hand woodblocks, the chapbook carried a miscellany of anecdotes, romantic tales, verses, riddles, puzzles, and jokes. It commonly measured 145 × 90 mm (5¾ × 3½in) and contained from four to twenty-four pages. More often than not the booklet was sold unstitched and untrimmed, the reader being required to cut the pages and stitch them together on the kitchen table. The chapbook had clear advantages over the broadsheet: for the customer it had the distinction of being a 'book'; for the chapman it had the advantage of easier storage and portability and was far less fragile.

Because of their use of antiquated type and wood blocks, chapbooks are not very easily dated. Illustrations may have been made up to a hundred years before the time of printing, and watermark dates are rare. The chapbook printer's only clear concession to changing fashion is the abandonment at the end of the 17th century of the black-letter, the 'old English' typeface that had been popular in Britain since the time of Caxton. But here too the change was nearly a century behind the times and the borderline between the old style chapbook and the new is indistinct.

The success of the chapbook led to its imitation by those who sought to wean the new reading public on to higher things. Various religious organizations began to put out publications in the same style, among them was the series of *Cheap Repository Tracts,* devised – and in large measure written – by Hannah More, poet, essayist, and social worker. The intention of this series appears to have been not only to bring the common man to religion but to divert him from political dissent. The chapbook gave way in the later 19th century to the industrialized popular literature of penny magazines and newspapers.

Major publishers of chapbooks in Britain were the Rushers (father and son) of Banbury and James Kendrew of York. Also prominent were William Davison of Alnwick, John Marshall of Newcastle, and F. Houlston & Son of Wellington. Glasgow had a number of printers and publishers of chapbooks, and in London there were some fifty, of whom Darton & Son, J. Evans & Co., Ann Lemoine, and John Roe were prominent.

American booksellers and printers often imported English chapbooks for distribution or reproduction. However, local printers did produce uniquely American versions, often based on 'Frontier adventure' tales. Noted publishers were Thomas and John Fleet of Boston, Samuel Wood & Sons of New York, and Wrigley & Berriman of Philadelphia.

REFERENCE Victor E. Neuburg, *Chapbooks* (London: The Vine Press, 1964); Harry B. Weiss, *A Book About Chapbooks* (Trenton, NJ: Edwards, 1942)

COLLECTIONS British Museum, London; Cambridge University Library; Harvard College Library, Cambridge, Mass.; New York Public Library

Charity election card

During much of the 19th century, admission to overcrowded orphanages and charity schools in Britain was by ballot, voting being confined to governors of the charity and its subscribers. It was customary for friends, parents, and guardians of candidates to print 'election addresses' in the form of cards or papers, seeking support for their nominees.

The appeals bore the name of the candidate as a main title, with the name of the charity and a description of the case, followed by a list of notable referees. The cards, 75 × 100mm (3 × 4in), were handed to potential supporters; papers, 205 × 130mm (8⅛ × 5⅛in) folded, were sent by post or put through letterboxes, sometimes with the personal superscription of the sponsor.

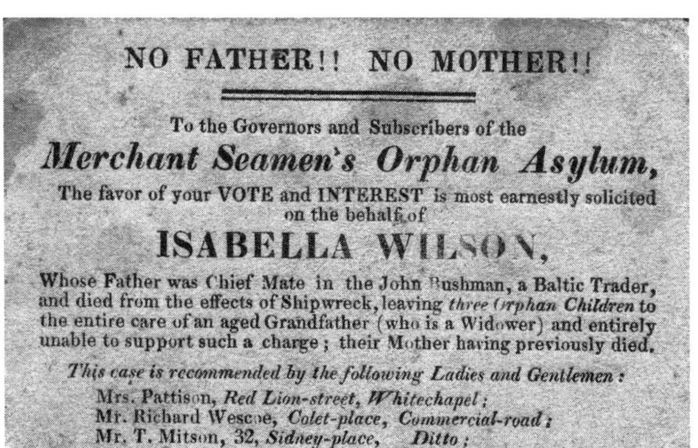

NO FATHER!! NO MOTHER!!

To the Governors and Subscribers of the

Merchant Seamen's Orphan Asylum,

The favor of your VOTE and INTEREST is most earnestly solicited on the behalf of

ISABELLA WILSON,

Whose Father was Chief Mate in the John Bushman, a Baltic Trader, and died from the effects of Shipwreck, leaving *three Orphan Children* to the entire care of an aged Grandfather (who is a Widower) and entirely unable to support such a charge; their Mother having previously died.

This case is recommended by the following Ladies and Gentlemen:

Mrs. Pattison, *Red Lion-street, Whitechapel;*
Mr. Richard Wescoe, *Colet-place, Commercial-road;*
Mr. T. Mitson, 32, *Sidney-place, Ditto;*
Mrs. Pattison, 2, *Grenada-terrace, Ditto;*
Mr. E. Dempsey, 23, *Sutton-street, Ditto.*

Charity election card, mid 19th century. Letterpress. 60 × 90mm (2⅜ × 3½in)

REFERENCES Norman Alvey, 'The great voting charities of the Metropolis', *The Local Historian*, vol. 21, no. 4 (November, 1991)

Charity petition

In the 18th and 19th centuries charity was generally dispensed either as accommodation in almshouses or as cash donations. Applications for consideration for charity were commonly made in the form of a petition. The document was signed by a group of sponsors who recommended the application, or by the applicant in person supported by an individual appointed to attest it.

Typical of the former are mid 19th-century addresses to the charity trustees of the City of York, in which the application is cast either as a formal petition ('The humble petition of Mary Lawson … widow of the late John Lawson … sheweth …') or as begging leave to recommend the applicant ('We the undersigned are desirous of recommending…'). Signatories, generally headed by vicars and churchwardens, are in the main professional people and local tradesmen, their occupations sometimes designated after their names. Signatures may number from half a dozen to thirty or forty. Petitions sometimes simply refer to the applicant as a 'proper and worthy object' or may present an extended account of qualifications and need.

Petitions presented in the applicant's own words (though not necessarily in his or her own writing) spell out details of misfortune, in some cases at length, in others briefly. From among petitions after a big fire in London's Artichoke Lane in April 1792, we may note two examples.

> [Jacob Seppet writes]: Jacob Seppet haveing sustained great damage by the late fire in Artichoke Lane humbly hopes it will be taken into Consideration.
>
> [Mrs Blenkinsop writes]: Mr Cockshead I Bag Pardon for givin you this Trouble but hopes your good Hart will Exscuse me when I nform you I am A Sufferer by the Late Fire in Hartychocke Laine No 30. We moved all our Goods and in Moving Broke and Lost Sevrell Yousfull Artickls tho to no Greet Amont but have no Inchourance. My Greatist Los and Trouble is by Sending my 5 Dr Children in to Wapping at that Early Oure in the Morning [illegible] and 2 of them has Never Loucked up Since. The Youngist But wone I am Afrade Will never be Restored in health to me A Gane. I have only to Say Good Sir if you Would Plase A Sist me with a Trifell it will be of the Greatist Sarvis to a Distress'd Famley and most thank fully Receved By Sir Your Humble svt Ann Blenkinsop.

The Artichoke Lane documents appear among a collection of some fifty such items relating to the same incident. Many are cast in the form of simple inventories, but the words 'petition' and 'petitioner' occur frequently and the general tone is of diffidence and humility ('Pardon the Trouble Good Sir…', 'Honoured Ladys and Gentlemen …', 'From your humble Pettishener…' etc.).

Charity sermon hymn sheet

The parish charity school of the 18th and early 19th centuries was supported by voluntary subscription and by special collections in parish churches and chapels at services dedicated to the purpose. Sermons on these occasions, delivered in the presence of the children themselves, took the form of appeals in aid of the charity concerned, the children contributing a hymn of gratitude before or after the address.

The children's hymn was printed on a sheet announcing the occasion, together with the details of the time and place and the names of officiating clergy. The sheet, commonly foolscap, also carried a brief report of the charity's work for the year, together with an analysis of numbers of pupils provided for and a plea for further help. In some cases, where pupils also did handwork as part of their education, suitable commissions were solicited.

Sometimes the foolscap item was replaced by a larger, more impressive, sheet. The Christ's Hospital authorities published an elaborate decorated broadside, 565×440mm (22¼×17⅜in), showing the words and music of a psalm of thanksgiving to be sung 'according to ancient custom' by the children of the hospital for their founders and benefactors. Two separate services in Easter week were set aside for the purpose, and the broadside showed an annual report not only for Christ's Hospital but also for St Bartholomew's Hospital, St Thomas's Hospital, Bridewell Hospital, and Bethlehem Hospital, all 'under the pious care of the Right Hon. the Lord-Mayor, Commonalty, and Citizens of the City of London'.

Charity subscription list

Appeals for money in the 19th century were made institutionally on behalf of social-service projects, schools, orphanages, hospitals, etc.; and personally on behalf of distressed, afflicted, or bereaved individuals.

Institutional appeals appear as extensive printed documents, often as four-page foolscap folders, and commonly devote a major portion of their space to a listing of subscribers and the sums donated. A typical example, published by a charity committee in a newly-formed ecclesiastical district in Devonport in 1847, outlines the need for a new church and school in an area of ungodliness ('There are streets in St Stephen's district incessantly ringing with blasphemous oaths ...'). After reciting extensive details of depravity and want, the text lists the names of some 270 benefactors already committed to contributions from 10*s* to £100. Also listed are the names of those ready to receive donations on behalf of the committee.

Appeals on behalf of individuals also appear as printed papers, generally presenting a two- or three-paragraph outline of the misfortune in question. Circumstances range from rail disasters to industrial injury, from shipwreck to desertion. An undated single sheet from Wales, c.1870, recounts the loss of men from a boat on Carnarvon Bar: 'On Sunday morning, the Pilot boat was found drifting into the Straits, bottom up ... proof that the whole five persons have perished.... By this sad event three wives have been made widows and their children fatherless; their cases are most distressing, and such as call for immediate relief ...'.

In most cases the appeal allows blank space for the addition of further names to the printed list of subscribers. Examples are to be found in which such additions have been made.

Charity ticket

Soup, meat, coal, bread, and other commodities were made available to the poor in the 19th century through the controlled distribution of printed tickets by charities.

The tickets, entitled 'Bread ticket', 'Coal ticket', etc., as appropriate, measured some 90 × 110mm (3½ × 4⅜in) and normally specified in print the value of the goods to be supplied and

Whitby, Jan. 28th, 1865.

SUPPLY the Bearer of this Ticket (not transferable) with a Bag of Coals, value One Shilling, or with One Shilling's worth of Groceries or Flour.

H. S. THOMPSON.

This Ticket to be presented for payment to Messrs. Gray & Pannett within two months.

Charity ticket, Whitby, 1865. Letterpress. 62 × 90mm (2⅜ × 3½in)

the name of the issuing charity. Handwritten details specified the name of the recipient, the date, and the signature of the 'provider' (the vestry clerk or churchwarden). Sometimes the cards were for exchange only at specific shops, whose names also appeared as a handwritten addendum.

Use of the tickets obviated the handing over of money (which might have been spent unwisely) and ensured that only the goods specified were supplied to recipients. Used tickets were returned by shopkeepers to the issuing charity in exchange for cash. In many cases, where the terms of a charity prescribed a specific annual date for distribution, tickets were used for the same supplier and recipient year by year, the dates being successively altered by hand. Often the distribution was confined to a given group of almshouses, and formed part of the charity under which the almshouses had been set up; in this case the ticket was made out not to a named recipient but to an address.

The 'ticket' principle was also used by charities and authorities in disaster situations, soup being the most common commodity offered. Here the tickets embodied a simple rationing system, ensuring a single portion for each applicant. Tickets, or 'warrants', were also issued for a night's lodgings at 'travellers' halls'. One such ticket, datelined Rochester, Kent, April 1831, which related to a charity founded in 1579, entitled the holder to four pence for subsistence and points out that 'the additional comfort of fire and candles is given in Winter months ...'.

The device was later used extensively for controlling and financing admissions to hospitals. Here the benefactor, in return for an annual subscription, disposed of a specific number of admission applications, to be filled in and handed to the needy as required (*see* HOSPITAL RECOMMENDATION DOCUMENT).

In another system, the benefactor subscribed to a 'Strangers' Friend Society' or the like. Having located a needy family at a given address, the subscriber filled in a form recommending that the 'visitor' investigate the case with a view to helping. Here, however, the 'warrant' was delivered to the institution.

Charm/curse

Belief in the miraculous properties of words is deep-rooted, and – for good or ill – is still widespread. 'Cussing and swearing', as well as prayers for help and protection, are commonly seen as a form of everyday human behaviour. This was no less so in former times, when the mere speaking or inscribing of words appeared to have satisfied a basic need. As scores of written fragments testify, the visible word held a special magic – a power derived, presumably, not only from its greater duration in time but from its tangible existence.

Typical of these are the inscribed curses and charms that former cultures used as amulets – and sometimes also as pharmaceutical pills and plasters. (We may reflect upon the meaning of the word 'pharmacy', which derives from the Greek, *pharmakon*: magic charm.) In a 14th-century medical treatise (Ida B. Jones, *Études Celtiques*, vol. 7, fasc 1, 1955) we find:

For the bite of a serpent or a sick dog write these words round the bottom of a vessel made of sycamore, and take clean water and delete that writing, and give (the water) to the bitten person to drink before he goeth to sleep: + Zable + leo + fortis + decim + cephans +

For the bite of a sick dog: write these words on a slice of barley-bread and butter and give it to the man to eat three days [successively] as first food: In nomine Patris + Filii ++ Spiritus Sancti + Pater Noster + twice + Gabriel + Michael + Raphael + Pard + Gard + Adonay + Kyrios + Dominus + Messyas + Sospitator + Sother + Saluator + El + theos + Ysayas + Geremias + Ezegias + Daniel + Alla + Matheus + Marcus + Lucas + Johannes + M + S + Esyn + Daniel + Emanuel + Dei + amen +++

The history of medicine abounds in mentions of charms and spells, not only as resorts of desperation but often as part of 'orthodox' therapy. Forms of prayer were included in instructions to the public in times of plague (*see* PLAGUE PAPERS), and the wearing of cabalistic signs and texts was widespread. In the numerous plagues of London in the 16th and 17th centuries it was the custom, and at some periods a statutory requirement, that stricken families should mark their street door with a cross and the words 'Lord have mercy upon us'. Clearly, the idea was not only to mark the house as a warning but to invoke divine assurance. At various stages it was required that the warning be on 'a large sheet of paper, printed with a great red circle of the circuit of a foot and breadth of two inches and the words Lord have mercy upon us printed in the midst'. The edict is among a number preserved in the Domestic State Papers at the Public Record Office, (SP Dom, Eliz. vol. 98, doc. 38). It bears a marginal sketch showing the required device.

The connection between prayer and prophylaxis appears at every level. The homely 'Book of remedies', handwritten and passed from one generation's kitchen to another, may also show this dual view. One such example (c.1750), has sixteen pages, measures 100 × 80 mm (4 × 3⅛ in) and has nine manuscript entries: 'Chill in a Breast', 'To Cleanse a Cow', 'To destroy Rats and Mice', etc. Also included are three forms of words: 'Charm for Red Water', 'A Charm for the Tooth Acke', and 'A Charm to stop Blood by saying it three times following'. This last appears as follows:

Our Saviour was of a Virgin born, was baptized in the River Jordan, was crucified upon the Cross, even as his blood was stopt, so shall thine M. or N. in the name of the Father and of the Son and of the Holy Ghost if for a person mind to say the right Christian name and surname' [M and N mark the point for pronouncing the sick person's name(s)].

In somewhat similar vein (though not necessarily pharmaceutical) is a paper found in a Dublin church in 1969:

St Jude. A Prayer. Say this Prayer for nine days and its never known to fail. May the Sacred Heart of Jesus be for ever Praised and Glorified for ever. May the blessed mother grant me my Request. May St Jude grant me my Request Amen. Please take this prayer and leave a copy in the church.

Specifically therapeutic, and of our own time, are printed prayers sold from tear-off pads by certain devotional supply stores in South America. These, appeals to such saints as Cosmo and Damiano and San Roque, are seen as an adjunct to the work of the physician.

Specifically non-therapeutic is the early Roman *Defixio*, an imprecation set out in writing and publicly posted up (Latin, *defigo*: fix in place), known to palaeographers as 'curse tablets'. Among the many Romano-British examples are lead tablets found in Bath, in which the writer sets a curse on three women (Germanilla, Velvinna, and Jovina), and five men (Exsupereus, Augustalis, Comitianus, Severinus, and Catusminianus) for taking away his girlfriend. He prays that all be struck dumb.

From the temple at Uley, Gloucestershire, comes a tablet invoking the god Mercury in the recovery of a linen cloth, and from a Roman site, in London, now Telegraph Street EC2, we have the first few lines of an imprecation directed at one Tretia Maria:

I curse Tretia Maria and her life and mind and memory and liver and lungs mixed up together, and her thoughts and memory; thus may she be unable to speak what things are concealed nor be able —.

The magical power of words may also be seen in some of the more colourful remedies of former times. Among the ingredients listed in recipes in one household notebook (c.1730) are: 'For the Falling Sickness ... Gall of a Living Dog ... Skull of a Christian ... Cat's Eare ... Lamb's Skin ... Spleen of a Sow ...'; for the scurvy '... in the Spring of the Year the Green of the Goose Turd ...'; against 'the Ricketts ... a Pint of Black Snails ...'. As with the recipes of the witches in Macbeth (Act 4, Scene 1), their mere intoning may seem to cast a spell. For better or worse, written or spoken, they cannot have entirely failed.

REFERENCES M. W. C. Hassall, 'Altars, Curses and other Epigraphic Evidence', in Warwick Rodwell (ed.), *Temples, Churches and Religion in Roman Britain: Recent Research in Roman Britain* (Oxford: BAR British Series 77(i), 1980); T. W. Potter, *Roman Britain* (London: British Museum Publications, 1983)

COLLECTION British Museum, London

Charter party

The expression 'charter party' is said to derive from the French *charte partie*: divided paper, in which one portion of a single sheet is given to each of two contracting parties as evidence of agreement (*see* INDENTURE).

The document has some affinities with a BILL OF LADING, which it often accompanies, but it records only an undertaking to hire a vessel for a specific voyage or period for transportation of a given cargo or cargoes. It is in effect a contract for hire, the terms, conditions, and other details being set out at length with each party to the transaction holding a signed copy.

In its part-printed form the document, like the bill of lading, enshrines a number of classic phrases ('The said ship being tight, staunch and strong ...') and often carries an outdated engraving of a sea-going vessel at its head. Its format is vertical, ranging from 320 × 200 mm (12½ × 7⅞ in) to 415 × 265 mm (16⅜ × 10½ in).

COLLECTIONS Historical Society of Pennsylvania, Philadelphia; National Maritime Museum, Greenwich; Southampton Maritime Museum

Cheese label

'Processed' cheese, a blended amalgam of so-called 'natural' cheeses, seasoning, and preservatives, was developed as a commercial product in the years immediately following World War I. Pioneer of the principle was the Gerber Cheese Co. of Switzerland.

Development of the cheese was closely linked with simultaneous changes in handling and packaging methods, the near-liquid consistency of the product allowing it to be formed into shape prior to cooling. The characteristic wedge shape derives from the segmenting of a cylindrical extrusion. Foil wrapping and labelling of individual portions is effected by machinery developed solely for this purpose, and the triangular label has become firmly identified with this product, and no other.

Processed cheese has a world market. In America it accounts for one-third of the cheese made in the country, and Switzerland and France also produce enormous quantities. Switzerland alone is said to have produced over 10,000 different brand labels. The triangular paper label is found more commonly in Switzerland and Britain; in America the format is often rectangular, and printed foil is more common than the paper label. In the former Yugoslavia, Hungary, and the Czech Republic the format is also generally rectangular, though the paper label predominates.

Cheese labels are commonly printed in two or three colours, major brands often by four-colour lithography. A few examples are known to have survived from the early 1920s. Dating of labels relies largely on design style, though searches through the trade mark registers may disclose precise dates. Specimens from the 1970s may be distinguished by code numbers, and from the 1980s European food labelling regulations required a statement of ingredients.

Among the most widely collected of cheese labels, particularly in France, are those for Camembert, a cheese manufactured in Normandy; they feature a wide range of subjects, including scenes of Normandy farms showing cattle grazing in lush pastures.

SOCIETY British Cheese Label Society

Chemist's label

The term 'chemist's label' commonly refers to labels used by the chemist to identify materials allegedly or actually of his own preparation (as opposed to the branded products of outside suppliers). Branded-product labels are normally referred to as 'pharmaceutical labels' (*see* PHARMACEUTICAL PACKAGE). Labels of both kinds may also relate to cosmetic as well as medical preparations.

The earliest chemist's labels appeared not on the product as delivered to the customer but on the ceramic, earthenware, or glass containers in which bulk quantities of chemicals were stored and displayed. Such labels, which date from the earliest beginnings of the apothecary, were lettered and fired directly on to the ceramics or painted on glass. Paper labels were also used. These were either stuck on the glass bottle or glued to the underside of a curved glass 'slip' which fitted the curve of the bottle. In a more refined version, the slip was hand-lettered in reverse on the back and fixed in a dished moulding in the glass.

In Britain in the early 1830s, Robert Best Ede's 'New and Cheap Series of Labels' appeared. These were among the earliest harbingers of pharmacy as a major business. Mr Ede's set of bottle labels was 'adapted to the pharmacopoeias of London, Edinburgh, and Dublin, including the new and recently-discovered remedies, intended for fitting up Chemists' Shops, Surgeries, Dispensaries etc., and comprising 540 large labels, and 400 small sizes, besides 170 duplicates and blanks, for those articles most liable to become soiled'. Mr Ede's up-to-the-minute service was augmented by provision of a 'very superior hard varnish prepared for the labels'. When a new edition of the *London Pharmacopœia* appeared in 1837 he announced a further range of 224 labels, again including duplicates and blanks for those most likely to become soiled, to take account of the changes. The changes involved the renaming of some chemicals as well as inclusion of 'new remedies and preparations'. It was recommended that during the changeover period both labels be used, 'both new and old exhibited at the same time'.

The design of the paper label echoed that of the traditional hand-painted version, the legend appearing in black on an upward-curving arc with, commonly, a broad black band at the foot and sides. (An additional link with the hand-painted label is provided by an outward curve at the foot of each side band, which imitates the action of the lettering brush as it completes its stroke.) The convention of the upward arc is itself explained by the earlier use of the brush. In executing the panel on which the lettering is to be painted, the artist rests the base of his palm on the foot of the bottle, moving the point of the brush laterally. The result is a perfectly symmetric upward arc. The hand lettering of labels did not die out abruptly. The 'medical labeller and writer' continued in practice at least into the 1870s, working not only on bottles but on shopfittings – drawers, fascias, show tablets – and other chemist's furnishings.

Paper labels were printed in sheets for cutting out, the sheets made up into books commonly carrying over 2000 labels each. Ede's range in 1837 was printed on bright yellow and green paper, but many suppliers printed on a gold/gamboge colour reminiscent of the gold used in painted labels. The curved paper label was still in use in the 1930s, more than a century or so after its inception, when it was 'revised and brought right up-to-date' under the title 'Latin label'. A set of 330 individual labels, 'cut to correct shape', from James F. Wilkinson of Manchester, cost ten shillings and sixpence.

The paper label eventually moved the customer to purchase, rapidly acquiring a role beyond that of mere identification. The design of the label, its decorative frame, its instructions for use, and later its extended text, had to inspire confidence.

The early years of the 19th century saw the emergence of a wide range of decorative and pictorial labels. Designs which rapidly became more or less standardized were produced by numerous printers, who sold them in large quantities direct to the chemist or to medical supply wholesalers. The labels bore a distinctly 18th-century air, often reflecting the origins of the pharmacist among pepperers and spicers, grocers, drysalters, and apothecaries. In a number of cases designs bear the footline 'Published as the Act Directs', thus providing a direct link with the Copyright Act of 1735 (8 Geo. II, c. 13) which ensured artists' rights in their work for fourteen years after publication. The designs were engraved on copper and, in the 19th century, were transferred to lithographic stones for printing in quantity (*see* TRANSFER LITHOGRAPHY).

The labels are printed in black, commonly measuring no more than some 65 × 50 mm (2½ × 2 in). They may be said to fall into two design categories: one predominantly pictorial, the other typographic. The pictorial style features the name of the substance as incidental to a landscape (e.g. as an inscription on a rock); the typographic style presents the wording as the dominant element in a decorative frame, panel, or cartouche.

Chemist's labels 'published' by Henry Silverlock, Doctors' Commons, London, second quarter of 19th century. Etched and printed intaglio (four from a set of at least eight on one sheet). Each image 60 × 42 mm (2⅜ × 1¾in)

Format varied according to the function of the label. For use on folded papers containing powders, the label was designed as an oblong, typically 48 × 60 mm (1 15/16 × 2⅜in), often with a rounded upper edge. Pastille and lozenge labels were designed as ovals (to fit the oval lozenge-box of the period) – portrait, or more commonly, landscape, and measuring some 45 × 60 mm (1¾ × 2⅜in). One design, in which wording was centred on a scallop shell, became widely used, surviving into the latter part of the 19th century as a more or less standardized presentation, redrawn, modified, and adapted by successive printers.

Preparations featured on the labels convey the pharmacopœia of the period. Titles include: 'Huxham's tincture of bark', 'tincture of fine turkey rhubarb', 'vitriolic aether', 'penny royal water', 'nitre lozenges', 'coltsfoot lozenges', and 'acidulated rose lozenges'. Others, less recognizably medical, reflect the pepperer and grocer connection: 'fine India soy', 'walnut ketchup', 'mushroom ketchup', 'fine salad oil', 'orange flower water', 'paté de jujubes', 'salt tartar', 'ginger powder', and 'capers'.

These early labels commonly bear no imprint or engraver's name, though 'Cox, Borough' (London) and 'J. Shaw & Sons, Fetter Lane' (London) are found. 'J Cross, Holborn' (London) is an infrequent 'sculpsit' signature. Most common by far is the name Henry Silverlock, Wardrobe Terrace, Doctors' Commons, London, whose imprint appears often simply as 'Silverlock' and occasionally in the form of a complete name and address. (The name Silverlock survived in the label field in the Andover firm of Suttley & Silverlock, 'Printers to Chemists and the Medical Profession' until the 1960s.)

The chemist's 'tie-on' label, a paper tag attached to the bottle closure with thread or wax, forms a category on its own. The device was in use in Scandinavia and parts of the Baltic area, including Russia and Northern Germany, from the 16th century. It is also reported from Hungary. Dr Margareta Modig (*Draco pro Medico*, 7, 1982) cites specific examples from the 18th century and reports their last appearance (as a promotional facsimile) in Finland, where they were abolished by law in 1973.

The tie-on label is depicted in paintings, prints, and caricatures of the 16th to 19th centuries; and even in Britain, where its use was minimal, it appears widely in caricatures for expressing cures for political ills. The labels, known in Sweden as 'hängsignaturer', were introduced to overcome the difficulty of applying a label directly to the surface of bottles of irregular shapes. In their commonest form they consist of a narrow paper, between 50 and 150 mm (2 and 6 in) in length, broader at its free end and tapering to a narrower measure at the point of attachment. In the earliest examples the paper curved freely, often becoming damaged by contact with liquids spilt on the side of the bottle; in later specimens the sides of the paper are folded to form a narrow flange, thus stiffening the paper and reducing contact with the surface.

It was the practice (in Sweden required by law from 1635) to enter details of the date, time, and place of preparation, and in 1688 the prescription also was to be entered. The tie-on label thus came to bear general details, including the patient's name on the front and the prescription on the reverse. In the latter part of the 18th century the labels were printed from copperplate engravings (later by letterpress) and were decorated with considerable elegance. A simple colour coding was introduced towards the end of the century (white paper for internal use, coloured for external), but practice appears to have varied from one country to another.

With the introduction of the mass-produced square-faced bottle the need for the tie-on label disappeared, but it remained in use in Sweden until 1927 and in Denmark until 1941. In Britain it disappeared in the early part of the 19th century. Few specimens survive.

The fashionable chemist of the mid 19th century was equipped with an 'own name' range of specially engraved labels, each conforming to an overall 'house-style' of its own, and adapted to specific sizes of bottle, paper, or pillbox. Typically, a matching set of such labels would comprise three sizes of 'blanks' in which the elaborately decorative border would frame handwritten details, to be filled in by the pharmacist or his assistant; three or four sizes of matching labels in which the frame encloses a printed name, address, and description ('Dispensing and Family Chemist'); and two or three sizes of pillbox, each framed with a perimeter design containing the name and address and a central blank for filling in by hand. Also part of the set was a PRESCRIPTION PAPER/ENVELOPE.

In mid 19th-century Britain the vogue for 'taking the waters' at such spas as Bath, Cheltenham, and Tunbridge Wells led to a concentration of chemists at these places. Many surviving labels, as well as the TRADE CARD, TRADE LIST, and prescription papers enshrine these resorts and the enterprise of their pharmacists. At least one chemist, T. Gilbert Batting, 'Family and Dispensing Chemist and Surgical Dentist' of Tunbridge Wells, improved his chances by positive action: 'A Messenger will be despatched daily at 11 a.m. and 6 p.m. to the Spa for Orders. Sundays excepted'.

Expansion of trade in the latter part of the century made it no longer practical to fill in blank labels by hand. Instead, the chemist ordered sets of typeset labels for preparations most in demand, each title appearing in a panel with its own standard name and address frame. In a typical case D. Davies and Co., 'Dispensing and Stock Chemists' of Caledonian Road, London, made use of some forty or fifty labels (including 'powdered rhubarb', 'sassafras oil', 'syrup of violets', 'oil of amber', 'powdered jalap', 'milk of sulphur', 'dill seed water', and 'syrup of squills'), all printed in black; printed in red were a dozen or so poisons ('paregoric elixir', 'syrup of poppies', 'hartshorn oil', and 'the application'). These labels measured around 30 × 60 mm (1³⁄₁₆ × 2⅜ in) and were printed on white gummed paper.

The typical label series of the period reflects not only the rapidly extending range of pharmaceutical stock-in-trade, including such items as 'marrow oil' and 'bear's grease' (for the hair), but often a variety of domestic and kitchen preparations ('furniture composition', and 'pickling vinegar'). The ultimate diversification of the American drug store was foreshadowed – though transiently – in the British chemist's mid-century move into Seidlitz, soda, lemonade and ginger beer powders; smelling bottles, night-lights, Congreves and wax matches; fire revivers, scouring drops for removing grease spots, black and red inks, peach and almond flavouring, mushroom ketchup, West Indian tamarinds, and aromatic fumigating pastilles.)

A label for a preparation from J. Lovett, chemist of Gloucester, expresses mid 19th-century diversification at its most enterprising: 'Concentrated essence of wood smoke – for preserving bacon, ham, tongues, hung beef, and all kinds of dried beef'. Directions for use indicate that instead of drying meats or fish in a chimney, the essence is to be applied with a common paint brush: 'Let it remain for two days and apply it a second time, and it will have acquired as much flavour as though it had been in a chimney for a fortnight'.

A major feature of 19th-century pharmacy was the pill, with its concommitant the pillbox and its label. The PILLBOX LABEL was produced in diameters from 15 mm (⅝ in) to 50 mm (2 in). Cream, ointment, and powder boxes, similarly constructed, were available in larger sizes. Production of circular or oval designs by letterpress called for special skills. Unlike the earlier engraved versions, in which wording was lettered on the curve by hand, the printer, using type, had to fit rectilinear pieces of metal into unaccustomed radii.

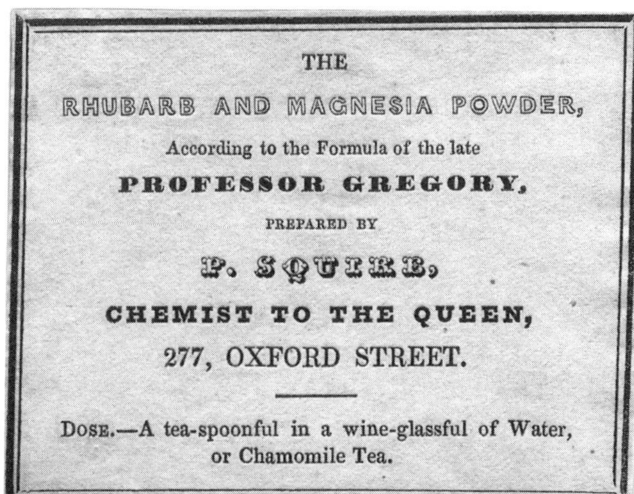

Chemist's label, P. Squire, Oxford Street, London, mid 19th century. Letterpress. 61 × 78 mm (2⅜ × 3⅛ in)

As with the PRESCRIPTION PAPER/ENVELOPE, continental chemists' labels tended on the whole toward multicoloured flamboyance. At the end of the 19th century stock labels were also widely used, but there was a much narrower range of named drug label. Accessory labels, such as 'Uso oftalmico' (ophthalmic use), 'Si agiti' (shake the bottle), 'Usage externe' (for external use), and 'Collutoire' (oral medication) were widely available, but only the commonest preparations – boric acid, cream of tartar, carbolic acid – had labels to themselves.

In continental Europe emphasis was put on supplying the chemist with labels of an elegance beyond anything that the local printer could economically provide, with the shopkeeper's name and address worked into a stock design of his own selection. Such labels allowed the local chemist to compete on apparently even terms with the flamboyant productions of the major firms. The labels featured 'elixirs' of various types: lotions, syrups, emulsions, and pomades – manufactured by the chemist himself or acquired in bulk from trade suppliers.

The pharmacist moved, via creams, lotions, and jellies, into cosmetics. The transition was gradual but clearly marked. 'Nutritive pomade' for the hair; 'camphor cream ice' for the face, neck, and hands; 'glycerine jelly' for chaps, chilblains, and roughness of the skin; these occupied a borderline area between medicament and cosmetic, but hair dyes, eye brighteners, and Cologne waters were indicators of a vast industry to come. Labels for these preparations, like those for the old non-proprietary remedies, were produced at first by individual shopkeepers, later by wholesale druggists and, towards the end of the 19th century, by manufacturers of branded products.

In America, during the rise of the wholesale druggist, own-name labels were commonly supplied free of charge to bulk purchasers. The principle was also applied to 'home-doctor' cabinets containing multiple cures. The cabinets were supplied free of charge with big orders, together with numerical remedy charts ('No 32 for disorders of the heart … No 28 for nervous prostration') and instruction booklets.

By the early years of the 20th century branded chemical preparations had begun to form the bulk of the chemist's stock, but the own-name element in labelling was retained in some cases by including the shopkeeper's name and address on labels in branded ranges. Labels incorporated a decorative panel at the foot, allowing insertion of the retailer's name in place of the decoration if required. A typical range was marketed by the London firm of Davy Hill & Son, Yates & Hicks, whose 'Squirrel Brand' was applied to some forty or fifty products from bay rum and sal volatile to 'Small Liver Pills'. The company's label designs, printed for the most part in black on white paper, were elaborately curlicued and floreated, with decorative borders and profusions of scroll and strap-work. They were available with or without the retailer's imprint, according to the size of the order.

In America, as in Britain, the patent medicine era brought its own packaging design genre. Here, the development of the 'bitters' business, in which the Hostetter family played a major part, brought many imitations – branded and otherwise. 'Bitters' (a term applied to a variable mixture, often largely alcoholic) were produced not only by famous-name manufacturers but anonymously in bulk for sale to general stores. For these products, bottled by the shopkeeper, label blanks were supplied. A typical example, measuring 127 × 90 mm (5 × 3½ in), declares itself as 'Oxygenated Bitters, a sovereign remedy for dyspepsia, phthisic and general debility'.

In Britain and America early 19th-century chemist's labels provide a telling conspectus of therapies, professional attitudes, and social conditions. 'Oxymel of squills', 'Steel drops', 'Gout pills', 'Cephalic snuff', 'Family aperient', 'Black draught', 'Magic liniment', 'Boiled oil anti-corpulent mixture', 'Head and stomach pills', 'Ointment of galls with opium', 'Nit pomade', 'Back-ache pills', 'Cure for deafness', 'Fine healthy leaches' – these terms evoke traditions in which for centuries little had changed but productivity and promotion.

In the period after World War II the custom-printed chemist's label became increasingly uneconomical to produce, and a practice developed among printers involved in multi-order production of combining work from a number of different customers on a single sheet. A typical gummed sheet from the 1950s (Suttley & Silverlock, Andover, Hampshire) measures 290 × 455 mm (11⅜ × 17⅞ in) and contains thirty-nine labels for seventeen different customers in places as far apart as Carlisle, Bristol, and Worthing. A manuscript note calls for a run of 2000 of the whole sheet and indicates the number of cuts required to separate the labels into single units ('39 labels; 72 cuts').

An addition to the general range of chemist's labels is the 'accessory label', the small extra item affixed to bottles, boxes etc. as indicators of special hazards or characteristics. Conventionally, the labels bear such legends as 'Shake the bottle' or 'Shake well' or 'External use'. Others carry indications of use: 'Eye lotion', 'Nose drops', etc. Dispensing chemists in the 1890s were recommended to record the use of such labels on specific prescriptions; a prescription delivered with a 'Shake well' label on one occasion, and without it subsequently, might be taken by the patient as an indication of negligence. Also widely used were direction labels: 'Two teaspoonfuls to be taken three times a day', 'A teaspoonful of this mixture to be taken three times a day', etc.

Poison labels were at one time used in Britain only at the discretion of the individual pharmacist. They were commonly printed in red or on a red or orange background. Many pharmacists thought that they were unduly daunting to the patient, who might be deterred from taking the prescription at all. However, the Pharmacy Act (1868) made the use of poison labels mandatory, and poison labels citing the Act duly appeared. America saw a similar law, and similar labels, in the same year.

Other accessory labels included the printed pillbox side-band, used in the manner of the government medicine-tax stamp as a wrap-round closure, and the gummed cork top, a printed paper disc used in lieu of the sealing wax formerly used to finish off the cork. Also widely used was the fluted paper bottle cap, a closure originally made by hand for each individual bottle (at one time in soft leather), but later mass-produced in paper and printed at the centre with the chemist's name and address. The cap was fixed in place at the neck with an elastic band. Final closure was effected by wrapping the bottle in a square of paper, plain or printed, and sealing the package with sealing wax. The practice of capping, wrapping, and sealing was designed to reassure the patient; the unbroken closure was evidence that the content had not been tampered with.

See also PACKAGING; TAXATION PAPERS (MEDICINE TAX)

REFERENCE *The Art of Dispensing* (London: 1888; 9th edn 1912)

COLLECTION Wellcome Institute for the History of Medicine, London

Cheque/check

Effectively, a cheque is a written, signed, and dated request to the signatory's bank to pay a stated sum to a specific recipient.

The earliest cheques were wholly handwritten, sometimes in fact a personal note from the owner of funds to their custodian. Among the earliest of such written instructions is a letter (1567) from Queen Elizabeth to Sir Thomas Gresham, authorizing and commanding him to pay one of her debts in Antwerp, but the earliest known formal 'drawn note' bears the signature of Henry van Acker. It instructs bankers 'Mr Morris & Mr Clayton' and is dated 1659; its request reads: 'Pray pay the bearer hereof Mr Delboe or order – four hundred pounds I say £400 for yrs Hen^y van Acker'. In a handwritten note to 'Mr Child' in 1689 the Earl of Castlemaine signs himself 'Yr assur'd friend, Castlemaine'. (Mr Child's bank was later to become a part of Williams & Glyn's.)

Provision of formal printed blanks for customers to fill in was an innovation of the early 19th century. (The use of the bank's printed cheque is still optional, and is a facility offered by the bank for the customer's convenience. As in the case of wills, the written declaration may be made on any substance by any method.) Basic ingredients of early cheques were: the name of the bank (but not the address); a dateline, generally including the name of the town of issue; the words 'Pay to' or 'Pay to the order of' and 'or bearer'; and space for the sum in words. Optionally, there also appeared space for the sum in figures; a number space (later a printed number); a printed PENMAN'S FLOURISH at the point of detachment from the counterfoil and, later, decorative motifs and illustrations. Tax stamps appear at various periods, as affixed revenue stamps, as feint colour underprints (US), and as colour or blind embossing (UK). Protection against alteration was introduced only towards the middle of the 19th century, when hatched panels were sometimes provided at number and date spaces, as well as in the area allocated to the sum in words. Various forms of 'chemical' printing later added to the difficulties of the forger. Soluble inks, introduced in the 1870s, showed obvious smearing if treated with liquids.

'Personalized' cheques, in which the customer's name is printed at the signature space on each cheque, became general in the 1950s and 1960s, though one very early example survives from Edinburgh in 1811. 'Pictorial' cheques, in which the whole of the background is occupied by a colour picture, appeared in the 1960s. In Britain, standardization of cheque layout was instituted among the five leading banks to facilitate automatic and computerized handling.

Early chronological 'runs' of British cheques convey not only sequences of mergers and takeovers but successive changes in printing technology. Three cheques from the period 1811–25 in Sherborne, Dorset, show a bank styled as 'Messrs Pretor, Pew & Whitty, Bankers' in the first instance, 'Messrs. Pretor, Pew, and

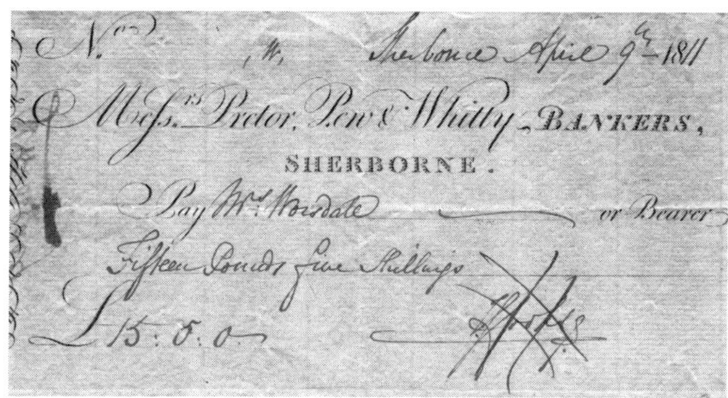

Cheque of Messrs Pretor, Pew & Whitty, 1811. Copper-engraved and manuscript. 90 × 184 mm (3½ × 7¼ in)

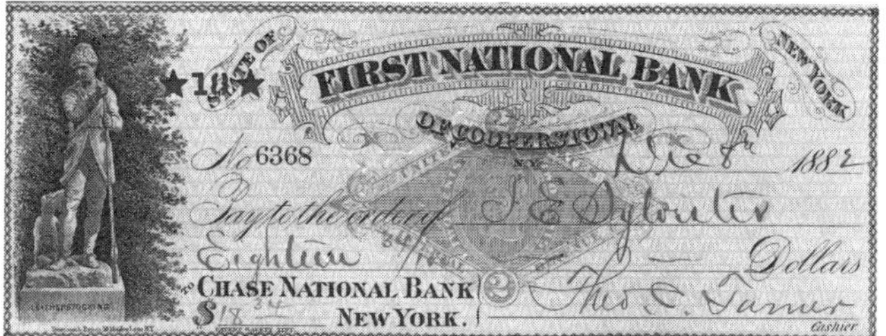

Cheque of the First National Bank of Cooperstown, New York, 1882. Printed by Dennison & Brown, New York, in three colours, the black engraved on stone. 82 × 215 mm (3¼ × 8½ in)

Whitty' in the second, and 'Messrs. S. Pretor, R. Pew, and B. Chandler' in the third. The printing method used for the first is copperplate engraving; in the second (1816) 'traditional' style letterpress; and the last letterpress using 'fat face' display forms in the then new style of typography.

The British cheque, though it was later to abandon some of its turn-of-the-century atmosphere, remained deeply attached to its black-letter and 'copperplate' titling. These features, still retained by the Bank of England and by Coutts Bank in the 1980s, were more or less standard cheque-form items in Britain until the mid 1960s.

The American cheque was early to reach a more relaxed appearance, moving into colour, decorative engravings, and typographic experiment. As in Britain, production of cheques was often in the hands of the printers of banknotes and share certificates, and something of the visual atmosphere of American SECURITY PRINTING pervades the American cheque. Cheque forms in both countries were initially engraved and printed by neighbourhood printers, but with the extension of business and the demand for high security the work went to bigger printers in the main cities. British companies closely involved in the development of cheque production in London include Robson Brooks & Co., McCorquodale & Co., Waterlow & Sons Ltd, and Blades East & Blades; in Edinburgh W. H. Lizars, Banks & Son, W. & A. K. Johnson, Smith & Ritchie, Scott & Ferguson. American cheque printers include Hooper Lewis & Co., Boston.

REFERENCE Ronald Myles Fitzmaurice, *British Banks and Banking* (Truro: Barton, 1975)

Child lost/found form

In the early 1830s the Gresham Committee, formed as a charitable trust under the Mercers' Company, introduced a scheme for restoring lost and found London children to their parents. They provided a notice board, for use by the public free of charge, on which written notices might be posted advertising details of the children concerned. The board was established at the Royal Exchange 'near the medicine shop', and persons receiving the printed announcement of the service were requested 'to fix it up in their shop-window, or other conspicuous place'.

Acting on this initiative, the managers of Spa Fields Chapel, Finsbury, set up their own notice board, producing specially printed forms on which details of children lost or found could readily be inserted by hand. The plan was also adopted in other London parishes. Pre-printed notices provided space for details ('where … when … sex… name, if known …' etc.), and in some of them inserted details were added in type by overprinting, thereby allowing widespread posting.

Children's advertising booklet

Small story books for children were a widely used advertising medium in the period 1880 to 1950. Generally of sixteen pages, about 180 × 75 mm (7⅛ × 3 in), and printed in three colours, they were given away in thousands, particularly at Christmas, by manufacturers of soaps and other household products.

Their popularity with children, who learnt the stories – and the brand names – by heart, led to the production of whole series of booklets. Best known in America were those put out by the Faultless Starch Co. of Kansas City, between the 1890s and the early 1930s. These booklets, thirty-six in all, carried stories featuring starch and sections of jokes, puzzles, and useful knowledge. The author of the stories was D. Arthur Brown; its illustrations were anonymous. In Britain J. and J. Colman, manufacturers of mustard, starch, cornflour, and other products, put out many millions of booklets. These covered a broad spectrum – fairy stories, 'comics', adventure, and instruction –

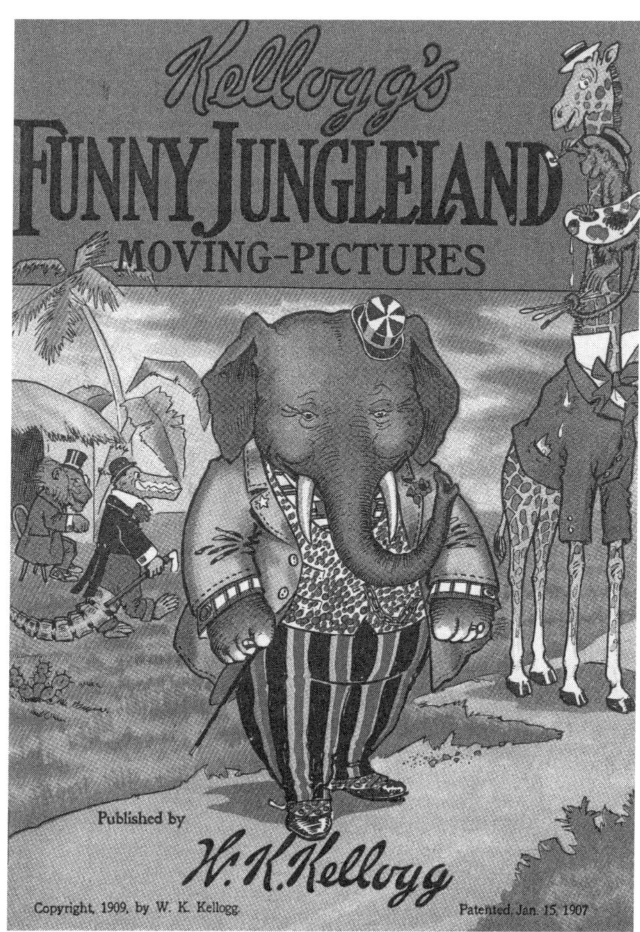

Children's advertising booklet, *Kellogg's Funny Jungleland: Moving-Pictures* (published by W. K. Kellogg, 1909). Letterpress, four-colour process. 203 × 150 mm (8 × 6 in)

and survived into the 1950s. The Colman books were illustrated by a wide range of artists, among them Alice B. Woodward and John Hassall; their authors were for the most part anonymous.

Chimney-sweep certificate

Early American cities, built largely of wood, were specially vulnerable to fire. Compared with other risks, the hazard of fire was taken specially seriously, more particularly as, in some areas, the chimneys themselves were constructed of wood. Chimney sweeping was seen as every housholder's civic duty, though many sought to evade it.

In New York and Boston, as in other towns, enforcement was a long-standing problem – as was the matter of recruiting sweeps to do the work. Chimney inspectors and 'fire commissioners' were appointed and efforts were made to set up a corps of approved sweeps, whose task was not only to clean chimneys but to report the progress of their work. In at least one area – Boston, Massachusetts – the appointed contractor for a time provided his customers with evidence of the work having been done. The certificate served to obviate arguments with inspectors, both as to the date and the nature of the work and the competence of the operator. The part-printed form was produced and distributed by John Vinton, employer of six chimney sweeps in the Boston area. A typical specimen, 76 × 152 mm

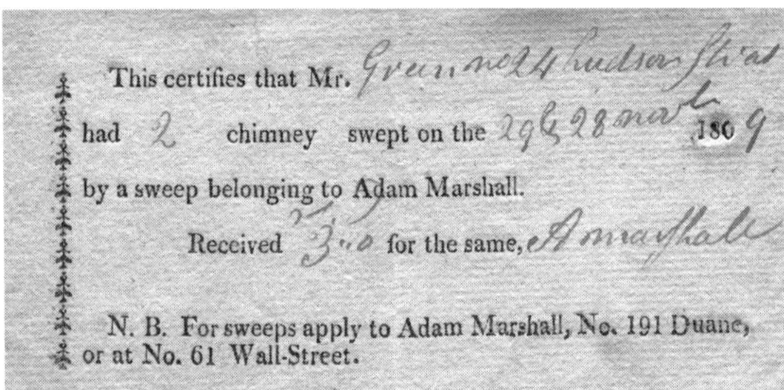
This certifies that Mr. [illegible]
had 2 chimney swept on the [illegible] 1809
by a sweep belonging to Adam Marshall.
Received [illegible] for the same, A Marshall
N. B. For sweeps apply to Adam Marshall, No. 191 Duane, or at No. 61 Wall-Street.

Chimney-sweep certificate, New York, November 1809. Letterpress and manuscript. 63 × 127 mm (2½ × 5 in)

(3 × 6 in), reads: 'This certifies, that Mr (West) had (stone) chimney swept, on (December 10) 180(7), by a sweep belonging to John Vinton. Receiv'd (50c) for the same (John Vinton). Please to apply for sweeps at the chimney-office, no. 100, Orange-Street, or at the office of the Clerk of the Market, under Faneuil-Hall'.

REFERENCE George Lewis Phillips, *American Chimney Sweeps* (Trenton, NJ: Past Times Press, 1957)

COLLECTION Baker Library, Harvard University, Cambridge, Mass.

Chop paper

The term 'chop paper' is given to the printed leaflet inserted in bales of raw silk by Chinese merchants in the latter part of the 19th century. The paper, sometimes elaborately watermarked, and printed for the most part in a single colour, bore the name of the supplier, a brief promotional text, and a distinctive image. The image served as a trade or brand mark (Chinese, 'chop': stamp or brand), and was a jealously guarded attribute of the company concerned. The language of the accompanying text was predominantly English (the British and Americans being the merchants' chief trading partners), and the burden of its message was invariably an injunction to trust the brand indicated and no other.

The majority of the papers measured some 140 × 220 mm (5½ × 8⅝ in), but there was also a larger size, approximately 200 × 300 mm (7⅞ × 11⅞ in), and several intermediate sizes. The papers were printed from wood blocks, from metal type, and from a combination of both. Paper was for the most part lightweight (in some cases very flimsy) and generally white.

Chop papers reflect the 'none-genuine-without-this-signature' syndrome of 19th-century European and American packaging. Pirating of brands was common, and merchants were continually inveighing against imitations, defecting partners, and other malefactors. Typical of the genre is a paper put out by Ching Tai Hong of Chin Sau in May 1875:

> One of the partners of the above hong [firm], which for some years past has selected the fine tatlees [raw silks] containing the chop known to Europeans as the 'Beautiful woman chop' has thought it best to separate himself from us at the commencement of the silk season, and to continue the production of the same chops, but at Nanting, instead of at Chin Sau. To prevent any minsconception on the part of the European buyers, we beg to inform them, that in future all silk that emanates from our hong at Chin Sau, will be fully equal in all respects to that formerly produced by our late firm, but will be distinguished ... by the insertion in each bundle of skeins, of a new chop paper bearing a picture of 'A man, a beautiful woman, and a buffalo' in addition to the original well-known chop paper.

The picture described appears in a panel adjacent to the text.

The majority of chops were less complex. 'Gold pheasant', 'Green pagoda', and 'Red elephant' are typical. Some merchants distinguished product grades by colour coding: for example, Soh Vow Sun Hong: No. 1, Blue elephant; No. 2, Yellow elephant; No. 3, Green elephant. The same firm's 'Extra No. 1' carried two chop papers, namely 'Red elephant' and 'Grasshopper'. Others printed the distinguishing mark once, twice, or three times in a row to indicate quality. As a protection against counterfeits, a number of firms relied on elaborately watermarked paper. The paper bore no printed message; it merely spelled out the company's name and town, and noted the year of the firm's founding.

Before insertion in silk bales, chop papers were folded and placed in sample envelopes containing a specimen of the product and bearing the merchant's name and brand mark, and sometimes the quality and crop number. These envelopes, made from handmade paper, and commonly measuring some

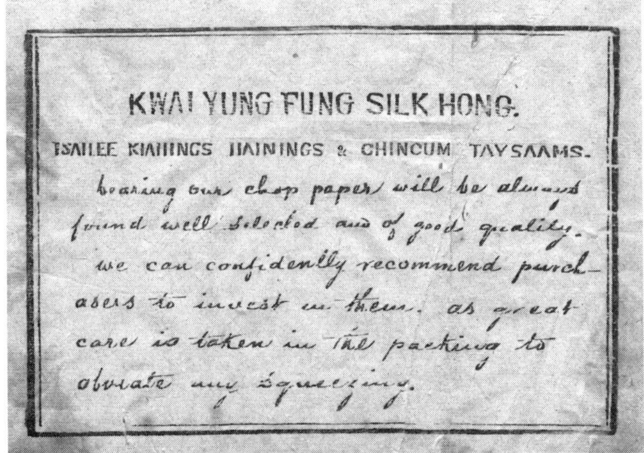
KWAI YUNG FUNG SILK HONG.
TSATLEE KIAHINGS HAININGS & CHINCUM TAYSAAMS.
bearing our chop paper will be always found well selected and of good quality. we can confidently recommend purchasers to invest in them. as great care is taken in the packing to obviate any squeezing.

Chop paper of Kwai Yung Fung Silk Hong. Printed in blue from a wood block. 125 × 170 mm (4⅞ × 6¾ in)

150 × 70 mm (6 × 2¾ in), were folded and sealed at the foot with a pasted paper strip and were similarly sealed at a central vertical join at the back. Fronts were printed, mostly in one colour, typically from hand-cut wood blocks. Surviving chop papers will generally be found to bear traces of the folding required to fit them into the sample envelopes.

Christmas card

The first Christmas card was said to have been devised in 1843 by Henry Cole, first Director of the Victoria & Albert Museum (then the South Kensington Museum), and designed for him by John Calcott Horsley (later RA). One thousand copies were printed for Cole under the pseudonym Felix Summerly, the surplus being sold at his Juvenilia shop the 'Home Treasury Office'. Printed lithographically and hand-coloured, they measured 83 × 127 mm (3¼ × 5 in) and sold in the shop for one shilling each.

This card was followed in 1848 by one with an etched design by William Maw Egley consisting of four Christmas scenes and the message 'Merry Christmas and a Happy New Year to you'. Both the Horsley and Egley cards conveyed festive rather than religious overtones, showing scenes redolent of 'A Christmas Carol' and Irving's 'Old Christmas'. The essential Christian aspect of the celebration appeared in later cards.

The Christmas card is said to have been introduced to America in the early 1870s by the German immigrant printer Louis Prang (*see* CHROMO). At the suggestion of Arthur Ackermann of London, Prang overprinted one of his chromolithographed trade cards with the words 'Merry Christmas', using the space normally devoted to an advertising message. This practice was subsequently followed by business houses on both sides of the Atlantic. This claim for Louis Prang is disputed: an earlier American card appears to pre-date his by some twenty years. A lithographed advertising card of R. H. Pease produced in Albany in about 1850 is said to have the added legend 'A Merry Christmas and a Happy New Year'.

Nevertheless, Louis Prang played an important role in the development of the American Christmas card. He instituted the 'prize card' scheme, offering four prizes annually (1880–85) for designs, and afterwards for essays written by women on the subject of Christmas cards. The practice survived into the 20th century: in London, Raphael Tuck and Sons, Hildesheim, and Hildesheimer & Faulkner offered prizes; Hallmark Cards also made a number of awards in late 1949 and the early 1950s.

The leading publishers of Christmas cards, some of whom were also printers, include (in Britain): Thomas De La Rue, Charles Goodall & Son, Hildesheimer & Faulkner, Siegmund Hildesheimer & Co., Joseph Mansell, Ernest Nister, Raphael Tuck & Sons, and Marcus Ward & Co.; and (in America): J. H. Bufford & Sons, John A. Lowell & Co., and Louis Prang & Co. (whose cards were marketed in Britain by Arthur Ackermann). The vast majority of Christmas cards were designed anonymously or were the work of little-known or otherwise unrecorded artists. Seddon (1992) lists the names or initials of around 400 designers, including some Royal Academicians who produced the occasional card. Some other significant artists produced Christmas cards, though in most cases not very many. Among them (in Britain) were Walter Crane, Robert Dudley, Birkett Foster, Kate Greenaway, John Leighton (Luke Limner), Beatrix Potter, and Louis Wain; and (in America) Rosina Emmet, Elihu Vedder, and D. Wheeler. Christmas cards by some of these artists are much sought after by collectors.

Christmas card designed by J. P. Beadle for the 7th Division of the British Army in World War I, 1917. Published by James Haworth, London. Photogravure. 102 × 152 mm (4 × 6 in)

The Christmas card also required writers, or, at the very least, texts. The Bible was the major source, but passages from Burns, Shakespeare, Shelley, Tennyson, and Wordsworth, and other major writers were widely quoted. In addition the Christmas-card trade generated a new kind of versifying copywriter, most of whom, though not all, were anonymous. One writer, Helen M. Burnside, wrote over 6000 texts between 1874 and 1900 for several publishers, and another, Samuel K.Cowan, 1005 verses for eleven different firms in one year alone, 1884 (Seddon, 1992, p. xix). Perhaps the most popular writer of verse found on Christmas cards was Frances Ridley Havergal, who died in 1879. Her religious poems were often quoted, and she also wrote specially for Christmas-card publishers.

The 19th-century Christmas-card industry expanded rapidly: chromolithography, lace paper, gold and silver, blind embossing, and all the delicate finery of the VALENTINE were enlisted in the production of increasingly decorative cards. Valentine 'blanks' were adapted for Christmas use with substitution of lovers' messages by Christmas greetings. By the 1880s Christmas cards had blossomed like valentines. Multi-layer cut-outs, with cribs, cattle, mangers, angels, and a Christmas star appeared as three-dimensional set-pieces. Shaped cards became popular: 'Christmas' birds, animals, and flowers were rendered in 'cut-out' cardboard with frost and tinsel trimming.

Toward the end of the century embellishments included fringes, tassels, mother-of-pearl, and satin padding. 'Mechanical' or 'animated cards' also appeared in which movement of a string or lever transformed the image; many of these were of great complexity, rivalling the works of Meggendorfer (*see* ADVERTISING NOVELTY).

The 20th century saw a marked decline in elaboration, not only because of changes in taste, but through the collapse of the 'stationery sweat-shop' in which poorly-paid women and girls had carried out much of the intricate work of assembly. Mechanized production and an apparently insatiable addiction to the Christmas-card habit brought a proliferation of simpler cheaper cards. The traditional themes, Dickensian on the one hand and religious on the other, continued largely unchanged, but there were occasional radical departures – notably in World War I – when patriotism was a dominant note; hope, largely with the return of peace, was a later theme. Similar, though less sentimental, were the Christmas cards produced in World War II.

By the 1950s, 1960s, and 1970s the annual wave of Christmas

cards had become a significant source of revenue, not only for manufacturers but for the postal service who observed a 'two-wave' pattern to the flow: the first having its peak some ten days before Christmas and the second, in response to the first, four or five days later. Over the last few decades the Christmas-card business attracted the attention of numerous charities, among them UNICEF, whose designs, unlike the award winning examples of the 1880s, were donated by their designers free of charge.

See also GREETINGS CARD

REFERENCES George Buday, *The History of the Christmas Card*, new edn (London: Spring Books, 1964); Laura Seddon, *A Gallery of Greetings* (Manchester: Manchester Polytechnic Library, 1992)

COLLECTIONS American Antiquarian Society, Worcester, Mass.; Boston Public Library, Boston, Mass.; Hallmark Historical Collection, Hallmark Cards, Kansas City; John Johnson Collection, Bodleian Library, Oxford; Manchester Metropolitan University Library

Christmas charity seal designed by Rockwell Kent, 1939. Printed in two colours by photogravure. The printed image of each seal 23 × 18 mm (⅞ × ¾in)

Christmas charity seal

The Christmas sticker, sold in aid of charity, and affixed as a seasonal gesture to Christmas mail, was the idea of Einar Holbøll, a postmaster in Denmark. It first appeared in 1904. The 'stamp' was not intended for postal use but nevertheless he applied to the postal authorities – and to his king – for permission to launch the idea.

The first issue bore the portrait of Queen Louise and sold for two ore. It raised a substantial sum for the Anti-Tuberculosis Association and was well received by the Danish public; as a result of its success it was decided to form a Christmas Seal Committee, the members of which determined to build a sanatorium for children with tuberculosis. The first, built in 1911, was called the Julemaerkesanatoriet or Christmas Seal Sanatorium. By the 1920s, sales of the Christmas seal in Denmark were bringing in more than 200,000 kronen a year.

The idea spread around the world. In 1907 it was introduced by Emily Bissell with great success in America, where its sales reached many millions. It generated the setting up of some 2000 state and local tuberculosis associations all over the country, all of which offered Christmas seals, each year beginning on Thanksgiving Day.

The Christmas seal spread gradually to other countries: Finland started in 1911; Switzerland in 1912; Czechoslovakia (as it was then) and Japan in 1924; France and Belgium in 1925; Poland in 1926; Korea in 1935; and Hungary in 1938. Great Britain entered the seal campaign in 1926; South Africa in 1929; Canada and Bermuda in 1931; India in 1943. Seals were also produced in Formosa, Iceland, Jamaica, Italy, Malaya, and Latvia.

These seals were commonly available in sheets, not merely in multiples but as pictorial presentations in which each portion of the sheet comprised a seal in itself and was also an ingredient in a larger whole. Much ingenuity was shown in thus disposing of large numbers of seals at one sale. The seals were also marketed in booklets.

A characteristic of most of the seals published after 1920 was the 'trade mark' of the double-barred cross of Lorraine. This device was introduced by a Frenchman, Dr Sersiron, who proposed it at an international tuberculosis conference in Berlin in 1902. It was adopted by the associations worldwide. The cross of Lorraine dates back through many uses (including adoption in World War II by the Free French) to the Crusades, and (except in Turkey and other Muslim countries where the star and crescent is used) connotes a crusade against the common enemy.

The Christmas seal idea was adopted by a number of other organizations; in America particularly it had much currency, appearing, among other causes, for the American Dental Association, the American Bible Society, and the Osteopathic Student Loan. With the radical decline in the incidence of tuberculosis in much of Western Europe, the Christmas seal lost its immediate relevance. It was 'inherited', however, by cognate organizations, latterly in Britain by the Chest and Heart Association (later the Chest Heart and Stroke Association).

The Christmas seal is designated among collectors as a 'Cinderella' stamp and has a following of enthusiasts. In America, *Dick Green's Catalogue*, published under the sponsorship of the Christmas Seal and Charity Stamp Society, lists every issue of every seal in every country with full particulars of each issue and notes on rarities.

See also 'CINDERELLA' STAMP

REFERENCES Bernard Reicher, *Bitte, bitte kleb'mich* (Frankfurt am Main: Institut für Stadtgeschichte, 1998); H. Thomas Steele, *Lick'em, Stick'em: the Lost Art of Poster Stamps* (New York: Abbeville Press, 1989); L. N. & M. Williams, *Cinderella Stamps* (London: Heinemann, 1970)

SOCIETY The Cinderella Stamp Club

Chromo [plates 3, 4, 11, 13–15]

Short for 'chromolithograph', the term refers to the popular lithographic colour print, mass produced and widely distributed, particularly in America, in the latter part of the 19th century.

In America the chromo is largely identified with the name of Louis Prang, a German immigrant who led the way in developing its production, popularization, and sale there. Strictly speaking, the term 'chromolithography' applies to any printing in which images are reproduced in colour by lithography (Greek, *chroma*: colour; and *lithos*: stone), but in the context of Prang and his followers the process was developed as a means of imitating oil paintings – works which, without the chromolithographer's intervention, would never have reached the walls of the poor. The paintings chosen for reproduction were of a distinctly popular cast, and it must be said that the chromo, both in subject matter and execution, was frowned on by the artistic élite. The word 'chromo' therefore came to be equated with ignorant sentimentality.

In the search for even greater fidelity of reproduction, Prang and other lithographers used increasing numbers of stones in their printing, a simple picture frequently requiring ten or twelve stones to render its various shades and hues. The extraordinary number of stones involved, and the ever-extending time required for their preparation, became in itself a matter of wonder and remarkable statistics were often quoted. In Prang's own promotional publication, *Prang's Chromo. A Journal of Popular Art,* one article (January 1868) refers to an image having to pass through the printing press as many as thirty times. This number was sometimes exceeded: McClinton (1973) reports that Prang's lithograph 'A Family Scene in Pompeii' by the Belgian artist Coomans required forty-five different stones. James Parton in *The Atlantic Monthly* (1869) refers to ever greater feats: 'Some landscapes have been executed which required fifty-two stones ...'. The implications of these numbers, when it is taken into account that each stone may have weighed as much as a man, are considerable. In many printing houses overhead lifting gear was used to move the stones.

The build-up of printing ink and the use of oils and varnish in imitation of oil painting led to images of substantial weight and thickness, and sometimes simulated canvas and paint texture brought works close to the realm of counterfeit. Some chromos were stretched on a canvas backing and sold in frames in the manner of paintings. Liberal use of varnish led to the use of the term 'oleograph', introduced from Europe. (In Britain the *Contemporary Review* in 1873 refers passionately to 'the detestable art of oleography'). In the long run, both Britain and America settled on the word 'chromo'.

Development of steam-powered presses in America in the 1870s, coupled with heavy promotion, resulted in increasing production, sharper competition, and lower prices. By the 1880s some stationery wholesalers were offering chromos as free gifts with every dozen packets of envelopes and notepaper.

Chromolithography was also very widely used in advertising. Typically the TRADE CARD, CALENDAR, POSTER, and SHOWCARD were produced by the process, and millions of chromolithographed GREETINGS CARDS also appeared. The process was also used for CERTIFICATES, REWARD OF MERIT cards, RELIGIOUS CARDS, and educational pictorial material. These items, however, though printed by substantially the same process, commonly employed a much smaller number of stones and made no attempt at simulating oil paintings.

Hand-stippling of chromolithographs to produce gradation and colour blending, was to be partly superseded from the 1880s in both America and Britain by the invention of mechanical ways of imitating such hand work. These methods were first patented by Benjamin Day in America in 1878. In their turn these methods were to be entirely superseded by the middle of the 20th century by half-tone effects produced by photomechanical means. The day of the chromo – and of the chromolithograph at large – was over.

See also CAN LABEL; CIGAR BAND/BOX LABEL; CIGARETTE CARD; FIREMAN'S MEMBERSHIP CERTIFICATE; SCRAP

REFERENCES Peter C. Marzio, *The Democratic Art: Chromolithography, 1840–1900* (Boston: Godine, 1979); Katharine Morrison McClinton, *The Chromolithographs of Louis Prang* (New York: Clarkson N. Potter, 1973)

COLLECTIONS Boston Public Library; New York Public Library

Church brief

Now obsolete in this sense, the term 'brief' was used in England until 1828 to refer to formal church collections for officially named charitable causes. Known also as a 'church brief' or 'King's letter' (Latin, *breve*: brief), the brief was originally a letter issued on the Pope's behalf by the Segretario dei Brevi, an officer of the Papal Chancery.

In England the term was adopted by the established church to refer to a letter of authority from the monarch, licensing a nationwide church collection for a designated charitable purpose. In its later use in America the term was modified to designate a letter patent 'from proper authority'.

The word first appears in Britain in the sense of a church collection licence in 1588 (Marprelate Epistles, 33), and it is clear from Pepys's complaint in his *Diary* on 30 June 1661 that both the term and the practice were well established in his time: 'To church, where we observe the trade of briefs is come now up to so constant a course every Sunday, that we resolve to give no more to them'. The issuing of briefs was at various periods delegated to the Privy Council, the Lord Chancellor, the 'Lord Keeper', 'The Secretary of Briefs', and 'the Clerk of the Briefs'. At a later period the brief took the form of a justice's letter.

The term 'Brief papers' refers in the main to the listings of briefs and collections in parish records, though there is a wide range of additional material, such as notices to parishes in arrears, and demands to appear at 'visitations' with accounts of briefs received and monies collected. Records of briefs and collections were at first inscribed in parish registers or appended as

RECEIVED 14 Aug 1813 of
the Minister and Church Wardens of St George
Middlesex
the following Briefs and Collections.

Hatherton	Fire		5	9
Kemberton	Do.		3	10
Elton	Church		9	6
Luddenden	Chapel		12	7
Radford	Church		16	4
St. Paul's	Do.	1	3	6
Wroxall	Fire		7	4
Brainton	Church		5	1
Child's Ercall	Do.		9	2
Fewston	Do.		7	8
Kingston	Do.		11	6
Barnacre	Fire		13	
Staines	Do.		11	6
Dawlish	Inundation		18	6
Mordiford	Church		8	6
Wetton	Do.		10	1
Gt. Burstead & Kingsley	Fires		3	1
Lower Wyersdale	Fire		2	7
Adderley	Church		8	7
Lugwardine	Do.		7	6
Quarnford	Do.		13	9
Howeth	Fire		3	3
Baddeley	Church		13	3
Cheswardine	Do.		12	1
Hindon	Chapel		16	6
Kingsley	Church		13	11
St. Helen's	Do.		14	
		14	3	10

For Messrs. STEVENSON & SALT.
P. Price

Church brief of St George's, Middlesex, 14 August 1813. Letterpress.
172 × 107 mm (6¾ × 4¼ in)

separate memoranda. In the 18th and early 19th centuries the system had become distinctly businesslike, the rights to collect being farmed out to individuals or companies known as 'farmers' or 'undertakers'. These undertook, for a consideration, to administer and carry out the whole operation. It was at this stage that printed forms began to appear, listing briefs. A typical example refers to briefs and collections at the Church of St George's, Middlesex, in a six-month plan in 1813 ('Hatherton: Fire; Kemberton: ditto; Elton: Church; Luddenden: Chapel ... Dawlish: Inundation'). The list shows twenty-seven such entries, with a blank column for insertion of amounts collected in each case. The completed forms were effectively receipts, and were signed at the foot under the printed name of the collecting company.

A practice evolved whereby congregations were called upon to contribute fixed amounts regardless of the nature of the need. In High Ercall, Shropshire, in 1788, it was agreed that twopence for each brief should be allowed out of the church rate except for fire 'and then something more as to be agreed by the parish'. In other cases the sum required to meet costs of damage or repair was used and the contributing church paid a specific rate per hundred pounds. Thus, in another document relating to St George's, Middlesex, the record appears as a handwritten double column. The first column shows the full amount required (in the case of the first entry – a fire at Lower Wyersdale – £256 10*s* 8*d*) and the second a sum equal to one shilling in the pound: 2*s* 7*d*. In each printed sheet, provided by the contractors J. S. Salt, the second figure only appears.

The system was subject to abuse. Competing 'undertakers' (notably Byrd, Hall & Stevenson and Robert Hodgson) engaged in public wrangles, and there was some evidence of malpractice, including forgery of briefs.

Church briefs were abolished by Act of Parliament (9 Geo. IV, c. 28) in 1828.

REFERENCES Wyndham Anstis Bewes, *Church Briefs or Royal Warrants for Collections for Charitable Objects* (London: Adam & Charles Black, 1896); *Notes & Queries*, 23 October 1875 (et passim)

Cigar band/box label

The printed cigar band is said to have been introduced in the early 1830s by Gustave-Antoine Bock, a German cigar manufacturer who sought to distinguish his own make from others, all cigars being at that time unbranded. In so doing, Bock was merely institutionalizing a custom of an earlier period, when the fastidious smoker wrapped a paper strip around the cigar to protect his gloves from stains the cigar might cause. The Bock cigar band (of which no specimen appears to survive) was the forerunner of countless millions of bands, brand labels of which proliferated with the expansion of the industry and increased in graphic splendour as competition mounted.

The decorative cigar ribbon, used in certain forms of cigar packaging, may be seen as a more elegant form of the tape used to bundle cigars in the factory prior to final inspection and boxing. The ribbons are traditionally in yellow, gold, or orange silk, though they are also found in red, blue, and green. Some were supplied in two colours: William Wicke & Co., cigar box and label specialists of New York (c.1880), offered them in red with yellow edges, yellow with blue edges, and yellow with red edges. Also available was a broad yellow ribbon with red, white, and blue edges. They generally bore wording, printed or woven in black (or black and a second colour), indicating the product's title or category (for example, Regalia de la Reina: Extrafina). Sometimes the name of the manufacturer is included (Cabine Selection: H. Upmann: Lonsdales: Habana). The ribbons vary in breadth from approximately 20 mm to 30 mm (13/16 to 1 3/16 in); the length was governed by the number of cigars enwrapped (normally twenty-five or fifty).

The cigar band was followed very shortly by the box label, this too achieving ever-mounting heights of elegance and distinction. Both items relied for their effect on a combination of chromolithography, embossing, and die cutting, all of which were at the time part of a rapidly developing new industry. The effects produced by these means were luxurious – if not always in impeccable taste. Chromolithographic printing used a dozen or so separate workings, and embossing and gold were virtually standard extras. The techniques, which originated in central Europe, were taken to other parts of the world – notably to the tobacco-growing areas. The production process generated a design idiom of its own. The cigar band commonly featured insignia, crests, and portraits of the great and famous. The box label, with its greatly expanded design area, explored every avenue of pomp and status symbol, including not only crests and portraits, but laurels, medallions, heroic figures, other classic images, and a wide range of nude or near-nude female figure arrangements.

The cigar band became an object of interest in its own right, and soon a 'collectable'. In America, bands were produced in sets (showing, for example, US presidents, Indian tribes, etc.). Many printers sold surplus stock directly to the collector, and interest was fuelled by the marketing of cigar-band albums for collectors. Custom-designed cigar bands also appeared. These featured advertisers' products or services (Coca-Cola, Dubonnet, Hotpoint Electric Range) and were also available as election campaign material. Special designs were printed for sports and social clubs; 'commemorative' bands were issued; and family celebrations were also the subject of specially-commissioned bands. Proliferation of designs was virtually unbounded. Systematic collecting of cigar bands gave way to their use for decorative display purposes. They appeared in montage on firescreens, wall panels, and other novelties. Apart from a minority of clearly definable manufacturers' brands, cigar-band designs may represent the enterprise of printers rather than cigarmakers. Cigar-band printers produced illustrated catalogues promoting their products – sometimes featuring many scenes of 'non-brand' designs. These carried such non-commital legends as 'Flor Fina', 'Regalia', 'Ne Plus Ultra', 'Tobacos Esquisitos', 'Reina', 'Pour La Noblesse', etc., and might be applied by the manufacturer or importer to any commercial cigar of his choice. It follows, of course – as with many other mass-market products then and now – that the same mass-produced cigar may appear in a wide variety of different guises.

The American cigar-band industry reached a climacteric in the early 1930s, when the Consolidated Lithographing Corporation of Brooklyn, New York, had acquired some seventy-five per cent of the market, printing 6500 different labels for about 4000 million cigars. The company also owned the International Banding Machine Company, whose cigar-banding machines were used by virtually every cigar manufacturer in America.

Cigar bands commonly measure approximately 90 mm (3 1/2 in) in length (approximately 10 mm (3/8 in) being an unprinted overlap for pasting). Bands are found measuring over 65 mm (2 1/2 in)

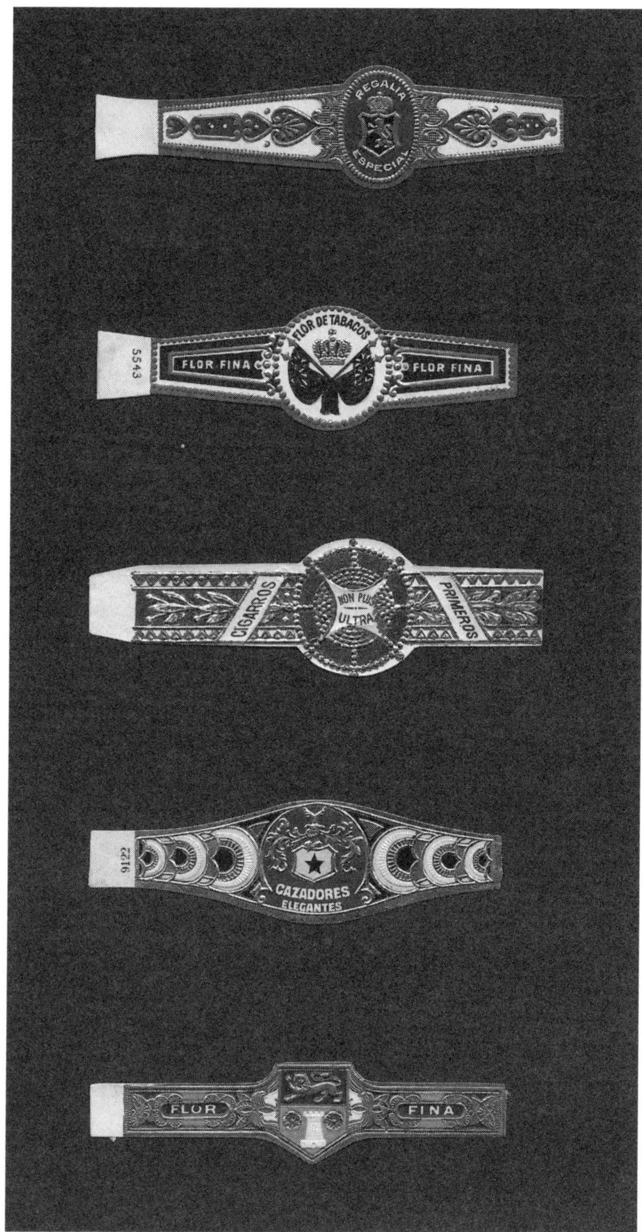

Cigar bands of uncertain date. Printed in one colour with gold embossing. The largest 23 × 86mm (⅞ × 3⅜in)

and as large as 180 or 200mm (7⅛ or 7⅞in) – these last were used for bundles of cigars sold as a single package.

Cigar-box labels are found in several positions and performed a number of functions: those used as the main title-piece on the lid and covering the inside of the lid (known respectively as 'outs' and 'ins'); flaps (hinged to the front of the box, and resting on the contents); seals (commonly oval, and used as a final closure covering the head of the lid pin); edging (a strip label used to finish the edges of the box and the lid); and, in the case of Cuban cigars, the government warranty seal guaranteeing the contents as the product of Cuba. Also found are end labels, used to identify the contents when boxes are stacked on shelves. These labels may carry an overprinted indication of the size of the cigar in question. Sizes are expressed in an arbitrary selection of Spanish-sounding names which vary from one manufacturer to another. Thus the smallest in the range of the Bolivar brand cigar are known as 'Demi Tasse' and the largest as 'Corona Gigantasa'. In the Upmann range the smallest is 'Aperitif', the largest a 'Churchill'. In the designation 'La Corona Corona', the first word is the brand name, the second indicates size.

As with cigar bands, cigar-box labels sought to express the ultimate in luxury, and their archetypal motifs and printing treatments were recognized all over the world as 'cigar-box graphics'. The vast majority of labels were in fact spurious; like cigar bands, they were proffered by specialist printers for the embellishment of any cigar the customer cared to apply them to. They were available as related four- or five-piece 'sets', comprising 'ins' and 'outs', flaps, seals, edging, etc., as desired. 'Brand names' featured on the labels were purely notional, Spanish phrases – 'Gran Fabrica de Tabacos', 'Elaboración Especial', 'Primera Calidad'; they conveyed nothing more special than atmosphere and their many gold medals and awards were fictitious. The 'Guarantee Certificate', also provided as part of a 'set', was a passable echo (though not an exact counterfeit) of the Cuban government warranty label.

A typical set, featuring an Hispanic beauty and the brand name 'Melina', offered an 'in' and 'out', a flap, and an oval seal in ten-colour chromolithography, with gold-leaf embossing, at 318 Reichsmarks per 1000. Executed by the 'new gold' process (bronze powder instead of gold leaf), the price was 233 Reichsmarks. American printers were no less enterprising, though in the main their package deal comprised only 'ins' and 'outs'.

The American cigar-box label appears in two identifiable styles. In the first, roughly pre-1900, as a home-grown version of the Cuban heyday, and in the second as an all-American 20th-century image of popular pleasure. It must be said that the latter was on the whole more competent than the former. Many of the Spanish-sounding names on classic labels are enigmatic ('La Zoos', 'Africora', 'La Balca', 'La Lunda', 'La Patura', etc.) and some are known to be inventions of the moment. 'La Palina' was coined from the name 'Paley' by Sam Paley, who originated the brand. The label shows 'La Palina', Mrs Sam Paley, in Spanish costume.

In the latest period, in which such names as 'Spirit of St Louis', 'Yellow Cab', and 'Rudolph Valentino' emerged, there remained a desire to invoke, if not Cuba, the European heritage. Among the more obscure American cigar titles were 'Blackstone', named after the celebrated British judge, and 'John Ruskin'. The magazine *Fortune* reported (February 1933) that dealers had been overheard telling customers that 'John Ruskin was the fellow that invented evolution'.

Brand-name proliferation in America was intense. The same basic product was in a continual state of renaming, restyling, and relabelling. Political figures, vaudeville stars, and other celebrities came and went – all duly celebrated in a 'new' cigar. To keep pace with the ever-increasing tempo of innovation the industry resorted to a form of name registration. The magazine *The Tobacco World* operated a registration bureau, issuing dated certificates recording 'a word or words as a trade mark and label for cigars ... to be published in the next succeeding issue of The Tobacco World'. The industry itself operated a similar scheme, issuing similar certificates under the aegis of the 'United Registration Bureau for the Tobacco Industries'.

From its earliest days, cigar packaging has featured the extravagances of chromolithographic effects, heavy embossing, and ornamental gold. Its heyday began in America in 1870 when cigar production reached 1000 million, rising later by successive steps of 1000 million in 1879, 1882, 1890, 1900, and 1902 to reach 7000 million in 1906. It was to reach its highest figure, 8200 million in 1920. It is said that in the 1880s there were 1400 cigar manufacturers producing a total of 20,000 brands. By the beginning of the 20th century it was reported that some 350,000 brand names had been registered. However, the totals of brand registrations did not necessarily correspond with the number of brands available at the time in question. Catchphrases, frivolous images – amusing, erotic, fantastic – all combined in an ever-changing kaleidoscope of popular appeal. Brand names, images, and general presentation also made much play with the product's Cuban origins. Such expressions as 'Perfectos', 'Superiores', 'La Rica Hoja', 'Flor Fina', 'Excelentes', etc. are frequent, regardless of the location of the maker and (it may be suspected) the origin of the leaf.

The cigar-box label, appearing on the ends, top, and sides of boxes, served as vital point-of-sale display material in cigar-stores, and the practice of displaying open boxes led to the use of the inside of the lid as an additional sales aid. The cigar band also, originally seen as a closure to the cigar's outer wrapping leaf, acquired display value. Printing and die-cutting of cigar bands became an industry as specialized as box label production. As in other fields, a multiplicity of printing firms was reduced by merger and absorption to relatively few. By the turn of the century leading names were The American Lithographic Co. and The Consolidated Litho Corporation. In Europe, the trade was largely concentrated in Germany, most of the printers concerned remaining anonymous. A reduction also occurred in the number of cigar firms. America's one-time 1400 companies had by the 1970s become 125.

In their heyday, cigar brands were produced in huge quantities and for many thousands of different 'brands'. A run of 100,000 of each design is thought not to have been unusual, and with brand designs in hundreds of thousands, overall numbers are high. One collector in the late 1970s claimed a total of 50,000 different specimens. Notwithstanding the close affinity of the cigar-box label and the cigar band, specialist collectors tend to view the two interests as separate.

See also SILK; UNION LABEL

REFERENCES Joe Davidson, *The Art of the Cigar Label* (Secaucus, NJ: Wellfleet Press, 1989); Joe and Sue Davidson, *Smoker's Art* (New York: Wellfleet Press, 1997); Julian Holland, *The Ultimate Cigar Encyclopedia* (Lorenz Books, 1998); Gerard S. Petrone, *Cigar Box Labels* (Atglen, PA: Schiffer Publishing, 1998)

COLLECTIONS New York Public Library; Smithsonian Institution, Washington, DC; University of South Florida, Tampa, Florida

Cigarette card

Cigarette cards were among the first items of ephemera to be produced specifically for collecting. Originating in America as cardboard stiffeners for the paper packs in which cigarettes were then sold, it was shortly realized that the faces of the blank cards might serve some promotional purpose. Initially the cards were used simply as advertising media, showing illustrations of the manufacturer's products, and in some cases advertising the cigarettes contained in the package itself. The celebrated 'Marquis of Lorne' card, reputed to be the first picture card ever published, simply showed a portrait of the Marquis whose name had been applied to the brand, with the name above and the word 'cigarette' below. The date of this card is uncertain, but cartophilic historians believe it to have appeared in 1879.

The notion of publishing a succession of cards, then adding information on the back, evolved in the following decade, first in America and then in Britain and elsewhere. With its competitively promotional role, the cigarette card took little root in countries where tobacco was a state monopoly; in such places, where they appeared at all, cards tended to be used as an instrument of state propaganda.

The production of cigarette cards became an industry. For many tobacco companies they were a major promotional device, with each new series a potential influence, for good or ill, on sales. By the 1920s and 1930s the companies (who in many cases were printers) were retaining artists, writers, and editors to generate a steady flow of informative miniatures. 'Cigarette-card knowledge' soon acquired a reputation for accuracy, and the few errors which crept in among many hundreds of thousands of cards are today coveted rarities.

Some manufacturers offered gifts in exchange for batches of cards; others exchanged a large complete picture for fifty separate portions provided in the set. In some cases a full list of the titles composing the set was printed on the reverse of the card; in others each card was numbered. By means known only to manufacturers it was arranged that certain cards of each set were 'rarer' than the rest, thus ensuring protractedly repeated purchases at the point of completion (in a number of cases such 'rarities' have subsequently proved to be virtually non-existent).

Sets pictured every conceivable subject, and include many novelties such as stereo cards; shaped cards; press-out booklets; cards printed on fabric, metal, plastic, and wood; silk embroidered cards; 'animated' cards; 'transformation' cards (in which a fold-out flap gave a choice of two versions of the picture); and miniature gramophone records. In one 1889 series each card in the set bore an actual postage stamp. Part of the appeal of the cigarette card as a 'collectable' – as a printed bygone no less than at the time of its original currency – is the fact that faced with the task of acquiring a set or sets, the collector is able to see the product as actually capable of completion. This characteristic has also made the cigarette card the subject of prodigious feats of research and documentation.

Apart from philately, no other collecting field has generated

Cigarette cards for 'Between the Act & Bravo Cigarettes' of Thos. H. Hall, New York, 1881. Printed by Heppenheimer & Maurer. Crayon lithography in black with two tints. 76 × 40 mm (3 × 1$\frac{9}{16}$ in)

such a literature of catalogue enumeration. Compiling records, which manufacturers themselves neglected to do, cartophilists have pieced together a retrospective picture of a publishing activity that circled the world and numbered many hundreds of thousands of separate units. Early cards were produced by chromolithography (*see* CHROMO), but increasingly in the 20th century by four-colour photomechanical methods, two or three complete sets to a sheet. Some monochrome photographic sets were also produced. Original ARTWORK FOR REPRODUCTION was preferred normally at three times linear size, and surviving specimens are still occasionally found.

Parallel with the development of the cigarette card (and in some instances pre-dating it) was a widespread use of 'serial cards' among manufacturers of other consumer products. Chromolithographed cards (known generally as 'chromos') had been put out by Bon Marché in Paris since the mid 1850s and the LIEBIG CARD had been current since 1872. Also widely distributed were chromos by Suchard and Cibils. Not all continental chromos were custom-made for specific advertisers: stock sets, mostly of eight units on a single sheet and bearing a series title and individual subject titles, were available for overprinting. In Britain, the chromos of Huntley & Palmers were well known, and in America the Armour Meat Company had a famous run of cards. All these were commonly larger than the normal cigarette card, averaging some 110 × 80 mm (4⅜ × 3⅛ in) against the cigarette cards' average of 68 × 36 mm (2⅝ × 1⁷⁄₁₆ in).

Cards following the cigarette-card format were later to be published by other concerns, among them magazines and newspapers, chain stores, industrial undertakings, marketing boards, launderers, cinema circuits, charities, stately homes, oil companies, football pools, travel agencies, safety organizations, and libraries. Commonly (and illogically) described as 'trade cards' to distinguish them from cigarette cards, these are sometimes confused in catalogue headings with the tradesman's card of the 18th or 19th centuries, an item produced not for collecting but as a business document.

See also SILK; TRADE CARD

REFERENCES Dorothy Bagnall, *Collecting Cigarette Cards* (London: Arco, 1965); Cartophilic Society of Great Britain, *World Tobacco Issues Index* (Windsor, 1956); Gordon Howsden, *Collecting Cigarette and Trade Cards* (London: New Cavendish, 1995); London Cigarette Card Company, *The Complete Catalogue of British Cigarette Cards* (Exeter: Webb & Bower, 1981)

COLLECTIONS Burdick Collection, Metropolitan Museum of Art, New York; John Johnson Collection, Bodleian Library, Oxford

SOCIETY Cartophilic Society of Great Britain

Cigarette pack

The cigarette, as distinct from the *cigarillo* or small cigar, is generally supposed to have been introduced into Europe (and thence into America) at the time of the Crimean War (1854–56) when British soldiers made its acquaintance through their Turkish allies and Russian prisoners of war. However, cigarettes were undoubtedly on sale in Britain before that date. Bacon Brothers of Cambridge and H. Simmons of Burlington Arcade, London, have business records showing sales of cigarettes in 1851, the year of the Great Exhibition.

The first branded cigarettes to be made in Britain were 'Sweet Threes', produced in 1856 by Robert Peacock Gloag (who had recently returned from service in the Crimea). Gloag had a small works in Deptford Lane, where hand-rolled cigarettes were turned out at about 1250 per worker per day. In Havana, Cuba, Don Luis Susini had been making cigarettes by machine since 1853).

Cigarettes were at first sold loose, by tens or dozens, or by weight. (Player's 'Weights' derive their name from this last practice.) They were wrapped in a square of paper in the same manner as tobacco and snuff, the ends of the package being folded over to form a closure (*see* CUBAN WRAPPER). Later they were slipped into small paper bags, and by the end of the 19th century printed envelopes were in use. These bore the name and trade design of the manufacturer, and were designed to take up to five cigarettes.

In Britain, the paper package was to become one of the standard forms of presentation, the cigarettes reaching the retailer ready-packed, often in a counter display box bearing a display label in its turn-back lid. The package, carrying five or ten cigarettes, was normally open at the top and sometimes had a scooped upper edge to allow easy access to the contents. It later evolved into a thin card container, closed at the foot and having a tongue-and-slit closure at the top. The majority of British manufacturers moved rapidly to the 'box', a rigid two-part card construction (known as 'hull-and-slide' or 'shell-and-slide'), in which the contents were held in a moveable tray within an outer sleeve. Construction was at first in the manner of a matchbox, the ends of the tray being fixed. Player's 'Navy Cut' and a number of other brands were presented in this way. Hinged trays, with tuck-in flaps, soon replaced rigid ends, and became virtually standard throughout the industry with the general introduction of the flip-top package in the 1950s. The hull-and-slide presentation was enhanced in the 1920s and 1930s by the introduction of a metal foil ('silver paper') liner, which was itself later lined with a tissue-paper liner. In the latter 1930s the upper area of the frontal portion of the foil was commonly separate, allowing complete removal for easier access. Cellophane-type outer wrappings appeared in 1931, and an 'easy-open' pullstrip came into general use in the latter part of the 1930s.

Packing in tens and twenties became general in the 1920s, but fives were commonly available from the turn of the century until the 1930s. Early brands are found with cigarettes in multiples of four (Faulkner's 'Kagga Whiffs'); six (Ogden's 'Lucky Star'); twelve (Player's 'Navy Cut'); and twenty-four ('Spanish Shawl'). Muratti's 'After Lunch' presented a single row of ten cigarettes. Novelty packings in the late 1930s include a mini-pack of four cigarettes with a pack of twenty as a bonus ('Four for your friends'); a twin-pack of ten cigarettes each for slot-machine sale as a packet of twenty (a halfpenny was included, as with the standard twenty pack, as change; most brands of the period sold at 11½*d* for twenty.) Also available from slot-machines was a single packaged cigarette 'Churchman' for one penny.

The rigid pack has remained dominant in Britain from its inception, whereas in America it soon gave way to the 'soft cup' presentation (a form, it is said, more comfortably adapted to the informal shirt-pocket than the hard-cornered hull-and-shell or flip-top).

Mechanical package production began in the 1880s, when hand rolling of cigarettes gave way to overall mechanization. The advent of James Bonsack's cigarette-rolling machine in America revolutionized the whole process, though in the event it was acquired and exploited by W. D. & H. O. Wills in Britain in some form for years in advance of its adoption in America. The Wills company acquired absolute rights to the machine in the UK from James Buchanan Duke, head of the American Tobacco Co., who held outright control of the machine in America. The association was to lead to the so-called 'tobacco war' and the formation in 1901 of The Imperial Tobacco Co. to counter Duke's 'invasion' of the British industry.

Manufacture of the two-part hull-and-shell package as a separate operation was in the later 1930s seen to be uneconomical, and research began into the production of a single unit pack. The result, in the 1950s, was the flip-top pack, of one-piece construction. Stronger, and yet effecting a materials economy of some fifteen per cent, and easier to use than any previous pack, the flip-top is produced from what is effectively a single sheet of printed card, cut and creased in a single operation, and folded, pasted, lined, filled, and film-wrapped in a continuous production flow. The principle is used virtually throughout the world for rigid-pack cigarettes.

The soft-cup pack has also achieved international currency, America's 'big three' – Lucky Strike, Chesterfield, and Camel – having brought the style to a world market. The pack is cheaper to produce than the flip-top, and conveys an air of friendly informality where the rigid pack tends to dignity. The soft-cup concept may be said to stem from the former practice of rolling cigarettes in paper wrappers and is not wholly distant from the draw-stringed tobacco bag of the turn of the century. This also bore a paper tax stamp, to be broken by the customer on opening, and we may note that a central paper seal remains a feature of today's soft-cup pack, even where no tax is payable. (It is also noticeable that this seal remains commonly unbroken, the smoker preferring to dispense cigarettes through the partially-opened closure rather than by breaking the whole of it.)

Cigarette-pack graphics tended to traditionalism, with brand loyalties surviving step-by-step changes in design detail; but in the 1960s, with health hazards ever more clearly spelt out, many old-established images disappeared and new 'clean-looking' brands were introduced. Thus, Player's branded sailor and lifebelt motif survived into the flip-top age (though much-modified – the traditional seascape background being replaced by areas of plain white and colour) and the design of Wills's classic 'Passing Clouds' was also 'cleaned up' for flip-top use. The latter brand was withdrawn, however, in 1973, one year short of its centenary.

The cleaning-up process – particularly the introduction of large areas of white or solid colour – has been widespread, and in America as well as Britain old-established brands have simplified their image. This process was started in the 1940s, when, in the post-war period, designers in many fields were employed to remove the curlicues and embellishments of their forebears' graphics.

Among cigarette-pack curiosities are packages custom-made for propaganda purposes ('Win with Nixon'); for amusement ('Brand X: For the man who is satisfied with nothing less than second-best'); and for advertising ('Miracle: The adjustable, all-in-one golf club'). Also to be recorded is a shell-and-slide pack bearing the large initials 'R N' and the legend '20 Cigarettes: Tipped'; on its back is a printed message: 'These cigarettes are supplied duty free for the exclusive use of officers and men of the Royal Navy and are not to be landed, given away or otherwise disposed of contrary to regulations'; on its side is a further message: 'Warning by H M Government: Smoking can damage your health'.

The health warning, first introduced in 1967, is now to be found on cigarette packs in many countries.

REFERENCES Alec Davis, *Package and Print* (London: Faber & Faber, 1967); Chris Mullen, *Cigarette Pack Art* (London: Hamlyn, 1979)

SOCIETY Cigarette Packet Collectors Club of Great Britain

Cigarette paper

According to Gaspar Gallo, tobacco historian, the first European to smoke a *cigarillo* (a small cigar, paper covered), was Don Juan de Grijalva on his arrival in Mexico from Cuba in 1518.

Five types of paper are recorded: 'Arroz' (rice), 'Pectoral' (chest), 'Brea' (tar), 'Trigo' (wheat), and 'Berro' (watercress).

Rice paper, a fine white, easily-burning paper, is in fact made not from rice but from the pith of certain trees, notably the *Fatsia papyrifera*. The paper, also known as 'Bible paper' (in France *papier mince*) has since been produced from other materials. 'Pectoral' paper was chocolate coloured (and may possibly have contained elements of cocoa); tar and wheat papers were yellow; watercress was bright green. Rice paper was considered merely as a good *cigarillo* paper. The others were thought to have therapeutic qualities and had the added advantage of being less flammable; used in cigarettes, they went out if not actually smoked – a major safety point. The *cigarillo* came to be known in Cuba as the *papeleta* or *papelete*.

The *papeleta* is said to have found its way through Turkey to British soldiers fighting in the Crimean War (1854–56), who brought the idea back with them to Europe. There is evidence however of cigarette paper production some fifty years earlier. Josepar Leonide la Croix was granted a licence to make 'fine paper' in Angoulême in 1799, and Jean Bardou appears as owner of the OCB Cigarette Paper Company in 1822, launching the first cigarette paper booklet under the trade name 'Job' in 1838.

The name 'la Croix' was to become identified with the trade name 'Rizla', in the name compounded of *riz* (French: rice) and la+ (the cross sign being incorporated in the company logo and appearing on every package). 'Rizla' and 'Job' are today the best-known names in what has become a world industry. Other names to emerge in the 19th century are, in France, C. Pradon ('Le Cosmopolite', 1874), Braunstein Frères ('Zig-Zag', c.1888); in Italy, S. D. Modiano (c.1893); in Spain Vincente Piccorelli, Francisco Abadie, and Miquel y Costas and Miquel (c.1878).

Admixture or impregnation with other substances was never far from the cigarette-paper industry's awareness. In addition to tar and wheat, which continued to be used intermittently, menthol and iodine were also used. Francisco Abadie's product (Barcelona, c.1880), was described as a 'pectoral and hygienic' paper, formulated on the patent of Vincente Piccorelli under the designation 'iodized cane sugar paper'. Wax-tipped 'papier ambre' was also introduced (Paris, 1912) to prevent paper sticking to the lips. The idea was also applied to commercially manufactured cigarettes in Britain under the name 'Sweethearts'.

In Britain the industry was represented in the 20th century by a number of smaller companies producing such brands as Archer (1935), Compton's (1950), Encore, Alexander & Alexander (1950), and Stella Dalam Products (1961). The first cigarette paper factory in Britain was opened in 1937 by Rizla Ltd, who had already acquired fifty per cent of the British market. The company's output supplied many foreign markets as well; by 1969 it had set up a major factory in Treforest, Wales, and others in Australia and Canada, with associates in a number of European countries. The French parent company eventually became a subsidiary.

Cigarette paper sales rise in times of economic stress, and demand was increased in World Wars I and II, in the depression of the 1930s, and in the recession of the 1970s and 1980s. The 1970s and 1980s also saw a renewal of interest in the product from smokers of cannabis and other substances, for whom a wide range of novelty papers appeared. Tastes also extended in other directions. Among these, the Rizla company offered 'Liquorice Double Wide', 'Sweetstraw', and promotional papers to accompany specific brands of roll-your-own cigarette tobacco. (The same company was also commissioned to supply unbranded papers for use by prisoners in British gaols: 'H M Prisons only'.) Also available were cherry paper, banana paper (made in Spain for Robert Burrow Associates Ltd, New York), multicoloured cherniak (Papeleras Reunidas, Spain), and maize paper (Miquel y Costas and Miquel, Spain). A plethora of papers led to a minor fad in cigarette-paper collecting. One wallet of papers presented a selection of different coloured papers under the title 'International Paper Collection ... Every Packet a Collector's Dream'.

Popular in the 1970s, imported into America from Italy, were printed cigarette papers bearing anti-establishment propaganda. The Patriotic Rolling Paper Co. Inc., put out a number of these, among them a miniature 100 dollar bill (the 'American State of Change') and a 'Stars and Stripes' motif.

Cigarette papers bearing messages, codes, etc., have frequently been used by resistance organizations and for espionage. In World War II the British authorities distributed sabotage instructions to resistance forces in forged cigarette paper packages, counterfeiting well-known German brands, complete with German government tax seals. In the more recent past, micro-printed codes have been found among cigarette papers in the possession of terrorists.

Cigarette papers are sold flat, in booklet form; flat or rolled over in slip-in wallets; interleaved in a pull-out dispenser; interleaved in a double dispenser; and in recent times as a continuous pull-out strip on a roll, allowing cigarettes of the desired length. Rigid card booklet and interleaf dispensers are found in earlier issues, sometimes rolled and fitted with elastic cords to hold their covers closed. Paper sizes, apart from the continuous roll paper, vary greatly. Typical is the standard Rizla paper, 37 × 70 mm (1 7/16 × 2 3/4 in), but sizes up to 70 × 93 mm (2 3/4 × 3 5/8 in) are also found.

Many papers carry a 'watermark' (today actually a thinning of the paper impressed into the substance between wood and steel rollers); some have corner cuts to facilitate rolling; in one Rizla variety each individual paper is provided with a built-in metal strip, which allows the cigarette to be smoked to the very end by holding the metal.

The roll-your-own cigarete has not always had the image of a home-made substitute. At about the turn of the 19th and 20th centuries the roll-your-own smoker could buy a silver cigarette case in a variety of styles. One style, specially designed, and bearing the company's name, was produced to take a booklet of 'Zig-Zag' papers. It cost 3*s* 6*d* and was stocked by the Army & Navy Stores, London.

REFERENCES Dard Hunter, *Papermaking* (New York: Dover, 1978); Gaspar Jorge Garcia Galló, *Biographia del Tabaco Habano*, with a foreword by Ché Guevara (Havana: Comisión Nacional del Tabaco Habano, 1961)

'Cinderella' stamp

So-called from its former relegation to the back of the philatelic dealer's stock book, and in America often described as a 'back of the book' stamp, the 'Cinderella' stamp is a stamp in all but national postal function. It is a stamp, but not a postage stamp. In the past, philatelists have classified any adhesive stamp that was not a postage stamp issued by a postal authority as a 'Cinderella' stamp. More recently, several types of adhesive stamp that would formerly have been described in this way have been identified separately, such as revenue or TAX STAMPS.

Paradoxically, the 'Cinderella' stamp does in fact include stamps with limited postal use, but this function must be considered as distinct from recognition for national and international use under the terms of the Universal Postal Union. Local postage networks, as in the Zemstvo system of Imperial Russia, and in the unofficial 'strike' mails in Britain in 1971, used stamps of their own – issues unrecognized by the National Postal Authority. (The Zemstvo system was used between big towns and rural areas; the National Post Authority accepted mail only between towns.)

Cinderella stamps are for the most part gummed and perforated in the manner of postage stamps (and often printed and produced by postage stamp manufacturers), but a minority are unperforated and uncoated. Gummed or otherwise, most (but not all) are intended for affixing; some few, as in the British glove-tax and hat-tax stamps at the turn of the 18th century, were designed to be pasted to fabrics.

American 'Cinderella' stamps of the inter-war years. The centre example lithographed, the others photogravure. The largest 64 × 45 mm (2½ × 1¾ in)

Cinderella stamps include Christmas and other letter seals ('Air Mail', 'registered', 'recorded delivery', etc.), trading stamps, savings stamps, TV licence stamps, telephone bill stamps, railway and bus parcel stamps, 'bogus' stamps (produced for amusement for non-existent countries), forgeries (produced to deceive the post office or the philatelist, or as 'black propaganda'), and publicity and advertising stamps. Also included in the category is a wide range of fiscal stamps.

Among 'fringe postal' stamps are those used in the 1870s and early 1880s by Oxford and Cambridge Universities for private postal service between and within their own institutions (*see* UNIVERSITY MAIL). Among notable forgeries are the 'Hitler/skull' stamp printed by the British in World War II, and the German versions of British stamps in which (among other alterations) the rose and thistle emblems of England and Scotland are converted into hammer and sickle and Star of David. Both countries produced the stamps for their demoralizing effect when covertly introduced into the other's postal system.

See also CHARITY STAMP; CHRISTMAS CHARITY SEAL

SOCIETY The Cinderella Stamp Club

Cipher label *See* CYPHER LABEL

City ordinance broadside

Newly-formed townships in the American West in the 1850s and 1860s formed boards of trustees, whose local by-laws – known as 'ordinances' – had the force of statute law.

Ordinances, divided into chapters dealing with specific subjects – 'Of Nuisances', 'Of the Prevention of Gaming and Disorderly Practices', 'Of Houses of Prostitution', etc. – extended often to some 1500–2000 words. They were published as printed broadsides and posted throughout the area concerned. In many cases, it may be concluded, the broadsides were produced as a symptom of self-importance on the part of the barely established communities, though many of their clauses showed an earthy acquaintance with conditions of the period. For example:

> (12 August 1868): Be it ordained by the President and Board of Trustees of Green River City, Dakota Territory. That it shall be unlawfaul for any person to carry concealed weapons of any kind within the corporate limits of said city .... That it shall be unlawful for any person to shoot or discharge any fire-arm ... within said corporate limits .... That it shall be unlawful ... to make loud and unusual noises, or to boisterously or uncivilly conduct himself ... or in any way disturb the peace of the citizens of said city as to fight or threaten to fight in said corporate limits ....
>
> (13 November 1851): Ordinances of the Board of Trustees of the Village of Ovid .... If any person shall be intoxicated so as to become noisy, quarrelsome or turbulent ... he shall forfeit a penalty not exceeding ten dollars ... and it shall be lawful for any constable to arrest any and all such persons and detain them until they shall become sober, and then take them before a justice .... No person shall keep in any store or dwelling more than twenty-five pounds of gun-powder ....

Ordinance broadsides were issued on behalf of Boards of Trustees over the names of the President of the Board and the Town Clerk. Printed in black in a three- or four-column layout, often within a decorative border, they commonly measured some 445 × 290 mm (17½ × 11⅜ in).

REFERENCES William Frost Mobley, *American 19th-Century Historical and Advertising Broadsides*...catalogue 1, (Wilbraham, Mass.: The Author, 1980); Keith Wheeler, *The Townsman* (Alexandria, VA: Time-Life Books 1975; rev. edn 1981)

COLLECTION American Antiquarian Society, Worcester, Mass.

Classroom label

The Lancastrian system of education, founded at the beginning of the 19th century by Joseph Lancaster, pioneered the concept of free universal schooling and, as a means of efficiency and economy, the application of the 'monitor' principle. The teacher taught the pupil-monitors, who then taught their fellows. By the use of monitors, Lancaster claimed, it was possible for one teacher to instruct 1000 pupils in reading, writing, and arithmetic for a year at a cost of only 7 shillings per pupil.

As part of his system, which was enthusiastically adopted in Britain, America, and elsewhere, Lancaster identified monitors with printed labels, which were pasted on cards and worn by those who bore the office. Lancaster went further, printing 'punishment' labels with such captions as 'Idle', 'Talking', 'Playing', 'Dirty boy', etc., to be worn as appropriate. Few, if any, used examples of the labels have survived, but unused specimens, unmounted, have been found in Britain. 'Monitor' labels have a decorative border and measure some 60 × 130 mm (2⅜ × 5⅛ in) or, in another version, 45 × 120 mm (1¾ × 4¾ in). Punishment labels, larger and bolder, carry no decorative border. They measure 120 × 140 mm (4¾ × 5½ in) and have space for details of the class to be filled in by hand.

REFERENCE Joseph Lancaster, *Improvements in Education, as it Respects the Industrious Classes of the Community* (London: Darton and Harvey, 1803)

Clipper-ship card *See* SAILING NOTICE/CARD

Club flyer

This, later strikingly colourful, form of entertainment advertising first appeared in Britain in the early 1980s in the shape of simple black and white photocopied flyers, usually hurriedly reproduced and distributed to advise potential customers that a rave was due to take place at a hitherto secret destination. However, the simultaneous arrival of the possibility of creating very sophisticated images swiftly and cheaply by means of computerized imaging and production techniques meant that they soon became a completely separate form of advertising. This was so not only for secret raves but also for popular music events of all sorts – especially at the 'underground' and non-mainstream end of the market. Club flyers also rapidly became an international (especially European) instead of a purely British phenomenon.

Essentially club flyers are a specialist form of the traditional throw-away bill, card, or leaflet, but presented in the style and manner of the market at which they are aimed. Thus both the imagery and the language used is often satirical (for example, Margaret Thatcher as an Edwardian callgirl), softly pornographic, psychedelic, or political. The standard of graphics is often high, as is the printing.

Designers of club flyers do not care to observe the laws of copyright, and graphic images of all kinds (even ones produced in the same year as the card) are considered fair game and transmogrified or cannibalized to good effect for an event often diametrically opposed to the original product being advertised. Much of the imagery has a serious political intent – but this is only obvious to the producers and those for whom they are intended. For example, in 1994 Jamie Reed produced a flyer incorporating Mickey Mouse, the McDonald arches, the Coca-Cola logo, and the Nazi swastika to protest against the Criminal Justice Bill which made dancing openly in large numbers a crime.

Many flyers use familiar washing-powder packet imagery as backgrounds (obviously a two-edged weapon as their effect depends on the reader having seen the originals – and knowing what they are). Tattoo imagery is rife as, of course, are the devices and images derived from all kinds of COMIC. Many are sophisticated pastiches of fashion drawings of the 1940s, 1950s, and 1960s and (like Student Union 'hop' posters of the 1950s and 1960s) some are very clever parodies of current film posters – although, unlike their more modest predecessors, this type of club flyer of the late 20th century was produced to the same high standard as the original.

That such a range of imagery is produced to a high standard of design and presentation is a perfect demonstration of the visually literate culture that has developed since around 1960 – a culture that depends for its effect on a wide range of ephemera of all periods being readily available as a source of reference. Many of the designers of club flyers will have studied graphic design either at school, or on specialist art and design courses at college and university. [DC]

REFERENCES *Highflyers: clubravepartyart* (London: Booth-Clibborn Editions, 1995); Nicola Ackland-Snow and others, *Fly: the art of the club flyers* (London: Thames and Hudson, 1996)

Coach ticket

Payment for early coach journeys was recorded by entry in a WAYBILL, by issue of a ticket, or by both. Tickets ranged in format and size from a large part-printed form of contract, signed at the foot by both parties, to a minimal slip of printed pasteboard, unmarked, unnumbered, and uncontrolled.

Typical of the 'contract' form of ticket are German and Italian specimens of the early 1800s in which a dozen or so more or less lengthy clauses set out the terms and conditions of the agreement. Italian tickets were commonly filled in in duplicate, each party retaining a two-signature copy.

ROYAL EAGLE COACH,
FROM
THE CROWN HOTEL, EDINBURGH,
TO
THE TONTINE, GLASGOW,
Every lawful Day, at a Quarter before 4 o'Clock Afternoon.
The 24 day of May 1809
No Passengers, Inside.
No 2 Ditto, Outside.

Coach ticket, Edinburgh to Glasgow, 24 May 1809. Letterpress on paper. 68 × 114 mm (2⅝ × 4½ in)

An Italian example, dated 3 March 1839, relates to a six-day journey from Florence to Rome, the coach proprietor undertaking to provide on each day 'A good fork breakfast, a good bed, fire, nightlight' and all passage expenses such as river, bridge, and other tolls, as well as the actual transportation of the passenger. The coachman also undertook to set off early each morning so as to arrive before nightfall at the overnight destination. This officially produced document, 305 × 210 mm (12 × 8¼ in), attempts to bring order to an operation notoriously hazardous and unpredictable. Other surviving versions from different regions bear the same basic wording with even greater sobriety of presentation.

Post-coach journeys, in which the passengers' role is subject to the disciplines of the service, produce tickets no less wordy though clearly less considerate of the traveller. A typical 'personen-schein', 230 × 185 mm (9 × 7¼ in), for the Hamburg–Bremen run in 1819, carries a 1000-word exposition of conditions of carriage, finishing with a clause pre-empting any claim by the passenger to ignorance of the content.

Switzerland's post-coach tickets, distinctly less long-winded, and often embellished with decorative borders and pictorial motifs, make one concession to the realities of coach travel. Where an early morning start is indicated, a sticker advises that passengers may be awakened, if desired. An 1838 example reads: 'Pour être reveillé à temps, on peut se faire inscrire chez le concierge, à la chambre des voyageurs, maison des postes, au fond de l'allée à gauche' (To be wakened in time, one may notify the porter in the travellers' room at the post office, at the end of the passage on the left).

Early French post-coach tickets, also less elaborate, nevertheless bore three or four paragraphs of small print. In an 1815 example the final paragraph disclaims responsibility for events of *force majeure* and armed robbery. Both Swiss and French tickets are modest in size, commonly of the order of 160 × 120 mm (6¼ × 4¾ in).

In Britain and America passenger control relied largely on the use of the waybill, though small tickets of pasteboard and paper, some bearing the holder's name in handwriting, were widely used in America. Combined coach and railroad tickets were also issued.

Coachmen's instructions

The 'Card for coachman' or 'Instructions for coachmen' was a measure designed to minimize traffic dislocation by carriages at state occasions. The guest was provided with a card for the driver directing him how to approach the setting-down point, how to leave the area, and where to rank in readiness for being called after the function. A typical card, used at the visit of the German Emperor to the Guildhall, London, in 1891, bore the heading 'Instructions for coachmen', the designation and date of the event, and the direction: 'After setting-down drive round and rank at once on the North Side of Cheapside, as directed by the Police'. It was signed by Henry Smith, Commissioner of Police.

In a development of the idea, the card had a tear-off counterfoil to be retained by the guest. This, numbered to correspond with the coachman's portion, was handed after the event to the uniformed carriage caller, who called the number to summon the carriage to the taking-up point. The modern equivalent to the card is a large windscreen sticker bearing drivers' instructions on the reverse.

Coal-seller's ticket

In Britain, particularly in London, the giving of short measure in coal was a widespread nuisance in the early years of the 19th century. A number of enactments sought to put a stop to this, many of them epitomized in part-printed certificates to be used at the various stages of handling coal between the mine and the ultimate user. Among the most common of these was the 'seller's ticket', required by law to accompany delivery of coal to the consumer, and to be filled in by hand with the total weight, number of sacks, and quality of the delivery. The law (originally

MIDDLE WHARF, GREAT SCOTLAND YARD.
No. SELLER'S TICKET.
Mr Wilson
TAKE NOTICE, That you are to receive herewith,
3 *Tons of* Wallsend *Coals,*
Tons of *Coals,*
Tons of *Coals,*
in 30 *Sacks, containing 224 lb. of Coal in each Sack.*
THE Act of the Second William the Fourth, Chapter 76, directs, "That with any "quantity of Coals exceeding Five Hundred and Sixty Pounds, a Paper or Ticket "describing the quantity; and if any particular sort is ordered or contracted for, the "sort of the Coals sent by the Seller shall be delivered to the Purchaser, or his Agent "or Servant, before any part of such Coals shall be unloaded; that a Weighing "Machine shall be carried with every Waggon, Cart or other Carriage, and the "Carman is required to Weigh, gratuitously, any Sack or Sacks of Coals which shall "be chosen by the Purchaser, or his Agent or Servant; and if any Carman refuses "to Weigh such Sack or Sacks of Coals as aforesaid, or drives away the Waggon, "Cart, or other Carriage, before the Coals are Weighed, or otherwise obstructs the "Weighing thereof, he is liable to a penalty not exceeding Twenty Pounds."
Dated this 17 Day of July 1833
Seller.
Carman.
Shaw & Sons, Printers, 137, Fetter-lane, London.

Coal-seller's ticket, London, 17 July 1833. Letterpress, printed by Shaw & Sons, London, with manuscript. 100 × 120 mm (4 × 4¾ in)

1, 2 Wm IV, c. 76, but modified by 1, 2 Vict.) also required that 'a proper weighing machine or proper scales and weights shall be carried with every waggon or cart or other carriage, and the carman is required to weigh gratuitously any sack or sacks of coals which shall be chosen by the purchaser', and further, that the accuracy of such scales and weights might be tested against sets kept for the purpose at every watch-house or police station'.

The ticket carried, as well as the basic structure of the form, an extended exposition of the law in question, as required by that law. The coal-seller's ticket remained in use in some parts of Britain into the late 20th century.

Coin disc/sticker

In the latter part of the 19th century the enterprise of advertisers extended into every available field of visibility. Advertisers managed to get their messages on to postage stamp edging, and on to the backs of postage stamps. E. S. Turner (1965) reports that Thomas Barratt, the Pears Soap publicity man, offered to print all the forms for the 1891 Census if the government would allow the back of the form to carry a Pears' advertisement. The offer was declined. Barratt also explored the advertising potential of coins. He imported a quarter of a million 10-centime coins from France – the coins were at that time accepted tender in England – and stamped them with the word 'Pears'. He issued them at fourteen to the shilling, but the Government bought them up, henceforth banning foreign coins from circulation in Britain.

Prior to this, Edward Lloyd of *Lloyd's Weekly Newspaper* had actually used British coins for stamping, paying half the wages of his employees with them. This also was stopped, officially on the grounds that such stamping constituted defacement, a criminal offence under the Coinage Offences Act of 1861.

Advertisers' fascination with coins remained, however, and Mellin's Food Co. ventured to produce relief-stamped silver-foil cardboard discs, each bearing on the silver side Queen Victoria's head, as in a genuine half-crown, complete with the inscription 'Victoria Dei Gratia Britt' and the date 1897, with a printed advertisement on the back.

Silver embossed adhesive stickers also appeared. They were made of paper, gummed, and bore a relief impression of a half-crown with an added legend 'Best value for money'. They were for use with pennies, an advertising message appearing on a similar sticker on the other side.

REFERENCES Henry Sampson, *A History of Advertising* (London: Chatto and Windus, 1874); E. S. Turner, *The Shocking History of Advertising*, rev. edn (Harmondsworth: Penguin, 1965)

Colouring book/sheet

Children's drawing and painting books originated in Germany in the early years of the 19th century. They emerged as one of the by-products of Alois Senefelder's invention of lithography (c.1798), at first appearing as uncoloured images for copying, later showing twin images, one coloured by the manufacturer, the other for the child to colour. Among many examples is *Der Kleine Zeichner und Mahler* (The little drawer and painter) put out by Carl August Friese in Pirna (1811). The booklet measures 133 × 240 mm (5¼ × 9½ in), and shows coloured drawings of figures etc. to the left, uncoloured to the right.

The printer's colouring was at first carried out by hand (free-hand or with simple stencils), often by cottage labour; but the advent of colour printing brought cheaper and quicker production. By the middle of the 19th century most such work was wholly printed.

Germany's lead in the field was exploited in a lively export trade, and the German drawing and colouring book reached most parts of Europe. The matter was made easy by absence of text; all that was necessary was an 'own language' printed cover or wrapper for each market. The books needed neither editorial introduction nor instructions.

In the 1840s appeared the sheet of colouring pictures (*Tuschbogen* or *Ausmalbogen*), incorporating numerous pairs of pictures, coloured and plain. Prominent among publishers of these was the firm of Oehmigke & Riemschneider of Neuruppin, who produced a wide range of printing matter for children.

The colouring book had a rebirth in the popular publishing boom of the turn of the 19th and 20th centuries, appearing as part of the TOY BOOK scene all over the world. In the 1920s and 1930s it was available in the classic 'coloured/plain' mode or as uncoloured outlines for filling in to individual taste. The 1930s brought a novelty variant, a 'magic' colouring book, in which colours appeared merely by the application of plain water. With the advent of television it suffered a decline, but has not wholly disappeared.

REFERENCE Heiner Vogel, *Bilderbogen, Papiersoldat, Würfelspiel und Lebensrad* (Würzburg: Popp, 1981)

Comic

The term 'comic' refers normally to a printed publication in which a narrative is presented as a connected sequence of pictures, usually drawings. In modern times secondary characteristics are the succession of sequences in instalments, featuring the same basic 'cast'; the use of more or less generally accepted visual symbols (such as air-stream lines to indicate movement); and wide ranging onomatopoeia ('vroom', 'pow', etc.).

The term is used loosely to refer to the individual strip-series appearing as a regular feature in a publication, to the magazine or newspaper supplement devoted largely to such strips, and to the 'comic book', a substantial paperback in similar idiom. (It will be seen that the word 'comic', in this last connection at least, may be a misnomer, many such publications appearing as 'crime' or 'horror comics'.) The convention of the balloon, in which dialogue is presented within the picture, stems from satirists James Gillray and Thomas Rowlandson, and later 'HB' (John Doyle), all of whom used the device extensively.

Early forerunners of the strip presentation were the series of humorous books lithographed by Rodolphe Töpffer in Geneva in the 1830s and 1840s and the 'Max und Moritz' series produced by Wilhelm Busch in Germany in the mid 1880s. In Britain, in 1876, came 'Ally Sloper', by Charles Ross. In none of these cases did text appear as speech balloons.

The comic paper era began in the 1890s. *Comic Cuts* appeared in 1890 ('cuts' referred to the illustrations, still given the name they had formerly had as woodcuts, though by this time the drawings were reproduced by photoengraving). *Funny Cuts* and *Chips* also appeared in 1890.

In 1896 America's first comic colour Sunday Supplement appeared in the *World*, featuring 'The Yellow Kid' by R. F. Outcault and the 'Katzen Jammer Kids' by Rudolph Dirks. The Sunday 'funnies' were to become an American national institution. The first successful daily strip was 'Mutt and Jeff' (1907) in the *San Francisco Chronicle*.

Britain followed suit with 'Tiger Tim' (1904), which appeared in full colour in the children's supplement to the *World & His Wife*. The first newspaper comic strip in Britain was 'Teddy Tail', though 'Pip, Squeak and Wilfred' began a thirty-six-year run in the *Daily Mirror* in 1919. Afterwards came 'Pop' (*Daily Sketch*, 1921), 'Dot and Carrie' (*The Star*, 1923). 'Jane', who became a national figure in the years of World War II, began her inadequately clad career in the *Daily Mirror* in 1932 and continued in character until 10 October 1959.

The idiom of the 'Comic', the comic strip, and the comic book has worldwide currency: it is found throughout Europe, the Americas and the English-speaking world, and in Japan, China, and the Soviet Union.

The advent of the 'horror comic' in the 1950s led to much controversy, Dr Wertham's book *Seduction of the Innocent* precipitating the setting up of a 'Comics Code Authority' whose strictures radically affected the industry.

In the late 20th century the comic has attracted much attention as a subject for social-history research and graphic analysis. In addition to its value as an unconscious indicator of attitudes and aspirations, it has been used as an explicit medium of social commentary.

REFERENCES Pierre Couperic and Maurice Horn, *A History of the Comic Strip* (New York: Crown, 1968); Dennis Gifford, *The British Comic Catalogue 1874–1974* (London: Mansell, 1975); Dennis Gifford, *Victorian Comics* (Allen & Unwin, 1976); Maurice Horn, *The World Encyclopedia of Comics* (Philadelphia: Chelsea House, 1999); David Kunzle, *The History of the Comic Strip*, 2 vol. (Berkeley: University of California Press, 1973–90); Frederic Wertham, *Seduction of the Innocent* (New York: Rinehart, 1954; London: Museum Press, 1955)

COLLECTIONS. Museum of Cartoon Art (Artwork) Port Chester, New York; British Institute for Cartoon Research, University of Kent, Canterbury

SOCIETY Association of Comic Enthusiasts, London

Commonplace book

The word 'commonplace' (first emerging in the 16th century as a rendering of the rhetorician's *locus communis*) was used to refer to a statement of generally accepted principle, or a 'general theme or argument applicable to many particular cases' (OED). The word retained this meaning at an academic level, and the term 'commonplace book' was applied, and still applies, to an album of notable passages worthy of record and reference. The word 'commonplace' went on to be used in a context of platitude, even of triviality. The concept of the commonplace book, which had become recognized as a jotting book for literati, was downgraded to include personal jottings and memoranda, jokes, puzzles, household notes, and recipes. The process appears to have been accelerated by the family-circle use of the inherited commonplace book as a household notebook, blank pages being filled with less weighty matter.

As it turns out, the family commonplace book is generally of far greater interest than the orthodox variety, the less weighty matter affording insight beyond the scope of literary extracts.

A representative example, 110 × 100mm (4⅜ × 4in), has forty pages, eleven of which are blank, the rest bearing manuscript entries, chiefly in ink, in a number of hands. Entries appear in random date order covering the period 1791 to 1846 and relate to members of the Reynolds family, the Moore family, and the Foleys. The contents include records of births and deaths; household and other accounts; records of payment of window tax, highway, and land tax; preachers stationed [in the neighbourhood?]; a fortnight's itinerary, Eggbrough to Haddlesey; remedies ('cure for spasmodic cholera', 'for the itch', 'for a weak constitution', 'for lice on cattle'; recipes ('how to make green paint', 'to make diadem plast', 'varnish for hatt case'). Also included is 'a cure for hard times: cheat the doctor by being temperate: cheat the lawyers by keeping out of debt: and cheat the demagogue, of Whatever party, by voting for the honest man'.

Spanning over half a century, this small booklet conveys a fragmentary image of lives and times long gone. It is one of a great number of such records, many of which survive among miscellaneous family papers and local collections.

Compliments slip

The compliments slip represents the irreducible courtesy of social and commercial correspondence. It offers a viable all-purpose alternative to the inclusion of nothing at all, and serves as a civilized form of greeting of the order of 'Best wishes' or other nominal salutation.

The compliments slip may also serve as a vehicle for a brief message. In this guise it is often seen as a substitute for a longer letter – informal in tone without sacrifice of dignity. It normally bears the words 'With Compliments' and in its commercial form is viewed as a public relations necessity. The item has no fixed determining characteristics, and ranges in size from a visiting card to a whole sheet of writing paper. Colours are at the discretion of the sender, but generally restrained effects are preferred.

Its origins lie in the earlier courtesy card left by a visitor. Around the turn of the 19th century it became both socially and commercially one of the mainstays of social courtesy as – in its modern form as a paper correspondence enclosure – it remains.

Compound-plate printing [plate 8]

The term 'compound-plate printing' refers to an anti-counterfeit printing system devised by Sir William Congreve and patented by him in 1820. Its chief virtue as a defence against forgery lay in its ability to print two separate colours in accurate register with each other – a feat which at the time taxed the skill of the professional printer, and which was in turn far beyond the capacity of the back-room amateur.

In Congreve's method the two-colour image was conveyed to paper by a single movement of an interlocking metal plate, selected parts of which were inked in one colour and other parts in another. Unlike the conventional processes of the time, in which each colour was applied in a separate working (with high risk of the second colour being misaligned), the compound plate printed two colours in a single working, each colour mechanically locked in register with the other.

The compound plate has two components. The main component has a printing surface pierced with cut-out apertures. The secondary component, backing the main plate, carries raised portions corresponding to the cut-outs. When the two components are brought together the combined unit presents a virtually unbroken printing surface. If this 'compound' plate is now engraved with an overall design, ignoring the changes of metal in the surface, it becomes possible to separate the two components, inking them in different colours and reassembling them as a single unit for a one-stroke colour impression. Effectively, the compound-plate printing process alternately separates and reassembles the printing plate, inking each portion in its own colour in the interval of separation, and restoring the two components to precise alignment for printing.

Perfect two-colour register was not the only anti-counterfeit aspect of the process. It was also virtually impossible for the counterfeit engraver to achieve on separate plates the flow of fine-line detail shown on the apparently continuous surface of the compound plate. It was additionally very unlikely, in the state of the art at the time, that the forger would have access to the techniques of compound-plate production.

Congreve, and later James Whiting and Robert Branston, who acquired the patent rights, made great efforts to promote the process for security printing, taking every opportunity to demonstrate its uncounterfeitability and urging its use in the production of tax and postage stamps and similar items. Typical of these extensions were Whiting's submissions to the authorities in connection with postal prepayment devices. His proposals, many of them embodied in printed specimens, totalled over one hundred. None was accepted.

The Congreve process (later to be identified in Britain exclusively with the firm of Whiting and Branston) did make some headway in the security field. It was used to print tax stamps on country banknotes, paper-duty labels, and (curiously, until the year 1920) medicine-tax labels.

An eccentric example of its use in the 'security' field is a 'Licence for a Hawker to Trade on Foot', dated 1863/4, printed in orange, green, and violet on lilac paper and bearing a blind-embossed tax stamp for £1. This item, measuring 400 × 270 mm (15¾ × 10⅝ in), presents an appearance approaching ostentation; unsuitable as it clearly was for its avowed purpose, it was equally clearly an excellent example of the work of 'Whiting, London', whose credit line it contained within its elaborate border. It can only be assumed that the extravagant item (though duly issued to Thos Palmer in Hemel Hempstead on 1 August 1863) was in fact a contrived Whiting promotion-piece – possibly designed and printed for the stamp office at nominal charge – and used as a specimen of his process.

The process received application in several marginal fields, in all of which the company sought to demonstrate its association with ideas of probity and authenticity. A notable success was its use in the elaborate invitation-tickets to the coronation of George IV (19 July 1821). These combined the technology of Whiting's printing and Dobbs's embossing, and were magnificent examples of decorative uncounterfeitability, which placed the process squarely on the side of the establishment.

Less portentously, and more noticeably, the lottery industry adopted the process for its better-quality promotional material, and the distinctive design element of the method became familiar to a wide public. Here again, it was identified (however mistakenly) with reliability.

Another major application was in the authentication of proprietary product labels. In the context of widespread pirating of successful products, leading manufacturers sought to protect their markets with anti-forgery devices. Chief among these was the maker's signature (forging of which was a serious criminal offence), but a number of firms adopted the compound-plate printed label as an additional protection. Before long the familiar Whiting design treatment appeared in a wide range of product labels. A typical selection of these labels appears in a Whiting & Branston specimen album now housed in the St Bride Printing Library, London. They include items for Eley's Patent Cartridges, Goodbarne's Purified Epsom Salts; Low's Highly Perfumed Brown Windsor Soap; Price and Gosnell's 'Union' Hairbrush; Robert Hendrie's 'Cocoa Shaving Cake' and 'Cowslip Pomatum'; and a variety of blackings, including those of Clayton & Co.; Jolly, Brown & Co.; Robert Warren; Darkers; Larnders & Co.; H. C. Handson; Salvert & Co.; Joseph Turner; and Richard Turner.

The 'compound-plate printing style', with its panels, lozenges, and arbitrary colour changes (and often with the additional ingredient of machine-turned decorative borders) became firmly established as a graphic design idiom. The treatment was imitated and echoed by printers using conventional methods, and long after technology had solved the problem of two-colour registration the 'compound-plate printing look' survived as an indicator of authenticity.

Compound-plate printing itself, promoted by its pioneers as a method 'for the prevention of forgery', was destined to play a less exalted role. The last of the Congreve presses, printing medicine-tax labels in a basement in Somerset House, ceased working in 1920 when that tax was abolished.

See LOTTERY PAPERS; REAM WRAPPER/LABEL

REFERENCES Maureen Greenland and Russell E. Day, *Compound-plate Printing* (The Foundation for Ephemera Studies, 1991); Maureen Greenland, 'Compound-plate printing – security with style', *Printing Historical Society Bulletin*, 43, Summer 1997, pp. 6–10; Elizabeth M. Harris, *Sir William Congreve and his Compound-plate Printing* (Washington: Smithsonian Institution Press, 1967); Elizabeth M. Harris, 'Experimental Graphic Processes in England 1800–1859' [part 1], *Journal of the Printing Historical Society*, no.4, 1968, pp. 34–86

COLLECTIONS St Bride Printing Library, London; John Johnson Collection, Bodleian Library, Oxford

Compulsive note

The term is applied to handwritten jottings and messages produced under pressure of emotion or circumstance, often without much hope of their being read, except perhaps by a stranger in the remote future. The category includes: the 'message-in-a-bottle' (a last despairing attempt to attract attention); certain kinds of suicide note; effusions from solitude; simple declarations of existence ('J. Smith was here'); and 'time-capsule' messages, secreted somewhere as a greeting to persons perhaps yet unborn.

The compulsion factor varies both in character and intensity, but a common element is the need to make a mark in life, even if only in secret. Typical secretions were found behind panelling during reconstruction work at Shrewsbury School in the late 1970s and early 1980s. They were published in the *Salopian Newsletter* in November 1982:

> This is to certify that Shrewsbury Royal Free Grammar school was on the 21st Day of May 1845 turned into a private School. The School Gates being locked & otherwise blocked to prevent us from going to the Races. Thank Heavens I leave this prison in three wks to my great joy.
> Richd H. Bourne, Top Sch: May 21. 1845 A.D.
>
> I William Gordon Patchett came to these Schools Midsummer 1861 as a day-boy and came as a boarder Midsummer 1863. I was in the Vth form when I came and am now in the Upper VIth. [Over which note has been written in a rough hand 'William Gordon Patchett is a shitt and a fool'.]
>
> C. J. Thomas came to Shrewsbury School April 11th 1861. Whoever finds this please put it back with the name of that person on it and the date. [There are added thirteen names, the latest being written in 1871.]
>
> J.C. Kay came to Shrewsbury School August 6th 1885 and

left July 31st 1867 5th Form (written day after Regatta day July 25th 1867).

Similar documents may be found as separate leaves among family papers, sometimes torn from copybooks or notepads. One such, dated 1 January 1893, appears as a single paragraph on a sheet from a school exercise book. Though dated, it is not a diary entry. It seeks only to serve as witness to a particular experience:

A bitterly cold day, frost very keen. Could not go out being right poorly, had to have the hot bag to my side all day, have not been able to go out during week owing to the absess in my back, it has been very troublesum for some time, and set in in earnist on Christmas day, and broke on the Thursday in Xmas week.

Also moved to pen and ink were Agnes and Joan Thompson, who in the exceptionally sunny winter of 1759 expressed their amazement on the flyleaf of a family bible:

Memerandum Jan ye 31:1759 our Garden was Licke a wood for flowers & ye Bees all out ye Same as in ye midel of sumer & ye Hagess all put out Green & ye Butter flies Flieing all round all this i Saw with my Own eys Witness my hand Agnes Thompson/Joan Thompson.

It may be argued that the motivation behind such messages resembles that of the buried 'time-capsule', in which the essence of today is conveyed as a *cri de cœur* or as a gift package to unknown friends in time to come.

REFERENCE Brian Durrans, *The Dialectics of the Time Capsule* (Conference Paper) (Edinburgh: 1990)

Copy-book

The noun 'copy' is ambiguous. As generally understood it refers to an imitation or reproduction of an original. In some usage however, notably in journalism, printing, and publishing, it refers to an *original,* a text, model, or pattern to be followed.

The term copy-book does not necessarily refer, as is often assumed, to a book in which imitations of given models are written by hand. The models themselves are described as copies. Thus, for example, a copy-book published in Philadelphia in c.1810, having no room in its pages for more than its printed texts, is entitled *An Alphabetical Set of Running Hand Copies.* A hundred years later William Collins's copy-book series, published in London, does provide room for handwritten addenda – and is nevertheless subtitled *The New Graphic Writing Copies.*

It is clear that the earliest copy-books were simply intended to provide styles and examples for the student to emulate. Many were produced by writing masters, among them the Italians Arrighi (1522), Tagliente (1524), Palatino (1540), and Cresci (1560), some of which ran to many editions. In England the great practitioners emerged in the 1600s. Martin Billingsley's *The Pen's Excellencie* appeared in 1618, and John Ayers published his *Tutor to Penmanship* in 1698. The same period saw the works of Pierre Hamon (1561) in Paris and Lucas (1608) in Madrid.

By the turn of the 16th century, when Shakespeare came to write in *Love's Labour's Lost* ('Faire as a text B in a Coppie Booke'), it may be assumed that the concept of the copy-book was universally understood, not as a book to write in but as an exemplar. John Brinsley's advice in his *Ludus Literanius* (1612) underlines the distinction: 'instead of setting of copies ... let everyone have a little copie booke fastened to the top of his writing booke'. In America in the 1890s the same sense of distinction appears: 'John J Marshall offers a combined copy-book and writing book under the title *Public School Writing-Book ... With an engraved copy for each page of the book, ruled with horizontal and perpendicular lines*'. The distinction is expressed as late as the turn of the century, when in Britain the Vere Foster copy-books carry the sub-title *Vere Foster's Writing Copy-Books.*

The 'writing copy-book' of more recent times represents a phase in a process of development in handwriting instruction. Unlike its forebears, the writing masters' and penmen's instructions, the copy-book of the 19th and 20th centuries emerged as an aid to the newly educated. Where Arrighi and Billingsley had addressed the leisured and the literate, the new penmanship was aimed at the elementary school and the aspiring employee.

The process of popularization may be said to have started in America in the early part of the century. In Philadelphia in 1815 Laning's *New-Invented Copy-Book* appeared, offering 'an easy guide to the art of writing by dotted full guides, half guides, and blank lines for exercise'. Around 1825, also in Philadelphia, appeared Alcock & Rand's *Patent Cupreo-Graphic Copy-Book* with thirty-two pages of ruled writing paper, each page headed by a copy in outline. There followed at irregular intervals a succession of such books. In 1826 appeared Chauncey Bascom's *A System of Penmanship* (Brattleboro) designed for the use of schools, with sixteen pages ruled and 'general directions interspersed among the copies'. The 1830s brought a more specific recognition of the student's role in learning. The expression 'writing book' began to appear, replacing or preceding the title 'Copy Book' or 'Copies'. A typical example is James French's series of six numbers entitled *Boston School Writing-Book, for the use of private and public schools... With copies to assist the teacher and aid the learner* (Boston, c.1840–42).

Among the earliest of Britain's elementary copy-books (spelt with or without hyphen, at choice) was a series put out in the 1860s by Griffith and Farran of St Paul's Churchyard. These were entitled *Danvan's Sure Guide to a Good Handwriting... A series of Twenty-Four copy books.* The first ten in the set bore feint-printed 'copies' to be over-written and blank interleaves for imitations. The format, 170 × 210mm (6¾ × 8¼in), had become more or less standardized and was to remain so until the copy-book virtually went out of use in the mid 1960s.

In 1865 appeared the first of Vere Foster's very successful copy-books. They also conformed to the standard format, and were at first printed by Marcus Ward & Co. in Dublin (after 1877 by Blackie and Son in Glasgow). They sold in millions throughout the English-speaking world and were still being published over a hundred years after their first appearance. A major feature of the Foster series was the provision of prizes in handwriting competitions. Expenditure on these is said to have helped to impoverish Foster, an enthusiastic advocate of education for the underprivileged. His zeal for his mission outstripped his pocket and he died in 1900 a poor man.

The heyday of the copy book brought others into the field. Among the many competing series at the turn of the century were Johnson's 'Eclectic'; Collins's; Darnell's; Gill's; Isbister's 'New'; Jackson's 'New Style'; Longman's 'Modern'; Nelson's; Jarrold's 'Empire'; Bemrose's; Chamber's 'New'; Cassell's; Moffat's; Townley's: most of these offering some two dozen specialities. The Vere Foster range alone covered specialities from 'Initiatory' to 'Shakespeare Quotations', from 'Plain and Ornamental' to 'Civil Service or Official' Style.

See also DRAWING BOOK

REFERENCES Ambrose Heal, *The English Writing Masters and their Copy-Books 1570–1800* (Cambridge: Cambridge University Press, 1931); Donald Mackenzie, 'Vere Foster's Copy Book', *Scottish Educational Journal* (11 May 1973); Ray Nash, *American Penmanship, 1800–1850* (Worcester: American Antiquarian Society, 1969); Tamara P. Thornton, *Handwriting in America: a Cultural History* (New Haven and London: Yale University Press, 1996)

COLLECTIONS American Antiquarian Society, Worcester, Mass.; British Library, London; Newberry Library, Chicago; Victoria & Albert Museum, London

Corner card *See* CAMEO CARD

Cotton bag

The cotton bag was widely used in the flour industry from the 1850s. In America it was superseded by the PAPER BAG during the Civil War as a result of a cotton shortage. It remained however in fairly general use elsewhere until the 1940s and early 1950s, and in Britain 7-pound flour bags were said to have been popular with country housewives who washed them out after use for service as kitchen cloths.

Bags ranged in capacity from 3 pounds to 70 pounds, the largest being used for farmhouse supplies and trade deliveries to bakers. They were printed, commonly in two colours on one side, from flexible rubber plates.

Cotton bags, stitched on one side and at the bottom, presented closure problems. Machine sewing, introduced at the beginning of the 20th century but never wholly satisfactory, was used on smaller sizes. Large sizes (including 7-pound bags) were stitched by hand. A perennial hazard was needle breakage, which meant that the contents of the bag had to be reprocessed to make sure that no portion of the broken needle was present.

The cotton bag remained in use for horticultural supplies, birdseed, dog biscuits, etc., in the 1950s and early 1960s, after which it was generally superseded by the plastic or combined paper/plastic pack. In America, the printed cotton bag was widely used by tobacco companies in the marketing of plug cut and loose mixtures. The bags, measuring some 100 × 60 mm (4 × 2⅜ in) to 120 × 90 mm (4¾ × 3½ in), were commonly rounded at the base and provided with a draw-string closure. Because of the risk of fraudulent reuse, the bags bore a warning: 'Every person is cautioned, under the penalties of law, not to use this package for tobacco again'.

Draw-string bags have also been widely used, both in Britain and America, for coin. Cotton bags are also found in limited use for such small items as uniform buttons, precision spare parts, etc.

Cover, postal

The term 'cover' is used by philatelists to denote the outer wrapper or container in which correspondence is posted, normally an envelope. Less accurately, the word may also be used to apply to the exterior of a single folded sheet, addressed for posting as a letter, though this is more correctly called an 'entire'. In general use the term refers to postally used items, but it may also include material such as an unused MULREADY ENVELOPE and unused pictorial and propaganda envelopes. Principal categories are as follows:

Air mail. Air delivery of messages is recorded in the 5th century BC at the siege of Potidaea, when tiny written scrolls were attached to besiegers' arrows and fired over the lines to agents within the city. Kites have also been used to fly messages, as have pigeons and balloons.

The first authentic record of an air-mail cover, specifically inscribed and used for the purpose, is a single surviving specimen from the flight of the American balloon Jupiter on 17 August 1859. Bearing the hand inscription 'via Balloon Jupiter', this was delivered by ordinary mail by the balloonist John Wise after an ascent from Lafayette, Indiana, and a nominal flight lasting several hours. James Mackay (1971) records that Wise thought it best not to state the destination of the balloon, offering simply a service 'to the place of landing' when mail would be placed in the nearest post office. Letters were accepted by the local postmaster and marked 'Prepaid' before being bagged for the flight. They were posted by Wise at Crawfordsville, some thirty miles from their starting place.

At the Siege of Metz by the German army in 1870 the defenders flew messages out of the city in unmanned balloons. The messages were written on flimsy slips of paper – *papillons* (French: butterflies) – and were designed to be mailed to specific addresses by the finder. Many thousands were despatched, but the only surviving example complete with its envelope is in the British Museum. Its cover bears the inscription 'Depèche expediée en ballon'.

The first air-mail covers used in quantity appeared at the Siege of Paris in 1870–71. They were privately produced and printed on tinted paper (green, blue, lilac, azure, and rose) bearing patriotic slogans in French and German, the arms of the Republic, and the legend 'Par ballon monté'. Though it is reported that 2 or 3 million letters left Paris by this means, relatively few have survived.

Air-mail covers (and postcards) appeared as souvenirs of a number of balloon, airship, and heavier-than-air flights in the period 1870 to 1910, but the world's first official air-mail flight was not until 1911, when on 18 February some 6500 letters and postcards were flown from the exhibition grounds at Allahabad, India, to Naini Railway Junction, five miles distant. The mail bore a 'First Aerial Post' postmark.

Early air-mail operations are recorded in covers from between London (Hendon) and Windsor (Post Office/Graham White Aviation Co., September 1911), between Swakopmund and Windhoek (German South West Africa, May 1914), and by Italian military aircraft between Brindisi, Italy, and Valona [Vlorë], Albania (May–June 1917). The first regular international air-mail service was inaugurated in Austria (March 1918), serving towns in Poland, Russia, and later Budapest. The first regular civil air-mail was started in Britain between Hounslow and Paris (November 1919). First transatlantic covers were salvaged from wreckage after Harry Hawker and Lieut. Cdr. Mackenzie-Grieve were forced to ditch on an unsuccessful flight in 1919. This was followed in June of the same year by the successful flight of John Alcock and Lieut. Arthur Whitten-Brown, who also carried mail.

The 'air letter', a lightweight printed correspondence form, originated in Siam [Thailand] in August 1932. This was devised by R. B. Jackson for use by Air Orient between Europe and the Far East. The form bore the title 'Air O Gram' and carried adhesive postage stamps as required. It was first used early in 1933. The idea was soon after adopted (on the initiative of another Englishman, Douglas W. Gumbley) by the Iraqi postal authorities and was subsequently taken up by Palestine (then under British mandate), and by the British authorities in World War II. The air letter was used for service personnel overseas and prisoner-of-war mail, and was later extended to civilian use. Though challenged by e-mail, it is in virtually universal use. It is known in most countries as an 'aerogramme' (and was thus styled at the thirteenth Universal Postal Union Congress, 1951–52), but Britain commonly retains the term 'air letter'.

The 'airgraph', introduced in 1941 as a wartime communications expedient, allowed the correspondent to write on a printed form which was mass microcopied, 100-feet lengths of negative being flown for printing at the receiving end. They were delivered by ordinary mail in window envelopes bearing the title 'Airgraph', the reproduced image of the sender's writing appearing in the address panel. The process, proposed to the Post Office by the Kodak company in 1932, and at that time rejected, transmitted some 350 million messages in four years of service in World War II.

Pigeon post services, which originated in Ceylon [Sri Lanka] in the 1850s for news transmission by the Ceylon Observer, had formal origins in New Zealand in 1897 when regular flights were begun between the Great Barrier Island and Okupu. Special stamps were printed bearing the words 'Great Barrier Island special post' (later overprinted 'Pigeongram'), and a further service between Auckland and Marotiri in 1899 used the same stamps overprinted 'Marotiri Island Pigeongram'. Examples of the message flimsies are rare, as are the covers in which they were delivered to recipients.

Among other air-mail covers are early glider, helicopter, and autogyro dispatches. Glider covers (commemorating club meetings) appeared in Austria, Germany, and Britain in 1923; covers for delivery by autogyro appeared in Britain in 1934, and by helicopter in America in 1946.

Catapult and rocket mails are also recorded in special covers. The French catapult mail of 1928 (and that of the Germans in the following year) was used to speed mails carried by transatlantic liners. Seaplanes were catapulted from their decks with mail when the ships were within a day's sailing of their destination. 'Catapult mail' covers survive from trips of the *Île de France*, the *Bremen*, and the *Europa*. Mail was also on occasion flown from land to the *Bremen*, the *Europa*, and the *Columbus* on their outward journeys. Rocket mail covers appeared in the early 1930s, when experimental firings were made in various places by the Austrian Friedrich Schmiedl, the Germans Reinhold Tiling and Gerhard Zucker, and in India in the 1930s and 1840s by the Englishman Dr Stephen Smith. Covers surviving from Zucker's firing in the Outer Hebrides are charred by the explosion that occurred on take-off.

The airship made a great impact on the public imagination in the 1920s and 1930s, generating a prodigious quantity of souvenir material and many thousands of flown covers. The British R-34, completed soon after World War I, was the first to cross the Atlantic, flying from East Fortune, Scotland, to Mineola, New York in five days in July 1919, and carrying just fourteen letters endorsed 'Per HMAS R-34'. The letters were dropped in a packet at Selman, Nova Scotia, where they remained undiscovered until 8 November 1919. A single letter is known to have been carried through to the airship's destination; it bore the cachet 'HMAS R-34 East Fortune/New York July 1919'.

Mail was flown on a large number of airship flights in the following years, and covers survive from Italy's F6 (1921), Germany's LZ-126 (1924), America's *Shenandoah* and *Los Angeles* (1925), and Italy's *Norge* and *Italia* (1926 and 1928). In 1928 Germany's *Graf Zeppelin* was completed and began a series of flights, including 144 ocean crossings, which by the time of her retirement in 1937 was to total 590, carrying in all some 235,300 pounds of mail. Zeppelin mail inspired special postage stamps, not only from Germany itself but from a number of countries visited on world tours. Zeppelin stamps were issued by Brazil, Cyrenaica [Libya], Egypt, Hungary, Iceland, Italy, Liechtenstein, Paraguay, Russia, and Tripolitania. The *Hindenburg*, commissioned in 1936, carried out ten scheduled Atlantic crossings before its disastrous touch-down on 6 May 1937. In the conflagration, which killed thirty-six people, the airship was completely destroyed. No mail from the trip survived.

Postal cover carried by the 'Hindenburg' on its first transatlantic flight from Friedrichshafen (Germany) to Lakehurst (New York State, America) on 6 May 1936, with air-mail and registered etiquette labels and two (superimposed) air-mail cachets. 114 × 162 mm ($4\frac{1}{2} \times 6\frac{3}{8}$ in)

Address, pre-street-numbering. Prior to the introduction of street numbering (*see* DIRECTORIES), which took place in Europe and America on a gradual basis during the latter part of the 18th century, postal addresses were informal, letters being inscribed with directions more or less elaborate as the case required. Inscriptions ranged from a minimal mention of name and town to a three- or four-line instruction.

Some of the more colourful of the longer inscriptions are recorded as minor collector's items. A listing published in *Notes and Queries* (5th series, 30 May 1874) quotes examples from 1714; William Hone's *Every-Day Book* (1827) has an example from the *Bolton Express*, reportedly put in at the post office in Manchester: 'For Mr Colwell that Keeps the Shop in Back Anderson-st to Bee Gave to Jack Timlen that Keeps the pigs in his own Sellar in Back Anderson-st the Irish man that has the Large family that B[rin]gs the mail from Mr Colwell and milk to Bolton'.

Descripive addresses ('over against the west end of the new exchange') continued to appear on many a TRADE CARD and BILLHEAD, in some cases after the advent of street numbering, the number being added by the engraver to an existing printing plate. Billheads may thus be found with identification expressed in multiple terms. A London grocer, John Vetch, appears in the 1770s as 'at the Three Sugar Loaves, the fourth door from the Minories, No 85' – the number plainly an addendum below the descriptive legend.

First-day. The term refers to an item postally used on the day of issue of the stamp it bears. Earliest examples of first-day covers are those posted on 6 May 1840, the day on which Britain's Penny Black postage stamp first appears. Though exceedingly rare, a number of these covers have survived. In the 1980s a specimen changed hands at £6000. The Penny Black first-day cover was in part pre-empted by an unofficial posting on 5 May 1840, but this unique specimen is not normally regarded as a legitimate contender for the title. There was considerable demand for the Penny Black at the time of issue, but those who acquired specimens generally soaked them off, discarding the letter together with the evidence of its date mark. It was only later that the stamp and cover were seen as a whole, and not until the end of the 19th century that the expression 'first-day cover' (FDC) began to be used.

The growth of interest in philately led to an increase in the production of special-issue stamps (mostly celebratory and commemorative) in addition to the standard 'definitive' sets in everyday use. The postage stamp began to be seen by issuing authorities as a source of revenue (because collectors put the stamps straight into albums, free of the commitment to carry mail).

The printed first-day cover, produced commercially to carry new issues for postal use, and bearing reference to a specific occasion, began to appear widely in the 1920s and 1930s. America led the way in 1909 with decorative covers for the issue of the 2-cent Hudson Fulton stamp, and in Britain the issue for the British Empire Exhibition also inspired a special cover. The 1930s saw growing popularity of the idea. In Britain, envelope designs of some distinction appeared for such occasions as the Silver Jubilee (1935) and the Coronation of King George VI (1937).

Proliferation of new issues from the 1950s to 1970s, particularly among countries with ailing economies, brought about a minor philatelic industry – the first-day cover business. Acting for the countries concerned, agents in Britain and elsewhere generated new issues, printing not only the relevant first-day covers and other promotional material but the stamps themselves. Many millions of such stamps reached the philatelist without even being within the borders of the country of issue.

First-flight. The first-flight cover records – by special label, cachet, or other mark – an inaugural flight between specified points. The category may be seen as a sub category of the first-day cover, but it is widely collected and studied as a speciality in its own right.

In a purist view the term 'first-flight' is taken to refer only to the first in a series of flights envisaged as becoming a regular public service, but in earlier years almost any first-time flight carrying a mailbag – or even a single letter – might have merited a first-flight cover, (*see above* **Air mail**; **First-day**). First-flight covers thus feature not only, for example, the inauguration of the London–Karachi Service (30 March 1923), but experimental balloon forays in the 19th century and the many aviation mailings and rallies of the early decades of the 20th century.

Some first-flight covers reflect the uncertainties of the technology of the period. One such example, a souvenir cover postmarked 'Newfoundland' 30 April 1919, and intended for the London office of the *Daily Express*, was twice frustrated by adverse conditions, eventually crossing the Atlantic by ship.

Among more recent first-flight covers are items carried to the moon. On 20 July 1969 Apollo 11 astronauts Armstrong and Aldrin cancelled a postal cover on the way back to earth, and on 2 August 1971 David Scott, leader of the Apollo 15 team, cancelled a cover while actually on the moon.

Maritime. In the early years of international mail it was the custom to entrust letters to the personal care of individuals (often sea captains), who for a consideration would post them formally at the port of arrival. Postage charges for the land journey were paid by the recipient. Letters thus handled commonly bore the inscription 'Ship' and sometimes the name of the ship concerned. It later became the practice to indicate the point of entry with a handstamp, together with the legend 'Ship', 'Ship Letter', or 'Loose Ship Letter', and – with the development of separate handling arrangements for mail to Britain from India – the inscription 'India Ship Letter'. Later, the date of arrival at the port of entry was included in the inscription.

With the coming of the adhesive postage stamp, ship-letter marks appear as cancellations. Thus covers may be found, for example, with Southampton Ship Letter cancellations on stamped covers from Spain and Africa; Liverpool marks on mail from America and Canada; and Edinburgh and Aberdeen marks on mail from Scandinavia and Iceland. At the turn of the 19th and 20th centuries international regulations were drawn up by the Universal Postal Union and a distinction was made between ordinary mail conveyed by ship and letters actually posted on board. The term 'Paquebot' was adopted to denote such mail. The word appears as a cachet or as a cancellation marking, sometimes with the words 'Posted at sea'.

Among the more bizarre examples of maritime covers are those from St Kilda in the period 1885 to 1930. From 1906 the islanders regularly floated mail to the mainland, the Post Office paying *2s 6d* to finders and forwarding letters to addressees. A similar service was used in the famous Tin Can Mail at Tonga (Pacific Ocean) instituted by Stuart Ramsay in 1921 and continued by Walter Quensell in the 1930s. Mail bearing special cachets and markings was floated out for pick-up by passing liners.

In a unique maritime example, on his round-the-world trip in 1967, Sir Francis Chichester carried fifty letters, each bearing the cachet 'Posted at sea' and postmarked to indicate a complete round voyage.

Military. Among the earliest surviving examples of British military covers are those of the Low Countries Campaign of 1743, in which soldiers' mail was for the first time treated as a special class. These covers bore the letters 'AB' (Army Bag) in a circle. The Netherlands Campaign of 1799 was the first occasion on which the British Post Office, as such, supervised collection and delivery of letters of service men in action. This mail was marked with a crown and the words 'Army Bag'. Letters also survive from the Peninsular War in which soldiers' mail reached England through Portugal, each letter being marked with the stamp of the British Post Office in Lisbon.

The first formally recognized prisoner-of-war letters appeared in the Napoleonic wars, when mail from French prisoners of war in England was stamped at the Transport Office at Chatham. Mail from Napoleon's armies had postmarks bearing such legends as 'Armée du Rhin' and 'Armée d'Espagne'.

In Britain's early 19th-century campaigns, army mail bore names of locations: 'P O Meywar F Force', 'Saugor Field Force P O', 'Central India Field Force', etc. Later, for reasons of security, army markings were less specific: 'Field Post Office', 'British Army South Africa', etc. Mail from warships also carried non-committal markings: 'From H M Ships/No charge to be raised', 'Post Office Maritime Mail'; and 'dumb' cancellations are often found in which locations or names are replaced by crosses, or cancellation is merely by inked cork or other improvised obliteration. Some military Post Office date stamps incorporate identifying code numbers, but these – again for security reasons – are frequently changed.

In the Crimean War, soldiers' mail was handled either locally through post offices in Balaklava, Constantinople [Istanbul], Varna, and other places through the Foreign Branch Office in London. Mail posted in the Crimea bore special cancellations (among them the well-known 'OXO' mark, a star between two zeros); letters distributed through London bore numerical cancellations from forty-five to forty-nine.

Boer War covers bear a variety of indications. A base Army Post Office at Cape Town handled most of the soldiers' mail and field post office units accompanied troops in action. Letters bear dated and numbered cancellations with 'Field Post Office: British Army South Africa' or 'Army Post Office South Africa', or (in some instances) named the office: 'Army Post Office: Elandsfontein'.

'Soldiers' and seamen's envelopes', issued for use by British troops in India in 1879, were the precursors of the 'Active Service envelope' and the 'Field Service Postcard', of which many millions were posted by serving soldiers in World War I. The postcard was adopted by most of the belligerents, a series of printed statements allowing the sender to strike out wording as desired: for example, 'I am quite well/I have been admitted into hospital', etc.

Prisoner-of-war mail, transmitted through the International Red Cross, forms another major category of military mail, each item bearing printed evidence of its function, together with markings showing freedom from postage charge but, in most cases, bearing censorship stamps.

Returned-to-sender letters convey their own story in cachet and handwritten annotation: 'Undelivered for reason stated' and 'It is regretted that this could not be delivered because the addressee is reported ...'. In one version the cachet bore the legend 'Certified missing prisoner of war or deceased', a Post Office obliteration mark being used to strike out whichever did not apply.

Private mail. The history of the early mails is effectively a history of competition between the state and private enterprise. From earliest times the monarch had retained control and supervision of communications, while private interests had sought to break the monopoly. Private posts arose at first not as communication undertakings but as services set up by organizations for their own use. Typical operators were monasteries, universities, and other academic institutions, for whom literacy was commonplace and communication essential. Later, as literacy and intercourse spread to the merchant classes, these too began to make their own postal arrangements.

Nevertheless, government control of the mails has in most periods been zealously guarded. Private postal services have been prohibited absolutely, tolerated under special conditions, or specifically licenced under contract to the state. In Britain the principle of state control is epitomized in a proclamation of Queen Elizabeth I of 1591, forbidding private transmission of letters to and from 'Countries beyond the seas', and by an Act of James I extending the prohibition to inland letters as well. State access to the mails as a means of counter-conspiracy is spelt out clearly in Oliver Cromwell's Post Office Act (1657). A government postal service, it declares, allows discovery and prevention of 'Dangerous and wicked designs... daily contrived against the peace and welfare of this commonwealth, intelligence whereof cannot well be communicated but by letter or escript'. As postal services developed, an additional motive for control appeared: the carrying of mails began to be seen as a source of revenue. On both counts – censorship and revenue – the state saw a centralized Post Office as an instrument of government and private mails as a threat.

Private mails fall in the main into two categories. On one hand are the services provided by private bodies for their own exclusive use (a mode in which the state service itself had begun) and, on the other, services run by private interest wholly or mainly for public use. Many such services were known to operate only on condition that they accepted private mails as well as their own. The 12th-century Metzger Post, possibly the first formally recognized private post, was organized by the Guild of Butchers in Germany for its own communications; it was required of each member that as he rode from place to place he be ready to carry mail as well.

Among the earliest surviving private post covers are those of the 'Thurn und Taxis' service, a postal enterprise run by members of the same family in western Europe from the middle of the 15th century until 1867. (The name is a Germanized version of 'Della Torre e Tassi', the names of the two Italian families who started the service, at first as an imperial mail only, later extending it to public use.) The covers are distinguished by 'Thurn und Taxis' adhesive postage stamps and concentric-ring cancellations.

In 1680 a private postal system was introduced by William Dockwra, who saw the need for a postal service within London. At the time, letters could be posted from Charing Cross to Edinburgh but not from Charing Cross to Hampstead. Dockwra set up no fewer than 450 receiving offices and 7 sorting offices, offering delivery to any London address within four hours. The service – an infringement of the Post Office monopoly – was suppressed after two years. His covers are scarce.

A private postal service appeared in Italy in the 1790s. This was known by the initials 'CFC' (*Compagnia fra Corrieri*). Letters carried by the service bore an oval handstamp with the letters 'CFC' and a coded indication of the office of origin.

In America in the early years of the 19th century private posts emerged as cheaper alternatives to the Government mail service. They sometimes evolved from the carriage of letters 'out of the mails' (as private commissions undertaken illicitly by Post Office mail-men), often as openly operating companies challenging the Government's monopoly rights. By 1844 more than forty private companies were operating in Boston alone. The period brought a plethora of prepayment handstamps and later adhesive stamps. (The first adhesive stamp to appear in the United States was issued by the City Despatch Post, a New York private mail company, 1 February 1842.)

The early 1860s saw a renewal of private mail operations, chiefly in postal services to the settlers of the raw West. The carriage of letters, gold dust, newspapers, and parcels was a profitable business – undoubtedly more reliable than prospecting itself. The period brought into being mail services of every calibre, including such companies as Adams, American, National, and Wells Fargo. It was at this period too that the Pony Express came into being. Each of these operators used identifying marks, on covers handstamped as a form of cancellation and often, additionally, as pre-printed devices on the envelope. The Wells Fargo company used pre-printed envelopes and issued specially printed envelopes for valuables. Also marginally within the category of private-mail covers are those bearing insignia of early American railroad companies. Of these, examples are sometimes found without stamps but bearing the inscripion 'RRS', denoting private carriage by the company in its own service.

Among 20th-century examples of private mail items is the 'Strike cover', used for transmission of mails by private bodies during postal strikes (*see* POSTAL-STRIKE LABEL).

Souvenir/commemorative. In a category of its own is the souvenir or commemorative cover, designed not necessarily as a vehicle for a first-day stamp but as an item published in its own right in celebration of a special event.

Typically, the decorative cover is produced on the occasion of an exhibition, fair, or festival, and is posted – often specially cancelled – from the site of the event. Great international exhibitions, such as the Columbian Exposition in Chicago in 1893, are recorded in this way, as are jubilees, centenaries, and other celebrations. Especially featured in the category are philatelic occasions: the exhibition in Manchester in 1909 and the fiftieth anniversary of Uniform Penny Postage in 1890 are examples.

Other events are also celebrated in covers, some of world significance, some of local interest only. These have ranged from the Versailles Peace Treaty Negotiations (1919–21) to the last voyage of the Queen Mary; from the annexation of Austria by Hitler (1938) to the first day of special cancellation (in 1974) at the Post Office at Sanquhar, Dumfries and Galloway, the oldest post office in the United Kingdom.

Souvenir and commemorative covers are produced commonly for any occasion likely to result in substantial sales, and in Britain the Post Office encourages such issues by providing special postmarks for use on the covers. Philatelic dealers may order quantities of the covers in advance for resale after the event.

Wreck/crash. Broadly speaking, the term 'wreck cover' is used to refer to covers salvaged from shipwrecks; 'crash cover' relates to railway and aircraft accidents. As a general rule the terms are applied to covers bearing an official handstamp cachet, naming the accident or wreck concerned; but the category also admits authenticated examples in which a manuscript note alone conveys the facts.

In the first wreck letter so far identified the inscription is in fact in handwriting: 'Bilboena, Stranded at Rottingdean 5 June 1817 : J B Stone Agent to Lloyds'. (The example is actually not a cover as such but a single-sheet folded letter.) Citing the *Bilboena* letter, Hopkins (1970) records confirmation of the mark in *Lloyd's Register* and names it as 'the earliest known cover bearing an official inscription identifying it with a wreck...'. Hopkins describes the first 'real' wreck cover, bearing a cachet printed apparently from metal type, as a folded letter dated 3 June 1829 addressed from Bath to Captain Ouseley in Fort William, Calcutta. The cachet reads: 'From the wreck of the Lady Holland'. The *Lady Holland* was wrecked off Bassan Island near Saldanha Bay, South Africa, on 13 February 1830.

Later inscriptions are almost invariably struck from metal, wood, or rubber stamps, or from movable type, impressed generally directly on the cover itself or on a separate slip and affixed as a label. The majority carry a minimum of information: 'Damaged by Seawater', 'Saved from the Wreck of the Colombo', 'Recovered from the wreck of the Carnatic'. Some are more explicit: 'Post Office Department: Office of third Assistant Postmaster General: Division of dead letters: This Letter was washed ashore from wreck of Steamship "City of Vera Cruz", which foundered at sea August 29 1880'.

Many examples show additional evidence of disaster: immersion-staining and discolouration, tearing, tattering, and crumpling, and scorching and charring. In many cases, stamps and labels have been washed off, and in some instances of burning all that remains is a portion of the front of the cover bearing the address – delivered, duly annotated, by the postal authority. Some cases of damage are exceptional. Hopkins (1970) reports examples of mail delivered with the manuscript note 'Stamp found eaten off by Snails' (Looe, Cornwall, 1964). In 1959 a mail bag thrown from a moving train at Salem Station bowled back under the wheels of a car at the end of the train; damaged mail from this mishap bore the handstamp: 'Run over by train at Salem, Ohio'.

See also CACHET, POSTAL; DISINFECTED MAIL; FEATHER LETTER; FREE FRANK; MULREADY CARICATURE; MULREADY ENVELOPE; POSTAL LABEL; POSTAL STATIONERY

REFERENCES A. H. Denney, *Militaria: Collecting Print and Manuscript* (St Ives, Huntingdon: Photo Precision Ltd, 1978); John Fisher, *Air Lift 1870* (London: Parrish, 1965); A. E. Hopkins, *A History of Wreck Covers*, 3rd edn (London: Robson Lowe, 1970); Peter Jennings, *Aerogrammes* (Chippenham: Picton, 1973); James A. Mackay, *Cover Collecting* (London: Philatelic Publishers, 1968); James A. Mackay, *Air-mails 1870–1970* (London: Batsford, 1971); Alan W. Robertson, *A History of the Ship Letters of the British Isles* (Pinner: The Author, 1955); R. M. Willcocks and Alan W. Robertson, *England's Postal History to 1840, with notes on Scotland, Wales and Ireland* (London: Willcocks, 1975)

SOCIETIES Forces Postal History Society; Cinderella Stamp Club (British Private Post Study Group)

Crate label

The crate label was evolved to bestow marketing identity on products that looked – and often actually were – indistinguishable. With the expansion of the orange-growing industry in California in the early 1880s the need for brand-selling became apparent and the hitherto unexploited crate was conceived as a mobile bill-board. There followed a development in graphic

Crate label for Hi Yu brand apples, mid 20th century. Colour lithography. 222 × 262 mm (8¾ × 10¼ in)

design that was to influence the marketing of fruit, and later of canned products, all over the world.

The design of the orange-crate label went through four stages. First came a fair representation of the grower's home ground, together with his name. Later, when the novelty of this waned, the grower was offered a choice of colourful stock designs to any of which he could add his name (though inevitably there was duplication of designs). In the third stage, 'artist-salesmen' worked out designs in the grower's home, mounting together a montage of clippings from magazines and reproductions and other scraps, to produce an on-the-spot 'unique' design. This montage was tidied up in the company's studio before being committed to four- or five-colour lithographic printing. In the fourth stage the companies called in graphic artists to produce designs. It must be said that though its impact was considerable, at no stage did the orange-crate label achieve design distinction.

Crate labels for apples and other produce appeared in a wide range of sizes and in recognizably similar vein. All were lithographed, initially from stone and later from metal plates. Most are varnished; some are lightly embossed.

Credit/cash card

The first credit cards were issued by Diners Club Inc. in New York in 1950. They were the idea of Frank McNamara, who had found himself without a wallet after entertaining business colleagues to dinner at a New York restaurant and sought some way of overcoming the difficulty in the future. In its first year the company had just 200 cardholders and provided credit facilities at two hotels and twenty-seven restaurants. By the early 1980s the number of Diners-listed establishments throughout the world was 500,000 and members exceeded four million.

The Diners Club card was followed by others, notably the American Express card (1958) (later to be styled a 'charge card'), and many bank credit cards.

Not all of today's cards are specifically *credit* cards. Some serve merely to identify the holder; others are used with cheques as a guarantee of indemnity; yet others are accepted in lieu of immediate cash, though the operating company offers the user no extended credit. They are known loosely by a variety of names – credit card, cash card, money card, charge card, cheque card, etc. – and may differ in the specific facilities they offer.

Early cards were of paperboard, but by the late 1950s the plastic card had appeared, together with embossing of the holder's name and card number. Imprinters for use in conjunction with embossing also appeared at this time. By the 1970s all cards conformed to an internationally recognized format, 54 × 86 mm (2⅛ × 3⅜ in), and the size was later adopted for other uses (e.g. kidney donor cards, library tickets, advertising novelties, TELEPHONE CARDS, etc.).

Use of the plastic card extended in the 1970s to a number of security applications, in which coded information on the card automatically allowed access to services. Typical uses are for keyboard cash dispensers and hotel-room key-cards. Here mechanisms are activated by coded perforations or by magnetic changes in the card. A development of the mid 1970s was the non-magnetic 'two-dimensional hologram card', devised for the Swiss company Landis & Gyr by a British scientist, Dr David Greenaway.

Some kinds of cards are sold to the user ready 'loaded' with a number of monetary units. These are progressively discharged when the card is used to operate, for example, a public telephone. The card is thrown away when it is wholly spent. The system, which was adopted for the telephone services of Switzerland, Belgium, and France in 1980, and initially experimentally in Britain in 1981, obviates storage and collection of large quantities of coins and is seen as a major step towards acceptance of the concept of electronic currency. The system is planned for use in automatic vending; gas, electricity and water metering; car-park control; and a wide range of ticket distribution applications.

The development of the plastic card has not been without problems. Security measures have been successively countered by forgers, and losses to operating companies were estimated in the early 1980s in America at $1000 million a year. Modern cards may incorporate up to a dozen distinct security features. These include absorbent-paper signature panel, intaglio printing, 'invisible' graphics, RAINBOW PRINTING, fluorescent inks, magnetic-strip coding, three-image holograms, and holographic side-by-side duplicates of photograph and signature.

The credit/cash card archive has notable gaps. Operating companies have been reluctant for security reasons to publicize the technology, and the cards themselves are commonly destroyed on expiry. There is thus only a sketchy physical record of this major phase in everyday economics, though it has become a popular field for collectors.

Crest/monogram

Stationery crests and monograms, vestigially surviving on personal stationery at the close of the 20th century, were much in use in Britain and elsewhere in the latter part of the 19th century. The vogue for collecting these items, and for displaying them in specially designed albums, was predominantly British and mainly middle-class. It depended for much of its appeal on implications of day-to-day correspondence with the affluent and influential, those whose status and income ran to more than ordinary writing paper.

Crest albums took their place alongside photograph, press-cutting, and autograph albums as parlour table conversation starters. Crests and monograms were for the most part embossed or die-stamped, often in colour, and were mounted as individual cut-outs on printed pages, each of which provided spaces for a specific number and type of specimen. Unlike the stamp album, which normally provided only rectilinear compartments, each crest-album page presented an overall design in which apertures appeared as decorative display frames. Page designs presented specific themes (e.g. military, naval, ducal, etc.) or neutral geometric patterns. The discipline of 'theme' pages was often disregarded, and many surviving albums display incongruities. One such example shows side by side on a military page the West End Silk Co. and the Camden Public Assistance Department. Album formats ranged from about 203 × 160 mm (8 × 6¼ in) to about 265 × 215 mm (10½ × 8½ in). Bindings of such albums were often elaborate, with heavy embossing and gilt titling; pages, printed in one or two colours on both sides, were of heavy cartridge or, in luxury versions, linen-jointed gilt-edged board.

Crest collecting was served by a minor industry, not only of album manufacturers, but of suppliers of specimens for display. Enthusiasts could speed the growth of their collections and effectively crash social barriers, through multiple sheets and

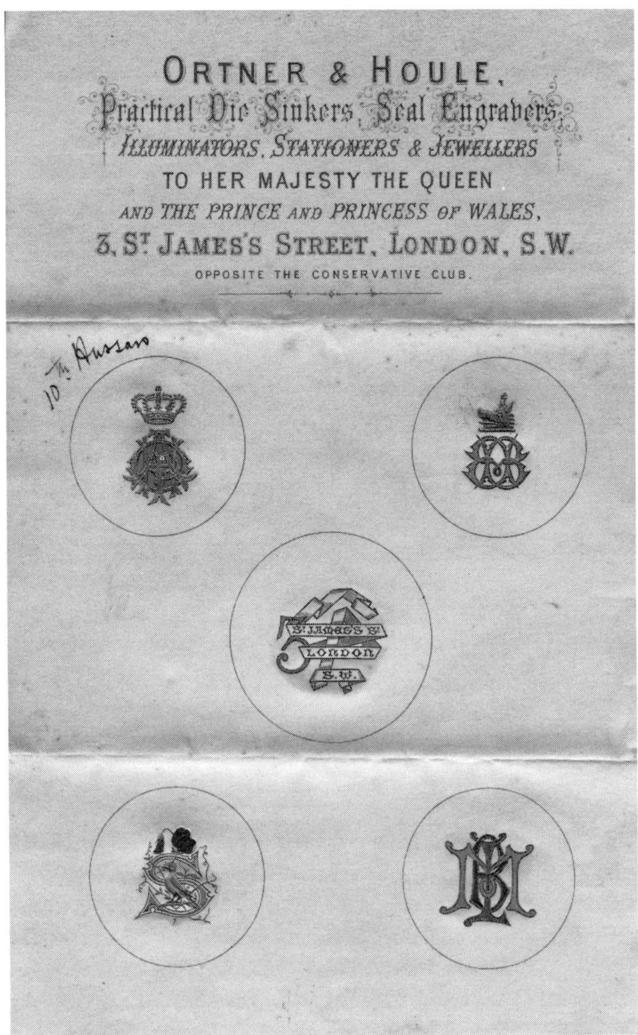

Specimen sheet of monograms by Ortner & Houle, die sinkers and seal engravers, St James's Street, London, late 19th century. Lithographed, with die-sunk specimens. 197 × 126 mm ($7\frac{3}{4}$ × 5 in)

packets available from album firms. One such source, William S. Lincoln of Holles Street, London, offered sheets of 'Royalty', 'Dukes and Nobility', and 'City Companies' at threepence per sheet. Mixed packets of several specimens were also available (72 varieties, one shilling; 32 varieties, sixpence). Apart from a few well-known institutional specimens these packets consisted of unattributed and apparently random combinations of letters: 'Packet No 1: P.H.D., G.S.G., R.H., R.H.S., H.D.P....'.

Sheets of royal and other prestigious crests and monograms were clearly preferred for this purpose, and it must be inferred that the shilling and sixpenny packets were made up of unauthorized over-runs from privately commissioned work of associated printers.

Cuban wrapper

In the period 1865–70 a number of Cuban cigarette companies marketed their products in bundles of fifty, each bundle wrapped in a decorative printed paper. The wrappers were folded over the cigarettes at top and bottom to form a cylindrical package, the paper being lightly pasted to form a closure.

Among reported issuing companies (Burdick, 1960/1988) are Luis Susini e Hijo; Julian Rivas; V. M. Ybor, and Anselmo y Del Valle. The wrappers appeared as collectable series (Arms of the Spanish Provinces, Butterflies, Views of the Paris Exhibition 1867, etc.) and were printed, with one exception, in full colour (Views of Europe appeared in black and white).

The wrappers measure about 150 × 300 mm (6 × $11\frac{7}{8}$ in), but the printed image occupies only a central panel of some 90 × 125 mm ($3\frac{1}{2}$ × $4\frac{7}{8}$ in). It is an archetypal forerunner of paper cigarette packs elsewhere, and was probably the basis for the new ubiquitous 'soft-cup' type pack (*see* CIGARETTE PACK). The idea was taken up for economy packing in a number of countries in World War II.

The Cuban wrapper is also thought to be among the world's first series-collectables.

REFERENCE J. R. Burdick, *American Card Catalogue* (East Stroudsbury, PA: Burdick, 1960; reprinted New York: Nostalgia Press, 1988)

COLLECTION Burdick Collection, Metropolitan Museum of Art, New York

Currier & Ives

The New York printmaking firm of Currier & Ives originated in 1835 when Nathaniel Currier began to publish cheap lithographic prints for the popular market; he specialized in subjects of contemporary appeal. Fires, catastrophes, innovations in rail and steamship transportation, and the exciting developments of the still youthful American nation were favourite subjects. He was joined in 1857 by James Merritt Ives, initially as accountant and general factotum, but soon as a prime creative force in the company. The two men worked together until Nathaniel's retirement in 1880, when his son Edward took over. Ives died in 1895, seven years after Currier's death, and was succeeded by his son, Chauncey Ives, to whom Edward Currier sold out in 1902. The business was liquidated in 1907.

The output of the firm was enormous. Estimates of the total number of print titles vary, but the figure of 7000 is quoted (Marzio, 1979) and in some cases print runs were of the order of 'several hundred thousands'. Unlike the equally successful Louis Prang prints (*see* CHROMO), Currier & Ives's pictures had few aesthetic pretensions and the firm did not, for the most part, attempt to reproduce the paintings of distinguished artists for their own sake. For the Currier & Ives partnership the product was essentially a form of pictorial journalism with a main accent on graphic presentation of current events and a fast turnover of titles and topics.

Again unlike the Prang output, which was mostly intended for framing, most Currier & Ives prints were seen as transients, each soon to be superseded by the next in a continuing process of release and distribution. Above all, the Currier & Ives print was cheap. Selling at $6 per hundred to stores, 'travelling agents', and peddlers, the prints were good value at the retail price of 25 cents each; and in a colour-starved and often illiterate society their news appeal made them specially desirable.

The news ingredient, though laced with admixtures of pretty pictorials (kittens and puppies, flowers and fruits, 'ladies' hands', etc.), was a continuing leitmotiv. In addition to major fires – fires at sea, railroad prairie fires and big-city fires – the partnership published such titles as 'The Trial of Effie Deans', 'High Water in the Mississippi', 'Ice-Boat Race on the Hudson', and 'Clipper Ship Dreadnought off Tuskar Light: $12\frac{1}{2}$ days from New York on her celebrated passage into dock at Liverpool in 13 days 11 hours, December 1854'. Graphic evidence of the company's news sense is the print entitled 'Across the Continent', a picture showing the first coast-to-coast train. Its appearance in 1868 predated the completion of the track by a year.

Currier & Ives prints appeared in a number of different guises. Earlier issues were wholly hand-coloured, others were part colour-printed and part hand-coloured; later titles were wholly colour-printed. 'Plain' or uncoloured prints were also produced. As a general rule, the firm's colour quality cannot be compared with that of the Louis Prang print. The Currier & Ives effect was achieved with a minimum of workings, adding the brightness of colours to a dominant black image. The multiple stipple effect of Prang's chromolithography was a technique that the partners were content to leave to him.

As Simkin (1952) has pointed out, Currier & Ives employed three distinct types of artist. In one group were creative artists whose work was copied on stone by lithographic craftsmen; in another were artists who drew directly on to the stone, avoiding the need for an intermediary; and a third group were the intermediaries, the craftsmen who, though uncreative themselves, were skilled in copying the work of others. It will be seen that in this context the word 'artist' may be ambiguous; the expression is best used to refer only to the original creative agent rather than to the skilled copyist.

Currier & Ives credit lines suggest that some ambiguity was also present in the minds of those personally concerned. Among a variety of credits we note, for example: 'Drawn by J B Smith & Son – on stone by C Parsons'; 'From nature and on stone by F F Palmer'; 'Sketched by Thomas Worth'; 'C Parsons Del[ineavit: (drew it)]; [signed] A F Tait'; 'J Ives Del [ineavit] – drawn by F F Palmer and J Cameron'. (This last is additionally complicated by the fact that Ives, though a partner, was not, so far as is known, an artist.) Whatever their specific functions, creative or copyist, none of the practitioners named in Currier & Ives credit lines may be said to be of the very first order. Their success, however, as purveyors of images to the American people, was unqualified.

Less widely known than their popular prints, though no less widely distributed, were Currier & Ives's 'commercial' prints, designs produced for specific advertisers or for generalized use as images for advertisers' overprinting. Typical of these is 'an American Railway Scene, at Hornellsville, Erie Railway', in which locomotives, coaches, and station buildings, carry advertising lettering.

The company also produced school mottoes ('God Bless Our School'), cards for use in school drawing lessons, school rewards, store mottoes ('to avoid a smash, sell for cash'), fire volunteer membership certificates, marriage and baptismal certificates, family registers, memorial cards, and trade cards.

REFERENCES Frederic A. Conningham, *Currier & Ives' Prints: An Illustrated Checklist* (New York: Crown, 1949; rev. Colin Simkin, New York: Crown, 1970); W. S. Hall, *The Spirit of America: Currier & Ives' Prints* (London: Studio, 1930); Peter C. Marzio, *The Democratic Art: Chromolithography, 1840–1900* (Boston: Godine, 1979); Harry T. Peters, *Currier & Ives: Printmakers to the American People* (New York: Doubleday, Doran, 1942); Colin Simkin (ed.), *Currier & Ives' America* (New York: Crown, 1952)

COLLECTIONS New York Historical Society; Library of Congress, Washington, DC

Cut-out toy

The TOY THEATRE is the best-known cut-out toy, but there have been large numbers of other cut-outs, ranging from the earliest and simplest of rectangular scraps to elaborate part-cut 'push-outs' and decorative pre-cut piercings for use with back-lashing. As with the toy theatre, the cut-out in general is typically a Northern European (indoor orientated) toy. It is found principally in Northern France, Germany, the Low Countries, Britain, and Scandinavia. Its heyday was from 1860 to 1920, though its origins go back to the begining of the 19th century and it was not wholly extinct in the late 20th century.

Sheets of 'toy soldier' images are among the earliest of prints produced for cutting out. Best known are those of Gustave Silbermann of Strasbourg whose six- or seven- colour productions included silver and gold, with twenty-six soldiers per sheet of approximately 300 × 520 mm (11⅞ × 20½ in), and twelve cavalry per large sheet of 420 × 470 mm (16½ × 18½ in).

In Britain, very much cruder sheets were available, commonly in black only, and measuring 440 × 310 mm (17⅜ × 12¼ in), at the end of the 19th century. By the 1914–18 war Pellerin et Cie of Épinal in France offered a wide range of 'civilian' cut-outs including, typically, railways, shops, street scenes, etc. In another cut-out toy novelty Pellerin produced 'silhouette' sheets bearing black and white portrait images of notabilities. Here the purchaser cut away the black area, stencil fashion, to produce an enlarged silhouette image on a screen by projection from a lamp.

The 'paper doll' sheet from which figures could be cut out and dressed in a variety of clothes had been available since the beginning of the 19th century, becoming popular in the 1870s. They appeared at first without means of affixing garments or standing up, but foldable tags and base flaps soon followed. Cut-outs for constructing animated figures appeared in Germany in the 1870s. In Britain, at about the same time, H. G. Clarke published a sheet by making figures for a 'Magic Punch and Judy'.

Cut-out sheets were popular as GIVE-AWAYS in magazines and other journals. Chromolithographed cut-out figures dressed in American college colours were put out as a promotion series early in the new century by the manufacturers of Enameline stove polish, and an animated series appeared as promotion for the Boston Sunday Clubs in the 1900s. Among 'pre-pierced' items were those of Demboul and Gangel, a range of perforated prints, predominantly black, with translucent coloured figures set in a tracery of 'Feux Pyriques et Diamanteaux'. When placed before a lamp or against a window the image conveys an impression of festive illumination.

A complicated form of cut-out is the model building con-

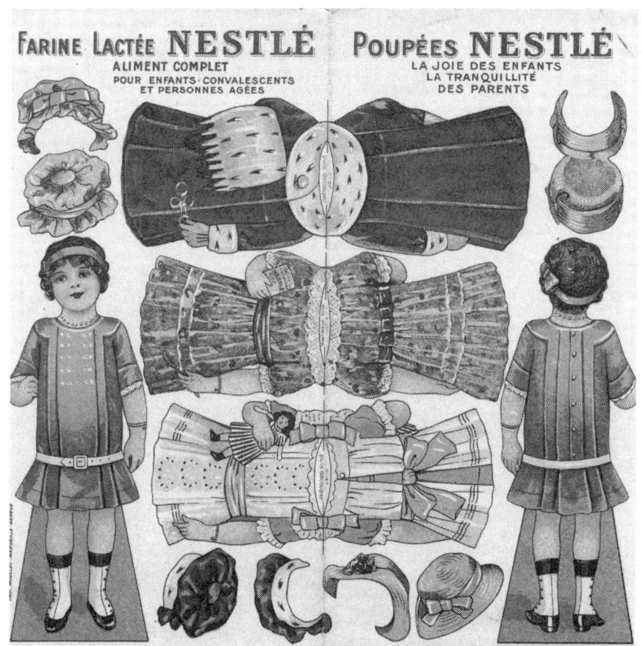

Cut-out toy, published by Nestlé as an advertising novelty, Paris, early 20th century. Chromolithographed by Moullot, Marseille and Geneva. 200 × 203 mm (7⅞ × 8 in)

struction kit, in which pierced and part-cut cardboard units slot together to form walls, roof, etc., often with a multiplicity of windows and doorways. In a classic 1890s example ('designed in England and made in our own works at Saxony') Buckingham Palace appears on an evening State Occasion: 'when all is finished' says the instruction sheet 'put the candles in the tin clips provided and place the lighted candles well under the funnels (roof lights) when the effect will be magical'. The assembled building measures 570 × 135 × 170 mm (22½ × 5¼ × 6¾ in), with an overall forecourt dimension of 700 × 255 mm (27⅝ × 10 in). The kit is contained in a manila envelope, 320 × 510 mm (12½ × 20⅛ in), bearing a single-colour illustration of the completed model under the title 'Buckingham Palace under a Flood of Lights'.

See also IMAGERIE POPULAIRE; SCRAP

REFERENCES Paul Martin, *Les Petits Soldats de Strasbourg* (Strasbourg and Paris: Compagnie des Arts Photomécaniques, 1950); Edward Ryan, *Paper Soldiers. The Illustrated History of Printed Paper Armies of the 18th, 19th & 20th Centuries* (New Cavendish Books, 1995)

Cutwork [plate 9a]

Sometimes known as 'papyrotamia' (Latin, *papyrus*: writing material; *tamias*: steward), the term 'cutwork' is normally applied to decorative paper items, produced generally by folding and cutting. The technique was introduced by German immigrants in Pennsylvania in the 1780s. It was based on the principle of cutting a folded piece of paper in such a way that, when opened out, each cut was repeated in a symmetrical pattern. The paper might be folded once, twice, or three or four times; cuts were made with scissors or penknife. The system produced a 'lace-paper' effect, often of great intricacy, and was used in the preparation of the love token and cobweb VALENTINE (the classic heart shape is a frequent feature). Many were cut so as to allow space, generally heart-shaped, for handwritten love messages, and the technique was also often combined with 'pin-prick' work, a fine multiple piercing of the paper in patterns for pictorial representations.

Small circular cutwork pieces, measuring no more than 60 or 70 mm (about 2½ in) in diameter, are also found. These are generally love tokens removed from heavy pocket watches of the 19th century. They were carried between the rear flap of the watch and the movement in the manner of a WATCHPAPER.

See also PAPER-CUT

REFERENCE Ruth Webb Lee, *History of Valentines* (New York: Studio Publications, 1952; London: Batsford, 1953)

COLLECTIONS Museum of the City of New York

Cypher label

Stamp tax, imposed on various categories of legal and financial documents, was first introduced into Britain in 1694. The tax required that proof of payment be firmly and irremovably affixed to the document in question. It was some time before a wholly tamper-proof method was devised. The cypher label, introduced in 1701, formed part of that method.

Parchment, on which the majority of documents of the time were inscribed or printed, was found to be unsuitable to receive the low-relief impression of the embossing tax stamp. To remedy this, a piece of paper was affixed to the parchment with glue prior to stamping. The low-relief effect of the embossing die was thus recorded simultaneously on paper and parchment together, the combined substances retaining the impression more effectively than parchment alone.

Cypher labels of King George III and Queen Victoria on documents dated, respectively, 1812 and 1856. Both printed intaglio, cut from sheets of multiple images. *Left:* 23 × 21mm (⅞ × $\frac{13}{16}$in); *right:* 21 × 18mm ($\frac{13}{16}$ × ¾in)

There was a danger of the affixed paper becoming detached, accidentally or otherwise, and it was later decided to make the fixture fully secure with a metal clip. This had prongs which pierced both paper and parchment and folded flat at the back of the document. The cypher label, a rectangular printed piece of paper, was pasted over the metal at the back to form a final closure, and the multi-layer unit thus formed received the impression of the tax stamp. The result was a fixing that was not only physically firm but virtually tamper-proof.

The cypher label measured approximately 25 × 20 mm (1 × $\frac{13}{16}$ in) and bore the cypher, or monogram, of the reigning monarch. Printed in multiples from engraved copper plates, the images also bore code marks indicating successive plate repairs. This coding device, universally adopted in Stamp Office printing of this kind, was a guard against counterfeiting. Slight changes in detail, resulting from hand-execution of the engraving, might otherwise allow forgeries to pass unnoticed. The labels were printed on variously coloured papers, which differed according to the nature of the document. Most common, and in use for over 180 years, was blue, which was used for deeds.

As with the plates for post-horse duty labels, hair-powder tax labels, hat-tax labels, playing card aces, and other such items, pulls from successive repairs and re-engravings of cypher stamp plates were filed for reference at Somerset House, London.

The labels appear in some variety; the varying cypher, code numbers, letters, and signs provide a multitude of variants within each group. As with duty stamps themselves, stocks of existing labels were often retained and used after the death of the monarch depicted. The cypher label on its own may therefore be an unreliable guide to date. The labels had no revenue validity in themselves; their function was as a security measure, specifically a closure, not a stamp in the fiscal sense.

See also TAXATION PAPERS

REFERENCES Samuel B. Frank and Joseph Schonfeld, with William A. Barber and Marcus Samuel, *The Stamp Duty of Great Britain and Ireland* (New York: Mamaroneck, 1970)

Dance programme

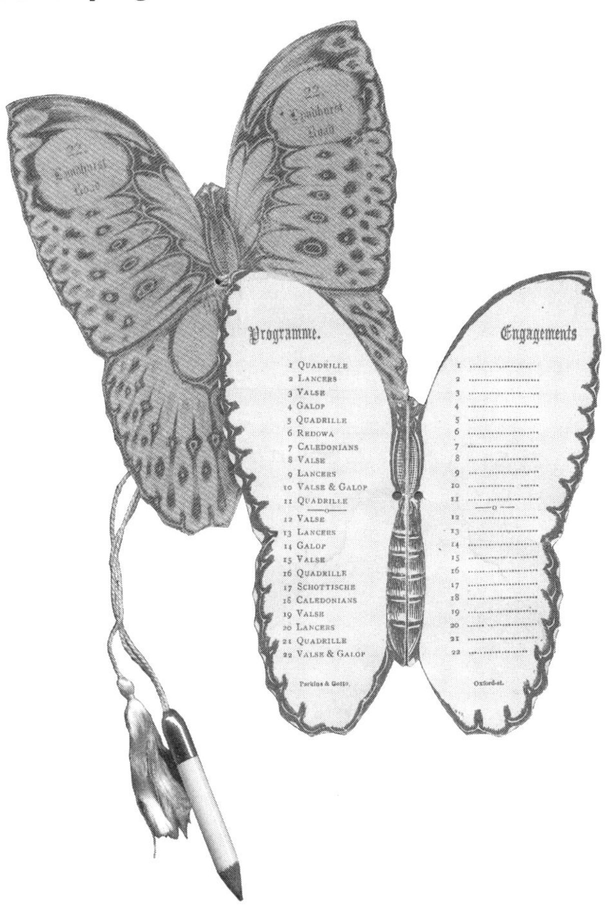

Programme for a dance at 22 Lyndhurst Road, London (?), 14 January 1875, with pencil. Printed letterpress in gold by Parkins & Gotto, London, on green coated card. 114 × 95 mm (4½ × 3¾ in)

The dance programme, commonly a four-page card folding to some 100 × 65 mm (4 × 2½ in), was used by lady guests to note their engagements in an evening's dancing. The card, sometimes supplied with miniature pencil attached, listed the dances – normally twenty in number – and provided spaces for entering partners' names. The convention was in vogue throughout the Victorian period and survived in some areas into the 1920s and 1930s, and for balls even later.

Cards were often designed and produced with great elegance, some of the 'Great occasions' programmes being printed in eight or nine lithographic workings with cord or silver embossing, and a silk tasselled pencil.

Dance token

In the American public dance-hall tradition, the dance token was sold by the management to a patron; the token was then proffered instead of cash to the partner of his choice. The system – but a short distance removed from the brass brothel token of the American West – ensured that cash transactions were kept out of the hands of the ladies themselves.

Dance tokens or tickets were produced in rolls, numbered and perforated in the manner of the cinema ticket. They sometimes carried the name of the establishment and the legend 'Good for one dance' as the central feature. In more elegant variations the treatment is elaborate, with a clear invocation of security printing.

A surviving example, 25 × 57 mm (1 × 2¼ in), printed in two colours with red numbering, was put out by the Rhodes Brothers for their casino on the *Pawtuxet* in the 'Season of 1901'. Here, it may be assumed, the token served as an inducement to enter the establishment, the cash element being taken care of by the tables.

Dart flight

Darts, as used in the British pub game, are equipped with tail-flights, feathered (as in the classic arrow), or a folded paper inserted in crossed slits in the tail. The mid 1930s saw the intro-

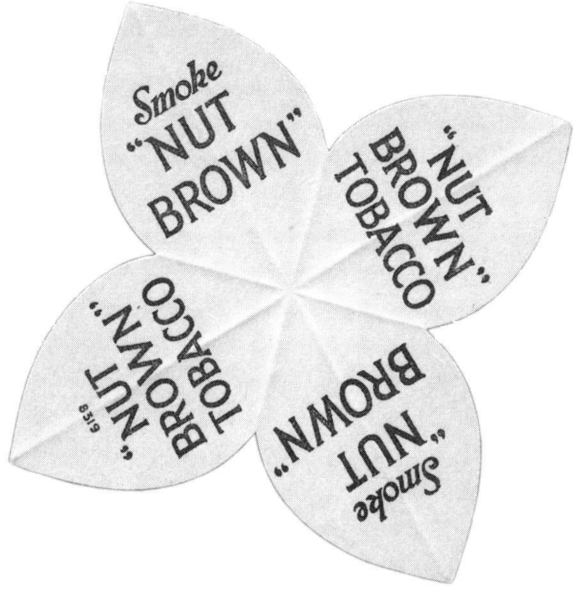

Dart flight, with advertisement for 'Nut Brown' tobacco. Letterpress, printed in blue. 95 × 95 mm (3¾ × 3¾ in)

duction of give-away paper flights bearing advertising for cigarettes, pipe tobacco, beers, etc., usually printed in a single colour on white or tinted card.

Death certificate

Systematic recording of births and deaths began in the early years of the 19th century. By the early 1830s registration had been adopted in ten European countries and five American cities. In Britain, nationwide registration was not introduced until the Births and Deaths Registration Act of 1836. This required not only registration of death but indication of cause. Since then, cause has become a universal feature of certificates of death – though there has been much difficulty in securing international agreement on a standard.

In Britain, under the Births and Deaths Registration Acts of 1874 and 1926, when a death occurs in a house, information of the death must be given to the Registrar within five days, and a medical certificate stating the cause of death must also be provided. The registrar then issues a certificate declaring that the death has been registered. It is the registrar's certificate that is normally referred to as the 'Death certificate'. Without this, or a coroner's order authorizing burial, or a certificate of stillbirth, burial or cremation may not take place. Details of the death certificate have changed (as with other certificates issued under the Registration Acts). Successive formats show a progressive tightening of controls in protection of the public interest.

In America, the term 'Death certificate' is applied to a more comprehensive registrar's document in which, in addition to such details as citizenship, colour or race, veteran status, etc., post-disposal information – name of cemetery or crematorium and date of interment or cremation – appears. Details required vary somewhat from one state to another. A few states register stillbirths on two separate certificates, one as a stillbirth, the other as a foetal death.

See also BIRTH CERTIFICATE; BURIAL IN WOOLLEN AFFIDAVIT; BURIAL PAPERS

REFERENCE *Population and Health Statistics in England and Wales* (London: Office of Population Censuses and Surveys, 1980)

Deck plan

The deck plan is an early feature of marine architecture, but it emerges as a document for public perusal in the early years of the 19th century when cabin allocation began to be made on a systematic basis. Prior to that period, sea passages were booked on a more or less haphazard basis, arrangements being made in most cases with the captain himself and without special promises as to accommodation, food, etc.

Passenger deck plans are rare before the 1840s. One surviving example, relating to the packet ship *Toronto A.1*, shows the poop deck and lower deck in two parallel diagrams, with the ship's designation inscribed in copperplate script at the foot. The vessel (650 tons; commander, Robert Griswold) was fitted with fifteen cabins on the lower deck, together with a ladies' cabin, a central dining table, store room, steward's room, and a single WC. The poop deck accommodated captain and mate in separate rooms, each with external WC, and a public sitting room. (The ship, used on the New York to London run, was about half the size of the *Britannia*, the first 'Cunarder', which in turn would have fitted easily within the lounge of the *Aquitania*, the 'Cunarder' flagship of the 1920s.)

The deck plan gained general currency with the advent of

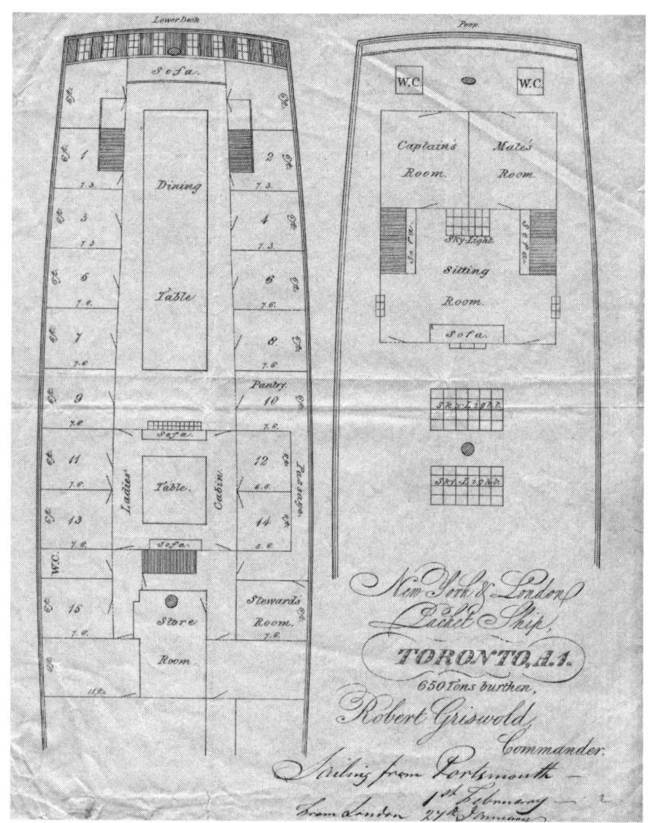

Deck plan for *Toronto, A.1*, a New-York and London packet ship, mid 19th century. Lithographed and manuscript. 250 × 203 mm (9⅞ × 8 in)

Samuel Cunard's transatlantic line, the British and North American Royal Mail Steam Packet Co., in 1840. Charles Dickens in his *American Notes* refers to drawings and a 'varnished lithographic plan' hanging in the agent's London office. Small deck plans (also called 'cabin plans') appeared as a more or less standard item on the reverse of pictorial trade cards featuring individual ships. Typical of these are cards issued by the Guion Line and the Inman Line. They commonly measure some 100 × 65 mm (4 × 2½ in).

As ships grew in size, cabin plans also grew. By the 1870s the cabin plans of White Star Line's six vessels – *Britannic, Germanic, Adriatic, Celtic, Baltic*, and *Republic* – were appearing as groups on folders, each diagram measuring some 200 mm (8 in) in length. By the 1930s, with sea cruises increasingly popular, shipping companies' promotion material featured cabin and deck plans in extensive detail. Some companies' plan folders opened out to as much as 910 × 1520 mm (35⅞ × 59⅞ in).

Decorated paper

'Marbled' and 'paste' papers were introduced into Europe from Persia and Turkey at about the end of the 16th century. Printed patterned papers became popular at the turn of the 17th century and remained widely in use until the first half of the 19th century. They were commonly used in bookbinding, both for covers and endpapers.

Marbling, though it was to be mechanized in the 19th century, remained a hand operation for centuries; it was often a closely guarded secret and sometimes the sole asset of a refugee or other immigrant practitioner. The process, in essence, consists of transferring colour patterns from the surface of a liquid (gum tragacanth) to paper; colours are applied to the liquid, and paper laid on the surface receives the resultant image. Innumerable permutations of colour, consistency, and speed of operation, as well as manipulation of the pattern by striping, combing, waving, etc., allow great variety of effect.

'Paste' papers rely for their effect on a covering of coloured paste (or colour on paste) in which manipulation of the surface by handwork or block printing produces patterning which is then allowed to dry. Examples of paste printing are found in book endpapers in the mid 16th century.

Printed patterned paper is produced by wood or metal block, lithography, or stencil, and may also be lightly embossed. In the 18th century small-pattern printed papers were used in large quantities as lining paper for boxes, cupboards, and chests, and was also used as wrapping material for toys imported into Britain from Holland. Holland's role as exporter of European goods led to the erroneous use of the designation 'Dutch', not only for the toys but for the wrapping too.

'Dutch gilt' or 'Dutch flowered' papers, also exported from Holland, were actually produced in Germany (in Augsburg, Fürth, and Nürnberg) and in Bassano, Italy. Dutch papers are characterized by free use of gold, many of the patterns evoking those of damask and brocade. They were printed from wood or metal blocks, and were also often embossed.

Of all decorated papers, Dutch gilt may most readily be recognized as falling within the category of ephemera. Though also occasionally used as endpapers, they commonly appear as loose wrappers on minor pamphlets, booklets, music, and the stock-in-trade of the itinerant chapman (*see* CHAPBOOK). They bore no label or other titling and enclosed the publication, including its own printed cover, in a purely decorative outer jacket. The paper was also used as a backing for the schoolchild's BATTLEDORE, the folded alphabet spelling cards of the late 18th and early 19th centuries. Dutch gilt paper was imported into America. Among a large number of American users was Isaiah Thomas of Worcester, Massachusetts, printer and publisher of numerous children's books (and founder of the American Antiquarian Society).

Paper size ranges from approximately 210 × 340mm (8¼ × 13⅜in) to 250 × 450mm (9⅞ × 17¾in). Designs are sometimes symmetrical, allowing a mid-line fold to correspond with the spine of the book. Printers' names are often to be found at the edge of the short sheet or worked into the pattern, though there was much pirating and interchange of designs, and many papers are unsigned. German papers may be commonly distinguished from those of Italy by being heavier in weight, even though designs may be virtually identical.

There was a revival of interest in printed patterned papers in Britain in the late 1920s and early 1930s. In 1920 Harold Curwen brought out a series of patterned papers based on the designs of Lovat Fraser, and in 1928 the Curwen Press published a collection of thirty-one papers in book form. This featured the commissioned work of Lovat Fraser, Albert Rutherston, Margaret Calkin James, Thomas Lowinski, E. O. Hoppé, Edward Bawden, Paul Nash, Enid Marx, Eric Ravilious, and Harry Carter.

REFERENCES Albert Haemmerle, *Buntpapier. Herkommen, Geschichte, Techniken, Beziehungen zur Kunst* (München: Verlag Georg D. W. Callway, 1977); Rosamond B. Loring, *Decorated Book Papers*, 3rd edn (Cambridge, Mass.: Harvard College Library, 1973); Ernst Wolfgang Mick, *Altes Buntpapier* (Dortmund: Harenberg, 1979)

COLLECTIONS Houghton Library, Harvard University, Cambridge, Mass.; Massachusetts Institute of Technology, Cambridge, Mass.; American Antiquarian Society, Worcester, Mass.

Degree certificate/diploma

The degree certificate or diploma has its origins in the document, issued by cathedral chancellors and others in the pre-university era, conferring the right to teach. Similar documents were in turn addressed by teachers to students.

With the emergence of the university (at first a more or less spontaneously generated 'guild' of teachers and students) the document began to be formalized, using universally recognized words and phrases in the then universal Latin of the world of learning. In the course of time, the certificate appeared as a printed form produced by copper engraving, lithography, or letterpress, and embellished with borders, cartouches, vignettes, and various devices of honour. Spaces allowed for the insertion of details by hand. An additional ingredient, by way of authentication, is the seal of the issuing body – originally in wax, later as a die-stamped impression – watermarked paper, and provision for the signature of one or more officers of the body concerned.

Throughout its history there has been an obvious desire to make the document impressive, in some cases by extravagance of decoration, in others by a dignified restraint. The influence of the engraver and calligrapher is dominant (Bartolozzi engraved Cipriani's design for the diploma of the Royal Academy, still in use in the 1980s). The penman's flourished titling, as imitated by the copper engraver, was at one period known as a 'Diploma Heading'. 'Copperplate' handwriting, itself derived from the engraved rendering of freehand script, is still widely used for inserting names, dates, etc., as is a form of italic handwriting using a broad pen. Conventions die hard: Latin, intelligible to a diminishing minority, is still used in certificates from some of the world's major universities.

The right to confer degrees – or 'licences to teach' – was derived from the pope, emperor, or king, but there is in Anglo-Saxon law nothing prohibiting conferral by self-appointed bodies. Nor is there any independent controlling organization to monitor such bodies and the certificates they issue. There are in existence large numbers of degree certificates of doubtful authority, commonly known as 'Bogus degrees'.

In December 1975, W. J. Dey, then Secretary of the University Entrance Requirements Department of the University of London, compiled and published (Dey, 1975) a list of some 240 'Institutions of doubtful standing', and the list has been added to in other publications subsequently. The bogus degree is widely found in America, its birthplace. In April 1983 action was taken by the Federal Bureau of Investigation against thirty-eight institutions (described unofficially as 'Mail-order colleges') for selling fraudulent diplomas. In Britain, one investigator reports (*Times Educational Supplement*, 3 December 1971) securing a certificate of proficiency in Estate Agency and Valuation for one Oliver Greenhalgh – later to be disclosed as his cat. In another investigation a 'Diploma of Naturopathy: ND' was acquired by submission of a four-page dissertation on diagnosis by the areolar method – health assessment by examination of the nipples. In a case reported in the *Sunday Times* (2 September 1984) one 'university' proprietor was alleged to have offered investigative journalists a job lot of 500 blank degree certificates for £4000 – an offer withdrawn when the enquirers declared themselves.

The bogus degree problem is of long standing. *The Pharmaceutical Journal and Transactions Advertiser* for December 1870 carried a small advertisement under the heading 'Degrees (foreign)': 'For Instructions for obtaining the above, Candidates may apply to Dr. S, 145, Packington Street, London N'. In the *Chemist and Druggist* for 15 May 1867 a correspondent reports receipt of an offer in the mail: 'Sir – The undersigned has for disposal a couple of well-written original medical MSS; also a Foreign Medical Diploma, MD. To be disposed of separately. A very rare chance. Yours &c, M.H–, Hoxton'. The editor of the *Chemist and Druggist* adds a note: 'We suppress the full name and address, not from any respect for the writer, but because their publication might by chance procure the diploma-monger a customer'.

It must be said that while many authentic degree certificates have their points of graphic and social history interest, it is the document of doubtful standing that sometimes claims the greater attention.

REFERENCES W. J. Dey, 'Institutions of Doubtful Standing', *ACU Bulletin of Current Documentation*, no. 21 (London, December 1975); Stewart H. Holbrook, *The Golden Age of Quackery* (New York: Collier Books, 1962); Lyndon Jones, 'Dishonoris Causa', *Education and Training*, November/December 1979 (London, 1979)

Dental papers

The emergence of dentistry as a scientific discipline is relatively recent, and dental publicity ephemera, with their many protestations of painlessness and efficiency, reflect the fact unerringly. They are perhaps most revealing when at their most zealous:

> Every instrument used by Mr Wigley is thoroughly aseptic by sterilization, and the same observance of perfect cleanliness should be continued by the patient. Caution: Never, under any circumstances, allow strangers or ignorant commission agents travelling from door to door to interfere with your teeth. Apart from the dreadful ignorance of men, who under all kinds of pretences foist cheap factory made teeth upon the public, there is the very great danger of allowing unknown strangers to attempt work they probably know nothing about with disease-laden appliances carried in a hand-bag. The perfect sterilizing and extreme care necessary is not possible to men travelling from house to house. Such important work should be done in a place completely equipped for the purpose.

This final paragraph, from a folder of 'instructions to the patient', Walsall (c.1916), conveys the professional still struggling with 19th-century attitudes, still living down the image of the itinerant or part-time tooth-puller.

The itinerant dentist, himself only a generation or two remote from his fairground forebear, was a recognized figure of the early part of the 19th century. In remote areas in America he travelled (as did his colleagues the writing masters, and later the photographers) with a TRADE CARD or handbill in which space for the name of the town was left blank for filling in on arrival.

The profession of dentistry, emerging over the course of the 19th century, contended not only with a legacy of ignorance (on the part of practitioner and patient alike) but on the all-too-obvious inadequacies of current techniques. Developments in anaesthesia were slow. Prosthesis for long remained experimental. Work on the control of caries, general preventive dentistry, and orthodontics (correction of growth abnormality) did not begin seriously until the first quarter of the 20th century.

The rise of dentistry as a profession was reflected in a prolific output of publicity material, much of it couched in terms of the

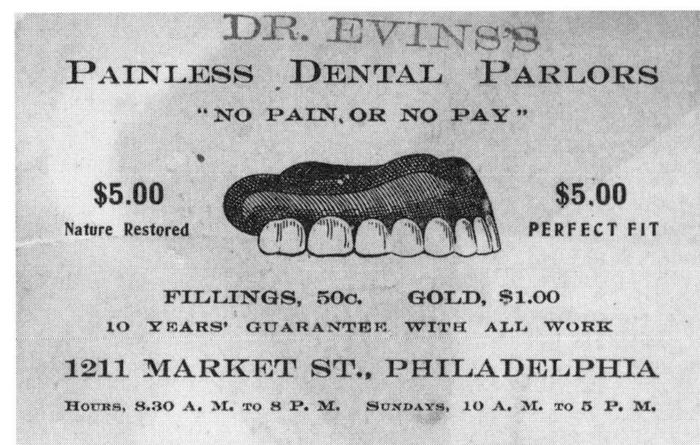

Dental card of Dr Evins, Philadelphia. Printed letterpress and overstamped with the dentist's name. 57 × 90 mm (2¼ × 3½in)

shopkeeper, and most of it highly competitive. It is in this promotion material (publicity forbidden in Britain by law in 1921) that the story is most graphically – if obliquely – conveyed, as in these examples:

> (Trade card: New England, c.1840) A. O. Dickey, Operative Dentist, Respectfully tenders his services to the Ladies and Gentlemen of (—). Decayed teeth filled, and Mineral teeth inserted on Gold-Plate, or Pivot, Kine and Sea-Horse teeth upon Ivory Plate, Clasp or Pivot from one to a whole set, and every other operation necessary to preserve and beautify the teeth, executed in the neatest and most durable manner and warranted.
>
> (Leaflet: Maryland, c.1880) Dr Eavey's Painless Dental Parlors ... teeth extracted positively without pain by the use of Vitalized Air or a local application on the gums.... My Vitalized Air is the original air as used all over the world ... all work done by experienced dentists and graduates. We are no floating dentists. We are here to stay ... .
>
> (Folder: Darlington, 1834) H. Barlow, Jun: Medical and Perfumery Warehouse. Chemist etc. ... an extensive assortment of genuine patent and cattle medicines ... bleeding and tooth drawing ... .
>
> (Folding card: Torquay, c.1890) J. M. Rendall M.P.S. Practical dentistry ... Patients waited upon at their homes, in town or country ... .Schools attended ... . Attendance on the Poor for Extraction 9 to 10am, free of charge ... . A reduction to servants ... .
>
> (Press announcement: Oxford Street, London, c.1840) Tooth-ache cured by fumigation ... Mr Lock continues to cure the tooth-ache, by fumigation, or Steam from Foreign Herbs, which has the effect of destroying the Nerve without causing any Pain to the Patient. The cure is effected in three seconds. The tooth remains firm in the socket, and will not decay any further. ... Charges moderate according to the circumstances of the patient ... .
>
> (Trade card: New York, c.1890) My sets of teeth cannot be beat for $4, $8 and $10 ... . My teeth have the approval of all who wear them, as being firm and easy in the mouth, giving the sunken cheeks a round, full and youthful appearance. ... Teeth extracted without charge if artificial teeth are to be inserted. ... Remember the number, 157 East 38th Street ... .
>
> (Magazine insert: Newcastle-on-Tyne, c.1895) They resemble nature so closely as to render detection impossible!!! Mr George Richardson, surgeon dentist ... inserts artificial teeth (by his New Painless Process) which, for com-

fort, durability and natural appearance, are unequalled... consultations free... country patients allowed rail fare, and fitted with sets or parts in time to return same day.

In addition to promotional material, the ephemera of the history of dentistry reveal increasing quantities of papers of organization and method. Folders and cards giving advice on post-extraction mouth hygiene, dental record charts, and 'visit-reminder cards' are increasingly in evidence, and in the 1920s and 1930s general dental hygiene education emerges as a major topic. Preventive dentistry may be said to date from the mid 19th century, but it was not until the beginning of the 20th century that public authorities in Britain (and private agencies in America) began to take the matter seriously. The benefits of organized dental care among troops in the Boer War, and of compulsory dental inspection and treatment for soldiers in most of the armies of World War I, led to the inception of clinics, dental infirmaries, and other treatment centres. These put out instructional charts and other printed matter, as did the expanding toothpaste industry.

In Britain the Dental Propaganda Committee, set up in 1923, produced posters and leaflets for use in schools, and general health education and industrial safety agencies also put out oral hygiene material.

REFERENCE William H. Helfand, *Crowning Achievements* (Philadelphia: Philadelphia Museum of Art, 1999)

COLLECTION Ars Medica Collection, Philadelphia Museum of Art; British Dental Association, London

SOCIETY American Academy of the History of Dentistry, Lindsay Club, 64 Wimpole Street London W1

Deposit label

In Britain in the period 1919 to 1939 a number of soft-drink manufacturers offered small sums for the return of empty bottles. Small printed paper labels were affixed to the bottles indicating the amounts in question.

Deposit labels, mid 20th century. Lithographed in red. Diameter 33 mm (1 5/16 in)

In most cases the design featured a single bold numeral followed by a small 'd' (the convention used in the pre-decimal era for 'penny' [Latin: *denarius*]), with a brief word of explanation in capital letters '2d left on this bottle', or '1d charged on this bottle and allowed for on return'. Some promised alternatives: 'If glass stoppered price 5d; if stopper lost price 3d.' The more costly soda syphon commanded one shilling, and made a slightly more circumspect offer: 'To ensure the safe return of this syphon when empty, one shilling is charged as a loan not as a sale'.

The reimbursement of a deposit on the return of soft-drink bottles continued for a time after World War II.

Dice-duty wrapper

Dice were taxed in Britain between 1711 and 1862. The duty was imposed with a view to discouraging gambling as well as providing revenue; it was increased from an initial 5*s* per pair to £1 per pair in 1804, at which level it remained until the repeal of the law in 1862.

From 1801 pairs of dice were sold in a sealed wrapper, a paper cover provided by the Stamp Office which constituted the duty stamp. The wrapper was printed from copper plates in red/brown on thin paper and in 1804 bore the words 'Stamp Office' and 'Duty one pound per pair'. The law also provided for the insertion of the maker's name on one face of the package: 'The Commissioners..., upon request of the maker provide an additional mark containing the maker's name, or other name to distinguish it, and cause the same to be made part of the said wrapper'. The wrapper was also printed with the mark of a crown in a circle of laurels.

As a further control measure, the dice themselves were required to be die-stamped with the impression of a crown. As with other Stamp Office devices (and indeed documents of most kinds) forgery was punishable by death. It is recorded that in 1724 one Anthony Walraven was sentenced to death for forging stamps on dice.

Die stamping *See* EMBOSSING/LACE PAPER

Dietary tables

Haphazard feeding of inmates in many institutions was gradually replaced in the 18th and 19th centuries by observance of a recognized scale of rations, which was commonly required to be printed and published. Scales of rations were also often required to be displayed, along with other regulations, within the institution concerned. Known as 'dietaries', these tabulated listings served on one hand to inform the inmate of his or her minimum feeding rights, and on the other to discourage corruption among supervisory staff.

The prison dietary was conceived in primitive terms, as was, in certain measure, that of the workhouse. Both were designed with a finely adjusted reference to living standards outside, ensuring that conditions inside were unmistakably worse than those without. Hospital, asylum, and school dietitians embodied the official view as to a healthy sufficiency; and army and navy diets represented the minimum provision consistent with avoidance of actual mutiny.

At the least oppressive end of the scale we may cite the 'Diet Table' (1810) of the Royal Military Asylum, Chelsea, for one child. As with most such tables, this deals with the week's arrangements day by day, meal by meal. For breakfast (every day of the week) the child receives '1/20th of a quartern loaf' of bread, 'one-sixth of a quart' of milk, and 'one-twentieth of a pound' of oatmeal. For supper, at a similarly economic level, there was bread, cheese, and beer on Sundays, Tuesdays, Thursdays, and Saturdays; bread and milk only on other days. Dinner offered variations from day to day: 'Sunday: beef roasted; potatoes; bread; beer. Monday: rice pudding; potatoes; beer. Tuesday: boiled beef in broth; potatoes; bread; beer'. Other days are in similar vein, with boiled mutton as a 'meat dish' on Saturday, pease soup and suet pudding as additional variants.

In the 1830s Andover Workhouse offered a diet of bread, meat, vegetables, soup, cheese, and the ubiquitous poor-house

DERBY COUNTY GAOL.—Scale of Di

	1 Class. Convicted Prisoners confined for any term not exceeding three days.			2 Class. Convicted Prisoners for any term exceeding three days, and not exceeding fourteen days. Prisoners of this class employed at hard labour, to have in addition one pint of soup per week.				
	Breakfast.	Dinner.	Supper.	Breakfast.		Dinner.	Supper.	
	Gruel.	Bread.	Gruel.	Gruel.	Bread.	Bread.	Gruel.	Bread.
	pt.	ozs.	pt.	pt.	ozs.	ozs.	pt.	ozs.
Sunday	1	16	1	1	6	12	1	6
Monday	1	16	1	1	6	12	1	6
Tuesday	1	16	1	1	6	12	1	6
Wednesday	1	16	1	1	6	12	1	6
Thursday	1	16	1	1	6	12	1	6
Friday	1	16	1	1	6	12	1	6
Saturday	1	16	1	1	6	12	1	6

	3 Class. Convicted Prisoners employed at hard labour for terms exceeding fourteen days, but not more than six weeks, and convicted Prisoners not employed at hard labour for terms exceeding fourteen days, and not more than three months.							
	Breakfast.			Dinner.			Supper.	
	Gruel.	Bread.	Soup.	Bread.	Cooked Meat.	Potatoes.	Gruel.	Bread.
	pt.	ozs.	pt.	ozs.	ozs.	lbs.	pt.	ozs.
Sunday	1	8	1	8			1	8
Monday	1	8		8		1	1	8
Tuesday	1	8		8	3	½	1	8
Wednesday	1	8		8		1	1	8
Thursday	1	8	1	8			1	8
Friday	1	8		8		1	1	8
Saturday	1	8		8	3	½	1	8

	4 Class. Convicted Prisoners employed at hard labour for terms exceeding six weeks, but not more than three months, and convicted Prisoners not employed at hard labour for terms exceeding three months.							
	Breakfast.		Dinner.				Supper.	
	Gruel.	Bread.	Cooked Meat.	Soup.	Bread.	Potatoes.	Gruel.	Bread.
	pt.	ozs.	ozs.	pt.	ozs.	lbs.	pt.	ozs.
Sunday	1	8	3		8	½	1	8
Monday	1	8		1	8		1	8
Tuesday	1	8	3		8	½	1	8
Wednesday	1	8		1	8		1	8
Thursday	1	8	3		8	½	1	8
Friday	1	8		1	8		1	8
Saturday	1	8	3		8	½	1	8

	5 Class. Convicted Prisoners employed at hard labour for terms exceeding three months.										6 Class. Prisoners sentenced by courts to solitary confinement to have their ordinary diet.
	Breakfast.				Dinner.				Supper.		
	Gruel.	Bread.	Cocoa.	Sugar or Molasses.	Cooked Meat.	Soup.	Potatoes.	Bread.	Gruel.	Bread.	
	pt.	ozs.	pt.	ozs.	ozs.	pt.	lbs.	ozs.	pt.	ozs.	
Sunday	1	6			4		1	6	1	6	
Monday		6	1	¾		1	1	6	1	6	
Tuesday	1	6			4		1	6	1	6	
Wednesday		6	1	¾		1	1	6	1	6	
Thursday	1	6			4		1	6	1	6	
Friday		6	1	¾		1	1	6	1	6	
Saturday	1	6			4		1	6	1	6	

Detail of a dietary table for Derby County Gaol. Letterpress, with red ruling, 1844. As shown, 160 × 390 mm (6¼ × 15⅜ in)

and prison gruel. (It was a common practice, for inmates over sixty, to replace breakfast gruel with a weekly allowance of 1 oz of tea, 7 oz of butter, and 8 oz of sugar.)

Gruel, much hated and often of doubtful content, was formally defined in the dietary tables of Derby County Gaol (1844) as containing 1½ ounces of oatmeal per pint [of water] and 2 ounces per pint if made in lesser quantities than 50 pints. On alternate days it was to be sweetened with ¾ oz of molasses or sugar, and seasoned with salt.

Dietaries, and their footnotes, throw considerable light on the detail of institutional catering. From a table published in 1839 we learn, for example, that in Grantham Union Workhouse 'on meat days, when from any cause the potatoes are bad, the men receive 6 oz of bread, and the women 5 oz in lieu of them'. A note on the dietary of New Bailey Prison, Salford (c.1844), prescribes that Saturday's stew be made from cows' heads, seasoned with pepper and salt.

'Private' poor-houses, run as businesses under contract from local authorities, also published ration details, though these were often sketchy as to quantities, and sometimes unspecific as to apportionment. They were commonly published under the title 'Bill of Fare'. One specimen from 'J Tipple's Receptacle for Parish Poor, Great White House, Hoxton' quotes food by the day, for example: 'Sunday: One Pint and a Half Gruel, Fourteen Ounces Bread, Twelve Ounces Meat Baked with Vegetables, and Small Beer'.

REFERENCES Ian Anstruther, *The Scandal of the Andover Workhouse* (London: Bles, 1973); Sir George Nicholls, *A History of the English Poor Law*, 3 vol. (reprint of rev. edn, London: Cass, 1967); Michael E. Rose, *The English Poor Law, 1780–1930* (Newton Abbot: David & Charles, 1971)

Directions for use

Before the end of the 18th century there were few devices whose use was so complex as to require explanation. Only in the field of folk medicine, with its often arcane concoctions and methods, were written instructions considered necessary. With the 19th century, however, an upsurgence of invention and innovation brought the need for detailed user-instruction. 'Directions for use' shortly became not merely a desirable adjunct to the marketing of a new product but an inherent component of its novelty – and hence of its sales appeal. The expression 'complete with full instructions for use', inserted in advertising copy on the price-line, became widespread.

Instruction sheets appeared as leaflets, as bottle-wrappers, and as package and box-lid labels. Loose leaflets sometimes included the elements of a TRADE CARD, serving as an introduction to a product as well as accompanying it.

Typical in this category is a leaflet, 210 × 175 mm (8¼ × 6⅞ in) (c.1770), bearing at its head the coat of arms of George III and the title 'Directions for using Baron van Haake's Composition for Manuring of land, which is to be sold at the Royal Letters Patent Tar and Pitch Manufactory, at Rochester; and at No 10, Bearbinder-Lane, near the Mansion House, London'. The text, after some two hundred words of combined plaudit and use-instruction, concludes in frankly pre-sale mode: 'The Price is a Shilling per pound weight; but to prevent trouble, not less than eight or ten pounds will be sold. Letters Post paid will be duly answered'.

In similar vein, though clearly devised for after-sales use, is a leaflet measuring 190 × 150 mm (7½ × 6 in) (c.1800), entitled 'Directions for cleaning'. It relates to Oldham & Co.'s patent polished steel stoves which were manufactured at their warehouse, the corner of Brook Street, Holborn, London. Here too the text runs to about two hundred words, but the instructions ('Mix some of the dark Powder with a little Sweet Oil …' etc.), presuppose that the product is already in the hands of the purchaser. Similar products bore brief instructions on the package: typical of these were such preparations as polishing powders, marking inks, and a wide range of pills, ointments, and other pharmaceutical products. Matches, also, carried instructions for use – and continued to do so for half a century after their introduction.

The more complicated inventions of the 19th century brought substantial editorial pieces, extending latterly to folders, booklets, and bound handbooks. At a mid-point in this development stands the Colt Revolver label with directions for loading and cleaning, 120 × 170 mm (4¾ × 6¾ in), which was pasted inside the lid of the company's products in the 1850s. Here, in the earliest days of mass production, is an exercise in technical copywriting, a combination of efficiency and informality: 'To take the lock to pieces, clean and oil … take a bit of paper, and number thereon – 1, 2, 3, 4, 5, 6, 7, 8, 9, 10; and, as you take to pieces, lay down the parts on the respective numbers until the whole is done; to re-assemble, reversing the order, putting in first what you took out last'.

Directories

Charles Lamb characterized directories as 'books which are no books', unjustly placing them with ALMANACS to be consigned to the waste paper basket at the end of each year upon publication of the new annual edition. This explains why they are today probably the rarest of books and qualify as ephemera. Their primary function was as instruments of commerce, giving lists of names with addresses and occupations. They are now of inestimable value to the biographer and genealogist and, particularly later ones, to the topographer.

Early directories were merely lists of names, as is made clear by the title of the very first, which was published by Samuel Lee in 1677. Called *A Collection of the Names of the Merchants Living in and about The City of London*, it consists of 1953 names and 'Habitations'; but, as house numbering had not yet been introduced, the addresses take the form of a brief indication of the thoroughfare. Though Lee claimed that his list was 'Very Useful and Necessary', it had no followers until 1734 when directories began to appear annually. They were all modelled on Samuel Lee's publication until 1763 when the first practical step towards the provision of a more useful directory was made by a Mr Mortimer who, in his *Universal Director*, added occupations to his names and addresses and included a section arranged under trades.

From that date onwards directories became more and more informative and useful, especially after 1765 when an Act was passed requiring all houses in London to be numbered and precise addresses began to appear. By 1768, when Richard Baldwin published his *New Complete Guide*, all such houses had been numbered.

A final feature of directories, the most valuable to the topographer, and one which would make a directory complete, had yet to appear. This was the inclusion of 'Streets, topographically described and arranged in alphabetical succession, with the names and occupations of the inhabitants'. The first directory to include this feature was Johnstone's *London Commercial Guide*, which was published in 1817; although it was not immediately copied, it set the standard for all future directories. In fact, many years were to pass before Johnstone's example was followed in London by Robson in 1832 and Pigot in 1838.

The *Post Office London Directory*, which had appeared annually since 1800 as a mere list of names, was acquired by Frederic Kelly in 1837. At first he appeared to be in no hurry to bring it into line with his more popular and formidable rivals Robson and Pigot. His 1840 edition, however, included a 'Trades' section for the first time, and 1841 was the first issue to include a 'Streets' section. Kelly's *Post Office London Directory* was now complete and its format remained, year after year, virtually unchanged, though its bulk increased considerably (the 1800 edition had some 324 pages; the 1900 edition 3515). It remains an invaluable research tool for historians, genealogists, and topographers and its replacement by *Yellow Pages* was a disastrous loss to scholarship.

The first British provincial directory was published for Birmingham in 1763. Though no copy is known to exist, it was advertised in the *London Chronicle* for 14–16 July 1763. A directory for Liverpool followed in 1766, for Manchester in 1772, and for Bristol in 1775. Unlike London directories, those published in the British provinces came out very irregularly and it was not until well into the 19th century that they were published annually.

The first two American directories were both published in Philadelphia in the same year, 1785. *Macpherson's Directory for the City and Suburbs of Philadelphia* contained 6250 names and William Bradford's directory a mere 3569. [PJ]

See also STREET VIEW; TELEPHONE DIRECTORY

REFERENCES Charles W. F. Goss, *The London Directories, 1677–1855* (London: Denis Archer, 1932); Jane E. Norton, *Guide to the National and Provincial Directories of England and Wales, excluding London, published before 1856* (London: Royal Historical Society, 1950)

SOURCES Guildhall Library, London; Bishopsgate Institute, London

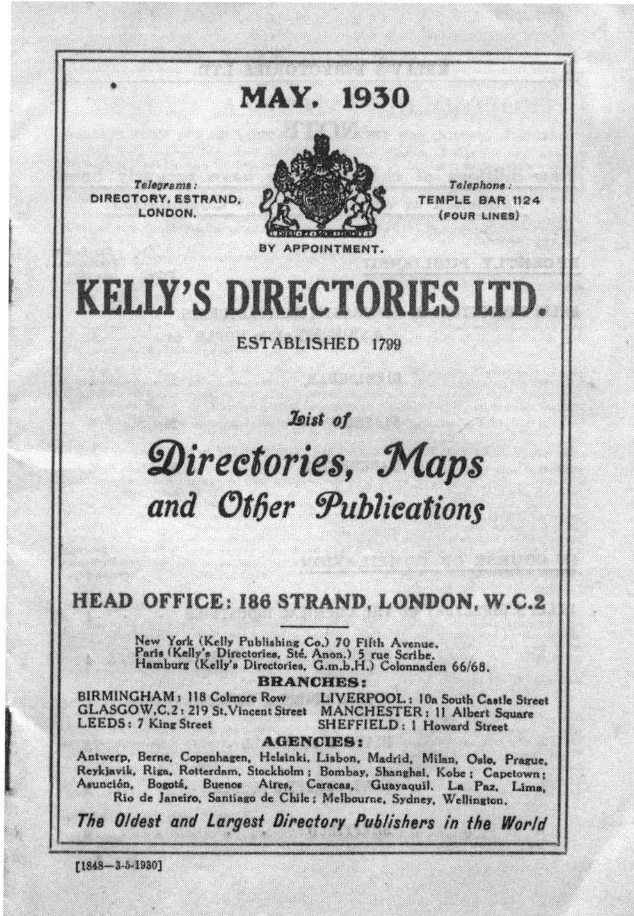

MAY. 1930

Telegrams: DIRECTORY, ESTRAND, LONDON.

Telephone: TEMPLE BAR 1124 (FOUR LINES)

BY APPOINTMENT.

KELLY'S DIRECTORIES LTD.

ESTABLISHED 1799

List of

Directories, Maps and Other Publications

HEAD OFFICE: 186 STRAND, LONDON, W.C.2

New York (Kelly Publishing Co.) 70 Fifth Avenue.
Paris (Kelly's Directories, Sté. Anon.) 5 rue Scribe.
Hamburg (Kelly's Directories, G.m.b.H.) Colonnaden 66/68.

BRANCHES:

BIRMINGHAM: 118 Colmore Row
LIVERPOOL: 10a South Castle Street
GLASGOW, C.2: 219 St. Vincent Street
MANCHESTER: 11 Albert Square
LEEDS: 7 King Street
SHEFFIELD: 1 Howard Street

AGENCIES:

Antwerp, Berne, Copenhagen, Helsinki, Lisbon, Madrid, Milan, Oslo, Prague, Reykjavik, Riga, Rotterdam, Stockholm; Bombay, Shanghai, Kobe; Capetown; Asunción, Bogotá, Buenos Aires, Caracas, Guayaquil, La Paz, Lima, Rio de Janeiro, Santiago de Chile; Melbourne, Sydney, Wellington.

The Oldest and Largest Directory Publishers in the World

[1848—3-5-1930]

'List of directories, maps, and other publications' issued by Kelly's Directories Ltd, May 1930. Letterpress, 8 pages, printed throughout in red and black. 177 × 121mm (7 × 4¾in)

Disinfected mail

Measures taken to control the spread of infectious disease in former times included interception and disinfection of mail at frontiers. In times of plague and other epidemics, which at some periods were frequent, letters from suspect areas were subjected by health authorities to 'treatment' and marked on the outside accordingly. Marking was effected by a variety of means, including wax and paper seals, handstamps, affixed labels, and manuscript notes. These had the dual function of explaining the often noticeable traces of the treatment and reassuring the recipient that the letter was safe to open.

Letters were treated by three basic methods: perforation, to let out the harmful 'miasma' and let in clean air; immersion or sprinkling with vinegar or sea-water (both thought to have prophylactic properties); and heating or fumigating. Traces of these measures are more or less readily apparent. In most cases a single method must have been used; in some, two or three.

Piercing was carried out by the use of spike-headed 'rastel' tongs, needles, or knives. Practice varied from one area to another, and it has been possible in some cases to relate specific types of perforation to particular places. Perforation, which normally penetrated the letter completely, is readily visible in cases where rastel tongs have been used. In many cases however the perforation takes the form of a fine slit, often so fine as to escape notice until the letter is handled, when manipulation may distend the cut. Piercing for disinfection may generally be distinguished from accidental damage by its presence in at least two places, commonly the same distance apart (though a single central cut is not unusual).

Disinfected mail sent from Naples, 7 September 1854. Manuscript with stamp 'Netta dentro e fuori'. As folded, 90 × 153 mm (3½ × 6 in)

Immersion in liquids has the effect of causing inks to run, sometimes to the point of producing illegibility, and in the case of vinegar – very widely used – causing a brown staining. Sprinkling from vinegar, less obliterative, produces a splash pattern of brown staining. Immersion in sea-water, commonly used in ports and quarantine harbours, had very bad effects on mail. As with all evidence of 'disinfection', however, the damage provided reassurance to the recipient.

Heat disinfection involved holding the letter over glowing coals. The effect here was to scorch the letter, leaving unburnt patches where tongs had held the item for treatment. In 'fumigation' the letter was exposed to sulphur fumes or smoke. Discolouration occurred in both cases.

In some instances, for added safety, letters were exposed to all three treatments. It was also not uncommon for letters on long journeys to be treated at two or more separate health stations in transmission.

Disinfected letters carried a wide range of marks and handstamps, in some cases these consisted mainly of the official stamp or seal of the certifying body, with or without location. Examples are: 'Provisores Salutis Venetiae' (Overseers of Health, Venice); 'Deputazione Sanitaria' (Sanitary Commission [Sicily]); 'Koeniglich Bayerisches Sanitäts Siegel' (Royal Bavarian Hygiene Seal). The town of Reggio provided a paste-on printed stamp – not unlike a postage stamp (though unperforated) – bearing the legend 'Uffizio di Disinfezione in Reggio' (Office of Disinfection, Reggio).

Other marks specifically referred to disinfection. Perforated mail from Italy claimed complete disinfection: 'Netta dentro e fuori' (Clean inside and out). Fumigated letters claimed only external treatment: 'Profumato soltanto al di fuori' (Fumigated only on outside). The word 'Disinfected' or its equivalent appeared on its own or with a location: 'Gereinigt: Lichtenfels; Disinfettata: Bologna; Disinfektiert; Purifée à La Coitat'. Specific treatment appears in a handstamp from Chile in 1887: 'Disinfectada por calor' (Disinfected by heat). Efforts at health controls through 'disinfection' spanned 300 years. Precautions centred largely on control of the movement of persons and cattle, but general goods, packages, and mail were a constant concern. Even imports of rags for paper-making were suspect. In the early 18th century British officers demanded health declarations on oath from masters of incoming ships. A Bible, kept for the purpose, was handed from shore to ship at the end of a boathook for the declaration. It was afterwards dragged through sea water to purify it.

Later scientific knowledge attributes the spread of the plague and cholera respectively to rat fleas and polluted drinking water. The measures taken to disinfect mail are now seen not merely as inadequate but unnecessary.

See also CACHET, POSTAL; PLAGUE PAPERS; PRATIQUE, PAPERS OF

REFERENCE Associazione Italiana di Storia Postale, *Bolli e Documenti di Sanità', dell'Area Italiana* ([Rome]): Italphil. S.R.L., Edizioni Studi Filatelici, [1981]); *Pratique: Quarterly Newsletter of The Disinfected Mail Study Circle*, London, 1974–

Display card

A 19th-century development in retail selling was the use of a combined show-and-display card, on which the product – usually small and light in weight – was threaded or pasted in quantity. The card carried a brand-name title and was punched and strung for hanging. The upper areas of small neighbourhood shops were often crowded with the cards which displayed such products as tap washers, corn cures, teapot spout guards, tubes of fixative, headache powders, pens, pencils, erasers, geometry instruments, blue-bags, kettle de-furrers, and similar items. Display cards also appeared in which products such as straps, dog leashes, key chains, etc. were strung from the lower edge of an abbreviated card, the card serving as a title-piece.

A typical example is a card displaying Parkinson's headache powders, or 'Head Powders' as they later became. The card measures 375 × 265 mm (14¾ × 10½ in) and devotes more than half its area to display space for the powder packets. The display space, revealed as packets are sold, carries slogans such as: 'Parkinson's BP drugs are always reliable', 'Fourteen prize

Display card for Joseph Gillott's 'Damascus' steel pen nibs (lacking the nibs), mid 19th century. Compound-plate printed in red and blue. 94 × 147 mm (3¾ × 5¾ in)

medals awarded to Parkinson's Baking Powder', 'Parkinson's Custard Powder in penny packets, delicious and nourishing', 'Parkinson's sell more sugar-coated pills than any other firm in England'. Evidence of the continued success of the product is provided by a series of three versions of the card, in which the style of the late 1880s gives way to that of 1900, and, later, of 1910. The price of the product, incidentally, remains unchanged at one penny for over a quarter of a century.

The early display card enshrines products sometimes not merely obsolete but obscure: the Parkinson company also used the principle to market 'colour polish in one penny blocks', and an anonymous company, based in Chalk Farm Road, London NW, displayed 'Bright lights preparation for oil lamps': the product consisted of a powder to be placed in the 'Bowl or Lamp each week'.

The display card originally appeared as a tentative experiment in the mid nineteenth century when steel pens were displayed on small cards, each item being threaded to a printed 'compartment' in the design. A dozen of Joseph Gillott's Damascus Steel Pens appeared on a two-colour Whiting and Branston card, 95 × 145 mm (3¾ × 5¾ in), in the 1850s and a dozen of Simpsons Scientific Steel and Gold Pens, with ink-retaining penholder, appeared on a display card, 215 mm square (8½ × 8½ in), in New York in the 1860s.

In the 1880s in Paris, small display cards were used to sell 'unbreakable' eye-glass cords. The card, 150 × 90 mm (6 × 3½ in), carried six specimens threaded to a chromolithographed design showing a cord being tested with a heavy weight.

See also MOTTO, SHOP-WINDOW; POINT-OF-SALE DISPLAY; SHELF STRIP; SHOW CARD

Distraint, papers of

Papers of distraint and attachment embody the legal concept of 'taking personal chattels from the offender into the custody of the injured party, in satisfaction of the wrong'. They normally have to do with to non-payment of rent, but may also relate to legal and other debts.

Early papers of distraint and attachment consist commonly of part-printed legal forms, each of which is devised to cover a specific phase or contingency in the process. Salient items are the 'Warrant of distress', authorizing the distraint to proceed; the 'Inventory of goods', in which chattels eligible for sale are listed; the 'Notice of distress', warning the debtor of impending appraisal and sale; the 'Appraiser's oath', a sworn valuation of the items listed in the inventory; the 'Complaint', of clandestine removal of chattels to evade listing; the 'Want of distress', a report indicating that no goods have been found suitable for distraint; and the 'Committal' of the debtor to prison. Other forms include search warrants for the discovery of concealed goods and an 'Information and complaint' that goods impounded for distraint have been 'rescued' and praying that a 'hue and cry' be levied for their recovery.

In America, the warrant of distress, known as a writ, was addressed to the Sheriff or his deputy, or to the Constable, and combined a warning of distraint with the alternative of apprehension. The sum in question was to be augmented by 'One Shilling Lawful Money more for this Writ, together with your own Fees' (Middletown, Connecticut, 1787), and the document commonly included the traditional injunction, 'Hereof fail not...'. Other American distraint documents, contemporaries of which are not normally found in Britain, are Sheriffs' signed

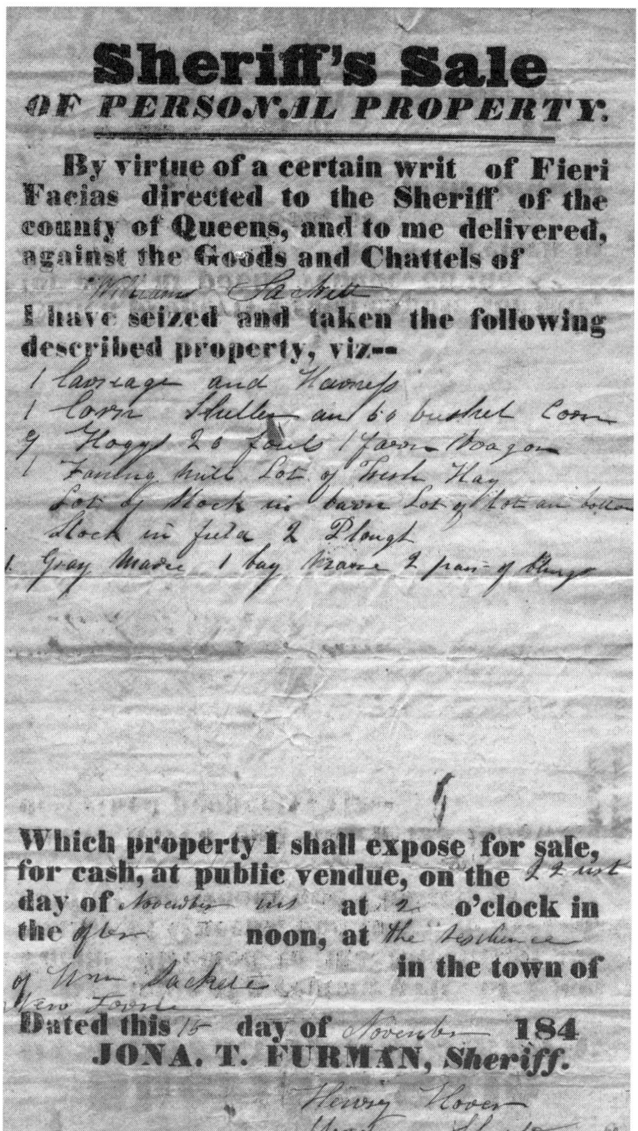

Sheriff's Sale

OF PERSONAL PROPERTY.

By virtue of a certain writ of Fieri Facias directed to the Sheriff of the county of Queens, and to me delivered, against the Goods and Chattels of William Sackett

I have seized and taken the following described property, viz--

1 Carriage and Harness
1 Corn Sheller and 60 bushel Corn
9 Hoggs 20 fouls 1 farm Wagon
1 Faning mill Lot of Fresh Hay
Lot of Stock in barn
Stock in field 2 Plough
1 Gray Mare 1 bay Mare 2 pair of

Which property I shall expose for sale, for cash, at public vendue, on the day of November at 2 o'clock in the after noon, at the residence in the town of of Wm. Sackett New Town

Dated this 15 day of November 184

JONA. T. FURMAN, Sheriff.

Henry Hover
Under Sheriff

Sheriff's sale notice, Queen's County, New York, 1840s. Letterpress and manuscript. 320 × 185 mm (12½ × 7¼ in)

certificates of sale proceeds, reports recording failure to sell goods distrained, and 'Sheriff's sale' public notices. Sheriff's sale notices quoted their authority in a writ of *fieri facias* (Latin: cause it to be done), a writ now obsolete which listed goods and other details by hand. The notice announced seizure of the property 'Which property I shall expose for sale, for cash, at public vendue...'. A typical example, 320 × 185 mm (12½ × 7¼ in), signed by Henry Hover, Under Sheriff of Queen's County, of an unspecified date in the 1840s, lists the property of William Sackett: '1 Carriage and Harness; 1 Corn Shelter and 60 bushel Corn; 9 Hoggs 20 fouls 1 farm Wagon; 1 faning mill Lot of Fresh Hay Lot of stock in barn..., Stock in field 2 Plough; 1 Gray Mare 1 bay Mare...'.

Doctor's bill

Many doctor's bills convey a medical and professional picture in some respects familiar, in others less so. Written on unheaded paper, and often covering a period of years, many of them resemble the submissions of a tradesman or artisan. Most of the surviving examples were in fact made out to the monied classes, those who could in the first place afford the services of a doctor and in the second afford to keep him waiting. Many of the bills were long and narrow in format, some extending to a depth of

400 mm (15¾ in) or so, and, as with long-standing tradesmen's bills, were also often extended to greater length by pasting two or more sheets together.

Entries itemized not only visits and consultations but treatments of various kinds, including bleeding and minor operations, and supply of medicines, dressings, glysters, leeches, and other remedies. A bill made out by 'Doctor Wood in Perth' to Lieutenant Stewart in the month of October 1776 details 'Oil for the Ears, Styptic drops, a Box of laxative pills, Thirty two doses Bark; Sixteen doses Ditto; a Glass Styptic Drops as formerly; a Box of Stomachic Pills and Thirty two doses Bark as formerly'. These items come to 18 shillings. An added item, clearly inserted subsequently, appears as 'To Advice at different times – £1'.

A bill made out to Christopher Hawkins Esq (location unspecified) covering the period 6 October 1781 to 3 January 1784 enumerates visits ('Journey & night') and the supply of, among other things, best lint, castor oil, peppermint water, opening tincture, sal volatile, draughts, opening pills, salt of wormwood, testaceous julep, laudanum drops, bladder opening pills no. 18, paregoric elixir, and one pound of green tea. A separate item, again added afterwards and showing no sum in the fee column, reads: 'Administering Glysters, making up Saline Draughts etc.: What you please'.

A companion piece to the Christopher Hawkins account is a separate bill for Hawkins's servants. This bill, covering the period from 6 September 1780 to 31 October 1783, includes such items as opening pills, a box, coachman; plaster to the arm, boy; 3 purges, John; Journey, Sarah, bleeding, drops, vomit, composing drops, decoction, nervous pills, a large box. The master's bill comes to £8 9*s* 8*d* the servants' to £2 12*s*, a total of £11 1*s* 8*d* over a period of some three years. The bills bear no evidence of payment.

A comparable account from Jersey in the 20th century presents the doctor's printed compliments to the patient and mentions a sum of £8 for professional attendance from 1946 to 1949. As a handwritten addendum the bill bears the word 'please!'. This bill also bears no mark of payment.

The doctor's bill of the 18th and 19th centuries, as well as reflecting early therapeutic techniques graphically, conveys the reality of the doctor's dual battle: on the one hand, against great odds, he struggles with disease; on the other, against almost equal odds, with the patient's reluctance to pay.

See also BILLHEAD

Donation list

In appeals in aid of charities and other causes, published lists of subscribers are seen both as kudos to the committees of management and encouragement to the doubtful. Their use appears in a wide range of contexts, institutional and personal. The 19th century, with rapidly developing industrial and social-welfare activity, but little social security, brought a multitude of appeals, many of them in the form of part-printed forms for the insertion of names and donations.

Surviving examples include the case of Robert Whitehead (c.1870), the subject of an appeal put out by E. Smitheman, station master at Witney, Oxford. The printed heading records an accident to Whitehead who had his thigh broken 'By the fall of a tree while loading timber in the Witney Station yard and is not likely to be able to do any work for some time to come ... a most deserving case ... he has a wife and five children who are at present left without any means of support whatever'. The appeal is printed on ledger-ruled paper, and allows room for the insertion of some thirty subscribers. The copy in question is blank.

A similar paper, headed in manuscript and dated 1896, comes from Mangotsfield Railway Station: 'Ladies and Gentlemen: A subscription is respectfully solicited for the purpose of giving the platform staff at Mangotsfield Station their Annual Christmas Dinner'. The appeal was answered by sixty-three people and a total of £7 19*s* 9*d* was raised.

Wholly-printed donation lists were also widely used, particularly in the earlier part of the century, commonly in appeals for the funding or continuing support of schools, hospitals, asylums, etc. These appeared for the most part as four-page documents, often with an extended introduction on the front page and the subscribers' list on the centre pages; the back was left blank for the recipient's address when the item was folded and sealed for posting.

Less formal donation lists, often compiled in neighbourhood appeals for the sick or bereaved, were kept in notebooks. These were also used in door-to-door swindles, the contributors' names and donations being punctiliously entered for fictitious causes – relief of disabled fireman, repair of churches, or setting up soup kitchens.

Donor card

The donor card, carried as an indication of the holder's willingness to supply blood or allow removal of organs after death for transplantation, is based in Britain on the Human Tissue Act of 1961, section 1 (1), which states that: 'If any person, either in writing at any time or orally in the presence of two or more witnesses during his last illness, has expressed a request that his body or any specified part of his body be used after his death for therapeutic purposes ... the person lawfully in possession of his body ... may, unless he has reason to believe that the request was subsequently withdrawn, authorise the removal of any part ... for use in accordance with the request'.

Britain's first formal donor system required the volunteer to apply to the British Medical Association or to the Ministry of Health for a form which, duly filled in, signed, and countersigned by a witness, constituted written authority.

The first British donor card for organs was brought into being through the initiative of Elizabeth Ward, herself the mother of a kidney patient. The card was distributed in 1972 through the Ministry of Health to hospitals, clinics, and doctors. A two-colour folder, opening to 150 × 105 mm (6 × 4⅛ in), provided space for the names, addresses, and signatures of both the holder and next of kin. The card related only to donation of kidneys. A second version, opening to a smaller format, 130 × 105 mm (5⅛ × 4⅛ in), was issued in 1974; this card was also conceived solely for kidney donation, but included a reminder of the possibility of corneal grafts and an invitation to apply for information from the Royal National Institute for the Blind.

In May 1980 a smaller version was distributed. Entitled simply 'Kidney donor', it was made of plastic, similar to a credit card, and measured 55 × 85 mm (2⅛ × 3⅜ in); it carried only the holder's name, signature, date, and the name and phone number of another person (the words 'next of kin' being omitted). The plastic card was shortly followed (June 1980) by one of similar format printed on ordinary card. Entitled 'Kidney donor/ Other donor', it covers kidneys, eyes, heart, liver, pituitary gland, and pancreas, with the option of deletions by the signa-

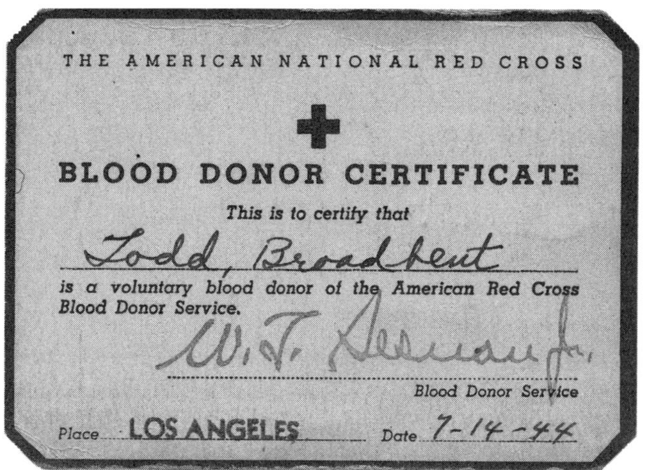
THE AMERICAN NATIONAL RED CROSS

BLOOD DONOR CERTIFICATE

This is to certify that

Todd Broadbent

is a voluntary blood donor of the American Red Cross Blood Donor Service.

W. T. [illegible] Jr.

Blood Donor Service

Place LOS ANGELES Date 7-14-44

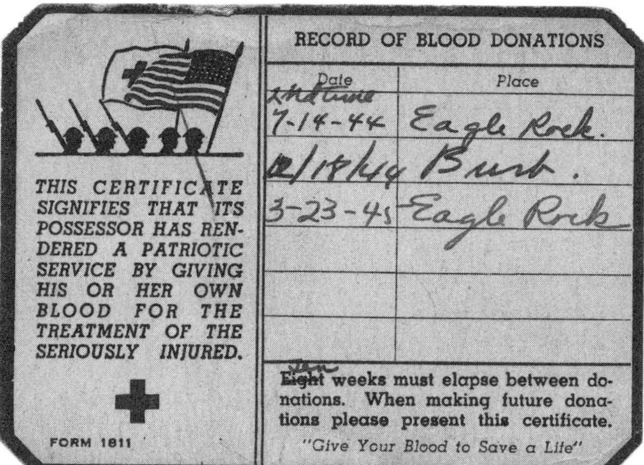
RECORD OF BLOOD DONATIONS

Date	Place
7-14-44	Eagle Rock.
12/18/44	Bush.
3-23-45	Eagle Rock

THIS CERTIFICATE SIGNIFIES THAT ITS POSSESSOR HAS RENDERED A PATRIOTIC SERVICE BY GIVING HIS OR HER OWN BLOOD FOR THE TREATMENT OF THE SERIOUSLY INJURED.

~~Eight~~ Ten weeks must elapse between donations. When making future donations please present this certificate.

"Give Your Blood to Save a Life"

FORM 1811

Blood donor card of the American National Red Cross, issued in Los Angeles, 14 July 1944. Lithographed in red and blue, with manuscript and stamped additions. 66 × 92 mm (2⅝ × 3⅝ in)

tory as desired. It also carries space for the name and phone number of someone to be contacted.

In the United States the development of a nationally recognized donor card was complicated by lack of uniformity in state laws concerning transplants. Donor cards had been provided by a number of organizations (eye banks, kidney foundations, and tissue banks) in the 1960s, but their legality was open to question in some states and there was confusion as to their interstate validity. After three years of consultation, the National Conference of Commissioners on state laws formulated the Uniform Anatomical Gift Act (1968), upon which, by the early 1980s, almost all states had based 'transplant laws'. In 1969 a meeting of the Ad Hoc Committee on Medical-Legal Problems agreed on the terms of a model uniform donor card.

The United States uniform donor card appears in a variety of formats, but its wording is constant. It provides the holder with the options of donating 'any needed organs or parts' or only specified organs or parts of the body for anatomical study. It also allows the holder to specify limitations or any special wishes. On its reverse, the card allows for the signature, birth date, date of signature, city and state of the holder, and the signatures of two witnesses produced in the presence of each other.

In neither Britain nor America is there a central file or other record of card holders. Those desiring to opt out of the system simply destroy the card. From the 1970s the view was increasingly being expressed that the system should be 'inverted', that is to say that permission to use organs after death should be assumed to be granted unless a card is carried indicating the contrary. The 'negative' or 'absence of objection' principle is in use in France and may well become universal. The present donor cards may thus be replaced by the non-donor-card.

Draft

The manuscript of James Elroy Flecker's 'The Golden Journey to Samarkand' reveals that the poet, as an afterthought in the opening lines, transformed his scene from morning to evening with the alteration of a single word. 'Our camels sniff the morning and are glad' becomes '... sniff the evening and are glad' – a change which, once revealed, must fundamentally affect the reader's view of the whole of the rest of the work.

No less than the altered literary manuscript in which the author's first and second thoughts appear simultaneously, the altered drafts of everyday texts provide subjects for study. Ordinary people in their handwritten works – job applications, letters of complaint, advertising, announcements, etc. – reveal much of interest through their corrections and amendments. The field is wide, and examples are fairly readily acquired.

Prior to the advent of office copying facilities (the copy press, carbon paper, etc.), it was customary for writers to retain for their own reference a fair copy of what they had written or, more commonly, the original rough draft, complete with additions and deletions. These are the raw material of the amendment-collector's study.

A typical example is contained in a handwritten draft from Hastings entitled 'Cry about removal – in case of an invasion from the French – 1803'. The term 'cry' applies to an official announcement, to be publicly proclaimed by a town crier; 'removal' refers to evacuation of horses and cattle from localities likely to become battle areas. In addition to its implicit drama, this document reflects by its alterations the thinking of the author.

Prior to the alteration, the text of the first paragraph reads: 'In case of Alarm, such of the inhabitants as are rendered incapable of taking an active part in the defence of their Country, either by age, sickness, or other Infirmity, are strongly advised to remain quietly at their own homes for the protection of their lives and property, both of which would certainly be endanger'd by any attempt to remove from the Town upon such an occasion'.

After alteration, the paragraph is strengthened: 'The inhabitants of this Place who are rendered incapable of taking an active part in the defence of their Country, either by age, sickness, or other infirmity, are strongly advised in case of alarm to remain at home for the preservation of their lives and property, which would be much endanger'd by any attempt to remove from the town upon such an occasion'.

The second paragraph, before alteration, reads: 'the owners of Horses and Oxen are hereby warn'd to have their cattle ready for driving away upon the first signal of an enemy; Any Cattle which shall be found near the Coast after a reasonable time allow'd for the removal of them, will be immediately destroy'd, in order that they may not fall into the Hands of the Enemy, and no compensation whatever will be made to the owners if it shall appear that they have neglected to conform to these regulations'.

In its altered version the paragraph makes minor adjustments to its final wording, but is more specific in its instructions: 'The owners of Horses and Oxen are likewise forewarn'd to have them ready for driving away into the Country by the road over Fairlight Down to Westfield & Bodiham upon the first signal; any Cattle of this description which shall be found near the Coast after a reasonable time allow'd for the removal of them, will be immediately destroy'd in order that they may not fall into the Hands of the Enemy, and no compensation whatever will be made to the owners unless it shall be made to appear that they have used their utmost endeavours to conform to these regulations'.

Drawing book

Early instructional drawing books consisted simply of a selection of reproductions for the aspiring artist to study and, if desired, copy on his or her own separate sheets. The earliest *Oxford English Dictionary* reference cites a 1755 publication, *The Complete Drawing Book, Containing Many and Curious Specimens.* The book is not described, but the title suggests that it offered, as with its successors for a century or so, no provision for the student to draw on the pages of the book itself.

Among early 19th century drawing books were those of William Pyne, who brought out a series of publications in the period 1803–15. These books mostly featured large numbers of figures in a multitude of trades, activities, and costumes, which were designed to be copied by landscape artists whose figure work was inadequate (*see* STAFFAGE). The first was a part-work entitled *Microcosm: or, a Picturesque Delineation of the Arts, Agriculture, Manufactures, &c of Great Britain; in a Series of above a Thousand Groups of Small Figures for the Embellishment of Landscape* (1803–6). The drawings were printed in black and hand-coloured. A second and complete edition appeared in 1806. Other such titles were *The Costume of Great Britain* (1808) and *Etchings of Rustic Figures for the Embellishment of Landscape* (1815). More directly instructional in tone was Pyne's *Rudiments of Landscape Drawing in a Series of easy Examples*, published in 1812.

The process of lithography proved ideal for the production of drawing books: one such set, the *New & Popular Drawing Books*, was published in the 1830s and 1840s by Tilt and Bogue of Fleet Street, London. Each number presented lithographs in black and a single tint, generally on sheets measuring 280 × 380 mm (11 × 14⅞ in). Bound in paper wrappers, they consisted of four sheets, but a full set of six, eight, twelve, or fourteen numbers could be bought as a cloth-bound volume or in a half-morocco binding. The sheets presented 'sketch-book' studies of groups of figures, landscapes, houses, shipping, 'and other picturesque objects', and each set featured the work of a single artist. Listed in an 1841 catalogue are the names of the following artists: Samuel Prout, W. M. Grundy, Andrew, Fairland, Julien, Worsley, Zeitter, G. Childs, Cooper, James Andrews, George Harley, and J. D. Harding. Titles include *Prout's Elementary Drawing Book, Sketch Book of Shipping and Craft, Julien's Studies of Heads* and *Zeitter's Studies of Animals and Rustic Groups.*

In a similar series the company published work by the best-known and most prolific of the British drawing masters of the period, J. D. Harding. One of his titles, it was pointed out, had been 'entirely drawn on Stone by Mr Harding *himself*, and printed under his immediate inspection'. Resemblance to the original sketches was complete, it was claimed: 'each Subject may be considered as a *bona fide* and first-rate Drawing'. It is clear that the drawings were produced as much for general application as for instruction.

The 'drawing copy-book', specifically produced for school children and providing space for drawing on the page, appeared in the 1860s. The term 'copy-book' was introduced by Vere Foster (*see* COPY-BOOK), whose 'writing copy-books' had wide success. A number of British firms, notably Cassell's, Collins, Blackie and Sons, and William Bemrose & Sons (all of whom had also published writing copy-books) followed Vere Foster's example and produced such drawing books. Blank spaces for the pupil's drawings became the general rule, and in many cases additional whole pages were left unprinted for working on.

As with the ordinary copy-book, the word 'copy' in 'drawing copy-book' referred not to the pupil's re-rendering of printed models but to the models themselves. Cassell's *Penny Drawing Copy Books,* each bearing printed models and blank spaces, added that completely blank books were issued 'in connection with these drawing copies'. Provision of blank paper, either within the body of the publication or as a separate unprinted book, remained something of a novelty in the latter years of the century. Vere Foster's drawing-book covers of the 1870s and 1880s carried specific references to the practice: 'With paper for copying'; 'Each book with instructions and paper to draw on'. By the turn of the century, however, blanks were the norm.

A variant of the drawing copy-book was the early colouring book. Designed for the home rather than the schoolroom, this presented pairs of identical lithographs, commonly on facing pages, one image being ready-coloured by the publisher, the

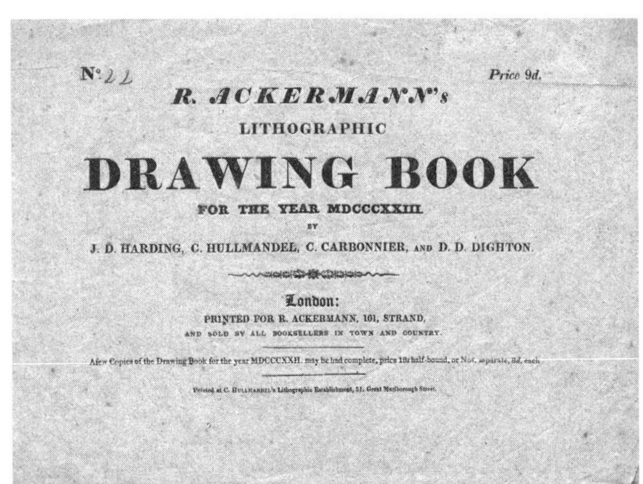

N°. 22 Price 9d.

R. ACKERMANN's

LITHOGRAPHIC

DRAWING BOOK

FOR THE YEAR MDCCCXXIII

BY

J. D. HARDING, C. HULLMANDEL, C. CARBONNIER, AND D. D. DIGHTON.

London:

PRINTED FOR R. ACKERMANN, 101, STRAND,

AND SOLD BY ALL BOOKSELLERS IN TOWN AND COUNTRY.

A few Copies of the Drawing Book for the year MDCCCXXII. may be had complete, price 18s half-bound, or Nos. separate, 8d. each

Printed at C. Hullmandel's Lithographic Establishment, 51, Great Marlborough Street.

Front wrappers of *R. Ackermann's Lithographic Drawing Book for the Year MDCCCXXIII*, no. 22 (London: R. Ackermann, 1823). Letterpress on buff paper. 195 × 283 mm (7⅝ × 11⅛ in)

Lithographed page from the publication shown on the left, 195 × 283 mm (7⅝ × 11⅛ in)

other in black only for colouring by the purchaser. In early examples where the publisher's colouring was done by hand – often by juveniles in multiple production – the purchaser's work may sometimes be seen to be on a par with that of the model. The genre developed rapidly in the 20th century, drawings being rendered in outline only, with or without pre-coloured models.

In America, the drawing instruction publication had its origins in the domestic self-improvement field. The 1830s and 1840s saw tentative pamphlets and prints in some numbers, together with 'drawing cards' for study and emulation. The cards, lithographed and sometimes hand-coloured, measured some 100 × 150mm (4 × 6in); they were sold in paper packets in sets, each set presenting varying stages of completion.

Among the first to exploit the drawing book concept on a large scale was Louis Prang, the Boston lithographic printer, who, in 1863, put out the first of a series of booklets under the title *Slate Pictures.* Prang's initiative was shortly reinforced by the arrival in America of Walter Smith, hitherto in charge of a number of schools in the English Midlands. Smith was appointed head of the Massachusetts Normal Art School, and devised original drawing-instruction materials of his own, among them a new set of white-line geometric cards, published by Prang as 'American Drawing Cards'. Smith's influence on American art education was considerable. His series of *American Text Books of Art Education,* published by James Osgood in the early 1870s, paved the way for a big expansion in the field – though Smith himself returned to England in 1882. By the end of the century in America publishing emphasis was on the domestic user, with such titles as *Young Folks' Drawing Book* leading the market.

REFERENCES Rafael C. Denis, 'A Preliminary Survey of Drawing Manuals in Britain c. 1825–1875', *Journal of Art & Design Education*, vol. 15, no. 3, 1996, pp. 263–75; Diana Korzenik, *Drawn to Art* (Hanover and London: University Press of New England, 1985)

Driving licence

The first recorded driving licence was issued by the Paris Commissioner of Police to two drivers, Messieurs Serpollet and Averard, on 17 April 1891. The document, a handwritten 'Notification', was addressed to the two men and related to two specific vehicles (both steam-driven) which had been submitted for examination to the Service of Mines on 16 August 1889 and 8 January 1891. The licence allowed the vehicles to be driven on the roads of Paris only.

In 1893 a Paris police ordinance (14 August, rule 1, paragraph 1) required that all persons driving motor vehicles submit to a driving test under the supervision of the Service of Mines, and in March 1899 cards were issued to drivers throughout France. These specified the type of vehicle the holder was entitled to drive and, in addition to personal details, carried an identity photograph.

Britain's first driving licences appeared in August 1903. They were issued by local authorities and were renewable annually. No driving test was required. They cost five shillings per year and were issued as single-sided sheets measuring 150 × 160mm (6 × 6¼in) from counterfoiled books. Failure to produce a licence incurred a fine not exceeding £5, but a duplicate was available in case of loss or defacement on payment of a fee of one shilling. The first member of the public to hold a driving licence was a Londoner, Mr Richard Cain, chauffeur and

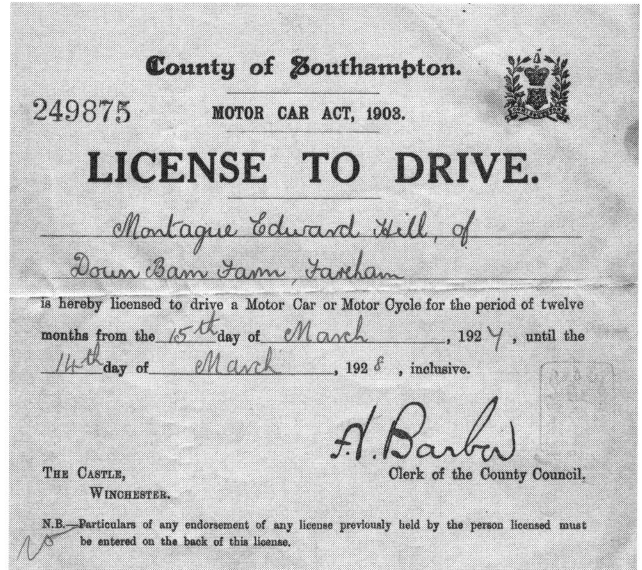
County of Southampton.
249875 MOTOR CAR ACT, 1903.
LICENSE TO DRIVE.
Montague Edward Hill, of
Down Barn Farm, Fareham
is hereby licensed to drive a Motor Car or Motor Cycle for the period of twelve months from the 15th day of March, 1927, until the 14th day of March, 1928, inclusive.
The Castle, Winchester.
Clerk of the County Council.
N.B.—Particulars of any endorsement of any license previously held by the person licensed must be entered on the back of this license.

Driving licence, Winchester, Hampshire (UK), valid from 15 March 1927 to 14 March 1928. Letterpress and manuscript, perforated along two sides. 162 × 181mm (6⅜ × 7⅛in)

bodyguard to the German Prince Hatzfeldt. It was dated 28 December 1903 – three days before the Motor Car Act became effective on 1 January 1904.

Booklet-type driving licences appeared in Britain in the early 1930s. They carried blank pages for pasted-in renewals and for endorsements recording traffic offences. (Endorsement had originated earlier as an entry on the back of the regular single-sheet licence.) The booklet format was widely imitated by overseas licensing authorities who, in many cases, also required an affixed photograph of the holder. The booklet was superseded in Britain in the 1970s by a computer-generated single sheet, which remained valid until the holder reached the age of seventy. Provisional driving licences appeared in Britain when the driving test was introduced in 1935. Provisional licence holders received a full licence on passing.

In America, driving licences were introduced slowly. By 1910 only a dozen states required licences, and Dakota, the last to do so, fell into line only in 1954. Some states issue 'Restricted permits' or 'Junior licences' to under-sixteens. North Dakota admits fourteen-year-olds.

See also FOREIGN ENGLISH; LICENCE

Dust wrapper

The detachable outer covering of a newly published book is described as a book jacket, dust jacket, or dust wrapper. In its present form the dust wrapper leaves the fore-edge free, its flaps being inserted between the cover and flyleaf, both front and back. In a number of earlier versions the wrapper encircled the book completely, covering the fore-edge as well. Originally its function was solely protective: unprinted, and made from rough paper or sometimes light card, it preserved bindings from damage in storage and transit.

The earliest recorded decorated wrap-round wrapper is from the United States, and appeared on a bound copy of *Atlantic Souvenir* for 1828. It is described by John T. Winterich in *Publisher's Weekly* (15 February 1930) as 'enclosed in a four-sided pasteboard sheath, the front and back of which reproduce, on green paper affixed to the pasteboard, the decorations of the covers of the book .... The parts ... covering the spine and fore-edge ... are blank'. A printed wrap-round jacket in paper appeared in America in 1857, but on both sides of the Atlantic the latter part of the century brought a general move to the present-day form.

The earliest surviving printed jacket in modern form appears on a copy of Heath's *The Keepsake,* printed in London in 1832 and published there by Longman in 1833. The design, printed in red on pale buff paper, is purely typographic, featuring only the title, date, description, and publisher's name on its front, and advertisements for other Longman books on its back.

Among other early examples are typographic wrappers for *Poems by W. W. Lord*, published in America in 1845, and *The Poetical Works of the late Richard S. Gedney,* published by Appleton & Company in New York in 1857. Bunyan's *The Pilgrim's Progress* (London: Longman, 1860) is held to be the first pictorial wrapper, though the image is unambitious.

The dust wrapper remained a tentative and intermittent phenomenon until the first decades of the 20th century. For the most part, it continued to be of plain paper, often unprinted, and sometimes provided with a cut-out spine window which allowed the title on the case to be seen. Slowly it began to bear perfunctory titling, and possibly a simple line illustration on the front. It was in 1902 that Britain's first truly pictorial wrapper appeared: this was for Kipling's *Just So Stories.* John T. Winterich in the *Publisher's Weekly* (1937), describes it as having a picture on the front reproduced from 'an illustration from the book'.

In 1906 appeared John Oliver Hobbes's novel *The Dream and the Business,* published in London by T. Fisher Unwin who, having some years previously taken the bold step of commissioning a general poster from Aubrey Beardsley, now adapted the design as a wrapper for Hobbes's book. It is from this moment of improvisation that the 'mini-poster' wrapper of the 20th century may be said to date. The 'blurb', introduced on wrappers by Harper and Dodd Mead in 1899, and described as such by Gelett Burgess in 1907, became a standard feature. With the general acceptance of the blurb in the early 20th century, the wrapper as a whole began to take on its present role as a point-of-sale promotion piece.

The wrapper is viewed by many bookmen as an intrusive addendum, to be thrown away without delay; by others it is seen as a valuable 'mint copy' adjunct, an essential ingredient of the volume as a collector's item. Among librarians, controversy as to whether or not the shelved book should retain its wrapper was keen in the closing decades of the 20th century, but in public libraries disposal is now the norm. In the sale room, it must be said, the hammer price of a wrappered book is commonly greater than that of the book on its own – in some cases by a factor of thirty, forty, or fifty.

Among a number of curiosity categories of wrapper are 'cancelled' specimens, withdrawn or barely issued, whose titles were for some reason called in; 'war economy' wrappers, in which designs are printed on the reverse of excess stock from other titles; editorial lapses ('... with a forward by...'); and home-made wrappers improvised from items such as manuscripts, wrapping paper, packaging, newspapers, etc.

REFERENCE Charles Rosner, *The Art of the Book-Jacket* (HMSO for the Victoria & Albert Museum, 1949); Charles Rosner, *The Growth of the Book Jacket* (London: Sylvan Press, 1954)

COLLECTIONS John Johnson Collection, Bodleian Library, Oxford; Department of Typography & Graphic Communication, The University of Reading; Victoria & Albert Museum, London

Eccentric advertising

The term relates to the category of satirical publicity material appearing occasionally in the period 1850 to 1900, produced in the form of handbills and put out by shopkeepers and tradesmen of a facetious turn of mind. The tone differs from the ordinary humorous or light-hearted (*see* TROMPE-L'OEIL ANNOUNCEMENT) in that the writer is clearly seizing on the opportunity for a self-indulgent exercise in flight of fancy. In some cases the work shows signs of dedicated effort, running at times to hundreds – and even thousands – of words.

In a typical example, distributed in Ramsgate in the latter part of the century by 'T Wilkinson, Household Furniture Remover', the writer takes two-thirds of his space to satirize the trade union movement, announcing 'The Amalgamated, Federated, Affiliated, Botherated, Extricated, Illuminated, Perforated, Underated, Overated [sic], Society of Toe-Rags, Mumpers, Moochers, Loafers, Cripples, Lunatics, Blind Men, Deaf and Dumb Men, Lazy Men and Beer Shifters'. The text, running to some 250 words, concludes with the union rate of working hours: 'Start at 12, Knock off at 1, and One Hour for Dinner'.

In another example, Harris, a Whitechapel clothier and trousers-maker, addresses the public in his trade vernacular, regardless of its obscurity. Describing himself as a 'Slap up tog and out-and-out kicksies builder', he offers 'Upper Benjamins, built on a Downy plan,... Fancy Sleeve Blue Plush, Pilot or Box-Cloth Vests, cut saucy,... Kerseymere or Fancy Doeskin Kicksies, any colour, cut peg-top', and a 'Pair of Moleskins, any colour, built hanky spanky, with a double fakemin down the sides and artful buttons at the bottom'. He adds that he also offers 'a decent allowance... to Seedy Swells, Tea Kettle Purgers, Quill Drivers, Mushroom Fakers, Counter Jumpers, Organ Grinders, Bruisers, Head Robbers and Flunkeys out of Collar'.

A classic of its kind is *Tanner's Commercialist,* a four-page folder put out in the mid 1840s by Richard Tanner, 'The Prince of Pen Makers'. In a 5000-word tour de force of surreal hyperbole the writer publicizes the 'Twenty-sixth Edition of his Epinicion Calamus Scriptorius', a document clearly devised as much for the amusement of the author as for the reader:

> The most proficuous and expetible invention has been assecuted by Richard Tanner – the primogenial maker – who, by much pensituated mosition of conamous pervestigation – percontation – and repertitious officination of the zotica – has collimated a quidative amalgamation of ternarious regulous, substituted with *wootz and the adamantines* – secerned and confricaed into filaceous canaliculations – and lamellated into the attenuation requisita – which by a chrysulco chymestical operation....

The passage quoted here continues as a single paragraph running to some 240 words, but is one of a dozen or so paragraphs forming the introduction to the writer's sales message. Other paragraphs of similar length consist almost wholly of such adjectives as 'laboriferous', 'obstruental', 'persiclitaed', 'sturditious', 'abnormous', 'immobilient', 'zigzagonal', 'sonectudinal', 'scaturiginous', 'polypotulous', etc.

It is evident that, for some citizens at least, advertising and the availability of the press brought a valued opportunity for getting into print.

Election papers

On both sides of the Atlantic the popular vote has produced immense quantities of printed ephemera, much of it – in the absence of detailed knowledge of the issues of the time – now obscure. The material serves, however, on the one hand to sharpen the recall of the political historian, and on the other to illustrate the mechanics of persuasion.

As compared with America, British election campaign material, though formerly rougher and notably plain-spoken, has tended on the whole to solemnity and wordiness. Proclamatory addresses and counter addresses, sometimes printed on successive days, may run to many hundreds of words. Only in the cut and thrust of SQUIB and popular satire do the proceedings approach the brilliance and excitement of the American campaign scene. American election material is geared to the notion of the occasion as a celebration rather than a battle. The scene was set in 1840 by William Henry Harrison's log cabin campaign, when the whole panoply of US-style electioneering began. Street parades, barbecues, slogans, music, buttons, and favours became firmly fixed in the public mind as the election idiom.

American campaign material proliferated: in addition to hand-painted banners, flags, and torches, the parties produced a multitude of badges, ribbons, medallions, and other novelties. These have remained a staple ingredient of campaigning ever since. Among less predictable items were lanterns, parasols, fans, gentlemen's white collars, all bearing campaigning images.

An additional item of the early American scene is the paper 'ballot', commonly known as a ticket, bearing the name of the

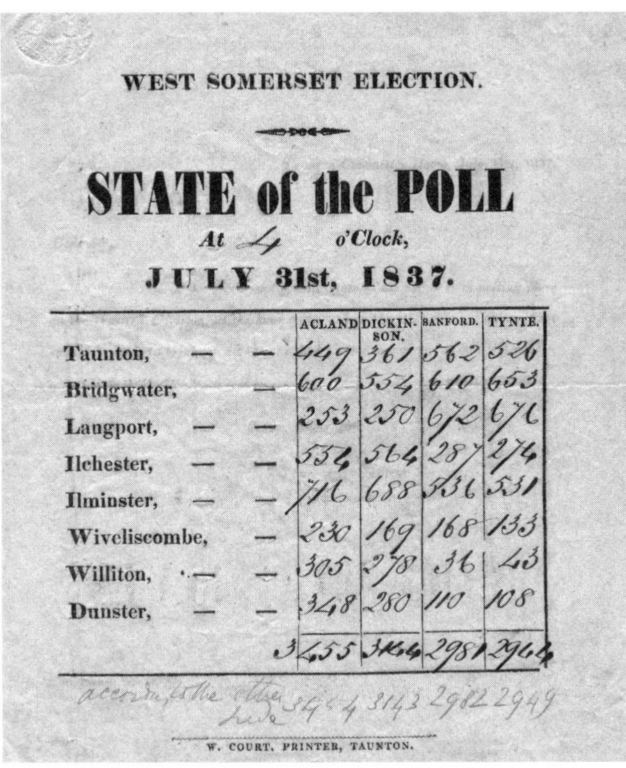

WEST SOMERSET ELECTION.

STATE of the POLL

At 4 o'Clock,

JULY 31st, 1837.

	ACLAND	DICKINSON.	SANFORD.	TYNTE.
Taunton, — —	449	361	562	526
Bridgwater, —	600	554	610	653
Langport, — —	253	250	672	676
Ilchester, — —	554	564	287	274
Ilminster, — —	716	688	536	531
Wiveliscombe, —	230	169	168	133
Williton, — —	305	278	36	43
Dunster, — —	348	280	110	108
	3455	3464	2981	2964

according to the other side 3464 3143 2982 2949

W. COURT, PRINTER, TAUNTON.

State of the poll notice at 4.00 pm on 31 July 1837, Taunton. Letterpress and manuscript, printed by W. Court, Taunton. 230 × 188 mm (9 × 7½ in)

candidate and the list of electors pledged to support him. This slip of paper was mailed to the electors or handed to them at the polling station. The electors registered their vote by signing the back of the paper and placing it in a ballot box (secrecy was out of the question: the vote was traceable through the signature, and the distinctive colours of the tickets allowed easy identification of votes by observers at the ballot box). Tickets measured between 115 × 65 mm (4½ × 2½ in) and 150 × 90 mm (6 × 3½ in). A number have survived. In 1888 a form of secret ballot was adopted. In this the voter was provided with a sheet of paper, divided into columns corresponding in number to the parties represented in the election. Column headings bore the names of the parties, a pictorial symbol as added identification, and a circle. Voters registered their choice with a cross in a circle, but lists of names in each column offered, if desired, an individual choice of candidates regardless of party. The paper was marked in secret, folded, and dropped in the ballot box. The system is now largely superseded by 'voting machines', which total votes instantly and deliver final totals immediately on completion of the vote.

Britain's electoral ephemera is embodied largely in broadsides, election addresses, candidate's cards, and (for the period when elections were held over a number of days) printed slips giving state-of-the-poll voting figures. Voting papers, begun in 1872 and secretly marked and destroyed after counting since 1874, do not appear to have survived.

See also BADGE; BALLOT PAPER; CAMPAIGN SOUVENIR

Electro-medical papers

The role of electricity in therapy has been perceived at a variety of levels since before the time of Mesmer, whose concept of 'animal magnetism' was finally discredited some two hundred years ago by a scientific commission of the French government.

With the emergence of electricity as the near-magical factotum of the 1880s, popular interest in the subject was renewed. Electricity was seen as the philosopher's stone. Henry Frith, in his *Coil and Current* (London: Ward Lock, 1896), described it as '... all pervading ... the Soul of the World, the basis of life. Electricity can do anything, and in time not far distant we shall be able to perform miracles with it'.

It was in this mood that the public turned to electricity as a cure-all. From the advertising ephemera of the period we see that the entrepreneur was not slow to respond. The word 'electricity' became the vogue-word of medical advertising, and such expressions as 'galvano-magnetic' and 'magneto-electric' came into general use. Typical of the enormous range of new products were: The Magneto-Electric Battery Co.'s Electric Body Belt and Electro-Magnetic Socks; Fraser's Electric Catarrh Cure; Ambrose Wilson's Magnetic Corset; The London Electric Fabric Co.'s Electric Garter; Pringle and Sons' Galvano-Magnetic Anti Rheumatic Ring; Dobbin's Electric Soap; The British Medical Institution's Dry-Cell Body Battery; Handyside's Electric Nervine Snuff; The Pall Mall Electric Association's Galvanic Generator.

By far the best-known of Britain's electro-medical manufacturers was the Medical Battery Co. Ltd, also known as the Electropathic and Zander Institute ('the largest electro-medical institute in the world'), whose president was Mr C. B. Harness. The company's principal business was in the sale of Harness's Electropathic Belt and Harness's Magnetic Corset, but customers could also be supplied with rupture appliances, the New Pocket Ammoniaphone (the perfect chemical inhaler), and treatment for corpulence and superfluous hairs.

Among the founding fathers of the electro-medical cult was J. L. Pulvermacher, whose appliances were on sale in London in the mid 1870s and who claimed to have been in business in the late 1840s. In advertisements for the products of his galvanic establishment in Regent Street he printed a testimonial for his Patent Volta Chain Batteries, signed in 1866 by six physicians, of whom three were physicians to the Queen, one was physician to the Prince of Wales, and one physician to the Hospital for Consumption at Brompton. Pulvermacher's principal product was the Electric Chain Band, with Chain-Batteries, Intensity Batteries, and other devices as supplements. His price list shows such items as Patent Adhesive Electro Generator, Electro Diffusing Bands and Belts, Galvanic Safety Heart Fastening, Pocket Galvanometer, Electro Diffusing Respirator, and Electro Generating Belts. Many of the items listed are described as being patented, and the British Patent Office records do indeed show Pulvermacher as the holder of two patents (nos 12899 and 13933; 1849 and 1852 respectively) for galvanic batteries, galvano-electric equipment, and telegraphic and lighting equipment.

Doctors themselves, it seems, were closely involved with electric devices. Prominent among electro-products were Dr Porter's Electric Magnetic Machine, Dr Carter Moffat's Electric Body Belt, Dr Williams' Electric Medicated Pads, Dr Bell's Self Restorer Belt, and Dr Scott's complete range of electrical aids: electric toothbrushes, hairbrushes, and housebrushes; curlers; insoles; electric plasters; and electric cigarettes.

Another all-electric range was available from Darlow & Co., including belts, kneecaps, chest protectors, lung invigorators, spine bands, necklets, wristlets, anklets and teething bands. Also available were The Electrolibration Co.'s 'Electropoise'

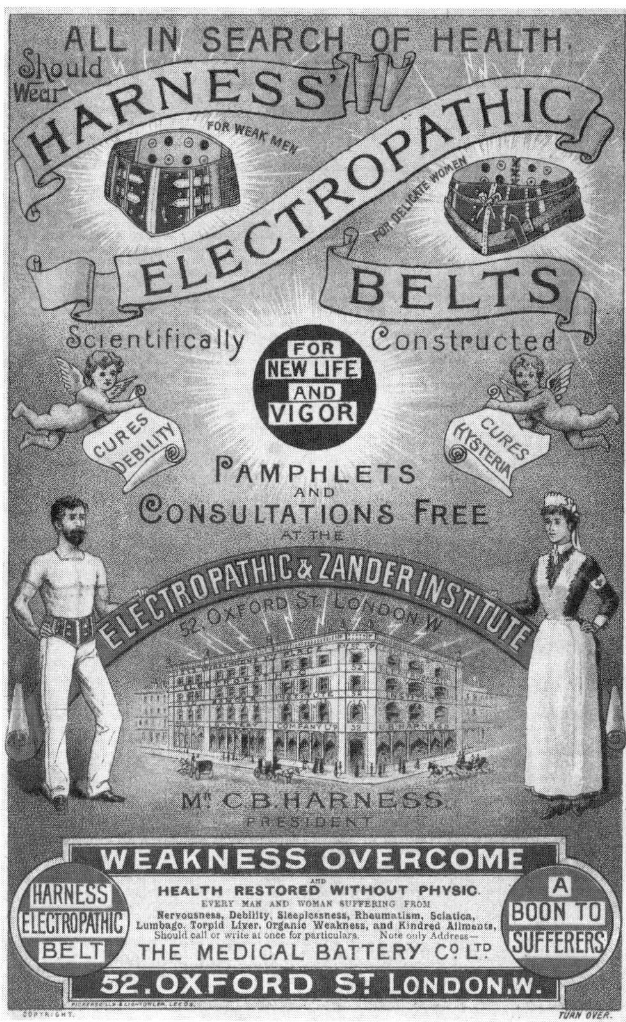

Advertisement for Harness' Electropathic Belts, Oxford Street, London. Chromolithographed by Pickersgills & Lightowler, Leeds. 220 × 140mm (8⅝ × 5½in)

('not a battery: no shock: pure atmospheric oxygen'), and the products of The Electro-Magnetic Truss Co.

Some advertising also offered consultations. The Magneto-Electric Battery Co. announced that their London Health Electrician could be seen daily, free of charge. Though unnamed, he is described as 'An M.B.A.M.E., PhD (formerly senior and principal demonstrator, Surgeon's Hall, Royal College of Surgeons, Edinburgh). Diseases for which cures were claimed covered a wide field. Lists of treatable ailments included melancholia, liver torpidity, paralysis, quinsey, blindness, cough, insanity, seminal weakness, pimples, dizzyness, diabetes, ague, constipation, cholera, cramp, loss of voice, swollen knee, toothache, spinal disease, diphtheria, disease of eye, and epilepsy.

Almost without exception, British firms in the electro-medical appliance business made use of the magazine inset for their advertising. The inset, a four-page folder, approximately 220 × 140mm (8⅝ × 5½in), was bound in with the pages of magazines or used on its own (*see* INSET, MAGAZINE). It was generally printed in black on a white or tinted paper, and usually devoted at least half of its space to the testimony of satisfied customers. Among exceptions are the full-colour chromolithographed single sheets of the Medical Battery Co. and for Harness's Electropathic Belts, which were used as magazine insets or on their own.

In America, medical electricity offered not only electric belts ('Great waves of joy and happiness go through the body', J. S. Beech Co., Chicago, Ill.), but Dobbins's Soap ('contains several substances wholly unknown to the trade'). Also available was Dr Thomas's electric oil ('positively cures toothache in five minutes ... deafness in two days ... coughs in 20 minutes') and, at Indiana's Mineral Springs, Magnetic Mineral Mud ('nature's natural and permanent cure of rheumatism in every form'). There was also W. G. Brownson's Electro-Chemical Ring, warranted to cure, among other things, diabetes, epilepsy, and cancer. Galvanic bands were available, as in Britain, with the added advantage of personal diagnosis and advice. A pencilled note on a printed instruction sheet says: 'Wear the galvanic bands on the throat a few nights, and then apply cold wet towel, and cover that with blankets and sleep in it. In morning rub the throat with coarse dry towel'.

Electricity also appeared in New York as a diagnostic aid. In a four-page folder (c.1863) the New York Electrical Institute announces: 'Good news for the sick; Any Disease Instantly Determined: Its Location Pointed Out, and its Progress upon the System Completely Developed'. By means of his 'New Electric Magnetic Machine', Dr Porter could provide visiting patients with immediate diagnosis and prescribe remedies, often curing the hitherto incurable in a single day. The folder enumerates 127 ailments, including insanity, 'Terpidity Kidneys', and five forms of cancer, which may be successfully treated; some, if not all, of these treatments were electrical. Dr Porter's terms were: 'Our Electrical remedies sent by Express on receipt of $2, $3, $5 or $10'.

The ephemera of electro-medicine provide an unbroken account of the field into the 1930s and, in some areas, beyond.

See also QUACK ADVERTISING

REFERENCES Stewart H. Holbrook, *The Golden Age of Quackery* (New York: Collier Books, 1962); Brooks McNamara, *Step Right Up!* (Garden City, NY: Doubleday, 1976); Dick Sutphen, *The Mad Old Ads* (London: Allen, 1968); E. S. Turner, *The Shocking History of Advertising!*, rev. edn (Harmondsworth: Penguin, 1965); Leonard de Vries, *The Wonderful World of American Advertisements* (London: Murray, 1973)

Electrotype

An electrotype is a faithful copy of an object made by the electrolytic deposition of copper. In printing, the process could be applied to the replication of both intaglio metal plates and relief wood-engraved blocks. In the field of ephemera it was primarily applied to WOOD-ENGRAVING, the most widely used pictorial process of the 19th century. Electrotype was invented around 1840 and by 1850 was in common use for the replication of wood blocks. As in other areas of letterpress printing it had to compete with the process of STEREOTYPE, and for over 100 years the two methods coexisted, stereotyping being considerably cheaper but less refined.

The name electrotype is derived from the process used in its manufacture. The development of the electric battery paved the way for experiments with electrolysis and its application to the copying of wood-engravings in the 1830s. A common method of making an electrotype began with taking an impression of the engraved surface of the wood block in a tray of wax. The surface of the wax impression is dusted with fine graphite powder, which conducts electricity; the tray is then immersed in a solution of copper sulphate and a thin layer of copper deposited on to the wax impression by electrolysis. The copper layer or shell is carefully removed from the wax and given strength and solidity by the back being filled with a metal similar to that used to make type. This plate is then trimmed and mounted on to a wooden base that is thick enough to raise the printing surface to the height of type. The accuracy of a copy made by this process is such that the resulting print is indistinguishable from one taken from the original wood block.

With the introduction of bigger and faster powered printing presses there was an increased risk of wear and accidental damage to a wood block and the loss of a valuable original. Making multiple copies of a block had obvious advantages; for example, the same image could be printed on several presses at the same time and copies of an engaving of a particular product could be distributed to a number of retailers around the country for inclusion in trade catalogues and advertisements. Manufacturers supplied STOCK BLOCKS in the form of electrotypes and thus images appropriate for all kinds of illustration became available for purchase by printers. [MA]

E-mail

Short for electronic mail, e-mail (or email) was taken up in the late 20th century with something like the enthusiasm shown for its more tangible forerunners in the 19th century, the Penny Post and POSTCARD.

E-mail is based on the Internet (an electronic communication network), which has precursors going back to the mid 20th century. Early applications of the Internet were of a specialist kind and related to the American space and defence programmes. The idea of using it for electronic mail emerged in the early 1970s, and the first international e-mail message was sent to a conference in Sussex in 1973 (as with the first British press telegram – which was about the birth of one of Queen Victoria's children – it concerned the birth of a child). In this period the now familiar @ sign (the commercial 'at') was introduced for e-mail addresses, though the Internet remained a system used only by the technologically privileged. It was not until the early 1990s, when it was able to take advantage of the desk-top computer and the emergence of the world wide web, that e-mail became a medium of mass communication. Estimates of its take-up vary enormously, but world-wide, e-mail users amounted to many scores of millions by the close of the 20th century.

E-mail messages are transmitted via the world's telephone system and are composed by the sender and viewed by the recipient on a computer screen. Messages are charged to the sender at the rate of a local telephone call (which is free in the USA). Each e-mail user chooses an electronic address through a service provider. In theory a user code enables messages to be kept confidential, but in practice it is possible for correspondence to be reviewed. E-mail therefore has a level of confidentiality that falls somewhat short of a sealed letter (when treated with customary respect), but considerably greater than that of a postcard.

The greatest advantage of e-mail is its speed: communication is almost instantaneous, regardless of the distance between the sender and the recipient. Because it is so convenient – particularly for the sender – e-mail is also used as a means of communication within an institution. A further convenience is the ability to send a message to any number of designated people at no extra cost. The idea of the 'paperless office', which was enthusiastically promoted a few decades earlier, may therefore become a reality; but at present many users of e-mail who view correspondence on screen prefer to print out on paper their more important 'in' and 'out' mail. Messages that are not printed out are likely to be erased sooner or later.

E-mail technology limits what users can do in terms of the characters available and the way in which text can be displayed, which means that messages (whether on screen or paper) look neutral and dull. Some users get around this problem by sending (electronically) what are known as attachments, which retain their graphic form. E-mail offers few visual attractions for collectors of ephemera, though it is possible that its range of graphic expression will increase in response to a demand for diversity.

Interest in e-mail as a genre lies more in the impact it has had on written language. In an attempt to make messages less formal and more conversational, a form of e-mail language has emerged. It reflects a relaxed view of users towards accuracy of grammar and spelling, and makes copious use of colloquialisms and acronyms. [MT]

REFERENCE B. Winston, *Media Technology and Society. A History: from the Telegraph to the Internet* (London and New York: Routledge, 1998).

Embossing/lace paper [plate 9b]

The techniques of embossing and lace-paper production have much in common. In the embossing process the surface of the paper is raised by mechanical pressure of a moulding tool. In the lace process, pressure of a moulding tool extends to full penetration, with actual removal of parts of the paper. The lace-paper technique was derived from faulty embossing work, in which excessive pressure fractured the paper instead of merely 'forming' it; the process was perfected by a paper embosser, Joseph Addenbrooke, in the mid 1830s.

Both processes, independently and in association, were the subject of a major printing development in the 19th century. They were used in 'ceremonial' items – banquet invitations, menus, etc. – in mourning cards (*see* FUNERALIA), and in an extensive range of popular greetings cards, notably the VALENTINE.

The technique of embossing derives from processes used in the preparation of seals and the minting of coins. A metal die, bearing a hollowed-out image of the desired low relief, is impressed against the surface of the material in question, forcing it into the configuration of the mould. The die is made by a process (known as die sinking) in which the image is engraved in the metal by hand or, at a later stage, by photomechanical means. Low-relief work was commonly done by hand. This last method, in which the highest points of the original are 'sculpted' correspondingly deep in the metal, is a highly skilled craft operation, and is becoming increasingly rare.

When embossing paper or other raw substances a secondary die is needed to force the paper fully into the cavities of the principle (or 'forward' die). A male component is made as an exact casting of the female die. It is built up of a semi-viscid cement or other substance; it duplicates in relief the hollows of the original and is precisely placed on the press to complement its pressure.

The process, which relies for its effect on the degree and delicacy of relief of the impress, calls for a pressure consistent with the capacity of the paper to deform without rupturing. Paper structure, thickness, and moisture content affect not only its receptivity but also its ability to retain stability after processing. The performance of the die is governed by its depth and the pressure provided by the male component. These interoperating factors, manipulated in primitive conditions, were mastered by trial and error.

The huge embossing press, commonly located in a basement, was hand-operated by the momentum of a horizontal flywheel, which exerted pressure of two or three tons on a central anvil set at floor level. Access to the anvil was provided by a floor-well; this was deep enough to accommodate a small boy, who placed cards under the die, removing and stacking them after each impact. Quality control was a matter for the flywheel operator, whose exertions governed the strength, depth, and spread of impact.

Embossing may appear in a number of variants. The effect may be produced by printing an image and afterwards embossing it; by embossing without a printed image ('blind embossing'); and by printing the background to an image, leaving the image itself embossed but unprinted ('cameo embosssing'). In embossing in gold and other metallic colours, the image is printed as a clear adhesive varnish to which metal leaf or powder is applied, the unwanted residue being brushed or dusted off afterwards.

Die stamping, a form of printed stamping, much used in 20th-century letterheads and business cards, is not commonly described as embossing. Here the relief and the printed image are produced in a single operation. The effect is superficially similar to embossing, as is that of the more recent thermographic process, in which a heat-positive ink is caused to swell on the paper surface without, however, affecting the paper itself.

'Blocking', another form of multi-plane printing, produces depressions in the printing surface, commonly forcing colour or metallic foils into the material. The process is widely employed in commercial bookbinding and was much used from the second quarter of the 19th century as decoration (often 'blind') on case-bound books. The process is not normally covered by the term embossing.

The formal history of paper embossing dates from 6 April 1796, when John Gregory Hancock was granted British patent no. 2102 for 'ornamenting paper by embossing or enchasing'. He was granted a second patent, no. 2783, 14 September 1804, for 'forcing or working the bolts of presses or engines used for cutting, pressing, and squeezing metals, horn, tortoiseshell, leather, paper, and other substances'. T. Lang and A. Muthenthaler were at work on the process in Germany at about the same period, but its major commercial application is identified with the rise of the firm of Dobbs & Co., 'ornamental stationers and pencil manufacturers' in the early years of the 19th century. Trading as 'H Dobbs' at 8 New Bridge Street, London, and moving through a variety of designations, partnerships, and addresses as the company developed, Henry Dobbs's enterprise was identified with high-quality embossing for the rest of the century. The company's work bears the embossed name 'Dobbs' in various formulations (Dobbs, Dobbs & Pratt; Dobbs & Co.; Dobbs, Bailey & Co.; Dobbs, Kidd & Co.). Discreetly concealed within the design, the credit line appears on a vast range of items, ranging from tickets for the coronation of George IV (*see* COMPOUND-PLATE PRINTING) to calling card envelopes and scholars' reward cards.

The company was closely involved with the firm of Whiting & Branston, whose efforts to exploit the 'compound-plate printing' process led to the production of elaborate items incorporating embossing as an adjunct to that process. Most of these items carry the Dobbs imprint as well as Whiting's, but it may also be assumed that even where there is no such attribution, these embossings are likely to be the work of Dobbs. Robert Branston and his son (also Robert) were themselves engravers, however, and some might possibly have been produced by them.

The Dobbs company also produced, in addition to 'special' embossings for specific customers, a series of all-purpose cards for general use. These were available in various sizes and tints. They provided a blank central panel within a decorative embossed frame and were used for overprinting as invitations, certificates, announcements, etc. They were also used in smaller quantities for handwritten messages and drawings. Much of Dobbs's production was geared to the rapidly growing 'album-filler' market, in which attractive items of all descriptions were bought by scrap collectors. Dobbs's album cards provided settings for handwritten mottoes, messages, and captions, the blank centres being framed by embossing or decorative perforation, or both. A less commercially successful venture was Dobbs's 'embossed tableaux' series. Also aimed at the album market, the series presented low-relief biblical or classical scenes on cards measuring between 265 × 370 mm (10½ × 14½ in) and 190 × 255 mm (7½ × 10 in). These multi-figure set-pieces featured such titles as 'Paul preaching at Athens', Leonardo da Vinci's 'Last Supper', and Titian's 'Woman taken in Adultery'.

A major undertaking, involving Dobbs as well as Charles Whiting, was a series of souvenir portraits of notabilities of the period. The series presented blind-embossed portrait profiles on coloured backgrounds and blind-embossed colour frames. The overall size of the printed image is some 180 × 150 mm (7⅛ × 6 in). The portraits are of William IV, Queen Adelaide, Queen Victoria, Duke of Wellington, Lord Grey, Lord Brougham, Lord Byron, Sir Walter Scott, and Thomas Moore (the Irish musician and poet). All are superbly embossed on the off-white absorbent board typical of the process, and all bear the imprint 'Whiting: printer' within the area of the design. There is no credit line for Dobbs, but the quality of the dies and the style of the decorative frames leaves little doubt as to their origin. Dobbs

Blind embossed portrait of the Duke of Wellington within an embossed border. Produced by Charles Whiting and marked 'Whiting patentee'. Image 179 × 144 mm (7⅛ × 5⅝in)

is known to have employed the foremost medallists to engrave his portrait dies, and those appearing in this set may well have been by members of the Wyon family and Henry Weekes.

The portraits, commonly referred to as 'the Whiting portraits', were apparently produced with an eye to publicity for Whiting's company. There is no record of their actually being sold, although Kendall and Son published an album in which they were pasted on to blank sheets. Complete specimens of the album are rare, but a detached title-page (itself printed and embossed by Whiting) is in the John Johnson Collection at Oxford. This carries the legend: 'Royal cameo: scrap book: embossed heads' and introduces eight of the engravings (the Queen Victoria portrait is absent). The heads were 'struck in steel at a cost of several hundred pounds'.

Surviving examples of the portraits show considerable variety in colour treatment, and it may be concluded that their production was on a more or less exploratory basis. Marcus Samuel (*Great Britain Philatelic Society Journal*, July 1974) lists numerous different colour combinations, four in the case of one of the William IV portraits. There is no record of printing quantities of these items, but in at least three cases they served as give-aways, two with newspapers and another with a magazine: 'Presented to purchasers of the Age Newspaper', and in the case of Walter Scott: 'Presented gratis with 1st number of the Story Teller or the journal of Fiction'. Of the two versions of the William IV portraits in the Marcus Samuel Collection, one carries no Whiting imprint but includes a manuscript note to the effect that copies were presented to readers of *The Atlas* newspaper. Use of these high-quality embossings as give-aways suggests production runs of some few thousands.

Though best known as embossers, the Dobbs firm also produced perforated cards for embroidery, 'ladies stationery', and a wide range of fancy goods. The company advertised itself on an embossed trade card in the 1820s as 'Under the Patronage of The President & Members of the Royal Academy' and offered 'Refined and Prepared Black Lead & Chalk Pencils of Various degrees of Hardness & Shade'.

Other London embossing specialists were Thomas De La Rue, Joseph Mansell, Windsor, and J. T. Wood. Much of the work of the smaller firms was concentrated on the production of mourning cards (*see* FUNERALIA). In America the dominant name was Samuel N. Dickinson of Boston, whose general printing, type casting, and stereotyping business was supplemented in the 1840s by sales of embossed cards, initially from Dobbs's dies, subsequently from his own.

Twentieth-century embossing is by comparison less refined in detail, shallower, and in relative terms very much more costly. Among today's leading practitioners are W. R. Royle & Son Ltd of London and Créations Fournier of Paris.

Lace paper was 'introduced' in London by a Dobbs employee, Joseph Addenbrooke in 1834. Successfully developing a technique which he hit upon by accident, Addenbrooke set up in the lace-paper business on his own account. His method, which was to become standard practice, consisted of using a sandpaper rasp on the paper when it was impaled on the cutting die, converting it to a perforated filigree. He was the forerunner of a number of such specialists, among them, notably, George Meek of Crane Court, Fleet Street (supplier of embossed and lace paper to Rimmel, the perfumed valentine firm), and Dobbs themselves, who became major producers.

Lace-paper work on a watch-paper valentine, with hand-coloured, intaglio-printed on-lay. Diameter 55 mm (2⅛ in)

A number of French companies entered the field during this period, producing lace-bordered letter paper, communion souvenirs, doilies, and greetings cards, many of them in the fashion of the later part of the century, extra-embellished by the addition of chromolithographed 'scraps'. Here the dominant names are Pépin Fils & Brouand, A Carrière, and Heste.

In America, the first lace-paper valentines were sold by Esther Howland, whose father's stationery shop in Worcester, Massachusetts, saw the beginnings of what was to become a major business. Actual manufacture of lace paper did not begin in America until very much later, Esther Howland's productions being composed largely of imported material.

As with embossing, modern lace papers are on the whole inferior to those of the 19th century, and are commonly confined to doilies for food and flower presentation.

See also GIVE-AWAYS; GREETINGS CARD; SCRAP; VALENTINE

Embroidery pattern

The earliest embroidery pattern books date back to the 16th century, when limited numbers of luxuriously produced publications provided for the needs of the few with leisure enough to make use of them. Prior to this (and for some 300 years afterwards) the ordinary needlewoman worked from a specimen strip of actual embroidery, developed and transmitted over generations. These pattern strips, which embodied an extensive repertoire of traditional designs, were the forerunners of the 'sampler' and the little girl's framed embroidery test-piece.

With the development of appropriate printing techniques, there emerged mass-produced pattern sheets for popular use. These sheets showed a basic grid of small squares, each representing a single stitch, with designs overlaid, either as a printed outline or as full-colour mosaics. As with earlier luxury productions, most of these publications originated and circulated in Central Europe, where minimal text, confined generally to colour titles, appeared in German, English, and French; but decorative alphabets for embroidery were also shown in Cyrillic script for Russian and other Slavonic markets. Such examples were commonly produced by lithography in the 19th century.

A typical format measured 225 × 195mm (8⅞ × 7⅝in), though 'Primers' were as small as 65 × 115mm (2½ × 4½in). In most cases the body of the booklet was presented as a double-sided concertina fold-out, 'tipped in' to a paper wrapper. Single-colour designs appeared on one side of the sheet and coloured ones on the other. The length of these patterns varied from 650 to 1500mm (25⅝ to 59in). Single-sheet fold-out patterns appeared in the 19th century, many of them as give-aways in women's magazines. Iron-on transfer sheets appeared after World War I and remain in use.

See also PAPER PATTERN

Enclosure badge

Issued to be worn as a visible sign of entitlement to be present, the enclosure badge was introduced as a security measure by the organizers of race meetings and other public events in the 19th century. It is still widely used, notably at such events as Royal Ascot, Goodwood, Henley Regatta, and the Royal Garden Party. Typically, badges take the form of shaped and embossed cards, printed in colour and designed with some complexity; they are threaded or pinned for wearing, and often leave space for the holder's signature.

The objective, as well as presenting a distinctive and attractive appearance, is to produce a design calculated to discourage counterfeits. In addition, a system of colour coding is often used to distinguish groups, enclosures, entrances, etc. Similar coding may be used for stewards, marshals, and other officials, as well as to distinguish ladies' badges from gentlemen's.

Die-stamped metal badges, enamelled in colours, were used in the early 20th century. This type of badge, more commonly familiar in clubs and societies as permanent badges of membership, also appeared as a mark of a single-occasion attendance. Typical of this type is a badge produced on the occasion of the First Scottish International Aviation Meeting in 1910. This badge, manufactured by Elkington of Glasgow, bore a low-relief image of a flying machine in gold with gold-lettered blue scroll-work forming a frame; a red-lettered golden scroll at the foot carried the word 'Official'. A meeting badge of the Royal Aero Club in 1915, however, appeared as a gold embossed red-leather disc bearing the words 'Membership card'. This badge, held by a cord in the lapel, also carried the member's signature on the reverse.

As an indicator of status and distinction, the enclosure badge has at times been an object of ceremonial veneration. Typical is a series of ivory cut-out badges, hand-painted and individually lettered, worn by Major General Lord Cheylesmore, Patron of the Royal Military Tournament in London at the turn of the 19th and 20th centuries. The design, which includes the royal crown and cipher and the date and name of the event, also bears the words 'Patron's box'.

Enclosure badges of the late 20th century were distinctly less elaborate than earlier versions, though the tendency to shaped cut-outs (shields, hexagons, etc.) persisted.

See also BADGE

Royal Ascot enclosure badges. *Left:* 1895, diameter 54mm (2⅛in); *right:* 1899, 60mm (2⅜in). Both letterpress, printed in four colours on card.

Engraved label

Metal seals, for use with sealing wax, were in widespread use in the first half of the 19th century. They were produced as miniature handstamps or incorporated in rings for the finger. Seals supplied to the customer were accompanied by a proof impression of the work in sealing wax.

A blob of wax bearing the impression was preserved in a small container, commonly a flat screw-top wooden box, measuring some 40–50mm (1–2in) in diameter, with a circular label pasted in the lid. The engraved label, more often than not itself a work of craftsmanship, was in effect a circular trade card, giving the supplier's name, address, designation, and, in many cases, additional specialities. The labels, printed for the most part in black, often appear on coloured paper, commonly green, red, or blue. They bear some similarity to the WATCHPAPER, with which they may sometimes be confused.

Label of Lewis, engraver and seal cutter, 3 Wall Street, New York. Intaglio engraved and printed in blue. Diameter 42mm (1¾in)

Entire *See* COVER, POSTAL

Envelope

The concept of the envelope as an outer container or 'wrapper' for letters is relatively modern. For generations it was customary to fold the letter paper itself into the form of a packet securing it with a seal. Britain's earliest recorded envelope was sent by Sir James Ogilvie in May 1696 to Sir William Turnbull, Secretary of State. It measured 76 × 108mm (3 × 4¼in). General use of envelopes or any other form of outer cover was discouraged by the system of postal charges, which were not only according to distance but at double rate if the letter consisted of more than a single folded sheet. The 'extra sheet' – the outer container – was not normally used until the 1830s, when S. K. Brewer, a Brighton manufacturer, began making them in modest quantities. They were also available in London at '2/6 for 100 to be had at 209 Regent Street' as stationer John Dickinson's daughter, Fanny, noted in her diary in 1837.

Early envelopes, or 'paper packets' as some called them, were sold flat without gum, the four corners being folded together by the sender under a seal.

With Rowland Hill's reform of postal charges in 1840 (a uniform charge of one penny per half ounce throughout the United Kingdom, regardless of the number of sheets), envelopes gradually replaced lettersheets and became popular. From January 1840 envelopes were sold by the Post Office for use by Members of Parliament, whose letters were carried free of charge provided they bore the sender's signature on the front. This privilege ended with the introduction of the new rate. In May 1840 the Post Office launched not only the world's first adhesive postage stamps but also prepaid lettersheets and envelopes. These were issued at one penny and twopence, and bore a decorative design by William Mulready. The MULREADY ENVELOPE was widely ridiculed and was withdrawn early in 1841. Though Mulready's design failed, decorative envelopes of all kinds flourished. Most of these were humorous, some were political, and a few featured topographical views.

The envelope for a while became a propaganda medium. Temperance, anti-slavery, free trade, and other causes were promoted, sometimes with the addition of 'seal' stickers bearing slogans.

Commercial advertisers adopted the medium of the pictorial envelope, particularly in the United States, where the use of colour flourished. By the 1860s the idiom was well established in America, and a wide range of topographical views were available, many of them with illustrated letter paper to match. When American railways were formally designated as mail carriers in 1837, letters at last bore rail cancellation marks, and later the name or logo of the carrying company. This identification later became a fully illustrated cover, often showing the train or general railway scenes. The Civil War saw wide use of the device, with images of gallantry, loyalty, and resolution appearing on both sides of the fighting lines.

Embossed prepaid envelopes were introduced by the British Post Office in January 1841, although the General Post Office at Sydney, New South Wales, had already adopted the idea in November 1838.

The vast increase in correspondence occasioned by the Penny Post led to a need for the mechanization of envelope manufacture. Warren De La Rue of the De La Rue printing company, and Edwin Hill (brother of Rowland), Supervisor of Stamps for the Government, jointly developed an envelope-making machine in the early 1840s. This was later improved by De La Rue, who added gumming to the machine's operation. The machine was one of the major attractions at the 1851 Exhibition in London, making 3600 envelopes an hour; the company distributed them to visitors free of charge as souvenirs.

Among envelope novelties and innovations have been a 'safety envelope' (1868), in which the perforation in the flap broke the paper if tampered with and spread gum on steaming; the 'window' envelope (1902); pressure closure (1933); and, during the paper shortages in both world wars, envelopes made from lined ledger sheets and other spare stock.

See also ADVERTISING ENVELOPE; ENVELOPE, ILLUSTRATED; ENVELOPE, STATIONER'S; MULREADY CARICATURE; PARLIAMENTARY ENVELOPE; POSTAL STATIONERY; SECONDARY USES OF EPHEMERA; STATIONERY, DECORATIVE

REFERENCE K. Huggins, *British Postal Stationery* (London: Great Britain Philatelic Society, 1970; reprinted with amendments, 1971)

Envelope, illustrated

Envelopes bearing illustrations or other decorative material appeared in Britain in 1840, the year of the first postage stamp. The heyday of the fashion was the period 1840–50, but it lasted spasmodically throughout the following century.

The illustrated envelope stems from the MULREADY ENVELOPE, which was launched by the Post Office as an attractive method of postal prepayment in 1840, but withdrawn in 1841 as a result of popular disfavour. The design was produced by William Mulready RA, and depicted a centrally posed Britannia, arms outstretched, extending the bounty of the post to the world at large. The composition served to frame a space for the address. The Mulready design brought forth a barrage of criticism, much of it expressed (and profitably exploited) in unofficial caricature versions (*see* MULREADY CARICATURE).

Other illustrated envelopes explored new styles and subject matter. One single issue item from Laurie & Knight of Edinburgh features the affairs of the Church of Scotland, and another, published anonymously and wholly seriously, celebrates Queen Victoria and Prince Albert. (This last, of which variants are reported, is said to have been used on one occasion as an invitation to a ball at Holyrood House.)

Scotland was a further source of illustrated envelopes. Robert Hume of Leith published several sets of humorous designs, and a set of 'musical envelopes' featuring Burns, Byron, Scott, and others, with their songs, music, and portraits. Hume also published 'Valentine envelopes' and a set of three 'Tourist envelopes' with views and a map as guides to Edinburgh, Stirling, and Ben Nevis. Also published in Scotland were 'Clerical Envelopes' of Ado Lesage, a further comment on Scottish Church affairs, and propaganda envelopes, put out by the Dundee firm of James Valentine, advocating Ocean Penny Postage and a number of other causes.

The illustrated envelope lost its impact as a medium of satire in the early 1850s and began to be adopted as a serious medium of propaganda. Elihu Burritt, America's 'learned blacksmith' and United States Consular agent in Birmingham, was an

Illustrated envelope, designed, engraved, and published by James Valentine, Dundee, c. 1840. Printed intaglio. 80 × 134 mm (3⅛ × 5¼ in)

earnest advocate of his League of Universal Brotherhood, and it was through his initiative that the Valentine family espoused the propaganda envelope. Subjects included not only Ocean Penny Postage, but anti-slavery, world peace and brotherhood, and temperance.

Other firms also took up the medium. Charles Gilpin, Bradshaw & Blacklock, and Myers in London, and John Gadsby in Manchester, put out illustrated envelopes, and subject matter extended to free trade, post office Sunday labour, and protests against the secret opening of mail by the Home Office. *Punch* ran a major campaign against Sir James Graham, the Home Secretary, who admitted to having ordered the interception of certain letters. The magazine published not only 'anti-Graham' envelopes but a series of propaganda letter seals for use on the backs of envelopes.

A side effect of the illustrated envelope craze was the emergence of the 'home-made' version. Amateur artists began mailing envelopes produced by themselves, contriving to combine address and postage stamps as elements in a pictorial presentation. The address might thus appear as wording on a street billboard, the stamp as a hanging inn sign. The formula was explored in an infinite number of combinations, the ingenuity of the design in many cases forming the sole point of the 'letter'. The heyday of the fashion was the period 1840–50, but it lasted spasmodically throughout the following century.

American use of the illustrated envelope became widespread in the Civil War. Sold as a single item, or with matching illustrated writing paper, the patriotic or sentimental envelope appeared in many hundreds of designs. Printed for the most part in two colours, and including flags, battle scenes, portraits of generals, and maps, it also featured themes in the vein of 'The Girl I left behind me'.

See also ADVERTISING ENVELOPE; AMERICAN CIVIL-WAR PAPERS

REFERENCES Richard Bodily, Chris Jarvis, and Charless Hahn, *British Pictorial Envelopes of the 19th century* (Chicago: Collectors Club of Chicago, 1984); Frank Staff, *The Picture Postcard and its Origins*, 2nd edn (London: Lutterworth, 1979)

Envelope, stationer's

The stationer's envelope was the stationery counterpart of the shopkeeper's PAPER BAG. It was produced on thin, low-grade paper and printed (commonly from metal type after manufacture) with an advertising message. Later examples, used by the multiple stationery groups and produced in large quantities, were printed from rotary rubber plates as part of the web-fed folding, pasting, and cutting process. (In the former case, the indentation that results from the printing affects both front and back sheets of the made-up envelope.)

Stationers' envelopes were produced in two main sizes, 110 × 160mm (4⅜ × 6¼in) for postcards, and 135 × 230mm (5¼ × 9in) for writing paper, almanacs, etc.

Unlike the large shopkeeper's bag, which normally carried no more than a bold illustration and a name and address, the stationer's envelope was often used as a medium for detailed product and service listing. Surviving examples convey the multiplicity of the Victorian and Edwardian stationer's stock-in-trade: in addition to 'Printing of every description' and 'Views in variety', they may offer coloured scraps, 'Fancy baskets, manilla bags, camp stools ... toys ... Bibles, Hymn Books', and 'Bazaar articles for presents'.

See also ADVERTISING ENVELOPE; ENVELOPE

Equivoque

Now virtually obsolete, the term was applied in the 17th and 18th centuries to ambiguity in the use of words (Latin: *Aequivocus, aecquus* equal; *vocare* call, name). It had a brief return to currency in the middle of the 19th century, notably in the context of deception. It was applied in particular to a written passage, commonly in the form of a letter, in which two opposed meanings appear, depending on the manner of the reading. In its innocuous form the wording is read in the normal way, line by line. At a second reading, in which one portion of the text is folded out of sight, the remaining portion provides a less complimentary passage.

A well-known example, allegedly written by Cardinal Richelieu to the Abbé Boufflers, professes to introduce Matthew Comprey, a friar. Comprey is described, in a full-line reading, as

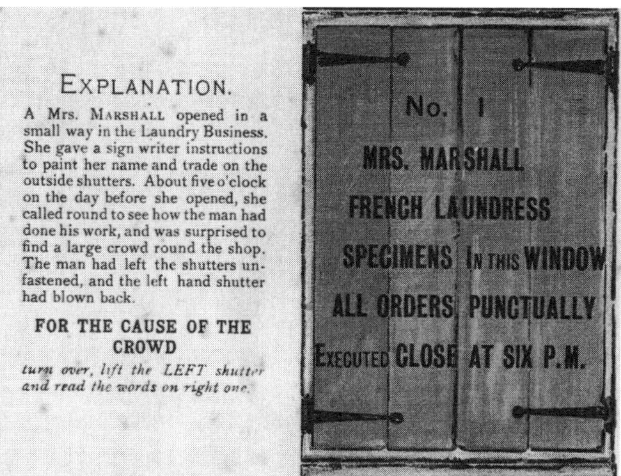

Equivoque from an uncut sheet, c. 1903. Chromolithographed by Gilbert Whitehead & Co. Ltd, London. One message reads across both shutters, another can be read when the left shutter is open (i.e. not seen). 110 × 77mm (4⅜ × 3in)

'one of the most sensible, as well as one of the least vicious persons that I have ever yet (among all I have conversed with) knew...'; a half-line reading appears as 'one of the most vicious persons that I ever yet knew...'. The effect is continued throughout the letter.

The Richelieu letter had wide circulation, appearing at intervals with variations, as manuscript sheets, in common prayer books, and as printed amusements. In one variant the letter is ascribed to Cardinal Mazarin, the recipient being the French ambassador at Rome.

A similar item is recorded as having been composed at the beginning of the French Revolution. Supposedly written by an aristocrat, it appears to welcome the new order. A modified reading invites the new order to go to the devil.

The device also appears in the form of love letters, in which the woman's true sentiments painfully emerge.

Erratum slip

In the 15th century, printers' errors were often corrected by hand on each copy of a book. Omitted lines might be hand-stamped from type at the foot of the page. Extensive errors were corrected by insertion of an extra leaf after the page in question. 'Cancels' were also used. These, named from the lattice-like crossing out of errors in manuscripts (Latin, *cancella*: grating) were paper strips pasted over errors. The word is also used to refer to any alterations to a book after its completion – for example, substitution of a complete four-page fold.

Errors in printed books were often so numerous as to fill out a page or two of correction entries. These appeared under such titles as 'Faults', 'Corrigenda' or, less directly, 'Ad lectorem' ('to the reader'), sometimes with a suggestion that the reader mark the corrections in ink. Numerous books from the 16th and 17th centuries are to be found thus corrected. Berry and Poole (1966) report the first example of a printed notice of errata in Venice in 1478. This is said to have been in an edition of *Enarrationes Saturarum Juvenalis*: the printer, Gabriele Di Pietro, apologizes for the errors, which were due to a workman's carelessness.

Printers not infrequently offer words of explanation for shortcomings. In Florio's translation of Montaigne's *Essays* (1691) six pages of corrections are accompanied by the observation: 'If any thinke he could do better, let him trie; then will he better think of what is done'. In 1624 the author himself comments (Featley, *The Romish Fisher Caught in His Own Net*): 'I entreat the courteous reader to understand that the greater part of the book was printed in the time of the great frost; when by reason that the Thames was shut up, I could not conveniently procure the proofs to be brought unto mee, before they were wrought off; whereupon it fell out that very many grosse escapes passed the press...'.

One printer, John Scott of St Andrews, dismisses a two-page list of errors with the suggestion that they present in any case no great difficulty: '... faults ... any gentil reider may esely persaif, and thairfor suld reid thame as weil as he can in the best maner'.

The true erratum slip, tipped or inserted into the pages of a book, came into general use in the 18th and 19th centuries. It may be said to represent a vestigial survivor of a more elaborate – and often more conscientious – declaration of shortcoming.

The erratum slip appeared also occasionally in the theatre. Printed in the manner of a cast-change notice, and distributed with the playbill or programme, the slip corrected a published error: 'Theatre Royal, Covent Garden, Thursday, October 27 1814; The Publick are respectfully informed that Miss Stephens will perform the part of Ophelia in this Play of tonight... Miss Matthans's name having been inserted by mistake'.

REFERENCES W. T. Berry and H. E. Poole, *Annals of Printing* (London: Blandford, 1966); R. B. McKerrow, *An Introduction to Bibliography* (Oxford: Clarendon Press, 1962)

Etiquette (postal) *See* POSTAL LABEL

Evidence, notes of

Notes of evidence taken at judicial hearings, enquiries, etc. are in most cases preserved with the general papers of the case as part of the official record. They are in any case regarded as confidential, and are not normally found in private hands. They are occasionally encountered as unidentified sheets among miscellaneous papers.

The notes may relate to court hearings, watch committee proceedings, or special enquiries. Most common are magistrates' notes, many of which provide fragmentary glimpses of the human condition:

> Feb 28 1770: Sarah John, Spinster, of Ystradvelty, aged 19, daughter to John Richard of [illegible] came voluntary before me and swore she is with Child and that Morgan [illegible] is the only true father thereof. NB He is about 60 year old and he first knew her abt ye middle of last August.
>
> June 25 1796: Israel seaman Sworn Saith that the Cow now in Dispute he has known from a Calf and has Notist her, being very Thrifty [thriving] and always understood that She belongd to Debe Williams and Beleeves she does.
>
> David Van Cott Senr Sworn Saith there was a Bill of Sale from Ambrose Seaman that Micah Williams had Bot 2 or 3 Cattle and was fully Satisfyd with Payment. Witness to the Bill of Sale: Nehemiah Collis, Thomas Jackson.
>
> Thos Jackson Affirms that he knows nothing about the Cow that is now in Dispute.

Execution broadside

Until its abolition in 1868, the public hanging was a popular focus of entertainment in Britain. By the 1820s, the number of capital offences on the statute book numbered nearly 500; these covered an unprecedented list of crimes, ranging from forgery to sheep stealing. Growth in the number of capital offences, frequency of executions, not to mention the size of unruly crowds, reached such a pitch that the establishment was persuaded to stop the practice. A leading voice in the mounting chorus of abolitionists was Charles Dickens. The last public hanging (of Michael Barrett, a conspirator in the Clerkenwell explosion of 1867) took place outside Newgate, London, on 26 May 1868.

Before this, hanging days had become virtually recognized as public holidays, and the occasions brought forth vendors of printed 'news-sheets' for sale amongst the immediate spectators, and afterwards to the public in general. These broadsides were prepared far in advance of the occasion, but they professed to carry up-to-date accounts of the crime or crimes in question, together with notes on the court proceedings, a description of the comportment of the prisoners, and their 'last dying speeches'. They also carried a supposed rendering of the gallows scene, using a STOCK BLOCK, the central portion of which was pierced to accommodate the requisite number of hanging figures (multiple hangings were common). No attempt was made at individual identification; women were distinguished by using a block for a male figure, cut out square at the knees to suggest a skirt. Distribution was withheld until the very moment of the fall of the trap, when vendors began shouting their news and running excitedly among the crowd.

Execution broadsides were notorious for their illiteracy. Like many other examples of street literature, they showed a fine disregard for printing and typographic niceties. They were liberally spattered with errors of all kinds, and used battered woodcuts (often bearing no relation to the subject of the text, and sometimes appearing upside down).

Their production was in the hands of a small number of printers, most of them centred about the narrow streets of the Seven Dials area of London. As well as hawkers, pedlars, and street vendors, this area attracted a coterie of down-at-heel scribes who could be relied on for a doggerel verse or an item of scandal at a moment's notice. Sometimes the fee was a glass or two of beer. Often the broadsides were printed in the presence of the writer.

See also BALLAD; BROADSIDE/BROADSHEET; STREET LITERATURE

facsimile
farthing novelette
fax
feather letter
fez label
film wallet
fire reward certificate
fireman's discharge certificate
fireman's membership certificate
firework/firecracker label
fish tally
flagday emblem
flap picture
Fleet marriage certificate
flicker book
fly-paper
fly-wagon bill
folk recipe
football programme
'foreign' English
forgery
form
form of prayer
Fraktur
free frank
frost-fair papers
fruit/vegetable sticker
fruit wrapper
funeralia
furniture label

Facsimile

Unlike the FORGERY, which is specifically designed to deceive, the facsimile is an open example of reproduction for its own sake, an attempt at duplication as a technological feat of skill.

For the student of the facsimile the attraction of the subject lies in its historical development as a technique, in analysing its varying degrees of expertise, and in the sometimes narrow margins by which the reproduction falls short of the original. It is also a matter of rueful interest – often of amazement – that poor-quality facsimiles may mislead even the apparently well-informed. For the unwary, a number of fundamental points may be made.

The most frequent source of the documentary facsimile is the book illustration, often printed on paper different from that of the body of the book, and in a different ink, tipped in as a frontispiece or separate addendum. Typical of these is the well-known 'Byron letter', a facsimile appearing in the Galignani (Paris) edition of 1837 and in its detached state perennially acclaimed as an original. Apart from considerations of paper and image quality, such items are recognized by traces of their detachment from the volume (commonly a paste-in tab, or its cut-off remnant) and by the eccentricity of their fold, which conforms not to their original use but to the dimensions of the book in question.

Most commercial facsimiles – certainly those of the 'frontispiece' type – make little or no effort to simulate paper detail, nor do they commonly reproduce the show-through effect of matter present on the reverse of the original. The colour shades, whether of ink, seal traces, or stains, are normally ignored, and indeed the average 'facsimile' presents a startlingly black and white image, devoid of the nuances and subtleties that distinguish the original.

Not least of the characteristics that may indicate a facsimile is its content. The document that combines popular appeal, historical association, and dramatic impact is clearly a candidate for reproduction. So is the document that is legible, brief, and single-sided. It follows that an item combining several of these features should be regarded as doubtful, regardless of the finer points of its physical appearance.

Early facsimiles, taken as tracings from originals, were produced by engraving and were commonly printed in black on any conveniently available white paper. With the invention of lithography at the very end of the 18th century, and particularly the widespread use of TRANSFER LITHOGRAPHY in the early years of the 19th century, numerous facsimiles were published of important historical documents, autographs, and letters (the last two often as collections in volume form). The value of the transfer process lay in the fact that the facsimilist could copy a letter or other document by working with greasy lithographic ink on translucent paper placed over the original. This gave much greater veracity than could be obtained by any other process at the time. All that had to be done after making the copy was to transfer the image to stone for multiplication. Among interesting documents reproduced by such means were King Charles's death warrant, the letter that led to the uncovering of the Gunpowder Plot, the signals used at the Battle of Trafalgar, all produced by Joseph Netherclift in 1833, and, most remarkably, Inigo Jones's 'Italian sketchbook' of 1614, copied by G. E. Madeley in 1831 from the original at Chatsworth.

The introduction of photomechanical processes in the second half of the 19th century gave a tremendous boost to the production of facsimiles, the most ambitious of which was a complete photolithographed facsimile of Domesday Book, published by the Ordnance Survey Office, Southampton, in thirty-five volumes, 1861–63. Later, photolithography was used for the rendering of half tones, and for the first time it became possible to reproduce paper surface as well as text, to distinguish variations of ink consistency, and to record show-through from the reverse of the document. Printing from such half-tone plates in shades of sepia and on cream-tinted paper produced greatly improved results.

With the introduction of collotype, developed in the 1870s from the earlier work of Alphonse Poitevin, half-tone reproduction was brought to a very high level of fidelity. The system, suited to runs of only a few thousand, and economically uncompetitive with other half-tone processes, was in use for about a hundred years. It was by collotype that the high-quality 20th-century facsimile was commonly produced. Early collotype facsimiles include the first folio of Shakespeare's plays published by the Clarendon Press, Oxford, in 1902, and such works as *The Servingman's Comfort,* printed in 1931 for the Shakespeare Association by Lund, Humphries & Co. These and similar productions sought only to represent the original item as an accurate photographic image against the white margins of the contemporary printed page. The reproduction conveyed most of the subtleties of the original (including show-through, pencilled annotations, folds, creases, and tears), but there was no attempt to present the sheet as a double-sided document, backed on the reverse of the paper by corresponding images and effects.

A landmark in the art of the facsimile was a series of portfolios published in Paris in 1938. Produced regardless of expense and printed in small editions, they contained a total of forty-five facsimiles, with their leaves tip-mounted on 'album' pages and faced on left-hand pages with textual comment, transcription, or both. Each portfolio, measuring 320 × 230 mm (12½ × 9 in), contains nine specimens and includes a contents page and a two-colour title-page. Titles are *Reliques émouvantes ou curieuses de l'Histoire; Quelques Reliques émouvantes de l'Histoire de France; Quelques Reliques émouvantes du Passé;* and *Some Stirring Relics of English History.* None of the portfolios has an imprint though (in the first two cases) acknowledgements are made to 'Charles Merriam' and, in that of the English volume, to 'Lady Kensley'. A fifth volume *Quelques pieux Souvenirs du récent Passé,* published to commemorate the 1918 armistice, acknowledges its cover design as being inspired by the 'Poilu' of Jean Boucher Marbre.

Detached specimens from the series are continually appearing, and the clarity of the facsimile work is good enough to produce a regular trickle of enquiries (sometimes through the police) as to their authenticity. The Department of Manuscripts of the British Library describes their quality as excellent, and adds that 'when removed from the volume they can certainly deceive the unwary'. They were produced by collotype and in most cases portray the nature of the original paper on both sides of the sheet. In some instances show-through is rendered, not only accurately but in precise register with the corresponding image on the reverse. In each case paper substance appears appropriate to the period of the document. Most of the specimens are ragged or irregular at the edges, and some are holed or broken at fold lines. In a number of cases unbroken fold lines appear not only as markings but as tangible creases, indicating their physical folding prior to mounting.

Side by side comparison with the originals reveals that the facsimiles are remarkably accurate in their rendering of the visual image, but in paper quality and condition they are notably less so. In one example, portraying a letter from the Duke of Wellington to General Dumouriez (*Some Stirring Relics of English History,* item 8), the facsimile shows two separate single-sided leaves, uniformly ragged, dirtied, and worn at all edges, whereas the original in the British Library is a double-sided single sheet, crisp and clean in all respects, and clean-cut at the edges.

Comparison of one version of a facsimile with another is also revealing, in that ragged edges and other irregularities vary substantially. One item, depicting Napoleon's letter of submission to the Prince Regent, appears both in *Some Stirring Relics of English History* and in *Reliques émouvantes ou curieuses de l'Histoire.* In the first, the sheet measures 200 × 155 mm (7⅞ × 6⅛ in); in the second, 225 × 170 mm (8⅞ × 6¾ in). In the first, the right-hand trim cuts into the text; in the second, it clears it. In the first, paper tone is fairly dark and fold lines appear faint. In the second, paper tone is light and folds are clearly apparent.

The art of the facsimile – certainly the multiple facsimile – is the art of the impossible. Not least of its problems, over and above that of the image itself, is the watermark; other matters that remain to be resolved are the 'feel' of the paper, its weight, its pliability, the sound it makes in handling – even its behaviour as it falls to the desk. However far from resolution these problems remained in the latter part of the 19th century, image quality has at least in one respect made advances over the Paris portfolios. Today's facsimiles in fine-screen lithography may also include the additional element of colour – present in subtle shades even in apparently monochrome originals. In the rendering of seals, stains, and matter added in secondary lines, this ingredient is vital.

Fanzine *See* 'ZINE

Farthing novelette

So called because of its use as a substitute for a farthing change by drapers and haberdashers in the period 1870 to 1914, the farthing novelette was the irreducible minimum in popular literature. It appeared in a series of titles, providing in eight-page miniature format stories of life in the aristocracy and upper middle classes. The booklets, described by Frederick Willis (*A Book of London Yesterdays*, London: Phoenix House, 1960) as 'smudgily printed pages of letterpress and a picture showing a scene in high society', were supplied to drapers at 2*s* 6*d* per gross (the same price as the pin sheets, widely used for the same purpose). As with the pin sheets, the shopkeeper made a profit on the novelettes – of 6*d* per gross.

See also CHANGE PIN-PAPER

Fax

Short for facsimile transmission, the fax is a means of transmitting messages and other documents by means of the telephone system. Whereas E-MAIL is limited to alpha-numeric characters, the fax will transmit any message, whether handwritten, typed, printed, or drawn, provided the marks are sufficiently black. An existing document is fed into a fax machine, which scans its marks and interprets them as digital signals for transmission using telephone lines. At the receiving end, the marks are reconverted to graphic form and printed out on paper, usually by means of toner. Most machines take A4 paper or American quarto, though some take paper twice these sizes. Copies can be made on plain or specially prepared paper.

The underlying technology of the fax goes back to developments in telegraphy in Britain and America in the 1830s and 1840s, to the sending of facsimiles of handwriting by phototelegraphy in France in the early 1860s, and to the invention of the telephone in the second half of the 1870s. It was not until 1968, however, with changes in regulatory practices in the American telephone industry, that facsimile transmission became a commercial reality. Thereafter it gradually built up a consumer base (1.2 million machines in America in the twenty-one years after 1968), though it was not until the 1990s that it took root more widely, both in America and elsewhere.

The first fax machines had a dramatic effect on office practice and began to be used instead of, and sometimes in addition to, traditional mail for transmitting letters, informal notes, and drawings. They are also widely used for the proofing of documents. Advertisers soon learnt to take advantage of the fax to send unsolicited (junk) mail. The relatively coarse resolution of output mechanisms means that there is some loss of definition, and documents sometimes get corrupted.

With the rapid take-up of e-mail by businesses and institutions in the second half of the 1990s the fax suffered something of a setback, though it still has a place when the graphic form of a message needs to be retained. For this reason it may be of greater potential interest for the ephemerist than e-mail. [MT]

Feather letter

The use of birds as message bearers is reported from earliest times (it is known that imperial despatches in China were carried by homing pigeons) and has an echo in the classic instruction to the European courier of the 17th and 18th centuries: *Volante; volantissime!* (Fly; as fast as you can!).

The feather, as a symbol of speed, was in some areas used as an indicator of special urgency, and Scheele (1970) reports its use in that sense in army mobilization orders in China about the first century AD.

The use of an 'express' indicator, forerunner of the 20th century LABEL, was revived in Sweden in the 1780s in the form of a feather ('flight') fixed in the wax of the letter seal. The device was widely recognized in Sweden, Norway, Denmark, and Finland in the period immediately prior to the advent of national postal services, though it was not adopted generally. Surviving examples are rare, even in Scandinavia.

See also CACHET, POSTAL; POSTAL HISTORY

REFERENCE Carl Scheele, *A Short History of the Mail Service* (Washington, DC: Smithsonian Institution Press, 1970)

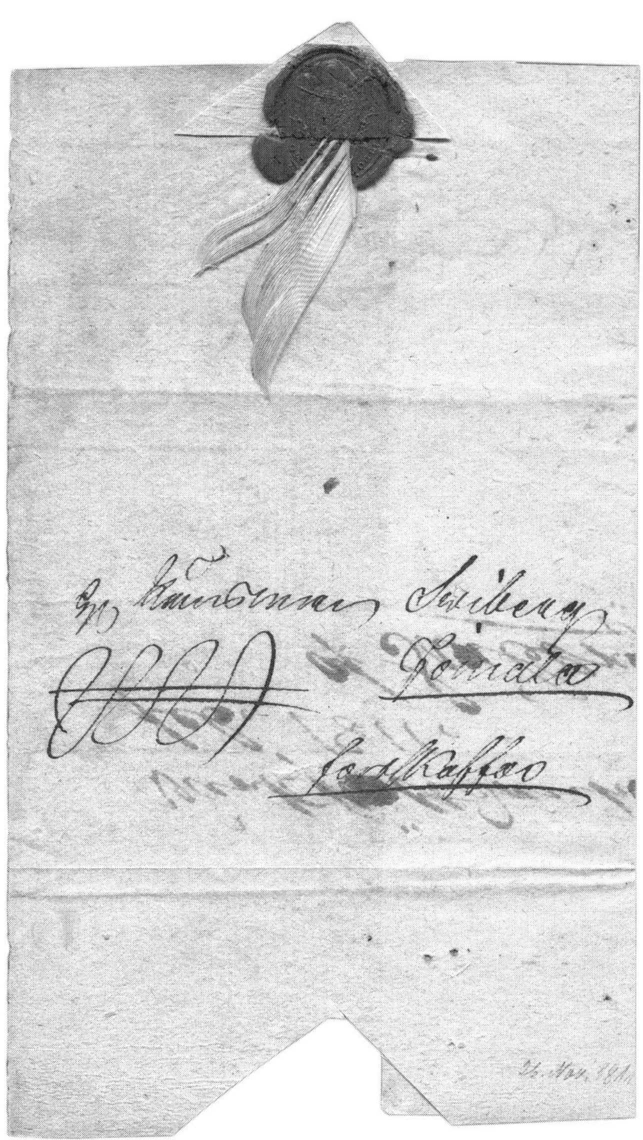

Feather letter, the sealed feather at the top, February 1811. Manuscript. 197 × 115 mm (7¾ × 4½ in)

Fez label

The survival of numbers of fez labels in mint condition is traceable to the 1925 prohibition by the Turkish Government of the wearing of the fez, formerly the national male headdress. The prohibition formed part of a major programme of reform ('Devrim') designed to westernize the country, the fez having become the symbol distinguishing Moslems from Christians and a mark of 'non-European' tradition.

Fez label, late 19th century. Chromolithograph. 113 × 239 mm (4½ × 9⅜ in)

Manufacture of the fez, said to have started in the Moroccan town of that name, had at the turn of the 19th century become a considerable industry in central Europe, the product being exported to most countries of the Muslim world. As with the British cotton industry, whose bale labels were designed to appeal to the taste of the overseas customer, fez manufacturers in Austria and what was then Czechoslovakia produced fez labels in similar vein, featuring images appropriate to the Middle and Near East.

Among their label output (printed, as in many of the British cotton examples, by chromolithography in continental Europe) are many showing specially Turkish motifs. One specimen features the Galata Bridge, with the old city of Constantinople (now Istanbul) in the background.

With the abolition of the fez in 1925 stocks of the Turkish labels became obsolete, and it is clear that many remained unsold in the years that followed. As with British bale labels, quantities of these emerge from time to time, most of them in excellent condition.

Fez labels measure approximately 255 × 115 mm (10 × 4½ in) and are printed in up to a dozen colours.

REFERENCE Helen Wilkins, 'The Fez and its Label', *The Ephemerist*, no. 90, September 1995

Film wallet

Developing and printing services for the amateur photographer became generally available in the early 20th century. Prints and negatives were at first delivered to customers in printed envelopes. Among many examples is a Kodak envelope bearing a simple typographic display of the company name ('Kodak Limited, successors to the Eastman Photographic Materials Co. Ltd: London, Paris, Berlin and Rochester, NY') and the recently registered trade name, in quotation marks: 'The Kodak'. Order details – customer's name and address, etc. – are provided for, together with a description of the camera used. Also to be filled in is a record of the number of negatives processed, and the number of successes or failures. The Kodak envelope appeared in several sizes, progressively smaller, and in turn bearing evidence of the company's expansion. The specimen noted measures 150 × 220 mm (6 × 8⅝ in); later versions

Kodak film wallet, mid 1920s. Letterpress on buff card. Front 115 × 76 mm (4½ × 3 in)

were reduced to 120 × 160 mm (4¾ × 6¼ in) and extend the company's operations to Berlin, Brussels, Glasgow, Liverpool, Lyons, Melbourne, Milan, Moscow, Paris, St Petersburg, and Vienna.

In 1908 the company announced the general introduction of 'Kodak Print Wallets' – 'a neat double envelope'. Wallets of this kind had been used by the company to send processed orders to retail shops but had proved so popular that they were made available, suitably printed with advertising, for retailers to supply to their own customers. Printed in black on grey paper, they had two pockets, 'one to hold the Kodak negatives, the other the prints'. Though introduced as a 'print wallet', the cover carried the title 'Kodak Film Case' in a decorative art nouveau frame. An almost identical presentation was used by Austin Edwards Ltd for their 'ensign' films – using, however, the expression 'print case'. In the proliferation of wallets that ensued the terms 'film and print wallet' and 'roll film and print wallet' appeared, settling down in the 1920s to 'film wallet'. By the 1930s the wallet had become familiar enough to need little more than a product title.

The 1920s and 1930s saw the development of the wallet as an advertising medium for both manufacturer and retailer. After World War II wallets carried details of snapshot competitions and other promotions. With the advent of mechanized processing in the 1950s and 1960s the format of the wallet changed to accommodate strips of negative rather than individual frames.

See also PHOTOGRAPHIC EPHEMERA

Fire reward certificate

To encourage prompt and effective attendance at fires in the 18th century, London Fire Brigades were offered incentives for speedy responses to alarms. Evidence of a brigade's arrival on the scene was attested by completion of a part-printed form 'pursuant to the statute in that case made and provided', with a signature duly appended by one of His Majesty's Justices of the Peace, an Alderman, or two of the Common Councilmen of the Ward.

The form, which was printed in a variety of formats, carried an instruction to the churchwardens of the parish to pay out the reward. Payment was on a sliding scale, according to whether the brigade was first, second, or third to reach the scene. In one version the form related to a single engine, with 'place' and payment entered accordingly; in another there was provision for all three contestants, with an extra allowance for the turncock whose responsibility was to supply water to the engine.

A typical three-in-one form reads:

London (August 6th) 17(94). These are to certify the Alderman, Deputy or two of the Common Councilmen of Ward (of Walbrook) That a fire happened this (morning) in the house (vaults of Mr Field) in the Parish of St (Mary Bothan) in the Said Ward and that (Daniel Ward) Engineer of St (Swithin) brought the first Engine (Jno Hardy) Engineer of St (Mary Abchurch) the second Engine and (the Sun Fire Office) the third Engine, all in good order and Compleat, to help extinguish the said Fire, a Plug was drawn and Water found on the Main belonging to the (Thames) which intitles the above Engineers and Turncock to the following Rewards according to Act of Parliament For the first Engine £1.10.0; second ditto £1.00; third ditto £0.10.0; turncock £0.10.0.

The form, which in this case measures 220 × 195 mm (8⅝ × 7⅝ in), is signed by two witnesses (Jno T. Keable and Samuel Howe), and by the Alderman, Deputy, or two of the Common Councilmen (Samuel Toulming and Robert Wyatt). The churchwarden is ordered to pay the rewards accordingly. The paper is receipted at the foot of the first arrival: 'Recd the Content, Daniel Ward'. The system was largely discontinued when London's fire-fighting services were brought under unified control in 1833.

REFERENCES G. V. Blackstone, *A History of the British Fire Service* (London: Routledge & Kegan Paul, 1957); Sally Holloway, *London's Noble Fire Brigades 1833–1904* (London: Cassell, 1973)

COLLECTION Guildhall Library, London

Fireman's discharge certificate

The early American firefighter was in some areas required by law to serve a period as a member of a fire company. The concept of the volunteer fire company had originated with Benjamin Franklin in 1736, and by the middle of the 19th century the neighbourhood team was a universal American institution.

Exemption from further service with his local company was in some areas granted to the American firefighter after a statutory period of duty. A certificate was issued to him, not only to mark his discharge but to honour his serving and to declare his freedom from further obligation. The certificate, which might measure up to some 500 × 380 mm (approximately 20 × 15 in), was designed in heroic vein, with symbolic figure groupings, calligraphic flourishes, and vignettes. It was perceived as a diploma of merit, a suitable subject for framing.

See also FIREMAN'S MEMBERSHIP CERTIFICATE

Fireman's membership certificate

Fire-company certificates of membership were a notable feature of the American firefighting scene of the 19th century. Elaborately illustrated with scenes of expertise and gallantry, these chromolithographed certificates provided an inspiring border design to the handwritten details of a holder's name, status, and date of joining.

They measured some 500 × 350 mm (19¾ × 13¾ in) and were designed for framing. Though produced in various forms by individual printers, the heroic style was universal and the chromolithographic treatment typical of the time. Variations were available for use as specific awards, memorials, etc.

The chromolithographed certificate, whose heyday was the period 1850 to 1880, had its precursor in the copper-engraved fireman's certificate of the late 18th century. One New York example, dated 2 July 1787 and measuring 210 × 250 mm (8¼ × 9⅞ in), was reproduced as a novelty in 1863 by A. Brown & Co., 47 Nassau Street, New York.

See also FIREMAN'S DISCHARGE CERTIFICATE

COLLECTION Insurance Company of North America, Historical Collection, Philadelphia, PA

Firework/firecracker label

In general terms the description 'firework' includes the firecracker, but whereas the European firework label specialist ranges over the whole field of pyrotechnics, the American tends to concentrate on the firecracker – specifically the Chinese 'banger', of which some seven or eight hundred different brand labels are known to exist, and which has featured in Fourth of July celebrations for upwards of a century.

Of all forms of printed ephemera, the pyrotechnic label is by definition one of the most vulnerable. Survivors are relatively rare. Collections necessarily include partially damaged specimens; but used labels, carefully salvaged, may sometimes survive intact. Labels in good condition may be derived (now rarely) from manufacturers' and printers' files, from display dummies, and from new fireworks prior to use.

Earliest records of fireworks point to their origins in China or India, but in Europe popular interest arose with public displays on occasions of national rejoicing. The public display, featuring elaborate set-pieces and multiple firings, has remained a standard entertainment into modern times.

In Britain, individual fireworks for home use emerged as a shopkeeper's item from the home-made squibs and crackers of the 17th century. Progressively governed by safety regulations, by the 1870s fireworks in Britain had become a widely available product, geared to a single annual celebration, Guy Fawkes' night (5 November). The retail industry greatly accelerated, though it did not wholly replace, the public display business. It was from the late 19th century that the product developed into a shop-counter 'package'. Prior to this time the firework had been a more or less anonymous cardboard cylinder, bearing only a minimum of identification in the form of a small printed or handwritten label. Henceforward it became an article of visual appeal using colourful labels and point-of-sale display material.

In the 1960s and 1970s, public concern for safety led to a decline in the shop-goods trade, with a progressive reduction in the number of firms in the field. By the early 1980s, after a number of take-overs, amalgamations, and closures, names still in business were Astra (founded c.1956), Benwell (1949), Brocks (c.1700), Pain (c.1860), and Standard (early 1930s). Of these, only Astra, Benwell, and Standard continued to supply loose fireworks. Names no longer current are Excelsior (ceased trading 1970), Guys (1957–58), Lion (c.1929–72), Rainbow (c.1955–c.1977), Wells (1837–1973), Wessex (1947–65), Wilders (c.1860–1977), and Wizard (c.1950–c.1960).

British firework label collections reflect not only the uncertain scene in the industry but changes in nomenclature, safety levels, pricing, and product range. For example, Pain's range of bangers once numbered thirty; by 1950 the figure was less than a dozen; by the mid 1960s it was four. Names became progressively more 'violent' (though explosive content was steadily reduced). 'Thunder Flash Guns' and 'Aerial Bomb Repeater' gave way to 'Space Bomb', 'Atomic Bomb', and 'Polaris Missile'. Some names, however – violent or otherwise – survived unchanged for a century: 'Pyramid Roman Candles', 'Devil-among-the-Taylors', 'Prince of Wales Feathers', and 'Jack in the Box' date from the 1860s and 1870s.

Britain's decimalization of currency in 1971 brought pricing changes, and rapid inflation resulted in a system of coding by

Firework label of Pain's Wessex fireworks, Salisbury (UK), third quarter of 20th century. Lithographed in five colours. 74 × 125 mm (2 7/8 × 4 7/8 in)

colour or letter. Labels of this period carry colour bands, or a single letter, or a repeated band of letters in lieu of prices. A 'size' system was also used in which single numerals showed price brackets. Firing instructions included such phrases as 'keep your head away', 'stand well back', 'stand clear' (as opposed to the earlier classic 'retire immediately', a relic of the 1870s).

The American firecracker is distinguished from the European firework by its concentration on sound alone. The individual unit, formerly up to 50 mm (2 in), but today commonly some 40 mm (1 9/16 in) in length, measures some 5 mm (3/16 in) in diameter and carries a thin paper fuse. Units are braided together to form a string of sixteen or twenty crackers which may be fired independently or as one. The cracker packs thus formed are wrapped in coloured paper and a colour-printed label is applied to each pack. Eighty packs are bundled together into a 'brick', each brick bearing a larger printed label.

These labels, latterly lacking in design appeal, were earlier of considerable charm and are today highly regarded by the firecracker label connoisseur. Pre-1920s labels are rarely found, though the genre had its inception in the mid 19th century, when Chinese firecrackers were first imported into America. (Although firecrackers have been banned in all but a few of its states, America still accounts for most of China's firecracker export sales.)

Labels from the heyday of the firecracker are notable for their pictorial images: animals, maidens, idyllic landscapes, flowers etc., bordered commonly by mosaic designs and accompanied by brand names and other wording in Chinese characters. In certain cases the more traditional firecracker companies put out labels in gold foil bearing hand-printed images.

In the late 1930s and the 1940s brands proliferated. Firework factories in Canton and other cities of southern China (and later Macau) launched brands by the score, and both the exporters and importers began to register designs with the US patent office. Such brand names as 'Black Cat', 'Camel', 'Peacock', and 'Zebra', still flourishing in the 1980s, made their appearance in this period. As with other brand-label proliferations (orange-crate labels, cotton-bale labels, cigar labels, etc., in which the product remained more or less standardized while names changed repeatedly), turnover in designs was prodigious. Many hundreds of long abandoned brands must have generated their quota of labels – yet to be uncovered.

In later times, taking the place of vanished titles, new images have appeared: 'Mini Bomb', 'Super-Charged Bomb', 'Thunder Bomb', 'H-Bomb', etc. are typical of such brand names.

A further sign of the times has been the advent of statutory safety warnings as part of the label design. The 19th century 'retire immediately' is now expressed more curtly as 'get away'.

REFERENCE Alan St. Hill Brock, *A History of Fireworks* (London: Harrap, 1949)

Fish tally

The fish tally is a printed paper/slip, generally some 50 × 125 mm (2 × 4⅞ in), bearing the name and port code number of a fishing vessel. It identifies the vendor, and is placed among fish in crates off-loaded at the dockside for auction.

Tallies, sometimes supplied in booklets of fifty or a hundred, are commonly printed letterpress in black on white paper, though red and blue are also seen on white or coloured paper. Survival rates are low; the normal life of a tally is limited to its brief journey to the auctioneer – in which time exposure to the crate's contents leaves it much the worse for wear. Fish tallies provide, as well as a conspectus of fishing craft, examples of unpretentious local printing, for the most part from much-used wood type. British Isles port codes, commonly appearing as a second line below the ship's name, were established in 1894 when the Merchant Shipping Act made registration of all fishing vessels a statutory requirement.

British fish tallies, second half of 20th century. Printed by a variety of processes and in different colours. The longest 39 × 141mm (1$\frac{9}{16}$ × 5⅝in); the deepest 51 × 128mm (2 × 5in)

Flagday emblem

The first formal street collections were held in Britain in the latter part of the 19th century. In October 1874 the Hospital Saturday Fund's first collection took place, with young women collecting money in 'missionary-type' wooden boxes. In the same month in 1891, the Royal National Lifeboat Institution celebrated 'Lifeboat Saturday' in Salford, Manchester, with a procession and marching collectors with long-poled money-bags extended among the crowds; money was also thrown into lifeboats in the procession. In 1896 Dr Barnardo's 'Waif Saturday' had its inception; tins and boxes were used to collect donations.

The first British street collection in which an item was given in return for a donation took place in London on 26 June 1912. The event was initiated by Queen Alexandra who was concerned to raise funds for London hospitals; she took the idea from a Danish priest who had sold roses from his garden in aid of orphans. Queen Alexandra's emblems were pink linen 'roses' manufactured by handicapped girls in John Groom's Crippleage (later John Groom's Association for the Disabled). The idea marked the beginning of Alexandra Rose Day, an annual event which has raised large sums over the years.

Flagday emblems from World War I. *Left:* 'Lewisham soldiers' Xmas pudding fund 1916', lithographed in red and blue, 28 × 39mm (1⅛ × 1$\frac{9}{16}$in); *centre:* 'Our day', lithographed in red, grey, and black 40 × 40mm (1$\frac{9}{16}$ × 1$\frac{9}{16}$in); *right:* 'RSPCA War Fund', lithographed in red, brown, black, and silver, 34 × 37mm (1$\frac{5}{16}$ × 1$\frac{7}{16}$in)

The notion of a 'flag day' derives from the enterprise of a Pontypool housewife, Mrs Harold George, who in August 1914 raised £10 by selling miniature red, white, and blue flags in aid of the Prince of Wales's National Relief Fund. On 5 September of the same year Mrs Agnes Morrison of Glasgow organized a 'Union Jack Day' in aid of the Soldiers', Sailors' Families Association and the Territorial Force Association. The term 'flag-day' is now applied regardless of the nature of the emblem, and the causes for which money is raised are multitudinous. The proliferation of the idea soon led to legal restrictions: in most countries no flagday may be organized without formal authorization.

World War I produced a vast range of appeals, each with its special day and emblem. Among less predictable causes were 'Cup Day' for providing cups of tea to soldiers on leave; 'Hut Day' for YMCA hostels; 'Fag Day for Tobacco for the Troops'; 'Splint and Bandage Day' and 'Crutch Day'. Flags were made of paper, card, or silk, mostly with pins for fixing; but later, to save metal, often as cards with slits for fixing to buttons.

Emblems have been produced in a wide variety of guises: among them, in Chicago in 1972, a doughnut (Salvation Army Doughnut Day) and, in Germany in 1937, a miniature 36-page illustrated booklet entitled *The Führer makes History.*

In spite of the immense quantities of emblems produced, some are exceedingly rare. Among these are the emblems sold in aid of the Cinematograph Ambulance Fund (a charity set up in World War I by cinema managers for the purchase of an ambu-

Russian flagday, 1916, official seller's emblem. Letterpress, printed in three colours. Diameter 70mm (2¾in)

lance) and an Irish shamrock motif dating from the time of the Easter Rising in 1916. Also scarce are the authorizing associations' cards, badges, and sellers' trays used in collecting.

REFERENCE Brian Love, 'Street-collection collection', *The Ephemerist*, no. 23, July 1979

COLLECTIONS John Johnson Collection, Bodleian Library, Oxford; Imperial War Museum, London; Brian Love, Charity file, c/o Ephemera Society, London

Flap picture

The flap picture, one of the many paper novelties to emerge in the early 19th century, featured an illustration in which a part or parts of a picture could be lifted to reveal an image underneath.

The device was used in a wide range of contexts – patriotic, satirical, sentimental, and, not infrequently, risqué. It was later exploited by advertisers as a promotion novelty and was extensively used in the GREETINGS CARD and VALENTINE. It survives today in Europe in Advent calendars, in which the recipient opens a single 'window' or other motif on each of the days leading up to Christmas.

Among the earliest flap pictures is a novelty series published in the form of a booklet 128 × 108 mm (5 × 4¼ in) in the early 1820s. Entitled 'The toilet', it shows a succession of items from a dressing table: a flask with the label 'A wash to smooth wrinkles' lifts to reveal the word 'contentment'; 'An enchanting mirror' proves to be 'humility'; 'An universal beautifier' is 'good humour'. An edition of the book appeared in New York in 1835.

In a more substantial production, published by Stacey Grimaldi in London in 1824, a boys' version of the flap book presented 'A set of armour for youth'. It consists of eleven 'framed' flap pictures, in each of which the title lifts to reveal the subject, for example: 'An admirable plume' – 'Loyalty'; 'A noble helmet' – 'Wisdom'. Appropriate homilies appear on facing pages.

In the 1830s political flap prints were produced showing a piece of furniture entitled 'The New Cabinet': the doors of the piece flapped open to disclose portraits of the latest government grouping. From the 1820s to the 1850s numerous separate flap pictures were published that related to the British royal family. A view of the Royal Exchange has a flap that covers William IV kissing Adelaide; a picture of a cravat entitled 'Prince Albert's Stock' opens to reveal a brood of royal babies; a window picture called 'The British Union' reveals the royal couple; and an untitled apple discloses Queen Victoria.

Fleet marriage certificate

In Britain, prior to the marriage act of 1753, laws relating to marriage ceremonies were relatively lax, both in form and observance. Among many abuses and irregularities was the marginal institution known as 'Fleet marriage', in which couples were married without banns or licence at any hour – often by unqualified 'parsons'. The Fleet Street area became notorious for its 'marrying shops', in front of which touts invited passers-by to instant matrimony.

The practice had arisen more or less legitimately from the presence in Fleet Prison of chaplains, whose services were available to prisoners, many of whom were debtors. The precincts of the prison (known as 'the rules') were later included in the 'special area' within which these chaplains and others – many of them in debt themselves – plied their trade.

Fleet marriages were a regular source of trouble: records, if maintained at all, were readily falsified or destroyed, and the facility was fully exploited by bigamists, fortune-hunters, seducers, and others. The ceremonies remained in great demand until their abolition: on 25 March 1754, the day before the Abolishing Act came into force, one Fleet register recorded a total of 217 weddings in one day.

Fleet marriage certificates, though they bore the Royal Crest and recorded that the marriage had been performed 'according to the rites and ceremonies of the Church of England', were of ambiguous validity. Though widely recognized as legal, they were not always admissible as evidence in courts of law, nor were the 'registers' in which the ceremonies were recorded.

The certificate commonly measured some 203 × 138 mm (8 × 5½ in): those issued in the prison itself bore the wording '... Married at the Fleet, London'; those in the 'rules' '... Married in the praecinct of the Fleet, London'. Certificates were also issued as *post hoc* verification of marriage. In one such 'praecinct' example, the signatory, 'John Evans, Minister, next dore to Mr Underwood a Brewer by the Ditchside', also testifies in handwriting: 'This is to certify whom it may concern that John Maun Hostler... and Mary Godwin' were married 'by James Colton, then Minister as Appears by his book, on the fifth day of January 1715...'.

Fleet marriage certificates are scarce, though a considerable number of register books have survived and are today lodged with The Public Record Office at Kew. [PJ]

See also GRETNA GREEN MARRIAGE CERTIFICATE

REFERENCES John Ashton, *The Fleet: its River, Prison and Marriages*, (London: T. Fisher Unwin, 1888); Mary Dorothy George, *London Life in the XIIIth Century* (London: Kegan Paul, 1925)

COLLECTIONS Guildhall Library, London; Museum of London

Flicker book

The flicker or flick book presents an illusion of movement through a succession of images, each showing a single phase of a complete action. The series is bound in the form of a booklet and viewed by letting the pages flick past the viewer's thumb (or, in mechanical versions, a release blade).

The flicker book has its origin in early research by motion-picture pioneers. Notable among these was a Philadelphia mechanical engineer, Coleman Sellers, who took a series of photographs in 1860 showing the action of hammering a nail into wood. The separate pictures, mounted on the blades of a paddle-wheel rotor and viewed from a fixed point, produced an effect of continuous movement. Sellers patented the device as the Kinematoscope on 5 February 1861.

Motion-picture development moved on to the 'roller-photography' stage (continuous film images for screen projection) and Sellers's idea simply became a novelty. In the 1890s Casler's 'Mutoscope' appeared: this involved a crank-handle viewer of the kind soon to become popular as 'what-the-butler-saw' machines of amusement arcades. A domestic version of the Mutoscope, known as the 'Kinora', was also produced. This was available in a variety of forms, all for table-top use; picture 'reels' were easily changed, and some models were operated by clockwork.

A modification of the idea was patented in Britain in the late 1890s by Henry W. Short as the 'Filoscope'. In this simpler, pocket version, pressure on a lever released a succession of pictures for hand-held operation.

In the same year the newly established *Harmsworth Magazine* printed a series of 71 'cinematograph' pictures in the top right-hand margin of its issue for November 1898 (vol. 1, no. 5). The series, filmed by Lumière & Sons, showed two children dancing. Explaining this 'novel expedient', devised to show the principle of the cinema to those who had never seen it, the editor instructed the reader to hold the magazine 'allowing the pages to escape rapidly from underneath the thumb'.

The flicker book as such appeared as an abbreviated version of the filoscope, containing, commonly, some thirty-six images and showing, in the main, cartoon episodes or sequences of dancing, sport, etc. In the 1920s and early 1930s 'instructional' flicker books appeared, portraying demonstration studies of tennis players, golfers, etc. in action. 'Two-way' flicker books also appeared in which the double-sided leaves produced a different sequence of images when the book was reversed.

REFERENCE Philip and Caroline Freeman Sayer, *Victorian Kinetic Toys* (London: Evans Bros, 1977)

Flyer *See* CLUB FLYER; LEAFLET

Fly-paper

The term refers to two kinds of paper products, the one sticky, the other impregnated with poison.

Mayhew reports that the street sale of sticky papers became general in London in the summer of 1848, and that there was a brisk demand for them from publicans and shopkeepers who bought them from streetsellers (who wore them, suitably studded with victims, in their hats). In the late 1850s and 1860s there appeared a new form of fly-paper, known variously as 'Papier Moure', 'Papier Mouche', 'Chemical Fly Catching Paper', or 'Chemical Fly Paper'.

Fly-papers were sold in 'parcels' or packets and as booklets, each of which was boldly printed with the supplier's advertising matter. They measured some 180 × 150 mm (7⅛ × 6 in) and in some cases were perforated for separation into four pieces 'so that each sheet contains enough for four apartments'. The sheets were designed to be soaked in water on a plate, with a little brown sugar added to attract insects. The solution thus produced was claimed to be harmless to anything but insects, but users were recommended to keep it away from children and animals.

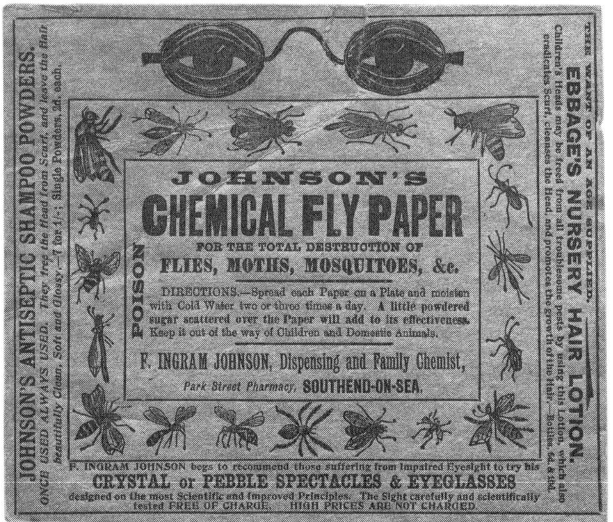

Johnson's Chemical Fly Paper. Letterpress on brown paper. 150 × 180 mm (6 × 7⅛ in)

Among leading suppliers were S. Maw, Son, & Thompson ('Papier Moure'); Matthew Tomlinson ('Papier Mouche – a substitute for Papier Moure'); Dixon, Dean & Co. ('One Penny per Book'); Mather's ('Spread each paper on one of Mather's Patent Trays'); Smithson's ('Chemical Fly Paper'); and Walls, Close & Co. ('Octagon Fly-Papers').

The *Pharmaceutical Journal*, in November 1859, reported a single sheet of 'Papier Moure' as containing 2.55 grammes of arsenious acid, 'quite enough to destroy human life'. The papers continued to be sold well into the mid 20th century and frequently featured (together with rat poison) in evidence in murder cases.

REFERENCES Advertisements: *The Druggist & Drysalter's Monthly Price Current*, 1868, passim ; *The Chemist & Druggist*, 1867, passim ; 'Papier Moure', *Notes and Queries*, 2nd series, 26 November 1859

COLLECTION Royal Pharmaceutical Society of Great Britain

Fly-wagon bill

By the early part of the 19th century, Britain's goods and parcels conveyance system had crystallized into a more or less coordinated national network. Working to a regular schedule, independent carriers in the major cities operated a service of covered vans or fly wagons. For each transaction in which unaccompanied goods were moved from one specified point to another, a bill was made out. The fly-wagon bill, a distinctive printed paper, formed not only a receipt but was sometimes an extended promotional piece. It often listed towns and villages served, time schedules, the names of porters and drivers in charge of the wagons, and the addresses of warehouses and other storage places. Prominently displayed on the bill was the name of the departure point, commonly an inn, and in many cases a woodcut picture of the four-horse wagon with its driver and guard. As with stage-coach material, the picture was a STOCK BLOCK only nominally resembling the team in question. In many cases the typeset name of the operator was dropped into a space in the block, thus conveying the impression of a specially-drawn representation of the operator's named vehicle. Some illustrations remained in use for decades. One operator showed in the late 1830s an eight-horse 'long wagon' with the broad wheels required by law in the mid 18th century.

The bills were generally printed in black on white paper but, unlike many common documents of the period, there were occasional excursions into coloured inks. Blue, red, and orange were popular and there were occasional lapses into yellow, a notoriously unsuitable colour for reading by candle or lamplight. Sizes varied widely from 150 × 110 mm (6 × 4⅜ in) to 230 × 190 mm (9 × 7½ in). The majority of used specimens are found to be pierced in the centre, having been filed on billspikes. An average print run appears to have been 2000.

The competitive nature of the business is reflected in slogans: 'Extra vans or wagons sent at short notice'; 'Goods carried in from all parts of London'; 'Paris via Calais: the only fly vans Direct to Dover from the White Hart Inn, Borough'. Files of bills reveal changes in routes, schedules, personnel, and ownership. Conditions of carriage, cited at increasing length and in progressively finer print, point to the hazards of the business. In 1843 the 200-word disclaimer on a Pickford and Co. bill occupied two-thirds of the printed area, though many operators were content to relegate such matter to the back of the bill.

The system paralleled the passenger coach network, often

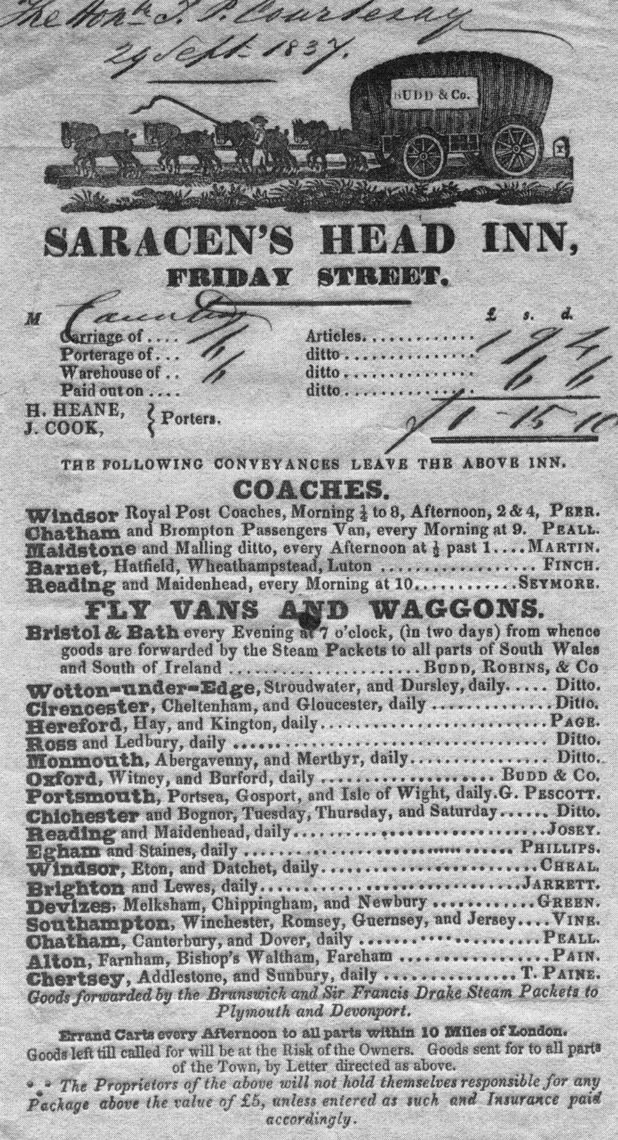

BUDD & Co.

SARACEN'S HEAD INN,

FRIDAY STREET.

M

		£ s. d.
Carriage of	Articles............	
Porterage of...	ditto..............	
Warehouse of..	ditto..............	
Paid out on	ditto..............	

H. HEANE,
J. COOK, } Porters.

THE FOLLOWING CONVEYANCES LEAVE THE ABOVE INN.

COACHES.

Windsor Royal Post Coaches, Morning ¼ to 8, Afternoon, 2 & 4, PEER.
Chatham and Brompton Passengers Van, every Morning at 9. PEALL.
Maidstone and Malling ditto, every Afternoon at ½ past 1....MARTIN.
Barnet, Hatfield, Wheathampstead, Luton .... FINCH.
Reading and Maidenhead, every Morning at 10............SEYMORE.

FLY VANS AND WAGGONS.

Bristol & Bath every Evening at 7 o'clock, (in two days) from whence goods are forwarded by the Steam Packets to all parts of South Wales and South of Ireland ....BUDD, ROBINS, & Co
Wotton-under-Edge, Stroudwater, and Dursley, daily..... Ditto.
Cirencester, Cheltenham, and Gloucester, daily ....Ditto.
Hereford, Hay, and Kington, daily.........................PAGE.
Ross and Ledbury, daily .... Ditto.
Monmouth, Abergavenny, and Merthyr, daily................. Ditto.
Oxford, Witney, and Burford, daily .... BUDD & Co.
Portsmouth, Portsea, Gosport, and Isle of Wight, daily.G. PESCOTT.
Chichester and Bognor, Tuesday, Thursday, and Saturday...... Ditto.
Reading and Maidenhead, daily.................................JOSEY.
Egham and Staines, daily .... PHILLIPS.
Windsor, Eton, and Datchet, daily...........................CHEAL.
Brighton and Lewes, daily...................................JARRETT.
Devizes, Melksham, Chippingham, and Newbury ....GREEN.
Southampton, Winchester, Romsey, Guernsey, and Jersey....VINE.
Chatham, Canterbury, and Dover, daily ....PEALL.
Alton, Farnham, Bishop's Waltham, Fareham ....PAIN.
Chertsey, Addlestone, and Sunbury, daily ....T. PAINE.
Goods forwarded by the Brunswick and Sir Francis Drake Steam Packets to Plymouth and Devonport.

Errand Carts every Afternoon to all parts within 10 Miles of London.
Goods left till called for will be at the Risk of the Owners. Goods sent for to all parts of the Town, by Letter directed as above.
**** The Proprietors of the above will not hold themselves responsible for any Package above the value of £5, unless entered as such and Insurance paid accordingly.*

Fly-wagon bill, September 1837. Letterpress with relief block and manuscript, printed in blue. 226 × 130 mm (8⅞ × 5⅛ in)

working out of the same inns and booking offices. As with coaching, there was an attempt to correlate services with shipping mailings and, later, railway services – which finally superseded wagons and coaches alike.

Folk recipe

The word recipe is the Latin *recipe* (take thou). Its use in the popular sense derives from its dominance in former times as the first word in a list of ingredients. It is thus that the word 'receipt' (past participle of a related form) was for long used instead of, or as an alternative to, the word recipe, though the usage is now obsolete.

Most early recipes bear the title 'receipt' or occasionally 'rect'. The word may be used in connection with the preparation of food and drink, the formulation of domestic cleaning agents, medicines, and the concoction of potions and poisons. In a world in which everyone was largely their own provider, the recipe or receipt was a valued heirloom property. The folk recipe is in a sense an heirloom – a crystallized outcome of generations of trial and error. For the student of social history it provides evidence of human dauntlessness.

The folk recipe appears in some profusion in the handwritten domestic account book. Here, in the hands of successive generations, are notes of abiding family importance: records of birth, marriages and death, income and expenditure, and recipes and remedies. Such books, sometimes merging imperceptibly into the COMMONPLACE BOOK in which the owner also transcribed verse and aphorisms, served as a general repository of wisdom and information.

Recipes often form a major part of these books. Entered more or less at random as required, and without organization or system, they present a kaleidoscopic conspectus of human ills and enterprise. A typical book carries these entries: 'Remedy for the itch for a large family'; 'For physic without pain'; 'Recipe for tincture of life'; 'How to make green paint'; 'To make diadem plaster'; 'Cure for spasmodic cholera'; 'For a weak constitution'; 'For burn or scald apply soft soap immediately'; 'For the jaundice, proved'; 'For lice on cattle'; 'For a cough'.

Many such books carry inserted scraps, sometimes pinned to the pages: 'Sir John Bernays Receipt to Cure Cloth for Covering Umbrellors'; 'To stop Mortification'; 'Muriate of Lime for the Evil or Leprosy'; 'Receipt for Surfeit water'; 'To destroy mice'; 'The only rect for the Plague'.

Football programme

At its first introduction, in Britain in the mid 1870s, the football programme presented little more than a diagrammatic line-up of players' names and a list of presiding officials. Printed in black on a white card, and measuring typically 150 × 130 mm (6 × 5⅛ in), the card carried the line-up on its face and details of venue, date, and kick-off on the reverse. It was generally priced at one penny.

Among the oldest surviving programmes is one for a Finchley versus Old Etonians match in 1879.

The football programme card derived in principle from the cricket scorecard, but shortly assumed its own identity; at the turn of the century it took the form of a double-sided paper leaflet measuring about 255 × 190 mm (10 × 7½ in). This larger format accommodated additional information, though the selling price continued generally at one penny as production costs began to be defrayed by the sale of advertising space.

In a further development, the single sheet became a four-page folder, page one serving as a 'cover'; the centre-spread carried the diagram, a nominal paragraph or two devoted to editorial comment and information, and advertisements. The back page often carried advertising. The four-page programme remained in use through the 1920s and 1930s (and in some cases into the 1960s), although during this period eight- and sixteen-page programmes also appeared. However, a new approach was adopted in the 1920s for major occasions only; this was an eight-, twelve-, or sixteen-page pamphlet, often with a two-colour cover and generally measuring some 200 × 130 mm (7⅞ × 5⅛ in). Here, as in the theatre programme, was a more heavyweight offering of editorial and advertising. Priced at threepence or sixpence, such pamphlets provided a more substantial record of the event and were clearly designed to be preserved as a souvenir (unlike the 'pre-pamphlet' specimens, which have rarely survived).

In 1948 Chelsea Football Club introduced a far more ambitious form of publication, a sixteen-page magazine, containing articles, pictures of teams and individual players, and action

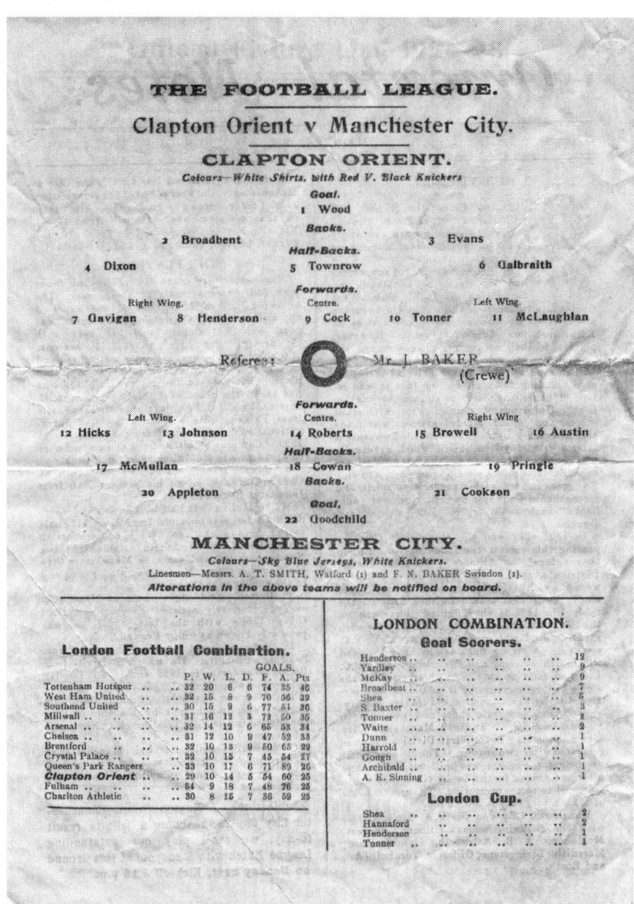

THE FOOTBALL LEAGUE.

Clapton Orient v Manchester City.

CLAPTON ORIENT.

Colours—White Shirts, with Red V. Black Knickers

Goal.
1 Wood

Backs.
2 Broadbent 3 Evans

Half-Backs.
4 Dixon 5 Townrow 6 Galbraith

Forwards.
Right Wing. Centre. Left Wing.
7 Gavigan 8 Henderson 9 Cock 10 Tonner 11 McLaughlan

Referee: Mr. J. BAKER (Crewe)

Forwards.
Left Wing. Centre. Right Wing.
12 Hicks 13 Johnson 14 Roberts 15 Browell 16 Austin

Half-Backs.
17 McMullan 18 Cowan 19 Pringle

Backs.
20 Appleton 21 Cookson

Goal.
22 Goodchild

MANCHESTER CITY.

Colours—Sky Blue Jerseys, White Knickers.

Linesmen—Messrs. A. T. SMITH, Watford (1) and F. N. BAKER Swindon (2).

Alterations in the above teams will be notified on board.

London Football Combination.

	P.	W.	L.	D.	GOALS. F.	GOALS. A.	Pts
Tottenham Hotspur	32	20	6	6	74	35	46
West Ham United	32	15	8	9	70	56	39
Southend United	30	15	9	6	77	51	36
Millwall	31	16	12	3	72	50	35
Arsenal	32	14	12	6	65	58	34
Chelsea	31	12	10	9	47	52	33
Brentford	32	10	13	9	50	65	29
Crystal Palace	32	10	15	7	45	54	27
Queen's Park Rangers	33	10	17	6	71	89	26
Clapton Orient	29	10	14	5	54	60	25
Fulham	34	9	18	7	48	76	25
Charlton Athletic	30	8	15	7	36	59	23

LONDON COMBINATION.

Goal Scorers.

Henderson	12
Yardley	9
McKay	9
Broadbent	7
Shea	5
S. Baxter	3
Tonner	2
Waite	2
Dunn	1
Harrold	1
Gough	1
Archibald	1
A. E. Sinning	1

London Cup.

Shea	2
Hannaford	2
Henderson	1
Tonner	1

Football programme of Clapton Orient Football Club for their game with Manchester City in the Football Association Cup, 6 March 1926. Page 3 (of eight). Letterpress, printed in blue by Henry Nevill, Hackney, London. 253 × 190 mm (10 × 7½ in)

shots of previous matches. The publication sold at sixpence – double the price of its predecessor. The idea was rapidly adopted by other clubs. With the advent of the programme-collecting cult (which it helped to generate), and with ticket voucher systems occasionally based on production of 'away-match' programmes, sales of programmes sometimes exceeded gate figures.

By the late 1990s, Chelsea's 'Official Matchday Magazine', a typical programme of its day measuring 235 × 160 mm (9¼ × 6½ in), ran to 64 full-colour pages and cost £2.50.

Britain, Holland, and Scandinavia are the chief centres of football-programme collecting. In Britain, the most sought-after, apart from rare 19th-century items, are pre-World War II programmes featuring British teams in international matches, and, from the same period, cup-final programmes and programmes relating to football clubs now defunct (e.g. Thames, Leeds City, Ashington, etc.).

The North American football programme scene is dominated by 'Soccer America', a mass-circulation publication which appears, duly modified, at specific MLS (Major League Soccer) matches throughout America and Canada.

SOCIETY Football Programme Directory, Wickford, Essex

'Foreign' English

Collected largely for their entertainment value, published examples of 'foreign' English are a striking testimony to the linguistic self-confidence of those who rush into print without seeking native advice. They have been delightfully parodied by Gerard Hoffnung in his stage and radio performances. The phenomenon dates from the beginnings of international commerce, in which English has been a dominant language, and in which the British have figured as major prospective customers.

Examples are frequent in tourism. In 1800 the Hotel Du Moulinet, Reims, issued this announcement:

> M. Desmaretz prays travellers not to believe the falze reports that some of his partners scatter by post boys (that they pay) in design of bringing forrigners to their house, in annoncing that he keeps no more his hotel. Stangers shall always find in this hotel all the advantages that a traveller could desire. They will be servee as by the past, et intent servants et lodged as the house which is renowned for the finest et best situated of the town can permit it....

More recently, in November 1931, the Hotel Engadinerhof, Pontresina, announced that

> ... every year I contributed something to the comfort of my hotel. So I Built the cosy Reading room, the big and homely Dining room the new part of the hotel with its Pleasant room and nice balconys ... and I augmented the number of the public baths with two new once ... I should also be very grateful if you would kindly inform all your friends about all news, happened in the Hotel Engadinerhof at Pontresina ....

Manufacturers' directions for use also provide fascinating examples. Early 1830s Dutch-made friction matches, in which the match was to be struck by quick withdrawal from between sandpaper sheets, carried the following instructions:

> ... the match is to be put between the paper sheets, the paper at the end of the match pressed, and to be drawn quick out, but so that the pressure does not touch the mass of the inflammation. Remark: It is not necessarij to throw the match awij if it don't tind bij wearing them well they must ijet inflame. If by long use the inside of the papr sheets worn out, it must be turned over and wasted in the same waij as above mentioned.

A French couscous packet of 1970 reads: '... let absorb the water during 8 to 10 minutes ... put it into a strainer with big holes, which can be adapted on a rather high pot ... boil the water, close the point of contact with a humid stuff, in order to obtain that all the steam goes up the Couscous and makes in this way the cooking of the Couscous ...'.

A driving licence issued by the Government of a Gulf State in the 1960s included this condition of issue: 'This licence is valid for driving Commercial vehicles of more than six passengers or less and Commercial trucks which total weight (With its load) is more than three tons or less'.

Forgery

Though it may be extended to cover coins, paintings, seals, dies, sculptures, antiques, and other objects, the term forgery here relates to items made of paper which were devised to defraud or deceive.

A forgery within this definition may be printed or handwritten or both; it may be wholly or partly false, it must manifestly have been produced with the intention to mislead, and its level of execution must be such as to be calculated to deceive an ordinary intelligent observer. These last two conditions thus exclude items produced by way of amusement and those whose execution is so crude as to rule out any possibility of deception.

Classically, forgeries have been of items of direct or indirect monetary value. Of these, currency notes are the commonest examples. Because of the importance of the note in the maintenance of a stable economy and the dangers of devaluation through inflated circulation, governments have been rigorous in maintaining its integrity. The crime of counterfeiting currency, in many periods punishable by death, remains a major offence. Mass forgery of enemy paper currency has more than once been carried out by government agencies as a weapon of war, and in the period of the French Revolution the British are said to have forged and distributed large numbers of ASSIGNATS in an effort to undermine an already ailing economy.

Forgery of BANKNOTES was widespread in Britain in the late 18th and early 19th centuries. Apart from the notes issued by country banks, which were complicated in design (and, additionally, backed by a two-colour stamp), banknotes were not difficult to counterfeit, and many thousands of forgeries were in circulation. Forgery of banknotes was a capital offence, and in 1763 the imitation of the watermark alone was made punishable by death. Nevertheless, the temptation to forge has been overwhelming.

With the introduction of £1 notes in 1802, forgery increased to new levels and the deterrent effect of hangings and transportations continued unavailing. The number of death sentences for forgery between 1797 and 1829 totalled 618. The scandal of the situation led George Cruikshank to produce his celebrated caricature note of 1819: 'Submitted to the Consideration of the Bank Directors and the inspection of the Public'. The note, signed by 'J. Ketch', the public hangman, featured a multiple hanging and symbols of death, imprisonment, and transportation. Public concern was eventually to lead to the substitution of transportation for the death sentence and a serious review of SECURITY PRINTING methods.

Forged notes, verified as such by the Bank of England, were for some time overstamped with the word 'forged' and returned to their owners, but later the forgeries were retained and destroyed.

Less readily 'convertible' subjects for forgery are taxation stamps and other fiscal devices. These too have been widely forged and in some cases equally rigorously defended. In Britain in 1805, Richard Harding, a playing-card maker, was sentenced to death for forging dutiable aces of spades, and in 1798 John Collins received the same sentence for forging hat-tax stamps.

Among the most spectacularly successful of fiscal forgeries was the case of the British 'shilling green', a postage stamp used on telegram forms by the Stock Exchange telegraph office in the early 1870s. The stamp came into use as a substitute for the earlier embossed stamps, which were struck directly on the forms, and the standard rate of twenty words for one shilling brought a marked increase in demand for this denomination. Its use at the Stock Exchange telegraph office allowed the telegraph clerk to issue it across the counter where, with only cursory inspection, it was immediately affixed to the form by the sender and passed back again. The clerk thus retained both form and stamp for cancellation, wire transmission, and temporary filing; after a statutory interval, they were destroyed. The forgery of 'shilling greens' came to light only in 1898, when Charles Nissen, a philatelic expert, was examining a batch of used forms that had escaped destruction. Nissen noticed an anomaly in one of the plate letters, and closer inspection was to reveal the existence of counterfeits of plates 'No 5' and 'No 6', each of which showed individual discrepancies from the genuine plate. Further research disclosed a major fraud in which, over a period of some two years, forged stamps had been used by the issuing clerk. The estimated total haul was in excess of £30,000, a figure in today's terms of several million pounds or dollars. No uncancelled version of the forgery was ever found. Nor was the culprit.

Postage stamp forgeries (which are properly the province of the philatelist) appear in three categories: those intended to deceive the Revenue; those simulating philatelic rarities and designed to deceive collectors; those produced in wartime for use in enemy mails or for propaganda purposes. In the latter class are World War II stamps printed in Britain for use in Europe and those produced in Germany for similar external use. 'Propaganda' forgeries fall into two groups: 'parody' designs, in which existing issues are grotesquely adapted, and subtly altered versions in which changes are apparent only on close inspection. In the first group, on the German side, is an adaptation of Britain's Silver Jubilee issue of 1935, in which the head of King George V is replaced by that of Stalin and with the words: 'This war is a Jewish war'; and from the allies a redrawn head of Hitler in which part of the face appears as a skull. In the second group is the German modification of Britain's 'King George VI low value' set, in which Jewish and communist emblems are discreetly introduced into the design. (There is some uncertainty as to the rationale of this design and its intended use, particularly as the set was produced and distributed on ungummed paper.)

'Straight' forgeries were produced for use by agents in enemy-occupied territory and for infiltration of enemy postal systems. In espionage, in resistance organizations, as well as in 'black' propaganda, production of false documents was an important war activity. Forged passports, identity cards, ration books, and general personal papers were manufactured in large quantities; there was also provision of 'counterfeit' boxes of matches, cigarettes, clothing labels, and other such clues to national background. Resistance material included miniature publications in 'disguise'. Though bearing innocent titles and opening pages, they carried instruction material for saboteurs, deserters, and malingerers. Also produced as vehicles for instructions were cigarette-paper packets, complete with 'local' manufacturers' trade names and publicity designs; these contained cigarette papers with guidance on rail sabotage. Fake bookmatches enclosed concertina-folded instruction sheets on the simulation of stomach ulcers, heart disease, etc.

'Black propaganda' forgeries, a significant feature in World War II, purported to come from within the enemy's own homeland. Items in this category sought to undermine civilian morale, by oblique and ostensibly innocent references to privilege among the ruling establishment or by apparently unintended disclosures of setbacks (*see* AERIAL LEAFLET). A typical 'black' forgery is a public notice prepared by the British for use in German-occupied Europe. The notice, a paper measuring 150 × 105 mm (6 × 4⅛ in), is addressed to *Wehrmacht* rail travellers. It warns that the enemy is everywhere: 'Assure yourself personally, by thorough search of this compartment, that no explosive charges, acid bombs or incendiary devices are concealed under the seats, in the upholstery, etc. Detain suspicious persons. Report statements immediately. – Army Traffic Board'. These notices were distributed on railways all over Europe, each bearing the name of the appropriate capital city as issuing office. In another dimension of warfare, the counterfeiting of escape documents by prisoners of war has a long and remarkable history, with passes, permits, identity cards and their appropriate rubber stamps prepared from virtually nothing.

Forgery has classically occupied the time of prisoners at many periods, both in civil and military gaols. French prisoners of war at Norman Cross in 1805 were found to have developed remarkable skills at counterfeiting banknotes. Two men, Nicholas Deschamps and Jean Roubilliard were sentenced to death at Huntingdon assizes for forging £1 banknotes, though they were reprieved and finally repatriated.

Peace-time forgery appears in a multitude of documents, including marriage and other certificates, licences, references, pedigrees, cheques, and passports.

To the collector (as well as to those whom the forgery is devised to deceive) verification of the item as a forgery is a matter of special interest. Even though the original function of the item has long lapsed, the cancellation mark 'forgery' has considerable impact. The word appears in unmistakable defacement on banknote forgeries of the early 19th century, and in France the counterfeit ASSIGNAT bears the stamped impression 'assignat certifié faux', and the declaration is signed by the Republic's 'verificateur en chef'.

Forgery of commercial printed matter was common in the mid and late 19th century, and Lea & Perrins, the manufacturers of Worcestershire Sauce, have a large collection of labels from all over the world which imitate the design and colour, if not the precise words, of this world famous sauce. The prevalence of forgery, or imitation verging on forgery, gave rise to the classic warning: 'None genuine without this signature'. This appeared on a wide range of products (many of them counterfeits themselves, which, through their mediocrity, had little or no fear of imitation). In a 'genuine' case of counterfeit in the 1890s ('one of many gross imitations which have recently come under their notice') W. D. & H. O. Wills, the tobacco company, published a magazine insert illustrating a true Wills label juxtaposed with that of 'a counterfeit detected in Copenhagen'. The matter was taken sufficiently seriously to warrant the company printing its labels on special paper '... every Label contains the Water-Mark of the Firm' (a watermark also present in the magazine insert bearing the message). No examples of the counterfeits in question appear to have been reported to date, however.

Forgery of 'collector's pieces' is not uncommon. Philately records many examples in which a minor manipulation of a detail may invest an item with exceptional scarcity value. Some 'scarce' items have required prodigious efforts of reproduction, involving many hundreds of thousands of words of typesetting and complex platemaking.

Typical of this category is the much forged *Daily Citizen* of Vicksburg, Mississippi, 4 July 1863, the last edition of a single-sheet newspaper printed, because of civil-war paper shortage, on the back of wallpaper. With the surrender of the town the printer and editor, J. M. Swords, was obliged to leave the paper uncompleted, with all but a few column inches of matter set up in type and virtually ready to print. Men of the union army completed the final column with a sardonic comment on the fortunes of war and an announcement that this was to be the last issue of the Vicksburg wallpaper *Daily Citizen*. They added that the issue would be 'valuable hereafter as a curiosity'.

The prediction proved to be correct. The Library of Congress, which holds four genuine copies of the issue, records that over thirty reprintings have been reported. In 1955 the Library listed the following points by which originals may be recognized, including: Type area: 429 × 232 mm (17 × 9⅛ in); Col. 1, line 1: Title THE DAILY CITIZEN, in capitals, not capitals and lower case, or capitals and small capitals; Col. 1, line 2: 'J. M. Swords, ... Proprietor' with a 'comma (or imperfect dot) and six periods'. It also refers to the wallpaper pattern itself as a possible identifying point, but explains that at least four patterns are known to have been used and that identification by this means is therefore uncertain.

The field of forgery must be approached with caution. Forgeries having in recent years become collectors' pieces, there has inevitably emerged the 'double-cross' in which forgeries are themselves forged. Classic examples of these are the allegedly spurious specimens of the book and pamphlet forgeries of T. J. Wise, whose deceptions now form a bibliographical category of their own.

See also AERIAL LEAFLET; BEER LABEL; BENEFIT TICKET; CIGARETTE PAPER; 'CINDERELLA' STAMP; COMPOUND-PLATE PRINTING; CREDIT/CASH CARD; DICE-DUTY WRAPPER; HAT-DUTY STAMP; VIOLIN LABEL

Form

The form is a means of gathering information in an orderly way for a particular purpose. It was originally called a 'blank form' in Britain and a 'blank' in America to indicate that parts of the document had to be filled in. The word 'form' emphasizes its structure, 'blank' its incompleteness.

The emergence of the form on a broad front coincides with the growing complexity of society and the need for authorities of all kinds to gather information and exercise control. It probably made its first appearance in such fields as taxation, censuses of population, the army, and maritime trade. By the end of the 18th century it had become an essential feature of the period identified in Britain with the growth of bureaucracy, and in France with the administrative reforms of the Napoleonic period.

The document we call a form (Latin: *forma*) reflects several other meanings of the word (for example, 'a set or fixed order of words', a 'formal procedure', 'the visible aspect of a thing') in that it elicits information in a set way, both in terms of its wording and appearance. The French *formulaire* and German *Formular* stem from the same root. The first use of the word form in the context of documents is not clear, but by the 1850s the Inland Revenue in Britain was issuing documents headed 'This form'.

The form displays some characteristics of a dialogue between two parties (sometimes more). In one kind of form information is called for by leaving gaps in a set text (e.g. I... of ...) for the form filler to complete; in a later approach, specific questions are asked of the form filler (either open-ended questions or choices from a set of possibilities). The second of these two kinds of forms might be called a questionnaire, an early example of which is 'Queries proposed by the Board of Agriculture to be answered by intelligent farmers' of around 1800. Some of the characteristics of a form as described above are shared by other named categories of document, such as CERTIFICATE, INDENTURE, LICENCE, PASSPORT, RECEIPT. A longstanding ambiguity of terminology is revealed by a document of 1780, which was described as a 'Form of the certificate of the amount of land tax'.

The earliest forms were entirely manuscript; that is, the set parts of the document and the user's response to them were

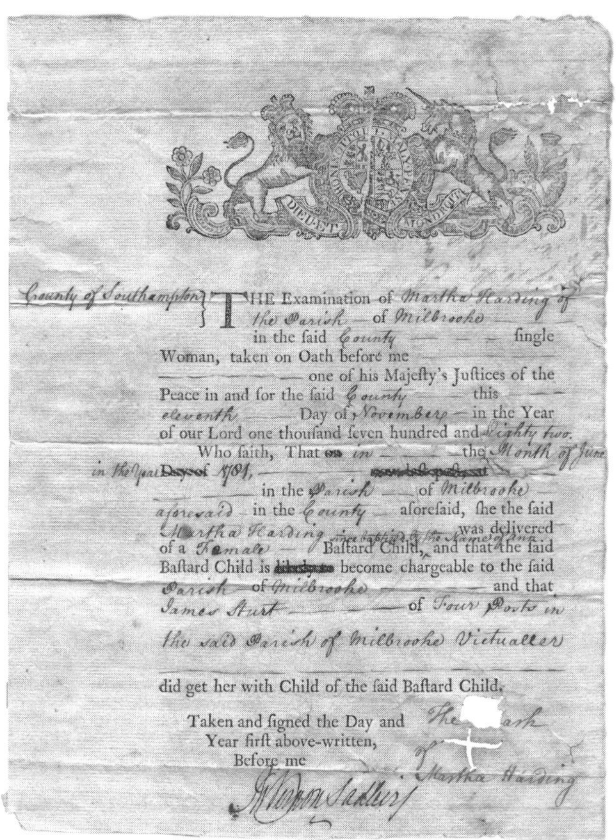

County of Southampton } THE Examination of Martha Harding of the Parish of Milbrooke in the said County single Woman, taken on Oath before me one of his Majesty's Justices of the Peace in and for the said County this eleventh Day of November in the Year of our Lord one thousand seven hundred and Eighty two. Who saith, That in the Month of June in the year 1781, in the Parish of Milbrooke aforesaid in the County aforesaid, she the said Martha Harding was delivered of a Female Bastard Child, and that the said Bastard Child is become chargeable to the said Parish of Milbrooke and that James Sturt of Four Posts in the said Parish of Milbrooke Victualler did get her with Child of the said Bastard Child.

Taken and signed the Day and Year first above-written, Before me

Paternity form, signed with her mark by Martha Harding before a Justice of the Peace, declaring that James Sturt was the father of her bastard child. Milbrooke, Southampton, 11 November 1781. Letterpress and manuscript. 255 × 190 mm (10 × 7½in)

handwritten. This method of production continued throughout the 18th century, though during this period, mainly in response to the need for more forms of the same kind, standard parts were printed. Utilitarian forms of the late 18th century were printed from type, but more prestigious ones, particularly those needed in smaller quantities, were printed from intaglio plates.

From the early 19th century lithographic forms began to replace intaglio-printed ones, as the lithographic process was cheap and lent itself to the production of short runs. The law stationer R. Cartwright of 1 Warwick Place, Bedford Row, London, pointed out in one of his advertisements of about 1840 that, when six or more copies were needed, it worked out cheaper to multiply a form from handwriting on lithographic transfer paper than to make individual manuscript versions. Forms were produced by TRANSFER LITHOGRAPHY throughout Europe in the first half of the 19th century, and particularly fine examples were issued in France, where the process continued to be used for this purpose well into the 20th century. The production of the standard parts of such forms was in keeping with the older manuscript practice, and also with the idea of the form as a dialogue between two parties.

Nevertheless, as forms began to be needed in large quantities, typesetting became the normal method of origination, initially for letterpress printing and, later in the 20th century, for lithographic printing. This established a clear difference between the standard wording and the responses of the form filler. Initially, as in the early days of the manuscript form, gaps were left in the standard wording for the user to complete, but in the course of the 19th century it became common practice for dotted or continuous rules to be printed as a guide to filling in. Another common element of forms of this kind, which survived into the 20th century, was the use of horizontal and vertical rules to divide information fields.

An abiding feature of the form, probably from the late 19th century onwards, has been the directive to form fillers to use 'capitals' or 'block letters' only. This reflects both the declining legibility of handwriting and the increasing demands placed on data handlers. Such directives survived the widespread take-up of the typewriter in the late 19th century, which, for a variety of reasons, did not lend itself to the filling in of forms.

Forms have traditionally been regarded as one of the least attractive fields of typographic design, and, with a few notable exceptions, have been ignored by those who wrote about or practised typography before the second half of the 20th century. However, from the 1970s forms began to attract attention in several parts of the world as a result of what can be regarded as a people's movement to make public documents easier to understand. Governments and businesses soon realized that it was in their interests to take note of such views since vast sums of money were being spent on devising, producing, and processing forms.

In the wake of public protests and some evaluation work, attempts were made in America, Australia, Britain, and elsewhere to make forms user friendly in both their language and appearance. This change in the attitude of those responsible for issuing forms happened to coincide with changes in print production methods that made it possible to produce forms with background tints, thus allowing parts that needed to be completed to appear white against a light-toned background. As a result, there emerged a new genre of form in the 1970s, clearer in meaning and less authoritarian in its use of words and graphic appearance, which departed radically in flavour from forms of the previous hundred years or so. It was an approach pioneered at much the same time by leading businesses and far-sighted government departments, and in Britain particularly by the Inland Revenue and the then Department of Health and Social Security.

Vast quantities of forms survive among other kinds of documents in the record offices of the world, but they do not appear to have been either collected or studied in their own right, even though they have played a major role in the administration of society for at least two hundred years. In Britain, and in France too, the range of forms in use was already considerable by the end of the 18th century. J. Tymbs, a Worcester (UK) printer who published the *Worcester Journal*, issued an advertisement in 1780 naming eighty-five different forms (and referring to others too) that were available from his office. Included among them are: 'Burial affidavits'; 'Exchequer writs', 'Land Tax Receipts', 'Orders of Removal', 'Parish Certificates', and 'Petitions for Insolvents'. Surviving work of the Ulverston printer John Soulby (junior) from the period 1819 to 1826 includes a good range of legal forms for use in the community; most of these were printed and reprinted in quantities of 50 for the local attorney, Remington, many of them relating to bastardy, paternity, and felonies. Tymbs and Soulby were probably typical of printers throughout the country.

Production details of British forms intended for nation-wide use in the 20th century were often printed in code form as part of the imprint (e.g. 50m 9/12 E & S: meaning 50,000 copies printed September 1912 by Eyre & Spottiswoode). Such codes reveal that some print runs were considerable, though they came to be dwarfed by those of the late 20th century, some of which ran to several million copies, and a few, such as the vehicle licence form, many more. The number of different kinds of forms also grew in this period, and to such an extent as to defy any reliable count. In the early 1980s, when British forms came under review from the Cabinet Office in response to a report by a committee chaired by Lord Rayner, the Inland Revenue estimated that it had over 8000 different forms, and the Department of Health and Social Security came up with an even more staggering figure of over 13,000.

Few can doubt the impact and significance of forms socially. Though disliked intensely by many who have to respond to them, and often inaccurately completed, they remain through the information sought, quite as much as through the responses elicited, a most useful barometer of society. [MT]

See also ARMED FORCES PAPERS; BASTARDY PAPERS; BURIAL IN WOOLLEN AFFIDAVIT; BURIAL PAPERS; CENSUS PAPERS; DISTRAINT, PAPERS OF; FIRE REWARD CERTIFICATE; FUNERALIA; GAOL PAPERS; HACKNEY PAPERS; HOSPITAL RECOMMENDATION DOCUMENT; HOUSEKEEPING ACCOUNTS; INDENTURE; LABOUR ACCOUNT; POOR-LAW PAPERS; SCHOOL RETURN; SUMMONS; TITHE PAPERS; WARRANT

REFERENCE 'Forms Reform: Second Progress Report to the Prime Minister by the Cabinet Office' ([London]: Management and Personnel Office, April 1984)

Form of prayer

Presented for use by the clergy in churches and chapels in England and Wales on specific occasions, forms of prayer date back at least to the reign of Elizabeth I (1558–1603). Traditionally they have been composed by the Archbishop of Canterbury at the monarch's command, and include prayers for divine intervention and for combined prayer and thanksgiving. They appear commonly as a printed four-page folder, the cover bearing the title and pages three and four (or three alone) setting out the words of the prayer.

The prayers relate to a wide variety of national occasions. Viewed as a corpus of printed record, they embody a kaleidoscopic miniature of rejoicing, apprehension, religious fervour, contrition, and chauvinism.

Of many scores of titles the following selection conveys the range of subject matter:

1626 A Short Forme of Thankesgiving to God For staying the contagious sickness of the Plague.

1746 Thanksgiving for the Suppression of the late Unnatural Rebellion, and Deliverance from the Calamities of an Intestine War.

1756 Fast for Blessing on our Fleets and Armies and humbling ourselves before Almighty God in deep sense of His late Visitation, by a most dreadful and extensive Earthquake, more particularly felt in some neighbouring Countries.

1759 Thanksgiving for Cease of Distemper among Horned Cattle.

1765 Thanksgiving for Safe Delivery of Queen, and Birth of a Prince.

1805 Prayer and Thanksgiving for Victory of the Fleet under Vice-Admiral Lord Viscount Nelson over the Combined Fleets of France and Spain.

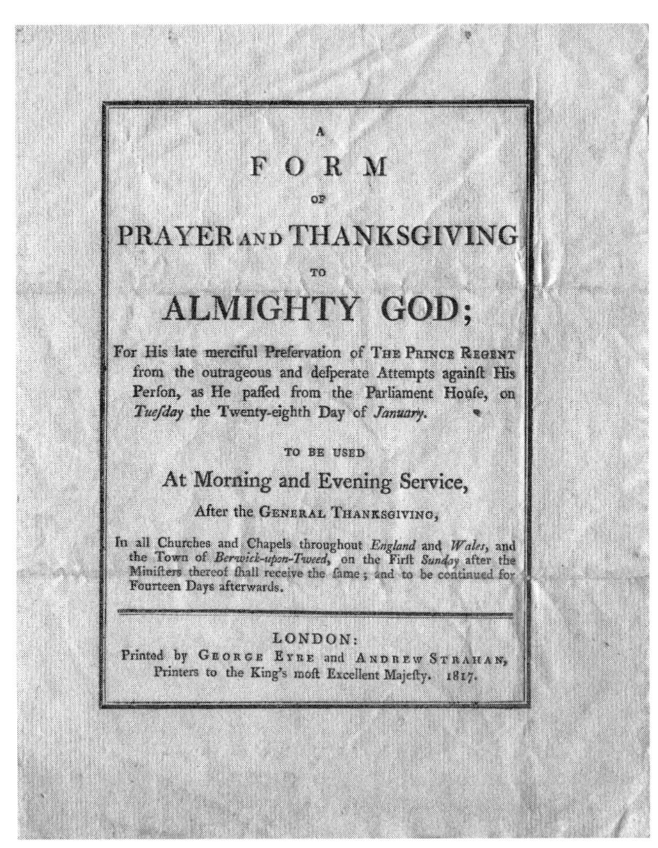

A
FORM
OF
PRAYER AND THANKSGIVING
TO
ALMIGHTY GOD;
For His late merciful Prefervation of THE PRINCE REGENT from the outrageous and defperate Attempts againft His Perfon, as He paffed from the Parliament Houfe, on *Tuefday* the Twenty-eighth Day of *January*.
TO BE USED
At Morning and Evening Service,
After the GENERAL THANKSGIVING,
In all Churches and Chapels throughout *England* and *Wales*, and the Town of *Berwick-upon-Tweed*, on the Firft *Sunday* after the Minifters thereof fhall receive the fame; and to be continued for Fourteen Days afterwards.
LONDON:
Printed by GEORGE EYRE and ANDREW STRAHAN, Printers to the King's moft Excellent Majefty. 1817.

Form of prayer and thanksgiving for the preservation of the Prince Regent, London, 1817. Letterpress, four pages, printed by George Eyre & Andrew Spottiswoode. 212 × 170 mm (8⅜ × 6¾ in)

1810 Thanksgiving for the Abundant Harvest.

1831 Prayers during the Continuance of our danger from the Pestilence now spreading over a great Part of Europe.

1846 Form for Relief from Dearth and Scarcity.

1848 Form for Maintenance of Peace and Tranquillity.

1856 Thanksgiving to Almighty God for His great Goodness in putting an End to the War in which we were engaged against Russia.

Forms of prayer of this kind are still occasionally issued in modern times.

From 1770, when the royal patent was acquired by Charles Eyre, forms of prayer were printed by the Eyres (Charles and George) in association at first with the Strahans (William and Andrew), and later with the Spottiswoodes (Andrew and William). The names Eyre, Strahan, and Spottiswoode appear in various combinations over a period of more than a century. Oxford and Cambridge University Presses had a similar right.

Forms of prayer may also be drawn up by other ecclesiastical bodies, as well as by independent agencies outside the church.

The concept of the form of prayer may be said to have its origin in the printed prayers published in times of distress by self-appointed counsellors. One such, cited in *Notes and Queries* (7 August 1858), is entitled 'A christian medication or praier to be sayed at all tymes whensoever God shall upset vs wyth anye mortall plague or sicnesse'. This example, 'Imprinted at London by W Alben, 1551', was apparently a private venture. Similarly, a 1636 plague broadside in Guildhall Library prints lists of the numbers of those buried in London in 1593, 1603, 1625, 1630, and 1636 with an extensive centre-piece of prayer: 'The humble Petition of England unto Almighty God ... for the cessation of this Mortality of Pestilence now raigning amongst us…'.

The prayer broadside, in its turn, may be not too distant a descendant of the written invocations recommended in the formulations of the early physicians. In a 15th-century medical treatise the following form of words appears: '+ In nomine Patris + et Filii + et Spiritus Sancti + amen. In nomine Domini Nostri Ihesu Xristi et caritas Dei fugite febres terciane cotidiane quaterne. Cruxifixus sub Poncio Pilato fugite febres + In nomine Patris + et Filii + et Spiritus Sancti + amen'. The words are to be used in the case of tertian ague in a woman. They are to be inserted on a paper and placed around the neck.

REFERENCES Ida B. Jones, 'Haffod 16: A Mediaeval Welsh Medical Treatise', *Études Celtiques*, vol. 7 fasc. 1 (Paris: Société d'Édition 'Les Belles Lettres', 1955); 'List of works in Guildhall Library relating to the Plague in London 1532–1858', *The Guildhall Miscellany* (September 1965); *Notes and Queries*, passim 1854, 1856, 1857, 1858; F. P. Wilson, *The Plague in Shakespeare's London* (Oxford University Press, 1963)

Fraktur [plate 10]

The Fraktur, a decoratively inscribed document celebrating a birth, baptism, or marriage, was introduced to America by the so-called 'Pennsylvania Dutch', German and Swiss immigrants who settled in Pennsylvania in the latter part of the 18th century, bringing with them a strongly religious background and their own folk art.

Fraktur is an abbreviation of *Frakturschrift* (Latin: *fractura*), the name given in Germany to type known in English as 'gothic', 'black-letter', or 'old English'. (The notion of 'fracture' relates to the manuscript and typographic form of characters, the predominantly non-vertical strokes of which were 'angled' or 'broken' instead of rounded.) The documents appeared as one-, two-, or three-colour designs, often on a tinted or coloured paper, and were of varying sizes and formats. They were generally framed for display and presented a distinct fusion of cultures; the text, in German, commonly refers to the event taking place in America in a specific state, county, and township – the last word sometimes appearing as 'taunschip'.

REFERENCE Donald A. Shelley, *The Fraktur-Writings or Illuminated Manuscripts of the Pennsylvania Germans* (Allentown, PA: The Pennsylvania German Folklore Society, 1961)

Free frank

The holder of the 'Privilege of Free Franking' was entitled, within limits from time to time prescribed, to free use of the mails.

The system originated as a benefit conferred on favoured subjects of the monarch, whose personal perquisite the mail revenues originally were. It was first codified by an order of the Council of State in Oliver Cromwell's time (1653–58) and was the subject of royal warrants on the restoration of the monarchy. Those entitled to the privilege, whether as specified individuals or by virtue of their office, were required to identify their letters on the front by means of a seal, or signature, or, during the period of the Commonwealth, by endorsement with the words 'For the Service of the Commonwealth'. During the Commonwealth period the privilege was extended to include members of both Houses of Parliament (Commons and Lords).

The system was a source of friction and controversy early on, and a series of acts, proclamations, and other measures sought in vain in the period 1705 to 1804 to bring it under control. It was clear, however, that free-franking legislation was virtually unenforceable. The privilege was widely abused. Holders of the right were found, for example, to be giving signed lettersheets to friends for their own use, enclosing quantities of mail within a single signed wrapper for private distribution, and evading the

Fraktur, certifying the birth and baptism of John George, son of Charles Deemer (?) and his wife Mary, Springfield, Bucks, Pennsylvania, 1830. Letterpress, printed in black and two colours by G. S. Peters, Harrisburg, Pennsylvania. 330 × 450 mm (13 × 17¾ in)

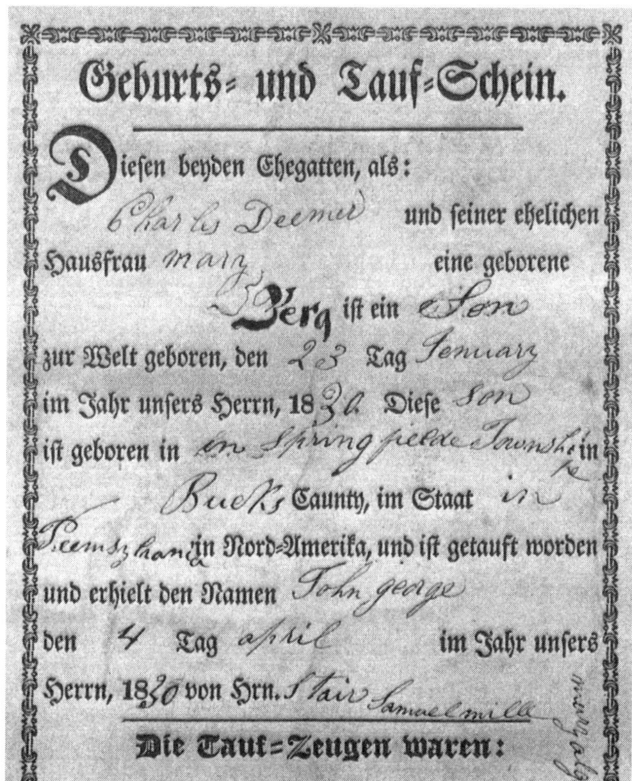

Geburts- und Tauf-Schein.

Diesen beyden Ehegatten, als:
Charles Deemer und seiner ehelichen
Hausfrau mary eine geborene
Berg ist ein Son
zur Welt geboren, den 23 Tag Jenuary
im Jahr unsers Herrn, 1830 Diese Son
ist geboren in Springfielde Township in
Bucks Caunty, im Staat in
Pennsylvanien in Nord-Amerika, und ist getauft worden
und erhielt den Namen John george
den 4 Tag april im Jahr unsers
Herrn, 1830 von Hrn. Stair
Die Tauf-Zeugen waren:

Detail, 122 x 101 mm (4¾ × 4 in)

limitations of the system in a variety of other ways. Evasion was sometimes by forgery of signature. Losses to the revenue were enormous. From 1764 onwards, as a measure of added control, free-frank mail from – or passing through – London or Dublin received a paid FREE handstamp (Edinburgh free franks were similarly handstamped for a few years). The design of the handstamp varied considerably, in some cases incorporating code numbers and letters denoting the franking officer, day or evening use, location, and date. Some scores of variants are recorded.

Free franking was abolished (with a number of exceptions still obtaining today) at the time of the introduction of uniform penny postage and the adhesive postage stamp in 1840.

A similar system was in operation in America for government officials, members of Congress and others, and was similarly abused. Free franking of mail in America was abolished (also with exceptions obtaining today) on 1 July 1873.

The system remains vestigially in force in Britain in the form of mail marked 'OHMS' (On Her[His] Majesty's Service), 'Official Paid' and, in mail from the monarch after 1902, the royal cypher cachet. Election candidates' printed communications are also free of postage, as are, in wartime, soldiers' active service letters.

In America free mail is allowed to members of Congress and other office-holders, including the President; business mail from government departments goes free under the superscription 'Official Business' and the name of the department concerned.

See also ENVELOPE, ILLUSTRATED; PARLIAMENTARY ENVELOPE

REFERENCES J. W. Lovegrove, '*Herewith My Frank…*' (Bournemouth: Lovegrove, 1975); Carl H. Scheele, *A Short History of the Mail Service* (Washington: Smithsonian Institution Press, 1970); R. M. Willcocks and Alan W. Robertson, *England's Postal History to 1840, with notes on Scotland, Wales and Ireland* (London: Willcocks, 1975)

Frost-fair papers

Prior to its removal, the narrow arches and broad footings of the old London Bridge caused serious obstruction to the flow of the Thames, and in freezing weather ice formed readily on the slow-moving water. Records of its surface freezing solid date from the 13th century, and first references to fairs and other diversions on the ice appeared in 1564, when some Londoners were recorded as playing football in mid-river, and others shooting at marks.

The frost fair became an accepted London institution, and by the late 17th and 18th centuries the event (depending on the length and strength of the freeze-up) reached major proportions. In the frost of 1683–84 there was a street of booths, puppet shows, bull-baiting, horse racing, and ox-roasting, and John

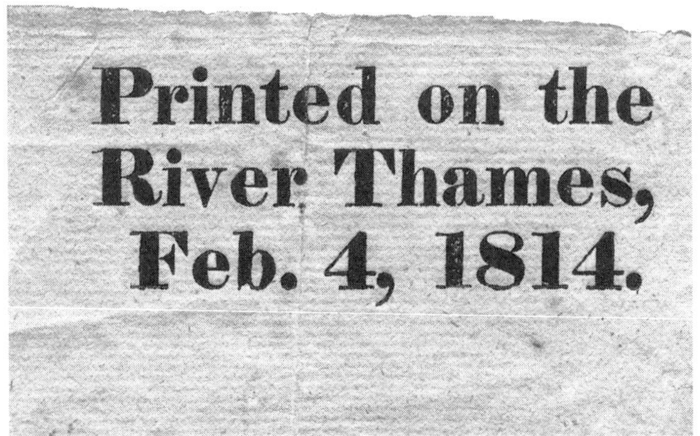

Frost-fair keepsake, printed on ice 4 February 1814. Letterpress. 62 × 108 mm (2⅜ × 4¼ in)

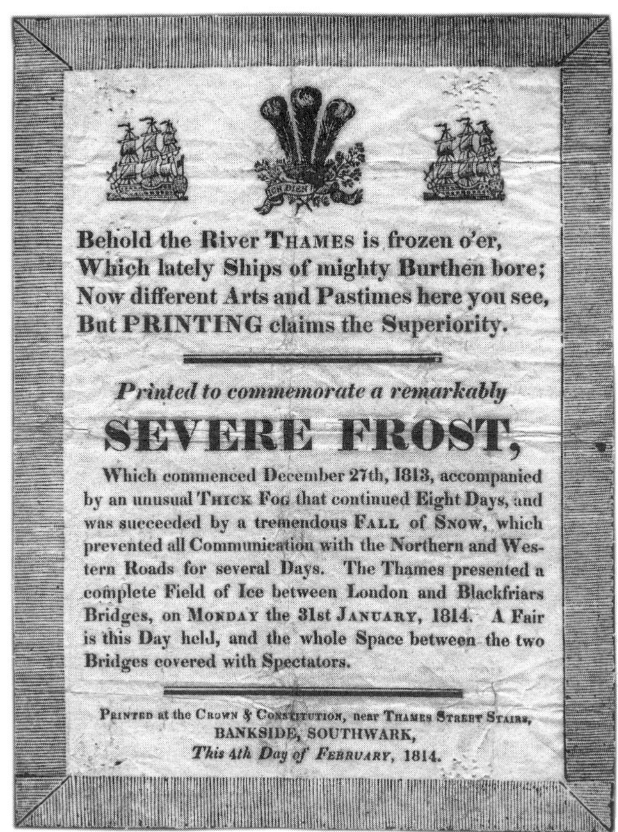

Frost-fair keepsake, 4 February 1814, Bankside, Southwark, London. Letterpress, printed at the 'Crown & Constitution, near Thames Street Stairs'. 205 × 155 mm (8⅛ × 6⅛ in)

Evelyn records in his diaries that 'ladyes took a fancy to have their names printed, and the day and the yeare set down when printed on the Thames'.

The printing press rapidly became a standard feature of frost fairs, and numb-fingered printers set up customers' names in pre-set decorative borders and printed them 'on the ice' at a few pence a time. In the frost of 1814, as well as donkey rides, swings, bookstalls, skittle alleys, merry-go-rounds, and other attractions, there were eight or ten printing presses offering cards, leaflets, and own-name mementoes.

Items printed on ice included crude woodcut illustrations, doggerel ballads, and small pieces of paper bearing no more than the words 'printed on the ice' or 'printed on the River Thames' and quoting the date. The appeal of the frost fairs extended to the famous. On Friday 16 February 1740, William Hogarth took his pug Trump for a run on the ice at Whitehall, recording the occasion with a souvenir bearing not his own name but that of his dog. In the 1684 freeze, King Charles II and five members of the royal family visited the fair and had their names grouped collectively on a single sheet. An extra member of the party, not yet quite present, but shortly expected, was the Princess Anne's forthcoming infant, described on the list as Hans in Kelder – 'Jack in the cellar'.

REFERENCE Ian Curry, *Frosts, Freezes and Fairs* (Coulsdon, Surrey: Frosted Earth, 1996)

Fruit/vegetable sticker

Introduced in January 1929 by Fyffes, the banana importers, the fruit (and later vegetable) sticker has become a worldwide convention. In the closing decades of the 20th century branded fruit and vegetables became a feature of all supermarkets and most smaller retailers. As with other commodities, public confidence in branded products is a major marketing factor.

The sticker was first used on produce in which the skin is not normally consumed. Items commonly bearing stickers include bananas, oranges, lemons, melons, tangerines, satsumas, clementines, mangoes, and avocado pears; but apples too now bear them. Other fruit and vegetable products are identified in labelled shrink-wraps, nets, etc.

The original Fyffes banana label appeared as a novelty at about the time of the introduction of dummy banana bunches used for display in fruitshop windows. The banana, first commercially introduced in the 1880s, was in the 1930s still not a mass-market product and the label and the display dummy formed part of a pioneering commercial campaign. Though substantially unchanged since its introduction, the Fyffes label has appeared in a number of modified forms.

The original design bore the company name in capitals, with the words 'blue label' above and 'brand' below. Its overall size of 23 × 30 mm (7/8 × 1 3/16 in) was larger than subsequent versions, most of which measure some 17 × 25 mm (11/16 × 1 in). From the 1960s the company name appears in upper and lower case and the country of origin is also shown. Examples are 'Jamaica', 'Ivory Coast', 'Surinam', and 'Belize'. Prior to the entry of Spain into the European Economic Community, Canary Island banana labels bore the word 'Canary'.

The earliest labels were gummed and applied to the bananas while they were still wet from washing. From the mid 1950s they have been self-adhesive and applied from a roll applicator. 'Pre-priced' labels, bearing a white tab for overprinting, appeared in the early 1960s. These were for use in distribution centres for supermarket sales. In Britain in the 1971 decimalization period such tabs showed prices in both old and new currencies.

'Chiquita' labels, used on the products of Fyffes' associated companies, are found on bananas sold in America and on the continent of Europe, and only rarely in Britain. The Chiquita label nominally indicates Honduras as the country of origin. The Chiquita banana was supplied as 'official fruit' to the 1980 Winter Olympic Games at Lake Placid and a series of thirteen different labels appeared in a collecting promotion. Other banana brand labels include 'Dole', 'Turbana', 'Onkel Tuca', and 'Bananos' (*bananos* is simply a rendering of the word banana, and cannot strictly be regarded as a brand name).

Spanish fruit growers' labels bear the sub-title 'Spania', the name of the Government-sponsored fruit export organization. The name stands in the same relation to Spanish fruit exports as 'Jaffa' to Israeli exports. Individual growers may use a number of different brand labels for the same product, reserving each for the exclusive use of a specific trade customer. Thus four or five brand labels may represent a single grower.

See also LABEL

Fruit wrapper

Individual wrapping of fruit began as a means of controlling the spread of fungal decay in product batches. As well as insulating the fruit, wrappers also provide a mutual cushioning in packing and storage, reducing risks of puncture or abrasion and thus of bacterial invasion.

Printed wrappers were first introduced, some time in the early 20th century, initially for oranges, later for lemons, grapefruit, pears, tangerines, mandarins, apricots, tomatoes, and other

Fruit wrapper (orange), Valencia. Printed in five colours on tissue paper. 230 × 184 mm (9 × 7 1/4 in)

produce. The designs are printed centrally on tissue papers ranging in size from 160 × 160 mm (6 1/4 × 6 1/4 in) to 200 × 200 mm (7 7/8 × 7 7/8 in). Lemon wrappers are not normally square; a typical size is 240 × 200 mm (9 1/2 × 7 7/8 in). Images generally incorporate brand names, the grower's name, and the country of origin, though occasionally they are purely decorative and carry no legend of any kind. Later specimens may bear the words 'treated with Diphenil' (a protective fungicide).

Printing is normally by rotary rubber plates in up to five (commonly three) colours, often with concomitant distortion and faulty register. The graphic design component partakes of the 'pop-trad-deco-naive'; it combines some of the elements of the BEER LABEL, the CRATE LABEL, and the fairground and the tattooist's booth.

The wrapper as brand identification has been somewhat eclipsed in recent years by the contact-adhesive FRUIT/VEGETABLE STICKER and by the introduction, in the case of citrus fruits, of fungicidal washes and 'finishing' treatments to enhance moisture retention, colour depth, and textural appeal.

COLLECTIONS Centre for Ephemera Studies, University of Reading; John Johnson Collection, Bodleian Library, Oxford; Department of Prints and Drawings, Victoria & Albert Museum, London

Funeralia

English-language items relating to funerals, burial, mourning, and commemoration are less common than formerly. Today's discreet drawing of a veil over death is in marked contrast with the directness of our forebears.

Invitations to funerals. Funeral invitations of the 17th and 18th centuries abound with wood- or copper-engraved images of grave-digging skeletons, skulls and crossbones, catafalques and coffins. Standard phraseology for over a century was 'You are desired to accompany the Corpse of (—) to the parish church of (—) on (—) next at (—) of the clock precisely and bring this ticket with you'. It must be said that the ticket's illustrations, with beckoning Father Time and Death himself to the fore, were less than comforting.

Invitations appear in various formats, commonly with a blank centre panel for insertion of handwritten details or for overprinting in type (sometimes even from a hand-engraved plate – prepared, presumably, virtually overnight). Treatments range from the most primitive of woodcuts to engravings of outstanding quality.

Early 19th-century funeral invitations are noticeably less ostentatious, confining themselves to a quietly typographic statement of subject, time, and place. The Victorian period brought renewed expression of emotion, this time in the form of mourning.

Undertakers' papers. A typical undertaker's estimate booklet, sixteen pages plus cover, 160 mm × 105 mm (6¼ × 4⅛ in), offers mid 19th-century funerals from 'No 1' at £28 to 'No 8' at £3.

'No 1' provides 'A Hearse and Four Horses, Two Mourning Coaches and Four with Feathers, Velvet Coverings and cloths for the Hearse and Horses, a Lid of Feathers, strong Inch Elm Shell, a stout Lead Coffin, an outer Elm Case covered with fine Black Cloth, finished three rows all round with best Black Nails, a Brass Plate of Inscription, with Handles, and other Achievements, a Wool Mattress, Burial Dress, Winding Sheet, Pillow, &c. Two Mutes in Silk Dresses, an attender with Silk Hatband, and Gloves; Men to bear the Corpse and attend as Pages, with Hatbands, Gloves, Truncheons, and Wands; use of best Silk Velvet Pall, Crape Hatbands, Hoods and Scarfs for Twelve Mourners.'

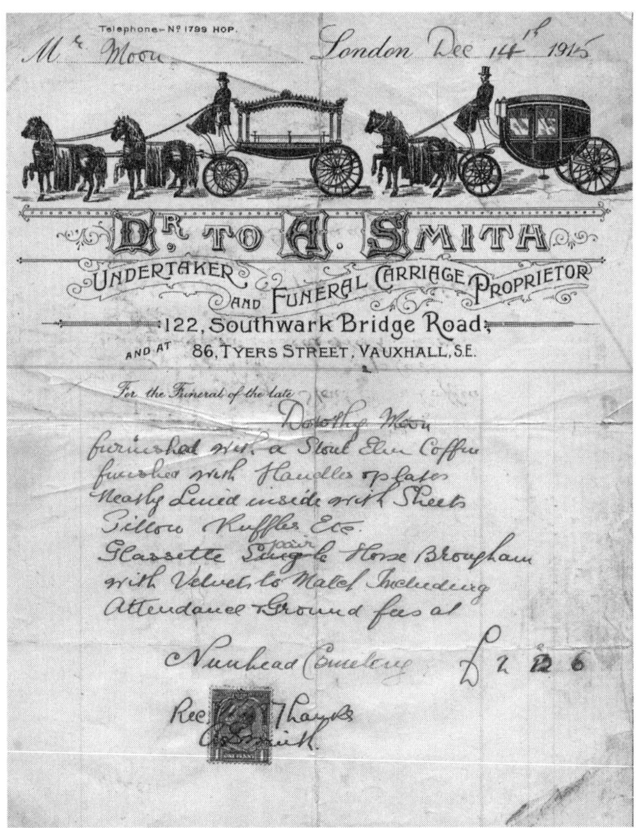
Telephone–No 1799 HOP.
Mr Moon London Dec 14th 1915
Dr. TO A. SMITH
UNDERTAKER AND FUNERAL CARRIAGE PROPRIETOR
122, Southwark Bridge Road,
AND AT 86, TYERS STREET, VAUXHALL, S.E.
For the Funeral of the late Dorothy Moon
furnished with a Stout Elm Coffin
finished with Handles & plates
Neatly Lined inside with Sheets
Pillow Ruffles Etc.
Glassette pair Horse Brougham
with Velvet to Match Including
attendance & Ground fees at
Nunhead Cemetery £ 2 12 6
Rec with Thanks
A. Smith

Undertaker's billhead of A. Smith, Southwark Bridge Row, London, 14 December 1915. Lithography and manuscript on ruled paper. 266 × 210 mm (10½ × 8¼ in)

Funeral 'No 8' provides 'A Strong Elm Coffin, covered with Black, finished neat, with Plate of Inscription, Handles &c., mattress, pillow and sheet; use of pall, dresses for six mourners, patent carriage and pair of horses to convey body and mourners, men to carry corpse, fittings for coachmen and attender.' A tailpiece also announces: 'Children's Funerals from twelve shillings and upwards'.

Undertakers' billheads, commonly decorated with representations of their turn-outs, and specifying costs of services rendered, are a productive source of detailed funeral information.

Monumental masons' papers. The memorial and headstone business generated its own ephemera. As with undertakers, specifications and invoices provide much detail, and promotional folders, leaflets, etc., throw light on sales psychology. A black-edged four-page folder, 205 × 130 mm (8⅛ × 5⅛ in), proffers the services of Messrs J. Underwood & Sons, Buckhurst Hill c.1880. In imitation handwriting the firm writes: 'Referring to the sad loss which you have recently sustained in your family; we take the liberty of calling your attention to our large variety of... designs suitable for commemorative memorials ...'. Also available, after due consultation, were hand-drawn miniature cut-outs showing proposed headstones, complete with name, dates, and verse.

Mourning outfitters' papers. A multiplicity of billheads and advertising from suppliers of mourning wear testify to the demand for due observance. In the early 1850s London's Regent Street had four major 'Mourning Houses' and most drapers and outfitters maintained mourning departments. In Britain, invoices for mourning clothes are among the most frequently encountered of family ephemera.

Funeral meeting announcement. In working-class communities, friends and neighbours of the deceased were invited to an evening of music at a pub, where a collection would be taken to defray the high cost of funerals. Cards, sometimes black-edged, bore the announcement, and in some cases related details of the bereavement and its economic consequences. Typography and printing quality are primitive, and were often the free gift of a printer's assistant or apprentice.

Burial card. To make provision for good funerals for themselves, many working-class people took out a form of insurance in which they paid a halfpenny or a penny per week into a 'Burial Society'. Their funeral expenses were underwitten by the organization, which was a form of friendly society. A typical card (1858) states: 'All applications for funerals made before twelve o'clock will be paid the same day if under £10; if above £10 within one week after all is found correct.' (A similar arrangement operated in some areas in respect of hearse hire alone. In 1795 a printed poster for the Oggleface [Ogilface] Friendly Society announced a cooperative scheme for hiring out a hearse – for payment – to non-members, with free use for subscription-paying members.)

Mourning stationery. Black-edged stationery was printed in Britain in various breadths of border, thus allowing for gradual diminution during the period of mourning. Two years' mourning was held to be appropriate for a widow, one year for a widower, and one year for a parent. The broadest band was commonly 12.5 mm (½ in), but the sombre effect might be increased by using notepaper of a light-to-mid-grey tint. Bandbreadths on the continent of Europe were commonly twice those of the British, the effect being increased by a double print-

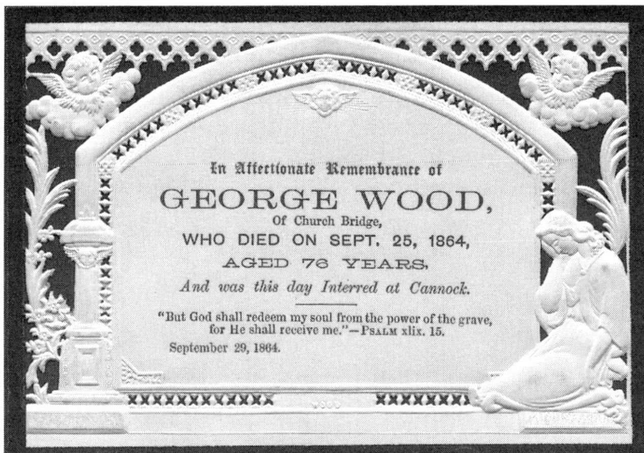

Memorial card, 1864. Letterpress, printed on card with embossed and lace-paper work by Wood. 78 × 114 mm (3⅛ × 4½in)

ing of the black, a glossy and narrower band appearing over the first matt printing.

In 1890, in an attempt to abolish the black edge in Britain (and to launch a possibly profitable new style), John Dickinson produced mourning stationery with only a triangle of black across the top left-hand corner. The idea failed. Black-edged stationery, for a time much in evidence in World War I, was at length tacitly dropped in the interests of public morale. It was never widely readopted in Britain, though the custom continues in many parts of Europe.

Memorial card. The Victorian response to bereavement was at once heartfelt and demonstrative, and the decorative memorial card, with its full-bodied expression of grief, conveys the matter neatly. Succeeding generations have had little patience with the card, but few critics conceal their admiration for its production expertise – and, within its own terms of reference, its beauty.

The memorial card, commonly about 75 × 115 mm (3 × 4½in), relied for much of its appeal on the austere extravagance of blind embossing. The process produced an uncoloured relief image of some delicacy, a quality seen in company seals and other formal documents, but exploited here for its portrayal of sculptural and monumental images. Tombs, funerary urns, angels, and mourning figures appeared as though in marble low-relief, printing ink being used only for the text of the announcement panel and the black border. Cards were produced as blanks for overprinting, or part-printed to allow for the addition of handwritten details. In some cases, part-printed cards were provided free of charge by the undertaker; these cards carried a fairly unobtrusive credit line, naming the undertaker and giving his full address. The cards clearly served as a valuable publicity medium. Embossed cards were also available as pierced 'lace' designs, the low-relief effect being enhanced by removal of the background (as in the contemporary VALENTINE and other forms of greeting).

In a further elaboration, cards might be mounted on larger 'frame' cards. These were similarly treated with low-relief and lace effect and were designed to be mounted on a black background for glazing and framing. The larger cards were of varying sizes and formats, and could also be used for direct overprinting instead of merely serving as mounts. Some of these appeared with the addition of silver (and, more rarely, pastel colours), but in the main, apart from occasional use of biscuit-tinted card, colour was absent. In some frame cards there was also a central aperture to allow inclusion of a photograph.

Memorial cards were printed and sold in the streets on occasions of general mourning, as at the loss of *HMS Captain* (1870) and the *Princess Alice* disaster (1878).

The great name in 19th-century EMBOSSING/LACE PAPER was Henry Dobbs, whose company, using various business styles, dominated the field for half a century. But the embossed memorial card business was the province in the main of Joseph Mansell, Windsor and, predominantly, J. T. Wood. In the final decades of the 19th century and on into the 20th century the most common form of mourning card was chromolithographed (usually in a range of grey or sepia colours and with a black border) for overprinting by the local printer.

Cemetery papers. Acute overcrowding of the floor vaults and burial grounds of London churches in the early 19th century led to legislation restricting further burials and the opening of 'private enterprise' cemeteries outside the then limits of the capital. The new cemeteries were run as businesses, and many items of cemetery ephemera of the period relate to their promotion, establishment, and administration. Among the first of the new establishments (1832) was Kensal Green, property of the General Cemetery Co., whose four-page promotional folder, measuring 225 × 140 mm (8⅞ × 5½in), includes a paragraph to allay fears of body-snatching: 'The lofty enclosure of this ground, and the effectual system of watching, by armed Patrols, afford perfect security from the danger of exhumation ...'.

Other cemetery papers include scales of charges and regulations ('Grave owners... are particularly requested not to employ [as gardeners] any persons soliciting orders in the grounds' and 'interments: third class ground – adult, unconsecrated ground, 12 shillings; under 10 nine shillings & sixpence; pauper seven shillings & sixpence; stillborn two shillings & sixpence'). The most frequently surviving cemetery paper is the BURIAL-RIGHT DEED, part-printed on vellum and entitling the holder to a burial plot 'to hold the same to the said (John Smith, his heirs and assigns for ever)'.

Mortuary and coroner's cards. A representative selection of ephemera relating to matters of mortuary and inquest includes the following:

Mortuary caretaker's instructions, Lewisham, March 1899; four-page folder, 215 × 140 mm (8½ × 5½in): 'The caretaker shall not allow any corpse brought from any place outside the district of the board to be placed in the mortuary ...'.

Coroner's disbursements, a list of fees payable at Southampton, July 1899; four-page card folder, 115 × 75 mm (4½ × 3 in): 'For finding a dead body, drowned or otherwise exposed, watching the same and giving notice to the nearest police constable ... five shillings; for removing any such Body so found as aforesaid and keeping it until the inquest... two shillings and sixpence...'.

Witness warrant, Marylebone c.1850, part printed form; unused, 155 × 195 mm (6 × 7⅝in): to Mr (—): Whereas, being credibly informed that you can give evidence touching the death of (—) now lying Dead in the parish of St Mary-lebone... you are hereby summoned... to give evidence... hereof fail not, as you will answer to the Coroner at your Peril ...'.

Coroner's certificate: foolscap, double-sided, part-printed form, unused, 1917: 'I certify that I held an inquest on the body of (—) and that the verdict of the Jury was as follows: (—)'. On the verso appears a second form authorizing, in this case, cremation.

Printed ephemera relating to the coroner's office consist largely of part-printed forms (many now obsolete) designed to meet the many varying contingencies of the function. Of the thirty-three such forms in use in Britain in 1845 the following extract, in its detailed provision for circumstances, is typical: '... not having God before his eyes, but being seduced and moved by the instigation of the devil, at (—) aforesaid, in a certain (—) at (—) aforesaid ... the said (—), being then and there alone, with a certain hempen cord ... which he then and there had and held in his hands, and one end thereof then and there put about his neck, and the other end thereof tied about a (—) of a certain (—) himself ... voluntarily and of his malice aforethought, hanged and suffocated ... against the peace of our said lady the Queen, her crown and dignity ...'.

State funeral papers. Apart from the primary ephemera generated by the internal organization and planning of a state funeral, a secondary wave reflects its impact on the public at large. Notices, posters, orders of procession etc. appear in profusion. Some survive as souvenirs; others, apparently less significant, only by chance. A typical chance survivor is a public notice posted in Blandford, Dorset, on the occasion of the funeral of William IV (July, 1837); the mayor declares that instead of cancelling the market (on which day the funeral is to take place) it has been agreed to hold it as usual, closing at 6pm 'and the remainder of the day observed with all the decorum such an event demands'.

Also unpremeditated is the survival of a notice posted by London County Council in January 1901. Headed 'Funeral of her late majesty Queen Victoria', it warns that the London Building Act, 1894, requires licensing of temporary structures. With the funeral only three days away, the council invites applications for licences and also warns that balconies intended to be used on the above occasion should be properly shored up to prevent risk of accident.

See also BURIAL PAPERS; BURIAL IN WOOLLEN AFFIDAVIT; DEATH CERTIFICATE; INVITATION

Furniture label

Early cabinet and furniture makers generally identified their products with initials stamped or branded in some inconspicuous part of the piece. Identification, legally required in France by an edict of 1745, was elsewhere voluntary. (Initials carved in relief or inlaid are invariably those of the owner, not the maker.)

In Britain from the beginning of the 18th century, and in France from about 1825, cabinet and furniture makers began to use a printed LABEL on their products. American furniture is rarely marked at all before the 19th century. Paper labels were for the most part printed from the same engraved plate as that used for the manufacturer's TRADE CARD, though a number of shaped labels (round, oval, etc.) are also found, some of them relief printed, which were clearly designed specifically as labels. In America it was also sometimes the practice to use advertisements from the columns of the local press as label substitutions. In some cases these announcements indicated readiness to accept 'country produce' in lieu of cash. One recorded example from the *Philadelphia Gazette* (1739) also offers side-lines which include, for sale, 'A likely negro woman fit for town or Country Business with a child about one year and a half old'.

Furniture label of Daniel Wild, cabinet-maker, St Paul's Church-Yard, London, still in place on the drawer of a piece of furniture of c. 1725. Letterpress with woodcut border. 59 × 88 mm (2¼ × 3½ in)

Furniture labels are subject to two major drawbacks. On the one hand they remain implacably attached to the wood, in which case they frustrate the label specialist; on the other hand they fall off, and become wholly separated from the item so that their evidential value to the furniture specialist is virtually nil. As with other examples of labelled items, the interests of the label collector must clearly defer to those of the specialist in the field in question. If, where furniture labels are discovered separately, there is the smallest possibility of restoring them to their original item, the effort should be made.

Game record

As an organized country pursuit, shooting for game in Britain has evolved its own conventions and disciplines, and of these the keeping of records is no small part.

Typically, the game record card carries the name of the person (or a blank to be filled in) and a listing of the kinds of game (grouse, pheasants, partridges, snipe, wild duck, etc.) in prospect. Blanks allow for entering details of the area (the specific location of the shoot), the number of guns in the party, the number of items in each category, the total bag, and the date. The card is commonly about the size of a postcard.

Some cards allow space for names of members of the party and a reference to the state of the weather. One such example, a folded card, bears the cover title 'Sandringham' and is dated 31 December 1936. It is made out to one of the party, the Hon David Bowes-Lyon, whose name appears on the listing inside. The others are 'His Majesty the King; the Duke of Gloucester; the Earl of Athlone; Hon Sir Richard Molyneux … Mr Arthur Penn; Mr Alan Lascelles'. The weather is entered as 'dull'. Kills are recorded as: pheasants 506, partridges 28, hares 70, rabbits 18, woodcock 6, snipe 1, wood pigeon 2; total bag 631. Wild duck, teal, and 'Miscellaneous' carry no entry.

More elaborate record cards are also found, often with pictorial renderings of game and 'rustic' column divides, the whole design surrounded by a coronet or other mark of standing. Lithographed, in some cases in three or four colours, they are large-format productions, measuring up to 150 × 235 mm (6 × 9¼ in), and provide space for a full week's shoot.

BEAT.	GAME KILLED.	
Commodore, Captain's Close & Dersingham Wood	Pheasnts	506
WEATHER.	Partridges	28
Dull	Hares	70
PARTY.	Rabbits	18
His Majesty The King	Woodcock	6
The Duke of Gloucester	Snipe	1
The Earl of Athlone	Wild Duck	
Hon. Sir Richard Molyneux	Teal	
Hon. David Bowes-Lyon	Wood Pigeon	2
Mr. Arthur Penn	Miscellaneous	
Mr. Alan Lascelles	Total	631

Game record card of the Hon. David Bowes-Lyon, 31 December 1936. Letterpress and manuscript, printed Harrison & Sons Ltd, London. Page size 115 × 75 mm (4½ × 3 in)

Game record card headed Cullen, the seat of the Earl of Seafield, mid 19th century. Lithographed in colour. 90 × 234 mm (3½ × 9¼ in)

Long-term printed records also appear, showing the results of named individuals or other statistical analysis. One such table sets out the performance of Earl de Grey in the years 1867–95, whose total bag for the period numbered 316,699. The figure included twelve buffalo, eleven tigers, and two rhinoceros. In another printed analysis, published by stags-head preservers MacLeay & Son of Inverness (1900), the firm records the 'points values' or quality ratings of the first 500 stags' heads received for preservation in each of the past ten seasons.

Associated game ephemera include the labels used for despatch of game by rail or post. These are commonly printed on linen or linen-based paper and bear the sender's address, space for an addressee, contents, and date of the kill and despatch. Some tags carry a printed salutation: 'With Mr Millar's compliments'. Others show a printed address: 'To be delivered to His Grace the Duke of Wellington's servant at Paddington Station', or 'Royal Household staff, Buckingham Palace, London SW1'. Also to be found are items relating to shooting rights, accounts, receipts for letting or purchase, and the transactional papers of shooting and estate activities.

See also GAME-LAW PAPERS

REFERENCE Lord Ralph Percy, *Debrett's Book of Game Cards* (London: Debrett, 1986)

Game-law papers

Britain's 19th-century game laws, in which property owners' rights against trespass poaching and depredation were stringently enforced, produced many marginal items of ephemera. Most notable is a large body of printed notices warning would-be intruders, the wording and design of which became more or less standardized throughout the country. From the numbers of such notices that survived in local printers' files it may be

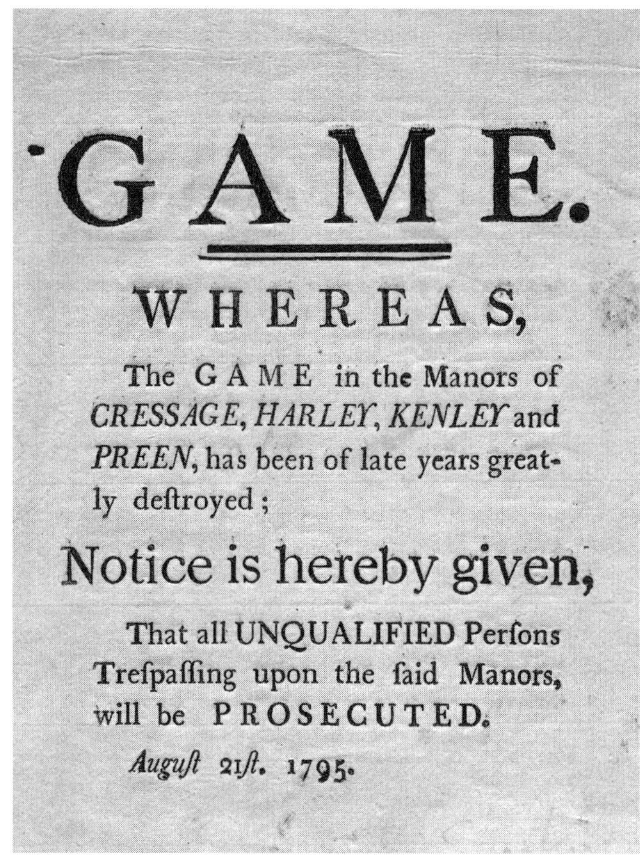
GAME.

WHEREAS,

The GAME in the Manors of CRESSAGE, HARLEY, KENLEY and PREEN, has been of late years greatly deftroyed;

Notice is hereby given,

That all UNQUALIFIED Perfons Trefpaffing upon the faid Manors, will be PROSECUTED.

Auguft 21ft. 1795.

Game notice warning of prosecution for trespass, Shropshire, August 1795. Letterpress. 195 × 147 mm (7⅝ × 5¾ in)

assumed that the large-character word 'game' remained as ready to the printer's hand as 'for sale', 'notice', and 'reward'.

A typical example is the warning, 250 × 190 mm (9⅞ × 7½ in), printed by G. Gitton of Bridgnorth, Shropshire, in August 1818: 'Game: Notice hereby given that all Persons who are found trespassing, or Destroying of Game, on the lands at Dallicot, the Lea, Morfe and High Grosvenor, in the Parish of Claverley, and County of Salop... will be prosecuted as the law directs'. From the same printer's output we see, one year later, the identical heading, subtitling, decorative rules, and imprints with a change of text extending its jurisdiction to the neighbouring parish of Tasley.

Not all game notices were so peaceably disposed: the battle between the landed gentry and their less privileged neighbours lasted for generations and was fought with increasing determination on both sides. One warning reads: 'Gentlemen, Tread Light! Man Traps are set in These Grounds!'. Some warnings distinguish between 'qualified gentlemen' who had a right to hunt or shoot, who were merely requested to desist for a season, and 'persons unqualified' who were threatened with prosecution.

Warnings also took the form of handbills, specifically addressed by handwritten superscription to named offenders, often neighbouring farmers: 'To Mr (—); We hereby give you notice, that if you hunt, sport, course, set, net, hawk, fish or fowl, or use any other Method to destroy the game upon any of the Lands manors, or vegatries, in our several occupations; that you will be deemed a Wilful Trespasser, and will be proceeded against as the Law directs...'. These warnings were delivered to the offender or nailed up at strategic points on the property.

In a related category of ephemera are announcements put out by groupings of owners who pooled their resources to prosecute those who trespassed on the property of any individual member. Thus, in 1821, the Dorchester Association for the Protection of Persons and Property issued the following announcement: 'Burglary and Felony: 120 pounds Reward... whereas... the dwelling house of Morgan Yeatman... was burglariously entered and a number of Silver Articles and several pounds in Money stolen therefrom... any person (whether an Accomplice or not) who will give Information...', and so on.

Associations of this kind proliferated in the early 19th century, but their advent had been forecast in the middle of the previous century when 'Noblemen and Gentlemen' entered into 'A Subscription for Preserving the Game all over England', offering specific rewards for information leading to the apprehension of 'unqualified persons who shall kill, destroy, sell, buy, carry, or have in their possession any sort of game'. In a notice measuring 370 × 250 mm (14½ × 9⅞ in) published in 1752, a society, as yet unidentified, lists its rewards and requests 'Noblemen and Gentlemen and other qualified persons' to advise it of stagecoach departures with any legitimate despatch of game, from their respective estates, in order that a check might be kept on illicit traffic.

Other forms of paper record the activities of specific persons. In the period 1832 to 1851 William Maxwell, successively of Cumberland, Northumberland, and Yorkshire, appears on five summonses as an alleged poacher. In each of the years 1864–67 however, presumably after a change of heart, he is named as authorized holder of a licence to kill game.

See also GAME RECORD

REFERENCE Maurice Rickards, *The Public Notice* (Newton Abbot: David & Charles, 1973)

COLLECTIONS Rural History Centre, The University of Reading

Gaol papers

The administration of prisons and prisoners has generated a large body of minor documents, ranging from DIETARY TABLES to death warrants, from prisoners' letters to gaolers' 'locking accounts'. Such documentation discloses, if not a keen concern for the prisoner's well-being, a preoccupation with accurate control and record. It is clear that, whatever the excesses, abuses, and inadequacies in practice, theory required both accountancy and accountability.

All the following directly or otherwise concerned the gaoler:

Assize orders. The assize order recorded the decision of the court in special cases (*see also* TRANSPORTATION PAPERS), the nature of the charge, and instructions to those responsible for the manner of the prisoner's disposal. One such decision in Wiltshire in 1798 records that William Eatle was convicted of murder:

> Let him be Hanged by the Neck until he be dead on Thursday the twenty sixth day of July instant and let his Body be delivered to Mr Robert Still, Mr John White and Mr Samuel Fisher, Surgeons to the Salisbury General Infirmary to be dissected and anatomized and let the Gaoler until the time of his execution as aforesaid confine him in some Cell or place separate and apart from the other Prisoners and no person or persons whomsoever except the Gaoler or his Servants have access to him without a licence from the Judge the Sheriff or his Under Sheriff and until the time of his Execution let him be fed with Bread and Water only except he shall be desirous of receiving the Sacrament of the Lord's Supper.

The assize order appears either as a wholly handwritten foolscap four-page folder or as a part-printed foolscap form completed in handwriting.

Commital papers. Part-printed or wholly handwritten warrants were issued by justices of the peace commanding that a named prisoner be gaoled. Typical is a warrant (1812) requiring the keeper of Lancaster Castle Gaol to receive one Anthony Physic, '... and him there safely keep until he shall give such security or enter into such recognizance as aforesaid...'. The recognizance in question relates to Physic's accountability to Ellen Gardner who, the form alleges, 'Hath declared herself to be with child... and hath charged (Anthony Physic) with having gotten her with child'. The child being likely to be born a bastard and to be 'chargeable to the Township', Physic is required to undertake to indemnify the township. This, states the form, he has failed to do. It may be observed that both the law and the printed form display some prescience in the matter of Anthony and Ellen; in mid 19th-century England there were no fewer than twenty-four legally recognized bastardy forms, each designed to meet a specific variant of the contingency. (It is worth noting, in the matter of legal forms in general, that the printed document has no authority or special capacity in itself; its existence is merely a facility to those whose task it is to set out facts according to law. Provided the basic wording conforms to the relevant requirement, it may be typeset, handwritten, or both.)

Warrant of release. Documents for the release of prisoners commonly cite the status of both the recipient and authority conveying the order, naming the prisoner, the grounds for his release and the date on which it is to take place. As with other WARRANTS the document may take various forms, from an elaborate part-printed document with seals and black-letter initials to a signed handwritten note. A discharge from Lancaster Castle Gaol in 1829 measures 400 × 320 mm (15¾ × 12½ in); it is a major calligraphic exercise and bears the seal of the diocese of Chester. It releases Betty Hughes, imprisoned for 'contumacy' and contempt (more specifically, repeated refusal to attend church); she is released on the strength of having 'submitted herself and satisfied the said contempt'.

A more modest handwritten work (c. 1830) from Thomas McClaughan, clerk to the justices at Salem, Massachusetts, discharges George Stewart from custody: 'Mr Wilson, Sheriff: Sir discharge George Stewart from jail on condition of James Stewart paying all the cost.' The document measures 90 × 200 mm (3½ × 7⅞ in).

Pardon. In Britain, as transportation to the colonies began to replace the death penalty in the early 19th century, the granting of pardons – with the reservation that the prisoner be transported – becomes more frequent. The part-printed document records His Majesty's 'Having been graciously pleased to extend His Royal Mercy to the said Offender', and concludes with a final space for the term of transportation. In one example Jonathan Bridge, convicted and 'condemned to death for beginning riotously to demolish a dwelling house', is now ordered to be 'immediately transported beyond the Seas for the term of (his natural life)'.

Execution papers. Gaol keepers, later to become prison governors, were charged not only with custodianship but with the minutiae of judicial despatch. Here, as in everything to do with prisons, the record was full and formal. The papers of Lancaster Castle Gaol, which include bills and receipts for a wide variety of tradesmen's services, also touch on the scaffold. An invoice

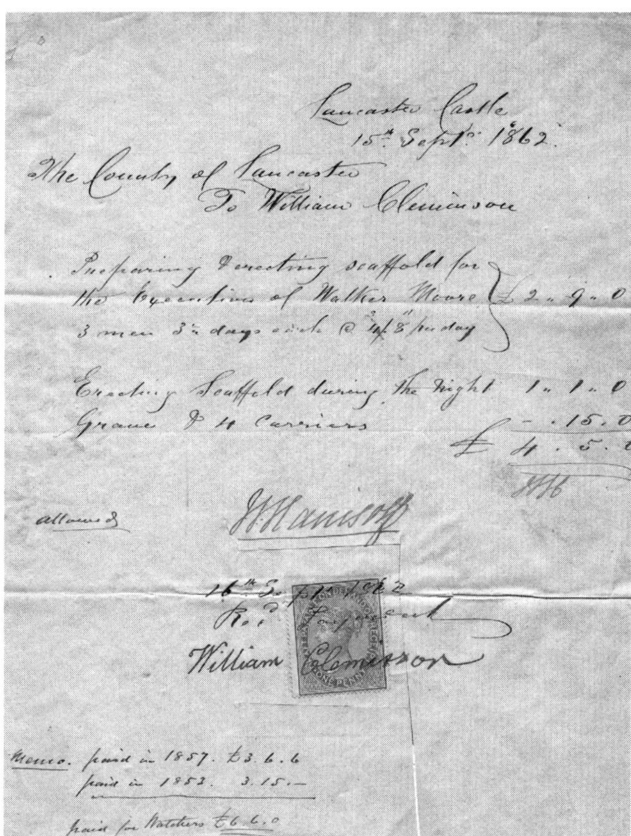
Lancaster Castle
15th Sept. 1862.
The County of Lancaster
To William Cleminson
Preparing & erecting scaffold for the execution of Walker Moore } 3 men 3½ days each @ 4/8 per day £2. 9. 0
Erecting Scaffold during the night 1. 1. 0
Grease & 4 Carriers –. 15. 0
£4. 5. 0
allowed
16th Sept. 1862
Recd Payment
William Cleminson
Memo. paid in 1857. £3. 6. 6
paid in 1853. 3. 15. –
paid for Watchers £6. 6. 0

Account for the erection of scaffold at Lancaster Castle Gaol, 15 September 1862. Manuscript. 231 × 190 mm (9⅛ × 7½ in)

reads: 'The County of Lancaster, August 29 1857; to William Cleminson and others preparing and erecting scaffold for the execution of Edward Hardman, and taking down... £2.11.6.'. The certificate of registry of death records: '(William Proctor) registrar of births and deaths... do hereby certify that the death of (Edward Hardman) was duly registered by me on the (29) day of (August) 185(7)...'. There follows a further invoice: 'County of Lancaster 29 August 1857; to William Cleminson and others for the interment of Edward Hardman after the execution £0.17.0. Settled 29 August 1857 William Cleminson'.

***Police Gazette* or *'Hue-and-Cry'*.** 'Hue-and-cry', a legal term of great antiquity, embodies the concept of the enlisting of the whole community in the apprehension of malefactors. The expression is subjoined to the title of the *Police Gazette* in a generalized listing of 'wanted' men, including escaped prisoners and deserters from Her Majesty's service. The publication appeared in various forms, probably from 1807 (and with the above title from 1828) to 1834, and relied for its wide appeal on offers of rewards. Apprehension of a deserter was at first worth ten shillings (raised to twenty shillings in 1866) and sums varying between £20 and £200 were offered in special cases. In one case, that of James Stephens, 'An active member of a treasonable conspiracy against the Queen's authority in Ireland', the whole of the front page of the publication, 450 × 290 mm (17¾ × 11⅜ in), was devoted to a proclamation offering £1000 for information and a further £1000 to the person or persons actually arresting Stephens. (A similar publication – circulated, however, only within the Metropolitan Police – was to appear at the turn of the century, when foolscap folders listed confidence tricksters and other wanted men, with the addition on the cover of a composite photographic print with numbered portraits.)

Reward notice. Closely related to the *Police Gazette* reward listings are reward notices published by Prosecuting Associations, groups of property owners who banded together to discourage the depredations of trespassers, poachers, and others. The reward notice, published cooperatively, privately, or by authority, is among the most prolific of 19th-century ephemera; it runs through the period as a continuing theme, part of the staple business of every local printer (*see* REWARD PAPERS).

Gaol notice. Printed notices on display inside prisons include prayers and other religious texts; disciplinary announcements, rules, and regulations, etc.; and staff and administration notices. A typical prayer card, 230 × 150 mm (9 × 6 in), comes from Derby gaol in the 1840s. The card, headed 'Prayer', begins: 'O Lord God Almighty, who has promised to hear the sorrowful sighing of the Prisoner, we humbly bow ourselves before thy Divine Majesty …'. Dining hall notices in Manchester gaol in the same period proffered forms of words for 'Grace before Meals' and 'Grace after Meals' in the same notice, 220 × 270 mm (8⅝ × 10⅝ in). Notices in the prison dining hall at Port Arthur(US) in the 1850s warned diners against 'not observing the strictest silence and decorum; not suspending their caps upon the racks provided …; not standing up during Grace before and after Meals …; not arranging their Mess Utensils according to the prescribed method after Meals …'.

Disciplinary notices are typified by an example from Pentonville prison (c.1843) in which inmates were informed of a three-tier behaviour system. Prisoners who behaved well (first class) were to be sent to Van Diemen's Land where continued good conduct would earn them a comforable and respectable position in life. Those who did not behave well (second class) would be sent to Van Diemen's Land under restraints and privations. Third class prisoners would be sent to a penal colony in 'Tasman's Peninsula' without wages, and deprived of liberty. Administrative notices include 'scale of dirt' charts, with variations of specific grades of prisoner. Derby County Gaol in the early 1840s provided 'convicted prisoners confined for any term not exceeding three days' with one pint of gruel for breakfast, sixteen ounces of bread for dinner, and another pint of gruel for supper.

Prisoners' correspondence. Officially sanctioned or not, messages from prison convey a graphic picture of inadequacy and deprivation.

> Lancaster, 1841 (pencilled message on a page torn from a prayer book): I received your kind presents which I am much obliged to you for it but it was a very unlucky present for me as one of the turnkeys caught me looking thro the window and searched me and found both tobacco and snuff and locked me up in Solitary 3 days on bread and water…
>
> Unnamed prison, November 1861: …Pray do then, my dear sir, if there is a possibility of relieving me out of this place, Do so…
>
> Maidstone Prison, 20 December 1861: I should be obliged by your seeing me…as I am anxious to know how I can proceed in procuring my discharge, and wish to explain my case to you…
>
> Bedford Gaol, January 1879 (written on the regulation four-page form): My Dear Wife, I am Very Sorry for getting into this trouble. I hope you will forgive and forget all…

A printed instruction on page one of the Bedford Gaol form includes the warning that 'All letters of an improper or idle tendency, either to or from Prisoners, or containing slang or other objectionable expressions, will be suppressed'. It adds that 'The permission to write and receive Letters is given to the Prisoners for the purpose of enabling them to keep up a connection with their respectable friends, and not that they may have news of the day…'.

Message forms were provided for those imprisoned for nonpayment of fines and costs or unable to find sureties for bail. They were to be filled in by the prisoner himself; they began: 'I am sorry to inform you that I am confined here…' and finished 'If you cannot succeed in obtaining my liberation, I will thank you to inform me as early as possible'. Another form, to be filled in by the governor at the prisoner's request, states that '(—) a Prisoner in my custody, wishes you to know that his Sentence of Imprisonment expires here on (—) at 9 o'clock in the Morning…'.

Calendar of prisoners. In British jurisprudence 'The Sheriff is to make a calendar [list] of the prisoners and deliver it to the justices…'. The list, contained in a document of from four to twenty or so pages, formed a 'running order' for trials to be held at the quarterly assizes when, according to law, visiting justices tried the cases of prisoners committed to gaol on serious charges during the preceding three months.

In a typical calendar (Liverpool Assizes, August 1847) lists are presented as double-page spreads with, on one page, headed columns for case numbers, name of prisoner and 'by whom and when committed', age, charge, degree of 'instruction', and, to be filled in by hand, the outcome of the trial ('event of trial'). Degree of 'instruction' was indicated by the use of N for 'neither read nor write'; R for 'read'; Imp. for 'read and write imperfectly'; W for 'Both well'; Sup. for 'Superior education'! On the facing page, blank columns provide space for handwritten details of previous offences and their respective sentences. A printed footline on the final page of the document, signed by the surgeon, attests to the prisoners' freedom from infectious disease. The document, which was completed at the conclusion of the trial by the clerk of the court, divides the charges into three categories of seriousness and lists cases in chronological order of commital. In the example cited, typical cases are as follows:

> Thomas Roach, 21 (R) Having at Manchester feloniously beat and assaulted Ann Donahoe, and with great personal violence robbed her of seven shillings and sixpence, her monies (previous offence: assault, Salford Gaol, Feb 1847; 14 days) Sentence: 10 years.
>
> Elizabeth Parr, 27 (R) Having, at Bury, stabbed and wounded Robert Grundy, with intent to do him some grevous bodily harm. (Previous offence: disorderly, Kirkdale Gaol, June 1838; 3 months. Common prostitute, Kirkdale Gaol, May 1845; 1 month. Felony, Kirkdale Sessions, 1847; acquitted.) Sentence: 12 months.
>
> Nicholas Leadbetter, 19 (R) Having, at North Meols, killed and slain Thomas Leadbetter. (Previous offence: not known.) Acquitted.
>
> Robert Pilkington, 56 (Imp.) Having, at Heaton, wilfully murdered Betty Pilkington. He is further charged with having feloniously cut and wounded Bridget Dean, with intent to do her some grievous bodily harm. (Previous offence: assault, Salford Gaol, 1843; 3 months.) Sentence: death.

Calendars of prisoners also took other forms. An example covering the gaols of Durham, Newcastle, and Morpeth for

1830 merely lists the prisoners, their ages, and details of their respective charges.

Miscellaneous. Gaol papers include a wide spectrum of marginalia, from contractors' and suppliers' accounts: 'poisoning rats; 24 chamber pots oil for tread mill' (Galway Gaol, 1841); to sketch plans for projected flower beds: 'The plots are edged with common daisies' (Perth County Prison, 1842). Visiting orders, prisoners' property lists, and many other ephemeral items contribute to the general picture.

See also CALENDAR OF PRISONERS; TRANSPORTATION PAPERS (PENAL)

REFERENCE Maurice Rickards, *The Ephemera of Crime and Punishment* (London: The Ephemera Society in association with the Solicitors' Law Society, 1983)

Garment label

The woven clothing label, bearing manufacturers' or suppliers' identification, was introduced into France and Britain in the 1870s. In France, those of Alexandre Elise are said to be the first; in Britain, Thomas Lomas of Manchester was advertising woven name and address labels for the trade in 1872. Shirt labels and underwear labels began to appear in Britain in the early 1880s

The technology of the woven name label stemmed from the activities of Thomas Stevens of Coventry, the Jacquard ribbon weaver who, in the depression of the 1860s, turned to the production of woven bookmarks and other novelties using the same methods. He later produced the famous range of souvenir woven pictures which he marketed under the name of 'Stevengraphs'. Other manufacturers applied the Jacquard principle to novelties, and in 1889 the former ribbon firm of J. and J. Cash introduced a personalized service of name tapes for individual shoppers. A number of large stores provided the additional service of sewing name tapes into purchases.

The manufacturer's name label, bearing not only details of provenance but care and cleaning instructions, became virtually universal after World War II. Pre-war labels, fewer in number, have for the most part disappeared with their respective garments, hence their scarcity. Surviving examples emerge, if at all, as rediscovered travellers' samples and in manufacturers' record books.

As with other categories of ephemera, the labels record not only developments in their own technology but the changing commercial and social scene; the labels of the early *haute couture* houses for example – Poiret, Worth, Paquin, Lanvin, Cheruit, Les Sœurs Callot – convey a world beyond recall. Inevitably the name label had its counterfeits, and in 1913 the *haute couture* houses of Paris sought to counteract New York's fashion piracy by forming the Syndicat pour la Défense de la Grande Couture Française to bring to an end the illicit use of their names and the counterfeiting of their labels.

The garment label reached new levels of significance in the late twentieth century, particularly in relation to youth culture. In this period garment labels such as those of Adidas, Gap, Levi, Nike, carried strong signals of acceptability, and, conversely, other labels did not.

See also LABEL; SILK

REFERENCE Ruven Feder and Jim Glasman, *The Woven Label Book* (Paris: Editions Yokar Feder, 1989)

Gift coupon

Advances in mass production in the late 19th century required a complementary increase in the techniques of the mass market. To help in creating and sustaining mass demand, manufacturers of popular consumer products instituted inducement schemes, offering rewards for long-term brand loyalty.

The cigarette- or chewing-gum card, introduced in America in the 1870s, formed an inducement in itself, and the serial-card idea has remained in use, if not in cigarettes, in a wide range of other products ever since (*see* GIVE-AWAYS). The notion of the gift coupon, to be collected and later exchanged in quantity for a 'present', originated in 1851, with soapmaker Benjamin Babbitt of New York. To meet the resistance of customers to paying for a wrapper in a product hitherto unwrapped, he overprinted the word 'coupon' on the wrapper. Twenty-five of the coupons were exchangeable for a lithographed picture. In Britain, the first recorded use of the gift coupon is in 'Discount tea tickets'. In 1876 Herbert Smith of Peterborough advertised the continuance of a scheme in which he offered 'ornamental articles' in exchange for tickets enclosed in tea packets. By the end of the century the idea was widely accepted, and coupon, ticket, token, and wrapper offers accompanied many consumer items. A typical offer is advertised in an 1890s American promotion leaflet listing ninety gifts exchangeable for varying numbers of tobacco tags, trade-mark stickers, and cigar bands. The Continental Tobacco Co. of St Louis, Missouri, offers gifts for tobacco tags in quantities ranging from 15 to 4000. At the lower end of the scale are a 10-cent package of sliced plug (15 tags), a pocket-knife (25 tags), and a baseball (100 tags). At the upper end, a Marlin repeating shotgun, take-down, 12-gauge (2000 tags), and a continental rug, nine feet by twelve feet (4000 tags). Tags are quoted at a specific equivalence rate with trademark stickers and cigar bands.

In similar vein is a card (c.1900) issued to customers of the store of McClennan & Co., general merchants, of East Bridge, New York. Here the customer is offered a 'handsome life-size crayon portrait', free with every ten dollars' worth of goods bought. Every purchase of five cents or over is marked on the card; when the record shows ten dollars the portrait may be ordered free of charge (except that the customer must buy a frame to go with it for $2.90). The card, which measures 68 × 112 mm (2⅝ × 4⅜ in), shows signs of having been overprinted with the name of the store, suggesting that the same scheme (presumably floated by the portrait and picture-frame suppliers) was on offer elsewhere. The makers of 'Century' bright golden chewing tobacco claimed to include not coupons, but actual dollar bills, in some of their product packages. Printed labels on shop-counter display boxes carried the legend: '$100 packed in this brand daily'.

It was, however, the coupon system that American companies favoured, and the example of Benjamin Babbitt was widely followed. Gum, tea, soap, clothing, and tobacco firms moved in with coupons, wrappers, and (later) box tops. The tobacco industry led the field; by 1910 some thirty American tobacco companies were running coupon schemes. Brown and Williamson, which became America's third largest tobacco company in the late 1970s, launched their coupon scheme in 1932 with Raleigh cigarettes; by 1936, with the addition of their Kool and Viceroy brands as coupon cigarettes, the firm's gift catalogue had expanded to thirty-six pages. The war effort significantly changed their focus, and in 1942 Brown and Williamson offered a $25 US War Savings Bond for 2500 coupons and a dollar's worth of War Savings Stamps for 133. By late 1943 the shortage of premium merchandise and the necessities of war brought the coupon program to a standstill. It started again, tentatively, in 1949 with Raleigh cigarettes. But by 1962, when Belair menthol cigarettes were added to the plan, the impact of the coupons helped sales increase three hundred per cent. In the late 1970s the company was operating one of the world's largest coupon schemes.

Other notable coupon pioneers in America were the Colgate Co. (which had started in the gift field with chromolithographed pictures in 1892); Borden, the milk company; and General Mills, whose forerunners, Washburn Crosby, had also started gift schemes in the 1890s. By the 1930s they were including coupons with Gold Medal Flour, Wheaties, Bisquick, and other products. In the 1970s and 1980s the company included coupons with some 125 products.

Canada's first use of coupons in cigarettes was in 1963, in a brand called 'Mark Ten'. A 'coupon war' ensued, but in 1970, by agreement, most incentive promotions were stopped, each competing company being allowed coupons in only one brand. In the event only one company continued with the idea of a coupon brand.

In Britain, the coupon principle was introduced somewhat later than in America (although the Lever Brothers Co. was running wrapper-covering competitions in America in the late 1890s). Nevertheless there was aggressive promotion, and in December 1909 the Rowntree Co. of York launched one of the first British 'Special price' offers. It issued a two-colour leaflet, measuring 140 × 220 mm (5½ × 8⅝ in), with a metal disc attached to it which was negotiable at stockists to effect a twopence reduction on any purchase of Elect Cocoa. The leaflet indicates that a free-gift coupon scheme is also in operation, and that the coupon contained in the twopence-off tin 'will count towards your collection'. Gifts were 'handsome free gift boxes of chocolates and pastilles'.

Coupon schemes proliferated in Britain, reaching their greatest popularity in the tobacco industry in the 1930s, when many homes contained at least one item exchanged for coupons. Illustrated catalogues, showing gifts and their coupon values, were commonplace. Cigarette coupons first appeared in Britain with Kinnear's 'Handicap' cigarettes in 1901, with a prize competition offering a weekend in Paris. The first offer of goods came with Ogden's 'Guinea Gold' cigarettes in 1902.

Comparable schemes are the Green Shield stamp and similar operations, which also issued catalogues and, in some cases, like their 19th-century forerunners, set up gift showrooms.

Give-aways

In addition to pictorial cards and gift coupons, products and publications have for long carried occasional extras by way of sales promotion. Known generically as 'give-aways', these have taken a multiplicity of forms, more or less ephemeral.

Newspapers and magazines have been the most frequent users of give-aways. Among the earliest recorded examples in Britain are the embossed souvenir portraits produced by James Whiting and Dobbs in the 1830s. One of these, showing the Duke of Wellington, carries a bold footline on the margin: 'Presented to the purchasers of The Age Newspaper'; another shows Walter Scott and has a minuscule footline within the decorative printed frame: 'Presented gratis with first number of *The Storyteller or the Journal of Fiction*'. Of the remaining sub-

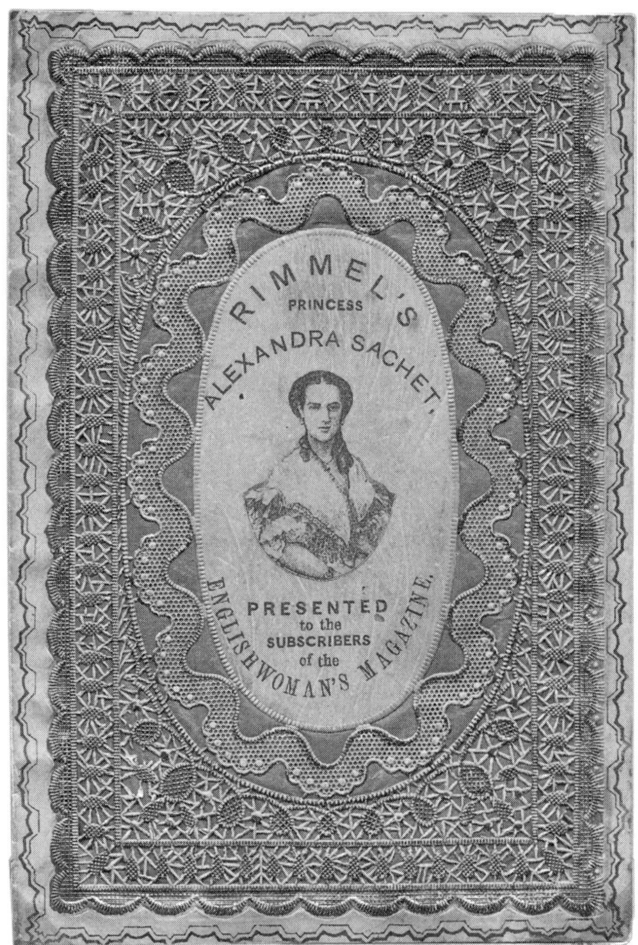

Give-away sachet presented to subscribers of the *Englishwoman's Magazine*, mid 19th century. Printed by lithography (the same design on both sides) in gold on glazed pink paper, with lace-paper work. A green sachet enclosed. 147 × 100 mm (5¾ × 4 in)

jects in the series – Lord Brougham, Lord Grey, Lord Byron, Thomas Moore, Queen Adelaide, William IV – the last is known to have been given away with *The Atlas* newspaper, although the fact is not mentioned on the item. These embosssed portraits may have been produced by Whiting largely as a publicity exercise for the promotion of his printing processes, and the inclusion of the William IV portrait with *The Atlas* may be accounted for by the fact that the proprietor of the newspaper was Whiting's father.

In more recent times give-aways have been included with magazines rather than newspapers. The practice became widespread in Britain during the period of the expansion of popular journalism, and most women's magazines at the turn of the 19th and 20th centuries included paper dress patterns as a matter of course. The give-away was widely used in the promotion of children's magazines in the 1920s and 1930s and again in women's magazines in the 1950s and 1960s. It has remained a stand-by feature of magazine promotion.

The give-away appeared in general trade, notably among grocers and tea and coffee dealers, in the 1890s. In America a major name in the field was C. D. Kenny, whose tea, coffee, and sugar stores were famous in fourteen cities as sources of 'free gifts'. Starting with elaborate chromolithographed trade cards, he moved to colour-printed gifts in tin – badges, plates, and plaques – and finally to such three-dimensional items as tea strainers, spice tins, and china figurines and ornaments. All bear the legend 'C. D. Kenny'.

In Britain in the same period, close identification of the dealers with give-aways led to the currency of the derogatory catchphrase 'given away with a pound of tea'. Some traders, aware of the declining image of both the product and the trade, reacted strongly. The solution is encapsulated in a leaflet put out by Patrick Thorn, tea-man, of Greyhound Road, Fulham, in which he inveighed against what had become known as 'present' tea: 'Do you *really* think, when you buy the so-called Present Tea, that you get two articles for the price of one? If you want crockery, buy crockery, but if you want tea, pay a fair price and see that you get value for money. We sell: *No faulty crockery! No trumpery toys! No trashy vases! No rag dolls! No penny whistles! No tin soldiers! No gimcrack presents of any sort* – but pure and fragrant tea'.

See also ADVERTISING FAN; ADVERTISING NOVELTY; BOOK-MATCH; CHANGE PIN-PAPER; CHILDREN'S ADVERTISING BOOKLET; CUT-OUT TOYS; EMBOSSING/LACE PAPER; EMBROIDERY PATTERN; GIFT COUPON; LIEBIG CARD; LOTTERY PAPER; NEEDLE-BOX PRINT; NEWSPAPER GIVE-AWAYS; PANORAMA, PAPER PATTERN

Gold-miners' papers, Australian

Most significant of Australian gold-rush ephemera is the 'gold licence' or 'miner's right', a key item in the prospector's often meagre possessions. Its survival to the present day is unusual. It was normally withdrawn on expiry (no new licence was available without surrender of the old); as a souvenir it had but bitter connotations in the vast majority of cases.

A typical specimen is a licence to dig for gold in the British colony of Victoria in the early 1850s. This cost the holder thirty shillings per month and entitled him to dig in an assigned area twelve feet square (16 square metres). The licence, bearing the Royal coat of arms and measuring 190 × 190 mm (7½ × 7½ in), was printed by John Ferres at the Government Printing Office and issued to the responsible commissioner in book form, counterfoils being retained as a record.

Conditions in the gold-strike areas were unstable. The sudden influx of numbers of adventurers brought problems, not least of them being law and order, and the cost of the licences, together with the authorities' rigorous control of their use, caused mounting resentment. A condition of issue was that each man should carry his licence for inspection at all times (it is noticeable that surviving examples are much creased), and frequent 'licence hunts' produced tension that led finally to the armed rebellion at Eureka Stockade in December 1854. Some twenty-five gold-miners and four soldiers were killed and a number on both sides were wounded. Fifteen of the surviving miners were tried for treason and acquitted. 'Gold licences' were abolished, the men henceforth paying a moderate duty on finds and a nominal annual fee for the right to dig.

Australian gold licences were issued from 1851 to 1855. They bore printed regulations that reflected the rigour of their control: '... every licenced person must always have his licence with him ready to be produced whenever demanded by a Commissioner or Person acting under his instructions, otherwise he is liable to be proceeded against as an unlicenced person. Every person digging for gold, or occupying land without a licence, is liable by Law to be fined, for a first offence, not exceeding £5; for a second offence, not exceeding £15; and for a subsequent offence not exceeding £30.... It is enjoined that all persons on the Gold Fields maintain and assist in maintaining a due and proper observance of Sundays'.

REFERENCE Robin May, *The Gold Rushes. From California to the Klondike* (London: William Luscombe, 1977)

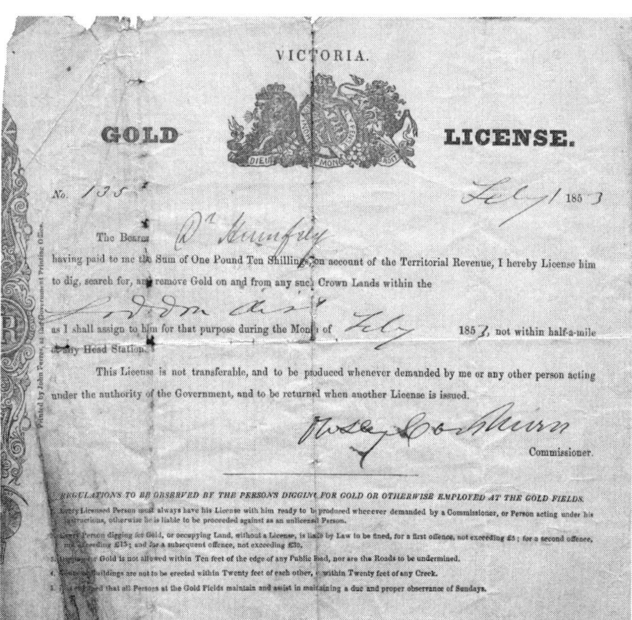

VICTORIA.

GOLD LICENSE.

No. 135 [illegible] 1853

The Bearer [illegible]

having paid to me the Sum of One Pound Ten Shillings, on account of the Territorial Revenue, I hereby License him to dig, search for, and remove Gold on and from any such Crown Lands within the [illegible]

as I shall assign to him for that purpose during the Month of [illegible] 1853, not within half-a-mile of any Head Station.

This License is not transferable, and to be produced whenever demanded by me or any other person acting under the authority of the Government, and to be returned when another License is issued.

[illegible]

Commissioner.

REGULATIONS TO BE OBSERVED BY THE PERSONS DIGGING FOR GOLD OR OTHERWISE EMPLOYED AT THE GOLD FIELDS.

1. Every Licensed Person must always have his License with him ready to be produced whenever demanded by a Commissioner, or Person acting under his instructions, otherwise he is liable to be proceeded against as an unlicensed Person.
2. Every Person digging for Gold, or occupying Land, without a License, is liable by Law to be fined, for a first offence, not exceeding £5; for a second offence, not exceeding £15; and for a subsequent offence, not exceeding £30.
3. Digging for Gold is not allowed within Ten feet of the edge of any Public Road, nor are the Roads to be undermined.
4. [illegible] Buildings are not to be erected within Twenty feet of each other, or within Twenty feet of any Creek.
5. It is enjoined that all Persons at the Gold Fields maintain and assist in maintaining a due and proper observance of Sundays.

Printed by John Ferres, at the Government Printing Office.

Gold miner's licence, issued by the State of Victoria, Australia, February 1853. Letterpress and manuscript, printed by John Ferres at the Government Printing Office. 190 × 195 mm (7½ × 7⅝ in)

Greetings card

'Greetings card' and 'greeting card' are both used as generic terms to cover the CHRISTMAS CARD, VALENTINE, and other cards bearing good wishes, congratulations, and similar messages. British usage is mixed, but tends to favour 'greetings' over the American 'greeting'. The plural form is adopted here, following the most recent Oxford dictionary practice (SOED) and the familiar postcard message 'Greetings from...'.

The greetings card emerged with the growth of the middle classes and the concomitant rise in prosperity and leisure time. Its success depended on the availability of an efficient postal service and – in its familiar, colourful form – relatively cheap industrial colour printing. The 19th century saw the valentine, Christmas card, New Year card, and general birthday card firmly established as forms of annual communication. Such cards are characterized by their graphic treatment: usually chromolithographed in numerous workings (*see* CHROMO), often with one or more additional features (embossing, cut-out shapes, on-lays, fringes, tassels, and movable parts), they aimed to appeal through their visual and tactile qualities. The messages they conveyed graphically were reinforced through their texts: often in verse, and frequently with hand-lettering rather than type, they plumbed new depths of Victorian sentimentality.

The late 19th century also saw the hesitant beginnings of the practice of sending cards in celebration of Rosh Hashanah, the Jewish New Year, which is the first day of the month of Tishri (and falls in September or October). Cards were sent on the occasion of Rosh Hashanah and Yom Kippur (which falls ten days later), together known as the High Holy Days. The practice was slow to develop and initially involved using ordinary calling cards with messages written on them by hand. With the growth of the greetings-card industry in the 20th century most American publishers issued a range of Jewish New Year cards,

Greetings card designed by Dorothy Malenschein for Hallmark Cards in 1939, originally as a Mother's day card but reworded in 1941 to become a friendship card. Though reworked, the design has been in print for over sixty years and has sold over thirty million copies. Photolithography. 97 × 139 mm (3⅞ × 5½ in). *Copyright Hallmark Cards UK.*

usually with some clear symbolic reference to the occasion. Similar cards published in Israel often celebrated the idea of peace or, in its early years, the State of Israel. More recently Pesach (Passover) and the Jewish holiday of Hanukkah, which commemorates the survival of Judaism and the heroism of Judas Maccabeus, have also been occasions for sending cards in some parts of the Jewish diaspora. In America, for example, Hanukkah accounts for more than 11 million cards annually, not all of them overtly religious.

Greetings cards are also sent by those of other faiths and cultures. The Sikh world celebrates the birth of its religion at Vaisakhi, which falls on 13 April. This is the most significant event in the Sikh calendar, but probably less an occasion for celebrations than the Hindu Festival of Lights, Diwali, which takes place at the time of the full moon at the end of October or the beginning of November and is associated with firework displays. Greetings cards are sent in connection with both occasions, though rather more so with Diwali. Some, though not all, are religious in spirit. They are not widely available outside India, and in Britain are imported for the benefit of Sikh and Hindu communities in, for example, Southall.

Muslims send cards on two main occasions: at the end of Ramadan, during a period of three days, when they celebrate Eid, and seventy days later at the Eid of the Sacrifice, when some make a pilgrimage to Mecca. The cards are not overtly religious; some feature mosques, but the majority are floral or scenic. The custom probably dates from the 1930s, and in recent years cards have been sold in most European countries and the United States. In Iran, secular greetings cards have been sent from at least the middle of the 20th century to celebrate the New Year, Noruz, which falls on 21 March.

The end of the 20th century saw the rise of the greetings card that met the needs of a variety of faiths with such bland messages as 'Happy holidays' or, in the newly emerging field of the E-MAIL card, 'Happy everything' and 'Happy whichever'.

The continuing rise in disposable income in the Western world in the 20th century, coupled with changing values in society, led to the celebration of virtually every situation in which greetings or best wishes were in order, whether expected or not. Developments in this period included the widespread use of the targeted birthday card, the beginnings of cards for 'Mother's day', 'Father's day', the ubiquitous 'Get well' card, and cards for family events, bearing congratulations 'on the birth of', 'on your engagement', 'on your wedding', etc. Cards were even sent to – and also as from – pets. Other cards related to the more menial aspects of life and featured such captions as 'On passing your driving test', 'On moving home', 'Your new job', 'Sorry you're leaving', and 'Why don't you write me?'

In the first half of the 20th century the typical greetings card lost some of the richness of its 19th century counterpart, partly because of the declining use of chromolithography and the introduction of new methods of production. It was left to the second half of the century to find a new direction for it by focusing on ideas – often conveyed through humour – in relation to specific groups or situations. Some such cards were overtly risqué, others explored the double entendre, particular human foibles, or current issues, such as 'girl power'. A further category of card, when taken at face value, even appeared to contradict the purpose of sending a message of good will.

Late 20th-century cards were often much more simply produced than their 19th century precursors. Many used line drawings, often in cartoon-like style, and flat areas of colour. Others reproduced major works of art or specially commissioned paintings – usually without any relevance to the particular message of the card – simply to delight the eye. Seductive images of this kind, often with a glossy finish, provided a late echo of the 19th century chromolithographed greetings card.

Building on 19th-century foundations laid by Louis Prang & Co. in America and several leading card publishers in Britain (*see* CHRISTMAS CARD), American publishers came into their own in the first half of the 20th century. In this period the following companies made significant contributions to the development of the greetings card: American Greetings Corporation (Cleveland, Ohio); Buzza Co. (from the late 1930s Buzza-Cardozo, in Hollywood, California); Hall Brothers Inc., later Hallmark Cards (Kansas City); Keating Co. (Philadelphia); Norcross Co. (New York); Rust Craft Publishers (Boston and Dedham, Mass.); and P. F. Volland Co. (Chicago).

Hallmark Cards Inc., now the largest greetings-card company in the world, was founded in 1910. It operates in more than one hundred countries and produces cards for different markets in over thirty languages. Its subsidiary, Hallmark Cards UK (established 1958), produces designs and messages to suit the British market, where it is the largest publisher of cards. It estimates that 2.7 billion greetings cards are sold in Britain every year, or 48 for every man, woman, and child in the country. Its 'Forever friends' series, designed by Deborah Jones, which features cuddly bears, is the most successful range ever and over 600 million cards have been sold world-wide. Most cards do not have a very long shelf life since tastes, situations, and markets change; but one Hallmark design featuring pansies has been available for over sixty years and is the world's best selling card.

As the 20th century came to a close, the estimated figures for cards sold in Britain (information supplied by Hallmark Cards) were: wedding cards 12 million; Father's day cards 15 million; Valentine's day cards 21 million; Easter cards 25 million; Mother's day cards 33 million; Christmas cards 1.5 billion. Christmas and New Year cards represented around 70 per cent of the total volume (though considerably less in value). Figures for America were proportionally lower, but amounted to an absolute figure for Christmas and New Year cards of 2.6 billion.

Greetings cards from the past, even 19th-century ones, have survived in enormous quantities. The practice of inserting cards into a SCRAPBOOK/ALBUM, which began almost from their inception, has led to a survival rate probably greater than for any other category of popular ephemera. But even without such deliberate preservation, cards have survived incidentally among the effects of people who held on to them as a continuing reminder of some occasion, or for fear of upsetting a loved one. It could be argued therefore that the main reason for considering greetings cards as ephemera is not so much that they are actually ephemeral as that they normally celebrate a particular day or passing occasion. [MT]

REFRENCES Ernest Dudley Chase, *The Romance of Greeting Cards* (Dedham, Mass.: Rust Craft Publications Ltd, 1956); Laura Seddon, *A Gallery of Greetings* (Manchester: Manchester Polytechnic Library, 1992); Ellen Stern, *The very best from the Hallmark Greeting Cards through the Years* (New York: Harry N. Abrams Inc., 1988)

Greetings telegram

The idea of a colourful 'special occasion' telegram form originated in Germany in the late 1890s.The first actual issue appeared in Denmark in 1907. Sweden followed in 1912, and other countries adopted the idea shortly after. Initially, a portion of the greetings surcharge was donated to charity. In the period 1912 to 1925 Sweden is said to have raised 3.5 million kronor in this way. By the 1930s greetings telegrams had spread to the whole of Europe, and to America, Australia, Canada, and the rest of the English-speaking world. Britain's first issue, designed by Margaret Calkin James, appeared on 24 July 1935, and America's first issue, introduced by Western Union, at about the same time

Britain's introduction of the service was in part an attempt to counter the 'bad news' connotation of the ordinary telegram, and partly to put new life into the failing telegram business. At its peak in 1913 the ordinary telegram service carried over eighty million messages a year, but by 1934 this number had more than halved. As elsewhere in the world, the telegram was being outflanked by a rapidly expanding telephone service and the promise of nationwide overnight delivery of mail.

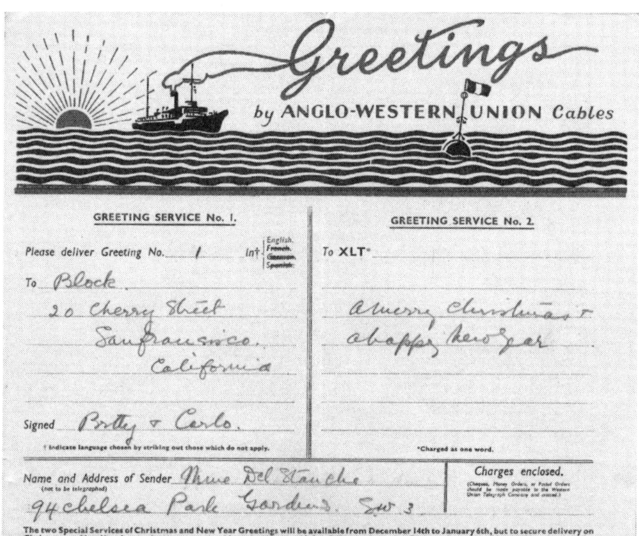

Greetings
by ANGLO-WESTERN UNION Cables

GREETING SERVICE No. 1.

Please deliver Greeting No. 1 Int† English.

To Block
20 Cherry Street
San Francisco,
California

Signed Betty & Carlo.

† Indicate language chosen by striking out those which do not apply.

GREETING SERVICE No. 2.

To XLT*

A merry Christmas & a happy New Year

*Charged as one word.

Name and Address of Sender
94 Chelsea Park Gardens. SW 3

Charges enclosed.

The two Special Services of Christmas and New Year Greetings will be available from December 14th to January 6th, but to secure delivery on Christmas or New Year's morning messages should reach a Western Union Office not later than 5 p.m. on December 24th and 31st respectively.

Greetings telegram form of Anglo-Western Union Cables for a message to be sent from London to San Francisco, 1930s. Letterpress. Printed in three colours, with manuscript. 178 × 215 mm (7 × 8½ in)

It took some time for the greetings telegram to fix itself in the public mind, and four years after its launch date the Post Office found it advisable to take whole-page magazine spaces to describe the idea:

WHAT is a Greetings Telegram?

A Greetings Telegram is a special telegram that comes in a golden envelope. The form is larger, gaily coloured. From time to time the design is changed. For celebrations of every kind, a Greetings Telegram is just the thing to lend your message warmth and wings.

HOW can you send one?

A Greetings Telegram may be handed in at a Post Office; or you can send it by telephoning through to 'Telegrams'.

HOW MUCH does it cost?

A Greetings Telegram costs only one penny a word, with a minimum of ninepence.

The British greetings telegram eventually achieved a market of many millions, and in the period 1935 to 1979 went through a total of seventy-nine designs. These covered birthdays, weddings, births, St Valentine's day, and two coronations (those of George VI, 1937, and Elizabeth II, 1953). Designers included such prominent names as Edward Ardizzone, Eric Fraser, Frank Newbould, Norman Thelwell, Rex Whistler, and Anna Zinkeisen

REFERENCE Ian G. Wilkinson, *British Greetings Telegrams* (Chesham, Bucks: Wilkinson, 1991)

Gretna Green marriage certificate

With the abolition of Fleet marriages in 1753 (*see* FLEET MARRIAGE CERTIFICATE), couples eloping from England resorted to Scotland, where the marriage law required simply that the pair should declare before witnesses their desire and consent to be considered as married. Publishing of banns was not required, nor was there a residential qualification, or a need for a MARRIAGE CERTIFICATE. The 'ceremony' might take place anywhere in Scotland before any officiating party at any time of the day or night. Such a marriage, though 'irregular', was regarded as valid on both sides of the border.

Notwithstanding the flexibility of these arrangements, eloping couples still sought some measure of formality, much of which evolved by chance. Gretna, as the first village in the journey over the border from Carlisle, became famous purely through its geographical location; the availability of the blacksmith led to his being called upon as celebrant; the 'certificate', a document of uncertain grammatical construction and no legal standing, came to be provided as an optional extra.

A number of other border villages shared in the clandestine marriage trade. Lamberton, at the eastern end of the border, was also a convenient refuge for runaways. But Gretna was preeminent. In 1856 the law was changed to require twenty-one days residence of one of the parties, thus much reducing the traffic; the practice was finally abolished in 1940 after the passing of the Marriage (Scotland) Act.

Among the officiating 'priests' at Gretna whose names may appear on certificates were Scott, George Gordon, Joseph Pasley 'Thomas Brown' (reputed to be Pasley incognito), Robert Elliot, David Laing, John Lynton, and Walter Coulthard. The wording of the certificate, in whichever version it appears, is ambiguous. In an early manuscript rendering (1793) it reads: 'this is to sartify all persons that may be concerned that (—) from the Parish of (—) in the county of (—) and (—) from the Parish of (—) and the county of (—) and both comes before me and declaryed themselves both to be single persons and now mayried by the form of the Kirk of Scotland and agreible to the Church of England, and givine under my hand this (—) day of (—). The 'priest' signs the document under or near the word 'witness' (not therefore as solemnizer but as spectator) with the parties themselves featuring as prime signatories. It is recorded, however, that as a sop to his clients in the 'ceremony' the celebrant read part of the liturgy of the Church of England; this form of words – the 'magic form of words' as successive operators privately called it – served to reinforce the couple's sense of validity.

With modifications and minor improvements in spelling and syntax – but with no discernible clarification of meaning – the document was later printed, and repeatedly reprinted. It bore the Royal Crest at the head and carried the dubious title 'Kingdom of Scotland'; its foolscap format 330 × 203 mm (13 × 8 in) gave it a further *cachet*.

Various estimates have been made of the number of Gretna marriages effected during the period 1738 to 1856, the 'heyday' of Gretna Green and its neighbours. Robert Elliot, who was one of the five 'marriers' officiating at Gretna between 1811 and 1839, laid claim to 3758 marriages. Registers (gratuitously maintained by a dozen or so operators over the period 1783 to 1865, and still preserved in various places in the district) record some 8300 such marriages. These registers had no statutory role, though they could be invoked as evidence of a 'ceremony' having taken place. [PJ]

REFERENCES Claverhouse [i.e. Meliora C. Smith], *Irregular Border Marriages* (Edinburgh and London: Moray Press, 1934); Mark Searle, *Turnpikes and Toll-Bars* (London: Hutchinson, 1930)

COLLECTION Ewart Library, Dumfries

Guest list

Dinner parties, weekend house parties, garden parties, receptions, wedding parties, state visits, and funerals are among the numerous occasions for which lists of those attending are recorded, either for publication or for private reference. They are to be found as manuscript jottings (often together with notes of catering arrangements) or as formally printed registers. Names generally appear, for semi-private occasions, in alphabetical order, and for public occasions according to the complex requirements of nationally or internationally accepted codes of precedence. Where major occasions are concerned, the residential location of those listed may appear, together with those of their respective attendants (equerries, ladies-in-waiting, servants, footmen, valets, grooms, dressers, pages, nurses, etc.).

Listings may sometimes reflect problems of accommodation. Elizabeth Longford records a list for the state visit of the German Kaiser to Hatfield House in 1891: the Rt Hon. Arthur Balfour was located in the 'Gate House: first floor, no.6' and the Hon. Eric Barrington 'Gate House: attic no. 1'. Similar difficulties appear repeatedly at Windsor Castle, where guests overflow into local hotels (The White Hart and The Castle) and valets are housed in box lobbies.

The list of those attending the funeral of Queen Victoria is a sixteen-page foolscap sheaf bearing 248 names, of which five are monarchs. 'His Majesty the King' (Edward VII) appears as a single entry on an otherwise blank front page. The list includes forty-four princes and princesses and twenty dukes and duchesses. Accommodation ranges from Buckingham Palace to Brown's Hotel, Dover Street.

REFERENCE Elizabeth Longford, *Louisa, Lady in Waiting* (London: Cape, 1979)

hackney papers
hand-knitting pattern
handwritten ephemera
harlequinade ('turn-up')
hat-duty stamp
hidden-name card
hold-to-light
holiday card
hornbook
hospital recommendation document
hostel admission ticket
hotel/tour coupon
hotel papers
house journal
household regulations
housekeeping accounts
hymn number card

Hackney papers

The ephemera of the cab trade may be said to divide into two distinct sections. On the one hand, by far the larger section, is material relating to control of the driver and his vehicle; on the other are papers arising from drivers' protests against control.

By the end of the 17th century in London, with the permitted number of coaches increased to seven hundred, and with five commissioners appointed to supervise them, hackney coachmen found themselves both over-numerous and over-disciplined. It is at this period that numerous printed appeals and petitions appeared calling for justice, not only for coachmen but for the numerous secondary trades and services their calling supported: 'Coach-makers, Harness-makers, Wheelers, Tire-Smiths, Curriers, Founders, Painters, Corn-chandlers, Farriers ... also a great many others in the country that serve them with Hay, Straw, Oats, Beans, Iron, Timber and Horses ...' (*The Case of the Poor Hackney-Coachmen, Humbly presented to the Honorable House of Commons*).

Other appeals came from hackney coachmen already overcharged for licences; from coachmen threatened with penury by withdrawal of licence for trivial offences; and from a body of 'two hundred ancient chair-men', deprived of licences by their being given instead to interlopers: 'We beseech your Honours to permit us to carry any Gentlemen in our own Chair by the Week, without any ... Molestation, or that you will be pleased to License One Hundred more ...'. Also addressed to the House of Commons were proposals from George Laverick, 'An ancient [i.e. former] Hackney-Coach-man and inhabitant in St Giles's for Thirty Five Years', suggesting means for preventing the 'Stop of Coaches in the Street ... which will be a great Advantage to said Hackney-Coachmen, as also to the whole publick'. Laverick proposed himself as a traffic warden to ease the flow of traffic by on the spot fining of offenders. The record is silent as to his success in the matter.

Controls were extended in the 19th century to hackney carts or other vehicles plying for hire for the carrying of goods. These vehicles, designated as 'carts, carrs and carrooms', were required to be driven only by licence holders and to be painted with the owner's name and cart number. Later, a system of branding was introduced in which a code letter, changed annually, was burnt into the woodwork of the vehicle. Lists of 'licensed persons' were printed and posted, showing their addresses and cart numbers. Also listed were carts not having been brought in for marking, together with their owners' names and cart numbers.

The essential ephemera of the hackney carriage are the FORMS relating to licensing, to agreements between drivers and proprietors, and to contact with passengers themselves.

LICENCE forms cover application for permission to operate a hackney carriage; the licence itself and a stamp office receipt showing payment of the carriage tax; and a 'Licence to drive a hackney carriage' (later to drive a carriage 'propelled by mechanical power'). An agreement between the driver and the proprietor generally stipulates a daily payment (or 'the earnings') for the use of a 'hackney carriage and one horse', indemnifying the driver to lodge his licence with his 'master' as a form of deposit.

For the hirer, two documents apply. One is an authorized statement of charges, 'the fare plate', to be displayed inside the vehicle 'in the most convenient place', in the case of a hansom 'on the inside of the splashboard'. The second document is the 'ticket'. The ticket (not to be confused with the metal number ticket worn by the driver) is a printed paper slip, which was handed to the hirer on request. It measured some 65 × 90 mm (2½ × 3½ in) and carried, on one side, the licence-holder's name and carriage number, and on the other a listing of the information shown on the fare plate. The ticket served not only as a confirmation of charges but, as stated on the name and address sign, as a 'reference in case of complaints, or property left in the carriage'. It remained in use until the first years of the 20th century.

Regulations governing hackney carriages in the latter part of the 19th century are embodied in the Metropolitan Public Carriage Act 1869 (32 & 33 Vict., c.115) and the London Cab Act 1896 (59 & 60 Vict., c.27). Their requirements, published as a

September 14th 1858

21, MELCOMBE MEWS, DORSET SQUARE.

I, Joseph Grant being a Licensed Driver of Hackney Carriages, agree with ROBERT TODD, a Proprietor of Licensed Hackney Carriages, to pay to the said ROBERT TODD the sum of 6, 6 ~~Shillings~~ per day, for the ~~use~~ earnings of a Hackney Carriage and one Horse, commencing before Eleven o'clock in the morning till Twelve o'clock at night, and One Shilling for every half-hour after that time, to be paid day by day so long as I continue to drive for the said ROBERT TODD; and I further agree to make good all damage done to the said Hackney Carriage and Horse which I am entrusted with, or any other damage I may do, and re-pay to the said ROBERT TODD any sum of money he may have to pay for me during my employment with the said R. TODD.

Signed Joseph Grant + Witness Wm Allin

Hackney carriage agreement between a licensed driver and a proprietor, London, 14 September 1858. Letterpress and manuscript, cut 'indentwise' through a 'cheque' device. Letterpress and manuscript. 94 × 180 mm (3¾ × 7⅛ in)

compendium in 1897, are detailed and extensive. The metal number ticket, already noted, was to be worn by the driver 'conspicuously upon his breast'. A 'check-string', a wire communications link between the interior and the driver, 'must be held in the driver's hand during the time of his driving any person in the carriage, so that it may be used for the accommodation of such person'. Feeding, foddering, shoeing, bleeding, cleaning, training or breaking horses 'to the annoyance of inhabitants or passengers' was an offence. So was 'furious or careless driving'. Among requirements for a Certificate of Fitness were: 'that all carriages fitted with noiseless or rubber-tyred wheels have bells affixed, either to the carriage or to the harness …'; and 'That seats, cushions etc. are stuffed with horsehair, wool or flock, and not with hay, straw, seaweed or whalebone shavings …'.

Among other examples of cab-trade ephemera are such items as the police commissioner's public cab-rank notice; the 1880s horse auction poster (Wise's Yard, Pimlico: '70 cab and omnibus horses … 16 sets of omnibus harness; 20 sets of cab harness'); and successive fare plates, latterly on paper, recording increased charges. Also part of the ephemera record are temporary conversion tables showing additions to be made to meter readings prior to their adjustment.

Ham radio card *See* QSL CARD

Hand-knitting pattern

The oldest extant knitting pattern is cited as 'The Order How to Knit a Hose' which was printed in London in 1655 (Rutt, 1987). There was, however, no general acceptance of the notion of a knitting pattern until the mid 19th century when the idea spread with the popularization of women's domestic literature. At this stage knitting features became common. Later, abbreviated shorthand instructions emerged for knitting as they have done for specifying moves in chess.

As with many other forms of handcraft, a sample of the work itself may often form a pattern from which further examples are generated. Thus the printed pattern – as for example in the case of knitting – emerged historically after the event rather than before it. This applies to crochet work too, but it is in knitting that we find it best exemplified.

REFERENCE Richard Rutt, *A History of Hand Knitting* (London: Batsford, 1987)

Handwritten ephemera

It may be argued that, if the individual documentary value of printed ephemera is high, that of handwritten ephemera is higher. Whereas the printed item has generalized social history content, manuscript material refers to a specific time, place, and occasion, and in that measure warrants, if anything, even closer study. Items of handwritten ephemera, like many printed items, are essentially documents of the moment. They are often brief, sometimes cryptic; more often than not they are produced without thought of more than transient validity. Typical items from the past are the FOLK RECIPE, INVENTORY, and ITINERARY.

There are also other handwritten items, less predictable and less easily allocated to a given category. Examples of these are the following:

Paper, 160 × 200 mm (6¼ × 7⅞ in); Stonehouse, Gloucestershire 15 August 1923: 'I hereby declare that I will desist from knocking, or making any other objectionable noise, either myself or by any of my employees, in my Bookbinding Shop, before the hour of 8 o'clock in the morning, and after the hour

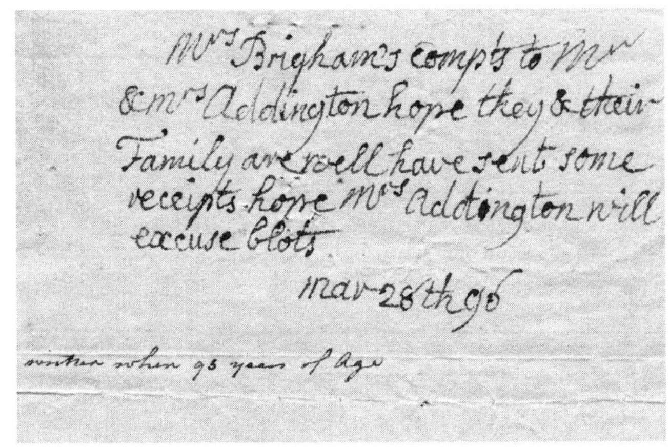
Mrs Brigham's compts to Mr & Mrs Addington hope they & their Family are well have sent some receipts hope Mrs Addington will excuse blots

mar 28th 96

written when 95 years of Age

Handwritten note of a ninety-six year old woman, 1796. 85 × 125 mm (3⅜ × 4⅞ in)

of 7 o'clock in the evening on any and every day from the above date [signed] G. Lewis'.

Paper, 325 × 205 mm (12¾ × 8⅛ in); Windsor, 7 July 1870: 'I, William Gould, being an inmate of Slough Union and formerly of Datchet Parish do hereby declare that I caught my wife Mary Gould in the act of committing adultery with a man who supplied her with coals and that this act of adultery was committed on my own premises when we resided at Datchet and I likewise declare that the aforesaid Mary Gould my wife is the Mary Gould now living at the Windsor almshouses. William Gould, His (X) mark'.

Paper, 305 × 180 mm (12 × 7⅛ in); 'Pitnacree [Pitnacrie] 27 February 1797: 'We the Proprietor and Tennants of Pitnacree make offer to Government free of any Expense of our Carts & Horses, that is one Double Cart & Driver from each plough in Case of Invasion to Convey Troops with their arms & Baggage Twenty miles through our district when ever required so to do. John Robertson, Ball[echin?], one plough, 1 Cart; Robert [?] Samnabrack, tow horses, one cart; Donald Robertson there, tow horses, one Cart; Charles McLaren in Pitnacree, one cart; Donald McLaren there. tow horses, a cart; Chas Stewart at Pitnacree a Cart'.

Paper, 35 × 135 mm (1⅜ × 5¼ in); [No date/place]: 'John March of Newbury is appointed to be a Captain of one of the Company for the Canada Expedition; and he forthwith to take care to list a Company under him'.

Paper, 135 × 210 mm (5¼ × 8¼ in) [No date/place] : 'This is to certify that this day the 5th day of February of 1884, we agreement [sic] has been entered into between M. M. Hitchcock and R. C. Crane and J. H. Stribling that if Congress in ten years from date prohibite that [sic] manufacture of intoxicating liquors, J. H. Stribling and R. C. Crane agree to make M. M. Hitchcock a present of a $50 suit of clothes; and if Congress does not pass such a bill to M. M. Hitchcock engage to write to B. C. Crane and J. H. Stribling individually acknowledging that he was mistaken. [Signed] M. M. Hitchcock; J. H. Stribling Jr; R. C. Crane'.

Paper, folded to 120 × 200 mm (4¾ × 7⅞ in); 12 April 1827: 'Sir, I beg leave to inform you that now I feel myself sufficiently well to travel I most earnestly solicit your assistance that I may leave England in the course of this week, for here I am determined not to stay one hour longer than I can possibly help. … Sir, your very grateful humble servant [signed] Ferdinand Parisa'.

Paper, 180 × 115 mm (7⅛ × 4½ in); […]head, 3 December, 1875: 'Sir Will you Pleas to Send And Let Mee Know What i am to Wright on the Wagon By return of Post it Would of Bin Writen today if i had of know Wot to Put on it Sin yrs &c Jacob Pike / to Mr Kerrel [?]'. It has to be assumed that Jacob Pike was a signwriter.

Paper, 235 × 190 mm (9¼ × 7½ in); Cowie, 5 September 1797: 'Sir, have sent you real good Whiskie seven Months old, I hope will please all that drinks it, none in the Country Like it. 4th: 1½ galls at 4/6: 6/9*d*; 5th: 5 galls at ditto £1.4.9. Total £1.11.6. Being in haste … your obedient humble servant [signed] Archd Mitchell'.

Not all ephemeral handwritten documents are self-explanatory. Some are incoherent or illegible. Others, explicit in meaning, leave much unsaid. Of this type the following are examples:

Paper, folding to 205 × 160 mm (8⅛ × 6¼ in); 20 February 1776: 'Dear Bache, Take of post Chaise and come to town directly. Yrs Ever [signed] W Phillips. Do not say you are coming to me'.

Paper, 160 × 155 mm (6¼ × 6⅛ in); [Addressee's name and address cut from sheet], 11 May 1752: 'My lady and I am very Sorry for ye Disapontement wch it will be both to your Ladyship & my Self but if I might have my Ld's whole Estate I could not Serve you for I think that every Servant goes in Danger of there Life. I hope your Ladyship will be so good as forgive me in Saying that I am Determined never to See my Ld more So I hope you will pleas to send me orders what I shall doe wth yr Keys for I cannot Stay Longer than the Latter End of the week for fear of his return. I am your Ladyships Duttyful Sert [signed] Eliz Metcalfe'.

See also ACCOUNTS, DOMESTIC; AMATEUR JOURNAL; ANONYMOUS LETTER; ARMY PAPERS; ARTISAN'S BILL/RECEIPT; DOCTOR'S BILL; EVIDENCE, NOTES OF; GAOL PAPERS; INVENTORY; MARROWBONE ANNOUNCEMENT; MENU; PLAGUE PAPERS; POSTAL DIAGNOSIS; PRESCRIPTION; RECIPE, FOLK; ROUND ROBIN; SCHOLAR'S LETTER; SERVANT'S 'CHARACTER' REFERENCE; SEATING PLAN, TABLE; SLAVE PAPERS; THREATENING LETTER; WILL; WRITING TABLET

REFERENCE Maurice Rickards, *This is Ephemera* (Newton Abbot: David & Charles, 1977)

Harlequinade ('turn-up')

The harlequinade (so-called from its frequent use of the harlequin as a central character) was a novelty story-folder popular in Britain for a period of some thirty years from its first appearance in 1765. Devised and published by Robert Sayer, who produced fifteen issues, the concertina-type folders present four vertical panels bearing illustrations of episodes in a narrative, with accompanying text verses.

Each illustration panel, measuring 185 × 80 mm (7¼ × 3⅛ in), is divided horizontally to make two flaps, attached respectively at the upper and lower edge. These, when lifted, reveal a further illustration showing a development in the narrative. In most cases, the drawing on one or other of the flaps appears to be a continuation of the picture beneath it, and lifting the flap has the effect of transforming the scene that first appears. Apart from its use of the transforming 'turn-up', in itself an innovation at the time, the harlequinade may be said to provide an early published example of the COMIC strip. The folders open out to 185 × 325 mm (7¼ × 12¾ in) and are printed in black on white paper. They sold at sixpence each, or one shilling hand-coloured, and were mounted and sewn into a wrapper, normally blue-grey in colour.

Sayer's success with the harlequinade led a number of other publishers to imitate the idea, but he remained the dominant supplier. The idea was also taken up in America.

See also MYRIORAMA

REFERENCE Peter Haining, *Movable Books* (London: New English Library, 1979)

COLLECTION Bethnal Green Museum of Childhood, London

Hat-duty stamp

Britain's hat tax was introduced by Act of Parliament (24 Geo. III, c. 51) in 1784 and was repealed (51 Geo. III, c. 70) in 1811. It applied to men's hats only. The law at first exacted threepence for hats selling at up to four shillings; sixpence for those between four and seven shillings; one shilling for those between seven and twelve shillings; and two shillings for those selling at over twelve shillings.

Persons selling hats were required to take out a LICENCE (two pounds in London; five shillings elsewhere) and to have the words 'Dealer in hats by retail' over their door. Commissioners of Stamps distributed hat stamps, which were printed on 'paper tickets' and required to be 'pasted or affixed … to the lining or inside of the crown' of the hats. Forgery of the 'tickets', as with all such fiscal devices of the time, was punishable by death. Penalties were imposed not only on the hatter for failing to use the stamp and to charge the tax, but also on the wearer of an untaxed hat. In addition, removal of a stamp for reuse was a punishable offence. The duty was nevertheless widely evaded, and a further law was passed in 1796 substituting stamps on 'silk, linen or other proper materials' for paper tickets. Shaped hat linings were required to be sent to the Stamp Office for printing with the official stamp, the linings to be fixed in hats in the ordinary course of manufacture.

Examples of hat-duty tax stamps, on either paper or on linen, are rare. Most of the labels disappeared as their respective hats were discarded. In any case the paper label, as with the glove-tax label, often became detached in use.

The paper ticket was printed from engraved plates in black, or green/blue on thin paper, measuring 25 × 76 mm (1 × 3 in). Its design, similar in character to that of the glove stamp and hair-powder stamp, bears a designation and value (e.g. 'hat duty six pence'), a crown, and the price range it applies to. Also included is a numeral indicating the impression number of the printing plate.

Stamped linings are reported as having survived in a number of hats and, very rarely, as detached silk or linen specimens (for the most part unused printer's proofs). They bear a crown, lion, and unicorn and, below the words 'Stamp Office', a panel shows details (as in the paper ticket). There is a variant for each of six tax levels, and numerals indicate plate impression numbers and any re-engraving. Proofs on paper were held for reference at the Stamp Office as a check on counterfeits; they appear as red/brown images, approximately 90 mm (3½ in) wide, on ribbed cream paper.

It is recorded that in September 1798 John Collins was caught with a forged printing plate, ready inked, with dampened linen ready to receive its impression. His hand bore the ink he had just wiped from the surface of the plate. He was sentenced to death.

See also TAX STAMP; TAXATION PAPERS

REFERENCE Marcus Samuel, 'British Hat Tax Stamps 1784–1811', *Philately* (London: January/February 1964)

SOCIETIES American Revenue Association; The Cinderella Stamp Club

Hidden-name card

The hidden-name card appeared in the 1880s as a part of the series of calling-card novelties that swept America during the rage for chromolithographs at the latter end of the century. The card, besides bearing a pre-printed chromolithographed design (with or without the addition of shaping, lapped corners, silk fringes, and other elements), also carries a hinged SCRAP concealing the bearer's name. At first sight the card appears to be purely decorative, since the name is visible only when the scrap is lifted.

As with the rest of the multitudinous range of chromolithographed 'fancy cards', the customer's name was printed to order on packs of twelve, twenty-five, forty, fifty, or a hundred, each set providing a variety of designs. The designs often show a hand with a bouquet, or clasped hands against a garland of flowers, and were sometimes treated with ground mica to add 'glitter'; a cherub or other portrait could be replaced (for 30 cents extra per dozen) by a photo miniature of the bearer 'gummed and perforated, similar to postage stamps'.

Prices for hidden-name cards with a name printed to order were commonly 15 cents per dozen, $1 for fifty. Very superior cards cost much more. One series, called by the Connecticut Steam Card Works the 'Gold leaf Victoria', is described as being of 'finest French satin enamel with pure gold leaf border and ornament... fringed with the best assorted combination silk fringe and backed'. The printed name is covered by 'a lovely Berlin scrap picture, with cherub's head peeping out through the centre of a resplendent gold and silver star clasp, that when lifted reveals the sentiment and colors within'. This type of card cost 90 cents per dozen. The hidden-name card (like the many other decorative calling cards of the American 1880s) was virtually unknown in Britain.

See also CHROMO; PRICE LIST; PUZZLE

Hidden-name card, late 19th century American. Chromolithographed, lightly embossed, cut out, and hinged to a card with a name printed on it. 60 × 95 mm (2⅜ × 3¾in)

Hold-to-light

A 'magic image' novelty based on the principle of the earlier 'protean view' (*see* TRANSPARENCY), the hold-to-light picture was widely used in Victorian popular printing. It involved the printing of a secondary image on the reverse of a primary image. When the print was viewed against the light, the composite picture presented a radical change. Thus, guardian angels were made to float above praying children, window lights appeared in daytime cities, volanoes erupted, and sunsets transformed a clear blue sky.

Hold-to-light advertisement for Pears' soap of the late 19th century. *Left:* seen by reflected light; *right:* seen by transmitted light. Chromolithographed by Grover & Co., Nottingham. 214 × 142 mm (8⅜ × 5⅝in)

Two factors were basic: one was the need for accurate front-to-back register; the other was translucency of the printing paper. Printers became adept at fine placing small but vital elements (scowls transformed to smiles; closed lids to bright eyes), and paper thickness increased without serious loss of the secondary image. It was a novelty that retained its appeal to the early 20th century, appearing in countless guises as 'puzzles' or 'teasers'.

A typical example of 1889 is a handbill advertising the Christmas issue of the *Graphic*. A sleeping woman is pictured with a verse: 'After feasting your eyes on my face so bright / Hold my portrait quite softly up to the light / You waken me then from the sweetest of slumber / To gaze with delight on your Christmas number'. When held to the light the portrait's eyes are seen to be duly open.

The principle had variants. In one version the secondary image was invisible by direct vision from the back, the image being concealed under a layer of blank paper. Another had blank paper on both sides, presenting the appearance of a totally blank card; the silhouette image within such versions was usually risqué. In a further variant, fragmented portions of a legend appeared on one side, the complementary fragments on the other; the wording thus made no sense until viewed against the light. An unusual presentation shows a blind-embossed image of angels surrounding the figure of the Madonna and Child. The statuesque lower relief is backed by an exactly corresponding chromolithographed rendering of the image, providing a colour half-tone confirmation of the three-dimensional grouping.

Holiday card

This is the term, still in use today, which was originally applied by American manufacturers of chromolithographed 'fancy cards' to cards suitable for use at Christmas, New Year, Easter, and for birthdays. Like many of the chromolithographed cards of the time, they bore no thematic image; they simply presented a decorative design, commonly of flowers, birds, cherubs, etc., and were overprinted with wording as desired. The scholars' REWARD OF MERIT was produced in the same way.

See also CHROMO; GREETINGS CARD

Hornbook

For the reader accustomed to thinking of a book as a presentation of a number of pages, the word hornbook may appear misleading. The hornbook, dating from the 15th century and perhaps the earliest of widely used teaching aids, was in fact a small alphabet sheet pasted on a flat wooden base, and covered with a sheet of transparent horn. A handle at the foot (often pierced for stringing to the pupil's waist) and strips of metal tacked at the edges of the horn to hold it in place, completed the device.

Its resemblance to a bat used in ball games (and its unofficial use as such) brought it the alternative name BATTLEDORE. Tuer (1897/1968) cites a Mr E. F. Shepherd from Staines, who recalled the words of an 1840s schoolgirl: 'Granny taught me to read, and [producing a hornbook] here's my horn-bat'. The name was later to be transferred to a folding card, also for classroom reference but no longer much suited for use in ball games.

The hornbook varied in size. The main panel, excluding the handle, measured anything from about 85 × 58mm (3⅜ × 2¼in) to twice that size. It also appeared in other materials with its alphabet and other inscriptions engraved directly into silver, ivory, bone, brass, leather, etc, using neither paper nor horn. It was also sometimes available as a novelty at fairs in the form of gingerbread, the child being rewarded with mouthfuls while learning.

The hornbook's text, commonly printed on parchment or paper, remained fairly constant. Essentially it set out the alphabet in lower-case and capitals, the Benediction and the Lord's Prayer, traditionally including a cross (Christ's cross or 'criss-cross') as the first character. The terms 'hornbook' and 'criss-cross' row came to be used to connote the level of the beginner, in ordinary speech as well as in education.

The hornbook was widely used in colonial American schoolrooms in the 17th and 18th century, often as an import from England, sometimes American-made. It is commonly seen as peculiar to English-speaking peoples, but it appears to have been known at least in Germany, Holland, and Italy as well. Sigfred Taubert in his *Bibliopola* (1966, p.45) has a 16th-century print by Carracci showing the basket of an itinerant printseller hung with hornbooks.

Once among the commonest of everyday objects, the hornbook has become a rarity. Since its disappearance in the early years of the 19th century it has been the subject of much scholarly research, notably by Tuer (1897/1968).

REFERENCES Beulah Folmsbee, *A Little History of the Horn-Book* (Boston: Horn Book Magazine, 1942); Andrew W. Tuer, *The History of the Horn-Book* (London: Leadenhall Press, 1897; reprinted New York: Blom, 1968)

COLLECTIONS Bagford Collection, British Library; John Johnson Collection, Bodleian Library, Oxford; New York Public Library

Hospital recommendation document

Printed forms issued by hospitals, infirmaries, and dispensaries, were used as a means of controlling acceptances for treatment. The forms provided a single solution to the two perennial problems of medical charity: on one hand they served to contain the tidal wave of demand, on the other they enlisted the aid of those who could afford to give.

In their most common form, recommendation documents ('tickets', 'letters', or 'cards') were made available to governors of hospitals, and to private individuals who supported the institution and received the printed blank in numbers according to the size of their donation. Benefactors were thus enabled to channel genuine cases among the sick and poor for treatment, avoiding out-of-pocket gifts to all and sundry. Typically, the subscriber received six printed forms per year for a guinea, or three every year for life for a single payment of ten guineas (in some cases special facilities were offered to subscribers' servants, who might be received as in-patients for one guinea per week).

The indigent patient took the completed form, on a named day of the week, to the hospital in question where, according to pressure of demand, he or she might or might not be admitted. One commentator, Dr J. Hunter (1779), wrote that 'Before a recommendation can be procured and the stated day come round, the sick person is either better or so much worse that he cannot be moved, or is perhaps dead'.

Recommendation documents – sometimes, though rarely, illustrated with a picture of the institution – appeared in many sizes, ranging from papers measuring 390 × 240mm (15⅜ × 9½in) to cards measuring 90 × 120mm (3½ × 4¾in). All bore a résumé of their use and instructions to prospective patients. In the 1840s the London Hospital's 'petition paper' pointed out that, except for cases of great urgency, no child under seven years of age, nor pregnant women, nor mentally deranged person would be admitted, nor would 'persons having measles, scarlet fever, small pox, itch or other infectious disease or the venereal distemper, or in a state of confirmed consumption, or deemed by the physicians and surgeons ... incurable'.

Out-patients were to 'preserve their ticket folded, under cover, with the printed side outwards, and not to omit bringing them'. In a typical example, a bold overprinting in red warns: 'the public are requested not to attend to this certificate if presented for the purpose of begging'.

Many recommendation documents required out-patients to bring with them a bottle, cork, and gallipot for medicines, and warned that non-attendance for more than fourteen days would render the ticket void. Some also pointed out that cured patients were to surrender their 'letter of recommendation' at the hospital in exchange for a 'letter of thanks', which they are to return to the governor who recommended them. This last had the effect of keeping the benefactor apprised of the patient's condition. In some cases a printed document was also sent, advising of the completion of the matter.

In one form or another the systems involving 'Recommendations' lasted well into the 1930s.

Hostel admission ticket

The 1890s saw the setting up of numerous charitable services for the workless and homeless in the form of hostels. Stemming from the provision of night shelters and free breakfasts, such hostels provided an alternative to the private-enterprise lodging houses, which were notorious for their squalor and overcrowding. The hostels were run by various bodies, including in some cases, local authorities, but notably by the Salvation Army and the Rowton House organization. Admission tickets to these were made available either directly to applicants at the entrance or for distribution by church workers and other charitable agencies.

The tickets, commonly costing sixpence, allowed the visitor a bed for the night. Cheaper still was the charge at the Salvation Army hostel at Blackfriars, London. For an inclusive charge of four pence guests could have supper, bed, and breakfast. Another halfpenny bought a shave (from a fellow guest). Also available from fellow guests were halfpennyworths of such commodities as broken pork pies, sausage ends, and the sweepings of the ham and beef shop counter. A halfpennyworth of cigar and cigarette ends, culled from the streets, could also be had.

The Rowton House 'chain' was started in 1892 by Lord Rowton. Visionary and philanthropist, he conceived the setting up of 'working men's hostels' which would improve on the facilities of the lodging house but at similar prices. The first Rowton House opened at Vauxhall, London, on 31 December 1892. The idea was afterwards imitated elsewhere in Britain and in Europe and the United States. The last Rowton House closed in 1982.

Hotel/tour coupon

Introduced in Britain in the 1870s by Thomas Cook, the hotel coupon freed the tourist from the burden of carrying cash while assuring virtually guaranteed services *en route*. It entitled the holder to meals and accommodation at listed hotels; it could be used without prior booking and required no signature or other verification. A typical set of three provided for 'plain breakfast or tea', 'table d'hôte', and 'bed, lights and attendance'. They were purchased in booklet or folder form, each day's set of three forming a perforated unit to be divided as required.

The idea was extended for use within the United Kingdom, a special 'English, Scotch and Irish Series' providing services in 207 hotels and meals on board Scottish steamers. Cook's coupons were also available for hotel service on railways abroad. A surviving example entitles the holder to 'early tea' on a train of the Royal State Railways of Siam. In another, the proprietor of the Railway Hotel, Nankow, Peking is requested from Cook's offices in Ludgate Circus, London, to provide the traveller with one sedan chair 'with four coolies from Nankow to the Ming Tombs and return'.

The coupon concept reached its logical conclusion with the introduction of the traveller's cheque by American Express in 1891.

REFERENCE Janice Anderson and Edmund Swinglehurst, *Ephemera of Travel and Transport* (London: New Cavendish Books, 1981)

Hotel papers

The origins of the hotel lie in the religious 'hospice' – which provided a charitable refuge for the traveller – and later the hostelry or inn. The inn was for centuries a doubtful luxury. It offered the only available overnight resting place in a world of comfortless carriages, primitive roads, and highwaymen.

Early evidence of travelling conditions and of the dominance of the horse as motive power is provided by items referred to on innkeepers' bills. Typical are such entries as 'Servants' eating etc.; horses hay and corn; fire in lodging room; post horses; tolls; lights; rushlights; hostler' (Bedale, c.1840). Other printed bills include 'carriage washing & greasing; post-chaise' (Richmond, c.1845); and 'saddler; blacksmith' (Ormskirk, c.1845). These entries conjure up a vivid picture of the rigours of their time and place.

Innkeepers' bills, commonly about 160 × 100 mm (6¼ × 4 in), are mostly printed in black and are single sided. They carry subtitles such as 'neat post-chaise careful drivers' and 'lock-up coach houses'. Some carry a little information about mileages to neighbouring towns. In cases where they are printed on both sides, the back is devoted to a comprehensive 'traveller's posting guide', which lists not only towns and distances but names of inns and their respective keepers (*see* ITINERARY). This information also appears in many cases on the backs of innkeepers' trade cards, which also form a major category of inn and hotel

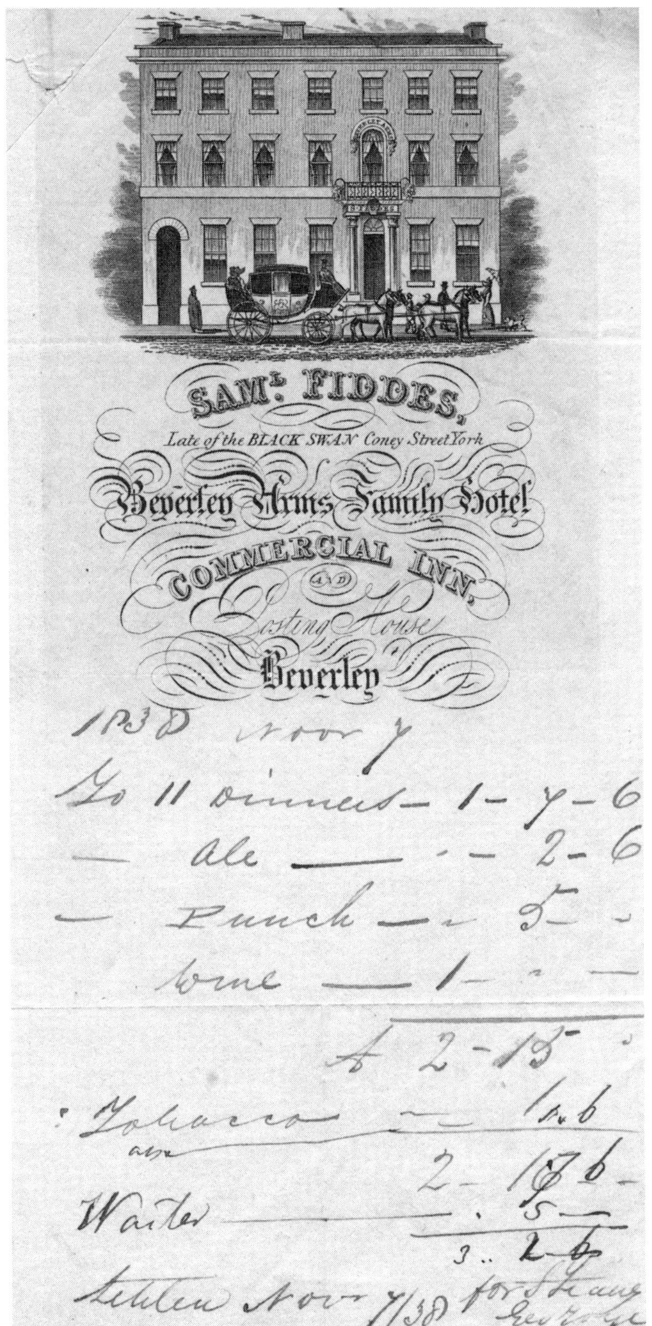
SAML. FIDDES,
Late of the BLACK SWAN Coney Street York
Beverley Arms Family Hotel
COMMERCIAL INN,
AND
Posting House
Beverley

1838 Nov 7
To 11 dinners — 1 - 7 - 6
— Ale — - - 2 - 6
— Punch — - 5 -
Wine — 1 - -
£ 2 - 15 -
Tobacco — 1/6
2 - 16 6
Waiter — 5
3 .. 2 6
Settled Nov 7/38 for S Fiddes George

Hotel bill of Samuel Fiddes, Beverley, Yorkshire, November 1838. Intaglio-printed heading and manuscript. 227 × 115 mm (9 × 4½ in)

ephemera. The inn catered almost exclusively for the traveller. A one- or two-night stay was normally as long as could be allowed on a journey that might, on the continent of Europe, take anything up to a month.

The hotel, the hostelry's successor, sought to provide a destination rather than a staging post. Many early hotel bills dispensed with the pre-printed listing of the inn, using instead a narrow-format blank, typically about 350 × 100 mm (13¾ × 4 in), and headed only with an engraved title-piece (with or without illustration), which was often printed from the copper plate of the proprietors' TRADE CARD. Details of charges were added day by day, end-of-page totals being carried forward to following sheets.

With the advent of the 'luxury' hotel in the late 1860s, hotel bills became more consciously elaborate. Many reverted to the use of printed lists of items, but provided space for extended stays. Hotels in continental Europe printed listings in English. In hotels of exceptional elegance, in which the gentry might be expected to make a really long stay, the bill was often prepared as a multi-page handwritten booklet.

One example of this, page size 310 × 220 mm (12¼ × 8⅝ in), covers the story of the Duke of Hamilton and his party of seven (plus two servants) for the period 22 November 1857 to 1 February 1858 at the Hotel Victoria, Nice. In a hand-sewn 56-page booklet (of which a four-page section is devoted to carriage-hire) expenditure on each item is listed separately. The list includes apartments for the servants for six days, their arrival in advance, their food, candles, firewood, etc., and records the temporary absence of the Duke and Duchess on a Christmas visit to the French Consul (Nice at that time was Sardinian) and the arrival of guests to join the party. Evidence of mishap appears: '1 broken lamp globe and glass funnel 7 francs, 1 broken tumbler 5 francs, 1 broken broom 4 francs'; also of mischance: 'nurse, 1 day 5 francs, nightlight 75c [27 times]'. Additional items listed are candles, matches, and writing paper; footbaths, hot and cold; and, on one occasion, 'a big bath'. The document also discloses that the Duke received a discount of 850 francs on his total bill of 16,784 francs.

Among the earliest forms of promotion for the hotel industry was the tariff, commonly a printed folder, listing the amenities and charges of individual establishments. The tariff card provides an illuminating guide to the development of the industry as a whole and, in successive cards for a single hotel, changes in specific terms and conditions. The advent of new amenities is carefully recorded, and they provide a sharp contrast with the survival arrangements of former times. The First Avenue Hotel, Holborn, offers: 'Sleeping apartment lighted by the electric light from fifteen shillings per day; eight course dinner, dessert and coffee, five shillings; sponge, hip or sitz bath in bedroom, sixpence.' Special rates for visitors' servants appeared widely on tariffs until the early 1920s. The tariff card for Fords Hotel, Richmond, Virginia, carries an amenity note in a two-word legend: 'Electric bells', and The Round Hill Hotel, Northampton, Massachusetts, informs guests that it is 'connected by telephone with the centre of the town' and has 'almost absolute freedom from mosquitos'.

The tariff card was backed by an increasing number of leaflets, brochures, and booklets, most of them illustrated, and many conveying images of elegance and extravagance beyond the normal reach of most potential visitors. The 'luxury hotel' concept arose from hoteliers' desire to attract the travelling aristocracy – customers who had hitherto been more inclined to stay with each other than at inns and lodging houses. Moreover, these splendours did not come amiss to the aspiring middle classes.

A major landmark in the travel field was the advent of Thomas Cook's *The Exhibition Advertiser and Excursionist* (1851) to promote the Great Exhibition of that year in Hyde Park, London. It continued to be published with this title until 1903 when it became the *Travellers Gazette*. Cook's first European excursion was organized in 1855, and as his business grew hoteliers in tourist resorts began to benefit from his popularization of holidays, and took to more overt advertising, principally by means of attractive labels. The ephemera of the hotel industry include Cook's 'Hotel coupons', which were valid as payment at a wide range of hotels for meals and accommodation.

See also HOTEL/TOUR COUPON; INN TALLY

House journal

Lloyd's List, first published in 1696 as *Lloyd's News*, may be regarded as the earliest of house magazines. The publication was introduced by Edward Lloyd, the London coffee-house keeper, as an information facility for his customers, though it was soon to expand into a national institution, thus outgrowing its original role.

More commonly considered the earliest house magazine was the *British Mercury*, published in 1710 by the Company of London Insurers (afterwards the Sun Fire Office) and delivered, to those policy holders who desired it, three times a week. The magazine was not much in demand however, and in 1716 the company replaced it with the *Historical Register*, a quarterly, which ran for some twenty-two years. Successive editors – Aaron Hill, David Jones, Alexander Justice, and Charles Gildon – received low payment and much criticism. Charles Gildon fell foul of the committee of management for publishing unfriendly references to the Moroccan ambassador, and was ordered thenceforth 'to never intermeddle with any Publick Ministers affaires . . . under penalty to be dismissed immediately'.

The next recorded house magazines date from the mid 19th century. The London and Dover Railway *Advertiser* appeared in 1844–45 and Thacker and Co.'s monthly, also first appearing in 1844, lasted until 1853. In America, the first was the *Mechanic*, put out by H. B. Smith Machine Co. of Vermont, 1847–1914. The oldest surviving American house magazine is *Protection*, published by the Travellers Insurance Company of Hartford, Connecticut. The oldest British house journal still published in the 1980s is National Cash Register's *National Post*, dating from 1899.

House journals proliferated to such an extent in the 20th century that they became essential components of the public relations activities of successful companies and institutions.

Household regulations

Household regulations had become reduced by the mid 20th century to a servants' timetable pinned up in the kitchen. Initially they appeared in the monasteries, castles, and palaces of the Middle Ages. In these major households, as in the armed forces, hospitals, asylums, and colleges, duties and responsibilities at every level were set out in detail. Regulations appeared under such titles as 'Rules and Orders' or 'Regulations and Instructions', and dealt in chapter and verse with each individual function in the structure of the household. Built on generations of experience, they sought not only to provide for every natural contingency, but to forestall any conceived wrongdoing. As a generalized body of order and control, they were clearly to be reckoned with. Within the close-knit communities concerned, they had virtually the force of statute law.

They present a considerable literature. Girouard (1978) cites Royal Household Regulations dating back to 1279 and 'Other Household Regulations' from the same period. 'Other' regulations include *The Northumberland Household Book c.1520* (London, 1770) and *Some Rules and Orders for the Government of the House of an Earle c.1605* (London, 1821). Also cited are two documents in the Huntington Library, California: 'Regulations of James Brydges, first Duke of Chandos, of Cannons, Middlesex, 1721'.

One of these documents includes a lengthy instruction to the 'Usher of the Halle'. In addition to sweeping and cleaning the

Poole's Family Account-book, and Ladies' and Gentlemen's useful Memoranda, for 1828 (Chiswick). Letterpress and manuscript, printed by C. and C. Whittingham. Page size 200 × 160 mm (7⅞ × 6¼ in)

place, and keeping out dogs, he is required 'upon Sundays and all other Times when Strangers are here as soon as he hears the Bell ring for Diner to repair to the Kitchin Door with his Gown on and Staff in his Hand and walk before the Clerk of the Kitchin and the Service into the Parlour, where he is to stay at the Lower end of the Room till the Dishes are sett upon the Table and this he is likewise to do as every Course is Served up'.

The 20th century brought domestic service almost to vanishing point, both in terms of personnel and extent of duties. By the end of the century the concept of household regulations survived only in the most august establishments. At the level of the one-servant family, vestigial as it was, there was even some doubt as to the desirability of written instructions of any kind.

See also HOUSEKEEPING ACCOUNTS

REFERENCE Mark Girouard, *Life in the English Country House* (New Haven: Yale University Press, 1978)

Housekeeping accounts

The great country houses of the 19th century, with their large staff and extensive estates, required more than kitchen-table accountancy, and the disciplines of estate management grew sharper as the century progressed. Records were kept not only in the form of account books, many of which survive in record offices and other archives, but as printed FORMS for the day-to-day use of staff. These often survive as discarded fall-out. Filled in, they provide an insight into the private life of the stately home, but even as unused blanks – which they more usually are – they convey much. Specially printed for the house in question, the layout and detail of individual forms varied, but typically they were foolscap in format and covered the activities of a single week or other stated period.

A case in point is a foolscap sheet, unused, watermarked 1841, and headed 'Expenses of Housekeeping at Exton Hall'. Divided vertically into columns headed 'Stock', 'Consumed', 'Added', 'Remains', 'Price', and 'Total', the form has horizontal divisions for 'Wines, &c', 'Groceries', 'Butchers' Meat', 'Bread and Beer', and 'Coals'. It allows for the insertion of the period covered. The listing under 'Wines, &c' may be taken to convey something of the levels of expectation at the house. It reads: 'Port, Steward's Room ditto; Claret; Hock; Sherry; Madeira; Calcavella; Mountain; Moselle; Hermitage; Grave; Vierge; Burgundy; Champaigne [sic] Malmsey; Paxarata; Guarachecho; Marcella; Rum; Brandy; Wax Candles.'

Similar forms for other establishments deal with transactions between 'The Farm' and 'The House', showing 'Milk from the Cows: Consumed in the House; Sold; Consumed in the Farm; Used for making Cheese; Butter made; Consumed in the House; Sold; Salted down; Cheese made; Consumed; Sold'.

See also HOUSEHOLD REGULATIONS

COLLECTION Rural History Centre, The University of Reading

Hymn number card

Designed for use on church hymn boards, these cards are usually printed as single white numerals on a black background or black ones on a white ground. They commonly measure some 80 mm (3⅛ in) in depth, and come in boxed sets trimmed top and bottom as required to fit into slots on wooden hymn boards.

Ice papers

In America, before the advent of the refrigerator (1913), urban ice delivery was widespread. Ice waggons made regular deliveries by the day, week, or month, the customer indicating by a window card how much ice was required on any particular day. A typical card was octagonal, allowing display in the window in four positions; in each of these appeared a large number: twenty-five, fifty, seventy-five, one hundred. A note in the centre of the card reads: 'When you want ice put this card in the window. The figures at the top of the card will show how much is desired'. The device obviated unnecessary journeys for the delivery man.

There were many hundreds of ice suppliers in the United States and the ice waggon was a familiar sight. The ice industry generated numerous categories of ephemera. These included not only the promotional handbill and TRADE CARD, but business stationery of all kinds: invoices, receipts, etc., and sometimes coupons which were supplied to the customer in booklet form, individual items being detached and handed to the ice man. The coupons could be cashed only in ice.

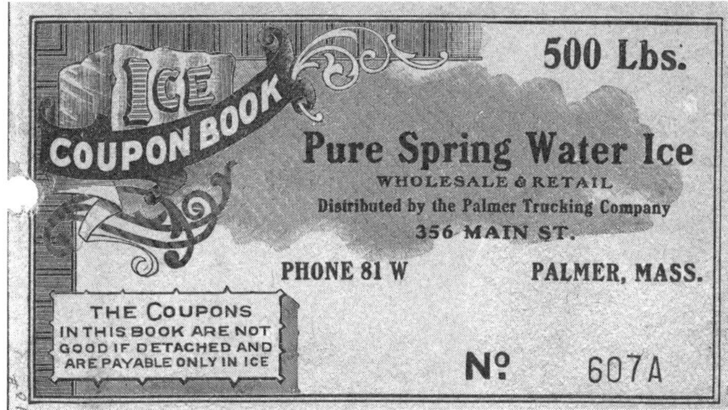

Cover of ice-coupon book issued by Palmer, Massachusetts, c. 1920. Letterpress on buff paper. 68 × 127 mm (2⅝ × 5 in)

Illuminated address

Illumination here relates to the elaborate calligraphic rendering of texts, with stress on colourful embellishment of capital initials and headings. The addresses referred to are the texts of thanks and appreciation often bestowed at 19th-century retirement or reward ceremonies. They normally appear as a single sheet measuring from 510 × 380 mm (20 × 14⅞ in) to 760 × 510 mm (30 × 20 in). In rare cases they may appear as a series of smaller sheets, for example 350 × 230 mm (13¾ × 9 in), bound in book form. The book form was also adopted as a means of conveying signatures accompanying the address.

The genre reached its highest point in Britain in the 1890s, and many lithographers and engravers ran profitable lines of businesses supplying the demand.

Essentially, the illuminated address consisted of a text panel and a massive decorative border. The text panel clearly had to be executed to order, but the border, a general effusion of floral ornamentation, was usually pre-printed by chromolithography. In many instances the border-work represented one-third to one-half of the overall design area, and the use of pre-printing (rarely recognized as such by the recipient) represented a major production economy.

Illuminated addresses reveal a remarkably high standard of skill in terms of execution, and occasionally the layout and treatment of the text show some sensitivity. On the whole, however, their design suffers from over-elaboration and overcrowding. Their texts are remarkable for their longwindedness and occasional lapses of spelling and syntax.

Imagerie populaire

The expression is applied not to popular prints in general but to a specific type of picture popularized in France over a long period and having its heyday in the second half of the 19th century. The prints, which had appeared originally in the Rhineland, found their full fame in the period 1850 to 1870 as the speciality of the printing house of Jean-Charles Pellerin, later Pellerin et Cie, which was established as a family enterprise at Épinal in 1796. The name of the town became so closely identified with the style that *images d'Épinal* became a generic term, regardless of whether the print was actually printed there or elsewhere. Metz, Nancy, Lille, Paris, and Strasbourg also had their *imagiers*.

Images d'Épinal continued to be produced through most of the twentieth century; the number of different sheets (all numbered) ran into thousands, and the total production of such prints must have been vast. They were commonly printed by lithography and crudely hand-stencilled, individual sheets measuring around 390 × 290 mm (15⅜ × 11⅜ in) – though sometimes in a landscape format. Some were published in volume form with such titles as *Album d'Images*. Typically, prints take the form of sequences of pictures with legends in comic-strip form. Some tell simple stories of contemporary life or of the past, others retell old fables and other stories; yet others show sets of caricatures or military subjects. A very common form of

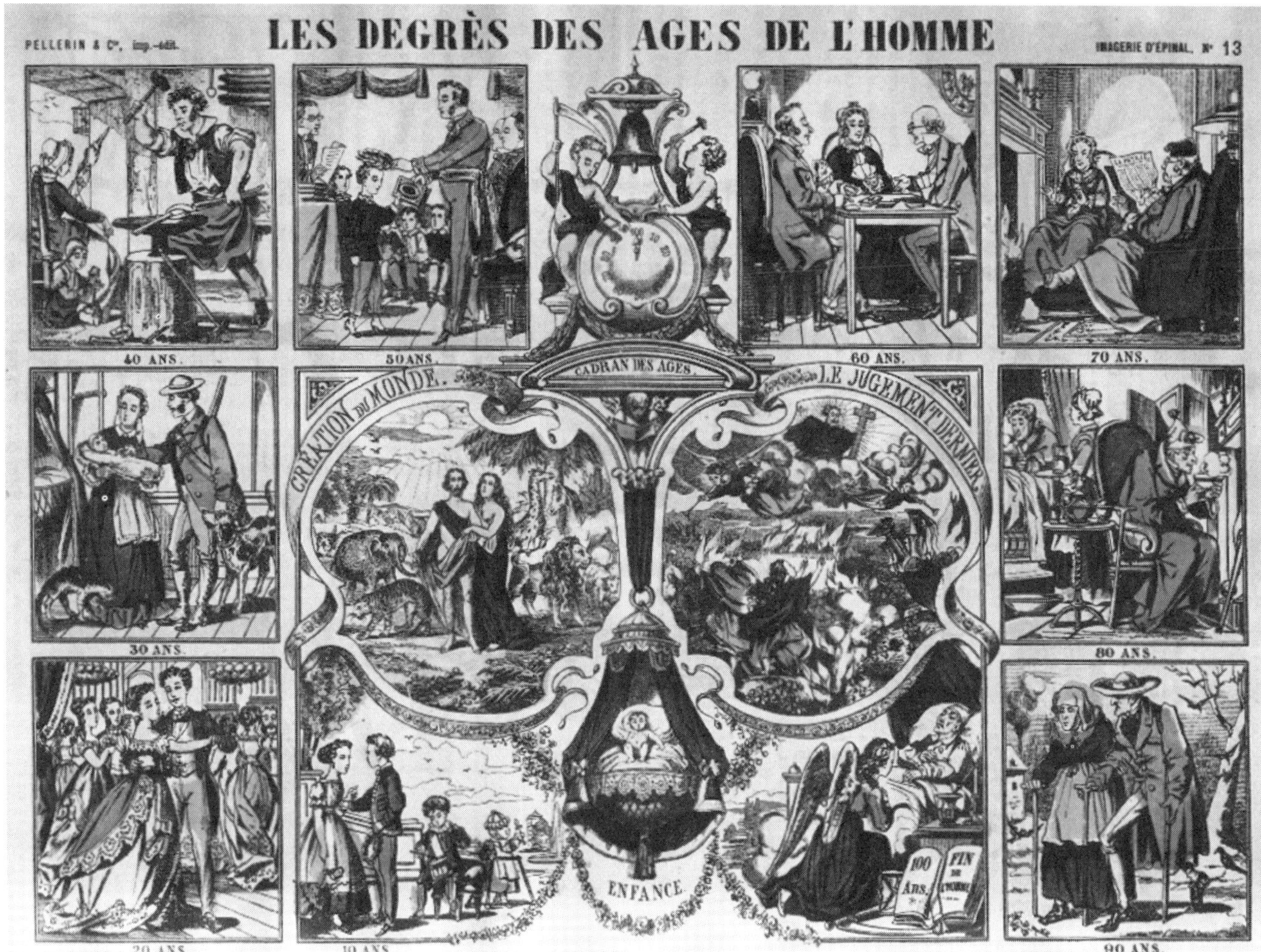

Imagerie d'Épinal, no. 13, 'Les Degrès des Ages de l'Homme', probably 1870s. Lithographed in black and stencilled in colour. 280 × 390 mm (11 × 15⅜in)

sheet depicted sets of soldiers (in multiples) to be cut out and turned into individual paper soldiers.

Imagerie populaire first emerged in the 15th and 16th century and pictured religious subjects, many of them saints and biblical figures. They came to be used not only as devotional images but protective icons, shielding their owners, and their families and cattle, from harm. The anti-religious sentiment at the time of the French Revolution put a stop to the trade in religious images, and printers found it prudent to diversify. There followed an upsurge of secular prints, including children's story illustrations, toy theatre material, 'comic-strip' adventure stories, cut-out toys and models, and historic and contemporary scenes.

Censorship had been a recurrent problem. Limitations were imposed on the publication of prints in the Napoleonic era, and images of the most innocent kind risked adverse interpretation. In the later years of the 19th century popular prints were often remarkably neutral, depending for their sales on the appeal of such subjects as 'The Opening of the Paris–Orleans Railway', 1849, and 'Cinderella', 1862.

See also CUT-OUT TOY

REFERENCES Denis Martin and Bernard Huin, *Images d'Épinal* (Québec and Paris: Musée du Québec and Réunion des Musées Nationaux, 1995); Edward Ryan, *Paper Soldiers: the Illustrated History of Printed Paper Armies of the 18th, 19th, & 20th centuries* (London: Golden Age, 1995)

Imprint, printer's

Under an Act of Parliament of 1799 (39 Geo. 3, c. 79) it was required that '... every person who shall print any paper or book whatsoever, which shall be meant... to be published... shall print on the front of every such paper, if the same shall be printed on one side only, and upon the first and last leaves of every paper or book which shall consist of more than one leaf... his or her name, and the name of the city, town, parish or place and also the name (if any) of the square, street, lane, court, or place, in which his or her dwelling house... shall be'. The Act prescribed a fine of twenty pounds for every copy of such paper not so imprinted.

The Act, avowedly for the suppression of sedition and treason, remains in force today. It was part of a long-standing effort to control Britain's press. Another of its provisions required printers to register with local justices, and receive certificates of approval before entering into business. An additional section required a copy of every paper printed to be 'carefully preserved for six months', with the name of the commissioning client inscribed on it, for production on demand from a Justice of the Peace. This last provision, which also remains in force today, has had the effect of preserving numerous files of printed work, many of which are valuable sources for the student of printed ephemera. The habit of keeping file copies became so ingrained that items were often kept long after the statutory six-month period.

The section of the Act dealing with the imprint specifically exempts certain items. These include papers printed for parliament, impressions of engravings, trade cards and professional stationery, and auction papers. Later Acts exempted banknotes, bills of lading, certain legal documents, insurance papers, receipts, and some other items. Many of these are in fact found with imprints: fear of prosection led printers to take no chances. Under the 1961 Printer's Imprint Act, formal exemption was granted to papers which do not contain 'words grouped together in a manner calculated to convey a message', thus additionally excluding such items as cloakroom tickets and price tags.

It may be noted that case law provides the printer with an additional incentive for including an imprint. An action decided in 1822 established that without their name appearing on the item printers cannot claim costs for work and materials.

Printers' imprints also occasionally provide gratuitous trade information. An example from around the 1870s advertises the printer's services: 'Bills this size (and paper) printed for 1/6d per 1000'. The legend precedes the normal printer's address, in this case Leadenhall Street, London. Later examples include offers of apprenticeship details and, in some cases, references to extramural printing.

See also IMPRINT, PUBLISHER'S

Imprint, publisher's

A distinction is drawn in book publishing between the printer's imprint and the publisher's imprint. In modern times it is customary for the publisher's imprint to appear at the foot of the title-page as the responsible issuing body. On the verso of the title-page the name of the publisher appears again, together with details of publishing dates, copyright, etc. Beneath this, often at the foot, appears the printer's imprint. If the law is strictly observed, the printer's name also appears on the last page of the book (*see* IMPRINT, PRINTER'S).

The above distinction expresses the separation of functions between publisher and printer, the printer serving only as contractor to the publisher. The expression 'publisher's imprint' therefore relates to the prime mover, regardless of who set the type, printed, and bound the book. The printer in this respect stands in the same relationship to the publisher as the author – an outside supplier.

In the early days of printing this separation of functions did not exist; printer and publisher were one. In this period it was customary for the imprint, or colophon as it was then called, to appear at the back of the work, as it had been with scribes in handwritten books (Greek, *kolophon*: summit, finishing touch). It was during the 16th and 17th centuries that it moved to the front.

The publisher's imprint might be thought to lie outside the field of the ephemerist, but there are two aspects of the matter that are relevant. There exists, in the first place, a larger body of 'book-like' ephemeral material – the ALMANAC, CHAPBOOK, jest book, NEWSPAPER, pamphlet, SONGSTER/SONG-BOOK, etc. – in which the publisher's imprint is a significant feature; and secondly, in many of these cases, contrary to current practice, printer and publisher are one.

In these areas the study of publishers' imprints, as with printers' imprints in the case of single-sheet ephemera, is a useful aid in ephemera research. Typical of many printer-publisher entrepreneurs was William Dicey, a 17th-century jobbing printer and highly successful printer and publisher of chapbooks. Like many of his colleagues, he added patent medicines to his stock-in-trade, and by the 1720s was a national name. Similarly, in New York in the mid 19th century, the name of William H. Murphy appears as publisher on miniature 'songsters' ('national and patriotic songs as sung by the principal vocalists'). He too was a jobbing printer, bookseller, and stationer, and diversified into valentines, envelopes, steel pens, wafers, sealing wax, and ink. Like Dicey, he offered 'a large assortment of all the patent medicines of the day...'.

In pamphlets and political tracts, too, publishers' imprints may offer a field of research. In numerous periods of suppression the writers of unpopular or illegal printed matter have been at pains to conceal their whereabouts, falsifying imprints accordingly. This was particularly so in periods of religious persecution, though falsification of imprints was also done for commercial reasons. In America prior to the revolution, when a British imprint continued to sell better than the home-produced article, it was not unheard of for American-printed publications to bear London imprints.

Improvised currency

The distinction between improvised currency and other emergency issues (referred to as *Notgeld:* German, emergency or token money) lies in its use of other items (e.g. playing cards and postage stamps) or unorthodox materials and methods (e.g. typewritten cards) as temporary substitutes. Opinions vary on points of detail, but the orthodox currency note, albeit a 'special' or 'emergency' issue, may be seen to fall more properly within the field of notaphily than of ephemera studies.

Typical examples of improvised currency are the Canadian playing card issues of the late 17th century (*see* PLAYING CARD, SECONDARY USES), the postage stamp substitutes of the Spanish Civil War, and the hand-signed typewritten makeshifts used in the siege of O'Okiep in the Boer War.

Canadian playing-card money, introduced by Jacques de Meulles, the Intendant of the French garrison in Québec, as a means of paying his troops when coins were scarce, began as an improvisation. In the event it became institutionalized, forming the dominant element in the colony's economy for seventy-five years. It also served as a model for others, emerging in France in the revolutionary period as a 'billet de confiance' (a substitute for the discredited ASSIGNAT), and also in the Dutch colony of Surinam, where shortage of coin forced the Governor to find a substitute. The playing card appeared again as currency in Germany and Austria during the inflation period after World War I.

Though at first sight a curious choice as a currency substitute, the playing card has a number of built-in qualifications for the role. It is familiar to the public at large, more or less uniform in substance and format, robust enough to survive repeated handling over a long period, and may readily be halved or quartered to furnish portions of the single unit.

The postage stamp is less well adapted to use as currency, although its acceptance as a token of value is a major advantage. At one time or another it has been authorized as improvised legal tender in thirty-four countries. The problem of wear and tear has generally been solved by affixing the stamp to a card, on the reverse of which was printed the formal authorization for its use as currency and instructions for use. In some cases the stamp has been printed directly on to the card, as in Spain in 1938.

Stamp money has also circulated in other forms. In America it appeared (1862) in cardboard pockets, the stamp inserted, the denomination printed on the outside. In Germany and Austria postage stamps were inserted in slits in cardboard mounts. America in the 1860s used a metallic container with a transparent front; in other countries transparent envelopes have been used.

Typewritten and handwritten improvisations of currency are commonly asssociated with siege conditions. French forces controlling the town of Mainz in 1793 issued internal currency during the siege of the city by the Austrians. Among a number of improvisations were assignats with revised handwritten denominations on the reverse. In the siege of Coburg by Napoleon's forces in 1807, cardboard notes consisted of a handwritten value, with a handstamp on one side and a handwritten date of issue on the other. Hand-signed typewritten notes from the O'Okiep siege in April–May 1902 bore the words 'On His Majesty's Service, O'Okiep Siege Note'. A single £1 denomination example survives.

See also PLAYING CARD, SECONDARY USES

REFERENCES Yasha Beresiner, *A Collector's Guide to Paper Money* (New York: Stein & Day, 1977; London: Andre Deutsch, 1977); Ruth McQuade (ed.), *Intrapam '81: the Congress Record* (Willowdale, Ontario: International Paper Money Historical Society, 1981)

SOCIETY International Paper Money Historical Society

Indenture

The term derives from Latin (*indentatus*: toothed) and refers to the irregularly indented edge of a document which, having been cut from a duplicate document correspondingly indented, forms its undoubted partner. In arrangements between three parties the document was inscribed in triplicate and divided by two irregular cuts. The device was used in the making of agreements of all kinds, though the term most commonly refers to undertakings between master and apprentice. In its terminology and presentation the apprentice indenture tellingly conveys the master/servant relationship of former times.

In the majority of cases the wording of the document is pre-printed, with appropriate breaks to allow insertions in handwriting, though wholly handwritten versions are common. The wording, sanctioned by usage over time, and in many cases laid down by statute, remains more or less constant. An indenture or apprenticeship to a Thames waterman in 1767 states:

> This indenture witnesseth that John Wills the son of Wm Wills… in the Parish of Hammersmith in the county of Middlesex doth put himself apprentice to John Shapley of the Parish of Chelsea… Waterman and lighterman, to learn the art, and with him to dwell… from the Day of the Date hereof unto the full End of the Term of Seven Years… During which Time the said Apprentice his said Master faithfully shall serve… his Secrets keep, his lawful Commandments every where gladly do: he shall do no Damage to his said Master, nor see it be done of others… he shall not waste the Goods of the said Master nor lend them unlawfully to any: he shall not commit Fornication, nor contract Matrimony within the said Term: he shall not play at Cards, Dice, Tables or any other unlawful Games… he shall not haunt taverns or playhouses, nor absent himself from his Master's service day or night, unlawfully.…

In return the master undertakes to 'teach and instruct' the boy and 'to find him meat, drink, apparel, lodging and all other necessaries, according to the Custom of the City of London…'.

Thirty years later, in the Commonwealth of Massachusetts, it is required of an apprentice that he 'his said Master well and faithfully shall serve, his Secrets keep etc etc', but fornication is omitted in favour of 'Acts of Vice or Immorality which are forbidden by the Laws of the Commonwealth…'. In the town of Windsor (UK) in 1891 all such prohibitions are omitted and the

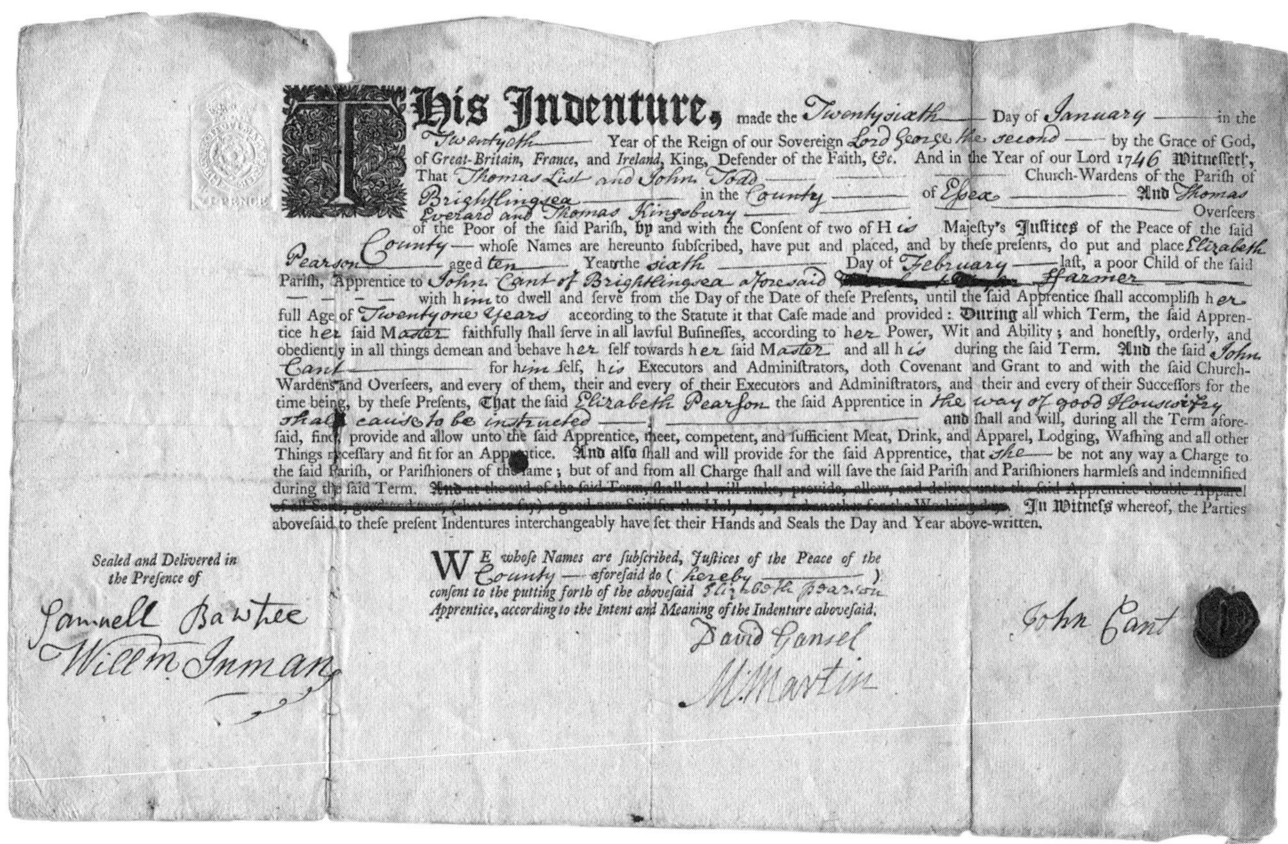

This Indenture, made the Twentysixth Day of January in the Twentyeth Year of the Reign of our Sovereign Lord George the second by the Grace of God, of *Great-Britain, France,* and *Ireland,* King, Defender of the Faith, &c. And in the Year of our Lord 1746 Witneſſeth, That Thomas List and John Todd Church-Wardens of the Pariſh of Brightlingsea in the County of Essex And Thomas Everard and Thomas Kingsbury Overſeers of the Poor of the ſaid Pariſh, by and with the Conſent of two of His Majeſty's Juſtices of the Peace of the ſaid County whoſe Names are hereunto ſubſcribed, have put and placed, and by theſe preſents, do put and place Elizabeth Pearson aged ten Years the sixth Day of February laſt, a poor Child of the ſaid Pariſh, Apprentice to John Cant of Brightlingsea aforesaid Farmer with him to dwell and ſerve from the Day of the Date of theſe Preſents, until the ſaid Apprentice ſhall accompliſh her full Age of Twentyone Years according to the Statute it that Caſe made and provided: During all which Term, the ſaid Apprentice her ſaid Master faithfully ſhall ſerve in all lawful Buſineſſes, according to her Power, Wit and Ability; and honeſtly, orderly, and obediently in all things demean and behave her ſelf towards her ſaid Master and all his during the ſaid Term. And the ſaid John Cant for him ſelf, his Executors and Adminiſtrators, doth Covenant and Grant to and with the ſaid Church-Wardens and Overſeers, and every of them, their and every of their Executors and Adminiſtrators, and their and every of their Succeſſors for the time being, by theſe Preſents, That the ſaid Elizabeth Pearson the ſaid Apprentice in the way of good Houswifry shall cause to be instructed and ſhall and will, during all the Term aforeſaid, find, provide and allow unto the ſaid Apprentice, meet, competent, and ſufficient Meat, Drink, and Apparel, Lodging, Waſhing and all other Things neceſſary and fit for an Apprentice. And alſo ſhall and will provide for the ſaid Apprentice, that she be not any way a Charge to the ſaid Pariſh, or Pariſhioners of the ſame; but of and from all Charge ſhall and will ſave the ſaid Pariſh and Pariſhioners harmleſs and indemnified during the ſaid Term. ~~And at the end of the ſaid Term, ſhall and will make, provide, allow, and deliver unto the ſaid Apprentice double Apparel of all Sorts, …~~ In Witneſs whereof, the Parties aboveſaid to theſe preſent Indentures interchangeably have ſet their Hands and Seals the Day and Year above-written.

Sealed and Delivered in the Preſence of

Samuell Bawtree
Willm Inman

We whoſe Names are ſubſcribed, Juſtices of the Peace of the County *aforeſaid do* (hereby) *conſent to the putting forth of the aboveſaid* Elizabeth Pearson *Apprentice, according to the Intent and Meaning of the Indenture aboveſaid.*

David Gansel
M. Martin

John Cant

Apprenticeship indenture relating to a poor child of the parish of Brightlingsea, Essex (UK), 1746. Letterpress and manuscript, cut 'indentwise' and sealed. 195 × 315mm (7⅝ × 12¾in)

clause appears as 'in all things as a faithful Apprentice shall behave himself towards his said Master…'.

Perhaps most significant of all are indentures for 'Parish Apprentices'. These released the parish authorities from responsibility for maintaining the child – in most cases an orphan – by binding it apprentice to a local employer. The earliest age at which children could be thus bound was nine. This is often the age found entered on the document, although in many cases the entry says 'apparently aged 9 years'. The apprentice indenture was only one of many documents dealing with apprenticeship, both private and parish. There was a prescribed form for every eventuality, from a charge of a child absconding, to the employer starving a child. In 1845 in Britain there were forty-eight such documents, and they provide an important source for the historian of child labour.

Indentures were impressively presented documents, commonly inscribed or printed on vellum, and with witnessed signatures and seals. Later ones were produced by specialist law printers from whom the whole range of statutorily worded documents could be obtained.

See also FORM

Indulgence

Indulgences, defined by the Roman Catholic Church as 'remissions before God of the temporal punishment still due to sin after the guilt has been forgiven', were granted long before the advent of printing. The earliest surviving printed specimens date from the middle of the 15th century. One example, which is not only the earliest known piece of printed ephemera but the earliest dated specimen of printing, was produced probably by Gutenberg or by his partners Fust and Schöffer in 1454. It was issued by Pope Nicholas V to those taking part in the war against the Turks.

Because of its widespread exploitation as a fund-raising device the granting of indulgences was vehemently opposed by Martin Luther (1483–1546), and was one of the primary causes of the Reformation. The indulgence fell into disrepute, and its sale or exchange for alms was prohibited by Pope Pius V in 1567. Nevertheless, the practice of granting indulgences continued.

Few early indulgences survive. Their evidential value lies not only in their historical context but in their embodiment of the work of the pioneer printers Johannes Fust, Peter Schöffer, Johann Gutenberg, William Caxton, and Wynkyn de Worde.

COLLECTION British Museum, London

Inn tally

An inkeeper's bill. The term 'tally' derives from the use of a notched stick (Latin, *talea*: stick) to record a number or transaction. In former times the notched stick was split lengthwise, which gave both parties proof of account when the two portions were placed together and tallied. The word survives as a noun only in a few restricted senses. FISH TALLY is still in common use; 'inn tally' survives only as an archaism, a specialist substitute for the more cumbersome 'innkeeper's bill'.

THOMAS DUNN,
Roos.

	£.	s.	d.
Breakfast			
Dinner			
Supper			
Brandy			
Rum			
Gin			
Ale			
Porter			
Tobacco			
Horses' Hay and Corn			
£.			

Allanson, Printer, Hull.

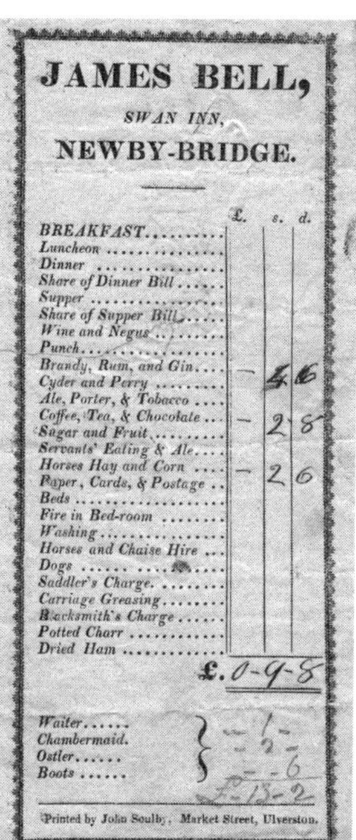

JAMES BELL,
SWAN INN,
NEWBY-BRIDGE.

	£.	s.	d.
BREAKFAST			
Luncheon			
Dinner			
Share of Dinner Bill			
Supper			
Share of Supper Bill			
Wine and Negus			
Punch			
Brandy, Rum, and Gin			
Cyder and Perry			
Ale, Porter, & Tobacco			
Coffee, Tea, & Chocolate			
Sugar and Fruit			
Servants' Eating & Ale			
Horses Hay and Corn			
Paper, Cards, & Postage			
Beds			
Fire in Bed-room			
Washing			
Horses and Chaise Hire			
Dogs			
Saddler's Charge			
Carriage Greasing			
Blacksmith's Charge			
Potted Charr			
Dried Ham			
£.			

Waiter
Chambermaid.
Ostler
Boots

Printed by John Soulby, Market Street, Ulverston.

Inn tallies of the 1820s.
Above: Thomas Dunn, Roos, 1826; printed letterpress by Allanson, Hull, 156 × 102 mm (6¼ × 4 in).
Right: James Bell, Newby-Bridge, printed letterpress by John Soulby (junior), Ulverston. 200 × 82 mm (7⅞ × 3¼ in)

The inn tally, showing the customer's account for bed, board, drinks, etc., was initially a handwritten slip, but early in the coaching era it appeared as a more or less standardized printed form, listing all the customer's possible purchases. Charges were entered by hand as necessary, the total appearing at the foot. It is the most widely recognized of coaching ephemera, and was among the staple products of the local printer's press. Measuring generally about 180 × 100 mm (7⅛ × 4 in) and commonly bearing a more or less perfunctory typeset heading, the tally was seen as a fixed formula, the heading only to be changed to suit the innkeeper. In a series of examples in Barrow-in-Furness Public Library the elder John Soulby has used virtually

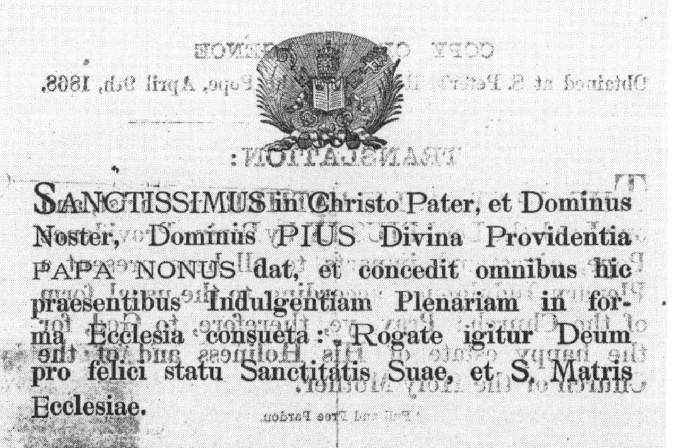

SANCTISSIMUS in Christo Pater, et Dominus Noster, Dominus PIUS Divina Providentia PAPA NONUS dat, et concedit omnibus hic praesentibus Indulgentiam Plenariam in forma Ecclesia consueta: Rogate igitur Deum pro felici statu Sanctitatis Suae, et S. Matris Ecclesiae.

COPY OF INDULGENCE
Obtained at S. Peter's, Rome, from the Pope, April 9th, 1868.

TRANSLATION:

THE MOST HOLY FATHER in Christ, and our Lord, the Lord PIUS IX by Divine Providence Pope, gives and imparts to all here present a Plenary Indulgence* according to the usual form of the Church: Pray, ye, therefore, to God, for the happy estate of His Holiness and of the Church of the Holy Mother.

* Full and Free Pardon.

Copy of an indulgence obtained from the Pope at St Peter's, Rome, 9 April 1868. One side of the sheet is printed in Latin, the other in an English translation. Letterpress. 194 × 254 mm (7⅝ × 10 in)

the same standing type (save only differences in the listing of soda water) in tallies for four local inns. The decorative border too, apart from dimensional adjustments, remained the same.

One feature in which tallies differ distinctly from one another is the mileage table, a listing of distances to other places, normally within a radius of some 25.5 miles. This appeared beneath the title-piece or at the foot of the tally, providing some half dozen distances.

See also BILLHEAD; HOTEL PAPERS; TRAVELLERS' GUIDE

COLLECTIONS Barrow-in-Furness Public Library; Rural History Centre, The University of Reading

Inset, magazine

The magazine inset is a separately printed card or leaflet, generally in colour, that is bound in with the pages of a magazine. The term may be ambiguous, because of its use to mean 'a smaller image let into a larger picture', but it is to be preferred to 'insert', a term often used in error for 'inset'. The word 'insert' refers to an item *placed within the pages* of a publication: that is, without being bound in.

The inset was a common feature of magazine publishing in Britain in the years 1890 to 1910, when national advertisers made extensive use of its impact in terms of colour in monochrome publications (full colour in the body of the publication itself being beyond the production means of the magazine at the time).

The device appears to have originated in the use of existing LEAFLETS as inclusions (inserts) to take advantage of the expanding magazine circulations of the period, binding-in being a safeguard against loss in distribution. Later, leaflets were produced as dual-purpose items, on the one hand for shop-counter use, on the other as insets. Finally, insets were produced in their own right, having a broader margin to the left than to the right to allow binding without loss of effective image.

Insets that have been carefully removed from their binding remain virtually intact, but the majority, torn or cut out hurriedly, are often found to be damaged (*see* LOTTERY PAPERS). This is true whether they were originally stitched into the magazine, or 'tipped in' with a line of glue along the spine edge.

Some advertisers favoured four-page versions; these were tipped in rather than bound. Pears' Soap, pioneer advertisers in all media, used both methods. Best-known of the insets was a series for Lux by John Hassall; Oxo and Bovril were also major users of such items.

Many insets were produced with an eye to the juvenile and drawing-room SCRAPBOOK/ALBUM, where large numbers of them continue to be found. Among the earliest exponents of the 'piggyback' concept, in which a leaflet appears under the aegis of a periodical, was London's Thomas Bish, one of the state lottery operators of the early 19th century. In a surviving example, a Bish leaflet advertising the draw of 8 September 1812 is pasted on to the outside back cover of a publication.

Magazine inset for Maypole soap, late 19th century. Chromolithographed by F. Waller & Co., Hatton Garden, London. 117 × 184mm (4⅝ × 7¼in)

REFERENCE Edmund Williams, *The Story of Sunlight 1884–1984* (Unilever plc, 1984)

Inventory

The listing of property (with or without valuation) has been a constant feature of organized life throughout history. The earliest surviving records either take the form of, or include, inventories.

A PAPYRUS of about AD250 lists the effects of a deceased husband:

> ... a lamp-stand, perfect, with an Eros and a lamp, valued at [.] 6 drachmae; a copper dish; a frying pan;... in clothing a tunic new from the fuller, with a Laconian stripe, worth a stater; a shawl, likewise white and with a Laconian stripe, worth a stater; a shawl, likewise white and with a Laconian stripe, worth 2 drachmae; another tunic, half worn; a new linen shirt with two stripes; a new linen kerchief; white linen cloths 12 in number, worth, at 8 drachmae each, 96 drachmae; a chisel for planing; a ploughshare, likewise perfect; a wooden bedstead, perfect; and property held in common with his brothers: a leaden cauldron, perfect, for boiling linen; a basin, perfect; a small cauldron; a small jar; and the slaves of my daughter's father, whom he holds as common property, 5 in number ... and the children of the latter....

Inventories offer other kinds of evidence. An inventory preserved at Traquair House, Peeblesshire, lists 'popish trinkets' found in the hiding place of a recusant priest. It lists vestments, images,crucifixes, eucharist cups, and a box of 'relics' containing, among other things, several pieces of bone 'tyed with a red thread, having written upon them the Saint they were said to belong unto', beads, 'a pot full of Holy Oyl', candles, wafers, and 'an hundred other Popish books great and small'. The listing concludes with a footline, '... all which were Solemnly burnt at the Cross of Peebles'.

In the course of normal life, inventories are made on occasions such as a change of location or status; a sale; entering or leaving an institution, such as a school, workhouse, hospital, or prison. Auction catalogues are a familiar form of inventory, as are records of business and estate disposals. A listing of house contents, room by room, may provide a graphic conspectus of a household and its members.

The value of such records can be illustrated by the inventory of the entire contents of the Hackney parish workhouse in a lease of 1764, among which are the following entries:

> HALL a steel stove, shovel, tongs, poker and fender, a large Copper Tea Kettle, five tables, six leather Chairs, two matted ditto, a Clock in a black Case, two looking glasses, a Mahogany tea Chest and a Coffee Mill, two slates, a pair of bellows, two bird cages and a parcel of Crockery Ware.
>
> KITCHEN AND SCULLERY a large range iron back and fenders, a heater stove as fixt, a Jack as fixt, four spits, a pair of spits, sacks, a pair of tongs, two Iron frying pans, ten Candlesticks, seven pewter Dishes, nineteen plates, one cheese plate, two funnells, a Cullender and twelve spoons, two lead

tobacco potts, three pottage potts and covers, two tea Kettles, a Coffee pott, a drinking pott, eight sauce pans, one cover, a Copper warming pan, a brass ditto, three stue pans, a brass Kettle, a Dinner Bell, two large Copper Canns, two tables and a desk, a kneeding trough, a pair of steps, a feather Bed and bolster, three ruggs, three blankets, eight brass Candlesticks, a tinder Box, a Chafendish, a pepper box, two drugers, a pestle morter, four box Irons, eight heaters, five stands, two flat irons, two hanging irons, an iron beam and Scales, a hundred lead weight, two small brass ditto, a Copper, and Iron work....

WASH HOUSE Yard a Copper ... two washing formes, three Cloths horses ....

The question arises as to whether such documents should be considered as transient ephemera or part of an archive. Certainly their relevance is transient, though their measure of interest may increase with the passing of time. To the social historian their evidence may be of more than purely local importance.

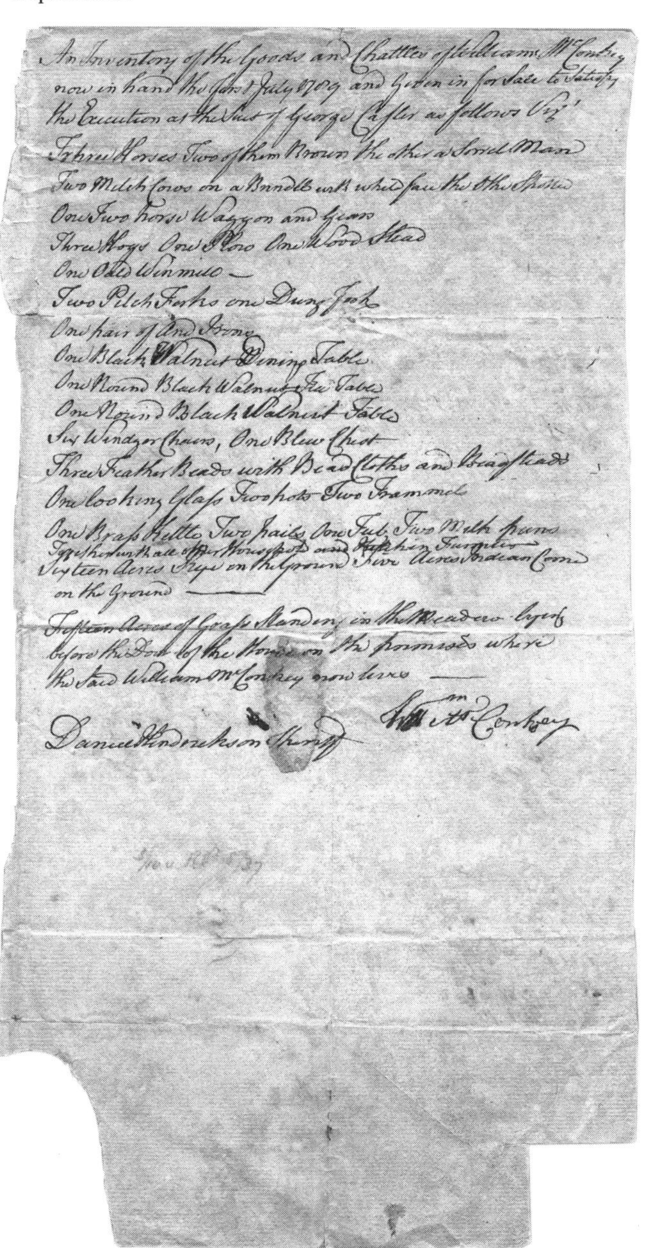

An Inventory of the Goods and Chattles of William McConkey
now in hand the [illegible] July 1789 and Given in for Sale to Satisfy
the Execution at the Suit of George [illegible] as follows Viz'
Three Horses Two of them Brown the other a Sorrel Mare
Two Milch Cows on a Brindle with white face the other Spotted
One Two horse Waggon and Gears
Three Hogs One Plow One Wood Stead
One Old Winmill —
Two Pitch Forks one Dung Fork
One pair of And Irons
One Black Walnut Dining Table
One Round Black Walnut Tea Table
One Round Black Walnut Table
Six Windsor Chairs, One Blew Chest
Three Feather Beads with Bead Cloths and Beadsteads
One looking Glass Two pots Two Trammels
One Brass Kettle Two pails One Tub Two Milk pans
Together with all other Household and Kitchen Furniture
Sixteen Acres Rye on the Ground Five Acres Indian Corn
on the Ground —
Fifteen Acres of Grass Standing in the Meadow lying
before the Door of the House on the premises where
the Said William McConkey now lives —

Daniel Hendrickson Sheriff   Wm McConkey

Inventory of the 'Goods and Chattles' of William McConkey, 1789. Manuscript. 170 × 315 mm (6¾ × 12¾ in)

Invitation

The history of the invitation runs parallel with, and partly overlaps, that of the ADMISSION TICKET. Among the earliest of printed invitation cards were those in which the recipient was 'desired to accompany' the corpse at 17th and 18th century funerals. This form of words, which specified the name of the departed and details of the ceremony, commonly concluded

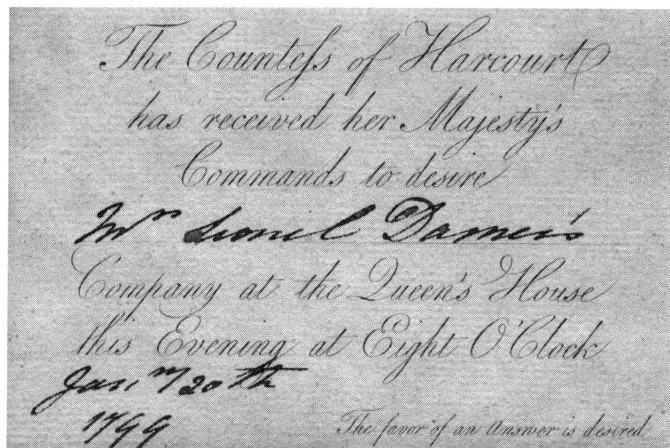

The Countess of Harcourt
has received her Majesty's
Commands to desire
Mr Lionel Damer's
Company at the Queen's House
this Evening at Eight O'Clock
Jan. 20th
1799
The favor of an Answer is desired.

Invitation, 20 January 1799. Engraved and printed intaglio, with manuscript. 79 × 121 mm (3⅛ × 4¾ in)

with the phrase: '... and Bring this Ticket with you'. In later versions, the holder was 'requested to accompany the funeral of...'. In America, the actual word 'invitation' occurred only rarely, but in the mid 19th century the notion of invitation was explicit in the standardized opening: 'The friends of (—), and the public generally, are invited to attend the Funeral of (—)...'. Later funeral invitations, particularly those for Masonic ceremonies, were regarded frankly as tickets. They often bore the expression 'Admit the bearer ...', and sometimes also the word 'ticket' (*see* FUNERALIA).

In addition to funeral invitations, the 17th century also saw the introduction of the formal request for 'The honour of your company at dinner'. Items of this kind were commonly issued by professional societies and institutions to their members. One such invitation, dated 1680, is addressed to no specific group. It serves to introduce one of a series of public relations exercises in which the host requests attendance at a meal provided by his cookery students and reads: 'The Honour of your Company is desired with ye Ladies & Gentlemen Practitioners in the Art of Pastery and Cookery Scholars to Nath. Meystnor, to dine at (—) on Thursday the (—) and bring this ticket with you.' The card, measuring some 200 × 150 mm (7⅞ × 6 in), is decorated with gastronomic illustrations. It provides spaces for the insertion of both time and place, but no provision for the name of the recipient; the salutation, part of the engraved design, simply reads 'Madam'.

Eighteenth-century invitations tended to revert to the formula 'You are desired to attend', or, sometimes, even less cordially, 'You are hereby notified of a meeting'.

COLLECTION John Johnson Collection, Bodleian Library, Oxford

Iridescent printing

Iridescence is the colour characteristic in which changes of hue or shade are seen to occur as the viewpoint changes or as the angle of lighting is varied. The effect is found in the plumage of certain birds, in the wings of some butterflies and beetles, and in mother-of-pearl. It is a diffraction phenomenon, caused by the breaking up of light rays reflected from finely ribbed or particulated matter.

Iridescent effects were explored for a while in the printing of decorative lithographed trade cards, menus, and invitations, notably in Belgium in the period 1840 to 1865. Essentially, the process consisted of printing in a varnish or ink, and dusting the resulting image with metallic powders of varying colours before it dried. The finely particulated powders imparted not only their own body colours to the image but a form of iridescence as the angle of viewing or the lighting varied. The powders, known generally as 'bronzes', were available in yellow, orange, lilac, red, green, lemon, silver, and bronze of various shades. The designs are commonly characterized by extreme delicacy of colour merging, and are enhanced by changing the angle of viewing. Hand-application of the powders meant that, although the image remained constant from one impression to the next, coloration detail varied considerably. Comparison of 'duplicates' discloses colour variation both as to area and intensity.

Printing stock was white-lead coated board (French: *carte porcelaine*), an 'enamel' card widely used at the time in Britain too. The powdering process lasted well into the 20th century, but was eventually abandoned because of the perceived danger to operatives' lungs.

See also TRADE CARD

REFERENCE Georges Renoy, *Bruxelles sous Léopold Ier: 25 Ans de Cartes Porcelaine 1840–1865* (Brussels: Crédit Communal de Belgique, 1979)

Itinerary

Travel aids prior to the advent of the coaching era were unreliable and limited in number. In Britain, road maps did not appear until the late 18th century, and signposting emerged only slowly in the course of the 19th century. Journeys were commonly undertaken on a pre-arranged point-to-point basis, stopping places being no further apart than a reasonable day's riding range. Plans for journeys were drawn up with some care, at first in handwriting and later, with the emergence of a network of posting inns, by reference to printed TRAVELLERS' GUIDES.

Handwritten itineraries convey varying degrees of detail. In their simplest form they list towns and distances in two columns. More conscientiously (commonly for the use of a friend or relative), they also name inns and innkeepers and include a column of comment and recommendation: 'Ferrybridge: Swan & Angel, the 2 best inns in England'; 'from Ferrybridge you may go to York by Tadcaster – Swann Inn, York; Backhouse's (I forget the sign) at Tadcaster…'. Crosses and other devices indicate 'best sleeping houses' and 'remarkable places'. The listings have clearly been set aside for repeated use; many of them have the personal quality of kitchen recipes.

In wider-ranging documents advice is proffered to ambassadors and others involved in frequent transmission of dispatches. A handwritten 'note', evidently prepared for Lord Stuart of Rothesay during his ambassadorship in Paris (1815–30), outlines posting arrangements:

> Despatches intended to be forwarded to Paris by express from London are generally sent to Calais by regular mail and thence… by special courier… a sum of 200 frs is allowed for the expenses of the run from Calais to Paris… 34 postes at 3 frs per poste make 170 frs for the horses and postillions and the remaining 30 frs are at the disposal of the courier… the horses on the road are wretched in the extreme; a courier who does the 64 leagues (160 miles) in 16 hours is a specie of prodigy….

The printed travellers' guide appeared as an adjunct to the innkeeper's billhead or INN TALLY, sometimes listing stops on journeys of 300–400 miles. Later, with the development of the hotel industry, the great establishments provided comparable information for the travelling gentry. In a broadside measuring 430 × 340 mm (17 × 13⅜ in) for the Hotel de Belle Vue in Brussels, c. 1840, engravings of the building are surrounded by itineraries from the capital to a dozen major cities, among them Amsterdam, Paris, Berlin, and Vienna. The lists cite some seventy establishments, the great majority of which are hotels.

See also HOTEL PAPERS; TOURING MAP

jigsaw puzzle
joke ephemera
jumping jack
jury papers

Jail papers *See* GAOL PAPERS

Jigsaw puzzle

The origins of the jigsaw puzzle are closely related to the vogue for educational BOARDGAMES that began in Britain in the mid 18th century. John Spilsbury, a young London cartographer, published in 1762 a 'dissected map of England', which was mounted on mahogany and cut into separate counties for reassembly by children as a learning aid. By the 1780s the idea had been taken up by other publishers, some of whom adapted it for different educational purposes. Historical chronologies, tables, and 'Pilgrim's Progress' and similar pictures appeared, though maps continued dominant into the 1860s.

These puzzles were expensive. Hand-cut and hand-coloured, they remained an upper-middle class item until the introduction, in the 1830s, of white wood. This was used for boxes as well as puzzles, and brought prices down considerably; thereafter, brightly coloured puzzles and box labels began to attract popular attention.

By the end of the 18th century the educational element had much diminished, and puzzles began to be bought for their amusement value alone. Prominent among a new wave of publishers were William Darton and John Wallis. Later, John Betts and William Spooner produced a large number of puzzles, as did the Barfoots (father and son). Many publishers, who already had a grasp of the boardgame market, produced puzzles which, when made up, could be played as a boardgame. Others utilized popular 'children's prints', forerunners of the chromolithographed SCRAP.

James Richard Barfoot and James Widdowfield Barfoot, both of whom had exhibited at the Royal Academy, provided a bizarre note in the history of the jigsaw puzzle. To conceal their involvement in a business of which neither was professionally proud, they produced their great range of puzzles from a secret workshop in their garden, using retailers as their outlet. Their puzzles, otherwise unmarked, carry one distinguishing feature – pink roses incorporated in the picture.

The interlocking of pieces, though introduced in Britain almost from the start, was confined to the outer frame of the puzzle for over half a century; centre parts, though of irregular shape, had no interlock. Continental puzzles were already wholly interlocking by the early 1830s. Many early British manufacturers, conforming to the convention of the 'separate county of the dissected map', cut the puzzle so as to present individual pictures, buildings, etc. as separate pieces, but later the practice was indiscriminate. In America, however, the separate figure approach was widely retained. In America, too, arbitrary shapes such as letters, numerals, profiles, etc. were cut without reference to the elements of the picture.

Birthday card jigsaw puzzle with its envelope, 1930s. The puzzle four-colour process. 100 × 129mm (4 × 5⅛in)

The advent of plywood in the early 20th century revolutionized jigsaw-puzzle production and allowed for much greater intricacy. In Britain, Raphael Tuck extended the market, making a special appeal to the adult. By 1915 the firm was selling 'The House of Lords', a puzzle of 1200 pieces. The 1930s brought cardboard and refinements in die-cutting, with the result that production costs decreased dramatically. Jigsaw puzzles were sold for sixpence at Woolworths, and Raphael Tuck produced postcard-size puzzles for one penny each.

British jigsaw puzzles have generally been sold loose in boxes, most of them bearing the complete picture on the label (though some advertising-novelty puzzles and 'penny puzzles' were presented on a cardboard backing as a completed picture with transparent covering). Continental puzzles have generally been sold as complete pictures, some from France and Germany in multi-layer packs containing a number of puzzles.

The American jigsaw puzzle came as an import from Britain. W. B. Gilley advertised 'Dissected maps' in 1819 and F. & R. Lockwood offered 'Travellers' tours of the United States', 'Travellers' tours of Europe', and 'Travellers' tours of the World' in the form of dissected maps. The first jigsaws to be made in America appeared in the 1850s and 1860s. Thomas S. Wagner of Philadelphia produced a 'Rowboat Excursion' scene in 1860, and the 1880s brought puzzles from a number of firms, including Milton Bradley, McLoughlin Brothers, and Parker Brothers of Salem, Massachusetts – the firm which later launched the board game Monopoly.

The American jigsaw puzzle ('Pastime puzzle' or 'Puzzle picture') came into its own during the years of the depression, when many people sought distraction, occupation, and constructive entertainment. With the introduction of die-cut stamping in 1900 (thirty years in advance of Europe), the American jigsaw puzzle became cheaper to produce and reached an expanding and mass market. The 'upper class' association prevailed, however, in puzzles custom-made to the orders of the rich and famous. Some 'exclusive' manufacturers even produced mahogany puzzles comprising, in some cases, many thousands of pieces.

REFERENCES Linda Hannas, *The English Jigsaw Puzzle, 1760–1890* (London: Wayland, 1972); *Two Hundred Years of Jigsaw Puzzles* (exhibition catalogue with introduction by Linda Hannas) (London: London Museum, 1968); Tom Tyler, *British Jigsaw Puzzles of the Twentieth Century* (Shepton Beauchamp, Som.: Richard Dennis, 1997)

COLLECTIONS Bethnal Green Museum of Childhood, London; Smithsonian Institution, Washington, DC

Joke ephemera

Joke ephemera, unlike 'spoof' items of ADVERTISING NOVELTY (mock banknotes, etc.), seek mainly to amuse. They are produced on the one hand by commercial publishers for sale, and on the other by private enthusiasts for amusement.

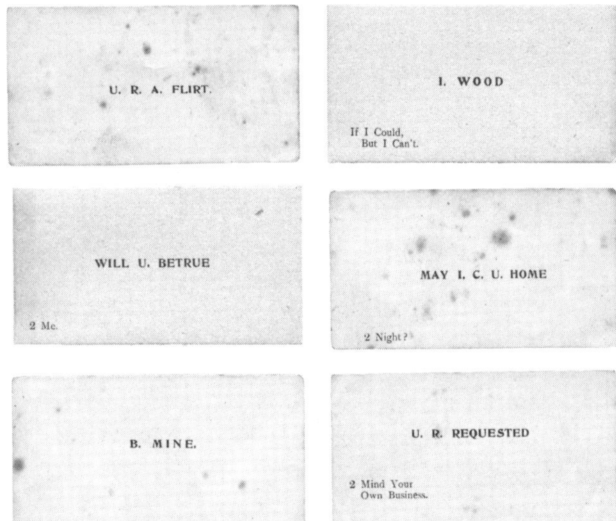

Joke visiting cards of the 1930s. Letterpress. Each 40 × 76 mm (1⁹⁄₁₆ × 3 in)

Typical items are joke visiting cards: 'Ray Gribble, Retired: No address; No phone; No business; No worries; No money; No prospects'. A leaflet appeared in the 1970s bearing no other wording than: 'Please keep our streets tidy; put this in a litter bin when you have read it'. A private printer in Annapolis, Maryland, produced a letterhead for 'The Committee for Selective Intolerance, a division of the Indiana Institute of Hypocracy'; the committee is defined in a footline as 'a charitable organization distinguished for its neighborly and companionable familiarity with the successive stages of elaboration through which the emotions of bigotry are transmuted into functional broadminded prejudice'.

Jumping jack

The subject of a great vogue in France in the 18th century, the jumping jack or *pantin* consisted of a cardboard articulated figure, printed or hand-painted in colour, and animated by a wire or string. *Pantin* is now used (additionally) to mean puppet in a pejorative sense; the word is said to derive from the name of a village near Paris, whose inhabitants were reputedly noted for their dancing.

The toy emerged as a juvenile novelty in the early 1700s, but in the period 1747 to 1756 was taken up as a fad among adult Parisians. It was at first a home-made gift, exchanged among the fashionable and distinguished, but was soon manufactured as a popular novelty. It also appeared in the form of paper sheets for pasting on card, colouring, and cutting out. Edmond Barbier wrote in his *Journal* in 1747 that *pantins* specially painted and devised by such academicians as Boucher sold for very large sums, and that the craze had overtaken everyone: 'one cannot go into any house without finding a *pantin* hanging by the mantelpiece'.

The *pantin* was used as an instrument of satire, lampooning the famous and notorious, and was so widely popular as to become a nuisance. It is said that at one stage there were serious proposals for it to be banned. It was revived in the evolving mass-production era of the 19th century, and survived in various forms in a number of countries into the early years of the 20th century.

Jury papers

Trial by jury is 'the Englishman's birthright' (Richard Burn, *Justice of the Peace and Parish Officer*, 29th edn, London: Sweet, 1845), and has been viewed through the centuries as 'the grand bulwark of every Englishman's liberties before the law'. An essential feature of the jury system is the jury list, typeset or handwritten, which lies close to the heart of many legal actions and identifies the individuals charged with deciding the issue in specific cases. Service on juries is viewed on the one hand as a privilege and on the other as a duty. Members of the jury are summoned to appear on given dates, the jury summons having the same force of law as any other legal SUMMONS.

The jury list and its attendant papers are usually prominent among accumulations of courtroom ephemera. As with many legal papers, archaisms abound, though less so in America than in England. Supporting documents may include such information as car parking facilities and relevant public transport systems. Paradoxically, 'old English' type, still identified with religion and the law, survives in the titling of the American jury summons whereas it has been largely abandoned in Britain.

In neither country has the wording, lay-out and general presentation, the force of statute; in both cases these characteristics have gained acceptance through long usage.

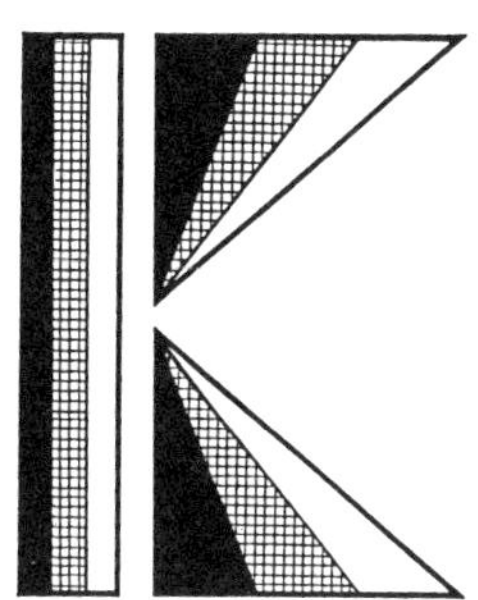

Keepsake

The term 'keepsake' was applied to literary annuals, also known as 'gift-books', which were produced as personal mementoes in Britain in the 1820s and 1830s. These anthologies of poems, steel engravings, and other fragments, among them *The Keepsake* (1827–56), were notable for their sentimentality. The word 'keepsake', in the sense of 'over-pretty', was coined in 1871 and remained current until the turn of the century.

In the context of ephemera, the term 'keepsake' commonly applies to the specially printed paper or card produced as a memento of a visit or other occasion, often for a named recipient. The convention derives from an early custom among printers of setting up a decorative name card for distinguished visitors, sometimes inviting recipients to operate the press, or even set the type, themselves.

The printer's keepsake generally consisted of a border composed of type ornaments, which framed the space in which the recipient's name appeared. Bestowal of the keepsake was not wholly disinterested as it was commonly expected that the visitor would make some small payment for the privilege of being received. The item may be viewed as a form of unofficial receipt. It was doubtless this custom that prompted the enterprise of London printers in setting up presses on the ice when the Thames froze over, printing 'own-name' mementoes for visitors at sixpence a line (*see* FROST-FAIR PAPERS).

The printer's keepsake has much in common, and is sometimes confused, with the BOOK LABEL, an item with similar features. It is in fact possible that the book label, a humbler version of the engraved BOOKPLATE, emerged as a useful by-product of an otherwise one-off conceit.

The keepsake survives in the 20th century as a souvenir of printing exhibitions, book and ephemera fairs, and other such promotions where, with or without the recipient's name, a memento is printed on the spot.

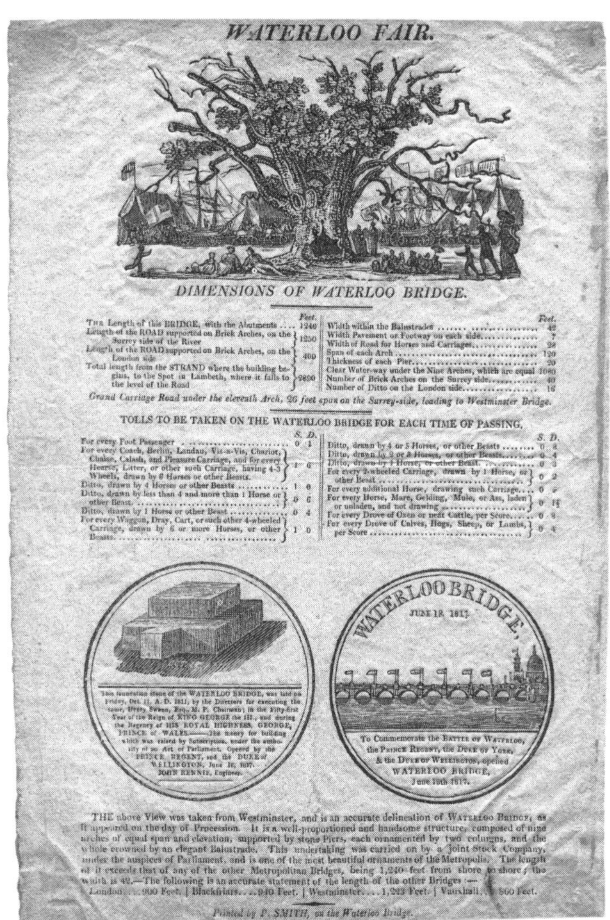

WATERLOO FAIR.

DIMENSIONS OF WATERLOO BRIDGE.

	Feet.
THE Length of this BRIDGE, with the Abutments	1240
Length of the ROAD supported on Brick Arches, on the Surrey side of the River	1250
Length of the ROAD supported on Brick Arches, on the London side	400
Total length from the STRAND where the building begins, to the Spot in Lambeth, where it falls to the level of the Road	2890
Width within the Balustrades	42
Width Pavement or Footway on each side	7
Width of Road for Horses and Carriages	28
Span of each Arch	120
Thickness of each Pier	20
Clear Water-way under the Nine Arches, which are equal	1080
Number of Brick Arches on the Surrey side	40
Number of Ditto on the London side	16

Grand Carriage Road under the eleventh Arch, 26 feet span on the Surrey-side, leading to Westminster Bridge.

TOLLS TO BE TAKEN ON THE WATERLOO BRIDGE FOR EACH TIME OF PASSING.

	S.	D.
For every Foot Passenger	0	1
For every Coach, Berlin, Landau, Vis-a-Vis, Chariot, Chaise, Calash, and Pleasure Carriage, and for every Hearse, Litter, or other such Carriage, having 4-3 Wheels, drawn by 6 Horses or other Beasts.	1	6
Ditto, drawn by 4 Horses or other Beasts	1	0
Ditto, drawn by less than 4 and more than 1 Horse or other Beast.	0	6
Ditto, drawn by 1 Horse or other Beast	0	4
For every Waggon, Dray, Cart, or such other 4-wheeled Carriage, drawn by 6 or more Horses, or other Beasts.	1	0
Ditto, drawn by 4 or 5 Horses, or other Beasts	0	8
Ditto, drawn by 2 or 3 Horses, or other Beasts	0	4
Ditto, drawn by 1 Horse, or other Beast.	0	3
For every 2-wheeled Carriage, drawn by 1 Horse, or other Beast	0	2
For every additional Horse, drawing such Carriage	0	[illegible]
For every Horse, Mare, Gelding, Mule, or Ass, laden or unladen, and not drawing	0	1½
For every Drove of Oxen or neat Cattle, per Score	0	8
For every Drove of Calves, Hogs, Sheep, or Lambs, per Score	0	4

This foundation stone of the WATERLOO BRIDGE, was laid on Friday, Oct. 11, A. D. 1811, by the Directors for executing the same, Henry Swann, Esq., M. P. Chairman; in the Fifty-first Year of the Reign of KING GEORGE the III., and during the Regency of HIS ROYAL HIGHNESS, GEORGE, PRINCE of WALES.——The money for building which was raised by Subscription, under the authority of an Act of Parliament. Opened by the PRINCE REGENT, and the DUKE of WELLINGTON, June 18, 1817. JOHN RENNIE, Engineer.

WATERLOO BRIDGE, JUNE 18, 1817.

To Commemorate the BATTLE OF WATERLOO, the PRINCE REGENT, the DUKE OF YORK, & the DUKE OF WELLINGTON, opened WATERLOO BRIDGE, June 18th 1817.

THE above View was taken from Westminster, and is an accurate delineation of WATERLOO BRIDGE, as it appeared on the day of Procession. It is a well-proportioned and handsome structure, composed of nine arches of equal span and elevation, supported by stone Piers, each ornamented by two colums, and the whole crowned by an elegant Balustrade. This undertaking was carried on by a Joint Stock Company, under the auspices of Parliament, and is one of the most beautiful ornaments of the Metropolis. The length of it exceeds that of any of the other Metropolitan Bridges, being 1,240 feet from shore to shore; the width is 42.—The following is an accurate statement of the length of the other Bridges:— London....900 Feet. | Blackfriars....940 Feet. | Westminster....1,223 Feet. | Vauxhall....800 Feet.

Printed by P. SMITH, on the Waterloo Bridge.

Keepsake printed on Waterloo Bridge by P. Smith to commemorate the opening of the bridge, 18 June 1817. Letterpress with wood-engravings. 350 × 190 mm (13¾ × 7½ in)

Keepsake, novelty

The popular success of the FROST-FAIR PAPER led to similar printing enterprise on other occasions. The 'Grand Jubilee' in 1814 was a notable case in point. Printers who only a few months previously (February 1814) had been printing souvenirs on the frozen Thames appeared with their presses in Hyde Park, scene of the national celebration of peace with France in August 1814. Here visitors were able to buy keepsakes, with or without their own name set in type, recording the three-fold rejoicing: 'Glorious Peace, The Centenary of the Illustrious House of Brunswick and the Glorious Battle of the Nile'. Some cards bore victorious verse; others described the Hyde Park event, 'the Largest Fair, for every kind of Amusement, that was ever known in this or any other Country', and the additional attractions in St James's Park, Green Park, and Kensington Gardens. Also for sale, printed on the spot, were illustration sheets showing the Temple of Concord 'for the display of magnificent fireworks' and souvenir watchpapers.

As with the frost-fair items, few of the Grand Jubilee cards bore a formal imprint, though all indicated the site of their origin. A number carried fictional or grandiose imprints:

'Printed at Blücher's Press in Hyde Park', 'Printed and published by G. Davis, at the Royal Jubilee Printing-Office, in Hyde Park'. Apart from Davis, Samuel Bell was among the few printers personally identified.

The ceremonial opening of Waterloo Bridge was the next occasion for on-the-spot printing, this time however with only one printer in the field. An illustrated foolscap broadside, 'Printed by P. Smith, on the Waterloo Bridge', sets out the dimensions of the structure and details of its inception. Further versions of the broadside also appeared, listing toll payments and penalties for evasion. On-the-spot printing had its enthusiasts: the John Johnson Collection, Bodleian Library, Oxford, includes a specimen of the Waterloo Bridge item bearing the handwritten footline 'Printed by G Pryer on the above bridge, July 2' and an 1814 Hyde Park jubilee keepsake in which the typeset name, inserted for the occasion, is 'G. Pryer'.

'Printed on the Spot by Permission' is an imprint appearing on a leaflet, 230 × 155mm (9 × 6⅛in), commemorating the inauguration of the statue of Achilles in Hyde Park in 1822 (the first undraped male statue in London). The printer's name is given as 'J Quick'.

King's evil certificate

In the *London Gazette* for 18–21 November 1672 appears the following proclamation:

> His Majesty has commanded that Notice be given, That no Persons whatsoever do come to be Healed of the King's Evil unless they bring a certificate under the Hands and Seals of the Minister and Churchwardens of the Parishes where they inhabit: That they have not been Touched before: And His Majesty Requires, That the Ministers in their respective Parishes do keep a constant Register of such Persons to whom they give these Certificates.

The certificate was introduced to relieve the pressure of applications at 'Services of touching' or 'Healing', and to restrict numbers to first-time patients only. The numbers involved were considerable. In the period from 1672 until his death in 1685, Charles II is said to have 'touched' many thousands, and in his whole reign some 90,000. It appears, however, that not a single example of the certificate survives.

The King's Evil (scrofula) had been allegedly curable by the touch of a consecrated king since the time of Edward the Confessor (reigned 1042–66) in England. Under Henry VII, and until 1715, a form of service for healing was included in the prayer book. 'Touching for the Evil' was viewed by the monarchs concerned with mixed feelings, though the facility was nonetheless publicized from time to time. In a broadside issued at Whitehall in 1683 the court proclaimed that His Majesty was pleased to declare 'His Royal Will and Pleasure' in the matter of their 'Sacred Touch and Invocation of the Name of God'. Times were announced at which he would officiate, principally in the cooler months, 'Being times more convenient for the Temperature of the Season and in respect of contagion which may happen in this near access to His Majesty's Sacred Person'.

Sufferers received 'Healing medals', to be worn at the knee on a ribbon. The ceremony once involved the monarch in a personal act of ablution of the patient's flesh, but under Henry VII this was omitted. Dr Johnson (at the age of two and a half) is said to have been among the last to be 'touched'.

REFERENCE *Notes & Queries*, series 3, 19 April 1862, p. 314; 21 June 1862, p. 497

Kite bag

The kite bag is a conical paper container, formerly widely used by shopkeepers for dispensing sweets, powders, and similar goods. It is machine-made from a square of paper, opposing corners being folded inwards and pasted along the overflap, the fold at the apex forming a powder-proof base. The triangular flap at the mouth of the cone is folded over the contents as a simple closure.

The kite bag is a direct descendant of the 'corner', 'cap', or cartouche, first used in the 16th century by apothecaries and grocers and consisting of a cone of paper twisted at the base. The shape had also been used for filter papers.

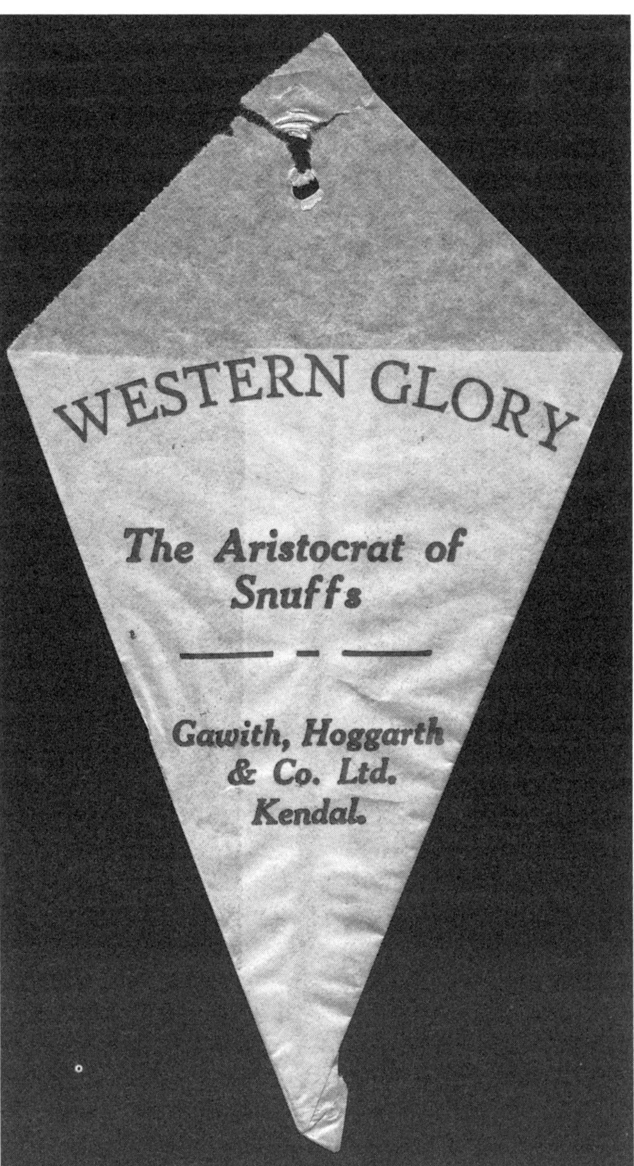

Kite bag. Letterpress. 200 × 124mm (8⅝ × 4⅞in)

Kite-bag production was first mechanized in the 1870s. Made from the cheapest light-weight paper (known, from this application, as 'cap' paper) and commonly printed in a single colour with the name of the trader, the bags were used for confectionery, sherbert, snuff, seeds, and other such products. As with the shopkeeper's rectangular PAPER BAG, they were supplied strung in hundreds for convenience in the shop. With the advent of factory packaging, the kite bag virtually disappeared, though it survives in Britain for fish-and-chip shop use.

Label [plates 2–4, 15]

In addition to its main current use, the word 'label' is or was applied to features of medieval documents: the strip of ribbon or other material that carries the seal on a document, and the strip of paper or parchment attached to a document as a supplement (obsolete). It is mainly used now to refer to a piece of paper, card, plastic, metal, or other material that is attached to an object to identify its contents, nature, ownership, destination, or other characteristics. Most commonly, it relates to the identification of products in bottles, jars, cans, and boxes; brand names woven in fabric and applied to clothing; and stickers or tags attached to luggage. Over forty headings that incorporate the word label are described in this encyclopedia. Somewhat oddly, other items of ephemera that fulfil similar requirements in that they are marks of ownership or indicate responsibility, the BOOKPLATE, BOOKBINDER'S TICKET, and WATCH PAPER, are not normally called labels.

By extension, 'labelling' and 'labelled' have come to be applied more generally to identification and description, as in 'food labelling', which may refer to aspects of packaging rather than specifically to a label. In recent years the word has been used to refer to the commercial 'branding' of a product, and the expression 'designer label' to products that have achieved design recognition in the market place, particularly in the eyes of the young.

The earliest surviving labels date from the mid 16th century; they were used to identify paper and fabric and were printed from wood blocks or copper plates. Such examples are extremely rare, but by the end of the 17th century and on into the 18th century certain kinds of products, particularly tobacco, snuff, and tea, commonly bore a monochrome, usually decorative, label. The emergence of the label for a wider range of products reflects changes in shopping following the spread of industrialization in Europe and America in the early 19th century. Among products of this period that regularly carried labels, many of them shaped and some printed in colour, are: beer, blacking, medicine, perfume, pomade, needles, nibs, and sauce. A characteristic of many of these labels is the signature, which was used as a mark of authenticity. Lea & Perrins, for example, who manufactured Worcestershire sauce, adopted this practice in the first half of the 19th century, and continued with it for over a hundred years.

In this period too there emerged the CAN LABEL, which followed Peter Durand's British patent (no. 3372) of 1810 (American patent 1818) for the use of tinplate for preserved-food containers. The first canning factory was set up in Britain in 1814; others followed in America, France, and Germany in the 1820s.

As the 19th century wore on, the custom of selling goods directly from shelves, bins, and sacks without any obvious identification began to decline. After the middle of the century, as Rickards has written, 'the buyer at last had a link with the source of the goods, and the label, pasted on the package, became a talisman.' (Rickards, 1988, p. 118). This change was gradual, but with the wider distribution of goods both nationally and internationally, the label became a prime means of selling certain kinds of products, such as biscuits, cigars, ink, medicaments, and perfume. Colour was essential in this battle of the brands, and label printers were quick to take advantage of the facilities offered by the rising process of chromolithography. Already in the late 19th century the stage was set for the explosion of packaging in the 20th century.

Most decorative early labels were printed intaglio from copper plates or in relief from woodcuts; undecorated ones were usually printed from type, often with simple borders. When small labels were needed in quantity, several were printed together at one pass of the press. In the course of the 19th century labels were increasingly printed lithographically, either monochrome or, after the middle of the century, in several or many colours. One of the reasons for the success of lithography in the field of label printing was the technique of TRANSFER LITHOGRAPHY, which made it possible to produce multiple versions of an identical image by transferring prints from a master to another stone, thus increasing output at the printing stage.

Many labels were, and still are, printed in enormous quantities. However, their survival rate is not high once they have found their way on to the item they identify. Pots, bottles, and boxes of the 19th century with their labels still on them are by no means common. Most labels that survive in collections of ephemera do so because they were surplus to requirements and probably came in bulk from their printer or the manufacturer of the product.

Initially most labels were applied by hand: Dodd (1843) describes in graphic detail the extraordinary speed with which blacking labels were stuck down in the first half of the 19th century. By the end of the 19th century machines were in use for both the gumming of labels and their application to objects. [MT]

See also ACCOUNT-BOOK LABEL; AIR-TRANSPORT LABEL; AMBROTYPE LABEL; BAGGAGE STICKER; BEER LABEL;

BISCUIT/CRACKER LABEL; BOOK LABEL; BOOK-DONOR LABEL; BOOK-PRIZE LABEL; BOOKSELLER'S LABEL; BROOM LABEL; CANDLE LABEL; CHEESE LABEL; CHEMIST'S LABEL; CHROMO; CIGAR BAND/BOX LABEL; CLASSROOM LABEL; COMPOUND-PLATE PRINTING; CRATE LABEL; CYPHER LABEL; DEPOSIT LABEL; ENGRAVED LABEL; FEZ LABEL; FIREWORK/FIRECRACKER LABEL; FRUIT/VEGETABLE STICKER; FURNITURE LABEL; GARMENT LABEL; LINEN-BUTTON LABEL; NEEDLE-BOX PRINT; PAPER-DUTY LABEL; PEN-BOX LABEL; PERFUME LABEL; PILL-BOX LABEL; PIN-BOX LABEL; POSTAL LABEL; POSTAL-STRIKE LABEL; RAILWAY LUGGAGE LABEL; REAM WRAPPER/LABEL; SEIDLITZ-POWDER LABEL; SHOEMAKER'S LABEL; STATIONER'S LABEL; STICKER; TAG LABEL; TEXTILE LABEL; TRADE LABEL; UNION LABEL; VIOLIN LABEL; WINE LABEL

REFERENCES Alec Davis, *Package and Print* (London: Faber & Faber, 1967); George Dodd, *Days at the Factories* (London: Charles Knight & Co., 1843; reprinted Augustus M. Keeley, 1967); John Lewis, *Printed Ephemera* (Ipswich: W. S. Cowell, 1962); Robert Opie, *The Art of the Label* (London: Simon & Schuster, 1987); Maurice Rickards, *Collecting Printed Ephemera* (Oxford: Phaidon/Christies 1988)

COLLECTIONS John Johnson Collection, Bodleian Library, Oxford; Bella C. Landauer Collection, New York Historical Society; Museum of Advertising and Packaging, Gloucester

Labour account

Known also as a time sheet, or service record (US), the labour account is a part-printed form, ledger page, or file card in which an employee's work performance is entered, usually with details of fines, deductions, and the final balance of wages due.

The labour account came into general use in the 1840s and 1850s. Surviving examples provide detailed evidence of wage rates and, in some cases, special working conditions. An 1855 example shows payments of 2*s* 6*d* a day for six days' work by John Rainford, in the employ of John Shaw Leigh of Clayton Square, Liverpool, for 'ditching the Plantation'. The sum of 13*s* 6*d* appears to have been signed for on behalf of Rainford.

In an 1858 example, Alfred P. Rockwell, a Cornish tin miner, is shown to have worked the 'tribute pay' system in which the employee receives a fixed proportion of the value of the product brought to the surface (less employer's charges): 'Mixing & Dividing & Grinding; Box and Drawing; Smith's Cost; Candles & Materials; Powder; Doctor'. On 23 April 1858 Rockwell received £79 8*s* 1*d* less £9 for the items listed, less £42. 5*s* 6*d* 'subsistence', less £42 5*s* 6*d* 'debt', less 'club' (presumably burial-club contribution) 6*s*, leaving a balance of £22. 16*s* 7*d*. The record does not state the period covered, but it may be inferred that it relates to a year's work.

A repair shop service card of the 'West Virginia Central and Pittsburg Railway Company' for 3 June 1907 records a total of ten hours' work on engines 304 and 309 by workman W. E. Staub, whose earnings for the day (7am–12am; 2pm–6pm) were $2. The reverse of the card provides a form listing materials that might be used on the job; though not filled in, it includes forgings, bolts, nuts, washers, nails, journal bearings, air brake, wheels on axle, yellow pine, oak, spruce, poplar, and hickory.

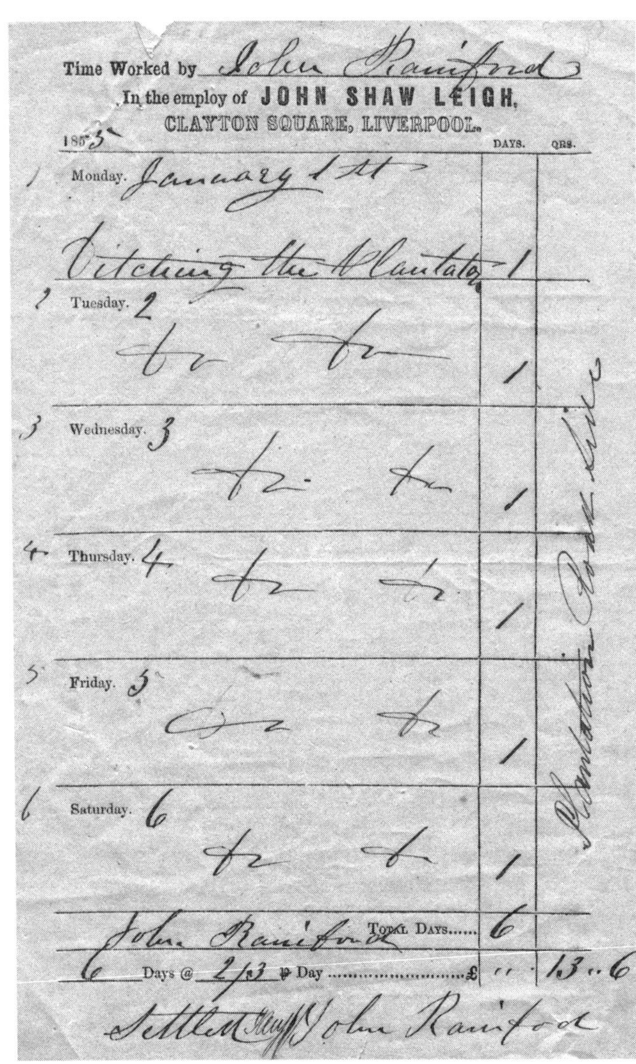

Time Worked by John Rainford
In the employ of JOHN SHAW LEIGH,
CLAYTON SQUARE, LIVERPOOL.
1855

	DAYS.	QRS.
1 Monday. January 1st Ditching the Plantation	1	
2 Tuesday. 2	1	
3 Wednesday. 3	1	
4 Thursday. 4	1	
5 Friday. 5	1	
6 Saturday. 6	1	
John Rainford TOTAL DAYS......	6	
6 Days @ 2/3 ₱ Day ......£	" 13 . 6	

Settled John Rainford

Labour account listing the time worked by John Rainford for ditching work, Liverpool, 1855. Letterpress and manuscript. 225 × 142 mm (8⅞ × 5⅝ in)

Lace paper *See* EMBOSSING/LACE PAPER

Lavatory paper

The development of lavatory paper as a commercial product began in the 1840s. Prior to that, it must be assumed, mankind was left to its own devices: the written history of the lavatory itself goes back at least to the 14th century (Chaucer, *The Marchauntes Tale*), but on this other matter history is largely silent. Research discloses a reference by the Arab writer Abu Zaid Hasan al Siraff (fl. 916) to this use of paper in India and China in the 9th century; and Rabelais has a passing comment on it in chapter thirteen of *Gargantua* (first published in 1534).

Newspapers in particular provided a ready source of lavatory paper for centuries, and it was the rise of popular literature in the 19th century that led to the widespread and long-lasting custom of hanging printed sheets from a nail in the privy. To counter this, early lavatory-paper manufacturers made much of the dangers of printing ink. J. C. Gayetty's Medicated Paper for the Water Closet, invented and introduced by Mr Gayetty in 1857, was still inveighing against improvisation at the turn of the century. Not only printers' ink, but the bleaches used in making unprinted papers, were cited as dangers: 'Printer's ink is also a rank poison, and a persistive use of printed paper is sure eventually to induce an aggravated stage of the above disease [piles].' Vitriol, lime, and potash, present in bleaches, also caused the complaint which, on the other hand, reacted well to the soothing medications present in Gayetty's paper – 'a perfectly pure article'.

Gayetty's paper was sold at $1 per 1000 sheets (50c per 500) and was marketed in an eyeletted cardboard container for hanging on the wall. Sheets measured 210 × 140 mm (8¼ × 5½ in), about double the average size of the perforated segments of

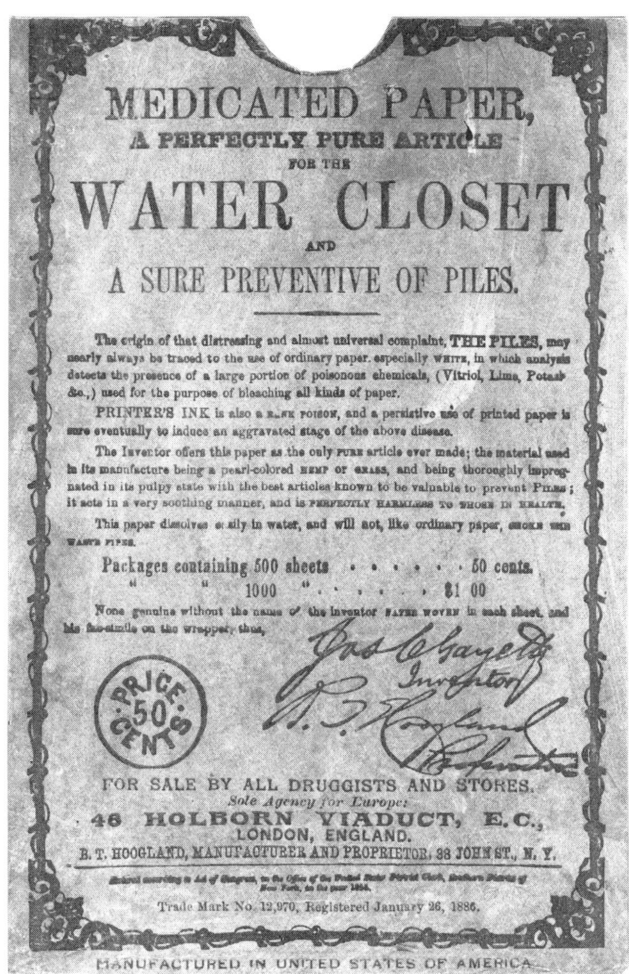

Package for Gayetty's medicated toilet paper, prepared by B. T. Hoogland, New York, late 19th century. Letterpress on yellow paper. 212 × 140mm (8⅜ × 5½in)

today's toilet-roll sheet. In addition to appearing on the pack as a signature, the name J. C. Gayetty formed the water-mark 'and when held to the light can be seen'. An additional selling point for Gayetty's paper, important in the increasing use of the water closet, was its solubility: 'The paper dissolves easily in water, and will not, like ordinary paper, choke the waste pipes'. The paper, manufactured and distributed under licence by B. T. Hoogland (whose signature also appeared on the pack), was available in Europe through 'All druggists and stores'.

A possible British forerunner of Gayetty was G. W. Atkins & Co., who came into prominence in the 1890s, and claimed to have held royal warrants from all crowned heads since 1817.

Packs containing separate sheets for hanging continued as a more or less standard product. Threaded with a corner loop or in hanging containers, they were available until World War II. Typical examples were 'Bronco', 'Drayton Mill', 'Mikado', 'Novio', and 'Virilla', most of which retained roughly the same large dimensions as the Gayetty paper. The hanging container began to be superseded at about the end of the 19th century by wooden or japanned metal holders which allowed one-at-a-time removal of interleaved sheets. In turn, they were replaced by porcelain dispensers ('Jeyes' – the House of Hygiene') with frontal dispensing. Bakelite dispensers were also used. Interleaved sheets, supplied in cartons, and dispensed from porcelain holders continued in use in the 1990s.

The brand names of the separate-sheet products of the 1880s and 1890s were carried forward into the toilet-roll era, some of them to survive into the latter part of the 20th century. Notably absent among survivors was a range of Japanese brand names, in Britain 'Mikado', 'San Toi', and 'Japanese Tar'; in America 'Japacrik' (which disappeared in World War II) and 'Anzora' (a name that was also applied to a popular hair cream, which likewise disappeared in World War II).

The toilet roll appeared in the early 1870s (Seth Wheeler introduced it in New York in 1870), and by 1890 a number of specialist firms were manufacturing the product. Among the most successful in Britain was W. W. Colley & Co. of Hatton Garden, sole patentee of Terebene perforated paper. Colley won a prize medal at the Paris Exhibition of 1889 and the firm's toilet rolls were used in lavatories at the exhibition, including the newly erected Eiffel Tower. Terebene was widely used in toilet rolls; so was eucalyptus. Jeyes Fluid was a well-known proprietary name in what was referred to as 'sanitization'; but many papers were merely described as 'medicated'.

Perforation or rouletting of rolls into separate sheets was not widespread until after World War II. Paper quality, texture, and thickness varied widely. Today's two-ply coloured papers were not in general use until the early 1960s. The toilet-roll wrapper-label, universal until the 1960s, began to disappear with the introduction of multiple-pack polythene shrink-wrap packaging. Sales appeal, formerly preoccupied with strength and medication, now concentrates on colour and softness.

Printed legends, which had been a common feature of individual sheets, also tended to disappear, though many public utilities and other undertakings continued to identify their property. Among those recorded as having done so on each sheet are, in Britain, Associated British Cinemas, Barclays Bank, Central Electricity Generating Board, London Transport, National Coal Board, London School of Economics, and the United Kingdom Atomic Energy Authority. Papers marked 'Council Property' and 'Government Property' are in widespread use.

Printed images survived widely in 'fun' toilet rolls. They take the form of different cartoon jokes on each sheet, and are a survival of novelty paper used for propaganda purposes in World Wars I and II. Other latter-day novelties include family coats of arms and crossword puzzles.

REFERENCE Ian Maxted, 'Sic transit gloria cloacarum', *The Ephemerist*, no. 71, December 1990, pp. 364–65.

Leaflet

Formerly known as handbills (and in America as flyers), leaflets were the most widely used form of printed publicity in the 19th century. Their popularity derived from their cheapness to produce and distribute, the immediacy and the topicality that the simplicity of their production allowed, and the ease with which distribution could be localized in a desired selling area. Additionally, in London at least, in streets full of hawkers who sold their wares, anyone who handed out items for nothing made a welcome change.

The leaflet has a twofold family connection. It is related on the one hand to the TRADE CARD, a modest slip designed initally to carry only a name and designation, later blossoming into sales copy; and on the other to the WINDOW BILL, PROCLAMATION, and large-scale POSTER. A cross between them, the leaflet carried messages not merely into shops and on to public walls and hoardings, but into the very hands of the passer-by.

The leaflet was pre-eminently the advertising medium of the

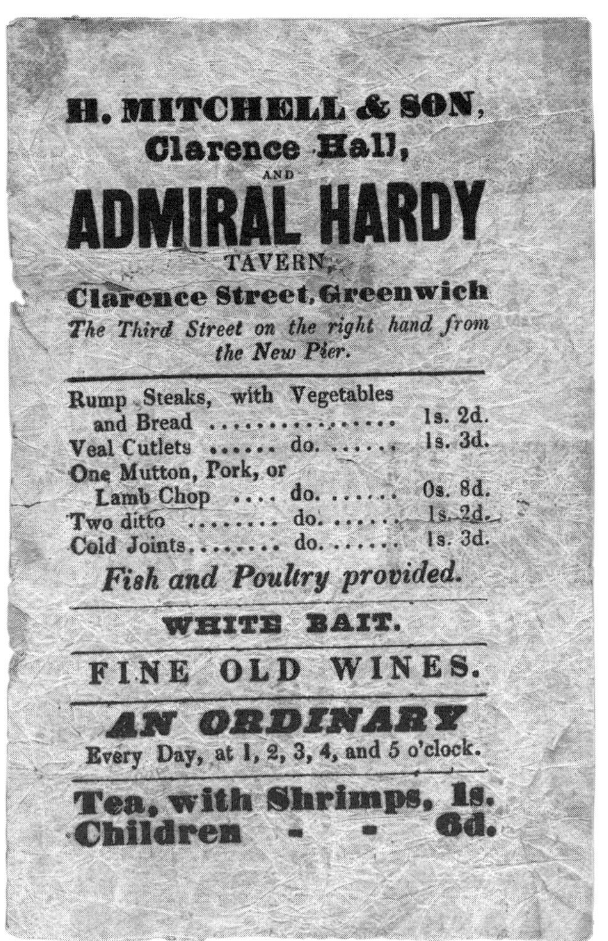

Leaflet of H. Mitchell & Son, Clarence Street, Greenwich, London, mid 19th century. Letterpress. 126 × 83 mm (5 × 3¼ in)

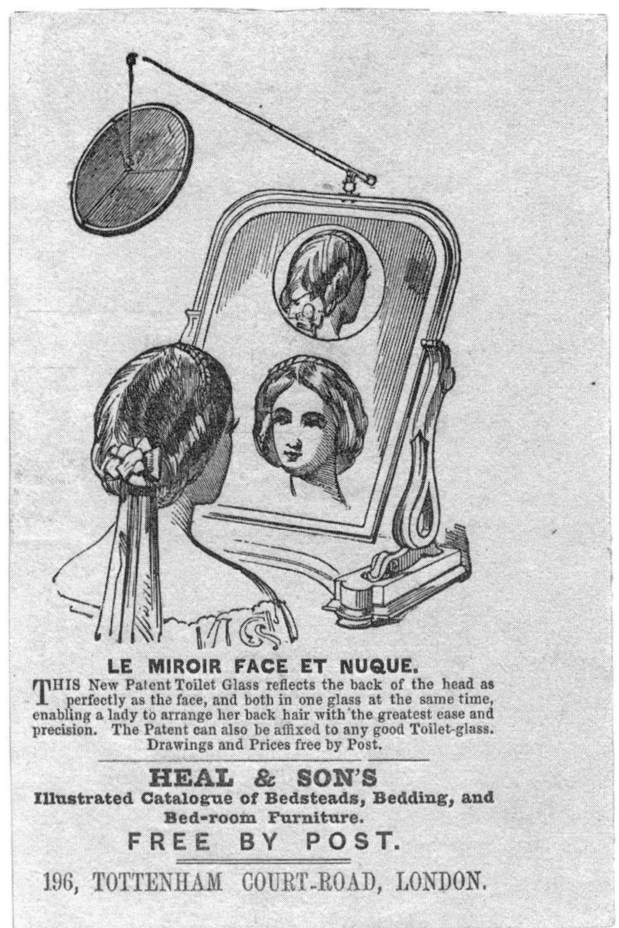

Leaflet of Heal & Sons, Tottenham Court Road, London, late 19th century. Letterpress, with wood-engraving. 130 × 87 mm (5⅛ × 3⅜ in)

smaller tradesman and shopkeeper. Major users were clothiers, ironmongers, grocers, dairies, bootmakers, tearooms, coffee houses, and dining rooms. Also prominent in leaflets were proprietors of popular spectacles and entertainments (exhibitions, pleasure gardens, etc.) and rag, bone, and bottle dealers (whose announcements were slipped under doors and in letter boxes with an intimation through a CALL-BACK HANDBILL of a return visit for collection). The most favoured size was approximately 190 × 135 mm (7½ × 5¼ in), with more elaborate announcements at approximately 255 × 190 mm (10 × 7½ in). Most were printed black on white paper, though American leaflets tended to favour tinted papers.

Hand-distribution of leaflets became something of a public nuisance, with much intrusion on passers-by and liberal scatterings of waste paper in the streets. The litter was caused not only by reluctant recipients but by distributors who, tired of handing out, discharged their loads indiscriminately.

The introduction of magazine insets or inserts in the latter part of the century led to a blurring of the distinction between single-sheet leaflets and four-page folders, many of which were used arbitrarily for both purposes. Two- or three-colour leaflets, many with wood-engraved illustrations or, later, chromolithographed designs, also appeared in both roles, though as leaflets their use was restricted to shop-counter display rather than general street distribution.

'Novelty' leaflets, designed to ensure a lengthy publicity life, presented puzzles, optical illusions, and, in the latter part of the century, chromolithographed HOLD-TO-LIGHT novelties. In this last category, a recapitulation of the earlier 'Protean view' novelty (*see* TRANSPARENCY), an advertising image appearing on the front of the leaflet was augmented or modified by a secondary image printed on the back; the aggregate image became apparent only when viewed against the light.

The leaflet was, and continues to be, well suited to the advertising of neighbourhood events, in which householder and passer by may be induced to take an impulse interest. Door-to-door and hand-to-hand distribution conveys a sense of special urgency and immediacy. Thus, in most collections of leaflets, there appears much 'special occasion' material, including bargain offers, grand openings, meetings, and entertainments and spectacles; in the 19th-century freaks, curiosities, and other transient shows account for a significant proportion of the total count.

See also ADVERTISING NOVELTY; AERIAL LEAFLET; CHOP PAPER; CLUB FLYER; INSET, MAGAZINE; LOTTERY PAPERS; PRICE LIST; PROSPECTUS, PUBLISHER'S; SAILING NOTICE/CARD; SALE CATALOGUE; SCHOOL PROSPECTUS; TRADE ADVERTISER

Lecture ticket

Students admitted to courses of study in university medical faculties and teaching hospitals in the 19th century were provided with tickets of authorization. The tickets, printed on card measuring some 77 × 115 mm (3 × 4½ in), were valid for specific periods, commonly one year, and carried the course subjects as a main title under the instructional heading. They were signed by the lecturer concerned or by the head or secretary of the faculty and bore the inscribed name and number of the student. They were printed in a single colour (black, or the much-favoured sanguine of the period) from copperplate engravings or were heavily impressed from type on heavyweight cardboard stock, sometimes colour-tinted.

Typical course-titles include: 'Anatomy and surgery' (University of Edinburgh, 1807–8); 'Theory and practice of physic' (Harvard University, 1838); 'Practical anatomy' (University of Pennsylvania, 1843); 'Lectures on chemistry' (Guy's Hospital, 1836). Other tickets were cast in more general terms: 'Conversations in anatomy and surgery' (University of Edinburgh, 1829); 'Admit Mr (—) to the public dissecting rooms' (Glasgow Medical School, 1827); 'Lectures on materia medica' (Harvard University, 1837); '(—) pupil to the Westminster Hospital for (—) months from (—) [signed] surgeons' (1826). A French example of the same period admits to the Faculty of Medicine at the University of France. It bears the legend on the reverse: 'Défense d'entrer dans l'intérieur de la Faculté avec canne ou armes'. Cards in similar style were also issued to students completing courses. A University of Glasgow card bears the title 'Ticket for the dissecting room' above the declaration: 'I certify that (Mr Thos. O Ward) attended the above course from (Nov 1 1826–May 1 1827): [signed] (Thos. Marshall MD, Demonstrator)'.

Tickets of admission to university courses in other subjects are also found: 'Faculty of Law… lectures on Scotch law' (University of Glasgow, 1853–54), as are tickets certifying attendance: 'I certify that (Mr William Lockart) attended the above [Greek] Class' (University of Glasgow, 1847–48). These particular tickets were produced lithographically and reflect the growing use of the process for this kind of work.

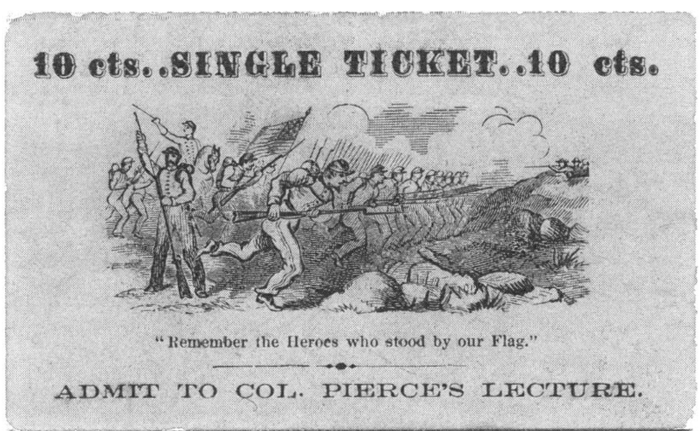

Ticket for Colonel Pierce's lecture, c. 1865. Letterpress with wood-engraving, printed on blue card. 53 × 90 mm (2⅛ × 3½in)

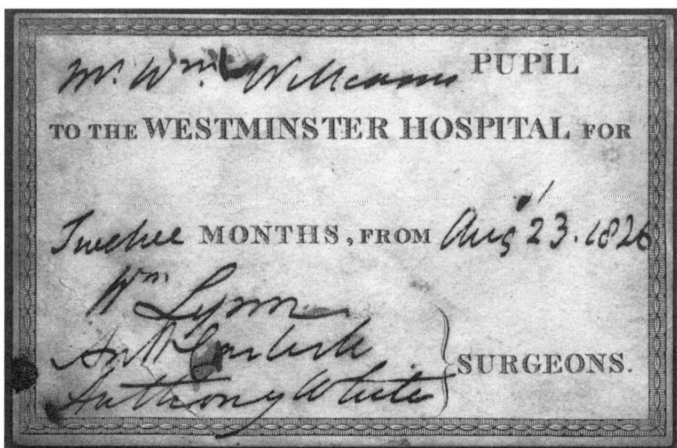

Ticket for admission to a course at Westminster Hospital for 12 months from 23 August 1826. Intaglio printed and manuscript. 75 × 117 mm (3 × 4⅝in)

At Cambridge University tickets were issued for intercollegiate lectures in the 1870s so that students' fees could be recouped from colleges.

Letter seal

Prior to the advent of the gummed ENVELOPE, letters were sealed at first with wax (which bore the imprint of the sender's seal), and later with sealing WAFERS, small discs of isinglass which were moistened and used to close the four flaps of the ungummed envelope upon each other. Also in use as letter seals were paper slips, some blank, some bearing the printed initials

Letter seals, mostly mid 19th century. Produced by a variety of methods, including embossing (with or without colour printing), printing in gold, and chromolithography. The largest with a diameter of 16 mm (⅝in)

of the sender and some, in Britain, bearing legends or propaganda messages, many of them relating to the repeal of the Corn Laws and to the Temperance Movement. Similar seals, with distinctly different wording, were sold for use on valentine envelopes and other love missives. The seals were sometimes sold in multiple sheets, invididual items being cut out and pasted down by the user. The separately applied seal continued in use long after the introduction of gummed envelopes; it had an echo in the flap of the gummed envelope, which retained – until it disappeared in the early 1920s – a projecting tongue.

The paper letter seal remained in widespread use in central Europe well into the 20th century, particularly in the context of official correspondence from central government and local authorities. Commonly circular in shape, and measuring some 40 mm (1½in) in diameter, it was usually die-stamped, generally appearing white on a single-colour background, with the title of the organization spelt out in a peripheral ring and a coat of arms or other device in the centre. Most letter seals were finished with scalloped edges or, in direct invocation of their wax forerunners, given irregular wavy edges. Such seals were in general use in Austria, Czechoslovakia, Germany, Hungary, Poland, and Romania, and were everywhere imitated by trade federations, banks, institutes, hospitals, and public utilities, as well as by doctors and lawyers. Many commercial concerns also adopted them, but with the intrusion of monogrammed trade marks and other 'selling images' the original concept weakened, finally disappearing after World War II.

Letterhead

The origins of the letterhead are closely allied to those of the TRADE CARD and BILLHEAD, from which it may be said to derive. As many surviving examples show, the billhead – and even the trade card – did frequent service as carriers of messages; it was clearly only a matter of time before the billhead shed its classic opening words 'Bought of' and emerged as a letterhead in its own right.

The development was gradual, however. Whereas the invoice was a vital document of business record, the business letter was a comparative rarity before the industrial age. Only in the mid 19th century, with the rising tide of commercial enterprise and the advent of postal reforms, did the concept of business correspondence begin to crystallize. And only in the last decades of the century did the letterhead in its modern form appear – with telephone number and telegraphic address added in the first years of the 20th century. The term 'letterhead' first appeared, as a commercial substitute for 'letter paper', in America in 1890.

No less clearly than other forms of printed ephemera, successive design phases of the letterhead reflect both the developing technology of printing and the received aesthetics of their time. In some cases, however, techniques may exist in parallel, producing radical contrasts of style within the same period. Thus, for much of the 19th century, the emergent billhead/letterhead appears at one level with the horizontal discipline and sobriety of movable type and at another with the hand-drawn panache of copper-engraving and lithography.

The advent in the 1850s of the American jobbing platen, a printing press offering hitherto unheard of accuracy of register, brought a complete reassessment of the role of the printer as designer. The new machine's precision brought forth from typefounders a spate of ornamental typefaces, borders, decorative panels, and cartouches designed to exploit its virtues. The result, much of it more whimsical than wholly prudent, was described as 'art printing'.

The style is enshrined in successive issues of the *Printers' International Specimen Exchange*, published in London between 1880 and 1898, in which enthusiastic practitioners explored their skills. Later volumes also record a further new design wave, the 'Leicester Free Style'. Characterized mainly by asymmetry of layout, and named after its place of origin (specifically the De Montfort Press, Leicester), the style was soon to give way to a fresh burst of creativity from the lithographic field, in which the artist's hand was again given free play. By the end of the 19th century, the lithographed letterhead, billhead, and indeed most of the items in the stationery range, had begun to convey their messages with a new exuberance. In swirling curves of shadowed lettering, in heavyweight strapwork and decoration reminiscent of the fairground, the style demanded every trick denied or made extremely difficult in letterpress.

It was in this period that the letterhead achieved ascendancy over the billhead. With the passage of time, the billhead was to become little more than a visual afterthought, a second-class version of a more distinguished senior partner.

The first decades of the 20th century saw a diminution in the weight and impact of the letterhead, reducing its scale to match the needs of the typewriter, by now the normal instrument for the production of the letter. Design phases moved through successive periods of restraint, the New Typography associated with the Bauhaus making way for the austerities of the 1950s and 1960s. During the 1940s, 1950s, and 1960s the emergence of the commercial 'house style' brought a growing focus on the company 'logo', and this was often the only decorative ingredient in an otherwise purely typographic presentation. Only in later decades did a more consciously decorative trend return, sometimes as nostalgic pastiche, sometimes through a revival of embossing.

Business stationery in Europe underwent a major transformation in the 1960s, when the earlier quarto, octavo, and foolscap formats were replaced by the international 'A' range of paper sizes. In this period the layout, folding, and general presentation of business correspondence became the subject, for the first time, of informed typographic advice and agreed standards. The change was confined to Europe; the format of the American letterhead and its derivatives remained unchanged.

REFERENCES Graham Hudson, 'Printed Ephemera and Design History', *Art Libraries Journal* vol. 6, no. 1 (London, 1981); John Lewis, *Printed Ephemera* (Ipswich: W. S. Cowell, 1962); Peter Pickard, 'The History of the Letterhead', *Printing Review*, vol. 75, Autumn 1957, pp. 5–20

Licence

A licence is an authority to do some act that would otherwise be unlawful. This is an abstract concept but the term is also used for a document that evidences the granting of a licence, and this is what mainly concerns us here. It is worth noting that simple licences are often granted orally and may well be implied. These leave no written record. British milkmen would probably be surprised to learn that they have an implied licence from customers to walk up their garden path to deliver milk, an act that would otherwise be a trespass.

Licensing has many functions. It may be purely commercial, as in the case of a licence to operate a process that is the subject of a patent. It is also used to restrict the performance of an activity to those whose competence has been assessed, as with a driving or pilot's licence. It may be used to control the numbers engaged in a particular occupation in a given area, as in the case of the licensing of market traders or premises for the sale of intoxicating liquor. It may be to ensure that the whereabouts of dangerous materials or equipment are known to the authorities, that they are in the care of responsible persons, and that proper safety precautions are observed. Examples are licences for the storage of explosives or petroleum and for the keeping of firearms. Control of some aspects of trade is exercised by the issue of import and export licences, which cover the movement of specified goods to named customers. Finally, licensing is used as a convenient means of levying a tax, as with the road fund licence.

Many licences are now statutory and issued by central or local government. The issue of a licence is normally recorded in a central register, inspection of which may be open to the public or restricted to certain groups of people, such as the police or Customs and Excise officials. The licence itself usually contains the same information as that recorded in the register and is kept or displayed by the licensee as evidence of having complied with the regulations. The licence may sometimes be called a CERTIFICATE or permit. The licence document may serve more than one purpose. For example, a THEATRE TICKET is a licence to occupy a seat in the theatre for the duration of the performance but it also serves as a RECEIPT for the purchase money.

Licences have a long history stretching back for at least eight hundred years. Some of the earliest were issued by the monarch to allow named persons he wished to reward to hunt in the royal forests. These are recorded in British Close Rolls. Licences to crenellate allowed the licensee to fortify his house, and would be granted by the monarch only to those he could rely upon to be his supporters.

By the late 18th century licensing had become a significant source of tax revenue in Britain. Among the occupations that required a licence were: auctioneering, brewing, calico printing, candle making, coach building, dealing in brandy, glass making, malting, paper making, selling of gold and silver plate, soap making, starch making, sweets (fruit wine) making, tanning, tea, coffee and chocolate selling, and wire drawing. The fees for these licences ranged from £2 to £10 annually, which were considerable sums for the period. The developments of the 20th century have given rise to many new licences, for example software licences, television receiving licences, and residents' parking permits.

Most official licences issued over the past century and a half are printed forms completed in manuscript or, in later years, increasingly in typescript. Single colour, elegant printing has given way to multicolour, elaborate designs, a trend paralleled by both postage stamps and banknotes.

Licences can be interesting documents in their own right, often giving rise to intriguing questions for the collector. What, for example, persuaded the British authorities to reduce the annual fee for a licence to keep one male servant, which was really a tax levied on those thought well able to afford it, from 25 shillings at the end of the 18th century to only 15 shillings at the start of the 20th century? In 1914 a licence for a carriage with less than four wheels allowed it to be drawn by horses or mules. However, if the unladen weight was less than one ton or greater than five tons it could, alternatively, be drawn by a motor car. Why were cars not allowed to draw carriages weighing between one and five tons?

Licences form a valuable resource for the social historian indicating, as they do, which activities the central and local authorities wished to control at any period and which they thought could withstand a degree of taxation. They are rarely collected and surviving examples are likely to be found scattered among other documents in record offices. [AA]

See also DRIVING LICENCE; FORM; HACKNEY PAPERS; PASS/PERMIT; PASSPORT; STAGE-PLAY LICENCE

REFERENCES R. and J. Burn, *The Justice of the Peace and Parish Officer*, 16th edn (London: T. Cadell, 1788); Charles Toase, *Aids to Reference Service: no.2, Licences and Current Offical Registers* (London: The Library Association, 1960); S. and B. Webb, *The History of Liquor Licensing in England* (London: Longmans & Co., 1903)

Liebig card

From its inception in 1872 the Liebig card was for a century the best-known advertising item in Europe. Introduced as a promotional GIVE-AWAY by the firm of Lemco ('Liebig's Extract of Meat Company'), the cards appeared in sets commonly of six or eight. By 1974, when they finally ceased publication, the total number of sets had reached 1866. A dozen or so additional sets were prepared which, for reasons unknown, were never issued.

International expansion of the company brought the product – and the cards – into virtually every European country, as well as to South Africa and the United States. Printed and prepared variously in Belgium, France, and Germany, they appeared in Czech, Danish, Dutch, English, Flemish, French, German, Hungarian, Italian, Russian, Spanish, and Swedish – though 'publication' was formally from the company's national offices. Most sets are to be found in more than one language.

Liebig was the parent company of Oxo and Fray Bentos, and in some cases the cards also advertise the product under the name of 'Oxo' and (less commonly) 'Sapis'. Most cards, after a number of costly prosecutions for 'passing off' in the 1870s, carry the signature of the company founder, Baron Justus von Liebig, as evidence of the product's authenticity, together with injunctions to the buyer to beware of counterfeits.

Liebig card from the series 'A travers champs et forêts' issued by the Compagnie Liebig, Antwerp, late 19th century. Shown front and back. Chromolithographed front. 71 × 105 mm (2¾ × 4⅛ in)

Liebig cards were first issued in France, where the company followed the then current pratice of overprinting their advertising message on 'stock' cards, which were available from specialist printers who supplied traders at large. Many of the earliest Liebig issues are therefore pictorially identical to other manufacturer's cards, only the text being specific to Liebig. Unlike the later Liebig issues, some of these cards appeared in sets of ten, twelve, sixteen, or twenty-four.

Soon afterwards the company embarked on producing its own cards, rapidly establishing a reputation for attractiveness and, in the course of time, their content. For many, the Liebig card was to acquire the status of universal mentor, offering a stream of useful and entertaining information. Design and production standards were consistently high, and many sets were collected for their pictorial beauty alone. Printed in huge quantities, and requiring up to twelve printings for each individual image, the cards are excellent examples of commercial chromolithography.

Liebig cards were at first given to customers over the counter, but were later issued in complete sets in return for coupons cut from the product wrapper. Their success provided a model on which many 20th-century give-aways were based. Other continental firms, both before and after the Liebig success, used the give-away card. Bon Marché, Cibils, Lindt, Memmenich, Stollwerk, Suchard, and Van Houten are prominent names, but the Liebig card became – and remained – pre-eminent.

As a promotional item, the Liebig card may be seen to have

passed through a number of development stages. The earliest examples, pre-printed, bore no product image. With the advent of the specially-produced 'company card', the product appears as a dominant element, either as a large inset or as a major item within the principal illustration. Later, the product appears as a marginal addendum, often wholly isolated from the main image.

The Liebig company also produced cards for hotels and restaurants. These were larger than the normal Liebig card and carried space for the insertion of the menu by hand; they were also available in collectable sets, each item designed for the diner to take away. Here the pictorial element inclined specifically to the decorative, though an image of the product remained a constant feature.

Other cards were produced for restaurant and hotel dining parties. These, too, had decorative illustrations and were designed to be kept as a souvenir; they appeared in sets of six and commonly bore the expression 'Bon appetit!' and provided space for the diner's name.

The Liebig company issued a number of other promotional items, including calendars, cookery books, postcards, playing cards, reward cards, games, and toys, as well as billheads for use by grocers and a wide range of general point-of-sale material.

In recent years there have been a number of 'reissues' of Liebig card sets, produced by the four-colour process of today's technology. Typical of these are sets produced in association with the present company Brooke Bond Liebig Italiana S.p.a. Printed in sets of six, they bear the words 'Ristampa 1978' (reprint 1978), though it must be said that the quality of reproduction poses little risk of confusion with the originals.

REFERENCES *Catalogue of Liebig Trade Cards* (Hendon: Murray Cards, 1980); *Figurine Liebig: Catalogo Generale* (Milan: Sanguinetti, 1981)

Lighthouse-dues papers

Responsibility for the maintenance of lighthouses, originally a burden borne by charitable groups (notably religious ones), in time passed to the mariners whose safety they ensured. 'Light dues', a levy similar in principle to port dues and graduated according to tonnage and nationality of the vessels concerned, became payable by all shipping entering or leaving ports, or even passing by. Ships in transit were boarded and charged at sea.

The system, which was open to serious abuse, bestowed on private individuals the right to collect dues. They undertook to maintain light from houses and to return the balance to the issuing authority. They often used arbitrary methods for assessing payment and were less than punctillious in making returns.

The ephemera of lighthouse dues consist in the main of two distinct classes of document: the certificates of appointment of collecting agents and the receipt forms that record payment of dues. The earliest surviving examples date from the 1680s.

Certificates of appointment, generally landscape in format and measuring approximately 130 × 180 mm (5⅛ × 7⅛ in), bore the insignia of the issuing authority (normally Trinity House) and some two hundred words of contractual text.

Receipt forms, approximately 140 × 165 mm (5½ × 6½ in), were distinctive in that they often carried a woodcut or engraved illustration of the lighthouse in question. In this respect they represent a significant category of ephemera that often provides reliable pictorial records of structures for which no other illustrations are available. To the historian of lighthouse technology the evidence they provide may be of great

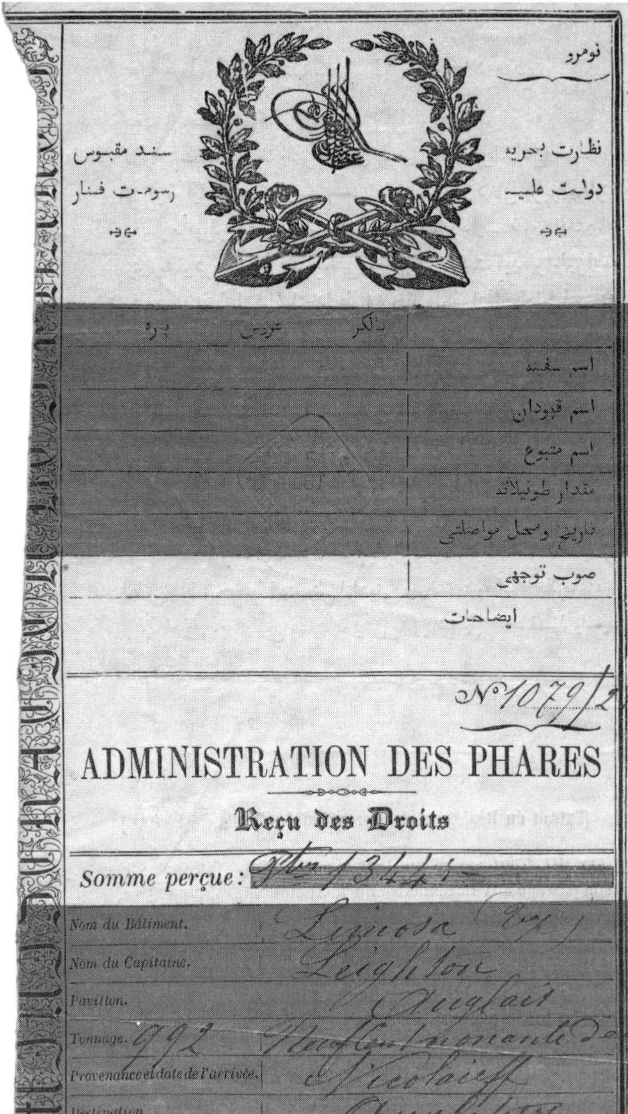
No 1079/2

ADMINISTRATION DES PHARES

Reçu des Droits

Somme perçue:

Nom du Bâtiment.

Nom du Capitaine. Leighton

Pavillon. Anglais

Tonnage. 992

Provenance et date de l'arrivée. Nicolaieff

Destination

Receipt for lighthouse dues, Constantinople, 15 July 1882. Letterpress and manuscript, with two stencilled bands in pink. 266 × 134 mm (10½ × 5¼ in)

importance. In one classic case, 'before' and 'after' illustrations show details of modifications in structure: on a late 18th-century receipt the Mumbles lighthouse appears as a 'double brazier' light, whereas on an early 19th-century version it is shown after its conversion to oil.

REFERENCES Douglas B. Hague and Rosemary Christie, *Lighthouses, their Architecture, History and Archaeology* (Llandysul: Gower, 1975); John Lewis, *Printed Ephemera* (Ipswich: W. S. Cowell, 1962)

COLLECTIONS Royal Institution of South Wales, Swansea; Trinity House, London

Linen-button card

Buttons are said to have been sold on cards in the early 17th century, but widespread marketing in this form emerged only in the late 18th and early 19th centuries when the 'Dorset thread button' appeared. This was a laundry-proof improvement on earlier breakable buttons. Essentially linen-based, it had an outer thread-covered ring of wire and a body composed of transverse linen threads. Production of the buttons became a major cottage industry, not only in Dorset but central and northern England too. The buttons were marketed on unprinted coloured papers, the colour denoting their quality. The Dorset button industry disappeared almost overnight with the introduction of linen-button making machinery in 1851.

The linen button was proof against boiling, mangling, and ironing. It appeared in a number of forms: with or without integral shank, eyeletted or blank, covered with one, two, three, or four layers of linen, linen-backed or unbacked, and in sizes from less than 6.0 mm (¼in) to 60 mm (2⅜in). It was a universally recognized household item, a feature of every sewing box as a standby for use on shirts, pyjamas, underwear, overalls, pillow-slips, and, in northern Europe, duvet covers. Many millions of linen buttons were produced in the English Midlands, notably in Birmingham and Manchester. At one stage it was reported that sixty per cent of Britain's button production (much of which was exported) was in the ubiquitous linen button.

The linen button was marketed as a branded product on cards measuring some 120 × 70 mm (4¾ × 2¾in). Printed in one, two, or three colours, the cards presented buttons, generally in sets of 6, 9, 12, or 24, with decorative title-pieces and ruled columns or rectangles as display areas. Decorative buttons were presented on display cards into the second half of the 20th century, but these make their appeal more through the buttons themselves than their display. The linen-button card, which was a more or less standard product, relied almost wholly on its decorative presentation.

Apart from brand names ('Beat-all', 'Briton', 'Climax', 'Excel', 'Owl', 'Snowdrop', 'Wreath and Lion', etc.), linen-button cards simply bore selling phrases ('Strong and durable', 'Best English make', 'Superior quality'). The diameters of buttons were expressed in lines: ten lines equalled 6.0 mm (¼in). Sizes ranged from eight lines to a hundred, the average being twenty lines. Cards are sometimes found in which the wrong size button appears, and in some cases the size designation has been altered by means of a sticker. Unbranded button cards also appeared, sometimes in multiple sets of dozens, with divisions allowing a dozen at a time to be cut off for sale as required.

Towards the end of the 19th century novelty cards appeared with buttons in a range of sizes, typically eighteen to twenty-six lines. In one example, the 'Ivy Set', each size was presented on a separate cut-out ivy leaf, five leaves and a title card being eyeletted together fanwise to form an interlocking circular display.

It is recorded that Will Thorne, founder of the British union that came to be called the National Union of General and Municipal Workers, worked at home as a child with his sisters and widowed mother sewing linen buttons on to cards. They sewed the buttons twelve to a card, provided their own needles and thread, and were paid at the rate of 1½*d* per 144 cards. Will Thorne was later to convene the meeting that led to the formation of the British Labour Party.

See also LINEN-BUTTON LABEL

COLLECTION The Button Museum, Ross-on-Wye, Hereford

Linen-button cards of the early 20th century. *Left:* lithographed in three colours, 121 × 72 mm (4¾ × 2⅞in); *right:* lithographed in two colours, 154 × 79mm (6⅛ × 3⅛in)

Linen-button label

Starting in Britain in 1841 with a handful of manufacturers (notably William Ashton, John Aston & Co., J. Chatwin and Sons, William Elliott and Sons, and Green, Cadbury & Co.), the linen-button industry rapidly spread among a number of family firms. Intermarriage and amalgamations led to a succession of double- and treble-barrelled titles. Brand names proliferated, not all of them the property of the manufacturers; many were used by non-manufacturing distributors who sold the buttons as their own. Patents too were often claimed by distributors, when in reality patent rights lay with the manufacturer.

The story is reflected in the multitude of paper labels used by the industry. The labels, appearing variously in display box lids and on the backs of LINEN-BUTTON CARDS, conformed to a design genre featuring the shadowed titles, arched panels, floral fill-ins, and circular trade marks of the period. Printed in two or four colours, with a high incidence of gold, the labels measured some 80 × 60 mm (3⅛ × 2⅜in). A few were circular.

Unlike the button card, the label tended to be marginally more explicit on the matter of provenance. Manufacturers and distributors names appeared in a number of designs. Among these were (as manufacturers): John Aston & Co.; Green and Co.; and Plant and Green; and (as distributors): Copestake, Crampton and Co.; Olney Amsden & Sons; J. & N. Philips and Co. Ltd; and Rylands and Sons Ltd. Brand names of the period include 'Atlas', 'Beat All', 'Bell', 'Briton', 'City', 'Climax', 'Crossed Swords', 'Doddington', 'Empire', 'Erin', 'Excel', 'Fashion', 'Globe', 'Ideal', 'Ivy', 'Lily', 'Manor', 'Newcastle', 'Owl', 'Paragon', 'Perseverance', 'Pilot', 'Pioneer', 'Regal', 'Royal', 'Shakespeare', 'Snowdrop', 'Victor', 'Wreath and Lion', 'XL', and 'XLCR'.

In 1907 a major amalgamation took place, bringing into a single firm – 'Buttons Ltd' – most of the major names of the day, among them John Aston; Green, Cadbury & Co.; J. Chatwin and Sons; Dain, Watts & Manton; William Elliott and Sons; Green and Co.; John Manton Shakespeare & Co.; and Plant and Green. The new company continued, however, to market buttons under the old brand names and with the labels unchanged. In spite of the uniformity of the product, individual brand loyalties remained strong. It is estimated that at one time the label range of Buttons Ltd numbered a hundred. The company continued to produce linen buttons until the 1930s.

SOCIETIES British Button Society; Button Society (US)

Lithography *See* CHROMO; CURRIER & IVES; SHEET-MUSIC COVER; TRANSFER LITHOGRAPHY

Lobby card

Also known simply as 'lobbies', lobby cards get their name from their point of display, the cinema entrance hall, where they advertised the attraction within, both current and forthcoming.

They were produced in huge quantities, and formed a major portion of the promotional 'package' that accompanied the marketing of every movie. They were produced in sets of eight or more, including a general title-piece, which was often based on the poster for the film. The complete set was designed to convey the film's subject matter, its key scenes, and its stars. The cards measured a standard 280 × 353 mm (11 × 13⅞ in), and were printed in colour (regardless of whether the film itself was in colour); they were commonly displayed in slip-in frames, more or less in the sequence of the movie story.

Standardization of their format emerged in the early 1920s. Some pre-World War I lobby cards (now rarities) were upright in format. Notable examples, dating from 1913, are in the Michael Hawks Collection; they advertise productions of the '101 Bison Feature' company, and bear the logo of Universal Films.

As with the film poster, design and production of the lobby card was subject to the contractual limitations of the movie industry. The relative sizes and sequence of stars' names and the placing of supporting cast-lists were both closely controlled. Designs were effectively the joint work of the executives and stars concerned. It was thus unusual for lobby cards (or film posters) to attract the talents of major graphic designers, though the signatures of such men as Norman Rockwell and Vargas occasionally appear on them. For the most part, early lobby cards were concocted from paste-ups of tinted photographs and the hand lettering of small-time commercial artists. The convention never really disappeared.

The lobby card traces the development of the movie industry, reflecting the rise and fall of stars, studios, and distributors as well as its technology in sound, colour, and special effects. Graphically its roots lie in the circus poster, the cover of the early 20th-century novelette, and the store-window showcard.

REFERENCES John Kobal, *50 Years of Film Posters* (London: Copperstone, 1972); John Kobal, *Foyer Pleasure* (London: Aurum Press, 1982); Kathryn Leigh Scott, *Lobby Cards: The Classic Films* (Los Angeles: Pomegranate Press, 1987)

COLLECTIONS British Film Institute, London; Library of Congress, Washington DC; Hollywood Studio Museum

Lord's prayer

This prayer was seen as a particularly suitable text for calligraphy or typographic rendition. It appeared both as a devotional text and as a worthy exercise for the executant in many countries, and was rendered in every available style and medium. A typical large example measuring 345 × 255 mm (13⅝ × 10 in), is a multicoloured lithograph with the comment that 'Each line of words across the engraving is varied in size and style so that all the choicest and most fascinating styles of type are represented'. Its smaller sizes of lettering approach the microscopic.

See also MINIATURE TEXT

Lottery papers [plate 8]

The use of the lottery as a means of raising revenue for the state began in France in 1533. The first English lottery was held in 1569, when tickets were sold at the west door of St Paul's Cathedral, the profits going to the repair of the harbours of England. Later, lotteries were held for various projects. In 1612 the Virginia Co. derived revenue from a lottery, and lottery funds contributed to the founding of a number of major American colleges, among them Harvard and Yale. The foundation collections of the British Museum were partly financed by a lottery.

The lottery as an institution, sometimes itself corrupt, and often inducing corruption, has been the subject of continuous controversy. The Louisiana State Lottery, set up in 1869 to raise funds for the New Orleans Charity Hospital, was abolished by law, as were all American lotteries, in 1892. The Irish Hospitals' Sweepstake, established in 1930, raised a total hospital revenue of over £120m, even though it had been illegal in Britain since its inception. (Specifically, the *sale* of these tickets in Britain is illegal, although their purchase is legal.) In America the postal transmission of sweepstake tickets – and any lottery ticket – is illegal.

State lotteries in Britain were abolished in 1826, though localized lotteries, restricted in prize-money and frequency, were made legal in the early 1970s. The British Premium Bond Scheme is not a lottery; the bondholder's 'stake' remains the individual's property after the draw; in a lottery the stake is relinquished. A state lottery, the 'National Lottery', was re-established in Britain in 1994, and the first contract to run it was awarded to Camelot. At the outset, draws were made once a week, later twice; prizes vary from between £1 million to over £20 million according to the number of winning draws.

Lottery items most commonly collected are those appearing in Britain in the decades immediately preceding the abolition of the lottery in 1826. The period coincides with the beginning of mass-publicity methods and the introduction of flamboyant printing types and similar wood-engraved letters. The range includes lottery tickets, background organizational material, announcements of results, leaflets, magazine insets, and promotional cards, in addition to a sprinkling of anti-lottery propaganda. Though financed and administered by the government, responsibility for the ticket sales and promotion was farmed out on a commission basis to private firms, known as 'contractors' or 'lottery office keepers'. There had originally been thirty of these, but by 1823 only fifteen licensed offices remained. Chief among them were Thomas Bish, George Carroll, Hazard & Co., Richardson, Goodluck, & Co., and J. and J. Sivewright ('Goodluck' was a name acquired by the company for a 'nominal partner's fee' of £50 a year from a Mrs Goodluck, whose name it really was).

Most of the 'contractors' had premises in Cornhill or Oxford Street. Cornhill had at least six offices; Oxford Street had three. Though mutually competitive, many of the leading firms used the same printers for their publicity material. Notable among these were Evans & Ruffy of Walbrook, Gye & Balne of Gracechurch Street, and Whiting & Branston of the Strand. Whiting & Branston had acquired the rights to the COMPOUND-PLATE PRINTING process that Sir William Congreve developed for security printing. They had used it to print invitations and tickets to the Coronation of George IV, and the process had become identified in the public mind with security and integrity. As it turned out, the compound-plate printing process was used for producing publicity material for lotteries rather than the tickets, which were fairly readily tampered with.

Whiting & Branston's lottery publicity items, some of them incorporating elaborate blind embossing, are superb examples of 'ceremonial' printing. The company's name usually appears not as a separate typeset footline, but discreetly incorporated into the design. The material appears chiefly in the form of cards in two sizes, 285 × 125 mm (11¼ × 4⅞ in) and 115 × 80 mm

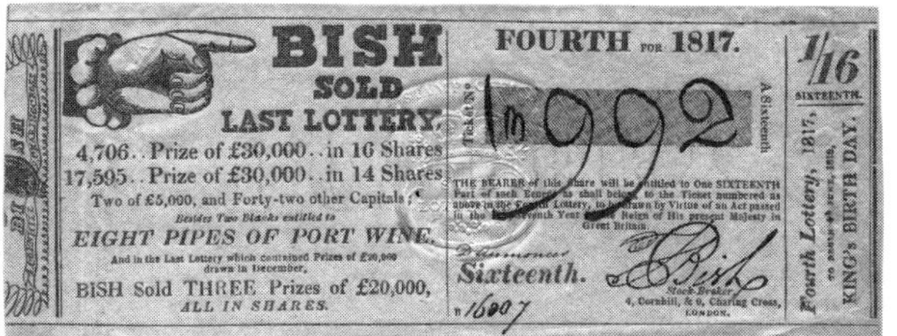

Lottery ticket of T. Bish, London, 1817. Letterpress (printed in red and blue) and manuscript. 69 × 181 mm ($2\frac{3}{4} \times 7\frac{1}{8}$ in)

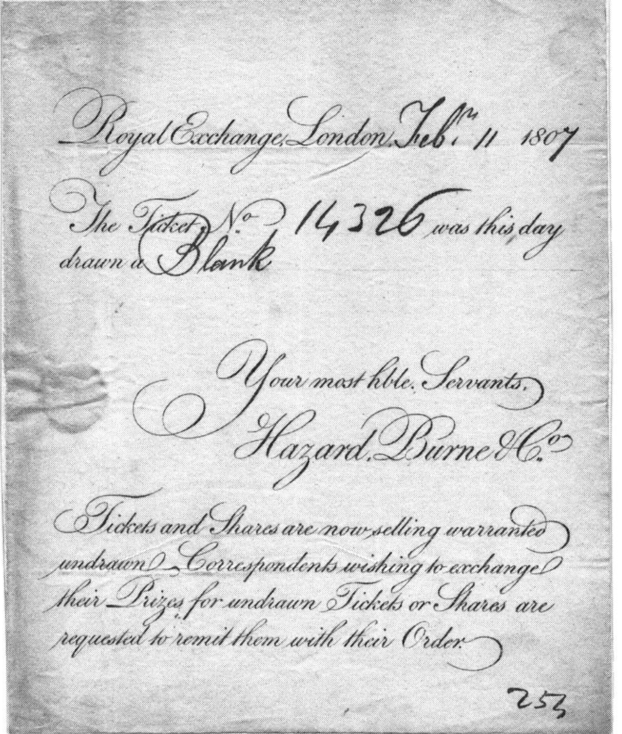

Royal Exchange, London Feby. 11 1807

The Ticket No. 14326 was this day drawn a Blank

Your most hble. Servants,

Hazard, Burne & Co.

Tickets and Shares are now selling warranted undrawn. Correspondents wishing to exchange their Prizes for undrawn Tickets or Shares are requested to remit them with their Order.

253

Lottery notification by Hazard, Burne & Co. of a 'blank' draw, 11 February 1807. Engraved and printed intaglio, with manuscript. 195 × 164 mm ($7\frac{5}{8} \times 6\frac{1}{2}$ in)

($4\frac{1}{2} \times 3\frac{1}{8}$ in), printed in three or four colours and with blind embossing. The basic design treatment features an elaborately engraved colour background, with inset panels in extra colours showing textual details. This approach allowed for the use of any of the contractors' names in the panels, which meant that the same design appears in different guises.

In a series of Whiting & Branston leaflets in similar vein, a wood-engraved design appears as a centrally-placed two- or three-colour motif on a white background without blind embossing; in most cases metal type is used in addition to wood-engraved lettering to convey the message. Lottery leaflets were used as street handouts or as magazine insets, and often appear with evidence of 'binding in' at their left-hand edge.

Large numbers of lottery leaflets – which were also used as insets – were produced as one- or two-colour throw-aways by Gye & Balne and other printers. They generally measure around 230 × 150 mm (9 × 6 in). In style they are robust (rather than in the style of SECURITY PRINTING), and carry large wood-block numerals showing prize monies in the manner of 'Reward' notices (*see* REWARD PAPERS). Through their frequent use of a second colour – principally red – they established an idiom of their own. As with the decorative Whiting & Branston productions, layout and wording were often identical for one or more contractors, only the names and addresses differing. Lottery leaflets are sometimes to be found printed on the backs of playbills – possibly by way of paper economy or to serve a dual function. Last-minute 'reminders' leaflets also appeared, often in horizontal format, 120 × 190 mm ($4\frac{3}{4} \times 7\frac{1}{2}$ in). They urged haste before the draw took place, and appreared in the few days preceding (or even on the morning of) the day of the draw.

Lottery publicity explored every technique of contemporary popular literature. Give-aways included puzzles, jokes, cartoons and caricatures, jingles and poems, mock valentines, and other attention-getting novelties. In many respects lottery campaigns of the period were well in advance of their time. In scope, ingenuity, and not least in volume, their operations far exceeded anything that advertising had hitherto conceived. Leaflet production figures soared. It is reported that at the height of the lottery boom one firm alone spent £36,000 a year on printing, a figure equal to over £10 million in late 20th-century terms.

Lottery tickets, commonly measuring some 65 × 170 mm ($2\frac{1}{2} \times 6\frac{3}{4}$ in), were usually printed in two colours (red and black, or red and blue) or in blue alone. Individual tickets were cut with scissors from bound booklets. Most tickets bore an embossed 'State Lotteries' stamp and, after 1814, a 'lottery' watermark. They also bore folio and ticket numbers (both handwritten) and the signature or initials of the issuing contractor. Numbered counterfoils remained in the book. Characteristically, owing to the corrosive effect of the writing ink then current, surviving tickets show signs of 'etching' in the handwritten areas. As a measure against fraudulent alteration, handwritten numerals adopted eccentricities: 'zero', for example, carried a straight line above and below the character, and 'thousand digits' were followed by a small 'm' to prevent insertion of extra figures. Tickets were sold in single units, halves, quarters, eighths, and sixteenths, the portion being marked in both words and figures in print.

Early tickets, like their corresponding leaflets, were less flamboyant and were usually printed in a single colour. Many 18th-century tickets were for private lotteries. Here the prizes were possessions: a house, silver plate, or jewellery. In London in the early 1770s, lottery prizes were offered as a sales inducement by shopkeepers, tailors, dressmakers, barbers, and shoeblacks. Though often undated, tickets from before around 1810 are on the whole distinguishable by their use of the 'long s' (ſ), which was used initially and medially, but not finally. Many early 18th-century lottery tickets were very crudely printed. A Mr Sydenham, who ran a London 'Land lottery', complained about other lotteries that it was 'difficult and troublesome for the adventurers to search and find out what prizes they have come up in their tickets, from the badness of the print, the many errors in them . . .'.

Another category of lottery paper, rarer than others, is the lottery notification certificate, which was sent to all ticket holders by the lottery agents informing them whether they had drawn a prize or a blank. These certificates were printed forms on which the date, ticket number, and value of the prize or simply the word 'Blank' were filled in by hand. The magnitude of this adinistrative task may be judged by taking as an example the lottery of 1771, when 50,000 certificates had to be filled in and sent out, the draw resulting in 16,690 prizes and 33,310 blanks.

As the date of the abolition of lotteries in 1826 approached, official-looking printed bills appeared warning the public that, after that date, lotteries must cease. Bearing the royal crest at the head and 'By Order of Government' at the foot, these bills were in fact produced as a final promotional effort by the contractors themselves. Many of them were printed by James Whiting, father of the senior partner in Whiting & Branston.

Not all lottery material was promotional. In one surviving leaflet, an anonymous protestor draws attention to simple mathematics: 'In the lottery to be drawn on Valentine's Day, there are fifteen thousand blanks'. He goes on: 'Of the five thousand prizes', the total number in the draw, 'four thousand eight hundred and sixty are prizes of fifteen pounds only… so that there are only 140 chances in twenty thousand of an adventurer who buys a ticket or share getting back his own money…'. Many similar calculations must have been made with the mounting awareness of the lottery's evils. Its demise in early 19th-century Britain was welcomed even by its addicts.

See also TRADE RHYME

REFERENCES John Ashton, *A History of English Lotteries* (London: Leadenhall Press, 1893); C. L'Estrange Ewen, *Lotteries and Sweepstakes* (London: Heath Cranton Ltd, 1932)

COLLECTIONS Guildhall Library, London; John Johnson Collection, Bodleian Library, Oxford

Lunacy papers

Changing attitudes to mental disorder are graphically expressed in the ephemera of asylums, lunacy commissions, and lunacy legislation. Among the earliest lunacy papers are pamphlets and papers containing general orders for the control of specific asylums. A pamphlet printed in 1778 for Bethlem Hospital, 200 × 125 mm (7⅞ × 5 in), reflects attitudes and conditions at that time. The duty of the porter on 'The Women's Side' was: 'that he shall light the fire in the stove room and assist in carrying the women thither; that he shall assist the Gallery Maids in bathing, bleeding, shaving and giving the Patients their medicines, and also in removing the straw and cleaning the cells… that the feet of every Patient in chains or straw, be carefully examined, well rubbed and covered with flannel every night and morning during the winter season; and if necessary, that immediate notice to be given to the Surgeon…'. The duty of the Surgeon was: 'To attend all such persons who have any accidents or disorders… and to be particularly attentive to them during the Winter, mortifications are very frequent proceeding from the coldness of the season…'.

In the thirty-page Perth Royal Asylum annual report for 1828, 205 × 130 mm (8⅛ × 5⅛ in), appears the injunction that 'No keeper is allowed at any time to deceive, terrify or irritate, by mockery, by mimicry, or by allusions to anything ludicrous in the present appearance or past conduct of any of the patients. They must not indulge or express vindictive feelings, but, considering the patients as utterly incapable to restrain themselves, must forgive all petulence or sarcasms, and treat with equal tenderness those who give the most and least trouble…'. The 1867 annual report of the town of Dorchester, Massachusetts, 145 × 230 mm (5¾ × 9 in), points out that '…the amount of expenditure for these unfortunates we cannot control. These persons cannot be properly provided for at our almshouse…'.

The provision of private accommodation for lunatics is documented in a single-sided prospectus (c.1840), 220 × 180 mm (8⅝ × 7⅛ in), advertising Gate Helmsley Retreat, near York, 'for the reception and recovery of a limited number of Persons of Both

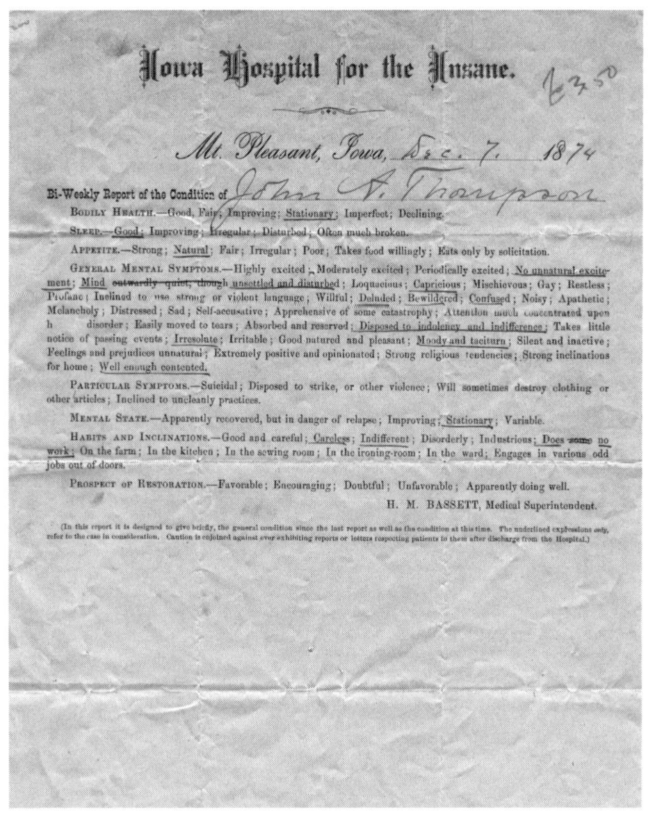

Iowa Hospital for the Insane.

Mt. Pleasant, Iowa, Dec. 7. 1874

Bi-Weekly Report of the Condition of John N. Thompson

BODILY HEALTH.—Good, Fair; Improving; Stationary; Imperfect; Declining.

SLEEP.—Good; Improving; Irregular; Disturbed; Often much broken.

APPETITE.—Strong; Natural; Fair; Irregular; Poor; Takes food willingly; Eats only by solicitation.

GENERAL MENTAL SYMPTOMS.—Highly excited; Moderately excited; Periodically excited; No unnatural excitement; Mind ~~outwardly quiet, though~~ unsettled and disturbed; Loquacious; Capricious; Mischievous; Gay; Restless; Profane; Inclined to use strong or violent language; Willful; Deluded; Bewildered; Confused; Noisy; Apathetic; Melancholy; Distressed; Sad; Self-accusative; Apprehensive of some catastrophy; Attention much concentrated upon h disorder; Easily moved to tears; Absorbed and reserved; Disposed to indolency and indifference; Takes little notice of passing events; Irresolute; Irritable; Good natured and pleasant; Moody and taciturn; Silent and inactive; Feelings and prejudices unnatural; Extremely positive and opinionated; Strong religious tendencies; Strong inclinations for home; Well enough contented.

PARTICULAR SYMPTOMS.—Suicidal; Disposed to strike, or other violence; Will sometimes destroy clothing or other articles; Inclined to uncleanly practices.

MENTAL STATE.—Apparently recovered, but in danger of relapse; Improving; Stationary; Variable.

HABITS AND INCLINATIONS.—Good and careful; Careless; Indifferent; Disorderly; Industrious; Does ~~some~~ no work; On the farm; In the kitchen; In the sewing room; In the ironing-room; In the ward; Engages in various odd jobs out of doors.

PROSPECT OF RESTORATION.—Favorable; Encouraging; Doubtful; Unfavorable; Apparently doing well.

H. M. BASSETT, Medical Superintendent.

(In this report it is designed to give briefly, the general condition since the last report as well as the condition at this time. The underlined expressions *only*, refer to the case in consideration. Caution is enjoined against ever exhibiting reports or letters respecting patients to them after discharge from the Hospital.)

Iowa Hospital for the Insane. Weekly report of the medical superintendent on a patient, 1874. Letterpress and manuscript. 266 × 207 mm (10½ × 8⅛ in)

Sexes afflicted with disorders of the mind'. It reports that 'Great care has been bestowed upon the domestic arrangements, so as to render them calculated to promote the comfort, security and recovery of the inmates…'.

Conditions in private lunatic asylums were a matter of continuing concern. A London public notice (c.1840) reads: 'Private Madhouses! James Wells to the public. Letters or communications addressed to me (post paid) relating to crimes and cruelties practised in these English *Bastiles* and earthly *hells* called private madhouses, shall have my very best attention, and most serious consideration, with a view to strict legal investigation'. Later documents convey a new, though no more humanitarian approach. A note from Isaac Fell of Shaftesbury Park, London, in 1890 informs the recipient: 'I am exceedingly sorry to have to inform you that your friend… was charged at Tunbridge Wells Town Hall last week with being a Wandering Lunatic, and committed to Barming Heath Lunatic Asylum. Please to inform his friends…'.

In some asylums attempts were made to analyse the 'causes' of lunacy. Among thirty-five causes listed in a statistical table at Colney Hatch Asylum in 1851 were 'bad company', 'sudden loss of several cows', and 'over-excitement at the Great Exhibition'. Lunacy, though little susceptible of therapy, was nevertheless successfully treated on occasions. On 29 April 1709 the Keeper of the Gaol at Lancaster Castle received instructions from Justices Thomas Lyon and Edward Owen to release one William Hall of Warrington, hairdresser, imprisoned on a charge of being a dangerous lunatic: 'Now it appearing unto us upon examination that the said William Hall is so far recovered from his lunacy that he may be permitted to go at large, these are therefore to authorize and require, you the Keeper… to discharge and set at liberty the said William Hall…'.

magazine sample sheet
manual alphabet card
marriage certificate
marrowbone announcement
match-tax stamp
medicine-show papers
menu
milk-bottle closure
miniature newspaper
miniature text
mock money
moral-lesson picture
motto, shop window
Mulready caricature
Mulready envelope
myriorama

Magazine sample sheet

Sample pages, featuring forthcoming covers and story openings, were printed by some magazine publishers as promotional items in the latter part of the 19th century and the early years of the 20th century. Given away a week or so in advance of publication, the sheets provided a tempting foretaste of the issue to come, breaking off in the middle of the first part of the opening story with a paragraph urging the reader to enjoy the complete text on publication day.

SUNDAY STORIES

MARY TRUE.

By H. ESCOTT-INMAN.

PROLOGUE.

Saturday, the best day of all the working days of the week; Saturday, when mother has hustled round all the morning getting things forward, so that the place shall be as neat and clean as a new pin when father comes home at mid-day. There was not another day in the week, except Sunday, that Mary True loved so much as she did Saturday. Not that she was afraid of work—no one could ever accuse Caleb True's wife of that—but, then, Caleb's work was so dangerous, for he was a steeplejack. It was all right for him to laugh, and say there was no danger in it: Mary was always possessed of a deadly fear, and it was such a relief when Saturday came, and he was home, safe and sound, after another week's perilous toil.

To and fro she went in her little house—ah, how proud she was of it!—singing softly to herself, helped by her two girls, Mary, the eldest, named after her mother, eleven years of age, and Alice, her sister, just one year younger.

"There's little pleasure in the house
When my good man's away."

So she sang to herself; and then "Mary!"

"Yes, mother!"

"Run to the gate, girl, and see if your father's coming down the road. It is time he was home, and dinner's done to a turn."

The child obeyed, and hardly had she got to the gate before she uttered a shout, and rushed down the road. The good wife understood—her husband was nearing his home. And then in came big, burly, broad-shouldered Caleb, laughing as gaily as the merry child who clutched at his hand, and greeted his wife with a vigorous kiss.

Magazine sample announcing 'Mary True', which was to appear with the issue of 10 February 1910 of *Sunday Stories*. Letterpress, printed in red and black on newsprint.
350 × 225 mm (13¾ × 8⅞ in)

An early example of the sheet shows the front page and page two of issue no. 123 of *Munro's Girls and Boys of America* (New York, 5 February 1876). On a conjunct sheet, inverted, appears a further two-page sample; this features the same masthead and dateline but a different story. Both stories were to be found complete in the next issue. In both cases the opening text runs to some 5500 words. Two British examples, dating from 1910, present previews of issues of *Sunday Stories* and *Sunday Companion*, each promising a full denouement in its next issue and featuring a dramatic two-colour illustration on its mock 'cover'. Here the texts run to 7500 and 6700 words respectively.

Manual alphabet card

Cards showing the alphabet in the sign system of the deaf were in widespread use until the middle years of the 20th century. They were commonly used, not for instructing the deaf, but as a means of helping them make friends with the hearing. In a majority of cases they bore an appeal, sometimes for 'the deaf and dumb' (c.1930), sometimes for an organization such as 'The Edinburgh Deaf and Dumb Benevolent Society Reconstruction Fund' (c.1950). Some take the form of a personal approach from the individual proffering the card: 'Best Wishes To All! I am out of work for the present, and to make a living I offer to my friends and the Public this Alphabet… for the convenience of those who wish to speak with the Hand and hear the Eye… Very truly yours, Thomas Wallace, Deaf Mute' (New York, c.1880). The use of cards in this way in Australia goes back at least to the middle of the 19th century.

In 1856 George W Baker, a deaf mute of Rochester, New York, produced the American (single-handed) alphabet as centrepiece to an editorial survey of the lives of Abbé de l'Epée and Laura Bridgman. The chart was topped with an illustration showing the institution for the deaf and dumb (Fanwood, near Washington Heights, New York), the whole production measuring 370 × 435 mm (14½ × 17⅛ in).

The practice of 'signing the alphabet' has diminished in recent years. Officially, it is viewed with disfavour: it tends to identify the deaf with inadequacy, and the chart itself fails to encourage lip-reading, a method held by many to offer far greater long-term benefit.

Marriage certificate

As with the BIRTH CERTIFICATE, the marriage certificate is commonly a copy of a formal entry in a register, either ecclesiastical

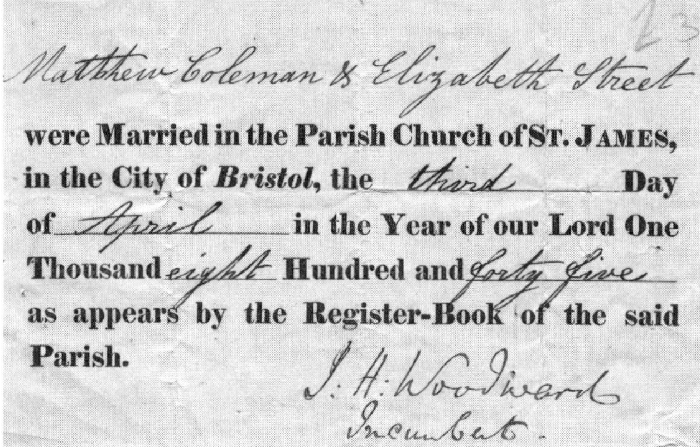

Matthew Coleman & Elizabeth Street
were Married in the Parish Church of St. James, in the City of *Bristol*, the *third* **Day of** *April* **in the Year of our Lord One Thousand** *eight* **Hundred and** *forty five* **as appears by the Register-Book of the said Parish.**
J. H. Woodward
Incumbt.

Marriage certificate, Parish of St James, Bristol, 3 April 1845. Letterpress and manuscript. 98 × 160 mm (3⅞ × 6¼ in)

or secular. To be valid, the document must be signed, sealed, or otherwise certified as a true copy, by the officiating minister, his curate or other representative, or the civil Registrar.

In Britain, until the passing of the Marriage Act in 1837, marriages were to be registered only by officiating clergy; but with the establishment of the office of Registrar General, facilities became available for civil registration.

See also FLEET MARRIAGE CERTIFICATE; GRETNA GREEN MARRIAGE CERTIFICATE

Marrowbone announcement

The custom of 'rough music' at weddings and other occasions dates at least from the 16th century and was widespread in Europe, and later in Canada and America, into the 19th century.

The practice was known variously as 'charivari' or 'shivaree' (US, sherrie-varrie), and featured a discordant performance on domestic utensils, trade tools, and any other object that came to hand. The tradition appears to have begun as an expression of enthusiasm and approval; later it was reserved for unpopular occasions, particularly ill-matched marriages, wife beating, and the precipitate remarriage of widows or widowers. In many areas it became a more or less standard demonstration of derision or disapproval.

In Britain in the 17th, 18th, and 19th centuries it became generally accepted as a good-natured embarrassment at weddings, which the couples concerned were often keen to escape by bribing the performers to desist. On occasions the practice caused annoyance, sometimes even scuffles, between the intruders and the officially engaged musicians. (William Hogarth, in the marriage scene in his 'Industrious Apprentice', depicts such an encounter.) Many different 'instruments' were used. Classic combinations were bellows and tongs, tongs and bones, saltbox (and rolling pin), and marrowbone and cleaver. This last, the speciality of butchers, is well known and documented, as is the practice of 'banging out' printers with the traditional wood and metal equipment of the trade.

The marrowbone announcement, a handwritten note sent to the selected victims, is a common surviving witness to the 'rough music' tradition. The form of words used shows remarkable consistency. Phraseology and structure follow a set pattern, clearly indicating a common archetype.

A typical rendering, recorded in Pentonville in 1816, reads as follows:

> Honoured Sir. With submission, we the Drums, Fifes and Marrow-bone and Cleaver Men presents our respectful Compliments to you on your Happy and Honourable Marriage of your Amiable Daughter. Wishing Health, Happiness, and Long to Live – Hoping for to receive the usual Gratuity given by Gentlemen on these Joyful and Happy Occurrences, Sir, from your most obt Servts, Waiting your pleasure.

As far as is known, the following example survives only as a printed account in *Notes & Queries* (3rd series, vol. v, 30 April 1864). The original manuscript (undated) was printed by the journal thus:

> Honoured Sir, with permission, we the marrowbones and cleavers and drums and fifes payes our usal and customary respects in wishing Sir you and your amiable lady joy of your happy and honourable marrige hoping Sir to receive a token of your goodness as is customary on those happy occasions. Sir we being in waiting your goodness and are all ready to perform if required.

In a version adapted to another form of celebration there is a mention of an additional common component – the names of alleged previous subscribers and their donations. This example (*Notes & Queries*, 8th series, vol. III, 1 April 1893) was 'written in a tolerably good handwriting' and addressed to a viscount in Bolton Street, London, on his elevation to the peerage on 23 July 1810:

> My Lord, – May it Please your Lordship with Permission. We, the Kings Royal Bell Ringers and the Marrowbones and Cleavers Payes our Usal and Customary Respects in Wishing your Lordship Joy of Comenge to your Titles and Estates and your Safe arrival to toun hoping to Receive a Token of your Lordships Goodness as We have from other Noblemen on the Like Honourable Occcasions. Being in Waiting your Lordships Goodness and have our Book of other Noblemen's Names to Shew. Having our Marrowbones & Cleavers all Ready to perform if Required.

Match-tax stamp

A tax has been imposed on matches at various periods in most parts of the world, and in many cases match boxes have carried stamps on bands ('banderoles') specifying the amount of the tax. Countries levying a match tax have included Argentina, Brazil, Canada, Columbia, Cuba, Dominica, France, French Indo-China, Greece, India, Iraq, Italy, Mexico, Pakistan, Portugal, Russia, Spain, Uruguay, the United States of America, and Vietnam. The match-tax stamp at large was designed and printed in the idiom of the postage stamp and appeared in a variety of sizes and formats, often perforated.

A match tax was extensively applied in the United States after the Civil War and remained in force until the mid 1880s. Rail transportation of matches was prohibited there by law and local manufacture proliferated, 'own label' tax stamps appearing in great variety. As with certain other commodities (i.e. tobacco, perfumes, and medicines) manufacturers were permitted to design and print their own tax labels. With frequent changes of ownership, a high rate of new stamps, and an endemic sense of the value of publicity, production of the American 'own label' match-tax stamp became almost an industry in itself. Of the 180 or so American match manufacturers that flourished in the 19th century, a significant number produced outsize stamps with advertising material and a portrait of the company's founder.

In Britain, a tax on matches was proposed, and some tax stamps were even produced (in April 1871), but no such tax was ever levied. Its attempted introduction in 1871 is an event of historic interest in the development of the British match industry. In that year Sir Robert Lowe, then Chancellor of the Exchequer, proposed a tax of one halfpenny on a box of a hundred wooden matches and one penny on a hundred wax matches or fusees. Revenue from the tax was estimated at £550,000, which it was hoped would defray the budgetary deficit of £2,800,000. In anticipation of its immediate acceptance, Lowe's department had printed and distributed the proposed stamp, a narrow vertical design bearing a flaming torch and the words *ex luce lucellum* (Latin: from light a small gain). Lowe's Latinism was to prove a major source of irritation: the *Illustrated London News* reflected public opinion in its reference to the words as 'a bit of quibbling Latin'.

Bryant & May, the country's best-known match manufacturers, were, not unnaturally, among leading opponents of the measure, but they nonetheless anticipated its adoption by preparing a new brand, the Exchequer Match, which bore an unflattering portrait of Lowe.

In the event, the tax proposal met with general hostility (not least from London's thousands of poorly-paid match workers). Lowe was obliged to abandon the proposal, and, amid general rejoicing, the stamps were destroyed. Bryant & May abandoned the Exchequer Match, introducing instead the Chancellor Match, which bore a reproduction of the abandoned stamp and the words 'Match Tax Bill. Introduced – 20th April, 1871. Withdrawn – 25th April, 1871'. A year later a commemorative drinking fountain was inaugurated in Bow Road, near the Bryant & May factory, celebrating the Bill's defeat.

The magazine *Punch* (April/May, 1871) carried a mock advertisement: 'To waste-paper dealers. – To be Disposed of: An immense quantity of unmatched Classical Literature, the writer having no further use for it, and the authorities of the House compelling immediate clearance . . . . This is an opportunity that will never occur again, as Mr. L. L. has resolved in future to get his Tax first, and consult the Classics afterwards'.

See also TAX STAMP; TAXATION PAPERS

REFERENCES Patrick Beaver, *The Match Makers* (London: Henry Melland, 1985); *Matchbox Collections Encyclopedia* (Camberley: Luker, 1979); Joan Rendell, *The Match, The Box and The Label* (Newton Abbott: David & Charles, 1983)

Medicine-show papers

The American medicine show was an entertainment that was used as a vehicle for the sale of popular remedies. Combining the characteristics of travelling circus and market-place quack, the show was constantly on the move, staying only long enough to draw a crowd and reap a harvest of sales. Most shows were one-day stands, though some, in a booked public hall or 'opera house', lasted three or four days. The idea derived from Europe, where the itinerant quack often used music, jugglers, clowns, etc. as aids in attracting attention.

The medicine show started in America in the 1850s. By the 1880s it had become a recognized feature of back-country life. As the concept of mass-marketing developed, manufacturers of nostrums began to offer their wares to medicine-show men, providing not only a packaged and labelled product but a supply of novelties, leaflets, posters, and other printed material in support. There was also advance publicity and point-of-sale promotion for the show itself. It came to be known generally as 'paper'.

The term appeared frequently in publicity directed at prospective agents. 'Our paper', announced a leaflet of the De Wolf Comedy Co. in the 1880s, 'is entirely different from that used by any other medicine company and is neat, catchy and original . . . we furnish all paper free, and if you always let us know just what you want, your wants will be cheerfully supplied'. Soap manufacturer Dr E. D. Wardes, of Corry, Pennsylvania, offered 'own name' facilities: 'If you will send in gross orders I will have your name printed on the paper'. His paper list included one soap circular, one wonder-worker sheet; one modern miracles sheet; one window hanger; one dodger ('tonight'); one dodger ('coming'); and eighteen different lithographs. Other companies offered admission tickets (two cents, five cents, and ten cents) and voting forms for 'Most beautiful baby' and 'Most popular lady' contests.

The medicine show developed into a major entertainment with intermittent selling 'spots', foreshadowing the commercial-radio and TV presentation. The German Medicine Company's publicity provided 'New acts, new papers, new features . . . starring specialties, dainty dancers, clever comedians, sweet singers . . . an unrivalled array of bright and catchy amusement . . .'. Other attractions provided by the company were 'Amateur nights' and ladies' wood-sawing contests and nail-driving.

In many medicine-show bills that included such items as contortionists, wire walkers, mind-reading, 'fancy rifle shooting', and Indian marriage ceremonies, there was no mention of the medicine concerned. In others, there was equal stress on the show and the product. In some cases the entertainer and the physician were one. 'Doctor Howard' of Mount Olive, North Carolina, advertised a free open-air show in which he starred as 'the Great Southern Ventriloquist' with 'his two little wooden boys', who would 'talk, spell, laugh and sing'. His announcement added the information that, with his 'infallible medicines', he also treated liver complaints and dyspepsia, sick headache and sour stomach, chills and fever, nervousness, fits, etc., and 'also removes all kinds of worms from the human family'.

Medicine-show papers fall into two categories. On one hand are the items provided under the heading of 'paper'; on the other are the ancilliaries, the promotional leaflets describing the paper, and the forms, price lists, contracts, and other items involved with the business as a whole. Typical items in the second category are hand-printed forms for advance booking of hotel rooms for the medicine-show troupe ('All rooms to be reasonably furnished; Doctor's room to have fire; plenty of fuel furnished'); questionnaire forms seeking advance quotations for hall rental ('Has a Medicine Company been in your town; if so how long ago?; Have you stage and scenery?; Very lowest price per week?'), and telegraph code slips for the bulk ordering of specific products. Also in this category is a vast range of labels and packaging, many of which were produced by the manufacturers themselves. As with 'paper', they were also available with the agent's own name instead of the supplier's when ordering in large quantities.

The outward appearance of the medical product, however modest its content, was a matter of much concern. Dr Wardes's 'Wonder worker', 'Modern miracles', and other products were presented with due regard to their appeal. 'These remedies,' says Wardes's trade leaflet, 'are put up in showy and attractive bottles and large, name blown in, cartons are elaborate and striking'.

The Pure Food and Drug Act of 1906 and other legislation brought much revision of labelling, though to little effect. The word 'cure' was outlawed and the weight of the preparation, and later the formula, had to appear on the label. Later still a listing was required of the ailments for which the product was intended.

The medicine show continued to flourish, however, with labels and leaflets proclaiming products 'Guaranteed under the Food and Drug Act'. It survived vestigially into the 1920s and early 1930s.

See also QUACK ADVERTISING

COLLECTION Ars Medica Collection, Philadelphia Museum of Art

Menu

Over long periods the social history of the table is little documented; where it is, there is evidence of considerable change. The last 150 years, for which the menu provides a fairly detailed record, have seen changes in dining habits almost from one generation to another. Prior to the 1830s, which marked the emergence of the restaurant and hotel, the image of the menu is hazy; evidence of changing fashions in eating in earlier times comes from other sources.

The earliest menus are believed by some authorities to have been handwritten instructions to the kitchen, a copy of which may have been retained by the host, and perhaps made available for reference at the table. Mrs Beeton (*The Book of Household Management*, 1907 edn, p. 1715) cites a story, perhaps apocryphal, of a banquet given in 1541 by the Duke of Brunswick. The Duke was seen from time to time to consult a paper resting on the table at his side. One guest, more curious than the others, ventured to ask the reason, 'whereupon the Duke explained that it was a list of the dishes to be served, and which he consulted... in order to reserve his appetite for those dishes he liked best'. Mrs Beeton goes on to say that 'For many years the menus must have resembled the smaller play-bills formerly in vogue, for they were gaudily decorated with gastronomical symbols, and so large that two were needed for a dining table. The peacock, a whole pig roasted, a boar's head, and the baron of beef, which constituted the substantial fare of the Tudor era, could not provide very artistic subjects for ornamentation; but in course of time the menus not only became smaller, but they also increased in artistic and intrinsic value...'.

Another view, however, sees the advent of the menu as a concomitant of the introduction, sometime in the 1860s and 1870s, of *service à la Russe.* In this, instead of partaking of 'communal' dishes set upon the table, guests were individually served from a sidetable. Apart from minor decorations (flowers, candles, etc.) cutlery, napery (linen), and glasses, the table remained clear of all but each individual's own dish throughout the meal. In this form of service each course may offer one or more alternatives, and the guests acquaint themselves of their options from a menu in advance. The menu gained wider currency as *service à la Russe* was introduced for banquets and other public occasions; it was also adopted by hoteliers and restaurateurs who sought to attract the hitherto house-bound upper classes.

The 'bill-of-fare' emerged at much the same time as the menu. The term was normally confined to the common eating house, but was also used in earlier times to refer to the overall 'shopping list' of the host. William Hone in *The Table Book* (1838) records the Christmas 'bill-of-fare' of a Bristol innkeeper, John Weeks (1800), which enumerates 150 items, including a 120 lb turtle; 1 bustard; a roasting pig; 98 gudgeons; 122 eels; 42 hares; 17 pheasants; 87 wild ducks; hogs' puddings; 5 house lambs; 1 boar's head; 81 woodcocks; 149 snipes; 1 cuckoo; 121 larks; 3 pork griskins; 430 mince pies; 52 barrels Pyfleet and Colchester oysters; and 4 pine apples.

The study of menus, and in some measure of the bill-of-fare, may be said to fall into four main fields: cuisine and gastronomy, design and presentation, price record, and association. Some specimens reflect aspects of all four fields; others, more commonly, of one or two.

In terms of cuisine and gastronomy, menus from successive epochs reflect the evolution of the table, both in terms of content and quantities consumed. The most marked of changes in the last hundred years has been the reduction in the numbers of courses. In the 1860s ten or eleven courses were considered normal; in the early 1920s a complete dinner consisted of eight courses. The Victorians could smile at outlandish items of documented Norman meals (boar's head, swan, mallard, teals roasted, pasties of pork, etc.), but it must be said that their own menus may contain items hardly less curious today. In Cassell's *Etiquette of Good Society* (1886), a list of recommended middle-class dinner-party menus includes the following: stewed pigeons with cherries, salmi of larks, quenelles of rabbit, quails, ragoût of sweetbreads, plovers' eggs, ramekins, curried ox-palates, oyster patties, snipe, iced asparagus, and strawberry water. In marked contrast, and no less redolent, are items of the same period in village dinners and other such functions. Here cowheel pie, marrow pudding, pigeon pie, negus, and grog are common entries.

In both Britain and America there has been a clear-cut division between the concept of native or 'home' cooking and the cuisine of the continent of Europe, a distinction clearly reflected in the content and terminology of the hotel and restaurant menu and, in later years, that of the private dinner party. Only in the 1950s did a trend emerge in British hotels and restaurants to add English translations (and sometimes extensive descriptions) to French menu listings. In American menus,

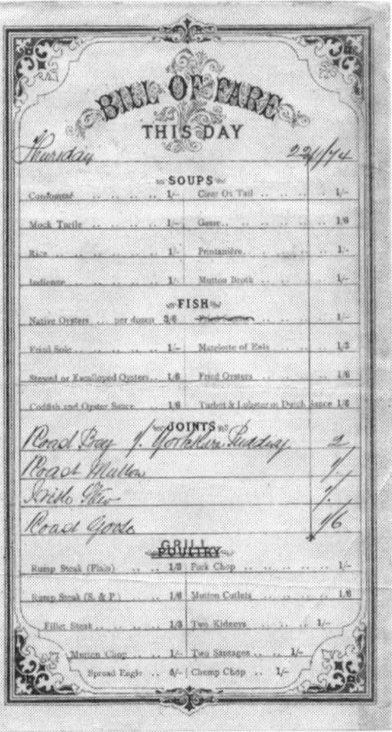

Bill of fare of Spiers & Pond, refreshment contractors to the Metropolitan, Chatham & Dover, Great Eastern & Midland railway companies, for Thursday 22 January 1874. Lithography and manuscript, printed by Waterlow & Sons, London. *Left:* the front printed in green and gold; *right:* the back printed in green, red, and gold. 250 × 143 mm (9⅞ × 5⅝ in)

French has appeared only rarely. With the rise of tourism, menus in many parts of Europe have become multilingual.

Menus appear in a wide range of style and formats. For major restaurants and hotels, ship's dining rooms, and for special dinners and banquets, they are generally overprinted on preprinted blanks. For ceremonial occasions (Buckingham Palace, Guildhall dinners, etc.) menus have been printed on silk, with fringing, tassels, and other embellishments, including embossing. In the heyday of the CHROMO (c.1860–1910) large numbers of full-colour pictorial designs appeared. Printed for the most part in Germany, these bore no title (and were thus marketable internationally) and featured flowers, girls, and other decorative elements as title-pieces to the blank area of the design. Many were also embossed and pierced in a more or less intricate frame treatment; in many cases this made them unsuitable for overprinting, which meant that they were completed by hand. 'Place-card menus' also appeared (*see* PLACE CARD). These were for private dinner parties, and provided for a brief handwritten listing of courses, with the guest's name on a separate panel.

Restaurant and hotel menus are of special value for the historian of food as, in addition to documenting changing fashions in cuisine, they provide direct information on price levels.

Menus may encapsulate not only dinners and diners but their designers. Menus designed by Alphonse Mucha, Charles Dana Gibson, H. M. Bateman, and Edward Ardizzone are of particular interest, as are those produced for the Double Crown Club in Britain (which, since the club's foundation in 1924, have been designed and printed by members of the club). 'Special-occasion menus', often bearing the signatures of those present, may also become collectors' items.

REFERENCE W. E. L. te Meij, *Cartes menu, Menu Cards, Menukarten, Menukaarten, 1812–1951* (['s-Gravenhage], 1979)

Milk-bottle closure

In the 19th century people who lived in the ever-expanding big towns got their milk from suburban farms or from cowkeepers who kept cows in stalls behind their shops. Milk was delivered to customers from pails or other vessels. Later, it was trundled through the streets in 'churns', big containers mounted on a variety of wheeled carts that were drawn by hand or horse. In each case the milk was dispensed into smaller containers before reaching the customer's own receptacle.

Whatever the detail of the method, it was obvious that this open-air distribution was a health risk. It was not until the beginning of the 20th century, however, that milk began to be delivered in bottles, and even then not in rural districts. The method of closure was at first a difficulty, but after experiments with wired-on caps and swing stoppers a recessed disc of card became standard. It remained in use for some forty years. It was improved in the early 1930s by provision of a lifting tag for removal and a press-in aperture to facilitate pouring.

The milk-bottle disc became a minor promotional medium, used not only for the supplier's name and address but for slogans and commemorative motifs on great national occasions. In some cases discs were imprinted with the day of the week of delivery. Frequent injunctions were to 'Keep it cool' and 'Kindly wash and return bottles daily'. Aluminium foil closures were introduced in Linköping, Sweden, in 1914. These were to supersede the disc closure, though it survived for some years as a closure for cream and ice- cream tubs.

Miniature newspaper

With the advent in 1872 of Charles Gillot's photomechanical line block, which gradually began to supersede the then orthodox wood-engraved block, it became possible to produce miniaturized versions of typeset matter. Miniature bibles led the way, but the newspaper industry was not slow to realize the promotional value of micro-versions of its own publications. By the end of the 19th century few British papers had failed to put out one or more such issues, either in celebration of some national event or anniversary, or as a standard gift to readers who visited the plant to see the paper being printed.

The best-known of these was the issue of *The Times* for 1 January 1924, specially printed to a scale of one inch to a foot for inclusion in the Queen's dolls' house, Queen Mary's contribution to the British Empire Exhibition at Wembley. The newspaper took its place in the dolls' house in company with similarly diminutive versions of *Who's Who*, *Whitaker's Almanac*, *Bradshaw*, and the *ABC*. The publishers of *The Times* printed many thousands of copies of the item, giving them away to visitors to the Wembley Exhibition and subsequently at showings of the dolls' house elsewhere in the 1930s. The version for general distribution differed, however, from the dolls' house specimen in size. It was felt that mothers might be anxious lest children strained their eyes in reading the one-inch-to-the-foot version, and a two-inch-to-the-foot reproduction was used.

The collector of miniature newspapers must bear in mind that the masthead date shown on a specimen may bear little or no relation to its actual publication date. Miniatures of the London *Daily Telegraph* exist for various issues with dates as far back as June 1855 (no.1), but those for dates prior to the 1870s could not of course have been printed on the dates indicated.

Newspaper companies' files of miniatures are incomplete, and in some cases non-existent. Such items were issued spasmodically – often in varying scales of reduction – and no complete record appears to exist of them. The number of issues comprising a 'complete' collection of any title is thus impossible to establish.

Typical examples are the 50,000th number of *The Times* (25 November 1944), measuring 280 × 205 mm (11 × 8⅛ in), and an issue of the *Daily Telegraph* (20 June 1970), measuring 139 × 100 mm (5½ × 4 in). The story of the micro-filmed front page of *The Times* being pigeon-posted into besieged Paris in 1871 may have been apocryphal. The London Stereoscopic Company printed the story on a promotional card, but new research in the archives of the Musée Postale in Paris suggest that it was false. *The Times* of 30 January 1871 carried the story, but published an expression of doubt on 4 February 1970.

Miniature text

The 19th-century engraver's ability to work in microscopic detail led to a generalized craze for miniature inscriptions, principally of prayers and other religious texts, and occasionally of messages of affection. The fad found expression in handwritten or engraved mementoes, particularly as decorative keepsakes for carrying in pocket watches with (or in place of) a WATCH-PAPER. The text, occupying a circular area of about 15 mm (9/16 in), formed the central feature in a more or less complex geometrical design, which sometimes included a decorative filigree pattern. Most favoured texts were the LORD'S PRAYER and the

Creed; more ambitious works featured the Ten Commandments, sometimes in different languages.

Skill in the exercise lay not only in producing legible characters at so small a size, but in disposing the text so as to occupy completely the space allotted to it. Some professional engravers were able to reduce the texts to the extent that, as part of a decorative design, they might even escape notice altogether.

The miniature text was also used for the production of novelty pictures, in which all or part of the image proved on close inspection to be composed of an extended text, the wording being so small as to appear merely as varying tones of grey.

The idea of the miniature text took another direction in the 20th century when pen draughtsmen at the Ordnance Survey Office in Southampton practised writing the Lord's Prayer small enough to fit several times on to a silver threepenny piece, the smallest British coin. It is claimed that Tommy Muir achieved the astonishing feat of fitting around twenty complete texts of the prayer within such a tiny area using a sable brush that tapered to two or three hairs.

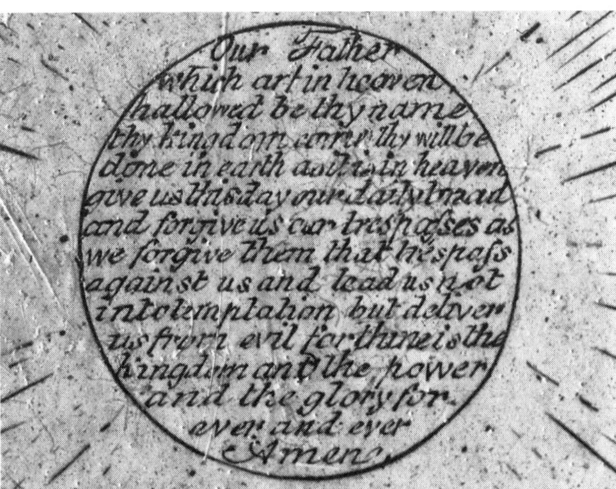

Above: miniature text of the Lord's Prayer, published by De La Rue James & Rudd, London, mid 19th century. Engraved on steel by W. Palmer and printed on coated card. 140 × 85 mm (5½ × 3⅜ in). *Below:* detail of the centre circle, diameter 4 mm (5/16 in)

Mock money

The term 'mock coin' refers to items simulating coin of the realm but having no claim to monetary function. The mock coin differs therefore from the trade token, 'Emergency money' (*Notgeld*), the *jeton*, and the counterfeit coin, all of which are designed for use in conjunction with, or as substitutes for, official coinage (*see* IMPROVISED CURRENCY).

The mock coin flourished in the second half of the 19th century, chiefly in the guise of an ADVERTISING NOVELTY. It appeared in the United States as a presidential campaign novelty, and in France as a political 'squib'. In Britain, a hollow 'locket halfpenny' allowed for the insertion of a photograph. Mock coins were also used for stage money and toy money, and, when foil-wrapped as 'chocolate money', are eaten.

In Britain, the best known of 'advertising coins' was that distributed by Mellin's, the baby-food company, in the 1890s. This took the form of a cardboard disc, bearing on its face an embossed silver-foil image of Queen Victoria. Among late 20th-century uses was a pay-packet novelty insert bearing a safety slogan for railway trackmen.

Moral-lesson picture

The moral-lesson picture, a late 19th-century teaching aid, commonly appeared as a linen-mounted, chromolithographed chart for hanging on the classroom wall. These charts measured some 750 × 500 mm (29½ × 19¾ in), were usually varnished, and were often provided with rolling rods at top and bottom. They presented scenes from which the child was expected to draw conclusions: subjects were, on one hand, prudence, industry, hygiene, health, and safety; on the other, danger, cruelty, untidiness, etc.

A typical series of six, published by the Educational Supply Association in London in the 1890s, carried the titles 'Kind and tidy children', 'Cruelty to animals', 'Industrious children', 'Dishonest and untidy children and mockers', 'Danger of stone throwing', and 'Danger of playing with fire'. The 'Industrious Children' picture showed a scene of assiduous constructiveness, with young figures smilingly occupied with needlework, ironing, woodwork, reading, etc.

In another presentation, measuring 800 × 610 mm (31½ × 24 in) and published in Paris by Mobilier et Materiel Scolaires Deyrolle, the newly recognized hazards of road traffic are shown. In four scenes, three featuring horse-drawn traffic and one showing the electric tram, accidents are graphically illustrated with directives such as: 'Do not run behind, or sit on the back of carriages', and 'on a bicycle, do not hold on to another vehicle'.

The scholastic moral-lesson picture is a close relation to the allegorical CHROMO of the 1880s and 1890s, in which religious reformers conveyed the choice between good and evil, hope and despair. In one example, 'The Broad and Narrow Way' (Matthew vii. 13, 14), pilgrims are seen on two paths, one through the pleasure gardens of self-indulgence to disaster and destruction, and the other through the valley of righteousness and respectability to heaven. General Booth, founder of the Salvation Army, used a similar technique in a pull-out frontispiece (1890) to *In Darkest England*, 430 × 280 mm (17 × 11 in). Here the present despair appears as a sea of shipwrecked survivors, with the Salvation Army bringing a hopeful tomorrow through rescue, training, farming settlement, and education.

Motto, shop window

The term 'motto' was applied in Britain at or around the turn of the century to the small display cards used in haberdashers, drapers, men's outfitters, etc. in praise of merchandise. 'Very smart', 'chic', and 'latest style' were typical of the genre; other examples conveyed specific information, such as 'in other colours', 'guaranteed waterproof', and 'a small deposit secures'. Many of these cards were hand-lettered, either by the display staff of larger stores or in commercial studios, but the majority were printed and available as stock items from display suppliers.

Mottoes commonly measured about 25 × 150 mm (1 × 6 in), but much larger sizes were available for suits and overcoats (sometimes providing space for prices). Typical of the latter is a range bearing the words 'choice', 'stylish', 'elegant', and 'quite new', printed in gold on a white card measuring 75 × 240 mm (3 × 9½ in) and in a larger size measuring 100 × 250 mm (4 × 9⅞ in), bearing the legend 'Trousers to measure 18/6 [i.e. 18 shillings and 6 pence]'.

Shop window motto, British, c. 1900. Letterpress on cream coated card. 104 × 245 mm (4⅛ × 9⅝ in)

Mulready caricature

The ill-starred MULREADY ENVELOPE, though it brought the postal authorities into ridicule, had a number of less negative side-effects, not least of which was the appearance of a lively series of caricature versions. These may be said to have paved the way for the propaganda envelope, the pictorial envelope, and the ADVERTISING ENVELOPE.

Mulready caricatures began to appear within a few weeks of the release of the Mulready envelope in May 1840. Public derision of the design, as reflected in much of the press of the day, was instant and intense. It seems likely, however, that hostility was based on more than aesthetic grounds. *The Times*, among the most acid of Tory critics of a Whig administration, could not resist bringing in politics on 2 May 1840: 'We never beheld anything more ludicrous… Britannia is seated in the centre, with the lion couchant (Whigish) at her feet…'; and again on 4 May: 'He appears as sulky, as hungry, and as discontented as a Whig out of place…'.

The first of the caricatures, published by Fores of Piccadilly,

Mulready caricature, 'Fores's comic envelopes No 1', drawn by John Leech, 1840. Printed by J. R. Jobbins and published by Fores, London. Image 113 × 158 mm (4⅜ × 6¼ in)

was by John Leech and appeared within a week or two of the official design; like its early successors, it took the form of an envelope for actual use. The design lampooned not only the Mulready envelope but the government. Other caricatures followed rapidly. Before the end of the year two of the brothers Doyle, Richard and James, had produced ten more designs for Fores, and William Spooner of the Strand had published the first of four series of fourteen lampoons in July 1840, most of which had political overtones. Caricatures of the envelope were also produced in London by Thomas White of Wych Street and J. W. Southgate of the Strand, and elsewhere by W. H. Mason of Brighton, Robert Hume of Leith, and John Menzies of Edinburgh.

Though their vogue passed, Mulready caricatures, together with other illustrated envelopes of the period, shortly became collectors' pieces. In the late 1860s, almost thirty years after the appearance of the Mulready envelope, a Brussels stamp dealer issued numerous examples bearing the name F. Deraedemaeker.

See also ENVELOPE, ILLUSTRATED

REFERENCES Ritchie Bodily, Chris Jarvis, and Charless Hahn, *British Pictorial Envelopes of the 19th Century* (Chicago: Collectors Club of Chicago, 1984); David Lidman, *Treasury of Stamps* (New York: Abrams, 1975); Robson Lowe, *The British Postage Stamp*, 2nd edn (London: National Postal Museum, 1979); A. G. Rigo de Righi, *The Story of the Penny Black* (London: National Postal Museum, 1980); Frank Staff, *The Picture Postcard and its Origins*, 2nd edn (London: Lutterworth, 1979)

COLLECTION National Postal Museum, London

Mulready envelope

The inception of Rowland Hill's universal Penny Postage in Britain in May 1840 was countered by the introduction of two methods of prepayment: the postage stamp and the Mulready envelope and lettersheet (commonly referred to as 'Mulreadys'). Both were validated for postage on 6 May 1840, and were sold at post offices at one penny and twopence for the Mulreadys and one penny for the stamp. Twopenny stamps appeared two days later.

The new system superseded a complex and costly service in which mail was charged by distance and the number of sheets comprising the letter. Whereas formerly the postage fee was payable, if desired, by the recipient, under the new regulations prepayment of postage was encouraged. The specially-printed envelope, designed for the Post Office by William Mulready RA, was a form of receipt for prepayment: the penny envelope,

Mulready envelope (unused), with notification of pre-payment: 'Postage one penny'. Designed by William Mulready R.A. and cut in brass by John Thompson. Relief printed from stereotype plate by W. Clowes and Son on Dickinson's security paper with silk thread, 1840. 85 × 130 mm (3⅜ × 5⅛ in)

printed in black, could be used for a letter of half an ounce to any address in the British Isles; the twopenny envelope, printed in blue, carried up to one ounce.

The postage stamp, designed by Henry Corbould from a portrait relief of William Wyon, was initially described as a postage label. It was designed to be affixed to letters and packets as an alternative to use of the Mulready. Contrary to expectation, the stamp rapidly overtook the Mulready in popularity.

The Mulready appeared in two forms: as a letter-sheet to be written on, folded, and sealed; and as an envelope to be used as a separate outer cover. The term 'cover' is commonly applied to both forms. The concept of a cover, as opposed to a stamp, was favoured by Rowland Hill, and had been a prominent feature among the 2600 submissions for the Treasury's 1839 competition for ideas for postal prepayment. None of the competition entries proved acceptable, however. After rejection of a sketch commissioned from Henry Corbould, William Mulready, a distinguished royal academician, was asked to produce a proposal. His design, in allegorical idiom, depicted Britannia as a goddess of communications, transmitter of messages to the peoples of the world. The design, 'much approved' by the Royal Academy, and passed for publication by the Queen, was duly issued. It was universally disliked, however, and much satirized (*see* MULREADY CARICATURE).

The envelope was withdrawn at the end of January 1841, to be replaced by the first of a series of official Post Office envelopes with embossed postage stamps. Shortly afterwards, the plates were destroyed; in 1844 the lettersheet was also withdrawn and replaced by one with an offical embossed stamp. In 1862 large remaining stocks were burnt, it is reported, in furnaces specially constructed to deal with the quantities involved.

Among Mulready rarities are examples posted in the week preceding the official start of the service, covers pasted in multiples as wrappers to make up additional postage for extra-weight packets, and covers bearing numbers of postage stamps to allow transmission overseas.

First essays for the letter-sheet bear indications of exploratory postal thinking. Among the user instructions on the side panels of an example in the National Postal History Museum, London, is a suggested paragraph dealing with postmasters' receipts: 'Receipts for letters : Forms on which postmasters will acknowledge the receipt of letters when posted may be bought as follows – At the Stamp Office, at (—); at the Post Office at (—)'. In a further proposed paragraph, 'carriers and others' are informed that they may legally convey letters properly stamped, provided the date of the day on which they are conveyed is legibly written in ink across each stamp – the figure of Britannia being considered as the stamp. Neither paragraph appeared on the covers as finally published.

See also COVER, POSTAL; POSTAL STATIONERY

REFERENCE Robson Lowe, *The British Postage Stamp*, 2nd edn (London: National Postal Museum, 1979)

Myriorama

Popular in the 1820s, often as a children's toy, the myriorama (Greek: *many views*) originated in Germany. It consists of a printed panoramic view, divided vertically into separate strips and capable of rearrangement to form a variety of differing scenes. The term was coined by analogy with the panorama and diorama, and is attributed to Clare of London (1824). Clare's set of sixteen cards, *Myriorama or Many Thousand Views*, was claimed to be capable of 20,922,789,880,000 permutations.

Individual strips commonly measure some 165 × 65 mm (6½ × 2½ in), the whole picture extending in length to include up to twenty-four strips. The subject, generally engraved or lithographed in black and hand-coloured, typically shows a lake-shore with trees, figures, and animals in the foreground, island-castles and ships in the middle distance, and a background of mountains. An early example (c. 1810) comprises five strips, but later specimens generally have ten or a dozen.

The card strips were usually sold in paper wrappers or in 'tray and lid' boxes, centrally divided to present two 'decks' side by side. Typical sets were 'Polyorama' by Hodgson and 'Myriorama' by Samuel Leigh, both with cards measuring 203 × 70 mm (8 × 2¾ in). In another set, produced by Robert Havell (junior) of Newman Street, Oxford Street, London, eighteen broader cards, 203 × 160 mm (8 × 6¼ in), presented an infinitely variable panorama of the Thames in a miniature portfolio complete with a cut-out foreground frame. The frame represented Pope in his garden grotto, through which, with some inconsistency, each identified and numbered section of the panorama might be viewed.

Similar 'changeable landscapes' were produced in France and Germany. A variant of it appeared in France in the 1830s, which combined the landscape sections with words and syllables for the construction of whole sentences. The set, described as 'Le syllabaire pittoresque', was printed on cards measuring 75 × 28 mm (3 × 1⅛ in) and boxed to show four decks side by side.

See also HARLEQUINADE; PANORAMA, ENTERTAINMENT

neck paper
needle packet
needle-box print
news bill
newspaper
notice to quit
nuisance papers

Neck paper

This expression refers to a notice, commonly derogatory, worn round the neck by an alleged wrongdoer. It may be seen to relate to the sardonic legend 'Jesus of Nazareth, King of the Jews', which was said to have been posted above the head of Jesus at his crucifixion. The superscription is reported to have appeared in Latin, Hebrew, and Greek. The 20th century saw a related device in Nazi Germany, where Jews might be forced to carry round their neck a placard bearing the word 'Jud'.

Neck papers also became a feature of certain early scholastic systems, in which backward or offending pupils were obliged to wear notices. The Lancastrian method, introduced in Britain in the early 19th century, in which brighter pupils were trained to teach whole groups of their fellows, relied heavily on the schoolroom use of printed neck notices such as 'Lazy' and 'Impolite'. Charlotte Brontë describes such a use in a passage in *Jane Eyre* (1847): 'Next morning Miss Scratcherd [the teacher] wrote in conspicuous characters on a piece of pasteboard the word 'Slattern', and bound it ... round Helen's large, mild, intelligent, and benign-looking forehead. She wore it till evening, patient, unresentful, regarding it as a deserved punishment'.

The neck paper was commonly used in Irish and Welsh schoolrooms to discourage the use of native languages. Pupils who used native words were obliged to wear a notice around the neck. They wore it until they in turn heard another offender, to whom they passed it on. The notice passed from one child to another until, at the end of the day, the last recipient received a special punishment from the teacher. In Wales the label was known as the 'Welsh Not'. The use of the word 'Not' is thought to have been derived from the word 'Note', here bearing the dictionary meaning of 'a stigma or mark of censure'. The letters WN were used as an abbreviated form of the notice, and were sometimes inscribed on a tablet of wood or slate.

Similar neck papers were worn by prisoners held in the pillory. The wearing of a neck paper was also imposed on criminals while serving their sentences, the text giving details of their offences.

Another form of neck-worn legend related not to offences but to the immunity of the wearer when appearing before a common law court. Immunity was claimed under a convention which came to be known as 'Benefit of Clergy'.

A relic of the later Middle Ages, Benefit of Clergy stemmed from the division of judicial powers between the ecclesiastical courts and those of the state. The courtroom aspect of the matter lay in a 'neck verse' worn by the accused. The text of the verse was from Psalm 51; it read: 'Have mercy upon me, O God, according to thy loving-kindness; according unto the multitude of thy tender mercies blot out my transgressions'. The ability to read these words (or to appear to read them) was held to be evidence of ecclesiastical learning, thus making it improbable that the accused was guilty. *Legit ut clericus* (Latin: he reads like a clerk) was the phrase used in pronouncing judgement. In some periods crimes were categorized according to their seriousness as 'clergyable' and 'unclergyable'. Actual examples of surviving neck verses have apparently yet to be reported, but their existence and use in the 15th and 16th centuries is undisputed. The custom was phased out in the 18th century and was finally abolished in 1827.

Needle packet

Commercial production of hand-sewing needles, with branded products in labelled packets, began in the early years of the 19th century in the Redditch district in the English midlands. Needles were packed loose in narrow folded papers, the free ends of which were again folded to make retaining flaps, the shorter being inserted within the longer. The longer flap extended the full length of the packet thus formed, and to this was pasted a vertical-format printed label. The folded paper was generally brown in colour; the labels were hand engraved and printed in a single colour, commonly black or brown.

Other packs displayed the needles in a slip of fabric, which was pasted to the paper or held at its head and foot by (printed) retaining tabs. In another version, the slip of fabric was pasted to a paper base, which in turn was held to the body of the packet

Early 20th-century needle packets of Abel Morrall, Redditch; Kirby, Beard & Co., London; W. Woodfield & Sons, Redditch. All lithographed. The smallest 40 × 20 mm ($1\frac{9}{16} \times \frac{3}{4}$in)

by a central retaining band. In later packs an envelope-type outer cover held the product, with its overlapping flaps and a tab-and-slot closure carrying brand designs and designation. Rigid envelope-type packs were also used, in which an inner paper folder was withdrawn to give access to the contents, which were either loose in the folder or stuck into crimps in the paper in the manner of pins.

Label texts convey the essential facts of a developing needle technology. 'Egg-eyed' needles (as opposed to earlier types, in which the eye was merely a drilled hole) had elongated eyes to allow less obstruction as the needle and thread passed through fabrics. They were also called 'long-eyed'. One manufacturer produced 'newly invented gazelle-eyed' needles; in addition to their elongated eyes, they had the advantage of a sloping bevil at each end to facilitate the passage of the head through fabric. This was to become a standard feature of needles in general.

The Kirby, Beard Co. (well-known also for pins) introduced the 'scientific needle'. This was 'so formed that the eye when threaded only equals the size of the body of the needle, and works in consequence most easily and rapidly'. Needle sizes were indicated by numerals and specialist manufacturers' terms (in descending order of size: darners, straws, sharps, long-eyed sharps, ground-downs, betweens, and blunts). General label slogans include: 'Rust entirely prevented' (T. Hessin & Co., Redditch); 'This method of wrapping needles… patented…' (H. Milward & Sons); and 'No friction: no stop: rapid work' (Kirby, Beard & Co.). Leading names in the industry are John James & Sons, Lewis & Baylis, Milward & Sons, Abel Morrall, W. Woodfield & Sons, all of Redditch.

Apart from Britain, the only other centres of large-scale needle production are China, Germany, Hong Kong, and Japan.

REFERENCE John G. Rollins, *Needlemaking* (Aylesbury: Shire Publications, 1981)

Needle-box print

Often referred to as 'needle prints', needle-box prints are commonly the work of the printer, George Baxter, his licencees, associates, or imitators. They form part of a small group of Baxter or Baxter-derived items in which the product appeared as a decorative ingredient rather than as an *objet de vertu* in its own right. Baxter prints in the latter category appeared in considerable numbers, many of them reproducing well-known paintings, and providing, in miniature form, 'facsimiles of the great masters'. The full Baxter story, which involves processes, personalities, and some uncertainty, is beyond the scope of the needle-box specialist, but a number of salient facts may be briefly mentioned.

George Baxter flourished in London in the period 1830 to 1860. At a time when colour printing was still largely experimental, and accurate register of fine colour details virtually impossible, he devised a method of colour reproduction for which he was granted a patent in 1836. The method, which Baxer applied mainly to the production of small-scale work, attracted widespread attention and was to lead to the production of large quantities of prints from a total of around 400 subjects. His method was to begin by producing a monochrome print of an original from an intaglio plate (usually an aquatint with etched outlines). He would then add as many colours as were necessary to produce an accurate copy of the original by

Set of needle-box prints by Le Blond & Co., using the Baxter colour-printing process, c. 1850. Untrimmed set, 93 × 131 mm (3⅝ × 5⅛ in)

successive workings from relief blocks. This usually involved between eight and twelve workings, occasionally many more. Though Baxter produced some very big prints, most of his work was on a small scale, and many of his prints are no larger than a postcard.

One of his major achievements was to solve the problem of register, in which each of a series of successive impressions is required to align precisely. This allowed him to produce prints showing extremely fine detail. Baxter's own explanation of his solution to the register problem, as outlined in his patent specification, is (perhaps intentionally) vague. So are his references to the quality of the inks he used. It is perhaps in those areas that the key to his success lies – and the key, moreover, to the relative failure of those to whom he later granted licences. It is generally conceded that his licencees – and indeed Abraham Le Blond, who later acquired and worked from many of his actual plates – often fell short of Baxter in the quality of their work. It may be concluded, as more than one commentator has suggested, that Baxter's real 'secret' lay in the exceptional care he took, and in his use of high-quality materials.

The Baxter specialist's preoccupation with authenticity (which of the plethora of prints is a 'true Baxter', and which by a licencee or imitator) is made more difficult by the presence of an extensive range of 'Baxter-type' pictorial labels, of which the so-called needle prints are an example. Baxter himself produced, in the period 1847–50, prints not only for needle boxes, but for notepaper, Sunday School attendance cards, handkerchief cases, and sheet music. His licencees – Le Blond, Bradshaw & Blacklock, William Dickes, J. M. Kronheim & Co., Joseph Mansell, and Myers & Co. – also produced such items of various quality, most of them bearing no mark of origin.

Typical of these 'anonymous' Baxter-type prints is a range of pictorial motifs that are unrecorded in formal Baxter listings. Used in embossed fabric-labels, they are cut to fit within a variety of frame-shapes and represent the Baxter print in a semi-industrialized application.

Baxter's own needle-box prints are the best known productions of his 'commercial' phase. The needle boxes measured some 50 × 25 × 10 mm (2 × 1 × 3⁄8 in) and were usually supplied in batches of ten in a larger box, some 150 × 110 × 15 mm (6 × 4 3⁄8 × 9⁄16). Both the large outer box and the smaller ones bore appropriately-sized pictorial labels, some of which were specially produced for the purpose, others being cut down from prints designed for other uses. Illustrations depicted such subjects as royalty, royal occasions, flowers, the Great Exhibition, biblical scenes, Crimean War personalities, classical figures, and landscapes. To facilitate production, the smaller needle-case prints were printed in multiple sheets, which were also sold separately for cutting into separate units as Sunday School cards or scrapbook items.

Needle prints were also produced by Le Blond & Co. They printed only two sets, both in very large quantities. Many survive in uncut sheets, but complete boxes are scarce. Bradshaw & Blacklock also produced needle-box prints, as did Mansell and Kronheim.

Apart from his needle-box prints, Baxter made only one other effort in the purely commercial field. He produced a series of portrait prints, commissioned by the *Patriot* newspaper as give-aways for regular subscribers. However, of these 'large and important portraits', Baxter was able to deliver only three (John Williams, Robert Moffatt, and William Knibb), and the scheme lapsed.

Baxter described himself as 'patentee in Great Britain, France, Germany, Belgium, etc.', and is known to have held an Austrian patent. There is, apparently, no record of his licences being taken up on the continent, although it is thought that Moons and Crosby of Boston, Massachusetts, may have held one.

The needle print, as such, appears to have remained a purely British institution.

REFERENCES C. T. Courtney Lewis, *George Baxter, the Picture Printer* (London: Samson Low, 1924); Max E. Mitzman, *George Baxter and the Baxter Prints* (Newton Abbot: David & Charles, 1978)

COLLECTIONS Department of Prints and Drawings, British Museum; Denis Knight, c/o Ephemera Society, London; Lewes Library; Maidstone Museum and Art Gallery; Museum of Reading (UK)

News bill

Bills describing the content of a newspaper first appeared in Britain in the 18th century as small handbills. The first 'poster-style' bills were used to introduce special issues in the middle of the 19th century. Early news bills, instead of headlining a single major item of news, sought to convey an impression of multiple content. A surviving example for 'Bell's Weekly Messenger' (6 January 1844) in a landscape format of 500 × 750 mm (19 3⁄4 × 29 1⁄2 in), lists no fewer than twenty-four news items plus 'Reviews, The Church, Theatres, Horticulture, Assizes, Law, Police, Accidents, Central Criminal Court, Place of Trade, Price Current, Provincial News, and a comprehensive Miscellany'. Regular postings of such bills did not become common

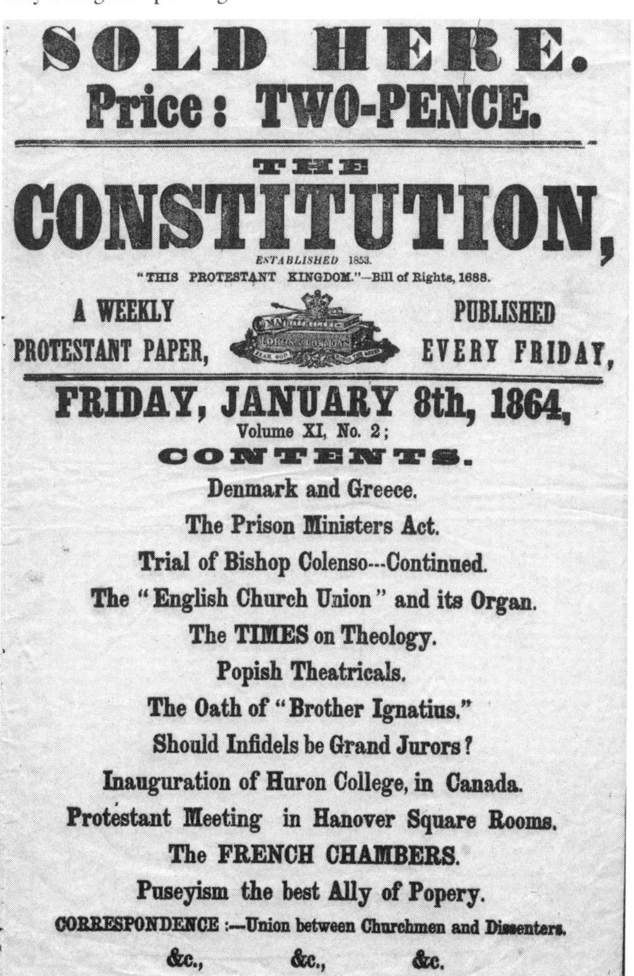
SOLD HERE.
Price: TWO-PENCE.
THE
CONSTITUTION,
ESTABLISHED 1853.
"THIS PROTESTANT KINGDOM."—Bill of Rights, 1688.
A WEEKLY PROTESTANT PAPER, PUBLISHED EVERY FRIDAY,
FRIDAY, JANUARY 8th, 1864,
Volume XI, No. 2;
CONTENTS.
Denmark and Greece.
The Prison Ministers Act.
Trial of Bishop Colenso---Continued.
The "English Church Union" and its Organ.
The TIMES on Theology.
Popish Theatricals.
The Oath of "Brother Ignatius."
Should Infidels be Grand Jurors?
Inauguration of Huron College, in Canada.
Protestant Meeting in Hanover Square Rooms.
The FRENCH CHAMBERS.
Puseyism the best Ally of Popery.
CORRESPONDENCE:—Union between Churchmen and Dissenters.
&c., &c., &c.

News bill for the *Constitution*, 8 January 1864. Letterpress. 380 × 253 mm (14 7⁄8 × 10 in)

until the 1890s, when weekly papers began to produce news bills carrying up to a dozen or so headlines. Sizes were 763 × 508 mm (30 × 20 in) and 508 × 381 mm (20 × 15 in).

Multi-headline bills continued in use into the 20th century, though major news items, such as the Relief of Mafeking [Mafikeng] and the Death of Queen Victoria received the now familiar treatment of two or three words in outsize wood-type capitals. Improved production speeds, following the introduction of curved wood type for use on rotary machines, led to the use of contents bills for dailies as well as for the more leisurely weeklies. By the end of the first decade of the century fresh contents bills were appearing night and morning. Each newspaper established its own printing colours for its bills and provided newsagents with display boards to promote their use. Some bills were overprinted on to waste printed sheets of newspapers. Street vendors carried the bills apron-fashion, sometimes displaying two or even three side by side.

The bills disappeared in World War II to be replaced by chalked headlines on improvised blackboards. In the early post-war period they reappeared with hand-executed brush lettering and, later, silk-screened hand lettering. Major news of a predictable kind was anticipated by the production of stockpiles of conventionally printed bills ('De Gaulle Dies', 'The Queen Ill', 'Princess Margaret Surprise', 'Middle East War Latest', 'Rail Crash', etc.).

The news bill is a predominantly British institution. Smaller versions were earlier used in the United States and are currently found in Europe, but Britain, and particularly London, led in their widespread daily use until the passing of two of its three evening newspapers.

REFERENCE Sarah Whitcombe, 'Sensation on the Street', *Penrose Annual*, 62, 1969, pp. 177–187

COLLECTION John Johnson Collection, Bodleian Library, Oxford

Newspaper

Of all ephemera, the newspaper offers perhaps the most prolific, if not always the most reliable, source of record. The field is vast in terms of period, location, and circumstance, and a study of the subject as a whole is virtually impossible. Historically the newspaper may be seen as a continuing struggle for freedom of expression; as a record of a developing technology; as an evolving medium of information, persuasion, and entertainment; and as a generalized reflection of the human condition. But developments in electronic communication, particularly in the form of television and the Internet, foreshadow a time, before too long, when a newspaper of any sort may well be viewed as a curiosity. Already, at the beginning of the 21st century, newspaper archives recall not only yesterday's news but yesterday's technology. The student of the newspaper commonly approaches the subject, whether as collector or as detached observer, from one of a number of specific viewpoints. Among these may be cited the following:

First and last issues. First issues of newspapers, especially those from the more distant past, commonly present a striking contrast, not only in content and editorial treatment but in visual style, with their later or current treatment. Juxtaposition of first and last issues has the effect of expressing a wide spectrum of change within limited physical compass. Collectors of first and last issues may also include some intervening changes in title, format, or masthead, in order to trace the morphology of the journal as an evolving product.

Mastheads. Newspaper title-pieces may be seen as encapsulations of the journals themselves, expressing through their typographic style, coats of arms, logos, or other devices the spirit of the individual paper's character and, collectively, the general design trends of the day, classes of readership, and national characteristics.

Headlines/front pages. The 20th-century front page, particularly that of the popular paper, with its banner headlines developed as a 'news-package wrapper', acquired an idiom of its own. It can often carry, in retrospect, an impact as powerful as on the day it appeared. A collection of key front pages, though shorn of their context, provide a graphic historical review of the past: election landslides, kidnappings, coronations, assassinations, space adventures, *coups d'état*, hijacks – their headlines embody their time in both content and form.

Commemoratives. Special editions of newspapers, published as mementoes of national occasions (of mourning, celebration, major sports events, etc.) are also collected. However, as with most ephemeral items produced specifically for retention, they prove for the most part less rewarding in retrospect than the unselfconscious throw-aways of everyday life. Items produced

Proofs of early 19th century mastheads for newspapers, probably engraved on brass. *Above:* 41 × 228 mm (1 9/16 × 9 in); *below:* 60 × 235 mm (2 3/8 × 9 1/4 in)

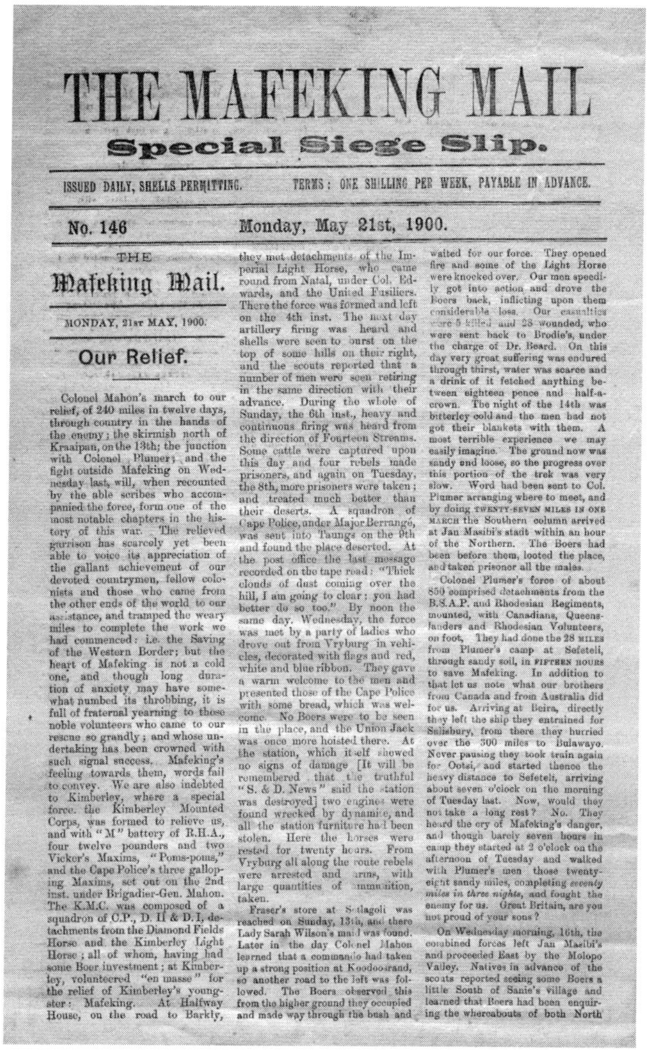

THE MAFEKING MAIL
Special Siege Slip.

ISSUED DAILY, SHELLS PERMITTING. TERMS: ONE SHILLING PER WEEK, PAYABLE IN ADVANCE.

No. 146 Monday, May 21st, 1900.

THE
Mafeking Mail.

MONDAY, 21st MAY, 1900.

Our Relief.

Colonel Mahon's march to our relief, of 240 miles in twelve days, through country in the hands of the enemy; the skirmish north of Kraaipan, on the 13th; the junction with Colonel Plumer; and the fight outside Mafeking on Wednesday last, will, when recounted by the able scribes who accompanied the force, form one of the most notable chapters in the history of this war. The relieved garrison has scarcely yet been able to voice its appreciation of the gallant achievement of our devoted countrymen, fellow colonists and those who came from the other ends of the world to our assistance, and tramped the weary miles to complete the work we had commenced: i.e. the Saving of the Western Border; but the heart of Mafeking is not a cold one, and though long duration of anxiety may have somewhat numbed its throbbing, it is full of fraternal yearning to those noble volunteers who came to our rescue so grandly; and whose undertaking has been crowned with such signal success. Mafeking's feeling towards them, words fail to convey. We are also indebted to Kimberley, where a special force, the Kimberley Mounted Corps, was formed to relieve us, and with "M" battery of R.H.A., four twelve pounders and two Vicker's Maxims, "Poms-poms," and the Cape Police's three galloping Maxims, set out on the 2nd inst. under Brigadier-Gen. Mahon. The K.M.C. was composed of a squadron of C.P., D. II & D. I, detachments from the Diamond Fields Horse and the Kimberley Light Horse; all of whom, having had some Boer investment; at Kimberley, volunteered "en masse" for the relief of Kimberley's youngster: Mafeking. At Halfway House, on the road to Barkly, they met detachments of the Imperial Light Horse, who came round from Natal, under Col. Edwards, and the United Fusiliers. There the force was formed and left on the 4th inst. The next day artillery firing was heard and shells were seen to burst on the top of some hills on their right, and the scouts reported that a number of men were seen retiring in the same direction with their advance. During the whole of Sunday, the 6th inst., heavy and continuous firing was heard from the direction of Fourteen Streams. Some cattle were captured upon this day and four rebels made prisoners, and again on Tuesday, the 8th, more prisoners were taken; and treated much better than their deserts. A squadron of Cape Police, under Major Berrangé, was sent into Taungs on the 9th and found the place deserted. At the post office the last message recorded on the tape read: "Thick clouds of dust coming over the hill, I am going to clear; you had better do so too." By noon the same day, Wednesday, the force was met by a party of ladies who drove out from Vryburg in vehicles, decorated with flags and red, white and blue ribbon. They gave a warm welcome to the men and presented those of the Cape Police with some bread, which was welcome. No Boers were to be seen in the place, and the Union Jack was once more hoisted there. At the station, which itself showed no signs of damage [It will be remembered that the truthful "S. & D. News" said the station was destroyed] two engines were found wrecked by dynamite, and all the station furniture had been stolen. Here the horses were rested for twenty hours. From Vryburg all along the route rebels were arrested and arms, with large quantities of ammunition, taken.

Fraser's store at Setlagoli was reached on Sunday, 13th, and there Lady Sarah Wilson's maid was found. Later in the day Colonel Mahon learned that a commando had taken up a strong position at Koodoosrand, so another road to the left was followed. The Boers observed this from the higher ground they occupied and made way through the bush and waited for our force. They opened fire and some of the Light Horse were knocked over. Our men speedily got into action and drove the Boers back, inflicting upon them considerable loss. Our casualties were 5 killed and 28 wounded, who were sent back to Brodie's, under the charge of Dr. Beard. On this day very great suffering was endured through thirst, water was scarce and a drink of it fetched anything between eighteen pence and half-a-crown. The night of the 14th was bitterley cold and the men had not got their blankets with them. A most terrible experience we may easily imagine. The ground now was sandy and loose, so the progress over this portion of the trek was very slow. Word had been sent to Col. Plumer arranging where to meet, and by doing TWENTY-SEVEN MILES IN ONE MARCH the Southern column arrived at Jan Masibi's stadt within an hour of the Northern. The Boers had been before them, looted the place, and taken prisoner all the males.

Colonel Plumer's force of about 850 comprised detachments from the B.S.A.P. and Rhodesian Regiments, mounted, with Canadians, Queenslanders and Rhodesian Volunteers, on foot. They had done the 28 MILES from Plumer's camp at Sefeteli, through sandy soil, in FIFTEEN HOURS to save Mafeking. In addition to that let us note what our brothers from Canada and from Australia did for us. Arriving at Beira, directly they left the ship they entrained for Salisbury, from there they hurried over the 300 miles to Bulawayo. Never pausing they took train again for Ootsi, and started thence the heavy distance to Sefeteli, arriving about seven o'clock on the morning of Tuesday last. Now, would they not take a long rest? No. They heard the cry of Mafeking's danger, and though barely seven hours in camp they started at 2 o'clock on the afternoon of Tuesday and walked with Plumer's men those twenty-eight sandy miles, completing *seventy miles in three nights*, and fought the enemy for us. Great Britain, are you not proud of your sons?

On Wednesday morning, 16th, the combined forces left Jan Masibi's and proceeded East by the Molopo Valley. Natives in advance of the scouts reported seeing some Boers a little South of Sanie's village and learned that Boers had been enquiring the whereabouts of both North

Front page of *The Mafeking Mail, Special Siege Slip*, no. 146, 21 May 1900. Letterpress, printed and published by Townshend & Son, Market Square, Mafeking. 330 × 204mm (13 × 8 in)

for keeping are by definition common: it is the issue of the newspaper for the day before, or the day after, the commemorated event that will have been discarded – and is therefore likely to be scarce.

Improvised newspapers. Newspapers produced in emergency or under special difficulties form a special group. These include the so-called 'trench newspapers' of World War I; 'Siege' newspapers such as *The Mafeking Mail* ('Issued daily, shells permitting. terms: one shilling per week, payable in advance'); 'strike editions' of major newspapers, produced by various means in the absence of normal editions; and single-sheet extras such as those produced by the German press for free distribution in the early weeks of World War I.

Mock newspapers. This category includes papers containing 'spoof' news, such as an April-fool front page of a European newspaper of the 1930s reporting the capture of the Loch Ness monster, and the World War I issue of the *New York Times*, put out by the War Bond Authority, with a front page story of a German air raid on New York. Also in this group is the London *Daily Mail's* issue for AD 2000, published in 1928. The story of a transatlantic balloon flight, engineered by Edgar Allen Poe in 'The balloon hoax' (1844), is a further example.

Language minority newspapers. America's first foreign-language newspaper appeared in German-town, Pennsylvania in 1739; *Die Londoner Zeitung* (published in London in the 1930s) and the *Dziennik Polski* (which began publication in London in 1940) are latter-day UK examples. Immigrant newspapers proliferated in America in the 19th century: by 1917, when US foreign-language newspapers had reached their peak, there were as many as 1500. Many still exist, though their number is diminishing.

Ships' newspapers. Printed on board as an additional service for passengers in the luxury liner era of the 1920s and 1930s, the ship's newspaper – with such titles as *Ocean Mail* – was past its prime by the close of the 20th century. The QE2's newspaper, which was keyboarded in Fleet Street and transmitted by radio to be computer-composed on board, marked a technological highpoint. *See also* SHIP'S NEWSPAPER

Curiosities. Collecting categories among newspaper curiosities are numerous. Misprints, both in text and headlines, and even occasionally in mastheads, are specialist interests (the Spanish newspaper *Diarío de Almeria* appeared on one occasion during the Spanish Civil War as *Diaría de Almerio*). Also collected are headlines which prove to be untruths: 'All saved from Titanic after collision' (The New York *Evening Sun*, 15 April 1912); 'Dewey defeats Truman' (*Chicago Daily Tribune*). Published corrections or apologies form another category. Typical is a 'correction' item in *The Times* of London in the mid 1970s: 'The caption to a photograph published on May 26, described the centrepiece in an exhibition of Henry Moore's work as a sculpture. It is in fact an elephant's skull'. Intimations of production disasters are collected (more particularly by newspaper personnel). A note at the foot of page seven of the St Lucia newspaper *Daylight* (Friday, 28 October 1898), in explanation of its reduced format and a blank back page, cryptically declares: 'While going to press we met with an accident, therefore this size'. Newspapers bearing blank spaces, indicating censorship or withdrawal of labour, form another specialist collector's group.

See also NEWS BILL; TAX STAMP (NEWSPAPER DUTY); UNSTAMPED NEWSPAPER/PERIODICAL

COLLECTION British Library (Colindale), London

Notice to quit

The term 'Notice to quit' most commonly applies to tenancy and has done so since the mid 19th century; it is an invitation, either to a sitting tenant terminating a tenancy or to an em-

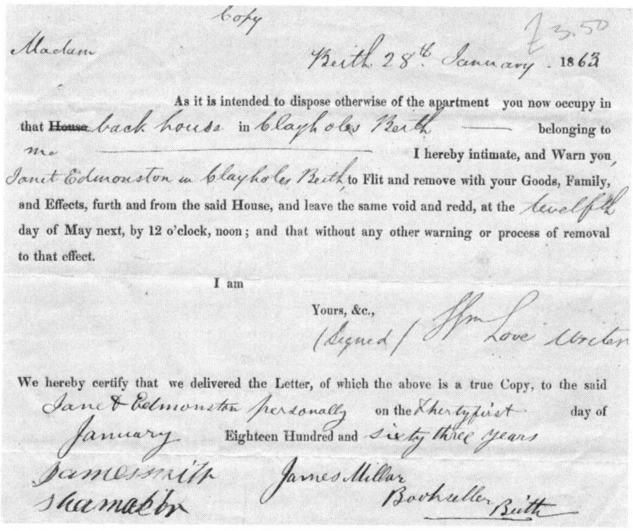

Copy

Madam Beith 28th January 1863

As it is intended to dispose otherwise of the apartment you now occupy in that ~~House~~ back house in Clayholes Beith — belonging to me — I hereby intimate, and Warn you, Janet Edmonston in Clayholes Beith to Flit and remove with your Goods, Family, and Effects, furth and from the said House, and leave the same void and redd, at the twelfth day of May next, by 12 o'clock, noon; and that without any other warning or process of removal to that effect.

I am
Yours, &c.,
(Signed) Wm Love Weaver

We hereby certify that we delivered the Letter, of which the above is a true Copy, to the said Janet Edmonston personally on the thirty first day of January Eighteen Hundred and sixty three years

James Smith
Shoemaker
James Millar
Bookseller Beith

Notice to quit (copy), Beith, Scotland, 28 January 1863. Letterpress and manuscript. 164 × 207 mm (6½ × 8⅛ in)

ployee regarding termination of employment. The document was at first handwritten, but it rapidly became a jobbing printer's standard item, the wording of which remained and remains unsettled. Its function is to give notice of the termination of an agreement on or before a specific date.

Many such documents contain qualifying clauses relating to the occasion of the tenancy, such as this one from Spalding (UK) of the 1850s:

> To put into proper tenantable repair and condition and to paint with two coats of the best paint in oil, the woodwork of the outside of the farm house and farm buildings and also the gates palings and posts belonging thereto...and likewise to paint the woodwork of the inside of the dwelling house with two coats of the best paint mixed with oil and turpentine in the usual way....

Another undated document from Beith, Scotland, reveals its own regional wording: '...I hereby intimate and warn you ... to flit and remove with your goods family and effects, furth and from the said house and leave the same void and redd ...without any other warning or process of removal to that effect ...'. Other notices are intimations from the tenant to the landlord: 'I hereby give you notice of my intention to quit...which I now hold of you...'. This notice clearly requires the tenant to acknowledge and confirm his forthcoming departure.

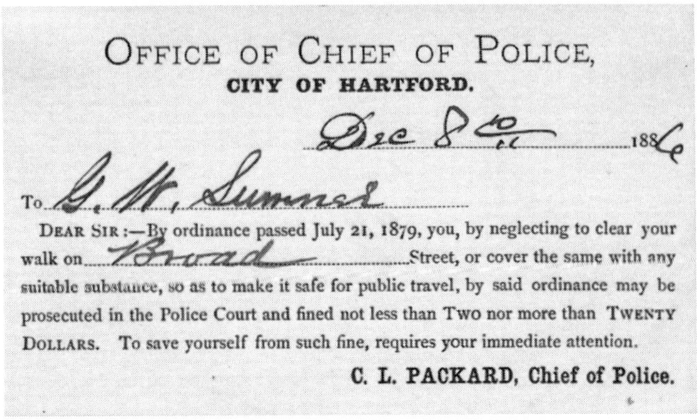

OFFICE OF CHIEF OF POLICE,
CITY OF HARTFORD.

Dec 8th 1886

To G. W. Sumner

DEAR SIR:—By ordinance passed July 21, 1879, you, by neglecting to clear your walk on Broad Street, or cover the same with any suitable substance, so as to make it safe for public travel, by said ordinance may be prosecuted in the Police Court and fined not less than Two nor more than TWENTY DOLLARS. To save yourself from such fine, requires your immediate attention.

C. L. PACKARD, Chief of Police.

Notice of a nuisance, City of Hartford, 8 December 1886. Letterpress and manuscript. 63 × 109 mm (2½ × 4¼in)

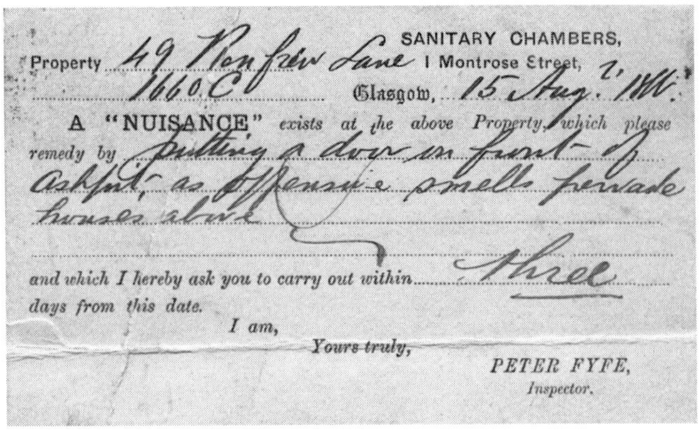

SANITARY CHAMBERS,
Property 49 Renfrew Lane 1 Montrose Street,
1660 C Glasgow, 15 Aug. 1888.

A "NUISANCE" exists at the above Property, which please remedy by putting a door in front of ashpit, as offensive smells pervade houses above

and which I hereby ask you to carry out within three days from this date.

I am,
Yours truly,
PETER FYFE,
Inspector.

Notice of a nuisance, Glasgow, 15 August 1888. Letterpress and manuscript. 75 × 120 mm (3 × 4¾in)

Nuisance papers

A common nuisance was defined in Richard Burn's *Justice of the Peace and Parish Officer* (21st edn, Cadell & Davies, 1810) as 'an offence against the public, either by doing a thing which tends to the annoyance of all of the King's subjects, or by neglecting to do a thing which the common good requires'. Annoyances to the prejudice of individuals are not punishable by public prosecution but through private actions of the persons aggrieved.

Nuisances may take a wide variety of forms. Classically they have included: 'bawdy houses, gaming houses and stages for rope dancers'; playhouses if they attract 'such a number of coaches or people as prove generally inconvenient to the places adjacent'; 'obstruction of neighbour's daylight'; 'making offensive smells or noises'; 'making great noises in the night'; and 'erecting a dovecote without licence from the lord of the manor'.

The 'common scold' was also liable to prosecution as a common nuisance. One such was convicted in the 18th century 'for being a common or turbulent brawler and sower of discord amongst her quiet and honest neighbours, so that she hath stirred, moved and incited divers strifes, controversies, quarrels and disputes amongst His Majesty's liege people, against the peace ...'.

Papers relating to the common scold are rare, but it is clear that the notion of action against her survived into the first decades of the 19th century. One handwritten fragment datelined Blackburn, 12 October 1840, sets out a complaint which is clearly a prelude to prosecution: 'Gents: This is to certify that we the undersigned being neighbours to the said Mrs Sarah Bagley of Fish St, we can prove our own personal observations that she is a very uneasy neighbour and is never free from broils and disturbances arrising from the natural disposition to quarrel as well as from the impetuosity of her tempers as witness our hands: James Lonsdale; Richd Bell; John Whiteside'. This document is cropped immediately below the last signature, and it is evident from fold-creases that the sheet was originally foolscap in size; it may therefore have had many more than the three signatures.

Another form of nuisance appears in a manuscript item from New Hampshire dated 1891. This is a receipt written by S. W. Hulman 'For the town of Hillsborough'. It reads: 'Recd of C Nilson Esq ten dollars to settle claim of town of Hillsborough, through Board of Health ... for leaving dead hog in the Contoocook River'.

Oath

The oath is a solemnly sworn declaration made in the presence of a duly authorized officer. It may take the form of an oral recital of a prescribed form of words, completion in writing of a part-printed form, or a wholly manuscript document. It is a requirement that the words contain an appeal to God (or something sacred) and, in the case of the written deposition, that the name and status of the administering officer and signatory be given. In Britain, provision is made for a modification in wording in the case of non-Christians and Quakers; others may merely 'affirm'. A primary function of the oath has been the securing of allegiance to the monarch, church, or other authority.

Classic forms of words appear in the British 'Oath of Allegiance': '[I] do solemnly promise and swear that I will be faithful, and bear true allegiance to His Majesty King George: So help me God'; and in the 'Oath of Supremacy', in which the signatory inveighs against the See of Rome and declares that 'no foreign prince, person, prelate, state or potentate hath or ought to have, any jurisdiction, power, superiority, pre-eminence or authority, ecclesiastical or spiritual, within this realm: So help me God'.

Other forms of words embody the 'Oath of Abjuration', in which alien claims to the throne of England are rejected; the 'Declaration against transubstantiation', a denial of the transformation of communion bread and wine into the body and blood of Christ; and the 'Declaration against Popery', an oath in which the believer dismisses not only transubstantiation but 'the invocation and adoration of the Virgin Mary or any other saint as superstitious and idolatrous'.

Other oaths relate to the duties of members of Courts Martial; to entry into the Royal Navy, Army, Militia, or East India Company; to the appointment of constables, headboroughs, etc.; and to employers' declarations about absconding apprentices.

In the City of London, Wardmote Inquests demanded detailed reports from constables or 'officers and nuisancers' in these areas, and others were required from those concerned in making formal presentations. The wording of the oaths was included in broadsheets, c. 1855, outlining the duties of constables. Also published by the City of London at the same period was a form of words for use in the swearing-in of coal-meters, the officers appointed to weigh coals brought into the city by ship from Newcastle. This oath was devised to be read over to the applicant for office, his role being merely to indicate assent. The document, 165 × 210 mm (6½ × 8¼ in), carries the arms of the city and the title 'Coal-meter's oath'. It reads:

> Ye shall swear that ye shall indifferently measure all coal that to you belongeth for to measure, and just measure ye shall give to every person, as well as to poor as to rich, without partiality shewing or favour; and ye shall buy no Coal but only to your own use, and in no wise to utter or sell again, as long as you stand in your office; also ye take no more for your labour in the measuring or metering of Coal but as of old time it hath been ordained and used. And this ye shall do, as God help you.

A typographically similar document, in which only the word 'coal' is altered, appears as an oath to be taken by corn-meters.

There are also surviving examples of early trade unionists' 'Illegal oaths', though they are rare. The wording of one of these, featured in Rex v Marks and Others in 1802 (3 East, 158), is recorded as: 'You shall be true to every journeyman [wool] shearman, and not to hurt any of them, and you shall not divulge any of their secrets, so help you God'.

Opticians' papers

Though not as commonly found as DENTAL PAPERS – and by no means as disconcerting in content – opticians' papers document both the increasing specialization and professionalization of the optician and changing tastes in spectacles. Understandably, opticians are not needed quite so desperately as dentists, and this may partly account for the fact that there were far fewer of them in 19th-century London. In the 1850s, London directories list between around 150 to 200 opticians, and almost twice that many dentists.

The origin of spectacles is obscure. They are mentioned before 1300 AD as being used by monks, and a manuscript survives (Swiss breviary, c. 1400) with its front board hollowed out to take a pair of spectacles. As early as 1629 the Worshipful Company of Spectacle Makers was granted a royal charter to regulate standards in spectacle making in Britain. In the 18th century and on into the 20th century the work of opticians was closely associated with that of instrument makers, and particularly those who made optical instruments. In 1826, J. Davis, who described himself as a 'working optician' from Glasgow, announced on a rather handsome poster that he was opening a shop in Ulverston in the north of England. The poster provides information about the range of optical appliances available from such shops in the 1820s, in what was then a fashionable market town with maritime interests. Davis offered the following:

Optician's test chart of E. & R. Simmons, wholesale opticians, London, late 19th century. Letterpress, mounted on card and hinged with linen. Each page 280 × 210 mm (11 × 8¼ in)

> A Large & very Valuable Assortment of Telescopes, Microscopes, Opera, Reading, Hand, Claude Lorraine, and Eye Glasses; Mariners' Compasses, Sextants, Quadrants, Camera Obscuras, and Luciters, Diagram & Landscape Mirrors, Thermometers, Barometers, Storm Glasses, Spirit Levels, Magnets, new improved Folding Eye Glasses, Patent Kaleidoscopes, Instrument Cases, Measuring Tapes, Ivory and Box Rules, Sun Dials, Globes, Pantographs, Prisms, Air Pumps, Theodolites, Electrifying Machines, new improved Phantasmagoria, Magic Lantern with Copper-plate Sliders &c. &c.

Beneath this list Davis refers to 'His improved spectacles, in Gold, Silver, and Tortoise Shell Mountings'.

More typical of the range of ephemera associated with the optician are the TRADE CARD and other promotional material, the appointment card, and the test card.

One advertisement of the 1830s lists the spectacles available from John Thomas Hudson, optician and spectacle maker of Henrietta Street, Cavendish Square, London. At its head is an image that, with variations, appears on many opticians' advertisements: a pair of spectacles enclosing disembodied and staring eyes. The advertisement describes a range of spectacles, each with four different sorts of lenses: 'concave pebbles', 'convex pebbles', 'concave glasses', and 'convex glasses'. At the top of the range are 'Golden Spectacles with concave pebbles' at £2 4*s* 0*d*; at the cheaper end, 'Strong steel spectacles for artizans with convex glasses' at 3*s* 6*d*, and 'Spectacles to correct squinting, in children' at 7*s* 6*d*. Hudson's price list appears on the publishers' announcement of his book *Spectaclænia: or the sight restored, &c. by the use of spectacles* (London: Simpkin and Marshall, 1833), which ran to at least ten editions.

An early 20th-century trade card of Heaton Caffin, an optician with five premises in London, provides on one side a simple test as a means of encouraging trade. The test involved reading a short passage of small type from a distance of ten inches, and the much more demanding task of identifying seven capital letters (F V T K P R H), each 6mm high, from a distance of sixteen feet. Failure to read the latter – it is shrewdly pointed out – 'proves that your eyes are in some way defective' and that 'it would be advisable to have them tested by a qualified Optician'.

Advances in spectacle manufacture and the clinical measurement and diagnosis of eye defects led to the formation of several optical associations (e.g. The British Optical Association in 1896). Until the late 19th century opticians were mainly dispensers of spectacles, but in the 1890s a distinction began to be made between ophthalmic (examining) opticians and others who merely dispensed spectacles. In the late 20th century the American term 'optometrist' was formally adopted in Britain for the 'ophthalmic optician'. Training also developed, and in Britain had become compulsory for ophthalmic opticians by 1920. From the 1890s it became customary for appropriate qualifications to be displayed on promotional material and, frequently, on a framed CERTIFICATE. A trade card of Black & Co. of Hove and Brighton, dating from the second quarter of the 20th century, provides an example of the former. The firm described itself modestly as 'Eye Specialists', but was clearly at pains to show its credentials: the name 'H. Milner Black F.S.M.C.' is accompanied by a coat of arms bearing the words 'Lux in tenebris' (Latin: light amid the shadows) with, beneath it, the note 'Fellow of the Institute of Ophthalmic Opticians. Just elected Member of its Council'.

An alternative approach to advertising, appealing to the emotions, is seen on a chromolithographed trade card used by A. Hirsch & Co., manufacturing opticians of 333 Kearny Street, San Francisco. It shows a bespectacled young girl, needle and thread in hand, with the unconvincing copy line: 'Papa buys his Spectacles and Eye Glasses from A. Hirsch & Co.'.

From a typographic point of view the most distinctive category of opticians' ephemera are sight-testing charts, which have features in common with both the ABC PRIMER and the printer's type specimen (*see* TYPOGRAPHICA). These charts are of two basic kinds: one that tests visual acuity (distance vision) and another that assesses ability to read standard print. The first goes back to the early 19th century when random-size letters were used to check visual standards; the method for testing distance vision used today stems from H. Snellen (1834–1908), who devised a chart around 1862 consisting mainly of single letters arranged systematically in decreasing size. The second kind of chart consists of paragraphs of text in different sizes: Heinrich Kuchler (b. 1818) devised a chart of this kind using black-letter type in 1843 and Eduard Jaeger (1818–84) produced a version in roman type which, in essence, is still in use. An example of a chart derived from Jaeger was issued on two hinged boards by E. & R. Simmons, 'Wholesale Opticians' of 57 Red Lion Street, London, probably at the end of the 19th century. It is headed 'Test-types in use at the Royal London Ophthalmic Hospital, Moorfields' and shows a scheme 'Corresponding to the "Schrift-Scalen" of Prof. Edwd Jaeger, of Vienna'. The chart displays twelve sizes of type, the first of which has its capital letters 1.0 mm high, the last its ascenders 33 mm high. The sizes are designated, using the traditional terms of the printing trade, from Brilliant to 8-line Roman. The wide range of sizes allowed for the testing of both the normally and partially sighted.

Over the last half century eye tests for distance vision have been replaced by changeable illuminated panels, though opticians still use hand-held printed cards with paragraphs of text in different sizes for testing continuous reading. [MT]

REFERENCES Arthur Linksz, 'The Development of Visual Standards: Snellen, Jaeger, and Giraud-Teulon', *Bulletin of the New York Academy of Medicine*, vol. 51, no. 2, February 1975, pp. 277–285; Hugh Orr, *Illustrated History of Early Antique Spectacles* (Beckenham, Kent: The Author, 1985)

COLLECTION British Optical Association, The College of Optometrists, London

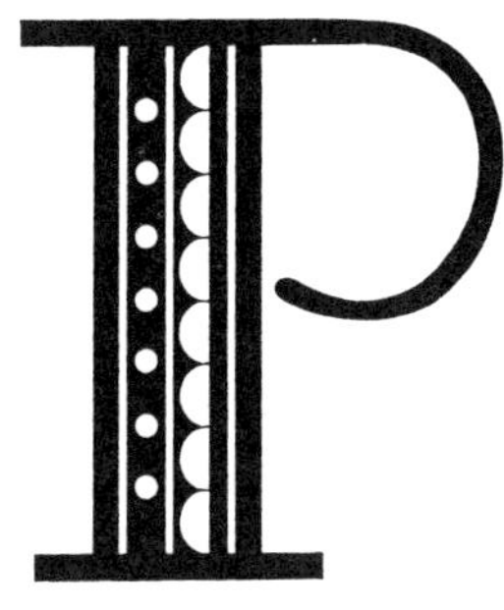

Packaging [plates 2b, 15]

In general terms the word packaging refers not merely to a container but to a commercial container of identifiable content and design, produced as part of a multiple sales operation. Among the earliest of product containers were the glass and ceramic pots of the apothecary. These however were commonly used for storage and display in the dispensary; it must be assumed that containers for take-away sales were improvised, either by the vendor or by the customer. Use of improvised bottles was not wholly unknown in the 20th century: the jug-and-bottle trade of the British pub, as well as the milkman's churn and dipper, are still within living memory.

Among the first of the purpose-made containers for liquids and pastes were the beer bottle, the stone bottle for ginger beer or ink, and the ceramic pot for pomade, ointment, and blacking. Such containers, marked by moulded impression, transfer printing, or pasted label, led in turn to the cola bottle, the plastic dispenser, and the aerosol.

The box, carton, tin, and collapsible tube generated their own line of succession, principally the paper package. Unlike the more enduring (and reusable) pot and tin, it survives only by exception. The very act of opening it begins its destruction, and by the end of its useful life it is normally damaged beyond retrieval. Barely, if ever, is it a candidate for reuse.

Early shopkeepers, if they wrapped their wares at all, did so only nominally. One 17th-century London tea-man's advertisement suggests that the customer should come provided with 'a convenient box'. Squares of paper, normally reserved only for the most unmanageable of commodities, were the universal standby. In this way, for those who shopped without convenient boxes, the problem of wrapping such products as pins, needles, snuff, tobacco, ink powder, sago, and the like was solved.

With the rise of shopkeeping and the growth of competition, it was only a matter of time before the square of wrapping paper carried a printed distinguishing mark. Later the printed paper became part wrapper, part trade advertisement; the mid 19th-century chemist's powder paper was sometimes printed not only with his name and address but also with an extensive list of his stock-in-trade.

Among the earliest of the 'unmanageable' products was the pack of cards, whose numerical integrity was vital. For these, a retaining wrapper was imperative – and had been so almost from the emergence of the PLAYING CARD as a commercial product. The PLAYING-CARD WRAPPER, printed with maker's name and image, is possibly the oldest form of paper package. The word 'paper', as in 'tobacco paper', 'powder paper', etc., commonly applies to paper folded on itself to form a flat container; a wrapper commonly forms a package in three dimensions.

The shopkeeper's printed PAPER BAG, a development of the 1860s, emerged as a logical extension of the tobacco paper. A more significant feature of the growth of the consumer market was the LABEL, an all-purpose marker for bottle, pot, packet, box, or carton. The label, custom-printed for the specific shopkeeper, or supplied for general use throughout a given trade, was a harbinger of an industry which today forms an integral part of mass-manufacturing technology.

Also a feature of 19th-century packaging – short-lived, but in its time more or less universal – was the printed COTTON BAG. In general use for flour, seed, rice, and other such products, it was largely superseded by paper during the cotton shortage of the American Civil War. It survived in minor applications (birdseed etc.) into the mid 20th century.

Another form of 20th-century packaging was the cylindrical paper box, which was closely related to the 17th-century circular BANDBOX and the colonial American 'painting box' (used, respectively, for storing collar bands, and herbs, spices, and the like). In its most abbreviated form it appeared as the pillbox. Taller versions were also made, normally for tapers and matches, but also for hairpins, bottles of tincture, marking ink, etc. The cylindrical form was widespread largely because of its relative ease of construction. Its main advantage lay in its avoidance of the difficulty of producing square-cut corners, a problem whose solution was to await the introduction of reliable creasing, folding, and cutting machinery. A sheet of paper, pasted and rolled to form a tube, provided a simple yet rigid basic structure. A second, outer, tube supplied additional thickness and strength. Sliced into narrow sections, with the outer thickness commonly divided between lid and base, top and bottom discs were pasted in place to complete the structure. Thin lining paper, often lapping the rims, was added. Black or coloured paper encircled the finished pillbox. In later versions, side-members were die-cut as strips, formed into bands, and pasted over with cover paper. Similar shaped containers were also produced in wood chip (familiar in matchbox construction), in solid turned wood, and later in tin-plate.

The 'pillbox' was also used in the marketing of such products as boot-buttons, hooks and eyes, sealing WAFERS, and paper fasteners. Larger round boxes were used for cuff and collar sets, talcum and toilet powders, hats, and Edison's cylindrical phonograph records.

See also BISCUIT/CRACKER LABEL; BOOKMATCH; CAN LABEL; CHEESE LABEL; CHOP PAPER; CIGARETTE PACK; CIGARETTE PAPER; CUBAN WRAPPER; KITE BAG; MILK-BOTTLE CLOSURE; NEEDLE PACKET; NEEDLE-BOX PRINT; PEN-BOX LABEL; PHARMACEUTICAL PACKAGE; PILLBOX LABEL; PIN PAPER; PIN-BOX LABEL; PLASTER PACKAGE; RAZOR-BLADE WRAPPER; REAM LABEL; RECORD COVER; SEED PACKET; SEIDLITZ-POWDER LABEL; TOBACCO PAPER; WINKLE BAG

REFERENCE Alec Davis, *Package and Print* (London: Faber and Faber, 1967)

COLLECTIONS Museum of Advertising and Packaging, Gloucester; Museum of Reading (UK); Reading University Library

Panorama, entertainment

Panoramas – giant 360-degree illusionistic paintings exhibited in specially designed rotundas – were the invention in the mid 1780s of Robert Barker (1739–1806). The word panorama (Greek: all-embracing view) was coined by a classical friend of his and came into use in 1791. Barker's first panorama was a painting of Edinburgh, which he took to London in 1788. Rotundas built according to the Barker patent were erected in Leicester Square and the Strand, and in them panorama paintings of cities and battles were exhibited. In due course similar buildings were erected in Birmingham, Liverpool, Edinburgh, and Dublin, and in numerous towns overseas.

To achieve maximum pleasure when viewing a panorama it was advisable for visitors to purchase a descriptive booklet. The frontispiece to this booklet invariably consisted of a folded key. Until 1819 the key's image in Barker's booklets was circular and unintentionally resembled an ANAMORPHIC IMAGE. From 1819 the key consisted of a pair of horizontal pictures, one over the other, printed on a single sheet. Booklets and keys for the panoramas of the Barkers and their successors, the Burfords, are widely collected and now fetch high prices. Less common are the Barker and Burford handbills advertising individual panoramas, which were presumably distributed in the streets.

A rival entertainment to the 360-degree panorama was the diorama (Greek: double view), invented by Louis Jacques Mandé Daguerre (1787–1851). At the diorama the image changed, being transformed by the adjustment of light directed on to the painting, front and reverse, by a clever system of blinds and shutters. Like the 360-degree panorama, it called for a specially designed building. Diorama ephemera consist almost entirely of descriptive booklets. Also related to the panorama was the cosmorama (Greek: world view). This consisted of a series of small panoramas viewed through windows (in fact lenses) set into the walls of a room. The principal cosmoramas were in Paris in the Palais-Royal, and in London at 209 Regent Street, but cosmoramas were frequently provided in bazaars and arcades as a distraction for shoppers. Descriptive booklets were available at the most classy cosmoramas. In addition to exhibiting cosmoramas, the Cosmorama in Regent Street provided space for a variety of non-panoramic shows that were announced on handbills, such as 'Xylopyrography, or the Art of Engraving on Char'd Wood', and paintings from Thomas Lawrence's personal collection. A 'Singing Mouse' exhibited at the Cosmorama excited the admiration of all who heard it.

The most widespread and popular rival to the 360-degree panorama was the moving panorama (sometimes incorrectly, and misleadingly, called diorama). It became popular in Britain in the 1810s and continued to be popular in the English-speaking world for another hundred years. The moving panorama consisted of a canvas of very great length, which was cranked from one giant spool on to another. It could consist of one continuous image or a sequence of tableaux. Such panoramas were a feature of pantomimes at the theatre, but more commonly they were shown in assembly rooms, mechanics institutes, corn exchanges, temperance halls, athenaeums, and concert rooms. Their showmen toured from town to town, transporting them sometimes in pantechnicons or in specially adapted trains. From the 1840s it was usual for the moving panorama to be presented by a lecturer or 'cicerone'. Music – a piano for the simplest, but more usually a brass band – provided the necessary atmosphere. Towards the end of the 19th century it was common for each panorama show to be accompanied by a troupe of entertainers – vocalists, jugglers, ventriloquists, acrobats, and tight-rope walkers.

The quantity of ephemera generated by moving panoramas was enormous. In Britain two dynasties of panoramists dominated the scene for many years – the Hamiltons and the Pooles. When the Pooles's myriorama (i.e. panorama: for the conventional use of the word *see* MYRIORAMA) visited a town such as Leeds or Manchester it was said that their agent employed forty to fifty sandwichmen, window-billers, hand-billers, and ticketers to publicise it. It has been calculated that in a four-week season in Manchester Pooles's agent pasted up 11,000 posters and distributed up to a million half-price tickets. (The half-price ticket artfully conveyed the idea of special privilege, but in fact very few visitors seem to have been charged the full rate. Half-price panorama tickets were so common that they were collected by schoolboys).

Even as early as the 1850s panoramists' handbills could be inventive. S. C. Brees, whose New Zealand panorama did more, *The Times* claimed, to promote emigration than a thousand speeches and resolutions, showed Brees rubbing noses with a Maori warrior and saying, 'Tar Nar Qoi Ar Re-Mi [You smell, but so do I]'.

Arriving at the actual panorama performance, the visitor could buy a programme. This would describe each of the panorama's tableaux, and also provide the words of the various songs that would be sung during the performance. At Albert Smith's 'Ascent of Mont Blanc' the audience could also purchase fans carrying a scene from the panorama, Mont Blanc roses with a scene on each petal, and a Mont Blanc Quadrille and a Chimouni [Chamonix] Polka, both with attractive lithographed covers. For his 'Excursions on the Continent' A. W. Hamilton provided his audiences with an elaborate timetable and encouraged them to make use of it during performances. The showmanship of moving panoramists was cruelly mocked in Artemus Ward's spoof panorama: 'Artemus Ward Among the Mormons'. Ward's handbill claimed his panorama was even 'worse than panoramas usually are'. And he insisted that no one should say they liked his lecture either, 'unless he wished to be thought eccentric; and nobody must say he doesn't like it unless he really is eccentric. This requires thinking over, but it will amply repay perusal'.

Albert Smith and the Poole family wrote their letters on elaborately designed headed notepaper which unashamedly advertised their panoramas. The Pooles also used elaborately designed chromolithographed envelopes, which fulfilled much the same purpose.

From the 1820s moving panoramas gave rise to numerous small paper panoramas, the most expensive of which were printed in aquatint and pulled out of elaborate lacquered cases. In the cheaper range were those designed for toy panorama prosceniums. The kit, if complete, would include text for the child who was assigned the role of 'cicerone'. In the 1870s H. G. Clarke sold a paper panorama of the Thames embankment, uncoloured one penny or sixpence coloured, and a similarly priced panorama of the Lord Mayor's Show, complete with instructions on how to construct your own toy panorama proscenium for performance. Panoramas of the Lord Mayor's Show, crudely printed and often hand-coloured, were sold in the streets of the Cities of London and Westminster on 9 November, and continued to be until well into the 20th century. The hawker's cry was:

Buy my panorama –
My penny panorama –
My penny panorama of
The Lord Mayor's Show [RH]

See also PANORAMA, NEWSPAPER GIVE-AWAYS

REFERENCES Richard Altick, *The Shows of London* (Cambridge, Mass.: The Belknap Press of Harvard University Press, 1978); Ralph Hyde, *Panoramania!* (London: Trefoil Publications Ltd in association with Barbican Art Gallery, 1988)

Panorama, newspaper give-aways

During the Victorian period, wood-engraved paper panoramas, chiefly of towns, were presented by weekly illustrated newspapers to their subscribers. The first, 'London in 1842', was issued by the *Illustrated London News* on 7 January 1843 with descriptive notes and a key. No WOOD-ENGRAVING this large had ever been attempted. After the *Pictorial Times* was launched in 1843 it distributed a handbill promising to give to its readers 'the largest engraving in the world', a panoramic view of the Thames from the Houses of Parliament to the Tower of London. It kept its promise on 11 January 1845 with an engraving of 89 × 1080 mm (3½ × 42½ in). An extension of this panorama, continuing the image to the Isle of Dogs, crossing the river at Greenwich and returning as far as Deptford, was issued two years later. Not to be outdone, the *Illustrated London News* responded with its own 'Panorama of the Thames in 1845', and announced that it was embarking on a series of panoramas of the principal cities of Europe, all to be presented gratis to readers. This it did until 1873. In addition it published a panorama of the Crystal Palace in 1851, and its last panorama, one of New York City, in 1876.

The *Illustrated London News*'s principal rival in the last quarter of the 19th century was the *Graphic*. Between 1876 and 1895 it too issued large panoramas of great cities – except for Constantinople [Istanbul], Sydney, and Cairo, all of them European – and followed the *Illustrated London News*'s practice of supplying descriptive notes and a key. Many of the *Graphic*'s panoramas were the work of the architectural artist H. W. Brewer. For the views of London and Liverpool Brewer collaborated with W. L. Wyllie, and for the one of Rome with H. E. Tidmarsh. The *Graphic*'s final panorama, also by Brewer, was 'Plymouth, Stonehouse and Devonport'; it was printed as a half-tone by Angerer & Goshl in 1895. The *Pictorial Times*'s Thames panorama (1845), and the *Illustrated London News*'s panoramas of London (1843), the Thames (1845), and the Crystal Palace (1851) were all later reissued in more permanent (non-ephemeral) formats and sold to non-subscribers. [RH]

See also PANORAMA, ENTERTAINMENT

REFERENCES Ralph Hyde, *Gilded Scenes and Shining Prospects* (New Haven: Yale Center for British Art, 1985); Ralph Hyde, 'Panoramas and the Illustrated Weeklies', *Map Collector*, September 1985, pp. 2–7

Pantin *See* JUMPING JACK

Paper *See* BLOTTING PAPER; CIGARETTE PAPER; CUT-WORK; DECORATED PAPER; FLY PAPER; LAVATORY PAPER; PAPER BAG; PAPER CLOTHING; PAPER DOLL; PAPER NAPKIN; PAPER PATTERN; PAPER-CUT; PAPER-DUTY LABEL; REAM WRAPPER/LABEL; THREAD PAPER; TRANSFER LITHOGRAPHY; WAFER; WATERMARK; WRITING PAPER

Paper bag

The earliest forerunners of the shopkeeper's printed bag were the 'papers' in which a limited number of commodities (tobacco, snuff, tea, etc.) were dispensed in the 17th and 18th centuries. For many decades, all that the shopkeeper expected to supply was the coarsest of wrapping paper. Packaging of any kind was a novelty.

In the 1840s and 1850s, however, printed hand-made paper bags began to appear. Like the more ambitiously produced

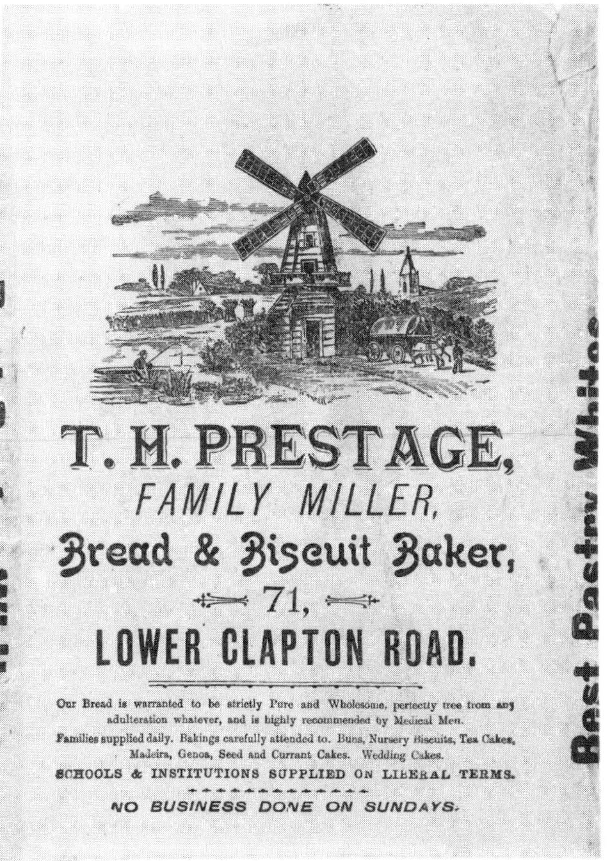

Paper bag, early 20th century. Relief printed in blue. 276 × 215 mm (10¾ × 8½ in)

TRADE CARD and BILLHEAD, many were embellished with pictures of the shopkeeper's premises and included its address. Here, even more noticeably, there was artist's licence in the rendering of scale. Shop premises, however small in fact, appeared enormous in the presence of the Lilliputian figures of customers, their carriage at the kerb, or the establishment's delivery horse and cart. It must be borne in mind that such drawings would have been sketched *in situ* by printers' representatives and handed over to engravers who had probably never seen the premises, and that pedestrians and vehicles would have been added as stock images by the engraver.

Machine bag-making, introduced by Francis Wolle in Bethlehem, Pennsylvania, in 1852, took a long time to become established; even by the turn of the century many bag producers, though partially mechanized, still employed hundreds of people in hand production. The flat-bottomed paper bag was invented by Margaret Knight of Springfield, Massachusetts in 1869. Elisha Robinson, of E. S. & A. Robinson of Bristol, bought the patent while on a trip to America in 1873. Seen as a novelty, it did not become standard.

The idea of 'sets' of bags (as with snuff and tobacco papers and, later, cigarette cards) became fashionable; the shopkeeper's name and address remained constant, whereas the pictorial element – a local view or national hero – might change with each purchase. Picture puzzles and pictorial jokes were later introduced and by the early 20th-century, with the advent of letterpress rotary printing from flexible rubber plates, there were excursions into simple three- and four-colour work.

Present-day shopkeepers' bags are produced by the same process, mostly in only one or two colours. Many are supplied at reduced cost by manufacturers whose products they advertise. Their use, where many products are already packaged, is increasingly a security measure providing evidence that the goods they contain have been checked and paid for.

See also AIR-SICKNESS BAG; KITE BAG; PACKAGING; WINKLE BAG

Paper clothing

Makeshift paper hats, made up and fitted by the wearer, were traditional headgear among workmen in a number of trades, particularly printers, stonecutters, and carpenters. The hat was often made from discarded printed sheets, wrapping paper, or newspaper. Tenniel's picture of the carpenter in the story of the Walrus and the Carpenter in *Alice in Wonderland* exemplifies the tradition. So does the portrait of Eric Gill, the lettercutter, included in his autobiography.

Paper had been used by milliners in the making of bonnet-brims since the early years of the 19th century, but it was not until the 1850s and 1860s that paper emerged as a material with wider application in clothing. Paper shirts, collars, and cuffs, often embossed with false linen texture, stitching, and seaming, came into general use. In Germany, paper garments were used by undertakers for clothing the dead. Paper collars, cuffs, blouses and shirtfronts remained in use for this purpose until the end of World War I. Paper clothing was at first adopted for the poor as a matter of economy, but wartime shortage made the practice a patriotic duty. In 1917 it was officially recommended.

For ordinary everyday use paper collars and cuffs became widespread, though wearers were disinclined to admit to using them; their similarity to linen made them more or less indistinguishable. The paper collar and cuff market was threatened by the advent of celluloid which was stiffer and washable, but highly flammable. An attempt was made in America in the 1880s to combine features of the substances: paper with the rigidity of celluloid and celluloid with the linen texture of paper.

Paper caps for maids, early 20th century. *Above:* blind embossed, 119 × 403 mm (4¾ × 15⅞in); *below:* relief printed, 124 × 410 mm (4⅞ × 16⅛in)

In Britain, the traditional waitress's headgear was available in embossed and perforated paper, with slits for threading a retaining ribbon in the orthodox style. Cuffs were available to match. A further phase emerged in the 1920s and 1930s with the advent of the American soda fountain and sandwich counter, which led to the introduction of the 'service cap' for counter staff. The cap was reminiscent of an American sailor's hat. It was adjustable to any headsize, disposable, and capable of being imprinted with a trade name or logo. The catering cap, available in various styles, became a virtually standard feature of the fast-food industry around the world and succeeded in meeting the combined requirements of food hygiene and marketing.

The disposable paper dress, selling for as little as £2, had a brief popularity in Britain in the flower-power era of the late 1960s.

Paper doll

Among the earliest paper dolls were dressmakers' sketch cut-outs, which were individually produced to provide customers with a preview of garments to be commissioned. In a typical selection of such dolls the figures (measuring some 150 mm (6 in) in height) are first drawn in pencil and colour wash on cartridge paper, then cut out and provided with fold-out tabs at the rear of the base to allow them to stand up.

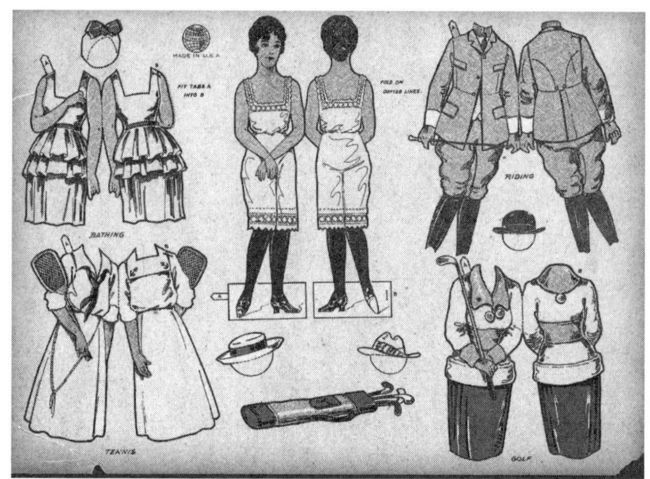

Paper doll sheet (tennis, bathing, riding, and golf), made in the United States, early 20th century. Lithographed in three colours. 191 × 267mm (7½ × 10½in)

The earliest printed paper dolls were featured in children's story books published by S. & J. Fuller from their 'Temple of Fancy' in Rathbone Place, London, 1810–12. Best-known is 'Little Fanny' (from *The History of Little Fanny*) who had seven costumes, a single transposable head, and a number of hats. The cut-outs were included as loose insets at appropriate stages of the story, the whole book being packaged in a slip case measuring 127 × 107 mm (5 × 4¼ in).

The first known American paper doll to be commercially published was issued by J. Belcher of Boston, Massachusetts, in 1812. Reminiscent of its British precursor, it bore the title 'The History & Adventures of Little Henry'. Another early American example, a boxed set of costumes with a separate head, was published in 1854 by Crosby, Nichols & Co. of Boston and called 'Fanny Gray'.

In the 1830s a more elaborate paper-doll book appeared, this time as an educational toy, entitled *The Paignion* (Greek: plaything, toy, game). Published by F. C. Westley of Piccadilly, London, the book (measuring 146 × 140 mm (5¾ × 5½ in)) carried twelve illustrations with slots ('The Zoological Gardens', 'Chemist', 'Theatre', etc.) into which a total of sixty-five cut-out figures might be inserted.

Paper dolls appeared in Europe, mainly in association with the TOY THEATRE, in the 1850s. In another development, cut-out paper figures were provided with a slatted wooden base and 'slip-over' costumes. The costume cut-outs were folded double at the shoulder line to form the front and back of the costume, the head of the doll passing through a cut in the fold. In an 1880s example of this principle, 'Dotty Dimple' is provided with costumes in a toy 'trunk', together with further printed items to cut out. The figure itself is packaged in the trunk.

'Animated' paper dolls appeared in Germany and Austria in the early part of the 19th century. Mounted on card and operated by lever, they performed simple movements. In a typical example a matching pair show, on one card, the bow of the gentleman and, on the other, a lady's curtsey. The devising of lever-operated animations shortly became a speciality and the trend continued, reaching its culmination in the work of the German Lothar Meggendorfer at the end of the century.

See also ADVERTISING NOVELTY; CUT-OUT TOY

REFERENCES Anne Tolstoi Wallach, *Paper Dolls* (New York: Van Nostrand Reinhold, 1982); Blair Whitton, *Paper Toys of the World* (Cumberland, MA: Hobby Horse Press, 1986)

Paper napkin

The first appearance in Britain of the printed souvenir table napkin was in July 1887, when a quantity of decorated blanks, brought from Japan, were overprinted by John Dickinson Ltd for their annual dinner.

The fashion caught on, and before long large quantities of the flimsy squares were being imported. They carried a decorative border, which was printed in up to five colours in Japan; the locally printed commemorative message and image occupied the centre area, often overlapping the colour border. Most of the border designs were fairly delicate, but the overprinting was commonly primitive. Sizes were of the order of 330 mm (13 in) and 420 mm (16½ in) square. These napkins (or 'handkerchiefs') were sold in the streets on ceremonial and processional occasions; they form a direct link with the STREET LITERATURE of earlier times and display a similar disregard for niceties of typography and spelling. The genre was the speciality of a number of printers, among them S. Burgess of the Strand and Mathews of Hoxton.

Paper napkin, shown here folded twice with its transparent label, mid 20th century. Printed in three colours on crêpe paper. Full size 355 × 355 mm (14 × 14 in)

Advertising leaflets on flimsy paper were also produced on which better-class printers overprinted publicity messages on 'novel Japanese papers... specially produced for these purposes... imported direct from Japan'. James R. Crompton & Brothers of Queenhithe offered a choice of thirty-three border designs.

Paper pattern

Early patterns for garments appeared as scale diagrams in instruction books. The first recorded example is a pattern for a lady's riding habit, printed in *La Tailleur Sincère* (1671). Similar pattern diagrams appear in *L'Art du Tailleur* (1769) and *L'Art de la Lingère* (1771). Until the end of the 18th century, however, fashion information was conveyed largely by means of dressed dolls, paper cut-out figures, and fashion plates in magazines.

In the early 19th century the use of paper patterns was beginning to develop (though the dressmaker often cut cloth patterns for her customers, afterwards using the pattern as a lining). By the 1820s a number of London drapers and trade fashion suppliers were selling full-size dress, hat, and bonnet patterns to the trade. These patterns were designed specifically for the professional; paper patterns for the home dressmaker appeared only in the 1840s and 1850s with the rise of the illustrated ladies' journal.

Inserted in magazines as part of their editorial service or as free-gift extras, patterns soon achieved wide popularity. Among the earliest of the pattern dispensing journals was Dresden's *Bekleidungsdienst für Damen* and *Allgemeine Musterzeitung* which first appeared in 1844. First in Britain was the *World of Fashion* in 1850. Pioneer of the free-gift approach was Samuel Beeton, husband of the celebrated household management writer. Mr Beeton's *Englishwoman's Domestic Magazine* carried a give-away paper pattern in its first issue in 1852.

Butterick's Patterns, an exclusively pattern-purveying service, began publication in Britain in 1863, and Weldon's, a more popularly-based competitor, started in 1879. In America, *McCall's Patterns* appeared in 1870 and *Vogue*, which also provided patterns (and additionally in the *Vogue Pattern Book*), was first published in 1892.

In early 20th-century Britain mass-circulation women's magazines competed in increasing numbers for readers. Typical of the 'practical fashions' journal was *Fashions for All*, published by the Amalgamated Press, whose double Christmas number of 1910 included six free patterns: a Lady's Evening Blouse, A Lady's Day Blouse, A Lady's Lining Bodice, A Lady's Evening Skirt, A Girl's Cloak (4 to 6 years), A Boy's Coat (2 to 4 years). The first issue of *Woman's Weekly* in 1911 offered, in addition to prizes of furs, eight-guinea silk blouses, and lace collars, the first of a series of paper patterns (blouses, chemise, skirt, camisole, knickers, nightdress, and under-bodice), the whole set provided with 'a big envelope, specially made to keep them in'.

A 20th-century variation on the paper pattern theme, resurrected in the 1970s by Clothkits of Lewes, was the patented innovation of the Traced Garment Company of Manchester. This allowed fabrics to be supplied with patterns printed directly on them ready for cutting out. Printed in washable blue inks, the pattern traces disappeared on the first laundering of the made-up garment. Designs were issued for ladies' and children's underwear, in four sizes – 'clear and distinct on each garment' – ready for the home worktable.

REFERENCE Janet Arnold, *Patterns of Fashion* (London: Macmillan, 1972)

Paper-cut [plate 9a]

The term paper-cut is commonly applied to hand-cut 'paper lace', a craftwork or peasant art of great antiquity. Images and patterns, often of great delicacy and complexity, are cut with a blade or scissors from lightweight paper (often coloured) and used as decoration on windows, lanterns, lampshades, fabrics, and furniture.

The paper-cut is first recorded in China during the Han dynasty (140–86 BC) and examples survive from the 7th century. A revival of interest in China in the latter part of the 20th century brought the craft to the world's attention. The hand-cut (*jian zhi*) has become a widespread minor industry in Kiangtu, Nantong, and Kweichow, and the cuts are sold in paper packets all over the world. Their delicacy and intricacy represent a high level of popular expertise and aesthetic awareness.

The paper-cut has appeared in numerous peasant cultures. In addition to various parts of the Far East, it is still found in Poland, Holland, Switzerland, and Mexico. In North America the craft is identified with the Pennsylvania Dutch, who introduced it from Europe. Each of the regions concerned possesses its own style and special applications. In Poland, paper-cuts (*wycianki*) are often used as Christmas decorations; in Switzerland and Holland symmetrical designs are produced by cutting folded paper, the unfolded pattern presenting a mirror image effect. Among the specialities of the Pennsylvania Dutch was the cutting of keepsakes or 'love tokens'. These, sometimes of minute intricacy, were often small enough to be carried inside the back flap of a pocket watch as a WATCHPAPER.

Related to the paper-cut (with end-products that are distinctly less than ephemeral) is a craft with 19th-century origins, *découpage* (cutting-out), in which coloured prints are pasted on to furniture, screens, boxes, trays, vases, etc.; and the craft of *potichomanie* (porcelain-vase mania), briefly popular in the 19th century, in which cut-outs were pasted on to the inside of glass vases, an interior coat of paint afterwards providing a colour background reminiscent of porcelain.

The SILHOUETTE, another form of paper-cut, was particularly popular in France in the 18th century. Cut out of thin black paper and mounted on white (or conversely produced as a 'hollowcut'), the portrait outline was a smart performer's trick that came close to acceptance as an art. Among notable practitioners were Joseph Sansom, Charles Willson Peale, John Vogler, Francis Torond, W. Phelps, John Miers, Johann-Jakob Hauswirth, Christina Luise Duttenhofer, and Augustin Edouart. A number of celebrities, of whom Goethe was one, cut silhouettes as a pastime.

See also CUTWORK

COLLECTION Historical Society of Pennsylvania (Paper and Silhouettes) Philadelphia

Paper-duty label

A duty on the manufacture of paper was first imposed in Britain in the reign of Queen Anne in 1712. It was finally removed in 1861.

The duty was administered by the Excise who, from 1802, supplied manufacturers with specially printed labels for use on the outside wrapper of each completed ream. Excise officers inspected record books and personally date-stamped and signed each label when it was affixed to the main wrapper. The system was reinforced by use of a 'charge stamp', a handstamp indicating that the duty had actually been charged to the manufacturer and, where applicable, an 'allowance stamp' showing that the consignment was free of duty by virtue of exportation or use by a university (the only categories exempt from such charges).

Paper-duty labels have not survived in any quantity. Of those issued between their inception in 1802 and the issue of 1821 not one is known. Subsequent issues are of five main types, one of which (here referred to by date c.1847) emerged only in 1982. The types are:

(c.1821) Decorative three-sided frame; departure stamp space at left; 'G IV' coat of arms at foot. Printed black/red; 144 × 124 mm (5⅝ × 4⅞ in)

(c.1841) Similar to the above but 'VR' coat of arms at foot and 51-word instruction and warning (white out of black) in vertical panel black/red; 147 × 127 mm (5¾ × 5 in)

(c.1847) Three-sided frame, central area black tint with regular pattern in rows and columns; 'VR' coat of arms in vertical panel; 27-word instructional text at foot. Black/red; 147 × 130 mm (5¾ × 5⅛ in); vertical black panels added left and right; bearing (left) 53-word instructional/warning text in white, and (right) a similar 25-word text

(c.1849) Four-sided frame; central area as above; 'paper label' in left-hand vertical panel; instruction/warning ('notice to stationers and the public'); elongated lozenge on right in black/blue; 152 × 145 mm (6 × 5¾ in)

Not included in the above listing are minor variants within each of the basic types. These are to be found in Chandler (1981).

In 1821 the British paper-duty label began to be printed by the Excise Printing Establishment from Congreve COMPOUND-PLATE PRINTING plates, but in 1841 the plates were handed over to Perkins, Bacon & Petch, together with the Congreve machines. The company bought the equipment under the terms of their contract, repairing, renewing, and redesigning plates as this became necessary. These labels replaced those produced by Jacob Perkins's 'siderographic' [Greek: steel drawing] process, in which machine-generated patterns were multiplied on steel as decorative borders and backgrounds.

Perkins, Bacon & Petch, later to become Perkins, Bacon & Co., continued to print ream labels in the 'compound-plate printing' style, even after the paper duty had been abolished. At least one surviving label shows the style used purely decoratively for Hollingworth's Turkey Mill at Maidstone. Using the bi-colour motifs of the traditional paper-duty label, the legend merely specifies the content: 'One ream of paper: watermarked: full weight 19 lbs'; only its numerals are overstamped (on a white lozenge provided as a background).

REFERENCES John H. Chandler, *Newspaper & Almanac Stamps of Great Britain and Ireland* (Saffron Walden: Great Britain Philatelic Publications Ltd, 1981); Joan Evans, *The Endless Web: John Dickinson & Co. Ltd., 1804–1954* (London: Jonathan Cape, 1955); Elizabeth Harris, 'Experimental Graphic Processes in England 1800–1859', *Journal of the Printing Historical Society*, no. 4 (London: 1968), pp. 33–86

COLLECTION John Johnson Collection, Bodleian Library, Oxford

Papyrus

In general use for writing as far back as 3000 BC, papyrus was for centuries the main surface of record, not only for books and manuscripts but for the minor documents of everyday life. It is in the form of papyrus that the world's most ancient ephemera survive.

Its survival has depended solely on climate. Of all the areas in the world where papyrus was used – and afterwards often left in rubbish dumps – only the dry sands of Egypt offered protection. Excavated thousands of years later, the material brings us news of a period about which, by a chance of climate, we know more than we do of many more recent times.

Papyrus was made from a two-layer laminate of strips of leaves of a papyrus plant (*Cyperus papyrus*), the layers crossing at right angles. Soaked in water, the strips adhered to each other and were dried, pressed, and hammered smooth. The result was a more or less satisfactory, but fragile, writing surface.

It was used for virtually the whole range of documentation, from dynastic histories and proclamations to personal missives and memoranda. As with paper in modern times, it was the major medium of government, bureaucracy, and civic and regional control. Much of the administration of the Roman Empire depended on it. Books and literature too were written on papyrus, the pieces being pasted together to form a continuous roll, rotulus, or biblion (book). Many of the great writers of the ancient world survive in part on papyrus; so does a huge quantity of other material.

The existence of this great mass of documentation became known to the western world only as late as the 1770s – and then almost by accident. The first example to reach Europe was bought from villagers by a traveller in 1778. It was an account of a compulsory labour scheme for irrigation in AD 192. It is said that the villagers who sold it offered a great many more specimens at the same time, but that the buyer felt that one was enough – so the rest were destroyed. Since then, many thousands of papyrus documents have been found. Some 40,000 have been translated and published, reportedly less than twenty per cent of those known to exist.

Typical of the ephemeral items already published are the following, drawn from Hunt and Edgar (1932–34):

Horus to Apion (late 1st century AD):

> Horus to the most honoured Apion greeting. Regarding Lampon the mouse-catcher, I paid him on your account 8 drachmae as earnest money to catch mice in Toka. You will kindly send me this sum. I have also lent 8 drachmae to Dionysius, president of Nemerae, and he has not sent them back; this is to inform you.

Petition of a lentil cook (3rd century BC):

> I do my best to pay the tax every month in order that you may have no complaint against me. Now the folk in the town are roasting pumpkins. For that reason then nobody buys lentils from me at the present time. I beg and beseech you then ... to be allowed more time ... for paying the tax to the king. For in the morning they straightway sit down beside the lentils selling their pumpkins and give me no chance to sell my lentils.

Appianus to Heroninus (AD 256):

> When one dispatches even the smallest load, he ought to send it with a letter stating what has been sent and by what carrier. And the goods which you despatched were not so many as to require a man and a donkey to leave their work for them, only four baskets of rotten figs. And it was evident from the poorness and dryness and parched appearance of the figs that the estate has been neglected. But about this we shall have an account to settle between ourselves.

A flute-player's contract (AD 322):

> I acknowledge that I have contracted and agreed with you the landlord to present myself at the village of ... at the vintage of the vineyards ... and without fault assist the grape-treaders and the other workers by my flute-playing and not leave ... until the completion .... and for the flute-playing and the entertainment I shall receive the prescribed fee....

Invitation to a festival (3rd or 4th century AD):

> Greeting, my lady Serenia, from Petosiris. Make every effort, dear lady, to come out on the 20th, the birthday festival of the god, and let me know whether you are coming by boat or by donkey, in order that we may send for you. Take care not to forget, dear lady. I pray for your lasting health.

Note from Victor to Theodore (6th or 7th century AD):

> Will your true brotherliness have the goodness to send me day by day some asparagus, for the vegetables here are rotten and disgust me....

Sarapammon to Piperas (3rd century AD):

> I sent you a letter by the baker, and perhaps you know what I wrote to you. If you persist in your folly, I wish you joy; if you are repenting, you yourself know. Let me tell you that you owe me seven years' rents and revenues, so unless you send remittances you know the risk you run.

Hermias to Horus (112 BC):

> Lucius Memmius, a Roman senator, who occupies a position of great dignity and honour, is sailing up from Alexandria ... to see the sights. Let him be received with special magnificence, and take care that at the proper spots the guest chambers be prepared and the landing-places to them be completed, and that the gifts ... be presented to him at the landing-place, and that the furniture of the guest-chamber, the titbits for ... the crocodiles, the conveniences for viewing the Labyrinth, and the offerings and sacrifices be provided; in general take the greatest pains in everything to see that the visitor is satisfied, and display the utmost zeal....

Many thousands of papyri, still in course of examination, are in museum and library collections all over the world. The largest single collection is said to be that of Archduke Rainer in Vienna, with over 100,000 items. There are major collections in the Egyptian Museum in Cairo, in the British Museum, and in the Universities of Oxford and Michigan. There are also big collections in Berlin, Florence, Heidelberg, Manchester, Milan, Paris, and Strasbourg, as well as at Columbia, Cornell, and Princeton Universities.

REFERENCES M. L. Bierbrier (ed.), *Papyrus: Structure and Usage*, British Museum Occasional Papers no. 60 (London: British Museum, 1986); A. S. Hunt and C. C. Edgar, *Select Papyri* (London: Loeb Classical Library 1932, 1933; reprinted London: Heinemann, and Cambridge, Mass.: Harvard University Press, 1970, 1977)

SOCIETY Egyptian Exploration Society, London

Parking ticket

Tickets are provided for motorists either as evidence of payment for a parking facility or as an essential element in the automated control of parking. They became an inescapable aspect of urban motoring in the second half of the 20th century as the increase in the use of cars led to the need for parking controls on the street and for more off-street parking.

In Britain, the designated and controlled car-parking area followed on from the success of the popular (£100) car at the end of the 1920s. Colonel and Mrs Lucas are credited with the idea, and the first car parks were created to serve sporting events in and around London in the early 1930s. After World War II the need for car parks in towns and near tourist sites and places of entertainment grew rapidly. By the end of the century Britain and Europe's largest parking organization, National Car Parks (founded in 1958 as a result of a business amalgamation), was accommodating 100 million cars every year. The first of the company's many multi-storey car parks was opened in 1962.

Initially, payment for off-street parking was controlled by car-park attendants, who issued a receipt in the form of a ticket and may even have guided the motorist to an appropriate parking space. Early tickets were torn from a perforated roll and often bore a large printed numeral that indicated the cost of the parking. Later tickets came in rolls that could be punched on a machine and were produced by companies that specialized in bus tickets (such as Bell Punch Corporation and Henry Booth & Co.). From the early 1960s, with the introduction of automatic machines that printed and delivered tickets at the point of issue and, among other things, indicated the times of issue and expiry, the attendant became almost redundant. The human element survives in automatically controlled car parks as a fall-back when machines fail or drivers get into difficulties, and also for security.

The control of on-street parking using coin-operated parking meters began in Oklahoma City in 1935. Britain's first machines – imported from America – were installed by Westminster City Council in July 1958; Bristol was the second British city to have them (in 1961). The use of such machines reached its peak in Britain in the 1970s, but subsequently meters began to be replaced by 'pay and display' machines, which produced ephemera in the form of tickets. In Britain this pay and display method of controlling parking began outside London (for example, in Edinburgh and Hull); it proved to have many advantages over the parking meter and became widespread in the course of the 1990s. Parking meters are now a rarity in Britain. The human element survives for on-street parking in the form of the much maligned traffic warden. Perversely, the term parking ticket is also commonly used in Britain to describe the 'Penalty charge notice' issued by traffic wardens to inform drivers that they have parked illegally or overrun their time.

Parking tickets take different forms according to their use and are mostly made of paper or card (specially coated when intended for outdoor machines). Those obtained on entry to a car park in order to activate a barrier at its exit (barrier tickets) are normally made of card and have a machine-readable strip. Those designed for display in the vehicle as evidence of payment (pay and display tickets) come in two main forms: either on card for placing on the dashboard, or, more commonly now, with a self-adhesive backing sheet for application, face out, on the inside of the windscreen. The machine reading of magnetic stripes on car-parking tickets was first seen in Britain in the mid to late 1980s (when car parks at Abingdon and Havering used the 'Zeag' system). From the early 1990s machine-reading of cards became common, and by the end of the century it had become the norm. Britain's largest producer of car-parking tickets, Advantage Ticketing, produces all its tickets by offset lithography (with ink-jet printing for the numbers and adhesive magnetic-stripe labels bought in from a supplier). Many tickets now carry advertising matter, and some entitle the motorist to commercial concessions.

Parking tickets are as characteristic of the late 20th and early 21st centuries as any items of ephemera. Though not without interest individually, collectively they provide evidence of the extent to which the car has come to dominate the city. They do not appear to be widely collected, except by those submitting claims for expenses. Their normal fate suggests that early examples are likely to have gone unrecorded. [MT]

COLLECTION British Parking Association

Parliamentary envelope

For a short period before the introduction in Britain of the uniform Penny Post in January 1840, members of parliament and certain other privileged persons were permitted to use the postal service free of charge. The practice, stemming from the middle of the 17th century, allowed the sender to sign his name on the front of the letter. Abuses of the system, in which privilege holders distributed signed blank papers for use by friends, led to a tightening of the regulations in the 18th century, but by the beginning of the 19th century losses in postal revenue were so great that it was clear that the privilege had to be abolished.

The opportunity was taken – with the introduction of uniform penny postage – for the Post Office to provide Members of Parliament with specially printed envelopes, free of charge, to be signed and addressed by the member himself as before, but accepted for posting only at the Palace of Westminster (where Parliament sat).

'Post-paid' parliamentary envelopes appeared in a number of versions: 'To be posted at the Houses of Parliament only' (1*d* & 2*d*); 'To be posted at the House of Lords only' (1*d* & 2*d*); and 'To be posted at the House of Commons only' (1*d*).

The envelopes were withdrawn after only fourteen weeks on 1 May 1840, the day of the inauguration of the MULREADY ENVELOPE and the first one penny stamp (both of which became valid for postal use on 6 May 1840). Because of the brief period of their validity, few parliamentary envelopes are to be found. Those from the House of Lords are exceptionally rare.

See also FREE FRANK

REFERENCES K. Huggins, *British Postal Stationery* (London: The Great Britain

Philatelic Society, 1970; reprinted with amendments, 1971); Robson Lowe, *The British Postage Stamp*, 2nd edn (London: National Postal Museum, 1979); A. G. Rigo de Righi, *The Story of the Penny Black* (National Postage Museum, 1980); R. M. Willcocks, *England's Postal History to 1840* (London: Willcocks, 1975)

Pass/permit

Passes and permits exist in great variety. Though they have a common denominator – the notion of privileged access – they operate in a wide range of disparate contexts. It is in this multiplicity of purpose, associated with the implication of special exemption, that the collector may find appeal.

Printed in every conceivable style and size, ranging from a slip of pasteboard to a foolscap sheet in linen or vellum, the pass or permit may allow or admit the holder to a Buckingham Palace garden party; to visit relations in Eastern Germany; to dig for gold in Australia; to enter an earthquake area; to be out after curfew; or to be present in the White House.

A typical collection of passes or permits may include such items as the following:

'Pass for devastated area', issued in Halifax in 1917, by the Nova Scotia city's Chief of Police. The pass was used after a harbour disaster, when an ammunition explosion caused by a collision resulted in a death-toll of 2000. Pasteboard; 45 × 90 mm (1¾ × 3½ in).

'Miner's right', issued in Western Australia, 1898, permitting the bearer, under the Goldfields Act of 1895, to dig for gold. Printed on linen; 115 × 205 mm (4½ × 8⅛ in).

'Permis de porte d'armes de chasse', dated 1832, allowing the holder to use a gun in the area of the Gironde, signed by the

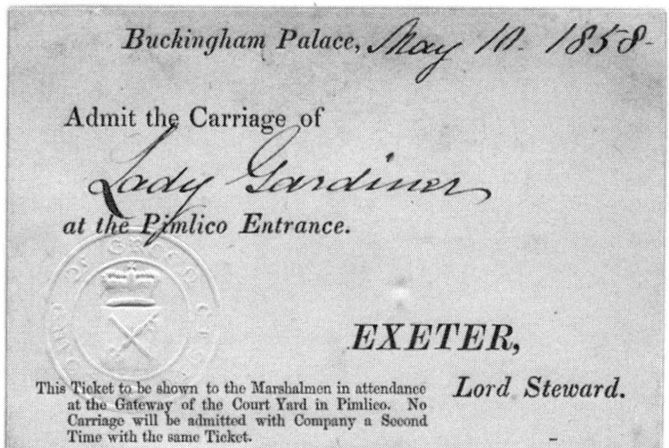

Carriage pass for Buckingham Palace, 10 May 1858. Letterpress and manuscript, with embossed stamp. 75 × 114 mm (3 × 4½ in)

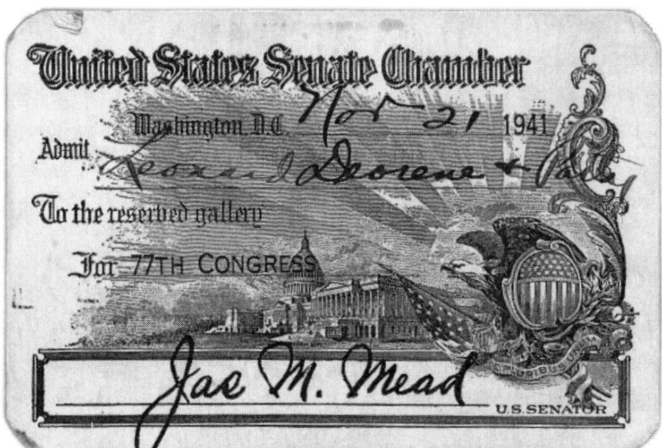

Pass to the United States Senate Chamber, 21 November 1941, relief printed on card. 70 × 105 mm (2¾ × 4⅛ in)

Prefect of Police 'au nom du Roi'. The paper is watermarked Charles X Roi de France, but the royal arms at the head of the document are obliterated. The 'July revolution' of 1830 had removed the King. Paper; 410 × 315 mm (16⅛ × 12⅜ in).

'Pass', issued in the 1930s by the management of the Grosvenor Hotel, Victoria Station, London, entitling female staff 'living in' to remain out until midnight ('Pass must be handed to the head porter on arrival'). Paper; 100 × 135 mm (4 × 5¼ in).

'Authority', given by the Director of Recruiting under Britain's National Register in 1915. The permit allows the holder 'to call upon men who, according to the National Register, are eligible for enlistment'. Card; 100 × 130 mm (4 × 5⅛ in).

'Visitor' pass issued in June 1976 by the office of Population Censuses and Surveys, London. Self-adhesive paper; 50 × 50 mm (2 × 2 in).

'News correspondent's permit' entitling the holder to move to forward areas of fighting in the American Civil War, 1861. The verso carries wording signed by the holder and reads: 'It is understood that the within named and subscriber accepts this pass on his word of honor that he is and will be ever loyal to the United States, and if hereafter found in arms against the Union or in any way aiding her enemies, the penalty will be death'. Paper; 110 × 220 mm (4⅜ × 8⅝ in).

See also ADMISSION TICKET; PASSPORT; PRATIQUE, PAPERS OF; RAIL TICKET

Passport [plate 5]

The passport, originally a personal letter from a monarch, pope, sultan, etc. introducing and commending his subject, later evolved into a part-printed document of identity – an optionally available protection for the traveller who might stand in need of it. At a later stage still, the passport changed from a desirable traveller's aid to an obligatory travel document. While every citizen had a right to a passport, exit and re-entry without it was prohibited. In a further stage in the mid 20th century, property of the document was transferred to the issuing authority; the passport could be withheld or withdrawn at the will of the authority.

A complementary convention was the visa, in which the request for protection expressed in the passport was endorsed by representatives of the country of destination. This too became modified in the course of time, finishing as a privilege rather than a courtesy.

The 'booklet' format of the 20th-century passport had its forerunner in the United Kingdom in 1915 when a single sheet measuring 340 × 535 mm (13⅜ × 21 in) was folded to make twenty pages, 170 × 110 mm (6¾ × 4⅜ in), and bound into a cardboard cover. For the first time it carried a photograph of the holder. This new-style passport was valid for two years from the date of issue and was renewable for up to a total of ten years. In cases where the whole of the space of the single sheet had been covered by visa stamps, the sheet was officially disbound from the outer cover and stapled to a fresh cover, complete with a new sheet (which carried updated details, photograph, etc. of the holder), forming a double-layer folding sheet of a total of forty panels. The charge for the 1915 passport was five shillings.

In 1920, at a League of Nations Conference in Paris, most member countries agreed to adopt the 'booklet' format with a fixed number of pages, a photograph of the holder and provision for details of height, hair colour, etc. As with the former

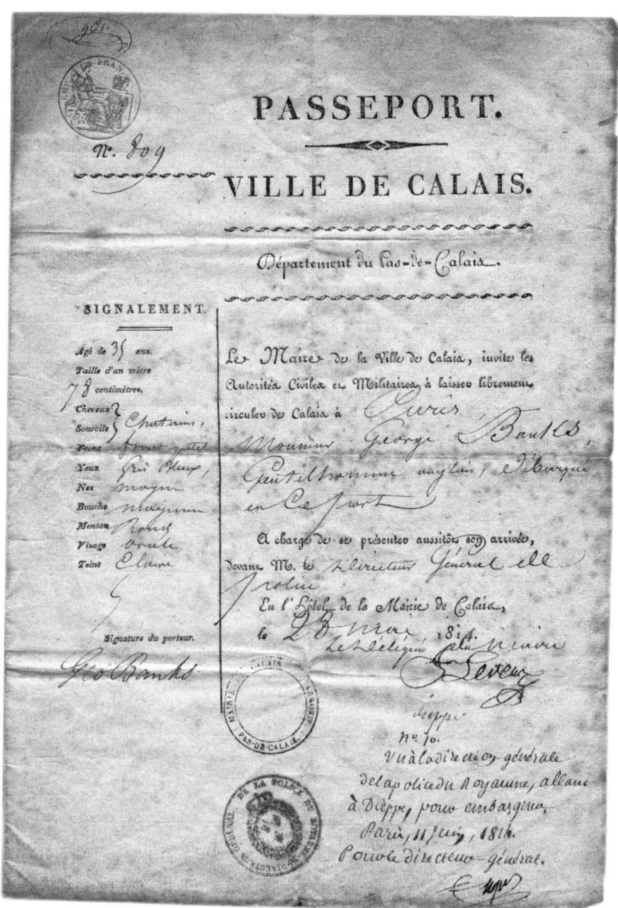
PASSEPORT.

N°. 809

VILLE DE CALAIS.

Département du Pas-de-Calais.

SIGNALEMENT.

Agé de 35 ans.
Taille d'un mètre
78 centimètres.
Cheveux
Sourcils
Front
Yeux
Nez
Bouche
Menton
Visage
Teint

Signature du porteur.

Le Maire de la Ville de Calais, invite les Autorités Civiles et Militaires, à laisser librement circuler de Calais à Paris Monsieur George Banks, Gentilhomme anglais, débarqué en ce port

A charge de se présenter aussitôt son arrivée, devant Mr. le Directeur Général de police

En l'Hôtel de la Mairie de Calais, le 28 mai 1814.

Passport of the town of Calais, issued to George Banks, 1814. Letterpress and manuscript. 305 × 212 mm (12 × 8⅜ in)

single-sheet version, blank space in the pages of the booklet were used for visas, entry and exit stamps, and other endorsements, providing a full record of the holder's movements.

The early history of the passport is fragmentary and examples are scarce. An Act of Parliament in 1436 contains a reference to passports and provides that 'in all Safe Conducts to be granted from henceforth to any Person or Persons, the Name of them . . . shall be expressed.' One of the earliest passports extant dates from 1641 and was signed personally by Charles I. Up to the time of Charles II all British passports were signed by the monarch, but during Charles II's reign a second form was introduced, issued by the Secretary of State. The two forms continued in use until 1794. From that time all passports were issued over the signature of the Secretary of State, though later examples carried a facsimile signature. The signature was dropped altogether in the 1950s. The last surviving example of a passport signed by the sovereign was issued to 'Robert Liston Esq, Ambassador to the Ottoman Porte' in March 1794.

British passports dating from before 1772 were worded in Latin or English. After that time and until 1858 they were in French or in French and English. Since 1858 they have been predominantly in English with (since 1921) some French translation.

The earliest single-sheet passport was elegantly engraved on a fine white watermarked paper, measuring some 420 × 270 mm (16½ × 10⅝ in), and bore visas and other endorsement stamps, commonly on the reverse but occasionally also on the margins of the face. No small part of the early passport's significance is in the legation and embassy handstamps of states no longer in being: mid 19th-century passports may bear the imprimatur of the Kingdom of the Two Sicilies, Sardinia, Bavaria, Saxony, Tuscany, Württemberg, or of the Hanseatic towns of Lübeck, Bremen or Hamburg.

In Europe in the early part of the 19th century was added the now commonplace list of details, such as age, height, colour of hair, etc. This appeared as an addendum engraved in the left-hand margin of the sheet, though it was in many cases ignored in practice. The list included, typically, age, height, hair, forehead, eyebrows, eyes, nose, mouth, chin, countenance (visage), complexion, and distinguishing marks.

Passport practice was by no means uniform. In France in the 1860s regulations required that the foreigner surrender his passport to the local authority on arrival. If found to be in order it was forwarded to the Paris police, a French passport being in the meantime handed to the visitor. This, entitled *passe provisoire*, is retained until the visitor reaches his prescribed destination (which he must not change), at which time his own passport will have been dispatched from Paris, duly stamped, and ready for him to receive in exchange for the *passe provisoire*. These regulations appear as a 500-word letterpress endorsement in English on the back of a French-language English passport (signed Granville) as early as 1840.

The earliest American passport (1796), a single sheet, somewhat smaller than the British format, was printed from script type and bore the title legend that was to appear on all American passports for at least a century: 'To all to whom these Presents shall come, Greeting'. It was issued and signed by the Secretary of State, Timothy Pickering, at Philadelphia. A latter letterpress passport (1811) bears the same legend under an inaccurately drawn wood-engraving of the American eagle and the words 'United States of America'. By 1820 passports were engraved on copper, and a left-hand column provided space for description details, as with the British version. The reverse was used for legation and consulate endorsements. Passports of this kind were in use until around the time of the Civil War.

Passports with covers were not introduced to America until the end of World War I, the first examples dating from January 1918. Early covers were in cream or green cloth and protected the document when it was folded in four. The first passports in proper booklet form, with a sequence of leaves, were introduced 22 March 1926 and had red cloth-covered boards with the words 'Passport/United States of America' blocked in gold on the front cover and an aperture at the top for the passport number.

The Nansen passport, introduced by Fridtjof Nansen, the Norwegian explorer and humanitarian, was instituted in 1920 when the League of Nations entrusted him with the task of repatriating prisoners of war from Russia. The Soviet Government would not recognize the League but agreed to deal with Nansen as a private person. The Nansen Relief organization issued an identity card to prisoners of war who had become stateless. The card, which was respected throughout the world, remained in use in modified form until it was replaced by a similar travel document in 1960.

The European Community passport, proposed since 1975, was the subject of much discussion and only very gradual stages of agreement. In the early 1980s however it was agreed among

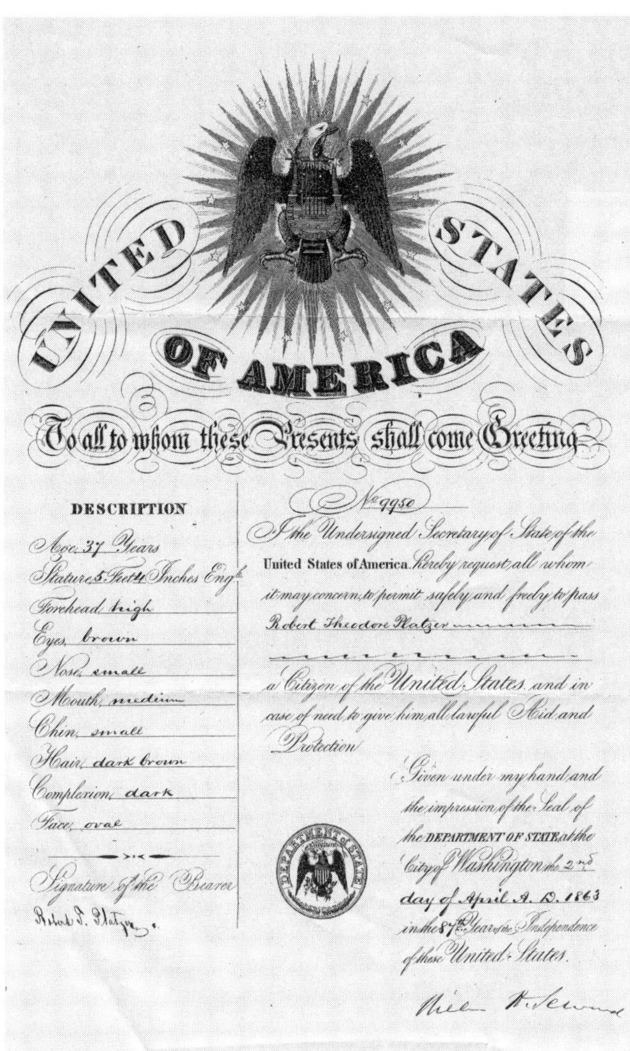

UNITED STATES OF AMERICA

To all to whom these Presents shall come Greeting

DESCRIPTION

Age 37 Years
Stature 5 Feet 4 Inches Eng
Forehead high
Eyes brown
Nose small
Mouth medium
Chin small
Hair dark brown
Complexion dark
Face oval

Signature of the Bearer
Robert T. Platzer

No 7950

I the Undersigned Secretary of State of the United States of America hereby request all whom it may concern to permit safely and freely to pass Robert Theodore Platzer a Citizen of the United States and in case of need to give him all lawful Aid and Protection

Given under my hand and the impression of the Seal of the DEPARTMENT OF STATE at the City of Washington the 2nd day of April A.D. 1863 in the 87th Year of the Independence of these United States.

United States passport, issued 2 April 1863. Approximately 430 × 280 mm (17 × 11 in)

the ten countries that its cover colour should be 'burgundy' (a colour free of national connotation) and that the words 'European Community', in the bearer's own language, would precede the name of the country concerned. Below these would appear the country's symbol. Other matters, such as uniform listing of identifying details, security measures, etc. were agreed in time for its introduction in July 1988. The last British blue passports were issued in April 1993. [MR and SW]

See also PASS/PERMIT

REFERENCES Gaillard Hunt, *The American Passport* (Washington: Government Printing Office, 1898); *The United States Passport, Past, Present, Future* (Washington: Passport Office, Department of State, 1976)

Pastiche, printer's

In the field of printed ephemera the word 'pastiche' is applied to a contrived assemblage of existing visual remnants to form a 'new' presentation. Typical examples are the mock Victorian and Edwardian items popular in the 1970s and 1980s, in which out-dated printers' blocks and type appeared in 20th-century contexts. The result normally differs from a FORGERY or a counterfeit in that it seeks to amuse rather than to deceive, though there is sometimes a risk that the uninformed will fail to recognize the pastiche, taking it for an original work.

The vogue for 'old-time' pastiche received much impetus in the mid 20th century, not only from a wave of generalized nostalgia, but from the emergence of cheap photolithographic and photocopying processes, which allowed for the 'pasting-up' of printed images without the need for blocks, plates, or type.

The value of pastiche ephemera as evidence for the social historian is limited. In the majority of instances its reconstruction of former modes is unreliable and its approach is in the main a form of satire. All that may reasonably be deduced from such ephemera is that its producers, at the time of its appearance, felt themselves safely distanced from the period or style it evoked.

Patterned paper *See* DECORATED PAPER

Peal card

Since the 1870s, British bellringers have recorded the successful completion of a peal by means of a card showing details of the date and place of the peal, its nature and duration, and the names of those participating.

The card commonly measures some 75 × 115 mm (3 × 4½ in). In most cases the run is no more than a dozen (one for each of the ringers listed); occasionally, to allow for presentation to friends and relatives, it may extend to twenty. For special occasions there may be an even longer run, and for occasions of national rejoicing the card's size may be increased to some 200 × 250 mm (7⅞ × 9⅞ in). Cards are sometimes framed and displayed in the belfry of the church where the peal was rung.

The custom arose from the practice of publishing peal records in *Bell News* (from 1881) and in the journal's successor *Ringing World*. The records were transferred to cards at the request of the individual teams of bellringers; at first they quoted the journal as their source, though subsequently they did not. The printing of the cards has been carried out by a limited number of printers, one late 20th-century specialist being Mrs Sue C. Sotheran, general printer of Redcar, Cleveland, who is herself a bellringer.

Peal cards are found in very small numbers in other parts of the English-speaking world, including the United States, though many of these are also printed by the firm of Sotheran.

Peep-show

In popular usage the term peep-show applies to a multi-plane presentation, commonly extendable concertina-fashion, devised to convey an impression of scenic depth when viewed through a peep-hole. The toy is a close relative of the 18th-century German Christmas crib, in which a similar effect is produced, though with a smaller number of planes. There are references to the peep-show effect in antiquity, and the travelling peep-show man of the 18th century carried viewing cabinets which, in all except concertina construction, were prototypes of the mass-produced toys of the 19th century.

The Victorian printed peep-show commonly portrayed scenes of topical interest, exploring whenever possible the fascination of recessive planes and long vistas. Popular subjects were royal occasions, in which variety of detail, depth of perspective, and regal grandeur were combined. The early 1850s saw a number of such publications. Typical were *Forbes's Telescopic View of the Visit of Her Majesty to the Great Exhibition* (1851), and *Bailey Rawlins' Expanding View of the Queen's Visit to the Civic Entertainment* [at the Guildhall] (c. 1852). Earlier, the completion of the Thames Tunnel at Rotherhithe had provided appropriate subject matter for peep-shows, including one depicting its twin carriageways extending apparently to infinity, with carriages, riders, and pedestrians making their way under the river.

The printed peep-show was generally supplied in an illustrated slip-case and measured some 190 × 215 mm (7½ × 8½ in) face on, but smaller productions also appeared. The Thames Tunnel peep-show, for example, measured only 115 × 140 mm (4½ × 5½ in). The depth of peep-shows when extended was anything between 485 mm (19in) and 635 mm (25 in).

Peep-shows are still occasionally produced, and one was issued on the occasion of the Silver Jubilee of Queen Elizabeth II in 1977. It showed a processional vista of The Mall with Buckingham Palace at the farthest point and flanking decorations in the foreground, with successive planes showing the royal coach and horseguards.

Pen-box label

The word 'pen' originally referred to the quill feather, the 'nib' being the shaped and sharpened end when it was cut for writing. Ambiguity arose in the early 19th century when steel substitutes (which included an integral metal shaft for use with a holder) were also described as pens. When, in a further development, a shortened version, the 'slip' pen – or 'nib' – was introduced, this too retained the name. The result, in spite of the widespread use of the word 'nib', was an unbroken succession of boxed products bearing the labelled designation 'pen': 'They come as a boon and blessing to men: The *Pickwick*, the *Owl* and the *Waverley* pen'.

The ambiguity is reflected in some of the earliest labels, which refer not to the new steel substitute but to the natural quill, its still flourishing predecessor. This item may be described on one label as 'quill nib pen', on another as 'quill pen nib'.

The 'quill nib' had been developed by Joseph Bramah as a mass-produced version of the traditional quill, which had been the universal writing instrument for centuries. His innovation paralleled the work of other pioneers, notably Peregrine Williamson in America and John Mitchell, James Perry, and Joseph Gillott in Britain, who sought a practical steel counterpart. Success in both fields led for a brief period to neck-and-neck market shares. Box labels of the period reflect the gradual eclipse of the quill, though it remained in general use in some areas until the 1850s and 1860s and marginally till the end of the century. It is still used by some calligraphers and illustrators.

The earliest commercially-produced quills, cut to some 160 or 170 mm (6¾ in) in length, had been sold for use with holders. These luxury items were packed in twenty-fives or thirties in card or wooden boxes, shaped and slit ready for use. In a typical French example a cardboard box measuring some 80 × 180 × 55 mm (3⅛ × 7⅛ × 2⅛ in) bears a printed label with a line illustration of the product and a legend. A slide-top wooden box, designed to hold twenty-five shorter quills and measuring 60 × 130 × 25 mm (2⅜ × 5⅛ × 1 in) bears an engraved oval label, 30 × 52 mm (1³⁄₁₆ × 2 in), with the legend: 'Willm Palmer, son and successor to the late Thos Palmer, pen cutter to the Royal family; Royal Pen Manufactory, East Grinstead'. A smaller label, 15 × 40 mm (⁹⁄₁₆ × 1⁹⁄₁₆ in), reads: 'Gentlemen's pens' (the appropriate counterpart for ladies was also available). Later, quill-pen box labels (for quill 'nibs') developed along the lines of the metal-pen label, measuring some 40 × 55 mm (1⁹⁄₁₆ × 2⅛ in).

The rise of the metal pen was spectacular from the 1840s onwards. Mechanized production brought a plethora of manufacturing companies, distributors, trade names, and range names. Leading British firms were C. Brandauer; Joseph Gillott; Hinks, Wells & Co.; D. Leonardt & Co.; MacNiven & Cameron; William Mitchell; Perry; A. Sommerville – most of them centred on Birmingham. America's major company was Esterbrook of Camden, New Jersey; Germany's big names were Heintze & Blanckertz of Berlin, Mueller of Leipzig, and Sornnecken of Bonn.

Pen-box label, second half of 19th century. Printed in green and embossed. 42 × 139 mm (1¾ × 5½ in)

Vast increases in business correspondence, banking, accountancy, etc., as well as the growth of compulsory education, brought mass markets. With the arrival of the fountain pen and the typewriter in the late 19th century, and the ball-point pen and computerized accounting in the 20th century, the market dwindled; by the last quarter of the 20th century the 'dipping pen' had become a curiosity.

Box labels for pen nibs reflect the intense competitiveness of the market in its heyday. The initial rigidity of the metal nib (as compared with the quill) led early manufacturers to stress its flexibility. 'Elastic' pens, and 'double elastic' pens were not uncommon; 'ladies'' pens offered 'ease and grace', as did 'round writer' and 'round hand' pens. Other titles suggested professional expertise: typical were 'Banker's favourite', 'Reporter', 'Counting house', 'Librarian's', 'Post Office', 'Engrossing', 'Legal', 'Scholastic', and 'Mapping quill' (the last also made of metal).

Few companies' labels command special attention for their design, though some French examples carry colourful chromolithographed pictorial scenes. Notable British exceptions were those of the William Mitchell Co., whose distinctive trade mark, blind-embossed as a white image on a single-colour ground, is highly effective. Its heraldic device (unaccountably pirated from the City of London) remained in use until after the company's amalgamation with Hinks, Wells in 1921. Careful scrutiny will quickly distinguish 20th-century embossed labels from the originals; the later versions, though heavily in relief, lack detail.

The year 1921 was a watershed for the British pen industry. With the formation of British Pens Ltd most of the remaining companies were absorbed. As with the case of the William Mitchell Co., individual labels were retained virtually unchanged. Many are distinguishable by their wrap-round tabs, which carry the British Pens Ltd imprint.

Penman's flourish

The term refers to the calligraphic convolutions produced by the quill in and around lettering and writing. The flourish exploits the quill's capacity to render extreme differences of line thickness in the course of a single unbroken movement. In documents of ceremonial and security it served at once as a gesture of self-importance and as an anti-counterfeit device.

In its security role the flourish was used early on in INDENTURES, the design being cut through so as to divide a document into two or more parts. The irregularity of the cut and the complexity of the flourish ensured a unique correspondence between the separated portions. Imitated by the engraver and later by the typefounder, the device was widely used in an extended 'border' form at the line of separation in counterfoil books. It also appears in a wide range of security documents, among them the CHEQUE/CHECK, LICENCE, RECEIPT, and SHARE CERTIFICATE.

Historically there has been a continuing interaction between the penman's quill and the engraver's burin. Though at first merely working as an imitator, the engraver shortly was to vie with his mentor, originating his own flights of fancy, and broadening still further the range of line thickness in flourishes. This was, of course, easier for the engraver than for the penman; the penman was required to perform in a single *tour de force*, whereas the engraver could work and rework lines at leisure.

The so-called 'off-hand' calligraphic flourish, at the outset merely abstract, soon turned into a form of fanciful representation. The curves and spirals of the pen began to convey not merely exuberance but angels and cherubs, birds, and beasts. In many of the specimens produced by early writing masters from all over Europe a flourished text is embellished with human figures, leaping tigers, peacocks, phoenixes, and other creatures. The work of Morante and Van den Steene on the continent, and Edward Cocker and George Bickham in Britain, abounds with these images. Samuel Pepys's calligraphic collection at Magdalene College, Cambridge, contains similar examples, among them an anonymous design displaying his own name with flourished birdlife in support.

The professional flourish was revived in the early years of the 19th century when it reappeared in the repertoire of the American writing teacher. It became a standard professional trick for the itinerant penman and was adopted enthusiastically as a cultural parlour trick by others. In its heyday in America the pictorial flourish was confined very largely to representations of quills and birdlife, though there were occasional excursions into leaping frogs and, rarely, cherubs. The quill motif had wide currency, particularly among writing teachers, but the bird formed the central feature of the vast majority of American flourishes. It was but a short step to adapt the device to a practical purpose by adding a scroll or banderole bearing a name or title. This idea was adopted for the letterheads and other promotional items of business colleges, the institution's name being trailed from the beak of a flourished bird in flight.

It was however in private usage that the flourished namepiece chiefly scored in America. Penmen – all very newly qualified – advertised their services as purveyors of flourished calling cards, and offered to render customers' names calligraphically for a modest fee, either alone or as part of a more elaborate bird and banderole design. The cult of the flourish became widespread. By the end of the 1880s there were some half a dozen penman's magazines in print, and *The Penman's Directory* listed over 350 names and addresses of practitioners, virtually all of whom were concerned with the 'flourished card' business. A number of these offered correspondence courses in the art of flourishing; others advertised aids to the novice penman setting up as a teacher. There were 'display flourishes for exhibition purposes to aid in organizing classes... for those who have gained enough skill in writing to teach classes near their homes, but who have not yet acquired sufficient skill to construct large designs...'.

American penman's flourish, December 1885. The flourishes printed in four colours and gold, the inscription manuscript. 172 × 243 mm (6¾ × 9½ in)

Towards the end of the 19th century the flourished card began to be seen as a candidate for the American parlour SCRAP BOOK/ALBUM; but the penman's satisfaction at this new outlet was tempered with irritation at the activities of the 'specimen sponger', the collector who wrote asking for a free specimen on the excuse of a possible large order. It was inevitable that the flourished card should move into print, and the familiar formula of bird and scroll began to appear as local printers' STOCK BLOCKS. These bore a blank name space for hand insertion or overprinting and, unlike their predecessors, often appeared in coloured inks on coloured card. Hand-flourishing in America survived, if only fitfully, into the mid 1930s.

The flourish had but a marginal following in Britain. After the passing of Edward Cocker in 1675 there are few examples, handwritten or engraved. The end of the 18th century and the beginning of the next brought a minor revival of flourishing among engravers of innkeepers' trade cards and billheads, and some lithographic writers turned their hand to it also.

The art of flourishing in lithography was much more common in Germany than elsewhere. The finest specialist there was Johann Evangeliste Mettenleiter, who worked in Munich producing title-pages, title panels on maps, and independent broadsheet texts for display.

The expertise of the flourish artist – whether as penman or engraver – is largely confined to the classic subject matter of the trade. In cases where subjects depart from accepted formulae, it is evident that picture making is rarely the flourisher's strong point.

See also COPY-BOOK

REFERENCES David P. Becker, *The Practice of Letters: The Hofer Collection of Writing Manuals, 1514–1800* (Cambridge, Mass.: Harvard College Library, 1997); George Clulow, 'Penmanship', *Strand Magazine*, vol. VIII, pp. 697–703, London, 1894; Ambrose Heal, *English Writing-Masters and their Copy-Books* (London, 1931; reprinted Hildesheim, 1962); E. A. Lupfer, *Ornate Pictorial Calligraphy* (New York: Dover, 1982); Ray Nash, *American Penmanship 1800–1850* (Worcester, Mass: American Antiquarian Society, 1969)

COLLECTIONS: American Antiquarian Society, Worcester, Mass.; Houghton Library, Harvard University, Cambridge, Mass.; Newberry Library, Chicago

Pennant

Deriving from the Latin *penna*: feather, the word refers to a long tapering flag (also called a pennon) flown from a mast or standard as a mark of rank or distinction. Often pennants served as a rallying point for supporters of monarchs in battle. In 1244 Henry III is said to have given orders for a banner to be made in the shape of a dragon in red silk 'sparkling all over with fine gold, the tongue of which should be made to resemble burning fire and appear to be continually moving, and the eyes of sapphire and other suitable stones'. Pennants were also flown as a sign of rank from fighting ships (flagships) and from tents used as headquarters in military encampments.

A triangular tapering shape was not deemed to be obligatory (in fact many such flags were square in format and accommodated coats of arms). The tapering shape gained favour for use in competitive contexts. The shape survives to the present day, particularly in America, where it occurs as a more or less standard item of allegiance in schools, colleges, and universities. The suspended pennant, hung from a crossbar, has been adopted as a social grace: it served as a keepsake token, to be exchanged ceremonially at fraternal meetings, and as table decorations at conferences and luncheons.

The pennant was also popular in the 1950s and 1960s among airlines as counter-top markers. It has been used in election campaigns, sometimes showing the candidate's portrait, and, when bearing the name of a tourist attraction, is widely used as a souvenir.

Small pennant flags known as 'bannerettes' were a feature of outdoor displays in some of the religious revival meetings of the latter part of the 19th century. They bore scriptural texts or other such legends, printed from wood on thin white linen. Their upper edges were hemmed; other edges were roughly cut to shapes (points, etc.). Similar flags also bore single-letter units for display in wording as desired. The files of Robert Smail, printer, Innerleithen, Peeblesshire, include a religious pennant dated August 1885. It is cut to four points at its lower edge and measures some 560 × 280 mm (22 × 11 in); printed in red, its legend reads: 'Whatsoever thy hand findeth to do, do it with all thy might'.

Perfume card

The advertising perfume card had a widespread vogue in Europe in the period from around 1900 to around 1930. The card, impregnated with perfume, and measuring some 55 × 95 mm (2⅛ × 3¾ in) was intended as an adjunct to the handbag. It was effectively a sweet-smelling TRADE CARD, carrying, in addition to a decorative design, the perfumier's name and that of the perfume itself. The card often had rounded corners and was printed – on the name side in three or four colours and on the reverse in a single colour.

The cards were occasionally used as inserts in the pocket-type embroidery silk postcards of World War I. Though bearing a sentimental greeting on the reverse, they retained unmodified the main advertising image on the front. Perfume cards were also made available in quantities for charities, who overprinted their backs with appeals for funds and sold them, nominally at one penny each, but in fact for whatever sum was offered. The idea remained in use for fund-raising purposes throughout the 1920s. Notwithstanding its charitable message, the back also carried a printed reminder: 'The perfume with which this card is scented can be procured from all Chemists, Perfumiers and Stores'.

Chief among the companies producing the cards was Eugène Rimmel of London and Paris, for whom they were a logical extension of the perfumed ALMANAC and VALENTINE card, which they had pioneered in the mid 19th century.

The perfume card had a revival in the last decades of the 20th century when luxury companies such as Armani, Christian

Perfume card 'Sweet pea' of E. Rimmel Ltd (its reverse bears an advertisement of the County of London Electric Supply Co. Ltd). Printed in colours by lithography. 53 × 93 mm (2⅛ × 3⅝ in)

Dior, Gucci, Yves Saint Laurent, and Paloma Picasso produced cards for counter display. Frequently die-cut as shapely bottles, blind embossed and with discreet gilt lettering, they are designed to echo the high cost of the product they advertise. The introduction of perfume specifically for men or children is emphasized by either printing the card or shaping the card as, for example, a teddy bear.

REFERENCE M. Carbré, M. Sebbag, V. Vidal, *Femmes de Papier* (Toulouse: Éditions Milan [c. 1996])

Perfume label

The chemists' intimate association with the technique of distilling (by which many basic perfumes are produced) led to their early involvement with the business of perfumery. Among the first in the field was the London chemist and pharmaceutical trade supplier Robert Best Ede (*see* CHEMIST'S LABEL), whose interest in both fields was formally acknowledged in a 'puff' announcement in the *Morning Chronicle* of 21 September 1837: 'Mr Robert Best Ede, inventor of the Odiferous Compound... has taken the necessary oath, and been appointed by special warrant from the Lord Chamberlain's office, Chemist and Perfumer in Ordinary to Her Majesty'.

Mr Ede was not slow to exploit this distinction and shortly announced that his Odiferous Compound, 100,000 packets of which he claimed had already been sold, would shortly be put up in 'New and more attractive boxes, labels and wrappers'. His other product, an 'Esprit for the handkerchief, the toilet and the drawing room', an essence combining all the properties of the Odiferous Compound, was sold in labelled bottles with the royal testimonial (from the Queen and the Duchess of Kent) affixed to each.

Robert Ede's promotional enterprise was a sign of the times. The 19th century brought the pharmacist firmly into the perfume industry. It was to be some time, however, before Ede's 'New and more attractive boxes, labels and wrappers' became common.

Perfume-duty label

Perfume was subject to a tax in Britain in the period 1786 to 1800 (*see* TAX STAMP).

The duty was under the jurisdiction of the Controller of the Commissioners of Stamps, who also granted annual licences to purvey the products. The Commissioners provided licensed vendors with labels to paste on all 'packets, boxes, pots, bottles and phials', and forms on which to record their sales. Duty was paid according to the selling price of the product, labels being marked 'one penny', 'two pence', 'three pence', 'six pence', and 'one shilling' accordingly, and bearing the words 'Stamp Office' and 'Perfume Duty'. The labels measured 25 × 57 mm (1 × 2¼ in).

Petition

The right to petition stems from the corpus of democratic privileges secured by the British parliament and embodied in the Bill of Rights (1689) and the Act of Settlement (1701). It is seen as one aspect of the citizen's democratic right to freedom of speech, and of parliament's role as the instrument of the people rather than of the monarch. It remains, in modern times, one of the rights and functions of parliament to receive petitions; provision is specifically made for their reception in a container placed for the purpose behind the Speaker's chair in the House of Commons. In America, the right to petition is expressed in

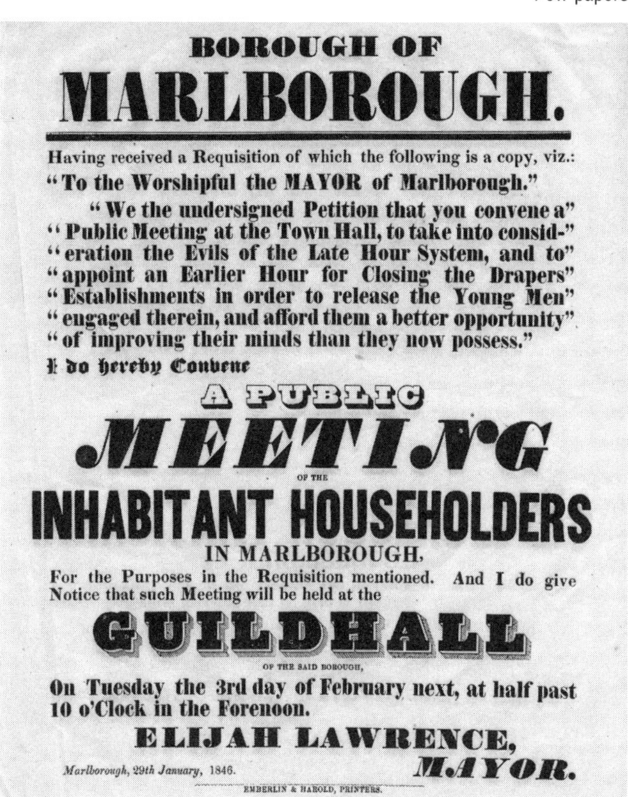

BOROUGH OF

MARLBOROUGH.

Having received a Requisition of which the following is a copy, viz.:

"To the Worshipful the MAYOR of Marlborough."

"We the undersigned Petition that you convene a"
"Public Meeting at the Town Hall, to take into consid-"
"eration the Evils of the Late Hour System, and to"
"appoint an Earlier Hour for Closing the Drapers"
"Establishments in order to release the Young Men"
"engaged therein, and afford them a better opportunity"
"of improving their minds than they now possess."

I do hereby Convene

A PUBLIC

MEETING

OF THE

INHABITANT HOUSEHOLDERS

IN MARLBOROUGH,

For the Purposes in the Requisition mentioned. And I do give Notice that such Meeting will be held at the

GUILDHALL

OF THE SAID BOROUGH,

On Tuesday the 3rd day of February next, at half past 10 o'Clock in the Forenoon.

ELIJAH LAWRENCE,

Marlborough, 29th January, 1846. MAYOR.

EMBERLIN & HAROLD, PRINTERS.

Notice of a public meeting concerning a petition about closing times, Marlborough, January 1846. Letterpress, printed by Emberlin & Harold. 280 × 226 mm (11 × 8⅞ in)

the First Amendment and is firmly established as part of the nation's constitutional structure.

The right to petition was often invoked in the 18th and 19th centuries. In Britain the petitions of the Chartists in 1838, 1842, and 1848, allegedly bearing an aggregate of over 10 million signatures, are perhaps the most notable examples of its use. The concept of the appeal to the governing power extends to lesser contexts however, and petitions have frequently been made to local authorities and other bodies in exercise of the same principle. The document commonly opens with the words, 'We the undersigned...', though in Britain parliamentary practice requires that a petition be expressed in 'respectful terms' (and, incidentally, be presented by a member of parliament).

Among major petitions in American history is that by American women for the abolition of slavery, drawn up in 1862. The printed preamble reads:

> To the Senate and House of Representatives of the United States: The undersigned women of (—) in the state of (—), believing that the cause of humanity and virtue will be advanced, and further difficulties in the National government effectually prevented by the extinction of slavery throughout our country, respectfully and earnestly petition that you will at an early day....

The petition as a social history record illuminates a wide variety of matters. It is used in campaigns of all descriptions, from demands for the release of prisoners, the closure of atomic plants, and the repeal of licensing laws, to calls for nursery schools and pedestrian crossings.

REFERENCE O. Smith, *The Politics of Language 1781–1819* (London: Oxford University Press, 1984)

Pew papers

In former times, exclusive rights to the use of specific church pews were granted to church-goers willing to pay for them. The custom provided a degree of privacy and privilege to worshippers who preferred not to mix with those whose standards of hygiene and comportment they felt they did not share. The custom also provided incumbents with no small part of their income.

Pews thus reserved were near the front of the congregation, the best positions being reserved for the Lord of the Manor and his family. They were locked and often bore a frame for the holder's name card. In some cases the term 'pew' also denoted an isolated compartment, having seats on three sides, in which a whole family might sit, as a self-contained unit. Pew rights were acquired either by virtue of the occupant having himself built and endowed the church (in which case no charge was made), by purchase in perpetuity, or by annual rental. More rarely, pew rights were sold by auction to the highest bidder. There is, however, doubt as to the legality of this practice.

The sale or renting of pews began in the early 16th century and was widespread, particularly in rural areas, until the end of the 19th century. It was a metropolitan custom too – and not only in Britain. American social historian James D. McCabe Jr, writing in 1872 reports: 'pew rent is very high in New York and only persons in good circumstances can have pews in a thriving church. In a fashionable church large sums are paid for pews'.

Items of pew ephemera include part-printed certificates of entitlement (generally foolscap), pew rent receipts (of varying format), reference to pews in the local church in auction particulars of large properties, and 'pew-openers' (handwritten receipts for annual or half-yearly payments for locking and unlocking of pews). These last are found as scraps of paper, often torn from a larger sheet, and in many cases signed with a cross or other such mark.

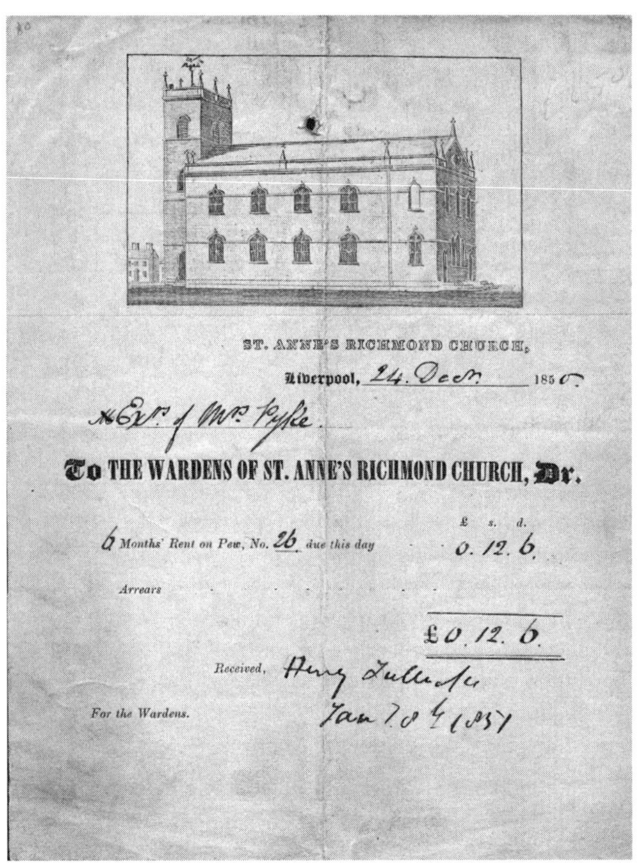

ST. ANNE'S RICHMOND CHURCH,

Liverpool, 24. Decr 1850

To THE WARDENS OF ST. ANNE'S RICHMOND CHURCH, Dr.

£ s. d.

6 Months' Rent on Pew, No. 26 due this day 0. 12. 6

Arrears

£0. 12. 6

Received, [illegible]

For the Wardens.

Invoice/receipt for rent of a pew in St Anne's Richmond Church, Liverpool, 24 December 1850. Letterpress and manuscript. 204 × 157 mm (8⅛ × 6¼ in)

Pharmaceutical package

Among many notable changes, the 19th century brought developments in three closely related areas: the pharmaceutical industry, promotion, and packaging. Expansion in each one of these fields may be said to have stimulated the other two; the triple alliance made much of the running in the emergence of the mass-market economy. Particularly in America, where scattered communications in remote areas brought access to new 'scientific remedies', nationwide distribution of cure-alls became a dominant industry.

Unlike the heavyweight products of hardware and furniture factories, health remedies presented few problems of transport and storage. Pills, potions, brews, ointment, liniments, lotions, syrups, and sarsaparillas were among the cheapest of all commodities to distribute. They were also among the cheapest to manufacture. For the most part, the manufacturer's greatest capital outlay was in advertising. The LEAFLET and ALMANAC were major outlets for this; so was PACKAGING.

As individual preparations were superseded on chemists' shelves by branded goods in packages, the public's awareness of centralized manufacturing developed. Soon, though the move to branded goods in other fields may have been less dramatic, pharmaceutical 'household' names appeared.

By the end of the 19th century few citizens, on either side of the Atlantic, can have failed to peruse a catalogue of proprietary cures. Typical of these were 'Fennings lung healers', 'Mother Seigel's curative syrup', 'Doan's kidney pills', 'Dr Pierce's favourite prescription', 'Stedman's soothing powders', 'Ayer's cherry pectoral', 'Warner's kidney and liver pills', 'Woodcock's wind pills', 'Owbridge's lung tonic', 'Lydia E. Pinkham's vegetable compound', 'Holloway's pills', and 'Carter's little liver pills'.

The glass bottle was the industry's primary packaging unit. Relief-moulded names and trade marks in the glass, together with distinctive colour and bottle shape, reinforced the individual brand image. But the paper LABEL carried most of the burden of identity. Labels were shaped to fit the front face of the bottle or, in the rarer case of the cylindrical bottle, wrapped round the whole of the body. The full wrap-round echoes the treatment of drug phials in the 17th and 18th centuries, in which the closure was a piece of parchment tied with string and a label that concealed the contents of the phial almost completely.

See also PILLBOX LABEL; PRESCRIPTION PAPER/ENVELOPE

Phenakistoscope disc

The earliest attempts at the portrayal of pictorial motion were those of the Belgian Joseph Antoine Plateau, who devised what he described as the phenakistoscope, a rotating disc bearing a series of separate pictures of motion. The word phenakistoscope derives from the Greek (*phenakistes*: deceiver; *skopein*: to view); it is spelt as shown here, not as widely misrendered 'phenakistiscope'. Viewed successively through slits in a second disc, which acts as a 'shutter' between pictures, the individual images are blended with an appearance of motion. The principle, on which the motion picture of today is based, exploits Roget's theory (1824) of the persistence of vision.

In another version of the device, slit and image appear on the same disc, the illusion being revealed through the slits by a rear mirror. The disc, measuring some 260 mm (10¼ in) in diameter, and printed in three or four colours, was spun on a wooden spindle inserted in a centre hole. Similar discs, lacking slots, were used as the basis of the ZOËTROPE.

See also THAUMATROPE

Photographic ephemera

The early years of photography, from its announcement to the world by William Henry Fox Talbot and Louis Jacques Mandé Daguerre in 1839, were dominated by the gifted and wealthy amateur. It was not until the late 1850s that professional photographers offered their services in many provincial towns. The itinerant photographer circulated handbills such as one for J. A. Foster, New England, of the 1860s in which he 'takes this opportunity to inform the inhabitants of the village and vicinity that he is now prepared to take Original Daguerrotypes Or to Copy Daguerrotypes or Pictures. All will remember to call at his Saloon without delay, as his stay in the village will be limited'. From the middle of the century advertisements appeared regularly in periodicals and newspapers, but the back of the CARTE-DE-VISITE, and later the cabinet photograph, endorsed by the photographic image, provided a major advertising outlet for photographers throughout the century.

In 1853, a prospectus for the *Journal of the Photographic Society* was issued; with just twenty-five members, including its President, the Society reflected the world of the leading amateur photographers, many of whom were eminent in other artistic and scientific fields. The rules of one of many local photographic societies, the Newcastle-upon-Tyne and North of England Photographic Society, published in 1860, are revealing: for example, rule 3 mentions both amateur and professional photographers, and also advises that ladies are admissible. A raffle ticket, for a photographic camera and lens, was included as an incentive to become a member.

Photography threatened the livelihood of many itinerant journeyman painters, and a broadsheet headed 'Pentography for the million!' is assumed to be a spirited response to the invention by one of them. The sheet (using the common misspelling of 'pantography') is undated, but the claim to produce a likeness in one minute should be compared with the ten to fifteen minutes required for exposure by the earliest photographic processes. Advertisements for equipment and processes began to appear from the very earliest years of photography, initially in periodicals; freestanding advertisements, like a lithographed sheet for Koch, produced on the occasion of the London exhibition of 1862, are much rarer. Advertisements of photographic suppliers were often inserted loose in periodicals; price lists are more likely to have been sent in response to a specific enquiry; instruction leaflets, such as 'The "Self-Pose" Attachment' costing 1*s* 6*d* or 'How to use the Coronet Box Camera', would have accompanied the item.

Concerts of dissolving views presented by means of the magic lantern were immensely popular throughout the 19th century and would have impinged on many people's lives; their popularity was often harnessed for evangelical purposes, and specifically in the battle against the abuse of drink. A ticket for the Grand Special Concert held at the Working Men's Teetotal Hall promised a show which included 'Dissolving Views of the 1889 Paris Exhibition' and '60 Views of the Exhibition and the Eiffel Tower'.

Enthusiasm for the new medium ensured that the characteristic image of the photographer beside his tripod, his head under the cloth covering his plate camera, appeared as a silhouette or in colour on many trade cards unrelated to photography as well as on SCRAPS. More elusive are the tiny photographic wafers, such as the gummed wafers of portraits of poets in their embossed envelope available from Ayling's of Oxford Street and Augustus Square, London, in the 1860s. Photographic bookplates were occasionally commissioned by bibliophiles in the late 19th and early 20th centuries; most are artistically unsatisfactory, though an appropriate one was produced for George Eastman, the American inventor of the first effective roll film and the Kodak camera in the 1880s.

Photography once again became the province of the amateur with the introduction of the light, hand-held camera in the 1880s. The exposed film was handed over to an agent, invariably a chemist, and the developed negatives and prints were returned in a decorative D&P (developing and printing) FILM WALLET. These wallets reflect changing fashions in dress and style through images on their covers. Tin lapel BADGES bearing photographic images were produced in the second half of the 19th century, and on into the 20th century, to advertise an exhibition or event, royal occasions, such as coronations and funerals, and, on both sides of the Atlantic, for campaigning politicians. Most commonly found are pictures of Boer War generals including Kitchener, Dundonald, Baden-Powell, and Lord Roberts. Other photographic ephemera of the 20th century include the trade cards handed out by itinerant street photographers who were regularly to be found in city centres and seaside towns.

Certain categories of printed ephemera of the second half of the 19th century, such as Christmas cards and writing paper, were often embellished with photographic prints. Some SHEET-MUSIC COVERS included photographs too, though more commonly photographic images were used as a source for lithographic draughtsmen to copy. Before half-tone blocks and plates came into common use in the early 20th century, photographs were occasionally applied to pieces of printed advertising. [JW]

See also AMBROTYPE LABEL; PHOTO-LITHOGRAPHIC VIEW; ROLL OF HONOUR

REFERENCES Heinz K. Henisch and Bridget A. Henisch, *The Photographic Experience 1839–1914* (Pennsylvania: Pennsylvania State University Press, 1993); Michael Pritchard, *A Directory of London Photographers 1841–1908* (Watford: PhotoResearch, 1986; reprinted 1994)

COLLECTIONS National Museum of Photography, Film and Television, Bradford, W. Yorkshire; Smithsonian Institution, Washington, DC

Photo-lithographic view

Prior to the general introduction of the 'screened' half-tone reproduction in the latter part of the 19th century, a photo-based process known as 'photo-lithography' was used in the preparation of pictorial souvenir albums. The term, which was also to be widely used to refer to the photomechanical production of lithographic printing plates, was later seen to be ambiguous, and was dropped. In present usage the distinction may be made by the use of a hyphen (as in album titles in which the word appears). 'Photolithography' – without a hyphen – commonly refers to the later process.

'Photo-lithographic views' may be identified by an essentially photographic base to which has been added an overall hand-working. The picture, commonly printed in shades of chocolate or 'sepia', appears as a combination of photograph and drawing. Buildings and other structures are rendered with extreme clarity, figures (which at that stage in the history of

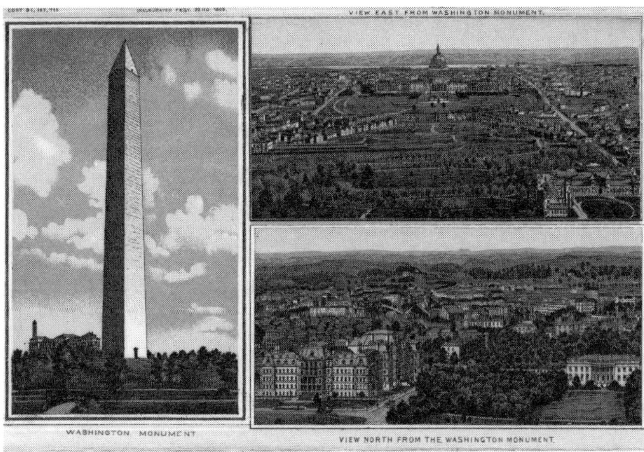

Photo-lithographic views from a 'Washington Album', c. 1890. Lithographed in shades of sepia. 18 × 234 mm (5⅞ × 9¼ in)

photography were blurred by movement) appear as conjectural reconstructions, commonly without conviction, often poorly drawn, and sometimes evidently inserted from imagination to fill an empty space.

The pictures were produced by means similar to those of chromolithography, in which an original coloured image was analysed into a series of hand-drawn colour workings (the separated colours being afterwards superimposed to produce a single full-colour image). In the photo-lithographic view a monochrome image is separated into five or six basic tones, each contributing to the multi-tone effect of the reconstructed picture. As with chromolithography, hatching, stipple, and other effects were used to produce tonal gradation. In chromolithography the whole of the work was carried out by hand; in the present process the original photograph was printed as a 'ghost image' on five or six separate stones, each image then being worked over manually according to its tonal role in the final reproduction.

The process originated in Germany, and depended largely for its production on the skills of chromolithographic craftsmen and artists. Its heyday was the period 1880 to 1890; by the early 1890s it had been used for view albums (but for little else) in many parts of the world. The typical album consists of a series of images, often in a variety of sizes, on concertina-folded sheets within cloth- or paper-covered boards. Some extend to as much as 3 metres (about 10 feet) or even more. One of the principal publishers in Britain was Charles, Reynolds & Co. of London, who produced over 100 sets of major British towns and resorts.

See also CHROMO

Phrenological chart

In the 19th century phrenologists used charts as an aid to summarizing their 'readings' of the configurations of the human head. The pseudo-science of phrenology, propounded by Franz Joseph Gall (1757–1828) and Johann Caspar Spurzheim (1776–1832), defined thirty-seven separate 'organs' of the brain, each of which was capable of specific degrees of development, ranging from 'very small' to 'excessive and tending to perversion'. The rating for each organ, evaluated according to a scale devised by the individual practitioner, was entered as a handwritten numeral at each of the relevant points on the chart. The chart superseded an individual handwritten assessment, which had formerly been drawn up in longhand for each sitter. It provided a complement to diagrams or models of the head showing locations of the organs in question. The expression 'phrenological chart' normally relates to the analysis of a sitter rather than to the diagram.

Charts measured anything from 600 × 420 mm (23⅝ × 16½ in) to 440 × 290 mm (17⅜ × 11⅜ in) and generally carried a space for insertion of the sitter's name. Typically printed in black, they came into general use in the 1830s and 1840s and continued until just after the turn of the century, when the practice of phrenology waned. The underlying idea was also adopted by practitioners of physiognomy (*see* PHYSIOGNOMICAL CHART).

Physician's directions

In the 17th, 18th, and early 19th centuries it was customary, if personal consultation was impossible, for the advice of a physician to be sought and given in writing. Often it was the apothecary, dispenser of drugs and potions, who was asked for diagnosis and treatment. He sought a second opinion, passing it on to the patient as agreed wisdom. The patient's enquiry would be carried by a messenger. Sometimes, the physician being away, a second-in-command would formulate a reply, the messenger carrying this back, together with medicines, as a temporary measure pending the return of his master.

Typical physician's directions occur in the correspondence of John Symcotts (1592?–1662) published in 1951 by the Bedfordshire Historical Record Society:

> For Mr Powers 2 May 1639: First take all the potion in the biggest glass on a morning fasting, cold and well shaken together, and 2 or 3 hours after a little thin warm broth sometimes, as it works, keeping warm within the house all the day and night after. And that night to bedward swallow down (without chewing) half the cordial in the bigger box and so rest.
>
> The next morning fasting take half the syrups in the least glass in a draught of warm posset ale wherein a few camomile flowers have been boiled, and the other half that afternoon about 4 o'clock, in like manner.
>
> The next morning about 6 o'clock swallow down (in anything you please) all the 4 pills in the less box, and observe the same order that day as when you took the potion. And that night to bedward take the rest of the cordial.
>
> Afterward draw up some of the water in the middle glass into your nostrils, warm every morning fasting and about an hour before supper, so long as it lasts.

Other examples include the following:

Folded paper, unsealed: 125 × 205 mm (4⅞ × 8⅛ in)

> For a Cough: Put 10 knucklebones of Mutton and two ounces of Pearl Barley and two ounces Hartshorn Shavings into a Gallon of Water, and let it simmer till reduced to a quart. When t'is almost enough put in a burnt Crust. Take the fat very clean off when it is cold. Drink a cup of it warm every morning.

The paper is addressed to 'William R Dunbar Esq, Care of Harry Davidson Esq W1 Edinburgh'. An appended note reads: 'If not in Town to be forwarded'. A pencilled addendum dates the document 1808.

Folded paper, unsealed with blank conjugate leaf; 190 × 115 mm (7½ × 4½ in)

> Advice for Miss Hall: You will please to take a couple of Pills an hour before bedtime. Two table-Spoonsful of the Mixture (a cupful of water or tea if more agreeable) at seven in the Morning, & at bedtime, shaking the bottle. You are advised to Abstain from salted, seasoned or pickled Meats; from new

PHRENOLOGICAL CHART AND REGISTER,

By THOMAS BROWN,

PRACTICAL PHRENOLOGIST, HEXHAM.

Scripture and Phrenology are in perfect harmony on the subject of human imperfection, and history and experience prove that there are national characteristics, and also traits of character peculiar to individuals; such facts give proof to the science discovered, and its uses are "Man know thyself."

Definitions of the functions of the Organs and Register of their size.

N.B.—The ordinary functions of the faculties of an equally developed head are defined first, next the change effected when the organs are very small, and third, their perversion resulting from excessive development or morbid action.

The absolute size of each organ is registered in the column at the right of the definitions, from a scale of twelve numbers indicating degrees of size, which are expressed in words thus: 1, very small; 2, small; 3, rather small; 4, moderate; 5, rather dull; 6, full, 7, a degree larger than full; 8, rather larger; 9, large; 10, a degree larger; 11, very large; 12, excessive and tending to perversion.

CLASS I.

Affective Faculties—Propensities.

1. Amativeness—Love for the opposite sex, gives rise to sexual feeling.
Very small—Passive, continence.
Perversion — Licentiousness and immoral gratification.

2. Philoprogenitiveness—Love for children, pets, &c.
Very small—Indifference for children.
Perversion—Spoiling children by excessive indulgence.

C. Inhabitiveness—Love of home and country.
Very small—Migratory disposition
Perversion—Home sickness.

3. Concentrativeness — Power of bringing the mind to bear on a definite object until its aims are accomplished.
Very small — Discursive, changeable.
Perversion—To dwell on abstractions to the exclusion of external realities.

4. Adhesiveness—Friendship and sociability, produces attachment.
Very small — Carelessness about others.
Perversion — Inseparable attachment to unworthy persons and objects and extravagant grief at their death or removal.

5. Combativeness—Courage, self-defence. Prompts to overcome oppression.
Very small—Peaceableness, cowardice.
Perversion — Quarrelsome, courts opposition, and provokes resistance.

6. Destructiveness — Power to overcome and subdue the numerous agents of nature, and to destroy what is noxious for self-preservation.
Very small — Want of activity, meekness.
Perversion — Revenge, cruelty, murder, swearing, and general coarseness, defacing ornament and beauty.

A. Alimentiveness—Gives a desire for and ability to select suitable nourishment.
Very small—Abstemiousness.
Perversion—Gormandizing.

7. Secretiveness — Power to prevent the improper expression of the other faculties; produces a tendency to conceal.
Very small — Openness, too confiding
Perversion — Lying, hypocrisy, cunning, treachery.

8. Acquisitiveness — A desire to acquire and possess.
Very small—Carelessness for money and property.
Perversion—The miser, covetousness, selfishness, theft, gambling.

9. Constructiveness—Tendency to construct, to make, to fashion, gives a desire for and skill in the use of tools.
Very small — No constructive ability, awkward in the use of tools.
Perversion—Constructing instruments for unlawful purposes.

CLASS II.

Sentiments (common to man and the lower animals).

10. Self-esteem — Imparts confidence, self-respect, and dignity of character.
Very small—Humility. Want of confidence.
Perversion—Self-conceit, love of power, tyranny, dogmatism.

11. Approbativeness—Desires the good opinion of others, fame and distinction.
Very small — Regardless of the good opinion of others.
Perversion — Vanity, dandyism, love of display, excessively fond of titles and distinction.

12. Cautiousness—Circumspection, foresight of consequences and a tendency to avoid their evils, causes, timidity, &c.
Very small—Rashness.
Perversion — Excessively timid, foreboding, gloomy, apprehensive.

(Superior Sentiments).

13. Benevolence—A desire for the good of others, give to the needy.
Very small—Uncharitableness.
Over activity, yielding to the pitiful tales of impostors.

14. Veneration — Produces devotion and reference in general.
Very small—Lack of devotion and respect due to others.
Perversion—Fanaticism, excessive love of antiquity, &c.

15. Firmness—Decision of character, constancy, and perseverance.
Very small—Fickleness, indecision.
Perversion—Obstinacy, perverseness, wilfulness.

16. Conscientiousness — Induces sentiments of strict justice and truthfulness.
Very small — Unscrupulousness, neglect of duty.

17. Hope—Expectation, gives a tendency to anticipate what the other faculties desire.
Very small—Leads to despondency
Perversion — Absurd, expectancy, rash speculation.

18. Wonder—Produces a desire for the novel, faith, credulity, &c.
Very small—Distaste for the marvellous, scepticism.
Perversion—Leads to superstition, a belief in Astrology, witchcraft, &c.

19. Ideality—Love of the beautiful, refinement and perfection, poetic taste and feeling.
Very small—Want of poetic inspiration, homeliness of character.
Perversion—Dwelling mentally in the regions of fancy to the neglect of the realities of life.

B. Sublimity—Fondness for the sublime in nature. Grandeur—The great and magnificent.
Very small — Distaste for the majestic and grand.
Perversion—Tendency to perbolical expressions and exaggerated descriptions.

20. Imitation—Power to imitate the performance and productions of others.
Very small—Little power to imitate.
Perversion. Buffoonery—Mimicing the natural defects of others.

21. Wit — Mirthfulness, humour, and a sense of the ludicrous.
Very small—Gravity of demeanour, slow at repartee.
Perversion. Lack of gravity—Tendency to make fun on solemn occasions.

CLASS III.

Intellectual Faculties.

Group 1. Perceptive Faculties.

22. Individuality—Gives a desire for knowledge of objects and an aptitude for practical observation.
Very small—Want of desire and power to observe.
Perversion.—Impudent gazing

23. Form—To perceive clearly the forms of bodies and the power of remembering them.

24. Size—The power to judge of size, space, and distance, and to measure by the eye.

25. Weight—To judge of momentum and the rtlistance of bodies, and the laws of gravitation. Power of adapting animal movements to the laws of equilibrium.
Very small—Want of power to calculate on the weight of bodies by the eye.

26. Colour—To distinguish, mix, and arrange colours harmoniously. To enjoy colour
Very small—Inability to distinguish colours.

27. Locality—Takes cognizance of the relative position of objects and places, delights in landscape scenery, and imparts fondness for travelling.
Very small—Cannot localise objects. Weak memory for places.
Perversion — Excessive desire to visit fresh places, &c.

28. Number — Gives ability to calculate and perceive the relation of numbers.
Very small—Liability to err in ordinary calculation.

29. Order—Love of neatness and methodical arrangement.
Very small — Unmethodical, slovenly.
Perversion—Tormented at slight derangement.

30. Eventuality—Takes cognizance of phenomena, actions and events, and recollects them easily.
Very small—Remembers occurrences with great difficulty.

31. Time—Perception of duration, and marks the revolutions of time in chronological order. Ability to measure intervals of melody by the ear.

32. Tune—Imparts the power to perceive the relations of sounds, and to harmonize them, and delights in music.

33. Language—Ability to learn and make use of words, to express ideas and remember them.
Very small—Not fluent.

GROUP II.

Reflective Faculties.

34. Comparison—Perceives resemblances and differences, arranges and classifies and uses similitudes in writing and discourse. Is fond of analyzing.
Very small—No power to analyze and classify.
Over activity, redundancy of proverbs and similes.

35. Causality—Perceives the relation of cause and effect and gives logical talent.
Very small—Illogical, &c.

F. Intuitive Perception — Discernment of character, of the motives and dispositions of strangers at first interview.

T. HODGSON, PRINTER, "HERALD" OFFICE, PENRITH.

Phrenological chart of Thomas Brown, Hexham, c. 1872. Letterpress and manuscript, printed by T. Hodgson, printer, 'Herald' Office, Penrith. 440 × 285 mm (17⅜ × 11¼ in)

bread, or much Pastry; and from malt Liquors or homemade Wines. H. Cambridge St Sept 13th 1827.

REFERENCE F. N. L. Poynter and W. J. Bishop, *A Seventeenth-Century Doctor and his Patients: John Symcotts, 1592?–1662* (Luton: Bedfordshire Historical Record Society, vol. 31, 1950)

COLLECTION Wellcome Institute for the History of Medicine, London

Physiognomical chart

The physiognomical chart was a printed form in which personality traits and advice to the sitter were individually listed, being ticked as requisite by the physiognomist or 'reader of faces'. The study of physiognomy, initiated by Aristotle and developed notably by Lavater (1741–1801) had fallen into disrepute by the end of the 19th century. The chart, typically 210 × 130 mm (8¼ × 5⅛ in) folded, was nevertheless used by practitioners at fairs, garden parties, and carnivals. It encompassed the whole human condition from 'splendid thinking power' to 'brutal'; advice given ranged from 'study yourself more' to 'do not worry about the future or it will affect your nerves'. The chart was adapted from the idea of the PHRENOLOGICAL CHART, which it survived by a decade or so.

Pillbox label

The circular pillbox, which emerged in an age when popular medicine was a major growth area, was among the first and best-known forms of mass-produced PACKAGING. Its construction stemmed from the BANDBOX or hatbox, a cottage-industry product of the 17th century. It graduated from chipboard or veneer to paper or card and, less successfully, to solid turned wood.

Its widespread use had the effect of establishing the circular LABEL as a standard printed product, and led to the quest for solutions to the typographic problems it posed. Whereas the engraved label had allowed the designer freedom, the intractable solidity of metal type, and the difficulty of setting it in curves, made letterpress production difficult. Working within a containing outer ring, printers sought somehow to pack in the required wording, adjusting and packing out the rectilinear pieces of type as best they could.

The most commonly adopted solution was a peripheral text enclosed by a smaller containing ring. A central horizontal legend formed the main feature. In the semicircular spaces above and below were inserted whatever additional material might fit. The interstices were filled in with substances of the printer's improvisation, commonly *papier mâché*, prepared for the purpose at the composing stone. The resultant set-piece was far from stable, the *papier mâché* infilling being unreliable. With the advent of STEREOTYPE, it became the practice to convert the metal type to a solid stereotype block as soon as practicable.

The pillbox label was available in diameters from 15 mm (9/16 in) to 50 mm (2 in), and ranged in subject matter from wind pills to head and stomach pills, from aperient pills to back-ache and kidney pills. The format was also applied to pomades, unguents, and embrocations, in these cases in sizes from 28 mm (1⅛ in) to 57 mm (2¼ in), and to nit pomade, bears' grease, drawing and healing ointment, and mother salve. Powders (cephalic snuff, anti-acid tooth powder, etc.) were packed in circular formats; so too were leeches ('Fine healthy leeches from J Bateman, Chemist and Druggist, Stroud').

Best known of proprietary pills were 'Parr's life pills', 'Mother Seigel's operating pills', and 'Rackham's liver pills'. The Parr's life pills label, unlike most of its black forebears, was printed in green. Later on in the 19th century came pillbox labels in a variety of colours, many of them printed on coloured papers.

An adjunct to the pillbox label, commonly designed to harmonise with it, was the BAND/BANDEROLE, a printed strip devised to cover the sides of the box and to seal the lid to the body. By the end of the 19th century (and well into the 20th century) this closure was a more or less standard item. Its place was taken by the medicine TAX STAMP, a two-colour strip printed by the Congreve COMPOUND-PLATE PRINTING process and used until the repeal of the tax in 1941.

See also CHEMIST'S LABEL; PHARMACEUTICAL PACKAGE

Pin paper

Pins are typical of a number of fancy commercial products (including tobacco, snuff, and sago) whose purchase was made manageable by the use of papers, printed with the name of the supplier or manufacturer, and folded and tucked to form a packet.

An early invention, applied to a wide variety of such papers, was the triangular tag at the head and foot of the printed image, which indicated fold-over flaps; when the packet was made up, they formed the verso, the main rectangle of the design forming the front. (The same principle was also applied to the PLAYING-CARD WRAPPER, where provision was made for the thickness of the contents by incorporating rectangular side and end panels into the design.)

Earliest surviving pin papers date from the 17th century. Printing was largely from woodcuts; later from metal intaglio plates, and later still by lithography. Designs showed a marked conservatism, the general style remaining unchanged in some cases for well over a century. The dominant design element was a portrait, often of a monarch. Also much in favour were coats of arms, mock heraldics, and other ceremonial devices. In some cases, as with those of London pin-maker citizens George Worral, Thomas Weaver, John Woodward, and John Jeffries, the arms are genuine; they indicate membership of the Pinners' and Needlers' Company. Though superseded by labelled cartons

Pin wrapper, Best Royal Superior Improved Strong Pins, c. 1820. Letterpress, printed in red. As shown, 253 × 294 mm (10 × 11⅝ in)

and by papers in which pins were pierced in rows, the folded paper packet remained in use into the middle of the 20th century. Specimens are often found in which the paper has been cut down to include only the printed image; it should be noted that the complete paper normally extends to more than twice the linear dimensions of the 'face' image. When opened out, typical paper dimensions are 255 × 170cm (10 × 6¾in); when folded, 100 × 60mm (4 × 2⅜in).

See also PIN SYNOPSIS CARD; PIN-BOX LABEL

REFERENCES John Lewis, *Printed Ephemera* (Ipswich: W. S. Cowell, 1962); E. D. Longman and S. Loch, *Pins and Pincushions* (London: Longmans Green & Co., 1911)

COLLECTIONS British Museum; John Johnson Collection, Bodleian Library, Oxford

Pin synopsis card

The pin synopsis was a folding card or piece of strong paper, some 125 × 80mm (4⅞ × 3⅛in), which carried specimens of a pin-maker's full range. Examples of each size of pin were inserted in crimped paper pasted to the card, or simply into crimped paper; they were sometimes numbered and priced. Best known in Britain was the card showing a range of thirteen sizes of entomological pins sold by D. F. Tayler and Co. of Birmingham in the 1870s. The card appeared in various 'editions' showing different prices. The 'synoptical' presentation echoed the 'synoptical needle case' put out by William Whiteley and other shops at about the same time.

See also NEEDLE PACKET; PIN PAPER

Pin-box label

Mechanization of pin manufacture, brought to a successful commercial pitch in the 1830s and 1840s with the introduction of the 'solid-headed' pin, led to a great expansion in marketing and promotion; the pierced PIN PAPER and the pin box were its two chief manifestations.

Chief innovators in the 'solid-head' revolution were John Ireland Howe in America and Daniel Foote-Taylor in Britain. Prior to 1837, pin heads had been individually attached (by child labour) to the wire shaft – a process as costly as it was inefficient. 'D. F. Tayler & Co.'s solid-headed pins' were followed rapidly in Britain by 'Kirby, Beard & Co.'s 'ne plus ultra pins with solid heads'. 'Perfect solid heads' and 'immovable solid heads' became standard phrases in label text-matter.

Pin boxes measured approximately 40 × 65 × 15mm (1⁹⁄₁₆ × 2½ × ⁹⁄₁₆in) and carried an unspecified quantity (normally about 1 ounce) of pins. The push-on lid bore a label and was sometimes held in place by a paper band of some 20mm (¹³⁄₁₆in) breadth. Boxes contained quantities from a quarter-ounce to eight ounces.

Early enterprises produced labels of some elegance, and a number of companies (notably Kirby, Beard & Co.) used embossing and up to four colours, including gold, in designs reminiscent of expensive greetings cards. Later designs, however, were more economical, and printing was commonly restricted to one – at most two – colours.

As labels indicate, the range of pins was extensive, with a multitude of sizes, colours, qualities, and functions. One major London supplier sold twenty-one different types of pin in 1899. Among more common types were 'dress and nursery' pins, 'toilet' pins, 'glass-headed' pins, 'entomological' pins, 'country' pins, and (black) 'mourning' pins.

See also NEEDLE PACKET; PIN PAPER; PIN SYNOPSIS CARD

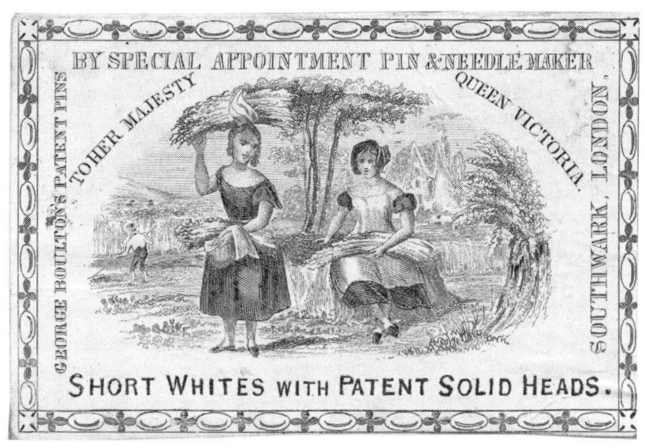

Pin-box labels, both printed intaglio, c. 1840. *Above:* George Boulton's Patent Pins, printed on white paper, 38 × 59mm (1½ × 2¼in); *below:* Hill & Co., Diamond Patent Mix'd Pins, printed on yellow paper, 38 × 52mm (1½ × 2in)

Place card

At formal dinners name cards are used to indicate guests' individual places, thereby ensuring an easy foregathering at the table and prudent juxtaposition of neighbours. They may be used in conjunction with a seating plan. The cards, plain or decorated, may be simple rectangles, or folded in an inverted v-shape to stand up. Somewhat larger cards are sometimes used to incorporate both a name and a brief menu.

Place card, early 20th century. Etched, with blind embossed name of the manufacturer, Parkins & Gotto, London. 58 × 103mm (2¼ × 4in)

The cards may achieve a high degree of elegance, often in the 19th century being decorated by hand to express a celebratory or other specific theme, sometimes featuring paper-lace and other embellishments reminiscent of the VALENTINE.

See also MENU; SEATING PLAN, TABLE

Place mat

The restaurant or lunch counter place mat originated in America and is now in general use as part of the promotional pattern of the catering industry at large. Printed in colours, and measuring approximately 260 × 345 mm (10¼ × 13⅝ in), the mat provides a point of interest, establishes the identity of the caterer, and sometimes offers menu suggestions.

The mat may be of more or less substantial plastic, but in the main it is a disposable paper item that has latterly been viewed by both proprietor and customer as a collectable. A footline on one mat reads: 'Take one with you if you wish – or we will mail free of charge'.

Plague papers

Early efforts to prevent and control plagues and epidemics are recorded in a variety of items of ephemera – some published by authority and some not. A large number are directly related to authenticated plague, but mounting awareness of the need for public and private hygiene produced 'prophylactic' ephemera both in and out of plague periods. With plague, and rumours of plague, a more or less continuing concern over many decades, distinctions may be academic. Ephemera related to plague include plague orders, remedies, BILLS OF MORTALITY, bills of health (*see* PRATIQUE, PAPERS OF), and unofficial plague remedies.

The term 'plague order' relates to the large body of formal instructions, furbishings, advice, and recommendations about plague issued in Britain in the 16th and 17th centuries. These were paralleled in various key centres in Europe, particularly in Italy, where they were known as *istruzioni* (instructions). The documents, at first written, later published as booklets and also posted in public, dealt with every aspect of prevention and containment. Their effect, it must be said, was minimal.

'Plague remedies', indistinguishable in their lack of scientific basis from those recommended by authority, proliferated. Handbills and posters appeared in multitudes offering 'infallible preventive pills', 'sovereign cordials', 'exact regulations for the conduct of the body in case of an infection', and 'approved remedies against the plague'. Also available were amulets and printed papers to be worn around the neck.

An inescapable ephemeral item was the paper, at first written and later printed, to be hung on the door of infected premises. In the City of London the paper bore 'a great red circle of the circuit of a foot and breadth of two inches and the words Lord have mercy upon us printed in the midst' (Public Record Office Domestic State Papers Elizabeth I, vol. 98 doc. 38). The paper was used in addition to the red cross already required to be painted directly on the door.

Other plague ephemera include applications for the holding of fairs, markets, theatre presentations, etc. (which were forbidden in plague years); prayer sheets and booklets; and squared paper worn on the heads of convicts, quacks, and profiteers. Less directly related items concern hygiene, public cleansing, scavenging, and constabulary oversight. Printed 'oath sheets' set out the solemn declaration to be made by those undertaking health control duties. Typical of these is the City of London's charge to scavengers (undated, but printed about the end of the 17th century by Samuel Roycroft 'printer to the Honorable City of London'): 'Ye shall swear, that ye shall diligently oversee that the pavements within your Ward be well and sufficiently repaired, and not made too high in noysance of your Neighbours; and that the Ways, Streets and Lanes, be cleansed of Dung, and all manner of Filth for the honesty of this City...'.

Plague papers are rare. Some items, such as the convicted profiteer's head-paper and the 'Lord have mercy upon us' street door bill, are not known to survive anywhere.

REFERENCES Carlo M. Cipolla, *Cristofano and the Plague* (London: Collins, 1973); F. P. Wilson, *The Plague in Shakespeare's London* (Clarendon Press, 1927)

COLLECTIONS Archivio di Stato, Florence; Bodleian Library, Oxford; Houghton Library, Harvard University, Cambridge, Mass.; Public Record Office, Kew

Plaster package

The application of plasters and poultices has been practised since earliest times; their effect was to serve as counter-irritants or analgesics in muscle and other pains. Among substances used in plasters were antharidine, lead, mercury, and opium, but the heyday of the commercial plaster (or earlier 'plaister') dates from the 19th to the early 20th century, when plasters of bella-

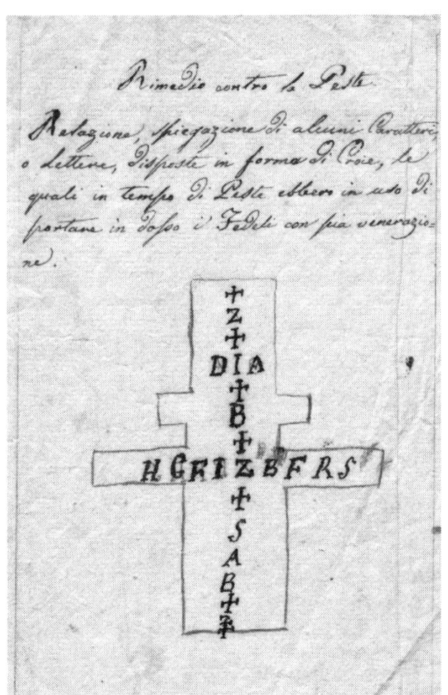

Rimedio contro la Peste

Relazione, Spiegazione di alcuni Caratteri, o Lettere, Disposte in forma di Croce, le quali in tempo di Peste ebbero in uso di portare in dosso i Fedeli con pia venerazione.

✝ Z ✝ DIA ✝ B ✝ HGFIZBFRS ✝ S A B ✝

Spiegazione dei Caratteri.

✝.Z.✝.D.IA.I.A.✝B.✝.Z.✝.S.A.B.✝Z.✝.
H.G.F.I.B.F.R.S.

Queste Sagre Lettere già manoscritte in carta pergamena da S. Zaccaria Vescovo di Gerusalemme, furono trovate alcuni centinaja d'Anni dopo nel Monastero di Trayles di Spagna, insieme colla Spiegazione della medesime, et orazione.

✝. Crux Christi salva me.
Z. Zelus Domus tuae liberet me.
✝. Crux vincit, Crux regnat, Crux imperat; per signum Crucis libera me Domine ab hac Peste.
D. Deus, Deus meus expelle pestem a me, et a loco isto, et libera me.
I. In manus tuas Domine, commendo spiritum meum, cor, et corpus meum.
A. Ante Coelum, et terram Deus erat et Deus potens est liberare me ab ista Peste.
✝ Crux Christi potens est ad expellendam pestem ab hoc loco, et a corpore meo.
B. Bonum est praestolari auxilium Dei cum silentio, et expellat Pestem a me.
✝. Crux Christi fugat Daemones, Aerem corruptum, et pestem expellat.
Z. Zelavi super iniquos, pacem peccatorum videns, speravi in te.
✝ Crux Christi, quae antea fuit in opprobrium et contumeliam; et nunc in gloriam et nobilitatem sit mihi in salutem, et expellat a loco isto Diabolum, et Aerem corruptum et Pestem a corpore meo.
S. Salus tua ego sum Dicit Dominus. Clama ad me, et ego exaudiam te, et liberabo te ab hac Peste.
A. Abyssus abyssus invocat, et voce tua expulisti Daemones; libera me ab hac Peste.
B. Beatus vir qui sperat in Domino, et non respexit in vanitates, et insanias falsas.

Italian plague papers headed 'Rimedio contro la Peste' (remedy against the plague) and 'Spiegazione dei Caratteri' (key to the characters). Manuscript. Page size 135 × 97 mm (5¼ × 3⅞ in)

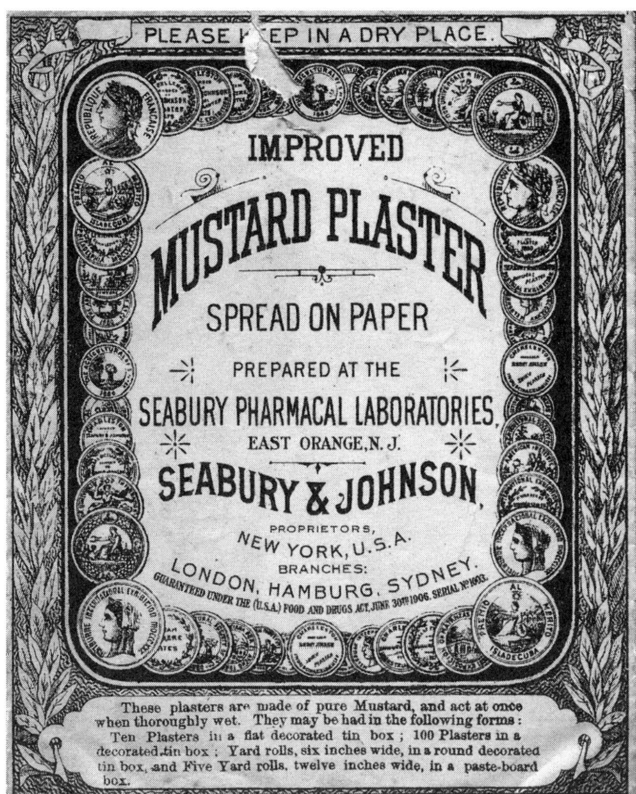

Improved Mustard Plaster package of Seabury & Johnson, New York, late 19th century. Lithographed on yellow paper. 124 × 102 mm (4⅞ × 4 in)

donna and capsicum were in common use and, somewhat later in the period, mustard plasters became popular.

The primary ingredient of the product was mixed with an adhesive plaster, which was spread thinly on paper or cloth. When dry, the product was cut to size and marketed in packets, envelopes, or tins, with or without paper or linen interlining. The most popular size for mustard plasters was about 120 × 90 mm (4¾ × 3½ in), but they were also available at 178 × 127 mm (7 × 5 in) and in rolls measuring 150 × 916 or 460 mm (6 in by 1 or ½ a yard). Notable manufacturers were Rigollot in France, Colman's in Britain, and Seabury & Johnson (later Johnson & Johnson) in the United States. Seabury & Johnson also manufactured belladonna plasters and belladonna and capsicum plasters. The plasters were soaked for a few seconds in water and applied to the affected part by means of a handkerchief or bandage (in case of headache, advised one instruction panel, 'apply at the back of the neck').

They were also known as 'sinapisms' (Latin, *sinapi:* mustard) and were often so labelled. Mustard was widely used therapeutically. In Britain, Colman's produced medical mustard bran (for use in poultices), bath mustard, and mustard oil. The oil, at first given away by the company, was widely held to be beneficial in cases of rheumatism. An article in *Truth* (3 December 1885) supported this view, and the company began to market the product in labelled bottles. Also available on a distinctly less scientific sales pitch was 'poultry mustard', which, when mixed with meal, was said to enhance the laying capability of hens.

The turn of the 19th and 20th centuries saw the rise and fall of the 'kidney plaster' ('for disorders of liver, bladder, and kidney; for pain in the back; for pain in the side').

Court plasters (so called from their origin in the black silk patch formerly worn by ladies at court) were used as a protection in cases of cuts, pimples, etc. They consisted of thin silk coated with isinglass, were cut to the required size, moistened, and applied to the skin. The isinglass (a derivative of fish glue) served as an adhesive. They were marketed in different 'skin' shades, some manufacturers offering a variety of shades within the same package. Sizes were commonly in the region of 60 × 30 mm (2⅜ × 1³⁄₁₆ in) and they were sold in card folders of about 85 × 50 mm (3⅜ × 2 in) or in envelopes. Notable manufacturers were Seabury & Johnson in America, and S. Maw, Son & Sons Ltd in London.

Playing card

Playing cards appeared in Europe after the mid 14th century, when the invention of wood-block printing on paper facilitated mass production. They were known in Spain by 1371; in Italy, France, and Switzerland by 1377; Germany 1378; Belgium 1379. In the 13th century, packs devised in China had four suits of nine cards representing sums of money, but without courts. When cards entered Spain and Italy via the Islamic world, the pack had been enlarged to 52 cards by the addition of tens, kings, and two other ranks, and the suits had become the parents of the Italo–Spanish signs of coins, sticks, swords, and cups, also to be used in France. In Germany and Switzerland suit signs developed into acorns, round bells, hearts/shields, and leaves/flowers. Around 1480, suit signs in France were replaced by the simple shapes that in English are called hearts, diamonds, spades, and clubs. The knights, who had ranked just below the kings, were replaced by queens.

Card games using fewer numeral cards soon developed, resulting in standard packs of 32, 36, 40, and 48 cards. In about 1440, the 52-card Italian pack was extended into the 78-card tarot pack by adding four queens and 22 picture cards intended as trumps in trick-taking games, followed by the 97-card Minchiate pack with 41 trumps. In the mid 18th century packs for tarot games, especially in Germany, changed over to French suit signs, and the former meaningless trump subjects were replaced by various sets of familiar images (such as animals or mythological figures), some of which became standard. Such packs were often reduced to 54 or even 42 cards (with only one numeral in each suit). Italian-suited tarot packs were first used for fortune-telling in 1783, in Paris, by a cartomancer who had previously used the 32-card French pack.

The joker appeared in the mid 19th century in America for the game of euchre. Since about 1950, 52-card packs tend to have three jokers, often of differing designs. Being surplus to the requirements of many games, jokers are often discarded by players to be snapped up as ephemera by joker collectors. Other collectors concentrate on back-designs, arranging them thematically by subject or type. Both activities are disliked by collectors of complete packs since the removal of cards ruins the unity, not to mention the value, of a pack, particularly of an artistically designed one.

Cards came into England from France. The earliest English reference to them was on Christmas Eve 1459, when French cards still had Spanish suits, as the words 'spades' and 'clubs' indicate. The earliest extant court cards in England date from c. 1500 and are elegant but vigorously executed. They came from Rouen, despite Edward IV's 1463 ban on importation.

The basic features of standard English court cards have stayed remarkably constant over four centuries, surviving conversion to double-headed cards in the 1850s. Cards were traditionally made by printing the court card outlines from wood blocks, colours and pips being added by stencilling. In 1832, Thomas De La Rue patented a method of printing card faces in oil colours from wood blocks or lithographic stones. The face sheets had further layers of paper pasted on the back, before being cut into cards, usually about 90 × 63 mm ($3\frac{1}{2} \times 2\frac{1}{2}$ in) in size. Cards had plain backs until the 19th century, allowing the backs of waste or discarded cards to be used as a ready-made source of pasteboard for other purposes. Decorative all-over back-designs appeared belatedly in England by the 1830s, but gave way to bordered formal and fancy designs when problems of ensuring registration of faces and backs had been solved. Advertising material began to appear on card-backs (and even face sides) in the late 19th century, initially in Belgium.

In the late 17th century, following a French initiative of 1644, there had been a spate of 'pictured cards' in which the face of every card was used to carry uncoloured, etched pictorial and textual information: propaganda, instructional, or satirical. The format was revived in the late 19th century for souvenir packs of photographic views, and is being increasingly used to display sets of 52 pictures on all sorts of themes. Corner indices, introduced in c. 1860, ensure that such cards can be used for play. During the 19th century there was a vogue for 'transformation cards' in which the suit-signs were incorporated into comic or sentimental pictures. In Germany, buyers of an 1804 pack, with literary courts, were recommended in an accompanying leaflet to use the blank backs of these charming but unusable cards as visiting cards. England was slow to experiment with specially designed court cards, but some attractive Victorian chromolithographic cards were produced, depicting historical royal figures. English makers were more inventive with cards without formal suits, which were meant to be used by children and/or adults for various social games such as 'Happy families' (invented 1861).

Novelties, such as circular cards (the norm in India) and other shapes, have had no lasting impact. Pips in four colours have made sporadic appearances, commendably as aids to players with poor eyesight. Packs with one or two additional suits have also been short-lived, as have packs with unusual suit-signs. Cards made entirely of plastic (after 1934) have met with little general approval, though today all playing cards are coated to give extra wear. [JB]

See also PLAYING CARD, SECONDARY USES; PLAYING-CARD DUTY; PLAYING-CARD WRAPPER

REFERENCE W. Gurney Benham, *Playing Cards* (London: Ward, Lock & Co., 1931); John Berry, *Playing Cards of the World: a Catalogue of the Worshipful Company of Makers of Playing-Cards on deposit at Guildhall Library* (London: The Author, 1995)

SOCIETY The English Playing-Card Society

Playing card, secondary uses

A little-observed aspect of the playing card is its use in connections other than card playing or divination. As mass-produced items printed to a more or less uniform size and on durable stock, and having – at least until the early 1860s – a conveniently blank side on which to print or write, the playing card did duty in a wide range of improvisations.

Though at first sight an extravagance, the secondary use was in fact confined to damaged or incomplete packs. Loss or impairment of a single card invalidated the whole of the remainder of the pack; the secondary use of such cards was thus not

✠

LEs Enfans de feu *CORNILLE SNEESSENS* annoncent la Mort de leur Mere MARI VAN CUTSEM, decedé le 13. Septembre 1775. dont l'Enterrement & Service ſe feront le 15. ditto à dix heures dans l'Egliſe Paroiſſiale de *St.* Gery.

R. I. P.

Chez Henry Vleminckx.

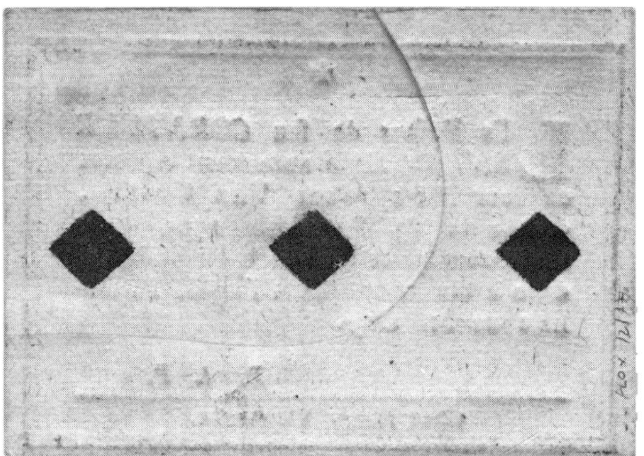

Announcement of death of Mari van Cutsem on 13 September 1775, printed letterpress (in the Low Countries) on the reverse of a stencil-printed playing card (shown below). 60 × 85 mm ($2\frac{3}{8} \times 3\frac{3}{8}$ in)

only a matter of convenience but of economy. Secondary use took two forms: physical alteration and written or printed addition. Typical of the first category were uses as bookmarks (where the card was cut with a v-shaped slit to allow for insertion over the head of the selected page), and cutting into halves or quarters as fractional units in money substitutes. Separate halves were also used in early maternity wards for mother/baby identification, one half being taped to each. A similar tag-label use was also common among lawyers and accountants for the identification of bundles of papers.

A further form of physical alteration was the cropping of corners, in the case of halves or quartered pieces, to balance existing rounded corners, and as an indication of cancellation. A rarer physical alteration is represented by an 18th-century coin collection cataloguing system, in which the impressed image of each individual coin appears obverse and reverse, duly annotated in handwriting on the front and rear faces of a single folded playing card.

Printed or handwritten additions, by far the commonest form of alteration, appear either on the complete card or as an integral unit on cut cards. Handwritten addenda present a wide variety of secondary use: personal notes, memoranda and messages, poetry, musical scores, IOUs, cheques and lottery tickets, shopping lists, charity tokens, visiting cards, invoices and receipts, rent demands. All these and more have appeared on the backs (and occasionally fronts) of playing cards.

Edward Gibbon, author of *History of the Decline and Fall of the Roman Empire* (1776–88), used playing cards to acknowledge gambling debts and also for an extensive series of catalogue cards recording items in his library. The series, under the title 'Library stock and reference cards', is now housed in the British Museum and comprises over 1000 different playing cards. Other notabilities recorded as having used playing cards for secondary purposes include Louis XVI, Jean-Jacques Rousseau, Louis Pasteur, Benjamin Franklin, and Queen Elizabeth I.

Printed additions to playing cards were at some periods as common as those in handwriting. A major field was IMPROVISED CURRENCY. In the 17th and 18th centuries in Canada playing cards introduced by the French authorities were used as money for the payment of troops. Issued in denominations of four francs, forty and fifteen sols, and cut in quarters, their introduction was covered by an ordinance proclaiming their legality and guaranteeing their redeemability. The cards became so widely accepted that at some stages completely blank playing cards, imported unprinted from France, were used instead of finished cards. There was a period from 1685 to 1759 during which there were two kinds of improvised currency in Canada – 'card money' and 'playing card money' – both equally valid.

Other uses of playing-card currency are found in France, Austria, Germany, and Surinam. In the French Revolution, when denominations of the new government's ASSIGNATS proved too high for everyday needs, 'billets de confiance' appeared. These small denomination 'notes', introduced by self-appointed organizations and individuals and relying on the probity of their issuers, were printed on the backs of playing cards. A handwritten 'endorsement' on the back of the card was countersigned, and a signature and number entered on the printed reverse. 'Playing-card money' was used not only as general currency but in some cases as commodity tokens. Bread, meat, and candles were obtainable from suppliers in specific districts against printed 'bons': 'bon pour quatre livres de pain, à delivrer par les boulangers de la section, est payable, les 1er et 16 de chaque mois par le trésorier sous-signé'.

As a sidelight on the use of playing cards as improvised money, a widespread tendency was for the 'court cards' to appear as higher denominations, their relative importance when playing cards being equated with greater financial values.

Printed alterations made to playing cards extend also to non-currency uses; these include wedding and funeral invitations, marriage certificates, ration coupons, summonses, and admission tickets. Less widespread, but no less fully authenticated, was the use of playing-card backs as a base for printed or stencilled language teaching aids, so that cards bearing separate syllables could be arranged to complete words and phrases.

See also PLAYING CARD

Playing-card duty

In 1694 the Government Stamp Office was created to impose 'duties on vellum, parchment and paper…toward carrying on the war against France'. In 1711 a duty of sixpence per pack was levied on playing cards in Britain, even if imported. The duty, made perpetual in 1717, was abolished on 4 August 1960. The initial duty was increased by sixpence in 1756, and again in 1776, 1789, and 1801, to a total of 2*s* 6*d*. In 1828 it was reduced to one shilling, and in 1862 to three pence.

The 1711 requirement to seal the maker's wrapper at his premises was met by applying an official 'label' already embossed at the Stamp Office. Initially this was probably a small piece of paper, all too easily removed for illicit reuse, since that practice was penalized in 1720. No example of this label has survived, though proof copies of the stamp exist. It was replaced by a large officially-printed and embossed label, designed to cover the back and ends of the wrapped pack, and impossible to remove undamaged. Such labels were used until 1744, again from 1765 to 1828, and (minus embossed stamps) from 1828 to 1862. From 1744 to 1765 the Stamp Office provided makers with combination wrappers and seals, though it is not certain how these were fastened.

In 1712 (when a reduced duty of a halfpenny was allowed for stock in hand) it was realized that, once the ephemeral label and wrapper were discarded, there was no sign that duty had been paid, nor of the amount. It was therefore decreed that the face side of one card should be marked. Handstamps of various designs were used for this purpose from 1712 to 1765, after c. 1715 on the ace of spades. In 1765 handstamps were replaced by engraved aces of spades, printed from plates of twenty dies at the Stamp Office on the maker's own paper. But the shilling duty was still collected by means of embossed sixpenny stamps on the sealing label and the maker's own wrapper.

Each of the subsequent additional sixpences was, unusually, denoted and exacted by means of legends added to the officially engraved aces of spades. In 1804 the three separate additional legends were combined into one legend – which has led to a mistaken idea that the duty was 1*s* 6*d* when it was 2*s* 6*d*, the first two sixpences being collected by embossed stamps on the seal and on the maker's wrapper.

From 1828, the reduced duty of one shilling was shown and exacted on the ace of spades alone, whose complicated design (known as 'Old Frizzle', and bearing the arms of George IV) was engraved by Perkins & Heath (Perkins, Bacon & Co. after 1 May 1829) and printed on the card-maker's own paper. However, packs continued to be sealed at the makers' premises, with official seals – but carrying no embossed stamps.

In 1862, the duty was reduced to three pence, no longer exacted on the ace of spades, but on paper tax-wrappers printed by the Perkins Company from engraved plates until 1883, and thereafter in revised designs by lithography. These wrappers, applied and sealed now by the makers themselves, bore legends about the penalties for infringement of the laws concerning their usage. These legends changed, as penalties changed, in 1883 and again around 1955. The tax-wrappers normally had a large oval hole through which could be seen the maker's own wrapper, later the transparent cellophane wrapper revealing the back-design of the cards.

After 1862, makers were free to devise and print their own designs for aces of spades. Many began by adapting the 'Old Frizzle' design, now bearing the royal arms of Victoria rather than George IV. Even today the ace of spades continues to display the maker's name, and to carry an elaborate design, often embodying his trademark or the brand name.

Taxation on playing cards has also been used in other countries, and involves handstamps, wrapper seals, or even marks cut into the blocks for printing the court cards and/or aces.

American playing-card duty stamps, abolished in 1960, took the form of perforated 'philatelic'-type stamps, printed by postage-stamp manufacturers. Though import duty was charged on playing cards from 1780, it appears that no stamp or other device was used to indicate payment. Perforated stamps, issued in 1866 to mark the Civil War 'Revenue Act', bore a portrait of George Washington and the legend: 'US Inter Rev Playing

Cards: one cent'. The stamps were intended, as were all documentary revenue stamps, for use only on the item specified, but their widespread arbitrary use on items of all kinds led to the legalization of playing-card stamps for other purposes. As with medicine, perfumery, and other American duty stamps in the latter part of the 19th century, individual manufacturers were later allowed to control the production of their own duty stamps. [JB]

See also PLAYING CARD; PLAYING-CARD WRAPPER

REFERENCE John Boynton Kaiser, *British Playing Card Stamp Duties and their Authorized Stamps* (The American Philatelic Society, 1960)

Playing-card wrapper

Playing cards share with pins, tobacco, snuff, and other such 'hand-full' products, the distinction of being among early products to be packaged. This distinction derived simply from the impracticality of selling such items loose (*see* PIN PAPER; TOBACCO PAPER).

From the start, however, playing cards could not be sold 'loose'; each deck consisted of a specific set of cards which had to be held together as a single unit. From the moment of their first collation into decks, therefore, the cards were packed in retaining wrappers. These bore the nominal maker's name rather than the shopkeeper's name. Playing cards may thus be seen as among the first – if not actually the first – manufacturer's pre-packaged products. In point of fact, many makers had their own shops, and some publishers (not themselves authorized *makers* – such as John Lenthall) did not give the name of the actual maker. From the late 17th century, novel packs were advertised in newspapers, which provide the best information for dating their first issue and the names of their makers/vendors.

As with snuff paper and TOBACCO PAPER, early playing-card wrappers carried a printed image in their centre with a broad margin to allow for folding round and under the contents. In the case of playing-card wrappers, because the dimensions of the contents were fixed, the central image conformed exactly to the format of the deck, and also included lateral side panels with text and end flaps with motifs.

The designs were robust woodcut images (executed presumably by the same hands that produced the cards themselves) and were printed in black, or, later, black and red. Early designs of wrappers for normal packs represented the 'marks' of the maker, referring to his shop sign and/or the quality of the products enclosed. The various qualities became known by popular names: 'Moguls', 'Harries', 'Highlanders', referring to the Great Mogul, Henry VIII, and the Valiant Highlander, still used in the mid 19th century. Pictorial packs had wrappers illustrating their subject matter. After 1828 makers had to register their wrapper designs at the Stamp Office. Gradually pictorial wrappers were replaced by ones simply carrying text.

The basic way of holding the wrapper in place was by a loop of thread. After 1711 the sealing label also covered parts of the thread, as specifically required by law. Even after 1862, when the entire pack in the maker's wrapper was sealed inside an official tax-wrapper, thread was still used around the internal wrapper. Paper wrappers and thread continued in use into the 20th century. Rigid cardboard slip-cases were in use by 1800, to be followed by boxes with push-on lids before 1828, and 'telescope' boxes and tuck-flap boxes made of thin folded card in the late 19th century.

By 1937, paper wrappers had given way to cellophane, which allowed the back design to be seen through the large oval aperture of the tax-wrapper. Various types of boxes were used, including boxes with hinged or drop-on padded lids. The simple tuck-flap box persists as the basic form of package. [MR/JB]

Pledge card

The pledge card provides testimony of a signatory's vow, notably of abstinence from alcoholic drink. The 'pledge' was a prominent feature of the temperance movement in mid-Victorian Britain, being frequently invoked as a means of instilling working-class discipline. It was the logical objective of campaigns carried out by numerous anti-drink organizations of the period.

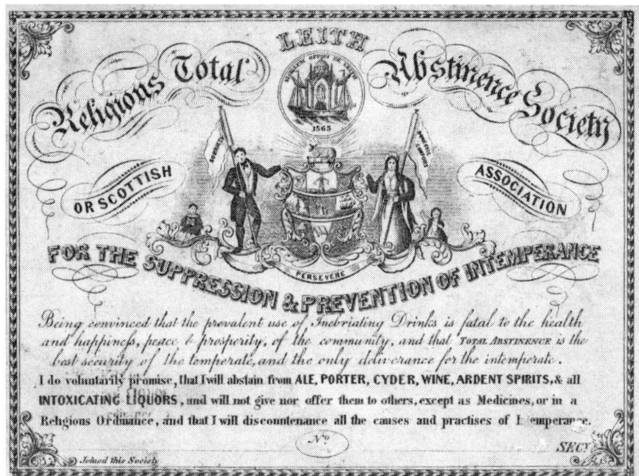

Pledge card of Leith Religious Total Abstinence Society, mid 19th century. Engraved (on stone?) by J. Carmichael. 94 × 127 mm (3¾ × 5 in)

The card appeared in many guises and sizes, but was invariably impressive. Wording varied greatly, but generally speaking the 'pledge' involved a 'promise to abstain from all intoxicating liquors as beverages' and that the signatory would 'neither give nor offer them to others'. The card was usually signed by the declarer and by the secretary or other official of the issuing body. In some cases the card bore graphic illustrations of the temptations of drink and its consequences, which were contrasted with others showing a golden drink-free future. In some cases, as in America, the certificate merely satisfied itself with a declaration of a signatory's membership of the total abstinence society, without commitment by one side or the other.

The pledge concept was later applied to other forms of promise. In World War I the National Boycott Pledge shows the figure of Britannia waving away a German sailing ship as it approaches. The pledge reads: 'I ... on my honour as a British Citizen solemnly pledge myself that for every month from the Date thereof that Germany continues the War I will not knowingly for one year buy enemy goods'. In similar vein a domestic window card announces: 'In Honour Bound we adopt the national scale of voluntary rations'.

See also TEMPERANCE PAPERS

Pocket mirror, advertising

Give-away pocket mirrors appeared in America at the beginning of the 20th century. They were at first paper-backed, and their publicity message was commonly a single-colour typographic legend showing little more than the advertiser's name and address. They were easily damaged, both by chipping of the mirror edge and by defacement or detachment of the backing. Efforts were made to improve the product by covering the backing with plain glass, thus sandwiching the paper message, but the problem was solved by the use of a printed celluloid 'casing' (a direct development of the method used in the production of the political pin-button).

The mirrors, mostly oval or circular, with backs printed by lithography in full colour, measured some 50–80 mm (2–3 in). Apart from the hazard of flammability, their life expectancy was much increased by the use of celluloid, and advertisers at every level distributed them in their thousands. As with the chromolithographed TRADE CARD, large-volume orders allowed commissioning of special artwork, but smaller advertisers could have standard pre-printed designs overprinted with their own message. Mirrors were given away by major advertisers – record companies, newspapers, shipping lines, etc. – and by local shops, hotels, and bars. Some bars distributed mirrors backed with risqué pictures, which were exchangeable as 5-cent tokens at the house in question.

Most of the designs were predictably crude, but there was also a wide field of 'respectable' female portraits in the chocolate-box idiom. A compromise middle ground was taken by offering 'old master' nudes. Many designs invited requests for further copies (at a few cents each), and some mirror manufacturers produced mirrors advertising themselves. Among recorded mirror manufacturers are Whitehead and Hoag Co., New Jersey; American Art Works, Ohio; Bastian Brothers, New York; Parisian Novelty Co., Chicago; Torsh and Franz, Baltimore; and the St Louis Button Company.

COLLECTION Warshaw Collection of Business Americana, Smithsonian Institution, Washington, DC

Point-of-sale display [plate 9b]

Earliest point-of-sale material stemmed from the use of product labelling on wooden boxes and cardboard cartons. A LABEL appeared not only for identification on the outer surface of the container but on the inside too, allowing the open lid of the container to serve as a sales aid. The device was to develop in the 1920s into an integral cardboard container with a cut-out motif in the lid, the cut-out forming a display unit when the forward flange of the lid was inserted behind the contents.

In addition to the WINDOW BILL and SHOWCARD a much-used point-of-sale display was the SHELF STRIP, a narrow printed pelmet for use on the front edge of shelves. These too were supplied by manufacturers. At first they carried a printed explanation on the back; one typical set of eight for the Allen Chocolate Co., dating from c. 1910, requested the 'customer' (i.e. the shopkeeper): 'Please fix this card strip by means of a couple of tacks to the edge of a shelf: it is hoped that customers will place the strip in a prominent position' (the last two words appear in capitals). The shelf pelmet appeared in card, metal, and, in the 1950s, in plastic.

Point-of-sale display material proliferated in the late 1920s, and shopkeepers received a continual flow of cardboard cut-outs, bottle and package crowners, and counter displays (many of them slotted, tabbed, and strutted) with diagrammatic instructions for their assembly. The 1950s and 1960s brought 'mobiles', hanging constructions consisting of threaded sets of cardboard cut-outs which moved with the flow of air.

With the advent of the supermarket and the demise of counter- and window-display techniques in grocery shops, point-of-sale ingenuity tended to move from display material to the package itself.

See also PACKAGING

Poison-gas papers

The development of war gases is reflected in the minor literature of the gas mask, specifically in military manuals, more generally in civilian and military instruction sheets.

The earliest British gas masks, used after the first German chlorine attack in April 1915, were little more than improvised pads of cotton, soaked in an unspecified chemical solution and held in place with ties over the nose and mouth. Printed instructions for their use – if any were issued – do not appear to have survived.

By the first days of June 1915, some five or six weeks later, the cotton pad or 'respirator' had been augmented by a so-called 'smoke helmet'. Printed instructions explained their use. The helmet, to be used first, was an all-enveloping head mask, the lower edges of which were to be tucked inside the shirt or tunic. The respirator, to be 'kept in reserve', was grasped at the pad by the teeth and tied back by 'veiling', covering the eyes. The instruction sheet was less than wholly encouraging: 'After it has been in use for some time, move the respirator to one side or the other so as to breathe through new portions of the cotton waste.... When the respirator no longer stops the entrance of the gas, apply a fresh one with the same precautions'.

Later instruction sheets, or 'gas defence cards', were more detailed and extensive, and showed some degree of confidence. The issue of March 1917 (SS 535) assured holders that they had 'nothing to fear from a gas attack, (a) if your respirator or helmet is in good order, (b) if you remain calm and carry out the measures in which you have been instructed'. An issue of January 1918, directed at officers, concerned previous gas defence cards and provided some 1500 words of instruction on drill and inspection.

The gas mask came to the civilian in the late 1930s. Britain's first civil defence anti-gas school opened in March 1936, and by the end of 1938 some 38 million people had been supplied with gas masks. 'Public Information Leaflet No 2, Your gas mask – masking your windows' was issued from the office of the Lord Privy Seal in July 1939; additional leaflets and booklets, official and commercial, gave advice on gas-proofing air-raid shelters, anti-gas clothing, gas detection and identification, and decontamination.

Instructions for the use and care of the civilian gas mask were printed on the underside of the cardboard carrying case supplied with it, and special instructions accompanied the masks devised for babies, small children, and invalids. Instruction sheets also advised on the gas-proofing of kennels, stables, cow byres, etc.

Poor-law papers

The term 'poor law' is no longer in use in Britain (and was at no time current in America), but for the ephemerist the expression 'poor-law papers' is taken to apply to items relating to locally administered measures of poor relief from 1572, when Britain's poor laws were instituted, to 1948 when they were suspended by centrally organized schemes of relief.

The ephemera of 'poor relief' reflect the principles attending its historical development. These are numerous, often mixed, sometimes mutally inconsistent and, from time to time, reflect different priorities.

One basic principle is that poor relief must seek to assuage not only hunger but anger: below certain levels of deprivation, the destitute become dangerous. Poor relief also assuages pangs of conscience: 'People ought not to be allowed to suffer'; 'Something must be done'. It must, in another aspect, be finely tuned to economic climate: relief must be seen to offer living standards distinctly lower than those obtaining generally. If it does not it will be abused, overloaded, and destroyed. In addition, it was held that abandonment of the notion of individual self-support would weaken the economy at large; relief must therefore err rather on the side of meanness than of generosity.

A final consideration requires that each locality should be responsible for its own poor only: a tendency to offer relief to outsiders would invite a general 'foisting off' of problems by one area upon another. It is on this last matter that the ephemera of poor relief most noticeably dwell. 'Settlement' was the term applied to the accepted domicile of the destitute, and little or nothing could be done for applicants until this point was established: in which locality were they legally resident? whose problem were they?

In a typical document (a part-printed four-page form, folded to foolscap) the story is traced of John Davis and his two children who, on 8 December 1760, were apprehended by the constable in the parish of Camberwell, Surrey, and brought to a Justice of the Peace as vagabonds. In a sworn deposition, signed with a cross, John Davis declares that the place of his last legal settlement was the parish of Ransputhwait [probably a corrupt Anglicization of Llansbyddyd] in Brecknockshire [Powis], Wales. The form elsewhere addresses sundry constables and overseers of the poor to 'convey the said vagabond (with his said children) to the parish of (St Magnus, London Bridge) that being the first parish through which (they) ought to pass in the next direct way to the parish of (Ransputhwait [?]) to which they are to be sent…'. The form goes on to instruct all officers along the route that Davis and his children are to be conveyed, together with the document duly annotated, out of each intermediate precinct successively until the party reaches its approved destination in Brecknockshire. Dog-eared and torn from its passage from hand to hand, the document carries the handwritten endorsement of each intermediate authority between Camberwell and Brecknockshire, dated and signed, requesting that the party be similarly passed forward. The paper records that Davis and his children arrived at their destination on Christmas day 1760, the 160-mile journey having taken sixteen days.

The matter of 'settlement' preoccupied local authorities and the poor in equal measure. Parish officers ('selectmen' in America) were in general as anxious to deny it as the applicant was to acquire it. In many cases the matter resolved itself into a dispute between one parish and another, each claiming the other to be responsible; in the meantime, pending resolution of the matter, maintenance of the pauper would be recorded as a charge against the parish allegedly responsible.

In a part-printed single sheet quarto form of 1842, the Overseers of the Poor of Bristol, Maine, are informed by those of Hallowell that 'An Inhabitant of your town (has) now become chargeable in this town as (a) Pauper. We conceive it necessary to give you this information, and to request that you order (his) removal, or otherwise provide for (him) as you may judge expedient. We have charged the expense of (his) support, which has already arisen, to your town, and shall continue so to do, so long as we are obliged to furnish (him) with supplies'.

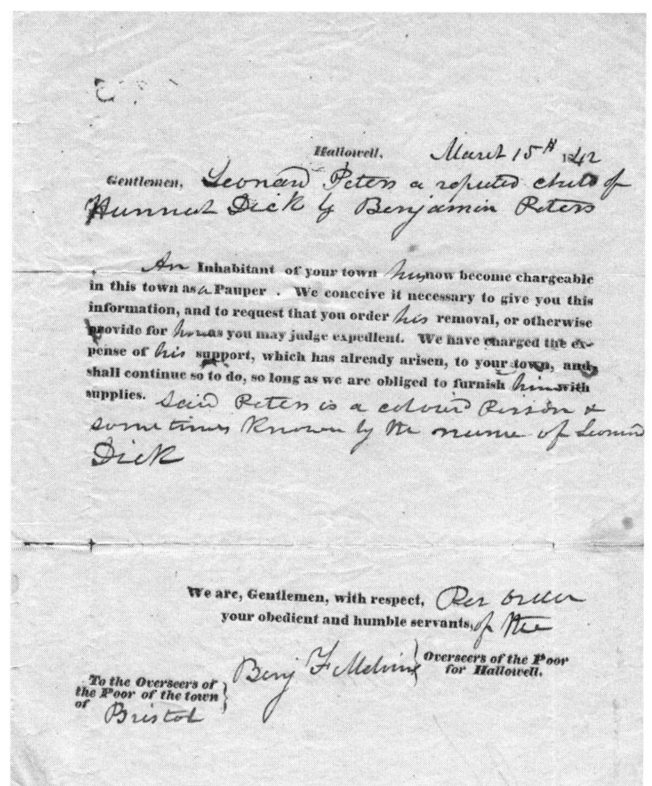

Hallowell, March 15th 1842

Gentlemen, Leonard Peters a reputed child of Hannah Dick by Benjamin Peters

An Inhabitant of your town has now become chargeable in this town as a Pauper. We conceive it necessary to give you this information, and to request that you order his removal, or otherwise provide for him as you may judge expedient. We have charged the expense of his support, which has already arisen, to your town, and shall continue so to do, so long as we are obliged to furnish him with supplies. Said Peters is a coloured Person & sometimes Known by the name of Leonard Dick

We are, Gentlemen, with respect, Per order your obedient and humble servants, of the Overseers of the Poor for Hallowell.

Benj F. Melvin

To the Overseers of the Poor of the town of Bristol

Notification from the Overseers of the Poor for Hallowell to the Overseers of the Poor for Bristol, Maine, concerning responsibility for a pauper, 1842. Letterpress and manuscript. 220 × 190 mm (8⅝ × 7½ in)

The 'inhabitant' named in the Hallowell form was an illegitimate child, a class of citizen of perennial concern to local authorities, and for whom pre-printed poor-law FORMS amply provide. In Britain in 1845 the number of such forms, each covering a special contingency in the matter of bastardy, was twenty-four. A parliamentary statistical return for 1834–37 showed the number of pauper marriages in a group of fifteen Cambridgeshire parishes as totalling 226; illegitimate births in the same period were 84.

See also BASTARDY PAPERS

Postal diagnosis

The postal diagnosis was a well-established instrument of the 19th-century quack medicine business, by which customers were invited to write an account of their complaints in their own words or, more conveniently, to supply yes/no answers to a questionnaire. In return they received an assurance that their case would respond to the therapy offered, together with injunctions to speedy action while the complaint was still treatable.

A typical response, from the Institution for the Cure of Deafness and Nervous Complaints, 9 Suffolk Place, Pall Mall, London, was posted on 11 December 1854 by Francis Robert Hoghton MD, 'Consulting Surgeon to the above Institution', Member of the London Royal College of Surgeons and Licentiate of the Apothecaries' Company. The letter, in the neatest and most legible of clerkly hands, reads as follows:

> I have given your Answers due consideration. It is my candid opinion that your Case will speedily yield to the Curative Principle lately discovered and practised only by Myself. It is one that I am daily I may say hourly in the habit of meeting with and in such scarcely an instance has occurred of failure, The majority of Cases being of a more inveterate nature than

the one described, the treatment is easy and can be applied by the most nervous or timid person without assistance and the benefit is great and immediately experienced it enables Persons extremely Deaf to hear with ease the usual tone Conversation at a great distance and permanently removes all distressing noises in the head and ringing in the ears. My charge for forwarding the means of cure in the case described will be £1.2/-. On receipt of that sum by Post Office Money Order or Postage stamps the same will be sent with plain directions for use to effect a perfect and permanent cure. I beg to remain Yrs respectfully F R Hoghton. PS The description of your case is entered in the Patient's Book, and if the means are applied as I will direct I can guarantee a perfect cure. Your early reply to this letter will oblige.

Though typically a product of the second half of the 19th century, the postal diagnosis survived in some areas into the 1930s. Telephone and internet diagnosis, introduced by the National Health Service in Britain at the close of the 20th century, provides an echo of the practice.

See also QUACK ADVERTISING

Postal history

Postal history relates to the carriage of letters in every aspect, including the use of postage stamps. Philately is the study of adhesive postage stamps and is concerned with values, shades of colour, printing methods, plate numbers, etc. Though closely related, and in some cases apparently overlapping, the two fields are commonly seen as separate. The subject matter in both cases is unarguably ephemeral. Philately cannot be viewed as a subsection or constituent part of any other field, and the same may strictly be said of postal history, which is also regarded as a speciality in its own right. In the case of postal history, however, a very broad coverage includes not only postal markings and endorsements on lettersheets and envelopes, postal rates, and seals, but much peripheral documentation: waybills, postmasters' reports and returns, postal-rate tables, broadsides, notices, and many other mail-related items.

Postal history ephemera may be reviewed in the following terms:

Post haste letter. Letters despatched by messenger or other private instrument in early times bore a manuscript note indicating degrees of urgency. Typical, in Britain, was the 17th-century expression 'Hast hast hast post with all speede' – the English version of the Latin 'Cito, cito, cito, citissime, volantissime' (swiftly, swiftly, swiftly, most swiftly, fly!) of the 13th and 14th centuries. Added inducements to speed included indications of the maximum allowable changes of horse on the journey ('stirrup' signs, penned in multiples), and in some cases the requirement that the messenger should endorse the correspondence with arrival times at points along the route. An additional inducement, appearing on some military and other state messages, was a penned symbol showing gallows – a warning of the consequence of failure. A small feather, fixed by the stalk in the sealing wax of a letter, was also used in some countries as an indication of urgency, suggesting that the carrier should 'fly' on his mission (*see* FEATHER LETTER).

'Private' post items. Special postal services were set up by members of institutions, trades, and other bodies – among them, initially, the royal court, monasteries, universities, merchants' guilds, as well as noble families who organized their own

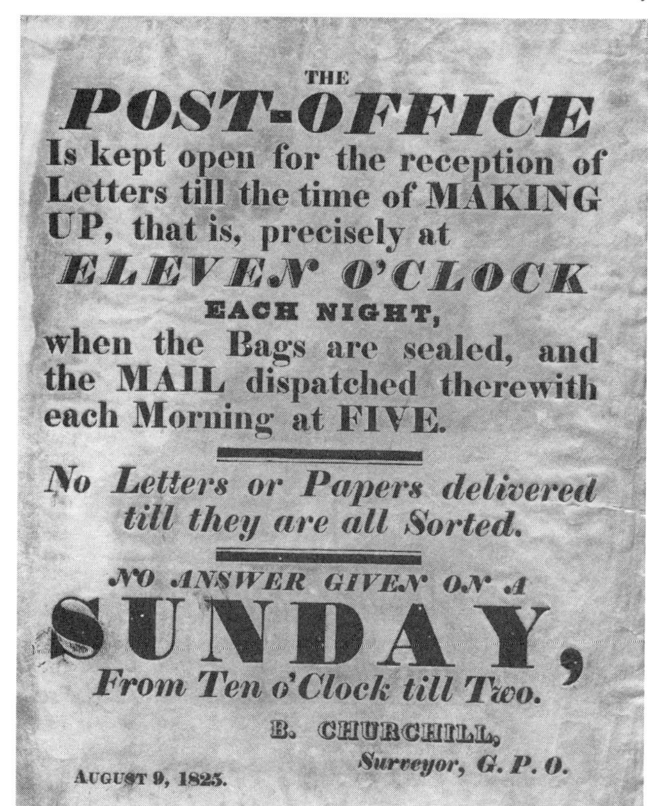

Post-office notice, 9 August 1825. Letterpress on bright orange stained paper. 332 × 275 mm (13⅛ × 10¾ in)

postal systems, charging generally by weight and distance (*see* UNIVERSITY MAIL). These posts were not unprofitable, and were often extended for the use of private persons.

Among examples of private post are those of the Viscontis and Sforzas in Milan in the 14th and 15th centuries and of the family of Della Torre e Tasso, whose postal services, started in Milan in the 15th century, spread through most of Europe. By the middle of the 18th century the enterprise was said to have 20,000 employees, and it lasted until the 1860s.

Other special postal systems, licensed by government but organized by individuals, include the 'Petite poste' of Paris, instituted under a privilege of Louis XIV by Renouard de Villayer in Paris in 1653 (of whose system of *Billets de port payé* unfortunately no trace remains), and the *Zemstvo* system in mid 19th-century Russia, in which an independent postal service extended the national network from towns to villages. London saw the inception of a penny-post system by William Dockwra, who provided a private service for the capital alone in 1680 (the national postal service operated only between London and the provinces at the time).

America's early postal history presents a somewhat similar pattern, with 'private' mails organized by ordinary citizens – often to evade the charges (and the postal censorship) imposed by the British. In 1692 an Act establishing a General Letter Office in New York imposed a substantial fine on anyone competing with the established postal service; nevertheless much correspondence continued 'out of the mails'.

In the 1860s American expansion into the West brought an intensive interest in communications. Private express companies vied with the United States Postal Services in letter carrying. Chief among these were such names as Adams, American, Majors & Waddell, National, Russel, and Wells Fargo. April

1860 saw the introduction of the Pony Express, the famous pony relay, which covered the 2000-mile run from St Joseph, Missouri, to San Francisco in ten and a half days (though it was superseded within 18 months by competition from the transcontinental telegraph).

Among more recent 'private' postal services have been those introduced by private enterprise, initially to replace national services withdrawn through strike action. Such services have grown considerably since the 1980s, particularly for urgent mail, though they have not yet replaced a national mail service in Britain or many other countries.

Private postal systems of every kind have used distinctive marks. By handwritten endorsement, handstamp, label, special postage stamp, or by provision of distinctive covers, each has recognizable signs and symbols, and the study and interpretation of these is part of the province of the postal historian.

'Unusual carrier' items. Mail has been carried by virtually every form of transport. Among less orthodox methods are balloon, pigeon, rocket, pneumatic tube, and tin can. Balloon mail had its first serious application in the Paris siege of 1870–71, when balloon mail from the city bore the printed cover line 'Par ballon monté'. In 1877 Samuel Archer King dropped stamped mail from a balloon over Gallatin, Tennessee; at least one item, addressed to Mrs Leonora Davies, of Harrodsburg, Kentucky, is known to have reached its destination. The cover bore the handwritten endorsement: 'Any one finding this will please put it in the nearest post office'.

Rocket-post trials in Austria and elsewhere in the 1930s brought their own small contribution of special covers (as did the Apollo11 and 15 moon-landings of 1969 and 1971).

Pneumatic-tube transmission, in which message-containers are pushed or pulled through tubes by air-pressure, has been in more or less continuous use since the middle of the 19th century. The first fully operational system was opened in London by the Electric and International Telegraph Co. in 1853, and similar systems, some of which remained in use in the late 20th century, appeared in Paris and other European centres and also in New York, Brooklyn, Boston, Chicago, St Louis, and Philadelphia. Some of these were used for public postal services, notably the one in Paris, which was inaugurated in 1866. Pneumatic letter-cards (*see* CARTE PNEUMATIQUE) were inserted in the City's 'ring' circuit, to be delivered locally by messenger immediately on arrival.

Among others in the 'unusual carrier' field is the tin-can mail. This originated on the island of St Kilda off Western Scotland in the latter part of the 19th century, when a marooned seaman successsfully floated a 'Mayday' message to the mainland in a miniature boat. The idea was adopted by the island's later inhabitants and tourist mailings continue in this way, letters in the special container bearing the rubber-stamped legend 'St Kilda tin can mail'. Another tin-can service was operating in the 1920s and 1930s from Niuafo'ou, an island in the Tonga group, where covers bore special handstamps and printed explanatory matter.

See also CACHET, POSTAL; COVER, POSTAL; DISINFECTED MAIL; FREE FRANK; MULREADY ENVELOPE; PARLIAMENTARY ENVELOPE; POSTAL LABEL; POSTAL STATIONERY; POSTAL SWINDLE; POSTAL-STRIKE LABEL; POSTCARD

REFERENCE Howard Robinson, *The British Post Office: a History* (Connecticut: Princeton University Press, 1948; reprinted Greenwood Press, 1970)

Postal label

The term postal label or etiquette refers to official labels of information or instruction affixed to postal items in addition to postal stamps. The term thus covers such categories as air mail, registration, express, and special delivery, but it excludes propaganda, advertising, commemorative and other non-official and postally irrelevant labels.

The earliest known referrence to a postal label, 'a label annexed to the packet', appears in 1582 in *Orders set Downe by Commandement of the Quenes Ma[jes]tie,* (SP 15 XXVIIA 124; SP 12 CLXX, 7). Among other things, such labels instruct postmasters to use 'a label of parchment or paper wherein the packet may be wrapped'. On the label, rather than on the packet itself, would be written the date and hour of its acceptance; these details would also be entered in a register, together with a description of the packet, as a permanent record of the service. In any subsequent query, the evidence of the label would make the matter easier to investigate. The concept of registration is already present in this instruction.

Registration (originally without compensation for loss) effectively begins with the 'money letter' of 1792. Under this system, letters were separately handled and their progress through sorting points was recorded in a written register. Various forms of outer wrapper later came into use, and in the late 1850s the blue-line indicator was introduced. The world's first registered envelope, bearing an embossed twopenny stamp and the words 'For registration only' was introduced in 1878. Adhesive stamps, to the amount required, were affixed to the envelope.

The registration postal label first appeared in Germany in 1870, and the idea was quickly adopted elsewhere. By the early 1880s labels were in widespread use in parts of Europe and the United States. France and Britain, however, followed later; France in 1900, Britain in 1907.

The basic design of the label was standardized by the Universal Postal Union Congress of 1882. Essentially, the design includes the name of the accepting office, the serial number of the letter as entered in the record, and a large capital R, commonly (but not invariably) at the left-hand side of the label. The whole is enclosed in a box rule, often with additional rules dividing the elements of the copy. In rare labels, especially in early examples, there was some attempt to produce elegant lettering and layout.

The printing of many later labels is perfunctory, and examples are found in which the image was simply handstamped and the serial number entered by hand. Colours are commonly blue or black, with occasional use of red as a second colour and of colour-tinted paper.

The air-mail label may be said to have had its origins in a form of label used on 26 February 1912, when postal items were flown between Boek and Brück, Germany, by Hans Grade. The label bore a decorative frame showing the countryside as seen from the air, the title 'Flugpost' (air mail), and a space for affixing the postage stamp. The expression 'Par avion' (by aeroplane) was first used as a handstamp on mail flown from Villacoubray to Bordeaux in October 1913, but it was in August 1918 that the first printed *par avion* label appeared. It was introduced by the French for a flight between Paris and St Nazaire. In conformity with the Universal Postal Union agreement that French be used as the officially recognized language, the words 'Par avion' have been in general use since that time (though single-language non-French versions are sometimes to be found). Semi-official air-mail labels have also appeared on experimental mails. Two from Austria, c.1930, are notable: one, in white letters on red, reads 'Mit Lufttorpedo/Par Aerotorpedo' (by air torpedo); another, in red and blue on tissue, 'Mit Rakatenpost/Katapultflug (by rocket post/catapult flight). Blue has been a dominant colour for the labels throughout the period, but earlier European issues appeared in black on colour-tinted paper.

Express labels may be said to owe their origin to the 18th-century Scandinavian FEATHER LETTER. They appear to have been introduced in central Europe in the 1880s, with, soon afterwards, the addition of the French word 'Exprès' to be adopted as an internationally recognized service by the Universal Postal Union. Early specimens bear single-language legends: 'Durch Eilboten' (German: By express messenger); 'Expressz' (Hungarian); and sometimes two-language (non-French) renderings: 'Durch Eilboten/Spěšně' (German/Czech). The United States adopted the system in 1885, and Britain in 1891.

A number of other categories of postal label, in use at various periods in Europe but virtually unknown elsewhere, are the following: 'Inconnu', 'Unbekannt', 'Neznámý' (Unknown); 'Parti', 'Elköltözött', 'Otputovao', 'Abgereist', 'Partito' (Gone away); 'Refusé', 'Nicht angenommen', 'Ne Prima', 'Nepřijato', 'Nem Fogadta el' (Refused); 'Non réclamé', 'Nicht gehoben', 'Nicht abgeholt', 'Nijetražio', 'Nevyžádáno' (Unclaimed); 'Décédé', 'Meghalt', 'Zemřel' (Deceased). These labels, in most cases bearing two words (the local rendering followed by the French translation) have survived in some numbers, but the full complement remains to be recorded.

Labels used for sealing letters damaged in transit were introduced in the United States in 1877, and also in Cuba and Mexico. It is not clear when the labels began to be used for this purpose in Britain.

Parcel-post labels appeared in Britain in August 1883. They bore the name of the specific post office concerned, and included spaces for the insertion of charges, code number, postage stamps, and date-stamp. In later versions the name of the issuing office was omitted, all offices using a standard label. In the United States a general parcel post was inaugurated on 1 January 1913 with a set of special postage stamps for use on parcels. The stamps proved unsatisfactory since the twelve denominations, though pictorially different, were of the same colour: carmine. Six months later, after much confusion, ordinary stamps were decreed valid for parcels. Parcel post labels were never used in the United States.

Censors' labels, used to reseal letters after interception, and generally bearing the examining officer's number, appeared on mail in World Wars I and II.

Postal stationery

Prepaid postal stationery was introduced in Britain with the MULREADY ENVELOPE in May 1840. This was replaced by an envelope bearing a pink embossed postage stamp of the Queen engraved by William Wyon, and a reticulated oval border (the work of Alfred Deacon), in the upper portion of which were the words 'Postage one penny'. Other values in a series from a halfpenny to one shilling appeared at intervals in the period 1841 to 1876. Changes of colour and shape provided distinction between values, and in most cases code-number signs in borders indicated the die number and date of issue. Envelopes embossed with a stamp appeared at first only in the official penny, twopenny, twopence halfpenny, and threepenny values, but with the introduction in 1855 of 'stamping to order' other values and value combinations appeared. Stamping to order allowed envelope manufacturers and stationers – and later postcard producers – to have their own materials embossed for postage.

As with tax-bearing papers, paper was brought to the Stamp Office to receive the designated impression. At a later stage, to relieve mounting congestion in the Stamp Office, arrangements were made for the embossing of stationery on manufacturers' own premises. This development led in turn to the introduction of the ADVERTISING RING (EMBOSSED), an added embossed collar featuring the special stamp. These were impressed as additions to ready-stamped stationery or incorporated with the official die for simultaneous stamping.

The registered envelope, embossed with a stamp, was introduced to Britain in 1878. Initially, the embossing appeared on the flap at the rear, representing a registration fee of twopence. Adhesive stamps, in payment of the normal postage charge, were affixed to the front. In later issues the embossed stamp appeared on the front, additional stamps being affixed beside it.

The prepaid POSTCARD was first sold in Britain on 1 October 1870, the year following its introduction in Austria-Hungary, where it had appeared at the insistence of Emanuel Herrmann and, earlier, Heinrich von Stephan. Printed in the normal letterpress manner or lithographed, it had a universal vogue. It was taken up by the North German Confederation and Switzerland in 1870; by Belgium, Denmark, Holland, Norway, and Sweden in 1871; Russia in 1872; and by France, Italy, Romania, Serbia, Spain, and the United States in 1873.

In Britain printed postcards, stamped to order at the Stamp Office, were sanctioned in June 1872. Stamping to order was also introduced in America at about this time. Wells Fargo, providers of a long-distance pony express, carried mail in envelopes bearing their own printed prepayment frank and the US Post Office embossed stamp. Adhesive stamps were added as needed to make up a given total.

The prepaid envelope, embossed with a stamp, had appeared in America in 1853, printed under contract by George F. Nesbitt

Pre-stamped British envelope for foreign postage, with a package band for a set of ten. The stamp embossed and printed grey/blue, 1890s. The envelope 78 × 139 mm (3⅛ × 5½ in)

& Co. First to go on sale were 3-cent and 6-cent values. The 10-cent version was available on the introduction of the 3000-mile rate in 1855. The embossings were similar in style to the British penny and twopence design, a white portrait head of Abraham Lincoln appearing within a reticulated oval frame.

In July 1875 Britain introduced the 'foreign postcard' for transmission abroad at the rate of one-penny-farthing, which was half the General Postal Union rate of twopence halfpenny for letters. This was superseded in 1878 when, with the inauguration of the Universal Postal Union, two classes of destination were recognized: 'A' and 'B'. The 'A' card cost one penny, the 'B' card three halfpence, both prepaid.

Letter-cards, folded and sealed at the edges with a perforated gummed strip, were first suggested by Akin Karoly of Belgium in 1882. They appeared in Britain in February 1892. In France, the letter-card also appeared as an advertising medium, the inside and rear pages being given over to advertisements which subsidized the purchase. This accounts for the official 15-centime stamp appearing with the words 'vendue 5 centimes'.

The letter-card principle was also used in Paris for the city's pneumatic post (*see* POSTAL HISTORY). Known as CARTES PNEUMATIQUES, and printed with a prepaid stamp, these sealed cards were sent in capsules through a system of air tubes between designated post offices. Delivery from the distant post office was by special messenger, free of charge. Similar systems operated at various periods in France, Germany, Austria, Italy, and – for bulk mail – Britain. In America, pneumatic postal tubes were installed in several towns, those in Boston and New York remaining in operation until 1950.

See also PARLIAMENTARY ENVELOPE; POSTCARD

REFERENCES H. Dagnall, *The Evolution of British Stamped Postcards & Letter Cards: their History & Documentation* (Edgware: The Author, 1985); A. K. Huggins, *British Postal Stationery* (London: Great Britain Philatelic Society, 1970, reprinted with amendments, 1971)

Postal swindle

A common feature of the 19th century was the fraudulent use of the mails. The best-known example of this kind was the begging letter: couched in respectful terms and written in a literate hand, it requested financial help for the victim of misfortune. The common denominator of all such items is the slenderness of the thread of introduction.

Henry Mayhew (1862, vol. 4, pp. 404–5) quotes an example: 'Although I have not the honour to be personally acquainted with you, I have had the advantage of an introduction to a member of your family, Major Sherbrook, when with his regiment at Malta…'. The point of contact is invariably not immediately verifiable and is often a friend or relative now dead. The link is established by the writer through discreet enquiry or by the study of press obituaries. Such letters proceed to relate a harrowing story of ill-luck and finally of swelled pride in this last despairing hope of help. There are decently restrained allusions to acts of assistance rendered by the writer to the relative referred to, together with glowing reports of the addressee's reputation for kindness. The gambit had limited variations and was operated by many practitioners as a full-time occupation. In many cases a successful first request was followed by others, increasingly engaging the commitment of the recipient in the writer's unfolding tale of disaster.

In another form of fraud the writer professed to hold information to the advantage of his victim: 'Sir, I am in possession of a List of Unclaimed Dividends, Legacies, etc etc amounting to 150 Million Pounds which I have compilled [sic] at great expence from various Public Documents. I notice one sum or more due to you, which I am willing to impart on Payment of 20/- for my trouble…'.

See also QUACK ADVERTISING

REFERENCE Henry Mayhew, *London Labour and the London Poor*, 4 vol. (London: Griffin, Bohn, 1862)

Postal-strike label

Private postal services, brought into being through disruption of normal services in industrial disputes, normally adopt an *ad hoc* stamping device. This may be a manuscript annotation, a rubber stamp, or an adhesive label.

The stamp commonly takes the form of a label. For reasons of economy, many issues have been printed on ordinary paper for pasting, but many are also found on adhesive paper. Few are perforated or printed in more than one colour (a second-colour ingredient is often provided by the use of coloured paper). Unornamented typography is common, though in strikes lasting long enough to allow for their preparation, pictorial designs have also appeared.

Pictorial issues tend to reflect the interests of the organizations issuing them. For example, a 'Soho Local Post' issue, produced in London's sex-shop area, featured a drawing of a female nude. Prominent users are printers and publishers; philatelic dealers seeking to create new stock-in-trade are not uncommon. Other pictorial issues have come from film companies, taxi services, newsagents, political parties, filling stations, schools, scout groups, bus companies, local authorities, philatelic societies, public relations consultants, employment agencies, hotels, churches, and private individuals. Many designs are based on 19th-century images, implying a return to simpler technologies. One set, issued in Britain during a postal strike, and showing a horse postman and an early steam train, is based on an 1876 American embossed envelope design commemorating Independence (1776).

The earliest postal-strike label appears to be one issued by the Fresno–San Francisco Bicycle Post in 1894. In France the Chamber of Commerce at Amiens operated a strike post and issued a stamp in 1909, and there have been later issues in Australia, Austria, China, France, Italy, and other countries.

The issues of Canada and Britain are those most commonly found. Disruptions in the Canadian postal systems have been frequent, and many of the major Canadian strikes have produced private stamp issues. In Britain, the disputes of 1962 and 1964, and especially that of 1971, brought forth numerous issues. In the 1971 strike the Post Office monopoly, hitherto rigidly enforced, was waived, and private posts were authorized on application to local postmasters. The matter of authorization may be regarded as academic, however. Many private posts, which performed a valuable service, did not seek authorization – and were not in fact closed down.

In many cases the aim was clearly to provide specimens for collectors, and the claim that the issue was 'authorized' may have been thought to lend weight to its value as a philatelic item. The collector has in mind too items which, though date-cancelled ('Emergency postal service'), have only rarely been used in the transmission of mail. It is noticeable that the overwhelming majority of surviving specimens are unused.

Britain's 1971 postal dispute, which lasted for seven weeks, generated the largest volume of private issues ever recorded. The figure remains largely conjectural, but is estimated to be in the region of 700.

REFERENCES A. Blair (ed.), *Stamp Year Book* (Croydon: 1972); A. Bondi, *Catalogue des Timbres de Grève des Postes* (Lyon: 1977); G. Migliavacca, *Francobolli e Timbri dello Sciopero Postale Inglese* (Turin: 1973); O. W. Newport, *The People's League Stamps and Markings* (Sidcup: The Author, 1962); Gerald Rosen, *Catalogue of British Postal Strike Stamps* (London: B.L.S.C. Publishing, 1971)

SOCIETY Cinderella Stamp Club (British Private Post Study Group)

Postcard

Pictorial postcards may be said to take their origins from the illustrated stationery of the Victorian era, when the pictorial element in personal correspondence became increasingly dominant (*see* WRITING PAPER, ILLUSTRATED).

At its inception, the postcard was proposed as a non-personal card. Heinrich von Stephan, an official in the postal service of the North German Confederation, proposed in 1865 a *Postblatt*, or 'post sheet', a plain card ready printed with a postage stamp and bearing on one side space for the address and on the other for the message. The idea in modified form had already occurred to John P. Charlton of Philadelphia, who obtained a copyright in 1861 for an unstamped postal card. Charlton's copyright passed to Hyman Lipman, who printed and published items as 'Lipman's Postal Cards', and continued to do so until the introduction of the first US Post Office prepaid cards in 1873.

Stephan's proposal for an unstamped postal card was rejected by his post office authorities. But a suggestion for a stamped card, submitted independently in 1869 by Emanuel Herrmann of Vienna, succeeded (*see* POSTAL STATIONERY). Postal authorities in various countries adopted the principle: after Austria in 1869 came Switzerland, Germany, and the United Kingdom (1870); Belgium, Canada, Denmark, Holland, Norway, and Sweden (1871); Russia (1872); and France, Italy, Romania, Serbia, Spain, and the United States (1873). In most countries, particularly in Britain, regulations concerning use of the postal card were complex and subject to frequent change. But over the next few years the success of the idea and its obvious benefit to postal revenue brought relaxation. By the end of the century postal authorities everywhere were accepting cards bearing an adhesive stamp, and measuring 90 × 140 mm (3½ × 5½ in). The address was restricted to one side and the message or picture to the other. In 1902 the backs of British postcards were divided, allowing for both message and address; other countries had adopted this approach by 1907.

German printers and publishers led the way in exploiting the new medium, and by 1908/9 the picture postcard craze was putting 860 million postcards through the British postal system every week. It is safe to say that the majority of these were sent not for their message but for their novelty. Before long, recipients realized that they were accumulating 'collections' of postcards, and the postcard album made its appearance. The presence of the album generated designs for additional cards, and many millions were bought and included without passing through the post.

The picture postcard soon became 'collectable'. Its status in the field of ephemera, as with CIGARETTE CARDS and other such items, is therefore ambiguous. The craze developed its own connoisseurs' clubs, whose journals encouraged collecting zeal.

Advances in mass-printing led to cheaper cards and higher sales, and by the outbreak of World War I the picture postcard had become an international institution. In every country soldiers left behind them photographs of themselves – produced by the photographer on a 'postcard' to add to the album. The 1914–18 war brought a new genre of card – the photomontage – in which the soldier's dream of home appears as a vision above his head. This was a respectable development of the 'naughty' French postcard, whose photographic fantasies also remained available for private acquisition. Another postcard feature of the period was the embroidered card, also a product of France (*see* SILK).

Folding postcards published by Manhattan Post Card Co., New York, late 1920s. Letterpress half-tone printed in black, with added colour workings. Both approx. 420 × 90 mm (16½ × 3½ in)

Advertisers were not slow to exploit the postcard's opportunities. With potential advertising space available free of charge in everybody's album, they produced large quantities of cards – many in collectable numbered 'sets', to encourage addiction. Typical, in Britain, were those produced by the Shell Petroleum Co., whose 1910–14 series numbered 100. (Some thirty-six of the series had a collectors' rerun in the late 1970s and early 1980s: the reproductions are distinguishable from the originals, if not by their printing quality, by the presence of the words 'Copyright Reserved').

Postcard collecting categories include such varied subjects as actresses, rail disasters, churches, hospital wards, windmills, airships, and shop fronts. Collections are also made of cards by named publishers or artists; cards relating to special regions; and cards produced by specific processes. Also collected are advertising and propaganda cards, risqué and obscene cards, and novelty cards of every description, including 'mechanical' cards, HOLD-TO-LIGHT cards, concertina pull-out view cards, fold-out cards, real-hair cards (in which a portrait is provided with actual hair), and cards printed on metal, wood, leather, and other materials.

As in some other collecting areas (notably series of GIVE-AWAYS), postcard collecting in the late 20th century saw a steady trend toward a structure of market values, publishing of price catalogues, and research into the full complement of issues in given collections. For curatorial and collecting purposes we may distinguish a number of clearly marked sectors. Among the more interesting are the so-called 'globetrotter' cards, souvenir postcards sold ostensibly to help meet the expenses of long-distance travellers. There was a vogue for these in Europe at the end of the 20th century: students, journalists, and married couples carried with them supplies of cards outlining plans for round-the-world journeys or treks into little-known parts, using them to appeal for funds to keep going. The cards bore half-tone pictures of the travellers, often in commanding poses, backed by a paragraph or so of promotional copy.

A further unusual category is the so-called TALL-TALE POSTCARD. This appeared in America in the period 1905 to 1915. It flourished at a time when simple photographic trickery, while partly accepted as such, still had the power to surprise. Thus came pictures of gigantic fish being landed by diminutive anglers, as well as corncobs ten feet long being hauled by teams of horses.

See also SECONDARY USES OF EPHEMERA; SPORTS PAPERS; VIEW CARD

REFERENCES Jefferson R. Burdick, *Pioneer Post Cards* (Franklin Square, NY: Nostalgia Press, 1964); Anthony Byatt, *Picture Postcards and their Publishers* (Malvern: Golden Age Postcard Books, 1978); A. W. Coysh, *The Dictionary of Picture Postcards in Britain 1899–1939* (Woodbridge: Antique Collectors Club, 1984); Tonie and Valmai Holt, *Picture Postcards of the Golden Age: a Collector's Guide* (London: Postcard Publishing Company, 1978); Frank Staff, *The Picture Postcard and its Origins*, 2nd edn (London: Lutterworth, 1979)

Poster [plates 6, 7, 16]

The poster has been viewed as a collector's item since the end of the 19th century, but the collector's life has been complicated by the fact that, once pasted up, the poster is effectively rendered inaccessible. Apart from illicit removal while still freshly posted (common practice in Paris in the 1890s), printers' and publishers' files have been the chief avenue of acquisition. There is thus, in any collection of posters, an inbuilt element of artificiality: few, if any, of the conserved specimens have actually fulfilled their role as posters.

The origins of the poster may be traced to the printed PROCLAMATION and PUBLIC NOTICE of the 15th century. Caxton's printed advertisement for a newly-published prayer book, posted up at Westminster in 1477, may be described as one of the first commercial posters. The pictorial poster emerged only slowly, starting in the late 18th century in Europe with army recruiting posters. At first they were in black and white, later in a single colour, or coloured by hand; they acquired full colour as a general rule only in the last quarter of the 19th century with the widespread use of colour lithography.

In France, Honoré Daumier and Paul Gavarni had designed posters in the 1830s and 1840s, but the heyday of the *belle époque* brought to the hoardings such names as Louis Anquetin, Pierre Bonnard, Jules Chéret, Alfred Choubrac, Jean-Louis Forain, Eugène Grasset, Henri-Gabriel Ibels, Henri de Toulouse-Lautrec, Édouard Manet, Alphonse Mucha, Jean Paléologue, Théophile Steinlen, Félix Vallotton, and Adolphe Willette.

In Britain the same impulse produced a less brilliant and rather later list of designers, among them Aubrey Beardsley, the Beggarstaff Brothers, and Dudley Hardy. America's contribution (also a little later) consisted of Elisha Bird, Will Bradley, Claude Bragdon, Will Carqueville, Edward Penfield, Charles Dana Gibson, Frank Hazenplug, Louis Rhead, Maxfield Parrish, Ethel Reed, and Charles Woodbury. In Italy leading names were Giovanni Beltrami, Luigi Bompard, Giovanni-Battista Carpanetto, Marcello Dudovich, R. Franzoni, Riccardo Galli, Adolfo Hohenstein, Giovanni Mataloni, Aleardo Terzi, and Aleardo Villa; and in Germany Thomas Heine, Emil Weiss, Joseph Witzel, and, later, Lucian Bernhard, Julius Gipkens, and Julius Klinger.

The poster came of age as a major social force in World War I, when poster artists from all the belligerents threw their weight into war propaganda. Among the most prominent of war poster designers were, in France: Jules Faivre, Charles Fouqueray, Lucien Jonas, and Georges Scott; in Germany: Lucian Bernhard, Julius Gipkens, Ludwig Hohlwein, and Jupp Wiertz; in Italy: Luciano Mauzan, Giovanni Capranesi, and Mario Borgoni; in Britain: Frank Brangwyn, John Hassall, Alfred Leete, Bernard Partridge, G. Spenser Pryse, and Septimus E. Scott; in America: Howard Chandler Christy, James Montgomery Flagg, Joseph Christian Lyendecker, Joseph Pennell, and Fred Spear.

The next (and possibly last) great wave of poster production occurred in the late 1920s and 1930s. This was the 'second golden age' of the medium, when, before the advent of television, the colour poster and press advertisement were joint spearheads of most major advertising campaigns. It was during this period that the last great names flourished – in some instances consolidating reputations already established, in others giving first showing to newcomers. Gregory Brown, Austin Cooper, Tom Eckersley, Abram Games, F. H. K. Henrion, E. McKnight Kauffer, Stan Krol, Frank Newbould, Tom Purvis, Fred Taylor, and Hans Unger were major figures in Britain. Italy produced Gino Boccasile, Leonetto Cappiello, Plinio Codognato, and Marcello Nizzoli; and France, Jean Carlu, A. M. Cassandre, Paul Colin, A. Moulin, and, later, Raymond Savignac. Established German designers included Ludwig Hohlwein, Jupp Wiertz, and Fritz Gotha; newcomers were Joseph Englehardt, Hermann Keimel, and Willy Petzold. Switzerland's contribution to the poster has been significant. Donald Brun, Augusto Giacometti, Ernst Keller, and Herbert Leupin are among key major names.

For the collector the poster provides interest at a number of levels: it may be viewed as a manifestation of popular aesthetics, as social history evidence, as an epitome of a particular period, as a conspectus of the development of printing technology, or as a mixture of all of these. Undoubtedly the period most favoured remains the so-called *belle époque* in France (roughly 1890 to 1914) with which such names as Chéret, Grasset, Toulouse-Lautrec, Mucha, and Steinlen are closely linked. In America the comparable *belle époque* (Penfield, Parrish, *et al*) was brief, derivative, and confined almost entirely to publicity for magazines and journals, a factor that tends to produce a certain similarity of approach. Other categories or collecting themes include specific product or company advertising, particular artists, war, political protest, and revolutionary posters.

Posters present special problems of storage and conservation, partly because of their size and period of production. Most specimens are printed on paper manufactured after the introduction of wood pulp as a raw material and are thus particularly subject to acidification, embrittlement, and discoloration.

See also 'CINDERELLA' STAMP; POSTER SLIP; SPORTS PAPERS; STOCK POSTER

REFERENCES Max Gallo, *The Poster in History* (London: Hamlyn, 1974); Bevis Hillier, *Posters* (London: Weidenfeld & Nicolson, 1969); E. McKnight Kauffer, *The Art of the Poster* (London: Cecil Palmer, 1924); Maurice Rickards, *Banned Posters* (London: Evelyn, Adams & Mackay, 1969); Maurice Rickards, *The Rise and Fall of the Poster* (Newton Abbot: David & Charles, 1971)

COLLECTIONS Boston Public Library, Boston, Mass.; Imperial War Museum, London; London Transport Museum; National Railway Museum, York; Victoria & Albert Museum, London

Poster slip

Pasted as an addendum across a pictorial poster or announcement, poster slips normally bear a one- or two-word phrase by way of update. Concerts, theatrical performances, and other shows may be proclaimed as 'Today', 'Tonight', 'Postponed', or 'Cancelled'. The wording generally appears as red or black lettering against a colour background. The slips commonly measure about 80 × 400 mm (3⅛ × 15¾ in), but vary with the size of the poster.

Other forms of poster slip were produced for putting on to 'off-the-peg' lithographed posters, which were produced by major suppliers, such as David Allen and Sons, of Belfast, Manchester, and London, to cover a range of applications. Commonly the slip was printed by letterpress and announced a particular performance, venue, and date(s).

Poster stamp *See* 'CINDERELLA' STAMP

Post-horse duty ticket

Britain's post-horse duties were in force from 1779 (19 Geo. III, c. 51) to 1869 (31, 32 Vict., c. 14). Earlier taxes had been imposed on hackney carriages (1637) and private carriages (1745), but the need to pay for the war with American 'rebels' induced the government to extend taxation to those who travelled 'post', that is to say by post-chaise or horse from one posting house to another. The posting system, operated largely by innkeepers, provided a network of stables throughout the country, allowing the traveller to change horses every dozen miles or so, riding with or without an accompanying postboy.

Post-horse duty was a sum over and above the cost of hire. It was charged by the hirer, who himself paid an annual licence fee of five shillings, and it varied according to the number of horses

Set of post-horse tickets, numbered in sequence, Lancashire, late 18th century. Letterpress with wood-engravings. Each ticket approx. 92 × 65 mm (3⅝ × 2½ in)

hired and the distance they travelled. The rate was initially one penny per horse per mile, or one shilling per horse per day. The day rate was raised to 1*s* 6*d* per horse in 1780, and in 1785 the mileage rate was raised to 1½*d* and the day rate to 1*s* 9*d*. There were adjustments in 1824; the mileage rate remained unchanged but day rates were increased on a sliding scale from 2*s* 6*d* per day for three days or less to 1*s* 3*d* per day for a period between thirteen and twenty-eight days. Alternatively, the hirer could pay twenty per cent of the hiring charge.

The duty tickets were produced by the Stamp Office for the Commissioners of Stamps, who distributed them to licence-holders. Central control of the system was difficult and measures were taken to combat abuses. In 1780 a system of 'exchange tickets' was introduced. These were surrendered at the first toll-gate on the journey in exchange for a ticket that took the bearer through all subsequent turnpikes (*see* TOLL/TURNPIKE TICKET). Tickets thus collected by the toll-gate keepers were sent to the Commissioners of Stamps for cancelling.

Also introduced at this time were 'certificates', to be used by travellers who hired horses for periods longer than two days and were now exempt from the tax. During the two-day period the certificates, measuring 65 × 100 mm (2½ × 4 in), were surrendered at the first toll-gate in exchange for a 'check ticket', measuring 80 × 120 mm (3⅛ × 4¾ in), which allowed free passage through all subsequent gates on the journey.

In 1788, in a further move to make the tax more effective, the Treasury was empowered to subcontract the operation, farming it out to the highest bidder. In 1837 this practice was discontinued and administration of the scheme was transferred from the Stamp Office to the Commissioners of Excise. From this time, until the abolition of the duty in 1869, inspection and collection was in the hands of Excise Officers. Tickets of this period bear the insignia 'EO' and the title 'Excise Ticket'.

Mileage tickets, initially engraved, but from the 1820s printed by letterpress, measured 90 × 63 mm (3½ × 2½ in). They were headed 'Stamp Office' and bore printed numerals indicating the number of horses concerned. Mileage was inserted by hand against the word 'miles'. Day tickets, of the same size, bore the same heading and a printed indication of the number of days of hire and the sum charged. Long-term tickets (one day to twenty-eight days), measuring 115 × 80 mm (4½ × 3⅛ in), were headed 'Stamp Office Ticket'. They provided space for licence-holder details, date, destination, and distance. In the case of hirings longer than two days, the hirer's name and address was to be written on the back of the ticket. Exchange tickets, of the same size as mileage and day tickets, were also headed 'Stamp Office', but carried the title 'Exchange Ticket', the name of the county in which they were issued, and the number of horses concerned. Space was provided for the name of the hirer and, in the case of tickets for more than a single day, the number of days.

In spite of the large numbers of post-horse duty tickets issued, very few are to be found. Most of the surviving examples are in fact file proofs, held at Somerset House for reference as an anti-counterfeit measure and removed from record books some time towards the end of the last century. Among other examples, actually issued and used, are tickets relating to Aylesbury, Buckingham, Evesham, Marylebone, Oxford, and Southampton.

REFERENCES H. Dagnall and John H. Chandler, *Post Horse Tickets, their Historical Background, Purpose & Use* (Edgware, Middlesex: 1988); Adolph Koeppel and Marcus Samuel, 'British post-horse Duty Stamps', *Stamp Collecting Magazine* (December, 1960)

SOCIETIES American Revenue Association

Pratique, papers of

The term 'pratique' (French: practice) refers to the process whereby incoming vessels received health-control clearance on arrival at seaports. The system was established at least as far back as the 14th century as a means of combating the spread of the plague (*see* PLAGUE PAPERS). It required the visiting ship to present papers certifying that its last port of call had been free of contagious disease, and that no disease had broken out during the voyage.

The document of *pratique*, signed by the authorities at the port of embarkation, was at first a handwritten note, but developed into a part-printed form bearing the insignia of the issuing authority and a more or less standardized form of words to the effect that the port in question was 'by the Grace of God free of any contagion or pestilence'.

The documents, which took various formats, were for the most part printed in Italian or French; there were also versions in Portuguese, Dutch, English, and (rarely) Latin. Handwritten details appeared in appropriate blanks, naming the ship and its master, the date of departure and, in many cases, listing names of crew members, along with their age and hair-colour. A similar procedure was also applied to some journeys by land, assuring inhabitants of the regions visited that the holder – sometimes also his flock of sheep – was from a plague-free area.

Closely allied to the system of pratique was quarantine, in which vessels of suspect provenance were moored outside port areas for specified periods originally, as the word implies, for forty days. Quarantine ephemera include printed sheets showing port regulations and government pamphlets outlining precautions against expected outbreaks of disease. Also associated with health-control systems was the government notice (BANDO) forbidding trade with infected localities; and, conversely, documents removing such prohibitions.

REFERENCES Carlo Cipolla, *Public Health and the Medical Profession in the Renaissance* (Cambridge: Cambridge University Press, 1976); Carlo Ravasini, *Documenti Sanitari* (Trieste: Minerva Medica, 1958); Société Internationale d'Histoire Postale, *Bulletin* 32/33 (1976)

COLLECTIONS Institut Pasteur, Paris; Smithsonian Institution, Washington, DC; Wellcome Institute for the History of Medicine, London

SOCIETY Disinfected Mail Study Circle

Premium plate *See* BOOK-PRIZE LABEL

Prescription

Normally the province of the medical collector (who needs no introduction to its conventions), the prescription is nonetheless a social history item of interest to the collector at large. For the non-specialist, a brief review of its basic elements may be of use.

The traditional prescription consists of six essential elements, expressed in the following order:

1 The superscription (the sign ℞ an abbreviation of the Latin, *recipe*: take thou);

2 The inscription: the names of the ingredients required, with quantities;

3 The so-called subscription: directions for making up the preparation;

4 The signature (Latin, *signetur:* let it be labelled) giving instructions to the patient;

5 The patient's name;

6 The name or initials of the prescriber and the date. Each of these elements normally has a line to itself.

The conventions of the prescription derive from antiquity, and it may be said that the origins of its signs and symbols remain undetermined. They have, moreover, changed in the course of time; for example, the symbol for drachm, which in modern times is rendered as 3. Unchanged for centuries are the Latin phrases (or their abbreviations) used in prescriptions. Typical of these are *ad partes dolentes* (ad part. dolent.): to the painful parts; *guttatim* (gtt): drop by drop; *tussi urgente* (tuss.urg.): when the cough is troublesome; *ter die sumendus* (t.d.s.): to be taken three times a day. A comprehensive list of these expressions may extend to some 300–400. Their use was only marginally a matter of concealing potentially harmful knowledge from the patient; they also express the supranational nature of the profession of healing. Even into the late 19th century the days of the week in a pharmacist's day book also appeared in Latin.

The admixture of Latin and the vernacular became marked in the 1840s and 1850s when proprietary preparations began to appear. Among the first recorded examples is 'Syrupus Ferri Citratis Bullock's' which was prescribed in Derby in 1845.

Study of prescriptions reveals changing trends in therapy. For example, it reveals the common use of opiates and emetics in the 18th century and of calomel, mercury, and antimony for treating children in the last part of the 19th century.

Prescriptions were often accompanied by letters of advice to the patient as reported in the *Chemist and Druggist* of 29 June 1929. In 1693 Dr John Skelton, of Leeds, wrote to Mr Thoresby:

> Sir, – Your Dyett must be of meat of easy concoction & of good juice, without variety of dishes & strong Sawces without onions, garlik, mustard, horse radich, anchoves & horspices & such things, your stomack must never be overburdened, nor your appetite totally Satiated, you must make but one meal a day, & that at noone & if you eate something at night it must be some light matter & not too late, you must eat nothing till the former meal be concocted… .
>
> At the end of your dinner you must take some times halfe a spoonful of a digestive powder which is described in the other paper, drinking nothin upon, if it is possible for a good while after, sometimes you can take at the end of your dinner, a preserved walnutt, a little bitt of quinces, marmelade, a little piece of orange or limon pill [peel] preserved, some few

raisins of the sunne, some few almonds. Your ordinary drink must be of good small beer or small Ale of convenient Age, neither too new, nor too stoale. You must avoide (which is a great pitty) wines of all sortes of all sortes of grapes without the double of water, & if you transgresse that rule let it be moderatly, avoide also too much drinking of Strong Ale, marsh beere, rum & such strong and heady liquors....

Rising Early is very conducible & being up, it is good to comb your head & to have it gently rubbed to open the pores only & to discusse [disperse] that numnesse which remaines after sleeping, you can rubb the nummed part with a little queene of Hungary water & a little round the affected part....

The custom of setting down detailed advice to the patient was maintained by the POSTAL DIAGNOSIS practitioners of the 19th century, who invited answers to questionnaires.

In a later, orthodox, but nonetheless unusual context, a printed prescription blank, published during the prohibition period by the US Treasury Department, allows a patient medicinal alcohol. Signed by a Los Angeles doctor, it prescribes 'Spts frumenti – 163 tablespoonful p r n' (fermented liquor, 16 drachms; tablespoonful *pro re nata*, as required, diluted). The prescription, designed in a style reminiscent of paper currency, and watermarked 'prohibition', carries the introductory symbol ℞ (take thou).

The illegibility of the 20th-century handwritten prescription – partially explained at the time by the need for confidentiality – was overcome in the closing decades of the century by the less personal, but very clearly presented, computer-generated prescription.

See also FOLK RECIPE; PRESCRIPTION PAPER/ENVELOPE; QUACK ADVERTISING

REFERENCES William Kirkby, 'The Evolution of the Prescription', *Pharmaceutical Journal*, vol. 82, 20 June 1936; G. Kasten Tallmadge, 'The Evolution of the Prescription', CIBA Symposia, vol. 9, no. 8, November 1947 (New Jersey); C. J. S. Thompson, *The Mystery and Art of the Apothecary* (London: Bodley Head, 1929)

Prescription paper/envelope

The paper (later an envelope) in which medical prescriptions were returned to the customers of pharmacies was for long an item as decorative as the BILLHEAD or TRADE CARD.

The printed area covered a rectangle of approximately 80 × 130mm (3⅛ × 5⅛in), allowing the blank margins to be folded underneath to form a container for the prescription. Unfolded, the sheet measured approximately 230 × 200mm (9 × 7⅞in). In many collections, and in chemists' and printers' files, the central area alone, cut from the full sheet, is retained.

The 'cover' design carried space for the customer's name, the date, and the number of the prescription as copied into the prescription book. It also afforded an opportunity for the chemist to advertise. Typical addenda, among the engraved flourishes and scrollwork, were: 'Prescriptions accurately dispensed', 'Member of the Society of Apothecaries', 'Physicians' prescriptions and family recipes prepared', 'Ship and Family Medicine Chests Supplied and refitted', 'Practical Chemist to His Majesty', and 'Cupping, Branding, the Application of Leeches etc, also carefully attended to by competent assistants'.

As medicine and pharmacy emerged from the professional uncertainties of the 18th century, dispensing chemists sought to assure the public of their integrity and reliability. Thomas Fardon of Bell Street, Henley, took the opportunity of observing: 'From the reprehensible practice of employing inexperienced persons to dispense Physicians' Prescriptions, or Family Recipes, accidents have occurred in many parts of the kingdom. As a means of security to those who favor him with their patronage, T. F. respectfully observes that Apprentices are not kept in his Establishment'.

Prescription heading of James Tucker, chemist and druggist, Gloucester. Intaglio-printed. 76 × 129mm (3 × 5⅛in)

In one phase, the publicity value of the prescription paper was further enhanced by the use of its verso as a comprehensive TRADE LIST, detailing the full range of the pharmacist's products and services. It appears likely that, notwithstanding their 'prescription' title, the papers were also used as unofficial containers for powders.

Continental prescription papers and envelopes aspired in some cases to very considerable decorative effect. Whereas British and American designs became distinctly less ornate with the coming of the envelope, the continental trend was to extreme elaboration. At the end of the 19th century the firm of Antonio Branini of Milan was supplying a range of some 400 pharmaceutical labels, some in four or five colours, including gold, each adapted as required for the individually named pharmacist; many of these designs were also available as prescription envelopes.

See also PRESCRIPTION

Press book, film

The press book plays a central role in the film industry's promotion and distribution structure and normally takes the form of a brochure. Its function is not only to enthuse the film exhibitor but to provide a selection of promotional material for local use by the cinemas concerned. Items covered commonly fall into two parts: general information on the film itself, and promotional advertisements – the last-named being the greater.

General information includes a cast list and credits, a more or less extensive synopsis of the story of the film, biographical details of leading members of the cast, and running time.

In the 'promotional-aids' section appear a wide variety of ready-made editorial items, which were designed for reproduction, without change, in newspapers and magazines. These include illustrated articles on the film, advance reviews, pictorial features, and single captioned pictures for use as general illustration material. Other items are press advertisements in a wide variety of formats (as printing blocks or photographs), posters, stills (both black and white and colour) for lobby and front-of-house display, trailers, and 'announcement' slides. Also presented are such marginal promotional ideas as children's painting competition pictures and listings of slogans or 'catchlines' for general publicity use in front-of-house displays.

The press book evolved from the simpler 'synopsis' folder or booklet, which was for long the industry's main promotional link with the cinema. The 'synopsis' took a wide variety of forms and formats, ranging from a single-sided leaflet to a multi-page brochure. The press book, which began to appear in the early 1930s, often reached considerable proportions. An example from the 1960s, published by Anglo-Amalgamated Film Distributors for the satire 'Carry on Cleo', measures 340 × 450 mm (13⅜ × 17¾ in), giving a double-page spread of nearly one metre (just over 3 feet) wide.

Synopses and press books provide an encapsulated (if one-sided) history of the film industry.

Pressed flowers

Plants, herbs, and ferns were popular in 19th-century parlours as subjects for display, study, and polite conversation. Specimens were dried, flattened between blotting paper under weights, and mounted in albums or on individual cards. Mounting was done with various forms of glue, by slips of paper gummed across the principal ribs of the specimen, and, in some cases, by natural adhesion under pressure. None of these methods was really satisfactory, and specimens often suffered either an overdose of glue or became detached. Examples do survive, however, showing a minimum of damage, even where the specimen appears as decoration on a greetings card or other fragile item.

Seaweeds too were collected and mounted on paper and card. The most popular varieties – and the most difficult to manage – were the most finely tendrilled. The specimen was floated in water with the mounting paper immersed beneath it. By bringing the mount gently up under it the seaweed could be arranged to advantage as it was lifted clear of the water. Seaweed had a greater propensity than plants to stick to paper, and simple pressure between blotting paper was often all that was needed. Certain glutinous kinds of seaweed were merely laid on the mount and lightly moistened from the underside of the paper. Other types would not stick at all; for these a light dusting over with 'a little isinglass dissolved in gin' was recommended.

Also popular as subjects for mounting were butterfly wings, which were detached and laid carefully on writing paper 'as in the act of flying'. A second piece of paper, soaked in clear gum water, was placed over the display and pressed gently down, causing the wings to adhere. 'The wings will then be firmly fixed', says the *Boy's Own Book* (1885), 'and you can afterwards draw the forms of the bodies between, and colour them after nature'.

Composite displays, featuring plants, ferns, seaweeds, and butterfly wings, were also prepared and commonly framed and glazed. Such displays also extended to sea shells and other three-dimensional items.

At some collecting levels, the pressing of flowers, seaweeds, and the like was seen as a serious study. The enthusiast was advised to arrange and label specimens systematically, using Latin names and formal division into genera, varieties, etc. Such collections are to be found, but on the whole surviving specimens appear as evidence of a pastime rather than study.

REFERENCES *The Boy's Own Book* (London: Crosby, Lockwood, 1885); *Encyclopaedia of Business and Social Forms* (Hartford, CT: Gately, 1880); James McCabe, *Every Boy's Book* (London/New York: Routledge, Warne and Routledge, 1856); Mrs Laura Valentine, *The Home Book* (London: Warne, 1860); J. G. Wood, *The Boy's Modern Playmate* (London/New York: Warne, 1891)

Price list [plate 12]

The origins of the price list may be traced to handwritten notes appended to the early printed TRADE CARD. In a logical development of the idea, some shopkeepers produced an enlarged trade card in which a list of priced goods was included as part of the design. An early example is the trade card (c.1790) of Robert Mallet of Dublin, who describes himself as 'Engine Leather Pipe, Bucket and Water Closet Maker to Several of His Majesty's Public Offices, the Bank of Ireland etc.'. Mallet lists sizes of engine, numbers of men required to operate each size, 'how many gallons discharged per min', 'at what number of yards distance', 'prices with six foot of suction pipe', and 'prices of leather pipe 40 foot each, with brass screws'.

The price list was not widely adopted until the more competitive days of the 19th century, when the trade card began to expand its role beyond that of simple identification to include prices. In its turn the price list developed into the latter-day LEAFLET, brochure, and book, ultimately carrying illustration, colour, and sales copy.

·SEASON OF 1891.·

Illustrated Price-List of Latest Styles of Concealed Name Cards.

As the expense of sending sample cards is so great, we take this method of introducing some of our leading styles. Of course we cannot, in this way, show you the beautiful colors or the fine finish as they REALLY ARE on the cards, but that you can judge by samples of other styles sent.

Do not be afraid to order from these illustrations, as they represent the same quality of cards as accompanying samples.

REMEMBER: These are all hidden name cards. The name is printed in the center of the card and the floral ornament can be raised at one end to show the name when desired.

NOTICE. Please select the style of card you wish and order by the number. Do not order half packs.

Style No. 664.—Assorted Designs. 12 for 15 cents.

Style No. 624.—Silk or Plush Ribbon and Bow. Name on small card which fits in envelope. 12 for 50 cents

Style No. 665.—Assorted Designs. 12 for 12 cents.

Style No. 601.—Assorted Designs. 12 for 20 cents.

Style No. 630.—Assorted Designs. 12 for 20 cents.

Style No. 616.—Assorted Designs. 12 for 20 cents. Motto concealed by a beautiful golden clasp.

Price list for hidden-name cards of Stevens Brothers, Northford, Connecticut, 1891. Four pages. Letterpress with wood-engravings. 305 × 242 mm (12 × 9½ in)

Price tag/ticket

In its heyday in the early 20th century the price-tag was a salient feature of displays that sought to show as many items as possible in one window. The majority of price tags were hand-executed, sometimes by in-house letterers, but mostly by outside suppliers who provided sets to cover every price requirement.

Such tags are of interest today partly for the low price ranges shown, but mostly for the naïvety of their hand execution. They were lettered at speed in large quantities and came from the same workshop-studios that produced the phrase tags – 'very smart', 'latest fashion', etc. – which were fixed to displayed items at random. Known in the trade as 'mottoes', phrase tags were also supplied in large quantities, often in slotted boxes for ready access.

'Price-and-praise' tags for outside use for grocery and vegetable display were available in metal and early forms of plastic. These too are collected for their identifiable period character. In Britain all pre-decimalization (pre-1971) price tags have a measure of nostalgia-interest.

See also MOTTO, SHOP WINDOW; SHOWCARD

Primer *See* ABC PRIMER

Printed handkerchief

The printed handkerchief or kerchief (old French, *couvre-chef:* head cover) became popular at the end of the 18th century, after the French innovation of printing calico from copper plates (1770) had got into its stride. In Britain, it was largely identified with commemorative celebrations and souvenirs, with a notable side-sector of political propaganda. In America, the printed kerchief (known as a 'bandana' from its Hindustan-Portuguese connection: Hindustani, *bandnu:* tie dye) was rapidly absorbed into the folklore of electioneering.

Early appearances of the kerchief in Britain relate to the introduction of the railways (campaigns for and against) in the 1830s and to the reform movement of about the same period. The 'Reform Apron', approximately 700 × 800 mm (27⅝ × 31½ in), worn by men in the reform processions, was in fact a printed kerchief with tapes. Examples are held in the People's Palace, Glasgow. Thomas [Tom] Paine, author of *The Rights of Man* and a hero of the reform movement, was celebrated in a printed square. In the latter part of the 19th century appeared mementoes of 'The Queen's Long Reign' (1887) and 'The Record Reign of Queen Victoria' (1897); the Boer War (1899–1902); and, in the 20th century, of the Delhi Durbar (1911) and the First World War (1914–18).

In America, the 'bandana' is known from the first years of Independence. It is said to have been introduced by an English immigrant printer, John Hewson, who settled in Philadelphia in 1773. Some early examples were even printed in England and France. Early bandanas are identified with presidential campaigns, notably of Andrew Jackson (1824, 1828, 1832) and Henry Clay (1824, 1832, 1844). William Henry Harrison (1840) was commemorated on a campaign bandana, as were Zachary Taylor (1848) and Franklin Pierce (1852). The bandana fell into disuse in the Civil War years but re-emerged in force in the 1870s and 1880s. It remained a standard campaign item into the 1900s and was still current in the 1960s and 1970s. Among numerous 20th-century specimens are ones featuring Hoover, Eisenhower, and Nixon.

The printed handkerchief has also been used to commemorate proclamations, declarations, and addresses, and to celebrate military campaigns (by means of battle maps). It is also found as a teaching aid (first-aid diagrams, deaf-mute alphabets, etc.). It was used in the 20th century as a convenient way of producing portable escape maps for prisoners of war. Small examples, secreted in hollow pencils, were manufactured for the services in World War II and can be seen at the Cumberland Pencil Museum.

Other ephemeral items printed on textiles include commemorative headsquares, scarves, and neckties; newspapers and almanacs of the 1830s (thus printed to evade stamp duty); advertising broadsides; and cigarette cards. Posters printed on linen have also appeared, notably in rural areas of America; they were designed for nailing to barn doors, fences, trees, and other sites where paper would survive less readily.

See also ALMANAC; ELECTION PAPERS; NEWSPAPER; RAG BOOK

REFERENCES Herbert Ridgeway Collins, *Threads of History* (Washington: Smithsonian Institution, 1979); Mary Schoeser, *Printed Handkerchiefs* (London: Museum of London, 1988); Edmund B. Sullivan, *Collecting Political Americana* (New York: Crown, 1980)

COLLECTIONS American Political Items Collection, Huntsville, Alabama; Museum of Costume, Bath; The People's Palace Museum, Glasgow; Smithsonian Institution, Washington, DC

Printing, 'primitive'

'Primitive' printing is a term used to refer to printed matter apparently produced without reference to normally accepted professional standards. The expression covers work carried out by professionals under exceptional difficulty, as well as the productions of untrained printers. Such work includes management-produced issues of newspapers published during labour disputes, publications printed under bombardment or siege conditions, 'underground' or illegal samizdat publications, 'pirate' versions – often editorially inadequate – of official programmes for public occasions, early settlers' printing-press items, and *ad hoc* souvenirs produced in unusual locations (as for example, mementoes printed in the middle of the ice-bound Thames during frost fairs).

Much of the appeal of primitive printing lies in its neglect – for reasons of haste, *force-majeur,* or naivety – of ordinary printing disciplines. It presents an often engagingly robust dismissal of the rules, sometimes with overtones of drama, sometimes merely in cheerful non-compliance.

See also AMATEUR JOURNAL; FROST-FAIR PAPERS; NEWSPAPER; PROCESSION PROGRAMME; STREET LITERATURE; 'ZINE

Procession programme

Among the earliest procession programmes are what might be called 'typo-diagrams', listings composed within the columnar format of newspapers. The procession programme as a separately printed item came to the fore in the early 19th century, and thereafter became the norm. Coronations and funerals predominate, but royal jubilees and peace and victory celebrations are also strongly represented.

Among the many solutions to the procession-programme design problem is the 'theatre playbill' format. In this the spectacle, whatever its length, is accommodated on a vertical strip of paper (sometimes more than one pasted together), finishing at the point when the programme is complete. Typical of this approach is the 1838 official order of procession of Queen Victoria's coronation. This document – part information, part souvenir – is over 1330 mm (4½ feet) deep. Printed in red and blue, and bearing the royal coat of arms at head and foot, it consists of two sheets pasted together to form a continuous whole.

The funeral procession programme, advisedly eschewing the playbill format, tends to the multi-column presentation of the newspaper, using a woodcut representation of a coffin, together with the words 'the body' (or 'the royal body') as a diagramatic centre-piece. In another form of treatment, one side of a broadsheet carries horizontal rows of woodcut illustrations showing numbered elements of the procession in profile, and the other an explanatory key.

'Pirated' programmes were a well-established street-sellers' item on processional routes. They were concocted from pre-event publicity in newspapers and were printed in haste – often illicitly by printers' apprentices – with misprints and solecisms in profusion.

COLLECTION Guildhall Library, London

Proclamation

The proclamation, a formal expression of the will of authority, is one of the oldest instruments of government. Its use in modern times is limited. In Britain, it signals the succession of monarchs, the dissolving and summoning of parliaments, declarations of war and states of emergency, the passing of laws of special importance, and the enforcing of existing laws. Apart from major state occasions there is no special circumstance, other than the assessed importance of the matter, that governs whether or not a proclamation is issued. In America, proclamations are issued by the President, by governors of states, and by mayors of cities. Here, too, publication is largely a matter of the exigency of the moment.

Traditionally a proclamation consists of two sections; the first, the preamble, establishes the reasoning behind the action outlined in the second. The first part thus classically starts with 'whereas…'; the second with the words 'now, therefore we…'. Both structure and phraseology are echoes of the classic form of published statute law, and it is as law that the printed proclamation has often been presented. Certainly it is as law that it has often been accepted, and in many periods government has been virtually exercised by proclamation.

The document itself was originally a visual confirmation of a declaration made by a crier. The paper, handwritten or printed, was read out and afterwards posted up as a formal reminder to the public. At one stage it was customary for the crier to send a copy of the paper back to the issuing authority, endorsing it with a declaration that he had duly cried and posted it.

The law has touched virtually every aspect of human existence at one time or another, from requiring that the dead be buried in wool to the suppression of coffee houses. The proclamation, as it highlights the law, has done no less. In a sample listing of proclamation subject matter we may include: an offer by Charles II (1679) of £10 per head for the apprehension of fugitive papists; an offer by His Excellency, William Shirley, His Majesty's Governor-in-Chief of Massachusetts (1755) of £40 for every male Indian scalp brought into Boston; and a warning by the Mayor of London (1684) of threats of punishment for those who set off squibs and crackers in the streets of the City. Among many hundreds of other subjects are the ejectment of French citizens living in Britain (London, 1803); a warning that looters will be killed (San Francisco, 1906); and instructions that 'enemy propaganda material found must be handed in immediately' (Jersey, 1940).

In Britain, early proclamations were printed largely in black-letter (Old English) type. The size of paper was consistent with the length of the text; it was normally left untrimmed, showing the deckle edge of the full sheet. The style of presentation was reminiscent of printed statutes, though in a much larger format; the royal crest, centred at the top, and a large decorative drop initial panel (factotum) were the sole embellishments. In an inversion of later practice, words to be stressed were printed in roman characters as opposed to black letter, thus producing a lighter rather than a bolder effect for important elements.

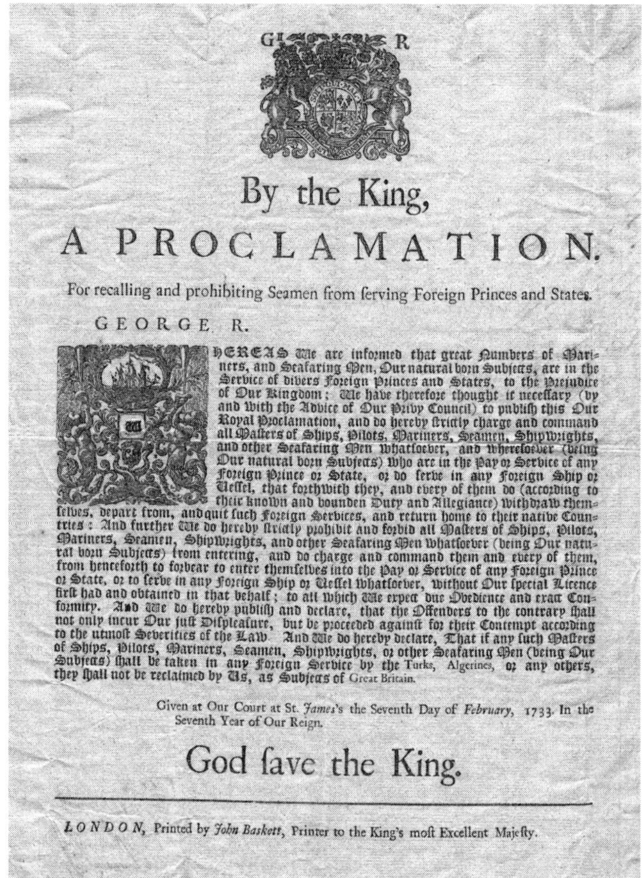

G R

By the King,

A PROCLAMATION.

For recalling and prohibiting Seamen from ſerving Foreign Princes and States.

GEORGE R.

WHEREAS We are informed that great Numbers of Mariners, and Seafaring Men, Our natural born Subjects, are in the Service of divers Foreign Princes and States, to the Prejudice of Our Kingdom; We have therefore thought it necessary (by and with the Advice of Our Privy Council) to publish this Our Royal Proclamation, and do hereby strictly charge and command all Masters of Ships, Pilots, Mariners, Seamen, Shipwrights, and other Seafaring Men whatsoever, and wheresoever (being Our natural born Subjects) who are in the Pay or Service of any Foreign Prince or State, or do serve in any Foreign Ship or Vessel, that forthwith they, and every of them do (according to their known and bounden Duty and Allegiance) withdraw themselves, depart from, and quit such Foreign Services, and return home to their native Countries: And further We do hereby strictly prohibit and forbid all Masters of Ships, Pilots, Mariners, Seamen, Shipwrights, and other Seafaring Men whatsoever (being Our natural born Subjects) from entering, and do charge and command them and every of them, from henceforth to forbear to enter themselves into the Pay or Service of any Foreign Prince or State, or to serve in any Foreign Ship or Vessel whatsoever, without Our special Licence first had and obtained in that behalf; to all which We expect due Obedience and exact Conformity. And We do hereby publish and declare, that the Offenders to the contrary shall not only incur Our just Displeasure, but be proceeded against for their Contempt according to the utmost Severities of the Law. And We do hereby declare, That if any such Masters of Ships, Pilots, Mariners, Seamen, Shipwrights, or other Seafaring Men (being Our Subjects) shall be taken in any Foreign Service by the Turks, Algerines, or any others, they shall not be reclaimed by Us, as Subjects of Great Britain.

Given at Our Court at St. *James's* the Seventh Day of *February*, 1733. In the Seventh Year of Our Reign.

God ſave the King.

LONDON, Printed by *John Baskett*, Printer to the King's moſt Excellent Majeſty.

Proclamation, George II, London, 7 February 1733. Letterpress, printed by John Baskett, 'Printer to the King's most Excellent Majesty'. 402 × 305 mm (15⅞ × 12 in)

The characteristic 'style' of the proclamation, with its air of austere authority, has been borrowed for use in a wide range of contexts. It appears in commercial posters and handbills, in satirical SQUIBS, as well as in appeals to insurrection. In its orthodox uses the style has wide international currency; its structure, phraseology, and layout bear a family resemblance regardless of language. Content, too, tends to standardization. A proclamation issued by Queen Anne in 1702 'For the Encouragement of Piety and Virtue and for the preventing and punishing of Vice, Profaneness and Immorality' is matched by one issued by Queen Victoria in 1837. The 1837 version, bearing the same title as its predecessor, uses a word-for-word re-rendering of Queen Anne's text, with only minor changes. Both preambles declare '…that it is an indispensable duty on Us to be careful, above all other things, to preserve and advance the honor and service of Almighty God, and to discourage and suppress all vice, profaneness, debauchery and immorality, which are so highly displeasing to God…'. And both conclude with the injunction: 'We do hereby strictly charge and command all Our Commanders and Officers whatsoever, that they do take care to avoid all profaneness, debauchery and other immoralities…'.

Similarities of wording also occur in the proclamations of George III and George V. Both monarchs (the first in 1800, the second in 1917) urged the nation to wartime economies in food consumption: '…and We do for this purpose more particularly exert and charge all heads of households to reduce consumption of bread in their respective families…' (George III seeks a reduction of one third; George V of one fourth). Both documents charge 'all persons who keep horses' to restrict the feeding of oats. Though more than a century separates these documents, the later version is virtually a reprint of its predecessor.

See also CITY ORDINANCE BROADSIDE; PUBLIC NOTICE

Prospectus, publisher's

The prospectus (literally 'preview') is among the oldest devices used by publishers in the marketing of books. It announces publication before the work is printed, extolling its virtue – often providing specimen pages – and inviting pre-publication orders and payment in full, or in part, forthwith. The prospectus may offer a reduced price to subscribers, and an additional inducement might include a listing of subscribers' names in updated prospectuses or in the book itself.

Signing up customers in advance gave both publisher and author a measure of confidence in the venture. In the case of scholarly or specialized works (which such books generally were) a certain cachet attached to the inclusion of one's name in the list; if the reputation of the author and publisher – and of the subscriber – were high enough there was satisfaction all round.

The first book to be published in England by this method appeared in 1617. It was John Minsheu's *Ductor in Linguas. The Guide into Tongues*, which was an extensive work covering nine languages and must have been both expensive to produce and difficult to sell.

See also MAGAZINE, SAMPLE SHEET

Prostitute's card *See* VICE CARD

Public apology

The public apology has at various periods been widely accepted as a form of restitution for offence. A printed 'submission', in the form of a press announcement, poster, or handbill, frequently served as a condition of discharge of the matter, expenses of publication being borne by the offender.

Examples from the 19th century commonly took the form of a handbill or PUBLIC NOTICE. Typical is the announcement of Richard Cousen of Bouth, Lancaster who, on 21 November 1806, apologized for throwing a 'certain Glass Bottle out of the Gallery of the Theatre of Ulverston, to the imminent Danger of the Audience and Performers' and promised 'never again to be guilty of such offence'.

In similar vein is a handbill from Great Grimsby, for the parliamentary election of 1895, in which James Duke expressed regret 'for having uttered certain slanderous statements regarding Mr Alderman George Doughty' and begged to withdraw them and 'apologise for having made them'. James Duke's withdrawal is capped, however, by his opponent's bold-type addendum: 'Tories, Beware!'.

Public notice

The printed public notice is a close relative of both the formal PROCLAMATION and the commercial POSTER, but it occupies a distinct middle ground between the two (with total authority on the one hand and mere seduction on the other). Historically the public notice partakes more of the proclamation than the poster. It adopts the autocratic look and language of command and, most commonly, severely warns. In this mode it is an instrument of control.

The notice is also a means of request, as it is in appeals for news of items lost, stolen, or strayed (with the offer of a reward), and calls for help for charity or works of communal enterprise.

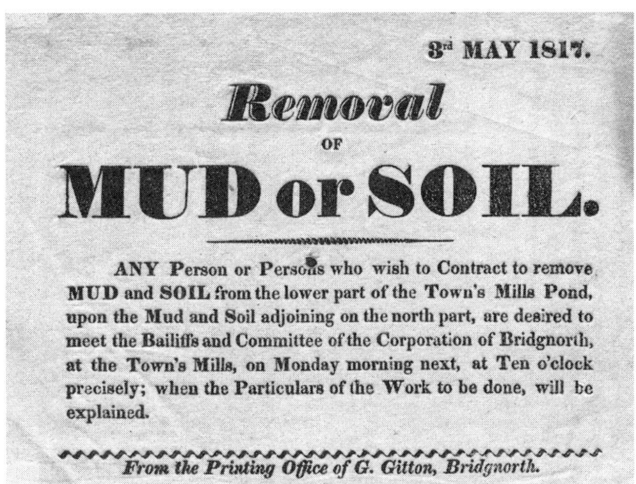

3rd MAY 1817.

Removal

OF

MUD or SOIL.

ANY Person or Persons who wish to Contract to remove MUD and SOIL from the lower part of the Town's Mills Pond, upon the Mud and Soil adjoining on the north part, are desired to meet the Bailiffs and Committee of the Corporation of Bridgnorth, at the Town's Mills, on Monday morning next, at Ten o'clock precisely; when the Particulars of the Work to be done, will be explained.

From the Printing Office of G. Gitton, Bridgnorth.

Public notice, Bridgnorth, 3 May 1817. Printed by G. Gitton, Bridgnorth. 160 × 214 mm (6¼ × 8½ in)

In a further category is the notice of protest and contention – the call to right wrongs, to vote this way or that, to overthrow the established order. In a fourth category appears the counterfeit: the device disguised as a public announcement; here the advertiser conveys a commercial message in the manner of authority, hoodwinking the reader into accepting it as 'official'. Finally, there is a small unclassifiable miscellany of public apologies, challenges, 'squibs', satires, jokes, and whimsicalities.

The public notice was for centuries the only medium of mass communication. In a barely literate community, and with newspapers in any case an expensive luxury, the simple printed announcement was the standard vehicle of warning, appeal, contention, and commercial information. With its extensive coverage of human affairs – local, regional, and national – it provides a uniquely detailed store of source material for social history.

Examples survive in considerable quantity – largely through conservation in printers' files where, as a legal requirement from 1799, a copy of each item produced was kept as a record (39 Geo.III, cap.79). Most such files have long been dispersed, but the few that remain more or less intact provide a fascinating survey of virtually every aspect of local life, sometimes over long periods. File copy specimens may be recognized by traces of binding, normally at the left-hand edge, and by handwritten annotations indicating quantities ordered, delivery dates, etc.

Typical of printers' files are those of the two John Soulbys, father and son, whose work in Ulverston in the north of England spanned the period from 1796 to 1827. The work of these printers, now housed in Barrow-in-Furness Library and the Rural History Centre, Reading, contains a wide spectrum of announcements, ranging from a forced PUBLIC APOLOGY to a reward notice for an escaped prisoner, released during the night by 'some evil disposed person or persons unknown' from an apartment of Dalton Castle.

Among the chief characteristics of the public notice are its uses of a 'telegraphic' form of typographic layout. For maximum impact salient words in the text are printed in large type faces, which convey the gist of the message at a glance and from a distance. The device was widely exploited after the introduction in the early years of the 19th century of bold and eye-catching display types from the foundries of, among others, Robert Thorne, William Thorowgood, and Vincent Figgins.

The dramatic impact of the 19th-century public notice stems in no small measure from its sensational associations. Most frequent catchwords of the genre are themselves compelling: warning, reward, lost, rescue, murder, burglary, felony, robbery, stolen, missing, caution. Even less urgent matters invite attention. In London in 1816 appeared a notice, headed 'Defamation', which reads: 'Whereas some evil disposed Person or Persons is employed in Circulating skandalous Reports injurious to the Character of Mrs Tuck, No 6, Queen-Street, Oxford Street, – who ever will give information of the Offender or Offenders, so that they may be brought to Justice, shall be handsomely Rewarded for their trouble'.

In more sober vein, though at the time unwittingly so, is a sale notice from Missouri in 1853. It announces a public sale of slaves, 'to the highest bidder six negroes… to wit: one negro boy about 20 years old; one negro girl about 16 years old, and one young negro woman, with three children…'.

See also AIR-RAID PAPERS; CITY ORDINANCE BROADSIDE; DISTRAINT, PAPERS OF; REWARD PAPERS; RIOT ACT

REFERENCES John Lewis, *Printed Ephemera* (Ipswich: W. S. Cowell, 1962); Maurice Rickards, *The Public Notice* (Newton Abbot: David & Charles, 1973); Maurice Rickards, *Rise and Fall of the Poster* (Newton Abbot: David & Charles, 1971); Michael Twyman, *Printing 1770–1970* (London: Eyre & Spottiswoode, 1970; reprinted British Library, 1998); Michael Twyman, *John Soulby, Printer, Ulverston* (Reading: University of Reading, 1966)

COLLECTIONS American Antiquarian Society, Worcester, Mass.; Bagford Collection, British Museum; Museum of Hartlepool, Cleveland (UK); Rural History Centre, The University of Reading

Punctuality card

The virtues of punctuality were propounded particularly from the 1830s to the 1860s in illustrated wall cards designed for schoolrooms, apprentices' quarters, and offices. Sizes varied, but a typical example, dating from c.1835, measures some 280 × 230 mm (11 × 9 in). Many were framed for permanent display.

Essentially the cards presented a text of some 150 words, with supporting pictorial elements showing the outcome of punctuality on one hand and unpunctuality on the other. The text consists of a string of maxims displayed as an exercise in calligraphic symmetry in the manner of an 18th-century gravestone or a displayed LORD'S PRAYER; major words and phrases were stressed by size and weight, and the whole contrived to fill out the shape of the panel it occupied. Wording varies in detail, but its basic structure and phraseology is substantially the same. It is clear that the text derives from an archetypal original or exemplar, though which, if any, of the surviving variants this might be is not apparent.

Illustrations, some obviously pirated, present contrasts between promptitude and lateness on such themes as: 'Indeed Sir, you are punctual', 'We are too late, the Bank is closed', 'Well, here we are in good time', and 'You are behind time, Sir, the mail is gone off'. In one redrawn example the royal monogram on the mail coach has been updated from GR to VR.

Texts, designs, and drawings are for the most part anonymous, but one example (published in the 1840s by D. Bogue of Fleet Street, London) bears the artist's name, T. C. Wilson, and that of the printer, C. Graf. Rock Brothers & Payne (well known for their illustrated stationery) published a version in the late 19th century, republishing it as a company memento in 1939. The original plate was made over to the Guildhall Library when Rock Brothers closed in 1980. The 1939 version bears the overprinted letterpress heading: 'A relic of a hundred years ago from Rock Brothers Limited, Wangye Works, Chadwell Heath, Essex', and the footline: 'reproduced from an original hand-etched [sic] plate designed by Mr W F Rock' (the founder of the firm).

Puzzle

Early advertising made extensive use of the puzzle or riddle as a means of claiming and retaining attention. Tobacco and snuff papers, lottery leaflets, magazine inserts, and handbills were chief among many media in which they were a common feature.

Prior to their use as GIVE-AWAYS, puzzles had been part of the commercial stock-in-trade of stationers, toymen, and printers; in the trade- and price-lists of the early 19th century they often

Puzzle card issued by Lyon, Elliott & Bloom, dealers in 'Staple and Fancy Dry Goods', Auburn, New York. Late 19th century. 75 × 117 mm (3 × 4⅝ in)

appear, together with 'songs and jests', 'acrostic cards', and other oddments, as puzzling cards. Many of them came to be preserved in SCRAPBOOK/ALBUMS. Printed in black on white card to a size of some 100 × 70 mm (4 × 2¾ in), they sold for a penny each, or less, and in many homes were the sole source of intellectual challenge.

Typical of the puzzle card genre is the 'anamorphic' puzzle (*see* ANAMORPHIC IMAGE), in which a word or phrase appears in unrecognizably attenuated characters, the meaning of which becomes evident only when the card is viewed obliquely.

Another form of puzzle was the American 'hidden object' trade card, in which a face, figure, bird, or beast was concealed within an intricate drawing. Also popular were the maze, the 'mystery' drawing (in which numerous dots were to be linked in pencil), the anagram, the acrostic, the REBUS, and other such puzzles. All these items appeared either as novelties in their own right or as collectable TRADE-CARD backs.

See also AMUSEMENT SHEET; HOLD-TO-LIGHT; JIGSAW PUZZLE; LOTTERY PAPERS

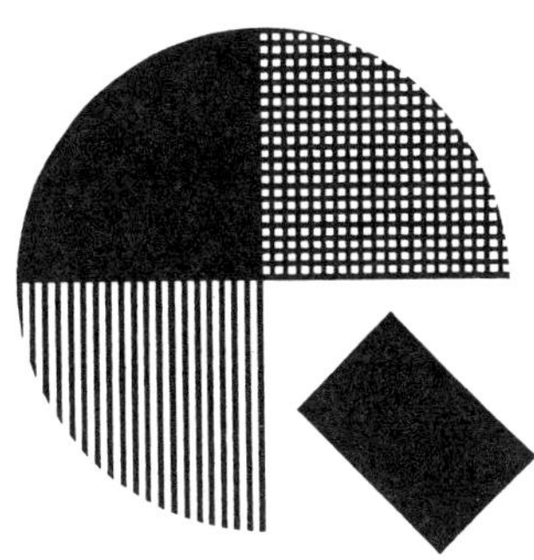

Quack advertising

Cures and nostrums are the subject of much of the earliest printed advertising. Defoe's *Journal of the Plague Year* refers to the plethora of 'Bills and Papers' of ignorant fellows that covered the walls of London in 1665. The emergence of the newspaper, with paid-for columns open to anyone with 'cures' to offer, immeasurably extended the field, and the rise of popular literature in the 19th century brought the matter to little short of a major industry. The public, too poor to afford professional medicine, ignorant enough to be 'blinded with science', readily responded.

Quack advertising, with its offers of cures for cancer, tuberculosis, and diabetes (not to mention fits, hysteria, diphtheria, and Bright's disease) remained largely unrestrained on both sides of the Atlantic until the beginning of the 20th century. Control came slowly in the 1890s. The more responsible magazines and newspapers began to exclude such material, and pressure from professional bodies – and eventually from governments – reduced the flood to a trickle.

Items relating to quack medicine advertising are multitudinous. A typical selection may include the following:

Leaflet (c.1900): Professor Eastburn AMS, Glasgow. 'Professor Eastburn stands alone!... Professor Eastburn is an Alumnus of the Great American Eclectic School of Medicine. Professor Eastburn... specially invites those ladies and gentlemen who have become tired of trying to be cured by the use of Mercury and other Mineral Poisons... ladies... young men... middle-aged men... those about to marry are specially invited.... A cure is guaranteed in every Case Undertaken... throat and lung diseases – consumption is curable: these diseases are treated by the use of oxygenic compound... of which Prof. Eastburn is the inventor... 13 Cambridge Street, Glasgow. Tram Cars from all parts of the City'. 220 × 145 mm (8⅝ × 5¾ in)

Part-printed form (1893): George Thomas Congreve, Peckham, London. '(Mr Albert Jenkins) In consideration of (your) circumstances, and on the distinct understanding that the price be not mentioned to any other person, I will let (you) have the 11/- bottle for (8/-)... or the 22/- bottle for (15/6) in either case carriage paid. This note must be sent whenever medicine is required. It will be returned to you for future use. Geo Thos Congreve'. 180 × 120 mm (7⅛ × 4¾ in)

Leaflet (c.1910), 4 pages: H. G. Root, Endsleigh Gardens, Euston Road, London. 'Fits, epilepsy or falling sickness... elepizone... a Sovereign Remedy for the cure of epilepsy... I believe it to contain more real merit and curative power than £5 worth of any other Fit medicine... 1 bottle 11/6; 3 bottles 30s; 6 bottles £2.14'. 220 × 140 mm (8⅝ × 5½ in)

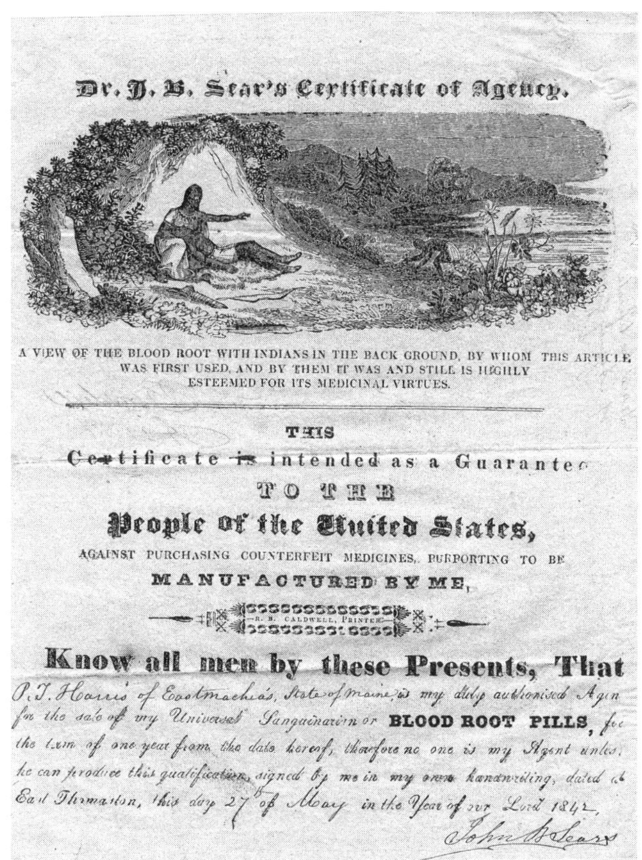
Dr. J. B. Sear's Certificate of Agency.

A VIEW OF THE BLOOD ROOT WITH INDIANS IN THE BACK GROUND, BY WHOM THIS ARTICLE WAS FIRST USED, AND BY THEM IT WAS AND STILL IS HIGHLY ESTEEMED FOR ITS MEDICINAL VIRTUES.

THIS
Certificate is intended as a Guarantee
TO THE
People of the United States,
AGAINST PURCHASING COUNTERFEIT MEDICINES, PURPORTING TO BE
MANUFACTURED BY ME,

R. B. CALDWELL, PRINTER

Know all men by these Presents, That P. T. Harris of Eastmachias, State of Maine, is my duly authorised Agent for the sale of my Universal Sanguinarian or BLOOD ROOT PILLS, for the term of one year from the date hereof, therefore no one is my Agent unless he can produce this qualification, signed by me in my own handwriting, dated at East Thomaston, this day 27th of May in the Year of our Lord 1842,
John B. Sears

Dr J. B. Sear's Certificate of Agency, East Thomaston (US), 27 May 1842. Letterpress with wood-engraving, printed by R. B. Caldwell. 250 × 202 mm (9⅞ × 8 in)

Leaflet (c.1910), 4 pages: 'Mr John Hern, Princes Road, Liverpool. 'Consumption, asthma, bronchitis, catarrh, coughs, colds etc. positively cured... Mr Hern has made astonishing cures of supposed "incurable" cases of Rheumatism, Bright's Disease, paralysis, epilepsy, corpulence etc... over ninety per cent of Mr Hern's cures have been effected by correspondence, a personal consultation being unnecessary... sufferers desirous of being treated should send six penny stamps for Mr Hern's booklet 'Help for the Hopeless' containing further particulars and a form in which to state case fully'. 220 × 140 mm (8⅝ × 5½ in)

Trade card (c.1895): Dr Thomas' Electric Oil. Agent Geo

Getchell, Maine. 'What it has done. What it will do. It will positively cure – toothache in 5 minutes; earache in 2 minutes; backache in 2 hours; lameness in 2 days; coughs in 20 minutes; hoarseness in 1 hour; colds in 24 hours; sore throat in 12 hours; deafness in 2 days; pain of burn in 5 minutes; pain of scald in 5 minutes; croup it will cease in 5 minutes, and positively cure any case when used at the outset'. 73 × 105 mm (2⅞ × 4⅛ in)

Self-measurement card (c.1904): Kimball's Anti-Rheumatic Ring, Oxford Street, London W. 'A speedy and permanent cure for rheumatism, neuralgia, gout, sciatica, lumbago etc'. 90 × 160 mm (3½ × 6¼ in)

Order form (c.1895): the Magneto-Electric Battery Company, Oxford Street, London W. 'Keep your feet warm and your circulation healthy by wearing our electro magnetic socks... which create a mild and continuous electrical current, producing, in accordance with physical laws, a high degree of warmth... NB These socks may be worn in addition to Dr Lowder's battery with great benefit and perfect safety...'. 105 × 140 mm (4⅛ × 5½ in)

Leaflet (c.1895): the Magneto-Electric Battery Company, Oxford Street, London W. 'Dr Lowder's electro magnetic battery. Most complaints effectively cured... suspended by a ribbon and worn on the chest... day and night, except with children under the age of 8, when it should be worn in the daytime only... why it should be worn by all, it purifies the blood, invigorates the whole system; builds up the most shattered constitution; prevents as well as cures diseases; strengthens the nerves; cures all aches and pain; is recommended by the medical profession; may be worn with perfect safety; requires no attention and does not get out of order; is simple in its application; costs less than a single visit to a physician; its price brings it within the reach of all... best remedy for indigestion, general debility; nervousness; biliousness; liver complaint; sore throat; rheumatism; hysteria or fits; paralysis; spinal disease; sick headaches; heartburn; pimples; swollen joints; sciatica; neuralgia; bronchitis; skin disease; quinsey; constipation; aches and pains; catarrh; boils; diphtheria; toothache; lumbago; asthma; pleurisy; ulcers; weak stomach...'. 230 × 150 mm (9 × 6 in)

The heyday of quack medicine lasted into the 20th century. In America the beginning of the end came after the campaign of Samuel Hopkins Adams whose investigative journalism, together with the efforts of the American Medical Association, brought about the passing of the Pure Food and Drug Act in 1906. In Britain, published reports by the British Medical Association – in 1902 and 1912 – led to the setting up of a House of Commons Select Committee on Patent Medicines. Its report, though muffled by World War I, spelled the beginning of the end of quack medicine in Britain – though it took another half century to apply the final touches to restrictive legislation.

See also ELECTRO-MEDICAL PAPERS; MEDICINE-SHOW PAPERS; POSTAL DIAGNOSIS

REFERENCES *Secret Remedies: what they Cost and what they Contain* (London: British Medical Association, 1909); Stewart H. Holbrook, *The Golden Age of Quackery* (New York: Macmillan, 1959; reprinted Collier, 1962); E. S. Turner, *The Shocking History of Advertising!*, rev. edn (Harmondsworth: Penguin, 1965); A. Walker Bingham, *The Snake-Oil Syndrome* (Hanover, Mass., 1994)

QSL card

Amateur radio enthusiasts, licensed to communicate with each other internationally on technical matters by Morse code, use combinations of letters for frequently recurring phrases. Most commonly used is the universal 'Q-code', which consists of three-letter codes beginning with Q (along with Z the least used letter in English). QSL stands for 'I am acknowledging receipt' and, with a question mark, 'Can you acknowledge receipt?'. The letters are also used to designate the card of confirmation which the operators exchange postally to record successful radio contact.

QSL cards took on a promotional role as the network of international communication expanded. Displaying prominently the operator's unique identifying call sign, as well as providing spaces for details of the successful contact, the cards carry graphic designs reflecting their sender's location and interests. The result has been the development of a distinct genre of postal ephemera. Collected and displayed by operators with an interest in representing a wide range of countries, the cards constitute an ever-widening medium of promotion – of the operator, the country of origin, and any sponsoring body willing to undertake the design, production, and printing costs.

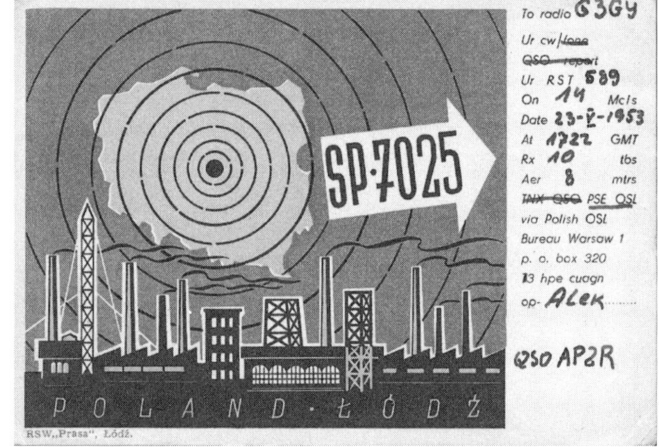

QSL card, message sent 23 May 1953 from Łódź, Poland. Lithographed in three colours by RSW 'Prasa', Łódź, with manuscript additions. 103 × 150 mm (4 × 6 in)

Sponsorship has become common, and ranges from major corporations to national governments. This has resulted in a marked improvement in design standards. Previously artwork and reproduction levels were moderate, if not amateur, reflecting the state of jobbing printing in their countries of origin, but the modern QSL card aspires to the standard of the four-colour picture postcard. The radio-information in the message area, filled in by hand, may be fronted by what at first glance suggests a wish-you-were-here card.

Radio operator call signs are formulated according to an internationally agreed codification, the initial letter(s) indicating the country or territory of the operator, for example: G = Britain; GM = Scotland; W or K = United States; VK = Australia. The handbook of the Radio Society of Great Britain provides information on the call sign system and its rationale.

COLLECTION Centre for Ephemera Studies, The University of Reading

Race bill

The early race bill, forerunner of today's race card, served the combined purpose of poster, handbill, and programme. In its classic form, during the period c.1750 to c.1850, it carried a bold headline announcing venue and date, a STOCK BLOCK showing two or three runners approaching the post, and a list of races, runners, owners, riders, weights, colours, and other details. Blank columns to the right allowed heat placings to be inserted by the racegoer, and these were often subsequently completed by the printer in type as a formal record of the races.

Format varied widely. The 'poster' style announcements were of the order of 440 × 280 mm (17⅜ × 11 in); the handbill variety were as small as 210 × 110 mm (8¼ × 4⅜ in). The majority, however, averaged some 250 × 190 mm (9⅞ × 7½ in). As with many of the products of the small jobbing printer, trimmed sizes were arbitrary, depending largely on the extent of the type-matter. Many of the bills were sold direct to the public by the printer himself.

Early race lists are of more than purely racing interest. They announce additional attractions in the form of theatre entertainments, illuminated gardens, special dinners and dances, single-stick matches, firework displays, musical concerts, and – before their official abolition in 1849 – cock-fights. An additional feature of the race list was the mention of one or more 'race ordinaries', fixed-price meals at local inns or public halls: 'an Ordinary the first day at the Antelope, the second day at the King's Arms. Dinner on the table each day at half-past two o'clock' (Sherborne, 1809); 'An ordinary every day immediately after the Races, provided by Mr Bodworth in the Exchange, which will be properly air'd for the Purpose' (Kersall Moor, Manchester, 1761).

Other incidental intelligence contained in the lists includes a warning that dogs on the course will be shot, that there is to be no crossing or jostling, and that booths and stalls may not be erected on the ground by persons who are in arrears with previous rental charges. Race cards of the mid 18th century, echoing the idiom of the street ballad, often carried a gratuitous verse or two of doggerel at the foot of the sheet.

REFERENCES John Lewis, *Printed Ephemera* (Ipswich: W. S. Cowell, 1962)

Rag book

The so-called rag book was printed on holland calico. It was described by its makers as 'virtually indestructible'. Devised for use by very young children, rag books could be sucked and

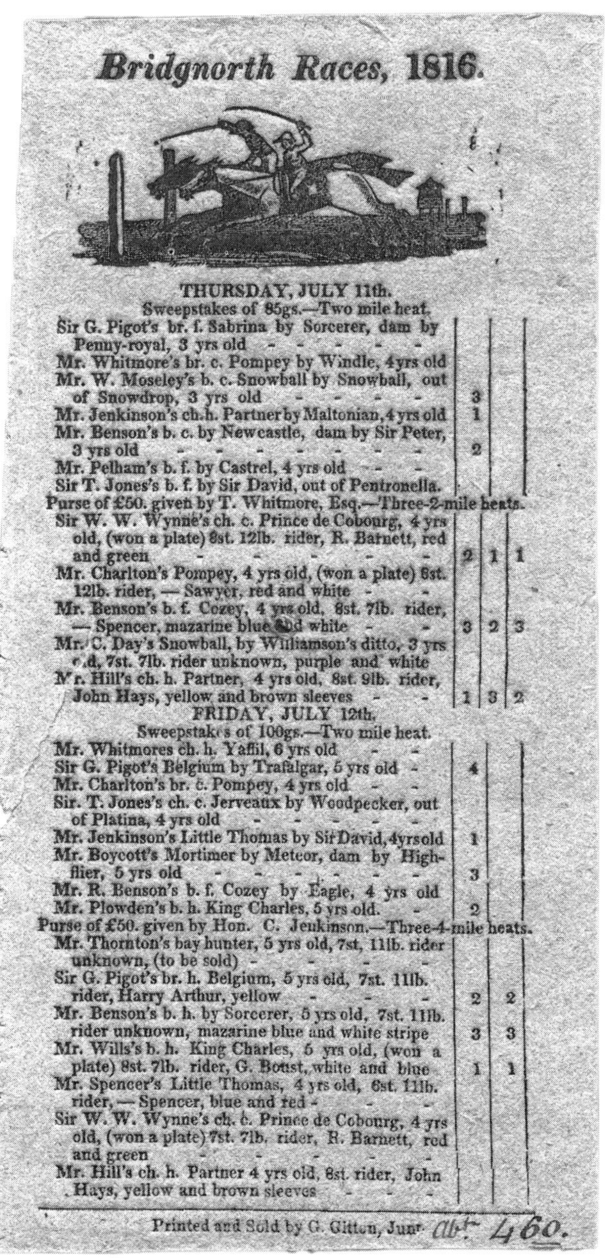

Bridgnorth Races, 1816.

THURSDAY, JULY 11th.
Sweepstakes of 85gs.—Two mile heat.
Sir G. Pigot's br. f. Sabrina by Sorcerer, dam by Penny-royal, 3 yrs old - - - - - - -
Mr. Whitmore's br. c. Pompey by Windle, 4yrs old
Mr. W. Moseley's b. c. Snowball by Snowball, out of Snowdrop, 3 yrs old - - - - - 3
Mr. Jenkinson's ch. h. Partner by Maltonian, 4 yrs old 1
Mr. Benson's b. c. by Newcastle, dam by Sir Peter, 3 yrs old - - - - - - - - 2
Mr. Pelham's b. f. by Castrel, 4 yrs old - -
Sir T. Jones's b. f. by Sir David, out of Pentronella.
Purse of £50. given by T. Whitmore, Esq.—Three-2-mile heats.
Sir W. W. Wynne's ch. c. Prince de Cobourg, 4 yrs old, (won a plate) 8st. 12lb. rider, R. Barnett, red and green - - - - - - 2 1 1
Mr. Charlton's Pompey, 4 yrs old, (won a plate) 8st. 12lb. rider, — Sawyer, red and white - -
Mr. Benson's b. f. Cozey, 4 yrs old, 8st. 7lb. rider, — Spencer, mazarine blue and white - - 3 2 3
Mr. C. Day's Snowball, by Williamson's ditto, 3 yrs old, 7st. 7lb. rider unknown, purple and white
Mr. Hill's ch. h. Partner, 4 yrs old, 8st. 9lb. rider, John Hays, yellow and brown sleeves - - 1 3 2
FRIDAY, JULY 12th.
Sweepstakes of 100gs.—Two mile heat.
Mr. Whitmores ch. h. Yaffil, 6 yrs old - -
Sir G. Pigot's Belgium by Trafalgar, 5 yrs old - 4
Mr. Charlton's br. c. Pompey, 4 yrs old - -
Sir. T. Jones's ch. c. Jerveaux by Woodpecker, out of Platina, 4 yrs old - - - - - -
Mr. Jenkinson's Little Thomas by Sir David, 4yrsold 1
Mr. Boycott's Mortimer by Meteor, dam by High-flier, 5 yrs old - - - - - - - 3
Mr. R. Benson's b. f. Cozey by Eagle, 4 yrs old
Mr. Plowden's b. h. King Charles, 5 yrs old. - 2
Purse of £50. given by Hon. C. Jenkinson.—Three-4-mile heats.
Mr. Thornton's bay hunter, 5 yrs old, 7st, 11lb. rider unknown, (to be sold) - - - - -
Sir G. Pigot's br. h. Belgium, 5 yrs old, 7st. 11lb. rider, Harry Arthur, yellow - - - - 2 2
Mr. Benson's b. h. by Sorcerer, 5 yrs old, 7st. 11lb. rider unknown, mazarine blue and white stripe 3 3
Mr. Wills's b. h. King Charles, 5 yrs old, (won a plate) 8st. 7lb. rider, G. Boust, white and blue 1 1
Mr. Spencer's Little Thomas, 4 yrs old, 6st. 11lb. rider, — Spencer, blue and red - - -
Sir W. W. Wynne's ch. c. Prince de Cobourg, 4 yrs old, (won a plate) 7st. 7lb. rider, R. Barnett, red and green - - - - -
Mr. Hill's ch. h. Partner 4 yrs old, 8st. rider, John Hays, yellow and brown sleeves - - -

Printed and Sold by G. Gitton, Junr. Abt. 460.

Race bill for Bridgnorth Races, 11 & 12 July 1826. Letterpress, printed and sold by G. Gitton (junior), Bridgnorth, with manuscript note that 460 copies were printed. 207 × 106 mm (8⅛ × 4⅛ in)

chewed without harm to book or child, and were also fast to washing. They were developed by the Dean family, who had been in the juvenile book business in the City of London since the late 18th century. In the late 19th century experiments were made in pasting printed paper pages on to calico, in the manner of maps, but this method was supplanted in 1901 by printing directly on to calico. The books, which ranged in price from sixpence to six shillings, were bound by sewing machine and trimmed with pinking shears to obviate fraying. Dean put great emphasis on indestructability; he is reported to have described children as 'wearing their food and eating their clothes'. His rag books had world success. ABCs and nursery rhymes appeared in many languages and Dean's list of published titles numbered over fifty.

The rag book idea was patented by Dean in most countries, though other manufacturers entered the market. In the early 1930s Raphael Tuck and Sons brought out 'Father Tuck's Inde structible Calico Books ... practically unspoilable ... printed direct on Tuck's Washable Calico'.

Rail ticket

The history of the railway ticket is in large measure expressed in the creation in the late 1830s and early 1840s of the Edmondson system, which has not been wholly superseded after over a century of worldwide application. Thomas Edmondson, former cabinetmaker and a newcomer to railways, was appointed stationmaster at Milton Station on the Newcastle and Carlisle Railway in 1836. Within a few years, first at Milton and later when working for the Manchester and Leeds Railway, he had devised a method of dealing with the issue and control of tickets.

The method was based on a pasteboard card measuring 30 × 57 mm (1 3/16 × 2 1/4 in), a size which was to become virtually a world standard. The card was part of an integrated system, incorporating ticket production and printing, dating machines, storage racks and dispensers, nippers for cancellation, and shredders for destruction after the ticket's use. In Britain in the 1970s and 1980s, by which time ticket-issuing had become almost wholly mechanized, the British Rail printing unit at Crewe was still producing some 100 million Edmondson-type tickets a year, and Edmondson dating machines were still in service for special-use issue on London's Underground.

Prior to the advent of Edmondson's system a number of others had been used: handwritten entries in a clerk's ledger (hence 'Booking Office'); numbered metal tallies (the number indicating passenger priority); and part-printed paper receipts for payment, the counterfoils being retained by the clerk. Also in use, for important passengers and Railway Company Directors, were special passes and tokens.

Many of these were items of some distinction in the early days of the railways; semi-precious metals and ivory tokens were not uncommon, and some of the passes conferring life travel privilege had the air of pocket awards of honour. The convention was maintained throughout the rest of the 19th century, not only for specially distinguished passengers but for 'company servants' and their families. Gold-blocked leather folders, even handwritten parchments, were at one time or another in use. The tradition was also continued in the handsomely printed season tickets and long-term passes issued to ordinary passengers. The Great Western Railway's season ticket in the 1920s and 1930s was a round-cornered heavyweight card engraved and printed by De La Rue & Co., printers of banknotes, stamps, and passports.

American special rail passes of the period 1860 to 1900 are among the most elegant items of ephemera the country ever produced. With three- four- and sometimes five-colour printings, and elaborately engraved scrollwork and vignettes, they added much to the railroad's public image. Some could be described as SECURITY PRINTING: at least one surviving pass confirms the Atlantic Mississippi & Ohio railroad as customers of the Continental Bank Note Co. of New York. Special passes were also often issued in America to members of State Legislature, politicians, newspaper editors, and (at half-fare) clergymen. The use and abuse of rail passes became widespread in America, as elsewhere. In the 1880s, to combat illicit transfer of passes, a number of companies introduced the identity photograph as an integral feature of the document.

The Edmondson ticket, in its multiplicity of destinations, passenger categories, and other variants, epitomizes the evolution and social impact of rail travel. Special-purpose tickets recall the conditions, occasions, people, and places – not to mention companies – of other times. Special occasions include such disparate events as 'Their Majesties visit reserved enclosure, Princes Street, Station: 9th July' (L M & S R: Edinburgh, 1937); 'Orange Demonstration Bruckless to Rossnowlagh and back' (County Down Railway Joint Committee, July 1950); Channel Cruise from Ramsgate Harbour' (New Mersey Steam Packet Company Ltd, 28 July 1948); and 'Admit one person for shelter (if available) at Finsbury Park (Picc.) Station' (London Transport in conjunction with the Local Authority, 1940). Passengers' categories include, from various periods and places, 'Harvestman', 'Fisherman', 'Commercial traveller', 'Lad', 'Hop-picker', 'Goldfields worker', and 'Corpse: adult/child/pauper'. Also recorded are 'Perambulator, unaccompanied', 'Third class dog', and 'Accompanied race horse'. Rail facilities for which Edmondson tickets appear are 'Platform', 'Dining room', 'Breakfast', 'Tray meal on forward journey', and 'Packed meal on special train'. Special Edmondson tickets were printed in fact for virtually any emergency railway requirement, sometimes in runs of only a few hundred.

The paper ticket, though widely abandoned in favour of the Edmondson system, remained in use throughout the Edmondson period. It has taken many forms, including several which, in some areas, have been adapted for bus and tramway use. Some smaller railways have adopted the early 'Stockton and Darlington' method, in which a part-printed form is completed by hand; others issued numbered paper tickets from counterfoiled books, with or without provision for handwritten details. Other small railways use the 'geographical' bus or tram system, in which a punched hole may indicate destination, date, time, class, and other details. 'Multiple' tickets, in which a multistage journey is represented by a series of perforated tear-off units, have also been widely used. For journeys involving extended inter-state travel, particularly in America, 'strips' of tickets were sometimes inordinately long. Strips up to 1.5 metres (about 5 feet) in length have been reported. Multiple paper tickets were later presented as booklets, each page corresponding to a stage in the journey.

The paper or thin card ticket returned towards the end of the 20th century with the computerized printing of travel details linked to electronic accountancy and record storage.

Railway ticket curiosities include: circular tickets (British North Borneo State Railways, 1938) on which seven single local-train journeys might be made on the system, each being marked off on a peripheral segment of the printed paper disc; 'spoof' tickets in which, typically, an apparent Edmondson ticket offers 'A Night on the Town' or 'A Happy Journey into the New Year'); and tickets bearing an affixed Tax Stamp (as at least for a period in the late 1930s in La Paz, Bolivia). Also occasionally found are railway tickets bearing unrelated face and reverse. In one example in the Graham Page Collection, a tenpenny London Transport ticket bears on its reverse the legend: 'This ticket is issued subject to the Bye-laws and regulations relating to the Corporation Bathing Establishment of the City'.

REFERENCES Maurice I. Bray, *Railway Tickets, Timetables and Handbills* (Ashbourne: Moorland Publishing Co., 1986); Gordon Fairchild, *A World of Tickets* (Brighton: Fairchild, 1972); William Fenton, *Railway Printed Ephemera* (Woodbridge: Antique Collectors Club, 1992); R. S. Gardiner, *History of the Railway Ticket* (Boston: Gardiner, 1938); Lionel Weiner, 'Passenger Tickets', *Railway Gazette* (UK) (1939)

COLLECTIONS Carlisle Library; John Rylands University Library of Manchester

SOCIETIES Railroadiana Collectors Association; Transport Ticket Society

Railway carriage panel

Carriage panels – decorative, informative, or both – have been a feature of British railway carriages since the late 19th century. They occupied the space above the seats in eight- or ten-person compartments, one, two, or three panels per side, framed and glazed, displaying system maps, landscapes, black and white photographs, reproductions of paintings in colour, and advertising matter.

They were first introduced by the Great Eastern Railway in 1884, when Thomas Worsdell, Superintendent of the Railway, installed black and white framed photographs in the company's carriages. The idea rapidly spread to other companies, and was adopted by railways in Europe at large. (North American railways did not take up the idea.)

Forerunner of the framed panel was the coloured transfer plaque, mounted centrally on the compartment wall, advertising the services of railway hotels. Designed in the manner of the heraldic transfers used on carriage doors (and probably produced by the same artists), the plaques used lettering on scroll and strapwork, with a liberal admixture of monograms, armorial devices, and gold. The Great Northern Railway's hotels at King's Cross, Peterborough, Bradford, and Leeds used such plaques to advertise their closeness to their respective stations, assuring passengers that 'Porters meet all trains and convey visitors' luggage to the hotel free' and that 'a spacious dining room is provided on the departure platform at King's Cross'.

Successor to the transfer plaque was a printed full-colour pictorial map, showing the ramifications of the company's network, with vignetted pictures of locomotives, steamships and other travel images. The map usually contrived to overstate the extent of the line, in some cases including other companies' adjacent lines with only a nominal colour change, in others presenting features on the map at varying scales to provide an added sense of scope (the system map was to return in the 1920s and 1930s, but by that time the treatment had become purely schematic, and was distorted to fit the format of the panel).

Also introduced in the early 1920s was the sepia photographic landscape, sometimes occupying the whole length of the panel, sometimes as a pair of ovals, showing scenes from the Company's regions. In World War II many of the panels were given over to air-raid and blackout instructions and general war-effort material, but the sepia photographs – many of them by that time notably out-of-date – remained in position for some years after the war. They were replaced in the early 1950s by colour reproductions of specially commissioned paintings. Chief among these was a series by G. Hamilton Ellis, artist and railway historian, who produced twenty-four scenes portraying the history of travel from 1840 to 1920. Other artists painted contemporary topographical views, among them J. E. Aitken, John L. Baker, F. W. Baldwin, F. D. Blake, Claude Buckle, H. J. Denham, W. Fairclough, E. T. Holding, R. E. Jordan, Charles King, R. M. Lander, Freda Marston, Frank Mason, Sidney Agnew Mercer, J. Merriott, Claude Muncaster, Gyrth Russell, Eric Scott, Frank Sherwin, L. R. Squirrell, Kenneth Steel, Henry Stringer, Edward Walker, and L. J. Wood.

By the mid 1970s the panels had been largely phased out, their place being taken by mirrors. In the late 1970s British Rail published a series of facsimile reproductions of early pictorial maps issued by the Southern Railway, the London & South Western Railway, the Southern Railway including the Isle of Wight, the London, Brighton & South Coast Railway, the Caledonian Railway, and the Great Eastern Railway.

REFERENCE P. B. Whitehouse (ed.), *Railway Relics and Regalia* (London, New York: Hamlyn for Country Life, 1975)

COLLECTION National Railway Museum, York

Railway ephemera *See* ARRANGEMENT OF CARRIAGES DIAGRAM; RAIL TICKET; RAILWAY-CARRIAGE PANEL; RAILWAY LUGGAGE LABEL; RAILWAY TRAVELLING CHARTS; TAG LABEL; TIMETABLE

Railway luggage label

In Britain, the railway label had its origins in the 1840s. Baggage, carried on the carriage roof in the accepted stage-coach manner, was becoming increasingly in danger of permanent separation from its owner, and by 1841 the London & Birmingham Railway was strongly recommending passengers to label their property with the name of the destination station. This company made no reference to the provision of labels, but by 1848 the Great Western Railway had begun issuing them and a few labels from that period have survived.

By 1923, the year when Britain's many railway companies combined to form the 'big four' (The London Midland & Scottish; the London and North Eastern, the Great Western, and the Southern), dozens of companies were issuing their own printed labels. Specimens from nearly a hundred of these have survived. Even after their disappearance as separate entities, the former companies' identity was often retained through local style and typographic layout.

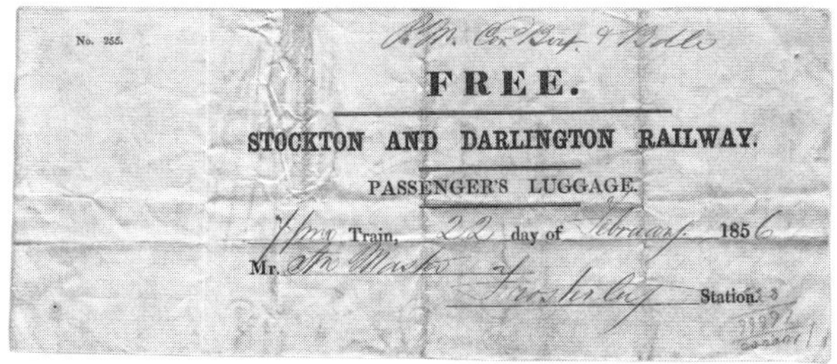
No. 355.
FREE.
STOCKTON AND DARLINGTON RAILWAY.
PASSENGER'S LUGGAGE.
Train, 22 day of February 1856
Mr.
Station.

Passenger luggage label for Stockton and Darlington Railway, 22 February 1856. Letterpress and manuscript. 99 × 240 mm (3⅞ × 9½ in)

Many early labels quoted not only the destination but the station of origin, a facility that posed problems of printing economics and distribution. Many bore the name of the system concerned, sometimes as a cryptic series of initials ('C R') and sometimes at full ceremonial length (East & West Junction & Stratford-on-Avon, Towcester & Midland Junction Railways). Some companies, however, such as the South Eastern and the later South Eastern & Chatham Railway, remained acronymous throughout their existence. These two companies were major users of colour-coding, however, and indicated some twenty different routes by colour and distinctive borders.

Parcel traffic produced labels of two kinds, one indicating receipt of payment, the other showing the amount to pay. They functioned as part of an accounting system as well as routeing guides. These too date from the 1840s. Provision was made in other labels for 'Luggage in advance', 'Delivered luggage', 'Collected luggage', and 'Carted luggage' (unaccompanied passenger-baggage). Generalized labels also appeared. These included such legends as 'Urgent', 'Fragile', 'Handle with care', 'Farm and garden produce', 'Valuable animals and birds', 'Livestock', as well as 'Left luggage' and 'Cloak room'.

Carriages too bore labels: 'Workman', 'Engaged', 'Ladies only'; and in wartime: 'This compartment not to be used', 'Reserved for wounded'. Wagon labels include indications of content and such injunctions as 'Shunt with care', 'Inflammable: place as near middle of train as possible and away from vehicles labelled "explosive"', and 'Not to go'.

As with many items of printed ephemera, railway labels often carry a coded printer's footline conveying production details, quantity, order number, printer's initials, etc. Dates may also be included (as for example 2/43 = February 1943). Additional dating clues may be derived from typographical evidence. The typeface known as Gill Sans, for example, designed by Eric Gill, first appeared in 1928 and was adopted for use in the printed matter of the London and North Eastern Railway shortly afterwards. Its use in luggage and goods labels, however, may not have occurred until some appreciable time later.

Passenger-accompanied baggage in America, even when carried in baggage compartments, was commonly tagged with a numbered metal token, a small version of which was retained by the passenger. The principle was later applied to numbered tear-off tags in which routeing and destination were written on the baggage by hand. The principle is also used for long-distance bus travel.

REFERENCE Trefor David, *Pre-Grouping Luggage Labels* (Cheltenham: Railway Print Society, 1981)

SOCIETIES Railway Print Society

Railway travelling chart

Publishers in the 19th century produced a range of printed pastimes for railway travellers. Chief among these were pictorial guides, panoramas, and charts depicting features visible from the carriage on specific routes. The travelling chart appeared as a booklet, or as a concertina fold-out, in which a central trackway is marked on either side with illustrated views or geographical and historical landmarks; the trackway itself shows viaducts, tunnels, cuttings, gradients, mileages, and stations. The fold-out chart was made famous by the publishers of the *Railway Chronicle* from 1846 to the 1890s. The charts they published 'For perusal on the journey', were described as 'Constituting a Novel and Complete Companion for the Railway Carriage'.

Railway travelling charts represented an updating of the 17th century 'ribbon' maps of John Ogilby, in which roads between specific towns in Britain appeared as semi-pictorial diagrams, and the book-form charts of Paterson, in which city-to-city routes appeared as typeset itineraries.

In America, where space and terrain did not admit such detailed treatment, booklets showed general views, often with conventional fold-out maps. These were sold independently or by the railway companies themselves. Some, like the railway companies' jigsaw puzzles, travelling cards, and other pastime-souvenirs were given free to passengers.

COLLECTION National Railway Museum, York

Rainbow printing [plate 16]

The term applies to a method of printing in a number of colours at a single working of the press. Inking rollers are charged along their length with different colours so that the inks merge with their neighbour to produce a graphic 'spectrum' effect. The principle may be applied to any form of printing in which inking rollers are used.

Because of the tendency of the inks to merge (and thus lose purity) the method was commonly used when only a relatively short printing run was required and where variation, as between one impression and another, was acceptable. The effect, introduced in the 1840s as an eye-catching novelty, was used chiefly as a background on which to overprint displayed text matter, though examples are also found in which lettering appears white reversed out of a rainbow ground.

Among early examples of rainbow printing is an admission ticket in the collection of the London Theatre Museum for the Theatre Royal, Drury Lane, which measures 90 × 130 mm (3½ × 5⅛ in). It has a white-embossed decorative border enclosing a rainbow-printed panel with overprinted wording. The ticket, for a 'Grand Neapolitan Carnival' on 22 May 1839, has no imprint, but bears design characteristics associated with the work of Whiting & Branston and Dobbs (*see* COMPOUND-PLATE PRINTING; EMBOSSING/LACE PAPER). An item in similar vein, clearly produced by the same printer/designer, is a pen label issued by Joseph Gillott at about the same time. It measures 52 × 95 mm (2 × 3¾ in) and bears a central overprinting of wording on a rainbow-printed background.

Rainbow printing was fairly widely used throughout the 19th century, especially for SHEET-MUSIC COVERS, and continued to appear as a novelty in the 20th century. In modified form it has been used in such items as local festival posters and labels for home-made wines. Colour merging is widely used in the printing of banknotes and other security documents. Here the merging of colour is under complete control, one colour-change being overprinted on another to produce an anti-counterfeit effect of great complexity.

A variation of the principle is applied in split-duct printing from machines. Here, there may or may not be merging of colours, the colours are applied simultaneously from the same roller in one working, separate colours being fed to various parts of the roller independently and, if required, far enough apart to obviate mixing.

Ration papers

Rationing of food and other commodities is essentially a military concept, imposing disciplines of consumption and conservation in times of shortage. The principle is extended to the

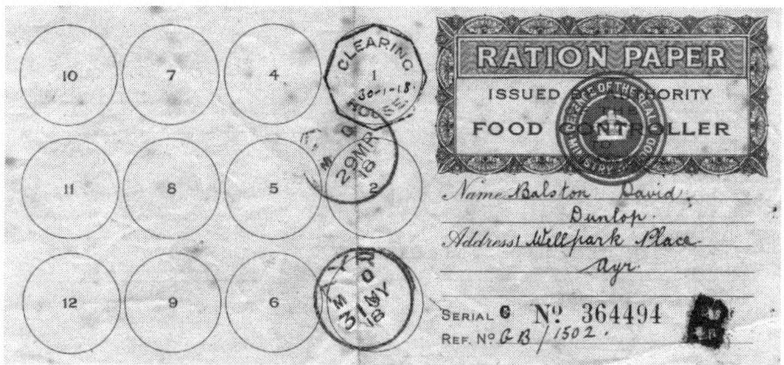

Ration paper, Ayr, stamped January to May 1918. Lithographed. 87 × 197 mm (3⅜ × 7¾ in)

civilian in localized siege conditions (Paris, 1870; Ladysmith, Mafeking, 1900), and to whole nations in total war. In these situations ration coupons, tickets, cards, etc. assume characteristics close to those of currency: their design, production, distribution, and exchange require security controls hardly less stringent.

Control of national ration systems is normally effected by linking individual registrations to a general census. This provides a statistical basis for provisioning as well as a control mechanism for conscription for military and civilian service. Possession of an identity card is normally essential in claiming entitlement to ration papers.

World War I saw the inception of rationing on a massive scale. Britain was slow to start, and rationing of meat, fats, and sugar became fully operational only in the summer of 1918. Ration books were abolished about a year later and 'registration' for sugar, an indirect form of rationing, had ceased by the end of 1920. Germany introduced rationing in the first days of the war (thus incidentally giving rise to the suggestion abroad that the country was already desperate) and other commodities followed, but subsequent failures of administration were to contribute to the collapse of 1918.

Rationing schemes in World War II, based largely on World War I experience, were brought into operation more or less universally at the outset. Britain's World War II food rationing began in January 1940 with butter, ham, bacon, and sugar; meat followed in March 1940, tea and cooking fats in July. Cheese, eggs, and milk were rationed in 1941, chocolate and sweets in 1942. Bread was not rationed until 1946. Many commodities, including meat, cheese, butter, and fats were not released from control until ten years after the end of the war. In America, patriotic moderation was the national call, as it had been in World War I, but in April 1941 the Office of Price Administation was set up, imposing controls on raw materials, and maximum prices. A 'Points' rationing system was administered by Local Ration Boards.

Ration papers have taken various forms. In World War I Germany and Austria at first issued separate cards or papers for each commodity, or 'composite' cards in which a double row of sections on four sides allowed punch control of eight commodities. Later, Germany introduced the 'Ration Book' (effectively a stapling-together of individual cards), and this was widely adopted, not least by the British who used the system when they brought in rationing in 1918. The booklet format reappeared in Europe in World War II, as it did in America under the Office of Price Administration.

Rationing invariably produces a 'black market', not only in commodities but in ration books themselves, and in most countries a printed notice on the document warned of penalties for infringement of the rationing laws. Counterfeiters were also deterred by the use of more or less complex SECURITY PRINTING measures. These include patterned colour underprinting and a single (black) printing on coloured-fibre security paper. Forgery of ration coupons was a major consideration for both sides in World War II, not only as it involved their own nationals, but because it was a potential means of economic disruption by the enemy. Forged German coupons were produced by the British in World War II for the use of their agents in Germany, if not for more extensive distribution.

War-time rationing must provide not only for everyday needs but for a wide range of 'non-standard' situations: evacuation, removals, members of forces on leave or in transit, special diets for invalids, children and nursing mothers, 'holiday' rations, supplies for foreign visitors, air raid victims, refugees and prisoners of war, farmers (self-supply 'coupons'). These and many other rationing contingencies require special cards, coupons, and documentation. Ration papers include all of these as well as notices, explanatory leaflets, declaration forms, registration cards, instructions to retailers and wholesalers, and other administrative items.

A harbinger of rationing in Britain in World Wars I and II is a Government leaflet published in December 1917, entitled 'The Rations'. Without actually implying a threat of rationing it enjoins (in capital letters) 'the utmost economy in the use of all kinds of food … by all classes and by all persons', and sets out a scale of adult rations per head per week, with varying rates for men and women and sub-divisions for those in heavy industrial or agricultural work, ordinary industrial or manual work (or 'domestic service'), in addition to those 'unoccupied or on sedentary work'. The weekly rations envisaged, in addition to bread, were 12 ounces of 'other cereals', 2 lb of meat, 14 ounces of butter, and 3 ounces of sugar. Bread amounts were to range from 8 lb for men in heavy industry to 3 lb 8 oz for women 'unoccupied or in sedentary work'. The concept of a ration differential, which was applied in Germany from the start, was not adopted in Britain.

Rationing is not only a wartime expedient. The ration book has appeared in a variety of peacetime emergencies – as, for example, in Spain in the 1950s ('colección de cupones de racionamiento'), and in Britain in 1957 (motor fuel ration book).

Razor-blade wrapper

In its first year of production (1903) Gillette's American Safety Razor Co. sold 51 razors and 168 blades. In the following year the figures were 90,000 razors and over 12,000,000 blades.

The razor-blade wrapper was a vital marketing aid. Its primary function was to prevent accidental cuts in distribution and storage. Secondly, it served to retain the film of protective grease that held rust at bay. Thirdly, it carried the new mass-market ingredient, the 'Brand-design'. By the 1920s the razor-blade wrapper had become a universally recognized item, each design seeking to bestow individuality on a product which had become very largely standardized. As with other articles of mass production, technology having reached a certain level of excellence, point-of-purchase choice became a matter of eye appeal.

After Gillette's first sober 'signed-portrait' design, wrappers broke into a plethora of visual stereotypes, enlisting every graphic genre from cigarette pack and match label to banknote and postage stamp. The original Gillette wrapper, measuring 44 × 22 mm (1¾ × ⅞ in), remained virtually unchanged (though there were seven-sided gentleman's models), which meant that the designer's scope was severely limited. Nevertheless, productivity was impressive. Today's major collections contain well over 20,000 different designs and specialists estimate an output of 30,000.

With the advent of the electric razor and the rise of cartridge-loading in 'conventional' razors, the point may be in sight when a definitive catalogue of razor-blade wrappers becomes a possibility. A start has been made in eastern Europe where collectors have compiled short-run editions of listings, largely in Polish and Czech. A catalogue has also been produced in Swedish and English, covering Swedish wrappers only (with elucidations in German). Full-scale research into factories, company histories, dating, etc. remains to be attempted.

Ream wrapper/label

The practice of marketing reams of paper in wrapping paper stems from the Middle Ages. At first the manufacturer's identity was written by hand on the wrapper, but printed marks soon followed, in many cases echoing the watermark of the sheets themselves.

Collectors and curators are normally interested in the marks as such, disregarding the full extent of the complete wrapper. Items in collections are therefore often found showing the mark only, the surrounding paper being trimmed off; in this way storage and display are facilitated, though purists prefer to retain the whole wrapper. Many specimens have come down to us with a crease across the image, which results from the use of waste wrappers as improvised files by early office clerks. The marks, of which there are many hundreds, have few pretensions to artistic merit, although they may be seen as a lively form of folk art and have undoubted value for historians of papermaking.

They are printed in black or red, usually on thick, poor quality paper or thin board. The printing stock was normally in shades of brown, blue, or grey, the colour deriving from the incidental mixture of old rags and blue clothing of sailors. Much of the grey base came from a regular intake of learned books claimed for repulping from the libraries of monasteries. In Holland the colour was referred to as *monnikegrauw* (monk grey).

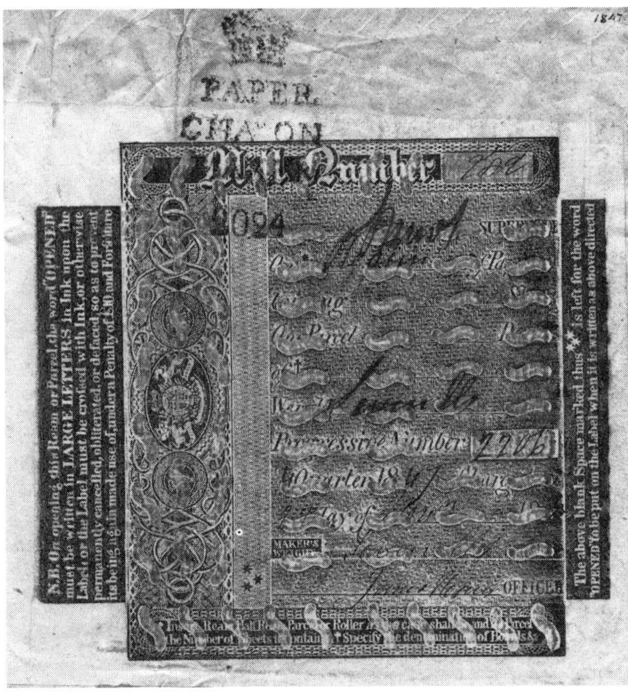

Ream label, printed in red and black by the compound-plate process, 1847. Paper 200 × 188 mm (7⅞ × 7½ in)

The images had a mock-heraldic air and included most of the well-known watermark symbols: posthorns, crowns, shields, ships, eagles, beehives, horsemen, and, suggesting the term 'foolscap', a jester's head. For the most part the designs of wrappers included the maker's name with, perhaps, a location: '*Papier fin fait par Pierre Dexmier*' or just a simple description: 'Fine paper'. 'Anonymous' wrappers were also produced so that the paper-maker could insert a name or not, as occasion required. Designs often incorporated punning allusions, playing on the maker's name or background (a tennis racket appears in the design for the Amsterdam firm of Raket); various other visual elements (angels, hourglasses, salamanders, etc.) still await explanation.

The woodcut style of European ream-wrapper marks had much in common with the robust simplicity of other early folk work. The style is found over a long period in playing cards, children's alphabets, street literature, and IMAGERIE POPULAIRE. The American ream wrapper, which first appeared in the early years of the 19th century, has an idiom of its own; it is more detailed and literal in its images and less influenced by pseudo-heraldry.

A tax on paper, first imposed in the reign of Queen Anne, levied 3½*d* per pound in weight on the product as it left the mill. Each packaged ream was required to carry a government excise label with details of its content filled in by hand. The manufacturer was also required to date the name label with a numbered stamp and to keep a record of despatches from the mill for inspection by the excise authorities. The penalty for failure to account for any labels delivered by the excise was £200. The tax was reduced to 1½*d* per pound in weight and, after much agitation, finally abolished in 1861.

The labels commonly measured some 150 × 120 mm (6 × 5 in) and were printed in two colours by COMPOUND PLATE-PRINTING, a security method in which interlocking plates separately inked with different colours are brought together for printing at one pass of the press. Engraved lines running through the design continue unbroken across the colour-change, producing a 'forgery-proof' image.

See also PAPER-DUTY LABEL

REFERENCES Joan Evans, *The Endless Web: John Dickinson & Co. Ltd., 1804–1954* (London: Jonathan Cape, 1955); Henk Voorn, *Old Ream Wrappers* (North Hills, PA: Bird & Bull Press, 1969)

Rebus

Also known as a hieroglyphic puzzle, the rebus was much in vogue in Britain in the 18th century, when it appeared as a novelty item in printsellers' shops. The puzzle presented a message in semi-pictorial form, using sections of objects in place of selected words or syllables. The device had been used since earliest times, conveying town or family names in cryptic form on coins and coats of arms, and may be ultimately traced to the ideographic and pictographic symbols of early Egypt and China.

The word *rebus* (Latin: by things) is said to derive from the expression *non verbis sed rebus* (not with words but by things). It is also said to have originated with the title *De rebus quae geruntur* (on things that are happening), to describe cryptic satires on matters of the day. The word has been used in this sense at least

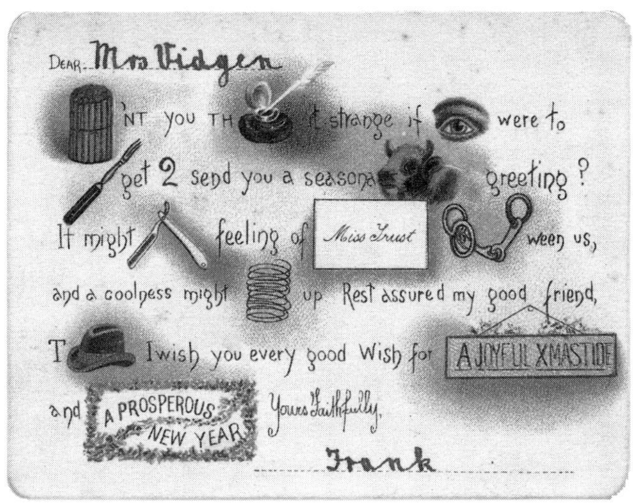

Rebus greetings card, early 20th century. Chromolithographed. 84 × 109mm (3¼ × 4¼in)

since the 15th century, and remains current today, but 18th-century usage favoured 'hieroglyphic puzzle' or 'hieroglyphic epistle'.

The hieroglyphic epistle, an open letter to a personality of the day, became a recognized form of political comment. Its enigmatic presentation served at the same time to intrigue the reader and to veil the directness of the message, which was often harshly critical. Formats varied widely, some examples measuring as much as 440 × 270mm (17⅜ × 10⅝in). Many carried decorative title pieces in borders as well as the small pictures within the text. The majority were engraved and printed intaglio, some simulating typesetting, others handwriting. Others used type interspersed with woodcut images.

In the 19th century the concept was taken up on both sides of the Atlantic as a medium of entertainment for its own sake, sometimes conveying moral and religious homilies. It also appeared on greetings cards, notably valentines. In France, sets of small numbered cards were available, each bearing a few words in rebus form, for sending in sequence as a continuing message.

The rebus had continuing currency in children's puzzles until the early years of the 20th century, and in America there was a widespread revival of interest in it in the 1930s when advertisers and magazine promoters used the idea in competitions, many of which offered big prizes.

COLLECTION John Johnson Collection, Bodleian Library, Oxford

Receipt

As an acknowledgement of monies received, the printed receipt provides a measure of accountancy control greater than that offered by the simple handwritten slip. The element of control applies not only to holders, by clearing them of further demand, but to those who receive on behalf of others, thus ensuring an open record of a transaction.

It is in this capacity, specifically in the levying of taxes, that the printed receipt first appeared. It was later adopted institutionally (by charities, hospitals, colleges, etc.) and by commerce generally. Additional security was achieved by the introduction of the counterfoil system, in which booklets of receipt forms provided a double record – one to be cut or torn out for the party making the payment, the other remaining with the recipient. Correspondence between the detached portion and the counterfoil was ensured by hand-numbering of the portions, by 'indenture' detachment (in which an irregular cut produces matching edges), and from the 1880s by mechanical numbering. Additional control over matching of the two parts appears in the use of elaborate printed flourishes and other patterning at the line of separation. Later refinements include watermarking and the use of other minor SECURITY PRINTING devices.

Among the earliest British printed receipts are LIGHTHOUSE-DUES PAPERS, in use in the late 17th century, and port dues receipts of the 18th century (covering storage, anchorage, and other charges). The 19th century saw a proliferation of charges for rates and taxes and their corresponding tax receipt forms. These covered highways; lighting and watching; paving and gravelling; sewerage, drainage, and cleaning; water; the poor; etc.

In America, receipt forms also refer to taxes on household furniture, on silver plate, watches, guns, and 'opening streets'; in Britain, to windows, hair powder, servants, greyhounds and armorial bearings.

ARMED FORCES PAPERS provide a rich source of receipt forms, in earlier times handwritten, according to prescribed formats, later as printed blanks. *The Seaman's New Vade-Mecum* (London, 1811) covers receipt forms for, among other items, 'Buckets', 'Dr James' fever powder', 'Condemned butter supplied to the boatswain', 'Extra wine for the sick', and 'A Deserter'. A United States army receipt dated 17 February 1864 acknowledges acceptance of forty-six mules and twenty-two horses; in the column marked 'Condition when delivered' is written the word 'Unserviceable'.

Receipt. Western Warehouses, Oxford Street, London, 13 August 1816. Intaglio-printed and manuscript. 97 × 238mm (3⅞ × 9⅜in)

The receipt is a major ingredient of papers, whether private, institutional or commercial. Though it is among the most commonly encountered of ephemera it often provides evidence beyond that of simple accountancy:

'(March 24) 19(24): Received of (MHS—) (four) dollars (court costs in adoption of v—d—w—) [Signed] (J. S. Thompson)'

'North Providence (Feb 1st) 188(9): M (Sawyer) to A. D. Swan, Dr: To (62½) qts milk at (7) cts per qt: $(4.38) to (8) qts (cream) at (35) ct per qt: $(2.80); $(7.18); received payment (A. D. Swan)'

'Port of Lynn-RS (March 9 1798) No. (105): For piloting the (sloop, Good Intent) of (Lynn) Capt. (Beaumont) up and down this channel… £(1.2.6.) Received (Jas. Middleton)'

'Baptist Free School, Tooks Court, Chancery Lane, for the religious education & clothing the necessitous poor of every denomination… Received of (Mr Roberts) the sum of (fifteen) shillings… being the amount of one year's subscription… (W. B. Kendrick)'

'Derby County and Borough Gaol and House of Correction. Received into my custody, the Bod(—) of (—) this (—) day of (—) 18(—) at (—) o'clock. (—) Governor'

'Providence, RI (July 7) 188(5) Received from Butler Hospital for the Insane (twenty five) dollars (for shopping and personal expenses) (Miss —)'

See also ARTISAN'S BILL/RECEIPT; PEW PAPERS; SALES-TAX TOKEN/ RECEIPT; TAXATION PAPERS; TITHE PAPERS; TOLL/ TURNPIKE TICKET

Recipe, folk

The word 'recipe' has only recently settled down to its present largely culinary use. As the imperative form of the Latin (*recipere:* to receive) it conveys the command 'take' (as in Mrs Beeton: 'Take three dozen eggs . . .'). The word is embodied in the symbol ℞ used in medical prescriptions, and was for long rendered as 'receipt' – in the general sense, medical or domestic, of 'formulation' (cf W. S. Gilbert: 'If you want a receipt for that popular mystery . . .').

The handwritten folk recipes of the 18th and 19th centuries carry the title 'Receipt' (or 'Rect') and cover formulations ranging from gooseberry tarts and syllabubs to complexion aids and bug exterminators. In the absence of formal sources of advice, recipes of all descriptions were passed from hand to hand (sometimes bearing the endorsement 'Proved') and kept as part of the small body of family wisdom in a kitchen notebook (*see* COMMONPLACE BOOK). Their virtues were enhanced by providing a source ('Sir John Berneys receipt to cure cloth for Covering Umbrellas etc', 'Dr Beddowes, from a convent in Hungary; To stop mortification. Equal quantities of Bark Rice and Charcoal made into a poultice . . .').

Earlier recipes also invoked the deity, enjoining the patient to prayer and, occasionally, spells and incantations. In the matter of major ills the tone was a mixture of confidence and desperation: 'The only rect. for the plague. Take three pints of muskadine and boil therein a handfull of Sage and a handful of Rue, untill a pint be wasted, then put these to a penny worth of long Pepper, half an ounce of Nutmegs all beaten together, then let it boil a little and put these to three penny worth of Treacle and two Nagens of the best Angelica waters you can get, keep this as yr life as above all Worldly treasure'.

It is clear that for long periods the handwritten folk remedy ranked equal in status to the doctor's PRESCRIPTION, the latter differing only in that it was presented in Latin. Certainly the domestic sector covered a wide spectrum. A list of typical titles includes: 'For a weak constitution', 'For burns or scalds', 'How to make green paint', 'Cholera morbus', 'Tincture of Life', 'To take rabbits alive', 'Remedy for the itch', 'Remedy for swine', 'For the jaundice, proved', 'Varnish for hat case', 'For the lice', 'For a cow's bad water', 'To kill fleas', 'Receipt for the surfeit of water'.

COLLECTION Rural History Centre, The University of Reading

Record, advertising

The earliest advertising records may be said to date from the advent of the commercial disc in the first decade of the 20th century. One surviving specimen put out by the Pathé Co. in 1905 carries music on one side and a printed advertisement for the company on the other, though this cannot be said to rank as a true advertising record since the publicity message is printed rather than audible.

Early advertising discs were made of the conventional shellac (sometimes of cardboard with a shellac facing), and, from the mid 1920s, of flexible lightweight plastic materials. At first they were made in a monochrome material (white, brown, or black) and had text and illustrations (printed in a single colour) that often extended over the whole of the recording surface as well as the central 'label' area. In the 1930s the printed image appeared in half-tone, monochrome or full-colour, the recording track being impressed on a transparent overlay. The diameter of the disc varied from the standard ten inches (255 mm) to $3\frac{3}{8}$ in (85 mm) with arbitrary intermediate stages depending on the length of the message.

Advertising record of Huntley & Palmers, Reading and London, 1930s. The record is mounted on card and shown with its envelope. 101 × 101 mm (4 × 4 in)

An early example, issued in Germany in the mid 1920s, was produced by a British firm, the Goodson Record Co., for Tietz, the Berlin chain-store. On a white flexible disc measuring some 245 mm ($9\frac{5}{8}$ in) an advertising message appears as a blue line image extending over the whole playing surface. The record is unusual in that, instead of an audible advertising message, it carries standard musical items (the 'Washington Post March' and 'Ramona'), and because the printed advertising is shared by the chain-store on one side and a gramophone-needle manufacturer (Fursten) on the other.

With the exception of a few spoken messages (for example, a charity message for Papworth Village industries, by the Duke of Kent) early advertising records were the musical forerunners of today's advertising jingle. This was an idiom unfamiliar in Britain until the coming of Radio Luxembourg, with its commercially-sponsored programmes, in the 1930s. In 1933 the Standard Motor Co. of Coventry put out a four-inch disc of 'The Song of the Standard', backed by a printed list of prices of six of the year's new models. (Most expensive was the Standard 'twenty' 6-cylinder saloon from £325, cheapest was the 'little twelve' 6-cylinder saloon from £189.)

Among examples of 'rigid' advertising discs is a 1930s Shellac/board issued by Siemens Lamps. A black 10-inch record bears the label 'Siemens Pearl and Opal Electric Lamps – the Popular Pair'; on one side is 'Forget-me-not' as a waltz by Mayhead Reaves played by the Opal and Pearl Dance Orchestra, and on the other 'The Popular Pair', a foxtrot by 'Jeanette' with 'vocal chorus played by the same orchestra'. The record is supplied in a paper cover bearing the advertising slogan 'Siemens – the lamps with a good record'.

Prominent names in the development of the advertising record are Durium in the United States, and Dubrico, Plaston, Goodson, Lyntone, and Livingston in Britain.

Record cover

The term 'record cover' refers to a printed paper or card envelope, commonly pierced with a central aperture to display the label of the record it contains. It is normally used in connection with the 78 r.p.m. production era. ('Record sleeve' entered into currency with the advent of the long-play disc towards the end of the 1940s.) The earliest commercial disc records (which were ultimately to supersede the cylinders of the 1880s and 1890s) were single-sided five-inch vulcanized rubber discs and were produced as toys by Kämmerer & Rheinhardt, of Waltershausen, Germany in 1889. Seven-inch records were introduced by the United States Gramophone Co. in Washington in 1894, and the company followed these with ten-inch records in 1900 and twelve-inch ones in 1903.

Earliest surviving covers are for ten-inch records; they were made of paper and printed in black. Because their contents were single-sided the label aperture appeared on one side of the cover only. Double-sided records were introduced in 1904, when covers were pierced accordingly. (Labels on discs first appeared in 1900.) By the 1920s most records were double-sided, but single-sided issues continued to appear until the mid 1930s.

Cover designs were largely devoted to advertising associated with equipment: 'graphophones' and 'phonographs' in America, 'gramophones' in Britain; needles ('the Songster', 'the polyphon Damascus', 'the Arrow', 'the Trumpeter') and, later, radio and radiograms.

Record companies issued their own standard covers, sometimes printing a catalogue selection on the reverse. In Britain in the early 1930s the Parlophone Co. issued a cover bearing its own standard design on one side and, on the reverse, a *News Chronicle* advertisement for its weekly record column by Christopher Stone, the pioneer disc jockey. A number of companies featured individual recording artists on their covers, regardless of the title of the record they contained. Also provided were substantial card covers for overprinting by retailers. These covers, produced not only by record companies but also by makers of gramophones and needles, were devised to contain both the record and its paper cover. Overprinted covers often carried details of retailers' other goods and services. The A1 Gramophone and Radio Stores of Walworth Road, London, advertised (c.1953) 'electric, incandescent and gas lighting accessories... all pendants fixed free of charge by experienced workmen'. Card covers, at first bound with gummed tape, were later machine-stitched. Printing was commonly in a single colour. Similar covers, unprinted, were later bound into a storage album to take sets of recordings of operas and other larger works. The colour-printed label on the covers of 'set' volumes was the direct forerunner of the 1960s 'album' cover.

Record cover, c. 1930. Lithographed on buff paper. 255 × 255 mm (10 × 10 in)

REFERENCE Peter Copeland, *Sound Recordings* (London: The British Library, 1991)

Relief printing for the blind

The first serious attempts at providing the blind with a reading system date from the 16th century. In c. 1517 Francisco Lucas of Saragossa devised a set of relief letters which were carved on thin tablets of wood. Rampazetto, of Rome, developed the idea, using incised letters and at the same time enlarging the size of the tablets. The idea lapsed, however, because blind people found the letters too difficult to read, and because, since the letters were immovable, a fresh tablet was required for each message. Other innovators included Girolimo Cardano in Italy, Pierre Moreau in France, Schonberger of Königsberg, and George Harsdoffer of Nürnberg.

The major figure in the field was Valentin Haüy who founded the world's first school for the blind in Paris in 1784. He introduced a method of relief printing using conventional large type. Apart from its cumbersomeness, the system had the defect that the blind could not use it for writing.

Haüy's books were among the first works for the blind to be used in Britain, but in the mid 1820s James Gall of Edinburgh devised a similar system, as did Edmund Fry of London. Fry's system was widely adopted and in a modified form appeared in a series of relief books published by John Alston of the Glasgow Institute for the Blind. Alston's system, again modified, was taken up by Samuel Howe, Director of the Perkins Institution in Boston. This became known as the Boston line letter.

Two shorthand systems were also introduced, one by Thomas Lucas and another by James Frere. These had only moderate success.

In 1847 Dr William Moon, who had himself become blind at twenty-one, introduced a system of simplified relief characters based on orthodox letters. The system, the first to be devised by a person who fully understood the problems of the blind, was easily learnt. It made rapid headway among a score or so of competitive systems.

It was another blind person, Louis BRAILLE, who came up with a different idea. In 1825 he devised a 6-dot system which, by 1834, he had virtually perfected. It was a system which, through its simplicity – and not least its capacity to be written as well as read by the blind – was to become the world's standard. With suitable modifications it is in use for most of the world's languages. Punched out from the rear in reverse (both in arrangement and sequence) the raised dots of Braille's system are produced either by a pointed stylus ('style') in conjunction with a perforated metal template or by a 6-key punch-head which traverses the paper in single character strips. In mass production, whole pages are printed from metal plates on high speed presses.

In the solid-dot process developed after World War II, plastic dots are deposited on the surface of thin paper, without penetration of the surface, thus reducing bulk by some 45 per cent. The solid-dot process has in turn given way to a system using the principles of typesetting, in which types are key-boarded on to a magnetic tape before being embossed at high speeds on to manila paper. Also widely used for diagrams, maps, and other 'pictorial' presentations is the thermoform process, in which a heated original is brought into vacuum contact with a thin plastic sheet, the image being permanently impressed on the plastic. This process, which is used by small office units and in institutions for the blind, allows short-run production of special items.

A retrospective collection of 'relief reading' material for the blind will include specimen type sheets showing the various systems (and their modifications) in use in the late 18th and 19th centuries, demonstration pieces, religious texts and other material produced by children in schools for the blind, maps and plans, and profile portraits of celebrities.

The Perkins Institution in Boston, which had workshops for the blind and also gave general instruction, put out price lists in orthodox raised type, showing rates for mattress renovating, laundering, etc. A typical example, measuring 360 × 275mm (14⅛ × 10¾in), dates from about 1910 and offers to give estimates 'for new work of all descriptions' and adds 'we sell brass and iron bedsteads'.

Modern 'relief reading' material includes newspapers, magazines, playing cards, music and maps, board games, typewriter keyboard charts, raised-line writing pads for use in handwriting, 'Taxi' call-cards for hailing taxis, and stickers for preserve jars.

Religious card

Widespread production of cards showing religious texts and moral lessons began in Britain with the inception of the Sunday School system in the 1780s. In America they appeared in strength in the 1820s, with the founding of the American Sunday-School Union.

The cards show, broadly speaking, two distinct phases of development. In the first phase, until about 1840, they reflect the design and production of the CHAPBOOK. Simple woodcuts, often hand-coloured, are accompanied by a scriptural text and a verse or two of 'improving' doggerel. Produced without finesse by jobbing printers, the cards were nevertheless received by children with some appreciation and were often used, by handwritten endorsement, as unofficial REWARD OF MERIT cards.

In the 1850s and 1860s, when the GREETINGS CARD industry began to get under way, design and production of religious cards of all kinds (including Sunday School reward cards) became the province of manufacturers of Christmas and birthday cards and valentines. All of the many decorative techniques developed from greetings cards were applied to moral and religious subjects. Thus the cards acquired chromolithographed illustrations, elaborate embossing and gold printing, as well as valentine-style paper lace, cut-out SCRAPS and, occasionally, even glitterwork and fringeing. The two streams met, of course,

Religious card, late 19th century. Chromolithographed, lightly embossed and die-cut to shape. 60 × 165mm (2⅜ × 6½in)

at Christmas and Easter; Jewish festival cards also partook of the chromolitho-cum-valentine idiom.

Small cards with religious texts were produced by the million, being printed in sheets of 50 or 100 different designs for guillotine separation. The vast majority featured flowers as illustrations, but some attempted to link picture with message: 'Jehova is my *rock* and my defence'; 'enter into his *gates* with thanksgiving'. Many bore simple imperatives: 'Swear not at all', 'Love not sleep lest thou come to poverty', 'Look to Jesus', 'Comfort one another'. Virtually every aspect of Christian theology was expressed. The cards were printed largely by chromolithography, with or without embossing of the image, in five or six colours, often with the addition of gold. As with many such items, these highly decorative cards, though published in Britain, were mostly printed in Germany.

The later 'moral lesson' cards, bearing clear indications of their greetings card background, form a class on their own. Measuring commonly some 110 × 75mm (4⅜ × 3in), they were the elegant progeny of the earlier 'chapbook'-type card. Instead of a primitive woodcut illustration, the richness of a Baxter or chromolithographic print provided a picture of some aesthetic quality; moreover, the verse, while sometimes less than inspired, was at least literate. An elaborate decorative border, always in colour, often embossed and sometimes in gold, completed an item which was attractive enough to find its way in large numbers into the SCRAPBOOKS/ALBUMS of the day. Typical titles for the cards are 'avoid the tale-bearer' (showing a youthful group, with a central figure pointing to a distant colleague), 'Christ, Lord of All' (villagers at a Church Service), and 'Christian Friendship' (a solicitous figure rests a hand on the forearm of a weeping friend).

Through the 1870s and onwards design styles followed closely those of the decorative arts at large and the greetings card industry in particular. There was, however, a single exception to this generalized interchange. The use of silver blocking on a maroon-coloured card, widely used for religious text cards in the latter years of the century, was used almost exclusively for that purpose, apart from minor incursions into the field of window cards ('Apartments', 'Dressmaking', etc.).

Scripture texts also appeared as wall decorations, both for school and home, in some cases in very large sizes. In Britain one major series of the 1890s offered chromolithographed illustrations of angels bearing scroll texts: 'Search the Scriptures', 'Praise ye the Lord', etc., each measuring 965 × 610mm (38 × 24in). Large embroidery cards, featuring secular as well as scriptural texts, were popular in the 1870s and 1880s. Texts such as 'Be not weary of well-doing' and 'Home, sweet home' were printed in colour on perforated card ready for working in silk or wool.

Also available, with or without texts, were sets of full-colour illustrations from the scriptures. The Religious Tract Society's *Scriptural Series* numbered thirty pictures; Phillips's *Scripture Prints for Schools and Families* appeared in a set of thirty-six, and *Varty's Preceptive Illustrations from the Bible* numbered fifty-two items. Similar sets were available in the late 20th century; one, showing the twelve Stations of the Cross, was printed in Italy and widely exported.

Religious text cards continued to be produced in the 20th century, though in simpler style, and smaller quantities than in the previous century. The larger texts of the late 19th century are exceptional, though they are still in production in some areas, principally as four-colour floral half-tone vignettes on a white ground with their text printed in a single colour. Hand-executed prayers are occasionally seen. The central control room in a New York Fire Station displayed one in the late 1970s: devised and executed by a local citizen, it read 'God Bless our Firemen'.

Religious cards of various kinds are still current and include 'get well' cards, baptism and confirmation cards, communion cards, sympathy cards, memorial cards, bookmarks and missal cards.

REFERENCE Colleen McDannell, *Material Christianity – Religion and Popular Culture in America* (New Haven and London: Yale University Press, 1995)

Removal card

The first recorded change-of-address announcements came from shopkeepers and tradesmen in the early years of the 18th century. They generally relate to removals actually effected rather than those planned. The announcement commonly appeared as a printed item featuring the trader's name as a headline, with or without a word or two of designation, followed by the key words 'Removed from' and the old and new addresses. The new address, in the days before street numbering, was often descriptive: '... the third door on the left hand in Long-Acre from James Street, Covent Garden'.

The cards or papers, which measured between 65 × 120 mm (2½ × 4¾ in) and 100 × 180 mm (4 × 7⅛ in), often carried a few words of promotional copy as in a TRADE CARD, and like it sometimes bear handwritten notes of purchases and receipt signatures.

The modern card, giving advance notice of a change of address, takes a wide variety of forms and may, whether commercial or private, strike an informal or humorous note. In one example, a personal card from a married couple in the 1970s, the announcement combined a New Year greeting with the announcement that as from 1 January they will be separating. Cartoon drawings, printed to the right and left of the card, show them making their ways in different directions to separate addresses.

Revenue stamp *See* TAX STAMP

Reward of merit

The reward of merit is a small paper or card, typically 65 × 100 mm (2½ × 4 in), given to school children for good conduct. It originated in America in the early years of the 19th century, initially as a single-colour printed slip, with a decorative engraving or woodcut, later as a two- or three-colour line lithograph and, in the 1880s, as a full-colour chromolithographed card. It carried dotted lines for the insertion of the names of pupil and teacher, and sometimes a printed phrase specifying the merit in question: 'Neatness in writing', 'Correct deportment', etc.

Illustrations bore little or no relevance to behaviour, good or bad, and were seen as merely agreeable pictures. The reward of merit is possibly the earliest example of the collectable 'set', each bearing a different picture or decorative motif. Some teachers designed their own reward cards: one handwritten American specimen reads: 'This is to certify that Daniel Presha is into two syllables'.

The American reward-of-merit card played a major part in primary education in the 19th and early 20th centuries. The cards appeared in many hundreds – indeed in thousands – of designs. There was some cross fertilization with the ubiquitous friendship cards, and with the advent of the chromolithographed SCRAP some reward cards received an additional colourful seal of luxury, transplanted direct from manufacturers' stocks of greetings-card accessories.

Reward-of-merit cards were a major sideline for the chromolithography industry; many commercial trade cards and personal calling card blanks required no greater adaptation than the addition of the words 'Reward of Merit' in place of a name. In some cases dual-purpose use brought odd results. Examples survive of reward-of-merit cards in which the printed words 'Reward of Merit' appear in the name panel on an unmistakeable friendship card above the legend 'Think of Me'.

The American reward-of-merit card also appeared as a simple 'moral text' card ('Be always learning'), and as a vehicle for pious verse. Some cards were designed as certificates: 'This is to certify that (—) is entitled to this acknowledgement for Perfect lessons for the period of (—) [signed] (—) Teacher'. Others took the form of bookmarks, and some, available in collectable sets, featured letters of the alphabet.

In another category, reward-of-merit cards mimicked currency or stockholders' certificates. One 'certificate', elaborately engraved with vignettes of happiness and learning, allocates 'four shares of stock to the holder' in the National Bank of Merit. A motto proclaims: 'God offers reward ... my teacher also ... they both encourage me ...'. The notion of paper currency is expressed in miniature 'notes' in denominations of '25 merits' or '50 merits' or, as in 'The Bank of Industry', the sum of 'one honor'.

In many cases the cards are tokens not only of academic encouragement but of regard. One handwritten example (c.1850) declares the recipient to be, simply, 'A fine little boy'. Reciprocal cards also exist. A printed specimen, elegantly embossed in gold and still retaining part of the album leaf on which it was mounted, carries a verse entitled 'To my Teacher'; its eight-line eulogy begins 'Affection prompts me this to send ...' and concludes 'Oh ne'er will I forgetful prove Of all thy kindness and thy love'. A handwritten caption on the album leaf reads: 'Given to me by little Trevor Eardley Wilmot. 1857.'

British reward-of-merit cards were late on the scene and were, on the whole, confined to the encouragement of regular attendance. 'Never absent, never late' was the key legend. This reflects the fact that grants made to elementary schools in Britain in the late 19th century were calculated mainly on the basis of average attendance figures. Weekly attendance tickets, printed in four or five colours by chromolithography and measuring some 60 × 80 mm (2⅜ × 3⅛ in), were available in sets

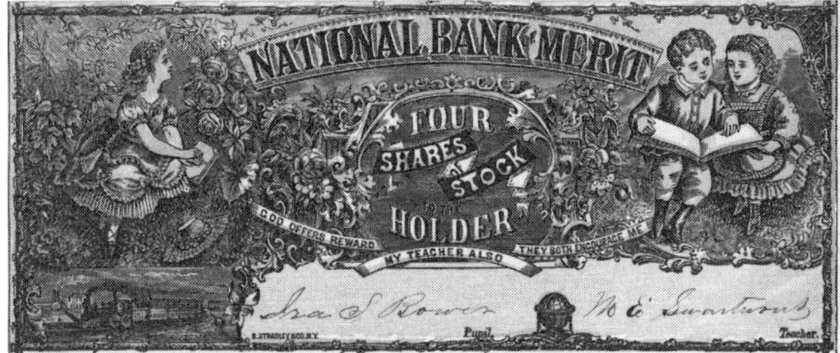

Reward of merit mimicking a share certificate. Lithographed in two colours by B. Stradley & Co., New York, late 19th century. 71 × 167 mm (2¾ × 6½in)

American reward of merit presented in October 1887. Lithographed in gold with a chromo-lithographed die-cut on-lay. 90 × 77 mm (3½ × 3 in)

of eight designs, which could be submitted as entitlement to longer-term cards or certificates. Typically, the cards showed 'capitals of the world' or similarly educational subjects. Few had the colourful appeal of the American reward of merit. E. J. Arnold and Son and the Educational Supply Association were Britain's principal suppliers of the cards, as they were of the plethora of examination certificates and certificates of merit that followed. Local education committees also provided sets of black and white topographical picture cards, 70 × 90 mm (2¾ × 3½in), for weekly attendance and, in exchange for these, post-card size, 90 × 140 mm (3½ × 5½in), for monthly attendance.

Commercial advertisers made a brief but concerted entry into the regular attendance card field at the end of the 19th century. They provided sets of cards to schools, featuring flowers, birds, butterflies, and similar subjects free of charge, deriving publicity from discreet product mentions, commonly on the backs of the cards. Colman's starch was among products advertised in this way.

In parts of America the attendance card took the form of a miniature certificate declaring the pupil's attendance record during a given term. An 1870s example from the state of Connecticut, a card measuring 80 × 120 mm (3⅛ × 4¾in), is designed in the formal style of a certificate and carries spaces for the teacher to fill in the school number, town, pupil's name, number of days present, number of days absent, and teacher's signature. The card also bears warnings: 'The law requires that all children between the ages of 8 and 14 years shall attend school at least three months in each year… six weeks at least of the attendance must be consecutive; it is not lawful for any person to employ a child under 14 years of age who has not attended School at least three months of the preceding year… the law requires Actual Attendance for Sixty days…'.

A British variant of the reward card theme was the BOOK-PRIZE LABEL, designed to be pasted, duly completed with the recipient's name and distinction, into prize volumes. These, measuring some 145 × 110 mm (5¾ × 4⅜in), were printed in up to a dozen colours and gold, principally in Austria and Germany, and supplied through E. J. Arnold and the Educational Supply Association.

The educational certificate, measuring beween 130 × 190 mm (5⅛ × 7½in) and 240 × 305 mm (9½ × 12 in), proliferated in Britain in the 1880s and 1890s. Printed almost exclusively on the continent, these imposing items were available as examination certificates, as awards for merit or regular attendance, and as blanks for general use. The chromolithographed educational CERTIFICATE, designed in the genre of the ILLUMINATED ADDRESS and the TRADE UNION MEMBERSHIP CERTIFICATE, was the first popular epitome of further education – the embodiment of turn-of-the-century self-improvement. By 1900 the production of gold-embellished multi-coloured certificates had become a minor industry. The Educational Supply Association offered upwards of sixty varieties of certificate; output continued into the 1920s and 1930s but largely ceased with World War II.

Educational certificates and rewards of merit had their closely related counterparts in Sunday schools. For the most part they were printed by the same printers, designed in much the same idiom, bore decorated texts and homilies, and rewarded regularity, diligence, and good conduct.

Small text cards, measuring between 20 × 40 mm (13/16 × 1 9/16 in) were printed in millions and given by Sunday schools, not necessarily as attendance rewards but as free-gift mementoes (*see* RELIGIOUS CARD). Many, however, were produced specifically as rewards. The *Christian Herald* produced a set in which each card, 40 × 65 mm (1 9/16 × 2½in), bore a text with an initial letter that formed part of the newspaper's title. The reverse of the cards carried the message: 'When the set of 15 Cards has been obtained, making the words CHRISTIAN HERALD, your Teacher will give you a large Picture Text Card as a reward for good attendance. Read Children's Weekly Supplement in CHRISTIAN HERALD each week'.

The reward-of-merit concept, with its underlying aim of inspiring loyalty and commitment, was in some instances rounded off with a final reward document. In the 1850s a 'leaving certificate' was given to departing members of a Sunday school in Troy, New York. It reads: 'This certifies that (John Harris) has been a member of the Sunday school attached to the North Baptist Church since (its organization) and at (his) request (he) is now honorably dismissed. May (his) subsequent life be a life of holiness, (his) death the death of the Righteous, and (his) last end like theirs. (A B Chadsey), Superintendent, Troy (April 21st) 18(50)'. In March 1930 the North Riding of Yorkshire County Council's Education Committee bestowed a card signed by head teacher J. W. Dodsworth to George Gilbert Roworth, departing pupil of Easingwold Church of England School. The text reads: 'On your leaving school to enter upon the more serious business of life, the Education Committee and your Head Teacher wish you every success in the future, and hope that you will always keep in your mind the honour and good name of your old school. Always remember that Cheerful obedience to duty, Consideration and respect for others, and Truthfulness in word and act are the Foundations of good Citizenship. Work hard, play hard, and never tell a lie'.

See also CURRIER & IVES

REFERENCE Patricia Fenn and Alfred P. Malpa, *Rewards of Merit* (Charlottesville, VA: The Ephemera Society of America, 1994)

COLLECTION American Antiquarian Society, Worcester, Mass.

Reward papers

Since earliest times, rewards have been offered for information leading to the recovery of missing property and/or the arrest of offenders. The idea relies heavily on the expectation of treachery among conspirators; for the most part it calls for information from those privy to the deed who may be persuaded to betray its secrets. It is a matter of record that while the approach may work well in minor matters, in the major man-hunt personal loyalty is often corruption-proof.

Big rewards were offered in Britain during the disorders of the 1830s for information on 'lawless and disorderly persons', but in spite of the large numbers of people involved, and the certainty that their identity must have been known to many, no claim was ever made. Similarly, among the many hundreds who knew the whereabouts of Australia's Ned Kelly and his colleagues in the man-hunts of 1879, the then enormous reward of £8000 also went unclaimed.

Reward notices may appear in the name of the Sovereign in person. A printed PROCLAMATION 360 × 290 mm (14⅛ × 11⅜ in) issued at the Court of Whitehall in December 1679 offers the sum of £10 'to any person who shall discover unto His Majesties Board of Greencloth any… Papist or suspected Papist being harboured in any of the King's Houses'.

In London during the 17th and 18th centuries printed reward notices were widely circulated. John Evelyn's diary entry for 11 June 1652 records that he was set upon and robbed by a street gang, and that when he was sufficiently recovered he 'got 500 tickets printed and dispers'd by an officer of Goldsmith's Hall, and within 2 daies had tidings of all I had lost except my sword…and some trifles'.

The 'official of the Goldsmiths' was the beadle of that livery company, who apparently ran the reward-notice distribution scheme as a personal sideline. The goldsmiths themselves were widely respected as experts in valuables at large. In addition to being gold- and silversmiths, they functioned as bankers, money changers, pawnbrokers, and dealers in precious stones. Their wide connections in these fields made their beadle specially suited as an information-exchange on loss or robbery.

The reward notices of the goldsmiths' beadle, some of which have survived, are printed paragraphs, set to a measure hardly broader than that of a newpaper column, and comprising some ten or twenty lines of text: 'May 15 1730: Lost this morning about Nine o'Clock, from Mr William Godfrey at the Bull in Old Bedlam, a Quart Silver Tankard, the weight 32 Ounces or thereabout, mark'd at the bottom and on the handle WGB: If offer'd to be sold, pawn'd or valu'd, you are desired to stop it, and give Notice to Mr William Godfrey as above, and you shall have One Guinea Reward. Benjamin Pyne, Beadle, at Goldsmith's-Hall'.

Printed in sets of three or four per sheet, each numbered notice was cut and delivered to appropriate recipients (pawnbrokers, jewellers, etc.) as well as to coffee houses, inns, and other public places for circulation and display. The Goldsmiths' Company's archives include a 'walk book' in which recipients' addresses were entered, presumably by the beadle, for use by messengers. It appears from the numbering of such notices that

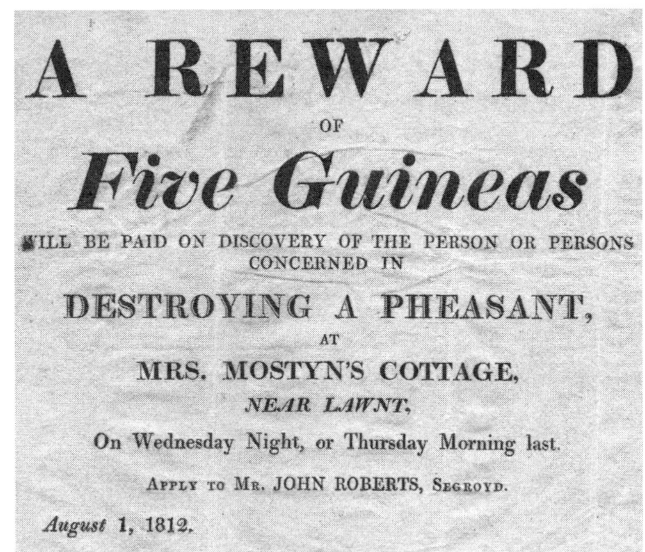

A REWARD
OF
Five Guineas
WILL BE PAID ON DISCOVERY OF THE PERSON OR PERSONS CONCERNED IN
DESTROYING A PHEASANT,
AT
MRS. MOSTYN'S COTTAGE,
NEAR LAWNT,
On Wednesday Night, or Thursday Morning last.
APPLY TO MR. JOHN ROBERTS, SEGROYD.
August 1, 1812.
THOMAS GEE, PRINTER, DENBIGH.

Notice of a reward for discovery of those responsible for destroying a pheasant, 1 August 1812. Letterpress, printed by Thomas Gee, Denbigh. 164 × 176 mm (6⅜ × 7 in)

200 DOLLARS
REWARD!
The "FAYVILLE STORE," at SOUTHBORO', was entered on the night of 23d inst., and robbed of $20 to $30 in Change and Plain Black Silks and Shoes to the value of $200 to $300.
The above Reward will be paid by the Proprietor of the store for the recovery of the property and the detection of the Thief or Thieves, or one-half for either, upon application to
SYLVESTER C. FAY,
FAYVILLE,
SEPT. 24, 1859. AGENT FOR THE PROPRIETOR.
Davis & Farmer, Printers, 18 Exchange St., Boston.

Notice of a reward offered by the 'Fayville Store', 24 September 1859. Letterpress, printed by Davis & Farmer, Boston (US). 305 × 235 mm (12 × 9¼ in)

the system was in use for many years. The 1730 item quoted above bears the number 11,898.

In general, however, reward notices were produced in large formats, appropriate for outdoor public display; they were often issued by way of the town crier, who posted them after publicly proclaiming their text (*see* PUBLIC NOTICE). Such notices appeared as proclamations in Boston, Massachusetts, in 1755, when the British Government required His Majesty's subjects 'to embrace all opportunities of pursuing, captivating, killing and destroying all and any ... Indians, the Penobscots excepted'. The text offered £50 for male Indian prisoners brought to Boston (£40 for scalp only); £25 for female prisoners and males under twelve; and £20 for scalps of females or males under twelve.

Printed notices appeared widely in connection with animals, stolen or strayed, and occasionally with lost children. In London on 10 November 1796 an appeal was posted for news of a twelve-year old boy, lost while attending the Lord Mayor's Show. The notice gives his description, an account of the circumstances, and concludes: 'whoever will bring him to his distressed Mother, Mary Fenner, at No 17 Mitre Court Buildings, in the Temple, or will give her Information respecting him, will be gratefully thanked, and rewarded for their Trouble. He need not be afraid of returning Home'.

Printing and posting of reward notices was a major function of the rural Protection and Prosecution Societies during the rural disturbances in Britain in the 1830s and 1840s. Such notices took two basic forms. In the first, the formation of the society is announced, and subscribing members are listed (each undertaking to contribute to the defrayal of costs in printing and posting notices, in payment of rewards, and in prosecution of offenders). The second form of notice offers a reward in the case of a specific offence.

In America, a major subject of the reward notice was the runaway slave. There was extensive use of press advertising (in which 'small ads' carried a standard title illustration showing a running figure, commonly with a stick and a bundle at his shoulder). Broadside notices also appeared. They too were illustrated with a running figure, and often carried extended editorial:

> $150 Reward: ranaway from the subscriber, on the night of the 2d instant, a negro man, who calls himself Henry May, about 22 years old, 5 feet 6 or 8 inches high, ordinary color, rather chunky built, bushy head, and has it divided mostly on one side, and keeps it very nicely combed; has been raised in the house, and is a first-rate dining-room servant, and was in a tavern in Louisville for 18 months. I expect he is now in Louisville, trying to make his escape to a free state (in all probability to Cincinnati, Ohio.) Perhaps he may try to get employment on a steamboat. He is a good cook, and is handy in any capacity as a house servant. Had on when he left, a dark cassinett coatee, and dark striped cassinett pantaloons, new – he had other clothing. I will give $50 reward if taken in Louisville; 100 dollars if taken one hundred miles from Louisville in this State, and 150 dollars if taken out of this State, and delivered to me, or secured in any jail so that I can get him again. William Burke, Bardstown, Kentucky 1838.

With the exception of those put out at the time of Abraham Lincoln's assassination in 1865, America's greatest spate of reward notices was to appear in the 1870s and 1880s, when the lawlessness of the Wild West provided frequent subject matter.

Ribbon, lapel

Ribbon has played a prominent role as decoration since early times. It is universally recognized as an embellishment and token of celebration. For the mass of the people it is used as the simplest form of colourful extravagance. A close relative of the flag or pennon (*see* PENNANT), its attributes are colour in motion and apparent gaiety. It has appeared in a multitude of popular contexts. In England it has been an essential feature of the maypole dance and a traditional decoration on coachmen's turnouts. It was worn by servants at hiring fairs as headgear and on the elbows and knees by morris dancers, and had a curious application as appendages to the headgear of parading recruiting officers; it was also attached to guitars, mandolins, and tambourines by street players. In pre-revolutionary Russia it was customary for beribboned young men to drive through towns on a farm cart, the ribbons indicating their availability as husbands.

Ribbons bearing printed legends began to appear in the early 19th century. Some of them, worn on children's hats, were of paper, crudely printed in gold. An example that survived the celebrations of 1800 bears the word 'PEACE'. By the end of the 19th century lettered ribbon, printed or embroidered, had become common. In the navies of many nations ships' names appeared on hatbands, and in America the printed or embroidered lapel ribbon became the universally accepted mark of political campaign allegiance.

The American campaign ribbon became a publicity item in its own right, often being pinned to the lapel by a metal clasp or, at a later date, by the ubiquitous button badge. In the course of time the two items, badge and ribbon, came to be considered as a single unit. Collectors may refer to the joint unit as 'badges' or 'ribbon badges'. The trend is found in related areas: ribbons used as awards may be pinned to the lapel with a rosette, brooch, or pin button, the whole device being seen as a single unit. Used in conjunction with metal, the award ribbon has some kinship with the traditional medal ribbon (the manufacture of which is itself a minor industry).

Lapel ribbons are widely used in America, both as campaign favours and tokens of award. They are thus found bearing a wide variety of legends. One specimen is lettered 'GUEST 18th Annual Parade of the Road Horse Association of New Jersey May 12 1917', another, 'Silver Laced Wyandotte Club of America BEST COCK'. Another, circulated in Ohio in the 1884 campaign for James G. Blaine, bears the cryptically local legend 'Don't Care A DAMN for the Mulligan Letters. Three Cheers and a Tiger for Blaine'.

In Britain, the lapel ribbon appeared less widely. Typical examples include 'God Bless our King and Queen' in the 1930s, and 'Eisteddfod Genedlaethol Cymru 1924 PONTYPWL [Pontypool] first prize'.

In Europe, the self-declared Empire of Austria-Hungary was the scene of its own form of souvenir ribbon. 'Vivat Österreich [Long live Austria]' was a patriotic war cry there in World War I, and the expression gave rise to the designation *Vivatbänder* for strips of decoratively printed silk portraying national figures. Scores of elaborate designs were issued, each celebrating a different person. Profits from sales were advertised as in aid of prisoner-of-war and other wartime charities.

The lapel ribbon falls within the category known in America as Political Textiles. The designation covers a wide range of printed, woven, and embroidered materials, including flags, pennons, banners, rosettes, and sashes, many of them woven on the principle of the Stevengraph.

In the 1990s a trend developed of showing sympathy and support for a cause by wearing a brooch made up of a folded ribbon measuring 10 to 15 × 140 mm (⅜ to ⅝ × 5½ in) attached to a safety pin. Among various colours worn are red ribbon for Aids awareness (1991), green for Sinn Fein political prisoners (also, in the US, for environmental causes), pink for breast cancer, and yellow for political hostages (Vietnam and, in April 1999, Kosovo).

See also SILK

Riddle book

Riddles were a prominent feature of parlour entertainment in the late 18th and early 19th centuries. They featured widely in party and nursery games and were used as space fillers in children's magazines and comics. Riddles also appeared as printed compilations in the form of booklets: numbered questions were answered by corresponding numbered solutions at the back of the book. Handwritten compilations also appeared. These were preserved as carefully as the printed versions and were kept as party standbys for future use. The intellectual level was often undemanding. Many riddles relied on tortuous puns and allusions: 'When is a door not a door? When it's a-jar'.

Ring-gauge card

The jeweller's ring-size gauge emerged as a standard trade item in the 1860s and was still in use in the late 20th century. Of POSTCARD format, and pierced with twelve holes in graduated and numbered or lettered sizes for prospective ring fingers, the card was normally printed in a single colour with decorative framings of the ring sizes and a panel for the jeweller's address. The card also served as an advertising TRADE CARD and was clearly intended to be kept for future reference. A small-print 'directions' panel reminded the customer that it was unnecessary to cut the card – 'reference to the lettered size is sufficient'.

Ring-gauge cards of considerable elegance were produced in the same basic format. Some 19th-century examples were printed in four or five colours by chromolithography, and are very different in effect from the utilitarian single-colour versions.

Ring-gauge card of the jeweller Arthur Ricketts, Lavender Hill, London, early 20th century. 90 × 150 mm (3½ × 6 in)

Riot act

'Reading the Riot Act' was in reality a reading of a brief portion of the Riot Act of 1714. The Act laid down a statutory form of words or 'proclamation' which was to be read aloud by a magistrate in the presence (and presumed hearing) of rioters. If within a period of one hour after the reading the rioters had failed to disperse, their action automatically ceased to be deemed a misdemeanour and became a felony punishable by life imprisonment. A further provision of the Act absolved the authorities from responsibility for death or injury caused in any subsequent action of the military brought in to aid the civil power.

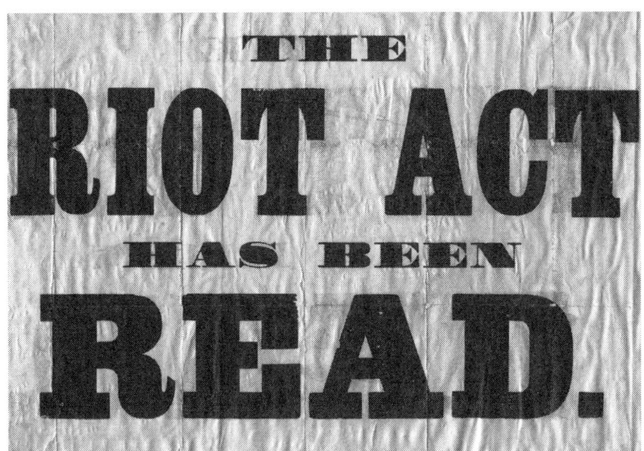

Riot Act notice, mid 19th century. Letterpress. 300 × 463 mm (11⅞ × 18½ in)

The proclamation is sometimes to be found as a handwritten memo, a hastily prepared slip to be held in the hand of the reader at the scene, bearing the words required by the Act. The text is as follows: 'Our Sovereign Lord the King chargeth and commandeth all persons, being assembled, immediately to disperse themselves, and peaceably to depart to their habitations, or to their lawful business, upon the pains contained in the Act made in the first year of King George the First for preventing tumults and riotous assemblies. God Save the King'.

Use of the precise wording of the proclamation was mandatory. A conviction in 1830 was quashed on appeal because the expression 'God Save the King' had been omitted.

The terms of the Act were modified on a number of occasions and the Act was finally repealed in 1980.

Roll of honour

The printed roll of honour (as a tribute to the living rather than the dead) appeared widely in Britain in the early months of World War I when service was still voluntary and the first 'rush to the Colours' had begun to subside. Published as a free insert in local newspapers, it gave the name of every local serving soldier, sailor, and airman, their town or village, and their regiment, division, or corps. A typical example, measuring 760 × 510 mm (30 × 20 in), printed and published in March 1915 by the *Buxton Herald,* appeared as a 6-column list showing some 1750 names from the town of Buxton itself, from Tideswell, and a score or so of neighbouring villages.

In another form of tribute, an item carried space for the insertion of a single name and photograph on a decorative frame. Typical of this approach is a 260 × 200 mm (10¼ × 7⅞ in) supplement given with the 13 March 1915 issue of the *War Illustrated.* Instructions printed in the photograph panel indicated a blank panel below: 'In space at foot write name and rank of soldier'.

Among other forms of printed recognition was a window disc bearing the legend 'Not at home – a man from this house now serving in His Majesty's Forces'; the disc carried a space on the reverse for the man's name. Also available was a twenty-page booklet, 115 × 90mm (4½ × 3½in), entitled *His War Record*. This provided space for his name, photograph, details of schooling, marriage, enlistment training, regimental honours, decorations and promotions, and most other predictable contingencies (including wounds, but excluding death) and ended on page 20 with spaces for the date of the signing of peace and a final single dotted line against the words 'arrived home'.

Printed rolls of honour for the dead of World War I also appeared but, after sporadic appearances in the columns of newspapers, they were soon seen to be both unmanageable and bad for morale. Full listings of Britain's war dead appeared in instalments in the Government's weekly casualty lists and in inscriptions on local war memorials in the early 1920s.

Post-war printed rolls of honour, commonly produced by local newspapers, were also used for public display, framed and glazed, on local memorials. Installed as a temporary measure, pending formal letter-cutting, some of these survived into the 1950s and beyond.

COLLECTION Imperial War Museum, London

Round robin

A round robin is a document, arranged and presented as a circle, in which names of signatories radiate from the centre, thus making it impossible to judge which was the initiating signature. The device is most commonly seen in connection with protests or complaints from members of a workforce or other group.

The format derives from mutinous groups in the armed forces who wanted to conceal their identity. The expression itself is thought to derive not only from the circularity of the document but from the word *ruban* (French: ribbon), which may have had some connection with naval terminology.

Use of the round robin has diminished, though it is still found among 20th-century documents.

Rules and regulations

Statute law seeks to regulate behaviour at large; rules and regulations are concerned with local details. To the social historian the local details are as rewarding a field of study as the overall picture, and the collector of rules and regulations provides essential source material.

Behind every list of formal 'do's and don'ts' is a history of human behaviour: each separate item enshrines one or more specific occasions when, wittingly or otherwise, someone ignored the will of the rule-maker. The list is thus evidence of an established order on the one hand and a detailed record of disorder on the other. On both counts it provides a graphic insight into conditions and attitudes which may vary as between one period, or one area, and another.

Rule 18 of the General Post Office's charge to mail-coach guards in 1829 states: 'it is the guard's duty always to have a bag of tools complete; and every week when they go to receive their wages the Postmaster has orders to examine their firearms to see if they are perfectly clean – barrel, lock and every part – that they have a blunderbuss and case, a pair of pistols and holsters, a powder horn, bullet mould ... etc etc'.

Rule 11 of the regulations for maid-servants at Robert Gordon's Hospital, Aberdeen, in 1823 requires that 'they shall throw no nastiness of any kind, or water, from the windows or doors of the House'.

Regulations for male casual paupers spending one night in

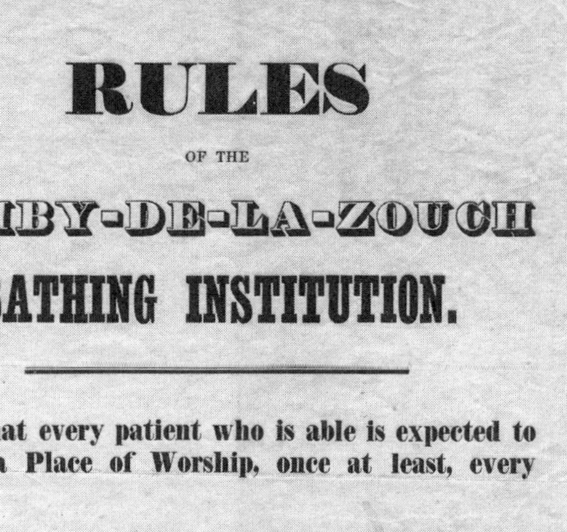

RULES

OF THE

ASHBY-DE-LA-ZOUCH

BATHING INSTITUTION.

I.—That every patient who is able is expected to attend a Place of Worship, once at least, every Sunday.

II.—That no patient be allowed to be out of the Institution after 8 o'clock in the Evening between Lady-day and Michaelmas, or after 6 o'clock in the Evening between Michaelmas and Lady-day.

III.—That if a patient sleep out [illegible] the Institution he is liable to forfeit his recomme[illegible]n.

IV.—That any patient frequenting a Public House is liable to be dismissed.

W. & J. HEXTALL, PRINTERS.

Rules of Ashby-de-la-Zouch Bathing Institution, mid 19th century. Letterpress, printed by W. & J. Hextall. 318 × 255mm (12½ × 10in)

British workhouses in 1892 require the following: 'The breaking of two hundredweight of stones, or such other quantity, not less than one and a half hundredweight, nor more than four hundredweight as the guardians, having regard to the nature of the stone, may prescribe. The stone shall be broken to such a size as the guardians, having regard to the nature thereof, may prescribe'.

Rule 186 of the General Instructions to Employees of the London, Chatham & Dover Railway in 1874 enjoins: 'Upon stoppage of a train at a station, and especially at a Watering Station, should any passenger require to alight for the purposes of nature, the Guard must immediately permit him to do so, always urging upon him the necessity for resuming his place quickly to prevent delay'.

New York's Third Avenue Railroad Company, in its rules for horse-tram drivers in the 1880s, instructs them: 'Never pass by passengers without shouting to them to take the car behind, at the same time pointing to the rear'. And in the same rule book, drivers are 'forbidden to pull on cars that are off the track'; instead they should 'request the passengers to move to the end of the car, and with the aid of other conductors and drivers lift the car on'.

Rule 6 of the Peace Dale Reading Room in 1857 reads: 'Smoking is not permitted in this room; and all who chew tobacco are expected to deposit their saliva in the spittoons provided for that purpose, and not upon the stove or floor of the room'.

Rule books, leaflets, and notices proliferate wherever communities and organizations are formed. They are among the most significant, if sometimes the most transient, of ephemera.

See also ARMED FORCES PAPERS; HOUSEHOLD REGULATIONS; LUNACY PAPERS; SCHOOL PROSPECTUS; SPORTS PAPERS

1 Page of an early 19th century guard book containing examples of commercial printing relating to the foundry of Edmund Fry of Bristol. This page shows a range of wood-engraved motifs, many of which relate to ephemera. Page size 435 × 280 mm (17⅛ × 11 in)

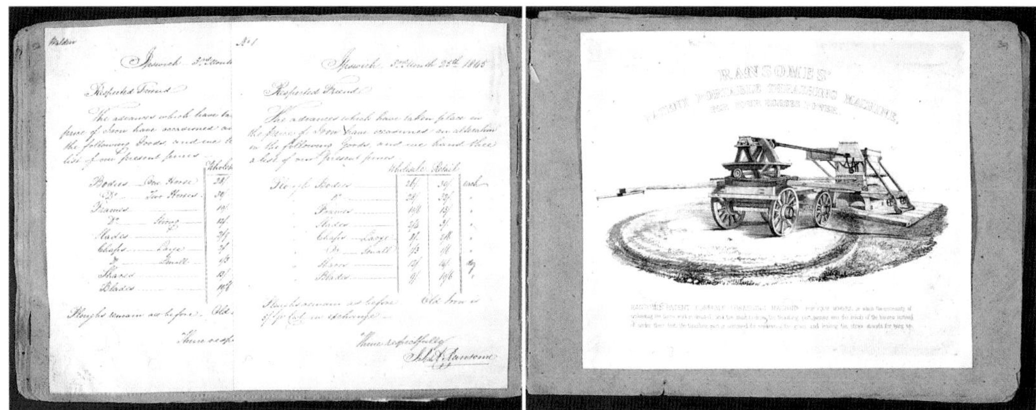

2a Two pages from one of the earliest of a large number of albums compiled by the agricultural and machine manufacturer Ransome & Co. of Ipswich as a record of their work. This album includes a range of lithographed and wood-engraved promotional ephemera of the mid 1840s. Page size 265 × 365 mm (10½ × 14 in)

2b Page from one of a series of seventeen albums, 1869 to 1962, compiled by the biscuit manufacturer Huntley & Palmers of Reading, containing labels, wrappers, publicity material, stationery, scraps, and items produced for internal use. This page shows material from 1883. Page size 395 × 475 mm (15½ × 20½in)

3 Page from an album consisting of over 2000 thread labels of various French and Belgian manufacturers, c. 1840–1880, compiled thematically in the late 19th century. The labels were printed in Lille, Marseille, and Paris, nearly all of them lithographically in colour. Page size 470 × 310 mm (18½ × 12¼in)

4 Page from an album consisting of a wide range of British advertising material, 1895–1905, mainly printed by chromolithography. Page size 510 × 300 mm (20⅛ × 11⅞ in)

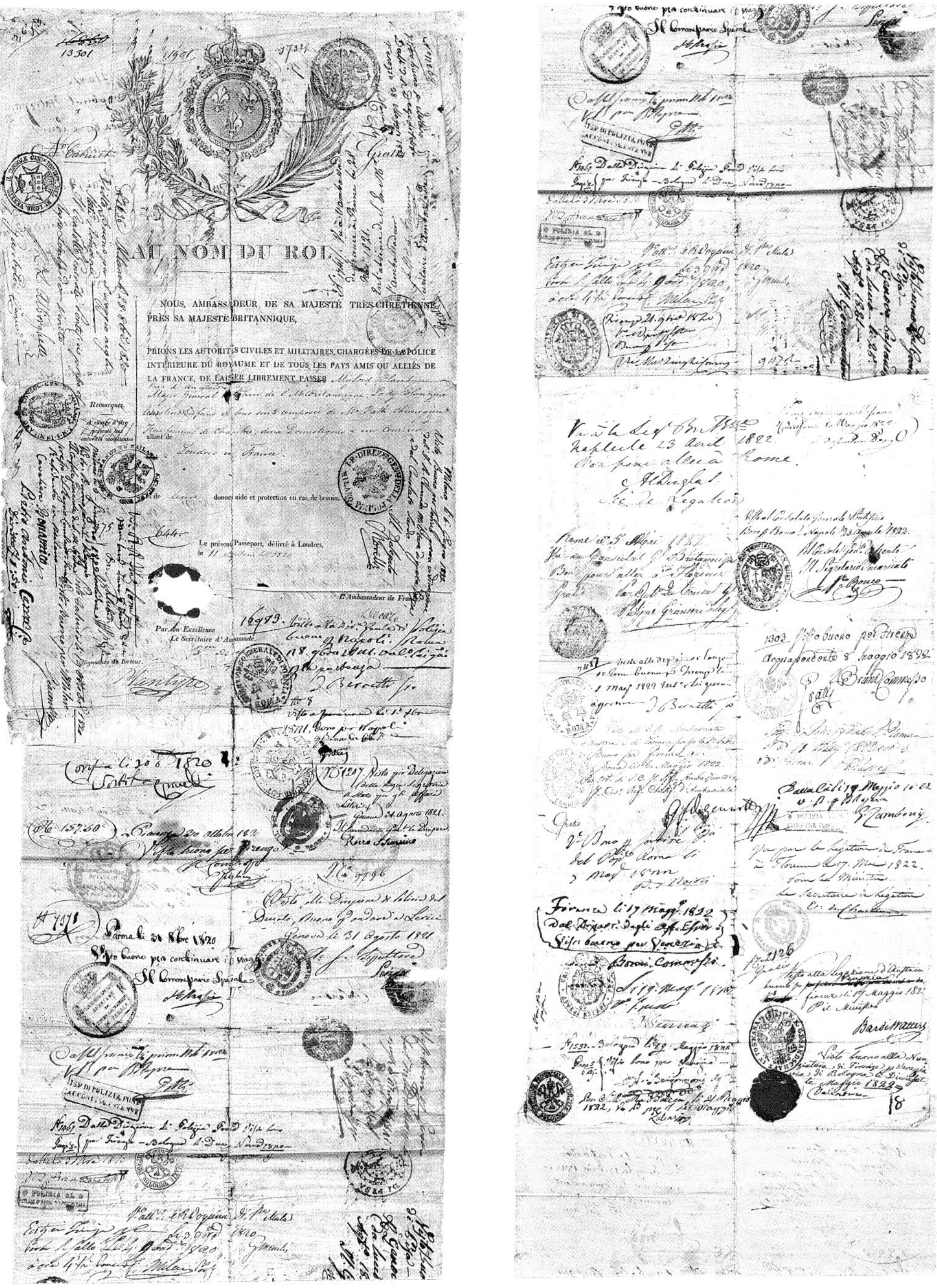

AU NOM DU ROI

NOUS, AMBASSADEUR DE SA MAJESTÉ TRÈS-CHRÉTIENNE PRÈS SA MAJESTÉ BRITANNIQUE,

PRIONS LES AUTORITÉS CIVILES ET MILITAIRES, CHARGÉES DE LA POLICE INTÉRIEURE DU ROYAUME ET DE TOUS LES PAYS AMIS OU ALLIÉS DE LA FRANCE, DE LAISSER LIBREMENT PASSER

allant de

Londres en France

donner aide et protection en cas de besoin.

Le présent Passeport, délivré à Londres, le 11

L'Ambassadeur de France

Par Son Excellence
Le Secrétaire d'Ambassade

Signature du Porteur.

5 Passport issued in London, 11 September 1820, for Lord and Lady Blantyre, their three children, and an entourage consisting of their surgeon, three chamber maids, two servants, and a messenger. They were travelling from London to France, and thereafter many locations in Italy (Rome, Parma, Genoa, Florence, etc.) between September 1820 and July 1822. Letterpress introductory sheet with three additional sheets pasted beneath carrying stamps and manuscript additions (on both sides of the sheet). Approximately 1525 × 260 mm (60 × 10¼in)

8th Time of the New Musical Comedy, and
75th Night of the Coronation!

THEATRE ROYAL, DRURY LANE.

This Evening, SATURDAY, November 17, 1821,
His Majesty's Servants will perform (EIGHTH TIME) a New MUSICAL COMEDY, in 2 Acts, call

MAID or WIFE?

Or, the Deceiver Deceived.

The Principal Characters by
Mr. E L L I S T O N,
Mr. H A R L E Y,
Miss S M I T H S O N, And Miss C O P E L A N D.
The OVERTURE and FINALE to the First Act, composed by Mr. T. COOKE.
The rest of the MUSIC composed and selected by the Author.
☞ *The New Musical Comedy of MAID or WIFE? is published, and may be had at the Theatre.*
After which, [SEVENTY-FIFTH TIME] The

CORONATION,

Which continues to maintain its unprecedented popularity, and is acknowledged to be the most correct and Splendid Exhibition ever produced on the British Stage.
It will be performed on *Tuesday, Wednesday, Thursday, and Saturday, in the ensuing week.*

Mr. K E A N,
Being anxiously engaged in the study of a new Tragic Character, will only perform twice next week——on *MONDAY* and *FRIDAY*.

The demand for Places for the new Musical Comedy of
MAID or WIFE? or the Deceiver Deceived,
requires its frequent performance; and, in consequence of the *Special Desire* for the representation of GIOVANNI in LONDON, the new Musical Comedy will, *this Evening*, precede the CORONATION.

To conclude with,

By Special  ***Desire.***

Giovanni in London.

Don Giovanni, Madame V E S T R I S,
Leporello, Mr. H A R L E Y,
Mr. Florentine Finickin, Mr. BARNARD, Mr. Deputy English, Mr. GATTIE,
Pluto, Mr. MEREDITH, Mercury, Mr. HOWELL, Charon, Mr. SMITH.
Firedrake, Mr. RANDALL. Drainemdry, Mr. WILLMOTT, Porous, Mr. W. H. WILLIAMS,
Simpkins, Mr. TURNOUR, Popinjay, Mr. VINING, Shirk, Mr. HUGHES, Spunge, Mr. DOBBS,
Proserine, Miss COOPER, Mrs. Leporello, Miss CUBITT, Miss Constantia Quixotte, Miss POVEY,
Mrs English, Mrs. ORGER, Mrs. Drainemdry, Mrs. HARLOWE, Mrs. Porous, Miss PHILLIPS,
Mrs. Simpkins, Mrs. MARGERUM, Squalling Fan, Mrs. BLAND,
Succubus, Miss VALANCY, Tartarus, Mrs. BEST,
In Act I. A PAS SEUL by Miss TREE.

On Monday, OTHELLO. Othello, Mr. KEAN.
After which, HIT or MISS. O'Rourke o'Daisy, Mr. Fitzwilliam, *his 2nd appearance on this Stage.*
On Tuesday, MAID or WIFE? or the DECEIVER DECEIVED. With the CORONATION.
And GIOVANNI in LONDON.
On Wednesday, GERALDI DUVAL. With the CORONATION. And MONSIEUR TONSON.
On Thursday, MAID or WIFE? With the CORONATION. And GIOVANNI in LONDON.
On Friday, (*1st time this Season*) HAMLET. Hamlet, Mr. KEAN, Polonius, Mr. Munden,
Queen, Mrs. Egerton, Ophelia, Miss Kelly.
On Saturday, The CORONATION, with other ENTERTAINMENTS.
On Tuesday, November 27, will be revived, the Tragedy of

D E M O N F O R T.

With a new arranged Fifth Act.
De Monfort, Mr. K E A N.

6 Theatre bill of the Theatre Royal, Drury Lane, 17 November 1821. Letterpress, printed in red and black. 330 × 192 mm (13 × 7⅝ in)

CRICKET

VICTORIA PARK CRICKET CLUB,

Patron---THE EARL OF CARLISLE.

A GRAND

MATCH

WILL BE PLAYED BETWEEN ELEVEN GENTLEMEN OF THE

ROYAL STANDARD BLACKHEATH

CLUB, AND ELEVEN GENTLEMEN OF THE

VICTORIA PARK CLUB,

On Tuesday, July 18, 1854,

ON THE GROUND IN THE

VICTORIA PARK

Wickets to be Pitched at 10 o'Clock.

DINNER and REFRESHMENTS will be provided by W. J. LEWIS, "Hosford Arms Tavern," Old Ford Road.

FORSAITH, Printer, 118, Bethnal Green Road.

7 Notice of a cricket match, Victoria Park, London, on 18 July 1854. Letterpress, with wood-engraving, printed in red and blue by Forsaith, Bethnal Green Road, London. 380 × 253 mm ($14\frac{7}{8}$ × 10 in)

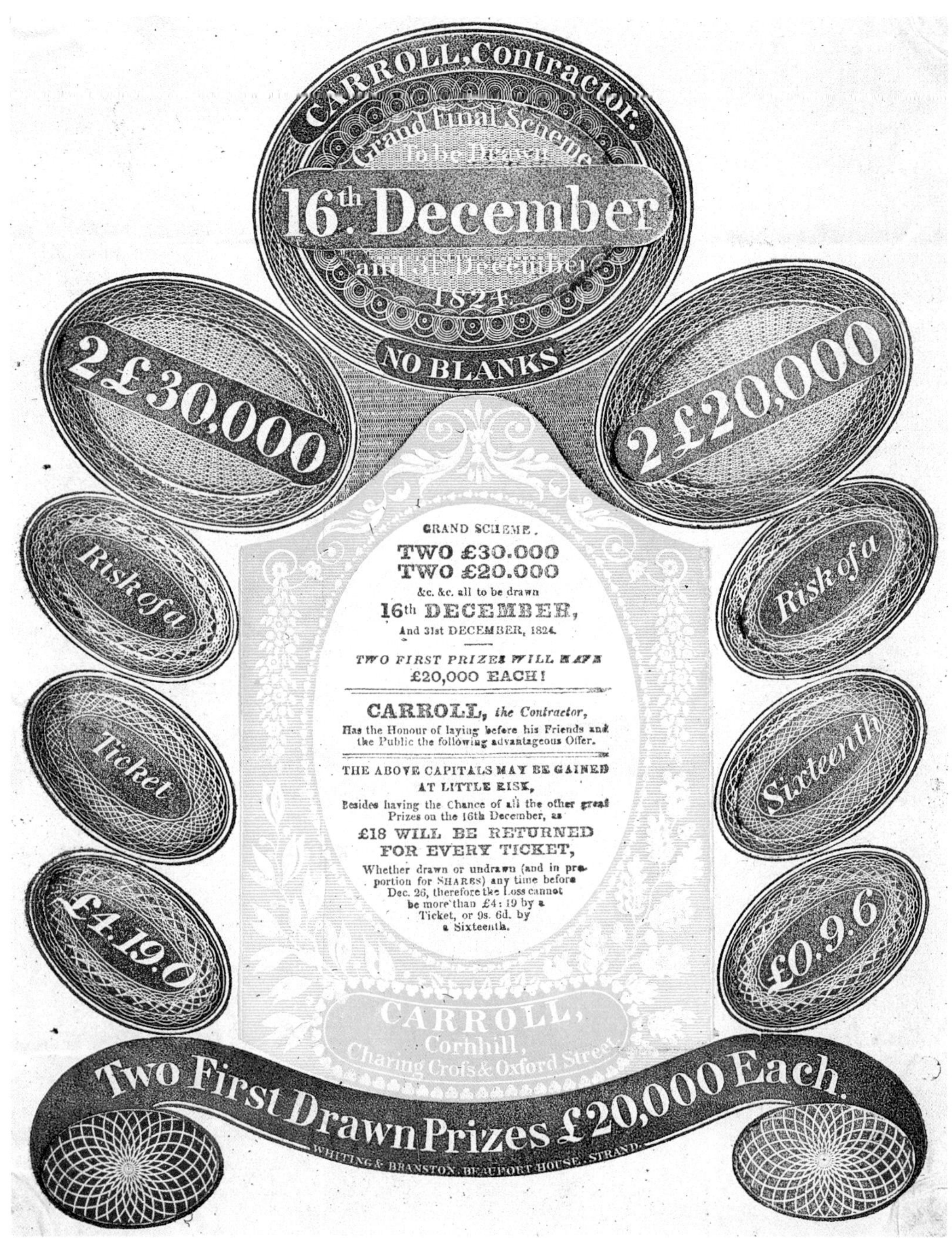

8 Lottery bill printed by Whiting & Branston, London, for the lottery contractor Carroll, 16 December 1824. The pink and blue parts printed at one pass through the press by the compound-plate process of William Congreve, the yellow parts printed separately. 215 × 169 mm (8½ × 6⅝ in)

9a Paper-cut valentine (the design produced by cutting the sheet when folded in four), British, second quarter of 19th century. Manuscript message in ink, the pattern coloured by hand with some gilding. 230 × 370 mm (9 × 14½ in)

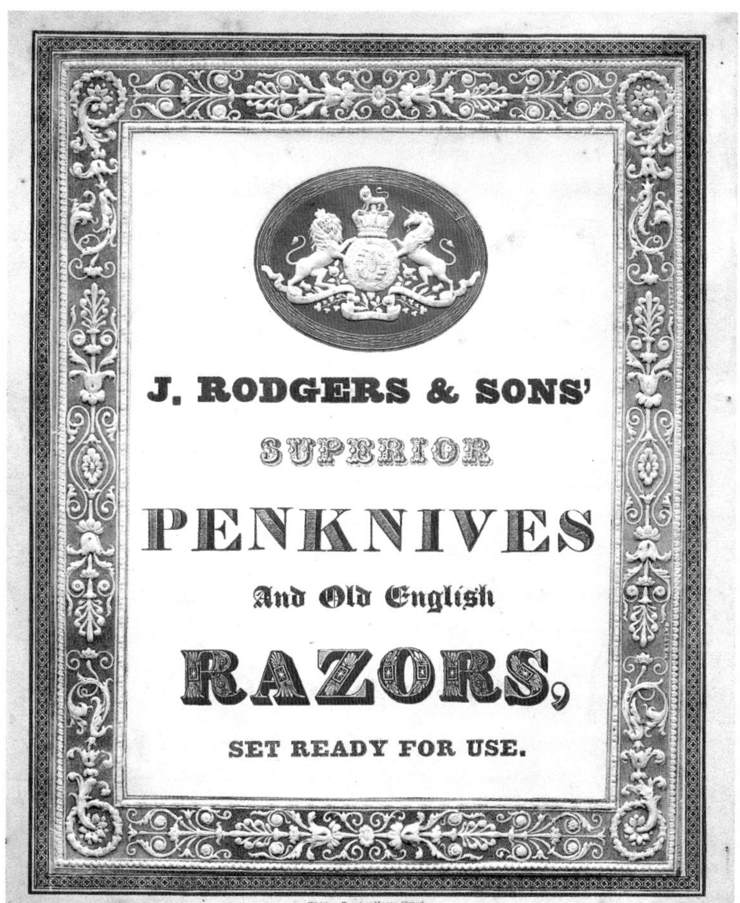

9b Showcard for the cutler J. Rodgers & Sons of Sheffield, 1820s. Printed in three colours and embossed by James Whiting, Beaufort House, Strand, London. 272 × 223 mm (10¾ × 8¾ in)

Geburts- und Taufschein.

Diesen
beiden Ehegatten,
Als: Philipp Michel
und seiner ehelichen Hausfrau —
Sussanna
eine geborne Fitting
ist eine Tochter geboren worden, den 6.
Januar im Jahr unsers HErrn, 1835
Diese Tochter ist geboren in Susquhanna
Townschip Dauphin County,
im Staat Pennsylvanien
in Nord-Amerika, ist getauft worden und
erhielt den Namen Leweine
den 5 Tag July.
im Jahr unsers Herrn 1835. von Hn.
Pfarrer August Lochman
Taufzeugen waren
die Eltern

Ich bin getauft, ich steh' im Bunde,
Durch meine Tauf, mit meinem Gott!
So sprech ich stets mit frohem Munde,
In Kreuz, in Trübsal, Angst und Noth.
Ich bin getauft, des freu ich mich,
Die Freude bleibt mir ewiglich.

Ich bin getauft in deinem Namen,
Gott Vater, Sohn und heiliger Geist!
Ich bin gezählt zu Deinem Saamen,
Zum Volk, das Dir geheiligt heißt.
O! welch ein Glück ward dadurch mein,
Herr, laß mich dessen würdig seyn!

Ich bin getauft, ob ich gleich sterbe,
Was schadet mir das kühle Grab?
Ich weiß mein Vaterland und Erbe,
Das ich bey Gott im Himmel hab:
Nach meinem Tod ist mir bereit,
Des Himmels Freud und Feyer-Kleid.

Allentaun, Pa. gedruckt und zu haben bei A. und W. Blumer.

10 Fraktur, certifying the birth and baptism of Leweine, daughter of Philipp Michel and his wife Sussanna, Susquehanna, Pennsylvania, 1835. Letterpress text with hand-coloured woodcuts and manuscript additions, printed and to be had from A & W Blumer, Allentaun [Allentown], Pennsylvania. 410 × 340 mm (16⅛ × 13⅜ in)

11 Contract of the marriage of Robert Davison and Martha E. Campbell, solemnized at Middleport, New York, 16 July 1863. Chromolithography and manuscript. Printed by T. Sinclair & Son, Philadelphia. 298 × 232 mm (11¾ × 9⅛ in)

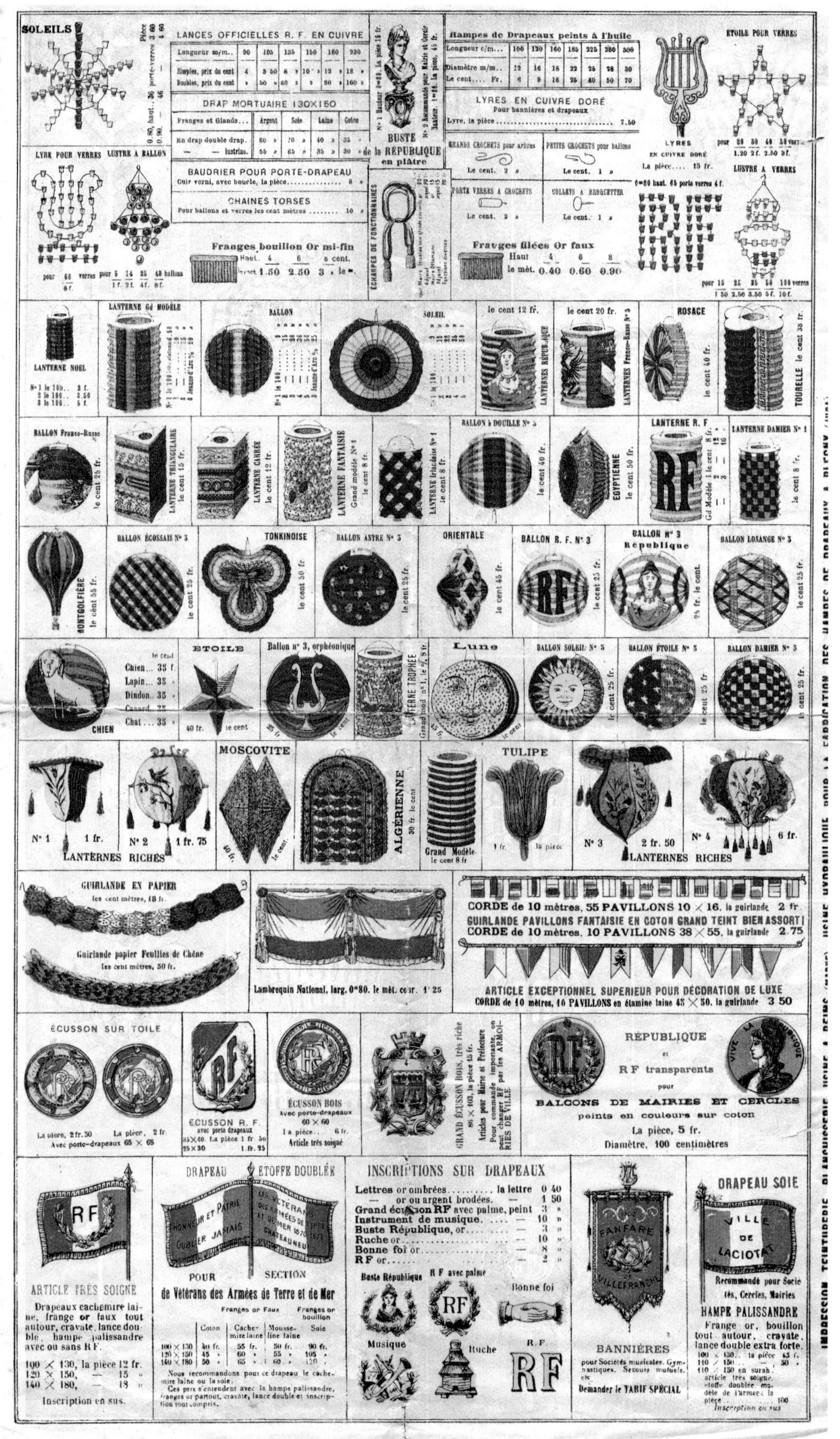

12 Rear page of a four-page price list of fireworks, illuminations, and decorations of the Atelier de Pyrotechnie Berthier & Cie, Monteux, Vaucluse, France, 1902. Lithographed in four colours. 445 × 265 mm (17½ × 10½ in)

13a Tobacco label of T. C. Williams Co.,Virginia, c. 1875. The copy line on the rock to the right reads: 'As the "Welcome Nugget" weighing 2217 ounces exceeds in purity and value any lump of gold ever found so this brand surpasses in quality any tobacco made'. Lithographed in seven colours. 270 × 270 mm (11⅞ × 11⅞in)

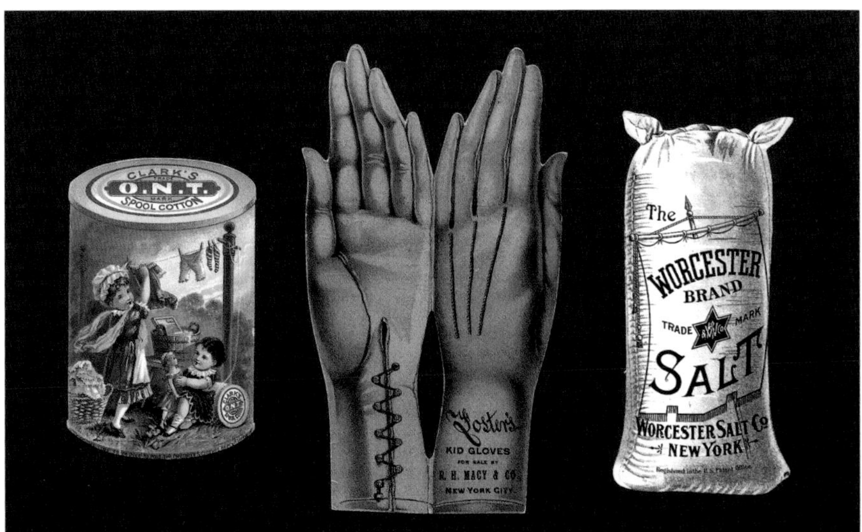

13b Shaped American advertising cards of the late 19th and early 20th centuries. All lithographed. *Left:* Clark's O.N.T. spool cotton, 110 × 70 mm (4⅜ × 2¾in); *centre:* Foster's kid gloves, for sale by R. H. Macy & Co., New York, 170 × 100 mm (6¾ × 4 in); *right:* Worcester Brand Salt Co., New York, 138 × 67 mm (5½ × 2⅝in

14 Certificate, awarded by the seed merchant Webb & Sons, Wordsley, Stourbridge,1904. Chromolithography and manuscript (for details of the award). 395 × 267 mm (15½ × 10½in)

15a,b Labels for different sizes of box for Price's 'Piano Candles', late 19th century. Chromo-lithographed. *Left:* 286 × 81 mm (11¼ × 3⅛in); *right:* 316 × 82 mm (12⅜ × 3¼in)

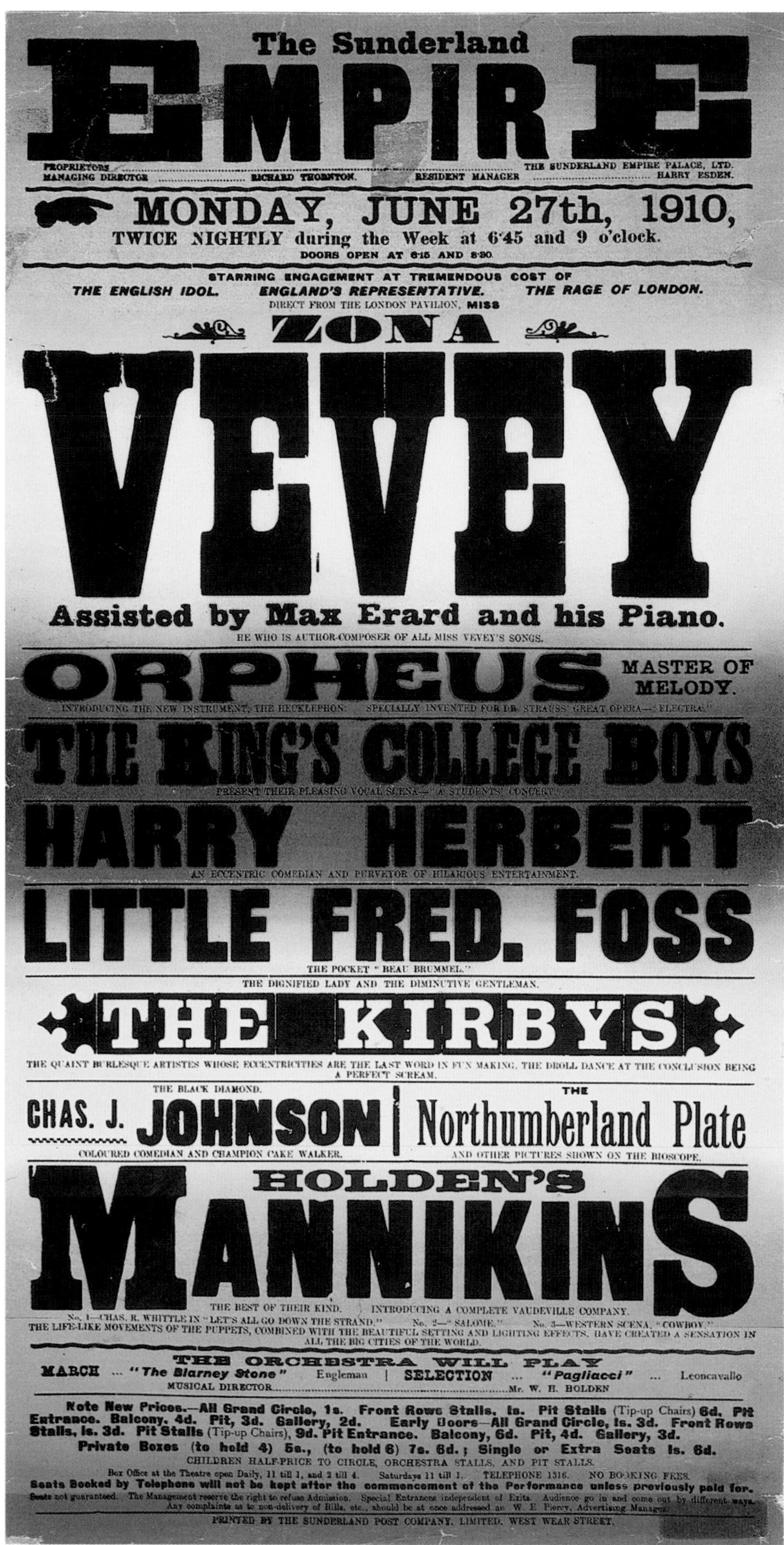

16 Theatre bill for the Sunderland Empire, 27 June 1910. Letterpress, with rainbow background, printed by the Sunderland Post Co. Ltd, Sunderland. 530 × 280 mm (20⅞ × 11 in)

Sabbath papers

Sunday observance was stringently imposed on the population of England during long periods. Under a law of Elizabeth I (1558): 'All... persons... shall...having no lawful or reasonable excuse to be absent, resort to their parish church or chapel... upon every Sunday... upon pain of punishment by the censures of the church'. In 1618 King James I publicly declared to his subjects, in what was called the 'book of sports', those games that were lawful: e.g. dancing, archery, leaping, and forbidding games such as bear baiting, bull baiting... and bowling 'by the meaner sort'. He laid it down that no shoemaker shall show, with the intention of putting on sale, any 'shoes, boots, buskins, startops, slippers, or pantofles' on Sunday 'on pain of three shillings and fourpence a pair'. A later Act of 1627 (3 Charles II, c. 1) required that 'no Carryer with any Horse, or Horses, nor waggon-men...nor Wayne-men...nor Drovers with any Cattell, shall...travell upon the said Day...Or if any Butcher by himselfe, or any other for him...shall...kill or sell any Victuall upon the said Day...[he] shall forfeit and lose for every such offence, the summe of sixe shillings and eight pence'.

Various modifications were made to these laws in the years following ('fish carriages shall be allowed to pass on Sundays and holidays whether laden or returning empty'), and failure to observe the sabbath was treated very much in the same way as the offence of BLASPHEMY and bad language.

Sunday observance has formed a notable sector of Anglo-Saxon legal systems for four or five centuries, and threads through ecclesiastical and statute law. The end of the 20th century saw only little change: Sunday working and opening is still a matter of contention in some areas of the British Isles, but widespread in others. Starting, as we have seen, from the offence of non-attendance at church the scope of the misdemeanour extends to a broad spectrum of activities.

In Essex in 1737 a typical document records in manuscript entries on a printed form that 'Moses Goodwin of Almsbury absented himself from the Public worship of God for the space of six weeks last past before the last Tuesday of March AD 1737'. It goes on to require 'the Sheriff or under Sheriff...or any of the constables of the town of Aylesbury to deliver the alleged offender to the Court of General Sessions'. The position is reflected in a notice posted in the 1980s by Scotland's Highland Regional Council at the harbour at Kinlochbervie: 'The use of the slipway is prohibited on the Sabbath Day. Except in an emergency. And then only with the harbourmaster's permission'.

At the end of the 19th century municipal by-laws were being made reinforcing recognition of the sabbath. Typically the City of Manchester in 1899 required that 'No person or persons shall on Sunday in any street within the City (a) cry out or call for sale any newspaper, journal or serial; or (b) advertise by any cry or calling out any newspaper, journal or serial; or (c) ring any bell or use any horse whistle or noisy instrument or create any noise whatsoever... vocal or otherwise for the purposes aforesaid or any of them'.

Sabbath-keeping was the subject of numerous items of ephemera produced in the 19th century; a petition published in the 1860s calls upon the public to support postmen in the call for banning of postal work on Sundays: 'Sunday Labour in the Post Office is totally unnecessary'. The appeal was distributed by the Working Men's Lord's Day Rest Association for presentation to parliament. The petition declared that this form of Sunday work was not only unnecessary but 'wrong in the sight of God'. Other ephemera take the form of handbills and tracts extolling the virtues of Sunday.

A major questionnaire regarding 'the Profanation of the Sabbath' was circulated in 1840 from Edinburgh. The printed form, folding to folio format, contained thirty-five questions directed to local ministers of the church. The questions sought to establish 'the chief causes of Sabbath profanation in your parish'. Subjects include the driving of cattle on the Lord's day: 'Whence they chiefly come; in what numbers; to what market; what are the market days, and by what roads do they travel'. The declarant is asked to state the average number of drivers; the number of parishioners who 'follow their ordinary labours on the Sabbath Day'; and the general effect 'on the minds of the parishioners of this evil practice'. The questions proceed through a detailed inquiry on mails, coaches and horses, their comings and goings and servicing, the number of tolls and toll-keepers involved, ferry connections, how many news-rooms and club-houses are open on the sabbath and what steps have been taken to dissuade the public from the 'vicious custom' of frequenting them. Further questions relate to the publishing of Monday newspapers (and their printing on the sabbath): how many mills, breweries and distilleries, coal mines, bakeries, milk deliveries and so forth are in operation. The manuscript answers to the questions reveal as detailed and conscientious attention to the matter as the questions. The coming of the railway and its attendant problems are clearly reflected: 'One [railway] between Dundee & Arbroath passes thro' this parish It is not open on Sabbath; but it is rumoured that this will soon be attempted; in which case I doubt not that the Presbyteries of Dundee [and] Forfar will endeavour to remove the nuisance'.

See also STUD CARD/NOTICE

Sailing notice/card

Early intimations of freight or passenger sailings appeared as small leaflets distributed or displayed in coffee houses, taverns, and other public places in seaports. Details of departure and arrival times were unspecific in the cases of 'collective' advertisements, in which a number of ships' masters issued combined announcements. Even the names of the vessels did not appear; the wording referred merely to 'vessels constantly loading' at a given location. As with the BILL OF LADING, marine insurance papers, and other such documents, phraseology expressed traditional mariners' caution: 'wind, tide and weather permitting' and 'if God permits' are common phrases.

The earliest sailing notices, dating from the late 17th century, were copper engraved, but by the middle of the 19th century most were printed by letterpress, with or without a WOOD-ENGRAVING or STOCK BLOCK. They took the form of announcements of specific sailings of individual vessels or forms issued by multiple ship-owners or agents in which details were added by hand.

A major difficulty, particularly on long voyages, was the requirement that ships be full, or nearly so, before sailing. Departure times thus depended as much on demand as on weather. Ship-owners were concerned to load and leave as rapidly as possible, not only to reduce unprofitable waiting time but to speed delivery. Sailing notices therefore sought to convey a state of immediate readiness to depart, regardless of the actual loading situation. When loading was within reach of an economically worthwhile voyage level, a sailing date was added.

By the mid 1840s sailing notices had settled down to a trade-card format: typically, in Britain, measuring about 80 × 115 mm (3⅛ × 4½ in), and in America 100 × 165 mm (4 × 6½ in). Unlike their paper forerunners, they were printed on card and came to be known as 'sailing cards' or 'despatch cards'. As shipping competition developed they became the commonest – though the most transient – of maritime ephemera.

In Britain, the cards remained largely typographic and rarely appeared in more than a single colour. In America, however, they burgeoned into colour, using three or four – and sometimes up to seven – printings.

The American sailing card (known as a 'Clipper-ship' card and roughly twice the size of the British version) was a highly competitive advertising medium, strikingly illustrated and replete with superlatives and indications of dramatic urgency. Descriptive phrases include 'fastest clipper afloat', 'beautiful extreme clipper ship', 'splendid out-and-out extreme clipper ship'; and performance figures, such as '110 and 118 days to San Francisco', are frequently quoted. Point-of-departure urgency is also stressed: 'now rapidly loading at Pier 11'; 'will be promptly despatched, having a large portion of her cargo ready to go on board . . . '. As competition further increased, a number of ship-owners began to promise more specific sailing dates ('early in May'; 'on or about December 20'). Finally, they took the bold step of announcing firm sailing dates, promising departure whether or not vessels were fully loaded. The heyday of the American sailing card was the period 1860 to 1890, the last of the clipper-ship years. The cards coincided with the era of the chromolithograph, but most were the products of a limited number of letterpress printers, chiefly in the New York and Boston areas, from which the trade chiefly operated.

Later sailing announcements, both in America and Britain, reverted to the handbill and small poster format. They advertised shipping services as well as individual ships, quoting more or less specific timings.

REFERENCE Allan Forbes and Ralph M. Eastman, *Yankee Ship Sailing Cards*, 3 vol. (Boston, Mass.: State Street Trust Co., 1948–1952)

COLLECTIONS The Bostonian Society Library, Boston; National Maritime Museum, Greenwich, London; The Peabody Museum of Salem, Mass.

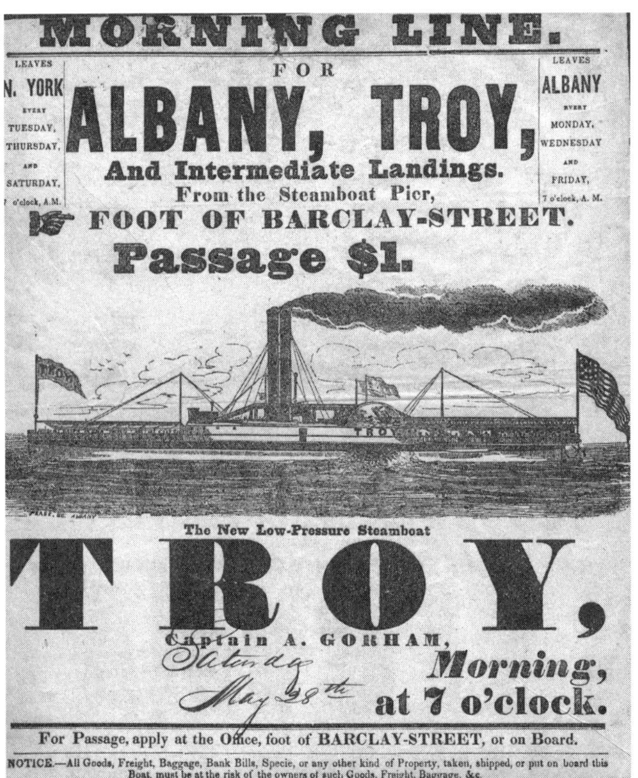

Notice of sailing from New York to Albany, mid 19th century. Letterpress with wood-engraving, printed by H. Ludwig, New York. 290 × 245 mm (15¼ × 9⅝ in)

Sale catalogue

Closely associated with the SALE NOTICE, the 19th-century sale catalogue occasionally formed part of the notice, lots being listed *in extenso* below the main title on a foolscap, or larger, sheet. For the most part, however, catalogues were in booklet form, of varying formats and numbers of pages. They offer important information on the detail of house contents, farming equipment, and other goods in domestic and commercial ownership in former times; in house sales, room-by-room enumerations of furniture and fittings provide an insight into everyday life in general. The typical catalogue starts in the servants' attics ('one bedstead, iron; one cane-seated chair; one washstand; one rug'), descends throughout the house with the cold eye of commerce, and finishes in the garden and outhouses ('one garden roller, faulty; one dog kennel and a miscellaneous lot of flower pots, sieves, watering cans etc.').

The majority of catalogues bear signs of the event itself, either customers' annotations or auctioneers' records. Inventories, handwritten and prepared either for valuation for probate or for sale by auction, are similarly useful sources of information. Because they list every individual object rather than groups of items in lots, they are particularly revealing.

Inventory notebooks for valuation normally measured some 160 × 200 mm (6¼ × 7⅞ in) and were bound in thin marbled boards. They were commonly used vertically, the list running from the foot of one page to the head of the next, the last page bearing a blind-embossed TAX STAMP ('one pound') at the point where valuation was noted.

Catalogues of the great auction houses are also collectors' items. Particularly when annotated, they furnish evidence of price levels and sometimes of the whereabouts of paintings, books, etc. as they pass from one purchaser to another.

The first recorded auction catalogue in Britain is that of William Cooper, who sold the library of Dr Seaman in 1676. America's earliest surviving auction catalogue relates to the sale of the library of Ebenezer Pemberton at the Brown Coffee House in Boston in 1717. Among many notable auction catalogues are those of the London sale of Marie Antoinette's pictures by Harry Phillips in 1798, and of a sale of Buckingham Palace furnishings in the offices of the palace by the same auctioneer in 1836.

See also SALE NOTICE

Sale notice

Known formerly as 'Particulars and conditions of sale', the sale notice advertised the disposal of major property, normally by auction. An important feature was its bold display (in the manner of a poster or PUBLIC NOTICE) of the description of the property on a page of at least foolscap size – sometimes larger.

The 'notice' revealed itself, however, as the cover of a four-page folder, opened as a double-spread. One page showed further details of the property – the 'particulars' – and the other the auctioneer's 'conditions of sale'. On the back page appeared a much compressed version of the cover display, disposed so that it showed the essentials when the document was folded for the pocket or for filing. Provision was also sometimes made for a 'Purchaser's agreement' to be signed on the spot by the highest bidder. In some surviving specimens the name of the purchaser, and the price paid, are entered in handwriting. In the case of more important properties, maps, plans, and perspective drawings were printed on additional sheets and inserted to make a six- or eight-page folder. The convention survives in principle to the present day. Like the public notice, which it resembled, the front page of the 19th-century sale folder presented a miscellany of the bold typefaces of the period, with emphasis on key words and phrases and – in most cases – a profusion of laudatory adjectives.

Sale notices provide not only detailed descriptions of properties which may no longer exist, but an indication of the tastes and aspirations of the property-buying public of the time. Notices published by George Robins, an auctioneer and estate agent from the 1820s to 1840s, are typical. In a notice of an 'excellent residence' (Tulse Hill, Brixton) he prefaces his description of the house ('adapted to the views of a family of respectability') with the intelligence 'that it is nearly in front of the admired property of the late John Blades Esq' and close to 'Lord Thurlow's admired domain'.

A mansion and estate at Evesham (1834) offers not only the property but a seat in parliament and 'a fine commanding spot, looking over … the respectable constituency which the new proprietor will necessarily represent at the next election'. A notice for 'valuable freehold houses and lands' (1841) includes a line intimating that 'coal has already been discovered'.

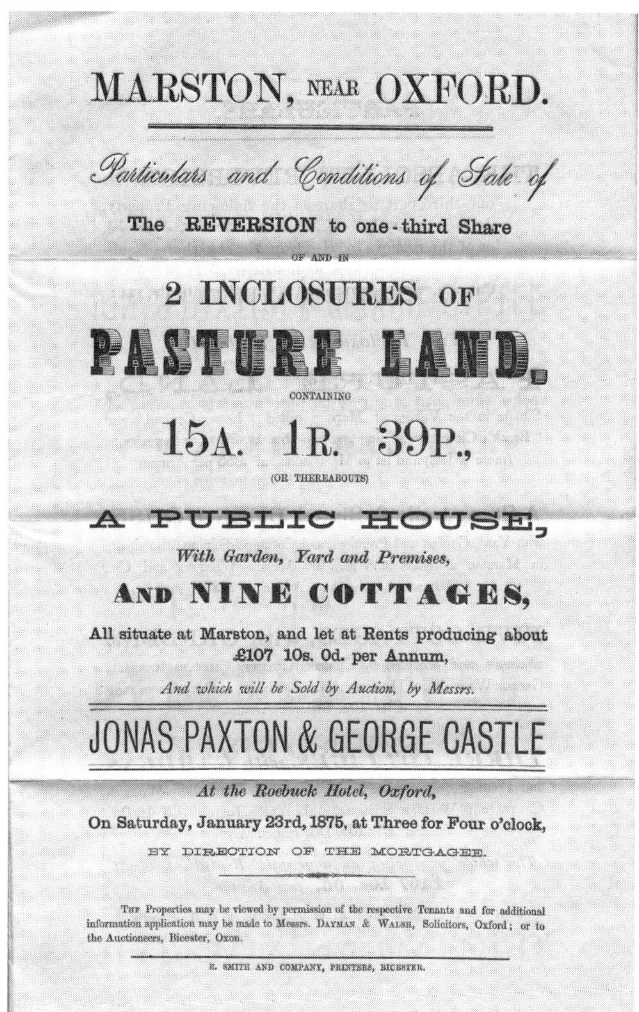

MARSTON, NEAR OXFORD.

Particulars and Conditions of Sale of

The REVERSION to one-third Share

OF AND IN

2 INCLOSURES OF

PASTURE LAND,

CONTAINING

15A. 1R. 39P.,

(OR THEREABOUTS)

A PUBLIC HOUSE,

With Garden, Yard and Premises,

AND NINE COTTAGES,

All situate at Marston, and let at Rents producing about £107 10s. 0d. per Annum,

And which will be Sold by Auction, by Messrs.

JONAS PAXTON & GEORGE CASTLE

At the Roebuck Hotel, Oxford,

On Saturday, January 23rd, 1875, at Three for Four o'clock,

BY DIRECTION OF THE MORTGAGEE.

THE Properties may be viewed by permission of the respective Tenants and for additional information application may be made to Messrs. DAYMAN & WALSH, Solicitors, Oxford; or to the Auctioneers, Bicester, Oxon.

E. SMITH AND COMPANY, PRINTERS, BICESTER.

Notice of Jonas Paxton & George Castle for a sale at Oxford (UK), 23 January 1875. Letterpress, printed by E. Smith & Co., Bicester. 387 × 245 mm (15¼ × 9⅝ in)

Other properties advertised on sale notices include shops, public houses, bakeries, mills, colliery equipment, almshouses, farming stock, and, occasionally, 'all the materials of the hustings and booths erected for the county election …'.

In America, a not uncommon item was the sale notice advertising auction of slaves (*see* SLAVE PAPERS). In many such cases the notice was a single one-sided sheet, unsupported by printed conditions and particulars, and simply inviting applications. Many surviving sale notices refer to 'sales by candle', in which bids were accepted only so long as an inch of candle remained alight. Other methods of timing referred to include a sand-glass and the time it took for a boy to run between two points.

See also PEW PAPERS; SALE CATALOGUE

Sales-tax token/receipt

First issued in the 1930s by various states of America (Alabama, Arizona, Colorado, Illinois, Kansas, Mississippi, Missouri, New Mexico, Oklahoma, Utah, and Washington), sales-tax tokens allowed payment of sums too small to be dealt with in conventional money. Tokens were generally issued in denominations of one-, two-, and five-tenths of a cent known as 1, 2, and 5 mille (the 'mille' equal to one thousandth of a dollar).

The tokens were commonly about 16 mm (⅝ in) or 23 mm (⅞ in) in diameter, sometimes centrally pierced, and made from metal, plastic, fibre, or card. Most carried die-stamped or embossed lettering, but those made of card were printed. One state only – Ohio – printed 'stamps' or ticket paper receipts printed in one or two colours on tinted and watermarked paper. These receipts, produced by the Columbian Bank Note Co., measured 35 × 37 mm (1 3/8 × 1 7/16 in) and were supplied in booklet form. They were printed in pairs; the left ('vendor's receipt') was retained by the shopkeeper and the right ('consumer's receipt') torn along a perforation and handed to the customer.

In the case of both the coin-like tokens and the paper receipts, the monetary value of the items was so small that the matter of security production hardly arose. Only the Ohio receipts, with their nominal ingredient of engraver's engine patterning, made any pretension to anti-counterfeit technology.

Sales-tax tokens and receipts remained in use for varying periods; most survived into the mid 1940s, though in Missouri tokens were used until 1960. 'Souvenir' and other unofficial tokens were issued by traders, numismatists, and others at varying periods. Among the most recent are promotional tokens put out by J. F. Schimmel of San Francisco, President of the American Tax Token Society.

SOCIETIES American Tax Token Society

Satirical print

The printseller, as shopkeeper or itinerant pedlar, was a widely recognized feature of everyday life in the 18th and early 19th centuries, and his stock-in-trade included images of irreverence as well as of the devotional and picturesque. Designed to provide passing comment rather than as works of art, satirical prints provided a more or less instant response to current affairs, lampooning not only modes and manners at large but particular personalities.

William Hogarth (1697–1764), painter and engraver, is a major figure in the field. In 1730 he produced the first of his sets of engravings depicting the social trends of the period. *A Harlot's Progress* (1733–34) showed stages in the career of its central figure, each picture in the series forming a unit complete in itself though integral to the anecdote as a whole. These works were followed by *A Rake's Progress* (1735), *Four Prints of an Election* (c.1744), *Marriage à la Mode* (1745), *Industry and Idleness* (1747), *Four Stages of Cruelty* (1751), and *Beer Street* and *Gin Lane* (both 1751). Hogarth was essentially a painter in the classical mould. His satirical and moralistic works, though overstatements, were only rarely caricatures. It is in his successors, Gillray, Rowlandson, and the Cruikshanks, that the spirit of ephemeral satire emerges.

James Gillray (1757–1815) was a true caricaturist, depicting his personal victims (George III, Charles James Fox, Pitt, Napoleon, etc.) with merciless exaggeration and irreverence. Unlike the studied 'set-pieces' of Hogarth, his work bears the dashed-off air of spontaneous creativity. It is reported that he often worked directly on the copper plate, unburdened by preliminary sketches.

Thomas Rowlandson (1756–1827), like Hogarth, was an artist in the traditional sense, working in water-colour. His humorous work was founded largely on his association with Rudolph Ackermann, who published his illustrations in the *Doctor Syntax* series: *Tour of Dr Syntax in Search of the Picturesque* (1812), *Dr Syntax in Search of Consolation* (1820), *Dr Syntax in Search of a Wife* (1821); and in *The English Dance of Death* (1816), and *Dance of Life* (1817). Rowlandson was fascinated by the excesses of his day, particularly by the tendency to overeat, and the characters of his satire are often portrayed not only as inadequate but as grotesquely fat.

George Cruikshank (1792–1878) was the best known of 'the three Cruikshanks'. Isaac, his father (1764–1811) was also an artist and caricaturist, and so was his brother, Robert Cruikshank (1789-1856). There had also been a grandfather Cruikshank, an out-of-work customs officer for whom art and alcohol had provided solace in unemployment. The three Cruikshanks worked in much the same fields, combining illustration with caricature and satire. Isaac, the father, died while the brothers were in their early twenties and George, the younger one, soon acquired the mantle of Gillray, who had by that time become insane. He was employed by Gillray's former publisher and mother-figure, Mrs Hannah Humphrey, to carry on with Gillray's work, completing unfinished plates and creating new ones in similar vein. Brother Robert, in the meantime, after being given up for lost at sea, returned to London to devote himself first to miniature painting and, for an intensive period (1820–25), to social satire and caricature, his particular targets being the fashion fads of the dandies of the period. Thereafter he turned to humorous illustration, for which, till his death in 1856, he established a major reputation.

It is to George Cruikshank, however, that the reputation for satire chiefly attaches. His subjects were the familiar targets of Gillray – Napoleon and Wellington, the Prince Regent and his affairs, the cotton laws and the property tax, Joanna Southcott and her divine pregnancy – and his hard hitting etchings became a national institution. A major single work, 'the greatest event of his artistic life', was Cruikshank's mock banknote, *Bank Note – not to be imitated.* It depicted gallows and hanging figures, and he engraved it as a commentary on the punishment of death for passing forged banknotes: a direct outcome, it is said, of his having seen the bodies of women hanging on a Newgate gallows. This satire was thought to have contributed to the movement for the reform of the law. In his later years Cruikshank espoused the cause of total abstinence. In 1847 and 1848 he produced two series of plates, *The Bottle* and *The Drunkard's Children,* anecdotes in the Hogarth mould, recording decline and fall in eight-stage sequences. With these works we see the return from satire to the pictorial moral tale, Hogarth's starting point of a hundred years before.

Prior to the rise of the popular press, the two key instruments of public comment were the pamphlet and the pictorial print. The pamphlet was the medium for the literate. For the mass of the public, however, the works of Hogarth, Rowlandson, Gillray, the Cruikshanks, and others were of immense influence. Between them they produced many hundreds of works, of which hundreds of thousands of copies were printed. Output was prodigious. Not all of the designs were engraved by the artists themselves, and hand colouring, where it was used, was carried out by teams of colourists, often hard pressed to keep up with demand in the case of best-sellers.

Pirating of successful designs was common. Hogarth was a major sufferer in this. His *Harlot's Progress* series was widely copied, the artist himself being deprived of large sums as a result. It was in large measure as a result of his representations that the Copyright Act of 1735 was passed. Often called 'Hogarth's act', it made copying of prints illegal for fourteen years after their original date of publication. This accounts for the footline often seen on prints of the period: 'Published as the Act directs . . .', with details of the publication.

The single-sheet satirical print disappeared in the second half of the 19th century, much of its function being taken over by the popular satirical periodical. But by this time much of its biting candour had in any case been lost.

In America, the political print is represented in the 18th-century work of Paul Revere, Henry Dawkins, and Nathaniel Hurd. The early 19th century saw the rise of William Charles and, in the 1820s, of David Claypoole Johnston, 'the American Cruikshank'. By contrast with Britain, output was small. The full flowering of the American caricaturist was to await the advent of the illustrated popular press.

Scholar's letter

Scholar's letters were written by 19th-century boarding-school pupils to their parents as exercises in calligraphy and the social graces. Couched in terms dictated by the school, they were also calculated to convey an impression of developing literacy, filial love, and gratitude for everything that the school, through the instrument of the parents, provided. The scholar's letter was in effect an ill-disguised institutional promotional piece.

An example written from Writtle School, Essex on 12 November 1801 declares in a fine copperplate hand:

Hon'd Mother, Were I to withold my sincere acknowledgments so justly due for the many advantages I have received, during a course of years, I should think myself unworthy of the Education which you have bestowed on me.

Learning is a valuable acquirement it forms the mind, enlightens the understanding, and makes men respectable in the eye of others; these advantages are derived from a virtuous Education. On the contrary A Man without Learning may be compared to a Stone just hewn from the Rock, before the Mechanic works upon it. his mind is unimproved by

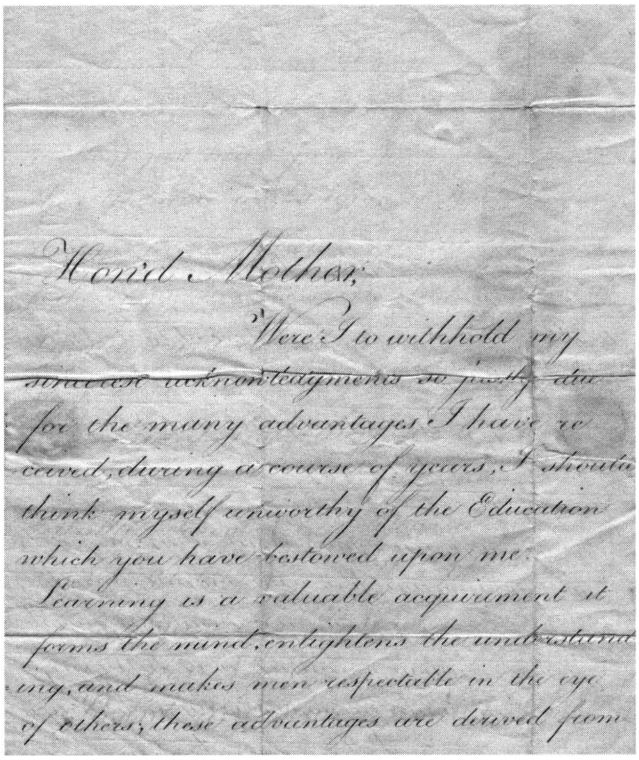
Hon'd Mother,
Were I to withhold my
sincere acknowledgments so justly due
for the many advantages I have received, during a course of years, I should
think myself unworthy of the Education
which you have bestowed upon me.
Learning is a valuable acquirement it
forms the mind, enlightens the understanding, and makes men respectable in the eye
of others; these advantages are derived from

Scholar's letter (first page only), written by William John Bright, Writtle School, 12 November 1801. Manuscript. 225 × 187 mm (8⅞ × 7½ in)

Science and he is subject to the impositions of every Imposter. Our Vacation will commence on Tuesday the 8th day of December. Accept my filial love and regard and believe me to be Hon'd Mother Your dutiful Son, Wm Jno Bright.

In similar vein, some seventy years later, a daughter wrote this from the Ladies Seminary, Beccles, Suffolk:

My Dear Parents, It is with pleasure I avail myself of the opportunity of addressing this letter to you, which I hope you will receive as a small testimony of my sincere gratitude for your kindness in allowing me the many advantages I enjoy, and trust the progress I have made will be an earnest of my diligence and assiduity in the pursuit of my studies, and likewise that the improvement in the different branches of my education will give you great satisfaction, and testify that the efforts of my preceptress have not been in vain. The vacation commences on the 19th inst. and terminates on the 23rd of July. With kindest love dear Parents I remain Your affectionate daughter Louisa Burwood.

The convention of the formal scholar's letter remained in fairly general use until the end of the 19th century, when it was modified, to the extent of requiring pupils to write in their own words (though often still under surveillance).

The poet and critic Matthew Arnold (1822–88), whose father, Dr Thomas Arnold, was the renowned headmaster of Rugby School, drew attention to the artificiality of the typical scholar's letter by juxtaposing an example with a letter written by 'an ordinary scholar in a public elementary school'. The two letters appeared in his 'General Report for 1867', which was published posthumously in *Reports on Elementary Schools 1852–1884* (London: Macmillan, 1889, pp. 122–124).

The 'ordinary scholar' was a girl of eleven years, who was educated in Arnold's own district:

Dear Fanny,—I am afraid I shall not pass in my examination; Miss C— says she thinks I shall. I shall be glad when the Serpentine is frozen over, for we shall have such fun; I wish you did not live so far away, then you could come and share in the game. Father cannot spare Willie, so I have as much as I can do to teach him to cipher nicely. I am now sitting by the school fire, so I assure you I am very warm. Father and mother are very well. I hope to see you on Christmas Day. Winter is coming; don't it make you shiver to think of? Shall you ever come to smoky old London again? It is not so bad, after all, with its bustle and business and noise. If you see Ellen T— will you kindly get her address for me. I must now conclude, as I am soon going to my reading class; so good-bye.

From your affectionate friend, M—

The 'scholar's letter' was the work of a boy (no age given) attending a 'private middle-class school':

My Dear Parents,—The anticipation of our Christmas vacation abounds in peculiar delights. Not only that its "festivities," its social gatherings, and its lively amusements crown the old year with happiness and mirth, but that I come a guest commended to your hospitable love by the performance of all you bade me remember when I left you in the glad season of sun and flowers.

And time has sped fleetly since reluctant my departing step crossed the threshold of that home whose indulgences and endearments their temporary loss has taught me to value more and more. Yet that restraint is salutary, and that self-reliance is as easily learnt as it is laudable, the propriety of my conduct and the readiness of my services shall ere long aptly illustrate. It is with confidence I promise that the close of every year shall find me advancing in your regard by constantly observing the precepts of my excellent tutors and the example of my excellent parents.

We break up on Thursday the 11th of December instant, and my impatience of the short delay will assure my dear parents of the filial sentiments of

Theirs very sincerely, N—

School/college bill

Many early educational bills were handwritten on unheaded paper. A typical example, dated 2 October 1768, appears on a sheet 115 × 190 mm (4½ × 7½ in) and records a payment of £6 19*s* 0*d* to 'John Lee, Schoolmaster' by Mr Gordon James for 'Mr James, halfe a Years Board & School due September 7 1768': this total includes 'shoes mend (three occasions), 'Pair Shoes', 'A Spellg Book', 'Coat & Breeches mnd', and 'Whitson Holodays'. In similar format is a handwritten bill to Mr Joseph Dean in October 1804 from 'The Preceptor of B. Academy' for '1 Qutrs Tuition of his daughter (1½ weeks absent) $1.74; washing, sweeping 0.99; Total $1.93'.

School bills were also often rendered in handwriting on the blank third page of the school's four-page printed prospectus of terms. James Hibard, who ran the Academy at 16 North Audley Street, Grosvenor Square, in the second decade of the 19th century lists items in Master Christie's bill in a fine scholastic hand: 'Tuition of Master Christie 1.1.0; pens and ink 2.0; copy book 1.0, English Grammar 1.0; French Fables 2.0'.

Printed bills provided for a wide variety of expenses over and above the more predictable items. In 1839 St John's College, Cambridge, listed Steward, Fellow's Butler, Cook, Bedmaker, Shoe-Cleaner, Launderess, Rent, Tuition, Public lectures, Barber, Grocer, Coal merchant, Bookseller, Fixtures, Furniture, Tailor, Hosier, Shoemaker, Hatter, Ironmonger, Upholsterer, Printer, Glazier, and Surgeon.

In 1837 Yale College listed, in addition to Tuition, Room

To the President & Fellows of Yale College, Dr.

1837 January 4

For Tuition, 11 —
" Room,—Rent and Sweeping,
" Ordinary Repairs, 87
" General Damages, 18
" Individual Damages,
" Fuel and Lights for Recitation Rooms, 1 —
" Catalogues, 10. 57 | 13 | 48

For Wood, at Purchase Price, viz:
" Nut, C. at $
" Birch,
" Oak,
" Pine,
" Sawing, Splitting and Carrying,
" Agent's Commission and sundry Incidental Exp's

For Ton Lehigh Egg Coal,
" do. do. Nut do.
" Bushels Charcoal,
" Delivering,

Recd payt. January 14, 1837
Wyllys Warner Treas

Payment is expected within one week after the close of vacation.

Yale College bill, 4 January 1837. Letterpress and manuscript. 177 × 165mm (7 × 6½in)

(rent and sweeping), such further items as Ordinary repairs, General damages, Individual damages, Fuel and lights for recitation rooms, Catalogues, Wood (sawing, splitting, and carrying).

St John's Middle School, Hurstpierpoint, included Seamstress and Drugs in its printed list (1865). Winchester College had Letterman and Scourer (1859), and Archbishop Horgain's School included use of Piano and Dilapidations (1879). Tipperary Grammar School listed Poor box (1868), and Eton College Bat-maker, Watchmaker, Carpenter, and China-Man (1865). In 1868 a printed letter from Eton's headmaster, J. J. Hornby, was included with the bill. It announced a discontinuance of separate charges for such items as 'Boys library', 'Mathematical stationery', 'Watching and lighting', 'Clark', 'Postman', and other such small payments. These would henceforth be consolidated in one standard payment. The letter also announced discontinuance of the double fee hitherto charged for noblemen.

Bills from private tutors, music teachers, and others were commonly handwritten, often with polite requests for dispatch. Miss Reichmann of 41 George Street, Hull, wrote in a re-rendering of a bill for music lessons from 10 June to 13 October 1864 that 'A settlement next week will oblige as Miss Reichmann has to make some payments'. Her request is dated – some two years after the lessons – 29 September 1866.

See also BILLHEAD

School list

It was the practice, particularly in the 19th century and in the early years of the 20th century, for schools and colleges to publish periodical pupil lists. ('Catalogs' in America; 'Election Lists' at Eton College). The lists appeared in various forms and formats; many American examples are broadsides; in Britain they took the form of single or folded sheets or booklets. They are normally found to relate to expanding or long-established and fully-subscribed institutions; those in decline preferred not to draw attention to diminishing numbers (and official records show that lists may be discontinued on this account).

School prospectus

The emergence of a commercially successful middle class in early 19th century Britain led to the setting up of large numbers of private schools, many of them of doubtful educational standard. Apart from personal recommendation, the printed prospectus was the school's only form of publicity, and considerable effort was expended in conveying an air of academic respectability and efficiency. Charles Dickens in *Nicholas Nickleby* (1838–39) did much to spotlight the duplicity of these documents.

Typically the school prospectus of the 19th century measured 250 × 200 mm (9⅞ × 7⅞ in) and carried its message on two or three of its four pages, leaving the back page blank to allow for folding and addressing for posting. The earliest versions favoured a centred 'title-page' arrangement, with a liberal sprinkling of typefaces and a mildly declamatory editorial style: 'Music, Dancing, Drawing and French, on the usual Terms, by the most approved masters ... the health, comfort and morals of the Young Gentlemen are objects of increasing solicitude ...'. Details about the number and qualifications of teaching staff are normally lacking, though there are often references to 'able assistants'. A popular – almost statutory – item on the educational agenda, after Latin, Greek, Arithmetic, and Algebra, is 'The use of the globes'.

The American version of the school prospectus appeared some years later, but the formula – and often the format – was the same. Its tenor is also similar though, as with the later British version, there was a move to a running text of some two to three hundred words, with continuation on page two, and lists of referees – if not actual testimonials – on page three. Later versions in both countries may run to eight pages and include extended outlines of studies and facilities, past students' successes, and possibly school rules and regulations.

Less detailed, but often no less informative, are the smaller-format folders, normally put out by schools with very restricted numbers: 'Miss Carr receives six young Ladies to Educate on the plan of a private family. She is assisted by Foreign Governesses…'; 'The Misses Morrish receive a number of Young Ladies to be instructed in every branch of a Sound English Education…'; 'A French Lady resides in the House'; 'Use of the Globes: Two guineas'.

Other establishments made do with little more than a TRADE CARD in which, for example, 'Mrs Brown begs to inform her Friends that she intends on the 4th of January 1841, opening a Seminary for the instruction of Young Ladies in the different branches of a female education… Writing, Arithmetic and Fancy and Plain Needle-Work attended to'.

Prospectuses were also produced by Church and other organizations seeking support for the building or rebuilding of schools. These carried engravings showing the proposed construction and names of persons who had opened the subscription lists.

Today's prospectuses, whether for state or private schools, play an essential promotional role. They have borrowed the marketing approaches of the commercial world and often make as liberal use as funds allow of the latest graphic idioms.

See also SCHOOL/COLLEGE BILL

School report

The practice of supplying parents with a review of pupils' progress dates back at least to the 18th century. The school report, commonly rendered at the end of each term, but sometimes monthly or weekly, is of special interest for its formal listing of subjects taught and marked: Farningham Academy in the 1830s provided not only Reading, Writing, English grammar, Arithmetic, Geography, French and Latin, but Orthography, Mapping, Tables, Dancing, and 'Problems' [i.e. mathematics]. The Grammar and Commercial School at Deptford in the 1850s included Surveying and Arithmetic (practical) and Arithmetic (mental).

Whereas English-speaking establishments list 'Conduct and order', 'Behaviour', or 'General deportment', as mark-earning subjects, continental schools are more explicit: the Notre Dame Convent in Antwerp (1915) offers marks for 'Politeness' as well as 'Conduct'; the Institut St Amand in Ghent (1929) lists not only 'Conduct' but 'Politeness and refinement' ('Politesse et distinction').

For many of the lesser establishments, in which pupils' fees were vitally needed revenue, report entries were often designed to reassure parents of progress – and thus to continue their patronage. The incidence of high marking may be attributed as much to commercial acumen as to scholastic success.

COÖPERATING MIRROR.

Weekly Report of the Conduct of

The Parent or Guardian is requested to sign opposite each week, and thus coöperate with the Teacher.

In Deportment, the lowest number denotes the best.
Parents and friends are always welcome visitors at the school-room

Published by Ide & Dutton, Boston Price $1. per hundred.

Weekly school report, Boston (US), 5 December 1853 to 4 March 1854. Letterpress and manuscript. Published by Ide & Dutton, Boston, at one dollar per hundred copies. 129 × 90 mm (5⅛ × 3½ in)

School return

The school return afforded 19th-century authorities a means of monitoring educational progress in areas under their control. Reports, often in the form of filled-in questionnaires, provided general or detailed information on school facilities in a given administrative region. The returns were rendered annually or on specific subjects, occasionally. They convey, in the nature of their questions no less than in their filled-in answers, a clear picture of the schoolroom standards of their time.

A questionnaire filled in by the Trustees of the 21-pupil school in district no. 6 in Johnston, Rhode Island, in 1856 is typical: it requires information on the nature of the neighbourhood, 'pecuniary resources', the schoolhouse building, appointments, attendance figures, subjects taught, schoolbooks used, teaching staff, inspection arrangements, etc. The section on the schoolhouse includes the following exchanges:

Furnished with a suitable playground (Yes); Out building (Yes); Material and condition of the building – material (Wood); condition – good, ordinary, bad (Ordinary); provided with a scraper (No); mat (Yes); water pail and cup (Yes); sink, basin and towel (No); old broom for feet (Yes); peg, hooks or shelves (Pegs); broom and dust-brush (Yes); number of school rooms and size of each (1); length (20ft); width (20); height (9);… provided with woodshed or shelter for fuel (No); shovel and tongs etc. (No); thermometer (No); bell (No); globe (No); clock (No); handbell for teacher (No);

blackboard, the size (if any) (6ft by 3ft); map of Rhode Island (Yes)

Other parts of the questionnaire reveal that the school disposed of thirty textbooks, and had only one copy of *Towers First Elements of Grammar*. The teacher, Miss Ira Merriam, was 17 years of age; she had been teaching for one year, and had no previous teaching experience; she received 20 dollars per month compensation. The school was inspected by one parent or other; average daily attendance was fifteen; the number of families served was twelve. There were no scholars in Reading (though there were fifteen in Spelling); none in History of the United States, General history, Etymology or Analysis of language, Definition, Mental arithmetic, Penmanship, Book-keeping, Algebra, Geometry, Natural philosophy, Physiology, Drawing, or Vocal music. Subjects taught (in addition to spelling) are listed as Alphabet, Geography, Composition, Grammar (one pupil), and Declamation (seventeen pupils).

A questionnaire circulated among Church of England Schools 'within the York call of the Archdeanery' in April 1839 covers more specialized ground. It seeks information on attendance in various categories of school and the nature of instruction offered. Questions include, as well as those on statistics, requests for opinions: 'Do you consider the Master of the Parish or National School sufficient for the fulfilment of his office? Is he competent to teach book-keeping, mensuration, etc. so as to be capable of undertaking the education of Farmers' or Tradesmen's sons? If competent, and permitted to do so, what number of such children could he possibly obtain at a charge of ten or fifteen shillings a quarter?'

In the return in question, which in this case relates to day schools for the poor and middle classes in which the church catechism is taught, these questions are unanswered, there being no such schools to report. In a later section, however, relating to education in general, there is the following exchange: 'What is the number of boys and girls in your Parish above the age of six who are receiving no education? (2) Do you attribute the defect to the want of means or will in the relatives? (To the want of means). Can you suggest any means by which education may be improved in your Parish? (No)'. The return is signed by the curate, Isaac Grayson, Holy Trinity Church, Kings Court.

Returns provided by teachers and clergy in Britain were superseded in the latter part of the century by personal visitation and reporting by local-authority and other inspectors.

See also ATTENDANCE RECORD, SCHOOL; SCHOOL LIST

Schoolboy's piece

Decorative printed sheets were published in the 18th and 19th centuries for scholars to fill in with their own handwriting as presents (notably at Christmas) for their parents. They were known variously as 'Schoolboys' pieces', 'School pieces', and 'Christmas pieces'. The sheets commonly measured 500 × 390 mm (19¾ × 15⅜ in) and carried a framing series of woodcuts or wood engravings, printed in black and, occasionally, coloured by hand. They generally featured a large landscape-format picture as a title piece, three smaller portrait-format illustrations forming a border on each side, and a garlanded motif at the foot which was designed to carry a hand-inserted date-line.

The illustrations were frequently of religious subjects, but another common theme was 'University Education' (1783): 'A Young Gentleman Delivering a Latin oration to the Professors and Heads of Colleges', 'Reading the Classicks', 'Translating Greek into English', 'Studying the Mathematics', and 'A Young Nobleman finishing his Studies'. Other themes illustrated were 'The London and Westminster Light Horse Volunteers' (1798); 'An East Indiaman just launched' (1800); and 'A Ballooning Event Monsr and Madame Garnarin and Mr Glassford ascending at Vauxhall, August 3rd 1802' (1802). Publishers included John Basire (Clerkenwell); William Belch (Borough); Carrington Bowles (St Paul's Churchyard); James Cole (Hatton Gardens); John Fairburn (Minories); Robert Harrild (Eastcheap); Edward Langley (Borough); Laurie & Whittle (Fleet Street); Robert Sayer (Fleet Street); and George Thompson (Bermondsey).

Scrap

The colourful decorative cut-outs, known in Britain as 'chromo-reliefs' or scraps, had their origins in Germany in the earlier part of the 19th century. They were called *Oblaten* or *Glanzbilder* ('wafers' or 'gloss pictures') and were originally used as decorative additions to sweetmeats and, later, to GREETINGS CARDS and VALENTINES. Their popularity as juvenile collectables spread rapidly, extending to the whole of Europe and America, and forming one aspect of the wave of German chromolithography that dominated the rest of the century.

The first scraps were not cut-outs. They were simply printed pictures, and were sold as multi-image sheets for cutting out with scissors. They were produced in very large quantities. A sheet published by Rudolph Ackermann and dated 1 January 1800 ('5 shillings plain, 10 shillings coloured') carried the intimation 'New Medallions and Transparencies every Week'. Other manufacturers, offering very much cheaper sheets, were John Betts, William Darton, J. Dickinson, S. W. Fores, and Edward Lacey. Other manufacturers or publishers are recorded in London in the same period. The pictures, which were etched, engraved, or lithographed, were bought for general decorative purposes as well as for albums. They were pasted on boxes, vases, screens, small items of furniture, windows, and lamps, and were also available as continuous strips, three to a sheet, for use as wall decorations. Sheets in this format were designed by Woodward in 1799 and etched by Thomas Rowlandson for an Ackermann publication, *Grotesque Borders for Rooms and Screens.*

Many scraps appeared in series form, such as a set of thirty sheets by George Cruikshank, published in 1830 under the general title *Scraps and Sketches*, John Fairburn's *Fairburn's Novelties*, and *Tregear's Humorous Scraps*, put out by Tregear & Lewis. Untitled sets were published by Burgis & Barfoot, Orlando Hodgson, and A. N. Myers & ('Educational Toy Importers') and London distributors of Julius Hoffman's lithographs for Thienemanns Verlag, Stuttgart.

Scraps at this early period may be seen as a sub-section of the popular print industry in which topical caricatures and lampoons, as well as topographical views and other pictures, were distributed by booksellers and printsellers throughout Europe. Use of these small prints as material for scrap books and albums was not at first envisaged, but they soon generated a renewed fad for the SCRAPBOOK/ALBUM. At first devoted to random fragments – poems, dried plants and ferns, silhouettes, feathers, sketches, and press cuttings – scrapbooks of the early 19th century began to include the offerings of the makers of small prints and, in due course, the new *Glanzbilder.* It was at this point that, in Britain, *Glanzbilder* came to be called scraps. The full-colour

Advertisement for one-penny scraps, late 19th century. Chromolithographed. The scrap, marked D.B. 575, loosely mounted on to a letterpress-printed sheet. 184 × 245 mm (7¼ × 9⅞in)

cut-out scrap was produced by chromolithography (*see* CHROMO), at first from stones, later from metal plates. Colour workings were commonly six to ten in number, but the larger, more elaborate specimens involved many more. Die-cutting and relief-stamping were carried out in one operation, and the characteristic glossy surface was imparted either incidentally by the build up of ink or by subsequent surface varnishing. The development from square-cut print to embossed cut-out took place in the 1860s and early 1870s. Individual subjects were presented in multiple sheets, each image held to its neighbour by narrow connecting tabs which usually bore the name of the manufacturer.

Pictorial content conformed to no rational discipline; all that was desired was an attractive picture, most commonly sentimental and sometimes exciting. The world of the relief scrap was for the most part a never-never land of hearts and flowers with occasional dashes of contemporary reality. Subjects thus ranged from angels on clouds and garlands of roses to fire brigades and the tragic death of Barnum's elephant. Scraps, though they became a worldwide cult, generally remained only a side-line for the printers who produced them. Major printers were German chromolithographic specialists, Albrecht & Meister, Zoecke & Mittmeyer, and Mamelok & Sohne (later the Mamelok Press Ltd in Britain), and Louis Prang in America. Most of these German-based companies produced material geared to the tastes of local markets, and presented it as, for example, 'Designed in Great Britain, printed in Germany'. Edward Elliot & Co. are recorded as the first to import the relief scrap into Britain (c.1852) and other prominent names in London were Raphael Tuck and Birn Brothers, who manufactured in Germany. As recently as the late 20th century scraps were still being produced by several printers, notably Mamelok Press Ltd in Britain, Paul B. Zoecke in Germany, and the Merrimack Co. in America.

REFERENCES Alistair Allen and Joan Hoverstadt, *The History of Printed Scraps* (London: New Cavendish, 1983); Estrid Faurholt, *De Kære små Billeder* (Sesam A/S, nd)

COLLECTION Alistair Allen Collection, Madame Tussaud's, London

Scrapbook/album

The scrapbook, like the scrap album, was devised for the display of a wide range of minor mementoes. It commonly housed such items as pressed flowers, paper cuts and silhouettes, dried sea-plants, feathers, puzzles, poems, and other natural and graphic ephemera. The scrapbook is closely related to the earlier COMMONPLACE BOOK, in which the owner recorded handwritten extracts from literature and popular wisdom, and which in turn generated the drawing-room 'visitors' book', a similar – though cooperative – record.

The scrap-collecting craze received no small part of its impetus from the publication of John Poole's *Manuscript Gleanings and Literary Scrap Book* (1826). In this book, Poole presented a bound volume of printed poems and engravings, together with a one-page introduction on the concept of the commonplace journal and the collecting and arranging of scraps. This was followed in 1832 by Henry Fisher's volume *Fisher's Drawing Room Scrap Book,* a further visual encouragement and exemplar for the scrap collector. Fisher later put out a series of *Drawing-Room Scrap Sheets,* decoratively printed for the reception of specimens and devised for binding as a personalized volume.

The scrap album, whose advent followed the growth of the scrapbook, provided the same facilities at a more sophisticated

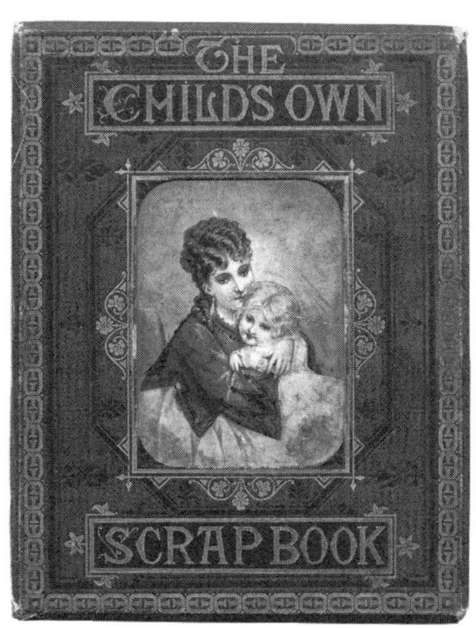

Scrapbook, autographed 1876. Gold-blocked cloth cover with chromolithographed on-lay and two of its pages of chromolithographed cards and scraps. Page size 220 × 180 mm (8⅝ × 7⅛in)

level. Its pages, though virtually blank, provided embossed or printed borders on a variety of tints; in addition, roundels, ovals, and rectangular frames offered display space for smaller entries. The idea was to be extended in the latter part of the century to the crest album, which also provided a decorative setting for its contents. Separate title-pages, elegantly designed and engraved, were also available for insertion in existing scrapbooks or for binding with loose pages in the manufacture of new ones.

The scrap mania was a major feature of middle-class 19th-century life, and publishers of scraps, scrapbooks, and albums were not slow to encourage and exploit it. Armed only with scissors and paste, the drawing-room practitioner could produce effects of apparent creativity and artistic merit, and the drawing-room album was a centre of much social interchange. From the 1820s to the 1840s the fad evoked a series of gently satirical prints on the theme of 'scrap-begging', in which every conceivable item of waste paper was seen as an item for the album. Scrap albums reveal a very broad miscellany, often including not only the products of the scrap publishers but decorative labels and advertising items – much of the material was badly cut or trimmed, but it sometimes provided undamaged specimens for the ephemerist.

Prominent among scrapbook and scrap-album manufacturers in Britain were J. L. Barritt, Bradbury & Wilkinson, De La Rue, W. H. Rock, and Rooney & Sons. Also active were George Chapman, Erdmann & Shanz, William Johnson & Sons, D. A. Lowthime, Frederick Macfarlane, Sidney Saunders & Co., Robert Sayer, Alexander Shapcott, Silber & Fleming, T. J. Smith Son & Co., James Speller (later Speller, Preston & Henry), and Charles Willson & Co.

See also ALBUM CARD; ALBUM FRONTISPIECE; SCRAP

Seating plan, table

Used in conjunction with individually-named PLACE CARDS at dinners and other such functions, table seating plans give guests guidance on where to sit.

Some plans follow protocol or convention (alternating genders), others are ingeniously devised to avoid incompatibility of neighbouring guests. Among typographically distinctive examples are the elegantly handwritten plans produced over the last thirty years by the designer John Miles for the Double Crown Club (London), and those of the Wynkyn de Worde Society (London) which, over the last few years, have been generated by computer from lists of members and guests.

Secondary uses of ephemera

Small items of ephemera, such as tickets, visiting cards, invitations, and flyers sometimes owe their survival to their use for a purpose other than the one originally intended. A ticket may have served as a BOOKMARK or a flyer as a surface on which to scribble a note. The latter may also find its way into a book for safe keeping and, over the years, books have provided as good a home as any for preserving small-scale ephemera. Larger items of ephemera have sometimes survived because a use was found for them as lining paper for bindings, framed prints, shelves, and drawers. Three-dimensional items (tins and cardboard boxes) have proved even more useful and may have had greatly extended lives as receptacles for buttons and other small items. Some of these secondary uses of ephemera may be obvious through the addition of manuscript notes, or deduced from fold marks, trimming, stains, and differential discolouration; others, such as the makeshift bookmark, may leave no trace of their later use.

The most widespread secondary use of ephemera, both before and after the introduction of LAVATORY PAPER in the 19th century, was extremely private and usually limited to the privy. It is known about through written, pictorial, and oral records: early manufacturers of lavatory paper referred to the advantages of their product over paper bearing printers' ink, and many still alive can recall the drawbacks of the latter. By contrast, SCRAPS – which were specifically produced and sold for reuse in scrapbooks and for applying to boxes and screens – have survived in enormous quantities, both in their published form and when applied. The art of découpage continues this tradition, though in the main using found items from magazines and other ephemera rather than purpose-made items.

Examples of the secondary use of ephemera fall into two main categories: the everyday, and in most cases personal and almost incidental reuse of the kind referred to above, and a systematic and sometimes official reuse for more general application, often as a substitute for currency in emergency situations. Playing cards were the major category of ephemera to serve as IMPROVISED CURRENCY (*see also* PLAYING CARD, SECONDARY USES). Other materials were used in the American Civil War, and as late as the 1950s in Italy sweets (including their wrappers) were provided as a substitute for small denominations when giving change. Other systematic secondary uses of ephemera include the reuse of printed sheets, usually, though not exclusively, in periods of war-time paper shortage. Printed waste sheets have been used for the end papers of books, for the NEWS BILLS of newspaper vendors, and for the production of envelopes (with the bonus that the printing reduced show-through).

Items of ephemera that reveal a secondary use, like marks of ownership in books, may be of significance for their association with the individuals concerned. One such item is a library slip, used by the British wood-engraver and writer Robert Gibbings in the 1950s as an informal 'calling card'. Items of this kind are highly collectable. Probably the most valuable of all such items of ephemera showing a secondary use – and possibly among the most valuable of all items of ephemera – is a coloured postcard of Leonardo da Vinci's painting of the Mona Lisa in the Louvre on which the French artist Marcel Duchamp added a goatee beard and a moustache. This unique reworked commercial postcard, which can be dated to 1919, now stands along with Duchamp's other 'ready-mades' of the period as one of the

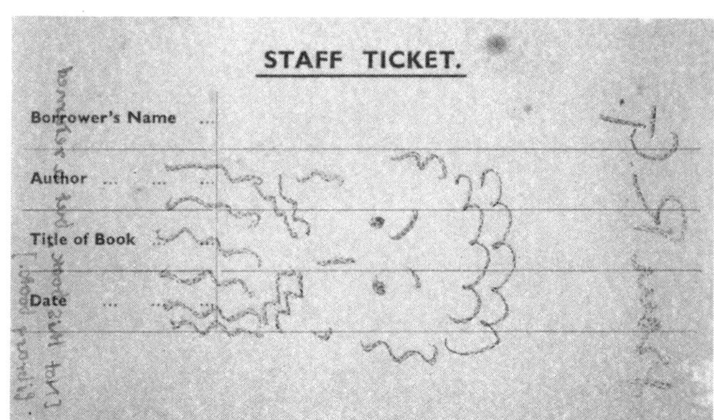

Library slip of Reading University Library, used as a 'calling card' by Robert Gibbings in the 1950s. Scanned with transmitted light to show the artist's pencil drawing on its reverse. 75 × 126 mm (3 × 5 in)

major landmarks of 20th-century art. This particular 'secondary use' turned a modest item of printed ephemera into a work of art which, over time, helped to redefine the nature of art. [MT]

See also SILK

Security printing

The term is widely and somewhat loosely used to cover the printing of items that need to be made 'secure' from FORGERY. This use may explain its derivation, though it is also possible that it has some connection with the financial sense of the word 'security' – a document held by a creditor as a guarantee of a right to payment. Most general dictionaries and specialist glossaries of printing ignore the subject entirely. By common usage, however, security printing has at its core a group of financial documents, such as a BANKNOTE, CHEQUE/CHECK, or SHARE CERTIFICATE, and other items that have a monetary value, including postage stamps and, even, trading stamps. By extension, the term is applied to the production of any printed item that has prevention of counterfeiting as a priority or important consideration, as in a LICENCE, PASSPORT, or RECEIPT.

Intaglio printing has been the principal process used for security printing since the 18th century. Originally the printing surface was engraved by hand; later it was often machine-engraved to give greater security; but from the end of the 19th century it was produced mainly by photogravure. However, what is called security printing amounts to more than the actual printing. It includes the design of the marks made on the plate, which need to be planned in such a way that any deviation from them in forgeries is relatively easy to spot. It also includes a strict control of materials and production as items pass through the workshop or factory, in order that every sheet of paper and every printed item can be accounted for. The parts of security printing that have to do more directly with manufacture relate to fugitive and other special inks, purpose-made paper (e.g. THREAD PAPER), the application of special printing methods (e.g. COMPOUND-PLATE PRINTING), and the use of such devices as matching-part documents, numeration for machine reading and, more recently, holograms. The underlying principle of all effective security printing is to produce documents that are so difficult and complex to manufacture that, even when forgers have the necessary skills, there are strong disincentives – over and above moral and legal ones – to using them. [MT]

See also ASSIGNAT; BANKNOTE, SPECIMEN; RAINBOW PRINTING; RATION PAPERS; STEEL ENGRAVING; WATERMARK

Seed packet

The original term was 'seed pocket'. The word 'pocket' first appeared in the sense of a paper envelope in America in 1842, though it had been in use in America and Britain to refer to a bag (of hops, flour, etc.) for many years before that date. In Britain, its use in this latter sense pre-dates its application as a feature of clothing.

Flower and vegetable seed 'pockets' were widely sold in Britain under that description until after the end of the 19th century. E. S. & A. Robinson, the Bristol printers, offered seedsmen a range of over 200 'pictorial card pockets', each chromolithographed design showing a named flower or vegetable in colour with, if desired, the seedsman's name on the front and sowing instructions on the back. General use of the term 'pocket' appears to have given way to 'packet' in the period 1900 to 1920, although 'pocket' remained current within the industry into recent times. In America, records indicate that seeds were sold in the 1790s in linen bags rather than paper. The Shakers (*see* SHAKER PAPERS) continued to refer to the paper packs they used for seeds as 'bags'. The oldest surviving American seed packet is held to date from the 1820s.

Seed packet of William D. Burt, Dalton, New York, first half of 20th century. Chromolithographed. As shown, 140 × 95 mm (5½ × 3¾ in)

Many British seedsmen used to sell their products in folded papers (after the manner of chemist's powders), but with the spread of the machine-made ENVELOPE in the 1860s and 1870s printed packets came into general use. At first the single-colour printed image was principally typographic, but decorative elements shortly appeared. Together with the seedsman's name and address, they differentiated between types of seed. They remained constant throughout a given seedsman's range, the seed title and sowing instructions changing only as required.

Typical examples are those of D. Strong & Son, Seed Growers, of Portland, Connecticut (c.1880), in which title and sowing instructions are framed in a decorative border, and of John K. King of Coggeshall, Essex (c.1880), bearing text plus a trademark and royal warrant.

Maiben & Bingham's Paper Bag Manufactory (c.1880) offered their 'very convenient envelopes', printed with their own trade name and decorative motif, and suggested that: 'The large quantities already supplied by them to Seedsmen throughout the country, and the general satisfaction they have given, warrant the belief that they will entirely supersede the old-fashioned and tedious method of wrapping'.

The popularization of chromolithographic printing in the

latter part of the century (*see* CHROMO) brought full-colour illustrations to the packets – often, as in the case of E. S. & A. Robinson already noted, without precise reference to the seedsman's own product. Blake & Mackenzie, the Liverpool printers, also brought out a series of chromolithographed pictorials for the trade, supplying in addition a counter container for the display of twenty-four varieties. The seed packet had become a 'mini-poster', a point-of-sale display item, and the principle was to continue in some areas into the mid 20th century. In the 1950s the John Dickinson Co. was producing a range of 300–400 colour-printed pictorial packets for overprinting with the seedsman's name. For large orders, printing plates were adapted to include the tradesman's name in a special working rather than overprinting existing stock.

The major seed companies were much concerned with accurate colour rendering, and even four-colour photomechanical reproduction did not always satisfy their needs. The older method of chromolithography – or a combination of both methods – lasted even into the 1960s. Writing in the early 1980s, John Attenburrow, past managing director of printers Dobson & Crowther, recalls workings of up to eight or nine colours, and in at least one case thirteen colours to achieve the desired effect. Seed packets of the mid 20th century put out by the Burt Co. of Dalton, New York, reflect a similar practice. Printed by the Genesee Valley Lithograph Co., they too show the characteristic stippled gradations of chromolithography.

Seidlitz-powder label

Seidlitz powders, widely used as a mild aperient and digestif, were named after the natural spring of Sedlice in Bohemia (now in the Czech Republic) whose waters their effervescence resembles. The powders, to be mixed in water just before drinking, are supplied in two separate folded papers, traditionally blue (containing sodium bicarbonate and rochelle salt) and white (containing tartaric acid). The papers are contained in an outer folder bearing a label or in a printed envelope.

As one of the few widely recognized remedies of the early 19th century, the product and its presentation and packaging became more or less standardized. Its 'directions for use' also varied but little: 'Dissolve the contents of the blue paper in half a tumbler of spring water, then add the contents of the white paper. Stir well and drink during effervescence'. Labels and envelopes were normally about 70 × 110 mm (2¾ × 4⅜ in), and their single-colour printing and graphic treatment commonly

Seidlitz powder label of G. Baldwin & Co., Walworth, London, late 19th century. Letterpress, the reverse gummed. 73 × 110 mm (2⅞ × 4⅜ in)

reflected a style from an earlier period. In Britain, the design was often embellished with the royal coat of arms; in other parts of Europe much visual play was made (as in many pharmaceutical labels) with Aesculapian symbols and alchemists' laboratory ware. In America, there were oblique (and misleading) references to Sedlice: their powder was described as '...possessing the medical properties of the effervescing springs in Germany'. Seidlitz powders were in general use until the 1930s and 1940s, but were superseded after World War I by mass-market proprietary drinks.

Sentiment card

The sentiment card flourished in America in the middle years of the 19th century. It was a recognized token of attachment, generally between young girls, though many that survive apparently bear adult male inscriptions. Smaller than the conventional calling-card – commonly about 40 × 70 mm (1 9/16 × 2¾ in) – it bore a floral motif, a pictorial illustration, or a motto.

Printing was by letterpress or engraving (or a combination of the two) and many were hand-coloured. Some designs provided space for the name of the bearer. The general standard of design was of an elegance far removed from the exuberance of the later chromolithographed calling card.

American sentiment cards, c. 1850. Wood-engraved, printed in blue and hand-coloured. Each 42 × 72 mm (1¾ × 2⅞ in)

The American sentiment card was paralleled in Europe by the German *Andenken-Bild* (keepsake image), which was a larger production, typically 90 × 105 mm (3½ × 4⅛ in). Featuring black-letter mottoes in hand-coloured wood-cut garlanded frames, they were sold in sheets of a dozen for cutting up.

Servant's award

Among the activities of the Agricultural Societies formed in Britain in the 19th century was the encouragement of loyalty and diligence in 'labourers and servants' on farms. With the setting-up of locally sponsored 'awards' or 'premiums' for workers, employers sought to counter the effects of the current agricultural discontent. Rewards in cash or kind, with accompanying certificates, were offered for a wide range of virtues. These ranged from long service to abstinence from liquor, and from Sunday School attendance to fat-pig rearing. Each award was made to a named inhabitant, details of his or her achievements being listed in the local press and, in many cases, in a leaflet issued by the Society.

A typical award of £2 was made in Glastonbury in 1869, 'to the Agricultural Labourer who since the year 1838, shall have brought up and educated the greatest number (above five) of his own legitimate children to the age of ten years, without parochial relief'. Another, in the same neighbourhood in 1843, bestowed £1 on a farm worker 'for having paid £5 into the Savings Bank during the year'. Winners' certificates took various forms. For the most part they were standard or near-standard basic designs, overprinted with suitable wording by the prime supplier or by a local printer. One series, supplied by Shaw & Jones of Fetter Lane, London, bore a selection of engravings of rural scenes with space for letterpress overprinting to show the name of the issuing society and lines for handwritten insertions of the recipient's name, achievement, and award. In other cases blind-embossed 'frames' (many of them supplied by Dobbs & Co., London) were overprinted locally, either with full details of each individual recipient or with blanks for handwritten completion.

Even by 19th-century standards, rewards were less than extravagant. In 1856, for 'having worked 30 years on the same farm & always maintained a good character', George Giles of Blandford received from the Blandford Agricultural Society for the encouragement of Industrious Labourers and Servants a coat and ten shillings. In 1882 George Riches received from the Suffolk Agricultural Association 'for having worked fifty years upon the same farm or with the same master or mistress' the sum of £2.

See also SERVANT'S REGISTRY PAPERS

REFERENCE Kenneth Hudson, *Patriotism with Profit* (London: Hugh Evelyn, 1972)

COLLECTION Rural History Centre, The University of Reading

Servant's 'character' reference

The employer's power to write good or bad references for a departing servant was a major factor in the domestic-service scene in Britain in the period 1814 to 1914.

Domestic service, one of the lowest rungs of the employment ladder, offered working conditions little short of slavery, and the employee's freedom to leave was counter-balanced by absolute dependence for another job on the 'character' provided by the employer. The employer was not obliged in law to provide references of any kind, and it was illegal to write good references where these were unjustified. Bad references, on the other hand, except where demonstrably malicious, were deemed to be 'privileged' and thus not actionable by law. In a final weighting of the balance against a servant, an Act of 1792 imposed a penalty of £20 on the falsification or counterfeiting of references 'contrary to truth and justice'. The reference was thus a crucial social document. A job applicant's failure to produce one, through whatever cause, was the inevitable prelude to disaster. It has been said that a common cause of girls' turning to prostitution was the 'dead end' effect of the absent reference.

The reference document itself, when it was positive, was more or less standardized:

> To whom it may concern: this is to certify that Mary Johnston has been in my employ as a servant for three years. During that time she has been honest, clean, conscientious and obliging. I have no hesitation in recommending her...

Less positive documents survive, however. A note from Lord Eldon to the Earl of Charlemont in 1843 goes into detail:

> I have just received your Lordship's letter of yesterday, respecting George Hayes, and I regret that I cannot answer satisfactorily your Lordship's enquiry whether he was 'faithful, sober, honest' and whether I 'parted with him for any fault'. My reason for parting with him was that I received information by letter that in paying for some blacking to a Mr Propert of South Audley Street he had brought me the bill for £1.16.0. out of which Mr Propert had had only £1.4.0 and had given up to Hayes 12 shillings. This Hayes and Propert most strenuously denied for some time, but at last when I thro' my solicitor and my own investigation got Propert to admit, Hayes could no longer deny...
>
> I dismissed Hayes immediately from my service, but during the day or two I permitted him to remain in my house as an act of charity I did not perceive that sense of shame which I had hoped and expected. As to his sobriety I cannot speak with confidence: I often had told him that I was sure there was something wrong in his conduct as he had no authority over the underservants....
>
> Hayes well knows that when a servant leaves me I never either understate or overstate the character they deserve, and I much wish that all gentlemen would do the same.... I assure your Lordship I write this with pain and regret, and even though it gives your Lordship the same, I cannot but express the wish that you would read it to Hayes...

Negative responses were commonly less detailed, though the *Ladies' New Letter Writer* (Dean & Co, London c.1840) recommended the following in the case of an unsatisfactory governess:

> Madam; in answer to your polite note in reference to the character and capabilities of Miss ... who lived with me in the capacity of governess to my children during the space of... I regret to say that a duty imposes itself upon me which, although requisite, is yet most unpleasant to my feelings; inasmuch as I feel obliged to state that the estimate which I formed of the capabilities of the lady were far from being of a satisfactory nature. I found her manners were extremely repulsive, and that, with the children, she had little or no command over her temper. In other respects I have nothing to say which would operate to her prejudice. Believe me, madam, your very obedient servant....

See also SERVANT'S AWARD; SERVANT'S REGISTRY PAPERS

Servant's registry papers

In the 18th-century Britain, organized hiring of servants in rural areas was largely confined to the annual 'Mop fair' or 'Hiring day', in which servants were engaged at an open-air market. With the general movement to towns in the 19th century the market was replaced by the 'Servants' agency' or 'Registry'. Though at first a philanthropic institution for the protection of the virtue of naive country girls, the agency soon became a commercial venture, run 'for the nobility and gentry' by respectable middle-class ladies.

In many cases registry premises served as meeting places for contracting parties. One leaflet declares that: 'Many servants attend daily from 11 to 2 o'clock for selection; but on Monday, Wednesday and Friday the number is very large indeed'. Fees

Westminster Central Mart,

CORNER OF SOUTHAMPTON-STREET, STRAND,

Is Open Daily, from 9 to 5 o'Clock, for the Purpose of

Hiring Servants

OF ALL DENOMINATIONS,

For Noblemen and Tradesmen's Families; and also for providing Situations for Servants of every Class and Description, who are furnished with proper Recommendations suitable to their Capacities.

From the system laid down and pursued in this concern, for the purposes above alluded to, it must, from its very nature, produce the most beneficial effects to every individual. The New Plans which the Proprietors of this Establishment have adopted, by having a daily Register of upwards of Five Hundred Applicants for Servants of every kind and denomination, will remove those inconveniences, particularly to Servants, which always attend Newspaper Advertisements.

Families from abroad, or from the Country, can be immediately furnished with suitable Servants of unquestionable character. And Servants wanting Places will be sent to Employers immediately.

Servants' registry bill, Westminster Central Mart, London, second quarter of 19th century. Letterpress. 142 × 229 mm (5⅝ × 9 in)

were normally charged to both parties; but as the century progressed, charges to servants diminished to next to nothing.

The ephemera of sevants' agencies consist in the main of handbills, commonly 250 × 150 mm (9⅞ × 6 in), directed on the one hand to employees, on the other to employers. There are also registration receipts, tariff lists, and display cards, most of which graphically convey the servant/mistress relationship of the time.

See also SERVANT'S AWARDS; SERVANT'S CHARACTER REFERENCE

REFERENCE Frank Dawes, *Not in Front of the Servants* (London: Wayland, 1973)

Servant's timetable

During the heyday of domestic service (c.1830 to c.1930) it was customary for the mistress of the house to turn for advice on duties and daily timetables to such works as Mrs Beeton's *Household Management* and the anonymous *The Management of Sevants*. However, these books gave only general recommendations, and the preparation of detailed instruction sheets was a matter for the individual employer. Pinned up in the servants' quarters, instructions sheets outlined a daily routine, sometimes in a fairly detailed way. They were, on the whole, much disliked by their readers and tended to be 'accidentally' damaged or destroyed in the course of employment.

Where they have survived they provide, in addition to an hour-by-hour account of the daily round, an insight into the social setting of the times. A typical example (c.1900) is a stained and faded handwritten paper, 230 × 180 mm (9 × 7⅛ in), bearing rusty pinholes, which reads:

> Before breakfast: 6.50 Den lay Breakfast table. 7.25, Get tea & call Mistress and Miss H. 7.40, own breakfast 8 a.m., Call Miss Nancy & Mr H. (shoes); Drawing room grate & floor. 8.40. Breakfast. After breakfast: Basins, Miss N's first. Then 3 rooms on 1st floor; own room & beds; bathroom & bottles. Sweep & dust 3 rooms on 1st floor. 11a.m. own lunch; 11.15. Miss N's & maid's rooms & stairs. 12.30. Dress and lay lunch. Afternoon: Silver. Ironing. Brass. Washing mats, etc. 4.30. Tea. 6.45. Dinner preparations. 9 to 9.30. Hot Water, turn beds down. Hot bottles. Turning out: Alternate Tues: Den. Miss H's room; Maids. Mr H's. Thurs. morn. help Mrs Watts in larger rooms. Fridays. Bathroom, landings & stairs.

Shaker papers

The founder of the Shaker movement in America was Ann Lee, daughter of a blacksmith from Manchester (England). She became associated with the Quakers ('who quaked at the name of the Lord') and applied many of their principles to the Shaker set, which she founded after emigrating to New England in 1774. Among the tenets of the group were reliance on simplicity, honesty, and celibacy – the last of which put an effective brake on the sect's expansion. Numbers nevertheless increased by means of adoptive apprenticeships, and by the 1840s there were some six thousand members.

The Shakers established 'cottage industries' dealing, among other things, in seeds, herbs, and eventually medicinal cures. The products were issued in packets, envelopes, and boxes, each of which was labelled in a more or less recognizable typographic style. This was characterized by extreme simplicity, printing being in black on a colour-tinted paper. Production of the labels was not by any means always the work of the Shakers themselves; in many cases they were printed to Shaker specifications

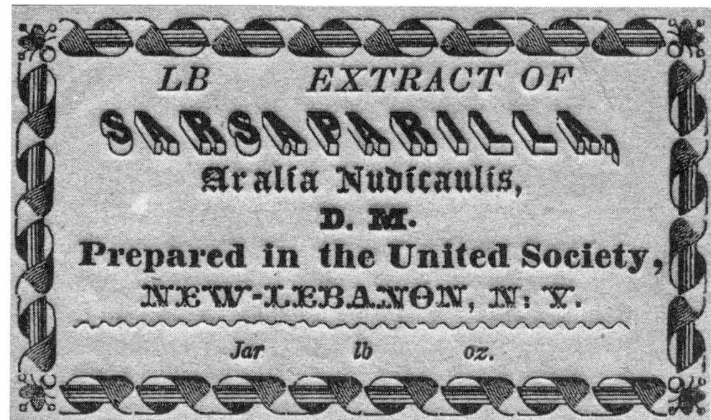

Shaker label for extract of Sarsaparilla. Letterpress on pink paper, mid 19th century. 46 × 78 mm (1$^{13}/_{16}$ × 3⅛ in)

by neighbouring printers. With the widespread use of multi-colour printing, designs became fulsomely illustrated, adopting most if not all of the commercial graphic conventions of the time.

A major Shaker activity was the manufacture of furniture, oval storage boxes, and women's bonnets, most of which also bore identifying labels. The sect inevitably diminished dramatically, but communities survived until late in the 20th century in New Hampshire, New England.

See also SEED PACKETS

REFERENCE Edward D. Andrews, *The Community Industries of the Shakers* (reprint of New York State Museum handbook 15, Emporium Publications, 1933)

Share certificate

The earliest surviving share certificates were engraved on copper and printed in black on parchment. A typical example, dating from 1809, certifies ownership of a single share in the Strand Bridge (renamed before its completion in 1817 Waterloo Bridge) and was engraved by 'R. Brook, Engraver to the Royal Family'. The document is in effect an INDENTURE, the left-hand edge of which has been cut in a random curve from a 'counterfoil' bearing the same number as that entered by quill pen on the engraved numeral panels on the main sheet. Apart from engraved flourishes across its indenture-cut, the document bears only one discernable security device. An oval motif is blind-embossed in the parchment, the area of the oval being covered by a corresponding area of gold foil. The embossed image, pressed through both foil and parchment simultaneously, shows an elevation of the finished bridge.

Share certificates are designed as documents of momentary value, and their manufacture calls for the forgery-proof characteristics of paper currency. It is not surprising, therefore, that with the beginnings of security engraving in the 1820s their printing and production became the province of banknote printers. The titles of such firms appear as footlines on most certificates: these include a small number of world-famous specialists – chief among them in America being the American Bank Note Co., the Franklin Bank Note Co., Western Bank Note and Engraving Co.; and in Britain, De La Rue Ltd, Bradbury Wilkinson & Co. and Waterlow and Sons Ltd. Most of the work of security printers was produced specifically to clients' requirements, each design being of unique and unrepeatable complexity, and each an individual engraver's work of art. With the proliferation of venture capital, however, and as a cost-cutting exercise, many of the motifs, borders, and illustrations on certificates were 'cannibalized'; they appeared in rearrangements and adaptations in more than one context, occasionally moving from someone's BANKNOTE to someone else's share certificate, and vice versa. Jacob Perkins' invention of 'siderography', which allowed images to be transferred from one steel plate to others, made such migrations commonplace.

Certificate design involved not only the anti-counterfeit factor (which led to much decorative intricacy) but the need to impress, which led to an atmosphere of ceremonial stability. As with currency notes, part of whose design function is to inspire confidence, the share certificate seeks to embody an image of reliability and assurance. In addition to its purely representational images of locomotives, oil wells, etc., the share certificate tended to feature allegorical figures: neo-classical groups with cornucopias, anvils, alembics, and other symbols of industry and enterprise. The idiom persisted well into the 20th century, and the same draped and laurel-wreathed figures appear in the 1920s and 1930s with telephone handsets, microphones, and model aircraft.

The essential ingredients of a share certificate are: the name of the issuing company, the name of the holder, the serial number of the certificate, the nature and number of shares held, the date of issue, and the signature of the responsible issuing officer. All other features contribute either to security, to impressiveness, or both. Cancellation of share certificates is often effected by punching holes or making excisions. Presence of these cancellations in 'collectors' items' is of no significance; but on the whole specimens are preferred where essential features (such as illustrations and signatures) are undamaged.

Set of three share certificates of the State of Louisiana, 1886. Steel-engraved, with stamped signature and numbers. The sheet 253 × 140 mm (10 × 5½ in)

'Bearer bond' certificates, not naming a specific holder, are provided with 'coupons' attached to the main document. These are designed to be detached at stated intervals and exchanged for interest payments. An additional slip, called a 'talon', also designed to be detached, is intended for exchange with a further certificate in which ownership is designated. The transferable Bearer bond has something in common with paper currency.

See also SECURITY PRINTING

REFERENCE Robin Hendy, *Collecting Old Bonds and Shares* (London: Stanley Gibbons, 1978)

SOCIETIES Bond and Share Society; Vereniging van Verzamelaars Van Oude Fondsen

Sheet-music cover

The pictorial sheet-music cover, which emerged as a genre in the early 19th century, soon became the vehicle for a wide variety of popular art. Apart from the pictorial POSTER, which developed somewhat later, no other category of ephemera provided artists with quite such a wide range of opportunities in terms of subject matter. In their heyday in the second half of the 19th century, sheet-music covers must have made just as great an impact in music shops and homes as record sleeves did a century later. Contemporary representations of music publishers' shops – some of which were printed on sheet-music covers themselves – show covers displayed in every window pane; and some music publishers' lists make special note of publications with illustrated covers, even as late as the 20th century.

The items discussed here are sometimes called music title-pages, because they display, at the very least, the title of the work, the name of the composer, and the publisher. In many cases they include the name of the writer of the words, information about where copies might be obtained, a dedication, a statement about other publications in the series, a printer's imprint, and a price. Early examples may include a publisher's number (plate number). They are printed as the front page of a publication and can therefore be said to serve as both title-page and cover. Strictly speaking some are not covers, since they were printed on the same sheet as one or more pages of the music. When describing 18th-century music publications, which generally have their publication details engraved using words and flourishes only, the term 'title-page' may be technically correct; but when describing the predominantly pictorial front page that emerged around the middle of the 19th century, 'cover' seems more appropriate.

The term 'sheet music' is applied to publications that are issued in loose sheets. Such publications are not normally extensive: many of them consist of no more than four pages, though some might run to eight or as many as sixteen. Most sheet music would be described as quarto in format, which strictly speaking means that it is the product of a sheet of paper folded twice, the second fold being at right angles to the first. In practice many examples of sheet music are small folios, the product of a sheet folded once at right angles to its longer dimension. But whatever the technicalities may have been, there was a remarkable similarity in the size of such publications over a long period of time and in various parts of the world. Measurements range from demy size, 370 × 266 mm (14½ × 10½ in) to around 308 × 235 mm (12⅛ × 9¼ in). The vast majority of sheet music falls within this range, though a few 19th-century publishers, particularly B. Schott's Söhne in Mainz, produced much smaller, octavo-format publications. In France there was something of a fashion for quarto publications in landscape formats in the middle of the 19th century.

In the context of ephemera, sheet music relates to popular publications that emerged after the invention of the piano in the 18th century and of the upright version in the early 19th century. Enthusiasm for the new instrument led to public concerts and, more importantly, to its introduction into middle-class homes. In the home it became the focus of the drawing room and of family entertainment. Much popular sheet music of the 19th century relates to the piano, with or without vocal accompaniment; later on in the century it responded to the popularity of the music-hall, the light operas of Gilbert and Sullivan, and the growing fashion for dancing, particularly the waltz.

It so happened that the piano's success came at just the right time for publishers to take advantage of changes in printing technology, and particularly the introduction of lithography. This entirely new kind of printing process, invented by Alois Senefelder in Munich around 1798, had a close relationship to music printing right from the outset. Initially it was not used extensively for printing music notation, except in Germany (by a few established music publishers: Johann André in Offenbach, Breitkopf & Härtl in Leipzig, Makarius Falter (Falter & Sohn) in Munich, and B. Schott's Söhne in Mainz), in Vienna (by the Chemische Druckerei), and in Italy (by several newcomers to music publishing). Its major application in music publishing was the printing of title-pages or covers. One of the curiosities of music publishing in the 19th century is that whereas most of the music pages were printed from intaglio plates or, from the 1830s, engraved on intaglio plates and put on to lithographic stones by TRANSFER LITHOGRAPHY, many covers to these pages were lithographed. There were two main reasons for this: first, lithography was likely to be cheaper than intaglio work, both in the origination of lettering and pictures and at the printing stage; secondly, that the process lent itself to the production of pictures along with text.

As public demand for popular music grew and print runs increased, and as colour printing began to be seen as an essential ingredient of publicity, production factors favoured lithography even more. The result was that the vast majority of sheet-music covers of the second half of the 19th century, and of the early 20th century too, were lithographed. Intaglio printing continued to be used for more serious, non-pictorial covers (particularly when the plates already existed); letterpress was used even less.

Some of the early lithographed publications of the music publisher Johann André in Offenbach, which date from the very first years of the 19th century, carry pictorial vignettes. A few years later a branch company that André established in Paris also produced lithographed title-pages or covers with vignettes, mainly for publications that were otherwise produced intaglio. Some other early publishers of lithographed music followed suit. The link between lithography and the covers of music pub-

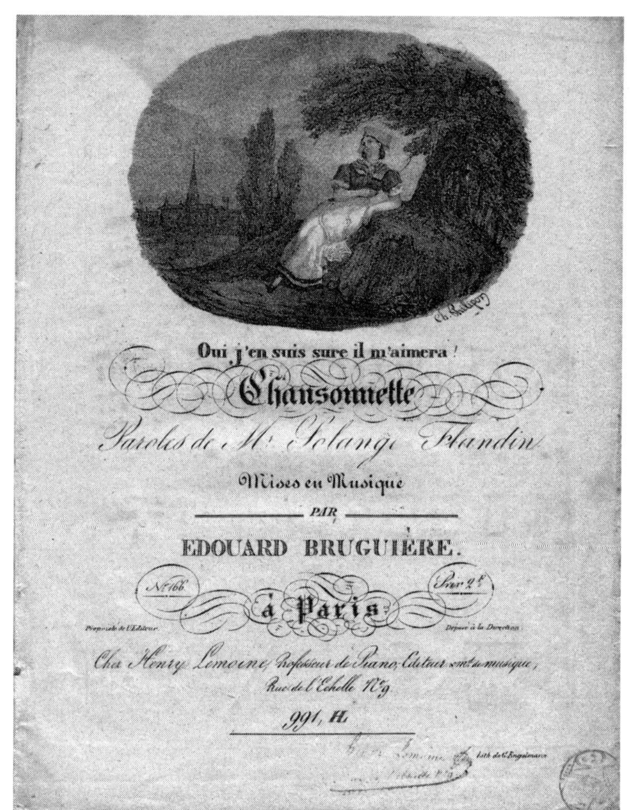

Sheet-music cover for Edouard Bruguière, 'Oui j'en suis sure il m'aimera!', Paris, c. 1825. Lithographed, the vignette drawn by Charles Philipon, printed by G. Engelmann. 332 × 255 mm (13⅛ × 10 in)

lications was therefore established right from the outset of the process.

The unsettled state of Europe at the time meant that the progress of lithography was somewhat delayed, and it was not until the 1820s that it made marked progress both geographically and technically. In this period the lithographed sheet-music cover began to be established as a genre. A typical example of the 1820s and early 1830s included a crayon-drawn vignette at the top of the page, normally occupying a third or it, occasionally as much as a half; below this would be elegantly displayed wording modelled on the conventions of copper-engraved lettering. Occasionally, examples are found with hand-colouring. In this period, too, some music was provided with a lithographed 'caption title', which took the form of a separately printed heading, consisting of a crayon-drawn vignette and lettering, at the top of the first page of intaglio-printed music. Gradually, however, the pictorial element of the lithographed cover became stronger. The Belgian artist J.-B. Madou and his printer J.-B. Jobard were innovators in this respect in the 1820s; but in the 1840s it became commonplace for sheet music published in Paris to have a crayon-drawn vignette occupying most of the page, with the words framing it at the top and bottom.

Another common approach in the middle decades of the 19th century was to add a second working to a cover lithograph, usually in the form of a beige or straw-coloured tint, to support a crayon drawing. A few early French and British publications used this approach in the 1820s; its popularity in later decades simply echoed a widespread fashion for tinted lithography. An element of colour was also introduced on occasions by adding a decorative border, printed in a single colour, around a black crayon-drawn vignette. A more significant development, both technically and in design, came with the introduction of colour lithography in the second half of the 1830s. Godefroy Engelmann, one of the leading lithographic printers in France, took out a patent for what he called 'Chromolithographie' in Paris in 1837; his leading competitor in Britain, Charles Joseph Hullmandel, developed his own colour printing methods for lithography at much the same time. Within a matter of a few years, what had been experimental in colour printing was the commercial norm.

Music covers soon responded to the new opportunities to produce work in colour, a turning point being a series of polkas and quadrilles produced by John Brandard for the enterprising musician, impresario, and publisher Louis Antoine Jullien (who had fled from France, bankrupted, in 1838). From then on colour gradually became the norm for the most popular publications. Its effect on the design of covers was to turn their imagery into rectangular, or other geometrically-shaped pictures. This was the norm in Britain in the 1860s, which is regarded as the heyday of the lithographed cover. A further development around the middle of the century was that representations of people, both full-figure and head only, were sometimes based on photographs; on occasions this was made explicit in imprints.

A common solution to the need to provide attractive, colourful covers at a reasonable cost was to turn to the technique of RAINBOW PRINTING. This allowed many different colours to be inked up on one stone at the same time, thereby reducing the number of workings considerably. British sheet music of the third quarter of the 19th century provides numerous examples of this technique; it is sometimes blatantly obvious because it forms part of the pictorial scheme, such as a sunset, but on other occasions is subtly disguised.

In the period during which the picture dominated text in British sheet-music covers, lettering moved back centre stage in a remarkable display of innovation. Having freed themselves from the copper-engraved traditions of earlier years, these largely anonymous designers took advantage of the scope offered by lithography and produced a small but exciting category of music cover that featured original and often bizarre lettering, sometimes to the exclusion of pictures.

Late in the 19th century, and on into the following century, it became common practice to print the whole of the surface of the cover, leaving no margins. This approach allowed designers to play on the highlights revealed by the white paper and to produce dramatic effects. In this same period designs became asymmetric, sometimes incorporated photographic images, and from time to time even attempted to capture the flavour of different cultures graphically.

Not all coloured sheet-music covers were chromolithographed throughout. Examples exist of covers with on-lays produced by photography, chromolithography, and the Baxter process (*see* NEEDLE-BOX PRINT). The Baxter prints were mainly produced for Jullien & Co. in the 1850s. Other covers show embossing, the use of gold printing, and the application of tinsel.

Artists did their best to reflect the themes of the publications they depicted. In the early 19th century this was often of a romantic kind; in the middle of the century, particularly in France, themes reflect the prevailing passion for historical topics ('Jean d'Arc: quadrille historique et militaire', 'François 1er; quadrille historique'). Most of the conflicts of the 19th century led to the publication of patriotic songs, including the Crimean War ('The Battle of the Alma', 'Sebastapol') and the Boer War ('Victory March'); there was even a British publication with the title 'The Confederate War March', which was dedicated to General Lee. Other publications focused on happier events, particularly those of a royal nature ('The Christening Song' [for Edward Prince of Wales], 'God Bless the Prince of Wales', 'Jubilee Gavotte' [for Queen Victoria]), and outstanding achievements ('The Great Eastern Polka', 'The Crystal Palace Quadrille', 'The World's Fair or a Voyage to Chicago 1893'). Yet others were religious. But perhaps the richest themes are those that touch on society in general, and depict its characters, fashion, entertainment, and modes of travel ('The Model Cabby', 'The Railway Guard', 'Costermonger Joe', 'The Croquet Gallop', 'The Rink Gallop', 'The Excursion Train', 'A Motor Car Marriage'). With the development of the music-hall, humorous topics increase and particular characters, well-known in their day, began to be depicted. Together, such covers provide a splendid pictorial record of how a period saw itself, or liked to be seen.

The composers and writers of lyrics for 19th-century sheet music must have run into thousands, and include many women. Most of the composers have failed to find their way into standard reference works on music, and the work of many of them is known only through surviving publications. The writers seemed to have fared even less well. The music that is remembered relates mainly to the music-hall (Harry Clifton's 'Polly Perkins of Paddington Green' and George Leybourne's 'Champagne Charlie'), to popular dances (the waltzes of the Strauss family and Emil Waldteufel), and to the operas of W. S. Gilbert and Arthur Sullivan.

Many publishers moved into the market opened up by the growth of interest in 'home music' and public entertainment, but some did so more than others. In the first half of the 19th century in Paris, Aulagnier, A. Colombier, Alphonse Leduc, A. Petibon, and A. Romagnesi, were leading publishers of sheet music with lithographed covers, though the most prolific firm appears to have been that of J. Meissonnier (J. Meissonnier fils, A. Meissonnier et Heugel). In London, Isaac Willis was a leading publisher in the field in the second half of the 1820s; later on John Blockley; Boosey & Co. (Boosey & Sons); Chappell & Co.; Robert Cocks & Co.; Hopwood & Crew; Keith, Prowse & Co.; Leoni Lee; and Metzler & Co. figure prominently.

As with publishers, many lithographic printers saw the commercial opportunities open to those working in this new area. Among the lithographic printers well-known for their work in other fields who produced covers in the 1820s and/or 1830s are: William Day; Engelmann, Graf, Coindet & Co.; C. J. Hullmandel; and G. E. Madeley (all in London); Godefroy Engelmann; Langlumé; Alfred Lemercier; and Thierry frères (all in Paris); and John Henry Bufford (in Boston). In addition, some printers appear to have specialized in such work. In the period of monochrome covers this was the case in Paris in the 1820s and 1830s with Mlle Formentin (Formentin & Cie) and, in the middle of the century, with Guillet and, even more evidently, Bertauts (whose imprints on covers of sheet music, 'rue Cadet 11', or similar, are particularly common). In Britain, at least three firms can be regarded as specialist printers of colour-printed

Sheet-music cover drawn by John Brandard for Albert Lindahl, 'Sebastopol. A Hymn of Praise', published by Jullien & Co., c. 1856. Lithographed in four colours and printed by M. & N. Hanhart, London. 345 × 250 mm (13⅝ × 4 in)

Sheet-music cover for C. F. Escher (Junior), 'Anemonies', published by C. F. Escher, Philadelphia, 1867. Lithographed in five colours by T. Sinclair, Philadelphia. 357 × 273 mm (14 × 10¾ in)

covers in their heyday: Concanen Siebe & Co. (Concanen, Lee & Siebe); M. & N. Hanhart; and Stannard & Co. (Stannard & Son, Stannard & Dixon). The firm of Hanhart continued into the 20th century, and from the 1890s was competing with the prolific printer and designer H. G. Banks.

It is the artists who contributed to sheet-music covers who are most remembered. The earliest of them, particularly those who worked in-house for publishers (such as Johann André), generally remain anonymous; but from the 1820s most pictorial sheet music is signed by the artist or lithographic draughtsman. In Britain, a particularly prolific producer of crayon-drawn vignettes in the 1820s and 1830s was Maxime Gauci, who worked for both Hullmandel and Engelmann, Graf, Coindet & Co. Other names that appear beneath vignettes of the period are those of Valentine Bartholomew (who was one of Hullmandel's managers) and R. J. Hamerton. In Paris, draughtsmen of rather more distinction undertook work for the music publishers. Among the more notable names that appear regularly on monochrome work are: Victor Adam, Jules Challamel, Jules David, Achille Devéria, Théophile Fragonard, F. Grenier, A. Menuet, Célestin Nanteuil, Ed. Rey, and Frédéric Sorrieu.

The major artists in the heyday of the colour-printed cover in Britain, were John Brandard, William Brandard, Alfred Concanen, A. Laby, H. C. Maguire, and T. Packer. Each tended to have his specialism in terms of subject matter, though John Brandard in particular produced a wide range of work. He began in the monochrome period when he drew some very delicate crayon lithographs for sheet-music covers. Thereafter he explored, successively, the possibilities of tinted lithography, rainbow printing, and colour lithography in five or six workings. His images embraced scenes of rural and domestic life, episodes of military courage, landscape and topography, figure subjects (military and fashion), and scenes from operas. He must have produced an enormous quantity of work, and this is reflected in its varied quality. The most innovative artist to apply his talents regularly to the sheet-music cover was Alfred Concanen (1835–86). His work varied in quality too, but his best designs are highly inventive, and in the 20th century he established a reputation as a minor master of popular art for his scenes of everyday life, railway subjects, and representations of music-hall figures. Some covers, signed 'Concanen & Lee' or 'Concanen, Lee & Siebe', acknowledge the fact that they were productions of the Concanen studio. The French poster artist Jules Chéret, who worked in London early on his career, produced several covers in Britain (for example, J. P. Clarke, 'The Witches' own Galop', signed and dated 1864).

The graphic style of the early lithographed sheet-music cover, established mainly in France and Britain in the 1820s, spread rapidly to other parts of Europe and to places as far apart as India and the United States. It was quickly adapted to American needs in the second quarter of the 19th century as lithography began to be practised commercially in its major centres of population, not infrequently by lithographers who had emigrated from Europe. Most major American lithographic firms, and many minor ones too, took on work for music publishers.

One of the leading figures was John Henry Bufford (1810–70). A pioneer of American lithography generally, he contributed to the development of the sheet-music cover in Boston and New York, first as artist, and then as a printer and publisher. In the 1830s and 1840s he produced numerous sheet-music covers, many of them plagiarizing British publications (not an uncommon practice at the time). His involvement with sheet music in various capacities spans the period of its development from monochrome crayon work on stone, to tinted lithography, and printing in many colours. The painter Winslow Homer is believed to have drawn many sheet-music covers for Bufford's firm in New York while he was serving his apprenticeship there (1855–57).

Among many others who printed sheet-music covers in America before the middle of the 19th century were P. S. Duval (Huddy & Duval) in Philadelphia; G. & W. Endicott (William Endicott & Co., Endicott & Co.) in New York; Pendleton's Lithography in Boston and New York; Thomas Moore and his successor Benjamin W. Thayer & Co. in Boston; and William Sharp & Co. in Boston.

A curiosity of the American sheet-music cover carries the title: 'United States Academy: Song of the Graduates 1852'. More significantly, its rather coy crayon lithograph of two young cadets is lettered 'Designed by Cadet Whistler'. James McNeill Whistler was a student at West Point at the time, and the assumption is that he provided the drawing for this image, which was then put on stone by a professional lithographer.

Popular sheet-music has survived in vast numbers, mainly because it was the custom in the 19th century to bind individual publications into albums. Many such albums still exist intact, some with the names or initials of the owner blocked on them, and with a manuscript list or 'register' of their content. Signatures and dates on individual publications suggest that they were frequently brought together some time after their issue or acquisition. In the second half of the 20th century, as a result of the growing interest in sheet-music covers, many albums were broken up. More seriously, some covers became separated from their music pages. Evidence of a publication's past existence in an album takes the form of holes in the back margin (the result of sewing items together) and of cropping. Items were often severely cropped in the course of binding, either because they had become dog-eared or in order to achieve consistency of size. Examples that have survived without sewing marks or evidence of cropping are therefore of special interest. [MT]

See also AMERICAN CIVIL-WAR PAPERS

REFERENCES William E. Imeson, *Illustrated Music-Titles and their Delineators* (London: The Author, 1912); A Hyatt King, 'English Pictorial Music Title Pages 1820–1885. Their Style, Evolution, and Importance', *Transactions of the Bibliographical Society*, 3rd series, vol. 4, pp. 262–272; Lester S. Levy *Picture the Songs: Lithographs from the Sheet Music of Nineteenth Century America* (Baltimore: Johns Hopkins University Press, 1976); Harry T. Peters, *America on Stone* (New York: Doubleday, Doran and Co. Inc, 1931); Sacheverell Sitwell, *Morning, Noon and Night in London* (London: Macmillan & Co., 1948); Dorothy and Sidney Spellman, *Victorian Music Covers* (London: Evelyn, Adams & Mackay, 1969); David Tatham, *John Henry Bufford, American Lithographer* (Worcester, Mass.: American Antiquarian Society, 1976); David Tatham, *The Lure of the Striped Pig. The Illustration of Popular Music in America, 1820–1870* (Barre, Mass.: Imprint Society, 1973); Michael Twyman, *Early Lithographed Music* (London: Farrand Press, 1996)

COLLECTIONS Lester S. Levy Collection of Sheet Music, Johns Hopkins University; Dorothy and Sidney Spellman Collection, Reading University Library

Shelf strip

The advertising shelf strip derives from the domestic shelf paper of the latter part of the 19th century. Shelf paper was bordered with decorative perforations and lace effects, the edging being turned down over the front of the shelf to form a trim. The idea was adapted for use by the small shopkeeper. Paper was replaced by American cloth with edging that was normally scalloped or crimped. By the 1890s, with shelf display a universal element in retail selling, the promotion potential of the shelf strip had been widely exploited. Manufacturers provided shopkeepers with advertising shelf strips as part of the general display material they offered. Strips were produced as flat cards for tacking on shelf edges, or as hinged cards, the hinged portion being slipped under goods on display. They were also made, flat or flanged, in metal.

The idea was widely applied. Manufacturers of foodstuffs, confectionery, tobacco, and other products often supplied separate strips for each of a range of their products. For example, around 1910 the Allen Chocolate Co. provided eight different strips including 'Allen's Chocolate Pineapple' and 'Allen's Queen Chocolate'. Firms with export interests provided strips in foreign languages: the Perry Pen Co. offered theirs in Danish, French, Norwegian, Russian, Spanish, and Swedish.

Shelf strips were also produced as stock items by display suppliers, chiefly for use in shop windows. They carried such generalized messages as 'Engagement and wedding rings' and 'Spectacles and eye-glasses repaired'. A forerunner of the advertising strip survives as a printer's proof in the archives of the De La Rue Co. (the University of Reading Library): dated 1852, it announces 'De La Rue & Co's Red Letter Diaries', and is believed to stem from the company's display arrangements for the Great Exhibition of 1851.

See also POINT-OF-SALE DISPLAY

Shipping

Shipping papers may be concerned with a whole shipping line, a single boat, or a specific voyage or cruise. They relate to both the carrying of freight and passengers and include items as varied as the BILL OF LADING, CHARTER PARTY, DECK PLAN, LIGHTHOUSE-DUES PAPER, SAILING CARD/NOTICE, and SHIP'S NEWSPAPER, in addition to all sorts of other ephemera relating to administration and advertising.

Particularly characteristic of the latter are the sailing lists of the companies responsible for transatlantic travel in its heyday in the first half of the twentieth century. The Cunard Line's publicity of the inter-war years is highly evocative of this major method of international travel across the seas before the coming of the jet. The pocket-size twenty-four page 'Cunard Line Sailing List', no. 3 for March 1926, advertises the activities of the whole fleet and bears on its cover a majestic four-funnel ship, probably the 'Mauretania', travelling full steam ahead. It provides details of the sailings of some eighteen ships to all parts of the world, including: Liverpool, Montreal, Nagasaki, New York, Plymouth, Reykjavik, Sydney, and Shanghai. Information is also provided about such things as baggage, insurance, money, on-board shop, passports, tax, and wireless. Among the ships in the fleet the largest, the 'Berengaria' (52,226 tons), offers 'Saloon, Second Class & Third Class'; some of the smaller ships 'Cabin & Third Class'; and the smallest, the 'Albania' (12,768 tons), 'Cabin Only'. The minimum transatlantic (westbound) rate for saloon passengers in summer and intermediate seasons was listed as £61. 10*s* (the cost for servants being £35. 10*s*).

An earlier Cunard Line publication, clearly one of a series that was modified to serve the needs of different ships, relates to a sailing of the 'Mauretania' from New York to England on 14 March 1919. Described as a 'List of Saloon Passengers', it prints the names of 96 saloon passengers (of a total of 314 passengers) and provides two pages of 'Information for Passen-

Cunard Line 'Sailing List', no. 3, March 1926. Front cover. Printed in relief in four colours. 160 × 95 mm (6¼ × 3¾ in)

gers', including the note that 'Professional Gamblers are reported as frequently crossing on Atlantic Steamers' and the warning that they should 'take precautions accordingly'.

In the 1930s the Orient Line presented their cruise passengers with attractive linen-covered folders entitled 'Records of a Voyage'. Inside were cards giving details of ports of call and arranged excursions, and in addition there was sufficient room in the pockets to retain the information leaflets and other ephemera for each trip. Wood-engravings commissioned from Robert Gibbings were used for the daily menus, and smaller images headed each informative excursion leaflet: a cruise on 'SS Orontes' in 1933 included images for Gibraltar, Corsica and Elba, and Naples and Pompeii, while in 1935 'SS Orontes' went to Australia with stops including Toulon and Aden. The Orient Line also commissioned Lynton Lamb to produce covers for their menus in the 1930s. He produced a series of seven cards to commemorate various national days and these continued in use until the 1950s; among their striking covers were those celebrating New Zealand Day, Empire Day, and St Andrew's Day.

An example of an American shipping line's advertising of the inter-war period is a colourful brochure of the 'Merchants and Miners Transportation Co.' (which had its head office in Boston). The company worked up and down the East Coast of the United States and claimed that its routes totalled 3895 miles. The routes are shown in the brochure on a detailed map and, summarily, on its front cover; on the back cover a young woman stands at a ship's rail, cloche hat firmly in place and cloak flying in the wind. The booklet traces the company's history back to its first side-wheeler in 1854. With the brochure came a schedule, effective from 1 September 1926, giving its routes and fares.

The advertising of individual ships emphasized their distinctive features, and particularly those relating to size, speed, and facilities. For example, the White Star Line claimed on the cover of one of its folders (1923/24) that the 'Britannic' was 'The world's largest cabin liner'. The statistics reveal that the ship was 712 feet long and that it weighed 27,000 tons; this was by no means the largest liner at the time, though it may have been the largest 'cabin liner', a distinction that may well have escaped most readers. A decade or so later a folder for the United States Lines adopted a similar approach and announced as 1933's biggest ship news: 'the new S.S.Washington, largest liner ever built in America! She and her sister ship, the Manhattan, are the fastest cabin liners in the sea. The Washington offers such ocean luxuries as smart shops … beauty parlor … sound pictures …gymnasium and swimming pool … spacious comfort in every cabin, and in every cabin real beds – not berths!'.

Items of ephemera that relate to particular sailings include passenger lists, sailing notices, and bills of lading; all had widespread use, the last two over several hundred years. Like other common categories of ephemera, they have changed in appearance in response to the introduction of different means of production. Items that relate to individual passengers on particular sailings include BAGGAGE STICKERS, immigration papers, maritime telegraphs, and, of course, tickets. Passenger tickets were often complicated, and in this respect were forerunners of airline tickets of the second half of the 20th century. One 19th-century example, called a 'Cabin passengers' contract', illustrates the point. It measures 178 × 254 mm (7 × 10 in) and was for a first-class cabin passenger on the 'Lincolnshire', sailing from the Port of London (Gravesend) to Melbourne on 23 December 1868. The cost was £150, and the conditions of issue are set out precisely – as the title of the ticket implies – in the form of a contract. These include conditions for completion of the ticket: 'All the Blanks must be correctly and legibly filled in, and the Ticket must be legibly signed with the Christian Names and Surname and Address in full of the Party issuing the same'. Other conditions relate to the passage itself: 'we hereby agree with the Person named in the Margin hereof that such Person shall be provided with First-Class Cabin Passage (exclusive of Wines, Beer, and Spirits), …with not less than Forty Cubical Feet of Luggage for each Person…'. [EG]

Ship's newspaper

The first ships' newspapers emerged as brief printed summaries of the formal ship's log. With the expansion of the travel and cruise industry this summary was developed editorially to resemble a conventional newspaper. Appearing under such titles as *Ocean Times* and *Atlantic News*, the papers were largely pre-set with non-topical news items, articles, and features, and were interlarded with stock illustrations of people and places.

Initially produced from metal type and blocks, the papers were latterly printed by rotary offset lithography. Text setting was carried out in on-shore offices and transmitted by radio link direct to the ship's keyboard. The resulting columns of text were cut and pasted in place along with headlines, which were set on board. Lithographic plates were then made from the pasted-down pages. The operation was carried out at night, delivery being made by slipping a copy under each cabin door at dawn.

See also NEWSPAPER

Shoe pattern

When shoes were made by hand, individually for each wearer, the shoemaker worked from a cut-out brown-paper pattern. The pattern bore the pencilled name of the customer and miscellaneous annotations to help in the final fitting. This method was better than the off-the-shelf provision of 'small', 'medium', and 'big', a system that industrialization brought into being.

Shoemaker's label

As with other clothing labels (hat and glove tax labels, manufacturer's woven labels, etc.), shoemaker's labels rarely survive the article they designate. Paper labels, most vulnerable of all, were widely used in shoes until the introduction, in the 1880s, of gold-blocking and printing directly on to their 'sock' or lining.

Printed paper labels, pasted to the sole of the shoe, first appeared in the 1750s, when shoemaking began to move from a bespoke trade to mass production for general sale. One example of this period identifies 'William Cooper, against Lincoln's Inn, Chancery Lane, London' as the maker. (Names also appeared as stamped impressions on the soles of shoes at about this time, as they had done in Roman times.) Another early label, from the 1760s, survives in a lady's yellow silk and silver brocade shoe by John Came, whose address is given as 'at the Blue Last, the Corner of Bow Church Yard in Cheapside'. In another survivor the Hull shoemaker Charlton ('from London') advertises 'Ladies' fancy slippers performed in the most fashionable style'.

It follows from its location in the shoe that, even when the shoe itself has survived, the legible life of the paper must have been very short. Labels survive therefore only in exceptional cases of conservation (in museums and similar collections) or as specimens from engravers' and printers' files. Where shoes do survive with labels intact, the label must remain in place as an integral part of the item, as should the FURNITURE LABEL.

In common with other labels with a long tradition, those from earlier periods are copper-engraved. They are roughly hand-trimmed, apparently with scissors, to conform to their decorative oval or circular frame. In some cases the same oval or circular image is also used on the shoemaker's BILLHEAD; it may appear either on its own or as an adjunct to a larger presentation of the name, address, and other details. Where the 'label' image appears as an additional element it nevertheless repeats most, if not all, the matter contained elsewhere on the billhead; sometimes it appears as a pasted-on 'sticker', possibly culled from a stock of pre-cut shoe labels.

Later shoemakers' labels were produced lithographically, often in two colours and occasionally in three or four colours, many using lettering reversed out of a coloured background or a gold image on coloured paper. Maximum size is some 45 × 35 mm (1¾ × 1⅜ in) with a mean average of some 35 × 25 mm (1⅜ × 1 in). Ovals and roundels are most common, though rectangular shapes also appear, and shields, horseshoes, and other shapes are to be found.

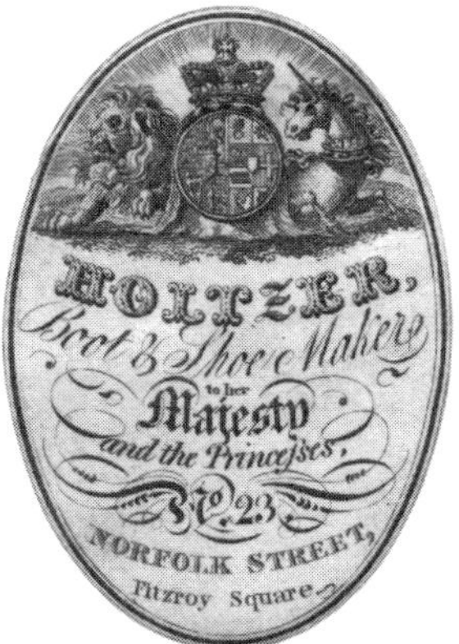

Shoemakers' labels. *Left:* Holtzer, London, mid 19th century, intaglio, 54 × 39 mm (2⅛ × 1 9⁄16 in); *right:* W. W. Kendall, Kansas City, early 20th century, relief-printed in three colours, 46 × 36 mm (1 5⁄16 × 1 7⁄16 in);

American shoemakers' labels are particularly colourful. A collection dating from the late 19th and early 20th centuries provides a conspectus of the country's shoe industry, though not all the names appearing on labels were necessarily those of manufacturers. Many were 'own-brand' distributors of other firms' products. Among names appearing are Bamberger Streng & Co.; Joseph Baum & Co.; Benedict Hall & Co.; Buck, Heflebower & Neer; California Tule Insole Co.; H. Childs & Co.; Cook & Seixas; Fairdean Bros; I. P. Farnum; Fuller, Childs & Co.; A. B. George, Weeks & Co.; H. & O. Manufacturing Co.; C. M. Henderson & Co.; Hills; Hinkle Nisbet & Co.; Hoosier; Hustons; W. W. Kendall Boot and Shoe Co.; Lawrence, Berry & Co.; Manss Bros & Co.; A. C. McGraw & Co.; Morse & Rogers; Noyes, Norman & Co.; O'Connell & Middleton; Orr & Lindsley Shoe Co.; Pfister & Vogel Leather Co.; Rosenberg, Flexner & Co.; St John Kirkham & Co.; Sharp, Clarke & Co.; Smith-Frazer & Co.; Sullivan; Tennent Walker & Co.; and Weil Connell & Winter.

REFERENCE June Swann, *Shoes* (London: Batsford, 1982)

COLLECTION Northampton Central Museum

Shopping bag *See* CARRIER BAG

Showcard [plate 9b]

With the development of retail trading in the 19th century the shopkeeper's premises became, as well as a store, a display area. The appeal of goods on show began to be supported by a range of display material. The PRICE TAG/TICKET was followed by the WINDOW BILL, SHELF STRIP and an increasing range of counter novelties. Not least among these was the showcard.

The showcard evolved in two forms: the 'special', devised and executed by the neighbourhood ticket-writer, and the mass-produced item distributed with stock deliveries by manufacturers. The position remained essentially unchanged until the latter part of the 20th century, though the scale of the exercise grew immeasurably, and the ticket-writer came to be superseded by mechanical lettering systems. With the advent of the supermarket, however, the concept of the showcard as sales aid gave way to the display appeal of PACKAGING.

The heyday of the hand-lettered showcard was approximately 1890 to 1939, though much earlier examples survive. Showcard lettering, closely related to signwriting (and often a branch of the signwriter's business), used two basic techniques. For larger work, letters were outlined quickly in single strokes, to be 'filled in' by an apprentice; in smaller work, letters were executed entirely in single strokes, using broader or narrower brushes as required. Speed of execution was not only an economic necessity: it also produced a fluency which a more laboured treatment would have lacked.

The printed showcard, supplied by the manufacturer with the product, stemmed from the new-found principle of factory packaging and labelling. Shelf stocks of labelled products were promotional displays in themselves, and products supplied in boxes could be placed directly on counters or in windows, the inside of the opened box-lid forming a ready-made display area for a printed 'poster'. As cardboard cartons replaced the earlier wooden boxes, display material was printed directly on to their surface (rather than being pasted on). This led to an innovation – the showcard – an item to be displayed on its own anywhere in the shop; with eyelets for hanging or, later, a strut to make it stand, the showcard assumed an independent existence. In a later development, small packaged products were pasted on to the card in quantity. This device, as with the open-carton display, allowed point-of-sale visibility and impulse purchase.

See also DISPLAY CARD; MOTTO, SHOP-WINDOW; POINT-OF-SALE DISPLAY; SHOWCARD, STOCK

Showcard, stock

Stock typographic showcards for use in shops became common in the years immediately following World War I. Typical, and possibly best-known, was the legend 'IMPOSSIBLE TO SHOW all we sell. If you do not see what you require, please ask for it'.

The cards, whose wording rapidly became standardized, carried a minimum of decorative presentation and were reprinted with only minor typographical updating over decades. A representative range in the mid 1920s included, in addition to that already noted, the following: 'ANY ARTICLE not in stock obtained to Order at Short Notice'; 'WEEKLY PAYMENTS TAKEN on Any Article. No Extra Charge'; 'REPAIRS of Every Description. Prompt and Cheap. Estimates Free'; 'CYCLES Cleaned and Overhauled. Enamelling and Plating. Accessories at Lowest Prices'; 'TENNIS RACQUETS Re-strung and Repaired'; 'WIRELESS OUTFITS and all Accessories in Stock'; 'ACCUMULATORS Charged and Repaired'. Also available was the 'cash' showcard. Wording varied, but one version was widely used: 'PLEASE DO NOT ASK FOR CREDIT as a refusal often offends'.

Other cards served specific trades: 'MORNING COFFEE'; 'ICES SOLD HERE'; 'We regret we cannot cater for people bringing their own food'. Some were merely incidental to shop-keeping at large: 'No pushchairs allowed in this shop'; 'Open'; 'Closed'; 'Gone to lunch'; 'Back in 10 minutes'. The cards, commonly eyeletted and strung, and often with rounded corners, were printed in one or two colours and measured some 255 × 305 mm (10 × 12 in). Stock showcards continued in use in the latter part of the 20th century, many of them (typically 'Open' and 'Closed') typographically unchanged since the 1940s and 1950s.

See also DISPLAY CARD; POINT-OF-SALE DISPLAY; SHOWCARD

Signal code, navy

The use of flags as daytime signals at sea began in Britain on a formal basis in Tudor times, but surviving signal listings, showing flag combinations and their meanings, date only from the late 18th century.

Hand-drawn colour diagrams with handwritten captions, commonly prepared by the flag-lieutenant, formed part of a ship's basic equipment in peace and war. Code systems in war were vital fighting tools; all were subject to change for security reasons, and capture of enemy signal codes was a notable objective. One English manuscript, dated 6 June 1812, shows changes registered as having been made in the French code of signals: numerical meanings appear in two columns against the flag diagrams, the first showing the new meaning and the second column the old. The vital function of war signals is underlined by a printed 'observation' on the front cover of a folded Admiralty form (c.1806) for the listing of 'Private signals for knowing each other by Day' and 'Private signals for His Majesty's Ships by night'. It reads:

> The captains and commanders, to whom only these Private Signals are to be delivered, are strictly commanded to keep them in their own Possession, with a sufficient weight affixed to them to ensure their being sunk, if it should be found necessary to throw them overboard. They are not, on any account, to allow them to be seen by any other Person; nor to suffer any Copy of them to be taken, even for their own use. As consequences of the most dangerous nature to His Majesty's Fleet may result from the Enemy's getting possession of these Signals, if any Officer entrusted with them, should in any degree fail in observing these directions, he will certainly be made to answer for his disobedience at a Court Martial.

One signal book (c.1830), which is typical of its kind, measures 175 × 105 mm (6⅞ × 4⅛ in) and has twenty-four pages plus a thick paper cover. Hand-executed throughout, it shows codes for specific boats (pinnaces, cutters, gigs, etc.), compass signals, and over 300 detailed operational signals for use on ships and boats. The code is based on ten different flags representing numerals 1 to 0. Displays of one, two, or three numeral flags correspond to single book entries. Such entries cover a wide range of contingencies including 'anchor immediately', 'ammunition is expended or destroyed', 'you are standing [i.e. steering] into danger', 'make all sail', 'spread yourself more', 'return at sunset', 'unable to obey signal or orders', 'wish to see carpenter', and 'want presents for natives'. Flag illustrations are commonly executed with great neatness in pen and watercolour, in many cases presenting not merely schematic diagrams but realistically 'rippled' flags with their undulations shaded.

REFERENCE W. G. Perrin, *British Flags* (Cambridge: Cambridge University Press, 1922)

COLLECTION National Maritime Museum, Greenwich

Silhouette

In its humblest form the silhouette is among the most ephemeral of popular novelties; at its most refined it may be seen as a minor art object, and in many cases as an heirloom.

The silhouette as a painted image appears on Greek and Etruscan pottery, Egyptian murals, and other works of art. In the 17th century the painting of shadowy portraits using a screen and candle had become a widespread fad. Professional 'profilists' rendered shadow pictures on materials of all kinds, often employing mechanical devices to reduce the image. But it is as a paper cut-out that the concept is commonly understood, and the period from c.1750 to c.1850 in which it chiefly flourished. The term derives from the name of the French Minister of Finance in 1759 who, it is said, cut profiles himself (an alterna-

Silhouettes cut from black paper and mounted on card. Signed and dated 'Scot-Ford 1929'. The cards were a gift from a mother and two sons (all represented) to the children's grand-parents. Each approx. 325 × 140 mm (12¾ × 5½ in)

tive derivation links the economy of the cut-out to the parsimony of Etienne de Silhouette's treasury policies).

As paper became more generally available, the fairground 'profilist' emerged, producing silhouette 'miniatures' in a matter of seconds. In London in the 1840s and early 1850s the 'penny-profile cutter' did a brisk trade in silhouettes ('mounted on card, twopence; bronzed, sixpence; framed, complete, one shilling'). The open-air silhouettist still practises occasionally today, cutting pictures among the crowds at holiday resorts and at fairs and country shows. The craft was finally eclipsed by the street photographer, whose advent, even in the heyday of the profile cutter, had much diminished the trade.

Outside the art field, the silhouette achieved a high degree of respectability. Moving from the fairground indoors, the more serious practitioners set themselves up in permanent quarters, sometimes offering great precision through the use of special apparatus. In the early 19th century, in his establishment in the State House, Independence Hall, Philadelphia, Charles Willson Peale provided 'physiognomies'; these were accurate outlines produced by photographic reduction and four-at-a-time cuttings in folded paper. Mechanized silhouettes were also produced in America by John Vogler, the Moravian horologist, whose equipment survives in Old Salem, North Carolina.

Prominent in the silhouette field was Johann Kaspar Lavater, the physiognomist, whose works on the 'characterology' of the human head had great impact in the latter part of the 18th century. He too devised equipment for greater accuracy of delineation. With the aid of Johann von Goethe (himself an enthusiastic paper-cutter), Lavater constructed a head-rest-cum-projection-screen, with pantographic reduction of the image.

Among Britain's notable silhouettists was Sarah Harrington of Bath, who also introduced technological innovations. Her patent machine for cutting 'hollow profiles' reversed the normal treatment: her silhouettes were cut in white paper, the outer area of which was retained and placed over black paper. Some professional silhouettists achieved fame. Most notable was Augustin Edouart (1789–1861), a refugee from France who worked widely in Britain and afterwards in America. He was responsible for some ten thousand silhouettes, many of them of celebrities. A number of other European silhouettists visited America. Best known of these were John André, Samuel Metford, and Master William Hubard, a 12-year-old boy prodigy from Britain (who was succeeded by the less gifted Master Hankes). Native-born American profile cutters included William Bache, William Henry Brown, Moses Chapman, William Doyle, Samuel Folwell, Henry Williams, and Charles Willson Peale.

Not referred to here are numerous well-known painters of silhouettes, whose work falls outside the field of ephemera.

REFERENCES Peggy Hickman, *Two Centuries of Silhouettes. Celebrities in Profile* (London: A. & C. Black, 1971); F. Nevill Jackson, *Silhouette. Notes and Dictionary* (London: Methuen, 1938)

Silk

The term 'silk' is loosely applied to printed textile items, more particularly to GIVE-AWAYS, that were once included in CIGARETTE PACKS and, less commonly, in special numbers of women's and girls' magazines. The term also covers satin, woven ribbon, twill, nylon, and (more remotely) canvas, velvet, lace, and even leather. Closely associated, and often included in collections of printed silks as a separate category, is the Jacquard-woven 'Stevengraph', popularized by Thomas Stevens of Coventry in the 19th century and still produced as souvenirs, keepsakes, and bookmarks in the late 20th century.

The silk CIGARETTE CARD appeared in the first years of the 20th century, the earliest known example featuring a series of butterflies and moths issued by R. J. Lea of Stockport in 1902. Foremost among silk-issuing cigarette firms were Godfrey Phillips Ltd, owners of the BDV (Best Dark Virginia) brand, who in the period 1910 to 1925 put out over 100 separate sets. These included army crests and badges, naval crests, flags, tartans, football colours, town and city arms, old masters, Great War celebrities, religious pictures, heraldry, etc. Other silk-issuing firms were: B. Muratti & Sons (fifty sets, 1902–39); John Sinclair Ltd (eight sets, 1914–15); Robert Sinclair Tobacco Co. Ltd (six sets, 1915); Singleton & Cole Ltd (one set, 1915); British American Tobacco Co. Ltd (seven sets, 1911–16); The American Tobacco Co. (seventy-nine sets, 1910; eighteen sets 'blankets', 1908; twenty sets 'leathers', 1908), Salmon & Gluckstein Ltd (one set, 1916); B. Morris & Sons Ltd (five sets, 1915–16); R. J. Lea Ltd (six sets, 1914–24); E. & W. Anstie (four sets, 1915); J. Wix & Sons Ltd (seven sets, 1923–39). Many cigarette-silks were issued with a cardboard backing to obviate creasing and as a production handling aid. In an additional promotional scheme, Godfrey Phillips Ltd ran a national needlework competition in which the company's silks were to be incorporated in domestic furnishings (cushions, firescreens, etc.), a secondary use for them that many smokers had already discovered.

The earliest-known silk picture given away with a periodical was issued with the Christmas number of the *Gentlewoman Magazine* in 1890. It shows a 'Gentlewoman' of 100 years earlier, and was the first of a series published annually until the magazine's closure in 1926.

Commemorative silks had been in vogue some half a century before the appearance of cigarette-card silks, and there was a well-established convention for the use of silk on ceremonial occasions for menus and theatre and concert programmes. Like their paper-printed counterparts, many of these short-run luxury productions were clearly devised as much for their prestige value to the printer as for the occasion itself. They were printed in numerous workings, sometimes in a combination of letterpress, lithography, and (later) collotype, and were often embellished with silk fringes. Also printed on silk were souvenir scarves and handkerchiefs, ceremonial sashes, decorative maps, boardgames, and cigar and cigarette wrappers for 'loose' sales. Silk was also used in the production of prisoner-of-war escape maps in both world wars, and in World War I for the first street-collection lapel flag. Notable printers on silk were Mardon, Son & Hall (Bristol) and James Walker Ltd (Dublin)

World War I saw the emergence in Germany and Austria-Hungary of a vogue for printed silks sold in aid of war charities. Known as *Vivatbänder*, they celebrated a wide range of persons, regiments, war exploits, and institutions: 'Long live the Defenders of Przemysl!', 'Long Live the Rulers of the Victorious Quadruple Alliance!', 'Long live Kaiser Karl I!'. Sold in the streets, in tobacconists, and on news stands, the silks were collected both as war-effort tokens and as *objets d'art*. Their designs, commonly printed in a single colour on a coloured silk, were of a high graphic quality, and many were contributed by notable artists of the time.

The embroidered silk postcard, popularly identified with World War I, is first recorded as a trade-school product in Austria in 1903. It appeared in Germany as a publisher's greeting item in Plauen in 1906 ('Gruss aus Plauen') and in the following year was introduced in Switzerland and France; in World War I it became an almost standard form of greeting from soldiers to womenfolk at home. The form survived with much reduced currency in the inter-war years. Peacetime examples are recorded in mails from soldiers serving in Gibraltar and the cards also had a limited use inside France. In World War II an effort was made to reintroduce them, but with no success. The latest recorded date on one (embroidered into the design) is 1945. The cards normally carry a blind-embossed border-mask which frames the embroidered silk organdie mounted beneath it. The embroidery was executed by hand on a cottage-industry basis, the designs being worked over lightly printed guidelines. The backs of the cards were commonly printed with the legend 'carte postale' and the publisher's name. Some fifty different publishers have been recorded, among them, in Britain, Birn Brothers (SCRAP importers) and Gale and Polden the Aldershot military publishers.

See also RIBBON, LAPEL

REFERENCE Geoffrey A. Godden, *Stevengraphs and other Victorian Silk Pictures* (London: Barrie & Jenkins, 1971)

Slave papers

Slavery as an institution – in America from the early 17th century to the end of the Civil War and in Britain for a time until its abolition in 1807 – has left relatively little in the way of minor paperwork, although the business, like any other, was transacted with its due concomitant of delivery notes, bills of lading, receipts, and other ephemera. What little survives, however, is not without impact. We may cite as typical the following:

Receipt handwritten, 105 × 190 mm (4⅛ × 7½ in): 'March 31 1812. Received of the Public Accountant the sum of Four Hundred and Ten Pounds on account of the Captured Negroes… K Macaulay'.

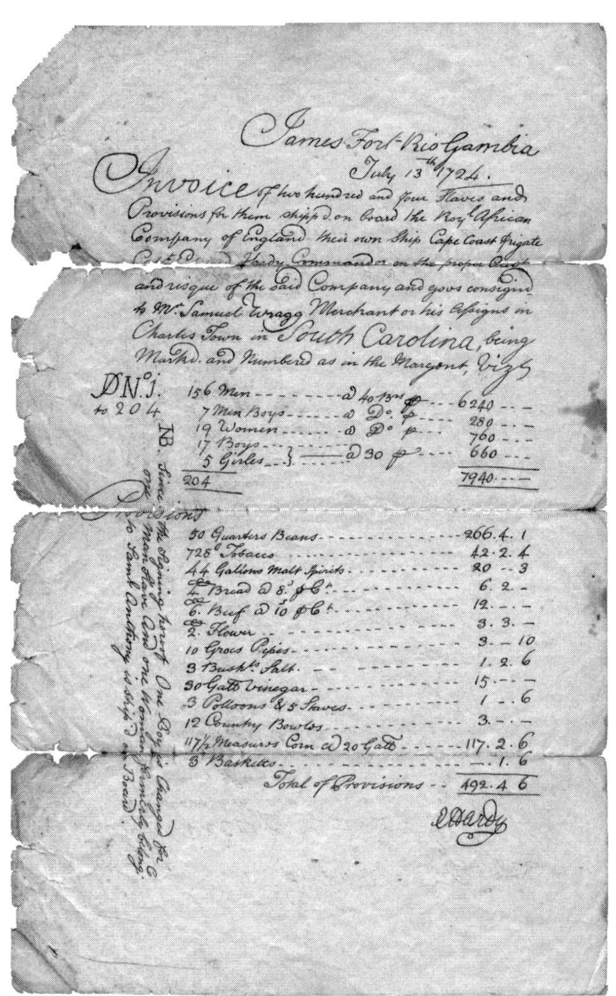

James Fort-Rio Gambia
July 13th 1724.
Invoice of two hundred and four Slaves and Provisions for them shipp'd on board the Roy.l African Company of England their own Ship Cape Coast Frigate Capt Edward Hardy Commander on the proper Acco.t and risque of the said Company and goes consigned to Mr. Samuel Wragg Merchant or his Assigns in Charles Town in South Carolina, being Marked and Numbered as in the Margent, Vizt.

DN.1. to 204
156 Men ---------- @ 40 Barrs ₽ --- 6240 - -
7 Men Boys ------- @ D.o ₽ --- 280 - -
19 Women ------- @ D.o ₽ --- 760 - -
17 Boys }
5 Girles } ------- @ 30 ₽ --- 660 - -
204 --- 7940 - -

NB. Since the Signing hereof One Boy is Changed for one Man Slave and one Woman ... Antony is Ship'd on Board.

Provisions
50 Quarters Beans ---------- 266.4.1
725l Tobacco ---------- 42.2.4
44 Gallons Malt Spirits ---------- 20 - - 3
Do 4 Bread @ 8s ₽ Ct ---------- 6.2. -
Do 6 Beef @ 10 ₽ Ct ---------- 12. - -
Do 2 Flower ---------- 3.3. -
10 Gross Pipes ---------- 3. - 10
3 Bushls Salt ---------- 1.2.6
30 Galls Vinegar ---------- 15. - -
3 Polloons & 5 Staves ---------- 1. - 6
12 Country Bowles ---------- 3. - -
117½ Measures Corn @ 20 Galls ---------- 117.2.6
3 Baskets ---------- - .1.6
Total of Provisions -- 492.4.6

EHardy

Invoice relating to 204 slaves and provisions for them, James Fort, Rio Gambia, 13 July 1724. Manuscript. 390 × 245 mm (15⅜ × 9⅝ in)

Letter, 4 pages, folded to 250 × 200 mm (9⅞ × 7⅞ in): 'New Orleans, May 10th 1818. I take the liberty of introducing to your acquaintance my friend Col. Davis, a planter of this country, and who visits your town partly with the view of purchasing negroes for his own use. I do this with the more pleasure, as it may have the effect of removing from him any suspicion of being engaged in such pursuits as a trader. Any facilities you can afford the 'Col' in effecting his object will be considered a favour conferred on me. The 'Col' was an officer of distinction in the late war: you will find him a pleasant companion and a well-informed gentleman… Wm O Winston'.

Manifest, handwritten, 390 × 250 mm (15⅜ × 9⅞ in): District of Alexandria, 1844, 'Manifest of negroes, mulattoes and persons of colour taken on board the Brig. Uncas whereof Nathaniel Boush is Master, burthen 155¼ tons, to be transported from the Port of Alexandria … for the purpose of being sold or disposed of, as slaves, or to be held to service or labour' [there follows a list of forty-three persons each with details of sex, age, colour, and owner's/shipper's name].

Letter, 4 pages, folded to 250 × 195 mm (9⅞ × 7⅝ in): Alexandria 27 June 1844, 'I have been requested by Judge Douglass to inform you that he will be here on Monday next, and wishes to see you in reference to the purchase of the servant woman you have for sale. As he would be unwilling to make the purchase without having first seen the woman, you had better send her up on Sunday, and she can stay at our house until the Judge's arrival… W G Cazenove'.

Inventory, handwritten, 380 × 320mm (14⅞ × 12½in): The estate of Thomas Hunt, Westchester, February 1741, 'A true and perfect inventory of all the goods ... taken apprised ... by us the subscribers [there follows a list of some one hundred items including] 'a beaver hatt; shorts and breeches ... one paire of silver shoo buckels ... two oxen; six cows; thirty one sheep ... sum cheani cups and boles; one chafin dish ... one crackt grinstone; on ox chaine; sum feathers; an old warming pan ... one negro man, Joseph; one Negren woman; one Negrow Boy ...'. In an estate of total value £246 the slaves are valued at £91 together.

List, handwritten, 4 pages, folded to 350 × 290mm (13¾ × 11⅜in): Liverpool 1797: 'Liverpool vessels sail'd for Africa in the year 1797.' [There follows a listing, in columns, showing name of ship, master, where bound, owner's number of slaves, and date of sailing. For the period 1 January to 20 October the document records seventy-one sailings and a total stowage space for 22,350 slaves.]

Other papers and ephemera relating to slavery include slave sale notices, schedules of compensation awarded to owners of liberated slaves, runaway slave reward offers, statutes relating to the number of slaves permitted to be carried in trading ships, parliamentary reports on the state of the trade, Admiralty papers on the intervention of traders and 'receipt of fugitive slaves', and abolitionist propaganda material of various kinds.

COLLECTION Wilberforce Museum and Georgian House, Hull

Society card

The society card was an American chromolithographed calling-card bearing the insignia of such organizations as the Freemasons, the Oddfellows, the Good Templars, etc. It was produced for over-printing of the bearer's name in black on a blank area (commonly to the right of the emblem).

Songster/song-book

The pocket songster or song-book had its origins in the 17th-century 'garland', one of the earliest forms of mass-produced popular literature. The garland appeared as a black-letter sheet or booklet of topical ditties, some sentimental, some scurrilous. Among the earliest surviving specimens of the garland is a 1631 edition of Thomas Deloney's *Garland of Good Will*, first published in London in the late 1590s.

The term 'songster' came to be applied to the song rather than the singer in the 19th century. The traditional use of the word is seen in the earliest surviving American example, *The American Mock-Bird*, which carries the alternative title *Songster's Delight*. Published in New York in 1764, the booklet offers 'A choice collection of entire new Songs, as they now are sung by the Best Singers at all the public Places of Diversion in England'.

The songster's heyday, on both sides of the Atlantic, was the first half of the 19th century. During this period it vied with the CHAPBOOK as a medium of popular entertainment, appearing commonly as a booklet of sixteen to thirty-two pages and bearing a coloured-paper wrapper. Its contents, which were only rarely accompanied by music, offered a miscellany of naval ballads, stage and comedy items, as well as dancing, hewing, and traditional songs. Many examples bore cover illustrations and some carried a contents list on their front cover. The back cover was commonly used to advertise other booklets in the series.

The songster later evolved into the vaudeville and music-hall song-sheet and, in the latter part of the century, the illustrated music sheet.

COLLECTION American Antiquarian Society, Worcester, Mass.

Sports papers [plate 7]

Professional sport can be seen as a branch of entertainment, though in recent years some sports have reached such levels of competitive intensity that entertainment no longer seems to be the main priority. Issues of prestige are at stake – individual, local, and national – to a much greater extent than they are with, for example, the cinema, theatre, music, and dancing. Nevertheless, sport shares with entertainment the need to advertise, issue tickets, and provide programmes, and such items form an important part of the ephemera of sport (*see* FOOTBALL PROGRAMME; RACE CARD). Even on this front, however, there tend to be differences. A poster for a sporting event is often no more than a bald announcement of a fixture: an entertainment poster usually aims to persuade; the one has tended to be sparse and typographic: the other to be pictorial and decorative.

The early British football (soccer) poster may be taken as an extreme example of sparse advertising for a sport. With some words in type a foot or so high, it simply announces that 'A' will play 'B' on such and such a date. Sometimes the home team is evident from the venue and taken as read. Posters of this kind, usually printed in a single colour, remained much the same for around a century. One such poster dating from 1890, measuring 1016 × 1524mm (40 × 60in), advertises next Saturday's game between Crompton and Oldham. Its language and typography make no concessions to the techniques of the advertiser, apart from its inducement 'ladies free'. In flavour it is almost identical to a poster photographed in Manchester in 1971 which reads 'Football at Maine Road [Manchester City's football ground] Football League: First Division Championship' then, in letters five times as large as any other on the poster, 'Leeds Utd.', followed by the date, 'Saturday 30th January'. Posters of this kind were the stock-in-trade of numerous letterpress printers, particularly in northern Britain, well into the second half of the 20th century. A poster of the 1880s advertising a game between Stoke and West Bromwich Albion for the Staffordshire County Challenge Cup lists the two teams in full and, overall, reflects the typographic style of an auction poster. Though common enough in their day, such old soccer posters are now far rarer than theatre or cinema posters because, as far as is known, few people bothered to collect them at the time. They are more

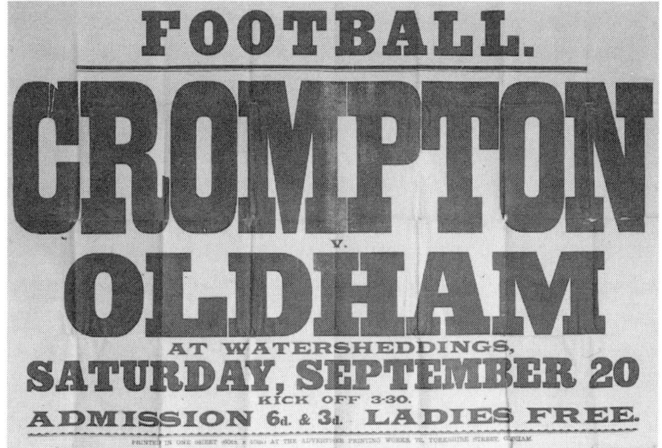

Soccer poster, Crompton versus Oldham, September 1890. Letterpress, printed in blue at the 'Advertiser Printing Works', Oldham, on a single sheet. 1016 × 1524mm (40 × 60in)

likely to be recorded through photographs of the urban scene than through actual examples.

There are good reasons to believe that records of sporting events go back to the beginnings of sport. Among graffiti found on the Athenian Agora is a fragment of a roof tile of the third century BC preserving what appear to be the headings of an informal listing of victories in a long race (equivalent to middle-distance races today) and 'the stone' (either weight-lifting or putting the shot). More formal records survive of the games of ancient Rome, which were written up much as results might appear in the press today, but were cut on stone. Fragments of a stone describing the Secular Games of 17 BC survive in the Museo Nazionale, Rome, with their reference to an ephemeral event, a chariot race, recorded for posterity by virtue of the medium.

Though strictly speaking an artistic and ritualistic spectacle rather than a sport, bullfighting can lay claim to a particularly long involvement with ephemera. Notices of bullfights have been produced more or less continuously, though in different forms, for over two hundred years. In Ronda, which boasts one of the oldest bull-rings in Spain, advertisements for bullfights of the 1790s were elegantly produced in small landscape formats by letterpress printers in neighbouring Sevilla. Only much later, particularly with the development of chromolithography in the last quarter of the 19th century, did the large pictorial bullfight poster emerge. These posters, hand-drawn on a series of stones (one for each constituent colour) continued to be produced for some time after World War II, and long after this method of lithography had been abandoned commercially elsewhere. In their dramatic depiction of, typically, the matador's encounter with the bull, they set the pattern for later, photo-mechanically produced, bullfight posters.

Sports have produced ephemera for which there are few parallels in other walks of life. Of special interest are 'blow-by-blow' records of sporting performances which, by their nature, vary from sport to sport and therefore take particular forms. Early paper records survive for medieval jousting contests, the hits of each contestant being marked, one by one it seems, as the contest unfolded. Other sports, referred to separately below, developed their own ways of recording results. The measured progress of a cricket match, often played over a period of days, may be recorded in several ways: officially in a specially prepared book by a 'scorer'; for their own benefit by spectators on a part-printed score sheet; and, more publicly and ephemerally, on a scoreboard. The scorecard of a golf match, on the other hand, though officially supervised, is also returned personally by the golfer; it is the individual golfer's responsibility to get it right, and errors incur penalties. In the 19th century archers 'pricked' their hits with a pointed tool on a score sheet. Virtually every sport has its own ways of recording its scores. Even those that do not leave behind a public trace of their methods of scoring, such as boxing, involve some person or a group of people in taking notes. Behind the scenes of most sporting events must lie the notes made by officials in the heat of the moment recording the outcome of encounters, hits made, speeds achieved, distances and heights jumped, and any infringements of the rules. Such records rarely see the light of day, and in some sports, such as rugby football, the notes of officials are deposited centrally after the match.

Some categories of sporting ephemera are found across a wide range of sports. Among them are the rules and regulations and membership lists of sporting clubs – in Britain most commonly athletics, bowls, cricket, football, golf, and tennis clubs, which sprang up across the country with the growth of leisure in the 19th and early 20th centuries. Rules for sports were established nationally, later internationally, by the regulating bodies of individual sports (in archery, for example, by the British 'Grand National Archery Society', founded in 1861, and internationally by the Fédération Internationale de Tir à l'Arc', founded in 1931). Such bodies set out in detail the official regulations for the conduct of a particular sport through 'Laws of the game' which, sometimes in diluted or modified form, and usually in pocket-size formats, worked their way down to the humblest level. The rules themselves are far from ephemeral, and in some sports have survived in broad outline for centuries, but the modest documents in which they were passed on to others certainly are. Typical of such rule books is a publication produced by the Royal Insurance Co. Ltd, Liverpool: *Rules of Golf: as approved by the Royal and Ancient Golf Club of St. Andrews, Scotland and the United States Golf Association effective 1st January, 1952*. Measuring 120 × 75 mm (4¾ × 3 in), it sets out on 93 pages the then forty-one rules of golf.

Another category of ephemera that applies across a range of sports is the fixture list, which would have been among the regular productions of the local printer from the second half of the 19th century until recent times. Commonly of pocket size, it set out in sequence the matches to be played by a particular club or team during the season. Early examples often have cloth covered covers, as though to emphasize the wear they would be subjected to by enthusiastic members; later ones were made more modestly of card alone. The files of the firm of Kitchin, a printer who worked in Ulverston in the north of England in the last quarter of the 19th century, show a regular production of fixture lists for the local cricket and football clubs, the designs remaining very similar over the years.

Other items of ephemera required across many sports range from the often elaborate CERTIFICATE of performance through to the modest numerals, on card or cloth, latterly often with a sponsor's name or logo, for attachment to a vest or pair of shorts. Certificates usually reward winners and those who fall just short of winning. Some, in the spirit of the founder of the modern Olympic games, celebrate the value of taking part: Cambridge 'Granta' Amateur Swimming Club, on a modest two-colour letterpress document, certifies that in July 1951 P. Andrews 'completed the swim through Cambridge' in a given time.

Yet a further category of sports ephemera, too great in scope to describe here, relates to the sports fan. It includes dealers' catalogues, the strategically marketed goods of the supporter's clubs and other franchized groups, the specialist sports 'ZINE, and the one-off banners and placards, often made by hand for the day and carrying some heartfelt slogan, usually banal, but sometimes perceptively witty.

A further spin-off from sport that produced printed ephemera in vast numbers is betting, a term mostly used to describe gambling on the results of races and other sports events. The practice goes back to ancient times in relation to, for example, chariot racing. Betting on horses remains by far the largest category of gambling relating to sport, and in many countries it is strictly controlled both on and off course. Betting tickets, once attractively printed in several colours on consecutive numbering machines as a guard against forgery, are the most common ephemera of gambling on horses. An even more recognizable item of betting ephemera is the British football pools coupon, on which people forecast the results of English and Scottish league and cup matches, match by match. The first such British football pool was organized in Birmingham in 1922, but it was not until the 1930s that the practice of filling in pools coupons became widespread. In the 1960s in Britain around ten million people filled in complex-looking coupons on a weekly basis, sometimes as a family or workplace activity. The appeal of the football pool was that it allowed ordinary people to gamble – with the prospect of winning what were then very considerable prizes – without considering that they were doing so. Several companies organized football pools, among the most important being Littlewoods and Vernons, but early coupons, frequently printed in millions of copies, are now not often to be found.

The appearance of sporting ephemera on a broad front in Britain coincided with the general increase in leisure activities of the late 19th and early 20th centuries and the growth of organized and professional sport. A working day of ten to twelve hours, with half a day off on Saturdays, left little time for sport, either as spectator or participant. Conventions governing activities on Sundays (*see* SABBATH PAPERS) also influenced the playing of sports. Initially, therefore, sporting events took place at times of festivities connected with coronations, celebrations of peace, and at least one major political event, the passing of the Reform Bill of 1832. A poster from Soham (Cambridgeshire), announcing celebrations of the peace of 1814, outlines a programme of 'Sports for the Day' (with prizes). The sports include donkey and pony races, climbing a mast, various races for particular groups (including a sack race and a wheelbarrow race), and the day was to end with 'A Grand display of fire works'. Cambridge celebrated the coronation of Queen Victoria (June 1838) in similar fashion with a programme of 'Rustic sports', as did the nearby town of Saffron Walden for the Marriage of HRH Albert Edward, Prince of Wales in 1863. Saffron Walden had already organized similar festivities to celebrate peace after the Crimean War – economically combining them with a celebration of the Queen's birthday – and announced a programme of 'Old English Sports' (donkey racing, climbing a greasy pole, sack and other races). Such ephemera reveal a strong strand of continuity in the 19th century. What is more, festivities of this kind continued in rural British communities almost unchanged in content well into the 20th century, and almost identical 'sports' to those announced on 19th century posters were enjoyed a hundred years later by those celebrating peace after World War II.

The nature of sport changed radically in the second half of the 20th century in response, principally, to the financial incentives offered by radio and television to cover their events. Consequently many previously amateur sports turned professional, some of them gradually and perhaps reluctantly. Most professional sport is now big business, and as such makes use of all the available techniques of marketing. Many of these involve the production of ephemeral material for sale at an event or through supporters' clubs. But even when not run strictly as business activities, sporting organizations have felt obliged to adopt the practices of the late 20th-century business world, with its emphasis on 'image'. Nowhere has this been more evident than in the modern Olympic Games, which is now seen as a source of national pride for the host nation and as a means of sporting and even economic regeneration. It has also been seen as providing a golden opportunity to promote a country's design industry. A turning point in this respect was the ill-fated Munich Olympics of 1972, for which a large design team under the direction of Ottl Aicher worked for several years to produce an exciting and innovative design scheme that was built on the colours of the rainbow. A lasting legacy of the Munich Olympics has been a set of sports symbols, which have been adopted, often loosely, by many other sporting bodies to the extent that the style itself has become associated with sport.

A further spin-off from sport that should be mentioned are the various kinds of diagrams evolved to describe actions and situations, and to record and analyse results. Though not in themselves ephemera, they provide a distinctive feature of some sporting ephemera. Descriptions of actions include sequences of drawings to illustrate the 'correct' way of executing a stroke (in cricket, golf, tennis, etc), and belong to the broader field of sequential instruction. Other diagrams relate to tactics and have a lot in common with war plans (both actually and in terms of the graphic conventions adopted), and are much used in analytical reports of games. Some sports have made good use of particular conventions of graphic statistics. One of these is the ray diagram, which is used by professional cricket scorers, but has also found its way into newspapers as an effective way of both highlighting and analysing an outstanding innings (e.g. Ian Botham's match-winning innings for England against Australia at Headingley in 1981 and Brian Lara's world record score of 501 not out for Warwickshire against Durham at Edgbaston in 1994). [MT]

The sample sports referred to below have been chosen not so much for their importance as sports as for the different categories of ephemera they have generated.

Archery. Archery has a long history. As a sport it grew out of the need in the Middle Ages to improve or at least maintain proficiency in battle. It can be sub-divided into clout shooting (at a long-range target set in the centre of a large target marked on the ground), crossbow shooting, field archery (with targets at unknown distances), flight archery (won by shooting the furthest), bow-hunting, and target archery. It is the last of these categories that provides the most ephemera, including constitutions of clubs, membership lists, regulations, advertising, fixture lists, and dealers' catalogues, in addition to items that are specific to archery. Handicap tables, based on an analysis of scores over a period of time, are also produced as a means of classifying archers (from 'third class' upwards).

One of the most unusual items relating to the sport are its scorecards. In the 19th century those for target archery were frequently printed in colour in a series of columns. Each column was headed with the name of the colour of the ring of the target, from the gold centre (which scored 9) and the red ring surrounding it (which scored 7), down to the outer white ring (which scored 1). The values were recorded in the appropriate column using a sharp tool called a 'pricker'. Such cards are highly distinctive. Among the most important firms producing them was the bowyer James Buchanan (1809–89) of Piccadilly, London, who by 1879 had been granted a warrant as archery manufacturer to the royal family. The scorecard that involved pricking was replaced towards the end of the 19th century by

SCORING J. BUCHANAN'S CARD.
215, PICCADILLY,

18 Yards. Ends.

Shooters	Gold 9	Red 7	Blue 5	Black 3	White 1	Hits	Value

Archery scorecard of James Buchanan, Piccadilly, London, second half of 19th century. Lithographed in four colours. 133 × 96 mm (5¼ × 3¾ in)

rather more utilitarian scorebooks and score sheets on which actual figures were recorded. Similar items are still being produced, printed in one colour. A single competition might require one score sheet, though national and international competitions lasting several days require whole books of sheets.

The most characteristic and distinctive category of ephemera specific to archery is the target face, consisting of five concentric rings (gold, red, blue, black, and white), which can measure up to 122 cm (4 ft) in diameter. Paper and cloth versions exist and there are special versions for archery darts, crossbow shooting, and field archery. In 1932 the Fédération Internationale de Tir à l'Arc (FITA) introduced a ten value scoring system (1–10), which involved dividing each of the traditional five rings into two zones of equal width, separated by a thin line. From the federation's foundation a year earlier rounds (combinations of arrows) have varied in the distances and numbers of arrows shot: its present round comprises three dozen arrows at 70, 60, 50, and 30 metres for women, and the same quantities at 90, 70, 50, and 30 metres for men. A target with a diameter of 80 cm is used for the 50 and 30 metres ranges. [FL]

Baseball. Of all sports, baseball is the one most closely associated with America. Originating from the game of 'One old cat' (which, like baseball, involved the use of bases), it developed in the second half of the 19th century into the country's national sport. In its present-day form it derives from rules formulated by Alexander Cartwright in 1845. In the same year the first organized baseball club was founded, and within twenty-five years the sport was being played professionally. Thereafter it became big business. In this respect it set the pattern for many other sports, particularly soccer, all over the world.

Baseball has generated vast quantities of ephemera relating to both the conduct of the game (rules, programmes, tickets, and advertisements of games) and general promotional material, much of it to do with supporters. The most widely collected of the latter are sets of baseball cards featuring individual players in striking poses or, sometimes, whole teams. Usually printed in colour (originally by chromolithography, later by photomechanical means), they date from the late 19th century. Their size varied little and was commonly around 100 × 70 mm; on their reverse was a panel of professional, biographical, and statistical information. They were produced by firms, such as Allen & Ginter and Topps, and were often issued with products, for example bubble gum (from 1933 when Goudey Gum Co. began issuing cards), bread, cigarettes, cookies, and dog food.

Scorecards, some of them carrying colourful baseball images on their front cover, were produced as promotional material, with the company's name and products overprinted on to an otherwise blank rear leaf. Scorecards were designed to be filled in by the spectator at the game, and include a pre-printed grid on to which details of batsmen and their hits can be entered.

Club and team promotional material (for example BUMPER STICKERS and PENNANTS) are other common examples of baseball ephemera. Pennants in particular characterize baseball and are widely displayed in children's bedrooms, college rooms, bars, and sports clubs, both as a demonstration of commitment and as a form of decoration. The tapering form of the typical pennant has led to some characteristic design features; they result from the difficulty of fitting the name of the club or institution, sometimes with a logotype or mascot, into such a constraining and challenging format.

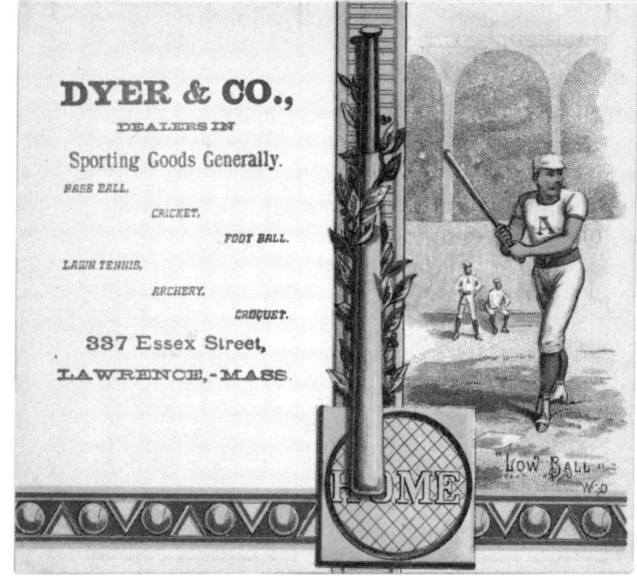

Baseball scorecard, signed 'WD', early 19th century. Chromolithography, overprinted with advertisement of Dyer & Co., Lawrence, Mass. 127 × 140 mm (5 × 5½ in)

Boxing. Fisticuffs in one form or another was a form of fighting known from the earliest times, especially in ancient Rome where it formed part of gladiatorial contests. But it was the activities of James Figg (d. 1734) in the early 18th century that marked the beginnings of modern boxing history.

Boxing ephemera were produced even in these early days of the sport. Figg, though not primarily a boxer but a 'Master of ye Noble Science of Defence', is recognized as the first prizefighting champion of England, and his friend William Hogarth engraved his trade card, which stands as the first piece of boxing-related ephemera. It is of the utmost rarity, though the image is well-known thanks to a reproduction of it dating from 1792 (which is quite common). Handbills of the period are also very rare, though one advertising Figg's New Amphitheatre, printed in 1726, was reproduced in Hone's *Every-day Book* in 1827.

One of Figg's pupils, Jack Broughton (1704–89), must be credited with regulating the sport, which until his time had consisted of brutal slugging matches in which the opponents battered each other with bare fists until one fell to the ground. He drew up the first set of rules for boxing in 1743, which remained in force for nearly one hundred years. These rules, 'To be observed in all battles on the stage', were printed in the form of a BROADSIDE/BROADSHEET. Late editions, often embellished with woodcuts of prize-fighters, are often to be seen framed in public houses around Britain. Broughton also introduced boxing gloves (at first called 'mufflers'), though they were originally used for sparring only.

Broughton's downfall came in 1750 when he lost a fight against Slack, the Norfolk (UK) Butcher. The Duke of Cumberland, who had backed Broughton, lost heavily on the bout and, thinking that he had been cheated, was instrumental in having an Act passed outlawing boxing. It remained illegal for almost 150 years, and throughout its 'golden age'. This accounts for the scarcity of early advertising bills and leaflets relating to the sport. Matches were held clandestinely and their location kept secret: punters were informed of them by word of mouth or by letter. 'Gentleman' John Jackson (1793–1845), ex-champion and proprietor of a famous boxing academy, had a special form printed for his clients: one copy of it, dated 5 June 1824, reads: 'I have the honor to acquaint you that a Fight will take place on (—) next, at (—) precisely at (—) o'clock, between (—)'.

Broadsides giving vivid accounts of the bouts, with all the gory details, were run off by Catnach and other Seven Dials printers, and were frequently embellished with the crudest of woodcuts (*see* STREET LITERATURE). In common with the EXECUTION BROADSIDE they often included 'portraits' of the protagonists, the same blocks being used for any number of individuals. The reports of results were no more reliable: it is said that on one occasion a bout was described in detail which had never taken place. Another popular feature of the 'golden age' of boxing was the production of pictorial commemorative handkerchiefs bearing images of prize-fighters and famous boxing matches. Frequently of head-scarf size, they were sometimes used by bare-knuckle fighters to keep their breeches up, and popular prints of the time show them tied around the waists of the boxers.

Throughout most of the 19th century organized tournaments and championships – which were attended by both the aristocracy and rowdy roughnecks – had to be held in remote country locations because of their illegality. They were frequently broken up by police raids, and in 1868 the railway companies were prohibited from carrying passengers going to prize-fights.

The more moderate members of the boxing fraternity decided to take the brutalization out of the sport and make it respectable. This led to the formation of the National Sporting Club, which opened at 43 King Street, Covent Garden, on 5 March 1891. In turn this led to the production of a wealth of ephemera in the shape of programmes, dinner menus, tickets and so on. Following the death of a boxer named Billy Smith on 24 April 1901, the members of the Club were indicted for manslaughter. They were found not guilty, and the ruling of Mr Justice Grantham effectively legalized boxing in Britain.

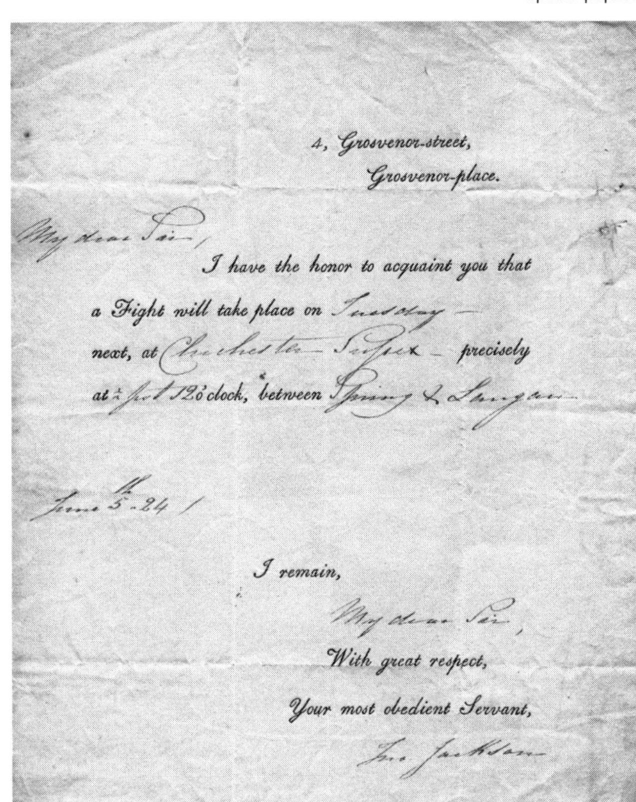

4, Grosvenor-street,
Grosvenor-place.

My dear Sir,

I have the honor to acquaint you that a Fight will take place on Tuesday — next, at Chichester Sussex — precisely at ½ past 12 o'clock, between Spring & Langan —

June 5-24 /

I remain,
My dear Sir,
With great respect,
Your most obedient Servant,
Jno. Jackson

Invitation to a boxing match between Spring and Langam at Chichester (UK), sent by the promoter, John Jackson, 5 June 1824. Letterpress and manuscript. 228 × 185 mm (9 × 7¼ in)

Posters now made their appearance to a more or less standard format, usually printed in garish colours, and with large type and photographic reproductions of the contestants. Because they mostly advertised small local bouts, which were of little interest once the match was over, they must be among the most ephemeral of posters. [PJ]

Cricket. The origins and early history of cricket are obscure, though it is clear that the game is among the oldest team sports. The earliest recorded set of laws of the game – the first of countless evolving examples – was drafted in 1744, which, coincidentally, is the year of the earliest surviving record of a match score. But long before this time competitive matches were being played, principally in the south of England, among them the first recorded county match (between Kent and London) in 1709. International matches followed much later, the first 'test match' being played between an English touring team and a combined Australian team in 1877.

All major cricket matches, and some less important ones too, would have required advertising. Initially this took the form of press announcements; later, small posters or notices were produced by local printers. Surviving cricket posters of the first half of the 19th century are less austere than posters produced later on for soccer matches, and some of them reflect the semi-pastoral origins of the game. Notices of the early nineteenth century exist for matches played at Lord's, the ground in London that later became the seat of the governing body of cricket, the MCC (Marylebone Cricket Club). Typically they measure less than 255 × 203 mm (10 × 8 in) and have the word 'Cricket' in capital letters at their head, followed by details of the venue and lists of the players in both teams. Among mid 19th-century examples of posters for other grounds are ones with wood-engraved vignettes depicting matches in progress. Some of these engravings show all the signs of having been used over and over again whether appropriate or not; on one poster, a single-wicket match is illustrated by a wood-engraving (already split in half) which clearly shows two batsmen. The poster advertises a match to be played at Garratt's Ground, Islington, London, in 1846, between gentlemen of the Copenhagen Club and City Club 'For £20, A side'. It lists the names of the four players in each team, and at its foot one of them, E. Paul, took the opportunity to advertise that his 'Cricket Bats, Stumps, and Balls, Leggings, Gloves, and every requisite for Cricket' could be bought at the ground. The wood-engraved vignette on this poster also appears three years later at the head of another surviving poster advertising a match at Islington, though for an eleven-a-side match.

Cricket requires the most assiduous record keeping. This was so even in its early days because it involved considerable sums of money in the form of wagers and prizes. Initially the scores of batsmen were recorded very simply by cutting notches on sticks. What was to become a complicated system of scoring on paper began with the introduction of ball-by-ball scoring in 1769.

The first recorded scoring for the benefit of spectators and players as the game progressed came with the introduction of a simple scoreboard, known as a 'telegraph', which was first used at Lord's in 1846; another London ground, the Oval, followed suit two years later. More complicated scoreboards that showed not just the overall score and number of wickets fallen, but also the individual scores of the batsmen, came in with 'Paget's patent scorer' (an invention of A. Paget & Co.), which was introduced at Lord's in 1886. The idea of purpose-made scoreboards spread, and individual numbers (white on black) began to be manufactured on separate sheets of metal for hanging on hooks. This practice is still widespread in village cricket in Britain. It seems likely that the custom of using white numbers on a black ground – which appears to be universal for cricket scoreboards – stems from an earlier practice of writing with chalk or 'blanco' (used for whitening cricket equipment) on black boards. In the 20th century large grounds, particularly those where test matches were played, used more refined systems with numbers on hinged flaps or canvas rollers, which allowed scorers to provide more information and yet keep up with the progress of the game. The first electronically controlled scoreboard was introduced at Melbourne in 1982.

In tandem with this public presentation of the progress of a match, an official 'scorer', amateur or professional according to the kind of match, records the score. Scorers are depicted on some 18th century prints seated at a table just outside the boundary of the ground. The early manuscript score sheet, often providing no more than a summary of the score, survived into the 20th century for local matches. By the beginning of the 20th century, however, pre-printed score sheets were available. Lithographically produced in book form, they helped scorers provide a more or less complete record of a match, including each ball bowled and each run scored in relation to every bats-

A GRAND MATCH!!
OF SINGLE WICKET
WILL BE PLAYED AT
Garratt's Ground,
COPENHAGEN HOUSE,
TUESDAY, OCTOBER 6, 1846,
BETWEEN FOUR GENTLEMEN OF THE
COPENHAGEN GROUND,
AGAINST FOUR GENTLEMEN OF THE
CITY CLUB,
Held at The NORTHAMPTON ARMS, ISLINGTON,
For £20. A side.
THE FOLLOWING IS A LIST OF THE PLAYERS.

COPENHAGEN.		CITY.	
Messrs. Dewdney Golding	Messrs. Rogers Paul	Messrs. Figg Hodson	Messrs. Clark Trestrum

*** Wickets pitched at Half-past Ten o'clock.

☞ Cricket Bats, Stumps, and Balls, Leggings, Gloves, and every article requisite for Cricket to be had of E. PAUL, on the Ground.

Wright, Printer, 10, Fulwood's Rents, Holborn.

Notice of a single-wicket cricket match at Islington, London, on 6 October 1846. Letterpress with wood-engraving, printed by Wright, Holborn, London. 405 × 270 mm (16 × 10⅝ in)

LILLYWHITE'S PRINTING TENT.
BY AUTHORITY AND UNDER
the PATRONAGE of the MARYLEBONE and OTHER CLUBS.
At LORD'S Marylebone Club & Ground against the Undergraduates of Oxford
return match Thursday, & Friday, July 5ht, & 6th 1855.

Marylebone Club	First Innings		Second Innings	
J. M. Fuller, Esq	c Peter, b A. Payne	8	c Fuller, b Marsham	12
T. W. Wills, Esq	c Fuller, b Marsham	5	run out	0
A. Haygarth, Esq	c Veitch, b C D Marsham	7	b A. Payne	0
Hon S. Ponsonby	c Veitch, b C D Marsham	22	b Fellows	0
J. Grundy	b Fellows	17	b Marsham	4
H. Royston	c Randolph, b Marsham	19	b A. Payne	13
C. Marsham, Esq	b Fellows	0	b Fellows	11
C. Du Cane, Esq	run out	0	not out	2
E. T. Drake, Esq	b A Payne	3	c Randolph, b A Payne	18
F. E. Stacey, Esq	b A Payne	0	b A. Payne	0
T. Nixon	not out	6	b Fellows	1
	b 21, l-b 6, w 4, n-b ,	31	b 17, l-b 5, w 2, n-b ,	24
	Total	118	Total	85
OXFORD	**First Innings**		**Second Innings**	
J. Sandford, Esq	c Drake, b Nixon	8	b Grundy	3
G. Fuller, Esq	b Grundy	2	b Grundy	3
R. Colley, Esq	c Ponsonby, b Nixon	9	c Grundy, b Royston	0
E. L. Bateman, Esq	b Nixon	2	b Nixon	8
H. Veitch, Esq	b Nixon	12	not out	9
A. F. Payne, Esq	b Nixon	4	c Grundy, b Nixon	0
B. M. Randolph, Esq	b Grundy	1	c Fuller, b Royston	38
A. Payne, Esq	c Du Cane, b Nixon	8	b Nixon	12
C. D. Marsham, Esq	b Royston	9	b Grundy	2
W. Fellows, Esq	c Haygarth, b Royston	30	run out	8
A. Peter, Esq	not out	0	c Haygarth, b Nixon	10
	b 3, l-b 4, w 1, n-b 2,	10	b 2, l-b 7, w 1, n-b ,	10
Umpires...... Adams & Chatterton	Total	95	Total	103

MATCHES TO COME.
Monday July 9, at Lord's...The Gentlemen of Kent & Surrey against Gentlemen of England
Thursday, July 12, at Kennington Oval. Marylebone Club (with two players) against the Surrey Club & County (with two players)...return match
Monday, July 16, at Lord's...Kent & Surrey against England.
Thursday, July 19, at Lord's...The Royal Horse Brigade against the I Zingari
Monday, July 23, at Lord's...The Gentlemen against the Players.
THE LATE WILLIAM LILLYWHITE.
Subscriptions towards erecting a MOMUMENT to this Player, limited to Five Shillings received at the Pavillion and at the above Tent, on the Ground.
Printed and Published, on the Ground by authority of the Proprietor, and under the distinguished Patronage of the M. C. C., by Frederick Lillywhite, price (in town) TWO-PENCE. Scores forwarded to any part, POST FREE for FOUR-PENCE
For other Matches, and "Cricketing Prints" &c. &c. turn over

Cricket scorecard, MCC versus Oxford University, 5 & 6 July 1855, at Lord's, London. Letterpress, printed on the ground in Lillywhite's printing tent, 153 × 113 mm (6 × 4½ in)

man and bowler. Such scorebooks have been kept by some clubs, both large and small, over very long periods, and provide lasting records of matches and a basis for club histories.

In addition, from the mid 19th century, simpler score sheets, generally called scorecards, have been printed 'on the ground' at Lord's, (from 1848) and the Oval (from 1847) for spectators to buy and complete for themselves. They included the names of both teams and provided spaces for the spectator to record the fall of each wicket, the nature of the dismissal, those responsible for it, and the score of the batsman. Their useful life as printed documents was often very short as they came out in several updated editions in the course of the day's play (keeping up, though somewhat slowly, with the progress of the match). A final edition appeared at the end of the day's play. This form of cricket scorecard, filled in by countless enthusiasts, young and old, naive and experienced, is among the most characteristic and evocative of sporting ephemera. [MT]

Football (American). This game relates only distantly to soccer, which in Britain is commonly and confusingly called football (and is run by a body called the Football Association). It derives more from the much older British game of rugby football (in which players handle an oval ball, and each other) than it does with soccer.

Though introduced to other countries, it remains essentially an American game. It began as a college sport, the first recorded game of inter-college football taking place in 1869 between the universities of Princeton and Rutgers. It remains a key sport in American universities, where it is seen as both a revenue earner and a promotional activity. The professional game was much slower to take root than baseball: it began in 1895, but did not really flourish until the 1920s. Thereafter, it soon led to the production of large quantities of ephemera, much of it in similar categories to those already produced in connection with baseball.

Sets of cards of football stars, both individual and in teams, were, in their heyday, just as collectable as baseball cards. In their size, and in their provision of panels of text on the reverse, they follow the baseball card model, the leading manufacturers being Bowman and Topps. Both baseball and football cards parallel the CIGARETTE CARD series of sporting heroes produced in Britain for cricket, golf, soccer, and other enthusiasts, though these cards include series of sports along with numerous other kinds of topics.

The PENNANT too is a common item of football ephemera in America, and probably just as widely used as the baseball pennant as a means of establishing allegiances to a team or institution

Golf. Though a serious competitive sport at all levels, golf carries with it the idea of a healthy activity undertaken in surroundings not far removed from what is perceived as a natural landscape. Because of this it has developed an image that has been cultivated by advertisers, who have used it to produce some very attractive peripheral ephemera. Golf as a theme was used on occasions to promote the independent rail companies in Britain from the 1890s to the 1940s, typically on posters as one of the pleasures offered by holiday resorts. For similar reasons golfing appears on baggage labels. Others with even less connection with the sport seized on its associations with healthy living. A calendar/blotter, issued by the Enfield (UK) firm Birkbeck Hygienic Laundry Ltd in the inter-war years of the 20th century takes this approach: it carries the copy line 'More time for the Open Air if you send your laundry to us' beneath a picture of an attractive young woman with golf clubs slung across her shoulder.

Golf also lends itself to humour, and has been used in this way on advertisements that, likewise, have little relation to the sport. Comic illustrations of golf appear in colour on advertising blotters of firms as varied as the British tobacconists and confectioners J. A. Charmbury & Son of Weymouth, and, in America, Park Place Auto Renting of New York City, and the Pawtucket Mutual Fire Insurance Co. of Lowville, NY. The humorous golfing POSTCARD is also common. Other items of ephemera that frequently depict golfers or refer to golf include the CIGARETTE CARD, 'CINDERELLA' STAMP, BOOKMATCH, BEER MAT (the last of these often advertising particular championships, clubs, and anniversaries). In addition, there have been many golfing postage stamps, including first-day covers for the Open Championships.

The most revealing and evocative ephemera that specifically relate to the sport are golfers' own scorecards, which, for stroke play, are completed hole by hole as the match progresses and submitted at the end of each round of a competition. Unglamorous though they are, they capture the achievements of the golfing day – particularly to those with a knowledge of the player and the course – more effectively than any other item of ephemera. Scorecards relating to major championships and outstanding performances are particularly rare. Cards for the Open Championship and Ryder Cup (established 1927) are highly collectable, as are other items associated with historic matches, such as players' badges, entry tickets, and dinner menus.

Golf has produced the standard range of sports club material, including membership lists, regulations, and so forth. Golf courses too have produced ephemera, but they differ from clubs in their need – at least in some parts of the world – to advertise. An American advertisement for the 'Highland Park Golf Course' emphasizes its growing facilities: 'The Only Public Links in Auburn Adjacent to and Overlooking the City/9 Holes in 1925 18 Holes in 1927' and 'Shower Baths and Locker Rooms'. Its colourful illustration suggests that golf in America was seen as a sport for the people at large rather than for an elite group, as it has been, and still sometimes is, in England (though not in Scotland).

Dealers' catalogues and stationery exist for golf as they do for other sports, and among the rarest of golfing ephemera are paper tees in booklets (not unlike books of raffle tickets). Though originally among the cheapest of golfing items, they are now highly regarded by collectors of golfing ephemera. [HRJG]

Rowing. Seamen of the ancient world raced boats, and in Britain there has long been a tradition for fishermen and pilots to do so around the coasts and for sailors from different ships to compete with one another. But the first evidence for actual matches between boat crews emerges from material relating to Thames watermen, the men who transported people and cargoes along London's river. Their races are reported in 18th-century newspapers, which indicate that actors often supplied the prizes.

Thomas Doggett, an actor and joint manager of Drury Lane Theatre, instigated the first sculling race in 1716. It was rowed by six watermen between London Bridge and Chelsea and is Britain's oldest annual sporting event. A ticket survives for a

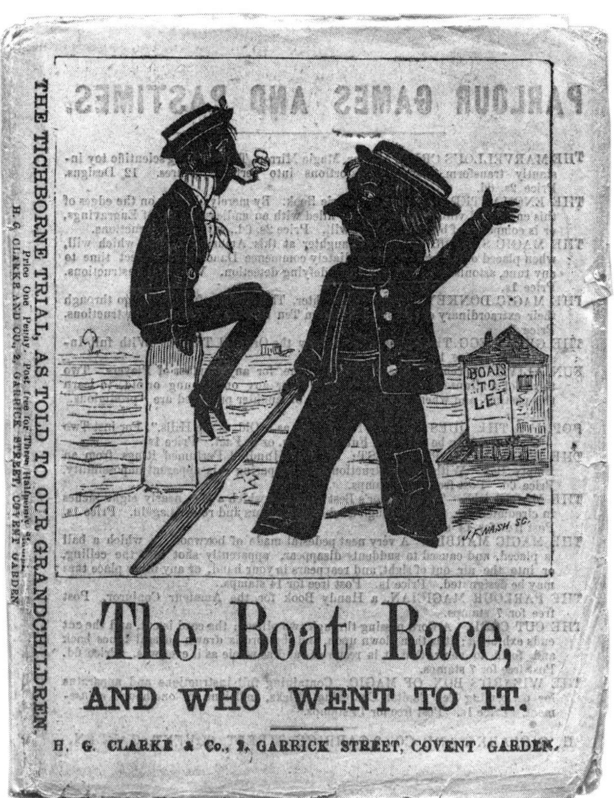

'The Boat Race, and who went to it', published by H. G. Clarke, Covent Garden, London, on the occasion of the Oxford and Cambridge boat race, mid 1870s. Front wrapper, printed in relief on beige paper. 150 × 120mm (6 × 4¾in)

fashionable regatta ball at Ranelagh Gardens on 23 June 1765 depicting Father Thames with attendants awarding medals to a pair of putti, each of which is shown racing a wherry. Unfortunately, it is not known whether the contestants in this smart event were professional Thames watermen or the liveried oarsmen who rowed barges kept by the nobility living beside the river.

In the north of England, professional watermen became folk heroes and enjoyed huge popularity and status. Their races, undertaken for wagers, were frequently reported in local newspapers and also in *Bell's Life*, the London sporting newspaper, the editor of which was frequently a stakeholder for the major races. Rowing feats on the river Tyne were celebrated through published songs, and with verse in the local Geordie dialect. In the 1840s crowds of between 50,000 and 100,000 thronged the banks of the Tyne to watch their hero, Harry Clasper, defend his international title against champions from London, Canada, America, and even Australia. Crowds were transported to matches by the Newcastle and Carlisle Railway, which published posters with details of the matches and of their special trains to them. One poster advertised a 'Great rowing match, on the river Tyne between Clasper and Newell on Monday, June 22, 1846' and states that 'In order to afford the Public a View of this Contest throughout, [a] Special Train will Start from the Newcastle and Redheugh Stations, and proceed along with the Boats on each Side of the River to Scotswood Bridge'.

19th-century newspapers regularly reported boat races. In 1804 the *London General Evening Post* announced an imminent 'rowing match for 200 guineas': a pair of military men, acting as impresarios, hired rowing gigs and crews of six men and a cox from the London and Gravesend watermen, who then raced each other. Heavy wagering was usual in such matches and often resulted in acts of sabotage and race fixing. In this instance it was reported that 'the Gravesend watermen have made a fine bargain, and they are sure to receive Four Guineas each man, should they prove unsuccessful, but if victorious, they trust to Major Warrington's liberality'.

More structured rowing contests evolved by way of Eton and Westminster schools to reach Oxford and Cambridge universities. Folding, hand-coloured keepsakes of university boat clubs survive from the 1840s; they present crews in boating costume, or in boats bearing college flags, and were handsomely published, in stiff blue covers, by local stationers. The first University Boat Race between Oxford and Cambridge was held in 1829. This annual event soon led to the production of numerous prints and souvenirs. A typical example of the latter is a chapbook of the 1860s entitled *The Boat Race and Who Went To It* (priced 6*d*), which described the event in doggerel and included crude woodcuts of the race and spectators. Another such memento is an informative, folding-paper chart of the course, dated 1877 and priced 3*d*. It has portraits of the crews, some in colour, and carries advertising material. An indication of its circulation can be gleaned from its statement that 'the charts were produced…on Geo. Mann & Co's 'Climax' lithographic machine, at the rate of 7,000 an hour'.

In Victorian England and throughout Europe an enthusiasm for rowing led to the development of regattas and town rowing clubs, both professional and amateur. In turn this led to a proliferation of ephemera of the kind common in other sports. Among such examples are menus for sumptuous club dinners, rule books, membership lists, receipts for subscriptions or equipment, scraps for albums, postcards, and tickets issued by steamers following the University Boat Race. Henley Regatta also provided material, though as a society fixture its ephemera had as much to do with social matters as with competitive racing. Wherever the British settled abroad an early instinct was to form a rowing club, and worm-eaten histories of clubs, fulminating instructional pamphlets, and badly printed regatta posters survive from local presses in Rangoon, Karachi, Shanghai, and other parts of the British empire.

In addition, the University Boat Race and Henley Regatta were used, often seasonally, to promote other services and products, and ephemera featuring these events include London Underground posters, matchbox labels, playing cards, ships' menus, boardgames, and advertisements for Cadbury's Cocoa, Guinness, Wills's Cigarettes, and Shell Oil.

Rowing ephemera takes many other forms, including sheet-music covers, postage stamps, certificates for the Olympic Games, and chromolithographed cards. The last-mentioned were mainly issued in Belgium and France by manufacturers of margarine, biscuits, chocolate, and meat extract, and depict men and women rowing. In America, where rowing was taken up just as quickly and enthusiastically as in Britain, the amount of surviving ephemera seems to be even greater, and rowing images are found on an even wider range of products, such as cigar-box and whiskey bottle labels, tobacco cards and felts, and sheet music. Often these articles are more decorative than their British equivalents. [DSC]

Tennis. Real, royal, or court tennis has been played for eight centuries. It has many descendants including rackets, squash rackets, field tennis, table tennis, badminton, and lawn tennis. A particularly interesting item of ephemera throws light on the history of the game: it is a label for a wooden box for Walter Clopton Wingfield's game *Sphairistike* (Greek: ball game), which was patented in March 1874. As few could pronounce the name, it was shortened to 'Sticky', and finally abandoned in favour of 'Lawn tennis'. The first press report on this new game was published in the *Army & Navy Gazette* in March 1874.

The success of lawn tennis depended on two 19th-century inventions: the lawn mower, which kept grass short and neat, and the rubber ball, which could bounce on it. The first Lawn Tennis Championship meeting was held on the croquet lawns of the All England Club at Worple Road, Wimbledon, in the summer of 1877. The Gentlemen's Singles event (there was no other) was supported by the *Field* magazine, which provided a silver Challenge Cup.

Lawn tennis soon caught on among the upper-middle classes in Britain, where it was considered a garden party pastime suitable for young ladies as well as young gentlemen. This called for special tennis gear, and *Pastime* magazine of 1 May 1895 advertised canvas tennis shoes in white or brown, tennis 'gladstones' in tan canvas or nut-brown cowhide, and the new cricket, boating, or tennis jacket. Advertisers were quick to seize upon associations with the lawn-tennis scene, and used it to promote products as diverse as soft drinks, flexible corsets, embrocations, and mustard.

Established firms that sold games and sports equipment, among them Slazengers and Ayres, show in their catalogues the number of rival lawn-tennis sets on the market. Such catalogues document the ways in which equipment for the game changed over the years. In the 1930s, for example, the introduction of the square-stem racket pinpointed 'a drastic change in racket construction to suit the fast forceful game of today'. Some product developments led to innovations in the design of ephemera: British Music and Tennis Strings Ltd packaged their 'Summit' and 'Cathedral' strings coiled in small square envelopes, and a small cardboard cut-out racket label was tied to English nylon 'Survon' tennis strings.

Confusion over the number of different sets of lawn-tennis rules then in circulation led the Marylebone Cricket Club to frame an official set in 1875. Other ephemera that relate to the actual playing of the game include the *Field* 'Lawn Tennis Score Sheet Book', dated 5 July 1880, which contained instructions to umpires, and the Lawn Tennis Association's 'Scoring Sheet', published by Slazengers in the 1890s, which came in a block with a rigid cardboard back and a tubular cover for a pencil.

The organization of tennis championships generates – as it has done in the past – draw cards, official notices, and the numerous tickets, programmes, passes, and badges for competitors, spectators, and the media for each and every day. Routine camera platform passes, competitor tea tickets, and perforated booklets of complimentary vouchers to the grounds may be contrasted with elaborate tickets to Wimbledon's Centre and No. 1 Courts. Early tennis ephemera of this kind are by no means common. The result of the Wimbledon draw in 1896 survives in the form of a single sheet, rescued from a noticeboard: it announced that 'The Winner of the First prize will be called upon to play Mr W. Baddeley, the present Champion, for the Championship, and the right to hold the Hundred Guinea Challenge Cup'. Equally rare are some surviving draw cards for the 1937 Davis Cup.

Lawn tennis lends itself to punning humour, particularly in relation to the language of scoring. Postcards and greetings cards are a favourite medium for this. Postcards use such expressions as 'Love match', 'The one I love', 'A deuce good time', and 'For a jolly good racket come here'; valentines show cherubs patting hearts across the net; and there are innumerable permutations of the idea of perfect partners and love doubles. In addition, greetings cards commonly show cats, rabbits, pigs, elephants, mice, and dogs playing tennis, and in the 1950s a photographic strip featuring a Chimps Tennis Tournament.

Many games based on lawn tennis emerged, but only one, variously known as Gossima, Ping Pong, and Table Tennis, has survived. A boxed ping-pong set of about 1900 describes the game as 'causing immense excitement and healthy exercise and is the nearest approach that can be, to the game of Lawn tennis as played out of doors'. Later indoor games include 'The Fred Perry Wimbledon Game' and 'Puzzling Pastimes Tennis Troubles', which describes itself as 'a clever and interesting game for afternoon and evening parties'. [HG]

REFERENCES John Arlott (ed.), *The Oxford Companion to Sports and Games* (London: Oxford University Press, 1976)); Sarah Baddiel, *Golfing Ephemera* (Chapman, 1991); John Barrett, *100 Wimbledon Championships – A Celebration* (London: Collins Willow, 1986); Keith Booth, *The Past, Present and Future of Cricket-Scoring* (Edinburgh and London: Mainstream Publishing, 1999); Neville Cardus and John Arlott, *The Noble Game of Cricket* (London: Harrap, 1969); R.W.Cox, *Sport in Britain 1800–1888* (Manchester: Manchester University Press, 1991); Christopher Dodd, *The Story of World Rowing* (London: Stanley Paul, 1992); Nat Fleischer and Sam André, *A Pictorial History of Boxing* (London: Spring Books, 1959); Fred Lake, *A Bibliography of Archery* (Manchester: Simon Archery Foundation, 1974); Fred Lake, 'James Buchanan the bowyer', *British Archer*, vol. 24, no. 4 (Jan/Feb 1973), pp. 167–168; Fred Lake, 'An album full of archers', *Picture Postcard Monthly*, no. 182 (June 1994), pp. 24–25; John M. and Martin W. Olman, *The Encyclopedia of Golf Collectibles* (Alabama: Books Americana, 1985); Dennis Signy, *A Pictorial History of Soccer*, 4th edn (London: Hamlyn, 1971); Tom Todd, *The Tennis Players: from Pagan Rites to Strawberries and Cream* (Guernsey: Vallancey, 1979); Glenys Williams, '150 years of Printing at Lord's', in M.C.C. v Rest of the World programme, 18 July 1988, pp. 53–55

COLLECTIONS Museo Taurino de la Real Maestranza de Caballeria de Ronda, Spain; M.C.C. Museum, Lord's Cricket Ground, London; The Wimbledon Lawn Tennis Museum, Wimbledon, London

SOCIETY British Society of Sports History

Squib

Satire (in the form of the BROADSIDE/BROADSHEET, HANDBILL, and SATIRICAL PRINT) was a prominent feature of early 19th-century public life on both sides of the Atlantic. Such items were described generally as 'squibs', and their subject matter ranged from elections and parliamentary politics to religion, local government, and personal vendettas.

Classics of the genre are the illustrated lampoons of Gillray, Cruikshank, and Rowlandson. The collaboration of Cruikshank and William Hone on the pamphlet *The Political House that Jack Built*, an illustrated pamphlet published in 1819, made political history. Its radical message, presented in the form of a parodied nursery rhyme, achieved instant success, selling over 100,000 copies in nearly fifty editions within a couple of years.

Parody is the keynote of the squib from the 18th and 19th centuries, much of it cast in the form of the mock public announcement, PROCLAMATION, or broadside. To the 20th-century eye many of its allusions appear obscure, but in many examples the intention and the effect is unmistakable. In local politics it was not unusual for one squib to generate another in reply, the term and allusions of the protagonists' satire becoming progressively more obscure. Mock proclamations were a favourite form, as were satirical warnings, reward announcements, and lost and found notices. Theatre, circus, and (later) music-hall bills were also much used formats.

Among a diminishing number of squibs in the 20th century is a 'proclamation' ostensibly by George V of England, but published in Ireland in 1914, addressed to 'Our faithful Irish subjects' and finishing 'God Save the King'. It urges Irishmen to enlist in the army: 'come and volunteer for the Army at once, and we will arrange that you will be sent to the Front and Killed…'. An Australian notice of 1915 carried the bold headline 'To Arms…', and beneath it appeared the words 'Capitalists, Parsons, Politicians, Landlords, Newspaper Editors and other stay-at-home Patriots. Your Country needs you in the trenches. *Workers* follow your masters!'.

Staffage

The word staffage (pronounced 'staffarge'), recorded from 1872, refers to drawings of figures suitable for copying and inclusion as pictorial 'accessories' in art students' landscape drawings and paintings. The idea originated with W. H. Pyne in a collection of etchings published under the title *Microcosm: or, a Picturesque Delineation of the Arts, Agriculture, Manufactures, &c. of Great Britain* (1803–6). The publication consists of more than six hundred groups of small figures for the embellishment of landscapes. The groupings show tradesmen and labourers engaged in a multiplicity of trades, each subject being a suitable addendum to an existing scene.

The idea proved popular, not only among students but for professional artists who, though possibly adept at landscape painting, were less confident at figure work. The groupings covered immense swathes of working life and include not only figures in action but the working of all manner of agricultural and industrial equipment. The pictures provide a rich conspectus of trades and industries of the early 19th century.

In another graphic series Pyne provided an overview of Britain's coaching life: tolls and turnpikes, carts and carriages, as well as countless drivers and passengers were portrayed for use by housebound artists.

Stage-play licence

Prior to its repeal in 1968, the Act of Parliament for regulating theatres (6 & 7 Vict. c. 68, sect. 12) required that no stage play may be performed publicly in Britain without the specific permission of the Lord Chamberlain. The Act was the last in a long history of legislation covering the theatre in Britain. (Controls were imposed in the Cromwellian period, when stage plays were seen as inherently immoral; earlier they had been viewed as sources of disaffection.)

Under the Act of 1843 the text of every play was required to be submitted to the Lord Chamberlain's office for approval – and, not infrequently, censorship. Licence to perform appeared in a number of formats. In one example ('Libel', at the Playhouse, London, March 1934) it is presented as a foolscap printed sheet, perforated at its upper edge for detachment from a pad, and bearing some similarity to a 19th-century single-sheet PASSPORT. Under the royal insignia a copperplate inscription declares that 'I, the Lord Chamberlain of the King's Household… Allow the performance of a new stage play… entitled ('Libel') with the exception of all Words and passages which are specified in the endorsement of this Licence and without any further variations whatsoever'. (In this case, no endorsement is

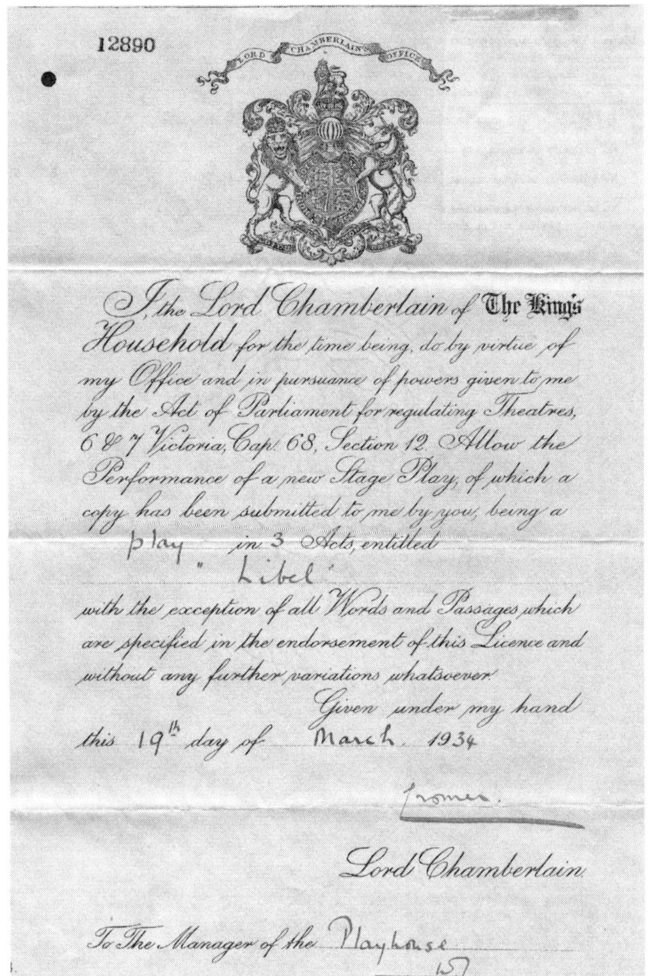

12890

LORD CHAMBERLAIN'S OFFICE

I, the Lord Chamberlain of The King's Household for the time being, do by virtue of my Office and in pursuance of powers given to me by the Act of Parliament for regulating Theatres, 6 & 7 Victoria, Cap. 68, Section 12. Allow the Performance of a new Stage Play, of which a copy has been submitted to me by you, being a play in 3 Acts, entitled "Libel" with the exception of all Words and Passages which are specified in the endorsement of this Licence and without any further variations whatsoever.

Given under my hand this 19th day of March 1934

Cromer.

Lord Chamberlain

To The Manager of the Playhouse

157

Lord Chamberlain's stage licence for 'Libel' at the Playhouse, London, 19 March 1934. Lithographed. 320 × 212 mm (12½ × 8⅜in)

present.) An attached slip adds that any alteration or addition to the play or its title must be submitted for approval, and that the licence must be forwarded to managers of theatres staging the play on tour. The licence is contained in a pre-printed envelope addressed to 'The management of the (Playhouse Theatre, Northumberland Avenue, WC2)'. It also bears the printed footline 'Lord Chamberlain', an oval rubber stamp in violet ink lettered 'Lord Chamberlain, St James's Palace', and is franked 'Official Paid'.

COLLECTIONS British Library, London; Theatre Museum, London

Stationer's label

Because of the historical combination of the trades of bookseller and stationer (often complicated by the additional roles of printer, librarian, publisher, etc.) it is difficult to place the stationer's label in a specific category of its own. To confuse the matter further, many of the larger 18th-century stationers' labels, though they have clearly been pasted in as labels, have equally clearly been conceived as TRADE CARDS. (Some are even large enough to qualify as handbills.)

Typical of the genre is an item from a Coggeshall (Essex) ratebook of the 1730s. Measuring 180 × 115 mm (7⅛ × 4½in), the label advertises the business of Charles Darby, stationer and bookseller 'at the Red Bible in the High Street, Colchester', and presents, under an illustration of an open book, a hundred-word paragraph of promotional copy. In similar style is a London label (trade card/handbill) of the same period from John

Gildersieve, stationer, 'Next to the Salutation Tavern in Lombard-Street'. Apart from a border of printers' flowers, the label is wholly verbal and reveals that Gildersieve '...Maketh and Selleth all Sorts of large books for merchants' accounts, shop-books, pocket-books &c he likewise selleth all sorts of Writing and Wrapping Paper; the Best Ink, Ink Powder, Quills, Letter Cases'. Items of this kind foreshadow the larger manufacturers' labels of the 19th and 20th centuries.

The early 19th-century stationer's label was somewhat less assertive, taking its cue perhaps (like the bookseller's label) from the reticence of the BINDER'S TICKET. Later, however, much enlarged, the stationer's label carried sometimes extensive advertising copy, including product lists, information on postage rates, and stamp-tax charges. The larger ACCOUNT-BOOK LABEL (from c.1850 to c.1914) reverts to the trade-card treatment and measures, typically, 180 × 130 mm (7⅛ × 5⅛ in). It sometimes shows an illustration of the firm's manufacturing and sale premises, a coat of arms, and other decorations, and may be printed on coloured paper with round-cut corners. This type of label is to be found on music folios and filing boxes of the period.

The stationer's label appears not only in unprinted books, but in diaries, almanacs, ruled notebooks, and on or inside the lids of quill and pen boxes, wafer boxes, and other containers.

See also BOOKSELLER'S LABEL

COLLECTION Roland Knaster Collection, Guildhall Library, London

Stationery, decorative

The term 'decorative stationery' is generally taken to refer to writing paper and envelopes bearing pre-printed or embossed ornament (as opposed to pictorial illustrations or advertising material). The genre appears to have stemmed from the decorative VISITING CARD of the 18th century, some versions of which carried framed cartouches and borders as a setting for the owner's name.

Ornamental writing paper began to appear in Europe in the latter part of the 18th century. Rare examples feature two-colour stencilled borders, but in the 19th century decoration was mainly applied in a single colour by lithographic printing, a treatment which remained current – particularly in America – into the middle of the century. Blind-embossed borders gained currency in Britain in the early 19th century. The London firm of Dobbs, possibly the greatest name in paper embossing, was at the centre of the trade, which rapidly established a popular market.

The middle and later years of the 19th century saw a huge development in the field of decorative printing. A combination of blind and colour embossing, lace-paper stamping, and chromolithography produced a tidal wave of decorative effects, which were widely exploited for VALENTINES and other GREETINGS CARDS, fancy labels, and decorative items of all kinds. Decorative stationery formed part of that development.

As with the greetings card, production of novelty writing sheets and envelopes received a fillip from the introduction of the Penny Post in 1840; and by the 1850s and 1860s manufacturers were vying with each other in the elegance and extravagance of their designs. Gold and silver embossing played a dominant role and, with the popularization of the chromolithographed SCRAP in the middle and latter years of the century, these too were added to the decorative ensemble, often as a visual title-piece in the left-hand corner of the writing sheet. This was an extension of the practice, widely successful in greetings cards and, in America, in the HIDDEN-NAME CARD.

Decorative envelope, mid 19th century. Embossed, lace-paper work, printed in gold, and hand-coloured. As shown, 127 × 143 mm (5 × 5⅝ in)

Decorative treatment was extended to virtually every form of domestic stationery, including message cards and invitations, as well as the envelope designed to go with them. By the 1880s and 1890s decorative stationery had become popular in most countries of Europe. In America, the decorative envelope appeared largely as an ingredient of the calling-card craze, cards being delivered, as in Europe, by hand in miniature covers. Writing sheets were commonly presented as a sheet folded to make four pages (the front page alone bearing decoration). Their size ranged from 280 × 210 mm (11 × 8¼ in) to 310 × 140mm (12¼ × 5½ in), and envelopes to go with them from 110 × 145mm (4⅜ × 5¾ in) to 70 × 105 mm (2¾ × 4⅛ in).

In Germany and elsewhere sales of decorative stationery, complete with pen holders and nibs, were sold in presentation boxes, the lids of which were also decorated with embossing, chromolithographs, and die-cuts.

See also EMBOSSING/LACE PAPER; WRITING PAPER, ILLUSTRATED

REFERENCES Christa Pieske, *Das ABC Des Luxuspapiers ... 1860 bis 1930* (Berlin: Dietrich Reimer Verlag, 1983); Frank Staff, *The Picture Postcard and its Origins*, 2nd edn (London: Lutterworth, 1979)

Stencil

The stencil has been used as a designer's aid since earliest times. Use of the word 'Stanesile' in multiple production is first recorded (OED) in 1707 in connection with the production of PLAYING CARDS, but it must be assumed to have been used for this purpose for some centuries before that date. Early cards were individually hand-painted, but in the 14th and 15th centuries they were printed in black from woodcut blocks with stencilling providing colour, both for numeral cards and for pictorial court cards.

The stencil also appears as a manufacturing aid in the porcelain industry, and in the production of books, wallpaper, and textiles. In the first half of the 19th century it was widely used by house painters and decorators as an alternative to patterned wallpapers, the designs being stencilled directly on to painted walls. It was also widely used in the hand-colouring of popular prints, often on a production-line basis, with prints passing from one operator to another for successive stencilling.

Stencilled book label, first half of 19th century. 75 × 117mm (3 × 4⅝in)

Later applications of the stencil idea include silk-screen printing, production of vitreous-enamel notices, typewriter duplicating, and multi-addressing systems. It survives in crate and bale marking, and in notices and signing. Stencilled wall notices, forerunners of modern stencilled graffiti, are mentioned in George Sala's *Dutch Pictures* (1861).

The metal-foil stencil, commonly of copper, and already well developed technically in France by the mid 18th century, was in use on stationery from the early years of the 19th century. It was provided in single word or letter units or as custom-made legends for specific purposes. Its use is occasionally seen on the VISITING CARD, TRADE CARD, and library BOOK LABEL. In alphabet versions the stencil might provide a single letter to a plate or a complete alphabet on one plate. A typical whole-alphabet example, produced in Germany in the 1860s, presents a two-plate set packed in a paper folded to 45 × 105mm (1¾ × 4⅛in).

Typical of special-purpose sets were 'Old English' words and phrases produced for solicitors. These offered a wide range of legal key-words for interpolation in hand-engrossed documents. One such set, sold by Shaw & Sons of London and available until the early part of the 20th century, provided thirty-six plates, including ones for 'Whereas', 'This is the Last Will and Testament', and 'Now this Indenture Witnesseth'. The sets were available in three sizes and were supplied in a tin stencil box, with ink and brush.

The most common use of the custom-made stencil was for personal or commercial name and address plates. In the American Civil War soldiers of both North and South carried their own stencils for use in marking clothing and equipment. They were normally made of brass and generally measured some 40 × 80mm (1$\frac{9}{16}$ × 3⅛in), though larger examples, some measuring as much as 50 × 140mm (2 × 5½in), are known. The plate bore the holder's name, company, and regiment and, in the case of a casualty, often served as an identity tag.

Stencils were commonly prepared by etching with acid, but they were also produced by punching with dies. Punching had the disadvantage of cockling the plate, making it less accurate in use, but it was popular as a do-it-yourself method, and in some areas generated a minor cottage industry. With only a small outlay for a set of alphabet dies, stencil cutters could offer trade cards and other small items at prices competitive with printing. A full set of dies contained not only letters and figures but various decorative motifs, as well as small curves and dashes from which the imaginative stenciller could compose pictorial images appropriate to a client's business.

See also TOY THEATRE

REFERENCE Eva Judd O'Meara, 'Notes on stencilled choir-books', *Gutenberg Jahrbuch*, 1933, pp. 169–185

Stereotype

Stereotype (Greek, *stereos:* solid; *typos:* type) is the process of making copies of a relief printing surface, such as a page of metal type or a wood block, by casting. Various methods have been used, all of which result in a solid metal printing plate. Before the introduction of casting and composing machinery in the 19th century, type was expensive and most printers could only afford to hold it in limited quantities. There were obvious advantages, therefore, particularly for the printer of popular books, in printing from casts made from typeset pages. These advantages can be summarized as follows: after stereotyping, type could be distributed into cases, unworn and ready for further use; replicas of pages of type could be put on several presses to increase speed of output; and stereotype plates were more convenient to store and reuse than formes of type.

Stereotyping has a long and obscure history, though the word 'stereotype' (now more commonly applied figuratively to mean anything constantly repeated without change) was not in use until the early 19th century. There are records of the process being used in the Netherlands from the late 17th century, and it was also practised in the 18th century by, among others, William Ged, Alexander Tilloch, and Andrew Foulis (in Britain), and Pierre and Firmin Didot (in France). The methods used varied, but one approach was to make moulds from plaster or sand, and then take casts by pouring molten metal into them. This particular method was advanced commercially by Charles Stanhope and Andrew Wilson in Britain in the very early years of the 19th century, and by the 1820s was being widely practised.

The plaster method began to be replaced in the 1830s by a faster and cleaner one that took up an earlier idea of using papier mâché to make the mould. Damped papier mâché was laid on to the surface of the type and forced against it, the deepest and smallest hollows being formed by beating the papier mâché with a stiff brush. The resulting 'flong' was then placed in a casting box and molten metal poured over it (as in the plaster method) to form a cast. The plate was later mounted type high for letterpress printing. This method proved to have a significant advantage over others in that the flong could be curved, thus producing plates that could be wrapped around cylinders. This technique prepared the way for the introduction of fast rotary presses for newspaper production in both Britain and America in the1860s.

Similar techniques were used for replicating blocks used in WOOD-ENGRAVING, but copies of wood blocks were mainly made by a process known variously as 'clichage', 'polytypage', and taking 'dabs'. This process was developed in the 18th century, when it was also used for replicating pages of text and, later, ASSIGNATS. It involved dropping or striking a relief block face down on to metal that was sufficiently molten to form a mould. Metal with a higher melting point than that of the mould was then poured into it to form a duplicate printing surface. From the late 18th century typefounders supplied printers with a range of pictures and ornaments produced by such means (*see* STOCK BLOCK); from the 1820s a few wood-engravers also offered such replicas of their work.

Stereotyping made pictorial and decorative images much more available to printers and helped to bring about the proliferation of illustrations in advertising, packaging, trade catalogues, and magazines in the 19th century. From the middle of the century the stereotype was superseded for high quality illustrative work by the ELECTROTYPE. Curved stereotyped plates continued to be used for newspaper production, however, until it changed from letterpress to photolithography after World War II (and in Britain not until the 1970s). [MA]

REFERENCES Horace Hart, *Charles Earl Stanhope and the Oxford University Press*, reprinted from *Collectanea*, III, 1896, with notes by James Mosley (London: Printing Historical Society, 1966); G. A. Kubler, *Historical Treatises, Abstracts & Papers on Stereotyping* (New York, 1936); G. A. Kubler, *A New History of Stereotyping* (New York, 1941); Michael Turner, 'Andrew Wilson: Lord Stanhope's Stereotype Printer', *Journal of the Printing Historical Society*, no. 9, 1973/4, pp. 22–65

Stevengraph *See* SILK

Sticker

Prior to 1880, when gum-coated paper was introduced as a generally available commercial product, the adhesive on most stickers and labels – and many postage stamps – was applied with brush and paste. The first ready-gummed postage stamps for general use, coated with glutinous 'cement', appeared in 1840 in Britain and 1842 in America; gummed envelopes in 1850.

Initially gummed stickers were used mainly in the office and for labelling packages, but their susceptibility to changes in temperature and humidity caused difficulty. They tended to curl unmanageably or to stick to each other in solid blocks. Non-curling gummed paper (in which the coating was broken into fine particles by flexing the paper over two blades) was introduced in 1905. The introduction of polyvinyl alcohol coating after World War II further enhanced resistance to curl and 'blocking' as did 'particle coating' in 1962. These developments made application of the sticker much easier, but it was the introduction of pressure-sensitive stickers (which, unlike paper, adhered readily to the rapidly increasing range of plastic products) that brought the sticker into universal use.

Early office uses included erratum slips, change-of-address labels, filing labels, outstanding account reminders, stationery stickers, address labels and envelope reuse labels. Other forms were school bookplates, circulating library book labels, stamp-album page titles, hotel baggage labels, and pharmaceutical labels. Self-adhesive stickers, first produced by Stanton Avery, in Los Angeles in 1935, extended the range to FLAGDAY EMBLEMS, conference lapel stickers, garment tags, supermarket price stickers, FRUIT/VEGETABLE STICKERS, cassette labels, slide numerals, personal address labels, shop-window stickers, windscreen and BUMPER STICKERS, and general propaganda stickers.

In the late 1960s and 1970s, gummed or otherwise, the propaganda sticker emerged as a familiar feature of the urban scene. The 'mini-poster', often barely larger than a postage stamp, became the medium of minority expression. It was affixed to lamp posts and other street furniture and appeared at strategic points on billboards – sometimes as comments on the larger work: 'this advert degrades women'; sometimes as a generalized injunction: 'Do something positive today to overthrow the system'.

See also BAGGAGE STICKER; COIN DISC/STICKER; LABEL

Stock block

The stock block (US: stock cut) showing generalized images as opposed to specific illustrations, has a history almost as old as printing itself. From earliest times printers have produced blocks with a life extending beyond a single one-purpose use, and indeed repeated use of blocks, without over-much concern for textual relevance, is a feature not only of early printing but of popular literature of later periods.

The true stock block, expressly designed for repeated use, may be said to stem from the large pictorial initial used at the opening of passages of text. Hand-cut in wood, or cast in metal, some versions had a space at the centre to take the first letter of the opening word of the passage. In this form it was known, appropriately, as a factotum (Latin: general purpose). The factotum remained in common use (for example in newspapers) throughout the 18th century, and in Acts of Parliament and other such documents, into the 19th century.

Also a feature of 18th-century newspapers, and said to have been introduced by Benjamin Franklin in his *Pennsylvania Gazette,* was the pictorial 'slug' for use in small advertisement columns as a visual index of subject matter. These slugs, occupying a depth of three or four lines of text, depicted sailing ships, stage coaches, houses for sale, and, in America, runaway slaves. Later came steamships, locomotives, and passenger and goods wagons in separate units (so that trains could be created of any desired length).

By the end of the 18th century typefounders were advertising a range of stock blocks in their specimen books. The original masters were engraved on wood; the stock blocks made from them were produced by striking the wood master into molten metal as it was cooling and then taking casts in type metal from these hollow forms. Other stock images took the form of STEREOTYPE and ELECTROTYPE blocks. As the 19th century progressed, a vast repertoire of such ready-made images became available from typefounders, most of them remaining in use long after their style was superseded.

The availability of stock blocks meant that the jobbing printer was able to increase his repertoire of images considerably to meet the needs of posters, handbills, billheads, and other general ephemera. Stock images available in the early 19th century included – as well as ships, coaches, and trains – horse-race scenes, stallions, motifs for bills of lading, almanac and calendar headings, and an extensive range of other trade and business symbols, some of them incorporating printed panels for insertion of the tradesman's name. Designs were widely copied. Many achieved a more or less fixed rendering, and were perpetuated by successive apprentice engravers.

In later years designs began to be updated. Sail gave way to steam, the horse to the automobile, the bicycle appeared, and shortly afterwards the aeroplane. The range of activity depicted became so great, and the styles and fashions so noticeably transient, that updating became more specific and more frequent. However, images remained unchanged in one or two restricted areas. In Britain, the butcher's billhead stock block, showing a bull's head or a group of sheep, survived in the late 20th century in virtually the same rendering as its Victorian forerunner.

By the end of the 19th century, with the advent of photomechanical processes, the stock-block business had become a major operation. Process engraving firms produced not only stock designs but in some cases stock photographic half-tones.

A 36-page catalogue put out by Garratt & Atkinson in the 1920s showed some 350 separate items for use in laundry advertising alone, over fifty of which were specially posed photographs of housewives admiring freshly delivered linen. The stock-block principle continued in the form of dry transfer and, later, computer 'clip art'.

See also FLY-WAGON BILL; STREET LITERATURE; STUD CARD/NOTICE

Stock poster

Stock posters – pictorial posters available from stock for overprinting with an advertiser's own wording – had a considerable vogue in the period 1870 to 1914. They provided the smaller advertiser with highly coloured designs in quantities below the normal threshold of economic production. Subject matter was geared to the activities and interests of the day. Emphasis was put on neighbourhood festivals; agricultural and horse shows; gymkhanas; fêtes and galas; bazaars and fun fairs; athletic events; dog, cat, pigeon, and poultry shows; firework displays; boxing, cycling and swimming events; brass band festivals; fire brigade displays; and theatrical performances. Also available were posters for ballooning events, parachute descents, and, in the latter years of the period, flying.

Posters ranged in size from 'crown', 508 × 381 mm (20 × 15 in), to 18-sheet 'double crown', 3048 × 2286 mm (120 × 90 in), and were available by the hundred for overprinting either by the supplier or by local printers.

Stafford & Co. Ltd, of Netherfield, Nottinghamshire, provided a selection of hundreds of different designs, together with 'slips' for pasting on them lettered: 'Tonight', 'Last night', 'Matinée', etc. They also produced general slips such as: 'To the show', 'This way', 'Gentlemen', 'Ladies only', 'To the band contest', 'No betting allowed'. Similarly, David Allen & Sons of Belfast, Manchester, and London offered over 700 examples of off-the-peg lithographic posters for theatrical and similar performances, together with a range of letterpress slips, in their catalogue for 1900. Other companies also specialized in the production of theatrical posters – also showing subjects of generalized application – for overprinting with titles, venues, and other details. Many of these posters are said to have occasioned changes in the action of plays they advertised, adjustments being made to accord with the detail of the episode depicted. Stock posters of this kind became increasingly lurid, and were eventually to attract the attention of the censorship committee of the British Poster Advertising Association.

Stock posters appeared in America too, though less commonly. The Calvert Litho Co. of Detroit produced them, as did the Russell-Morgan Printing Co. of Cincinnati and, in small measure, CURRIER & IVES. Subjects, as in Britain, were agricultural and other events, and to a modest degree 'Party girl' pictures, which served as vehicles for product advertisements.

See also POSTER

Street literature

Street literature is the term applied to primitive printed matter sold in the open air by hawkers rather than through orthodox publishing channels. Its sale was often accompanied by the crying-out of the text ('pattering' or 'chaunting'), and its literary level was robustly popular. Much of it originated in London in the area of Seven Dials. James Catnach, of Monmouth Court, was among its best-known exponents in Britain.

Haphazardly printed and spattered with typographic and grammatical improvisations, the publications were composed by a small coterie of 'authors' whose fee for each original work was reported to be one shilling (Hindley, 1871). Illustrations were produced by the printer from secondhand wood blocks, often bearing no relation to the subject matter. Exceptions were the illustrations of Newgate hangings, which were printed from standard blocks in which the details of the figures on the scaffold could be changed according to the number and sex of the malefactors named in the text. Murder scenes, as well as condemned-cell set-pieces, also did general service.

Hindley enumerates several distinct categories of the genre: 'Cock' or 'Catchpenny', 'Broadside, royalty and political', 'Street ballad', and 'Gallows literature'.

The **cock** is distinguished from its fellows by the element of pure fiction. Whereas the broadside, the ballad, and gallows literature may have been broadly founded on fact, the cock was wholly imaginative. Its objective was to incorporate as many scandalous and sensational elements as possible, at the same time suggesting that the story referred to people in the reader's own neighbourhood. Typical titles are 'Shocking Rape and Murder of Two Lovers', 'The Love Letter, The Lady's Maid!! The Secret Found Out!!! Or A Married Man Caught in a Trap', and 'The Secrets Revealed, or the Fashionable Life of Lord and Lady – who reside not one hundred miles from this neighbourhood'.

The **catchpenny** is of a slightly different stamp, and relied specifically for its appeal on a trick of headline. A classic example is Catnach's exploitation of continuing interest in the murder of William Weare in 1823, even after his murderer, John Thurtell, had been executed. Catnach published a paper, actually dealing with his own publishing activities, but headed 'We are alive again'. Leaving little or no space between the first and second words, he conveyed to the incautious a sensational headline. The item sold well. It earned a name – 'catchpenny' – which came to be applied to productions of this kind at large.

The **broadside, royalty, and political** category consists of satirical doggerel, irreverent addresses, political squibs, 'litanies', and 'catechisms'. Subjects include every topic of the day, including royal births and marriages, reform, rights of women, the Irish question, adulteration of food, the Poor Law, and the Sunday Trading bill.

Ballads (more formally 'Ballads on a subject') were written wholly in doggerel. Set to a more or less popular tune, they celebrated a specific item of topical interest. Typical titles are: 'Terrible Accident On The Ice in Regent's Park, and Loss of Forty Lives', 'The Naughty Lord and the Gay Young Lady', 'Funny Doings in the Convent', and 'The Suppression of Crinoline'.

They were written and printed at great speed, their sales potential depending as much on topicality as on any other merit. It is reported that in a court case in which a barman was convicted of robbing his master, the prisoner was found on arrival in gaol to be a woman. At 10 am on the following day the story was being sold on the streets under the title 'She/He Barman of Southwark'.

Though the 1820s to 1880s may be viewed as the heyday of the ballad sheet, the genre dates back at least to the mid 16th century. The Pepys collection at Magdalene College, Cambridge has many hundreds of examples from the 16th and 17th centuries, many of them virtually indistinguishable in style (apart from their black-letter typeface) from those of Catnach and his contemporaries.

Gallows literature reported public executions and alleged dying speeches and confessions. Also appended in many cases was 'a copy of verses' written by the author of the report or ostensibly by the condemned man in his cell. 'Execution ballads' were the most successful of all street literature. The murder of Maria Marten (1828) was said to have generated sales of over a million; those of Lord William Russell (1840) and Hannah Brown (1840) over 1.5 million each; and those of Patrick O'Connor (1849) and the Jermy's (1849) 2.5 million.

Street literature in general was ultimately to give way to its rapidly developing competitor, the popular press. For a long time, however, street literature held the advantage; where such items as hangings were concerned Catnach and his friends consistently 'scooped' the press by printing in advance of the happening. It was said that no sooner had the trap door opened beneath the malefactor than the broadside sellers began to shout their full account, last dying speech and all. While much of the general street literature industry centred on London, with a considerable 'export' trade to the provinces, gallows literature was produced by printers all over the country. John Harkness of Preston did a lively trade, as did printers in Brighton, Carlisle, Chester, Lincoln, and Portsmouth.

The study of street ephemera casts light on many aspects of social history, but exposes an apparent paradox. There is a vast body of evidence to indicate the popularity of such items, even from the relatively early days of printing; there is also much evidence to show that the majority of the population, at least until the beginning of the 19th century, was more or less illiterate.

See also BALLAD; BELLMAN'S VERSES; BROADSIDE/BROADSHEET; EXECUTION BROADSIDE; PANORAMA, ENTERTAINMENT

REFERENCES Charles Hindley, *Curiosities of Street Literature* (London: Reeves & Turner, 1871); Louis James, *Print and the People 1819–1851* (London: Allen Lane, 1976); Henry Mayhew, *London Labour and the London Poor*, 4 vol. (London: G. Woodfall and Son, 1851–62); Sheila O'Connell, *The Popular Print in England* (London: British Museum Press, 1999); Victor E. Neuburg, *Popular Literature* (Harmondsworth: Penguin, 1977)

COLLECTIONS John Johnson Collection, Bodleian Library, Oxford; Pepys Library, Magdalene College, Cambridge

Street view

John Tallis's series of street elevations, showing detailed renderings of buildings in London's major thoroughfares, provides a unique record of the London of the 1830s. The views were issued in eighty-eight parts between 1838 and 1840. Each part had an outer title wrapper printed on tinted paper, with advertisements on inside front and back covers; a four-page interior spread containing advertisements and directory information; and, as a centre-spread, a display showing two lengths of a given street, each length showing elevations of both sides. The views were flanked at one end by an illustration of a shop or other building in the street and at the other by a map of the immediate area. The opened centre-spread measured 135 × 440 mm (5¼ × 17⅜ in), the trimmed folded size (with slightly oversize wrapper) being 140 × 225 mm (5½ × 8⅞ in). In a second series of eighteen views, published in 1847 at 3*d* each, the trimmed folded size was 200 × 275 mm (7⅞ × 10¾ in).

In addition to the novelty of the style of their presentation, Tallis's street views represent an innovation in advertising. As well as naming public buildings, Tallis captioned many of the numbered building elevations with the title and designation of their shopkeeper occupants – a distinction for which Tallis made an appropriate charge. The flanking illustrations on each spread also produced advertising revenue; each picture was a detailed representation of a specific shop, suitably named on sign and fascia boards. It was the revenue from advertisers that allowed Tallis to publish at 1½*d* (occasionally 2*d*) per issue, and still make a profit.

The views offer an informative but fragmentary record of London. In the nature of the operation, Tallis's choice of streets was governed by the presence of potential advertisers; coverage is thus patchy. Nevertheless, Tallis's street views are among the rarest of London ephemera: few collections, public or private, contain the complete series.

REFERENCE Peter Jackson (ed.), *John Tallis's London Street Views 1838–1840* (London: Nattali & Maurice in association with London Topographical Society, 1969)

COLLECTION Guildhall Library, London

Stud card/notice

A printed announcement was circulated to owners of horses in a particular district indicating that a named stud horse would be available to serve mares during a given season. The card extolled the merits of the horse in question, citing his antecedents, progeny, and prize-winnings, sometimes at considerable length, and quoting fees for each service. Fees were commonly quoted with an additional small sum (usually about five per cent of the main fee) for the attendant groom. The card often indicated where and when the animal would be available and – where mares were to be brought to the horse – offered grazing at a nominal sum per night. One Tadcaster owner stipulated 'no business done on Sunday'.

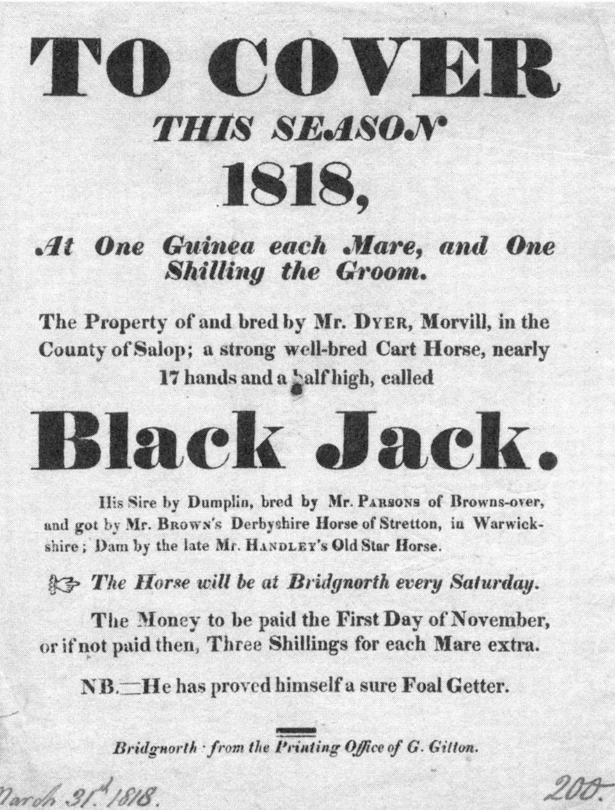

TO COVER

THIS SEASON

1818,

At One Guinea each Mare, and One Shilling the Groom.

The Property of and bred by Mr. DYER, Morvill, in the County of Salop; a strong well-bred Cart Horse, nearly 17 hands and a half high, called

Black Jack.

His Sire by Dumplin, bred by Mr. PARSONS of Browns-over, and got by Mr. BROWN's Derbyshire Horse of Stretton, in Warwickshire; Dam by the late Mr. HANDLEY's Old Star Horse.

The Horse will be at Bridgnorth every Saturday.

The Money to be paid the First Day of November, or if not paid then, Three Shillings for each Mare extra.

N.B.—He has proved himself a sure Foal Getter.

Bridgnorth: from the Printing Office of G. Gitton.

March 31st 1818. 200

Stud notice, Bridgenorth, 1818. Letterpress, printed by G. Gitton, Bridgnorth, with manuscript note that 200 copies were printed. 240 × 187 mm (9½ × 7½ in)

Announcements of the same kind appeared in respect of cattle; services of prize-winning bulls being offered on similar (though less costly) terms.

British stud cards were normally printed in black, and measured not more than 165 × 115 mm (6½ × 4½ in). As with many other examples of 19th-century ephemera the use of the word 'card' was often misleading. A stud 'card' might also be printed on paper and extend to the size of a small public notice and measure 300 × 200 mm (11⅞ × 7⅞ in) or more. Large stud notices, and to a lesser extent smaller stud cards, featured STOCK BLOCKS (or crude wood-engravings based on them) of a stallion with or without a groom. Several stock blocks appear over and over again, both within one printer's output and more generally throughout the country. Some of them became exemplars for local wood-engravers to copy and established a clear identity for the genre.

In America a poster format was commonly used, often with a large woodcut or stock block, decorative border, and displayed text matter. Typical dimensions are 450 × 300 mm (17¾ × 11⅞ in), but specimens twice this size are also found.

COLLECTIONS Rural History Centre, The University of Reading; Reading University Library

Sugar leaf

Commodity shortages in Britain in World War I led to the marketing of a number of substitutes, among them sweetening agents for use in tea, coffee, etc. In a surviving example, a sweetener is presented in the form of impregnated paper, perforated in the manner of postage stamps and bound into a small booklet for the pocket or handbag. The stamp-sized portions are white, unprinted, and intended for immersion in the beverage: 'The paper is harmless and will adhere to the cup… the composition of the sugar substitute is of such a character that the food value of sugar is equalled…'. The product bears the cover title 'Sweetleaf' and was manufactured under a provisional patent by Handoleaf, 104 High Holborn, London WC1.

Summons

In general terms a summons is a document directing a named person to appear at a given time and place for a specific judicial purpose.

In the ordinary sense of the word a summons requires the recipient to attend a magistrate's court 'to answer an information or complaint' laid by a third party. It is issued in the case of less serious matters and differs from a WARRANT for arrest chiefly in requiring attendance at a future date, as opposed to empowering immediate apprehension.

The word summons ('an authoritative call') appears in a legal sense in the earliest years of British constitutional history; it may refer to a command to the Great Barons at the time of Magna Carta, to feudal tenantry to meet to approve extra measures of taxation, to individuals to attend parliament, or to parliament as a body to sit. In modern times, it appears as calls to individuals to serve on juries, to attend as witnesses in Coroners', Magistrates', and County Courts; it is also used in specialized senses in High Court proceedings. In this last case, the summons is issued on behalf of the parties to the action, not by an outside agency.

The wording of the Justice of the Peace Summons has changed little since the 17th century, though early summonses were directed not to the person who had to appear but to the Constable, who was required to transmit the summons and to attend court on the appointed day 'to certify what we shall have done in the premises'. A further form of summons required the attendance of a witness for examination in a proceeding.

A jury summons ('You are hereby summoned to appear…') was, and remains, a printed form bearing space for the insertion of the name and address of the recipient. A coroner's summons was normally addressed directly to the person required as a witness: 'Whereas, being credibly informed you can give Evidence touching the Death of (—) now lying Dead in the Parish of St Mary-le-Bone…'. It was a traditional characteristic of these and other summonses, as in the writ and warrant, to conclude with the words 'hereof fail not' or 'hereof fail not, as you will answer the contrary at your Peril'. The format, layout, and typography of the summons were infinitely varied.

A Justice of the Peace summons, 185 × 230 mm (7¼ × 9 in), issued at Easingwold, North Yorkshire in 1862, addressed to Robert Wright of the Township of Stearsby, reads:

> 'Whereas… complaint hath this Day been made before the undersigned, one of Her Majesty's Justices of the Peace… that you (the said Robert Wright, being the duly hired servant in husbandry of Robert Cattley of the Township of Stearsby… to serve him until Martinmas next and having entered into such service have been guilty of misconduct and misbehaviour and especially did refuse to obey the lawful orders of your said master) these are therefore to command you, in Her Majesty's Name, to be and appear on (Friday) the (29th) day of (August inst) at Eleven o'Clock in the Forenoon at the (Magistrate's Clerk's Office)… to be dealt with according to Law.

In another example, from Great Yarmouth in 1896, the part-printed summons form relates specifically to one form of offence:

> To (George Lawson, St Peter's Road, tobacconist): Information has been laid before me this day by William Parker, of Great Yarmouth… Chief Constable, for that you on the (30th) Day of (August) in the year of our Lord one thousand eight hundred and ninety (six)… the same being the Lord's Day, commonly called Sunday and you being then a (tobacconist) and above the age of fourteen years, did unlawfuly do and exercise certain worldly labour, business and work in your ordinary calling of a tobacconist… the same not being a work of charity… you are therefore hereby summoned to appear…'.

tag label
tall-tale postcard
tax abstract
tax stamp
taxation papers
telegram/telegram form
telephone card
telephone directory
temperance papers
testimonial
textile label
thaumatrope
theatre programme
theatre ticket
thread paper
ticket
timetable
tinsel print
tithe papers
title-page
tobacco paper
toll/ferry rate-list
toll/turnpike ticket
touring map
toy book
toy theatre
trade advertiser
trade card
trade label
trade list
trade rhyme
trade union membership certificate
tramping card
transfer lithography
transparency
transportation papers (penal)
travellers' guide
trompe-l'oeil announcement
Tyburn ticket
typographica

Tag label

The tag label, eyeletted and strung for attachment, is as remarkable for the universality of its basic concept as for its multiplicity of application. Its structure, virtually unchanged for generations, derives from its function. Cropped corners at the attachment end minimize fouling of the tag on the object it is tied to; reinforcement of the string hole by a 'collar' of stronger material, card, paper, metal, or plastic reduces the risk of tearing; the classic threading of the cord in which the free ends are passed through a loop, after insertion in the hole, provides a quick, foolproof method of attachment. Like the wheel and the candle, the tag label appears to have emerged as a fully developed innovation.

It is used in virtually every country in the world to identify baggage, mail bags, parcels, bankers' coin bags, toy racing balloons, delivery notes, anatomical specimens, courtroom evidence, antiques, bundles for charity, racing-pigeon baskets, auction lots, postal packages, archaeological finds, game baskets, laundry boxes, and in a vast range of other everyday contexts. In time of war the tag label is used on cadavers, stretcher cases, wounded men's possessions, air-raid casualties, and child evacuees.

It is the precursor of the ubiquitous PRICE TAG/TICKET of the garment and other trades and appears in modified form as a tie-on label badge for identification at numerous out-door functions (*see* ENCLOSURE BADGE).

In one field, that of air travel, the tag label has largely given way to the self-adhesive rigid tag, which is quickly looped and sealed around baggage handles.

Book of railway tag labels for cyclists, early 20th century. The tags printed letterpress on manila card. 60 × 110 mm (2⅜ × 4⅜ in)

Tall-tale postcard

Known originally as 'freak' postcards, America's tall-tale cards were a visual version of the classic angler's tale. Using 'trick' photography (most of it transparently naïve) they commonly featured a fantasy world of outsize rural produce. Typically, farmers load a single monster potato on a wagon; a grower climbs a step ladder to a cotton plant; and a fisherman flees as a whale-size perch pursues him up the shore. The theme was constant and included claims to world records and such captions as: 'This is the way they come in these parts' and 'A fair crop this season'.

Tall-tale postcard, copyright by Edward H. Mitchell, San Francisco, with copy line 'I'm sending you a lemon from...'. Relief-printed from half-tone block with added colour workings. 87 × 138 mm (3⅜ × 5½ in)

The black-and-white cards had a vogue in America in the period 1905 to 1915, most of them emanating from the Great Plains, the huge agricultural area bordered by the Appalachians and the Rockies. They are thought by some to express the unfulfilled dreams of settlers who had been offered a land of promise and plenty, and had in fact found little or nothing. Printed in large quantities, the cards were overprinted for sale in specific localities: 'How we do things at Omaha, NEB'; 'The first one I landed in Jackson, Mich', etc.

Among a dozen or so principal practitioners were George B. Cornish; M. W. Bailey; William Martin; F. D. Conard (Kansas); M. L. Oakes (Washington); Archer King (Nebraska); and Alfred Stanley Johnson (Wisconsin). The genre became more or less extinct between World Wars I and II, though one or two full-colour examples appeared in the 1970s, notably those of Mike Roberts of Berkeley, California.

REFERENCE Roger L. Welsch, *Tall-Tale Postcards: A Pictorial History* (South Brunswick: A. S. Barnes, 1976)

Tax abstract

The 1820s in Britain saw the private publication of summaries of taxation rates for the use of solicitors, accountants, and the general public. One example was headed and laid out in the manner of a news-sheet measuring 645 × 455 mm (25½ × 18 in). Having first appeared in April 1823, it continued to be published regularly for some years.

The first issue was priced at 'One shilling... On Paste-board Two Shillings'. Its similarity to a newspaper was clearly intentional. The information it bore was presented as news; the title 'Walwyn's Original' was adorned with the royal coat of arms and its five columns dealt with New reduced taxes, Marriage Act repeal, House and window duty, Reduced horse duty, and Stamp duties.

Included within these sections is news of reduced duties, extensions of duties on licences which it had been intended to discontinue, and adjustments to taxes. The adjustments relate to armorial bearings; production of ale, beer, cider and perry; auctioneers; brewers; candles; coffee, tea, cocoa, nuts, and chocolate; gold and silver plate; hides and skins; and so forth. Mentioned elsewhere is an extensive range of products and services, including windows, horses, stage coaches, game certificates, carriages, apprenticeships or clerkship indentures, mortgages, and letters of administration.

Tax stamp

In Britain, the use of pre-stamped papers for fiscal purposes dates from the Stamp Duty Act (5 & 6 William & Mary, c. 21) of 1694. The principle, subsequently applied to a wide range of taxation, provides that documents embodying a taxable transaction should be stamped before anything is written or printed on them. Blank papers and parchments were supplied ready-stamped by the Stamp Office or brought to the Stamp Office by lawyers, stationers, etc. for stamping. In the case of ready-stamped papers a charge was made (by way of taxation) for the stamp itself; there was a separate additional charge to cover the cost of the paper. In the case of paper brought for stamping, the charge was for stamping only.

The word 'stamp' has undergone a change since its 17th-century application. Initially, the word referred to an applied impression, whether inked or 'blind'; later, it referred to a separate piece of paper which, bearing an impression, is affixed to a document, thus 'stamping' it (*see* CYPHER LABEL). Tax stamps, affixed or directly applied, are to be found on documents of great variety, including indentures, passports, leases, insurance policies, almanacs, licences, patents, bonds, letters of administration, playing cards, hair-powder tax labels, agreements, Newgate pardons, university degrees, mortgages, naturalization papers, and many others. Most such stamps bear the amount of the tax in words, expressed either as a sum or as a percentage; many also indicate the subject of the tax: 'Dog licence', 'Copyright of design', 'Consular Service', etc. A number of British tax stamps remained in use at the close of the 20th century. The embossed tax stamp on cheques, one of the most widely known in the 20th century, was abolished in Britain in 1971.

The list of items at one time or another subject to tax is long and varied. Initially the government derived revenue from beer, ale, wine, tobacco, raisins, currants, loaf sugar, cloth of gold and silver, and damask table linen. In 1797 the list included auctions, bricks, glass, hops, licences, malt, paper, soap, spirits, vinegar, starch, stone bottles, sweets and mead, tea, tiles, coconuts and cocoa, pepper, tobacco and snuff, coaches, salt, wire, candles, cyder and perry, hides and skins, and 'printed goods'. Some of these taxes are briefly referred to below.

Almanac/calendar. Payment of this tax, imposed in Britain from 1711 to 1834, was recorded on the title-page of ALMANACS and 'calendar books' as a printed device showing a central disc and crown (superimposed on crossed sceptres, rose and thistle emblems), the word 'almanac[k]', the year, and the amount of the tax in words.

The tax was high: the publisher of a 48-page almanac, 175 × 115 mm (6⅞ × 4½ in), was obliged to pay one shilling of its cover price of one shilling and tenpence in tax. As with the newspaper duty stamp, initiated a year later, the stamp was pre-printed in red by the Stamp Office on paper brought there by the publisher.

Banknote duty. *See* BANKNOTE-DUTY STAMP

Dice duty. *See* DICE-DUTY WRAPPER

Glove tax. The subject of a duty in Britain from 1785 to 1794, gloves and mittens were sold with a Stamp Office tax label inside the right-hand of every pair sold. The tax varied with the selling price. Labels were copperplate engraved in the style of other tax stamps (hair powder, perfume, etc., and measured approximately 23 × 35 mm (⅞ × 1⅜ in). The tax was widely evaded and produced, at best, a negligible yield.

Hair-powder duty. Britain taxed hair powder during the period 1786 to 1869. Initially, only the powder itself was taxed, but in 1795 users of powder were obliged to register and to acquire a licence at the cost of a guinea per year. Labels, engraved by the

Hair Powder Annual Duty, 1800.

STAMP OFFICE

CERTIFICATE.

For the Year 1800

No 13

April 16,

1800.

Office

District

This Certificate will expire on the fifth Day of April 1801.

Certificate of payment of hair-powder duty for 1800. Letterpress and manuscript, printed in red by Mount & Davidson, London. 150 × 197 mm (6 × 7¾ in)

Hair-powder tax stamp, c. 1800. Intaglio-printed in red. 28 × 59 mm (1⅛ × 2¼ in)

Stamp Office in the style of glove and other tax labels of the period, and measuring 25 × 57 mm (1 × 2⅛ in), were used to seal packets. The rate of the tax was one penny per pound weight for powder costing not more than two shillings a pound.

Hat duty. *See* HAT-DUTY STAMP

Match tax. *See* MATCH-TAX STAMP

Medicine tax. Initially designed as a tax on quack medicines (*see* QUACK ADVERTISING), Britain's Medicine Stamp Act came into force in 1783 and survived in various modified forms until 1941. It met with much opposition at first, but later came to be viewed by patent medicine vendors as a sales advantage. The presence of an official label on the package was thought to imply government approval. So much did this impression gain ground that in 1885 stamps began to carry the disclaimer: 'This stamp implies no government guarantee' or simply 'No government guarantee'. Nevertheless, the position remained ambiguous; in spite of such disclaimers the impression remained that the product had received official recognition. The matter was further complicated by the inclusion of the manufacturer's product name in the government-printed label: 'Mrs Winslow's Soothing Syrup', 'Thos Allcock & Co Porous Plaster'; later 'Zam-Buk-Rubitin' appeared as an integral part of the design of a Stamp Office or Inland Revenue Stamp label.

British excise stamps (at first cruciform, for use in sealing medicine bottle corks) were originally engraved on copper, but in 1823 they began to be produced by Congreve's COMPOUND-PLATE PRINTING process at Somerset House. The Congreve process, with its 'forgery-proof' two- and three-colour patterns, enhanced the impression of authority conveyed by the labels. Standard sizes were 25 × 105 mm (1 × 4⅛ in) and 30 × 135 mm (1³⁄₁₆ × 5¼ in).

The tax was widely evaded and gave rise to many counterfeits, despite the penalty of death for forgers. Among many malpractices was the export of used British bottles to America, where they were filled with a variety of fluids and labelled and sealed with counterfeit British tax labels. Such counterfeits are today prized by collectors.

American medicine-tax stamps were introduced by the Union as part of a major taxation operation to pay for the Civil War. The law governing them, passed in 1862, covered, among other things, proprietary articles such as pills, powders, tinctures, lozenges, bitters, and also extended to perfumery and cosmetics. The first stamps issued within the Act were produced by Butler and Carpenter, but in 1875 the National Banknote Co. of New York took over the contract, continuing with it as the American Banknote Co. (after amalgamation with the Continental Bank Note Co.), relinquishing it to the Bureau of Engraving and Printing in 1880.

As in Britain, provision was made (1863) for inclusion of the trade name etc., and brand proprietors were licensed to commission their own government-approved designs direct from Butler and Carpenter. This led to the emergence of a very wide variety of stamps and labels, perforated or otherwise, for products ranging from 'Dalley's Horse Salve' to 'Schenck's Mandrake Pills'.

The Act of 1862 was repealed in 1883, but the war with Spain in 1898 brought a new tax on proprietary medicines, perfumery, and cosmetics. Again there was resistance to the tax, and a shortage of stamps led to the makeshift use of postage stamps cancelled 'IR' (Internal Revenue), and to the production of provisional stickers bearing the words 'Internal Revenue Tax: 1 cent' and an explanation of the non-availability of orthodox tax stamps. The war was over before the tax system had been properly established, but the tax remained in force until 1901.

Further series of American medical and pharmaceutical tax stamps appeared in 1914, 1919, 1920, 1932, and 1941. Individual states later imposed their own taxes, among them Arkansas, South Carolina, Ohio, and Arizona. The American Government also applied stamp tax to narcotics (principally opium) and 'medicinal liquor' (in the prohibition era).

Narcotic tax stamps have also been issued in Japan. Other countries to impose taxes on medicine and pharmaceuticals are Argentina, Brazil, Canada, Chile, Cochin, Colombia, Ecuador, France, Italy, Japan, Monaco, Panama, Peru, Portugal, South Africa, Spain, Tunisia, Turkey, and Uruguay.

Newspaper duty. Appearing from 1712 to 1855 on all British newspapers, the tax stamp embodied the Government's concern to limit the influence of the popular press. Standing at a halfpenny per half sheet and a penny per whole sheet, the tax rose in 1757 by a halfpenny and was increased by further halfpenny increments in 1776 and 1789. In 1797 it stood at three-pence-halfpenny and in 1815 fourpence. The mounting tax burden served only to increase the number of open evasions. Prosecutions, though frequent, were useless. In the early 1830s many scores of untaxed journals appeared and the tone of the press at large became even more openly radical. The tax was reduced to a penny in 1836 and abolished in 1855. (Paper tax, a perennial burden to the press since its inception in 1712, was abolished in 1861. A tax on advertisements, instituted at the same time as the newspaper duty and similarly crippling, was abolished in 1853.)

Stamping was carried out by hand on blank paper delivered by the publisher to the Stamp Office. Prompt payment of sums of £10 or more entitled the publisher to a discount of three per cent. Images were at first handstamped, but copper-engraved images were later applied twenty-five at a time, the sheets being fanned out in three sets of five to print all the images in one operation of the press. Impressions were in red, though the shade sometimes darkened almost to black. Code numbers within or adjacent to the designs indicate plate and die numbers (and sometimes regional stamp offices); coded 'recut' blanks below the device record fresh cuttings of the plates as they wore down in use. Increases to the duty were indicated by the addition of an extra rendering of the word 'halfpenny'; by the turn of the century some stamps bore four such additions as well as the words 'three halfpence'. Some stamps also bore an indication of the discount rate per hundred.

Continually increasing production speeds brought problems in stamping; attempts at mechanization gave way in 1830 to a reversion to hand methods. By 1851 the Stamp Office was employing forty stampers. In 1853 *The Times* newspaper, together with a number of others, received permission to print the stamp on its own presses in the course of normal printing.

The newspaper tax stamp also served as a postage stamp. Newspapapers, folded and wrapped so as to show the stamp, were allowed free transmission through the post, though the practice was not formally legislated for until 1825.

Paper duty. *See* PAPER-DUTY LABEL

Perfume tax. Perfume, as distinct from general toiletries, has been taxed by Britain (1786–1800), the United States (1864–

83), Puerto Rico (1940–60), Portugal (1924), Chile (1920s), and Brazil (1899). Britain had imposed stamp duties on cosmetics in general before issuing a specific 'perfume duty' label in 1786. This, the earliest known perfume-tax stamp, was produced from a copperplate engraving showing a central crown-and-sceptre device within a lozenge, in the idiom of the hat-duty label. As with many such stamps, tickets, etc. of the time, the image, 35 × 150 mm (1⅜ × 6 in), was engraved in multiples on a single plate and cut from the sheet along dotted dividing lines, traces of which may appear at the borders. Designed expressly as a seal to be broken when opened, few have survived. Most known examples are proofs from Stamp Office files.

Playing-card duty. *See* PLAYING-CARD DUTY

Post-horse duty. *See* POST-HORSE DUTY TICKET

Wallpaper. Wallpaper was subject to duty in Britain from 1712 to 1836. Imported papers continued to bear tax until 1861, and import stamps showed the port of entry. The tax was payable at the rate of one penny per square yard of paper, control being applied within the manufacturer's premises by an excise officer who stamped the back of each sheet with the royal cypher and a code number. In 1786 a 'Duty charged remnant' stamp was introduced showing the port of entry.

See also CYPHER LABEL; REAM LABEL; TAXATION PAPERS; UNSTAMPED NEWSPAPER/PERIODICAL

Taxation papers

Taxation provides government with resources for the collective good. It is also used as a control mechanism, regulating the economy at large – and often the conduct of social groups. Traditionally, revenue has been derived at two levels, central and local, and the term 'tax' or 'duty' has normally applied to the former and 'rate' to the latter. The position is not clear-cut, however; the division between one field and the other is often blurred, changing in time and place. For the ephemerist, therefore, the expression 'taxation papers' may be taken to include items relating to rates as well as taxes.

Taxation has generated a large body of printed and handwritten ephemera, many of which have survived among family papers. Such documents may convey more than just the detail of former taxation structures; they also mirror details of bygone everyday life.

Typical of such ephemera are Britain's window-tax papers. This tax, first levied in 1697 to recoup losses from clipped coinage, is among the earliest of taxes to feature widely in surviving ephemera. It was at first imposed on all houses, with minor exceptions, at the rate of two shillings per year, with an additional four shillings for every ten windows in excess of the first ten. The rate increased throughout the 18th century, and at the first increase, in 1710, the practice of 'stopping up' windows to avoid tax began. Stopping up – to qualify for exemption – was required to be complete and permanent, employing the materials of which adjacent walls were built.

Inspecting commissioners were appointed to levy the tax. Visiting each building in their area, they counted windows, noted those stopped up, and any illegally 'broken out' since the previous inspection. The commonest items of window-tax ephemera are receipts ('for window money'), mostly handwritten on slips of plain paper approximately 80 × 200 mm (3⅛ × 7⅞ in), and, later, formal receipt slips, blank or part-printed, bearing a blind-embossed stamp. Formal receipt slips are sometimes watermarked with the word 'Receipt'.

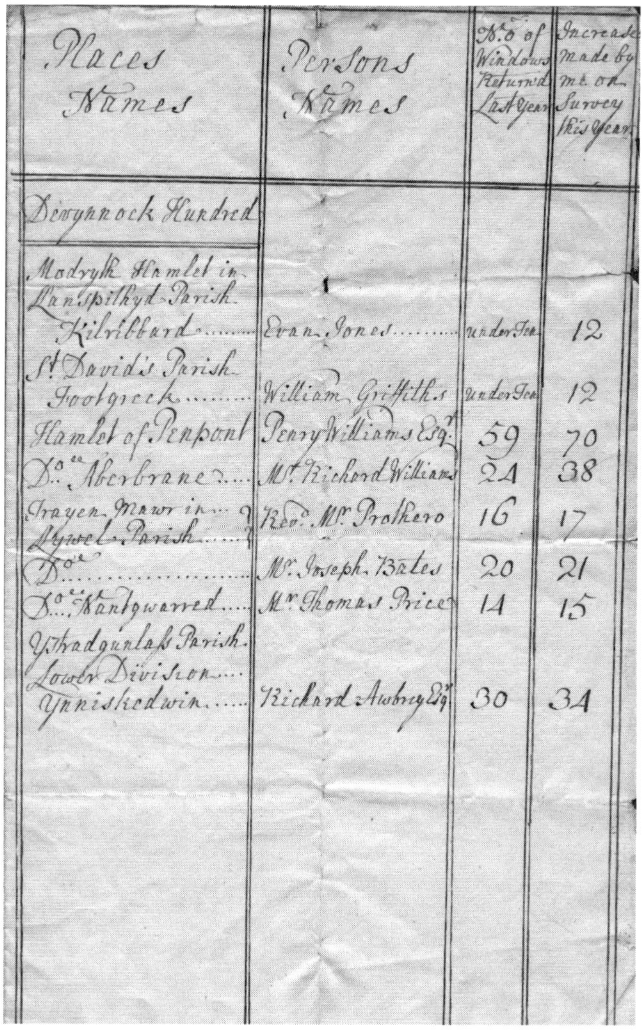

Places Names	Persons Names	No. of Windows Returned Last Year	Increase made by me on Survey this Year
Devynnock Hundred			
Modrydd Hamlet in Llanspyddyd Parish			
Kilribbord......	Evan Jones.........	under Ten	12
St David's Parish			
Footgreck........	William Griffiths	under Ten	12
Hamlet of Penpont	Penry Williams Esq.	59	70
Do. Aberbrane....	Mr Richard Williams	24	38
Trayen Mawr in Lywel Parish	Revd. Mr Prothero	16	17
Do.	Mr Joseph Bates	20	21
Do. Nantgwarred....	Mr Thomas Price	14	15
Ystradgunlais Parish Lower Division....			
Ynniskedwin......	Richard Awbrey Esq.	30	34

Window-tax return for Devynnock Hundred, Wales, late 18th century. Manuscript. 312 × 195 mm (12½ × 7⅝ in)

Less common are 'field records' in which the commissioners recorded their inspection findings. These are in most cases wholly handwritten. Other handwritten material, also relatively scarce, includes notices of appeal against assessment, as well as informal notes of protest: 'Sir: I perceive you have sent me a charge of ten windows which is more than I have. Whoever may be your informer has informed you wrong ... The Collector may look at them at any time ... I am your obedient Wm Farmer' (Weobley, Herefordshire, 1824).

Window tax was abolished, after much public agitation, in 1851, its place being taken in the fiscal structure by income (and other) taxes. Window tax levies are included among part-printed 'Assessed Taxes' forms of the 19th century. These forms, of varying format, give assessments on one side of the paper and general instructions on the other. Varying with changes in tax law throughout the century, the assessment list included in 1839: 'windows; servants; under-gamekeepers; waiters at taverns etc.; stage-coachmen and guards... carriages with four wheels drawn by more than one horse; – of two wheels drawn by two horses; additional bodies; horses, exceeding 13 hands; – not exceeding 13 hands; – rode by bailiffs; – rode by butcher; – let to hire; race horses; ... mules ... grey hounds; other dogs; packs of hounds; horse dealers; hair powder; armorial bearings'.

Local rates and taxes raised revenue for an increasing range of services in 19th-century Britain, including street-lighting, night-watch, paving, water supply, sewers, gaols, poor relief, burial grounds (and, in parts of the eastern counties, fen drainage).

In both Britain and America, part-printed receipts for payments, as well as specifying rate and subject matter, often bear additional printed information: 'NB Every inhabitant neglecting to have the footway of the premises swept every morning by nine o'clock, is liable to the penalty of five shillings' (St George's Pavement, London, 1804); 'All taxes paid on or before the last day of September, at 5 o'clock PM will be entitled to a discount of 4 per cent' (Roxbury, Vermont, 1841); 'Water Rent, New River Company... In Case of Fire, or deficient supply, send to turncocks' (Islington, London, 1860); 'Water Rates, City of Salem... Parties requesting the pipes thawed when frozen, must deposit... two dollars; if found to be caused by neglect or fault of the Water Board, the same will be refunded' (Salem, Massachusetts, 1879).

In the broader field of taxation, a vast body of part-printed papers records the development of primary levies – income tax, land tax, property tax, inhabited house tax, real estate tax – in some States of America, poll tax – and a host of variants on familiar themes. Differing not only in period but also in place, the tax story is complex; but through its minor documents it is clearly defined.

In a class apart, but relevant, is an intermittent barrage of printed protest, denouncing taxation in all its forms. One well-known 19th-century text, wording of which was modified to the individual taste of successive leaflet publishers, listed the full litany of tax injustice:

> TAXES: taxes upon every article which enters the Mouth or covers the Back... is pleasant to see, hear, feel, smell or taste, taxes on warmth, light or locomotion.... The dying Englishman, pouring his medicine, which has paid five per cent, into a spoon that has paid fifteen per cent, flings himself back on his chintz bed, which has paid twenty-two per cent, makes his will on an eight-pound stamp, and expires in the arms of an apothecary who has paid a hundred pounds for the privilege of putting him to death.

Protest against taxation resulted at one stage in more than the production of leaflets. In 1765 the British sought to impose a tax in the American colonies to raise money to pay for the maintenance there of some 10,000 British soldiers. The Stamp Tax, similar to Britain's own Stamp Tax of 1712, imposed levies on 'every skin or piece of vellum or parchment, or sheet or piece of paper'. The outcome, of this and a succession of other impositions, was the American Revolution.

In Britain, taxes on newspapers, on advertisements, and on paper itself, remained in force into the middle of the 19th century. Taxes on receipts and bank cheques were abolished in the 1950s. Taxes are still imposed on property transfer documents, leases, stocks, shares and similar securities in Britain and parts of Europe, and in the United States on new stock and bond documents and other papers.

The most commonly collected of tax stamps are Britain's newspaper tax stamps and patent medicine tax labels.

See also BANKNOTE-DUTY STAMP; DICE-DUTY WRAPPER; HAT-DUTY STAMP; LIGHTHOUSE-DUES PAPERS; MATCH-TAX STAMP; PAPER-DUTY LABEL; PERFUME-DUTY LABEL; PLAYING-CARD DUTY; POST-HORSE DUTY TICKET; RECEIPT; SALES-TAX TOKEN/RECEIPT; TAX ABSTRACT; TAX STAMP

Telegram/telegram form

Commercial use of the electric telegraph was initially a sideline of the railway companies. Having installed the system for their own administration and operational control, they made it available to the public for private messages. Early telegrams are thus found with railway stations named as offices of origin and receipt, and with additional delivery charges (for the journey from the receiving station to the addressee) noted as extras. The system became standard practice wherever railways were laid down.

With the formation of independent telegraph companies in the late 1840s, 1850s, and 1860s, the telegram took on a more 'commercial' look, advertising addresses of company offices and often carrying company logos. Accompanying leaflets also promoted telegraphic services. The British and Irish Magnetic Telegraph Co. pointed out in 1863 – well before the inauguration of the transatlantic cable in 1866 – that even America was within reach: 'Messages... may be forwarded... to catch the Mails calling at Queenstown, and Londonderry, and can be Telegraphed on to their destinations from the first Port at which the Vessels touch, on the American side'.

The much publicized speed of transmission caused frequent embarrassment, particularly on short journeys. Processing times for messages were often so lengthy that in some cases it was quicker to write the message directly on to a form and send it by messenger, by-passing the electrical system altogether. 'Short-haul' telegrams of the 1860s may thus be non-telegraphic.

Messages were written by hand at receiving stations until the introduction of tape strips in 1929, but in many areas handwriting continued in use into the 1980s. Tape strips were replaced by continuous roll telex paper in 1978. Repetition of doubtful messages cost the recipient half the total transmission charge (with a refund 'on application to the Secretary' in the event of there being an error in the original transmission'). Free repetition of doubtful words was instituted in 1935.

Telegrams appeared in a variety of sizes in the early years, but afterwards settled down to an average 140 × 220 mm (5½ × 8⅝ in). British forms in the early 1870s measured twice that size: 220 × 280 mm (8⅝ × 11 in). Early telegrams were delivered in distinctive coloured envelopes (the District Telegraph Company in London used a bright red envelope in the late 1850s), but public dislike for the 'bad news' image of the telegram caused these to be abandoned. A similar reaction to news of bereavements in World War I brought a change from the wartime light brown envelope to yellow. In a number of countries envelopes were not used, the telegram being folded inwards and paste-sealed. This practice continues in some areas. Decorative greetings telegrams were introduced in Britain in 1935. Among the first of these was one bearing a design by Rex Whistler. Since then the British Post Office has produced seventy-nine different designs, providing a selection for particular occasions. In later formats, tape strips were replaced by direct telex typing on a special sheet which was slipped into a decorative frame-folder.

The Western Union Telegraph Co., formed in the 1860s, was the main operator of telegraphs in the United States until the early 1980s, when other companies entered the field. Company logos feature on most US telegrams, as they do on those (in Europe) of Western Union International, a separate company formed in 1963. Cable and Wireless Ltd, the British company whose international telegrams carried the slogan 'Via Imperial', was formed in 1929 under the title Imperial and International Communications Ltd, and was renamed Cable and Wireless in 1934. The company, nationalized in 1947, no longer delivers messages in Britain, all telegraph traffic being handled by the Post Office. There is, however, Cable and Wireless delivery elsewhere, notably in Hong Kong, the Gulf area, and the Caribbean, where messages carry the Cable and Wireless logo.

The first American telegraph line was opened by Samuel Morse, who received an appropriation of $30,000 from Congress for a trial link between Baltimore and Washington. It became operational in May 1844. By the end of the Civil War some sixty or seventy telegraph companies had been formed. Among these were the New York and Boston Magnetic Telegraph (1846); New York and Washington Telegraph (1848); Magnetic Telegraph Co. (1848); New London, Norwich and Worcester Telegraph (1849); Western Telegraph Co. (1850); Rhode Island Magnetic Telegraph (1850); Washington and New Orleans Telegraph Line (1851); Chemical Telegraph (1851); New York and New England Union Telegraph Co. (1852); Cape Cod Telegraph Line (1853); Union Telegraph Co. (1853); Vermont and Boston Telegraph Line (1854); Maine Telegraph (1854); Electric Marine Telegraph (1859); Illinois and Mississippi Telegraph Co. (1860); Western Union Telegraph Co. (1862); People's Telegraph Lines (1864); Insulated Lines Telegraph Co. (1865); United States Telegraph Co. (1865); Franklin Telegraph Co. (1867); International Telegraph Co. (1868); Northern Telegraph Co. (1869).

See also GREETINGS TELEGRAM

COLLECTIONS American Antiquarian Society, Worcester, Mass.; New York Historical Society; Western Union Telegraph Company International Inc., London

Telephone card

In March 1876 Alexander Graham Bell inaugurated the first telephone with words to his assistant, 'Come here, Watson, I want you'. In the late 20th century the call was for something else: the craze for collecting plastic telephone cards, known as fusilately, had outpaced even stamp collecting by the year 2000. An estimated four million people scour public phone boxes for a discarded issue or go to fairs in search of a fine example.

The card, now commonly known as a 'phonecard', had a modest beginning. Introduced as a trial on the via Oriolo Romano in Rome in May 1976 by the Italian national telephone company SIP (now Telecom Italia), it surfaced again in the Hotel Frantel Windsor, Paris, in 1978 as a convenient perk for guests.

Vandalism of coin-operated phoneboxes and an increase in long-distance calls made from public spaces prompted the Belgian telecommunications network RTT to work with the technology giant Landis & Gyr to produce a telephone card for general use. Inaugurated in 1979, this convenient alternative to pockets full of change became an instant success.

Britain introduced similar cards on 27 July 1981 when Sir George Jefferson, then chairman of British Telecom (BT), initiated the service with a call from Waterloo Station, London. A rather hesitant BT press release of the same date has a 'questions and answers' addendum. Of particular interest is query number eight: 'Aren't you creating a litter menace? Won't the area around these phones be littered with discarded, used cards?' BT's answer placed full responsibility on users to do the decent thing and 'dispose of their cards properly'. As evidenced

British Telecom 'Phonecard 2000' commemorating the Millennium Dome in London. 54 × 85 mm (2⅛ × 3⅜ in)

by current accumulations of cards in phone boxes, proper behaviour is not the norm. British Telecom's nightmare has become the ephemerist's dream.

Telephone cards, commonly the size of CREDIT/CASH CARDS, 54 × 85 mm (2⅛ × 3⅜ in), use similar methods to expedite payment and detect fraud. Magnetic strips, silicon chips, and reactive optical devices make for efficient operation, but show little of the elegance of earlier SECURITY PRINTING.

Having spread globally with incredible speed, telephone cards are now issued (sometimes in collectable sets) for Christmas and Valentine's Day, commemorative events, promotional campaigns, and that one 'special' occasion. Composers, cities, athletic meetings, works of art, writers, exhibitions, face creams, gin distilleries, presidents and aerospace companies all vie for attention. In Japan, where the cult of the telephone card has reached epic proportions, personalized cards are commonly designed by individual collectors as gifts.

With little graphic matter sacrosanct, telephone cards echo the extravagance and fantasy, although often not the humour, of the American trade card of the 1880s and 1890s. And like such trade cards, they help to form a composite image of an era. [SB]

REFERENCES Yves Arden, *Telephone Cards* (Princes Risborough, Bucks: Shire Publications Ltd, 1994); Steve Hiscocks, *Telephone Cards. A Collector's Handbook* (Woking, Surrey: The Author, 1996); Vincent Vidal, *Les Télécartes* (Paris: Syros Alternatives, 1992)

Telephone directory

The first telephone company to issue a directory was the District Telephone Co. of New Haven, Connecticut. Their printed list appeared on 21 February 1878. London's first directory, published by the London Telephone Co., followed two years later. London's first two-volume directory appeared in 1931, and its first four-volume one in 1947.

Early telephone directories were slender pamphlets, often pierced at the top left-hand corner and provided with a ring or cord for hanging near the instrument A typical example is the Bell National Telephone Co.'s 'List of Subscribers', published on 1 January 1882 in Portland, Maine, and covering Portland, Lewiston, Biddeford, Old Orchard, Pine Point, Scarboro and other places. The booklet measures 215 × 110 mm (8½ × 4⅜ in) and runs to twenty pages plus a cover.

The twelve-page Portland section is headed by a note announcing that the latest total of subscribers in the area is 575. The figure is compared with that of 1 September 1879, when the total was only 113. The list gives names (alphabetically presented) of trades and occupations, but no addresses. Notes and hints to subscribers provide an insight into the state of the art at the time. Among fifteen helpful points the directory includes: 'All having "push button" bells call the central office by striking the button twice (and only twice). Then put the telephone to the ear and wait for the operator's voice.... When done speaking always hang the telephone on the hook'. 'Whenever trouble is noticed', the booklet advises, 'please call for I H Farnham (managing electrician)... and explain to him...'. It is pointed out that the system may sometimes get overloaded: 'There are often 15 or 20 calls come in at about the same time; when this occurs all cannot be answered on the instant, but will be attended to as soon as the operators can do it'. There is also a note on severe thunder storms, during which the subscriber is requested to 'refrain from using the telephone, as no calls will be answered by the Exchange'. A bold-type note warns that the service is for subscribers only: 'The use of the Telephone by parties other than the subscriber is strictly prohibited ...'.

The London Telephone Directory of 1904, a hard-bound volume of 1020 pages, 210 × 130 mm (8¼ × 5⅛ in), has a twelve-page preface outlining the service. Among assurances to the subscriber is a note referring to the company's methods of monitoring employee response: 'To ensure that calls are attended to promptly by the operators at the exchange, officers of the Post Office will from time to time, unknown to the operators, visit subscribers' premises and ask permission to call up the exchange. The number of seconds occupied before the operator answers will be recorded, and subscribers are earnestly requested to give the officer, on production of his card of authorization, every facility'.

In the closing decades of the 20th century increasing emphasis began to be put on the design of telephone directories to cope with the growing number of entries and the need for economy on the one hand and greater legibility on the other. Leading designers from several countries undertook such work (Colin Banks in Britain, Wim Crouwel and Gerard Unger in the Netherlands, the Hungarian designer Ladislas Mandel in France, and the British designer Matthew Carter in America). Pioneering work was done by Matthew Carter with the design of Bell type, and in the design of both type and directories by Ladislas Mandel (for several European countries) and Colin Banks for the British telephone books. The last project, undertaken in the 1980s with Ben Johnson of Gateshead as printers, led to Banks & Miles winning both the Royal Society of Arts and the BBC Green Awards for the compactness and legibility of the product.

A widespread tendency to throw directories away immediately on receipt of updated editions has meant that directories, particularly early ones, may now be among the scarcest of everyday ephemera.

COLLECTION BT Archives, London

Temperance papers

Nineteenth-century campaigns against alcohol were focused largely on obtaining written pledges of abstinence, sometimes in a 'Pledge Book', sometimes on PLEDGE CARDS or certificates. These last are the most commonly surviving temperance items.

The idea of a signed pledge dates back to the first years of the century in Massachusetts, but the movement gathered impetus in both America and Britain in the 1830s. In America, there were over a million members of the American Society for the

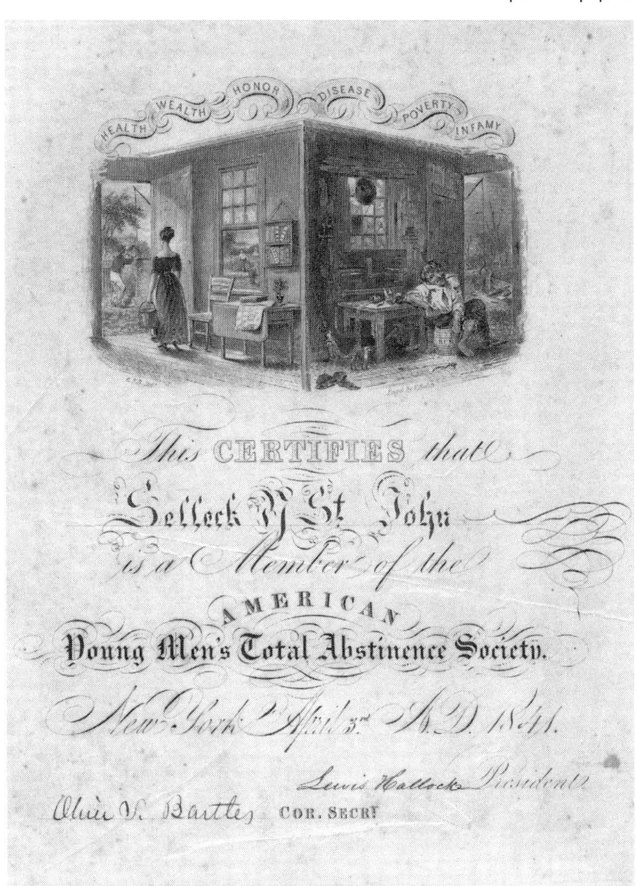

Membership certificate of the American Young Men's Total Abstinence Society, New York, 3 April 1841. Intaglio-printed. Engraved by V. Balch after E.F.B. 285 × 207 mm (11¼ × 8⅛in)

Promotion of Temperance by 1833. In Ireland, in the same period, Father Mathew of Cork was reputed to have 'pledged' over four million people (about half the total population).

The temperance movement was based largely on the churches, and the typical Temperance Pledge is expressed in religious terms: 'I promise, by Divine Assistance, to abstain from all intoxicating liquors as beverages...' (Gosberton, 1910); 'This is to certify that (—) having promised, with the help of God, to abstain from all intoxicating liquors as beverages, has been enrolled as a member...' (Dunkeld, The United Free Church Temperance Union, 1903). Earlier declarations were often more resounding: 'Leith Religious Total Abstinence Society – or Scottish Association for the Suppression and Prevention of Intemperance: Being convinced that the prevalent use of inebriating drinks is fatal to the health and happiness, peace and prosperity, of the community, and that total abstinence is the best security of the temperate, and the only deliverance for the intemperate, I do voluntarily promise that I will abstain from all porter, cyder, wine, ardent spirits, & all intoxicating liquors, and will not give nor offer them to others, except as medicines, or in a religious ordinance, and that I will discountenance all the causes and practices of intemperance...' (Leith, c.1845).

Pledge cards and certificates appeared in a wide variety of styles and formats. Early specimens are copper-engraved. Late 19th-century examples are reminiscent of scholastic awards, being lithographed in four, five, or six colours plus gold.

By the end of the 20th century, the signing of pledge cards and certificates had much diminished; the practice continued in certain localized areas (notably in Ireland), and often the pledge relates only to a given period (for example, up to the age of twenty-one) rather than to life-long abstinence.

Other temperance papers include handbills and posters announcing anti-drink meetings, educational booklets and handbills (known as 'tracts'), 'reciters', bearing lengthy temperance verse, and temperance calligrams in which, for example, the line at the foot of a typographic 'Tree of Dissipation' reads 'the root of all evil is drunkenness'.

Testimonial

In Britain in the 18th century it was possible for certain classes of people, not being 'vagrants, vagabonds, rogues or beggars', to request a local Justice of the Peace to furnish them with a written document or 'licence'. The document was given to 'shipwrecked persons, poor soldiers and mariners' and allowed them 'to pass to their own dwelling... in a convenient time' (thus escaping charges of vagrancy while on the way there). The document was known as a 'testimonial'. It was also available to people whose homes had been burnt down, making it easier for them to secure help 'towards repairing the damages sustained by the poor sufferers'.

Textile label

The printed textile label emerged as a concomitant of industrialized textile production in the first half of the 19th century. It appeared in a wide range of formats and had three distinct functions. It was used to identify bales of material in bulk, in bolts, and in individual fabric lengths.

Typical bale labels were those produced for British cotton exports, measuring between 155 × 110 mm (6⅛ × 4⅜ in) and 245 × 190 mm (9⅝ × 7½ in) and printed by chromolithography, or, later, by four-colour half-tone on high gloss paper. They took the form of pictorial trade marks, sometimes devoid of lettering, and featured animals, flowers, birds, and other colourful images as evidence of provenance. Though these labels were printed in Britain, their designs were geared to the tastes of the overseas buyer; in general appearance they conveyed a message of Africa, India, or the Middle and Far East.

Bale labels were fixed not only on the outside of the bale but at intervals in the layers of material within it. This had the effect of identifying the contents throughout its depth, even after the upper layers, with their respective labels, had been removed. Smaller labels with similar designs were used on bolts, and measured some 150 × 100 mm (6 × 4 in). They carried spaces so that bolt details (number and length in metres or yards) could be inserted by hand. Labels in both categories were in use from the 1890s to the 1970s.

In function, the British cotton export label has much in common with the Chinese CHOP PAPER. In design it is reminiscent of the Californian orange-crate label (though occasional exceptions include the work of such designers as E. McKnight Kauffer).

Allied to the bale and bolt label is the fabric label – heavily embossed, sometimes intricately cut out, and often decorated with chromolithographs or multi-colour woodcut illustrations. Some are productions of extreme elegance, conceived and executed in the luxurious idiom of the Victorian GREETINGS CARD (and often preserved in a secondary role as items in scrap albums). Similar, but on the whole less successful, are the cut-out gold embossed labels produced for Irish linen.

British and American fabric labels, produced for the home market, and often letterpress-printed in a single colour, convey little more than the necessary facts, eschewing decorative appeal.

Thaumatrope

The thaumatrope was a toy devised in 1826 by John Ayrton Paris, a medical doctor, in Penzance. It was based on the phenomenon of the persistence of vision, earlier demonstrated by Peter Roget (1824) in a paper to the Royal Society in London.

The toy consisted of a striped cardboard disc threaded on string, having one image (for example, a parrot) on one side and another (a cage) on the reverse. By first twisting, then gently pulling the strings, the disc is caused to spin; the two images blend, apparently placing the parrot in the cage. The effect had been pointed out by Sir John Herschel, who observed that a spinning coin appears to show both sides simultaneously.

The thaumatrope (Greek: *thauma:* wonder; *tropos:* turn) was sold as a 'Thaumatropical Amusement to illustrate the seeming Paradox of Seeing an Object which is out of sight, and to demonstrate the faculty of the Retina of the eye to retain the impression of an Object after its disappearance'. It was packaged in labelled boxes of four, six, or eight.

The term 'thaumatrope' was also applied to other optical toys, notably the PHENAKISTOSCOPE (or stroboscope) and the ZOËTROPE (or wheel of life). Huxley in his *Physiography: An Introduction to the Study of Nature* (1877) uses the term to denote a device '...by the help of which, on looking through a hole, one sees images of jugglers throwing up and catching balls'. The 1876 catalogue of A. N. Myers & Co. of Oxford Street, London, offers 'the Thaumatrope or Wheel of Life'.

REFERENCES Olive Cook, *Movement in Two Dimensions* (London: Hutchinson, 1963); Philip and Caroline Freemann Sayer, *Victorian Kinetic Toys and how to make them* (London: Evans, 1977)

COLLECTIONS Museum of the Moving Image, London; Science Museum, London; Smithsonian Institution, Washington, DC

Theatre programme [plate 6]

The 'bill of the play', the narrow printed sheet that also served as a POSTER, was the first theatre programme, and was sold to playgoers for reference during the performance. In late 18th century London the 'bills' were sold in the streets by orange girls, who displayed them on their stalls and baskets as sidelines, selling them at a penny each, or giving them as a bonus to those who bought oranges. At the time, the cry 'Bill of the play!' was among the many well-known cries of London, ranking with 'Cherry ripe!' and 'Sweet blooming lavender!'.

As theatre productions became more extravagant, playbills became longer. The printer merely added type matter to the foot of the bill, as required. Though varying only slightly in width, playbills are of arbitrary length, ranging from perhaps 300 mm (11⅞ in) to nearly twice that length. To make them more manageable and easier to print, excessively long bills were produced side-by-side on a single, broader, sheet, thus paving the way for the booklet format of modern times. For use in the theatre the 'double' bill was folded vertically back on itself, forming a double-sided paper, which was easily handled.

The long narrow format of the bills accounts for the development, in the first half of the 19th century, of highly condensed headline types. These offered maximum depth and boldness with minimum width. (A revival of one of these survives today under the designation 'Playbill'). This typographic convention had a secondary effect: bills for spectacles of all kinds – circuses, zoos, waxworks, exhibitions, and, later, music halls – adopted the same principle. From the 1860s, special printing types appeared for multicoloured printing, and two- three- or even four-colour workings were used to produce the classic music-hall poster – and were to lead, in the early decades of the 20th century, to the local cinema bill.

The theatre programme proper – sold only inside the theatre – developed from the simple four-page folder of the end of the 19th century to a multi-page souvenir booklet carrying editorial matter and advertising. In America, there was a passing vogue for a single-sheet broadside in which the programme formed the centre-piece with a surround of editorial-cum-advertising.

Theatre programme collections may be organized under a wide variety of headings. These include first nights, specific theatres, performer, plays, producers, etc., but most personal collections emerge as a cumulative record of one individual's theatre-going career. Of all ephemera items, the theatre programme is one of the least rare; playgoers tend to preserve them first as a reminder of an enjoyable occasion, and then almost by oversight. The same was probably true of the 'bill of the play'; these too have survived in very large numbers.

REFERENCES John Kennedy Melling, *Discovering Theatre Ephemera* (Aylesbury: Shire Publications, 1974); George Speaight, *Collecting Theatre Memorabilia* (Ashbourne: Moorland Publishing Co., 1988)

COLLECTIONS Elspeth Evans and John Lewis Collections, Reading University Library; Harvard Theatre Collection, Harvard College Library, Cambridge, Mass.; Theatre Collection, Victoria & Albert Museum, London

Theatre ticket

For the ephemerist, the term 'theatre ticket' relates to a paper printed item, not to the metal or ivory token (also described as a 'ticket') in common use at the end of the 18th century and after.

Many early printed theatre tickets have the air of 'souvenirs in advance'. Delicate engravings or elegant letterpress designs convey not only a contractual agreement but a distinct sense of occasion. Thomas Bewick, George Cruikshank, and other distinguished artists designed tickets in the late 18th and early 19th centuries. Of special elegance are tickets admitting to boxes, 'pass and repass tickets' (allowing readmission), 'benefit performance' tickets, season tickets, and certain complimentary tickets issued to influential friends by the theatre management. Many of these may have the added distinction of bearing the personal signature of the manager; tickets signed by Kemble, Kean, Macready, and other actor-managers are not uncommon.

At a less august level, complimentary tickets were also issued in an attempt to fill out audiences at failing plays. These tickets relate in the main to Monday or Tuesday performances, notoriously the least patronized of theatre evenings. Some complimentary tickets, available on any of the first four days of the week, expressly exclude Fridays and Saturdays – the best box-office days. In a number of (clearly desperate) cases the printed exclusion of Friday and Saturday has been cancelled in pen, indicating that even the best days needed reinforcements.

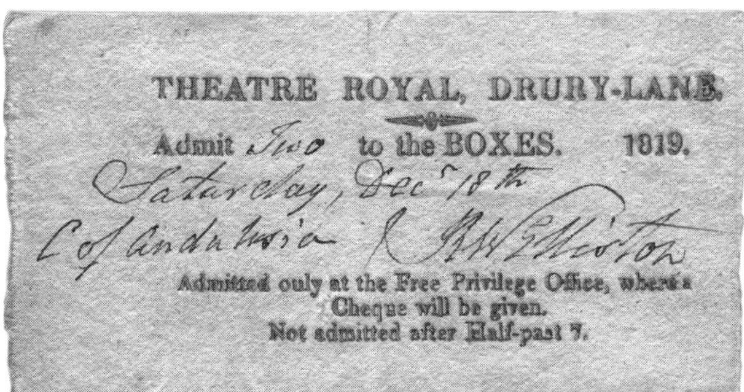
THEATRE ROYAL, DRURY-LANE.
Admit Two to the BOXES. 1819.
Saturday, Dec 18th
Admitted only at the Free Privilege Office, where a Cheque will be given.
Not admitted after Half-past 7.

Ticket for the Theatre Royal, Drury Lane, London, 1819. Letterpress, printed in red, and manuscript. 54 × 103 mm (2⅛ × 4 in)

American theatre tickets of the period follow the same general pattern, though their design is less assured. In many cases they are reminiscent of, on the one hand, professional diplomas and, on the other, early tradesmen's business cards.

In both Britain and America the numbering of places (apart from boxes) was generally speaking a late development; tickets rarely bore numbers in the first half of the 19th century, and experiments in organized advance booking were tried in Britain only after Queen Victoria had lent decorum to the theatre by commanding Christmas 'theatricals' at Windsor Castle. Prior to this, the theatrical world and its public had been noted for less than satisfactory behaviour. Theatre-going appears to have been either a formal affair – as suggested by the elaborateness of some tickets – or a matter of casual impulse. A complimentary ticket for the New Royalty Theatre, London (undated), bears the printed legend: 'Admit two ... This Evening'. Even with its colour-coded card to define the day of the week intended, the wording implies a none too rigorous control system.

Twentieth-century theatre tickets, numbered and counterfoiled, have few design pretensions and are collected for the most part merely as souvenirs, but they may carry incidentals worth noting. An orchestra stall ticket for *Cosí Fan Tutte* at the Royal Opera House, Covent Garden (c.1975) bears the small-print condition that the management reserves the right to '... request the holder of this ticket to leave the Theatre and take any appropriate action to enforce the right'.

See also AUDITORIUM SEATING PLAN; BENEFIT TICKET

COLLECTIONS Harvard Theatre Collection, Harvard College Library, Cambridge, Mass.; Theatre Collection, Victoria & Albert Museum, London

Thread paper

Measures taken by paper manufacturers to combat forgery have been numerous. They have commonly included the addition of 'foreign' ingredients in the paper-mix, often in the form of coloured fibres, threads, fillets, etc., to produce a distinctive substrate beyond the capacity of the forger to imitate.

A pioneer in the field was John Dickinson (1782–1869), founder of the paper and stationery firm that bears his name. He conceived the idea of incorporating continuous coloured threads in the substance of the paper, a device which lent itself readily to the continuous-roll production principle, introduced by Fourdrinier in the early 19th century. He derived the idea from the white strand in government cordage, introduced into the rope as a marker to discourage theft. Dickinson was granted patents in machines for producing his 'thread paper', one in 1829, embodying the idea in principle, and another in 1839, in which numbers of threads might be introduced into the paper simultaneously at three levels – in the middle of the thickness of the paper, close to one surface, and close to the opposite surface.

Dickinson's thread paper was adopted for use in exchequer bonds and certain other official papers from 1829, being manufactured under Excise control in high-security conditions at the inventor's works at Nash Mills in Hertfordshire. The campaign for postal reform and the Treasury's competition for a prepaid postal label or wrapper, spurred Dickinson to bring the idea to public attention. He prepared two specimens, a one penny lettersheet (which could be folded to make an envelope) and a twopenny lettersheet, both of which were printed on his thread paper. There were some 2600 entries for the competition. As it turned out, none of them – not even any of the four winning entries – was used. Dickinson's thread paper, however, was adopted for the printing of the MULREADY ENVELOPE and letter sheet, the idea that was finally to emerge, together with the 'postage stamp', at the end of the operation. The Mulready items incorporated blue and red threads, blue near the printed surface, red near the underside. The Mulready image was not a success with the public, and the thread component had barely registered before the design was withdrawn (*see* MULREADY CARICATURE). It was replaced by the plain penny or twopenny envelope bearing the embossed cameo head designed by Wyon, thread lines appearing diagonally across the upper right-hand corner of the envelope (under or near the embossing) and on flaps, or on flaps only. The method was not adopted for the adhesive postage stamp, although two issues, the embossed one shilling (1847) and the tenpence (1848), did use it.

Thread paper, manufactured under licence from Dickinson, was used for stamps in Bavaria (1849), Schleswig Holstein (1850), Switzerland (1854), and Württemberg (1857; 1864). Prussia used thread paper for embossed envelopes: three issues in 1851 and four in 1852 carried two red threads through the embossing, lower left to upper right; the issue of 1853 and a reprint of the 1852 issue in 1864 did not use thread paper.

By the 1860s the method had been abandoned virtually everywhere in favour of the watermark. The principle had a number of disadvantages. Difficulties of production were never wholly overcome, and the incidence of errors was high. Threads were said to be drawn out when sheets were cut up, and to become entangled in the perforating machine. It was claimed, moreover, that the visual effect of the threads could be easily imitated by merely drawing fine coloured lines.

The principle of thread paper survives in the second half of the 20th century in the metal strip within paper used for currency.

REFERENCES H. Dagnall, *John Dickinson and his Silk-Thread Paper* (Leicester: the Author, 1975); Joan Evans, *The Endless Web: John Dickinson & Co. Ltd., 1804–1954* (London: Jonathan Cape, 1955); Sir Rowland Hill, *Post Office Reform: Its Importance and Practicability* (London: G. Knight, 1837); Alan Huggins, *British Postal Stationery* (London: Great Britain Philatelic Society, 1971); Robson Lowe, *The British Postage Stamp*, 2nd edn (London: National Postal Museum, 1979)

COLLECTION National Postal Museum, London

Ticket

Tickets are a form of RECEIPT, a record of an entitlement to a service (commonly entertainment or transport) or of a transaction (as in a lottery ticket). Entries are included in this encyclopedia for some fifteen items of ephemera that might be called tickets. Others, though described as tickets, such as the BINDER'S TICKET (a small label applied to the inside of a binding as a mark of identification of the supplier), are only distantly related to the ticket as commonly understood.

Metal tokens survive from ancient Roman times, with the head of the emperor on one side and a number on the other, which may have been used as tickets for entry to an arena (though it is also possible that they were used as gaming tickets). Thereafter, tickets have been provided in all sorts of materials: paper, card, ivory, and even semi-precious metals. From the 18th century onwards, printing on paper and card became the most common production method. At one end of the scale there was the large, elaborate ticket for an exhibition or performance that approached the INVITATION in style, at the other the modest and often very small ticket recording a short journey or service, as in a bus or cloakroom ticket. More modest tickets, when printed by the traditional methods of the 18th and 19th centuries, would often have been produced as multiples on a large sheet for cutting up later (*see* TOLL/TURNPIKE TICKET).

Tickets of all kinds are among the most ephemeral of printed matter: they are frequently torn in half as a means of preventing their reuse and, in some forms of transport, holders of tickets are invited to dispose of them immediately in receptacles provided for the purpose. But even without such incentives for disposal, tickets are rarely preserved deliberately, except perhaps in recent times as a record of expenses to be claimed. Examples that have survived have done so incidentally, for example, through their use as a BOOKMARK.

The RAIL TICKET, which was needed in vast numbers and numerous variants, led to an entirely different system of production and control, using cards. The system lasted a century and a half and changed the look of the ticket radically. Both system and product were replaced in the closing decades of the 20th century by computer methods of control using, mainly, paper tickets. The business of ticketing for large-scale enterprises can now involve advance booking and collection from machines at the point of entertainment (in cinemas), credit-card purchase from machines (at railway stations), internet booking and the production of named, multi-sheet tickets (for air travel). But despite these technological advances, ticketing

London Transport special bus service ticket for the Festival of Britain, 1951. Shown front and back. Printed in relief in blue and black. 99 × 33 mm (3⅞ × 1⁵⁄₁₆ in)

requirements for small-scale events and services are met in ways not so very different from those of a century or so ago. [MT]

See also ADMISSION TICKET; BENEFIT TICKET; CHARITY TICKET; COACH TICKET; COAL-SELLER'S TICKET; DANCE TOKEN; ELECTION TICKET; GIFT COUPON; HOSTEL ADMISSION TICKET; LECTURE TICKET; LOTTERY PAPERS; PARKING TICKET; POST-HORSE DUTY TICKET; SALES-TAX/TOKEN RECEIPT; SHIPPING; THEATRE TICKET; WEIGHT CARD

Timetable

The earliest surviving timetables, whether handwritten or engraved, relate to times of tides at coastal and estuarial ferries. One 18th-century example, showing high and low water at the Bewmares–Penmaenmaure [Beaumaris–Penmaenmawr] ferry (North Wales), gives morning and evening times at each stage of 'the moon's age'. It also points out in a subtitle that 'marks are sett' on opposite sides of the crossing for the 'Safety of Travellers'.

Less certain, in a world of travel hazards, were tables relating to modes of transport. Early FLY-WAGON BILLS were specific as to departure times but vague about arrivals. The twice-a-week service from Glasgow to Carlisle in 1781 gave four o'clock every Wednesday and Saturday for departure on the hundred-mile journey, but promised only 'Monday and Thursday the following week' for arrivals. Publicity for horse-drawn transport remained non-committal on timings for decades. In the 1830s the waybill of the Citizen's Union Line and United States Mail promised a service 'through from Boston to Keene in thirteen hours', but times of arrival and departure at intermediate points were left to be filled in during, rather than before, the journey. In Switzerland – certainly not the easiest of coaching terrain – journey times remained doubtful into the 1860s and 1870s; printed timetables carried two columns, one headed 'Planned times', the other, left blank to be filled in later, 'Actual times'.

Bus and tram times, starting with George Shillibeer's schedules for his horse-bus service in London in 1829, displayed greater confidence. (Bus and train times continue to do so today, long after performance ceased to match promise.) Least specific, in the early days of public transport services, were shipping companies, whose advertised departures carried stereotyped reservations in the matter of winds and tides.

First among the methods of public transport to aspire to punctuality were the railways, whose timetables, initially published as newspaper advertisements in the areas served, soon appeared as handbills and reference cards. As punctuality relied partly on the passenger, timetables also requested travellers to arrive at stations at least ten minutes before time (twenty minutes if there was much luggage, or if horse and carriage were also to be taken on the railway). There was also a warning that, in order to speed the booking of passengers, the booking office would be closed 'when the Trains are in sight'.

From the 1840s to 1860s railway timetables began to appear in booklet form. The booklets, approximately 150 × 120mm ($6 \times 4\frac{3}{4}$in), sometimes extended to sixty-four pages and carried advertising. Timetables also appeared as broadsides, typically 250 × 300mm ($9\frac{7}{8} \times 11\frac{7}{8}$in), for public posting. Sizes were to increase throughout the period, and by the turn of the century reached 750 × 500mm ($29\frac{1}{2} \times 19\frac{3}{4}$in). Multiplicity of services and interconnections between increasing numbers of company lines brought typographic problems, and many travellers professed their inability to read timetables. (One timetable, published briefly in Britain by Kent in the 1850s, was called *The Intelligible Railway Guide*.)

A Tide Table for Bewmares Ferry
where marks are Sett from Penmaenmaure
to the Ferry side for ye Safety of Travellers

High water	Low water		High water	Low water
Morning			Evening	
Hours: min	Ho: min	The Age	Ho: min	Ho: min
10 - 30	4 - 18		10 - 30	4 18
11 - 18	5 - 06	1 - 16	11 - 18	5 - 06
12 - 06	5 - 54	2 - 17	12 - 06	5 - 54
12 - 54	6 - 42	3 - 18	12 - 54	6 - 42
1 - 42	7 - 30	4 - 19	1 - 42	7 - 30
2 - 30	8 - 18	5 - 20	2 - 30	8 - 18
3 - 18	9 - 06	6 - 21	3 - 18	9 - 06
4 - 06	9 - 54	7 - 22	4 - 06	9 - 54
4 - 54	10 - 42	8 - 23	4 - 54	10 - 42
5 - 42	11 - 30	9 - 24	5 - 42	11 - 30
6 - 30	12 - 18	10 - 25	6 - 30	12 - 18
7 - 18	1 - 06	11 - 26	7 - 18	1 - 06
8 - 06	1 - 54	12 - 27	8 - 06	1 - 54
8 - 54	2 - 42	13 - 28	8 - 54	2 - 42
9 - 42	3 - 30	14 - 29	9 - 42	3 - 30
		15 - 30		

Tide table for Bewmares ferry, Wales. Intaglio-printed. Late 18th century. 130 × 72mm ($5 \times 2\frac{7}{8}$in)

Pre-eminent among the publishers of railway timetables was George Bradshaw, whose guides, in tabular form, first appeared in 1839 and endured, in ever more compendious detail, until 1961. Bradshaw's publications, though fluctuating greatly in legibility, acquired a world reputation for reliability – in spite of the initial reluctance of railway companies to furnish detailed information in advance. Many timetable booklets were published as independent operations by local and national printers, whose revenue came from sales of advertising space as well as from sales of the publication.

American railway companies often published their own timetable booklets. In the early 1890s the Denver & Rio Grande Railroad Co. was issuing 120,000 copies of its timetables per year in booklets measuring 180 × 110mm ($7\frac{1}{8} \times 4\frac{3}{8}$in) and carrying over fifty pages of advertising. Timetables for individual 'named' trains appeared later. In 1924 the Pennsylvania Railroad System published a twelve-panel leaflet, folding to 155 × 85mm ($6\frac{1}{8} \times 3\frac{3}{8}$in), extolling the advantages of the 'Washington Broadway Limited' in its nineteen-hour service from Washington to Chicago and eighteen-hour run between Baltimore and

Chicago. Its brief timetable is surrounded by text and pictures showing the train's 'club car', barber shop, observation car, stenographic service, and ladies' maid and manicurist service.

Shipping companies ventured into timetable booklets in the 1870s. Reminiscent of the early railway booklets, they were printed in black on white, cream, or yellow paper. In the General Steam Navigation Co.'s booklet for April 1873, departure and arrival times are quoted as 'morning' or 'evening', and passengers are advised that carriages and horses intended for embarkation must be ready to embark two hours before departure. 'The packets', says a note, 'will start at the time specified, weather permitting' – although no time is specified.

Canal traffic, though less subject to weather hazards, was equally wary as to timings. Thomas Bache, a canal fly-boat operator on the Ashby canal in the 1820s, advised simply that 'Goods received in London and Manchester on Monday by Noon will be delivered to all Places on the Ashby Canal the following Friday'. Air timetables have remained circumspect from their beginnings, as is shown by *Guides des Voyages Aeriens* published in Paris in 1924. An Imperial Airways timetable for flights from London to Burma in 1933 quotes specific departure times but gives arrivals as 'morning', 'afternoon', or 'evening'. The full journey took nine days, with a rail link between Paris and Brindisi. The London–Capetown journey, with the same rail break, took eleven days. One stop on the Burma flight – Kuwait – is marked on the timetable with an asterisk: 'This call will be made only if inducement offers and circumstances permit'.

Airship timetables, also unspecific as to arrival times, were published for the 'Graf Zeppelin', which remained in service for nine years, and for the Hindenberg, which operated the first commercial transatlantic air service. The two craft carried an aggregate of some 14,000 passengers. Few timetables for their services survive.

Motor coach and long-haul bus operators, like those of the railways, have schedules that are built on minute-to-minute timing. The format for these, and for many modern timetables, tends to standardize around 210 × 100 mm (8¼ × 4 in), a third of the international A4 paper size that is widely used in Europe.

See also SERVANT'S TIMETABLE

REFERENCES *Railway Relics and Regalia* (London: Hamlyn, 1975); Michael Twyman, *Printing 1770–1970* (London: Eyre & Spottiswoode, 1970; reprinted, British Library, 1998)

COLLECTIONS (Bus) London Transport Museum, London; (Rail) National Railway Museum, York

Tinsel print

The tinsel print, a hand-coloured print embossed with metallic foil and other materials, is closely associated with the toy theatre, which was popular in Britain in the first half of the 19th century.

The practice stems from the vogue in 17th-century France of decorating prints with additional materials. These prints were chiefly of religious subjects (biblical scenes and saints), and were produced not only with gold and silver papers but with velvets, silks, and other fabrics. The idea was taken up by London's toy theatre makers as an additional option for their cut-out figures, a de luxe version of their 'tuppence coloured' products. The technique, which appears to have developed at first as a customer initiative, was best suited to the larger figures put out by the trade as souvenirs for theatre-goers. Celebrated players shown in typical roles had wide popularity in the 1830s and 1840s.

The prints, produced from an engraved plate measuring some 220 × 175 mm (8⅝ × 6⅞ in) and commonly printed on a sheet of about 300 × 225 mm (11⅞ × 8⅞ in), were later produced ready-tinselled. Many toy shops and stationers also sold ready-made addenda – breastplates, plumes, helmets, swords, jewelled necklets, etc., cut out and requiring only to be glued on to figures. In a later refinement of the process, portions of the print were cut away, allowing metallic foils and fabrics to appear in the apertures, often with padding from behind to enhance a three-dimensional effect. In some cases materials showed through from behind, in others they were applied to the front of the print.

Among those who sold tinsel-print materials in London were Ackermann and H. J. Webb, both of whom compiled extensive samples and stock books. Ackermann issued pattern cards 'for Embossed Ornaments in Gold, White or Other Colours'. Webb's stock book contained over 13,000 different ornaments and items of accoutrement. It is reported that some twenty different types of tinsel snow could be had of London's tinsel suppliers.

REFERENCES Robert Culff, *Pollock's Shakesperian Theatrical Portraits* (London: Pollock's Toy Theatres Ltd, 1975); George Speaight, *The History of the English Toy Theatre*, rev. edn (London: Studio Vista, 1969)

COLLECTIONS Cooper-Hewitt, National Design Museum, Smithsonian Institution (New York); Museum of London

Tithe papers

Tithes (literally 'tenths') were originally the tenth part of the increase or profit derived by inhabitants of a parish from the land they occupied. The tithe was payable, formerly in kind, for the maintenance of the church and its incumbent. Secularly viewed, the tithe was a tribute extracted from a tenant or subject: the Church saw it as an offering of first fruits to God.

The system changed in detail over the course of time. In Britain, fixed 'tithe rent charges' were substituted for goods; the Tithe Commutation Acts (1836 onwards) brought statutory order to a position that had become ill-defined by linking payments to an index based on corn prices.

Tithe ephemera consist in the main of receipt slips, commonly measuring 80 × 200 mm (3⅛ × 7⅞ in). They are found

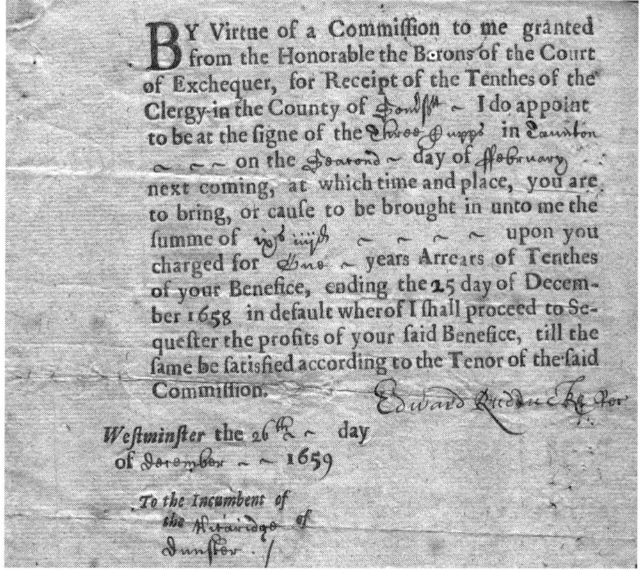

BY Virtue of a Commiſſion to me granted from the Honorable the Barons of the Court of Exchequer, for Receipt of the Tenthes of the Clergy in the County of [illegible] I do appoint to be at the ſigne of the Three Cupps in Taunton on the Second day of February next coming, at which time and place, you are to bring, or cauſe to be brought in unto me the ſumme of [illegible] upon you charged for One years Arrears of Tenthes of your Benefice, ending the 25 day of December 1658 in default wherof I ſhall proceed to Sequeſter the profits of your ſaid Benefice, till the ſame be ſatisfied according to the Tenor of the ſaid Commiſſion.

Edward [illegible]

Weſtminſter the 26th day of December 1659

To the Incumbent of [illegible]

Tithe demand, Westminster, 26 December 1659. Letterpress and manuscript. 140 × 157 mm (5½ × 6¼ in)

handwritten and part-printed from copperplates or type. Other examples are part-printed letterpress requests for payment and final demands, 180 × 120 mm (7⅛ × 4¾ in) folded, and part-printed letterpress complaints to justices seeking redress for non-payment, measuring 330 × 203 mm (13 × 8 in).

Further items include printed tables showing tithe rent-charge values based on corn prices and, in the 17th century, part-printed demands from rectors to parish priests claiming due share of tithe payments ('... in default whereof I shall proceed to sequester the profits of your said benefice...').

Tithe payments in one form or another survived in Britain into the 20th century. The system was formally abolished by Act of Parliament in 1936, but 'voluntary tithing', in which church members commit themselves to an annual gift equal to one-tenth of their income, continues in Britain as well as in the United States, and other parts of the world.

COLLECTION Rural History Centre, The University of Reading

Title-page

The title-page of a printed book represents the formal opening of the body of the book. It follows the front endpaper and the half-title, and on its two sides it should carry all the information the reader requires about the book's subject matter, provenance, antecedents, production, property rights, date, etc. Latterly its reverse has carried the book's ISBN (International Standard Book Number) and cataloguing information.The single leaf represents, as it were, the book's 'identity card'.

By all ordinary standards the title-page cannot be described as an item of ephemera, as the bound book is normally produced with a view to maximum permanence. There is one context, however, in which the title-page is undeniably and specifically ephemeral. This is its use, in former times, as a pre-publication advertisement.

In the Elizabethan period, and later, it was customary for title-pages to be printed in excess of the number required for the book itself, and for these to be posted up in advance of the book's appearance. In London they were nailed to public whipping posts, to the pillars in St Paul's Cathedral, and to the walls of the Inns of Court. It is said that at one period bookbinders' apprentices were sent round the town on Saturday nights posting up the title-pages of books that were to be completed in the following week. Title-pages were also posted up by booksellers, before and after publication, using the small panes of their shopwindows as display frames. It is thought that the very lengthy subtitles that appeared on title-pages may derive from their use as posters – though lengthy main titles were also a characteristic of many early books.

Widespread use of the title-page as a 'poster' is underlined by the story of a Mr Stevens, 'a gentleman of a typographical turn', who devised and printed title-pages 'of strange and ludicrous books speedily to be published which were never to be published, nor indeed had any existence; and these title-pages he dabbed up in the cool of the evening at the corners of the public streets to stir up the expectations of those who stopped'.

The title-page as a convention appeared only slowly; the handwritten book, and many early printed books, normally carried publishing details on their final page. The first decorative title-page appeared in Johann Müller (Regiomontanus), *Calendrium*, printed in Venice by Erhard Ratdolt in 1476. Decorative title-pages in succeeding centuries passed through design phases corresponding to their times employing, variously, woodcut, copper engravings, wood-engravings, and lithography. There was much plagiarism and indiscriminate multiple use of printing blocks and plates, the same border design serving as a frame for widely differing titles over long periods.

The collecting of title-pages of the kind undertaken by John Bagford (1650–1716) in connection with a projected history of printing must always be open to charges of vandalism. There is an assumption, not necessarily justified, that the item has been preserved at the sacrifice of a complete volume. The position is made no easier by the fact that, except in rare cases, the distinction between a true title-page and a bookseller's 'poster' is difficult to establish.

REFERENCES Edward Rowe Mores, *A Dissertation upon English Typographical Founders and Founderies*, 3rd edn (Oxford: Oxford University Press, 1961);Alexander Nesbitt (ed.), *200 Decorative Title-Pages* (New York/London: Dover, 1964); Marjorie Plant, *The English Book Trade* (London: Allen & Unwin, 1974); Melvin H. Wolf (ed.), *Catalogue and Indexes to the Title-pages of English Printed Books preserved in the British Library's Bagford Collection* (London: British Museum Publications, 1974)

COLLECTIONS Bagford Collection, British Library, London; St Bride Printing Library, London

SOCIETIES American Printing History Society, New York; Printing Historical Society, London

Tobacco paper

Tobacco was among the first commodities to be sold in printed paper wrappers. Among the earliest surviving dated examples is a specimen in the Guildhall Library, London. It bears an armorial device, the name of Thomas Lacy, Martin's Lane, Cannon Street, London, and the date 1669. It seems likely that printed wrapping papers for tobacco appeared some time before this, however.

The design element of tobacco papers was normally confined to the centre of the printed sheet, which was large enough to accommodate varying quantities of tobacco. The earliest designs were in the tradition of the BOOKPLATE, but later they took on the characteristics of the TRADE CARD and were often printed from plates actually designed as trade cards. Engraved pictorial designs were common in Germany, Holland, and France, although almost everywhere they gave way to the crude woodcuts that were to remain the common denominator of the tobacco paper from the mid 18th century to the 1940s.

Chief among its pictorial motifs were the black man, the sailor, and the sailing ship – all of which suggested the exotic origins of the product. (The 'negro' image became confused with that of the North American Indian, whose head-dress the negro often wore.) In Britain, there also emerged the image of the Scotsman, whose figure became identified with the tobacconist. David Wishart, a conspirator in the Jacobite rebellion, had a life-size effigy of a Scotsman outside his London tobacco shop; after the failure of the 1745 rebellion Wishart and his friends decamped. The figure became a trade symbol by accident and survived in a lifesize representation outside a Cheltenham tobacconist, Charles Dickins, in the 1950s.

The tobacco paper was the first advertising item to incorporate the 'series' concept, in which the customer receives variants in sequence as the tobacco happens to be purchased. Rhymes, mottoes, puzzles, and jokes, some illustrated and others purely typographic, appeared on tobacco papers and wrappers from the early 19th century to the beginning of the next. Others featured riddles, such as 'Why is a Churchyard like an Inn?' Answers are never given and it has to be assumed that the buyer, driven to desperation, returned to the tobacconist, who revealed the secret in return for another purchase.

The simple tobacco paper was superseded by the tobacco wrapper when the manufacturer took over the role of packager from the shopkeeper. The term 'wrapper' properly applies only to the manufacturer's version, though it is sometimes also used in reference to the shopkeeper's paper. Also occasionally misused is the term LABEL, which correctly denotes an item *affixed* to a package, not to the printed image on the paper itself. Confusion may also arise from tobacco papers having later been cut down to the limits of the printed image, thus creating the impression of a label or trade card.

As in other forms of early ephemera, tobacco graphics show evidence of plagiarism. Initially, when designs were commissioned by tobacconists independently, plagiarism was widespread – and largely ignored. Later, when the labelled wrapper had become part of the manufacturer's own product, the matter was taken extremely seriously. In the 1890s, W. D. & H. O. Wills issued a leaflet showing their own 'Best Birds Eye' label and a counterfeit design produced in Copenhagen. The leaflet itself and – as the company pointed out – the genuine label were printed on paper watermarked 'WD & HO'. (By this time the wrapper had evolved into a label, not for a package, but a tin.)

Tobacco papers were normally printed in black (occasionally red) on white or tinted paper; sizes vary between 120 × 120 mm (4¾ × 4¾ in) and 500 × 320 mm (19¾ × 12½ in).

REFERENCES Alec Davis, *Package and Print* (London: Faber & Faber, 1967); F. W. Fairholt, *Tobacco: its History and Associations* (London: Chatto & Windus, 1876); Sir Ambrose Heal, *London Tradesmen's Cards of the XVIII Century* (London: B. T. Batsford, 1925); John Lewis, *Printed Ephemera* (Ipswich: W. S. Cowell, 1962); Walter von zur Westen, *Reklamekunst aus Zwei Jahrtausende* (Berlin: Eigenbrodler, 1925)

COLLECTIONS Bagford Collection, British Library; John Johnson Collection, Bodleian Library, Oxford; Guildhall Library, London; Bella C. Landauer Collection, New York Historical Society

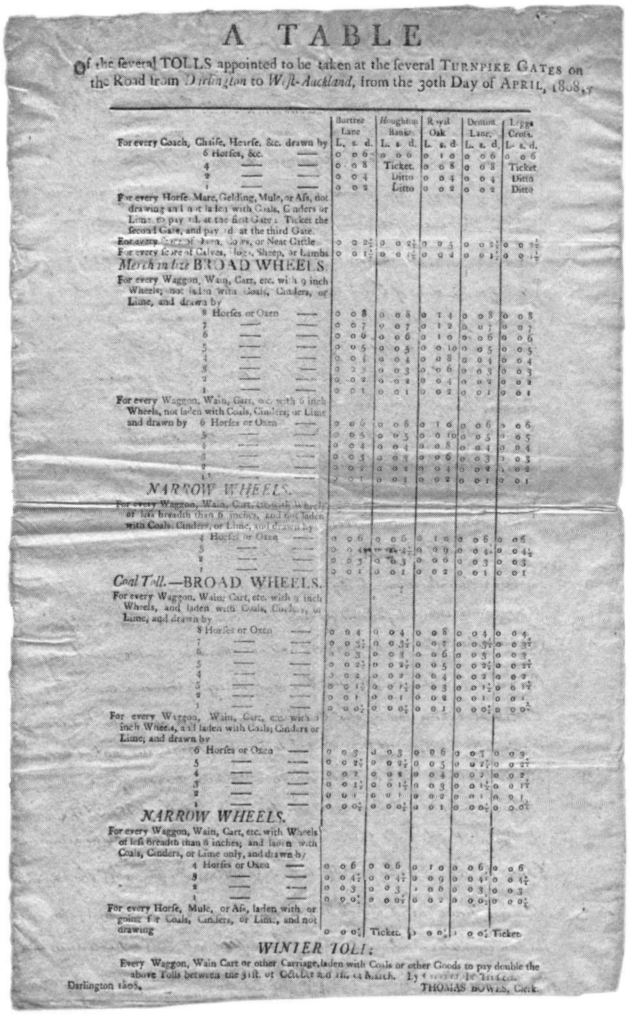

Toll/ferry rate-list

Rates of toll and ferriage, normally listed on noticeboards at the point of payment, are also found as printed broadsides or handbills. They provide information not only on charges, but on the nature of the traffic concerned.

The 1814 rate-list for the toll road at Peru, Vermont, for example, draws a distinction between the 'wheeled pleasure carriage' and the working 'wagon', the rates for the latter being considerably lower. Similarly, in winter, a sled or 'lumber sleigh' is cheaper than a 'pleasure sleigh'.

The rate-list for London's Waterloo Bridge (1817) includes not only individuals on foot (one penny each) and the usual range of vehicles – coach, Berlin, landau, vis-à-vis, chariot, chaise, calash, pleasure carriage, hearse, litter, etc. (one shilling and sixpence) – but droves of oxen or neat cattle (per score, eightpence) and of calves, hogs, sheep, or lambs (per score, fourpence).

A list published in 1838 by the North Union Railway Co., Preston, Lancashire, cites a long and detailed list of goods and products chargeable per ton per mile, culminating in a final catch-all: 'For all Cotton and other Wool, Hides, Drugs, Manufactured Goods and all other Wares, Merchandize, Matters or Things, one penny-three-farthings per Ton per mile'.

The rate-list of the Jersey City Ferry in November 1847 cites over ninety distinct categories of person, animal, vehicle, product, and commodity (priced in cents). These include 'A Wheelbarrow and one person' (9 cts); 'Sucking pigs' (2 cts); 'Bundles of sole and upper leathers' (1 ct); 'Tobacco in kegs' (6¼ cts); 'Kegs of nails' (6¼ cts); 'Fancy chairs' (2 cts); 'Common chairs' (1 ct); and 'Boxes of window glass' (2 cts).

Toll table for turnpike gates on the road between Darlington and West-Auckland, valid from 30 April 1808. Letterpress. 425 × 272 mm (16¾ × 10¾ in)

Toll/turnpike ticket

Toll and turnpike fees were charged when the large-scale building and repair of roads began in the early 19th century (though the principle had been exercised spasmodically for centuries). In Britain, acts of Parliament permitted private capitalization of the maintenance of specific roads, together with the right to charge for access or transit. The system flourished, with indifferent practical benefits to road-users, until the 1860s, when unpopularity, aided by the trend to centralization of control, made it no longer tenable. At the height of the turnpike era there were some 8000 toll-gates in Britain. In the United States and elsewhere similar systems operated. A 'Second turnpike era' started in America with the building of the Pennsylvania turnpike in 1940.

Toll tickets of the 18th and 19th centuries were normally squarish in format, typically 50 × 64 mm (2 × 2½ in), and printed black on white or tinted paper. They represented a receipt for cash paid at a toll-gate or turnpike (a swinging bar across the road). They were among the most commonplace – and now the rarest – of early 19th-century printed ephemera.

Most examples are crudely printed, though some earlier specimens reflect the creative zeal of the conscientious local printer. Tickets normally carry the name of the place of entry, and sometimes names of other points on the journey, space for the date to be written in, and sometimes also provision for recording details of vehicles, animals, etc. In some cases vehicles were charged by weight, a weighbridge reading being written on the ticket. There were also rarer cases, notably in the 18th century, before the 'turnpike explosion', in which a specially-dated ticket was printed each day. Other tickets, designated 'Sunday tickets', carried a special surcharge. Toll tickets were also issued for passage over certain bridges and at the majority of ferries. When 'frost fairs' were held on the frozen Thames, watermen even charged the public for walking out over the ice (*see* FROST-FAIR PAPERS).

Most of the Thames bridges charged a toll, their tickets being somewhat larger; some of them featured decorative, though crude, wood-engravings in which the tariff and the day of the week appeared as part of the design. As an added defence against fraud, paper colour was changed day by day. The bridges of Boston, Massachusetts, were similarly managed.

Except for the major bridge tickets, which clearly aspired to a measure of elegance, toll and turnpike tickets are roughly trimmed, and were probably cut from a multiple sheet by the tollkeeper.

See also POST-HORSE DUTY TICKET; WEIGHT CARD

Touring map

The folding pocket map, specifically designed for the tourist (as distinct from the traveller), emerged at the birth of the railway era, when for the first time it became possible for ordinary people to get away from their normal surroundings – simply for pleasure.

Touring maps reflect the developing story of travel and transport, through the periods of steam, cycle, and car. In the changing detail of their internal information and in the design of their covers they document a rapidly broadening touring scene.

Britain, because of its compactness and relative accessibility, developed the touring map in advance of the United States, where great distances limited travel for pleasure until well into the car and aircraft era. Among the earliest of Britain's touring maps was the series of county maps published in London by Longman & Co. and J. & C. Walker in the early 1840s. These maps, folded and tipped into hard covers, measured 120 × 90 mm (4¾ × 3½ in): they bore no cover illustration, but they were specifically produced for the use of the railway explorer and showed the latest line completions and stations. The coming of the railways generated large numbers of inland travel publications, including town and country guides, as well as 'Railway travelling companions' that described the view from the train as it passed along its route.

Folding touring maps, published in county editions, were available not only at bookshops but railway stations. Cassell's

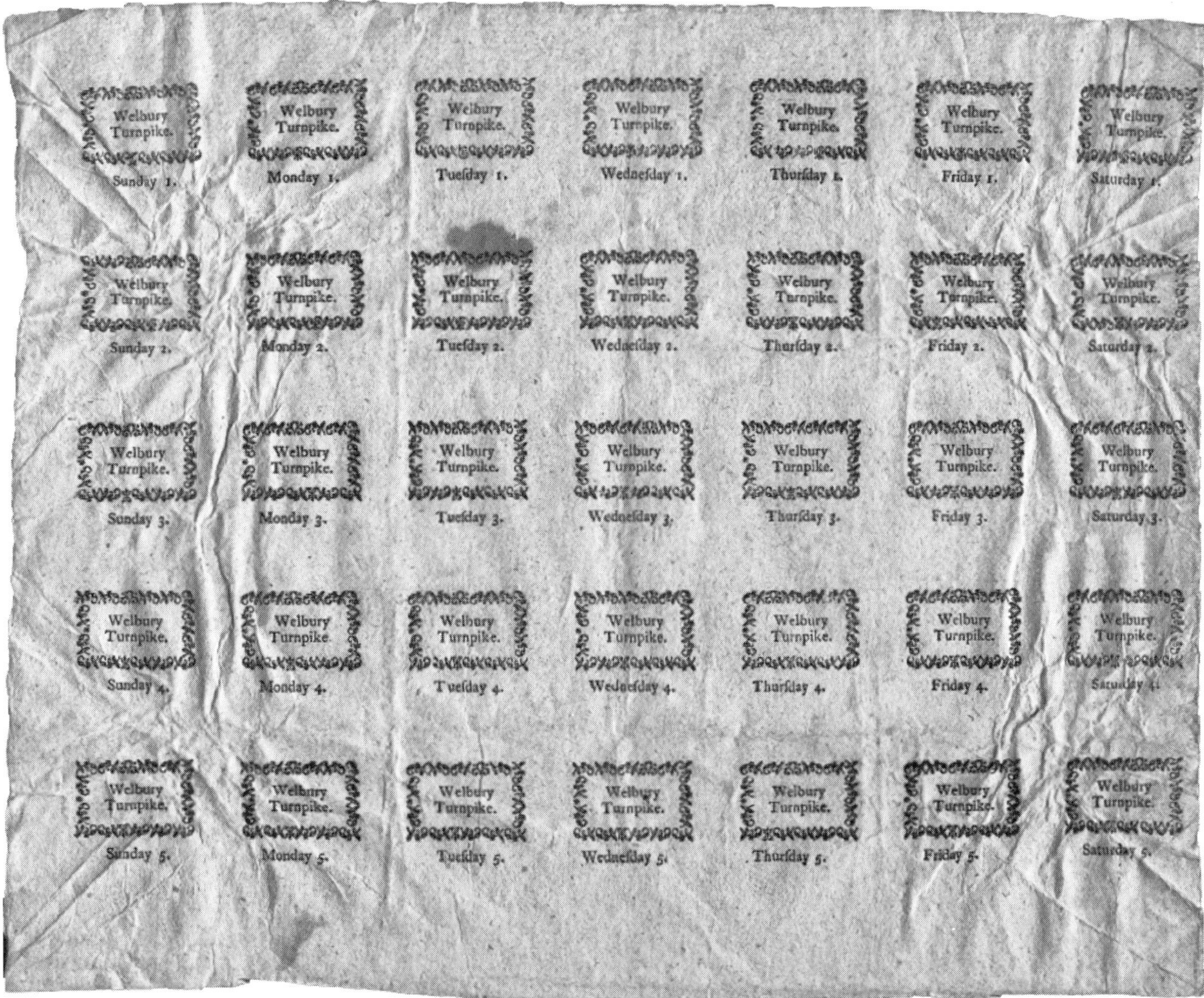

Set of thirty-five turnpike tickets, each for a different day of the week and month, c. 1800. Letterpress. Sheet size 265 × 325 mm (10½ × 12¾ in)

Road and Rail County Maps (early 1860s) had a two-part wood-engraved cover illustration showing, in one picture, country-goers relaxing in the open air and, in the other, riding in a railway carriage. The series comprised fifty maps 'in sheets, Threepence each, folded; and in a neat Wrapper for the Pocket, Fourpence each', and had been 'wrought out with such laborious fullness and exactitude ... that scarcely a Hamlet, and in many instances scarcely a Farm is omitted'. Their folded size was 180 × 110 mm (7⅛ × 4⅜ in), which soon became – and still remains – more or less standard.

Many 19th-century map publishers modified their productions to keep pace with changes, often overprinting old maps with new railways – or in some cases merely changing titles – to convey an impression of complete updating. The maps of a number of publishers remained in print throughout the period, either under their original styling or as incorporated in take-overs. George Frederick Cruchley, whose business had begun early in the century, survived (in name at least) into the 1890s. Some of his printing plates were bought up by Gall & Inglis of Edinburgh, who continued as publishers of touring maps for cyclists as well as railway travellers.

Cycling brought new impetus to sales of touring maps. So, in the early 20th century, did motoring. Bacon's 'County Maps' series conveys the changing scene with successive cover pictures of cyclists, lady cyclists, drivers, lady drivers, and annotations of 'rideable roads' and 'danger hills'. Many such turn-of-the-century maps continued, however, to show turnpikes and 'gentlemen's seats' – the country estates of the nobility and gentry.

Other British touring map publishing names included Ward Lock, W. & A. K. Johnston, and H. Grube. On the continent publishers included Freytag & Berndt (Vienna); Cartes Taride (Paris), and Kummerly & Frey (Bern). Not least significant, among those interested in motoring, were the publications of Michelin and Dunlop.

Magazines and other commercial interests also published touring maps. Typical are Hovis's 'Cycle Road Map' (showing 'free inflating stations'), and Bazaar Exchange & Mart's map 'For all Cyclists and Roadmen'. The Automobile Association and the Royal Automobile Club also issued maps. All these were produced by map specialists, such as George Philip & Son and Bartholomew & Son, who also published extensively themselves.

The history of the folding tourist map in Britain is closely linked with that of the Ordnance Survey, the Government's official map-producing agency. Virtually every touring map published in Britain was based, with or without permission, on Ordnance Survey publications. Today, with copyright observance strictly enforced, dependence on the Survey is complete.

The Ordnance Survey's own series of maps, first published in 1801, is the most detailed and exhaustive of its kind in the world. Two series of 1 inch to 1 mile tourists' and district maps published in the period 1919 to 1938 carried pictorial covers of particular interest. Most of the illustrations, generally in four colours, were by Ellis Martin and his assistant, Arthur Palmer. Another artist whose work appeared on map covers was John Willis, also a member of the Survey's staff, who was to become Director-General (1953–57). Much of the reproduction material for the full 'pictorial cover' series was destroyed in an air raid in World War II. A comparable post-war series, the 1:25,000 leisure series, with pictorial covers designed by Harry Titcombe, carries eighteen different pictures of regional birdlife by the same artist.

At the end of the 20th century only the Ordnance Survey and Philip remained of the famous British map publishing names of the previous century.

American touring maps are based largely on material supplied by the US Coast and Geodetic Survey, and other map-making agencies, both governmental and commercial. Maps issued by oil companies (free of charge until 1986) were widespread from the 1930s when intensive oil-company promotion began. British and European oil companies also publish touring maps as give-aways. [MR and TN]

REFERENCE John Paddy Browne, *Map Cover Art* (Southampton: Ordnance Survey, 1990)

SOCIETY The Charles Close Society for the Study of Ordnance Survey Maps

Toy book

The toy book, though it had its roots in a wide range of children's novelty publications in 19th-century Britain, was further popularized by the firm of Louis Prang & Co. in Boston in the 1860s.

The Prang Co. put out two series of books. In one, *The Christmas Stocking Library*, a picture story appeared on an extending 'panorama' or fold-out, each of whose twelve panels carried an illustration in oil colours and a four-line rhyming caption. The whole was folded into a colour-printed cover and the complete set of six titles was boxed as a Christmas gift.

In a second Prang series, called *Doll Book*, the whole publication was cut out in a shape appropriate to the subject. These books, featuring such characters as Robinson Crusoe, Cinderella, and Little Red Riding Hood, were boxed in threes as a Christmas gift. The company also produced a wide range of other 'shape booklets' as they were called, as well as shaped folding cards featuring leaves, shells, and other natural objects. These were enhanced by embossing. Shape books continued to appear for minor collections of illustrated verse into the early 20th century.

The toy book continued in Europe in the 19th century (much of the printing being done in Germany) and also remained popular into the following century. Publishers in Britain included the Raphael Tuck Co. – whose founder, like Prang in America, was a German immigrant of the 1830s – Routledge, and the Religious Tract Society.

REFERENCE Katharine M. McClinton, *The Chromolithographs of Louis Prang* (New York: C. N. Potter, 1973)

COLLECTIONS Florida State University, Tallahassee, Florida

Toy theatre

Originally styled 'Juvenile drama', the toy theatre was introduced in London in 1811 for the presenting of children's versions of the successful plays of the day. Miniature stage prosceniums, backcloths, and characters, printed on paper for cutting out, were supplied with simplified scripts for children to speak as they manipulated characters by wires from the wings.

Credit for the origination of the toy theatre is divided between J. K. Green and William West. There were several important later publishers, but the name of Benjamin Pollock is among the best-known in the toy-theatre world. He was the last surviving publisher of the plays in their original form. Pollock's shop in Hoxton, London, was world-famous, and he continued

Toy theatre characters, published by J. Redington, Hoxton Street, London, mid 19th century. Lithographed and hand-coloured. 170 × 215 mm (6¾ × 8½ in)

in business until his death in 1937. The firm continues as Pollock's Toy Theatres, Scala Street, London W1. Pollock's business had been founded by John Redington, a Hoxton compositor; Pollock, a frequent visitor to his shop, eventually married Redington's daughter, Eliza, and the couple continued the business after Redington's death in 1876.

Many of the prints still on sale in the late 20th century came from the original Benjamin Pollock stock, and surviving original copperplates have also been used for the production of fresh prints. 'Repros', made by copying original prints, are also available. Original prints are readily distinguishable from reproductions – principally by their better paper quality and clarity of image. Recent prints from the original plates are less easily recognized, however, and the difficulty is compounded by the fact that many of the originally marketed prints had been transferred from copperplate to lithographic stone for publication.

Coloured versions are no more readily dated, but a firm pointer to age is provided by indications of the use of a STENCIL. Although vast numbers were coloured free-hand (and recent free-hand colouring may be indistinguishable from earlier work even to the specialist), many were stencil-coloured. As this technique is not normally used in modern times, evidence of stencilling – 'stencil slips' or double outline – is likely to indicate an 'original'.

Prints also exist with the byline 'G Skelt'; these were privately reprinted in Jersey in the first half of the 20th century by George Wood (also known as George Conetta). The originals from which he worked were in fact the 19th-century productions of the Skelt family in London. Wood (or Conetta) adopted the name as a link with the past. Since none of the Christian names of the original Skelt family began with a 'G', prints bearing that initial are readily distinguishable as 20th-century reproductions.

Since their inception early in the 19th century, a total of some 300 toy-theatre plays have been published, of which the most famous is *The Miller and his Men* (1813). New plays, specially designed for performance by children, were published in the 20th century; among these was *The High Toby* by J. B. Priestley (1948).

The toy theatre is essentially a North European phenomenon, though there are publishers in France (notably Pellerin et Cie of Épinal) and Spain. Germany and Denmark are the principle European publishing countries.

REFERENCES Georg Garde, *Theatergeschichte im Spiegel der Kindertheater* (Copenhagen: Borgens Vorlag, 1971); Walter Röhler, *Grosse Liebe zu Kleinen Theatern* (Hamburg: M. von Schroder, 1963); George Speaight, *The History of the English Toy Theatre*, rev. edn (London: Studio Vista, 1969); A. E. Wilson, *Penny Plain, Twopence Coloured* (London: Harrap, 1932)

COLLECTIONS Frank Bradley Collection, Derby Museum & Art Gallery; Hinkins Collection and Stone Collection, Victoria & Albert Museum, London; Jonathan King Collection, Museum of London; Puppentheatermuseum, Stadtmuseum, München; Rare Book Library, Toronto University; Walter Röhler Sammlung, Institut für Puppenspiel, Bochum, Germany; Theatre Collection, Harvard College Library, Cambridge, Mass.; Ralph Thomas Collection, Department of Prints and Drawings, British Museum

Trade advertiser

Known under such titles as *Trade Advertiser, Commercial Advertiser, Tradesmen's Local Advertiser*, etc., the 19th-century advertiser was a forerunner of the 'controlled circulation' journal or freebie, a sheet distributed free of charge dedicated to advertisements for local businesses. The medium was widely used, both in Britain and America. It was closely related to the 'local guide', for which a charge was normally made, and in some cases it evolved into, or was merged with, a local newspaper. In Britain the suffix '–and Advertiser' formed part of the title of many local newspapers of the period and remains vestigially in use today.

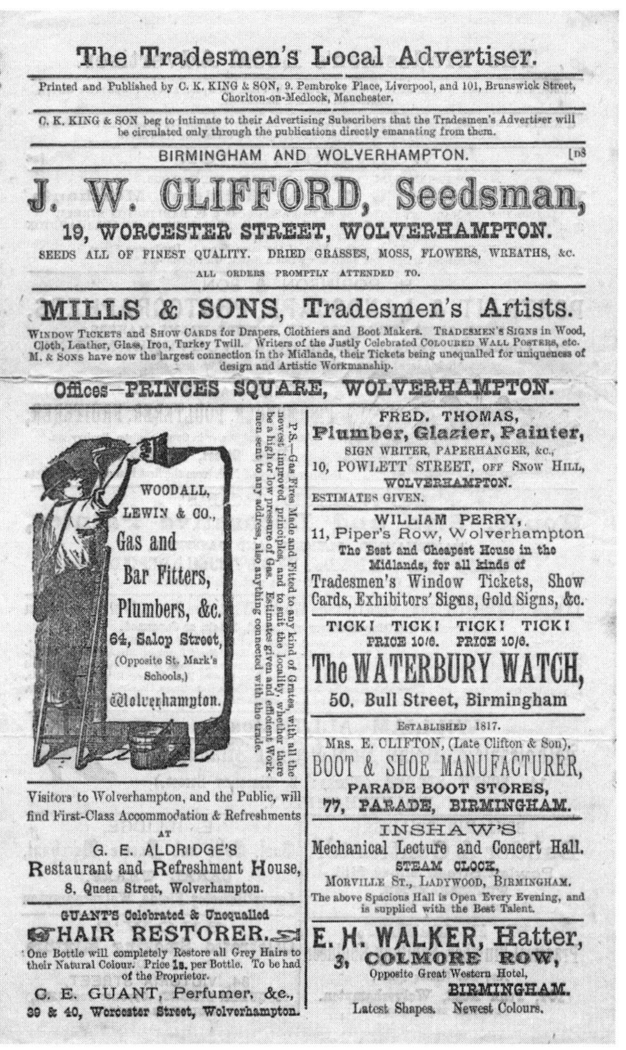

The Tradesmen's Local Advertiser.

Printed and Published by C. K. KING & SON, 9, Pembroke Place, Liverpool, and 101, Brunswick Street, Chorlton-on-Medlock, Manchester.

C. K. KING & SON beg to intimate to their Advertising Subscribers that the Tradesmen's Advertiser will be circulated only through the publications directly emanating from them.

BIRMINGHAM AND WOLVERHAMPTON. [n8

J. W. CLIFFORD, Seedsman,
19, WORCESTER STREET, WOLVERHAMPTON.
SEEDS ALL OF FINEST QUALITY. DRIED GRASSES, MOSS, FLOWERS, WREATHS, &c.
ALL ORDERS PROMPTLY ATTENDED TO.

MILLS & SONS, Tradesmen's Artists.
WINDOW TICKETS and SHOW CARDS for Drapers, Clothiers and Boot Makers. TRADESMEN'S SIGNS in Wood, Cloth, Leather, Glass, Iron, Turkey Twill. Writers of the Justly Celebrated COLOURED WALL POSTERS, etc. M. & SONS have now the largest connection in the Midlands, their Tickets being unequalled for uniqueness of design and Artistic Workmanship.
Offices—PRINCES SQUARE, WOLVERHAMPTON.

WOODALL, LEWIN & CO.,
Gas and Bar Fitters, Plumbers, &c.
64, Salop Street,
(Opposite St. Mark's Schools,)
Wolverhampton.

P.S.—Gas Fires Made and Fitted to any kind of Grates, with all the newest improved principles, and to suit the locality, whether there be a high or low pressure of Gas. Estimates given and efficient Workmen sent to any address, also anything connected with the trade.

Visitors to Wolverhampton, and the Public, will find First-Class Accommodation & Refreshments
AT
G. E. ALDRIDGE'S
Restaurant and Refreshment House,
8, Queen Street, Wolverhampton.

GUANT'S Celebrated & Unequalled
HAIR RESTORER.
One Bottle will completely Restore all Grey Hairs to their Natural Colour. Price 1s. per Bottle. To be had of the Proprietor.
C. E. GUANT, Perfumer, &c.,
39 & 40, Worcester Street, Wolverhampton.

FRED. THOMAS,
Plumber, Glazier, Painter,
SIGN WRITER, PAPERHANGER, &c.,
10, POWLETT STREET, OFF SNOW HILL,
WOLVERHAMPTON.
ESTIMATES GIVEN.

WILLIAM PERRY,
11, Piper's Row, Wolverhampton
The Best and Cheapest House in the Midlands, for all kinds of
Tradesmen's Window Tickets, Show Cards, Exhibitors' Signs, Gold Signs, &c.

TICK! TICK! TICK! TICK!
PRICE 10/6. PRICE 10/6.
The WATERBURY WATCH,
50, Bull Street, Birmingham

ESTABLISHED 1817.
MRS. E. CLIFTON, (Late Clifton & Son),
BOOT & SHOE MANUFACTURER,
PARADE BOOT STORES,
77, PARADE, BIRMINGHAM.

INSHAW'S
Mechanical Lecture and Concert Hall.
STEAM CLOCK,
MORVILLE ST., LADYWOOD, BIRMINGHAM.
The above Spacious Hall is Open Every Evening, and is supplied with the Best Talent.

E. H. WALKER, Hatter,
3, COLMORE ROW,
Opposite Great Western Hotel,
BIRMINGHAM.
Latest Shapes. Newest Colours.

Trade advertiser, late 19th century. Letterpress, printed and published by C.K.King & Son, Liverpool and Manchester. 255 × 156 mm (10 × 6¼ in)

The trade advertiser commonly took the form of a single sheet, printed on one or both sides, with single- or double-column display advertisements. Sheet size was of the order of 250 × 150 mm (9⅞ × 6 in). Space was sold to advertisers by the column inch. In many cases the publication appeared monthly. Its masthead was often dated, and sometimes bore a note specifying areas of circulation, the quantity distributed, and an indication that the sheet was free of charge.

The concept of collective local advertising was also applied in Britain to the MULREADY ENVELOPE and generally to stationers' envelopes, postcards, bookmarks, blotters, and calendars.

See also ADVERTISING ENVELOPE

Trade card [plate 13b]

The term 'trade card', already ambiguous in its first usage (historically it referred to an item of paper), has become doubly ambiguous through its use to denote multicoloured collectable give-aways. The bubble-gum card, and all its related phenomena, must be clearly distinguished from the original tradesman's name-and-address slip. The use of the term in its more recent sense will be considered in a later paragraph.

For the antiquarian ephemerist the trade card is the printed paper used by the early shopkeeper as an aide-mémoire for his customers. The paper later became a card, and the term 'trade card' came to be used for all such items, even though some were of paper.

The printed-paper version was an all-purpose jotter, bearing the tradesman's name and address – or, before the introduction of street numbering, a long-winded indication of where he was to be found. Printed from plates engraved by a local craftsman, it also served as an invoice and receipt form, as a homing guide for messengers, and as memorandum sheet for quotations, price lists, and other handwritten business fragments.

Prior to the 1760s the dominant item of shop publicity was the hanging signboard. But the obstruction it caused, and the danger it presented to passers-by in stormy weather, led finally to prohibition by law. Henceforth, signboards were to be fixed flush to the wall of the shop concerned. With his visibility thus impaired, the shopkeeper centred attention on his trade card, in many cases reproducing on it the sign he had been obliged to withdraw. Shortly afterwards, with the introduction of street numbering, he added the number to the information on the paper. His earlier designation: 'John Smith, Fishmonger in the Strand over against the Church of St Sepulchre' became 'John Smith, 72 Strand'. Notwithstanding this simplification, shopkeepers took care to retain the sign or symbol of their shop; widespread illiteracy placed a premium on their retention, though the signs themselves might bear no relation to the trade in question. Often these were second- and third-hand acquisitions from former tenants who might or might not have run businesses appropriate to the sign.

The evolution of the early trade card conveys these matters in detail. The trade card later evolved into the business card proper, the pasteboard slip still in use today. It also turned into more specialized items: the commercial BILLHEAD (for which it increasingly did duty),the LEAFLET, LETTERHEAD, POSTER, PRICE LIST – in fact, the whole spectrum of printed stationery and publicity material. The trade card may thus be seen as the foundation stone of commercial printed graphics.

From the trade card sprang not only stationery and general promotion material but POINT-OF-SALE DISPLAY, LABELS,

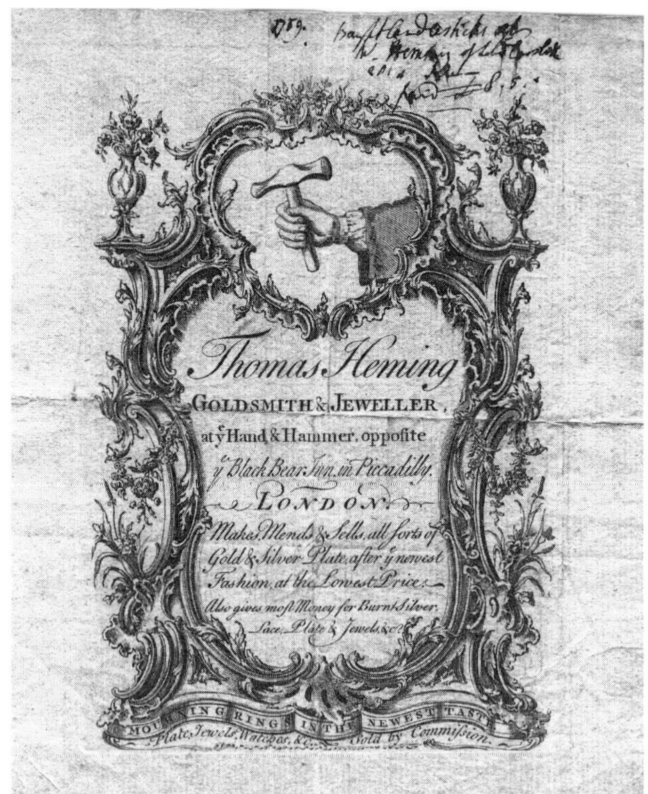

Trade card of Thomas Heming, goldsmith and jeweller, Piccadilly, London, mid 18th century. Copper-engraved. 195 × 165 mm (7⅝ × 6½ in)

PACKAGING, and the whole apparatus of mass-marketing.

The early trade card, with its wealth of incidental information on trades, locations, and terms of business, is a fruitful area of topographical and social history research. It is also a genre much admired for its often high aesthetic standards. The hanging signboard had been for many tradesmen a status symbol above and beyond commercial profit, and corresponding care was bestowed on the production of the trade card. The earliest trade cards were printed by letterpress from type, but the introduction of commercial engraving and, later, lithography allowed almost unlimited pictorial and decorative treatments. Even the humblest tradesman aspired to an impressive trade card: Hogarth, Bartolozzi, and Bewick are among the great names who accepted commissions to work on trade cards.

The tradesman of the day relied for most of his custom on the 'upper classes', whose modes and manners he sought to emulate. The 'tone' of the trade card reflects the deference – often obsequiousness – shown to the station of the customer. The approach could not fail to please: to 'Royalty, the Nobility and the Gentry' it was no more than fitting; to the aspiring middle class it was flattering.

Later trade cards, though clearly directed at a wider public, retained much of the same spirit, featuring coats of arms and other heraldic forms – even in the improbable context of fire-irons, artificial limbs, and bug destruction. In an alternative treatment the tradesman's wares were illustrated: a montage of hardware, or a single item, might appear with his name and address, and such slogans as 'Repairs done in the Neatest Manner', 'Families Waited on Daily'.

The decorative conventions adopted by trade engravers became more or less standardized. As with the STOCK BLOCK of the letterpress printer, 'stock images' appeared, copied from one to another. Trade engravers were, for the most part, skilled craftsmen rather than creative artists. They were competent copyists, reducing the often sketchy drawings of the originating artist to clearly defined impressions in printer's ink. Whatever their medium, they brought distinction and definition to images that sometimes lacked both.

As in other contexts, the respective contributions of trade-card artist and engraver are indicated in formal bylines: John Brown del[ineavit]; John Jones sculp[sit] (John Brown drew the picture; John Jones engraved it). Occasionally a third name indicates the 'conceiver' of the design: John Thomas inv[entavit]. It is not easy to apportion merit. Sometimes a single name may assume responsibility for all three functions. But certainly some trade-card images are the work of artists rather than mere craftsmen. Many designs are non-pictorial, presenting the tradesman's message simply as a cohesive symmetrical arrangement of flourished lettering. Here too a single unqualified byline may indicate designer, engraver, or both. But in pictorial and non-pictorial cards alike it must be remembered that a single name may be that of the proprietor of the printing establishment – not of the actual executant.

Among the trade-card elegancies of the 1840s and 1850s was the textured card, whose white high-gloss surface carried a low-relief patterning, often featuring a central frame within which the printed image appeared. Also strikingly simple – and exceedingly rare – is the device of the blind-embossed coat of arms. Peirce's card for Eastwood and Perrett of Windsor, 'by Royal Appointment Silversmiths and Jewellers', is a model of restrained ostentation. By no means all tradesmen who sported the royal arms were entitled to do so: many included the device as an unofficial 'extra'. But in the case of Eastwood and Perrett, with Windsor Castle close by, we may assume entitlement.

The engraved copper plates from which trade cards were printed were also available for other uses. One common application was as a billhead. In many invoices of the period – particularly those for hostelries – the characteristically long strip of paper may bear the whole of the trade-card image at its head, complete with the impression of the edges of the plate. The plates were also used to print advertisements in local trade guides, the plate being printed in a run of single sheets, each of which was bound in with the finished book. The image appeared as a small horizontal design on a vertical page, with white space above and below it. In a later development, larger vertical engravings were produced specially for the purpose; they occupied the whole of the page and were thus more effective for their function. They also gave rise to a new item of trade ephemera. Having, for safety's sake, had more printed than were required, the tradesman now found himself with 'overs '–which he used as publicity leaflets.

One trade-card phenomenon, apparently unique in printing technology, appeared principally in the 1840s in Belgium. Here the card was lithographed in iridescent inks, producing colour changes as the angle of view alters. The effect, which defies today's reproduction techniques, is remarkable. The delicacy of the designs, coupled with the fascination of the colour effect, makes the cards much sought after. The process appears to have been confined to a small group of printers, most of them in Brussels, with a few in Ghent, Liège, and Bruges. No similar work has appeared since, in Belgium or elsewhere.

In Britain, trade cards remained largely black and white, but in Europe, notably in Germany, Moravia, and Switzerland in the 1880s, multicoloured trade cards appeared. In America, with the arrival of immigrant chromolithographic printers, colour-printed trade cards became a familiar item on the commercial landscape.

The American trade card became radically different from the British in the 19th century. Essentially, it was a brightly coloured picture, devised as a collectable. Presented as a series of attractive GIVE-AWAYS, the cards were either produced for a firm or were overprinted with its name; the space on the back of the card was used for the main publicity message. The aim was to tempt customers to return to the same source continually, extending their collection of cards in the same series.

American chromolithographic printers supplied 'sets' of cards ready-printed with the tradesman's name or for overprinting locally. The Union Card Co. of Montpelier, Vermont, advertised: 'We will send you Fancy Advertising Cards, no two alike, With or Without Advertisement on them, for only Twenty-five Three Cent Stamps, Post Free to any Address'. This was a totally new concept – a departure from the 'business card' in the formerly accepted sense and a move into a field which was to become a major promotion industry. Big names in the business were: (in New York), Mayer, Merkel & Ottmann; Donaldson Brothers; and Major & Knapp; (in Buffalo), Clay, Cosack & Co.; (in Detroit), The Calvert Lithography Co.; (in Chicago), Shober & Carqueville; and (in Boston), Bufford & Sons, and Louis Prang. Prang dominated the chromolithography scene throughout the period, manufacturing not only trade cards but a vast range of greetings cards and popular fine art reproductions. The eventual outcome of the coloured trade-card 'explosion' was the CIGARETTE CARD, the bubble-gum card, and the whole range of commercially generated 'collectables' of the 20th century.

A similar idea was widely taken up in Europe – though less enthusiastically in Britain. The Liebig Co. led the way with an immense output of chromolithographed 'sets' (*see* LIEBIG CARD). These circulated in separate language issues in French, German, Danish, Italian, Flemish, and English and were still being published in the 1970s. Series ranged from 'The Fables of La Fontaine' to 'Aircraft of the World'. The total number of sets issued since their inception in Germany in 1872 is 27,000, representing some 162 million cards. Other companies operated similar schemes including Van Houten in Holland, Suchard in Switzerland, and Bon Marché in France.

In another development, manufacturers put out a wide range of novelty cards. Published in sets or singly, they featured cutouts, flaps, stand-ups, lever-operated animations and a host of other contrivances. The end of the 19th century, with its great extension of the concept of the mass market, brought a proliferation of these items – by that time barely recognizable descendants of the original engraved trade card (*see* ADVERTISING NOVELTY).

The term 'trade card' today refers to a widely disparate range of items: confusion arises when it is used to refer, for example, to a Liebig card when what is understood is an early 19th-century shopkeeper's business card. Ambiguous use of the term has become widespread, however, and there now appears little hope of sorting the matter out. Confusion may at least be minimized if the term is qualified or modified. The terms 'early trade card', 'chromolitho trade card', and 'commercial collecting card' appear to offer a measure of clarity.

See also CARTE-DE-VISITE; CHANGE PACKET; COVER, POSTAL (ADDRESS, PRE-STREET NUMBERING); DECK PLAN; FURNITURE

LABEL; IRIDESCENT PRINTING; RING-GAUGE CARD; TRADE LABEL; TRADE LIST

REFERENCES H. R. Calvert, *Scientific Trade Cards in the Science Museum Collection* (London: HMSO, 1971); Sir Ambrose Heal, *London Tradesmen's Cards of the XVIII Century* (London: Batsford, 1925; reprinted, New York: Dover Books, 1968); Sir Ambrose Heal, *The London Goldsmiths 1200–1800* (Cambridge: Cambridge University Press, 1935; reprinted, Newton Abbot: David & Charles, 1978); Graham Hudson, 'Printed Ephemera and the Industrial Historian', *Industrial Archeology*, vol. 12, no. 4 (Tavistock, Devon: Graphmitre, 1977); Robert Jay, *The Trade Card in Nineteenth-Century America* (Columbia: University of Missouri Press, 1987); John Lewis, *Printed Ephemera* (Ipswich: W. S. Cowell, 1962); Walter von zur Westen, *Reklamekunst aus Zwei Jahrtausende* (Berlin: Eigenbrodler, 1925)

COLLECTIONS American Antiquarian Society, Worcester, Mass.; Heal Collection, British Museum; Guildhall Library, London; John Johnson Collection, Bodleian Library, Oxford; Bella C. Landauer Collection, New York Historical Society; Pepys Library, Magdalene College, Cambridge

Trade label

The term trade label normally applies to an identifying paper, slip, or ticket affixed to the handiwork of a trade craftsman. The trade label partakes of the qualities of a TRADE CARD, and in some cases was printed unchanged from the copperplate used for the trade card.

The label appears on the backs of pictures and other frames, in the lids of instrument boxes, on the underside of furniture, in the lining of hats, shoes, and other garments, and inside clocks, musical instruments, and luggage. In many cases its presence is vital to the authentication of the item in question and may distinguish a nonentity from a 'valuable collector's piece'. It is viewed by many as an integral part of the item, to be retained undisturbed at all costs. On the other hand, in many less critical contexts (broken picture frames, wall mirrors, etc.) removal may appear not only permissible but imperative.

Trade labels came into use in the later 17th century and were a familiar feature of the 18th and early 19th centuries. They survive in the late 20th century chiefly among picture framers. The many users of trade labels include scientific-instrument makers ('mathematical, optical, nautical and philosophical'); music-instrument makers (including musical-box makers); balance makers; cabinet makers; bookbinders; booksellers; stationers and printers; carvers, gilders, framers and mount-cutters; picture restorers; looking-glass manufacturers; die-sinkers and engravers; screen makers; silhouettists; and photographers.

See also BOOKBINDER'S TICKET; BOOKSELLER'S LABEL; FURNITURE LABEL; SHOE LABEL; VIOLIN LABEL

Trade list

The term is used to describe an itemized trade card, enumerating categories of goods for sale. Flourishing at the end of the 18th century, the trade list forms an evolutionary bridge between the earlier general TRADE CARD and the PRICE LIST. The trade card provides the briefest summary of the tradesman's wares, the trade list indicates the full extent of his stock-in-trade (without mention of prices); it seeks to impress simply by scope and length, whereas the price list gives details of selected articles and their prices. Early trade lists, like the trade card, are decoratively engraved, often with illustrations of some of the items listed. In later trade lists there was little or no attempt at decoration or typographic display, items being listed in general categories, often in three columns, and generally on one side only of a single sheet. A typical trade list of a small-town general store in Britain in 1800 was 300 × 200 mm (11⅞ × 7⅞ in), but some were much larger.

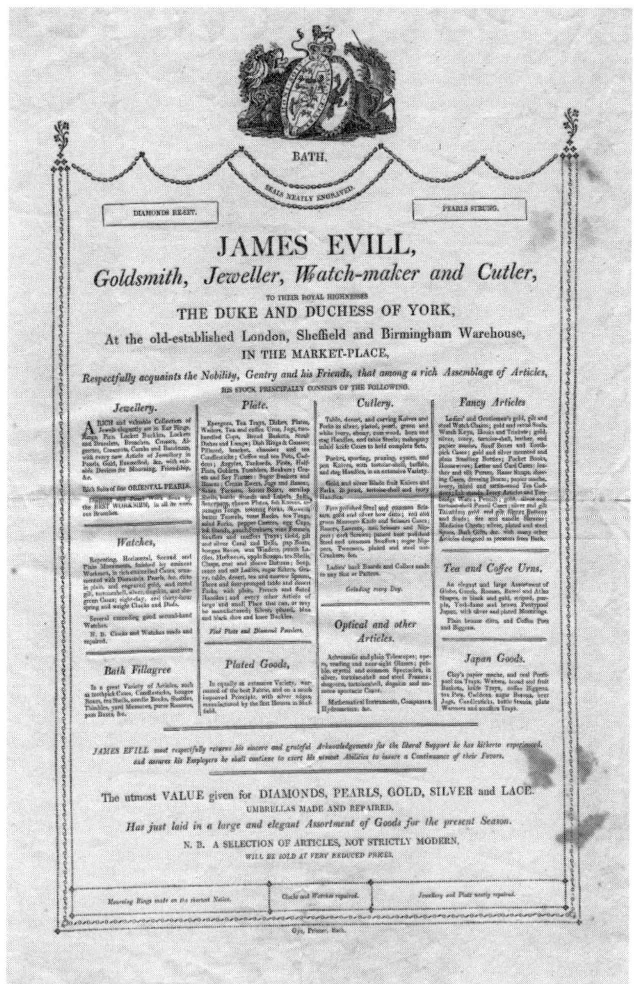
BATH.

SEALS NEATLY ENGRAVED.

DIAMONDS RE-SET. | PEARLS STRUNG.

JAMES EVILL,

Goldsmith, Jeweller, Watch-maker and Cutler,

TO THEIR ROYAL HIGHNESSES

THE DUKE AND DUCHESS OF YORK,

At the old-established London, Sheffield and Birmingham Warehouse,

IN THE MARKET-PLACE,

Respectfully acquaints the Nobility, Gentry and his Friends, that among a rich Assemblage of Articles,

HIS STOCK PRINCIPALLY CONSISTS OF THE FOLLOWING.

Jewellery. | *Plate.* | *Cutlery.* | *Fancy Articles*

Watches, | *Tea and Coffee Urns.*

Optical and other Articles.

Bath Fillagree | *Plated Goods,* | *Japan Goods.*

JAMES EVILL most respectfully returns his sincere and grateful Acknowledgements for the liberal Support he has hitherto experienced, and assures his Employers he shall continue to exert his utmost Abilities to insure a Continuance of their Favors.

The utmost VALUE given for DIAMONDS, PEARLS, GOLD, SILVER and LACE.

UMBRELLAS MADE AND REPAIRED.

Has just laid in a large and elegant Assortment of Goods for the present Season.

N. B. A SELECTION OF ARTICLES, NOT STRICTLY MODERN,

WILL BE SOLD AT VERY REDUCED PRICES.

Gye, Printer, Bath.

Trade list of James Evill, goldsmith, jeweller, watchmaker, and cutler, Bath, early 19th century. Letterpress, printed by Gye, Bath. 410 × 300 mm (16⅛ × 11⅞ in)

Such lists provide an insight into early retail trading. A significant feature is the multiplicity of goods stocked by the individual shopkeeper. The list of a 'grocer and tea dealer' in Salisbury (UK) in 1816 includes 'Sand Paper; Pipeclay and Pipes; Brushes and Baskets; Snuff and Tobacco; Gunpowder and Shot; Brimstone and Sulphur; Tape; Thread and Pins'. John Soulby (senior), a printer in Ulverston in the north of England, was not untypical of his trade in selling much more than stationery and related items. On a two-sided list of the early 19th century he included headings for 'Sundry articles from the Repository of Arts, in London', 'Music', 'Upholstery', 'Sundries' (including 'Pink Stain for Silk Stockings'), 'Patent Medicines' (with prices), and 'Perfumery, &c'. Patent medicines included 'Dixon's Antibilious Pills', 'Hooper's Female Pills', 'Ramsay's Anti-Odontalgia', and 'Taylor's Remedy' (for deafness).

Printers, by virtue of their craft, were regular users of the trade list, but the idea was adopted by grocers, haberdashers, pharmacists, and general traders. A notable variant was a list put out by Thomas Meers, the Whitechapel bellfounders: this detailed over four hundred churches in which the company's products had been installed, without mention of price.

REFERENCES John Lewis, *Printed Ephemera* (Ipswich: W. S. Cowell, 1962); Michael Twyman, 'A printer's travelling case of the early nineteenth century', *Printing Historical Society Bulletin*, 29, Winter 1990, pp. 10–12; Michael Twyman, *John Soulby, Printer, Ulverston* (Reading: University of Reading, 1966)

COLLECTIONS American Antiquarian Society, Worcester, Mass.; John Johnson Collection, Bodleian Library, Oxford

Trade rhyme

Rhymed advertising material, apparently composed by the tradesman himself, was a popular vogue of the 19th century. The device, a true forebear of the radio and television jingle, has its spiritual roots in the songs and ballads of early STREET LITERATURE. Specifically, it stems from the rhymed appeals put out by night watchmen, lamplighters and others, whose Christmas 'addresses' to householders were a feature of the 18th and 19th centuries (*see* BELLMAN'S VERSES). As with such items, the message of the early trade rhyme is commonly couched in personal terms, sometimes in the first person singular. In one early example, 'Lockett's Address to his friends at Dorchester, and its vicinity' (c.1790), the author introduced three columns of doggerel with the words: 'Shop Bills in Prose are now so trite,/So easy too for Folks to write,/So dull the Catalogue appears,/So grating to a Poet's Ears;/That I'm determined now to cross,/my little fav'rite Hobby Horse:/Just take a Sip at Helicon,/Recount my Wares, and thus just jog on...'. In the ensuing 150 lines the whole of Lockett's services and stock-in-trade are covered. These include commodities from verdigris and turpentine to cheese and tobacco, and services from printing to funerals. Rhymes – of varying degrees of tenuousness – include 'coffee' and 'off ye'; 'plates' and 'sheets'; 'credit' and 'did it'.

Rhymed advertising was a major feature of lottery promotions in Britain in the early 19th century, when leaflets bearing woodcut illustrations and rhyming captions were issued in huge quantities. Trade rhymes continued to be popular throughout the century and into the early 20th century. A leaflet put out by Harry Nice of Park Farm Dairy, Hampstead Road, London (c.1910), declares that 'The cheapest provisions are to be found/at Harry Nice's all the year round;/he meets the times in every way/by giving Lots of Money away;/on Saturday Next, I have just learned,/every purchaser of 1lb of butter/will have Two Pence Returned'.

Trade rhyme on a lottery bill of T. Bish, Cornhill and Charing Cross, London, early 19th century. Letterpress in wood-engraved surround. 124 × 213 mm (4⅞ × 8⅜ in)

Trade union membership certificate

Trade union membership, at first tentatively expressed in the 'Blank book' and TRAMPING CARD, was in the mid 19th century displayed in elaborate chromolithography in the form of 'emblems', certificates bearing the individual member's name and date of admission, and the signature of the union's general secretary. In the context of trade unionism, specifically in America during the period 1830 to 1900, the word 'emblem' came to be applied not only in its general sense of 'symbolic representation' but to the card or certificate that bore it. By the 1870s it was widely accepted as meaning the coloured certificate displayed in the homes of union members and, among a multitude of gold-framed mirrors and almanacs, on the walls of the upper rooms of pubs throughout the land.

The certificates, measuring some 560 × 460 mm (22 × 18⅛ in) and chromolithographed in numerous workings, were expressions not only of working-class solidarity but of craft pride and high moral purpose. Devised for each union individually, they sought to portray the traditions of the trade concerned. Most of them showed a central shield with 'supporters' (often craftsmen in working attire) and mottoes, many in English, some in Latin. Some unions, in traditional manner, published detailed explanations of the designs. They depicted scenes of care and compassion as well as workshop prowess. Many designs include the heavenly 'all-seeing eye', derived from freemasonry, and such symbols as the beehive (labour) and keys (knowledge) are common.

Declarations of goodness and non-aggression abound: 'In the Lord is All Our Trust' (Stone Mason's Friendly Society, 1868); 'Amore Uniti Sitis' (Be ye united in love) (Braziers and Sheet Metal Workers' Society, 1870); 'United to Protect Not Combined to Injure' (Amalgamated Society of Carpenters and Joiners, 1866). Later examples are less inspired: a central illustration of a planing machine on the certificates of the United Machine Workers' Association of the 1880s carries the legend 'Planing Machine'.

The heyday of the 'emblem' was the period 1870 to 1900. These were the years when trade unions multiplied (there were some 1300 unions in Britain at the time) and when chromolithography flourished.

Emblems were at first designed by worker-artists. William Hughes, himself a boilermaker, was commissioned by the founder members of the Order of Friendly Boilermakers to design their first emblem in 1834. Another worker-artist, James Sharples, produced the design for the Amalgamated Society of Engineers in 1852. On the whole, however, the work was given to professional artists, among them James Chant, Walter Crane, George Greatbach, John Saddler, and A. J. Waudby. Among the chief printer-designers of the 1880s (when production had got fully into its stride) were Gow Butterfield and Blades, East and Blades (the Blades, father and son, were ardent trade unionists). Alexander Gow was to emerge as the dominant figure in emblem production in the closing decades of the century. At least half the surviving specimens from this period bear his imprint.

As in other fields of Victorian graphic design, increased productivity brought much unobtrusive cannibalization. Figures, borders, slogans, and other elements appeared in only slightly modified form in more than one design. Actual photographs of union leaders, headquarters, machinery etc. began to appear as part of the design at the end of the 19th century. The certificates were commonly prepared for framing with a broad mount, the bevel of which was cut in curves or square to conform to and complement the general outline of the design. This treatment was also widely used in the mounting and framing of the ILLUMINATED ADDRESS.

The trade union membership certificate has many points in common with the trade union professional banner, which it often closely resembles. One of the recorded certificate artists, George Tuthill, was the celebrated banner-maker who was responsible, it is said, for more than three-quarters of all British trade union banners from 1837 onwards.

See also CARD OF THANKS; CHROMO; FIREMAN'S MEMBERSHIP CERTIFICATE

REFERENCE R. A. Leeson, *United We Stand: an Illustrated Account of Trade Union Emblems* (Bath: Adams & Dart, 1971)

COLLECTION Trades Union Congress Library, London

Tramping card

The tramping card was a tradesman's 'identity card', used by itinerant members of workers' clubs in the early 19th century to prove membership and entitlement to help from local clubs. Before the coming of the railways, Britain's employment fluctuations were more or less localized. It was therefore sensible for an unemployed craftsman to set out across the country 'on tramp' to find casual work in other areas.

In addition to the major trade unions, then only tentatively emerging as legal bodies, there were scores of small local groups, each committed to offering a few days' lodging to members on the road while they looked for work. Some societies provided members with a booklet guide to 'houses of call' showing itineraries and the amount of relief (in money, beer, and bed) available at each stop.

The tramping card bore an engraving of the society's insignia (forerunner of the devices used in processional banners), space for the bearer's name and membership number, and sometimes provision for entering the date and place of completion of his apprenticeship. In other cases the engraved device was printed on the otherwise blank sheet, with personal details added in handwriting in the blank space. Though described as a card, the document was often printed on paper, in a size and format that varied considerably. The printed image was black, though there was occasional use of a (single) colour.

The tramping card survived in various forms until the end of the 19th century (when it was known as a 'travelling card'), and is reported as being in use by travelling compositors in the printing trade as late as 1907.

REFERENCE Sheila Lewenhak (ed.), *The Early Trade Unions and the Prosecution of the Tolpuddle Martyrs*, Jackdaw, no. 35 (London: Cape, 1969)

Transfer lithography

The method of printing now known as lithography was discovered by Alois Senefelder in Munich in or around 1798. Originally it involved writing or drawing with greasy ink or crayon on slabs of compact limestone, hence the word lithography (Greek, *lithos*: stone; *graphein*: to write or draw).

Various branches of lithography were used for the printing of ephemera, but transfer lithography and, later, chromolithography (*see* CHROMO), were the two most important. From the outset, transfer lithography was developed by Senefelder in parallel with lithography itself. Instead of working directly on stone, writers and draughtsmen used much the same greasy materials on a specially prepared non-absorbent paper, known as transfer paper. These marks were then transferred by placing the paper face down on to the surface of a lithographic stone and pulling both through a press under considerable pressure. If all went well – and the process of transferring was not without its risks – the greasy marks on the paper were transferred to the stone intact. In practice, it proved difficult to transfer crayon drawings, and for this reason most drawn work intended for transferring was done in ink, either with a pen or brush.

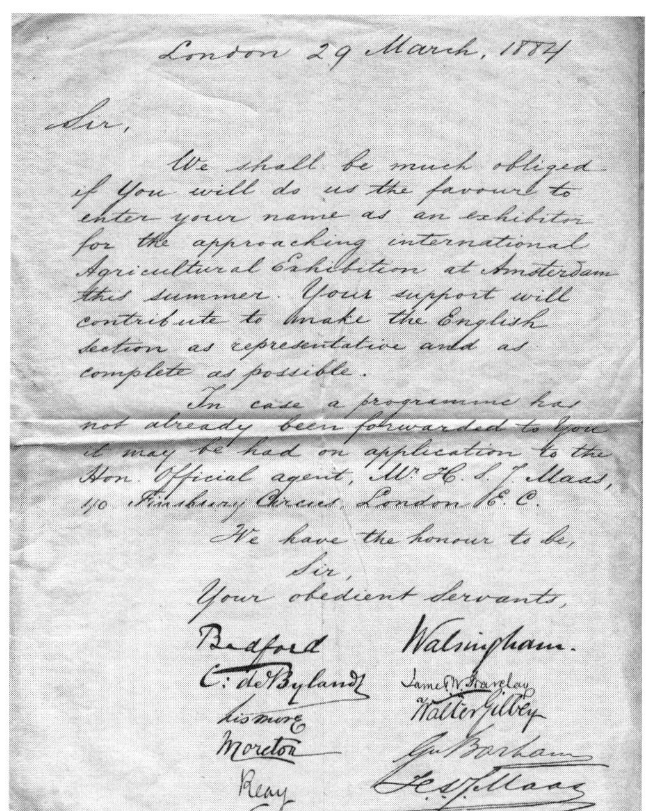

London 29 March, 1884

Sir,

We shall be much obliged if You will do us the favour to enter your name as an exhibitor for the approaching international Agricultural Exhibition at Amsterdam this summer. Your support will contribute to make the English section as representative and as complete as possible.

In case a programme has not already been forwarded to You it may be had on application to the Hon. Official agent, Mr H. S. J. Maas, 140 Finsbury Circus, London E.C.

We have the honour to be,
Sir,
Your obedient servants,

Bedford Walsingham.
C: de Bylandt James W. Barclay
Lismore Walter Gilbey
Moreton
Reay H. S. J. Maas

Circular, with facsimile signatures, inviting participation in an international agricultural exhibition at Amsterdam, headed 'London 29 March 1884'. Transfer lithography. 270 × 213 mm (10⅝ × 8⅜ in)

The main benefit of transfer lithography was that, for the first time in the history of printing, writing and drawing could be produced the right way round on a printing surface rather than in reverse. This facility led to its being taken up widely for the production of documents that needed a personal touch, the main application being circulars. Transfer lithography was also used for other kinds of ephemera, usually when economy was the main consideration and quality of production secondary. It was particularly suited to short-run work and was taken up by the printing trade wherever lithography was practised, for price lists, accounts, notices, invitations, facsimiles of signatures and documents, plans, music, and FORMS – in addition to circulars. It remained an important branch of lithography until it began to be replaced by photolithography in the 1860s.

The process was also used outside the professional lithographic trade for reasons of economy and, perhaps, security; both might account for its use by the University of Virginia for at least one of its examination papers in 1826. From the 1820s to the end of the 19th century small presses, designed primarily to cater for transfer lithography, were being marketed for in-house use by banks, railway companies, large stores, societies, and other offices. Senefelder designed and sold presses of this kind in Paris in the early 1820s, and in London Waterlow and Sons sold many hundreds of their 'autographic presses' for in-house use, mainly, it has to be assumed, for the production of ephemera. Presses of this kind, sometimes designed for use with metal plates rather than stones, did much to promote the use of transfer lithography as an office duplicating process (*see* XEROGRAPHY).

A further application of transfer lithography involved taking proofs from any kind of printing surface and transferring them to stone. This was sometimes done when text and illustrations needed to be combined: proofs taken from type could be transferred to stone and combined with illustrative work (either drawn on stone or transferred to it). This method gave both the authority of traditional type and the freedom and ease of lithographic drawing. However, the main advantage of transferring printed images was that numerous proofs of the same small image (usually a lithographic one) could be arranged on a large sheet of paper and transferred together to a stone. This method was frequently used for the production of ephemera, such as labels.

With the commercial development of chromolithography in the second half of the 19th century this application of transfer lithography became an essential part of the lithographic printers' work. It involved a high level of precision in the transferring, since each of the separate workings of a CHROMO produced by such means had to be arranged and transferred to the stone in exactly the right place in order to make perfect registration possible at the printing stage. [MT]

See also FACSIMILE; LABEL

Transparency

Rudolph Ackermann, shortly after opening his print shop in the Strand, London, published one hundred and nine transparent hand-coloured etchings between 1796 and 1802 and a book called *Instructions for Painting Transparencies* (1799). They all showed images which, when held to the light, acquired enhanced tonal range and luminous colour. The effect was achieved by adding to the back of the print broad masses of tone and colour with a brush to correspond with the outlines of the illustration. Added translucency was produced locally by application of varnish.

These Ackermann transparencies were the first to be sold as individual prints, but they were preceded, some thirty-five years earlier, by three novelty pages in a book of illustrations entitled *A Political and Satirical History Displaying the Unhappy Influence of Scotch Prevalency in the Years 1761, 1762 and 1763*. The book, published in two volumes by Mary Darly, featured the work of George Townshend. Beyond a reference on the title-page to '...humourous transparent and entertaining prints', the transparencies are presented without comment or instructions for viewing. One of them, revealing figures standing behind a screen, is coloured. The transparency pages are distinguishable only by their double thickness, the 'ghost' image being printed on a second sheet pasted to the first.

Ackermann's prints were followed by the publication in 1807 of a book by Edward Orme entitled *An Essay on Transparent Prints, and on Transparencies in general*. In this extensive work, with parallel texts in English and French, Orme showed examples of pictures before and after treatment and gave detailed instructions in methods. He also showed numerous 'practical' applications, including lantern shades, firescreens, and fans (the book makes no reference to Ackermann). In Paris in 1822 appeared a series entitled *Les Surprises*; it consisted of twelve separate hand-coloured lithographed transparencies in a slip-case measuring 65 × 52 mm (2½ × 2 in).

The transparency trade remained more or less dormant in London until the appearance in the 1830s of William Spooner's series of 'Protean Views'. In these prints the picture was not merely enhanced but transformed by backlighting. Typical was his view of Vesuvius, seen by frontal light as quiescent and in transparency as in spectacular eruption. Unlike Ackermann's prints, in which the secondary image was visible from the back, Spooner's prints carried a tissue paper covering at the back concealing the transformation until the print was held to the light. Their image size was more or less standard at about 134 × 180 mm (5¼ × 7⅛ in); their mounts, which bore a caption label, measured 230 × 286 mm (9 × 11¼ in). Spooner published two further series of transparencies, one of 'Transformations' (essentially the same formula as the Protean Views) and another of 'Scriptural Protean Views'. He published in all some ninety subjects. (He also published a novelty print for use in stereoscopes, in which a pair of figures facing in opposite directions appeared to transpose and face each other.)

Another publisher in the transparency and transformation business (not up to Spooner's standard) was William Morgan ('Improved Protean Scenery', 'Morgan's Dioramic Views', 'Morgan's Improved Transformations'). Transparencies also appeared in France later in the century. A variant of the transformation principle appeared fitfully in 1835–36 when Spooner and Morgan produced pictures in which the secondary image was revealed by heat. Both versions – light and heat – were also used later in the century by commercial advertisers.

'Transparent' cards were among the many novelties produced during the American calling-card craze of the late 19th century. They were available with or without the printed name of the bearer. Manufacturers' specimens bore the printed words 'transparency card'. The cards, which were of normal calling-card format, disclosed a hidden cartoon image when held to the light. The images were invariably faintly risqué, though manufacturers were constrained to refer to them as 'very comical images...creating a world of amusement'. A typical example shows a couple in embrace on a country walk; the caption reads 'there is no harm in kissing'. The transparency effect was produced by pasting a blank paper over the printed image on another sheet and trimming the resultant 'sandwich' to size. The idea originated in France, and the American trade referred to them as 'French transparent cards', regardless of where they were manufactured.

See also ADVERTISING NOVELTY; HOLD-TO-LIGHT; LEAFLET

REFERENCE Edward Orme, *An Essay on Transparent Prints* (London: 1807)

COLLECTION Hannas Collection, c.o Lloyds Bank, London

Transportation papers (penal)

In Britain 'transportation' refers to punishment by banishment to a convict colony. Transportation, for life or for shorter periods, formed a dominant part of the British penal code from the end of the 17th century until its abolition in the mid 19th century. The punishment was adopted as a humane alternative to hanging which, during the 18th century, had become the penalty for all but the most trivial crimes. By the end of that century the number of capital offences ran to over 160. Capital crimes included stealing a sheep and 'picking pockets above one shilling'. Imprisonment, apart from its use for the detention of insolvent debtors, was seen initially not as a punishment in itself but as a temporary lodging. It was used for those awaiting trial and for condemned prisoners awaiting execution.

Transportation was originally to Britain's colonies in America, but with the loss of these in 1776 and the discovery of Australia, convict colonies were set up in New South Wales and later in Van Diemen's Land [Tasmania] and Western Australia. Inadequate prison accommodation in Britain in the meantime led to the use of prison ships or 'hulks' anchored in the Thames and

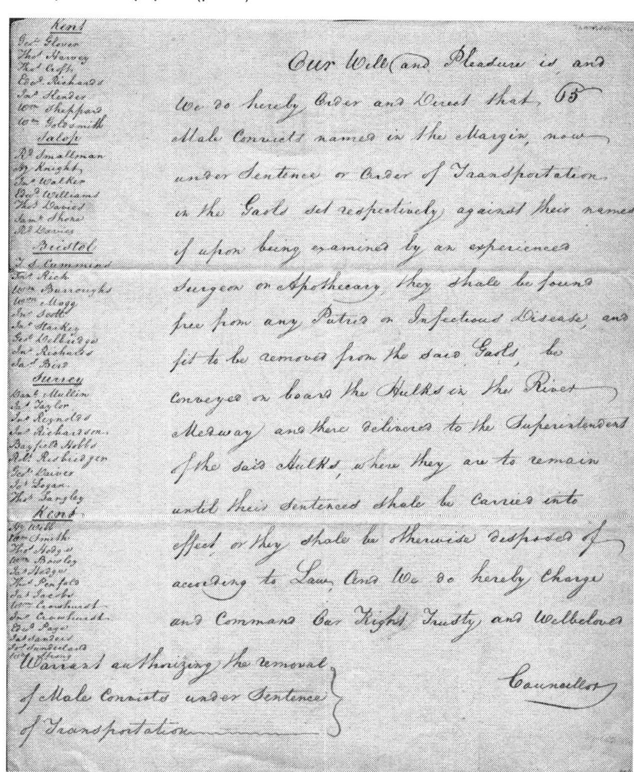
Our Will and Pleasure is, and We do hereby Order and Direct that 65 Male Convicts named in the Margin, now under Sentence or Order of Transportation in the Gaols set respectively against their names if upon being examined by an experienced Surgeon or Apothecary they shall be found free from any Putrid or Infectious Disease, and fit to be removed from the said Gaols, be conveyed on board the Hulks in the River Medway and there delivered to the Superintendent of the said Hulks, where they are to remain until their sentences shall be carried into effect or they shall be otherwise disposed of according to Law, And We do hereby Charge and Command Our Right Trusty and Wellbeloved

Counsellor

Warrant authorizing the removal of Male Convicts under Sentence of Transportation

Kent

Salop

Bristol

Surrey

Kent

Warrant authorizing the transportation of fifteen named male convicts, August 1829. Manuscript. 235 × 202 mm (9¼ × 8 in)

elsewhere. Here, in appalling conditions, prisoners served hard labour pending shipment overseas. Of a total of 8000 convicts so held in the period 1776 to 1795 no fewer than 1946 died on board. Later, regular sailings of convict ships carried many thousands to penal servitude, either in Government-operated schemes for road, bridge, and harbour building or, less generally, as 'prisoner servants' to private settlers.

Transportation papers consist in the main of a large body of forms, declarations, and permits, in which the prisoner's progress through the system is recorded. The majority are pre-printed and filled in by hand. Some are wholly printed, others wholly handwritten. Among a plethora of such items we note a number of key documents:

Parliamentary papers. These include reports of Royal Commissions, select committees of the House of Commons, correspondence, statistical returns, bills, accounts, and other miscellaneous items 'ordered, by the House of Commons, to be printed'. Typical are: 'Return of the Number of Persons who, Being under Sentence of Transportation, have in each Year since the Year 1800, Died in the Hulks' (1808); 'A Return of the Number of Persons, Male and Female, who have been Transported as Criminals to New South Wales since the Month of August 1811' (1813). These items, ranging from a single sheet to a 200-page paper-bound document, are uniformly of foolscap size. (The covers of all such official publications are blue – hence 'Blue books'.) The papers, of which great numbers were published, offer a vast corpus of detailed information on transportation and a variety of other matters of the time.

Assize order. The assize order, wholly or partly handwritten, records decisions and sentences of Courts of Assize. The document lists prisoners on trial, together with the charge and the court's decision. Cases are listed in order of gravity. A typical order (Wiltshire, 1805) includes the case of Fanny Barnett 'convicted … of feloniously, knowingly and wittingly … having in her possession … a certain forged and counterfeited Bank Note …. Let her be transported beyond the Seas for the term of fourteen years'. (Her case is preceded by that of Charles Sims 'attainted of stealing goods and monies above the value of forty shillings …. Let him be Hanged by the Neck until he be dead'.)

Single-sheet assize orders (part-printed, either by copperplate or letterpress, on foolscap paper) refer to one prisoner per sheet, recording the sentence of the court: 'It is thereupon ordered and adjudged … that the above-named (Joseph Bargery) be transported beyond the seas … for the term of (his life)' (Wiltshire, 1839).

Removal order. This was a part-printed form, normally a four-page foolscap document. It required the removal of convicts from gaol to hulk and delivery to the superintendent of the hulk of details of each prisoner's sentence including 'a Certificate containing his Age, and an account of his Behaviour in Prison and after his Trial, and the Gaoler's observations on his Temper and Disposition, and such information concerning his Connexions and former course of Life as may have come to the Gaoler's Knowledge'.

Captain's receipt. The acknowledgement of receipt of prisoners into custody on board the hulk was often a wholly handwritten document: 'Received this 24th day of August 1819 from H M Gaol at Horsham aboard the Hulk at Gosport the fifteen male convicts as under …'.

Remove warrant. This was a part-printed form, consisting of a single foolscap sheet, ordering constables in Australia to transfer a named convict from one penal establishment to another.

Remain pass. This was a part-printed, double-sided form, that was issued to a 'Prisoner Servant', allowing him to proceed 'to the House of (his Master) … there to remain in the service of (his Master) (Hobart Town, 1834).

Ticket of leave. A part-printed form, often of parchment, was given to convicts released in advance of their term to allow them to work for money at an occupation of their own choice. Conditions governing the issue of tickets of leave varied, and there was some uncertainty, even at official levels, as to the precise meaning of the term. At some periods the ticket of leave was confused with the 'conditional pardon', which at one stage replaced it.

The tickets (or, more properly, papers) varied in wording, style, and format. In one example, issued from the Colonial Secretary's Office, New South Wales, in 1819, the document bears the title 'Ticket of leave' and permits the holder (whose name and other details are filled in) to obtain employment within a given district in Australia. Another example, produced in evidence before the Parliamentary Select Committee on Transportation in 1856, bore the title 'Order of Licence to a Convict' and declared that Her Majesty was graciously pleased to grant the holder her royal licence 'to be at large in the United Kingdom … during the remaining portion of his said term of transportation, unless it shall please Her Majesty sooner to revoke or alter such Licence'. The back of the form bore a part-printed description of the holder, and a reminder that he must prove himself 'worthy of Her Majesty's clemency' and that 'If he associates with notoriously bad characters, leads an idle and dissolute life, or has no visible means of obtaining an honest livelihood, &c., it will be assumed that he is about to relapse into crime, and he will be at once apprehended, and re-committed to prison under his original sentence'.

The ticket-of-leave man was a well-known figure in the social order of the time. His licence was at once a protection against renewed punishment and a mark of shame to the seeker of employment. The document, once it had served its period of validity, was therefore quickly destroyed; few have survived. The system, begun in 1791, fell into disuse in the 1850s and 1860s.

See also GAOL PAPERS

REFERENCES Irish University Press series of British Parliamentary Papers, *Crime and Punishment: Transportation*, 16 vol. (Shannon: Irish University Press, 1968–71); A. G. L. Shaw, *Convicts and the Colonies* (Carlton, Vic.: Melbourne University Press, 1966); B. Coultman Smith, *Shadow over Tasmania* (Hobart: Welch, 1941)

COLLECTIONS Mitchell Library, State Library of N.S. Wales, Sydney; National Library of Australia, Canberra; State Library of Tasmania

Travellers' guide

This was the term applied to route information appearing on innkeepers' and hoteliers' trade cards. They listed the route from the inn or hotel in question to other places, giving the distances between each stop and the names of establishments and their proprietors.

The guide was an institution in Britain, America, and Canada, and in some parts of France and Belgium too. It was also a feature of the INN TALLY, distances being indicated in post-horse stops rather than kilometres or miles.

THE
TRAVELLERS' GUIDE
FROM
LONDON to EDINBURGH.

TOWNS.	INNS.	INNKEEPERS' NAMES.	Miles
To Barnet	Green-Man	Newman	12
Hatfield	Salsbury-Arms	Townsend	9
Stevenage	Swan	Cass	12
Biggleswade	Sun	Cass	14
Eaton	Cock	Walker	10
Alconbury-Hill	Wheatsheaf	Walker	13
Wansford	Haycock	Perceval	16
Witham-Common	Bull	Hardy	17
Grantham	George	Burbage	10
Newark	Kingston-Arms	Lawton	14
Scarthing-Moor	Black-Lion	Pearce	12
Barnby-Moor	Bell	Clarke	12
Doncaster	Angel	Belcher	14
Ferrybridge	Angel	Alderson	15
Wetherby	Angel	Clemishaw	17
Borougbridge	Crown	Stott	12
Northallerton	Golden-Lion	Hirst	19
Darlington	King's-Head	Scott	16
Rushyford	Wheatsheaf	Hoult	9
Durham	Waterloo-Hotel	Ward	9
Newcastle	Queen's-Head	Dodsworth	15
Morpeth	Queen's-Head	Sunderland	14
Alnwick	Swan	Wilson	19
Belford	Bell	Henderson	14
Berwick	Red-Lion	Donovan	15
Renton	Renton-Inn		12
Dunbar	George	Loriman	15
Haddington	George	Sang	11
EDINBURGH	Hotel		16
		Total Number of Miles	393

'The Travellers' Guide from London to Edinburgh', issued by F. Hirst, the Golden-Lion, Northallerton, July 1822. Letterpress. 167 × 105 mm (6½ × 4⅛ in)

Trompe-l'oeil announcement

Trompe-l'oeil is the expression normally used to describe paintings which, literally, 'cheat the eye' into believing that a two-dimensional rendering is in fact a three-dimensional object. The expression is also used to describe printed matter which attracts the attention by conveying at first sight a message more sensational, scandalous, or significant than is actually intended. The trick was much in vogue among mid 19th-century small-time advertisers. It relied on excessive typographic stress on selected words in a message, the remainder of the text being printed in small type. Typical is a San Francisco daguerreotyper's handbill proclaiming 'BABIES MADE FOR THREE DOLLARS'. On closer inspection the message turns out to be 'Mr Shew is prepared to take either improved or patent ambrotypes of BABIES, or children of any age... no matter how many attempts have been MADE by other artists without success... only come to Shew's... and you can get good pictures 'FOR THREE DOLLARS...'.

The gambit was confined to single-colour handbills and appears to have flourished for a decade or so in the 1840s and 1850s.

Tyburn ticket

This was the popular name for the certificate given to the prosecutor of a felon when the prosecution ended in a conviction and a hanging. The word Tyburn referred to an area near the present Marble Arch, London (said by some to centre on Connaught Square). The site marked the place of execution for many years and was synonymous with execution by hanging. The gallows, or Tyburn Tree as it was called, was a notorious location and at some stages had public stands built around it for spectators.

The Tyburn Ticket exempted the holder from all 'Parish and ward offices...wherein such felony or felonies shall be committed'. The tickets were much coveted as special privileges and were designed to encourage the successful prosecution of offenders. They were saleable (once only), their privileges being transferred to the new holder. They were instituted in 1699 by an Act of William III (10 & 11 Will. III, c. 23) and were finally abolished in 1818.

Though popularly described as tickets, they were in fact manuscript parchments specially inscribed for each case, using more or less the same form of words. At some stages the certificate also gave the holder rights in the matter of Benefit of Clergy. It is said that the sale of the ticket as a curiosity continued into the early years of the 19th century.

Typographica

The term 'typographica' relates to printed items concerned with the art and craft of printing, with special reference to type, letterforms, and the printed page. The expression has secondary connotations (*see below*), but it generally refers to such items as printers' and typefounders' type specimens, style sheets, corrected and uncorrected proofs, and examples of fine, curious, or primitive presswork (*see* PRINTING,'PRIMITIVE'). Collections of typographica often include related printing blocks, type, plates, etc., though these items are not, in themselves, normally regarded as ephemera.

Type specimens are among the most commonly collected of typographic ephemera, though there is some difficulty in drawing a line of demarcation between the clearly ephemeral single sheet and the less ephemeral bound volume of sheets. The

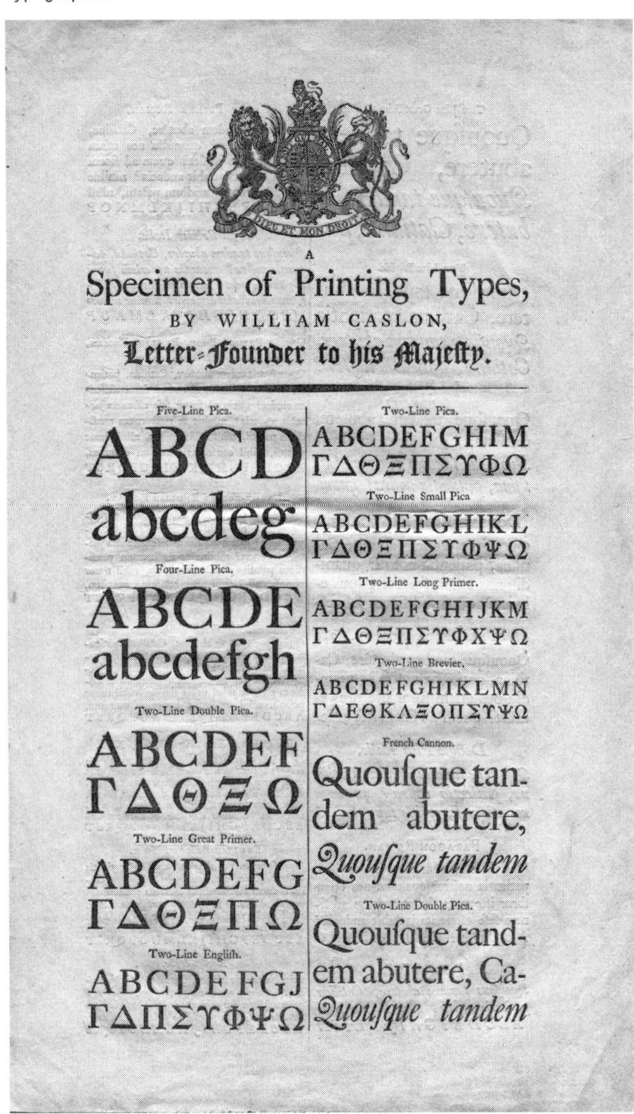
A
Specimen of Printing Types,
BY WILLIAM CASLON,
Letter-Founder to his Majesty.

Five-Line Pica.
ABCD
abcdeg
Four-Line Pica.
ABCDE
abcdefgh
Two-Line Double Pica.
ABCDEF
ΓΔΘΞΩ
Two-Line Great Primer.
ABCDEFG
ΓΔΘΞΠΩ
Two-Line Engliſh.
ABCDE FGJ
ΓΔΠΣΥΦΨΩ

Two-Line Pica.
ABCDEFGHIM
ΓΔΘΞΠΣΥΦΩ
Two-Line Small Pica.
ABCDEFGHIKL
ΓΔΘΞΠΣΥΦΨΩ
Two-Line Long Primer.
ABCDEFGHIJKM
ΓΔΘΞΠΣΥΦΧΨΩ
Two-Line Brevier.
ABCDEFGHIKLMN
ΓΔΕΘΚΛΞΟΠΣΥΨΩ
French Cannon.
Quouſque tandem abutere,
Quouſque tandem
Two-Line Double Pica.
Quouſque tandem abutere, Ca-
Quouſque tandem

‘A Specimen of Printing Types’ by William Caslon [III], 1786. Letterpress, first of eight pages. 415 × 260 mm (16⅜ × 10¼ in)

earliest type specimens were produced as single sheets, but by the early 19th century typeface production had become so prolific that manufacturers felt impelled to publish continually updated collection of sheets in volume form. The individual leaves that were used to form specimen books in the first half of the 19th century sometimes survive in their own right, and in this form are highly desirable. The system foreshadowed the cumulative loose-leaf specimen book common in the mid 20th century.

Most famous among early ‘single sheet’ specimens is one published by Conrad Berner, typefounder of Frankfurt, in 1592. It displays examples, in various sizes, of typefaces designed by Granjon, Garamond, and others. (Sizes are designated by name rather than number – ‘Canon’, ‘Petit Canon’, etc – the smallest being about 6-point, ‘non-parel’ [sic].) The sheets, which measure some 470 × 330 mm (18½ × 13 in), also show Greek and Hebrew types as well as decorative flowers and borders. Type sheets continued to appear on the continent, notably in Holland, until about the middle of the 18th century, when type ‘books’ began to take their place. Some of the earliest examples were produced in 1742 in France (Lamesle and Fournier); in 1743 in Holland (Enschedé); and in 1763 in England (Caslon).

More ambitious specimens with a much wider range of type faces and sizes, some of them for posters, appeared in the form of books in the 19th century. Notable in Britain were those issued by the foundries of Caslon, Figgins, Thorowgood, and Wood & Sharwoods. In the United States specimens were produced by, among others, Darius Wells, Mackellar, Smiths & Jordan, the Boston Type Foundry, and Dickinsons. At the end of the 19th century, responding to the challenge of mechanized typesetting (Linotype, Monotype, and later Ludlow) the combination known as the American Typefounders Co. emerged, producing type for display advertising. The company published a large number of colourful specimens showing its products in a publicity context. German, French, and British specimens reflect a similar interest in display faces in the period 1920 to 1960 and are among the most collectable of typographic items.

In another category altogether are the specimen sheets published as sixteen bound annual volumes by the *Printers' International Specimen Exchange* between 1880 and 1898. The volumes displayed examples of the work of contributing printers, most of the items being notional concoctions for fictitious clients. The sheets, when disbound, are occasionally described as ephemera, but they have only marginal validity as specimens of genuinely ephemeral printing.

The term ‘typographica’ is also applied to fragmentary items bearing letters, numerals, or both, some of which have no discernable function. Included in this wholly legitimate category of typographic ephemera, are such items as: the motor-coach or railway-carriage identification numeral – a single character on an otherwise blank sheet; the cryptically abbreviated packing-case sticker; the numbered cloakroom ticket or shelf label. For the enthusiast, these items may embody the quintessence of the typographic statement – the placing of significant characters on a sheet of paper; the fact that the message conveyed may be understood only by a minority may serve to enhance rather than reduce the appeal of the item. The collector in this category will try to acquire specimens ranging from those whose purpose may be apparent to those in which the enigma is complete; to the typographic eye, whatever their function, they have a validity of their own.

REFERENCES Harry Carter, *A View of early Typography* (Oxford: Clarendon Press, 1969); Nicolete Gray, *Nineteenth Century Ornamented Typefaces* (London: Faber & Faber, 1976); James Mosley, *British Type Specimens before 1831: a hand-list* (Oxford Bibliographical Society, occasional publication no. 14, 1984).

COLLECTION St Bride Printing Library, London

SOCIETIES American Printing History Society, New York; Printing Historical Society, London

unemployed appeal
union label
university mail
unstamped newspaper/periodical

Unemployed appeal

Unemployment in Britain after World War I brought poverty, unrelieved except by parish and personal charity. Begging in the streets became commonplace and thousands of ex-servicemen found themselves selling matches, bootlaces, and printed 'ballads' from the gutter.

The ballads, in the tradition of STREET LITERATURE, expressed their message in manifestly unprofessional verse, often to the extent of forty or fifty lines. They were offered for sale, commonly at one penny each, by individuals or by groups of jobless, many of whom sang as they moved along the street.

A typical one-man ballad, presented on a postcard, is headed 'A Disabled Soldier's Appeal; can you give this ex-serviceman a job or help him by buying this card price one penny'. An eight-verse poem 'copyright by ex-sgt F Scarborough' begins 'I heard my country calling in those darkened years of strife, and at once returned the answer, risking health and limb and life'. It finishes 'so now I ask your sympathy, for one who fought for you, that you will help where'er you can, the lads who proved so true'.

A group leaflet of the 1920s, measuring 255 × 195mm (10 × 7⅝in), has six verses under the title 'An appeal of the unemployed': ('Oh, list ye feeling Christians, You're aware where'er you go, There are thousands of good tradesmen, Borne down in grief and woe; Their families are perishing, Their prospects are destroyed, Then grant, oh! grant your sympathy, Unto the unemployed.'). The final paragraph declares: 'The bearers are a party of unemployed tradesmen who have been out of work for many weeks past; having large families we are compelled to throw ourselves at the feet of a sympathizing public, hoping they will take our case into consideration, and render us some small assistance, so that we may be enabled to obtain food and shelter for our wives and children, till trade mends, and for which, we return our most sincere and most grateful thanks'. The general tenor of this item reflects its 19th-century forerunners so accurately as to suggest that it might have been a direct copy.

In another approach – again in direct descent from 19th-century practice – cards and leaflets were left in letterboxes for 'sale' or retrieval at a later date with such messages as: 'Please buy this leaflet … I will call back later. Should be glad of any work' (*see* CALL-BACK HANDBILL). Packets of stationery, needles, and other items were also proffered: 'I have no other means and I cannot find employment … trusting not to offend … price twopence' and 'I am unemployed … No dole or pension, my only means of livelihood'.

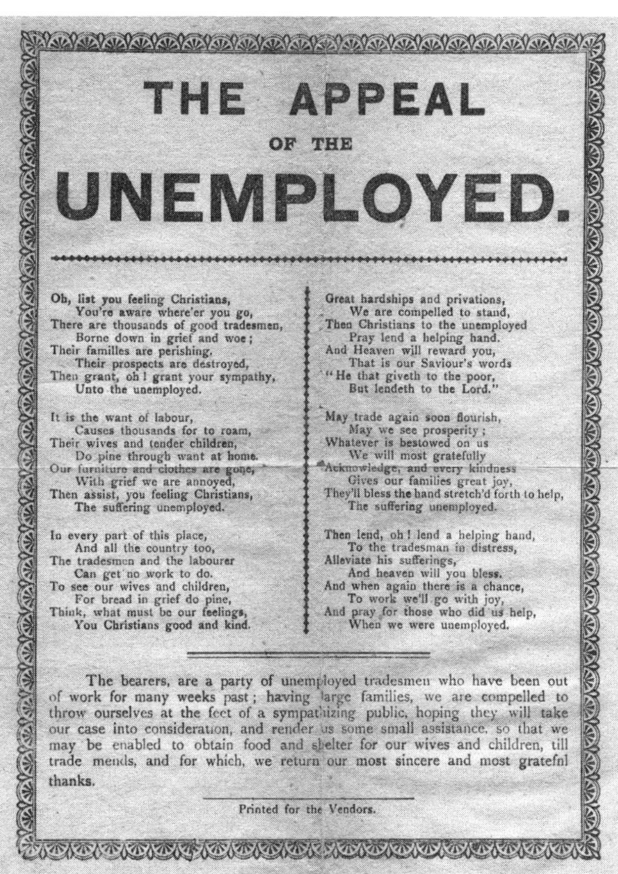

THE APPEAL
OF THE
UNEMPLOYED.

Oh, list you feeling Christians,
You're aware where'er you go,
There are thousands of good tradesmen,
Borne down in grief and woe;
Their familles are perishing.
Their prospects are destroyed,
Then grant, oh! grant your sympathy,
Unto the unemployed.

It is the want of labour,
Causes thousands for to roam,
Their wives and tender children,
Do pine through want at home.
Our furniture and clothes are gone,
With grief we are annoyed,
Then assist, you feeling Christians,
The suffering unemployed.

In every part of this place,
And all the country too,
The tradesmen and the labourer
Can get no work to do.
To see our wives and children,
For bread in grief do pine,
Think, what must be our feelings,
You Christians good and kind.

Great hardships and privations,
We are compelled to stand,
Then Christians to the unemployed
Pray lend a helping hand.
And Heaven will reward you,
That is our Saviour's words
"He that giveth to the poor,
But lendeth to the Lord."

May trade again soon flourish,
May we see prosperity;
Whatever is bestowed on us
We will most gratefully
Acknowledge, and every kindness
Gives our families great joy,
They'll bless the hand stretch'd forth to help,
The suffering unemployed.

Then lend, oh! lend a helping hand,
To the tradesman in distress,
Alleviate his sufferings,
And heaven will you bless.
And when again there is a chance,
To work we'll go with joy,
And pray for those who did us help,
When we were unemployed.

The bearers, are a party of unemployed tradesmen who have been out of work for many weeks past; having large families, we are compelled to throw ourselves at the feet of a sympathizing public, hoping they will take our case into consideration, and render us some small assistance, so that we may be enabled to obtain food and shelter for our wives and children, till trade mends, and for which, we return our most sincere and most gratefnl thanks.

Printed for the Vendors.

Unemployed appeal, 'printed for the vendors', c. 1918. Letterpress. 255 × 195mm (10 × 7⅝in)

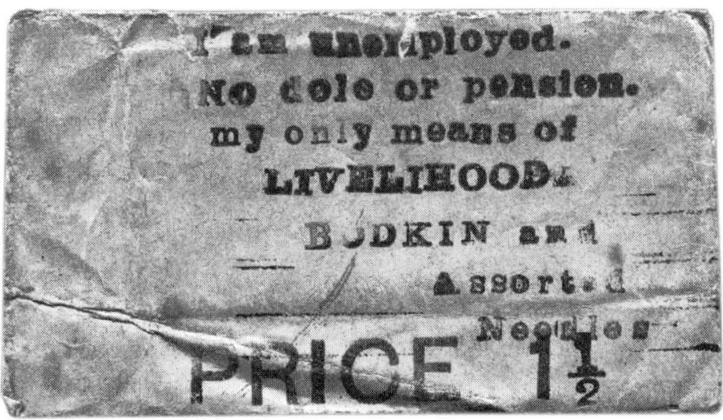

Packet containing a bodkin and assorted needles for sale by an unemployed person. Lettered in purple ink from two rubber stamps. 53 × 97mm (2⅛ × 3⅞in)

Union label

The union label was affixed to a product by the employees of a company as an assurance of quality and of the employer's good working conditions, and had its origins in the cigar industry. In the 1880s the Cigarmakers' International Union began issuing labels of this kind following an initiative of the White Cooperative Cigar Manufacturing Co. of San Francisco. The heyday of the cigar union label lasted from 1880 to 1926. The label in question was affixed to the base of the cigar box in a position where it would be torn by the opening of the box, and many people regarded it as being on a par with the revenue stamp. Its text was originally in sharp tones:

> This certifies that the cigars contained in this box have been made by a first class workman, a member of the Cigarmakers' International Union of America, an organization opposed to inferior rat-shop, coolie, prison or filthy tenement-house workmanship. Therefore, we recommend these cigars to all smokers throughout the world. All infringements on this label will be punished according to law. A. Strasser President CMIU of America.

This wording was modified two years later by a new president, George W. Perkins. In the new form it read in somewhat more conciliatory tones:

> This certifies that the cigars contained in this box have been made by a first-class workman, a member of the Cigarmakers' International Union of America, an organization devoted to the advancement of the moral, material and intellectual welfare of the craft....

Apart from the change in the president's name, the rest of the wording was unchanged.

At about the same time in America the union label idea was applied to garments, specifically hats. It was also introduced to Britain in 1894.

The British stamp, printed in black on pink paper and perforated in the manner of a postage stamp, was put out on the initiative of the Felt Hatters' and Trimmers' Unions from their headquarters in Denton, Manchester. At first it measured 45 × 40 mm (1¾ × 1⁹⁄₁₆ in), but it was later reduced in size to 26 × 22 mm (1 × ⅞ in) so as to resemble a postage stamp more closely. The labels were gummed to the leather linings of the hats.

Label of the Felt Hatters' and Trimmers' Unions, early 20th century. Lithographed in black on pink adhesive paper, perforated. 26 × 22 mm (1 × ⅞ in)

Advertising of the idea was extensive. Letters went to other trade unions and to retailers; posters and showcards were distributed; advertisements appeared in trade-union journals and general newspapers; and in Manchester there were street poster-parades featuring the label. By the end of April 1895 two million labels had been issued.

The campaign message proclaimed that the succcess of the stamp was due to the fact that 'men of honour, rich or poor' felt it was degrading to purchase goods made by sweated labour: 'This label is the Only Guarantee that your Head Cover is not

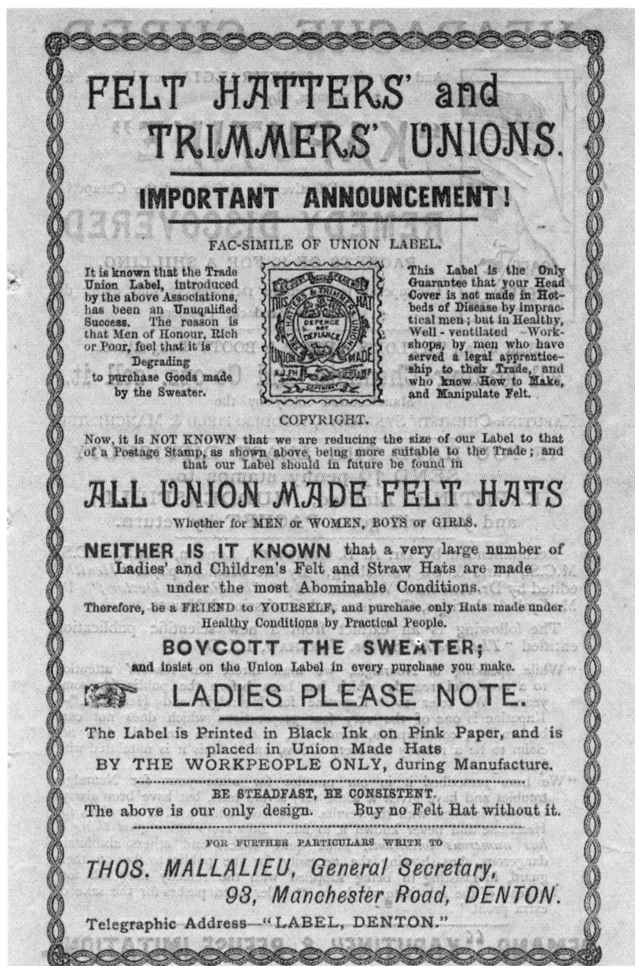

FELT HATTERS' and TRIMMERS' UNIONS.

IMPORTANT ANNOUNCEMENT!

FAC-SIMILE OF UNION LABEL.

It is known that the Trade Union Label, introduced by the above Associations, has been an Unuqalified Success. The reason is that Men of Honour, Rich or Poor, feel that it is Degrading to purchase Goods made by the Sweater.

This Label is the Only Guarantee that your Head Cover is not made in Hot-beds of Disease by impractical men; but in Healthy, Well-ventilated Workshops, by men who have served a legal apprenticeship to their Trade, and who know How to Make, and Manipulate Felt.

COPYRIGHT.

Now, it is NOT KNOWN that we are reducing the size of our Label to that of a Postage Stamp, as shown above, being more suitable to the Trade; and that our Label should in future be found in

ALL UNION MADE FELT HATS

Whether for MEN or WOMEN, BOYS or GIRLS.

NEITHER IS IT KNOWN that a very large number of Ladies' and Children's Felt and Straw Hats are made under the most Abominable Conditions.

Therefore, be a FRIEND to YOURSELF, and purchase only Hats made under Healthy Conditions by Practical People.

BOYCOTT THE SWEATER;

and insist on the Union Label in every purchase you make.

LADIES PLEASE NOTE.

The Label is Printed in Black Ink on Pink Paper, and is placed in Union Made Hats BY THE WORKPEOPLE ONLY, during Manufacture.

BE STEADFAST, BE CONSISTENT.

The above is our only design. Buy no Felt Hat without it.

FOR FURTHER PARTICULARS WRITE TO

THOS. MALLALIEU, General Secretary,
93, Manchester Road, DENTON.

Telegraphic Address—"LABEL, DENTON."

Announcement issued by the Felt Hatters' and Trimmers' Unions, with an illustration of their new, smaller 'Union label', early 20th century. Letterpress. 184 × 120 mm (7¼ × 4¾ in)

made in Hotbeds of Disease by impractical men; but in Healthy, Well-ventilated Workshops, by men who have served a legal apprenticeship to their Trade, and who know How to Make, and Manipulate Felt'.

Urging women also to boycott the 'Sweater', the Union claimed that 'a very large number of Ladies' and Children's Felt and Straw Hats are made under the most Abominable Conditions' and urged 'Be a friend to yourself, and purchase only Hats made under Healthy Conditions by Practical People'. It pointed out that the label 'is placed in Union Made Hats by the workpeople only, during Manufacture'.

The union in question remained in being during the 1980s, when the hat label motif still appeared on their stationery with the telegraphic address as 'Label, Denton'.

University mail

Postal communications in the Middle Ages, largely in the hands of state authorities, were augmented by the initiative of non-governmental bodies – monastic establishments, universities, trade guilds, etc. – whose scattered interests called for frequent and regular exchange of information. These unofficial services were often regarded with suspicion by the state, which saw in them a potential instrument of conspiracy.

In spite of attempts to suppress them, these services flourished; sometimes they extended to private individuals, producing revenues to support the work of the bodies concerned. The universities of Oxford, Bologna, and Paris were among those running their own messenger systems, and many contrived to do so until the 18th century, when state-operated international mails began to come into formal existence.

Among the survivors of the individual system were the universities of Oxford and Cambridge, who retained limited postal rights even in recent times. Their services were for use by members of the universities only and were contained within certain limited areas. The system was marked in the period from 1871 to 1886 by the setting up of post boxes, the scheduling of collection and delivery times, and the use of adhesive stamps. It was the use of 'postage' stamps that appears to have been the final straw for the Postmaster General, who in January 1886 claimed his exclusive rights to carry the mails. The universities conceded.

College stamps for university mail. All lithographed in a single colour. *Left:* St John's College, Oxford, slate blue, 1884; *centre:* Hertford College, Oxford, mauve, printed by Spiers & Son, Oxford, 1875; *right:* St John's College, Cambridge, vermilion, 1884. Printed image of the largest 26 × 20 mm (1 × ¾in)

The stamps, most of which were produced by local printers and stationers, were individually designed for each college. Issuing colleges were, at Oxford: Keble, Merton, Hertford, Lincoln, St John's, and All Souls; at Cambridge: Selwyn, Queens', and St John's. An own design, printed for Balliol College, Oxford, was never issued. A number of stamps also appeared as embossed impressions on postcards and envelopes. These were issued by Keble, Merton, and Hertford; the adhesive issues of Keble, Merton, and Balliol were themselves embossed.

There is in some cases doubt as to whether an item is a postal stamp or an impression cut from existing college stationery. The matter is complicated by the fact that, on one hand, some of the stamps in question were unperforated, on the other that the dies used for printing them may also have been used as ordinary stationery dies by the local printers concerned.

Cancellation of college stamps was in two cases only – those of Keble and Hertford – by a special obliteration stamp. The rest were cancelled by pen or pencil marks, initials, crosses, etc. At Keble it was reported that messengers tore up stamps rather than have the bother of sticking them on letters and parcels.

University mail was revived during the postal strike in Britain in 1971, and Oxford and Cambridge still operate their own (unstamped) internal mail systems.

REFERENCES Dimitry Kandaouroff-Deka, *Collecting Postal History* (London: Peter Lowe, 1973); Raymond Lister, *College Stamps of Oxford and Cambridge* (Cambridge: Golden Head Press, 1966); Carl H. Scheele, *A Short History of the Mail Service* (Washington, DC: Smithsonian Institution Press, 1970)

Unstamped newspaper/periodical

This entry relates to journals and NEWSPAPERS published in defiance of Britain's Stamp Duty laws. A tax on newspapers, originally imposed at a penny per copy in 1712, and progressively increased in the following hundred years to fourpence, was in 1819 extended to cover virtually any periodical appearing more frequently than monthly and selling at less than sixpence.

The tax had first been imposed as part of a general scheme of revenue, but, together with other related taxes (such as paper excise duties and taxes on advertisements, pamphlets, and almanacs), it was later used as a means of curbing the developing power of the press. More particularly it served as a gag on the radical press, whose agitation for reform reached a climax at the time of the 'Peterloo Massacre' (1819). By their opponents these taxes were known collectively as 'taxes on knowledge'. They formed the butt of reformist agitation until, after successive reductions and repeals, they finally disappeared in 1861 with the removal of the paper excise duty. Pamphlets and almanacs were freed from their specific duties in 1833 and 1834, advertisements in 1853, and newspapers in 1855.

The period 1830 to 1836 saw a proliferation of journals and periodicals, many of them openly flouting the law by appearing without the imprinted tax stamp. Henry Hetherington's *The Poor Man's Guardian* (London, 1831) bore the words 'Established contrary to "law" to try the powers of the "might" against "right"'. Hetherington was among 750 publishers and vendors who were prosecuted. He was thrice imprisoned, but contrived with the aid of friends to sustain publication. After six years of the 'war of the unstamped', the duty was reduced in September 1836 to a penny. The period is considered as crucial in the hisory of British journalism.

Not all the journals concerned were organs of protest. Among over 550 titles of the period (given here with the date of the first year of publication) are: *The Physician* (London, 1832); *The Literary Times* (London, 1835); *The Liverpool Dramatic Censor* (1834); *The Liverpool Temperance Advocate* (1836); *The Magazine for all the Boys* (London, c.1832); *The Maids, Wives & Widows' Penny Magazine, and Gazette of Fashion* (London, 1832); and *The Penny Christ* (London, c. 1833). Also unstamped was *The Ten Pounder* (Edinburgh, 1832), a Tory paper (the title derives from the borough elector whose vote relied on occupation of property to the annual value of £10).

Some unstamped journals ran for a decade or more. *The Penny Magazine* (1832), and *The Penny Cyclopaedia* (1833), both published in parts in London by the Society for the Diffusion of Useful Knowledge, ran for thirteen and ten years respectively. *The Saturday Magazine* (London, 1832) lasted eleven and a half years, *Figaro in London* (1831) eight and a half years, and *The Loyal Reformers' Gazette* (later *The Reformers' Gazette*) (Glasgow, 1831) seven years. Hetherington's own papers, *The Poor Man's Guardian* (London, 1831) and *Twopenny Dispatch, and People's Police Register* (London, 1834), ran for three and a half and two years respectively.

For the most part, however, unstamped titles were short-lived. Of 562 recorded launches in the period from January 1830 to December 1836, 57 lasted between five and forty issues, and a total of 118 appeared (or are believed to have appeared) only as a single issue. Survival rates for actual copies of some unstamped periodicals are also low. Titles of 72 journals are known only through references in editorials, advertisements, and correspondence.

The study of the unstamped press is made difficult not only by the scarcity of much of the material but by the strategems of publishers who sought to evade the law. Changes of title occur frequently. One publication, *An Address from One of the 3730 Electors of Preston, then Bolton, to the Labouring Classes of Great Britain and Ireland* (Preston, 1831), varied its title for each of over fifty weekly issues. Changes of publisher and printer were also used as a means of masking continuity, and unnumbered and undated issues masqueraded as single pamphlets. Two titles, *Berthold's Political Handkerchief* (London, 1831) and *Union* (London, 1831), sought refuge in editions printed on cotton.

The unstamped press ranged from the covert to the frankly jubilant. Hetherington's *The Poor Man's Guardian* carried a mock stamp at its masthead showing a printing press and the legend 'Liberty of the Press: Knowledge is Power'. It also revealed another Hetherington gambit, a note saying 'Lent to Read, without deposit, for Six months, charge one penny'. In an editorial paragraph he explained that he had 'hit upon an expedient to evade the law', thus protecting traders from risk of prosecution for 'exposing to sale' our 'newspapers'. Prosecutions continued, however, and Hetherington later abandoned the idea.

See also PAPER-DUTY LABEL; TAX STAMP (NEWSPAPER DUTY)

REFERENCES John H. Chandler, *The Newspaper & Almanac Stamps of Great Britain & Ireland* (Hempstead, Saffron Walden: Great Britain Philatelic Publications, 1981); Joel H. Wiener, *A Descriptive Finding List of Unstamped British Periodicals 1830–1836* (London: Bibliographical Society, 1970); Joel H. Wiener, *The War of the Unstamped: the Movement to Repeal the British Newspaper Tax, 1830–1936* (Ithaca: Cornell University Press, 1969)

vaccination papers
valentine
vice card
view card
violin label
visiting card
visiting craftsmen's papers
visitors' register

Vaccination papers

Vaccination, stemming from experiments by Edward Jenner in 1796, was primarily concerned with the prevention of smallpox by implantation of the virus of cowpox; but the term 'vaccine' is loosely used to refer to any bacterial implant inducing production of antibodies – and thus immunity. The ephemera of vaccination are concerned on the one hand with items relating to its advocacy and effective practice, on the other to documents of protest and rejection. The concept of vaccination, with its connotations of 'injection of disease', was met in many quarters with hostility. For decades the matter was a hard-fought issue between health authorities and a loquacious popular opposition, backed by a minority of medical opinion. The contenders produced their respective portions of printed paper, some of which are recorded here.

Reporting to the House of Commons in March 1912, the Board of the National Vaccine Establishment records the enlightened attitude of the continental clergy 'who were assiduous in recommending the practice to their Parishioners from the pulpit', and considers it as part of its duty in Britain to 'address the Bishops'.

A variety of classifications, declarations, warnings, and summonses continue the story. A medical certificate of 1855 records the successful vaccination of a 3-month-old baby; an 1870 certificate records an unsuccessful vaccination; a blank form allows the vaccination officer the option of declaring that the subject is 'in my opinion insusceptible of successful vaccination' or 'has already had the Small Pox'.

A declaration form issued by the Biggleswade Board of Guardians of the poor states that at a meeting 'it was unani-

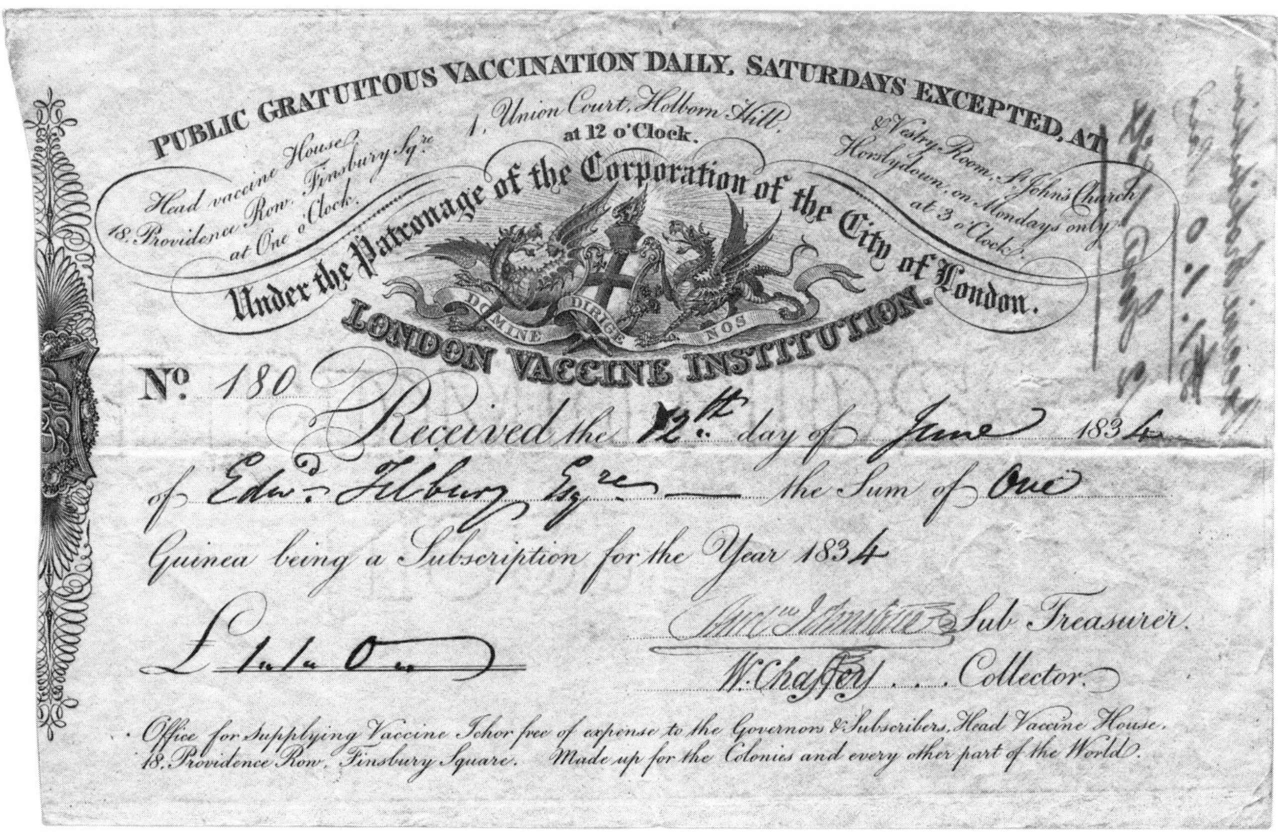

PUBLIC GRATUITOUS VACCINATION DAILY, SATURDAYS EXCEPTED, AT

Head vaccine House, 18, Providence Row, Finsbury Sq.re at One o'Clock.

1, Union Court, Holborn Hill, at 12 o'Clock.

& Vestry Room, St. John's Church Horslydown, on Mondays only at 3 o'Clock.

Under the Patronage of the Corporation of the City of London.

DOMINE DIRIGE NOS

LONDON VACCINE INSTITUTION.

No. 180

Received the 12th day of June 1834

of Edw.d Filbury Esq.re — the Sum of One

Guinea being a Subscription for the Year 1834

£ 1.1.0

[illegible] Sub Treasurer.

W. Chaffey Collector.

Office for Supplying Vaccine Ichor free of expense to the Governors & Subscribers, Head Vaccine House, 18, Providence Row, Finsbury Square. Made up for the Colonies and every other part of the World.

Receipt for a one guinea subscription to the London Vaccine Institution, 1834. Intaglio-printed. 127 × 200mm (5 × 7⅞in)

mously resolved ... that the relieving officer ... be directed to take proceedings against (George Odell) of the parish of (Clifton) ... for neglecting to have his child vaccinated ...'.

A warning by the Vaccination Officer of the Croydon Union in 1897 requires a father to have his child vaccinated within fourteen days 'failing which it will be my duty to take the proper steps for securing the enforcement of the law ...'. Eight months later a 'complaint and information' form issued by a magistrate requires the same father to attend court to answer the complaint and to show why the child should not now be vaccinated in pursuance of the law.

A certificate issued in 1925 at St Bartholomew's Hospital, London, declares that the bearer, having been duly instructed in the practice and principles of vaccination, and having studied on the occasion of six (and not less than four) attendances at the vaccination centre, is now believed to be 'Skilful and well-informed in all that belongs to the duties of a Public Vaccinator'.

Valentine [plate 9a]

The custom of sending loving greetings (often, but not always, anonymously) came to the fore in the late 18th and early 19th centuries, but in its delicately decorative form the 'valentine' dates from the introduction of the uniform Penny Post in Britain in 1840. It has little connection with St Valentine, but is believed to go back to ancient Roman customs.

By the 1870s the idiom of the valentine had become firmly established. Central to the industry was George Mark, of Crane Court, Fleet Street, whose processes of gilding and silvering, embossing, perforating, and cutting-out formed the basis of the technology. Dobbs, Kidd and Co., notable since the early years of the century for their expertise in blind embossing and perforating, were also heavily involved. London's 'fancy stationery' was exported all over the world, much of it to America.

Valentine, c. 1800. Designed, etched and engraved by F. Bartolozzi. 250 × 202 mm (9⅞ × 8 in)

Advertisement for valentines issued by W. Shaw, Brighton, late 19th century. Letterpress, printed by W. Shaw. 220 × 135 mm (8⅝ × 5¼ in)

The work was carried out in simple – often primitive – workshops. Gilding and silvering was applied over a moist varnish, metal leaf being pressed on to the surface and afterwards rubbed away with a cloth leaving the unvarnished areas clear. Relief and 'lace' effects were produced by heavy impressions from embossing dies and filigree cutting tools (*see* EMBOSSING/LACE PAPER). Men and boys operated the printing machines and embossing and cutting-out presses; girls pasted and assembled the components.

Multiple layers, using lace-bordered padded silks, were 'sprung' one above the other on paper hinges to produce three-dimensional displays, with printed poems, engravings, artificial flowers, feathers, mirror-glass – and, later, multicoloured SCRAPS – forming a central motif. Many of the more elaborate constructions, costing up to five guineas. were supplied in presentation cartons. The genre – frivolous, elaborate, and sentimental – established an idiom of its own; its basic ingredients overflowed into the general greetings and Christmas card field, but in the main it was a confection identified with 14 February – St Valentine's Day.

George Mark and his competitors manufactured the components; others put them together to form finished products. Notable among 'makers-up' was Eugene Rimmel, of the Strand, whose perfumes, famous in their own right, added a final touch of elegance and luxury to the greetings. His perfumed calendars and almanacs, also elaborately printed, were already well-established New Year mementoes. The Rimmel workshops employed between 80 and 150 women, according to the season; some of their lines included minor jewellery, bottles of perfume, confectionery, – and even small musical boxes, which played when the carton was opened.

In sharp contrast were the 'comic' valentines, crudely printed sheets with caricatures and insulting doggerel, posted anonymously to targets of irreverence. These productions, commonly combining woodcut illustrations with typeset verse, were often hand-coloured. They observed no general format, ranging from some 400 × 180 mm (15¾ × 7⅛ in) to 220 × 180 mm (8⅝ × 7⅛ in). Their vulgarity – and often viciousness – explored the lower end of the scale of sensibilities as assiduously as did lace paper and perfume at the upper end. 'Comic' valentines lampooned people in general and, in large numbers, trades and occupations. They had an extensive sale, both in Britain and America, and were succeeded, in slightly less virulent vein, by sets of postcards issued early in the 20th century by Raphael Tuck, Edward Stern, and the Illustrated Postcard and Novelty Co.

See also CHRISTMAS CARD; CUTWORK; EMBOSSING/LACE PAPER; GREETINGS CARD

REFERENCES Diane De Blois (ed.), *The Ephemera Journal*, vol. 3, 1990 [special valentine issue]; Ruth Webb Lee, *A History of Valentines* (New York: Batsford, 1952, London: Batsford, 1953); Laura Seddon, *Victorian Valentines* (Manchester: Manchester Metropolitan University Library, 1996); Frank Staff, *The Valentine and its Origins* (London: Lutterworth, 1969)

COLLECTIONS American Antiquarian Society, Worcester, Mass.; Jonathan King Collection, Museum of London; Manchester Metropolitan University Library

Vice card

Printed cards found in telephone boxes offering various sexual services and bearing the phone number of the advertiser are frequently referred to as prostitutes' cards. Prostitution itself is never suggested or implied, though 'Busty blonde model offers personal services' leaves little to the imagination, while various euphemisms such as 'Leather bondage', 'Divine domination', 'Water sports', 'Rubber fun' are employed which rely on the prospective client's knowledge of arcane sexual practices to give him some idea of what services he is likely to receive.

Vice cards began appearing as a result of the legislation in Britain which made it illegal for prostitutes to solicit in the streets. At first their numbers were insignificant, but by the 1990s they had increased to such an extent that Westminster City Council was forced by public opinion to do something about them. The Post Office Act of 1953 had prohibited unauthorized advertising in telephone boxes, but British Telecom were receiving an estimated annual revenue of £136,000 from calls made to the advertised numbers on the cards and were in no hurry to discourage them.

In 1992 Westminster City Council tried to promote an amendment to the London Local Authorities Bill to make it a criminal offence, with a fine of £400, to put the cards in phone boxes. The move was rejected by a House of Lords committee after lobbying by the English Collective of Prostitutes. The Peers ruled that the matter should be dealt with by national rather than London legislation. The suggestion that prostitutes should be allowed to advertise in Yellow Pages was rejected by British Telecom.

At this time an estimated 20,000 cards were being deposited each week in Westminster alone, and by 1994 this figure had risen to 50,000 out of an estimated total of 100,000 being placed in kiosks throughout London. 'Carders', a name given to the individuals, usually students and men on the dole who put the cards in phone boxes, were earning £350 a day by working for several clients. One prostitute, in a newspaper interview, claimed that it cost her £100 a day to advertise.

With increasing objections from local residents, Westminster Council, supported by British Telecom, mounted a joint campaign to clean up the phone boxes. Teams of officials, British Telecom cleaners, and private contractors removed 14,000 cards from Covent Garden and Leicester Square kiosks during a four day clean-up operation. Surprised by the magnitude of the problem, Westminster decided, in July 1994, to fund an intensive eight-week card removal programme to the tune of £20,000. The campaign was not wholly successful: as soon as the cards had been removed, the carders would replace them. Four years later it was estimated that 13 million cards were removed each year during routine cleaning of Westminster kiosks (the cards have to be weighed as there are too many to count). The number would have been appreciably greater had it not been for the 'cooperation' of enthusiastic collectors. In October 1998, after questions were raised in Parliament, the Home Office indicated its willingness to look at the problem.

Although this form of soliciting is a modern phenomenon it has historical precedents. In Victorian times London prostitutes had cards printed giving their address. They were placed in sealed envelopes which were discreetly dropped at theatres and places of entertainment. The envelopes carried messages which left little doubt as to what the prospective client would find if he visited the address on the card. One such envelope reads:

Illustrious stranger, break this seal,
Then at some fair one's footstep kneel
Appoint the time, and her invite
To join you for one magic night.

[PJ]

View card

The engraved view card, printed typically on enamelled stock, was the true forerunner of the picture POSTCARD. VIEW CARDS were produced in very large numbers, many for pioneer tourists (as English/French titling often indicates) and for the increasingly mobile upper-class visitors to spas and beauty spots. Their popularity is underlined by the huge range of their subject matter. In the mid 19th century, when stocks were at their high-

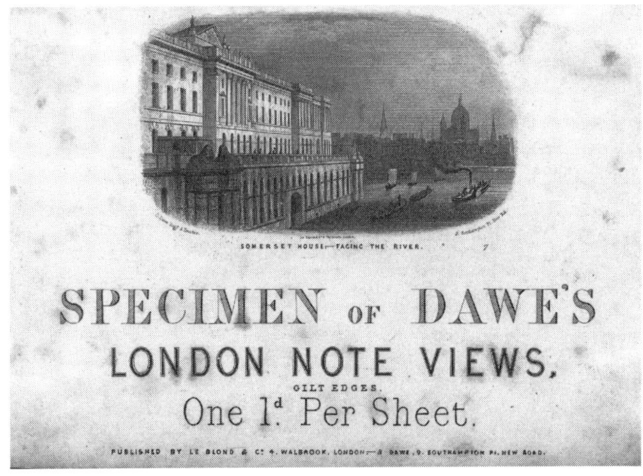

Specimen of Dawe's London note views, showing Somerset House, published by Le Blond & Co., London, mid 19th century. Steel-engraved and printed by G. Dawe. 120 × 167 mm (4¾ × 6½ in)

est, one supplier, J. T. Wood of London, was able to offer a range of '3,000 Views in London and the Towns in England, on enamelled cards'. A typical card, no. 204 in Wood's series ('St Paul's Cathedral, London/La Cathédrale de St Paul à Londres') measures 117 × 152 mm (4⅝ × 6 in), but smaller sizes, 90 × 135 mm (3½ × 5¼ in), are more common.

The views were generally printed on white card, though tinted stock was also sometimes used, and some specimens were hand-coloured and varnished. The treatment of the engravings is very similar to that of the images used on pictorial stationery of the period – a vignette with centre title and minuscule credits curving left and right – and many engraved plates clearly served both functions. The image, noted above, occupied the top half of the quarto writing paper of the time, 253 × 203 mm (10 × 8 in); and in its smaller form was used on 'note size' paper, 185 × 125 mm (7¼ × 4⅞ in).

See also STATIONERY, DECORATIVE

Violin label

In few other fields is the pasted printed label so closely related to matters of value; and throughout the history of the instrument, the violin label has been widely tampered with, transposed, altered, counterfeited, or simply stolen.

As with fine furniture makers, many of the early master craftsmen regarded their work as so recognizably pre-eminent that they disdained the use of the label. Others, less confident, were content to copy not only the style of the instrument but of the label too – even, in some cases, with specific names and dates. Genuine or false, the presence of a label or labels in isolation must in itself be a matter for some suspicion, and multiple sheets of labels (which do occasionally come to light) particularly so.

The violin proper emerged from a succession of earlier forms – violas, violin cellos, lutes etc. – and the date of the first violin is uncertain. The traditional position of the violin label (commonly below the left-hand sound aperture) places responsibility for its integrity more or less equally with the maker, repairer, or restorer, for whom access during assembly is relatively easy. It was among the less reputable of these craftsmen that, historically, the false violin label had currency.

Counterfeits ranged from the crude to the convincing. Some embodied typographical anachronisms, using typefaces uninvented in the period in question. Others were pure invention and provided labels for makers for whom no actual label ever existed; yet others provided printed labels for makers whose labels were invariably handwritten. It was also not unknown for trade handbooks, in which labels were listed and illustrated as guides to authenticity, to be used as material for the counterfeiter. Reproductions from these works were cut from the page with scissors and pasted into 'nameless' instruments. Some of these illustrated listings include an editor's introduction with a special warning of the penalties for this offence.

Many early violins are identified by branding rather than by label. Among these are instruments by the 18th-century maker Chappuy of Paris, who branded an 'N' on the base of the violin, but also sometimes used a label; Cuny, who branded 'Cuny à Paris' on the inside of the violin's back; and Jean Lambert, also of Paris, who sometimes used a label and sometimes a brand on the side of the instrument. In the 19th century Joseph Nicolas of Mirecourt and the Marquis de Lair, also of Mirecourt, both used branding only.

Ambiguously labelled violins are those of Giuseppe Odoardi of Ascoli; at his death at the age of twenty-eight he left some 200 violins, which were afterwards labelled as the work of Cremonese and Brescian makers. Jean Baptiste Juillaume of Paris produced a number of violins of his own design bearing his label, but also made such a success of 'reproductions' of old Italian masters that he made them in considerable quantity, selling them as originals. He imitated not only the violin's structure but the colouring of the wood, the composition of the varnish, and the labels. In the latter years of his life, when his own reputation was established, he began to put his own labels on the reproductions. He finished his career by making his own model, shortly to become world famous, of which he is said to have produced some 3000 examples. These bore his own label.

Equally ambiguous is the labelling history of the Stradivari violin. Antonio Stradivari of Cremona was a pupil in the workshop of Nicola Amati for whom, under Amati's label, he made many instruments. Setting up on his own in 1666, he made some 2000 violins in a period of sixty-four years. His work carried his own labels, some printed, others written by hand. His last printed labels bear the handwritten intimation of his age – ninety-four years. At his death, his unfinished violins were completed by his sons and pupils and were sold with the labels 'sub-disciplina di Ant Stradivari' or 'sotto la Disciplina D'Antonio Stradivari' ('according to the methods of Antonio Stradivari').

Handwriting appears on violin labels in fair measure, and a few are written wholly by hand. Those of Jakob Steiner (Jacobus Stainer), when they appear at all, are always found to be handwritten. Dates, which are almost invariably included, may be written wholly or partly by hand, the first two digits being printed. (Giovanni Paolo Maggini, it is recorded, never dated his labels.) Handwritten inscriptions also include references to repairs: 'Revisto e corretto da me, Antonio Stradivari in Cremona 1701' ('Examined and corrected by me Antonio Stradivari in Cremona in 1701').

Latin is widely used on the violin label. 'Fecit' and 'Reparavit' appear frequently for 'made it' and 'repaired it', as well as 'me fecit' (made me). Addresses too may be rendered in Latin: 'Ludovicus Guersan, prope comoediam Gallicam, Lutetia (Louis Guernsan, near the Comédie Francaise, Paris); 'Augustinus Chappuy, olim Parisiis, nunc Mirecurtio' (Auguste Chappuy, formerly of Paris, now at Mirecourt). The practice survives into the 20th century: a 1911 label reads 'Robert Robinson fecit: Portlanda: Oregona: USA'. In Central Europe, with the names Stradivari and Guarneri still to be competed with, the Latin phrase 'Ad formam' (to the shape of; following the pattern of) allows the greater name to accompany the lesser: 'Joh. Bapt. Schweitzer fecit ad formam Antonii Stradivarii, Pestini, 18(—)'. Similarly, but with rather more justification, Stradivari's former pupil Gagliano describes himself as 'Alumnus Stradivarius'.

Latinization was of course applied to the names of Guarneri and Stradivari, who are perhaps better known as Guarnerius and Stradivarius; Guarneri acquired the additional name 'Del Gesù' from his practice of including the letters JHS (Jesus, Hominum Salvator) on his labels.

Among the earliest surviving labels are those of Gasparo Da Salò, Brescia c.1575 (Italy); Ernst Busch, Nürnberg 1644 (Germany); Mathias Albani, Botzen 1644 (Austria); Nicolas Médard, Paris 1645 (France); Henry Jaye, Southwark 1629 (Britain); John Friedrich, New York 1883 (United States).

Labels measure around 20 × 70mm (¾ × 2¾in) and are usually roughly trimmed. Examples surviving in isolation are rarely undamaged.

REFERENCE Heinrich Bauer, *Practical History of the Violin* (New York: H. Bauer Music Co., 1911)

COLLECTIONS Museo Stradivariana, Cremona, Italy

Visiting card

Known formerly and more accurately in Britain (and in America too) as a calling card, the visiting card was in the early 18th century the mark of the elegant traveller, whose important social engagements required an appropriate imprimatur.

Its use originated on the continent of Europe, where it was the practice to proffer engraved pictorial cards with the bearer's name inserted by hand in a panel left for the purpose. Subject matter ranged from views of actual locations to allegorical scenes and set-pieces – rarely related in any way to the bearer. Professional people, whose visiting was more than merely social, went to the expense of having their names incorporated in the design.

The use of the visiting card paralleled that of the TRADE CARD, but in much of Europe the private card was at pains to avoid a commercial air. As the trade card moved more firmly into the field of decorative borders, illustration, and flamboyance, the personal version became ever more reticent; whereas the trade card increased in size, the visiting card became smaller. In some areas, notably Belgium and Holland, the bearer's name was so small and the tints of printing ink so light as to be only just legible. In Central Europe the idiom remained elaborate, if not flamboyant, with much experimental use of marbled backgrounds and tinted enamelled surfaces. Among the engravers and printers themselves, and among artists, architects, sculptors, and craftsmen in general, it was felt not inappropriate to sport a card of minor extravagance; but even here the trend was to tasteful reticence.

By the 1860s and 1870s most of Europe, including Britain, had wholly espoused sobriety in personal cards, and sizes had stabilized at 90 × 65mm (3½ × 2½in) for ladies and 90 × 32mm (3½ × 1¼in) for gentlemen. Gentlemen's cards, though smaller, were slightly thicker than those of ladies. In Britain, the etiquette of typographic style and layout was rigorously observed: the wording was engraved, printing was in black, card colour was white. A man's town address appeared in the lower left-hand corner, his club on the right; if he had a country address this went on the right, and mention of the club was omitted. Unmarried daughters living at home did not have cards of their own. They appeared compendiously on their mother's card. Sisters without parents used cards with their names listed in order of seniority, or simply as 'The Misses Smith'. If they had separate cards the most senior girl appeared as 'Miss Smith'; the others included their Christian names.

The 'leaving of cards' was a clearly defined convention. Generally speaking, the card was used not as an *accompaniment* to a call but as a graceful *substitute*. Cards were left when there had been no meeting – actual or intended – between the mistress of the house and the caller. If the lady were out or 'not at home' (not receiving), or the caller merely wished to indicate a courteous interest, cards were left with the servant who answered the door. The gesture indicated merely that a call had been made. It was laid down that the cards, in the case of a first call, should be three in number – one of the woman's and two of her husband's; her own card was for the mistress of the house and her husband's for both master and mistress. The only time cards were left at an actual visit was at its completion, when the visitor left two of her husband's cards on the hallway table on departure. She did not leave her own card as, having seen the lady of the house, she had no reason to proffer a substitute for her own presence.

The visiting cards of British ladies may often be found with a corner folded down. This indicated that it was left personally (rather than sent through the post); it had a secondary meaning: that all the ladies in the house are also included in the courtesy of the call. A gentleman's card, it follows, was never thus presented; there might well have been unmarried ladies in the household whom it would have been improper for him to have called on.

There were other conventions. In case of illness it was the custom to leave one's card bearing the handwritten legend 'to enquire', and in the case of death, in a family of remote acquaintance, a note of sympathy. Cards are sometimes found bearing the letters 'ppc' in handwriting at the bottom right-hand corner. This – 'pour prendre congé' (to take leave) – is an intimation that the caller is about to leave the district and wishes to signal his departure courteously, but without fuss.

In a further convention a miniature 'calling card', 20 × 45mm ($^{13}/_{16}$ × 1¾in), was produced on behalf of a new-born baby; it bore the child's name in the centre and the date of birth in the bottom left-hand corner and is sometimes found attached by a ribbon to the mother's card of 'thanks for kind enquiries and congratulations'.

The British visiting card was simple, though complicated in use. The American card was often much more elaborate and, on the whole, simpler in use; it admitted novelties of every kind, many in excellent taste, others less so. Printed in colour on tinted card, it was produced in a wide range of sizes, and included all sorts of features: unorthodox typefaces, borders,

Three visiting cards of the early 19th century, two of them signed by Barnes of Coventry Street, London. Intaglio-printed, the two on the right in blue. Each approx. 45 × 65mm (1¾ × 2½in)

cropped corners, chromolithographed flower pieces, textile trimmings, and even ferrotype photographs of the bearer. No trick was missed by an industry that sought to bring the calling card to the ordinary man.

As in the chromolithographed trade card, multicoloured 'frame' designs were available from stock. In many cases these closely resembled those used for trade cards. Mass-produced in up to eight or ten workings, the cards were supplied in thousands to local printers, who merely set up individual customers' names in type and overprinted in black. In the vast majority of cases, the legend consisted only of the name. Unlike the British version, there was neither designation nor address.

An American extension of the calling card, unknown in Britain, was the 'flirtation' card (or 'escort' or 'acquaintance' card). Designed as a method of encounter, it was slipped to prospective companions and carried not only the name of the bearer but an introductory verse and illustration. In a typical example, the name of Walter W. Kimball is flanked by a sketch of a respectable encounter on one side, and by an embrace on the other. 'Yours truly' and 'Please answer' are the twin captions, and the main message reads: 'Your coral lips were made to kiss, I stoutly will maintain; and dare you say my lovely miss, that aught was made in vain?'. Other versions in the same series offer different messages. In another, more discreet presentation, a chastely printed white card (presumably for use by ladies) carries the message: 'Acquaintance card; between ourselves. Can I have the pleasure of your company this evening? If I can, keep this card; if not, please return it'.

See also ACQUAINTANCE CARD; CHROMO

REFERENCES Edwin Banfield, *Visiting Cards and Cases* (Trowbridge: Baros Books, 1989); Achille and Henry Prior, *Biglietti di Vista Italiano* (Bergamo, 1911); F. C. Schang, *Visiting Cards of Celebrities* (Paris: Fernand Hazan, 1971); Victoria [pseud.], *Calling Cards* (New York: Hearst Books, 1992)

Visiting craftsmen's papers

A variant of the CALL-BACK HANDBILL, the visiting craftsmen's handbill offers services in the customer's own home. Typically, it promises attendance at residents' addresses to carry out the work in question. Watch-making and repairing was a frequent service, the work being carried out on the customer's kitchen table.

In some cases attendance was monthly or yearly by arrangement; in others, visits were unplanned and the customer was advised in the handbill that 'Mr S' [Simmons's] stay in this town will only be for this week and no longer'. The system was used not only by itinerant craftsmen but by permanently established tradesmen in shops.

The visiting craftsman was a feature of the outlying districts of Britain and America. The wording and general presentation of the handbills follow much the same pattern, and they normally carried blanks in which details of the visit, etc. were entered by hand. The system is still in operation in some parts of Britain where the 'craftsman' is a dentist or chiropodist.

Visitors' register

The development of tourism in the later years of the 19th century brought new trade, and in some cases prosperity, to hitherto unfrequented areas. The hotel and boarding-house business flourished, and local tradesmen were glad to serve the increasing numbers of visitors who came to stay, some of them regularly, season after season.

To cater for visitors' needs and to provide tradesmen with a likely advertising medium, many resorts published a Visitors' Register, a weekly listing of visitors and their respective hotel or boarding-house addresses. The register commonly appeared in the guise of a magazine or newspaper and ranged in extent from a single sheet to a substantial pocket-book. It carried articles, timetables, postal and other local information, as well as a sprinkling of news. It was bought and scanned with interest by visitors, who aspired to inclusion in the listings, and by tradesmen who kept an eye on the comings and goings of potential customers.

In the nature of its readership, apart from the actual listings, the content of the paper needed little change beyond a six- or eight-week cycle, at the end of which, with new readers displacing the old, the same material could be reprinted virtually unchanged. Topical editorial material, in the form of chit-chat paragraphs, was mainly lightweight. A typical item in the 'Oban Visitors' Register' (15 July 1891) reads: 'We observe a fruit stall has been opened by Mr Drummond, ex-Provost, in the Railway Station, the usefulness of which will no doubt be fully appreciated by the travelling public'.

The visitors' register, which appeared only during the summer months, was generally put out as a seasonal sideline by the printers and publishers of the local newspaper.

Wafer

A stationer's adhesive in widespread use in the 19th century as a substitute for sealing wax, the wafer was the generally accepted means of letter closure prior to the advent of the gummed ENVELOPE. It was also used to attach papers to each other, for mounting items in albums, and often for the posting of notices on walls and windows.

The adhesive of the wafer was commonly made from flour, gum, gelatine, or isinglass. It was coated on both sides of thin sheets of material, stamped out in the form of discs, to be moistened and pressed into place. In this form the wafer provided a double-sided adhesive as an interface between papers. It also appeared in single-sided form for use as a sealant in the manner of sealing wax, the body of the wafer lying partly on the overlap and partly on the paper below. In this form the upper non-adhesive surface of the wafer was used for a variety of graphic motifs, including monograms (as in the traditional wax seal), messages of affection, propaganda slogans and, later, commercial name and address panels.

Punch's anti-Graham wafers, published at the Punch Office in London, 1844. Printed in relief by Bradbury and Evans, Whitefriars, London, the wood-engraved surround in brown, the wafers in green. 280 × 223 mm (11 × 8 3/4 in)

The single-sided wafer was generally supplied in multiple sheets for cutting up. In some cases, particularly in cryptic messages of regard, the image measured barely more than 6 or 7 mm (5/16 in). In others, notably propaganda and commercial wafers, dimensions were of the order of 20 × 25 mm (13/16 × 1 in). Wafers were also available as metallic reliefs, as chromolithographed 'scraps', as golden filigree cut-outs, and as miniature photographs.

Message wafers ranged from the jocose ('Ah! tis only me') to the frankly sentimental ('My love'). Messages in the new shorthand, or 'phonography', had a vogue, and religious text-references also appeared. Campaign slogans included calls for temperance, world peace, and reform.

Most celebrated of the campaign wafers were those published from the *Punch* office, denouncing the Home Secretary Sir James Graham for his action in opening letters at the Post Office. At the insistence of the Foreign Secretary, Graham had exercised his right as Home Secretary to intercept and examine mail – in this case the correspondence of W. J. Linton and Giuseppe Mazzini, the Italian suspected of plotting against his own government. '*Punch*'s anti-Graham wafers' appeared as sixteen different illustrated slogans on a single sheet costing twopence. The sheet, measuring 282 × 222 mm (11 1/8 × 8 3/4 in), was decorated with images of prying bureaucracy, the wafer-panels bearing such motifs as a porcupine ('Hands off') and a lobster ('Not to be red without getting into hot water'). *Punch* also produced a MULREADY CARICATURE satirizing Graham.

See also LETTER SEAL

REFERENCE Michael Champness and David Trapnell, *Adhesive Wafer Seals* (Beckenham: Chancery House Press, 1996)

COLLECTION John Johnson Collection, Bodleian Library, Oxford

Warrant

A warrant is a document of authority. The term is applied in a wide range of contexts, as for example the following: travel warrant, money warrant, royal warrant, dividend warrant, extradition warrant. It has particular associations with jurisprudence and penology, as in distress (or attachment) warrants, gaoler's warrant, governor's warrant, release warrant, discharge warrant, death warrant, reprieve warrant, prisoner's remove war-

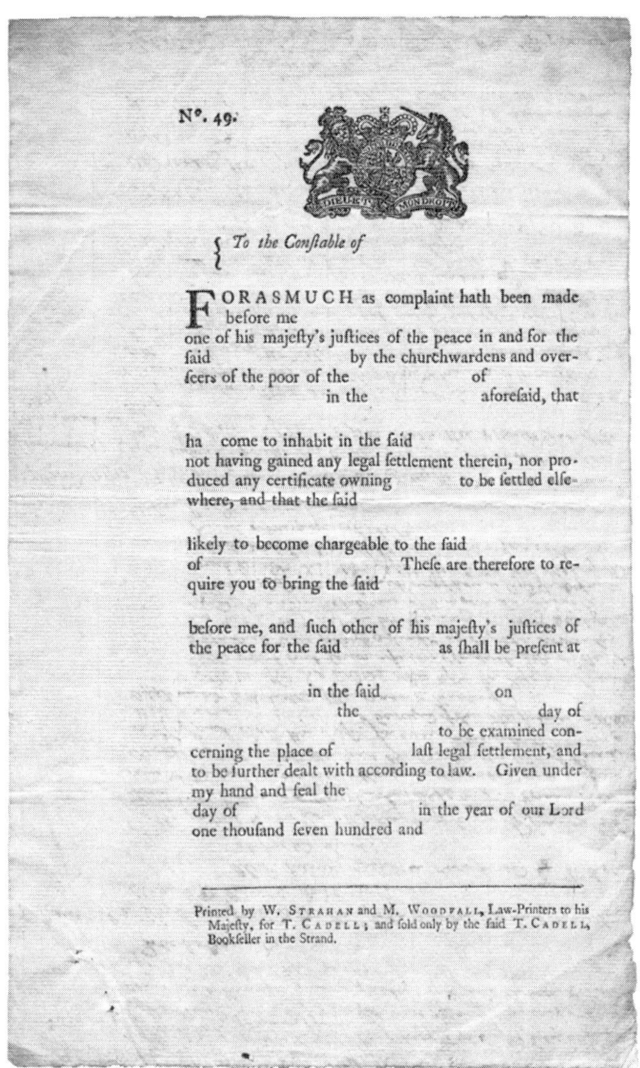

Nº. 49.

To the Conſtable of

FORASMUCH as complaint hath been made before me one of his majeſty's juſtices of the peace in and for the ſaid by the churchwardens and overſeers of the poor of the of in the aforeſaid, that

ha come to inhabit in the ſaid not having gained any legal ſettlement therein, nor produced any certificate owning to be ſettled elſewhere, and that the ſaid

likely to become chargeable to the ſaid of Theſe are therefore to require you to bring the ſaid

before me, and ſuch other of his majeſty's juſtices of the peace for the ſaid as ſhall be preſent at

in the ſaid on the day of to be examined concerning the place of laſt legal ſettlement, and to be further dealt with according to law. Given under my hand and ſeal the day of in the year of our Lord one thouſand ſeven hundred and

Printed by W. STRAHAN and M. WOODFALL, Law-Printers to his Majeſty, for T. CADELL; and ſold only by the ſaid T. CADELL, Bookſeller in the Strand.

Warrant form concerning illegal residence of a vagrant, late 18th century. Letterpress, printed by W. Strahan and M. Woodfall, law-printers to his Majesty, for T. Cadell, bookseller, Strand, London. 315 × 195 mm (12¾ × 7⅝ in)

rant, transportation warrant; in some instances (as in the State of Virginia) the term 'warrant' is used to refer to a Justice of the Peace summons.

In the majority of cases the term relates to a document conferring authority where none normally exists, thus securing the recipient against loss, damage, or disciplinary action. The notion is explicit in many such documents of command where, although the word 'warrant' is absent from the heading, a final phrase confirms '... and for so doing this shall be your warrant'.

Typical of such documents is an order of the Justices at Liverpool Quarter Sessions of 18 January 1836, measuring 335 × 205 mm (13⅛ × 8⅛ in). After a formal preamble, the Justices declare: '(William Spencer) having at this Session been convicted of (Felony) This Court doth therefore order and adjudge that the said (William Spencer) be committed to (His Majesty's Gaol the Castle of Lancaster) the Governor whereof is hereby required to receive and keep (him) in safe custody and to hard labour for the space of (twelve calendar months) ... (and that the said William Spencer during the said term be twice whipped for doing which this shall be the said Governor's Warrant)'.

A warrant may also be couched in general terms. A wholly handwritten example, dated Salem 6 July 1829 and addressed to the Sheriff, appears as a slip of paper measuring 85 × 200 mm (3⅜ × 7⅞ in). It reads: 'Mr Willson, Shrf: Sir Descharge George Stewart from Jail on condition of James Stewart paing all the cost. Thos McClaughry'.

In another handwritten example, dated 15 July 1788, and measuring 165 × 200 mm (6½ × 7⅞ in), an instruction is addressed to 'The High Sheriff of Wiltshire, his Under Sheriff, Gaoler and all others to whom it may concern'. It reads: 'Let the execution of John Clements be respited for one month, for which this shall be your warrant'.

See also GAOL PAPERS; SUMMONS; TRANSPORTATION PAPERS

Watchpaper

Originally blank discs of paper or fine linen, watchpapers were used by makers and repairers to keep the movements of pocket watches free of dust. In the latter part of the 18th century they took on the additional function of a TRADE CARD, carrying engraved advertisements, often of some elegance. Many early examples bore finely engraved classical and allegorical figures (Father Time was much favoured), but by the mid 19th century they had settled down to less fanciful designs and displays of wording. By the end of the century many were printed from metal type and had clearly abandoned pretensions to elegance.

The margin was often used as a sales-message area: 'NB – every description of foreign watches, clocks plain and jewellery neatly repaired'; and opportunity was taken to publicize sidelines, some of them indicating versatility. S. M. Philips, watchmaker of Norwich (c.1840), refers to his coaching office; other sidelines include 'fishing tackle maker' and 'umbrellas and parasols repaired'.

Most watchpapers were printed in a single colour on white or beige paper, the image measuring 50 mm (2 in) in diameter. Unused examples (or engravers' proofs) are found with their image centred on a rectangular paper; used papers have normally been cut round with scissors to fit the watch. The trimming is often less than careful. Additional scissor work may appear in a series of radiating snips around the edge of the disc to allow the paper to follow the concave form of the back of the watch. In some cases, engraved designs provide spaces for the cuts; typical of these are designs showing zodiacal signs and other calendar notes in a twelve-segment border pattern.

The watchpaper adopted much the same design conventions in America as in Britain, though American designs are more often found to bear the engraver's name. Among those recorded in American collections is that of Paul Revere. The American watch was also used to house a personal keepsake, in the form of a decorative memento. This item, sometimes executed by hand, but more commonly printed and available from stationers, was inserted in the watch with the watchmaker's label or used in its

Watchpapers of the early 19th century, intaglio-printed. *Left:* of Stimson, Bath, printed in black, diameter of printed image 45 mm (1¾ in); *right:* of H. Russell, Cripplegate, London, printed in brown, diameter of printed image 48 mm (1$^{15}/_{16}$ in)

stead. The design often incorporated a central disc bearing the Lord's Prayer or other religious passage (legible only under a magnifying glass), or expressions of affection and goodwill. A popular approach was to produce the outer areas of the design as a fine filigree or 'paper lace', often coloured, and sometimes embossed. The paper lace convention was reinforced by the intricate CUTWORK of the Pennsylvania Dutch, whose designs incorporated numerous traditional symbols of affection.

REFERENCE Dorothea E. Spear, *American Watch Papers, with a Descriptive List of the Collection in the American Antiquarian Society* (Worcester, Mass.: American Antiquarian Society, 1952)

Watermark

The watermark is produced by a controlled thinning of the paper during its manufacture. In its simplest form (still essentially the method in use today) the mark is formed by a wire, fashioned to the design shape, attached to the mould or roller on which the paper is made. The outline of the wire, impinging on the surface of the wet paper, appears as a lighter tone as a consequence of the greater translucency of the finished product. In a more advanced method, introduced in the 1850s, the mark appears not merely as a line effect but as an infinitely variable tonal image with a light-and-shade effect reminiscent of a photograph.

Wire watermark used in the manufacture of Ceylon and Colonial Government stamped papers, with a manuscript description. Size of watermark 84 × 115 mm (3¼ × 4½ in)

Watermarks were introduced as a form of trade mark. The first recorded watermark appears in Italy in 1271. In England they appear in Hertford (John Tate, Sele Mill) in about 1490, and in America (Rittenhouse) in 1699. Their use in France became general when trade marks were made compulsory in the 14th century. They were at first very simple, taking the form of crosses, triangles, and other shapes readily made from bent wire. In time the shapes became more complex, and included numerals and lettering. Manufacturers' initials began to appear from the 15th to 16th centuries, and city insignia and royal coats of arms were in use from the end of the 17th century. Dating had become general by the end of the 18th century, and was to remain so until the 1940s and 1950s. Watermark dates provide a useful, but not wholly reliable, help in document dating. Because paper was often stored for some time before it was used for printing, they may function only as 'not-earlier-than' guidelines (and even then not very accurate ones).

The light-and-shade watermark (for example a portrait profile) is produced from a low-relief wax model. Male and female plates are made from the wax by the ELECTROTYPE process and the plates are used to imprint the image on a fine wire gauze. The wire gauze, now bearing the same contours as the wax original, is used in the paper mould, producing corresponding variations in the thickness of the resultant sheet.

Apart from its value as a mark of origin, the watermark presented a major deterrent to the counterfeiter. The light-and-shade mark, particularly, is favoured in paper currency and high-value security documents. The simple line watermark has been used in a wide variety of anti-counterfeit documents, among them, less predictably, prohibition-era alcohol prescriptions and Chinese CHOP PAPERS. Colour watermarks, invisible until held to the light, were introduced experimentally by Sir William Congreve in 1818. They involved a sandwich effect, coloured-paper pulp being suspended between layers of white. Their practical application, however, was limited.

Watermarks have been designed for special occasions, centenary and other celebrations, and for use by individuals. Typical of these are the designs produced for the Caxton Quincentennial in 1976, for the American Bicentennial in 1976, and for the 'personalized' paper used by George Washington.

See also CAVALLINO; CIGARETTE PAPER

COLLECTIONS American Antiquarian Society, Worcester, Mass.

SOCIETY British Association of Paper Historians; Paper Publications Society

Waybill

The term 'waybill' was at one period applied to a printed or handwritten itinerary, listing the route to be taken by a traveller. More commonly it relates to the carriage of freight and lists goods in transit, their route, dates of despatch and arrival, charges for carriage, and records for payment. In the coaching era it applied also to passengers, whose names (and sometimes addresses) are listed. The document appears in virtually every field of transport, and the 19th-century waybill provides much information on the commercial development of canals, stage coaches, and railways.

Waybills appear in many formats, but the basic structure is common to most. A typical American coaching waybill of the 1840s measures 215 × 265 mm (8½ × 10½ in). As with many for-

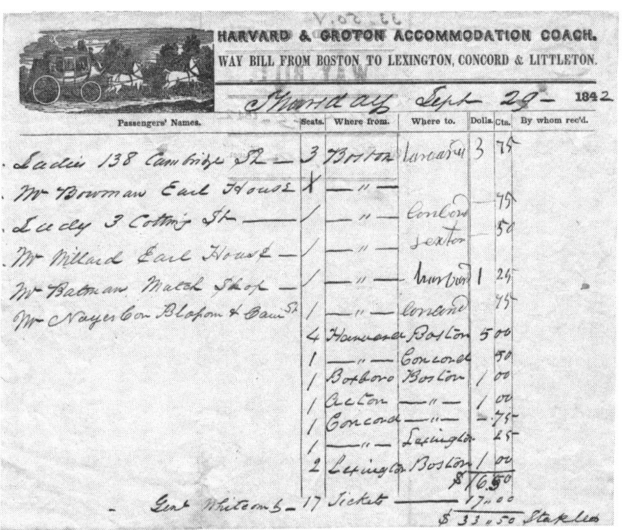
HARVARD & GROTON ACCOMMODATION COACH.
WAY BILL FROM BOSTON TO LEXINGTON, CONCORD & LITTLETON.
Monday Sept 29 1842

Passengers' Names.	Seats.	Where from.	Where to.	Dolls.	Cts.	By whom rec'd.

Waybill for the Harvard & Groton accommodation coach from Boston (US) to Lexington, Concord & Littleton, 29 September 1842. Letterpress, with wood-engraving and manuscript. 215 × 265 mm (8½ × 10½ in)

mal papers of the period, for convenience of handling and filing it was often devised to fold to a narrow format – approximately 215 × 95 mm (8½ × 3¾ in) – with a printed title appearing on one face of the folded document. (The method was applied to most business correspondence, the title being entered by hand at the head, and the documents taped in binders.) It is headed with a stagecoach wood-engraving and the words 'Harvard & Groton accommodation coach; way bill from Boston to Lexington, Concord & Littleton'. Beneath a handwritten dateline appear column headings: 'Passengers' names/Seats/Where from/Where to/Dolls/Cents/By whom rec'd'.

From a trip recorded on Thursday 29 September 1842 we learn that seven passengers left Boston: 'Three ladies' of 138 Cambridge Street for Concord: $3.75; a 'lady' of 3 Cotting Street, also for Concord: 75c ('outside'); Mr Millard of Earl House, for Lexington (50c); Mr Batman of the 'Match Shop' for Concord: $1.25; and Mr Nayes of 'Corner of Blossom and Cam St', also for Concord: 75c. One scheduled passenger, Mr Bowman, of Earl House, failed to appear. His seat, unpaid for, remained empty. On the return trip passengers are unnamed. Four travelled from Harvard all the way to Boston: $5.00; one from Harvard was dropped off at Concord: 50c; one was picked up at Boxboro for Boston: $1; one at Acton: $1; two passengers joined at Concord, one for Boston: 75c, the other getting off at Lexington: 25c. Two joined at Lexington for Boston at 50c each. The driver's name, entered below the title on the back of the form, was Harrington.

Weight card

A minor attraction at fairs and other holiday events in the period 1900 to 1940 was the 'I guess your weight' man. His scales were free of charge to those whose weight he failed to guess within set limits. The card, on which he afterwards pencilled the exact weight, was kept by the customer as a record and as a souvenir of the occasion. The cards measured approximately 50 × 70 mm (2 × 2¾ in) and often carried a message on their reverse advertising a neighbouring attraction. Similar cards, smaller and sometimes bearing 'character readings' on their reverse were delivered by penny-in-the-slot machines. Both types – more particularly the first – may be described as primitive printing (*see* PRINTING, PRIMITIVE).

The cards were in direct line of succession from the toll weighing machines of the 18th and 19th centuries, on which vehicles and their loads were weighed and subject to tolls according to their weight. Tickets of this kind, usually of paper, were printed with provision for handwritten details of date, vehicle, load weight, etc. to be added.

'Automatic' weighing-machine cards made their appearance in the early 1920s. They were pre-printed with advertising or other matter in up to four colours and were imprinted at the time of weighing with a date and weight. In Switzerland, particularly, they had a considerable vogue, being presented on a series basis to encourage the weighing enthusiast to weigh frequently and so collect a complete 'set'.

In the late 20th century, as now, electronic weighing machines allowed weight-watchers the chance to discover their present weight and also what was, according to their age, height, etc., their ideal weight. The information was delivered from the machine on a slip of paper.

See also TOLL/TURNPIKE TICKET

Weight cards from the years around 1900. Letterpress, with pencil and embossed additions. Each approximately 20 × 100 mm (¾ × 4 in)

Will

Apart from its primary function as a legal document, the will is a fruitful source of secondary information. As part of an archive it forms a possibly vital link in a biographical or regional narrative, and needs to be considered within its specific context. Discovered on its own, however, often as an unselected item among discarded papers, the will may be studied as a single ephemeral document. To the student of social and economic history it may reveal unexpected sidelights.

Common to wills at large are the elements of integrity and security. The document must be proof against removal or addition of any of its parts, either in its text or constituent pages, and it must be proof against alteration or misrepresentation. It must also be abundantly clear as to meaning. These needs have led over the centuries to the adoption of numerous conventions, verbal and physical, as safeguards. Among these, principally, are the inadmissibility of textual alterations, erasures, or corrections; signing in the presence of witnesses who, knowing the nature of the document, sign in the presence of each other; and the numbering and sealed-stitching of pages. Details vary from one country to another, and in America in certain cases from one state to another, but the general principle is constant: the document must admit no doubt as to the author's intention and identity.

There are three basic systems of will-making: the witnessed will, already noted, as in Anglo-American and British Commonwealth practice; the holographic will, in which the whole document, not necessarily witnessed, is written and signed by the testator; and the notional will, in which the document is drawn up and filed at the testator's request by an authorized legal practitioner – a 'notary' – who himself attests to its authenticity.

It is commonly held that the formalities of will-making have a function beyond that of clarity and security. Part of the purpose is to impress upon the testator the importance of the act, a matter not to be undertaken lightly.

It is doubtless for this reason, and perhaps because in Britain the proving of wills was formerly a matter for ecclesiastical courts, that early wills adopt a near-liturgical tone:

(1727) In the name of God Amen. I, William Hunt the Younger of Rodmorsham in the County of Kent, Yeoman, being at present in good health and of sound mind memory and understanding, God be praised for the same, but knowing

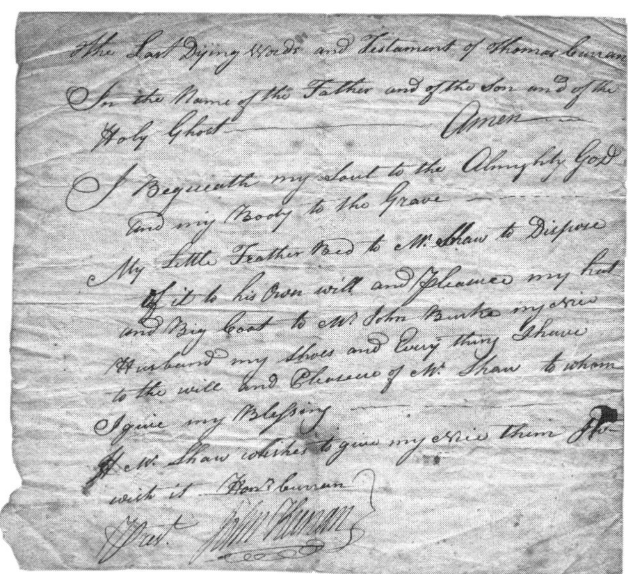
The Last Dying Words and Testament of Thomas Curran
In the Name of the Father and of the Son and of the
Holy Ghost ——— Amen——
I Bequeath my Soul to the Almighty God
and my Body to the Grave ——
My Little Feather Bed to Mr Shaw to Dispose
of it to his Own will and Pleasure my hat
and Big Coat to Mr John Burke my Niece
Husband my Shoes and Every thing I have
to the will and Pleasure of Mr Shaw to whom
I give my Blessing
If Mr Shaw wishes to give my Niece them I so
wish it. Thos Curran

The last dying words and testament of Thomas Curran, 18th century. Manuscript. 170 × 190 mm (6¾ × 7½ in)

it is appointed for all men once to dye … do for the quieting of my mind and settling that part of Worldly goods which God of his infinite goodness hath bestowed upon me do make my last will and Testament in manner following….

(1728) …First and principally I (William Frost-Grampton of Upton Gray, Southton [Southampton]) Comitt my soul into the hands of Almighty God relying on the merrits of my Blessed Lord and Saviour Jesus Christ for pardon and Remission of all my Sinns. And my Body I Comitt to the Earth to be decently buryed….

In some cases, notably about the start of the 19th century, there was an admixture of earthly concern. There had been rumours of people being buried alive, the victims reviving but being unable to escape. Thomas Hannam of Crondall was much perturbed:

(1803) In the Name of God Amen. I Thomas Hannam of Crondall in the County of Hampshire, Gentleman, do make and publish this my last Will and Testament in Manner and Form following (that is to say) My Soul I recommend to the Almighty who gave it hoping to be everlasting happy through the Merits of Jesus Christ our Blessed Redeemer as to my Body my Will and Desire is to be kept twelve days at least until my flesh and Body is turned if so to be often bathed with Spirits of Wine and Campher & to preserve my Body and my Will is to be buried in a wooden Coffin and the Lidd to be put on and taken off as pleasure as my dear Wife and Daughters were and that no Screws to be used in or about the Lidd or any Part of my Coffin and my Desire is not to have no leaden Coffin. Coffin only to be Wood as before mentioned and that single and no Nails or Screws to be used to fasten down the Led of my Coffin but to take on and off at Leisure or as occasion may require…. and my Will is and I do hereby desire that the Singers belonging to the Church… do sing at my funeral the Burial Psalm for which I give them the Sum of ten shillings and sixpence and my Will further is that my Coffin Lid is not to be fastened down by any means whatever….

Wills appear in a variety of formats and lengths. They range from a single foolscap sheet to thirty or forty tape-bound pages, and there are examples on folded parchment opening out to as much as 600 × 700 mm (23⅝ × 27⅝ in). Unusually small specimens are also found, one, undated, measuring no more than 170 × 190 mm (6¾ × 7½ in). It disposes briefly of a minimal estate:

The Last Dying Words and Testament of Thomas Curran: In the Name of the Father and of the Son and of the Holy Ghost Amen. I bequeath my Soul to the Almighty God and my Body to the Grave. My Little Feather Bed to Mr Shaw to Dispose of it to his own will and Pleasure my hat and Big Coat to Mr John Burke my Nieces Husband my Shoes and Every thing I have to the will and Pleasure of Mr Shaw to whom I give my Blessing. If Mr Shaw wishes to give my Niece them I so wish it….

Also of modest proportions is the will of one Tom Moley, dated 'Fall 1856'. In faded ink on crumpled paper measuring some 90 × 90 mm (3½ × 3½ in), it reads: 'I Tom Moley give my money amounting to 3 hundred dollars to my kittens Reada and Tabbe divided between them. Tom Moley'.

Bagley (1971) cites the will as an aid not only in supplementing the parish register and filling gaps in the family tree, but also in throwing light on the character, interests, and well-being of the testator: 'It cannot disguise the concern of a loving husband for his wife's future welfare, or the disapproval of an aggrieved father for an erring son…'.

Wills have survived in very large quantities, either in archives and record offices or as oddments in ephemera fairs and flea-markets. Their study, until now largely neglected, is potentially rewarding.

See also BURIAL PAPERS; INVENTORY

REFERENCE J. J. Bagley, *Historical Intepretation*, 2 vol. (Harmondsworth: Penguin, 1971)

Window bill, shop

The shopkeeper's window bill is related to the SHOWCARD. Initially, like the showcard, locally executed and worded to the requirement of the individual tradesman, it later became a standard printed item in Britain, available in a range covering a wide variety of trades. Printed chiefly in red, blue, and black on a white ground, the bills often used wood type and, occasionally, crudely executed woodcut illustrations in black. Their format was commonly landscape, typically 160 × 510 mm (6¼ × 20⅛ in), to allow posting in the upper areas of the windows where displays of goods were less crowded, but small portrait-format bills were also produced for spot posting in vacant spaces.

The bills began to appear in the late 1870s and remained in general use, often unchanged, until the late 1930s and, vestigially, into the late 1940s. Their subject matter and wording reflected the printer's concern to make them as widely applicable as possible and, taken together, they remind us of the period's multiplicity of small shops. Butchers, bakers, grocers, and general stores are well provided for; fringe areas include rag, bone, and bottle dealers, boot repairers, and window glass

Shop window bill, 1930s. Letterpress, printed in black and red (for the 'L' of Ladies'), printed and sold by Samuel Reeves, King's Cross, London. 157 × 455 mm (6¼ × 17⅞ in)

suppliers. Typical legends are: 'Brown boots dyed black', 'All kinds of wine, beer and doctors' bottles bought', 'Oil is cheaper', 'Something to eat and enjoy', 'Turkeys are cheap'.

As with the early showcard, manufacturers and suppliers later stepped in with illustrated window bills in full colour. Later still, they supplied display corner-pieces, pelmet strips, and border motifs to fit windows of any dimension – all publicizing branded products. These too are redolent of their time and are sought as collectors' items. Parallel with the development of manufacturers' window bills was the production by chain stores of 'company' bills for use in all their branches. Devised and sometimes also printed centrally, they were released simultaneously and through their uniform design contributed to the establishing of the concept of 'house style'. All these methods of window display continue, particularly for a special 'promotion' and at times of sales.

See also POINT-OF-SALE DISPLAY; WINKLE BAG

Window card, domestic

The 'private house' window card dates back at least to the 1830s. Charles Dickens mentions one in *Pickwick Papers*: 'Apartments furnished for a single gentleman'. The earliest such cards measured around 110 × 150 mm (4³⁄₈ × 6 in) and were printed in black on white from engraved copper plates. They were refined in appearance and illegible from a distance. Available with or without eyelets and a hanging cord, they were normally propped against the inside of the window on the ledge formed by the lower frame, or hung in the lower window from its catch. The cards were sold in a range bearing various legends: 'A bedroom, furnished' was among the commonest, but there was provision for much variation on the board and lodging theme.

Towards the end of the 19th century less reticent cards appeared, with bolder and wider-ranging legends: 'Pianoforte taught' was one such notice. The private citizen had gone into business. Still less reticent were others in the same series: 'Ironing done here', 'Washing and charing', 'Machine work done here', 'Mangling done here', and, over half a century after Dickens, 'Lodgings for a single gentleman'. The starkness of the bold lettering was offset by a nominally decorative second-colour border.

With the development of the seaside holiday industry there appeared larger (particularly longer) cards, approximately 100 × 360 mm (4 × 14⅛ in), bearing on one side 'Vacancies' and on the other 'No vacancies'. Normally printed in black on white and having rounded corners, they continue in use.

Domestic window card, no. 151 in the series, mid 19th century. Letterpress, printed and sold by J. Redington, Hoxton Old Town, London. 137 × 215 mm (5½ × 8½ in)

The domestic window card enshrines some of the least documented, but perhaps most widespread, forms of private enterprise.

See also ICE CARD

Wine label

The necessity to label wine bottles only became apparent in the late 18th century when major changes occurred which were to transform the industry. Among these were the introduction of cork bark for making tightly fitting bottle corks and the redesigning of bottles so that they could be binned, laid flat, for the contents to mature.

For centuries wine had been matured in wood, after which it would be transferred for consumption into pottery jugs, leather blackjacks or thick black glass bottles which had wooden or parchment labels tied to the neck. Smart households, university colleges, and taverns might have bottles with an embossed seal showing a coat of arms, date, initials or name; these usually identified the owner of the bottle, in order for it to be reclaimed, rather than the contents. The date referred to the year when the wine was made, and was likely to differ by many decades from the bottle date. In the 18th century, as the production of both glassmaking and wine improved, more elegant labelling was required; ivory, silver, or enamel was used to make the bottle 'tickets' or 'labels' which were hung round the neck to identify the contents of bottles and decanters in the dining room.

The earliest paper label appears to be one from a bottle of 1756 'Real Companhia' port which was given to the late André Simon. As interest in vintages and sources developed throughout the 19th century it became customary to label bottles, which were now sufficiently elegant to come to table. Two table wine labels dating from the first half of the 19th century are in the Musée du Vin, Beaune, France. Printers sometimes provided for flexibility in the use of a label by leaving a space for the last two digits of the date to be written in by hand. By the first half of the 19th century French and German labels were either engraved or produced by chromolithography and had become flamboyantly colourful and decorative with swags of fruit, coats of arms, and Bacchanalian characters. The beginning of the 20th century saw the first laws governing the information required on labels, although this can be an unreliable guide to dating and almost a century later there continue to be many anomalies. 1936 saw the addition of 'Appellation Contrôlée', and in the last quarter of the 20th century the European Community introduced legislation to standardize label information.

Since the 1950s the marketing explosion in wine buying from high street shops has made the design of the wine label one of prime importance. Legal requirements now dictate the printed content, and any extra optional information offered by the producer or wine merchant is usually placed on a less decorative back label. These latter, which began to appear in the 1940s, might include a guide to quality and use or a map and details of the wine-producing area. In addition, some wines will merit a neck label giving the vintage. Some of the most outstanding 20th-century labels come from Château Mouton Rothschild. The earliest surviving Mouton Rothschild label is a simple letterpress example dated 1859, but in 1923 Baron Philippe de Rothschild introduced a pictorial label. The initial design was not a success and the idea was dropped until 1945 when Baron Philippe began commissioning on an annual basis leading artists, among them Jean Cocteau (1947), Marie Laurencin (1948), Georges Braque (1955), and Salvador Dali (1958).

The custom of commissioning artists is now well established and work by artists is found both in wine merchants' lists (David Gentleman in 1961 and Edward Ardizzone in 1962–3 for Harveys, Bristol) and for labels such as the one designed by Reynolds Stone for the Breaky Bottom Vineyard, Sussex. [AT]

REFERENCES François Bonal, *Le Livre d'Or du Champagne* (Lausanne: Editions du Grand-Pont, 1984); Andrew Jones, *The Stories Behind the Labels* (Bathurst, NSW, 1994); Robert Joseph, *Art of the Wine Label* (Leicester: Windward, 1987); John Lewis, *Wine List Decorations 1961–63* (Bristol: John Harvey & Sons Ltd, 1964); Philippine Rothschild, *Mouton Rothschild: Paintings for the Labels* (Boston: Little, Brown, 1983)

COLLECTIONS The International Wine & Food Society, 9 Fitzmaurice Place, Berkeley Square, London; Musée du Vin de Bourgogne, Beaune, France; Waddesdon Manor (NT), near Aylesbury, Bucks

Winkle bag

The winkle-bag trade originated in Billingsgate, London, in 1874. It flourished mainly in the period 1910 to 1942, when the bags, in addition to the winkle-stall's name, bore a doggerel verse. This was written by Robert Collis Hancock, a bag manufacturer and printer of the bags, in whose company's hands the bulk of the business remained as a near-monopoly for over a century.

Robert Hancock is said to have started by selling PAPER BAGS from a basket on the pavement outside Billingsgate fish market; later he acquired the freehold of a shop in Fish Street Hill where he sold fishmongers' requisites in general, and supplied printed WINDOW BILLS for fish-and-chip shops, fish restaurants, and fish shops. The window bills ('Frying tonight', 'Choice new bloaters', 'Soles are cheap today') were bought from outside suppliers, but in 1910 he decided to print winkle bags himself. He bought and installed an old hand press, printing new verses on the bags each week, eventually building up a repertoire of some eighty or ninety different compositions.

When he died in 1942 his grandsons Robert and Thomas carried on the business, later installing a powered press. Thomas took over the verse-writing. The firm continued in the 1990s, manufacturing a wide range of printed paper bags. Winkle-bag production dwindled in parallel with the winkle trade in the years following World War II, though the firm still supplies bags – printed, but without verses – to a number of traders.

Originally printed from wood and metal type on a platen press, the Kraft wet-strength bags were later printed from rubber stereos, the image being added as a final stage in a continuous fold-cut-and-paste process on a bag-making machine. The Hancock Collis & Co.'s stereo file contains many of the names and verses of the winkle bag in its heyday. As in former times, the bags were supplied by weight and made in two sizes: ½ pint, 155 × 153 mm (6⅛ × 6 in), and 1 pint, 178 × 178 mm (7 × 7 in).

Few of the verse-bearing bags survive. Early examples carry the imprint 'R Hancock, facing Monument'. Later, the imprint appears as 'Hancock Collis & Co.', Billingsgate. Non-verse carrying bags have the imprint '315 Kennington Park Road, London SE11' and, later, 'Hancock Collis'. Among the names on surviving specimens are C. McCall, Chapel Market and Caledonian Road; F. Welsh, Pratt Street, Camden Town; J. Ovenell & Son, Deptford High Street and Billingsgate Market; W. Millson & Sons [no address]; W. F. Howlett & Sons, Bell Green, Lower Sydenham; E. Goodridge & Son, Plaistow; Bill Hugman, East Street, Walworth. Addresses of stalls are often given indirectly as, for example, 'outside the old green gate', Plaistow (E. Goodridge & Son); 'opposite Mason's Arms' (Bill Hugman); and 'facing gas works' (W. F. Howlett & Sons).

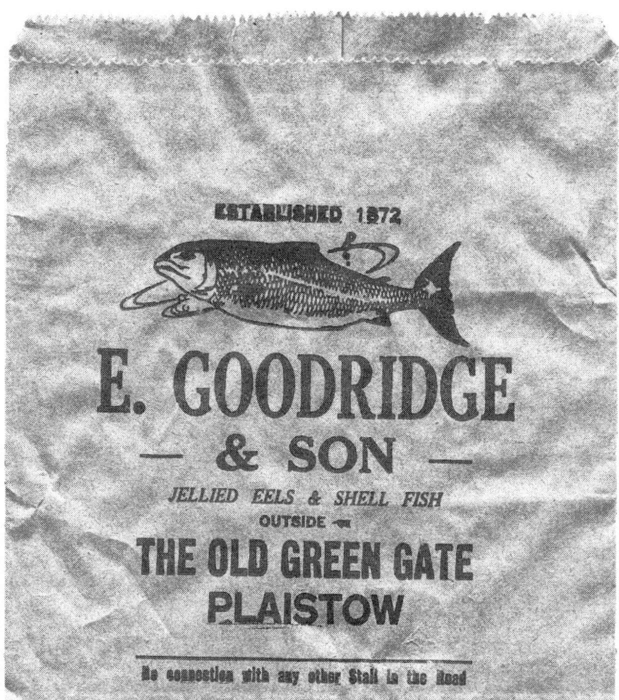

Winkle bag of E. Goodridge & Son, Plaistow, London, second half of 20th century. Printed in relief on manila paper. 190 × 175 mm (7½ × 6⅞ in)

Very few of the bags carry illustrations. Occasional exceptions show a stylized fish, and one example, of the 1890s, shows a well-dressed gentleman telling a hansom cab driver to 'Stop at H. Hickson outside the "Cambridge", Goodge St.'.

Wood-engraving [plate 1]

Wood-engraving was the most widely used process for printing pictures in the 19th century. It is a relief method in which the parts of a block of wood that are not to print are physically removed, leaving raised areas that receive ink and produce the marks that print. The great advantage of wood-engraving was that, like woodcutting, the block could be made 'type high' and be printed alongside metal type at one pass though the press.

There is often confusion over the use of the term 'engraving', which suggests to some people an intaglio process like copper-engraving (which involves forcing ink into the incised lines of a metal plate, wiping its surface clean, and squeezing ink out of the lines on to paper under pressure). The use of the term in relation to taking prints from wood arises from the fact that early wood-engravers tried to emulate the refinement and subtlety of the marks made in copper-engraving, and that they also used similar tools to those of copper engravers – the burin or graver.

Wood-engraving was cheaper than copper engraving for a variety of reasons: wood blocks were easier and quicker to print than intaglio plates; they could be printed on cheap paper and card; they withstood long printing runs and could be used on steam-powered presses. For these and other reasons, wood-engraving was used extensively for book, magazine, and catalogue illustration, and on posters and handbills, advertisements, packaging, and many other items of ephemera.

Wood-engraving is done on hardwood with a close and even grain, most commonly in the 19th century on English or Turkish boxwood. In contrast to woodcutting (in which a plank is cut along its grain) a wood-engraving block is cut across the trunk of the tree, so that the 'end grain' can be used for the engraving. Box is a very slow growing tree and its trunk is small in diameter. This means that blocks made from it tended to be small. Larger blocks were made by bolting several small pieces of wood together, or by gluing them (with tongue and groove joints for additional strength). Drawings were made either directly on to the block (in reverse of the intended printed image), or transferred to it using tracing paper. By the 1860s a photographic method was available whereby the block was coated with a light-sensitive solution and an image exposed directly on to its surface. The engraver then interpreted the image using a range of marks made by various cutting tools: effects of tone, shading, and volume could be achieved using fine parallel lines of different weight, sometimes swelling and tapering, and by varying the spacing between them. Later in the century the difficult task of reproducing the cross-hatched black lines of draughtsmen became increasingly common.

Thomas Bewick (1753–1823) is generally considered to have been the founding figure of wood-engraving. He was the first to recognize the full potential of the medium and developed it in terms of both artistry and technique. He is famed for his books on natural history, for which he produced sensitive and well-observed illustrations of birds and animals and numerous vignettes of everyday country life. Bewick was an engraver in both wood and metal and used his skills in wood-engraving to produce a range of ephemeral work (billheads, bookplates, and trade cards). He drew on the block and engraved the wood too, using a range of marks that exactly suited his drawing. He employed both a 'black-line' technique, in which unwanted wood was cut away to leave a line that would print black, and a 'white-line' technique, in which the engraved lines appeared white against a black ground. A combination of the two approaches provided a rich variety of tone and texture. Bewick passed on his skills to his apprentices, several of whom came to London where they helped to establish the beginnings of a wood-engraving 'industry'. By the middle of the 19th century there were hundreds of engravers in London, and others in the British provinces and the large cities of America. Some firms, such as the Dalziel Brothers and Joseph Swain in London, employed many engravers. It is sometimes possible to identify the work of an individual engraver, though more commonly the name at the foot of a wood-engraving is that of the firm.

In larger firms, to achieve greater speed and efficiency, individuals became specialists in different aspects of the process: 'artists on wood' were responsible for the drawing; other craftsmen, according to their experience and skill, cut outlines, skies, and foliage; the most experienced engravers usually undertook figure work. When speed was essential, as in newspapers and magazines, blocks that were bolted together could be dismantled and the sections distributed among several engravers; after the separate parts were engraved they were bolted together again and touched up by a foreman to disguise the joins. To achieve efficiencies in production, it was necessary for all the engravers working in a team to follow a similar style. As a result, the character and individuality of the wood-engravings of Bewick's day were lost. The goal for many engravers (particularly those working for *Punch*, the *Illustrated London News*, and other journals) was to copy as faithfully as possible the quality and lines of the original drawing. Work of this kind was known as 'facsimile' engraving. In other areas, such as the illustration of machinery and similar products, it was appropriate to develop a 'mechanical' style that achieved maximum precision and clarity. By the 1880s ruling machines were in common use; they allowed very accurate tints to be engraved, and with much greater speed and precision than could be achieved by hand. The introduction of such mechanical aids reduced individuality still further.

In Bewick's day most wood-engravings were printed directly from the wood block. However, with the introduction of powered printing machines, the possibility of wear and accidental damage to the block increased considerably. In the course of the first half of the 19th century it became increasingly common for copies of blocks to be made by means of the STEREOTYPE process, and from the middle of the century (in the case of quality work) by means of the ELECTROTYPE process. The normal practice throughout much of the century was therefore to retain the original wood block as a master and to print from a metal replica. In addition, wood-engravings were sometimes proofed on transfer paper and transferred to lithographic stone (*see* TRANSFER LITHOGRAPHY).

Towards the end of the 19th century, wood-engraving was challenged by the photographic methods of making relief blocks called, generically, process engraving. By the early years of the 20th century many commercial wood-engraving firms embraced the new photomechanical methods and some converted to them entirely. Nevertheless, wood-engraving as a commercial activity did not die out completely, and as late as the 1970s one or two British firms continued to supply specialist markets with engravings for engineering products, jewellery, watches, and similar work requiring precision.

Wood-engraving underwent a revival in the 1920s and 1930s, but mainly as a medium for artists and book illustrators, many of whom engraved their own blocks. In this period it was used in advertising and packaging to provide a touch of distinction; companies using wood-engravers in this period included the GPO (General Post Office), Shell-Mex, and the Orient Shipping Line. More recently, wood-engraving has been used to promote products such as whole foods, whisky, and a variety of ephemera associated with tradition, craft, and the countryside. [MA]

See also ARTWORK FOR REPRODUCTION

REFERENCES M. J. Andrews, 'Hare & Co., commercial wood-engravers: Jabez Hare, founder of the firm and his letters 1846 to 1847', *Journal of the Printing Historical Society*, no. 24, 1995, pp. 53–106; Iain Bain, *The Workshop of Thomas Bewick: a Pictorial Survey*, The Thomas Bewick Birthplace Trust, Cherryburn, Mickley, Stocksfield, Northumberland, 1989; [W. A. Chatto] and John Jackson, *A Treatise on Wood Engraving, Historical and Practical* (London: Charles Knight and Co., 1839; 2nd rev. edn, 1861); Leo De Freitas, 'Commercial engraving on wood in England 1700–1880: an economic art', PhD thesis, Royal College of Art, London, 1986; Rodney Engen, *Dictionary of Victorian Wood Engravers* (Cambridge, 1985); Kenneth Lindley, *The Woodblock Engravers* (Newton Abbot, 1970); W. J. Linton, *Wood-engraving: a Manual of Instruction* (London: 1884)

Writing paper, illustrated

Writing paper embellished with borders and decorations began to appear in Europe towards the end of the 18th century. The fashion emerged at the moment when the decorative VISITING CARD was on the wane. Some papers bore coloured borders,

Illustrated writing paper with the heading 'Bowling Green', New York, mid 19th century. Engraved on stone and printed by Charles Magnus, New York; hand-coloured. 255 × 210 mm (10 × 8¼ in)

others were blind-embossed; classical figures and allegorical scenes were common themes.

'Illustrated' or 'pictorial' writing papers began to appear in Europe in the 1830s; they flooded into Britain in the 1840s and soon began to cater for the standard 'wish-you-were-here' messages of holidaymakers. Views of watering places, beauty spots, country seats, and towns were engraved or lithographed for headed writing paper – often to be used, as the later POSTCARD, regardless of the visitor's presence at the place depicted.

The format of British illustrated writing paper was commonly double-page octavo, 190 × 115 mm (7½ × 4½ in), or double-page quarto, 230 × 185 mm (9 × 7¼ in). Illustrations were chiefly from steel engravings – which had in some instances done service elsewhere – or, less commonly, were produced by lithography. A minority were coloured, either by the printer, using simple wood blocks, or, later, by the recipient, by hand. Many have survived because, along with other pictorial printed items of the time, they were cut out and pasted by the recipient into albums.

In lighter vein was a long succession of humorous illustrations, most of them based on seaside-holiday situations – forerunners, in Britain at least, of the saucy seaside picture-postcard. Instead of typographical titles, they bore laconic captions.

The fashion for illustrated writing paper moved from Europe to America, where 'aerial views' of major cities were popular themes, along with views of Niagara Falls and other such spectacles. Unlike the European version, in which the illustration appeared as a vignetted ovoid, the American illustration was presented in rectangular form. The paper size, commonly 300 × 235 mm (11⅞ × 9¼ in), was distinctly larger than that of its European counterpart. A major feature of American illustrated stationery, both on writing paper and envelopes, was a wide range of illustrations showing incidents in the Civil War; this may be said to mark the first appearance of propaganda stationery.

Illustrations on writing paper are normally the product of three individuals, one or more of whom may remain anonymous. According to convention the name on the left designates the artist, that on the right the engraver or lithographer; in the centre is the name and, usually, the address of the publisher.

See also STATIONERY, DECORATIVE

REFERENCE Frank Staff, *The Picture Postcard and its Origins*, 2nd edn (London: Lutterworth, 1979)

Writing tablet

The early Roman writing *tabula* (Latin: tablet) may be divided into two categories, described by the palaeographer Marichal (1975) as *tablettes de cire* (wax tablets) and *tablettes de bois* (wooden tablets). Both are made of wood, the former being 'dished' to accept a coating of wax for inscribing with a stylus, the latter having a flat uncoated surface for writing on directly in ink. The flat version is also known as a 'leaf tablet'; its extreme thinness approximates more to a sliver of veneer than to a tablet in the usual sense of the term. The rigid, waxed version is also known as a 'stylus tablet'.

The stylus tablet could be reused, its wax surface being smoothed with the flat end of the stylus to provide a fresh writing surface. It could also be used as a more permanent document by fitting it with a thong-hinged cover and a form of sealed closure. It was suitable, depending on its size, for note-taking, accounts and computations, schoolroom exercises, business and social correspondence, as well as for contracts, wills, certificates, and extensive legal documents. It was also suitable for transmission by a messenger.

The leaf tablet was intended for one-time use (though examples are also found in which the first inked wording has been over-written), and its fragility and small size commonly confined it to more transient applications.

Dimensions vary: the stylus tablet averages some 100 × 200 mm (4 × 7⅞ in) and the leaf tablet some 100 × 60 mm (4 × 2⅜ in). The thickness of the stylus tablet is of the order of 10 mm (⅜ in), whereas the leaf tablet averages 1 mm (about 1/32 in). In some cases, as in the Vindolanda find at Chesterholm, Northumberland, leaves were so thin that four of them matted together were only 1 mm thick. While the two types of tablet were specifically intended for different uses, there are cases where there has been 'misuse': ink or stylus inscriptions appear on the under-wax surface of the stylus tablet and, occasionally, stylus markings on the leaf tablet. As with the PAPYRUS, both forms of writing tablet come within the designation 'ephemera', more particularly the leaf tablet, on which messages are more likely to arrive, and whose function is generally more transient.

The Vindolanda find, uncovered by Robin Birley in March 1973 and subsequently yielding over 200 examples, is the largest deposit of leaf tablets ever discovered. It also ranks as Britain's oldest known corpus of ephemera. The first tablets to emerge were described by Birley as 'two small thin fragments of wood which looked rather like oily plane shavings'. When gently prised apart they were found to bear writing on their inner surfaces.

The leaf tablets proved to have been thrown on a rubbish dump by soldiers of the Roman army at its pre-Hadrianic encampment between about AD 95 and 105. They provide a fragmented picture of the life of occupying soldiers in a winter garrison twelve hundred miles from home. They include portions of letters, inventories, military accounts and records, as well as a large number of fragments yet to be matched and identified. There are references to gifts of warm clothing from home including 'udones' – socks made of wool or felt – and 'subligaria' – Roman underpants: 'I have sent you... pairs of socks... from Sattua two pairs of sandals and two pairs of underpants...'. Another fragment acknowledges a gift of fifty oysters from Cordonovi: 'a Cordonovis amicus missit mihi ostria quinquaginta' (Cordonovi, assumed to be a place-name, has yet to be identified).

Quartermasters' records reflect the variety of soldiers' foodstuffs. These include venison, roe deer, young pig, and ham. The military unit bought flour, salt, and spices, as well as fish sauce and pork fat. Barley, probably for fodder, is also listed. The men drank beer and acetum, a sour wine mixed with water; proper wine was bought by the officers from the continent. Also mentioned are the building of bath-houses, the use of kilns, the work of shoemakers, plasterers, and wagoners, and, in less than complimentary terms, there are references to Britimenti (Little Brits). As well as the rigours and realities of army life there are indications of the forms and practices of polite society. A fulsome correspondent writes to his Prefect, Cerialis, seeking preferment for a friend:

> Karus to his Cerialis, greeting... Brigionus has requested me, my lord, to recommend him to you. I therefore ask, my lord, that if he has made any request of you, you consent to give him your approval. I ask that you think fit to recommend him to Annius Equester, centurion in charge of the region, at Luguvalium; by doing which you will place me in debt to you both in his name and my own. I hope that you are enjoying the best of fortune and are in good health....

Similarly polished is Flavia Severa's invitation to Lepidina, the commanding officer's wife, asking her to her birthday party. She adds her own greeting to the message as written by her sister: 'I shall expect you, sister, my dearest soul. I live in good health. Farewell'.

REFERENCES Alan K. Bowman and J. D. Thomas, *Vindolanda: The Latin Writing Tablets* (London: Society for the Promotion of Roman Studies, 1983); M. Greenland, 'Digging up Ephemera', *The Ephemerist* (September, 1986); Society for the Promotion of Roman Studies, London; Robert Marichal, Découverte de tablettes de bois écrites à l'encre à Vindolanda (Northumberland), *Journal des Savants* (Paris, 1975), pp. 113–20

COLLECTIONS British Museum; Chesterholm Museum, Hexham, Northumberland

SOCIETIES Friends of Vindolanda, Chesterholm, Northumberland

xerography
'zine
zöetrope strip/disc

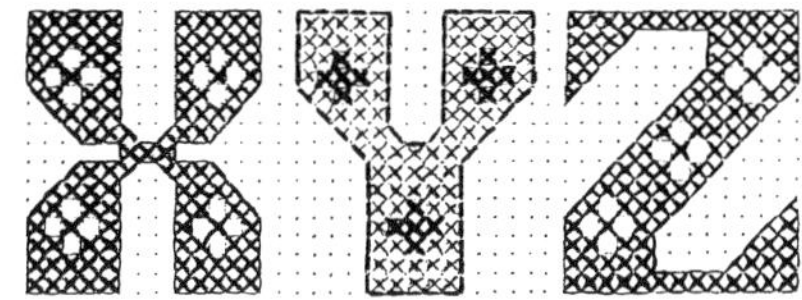

Xerography

Invented by Chester Carlson in America just before World War II, xerography stands in a line of document copying processes that started with James Watt in 1780. Watt took out a patent in that year for a method of making a limited number of copies of a document; it involved writing with a special ink that could be partially transferred, under pressure from a screw press, to one or more sheets of dampened flimsy paper. The copies, which had to be read from the back, were produced in vast quantities throughout the 19th century, and on into the next, and are most often preserved in bound files. The use of carbon paper, interleaved between sheets of flimsy copy paper, served much the same purpose and, with the widespread use of the typewriter, replaced Watt's method, lasting through to the closing decades of the 20th century. Both methods had severe limitations: they produced copies in very limited numbers, and, more significantly, they worked only when a document was specially produced for copying.

The first of these limitations was overcome more easily than the second, initially by TRANSFER LITHOGRAPHY, which flourished for short-run office printing for half a century from about 1820. Then came the 'Cyclostyle' stencil-duplicating process of Gestetner (covered by several patents in the 1880s), which was well suited to the typewriter and continued to meet most office duplicating needs beyond the middle of the 20th century. Its main competitors in later years were the jellygraph and spirit duplicating, the latter being a development of Watt's idea (but capable of taking hundreds of copies from a chemical master).

All these processes had the primary limitation that a master document had to be specially produced in order for copies to be made. One little-used lithographic process, developed in the 1840s, partially overcame this limitation. It was called Anastatic printing and was capable of resurrecting old documents – though only if they had been printed with greasy printing ink in the first place. A few spectacular examples are reported, some of which survive, but it did not live up to the promise of its name (Greek, *anastasis:* raising up).

The branch of photography that involved the use of negatives (the process announced by Fox Talbot in 1839) proved more promising, and opened up all sorts of possibilities for the reproduction of existing documents. Some contemporary writers – among them Baudelaire – even felt that this was one of the fields that photography should concentrate on, rather than the production of works of art. For the most part, however, early PHOTOGRAPHIC EPHEMERA were not of this kind. The development of photolithography (specifically photozincography) in Australia, Britain, and India at more or less the same time in the 1860s changed this. From its outset, the process found a fruitful outlet in the reproduction of documents, particularly those of great historic interest (*see* FACSIMILE). This development prepared the way for various photographically related duplicating processes that were developed specifically for use in the office or library to produce copies of routine existing documents. Such methods lasted into the 1960s when they were replaced by the major office copying process of the second half of the twentieth century – xerography.

The process was pioneered commercially by Rank Xerox and, with the lapse of its protection, was taken up by many other companies. Xerography satisfies the two basic requirements of a copying process referred to above and is used universally, both to make one or more faithful copies of an existing document and as a means of producing purpose-made documents in quantity. On the one front it challenges photography; on the other, offset lithographic printing.

Xerography – the word is now used with a small initial letter to describe the process rather than just the products of one company – is a form of electrostatic printing. It involves the projection of an image on to an electrostatically charged plate, which causes a powder (toner) to adhere to it selectively in response to the tone and shape of the image. The toner is then transferred to paper and fixed by heating. Early machines were slow and unreliable. Successive improvements led to increases in speed and quality, and facilities were introduced for enlargement and reduction, for controlling tone, for backing up sheets of documents, and for the collation of sets. All these improvements have been made without over-complicating the exercise of making copies. In the late 20th century colour xerographic machines were introduced that, for short-run work at least, make xerography a serious competitor to colour printing.

For the ephemerist, the quality of the best xerographic copying, particularly when done on carefully chosen paper, can lead to problems in the detection of an original from a copy. What in the 19th century would have been described as a high-quality facsimile can now be produced in a matter of moments by a relatively unskilled person using the latest xerographic equipment. This first began to be an issue when monochrome copies were made of typed or printed documents with no intention to deceive; it became a very serious matter in the 1980s when American dollar bills began to be copied in colour and passed off as originals.

Xerography has led to a veritable explosion of document copying in the last quarter of the 20th century. For example, in the library of one British university the weekly production of copies of documents in the early 1960s was counted in scores; by the end of the century (admittedly to meet the requirements of a population perhaps ten times as great) the weekly output in term-time reached scores of thousands. The impact of xerography on society has been phenomenal and the high-street copying shop (with its range of ancillary facilities) now offers the kind of service that used to be available in the 19th century when, conventionally, printers worked in the centre of towns. For the social historian – if not for all ephemerists – the xeroxed notice, handbill, window card, ticket and invitation, questionnaire, parish magazine and 'ZINE is just as significant as its handwritten or printed counterpart. [MT]

'Zine

The term ''zine' began to be used some time in the 1970s as a shortened form of 'fanzine' or 'fan magazine', terms in use at the time to describe duplicated, stapled, non-commercial and non-professional, small-circulation publications. 'Zines are created by 'zinesters' and disseminated to like-minded 'fans' whose interests may range from science fiction, sport, and music, to television, thrift shopping, and beer drinking. 'Zines are often politically self-conscious amateur publications, and they form part of an important network for alternative cultures.

The distribution of 'zines is primarily by mail order or through specialist music, book, and comic stores. They are advertised by word of mouth, sold at concert venues or specialist meets (e.g. science-fiction fairs) and reviewed in other 'zine publication guides (e.g. *Fact Sheet Five*, *Broken Pencil*, and *Zineguide*). By the mid 1990s, 'zines were brought into mainstream publishing with the appearance of compilation books of 'zine writing.

'Zines were born out of the tradition of political broadsheets, pamphlets, self-publishing and amateur printing of the 19th century (*see* AMATEUR JOURNAL; SQUIB), and of the underground publications of the 1960s. The contemporary format of 'zines is derived from publications produced by the science-fiction community of the 1930s in Britain and America. Fans of science fiction created and distributed publications containing their own fictionalized stories and critical commentary. The *Comet*, for example, was produced in 1932 and is usually recognized by historians of the field as the world's first fanzine. By 1940 the term 'fanzine' was being widely used by science-fiction and Hollywood movie enthusiasts as an abbreviated form for the fan magazine; but it was not until 1949, when the *New Republic* magazine adopted the term, that fanzines entered into mainstream consciousness.

As part of an active alternative culture, 'zine editors often consider their publications immune from conventional rules of publishing. 'Zines commonly violate copyright regulations and, sometimes, libel and obscenity laws. They do not necessarily follow the mainstream conventions of grammar, spelling, punctuation, and pagination, and sometimes appear to depart from them deliberately. The content of a 'zine typically consists of personalized commentary and opinionated essays, readers' pages, hand-drawn illustrations or 'comix', a section of reviews, poems and/or short stories.

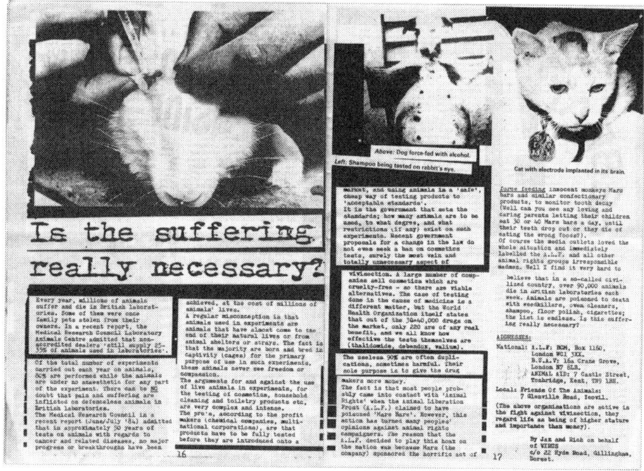

Is the suffering really necessary?

Every year, millions of animals suffer and die in British laboratories. Some of them were once family pets stolen from their owners. In a recent report, the Medical Research Council Laboratory Animals Centre admitted that non-accredited dealers 'still supply 25-35% of animals used in laboratories'.

Of the total number of experiments carried out each year on animals, 80% are performed while the animals are under no anaesthetic for any part of the experiment. There can be NO doubt that pain and suffering are inflicted on defenceless animals in British laboratories.
The Medical Research Council in a recent report (June/July '84) admitted that in approximately 50 years of tests on animals with regards to cancer and related diseases, no major progress or breakthroughs have been achieved, at the cost of millions of animals' lives.
A regular misconception is that animals used in experiments are animals that have almost come to the end of their natural lives or from animal shelters or strays. The fact is that the majority are born and bred in captivity (cages) for the primary purpose of use in such experiments, these animals never see freedom or compassion.
The arguments for and against the use of live animals in experiments, for the testing of cosmetics, household cleaning and toiletry products etc, are very complex and intense.
The pro's, according to the profit makers (chemical companies, multi-national corporations), are that products have to be fully tested before they are introduced onto a

16

Above: Dog force-fed with alcohol.

Left: Shampoo being tested on rabbit's eye.

market, and using animals in a 'safe', cheap way of testing products to 'acceptable standards'.
It is the government that sets the standards; how many animals are to be used, to what degree, and what restrictions (if any) exist on such experiments. Recent government proposals for a change in the law do not even seek a ban on cosmetics tests, surely the most vain and totally unnecessary aspect of vivisection. A large number of companies sell cosmetics which are cruelty-free – so there are viable alternatives. The case of testing done in the cause of medicine is a different matter, but the World Health Organization itself states that out of the 30-40,000 drugs on the market, only 220 are of any real benefit, and we all know how effective the tests themselves are (thalidomide, debendox, valium).
The useless 90% are often duplications, sometimes harmful. Their sole purpose is to give the drug makers more money.
The fact is that most people probably came into contact with 'Animal Rights' when the Animal Liberation Front (A.L.F.) claimed to have poisoned 'Mars Bars'. However, this action has turned many peoples' opinions against animal rights campaigners. The reason that the A.L.F. decided to play this hoax on the nation was because Mars (the company) sponsored the horrific act of

Cat with electrode implanted in its brain.

force feeding innocent monkeys Mars bars and similar confectionary products, to monitor tooth decay (Well can you see any loving and caring parents letting their children eat 30 or 40 Mars bars a day, until their teeth drop out or they die of eating the wrong foods?).
Of course the media outlets loved the whole situation and immediately labelled the A.L.F. and all other animal rights groups irresponsible madmen. Well I find it very hard to believe that in a so-called civilized country, over 90,000 animals die in British laboratories each week. Animals are poisoned to death with weedkillers, oven cleaners, shampoo, floor polish, cigarettes; the list is endless. Is this suffering really necessary?

ADDRESSES:

National: A.L.F: BCM, Box 1160, London WC1 3XX.
B.U.A.V: 16a Crane Grove, London N7 8LB.
ANIMAL AID: 7 Castle Street, Tonbridge, Kent, TN9 1BH.

Local: Friends Of The Animals: 7 Glenville Road, Yeovil.

(The above organisations are active in the fight against vivisection, they regard life as being of higher stature and importance than money).

By Jaz and Rich on behalf of VIRUS c/o 22 Hyde Road, Gillingham, Dorset.

17

Double spread from *Screed!*, no. 3, May/June 1985, published by Steve Screed in Yeovil, Somerset. 20 pages, the text typed, reproduced by xerography in around 200 copies. 210 × 148 mm (8¼ × 5⅝ in)

'Zines tend to adopt a do-it-yourself look, employing typewritten and handwritten methods alongside a 'cut-and-paste' technique in which text and image, often 'stolen' from the mainstream press, are combined. Early 'zines were produced using stencil-duplicating. With developments in reproduction technology 'zine producers turned to other methods, particularly XEROGRAPHY and, later, desktop publishing (DTP). They also looked at new methods of distribution available through the world wide web, and published electronic 'zines, known as 'e-zines'. While the latter remain true to earlier 'zines in content, their visual language is more aligned to that of professionally produced magazines and web sites.

The extent of printed 'zines is often determined by the costs of production and distribution. It is normally in the order of eight to forty pages, though some 'zines may reach 100 pages and have colour reproductions and card covers, which raises questions about what constitutes a 'zine. Print runs for 'zines vary widely: some may be counted in tens or scores; more popular publications run to 8000 or more; the average is probably around 250. The lifespan of a title also varies considerably, from one-off single issues to regular publication over a period of several years. It has been estimated that between 10,000 and 20,000 titles (some estimates are as high as 50,000) were circulated world-wide in 1997.

Though 'zines may be produced by anyone passionate about a subject, they have been most evident in America and Britain. Among the more influential titles are *Bam Balam* (1975), *Crawdaddy* (1966), *Bomp!* (1970), *Sniffin' Glue* (1976), *Search and Destroy* (1977), *Boys Own* (1986), *Dishwasher* (1990), and *Beer Frame* (1994). 'Zines are among the most ephemeral of serial publications. Because they do not often find their way into copyright and other libraries, many have become extremely rare; it is doubtful whether complete runs will ever be found of some titles. [TT]

REFERENCES Stephen Duncombe, *Notes from Underground: Zines and the Politics of Alternative Culture* (London: Verso, 1997); Teal Triggs, 'Generation Terrorists: the Politics and Graphic Language of Punk and Feminist Fanzines in Britain 1976–1996', PhD thesis, The University of Reading, 2000

COLLECTIONS Fact Sheet Five Collection, The New York State Library, Albany, NY; Institute of Popular Culture, Manchester Metropolitan University, Manchester; National Art Library, Victoria & Albert Museum, London

Zoëtrope strip/disc

The zoëtrope, a development of the PHENAKISTOSCOPE DISC, was invented in 1834 by William George Horner of Bristol and initially called the 'Daedelum'. The first model to appear on the open market in England was produced by Peter H. Desvignes in 1860. In America, William E. Lincoln patented the zoëtrope in 1867 and then assigned the rights over it to Milton Bradley, who popularized it.

Known also as the 'wheel of life' (Greek, *zoe:* life; *trope:* turn), it consists of a rotating drum, on the interior wall of which is placed a paper strip bearing images of figures in various stages of motion. When the drum is rotated and the images are viewed through slits an impression is conveyed of animation; the slits provide the intermittent shutter effect of a cinema projector.

Picture strips, printed in four or five colours, were available in great variety, each providing a cycle of continuous movement, either of figures or abstract patterns. The strips measured some 75 × 760 mm (3 × 30 in) and provided a complete circuit of the interior of the drum. Also available were printed discs, similar to those used in the phenakistoscope, which were placed on the floor of the drum. These commonly showed effects of movement in abstract patterns, cog-wheels, bouncing balls, etc.

Walter Frères of Paris were specialists in the design and production of these items, as they were for the phenakistoscope and the ANAMORPHIC IMAGE.

See also THAUMATROPE

REFERENCE Olive Cook, *Movement in Two Dimensions* (London: Hutchinson, 1963)

COLLECTIONS Museum of the Moving Image, London; National Museum of Photography, Film and Television, Bradford, W. Yorkshire

Collections and societies

Ephemera societies world wide

The Ephemera Society, 8 Galveston Road, London, SW15 2SA (tel/fax: 020 8874 3363)
The Ephemera Society of America, PO Box 95, Cazenovia, New York 13035, (tel/fax: 315 655 9139)
The Ephemera Society of Australia Inc., PO Box 346, Warragul, Victoria 3820, Australia (tel: 0356 234 275; fax: 0356 236 948)
The Ephemera Society of Austria, Verein für Alltagsgrafik, Bäumlegarten 5a, A–6973, Höchst, Austria (tel/fax: 0043 (0) 5578 76903)
The Ephemera Society of Canada, 36 Macauley Drive, Thornhill, Ontario L3T 585, Canada (tel: 416 881 7520)

Specialist societies

The specialist ephemera societies referred to after some entries have not been provided with addresses because experience has shown that their officers (and hence their addresses) change frequently. Information about many of these societies, and others not referred to, can be found on the world wide web.

Collections

The institutions referred to after entries are listed below with their addresses. Since no world directory yet exists for holdings of ephemera, major specialist collections may well have been omitted. Those referred to are simply examples of institutions known to hold relevant material, and their collections are not necessarily the most important of their kind.

American Antiquarian Society, 185 Salisbury Street, Worcester, Massachusetts, MA 01609
American Museum in Britain, Claverton Manor, Bath, BA2 7BD
Archivio di Stato di Firenze, Biblioteca, Piazzale degli Uffizi, 50122 Firenze
Archivio di Stato di Torino, Biblioteca, Piazzetta Mollino 1, 10123 Torino
Baker Library, Harvard University, Soldiers Field Road, Cambridge, Boston, MA 02163
Bank of England Museum, Bank of England, Threadneedle Street, London, EC2R 8AH
Barrow-in-Furness Public Library (County Heritage Service), Ramsden Square, Barrow-in-Furness, Cumbria, LA13 1LL
Bass Brewers Ltd, 137 High Street, Burton-on-Trent, DE14 1JZ
Bella C. Landauer Collection, New York Historical Society, 170 Central Park West, New York, NY 10024
Bethnal Green Museum of Childhood, Cambridge Heath Road, London, E2 9PA
Bishopsgate Institute, 230 Bishopsgate, London, EC2M 4QH
Bodleian Library, Broad Street, Oxford, OX1 3BG
Book Tokens Ltd, 272 Vauxhall Bridge Road, London SW1V 1BA
Boston Public Library, Copley Square, Box 286, Boston, MA 02117
The Bostonian Society Library, 3rd floor, 15 State Street, Boston, MA 02109
British Dental Association, 64 Wimpole Street, London, W1M 8AL
British Film Institute, 21 Stephen Street, London, W1P 2LN
British Institute for Cartoon Research, University of Kent, Canterbury, CT2 7NU
The British Library, 96 Euston Road, London, NW1 2DB
The British Museum (Department of Prints and Drawings), Great Russell Street, London, WC1B 3DG
British Optical Association, British College of Optometrists, 10 Knaresborough Place, London, SW56 0TG
British Parking Association, room 514, Impact House, 2 Eldridge Road, Croydon, Surrey, CR9 1PJ
BT (British Telecommunications plc), Telephone House, 2–4 Temple Avenue, London, EC4Y 0HL
The Button Museum, 13 Kyrle Street, Ross-on-Wye, Herefordshire, HR9 7DB
Cambridge University Library, West Road, Cambridge, CB3 9DR
Carlisle Library, 11 Globe Lane, Cumbria, CA3 8NX
Centre for Ephemera Studies, Department of Typography & Graphic Communication, The University of Reading, Whiteknights, Reading, RG6 6AU
Chesterholm Museum (The Vindolanda Trust), Bardon Mill, Hexham, Northumberland, NE47 7JN
Cooper-Hewitt National Museum of Design, Smithsonian Institution (New York), 2E 91st Street, New York, NY 10028
Cornell University Archives, Ithaca, New York, NY 14853
DeWitt College of Political Americana, Hartford University, 200 Bloomfield Avenue, West Hartford, Connecticut, CT 06117
Department of Typography & Graphic Communication, The University of Reading, Whiteknights, Reading RG6 6AU
Derby Museum & Art Gallery, The Strand, Derby, DE1 1BS
Design Museum, Butler's Wharf, Shad Thames, London SE1 2YD
Ewart Library, Catherine Street, Dumfries, DG1 1JB
Fan Museum, 12 Crooms Hill, Greenwich, London, SE10 8ER
Fisher Rare Book Library, Toronto University, 130 St George Street, Toronto, Ontario, M5S 1A5
Florida State University, Tallahassee, Florida, FL 32306
Guildhall Library, Aldermanbury, London, EC2P 2EJ
Hallmark Historical Collection, Hallmark Cards, 25th and McGee, Kansas City, MO 6414
Harvard College Library, Cambridge, MA 02138
Harvard Theatre Collection, Harvard University, Cambridge, MA 02138
Historical Society of Pennsylvania, 1300 Locust Street, Philadelphia, PA 19107
Hollywood Studio Museum, 2100 North Highland Avenue, Hollywood, California 90068
Houghton Library, Harvard University, Cambridge, Massachusetts, MA 02138
Imperial War Museum, Lambeth Road, London, SE1 6HZ
Institut Pasteur, Bibliothèque Centrale, 28 rue du Docteur-Roux, 75724 Paris

Insurance Company of North America, Historical Collection, Philadelphia, PA
Institute of Popular Culture, Manchester Metropolitan University, Manchester, All Saints, Manchester M15 6BH
John Johnson Collection, Bodleian Library, Broad Street, Oxford, OX1 3BG
John Rylands University Library of Manchester, Oxford Road, Manchester, M13 9PP
Lester S. Levy Collection of Sheet Music, Johns Hopkins University, Charles & 34th Street, Baltimore, MD 21218
Lewes Library (East Sussex County Library Services) Albion Street, Lewes, East Sussex, BN7 2ND
Library of Congress, Independent Avenue at 1st Street, SE, Washington, DC
London Transport Museum, Covent Garden Piazza, London, WC2E 7BB
Madame Tussaud's (Alistair Allen Collection), Marylebone Road, London, NW1 5LR
Magdelene College, University of Cambridge, Cambridge, CB3 0AG
Maidstone Museum and Art Gallery, St Faith's Street, Maidstone, Kent, ME14 1LH
Manchester Metropolitan University Library, All Saints, Manchester, M15 6BH
Massachusetts Historical Society, 1154 Boylston Street, Boston, Massachusetts, MA 02215
Massachusetts Institute of Technology, Cambridge, MA 02139
M.C.C. Museum, Lord's Cricket Ground, St John's Wood, London, NW8 8QN
Metropolitan Museum of Art, 1000 5th Avenue, New York, NY 10028
Musée du Vin de Bourgogne, Ancien Palais des Ducs de Bourgogne, rue d'Enfer, 21200 Beaune, France
Museo Stradivariana, Palazzo Affaitati, Via Palestro 17, 26100 Cremona, Italy
Museo Taurino de la Real Maestranza de Cabelleria de Ronda, Ronda, Spain
Museum of Advertising and Packaging, Albert Warehouse, Gloucester Docks, Gloucester, GL1 2EH
Museum of Cartoon Art, Comly Avenue, Rye Brook, New York, NY 10573
Museum of the City of New York, 5th Avenue at 103rd Street, New York, NY 10029
Museum of Costume, Assembly Rooms, Bennett Street, Bath, Avon, BA1 2QH
Museum of Hartlepool, Jackson's Dock. Marina, Hartlepool, TS24 0X2
Museum of London, London Wall, London, EC2Y 5HN
Museum of the Moving Image, South Bank, Waterloo, London, SE1 8XT
Museum of Reading, Blagrave Street, Reading, RG1 1QH
National Library of Australia, Canberra, ACT 2600
National Maritime Museum, Romney Road, Greenwich, London, SE10 9NF
National Museum of Photography, Film, and Television, Pictureville, Bradford, W. Yorkshire, BD1 1NQ
National Postal Museum, King Edward Building, King Edward Street, London, EC1A 1LP
National Railway Museum, Leeman Road, York, YO2 4XJ
New York Historical Society, 170 Central Park West, New York, NY 10024
New York Public Library, 5th Avenue and 42nd Street, New York, NY 10063
New York State Library, Albany, New York, NY 12230
Newberry Library, 60 West Walton, Chicago, IL 60610
Northampton Central Museum and Art Gallery, Guildhall Road, Northampton, NN1 1DP
Office for National Statistics, London, 1 Drummond Gate, SW1V 2QQ
Peabody Museum of Salem, E. India Square, Salem, Massachusetts, MA 01970
The People's Palace Museum, Glasgow Green, Glasgow, G40 1AT
Pepys Library, Magdelene College, University of Cambridge, Cambridge, CB3 0AG
Philadelphia Museum of Art (Ars Medica Collection), Benjamin Franklin Library, Parkway at 26th St, Box 7646, Philadelphia, PA 19101
Public Record Office, Kew, Richmond, Surrey, TW9 4DU
Puppentheatermuseum mit Abteilung Schaustellerie, Stadtmuseum, St Jakobs Pl. 1, München 2, Germany
Reading University Library, Whiteknights, Reading, RG6 6AE
Royal Institution of South Wales, c/o Swansea Museum, Victoria Road, Swansea, SA1 1SN
Royal Pharmaceutical Society of Great Britain, 1 Lambeth High Street, London, SE1 7JN
Rural History Centre, The University of Reading, Whiteknights, Reading, RG6 2AG
St Bride Printing Library, Bride Lane, London, EC4Y 8EE
The Science Museum, Exhibition Road, London, SW7 2DD
Smithsonian Institution, Central Reference and Loan Services, 10th and Constitution Avenue, NW, Washington, DC 20560
Society of Antiquaries, Burlington House, Piccadilly, London, W1V 0HS
Southampton Maritime Museum, Wool House, Bugle Street, Southampton, SO14 2AR
State Library of New South Wales, Macquarie Street, Sydney, NSW 2000
State Library of Tasmania, 91 Murray Street, Hobart, Tasmania 7000
Stationers' Hall, Ave Maria Lane, Ludgate Hill, EC4M 7DD
Theatre Museum, Russell Street, Covent Garden, London, WC2E 7PA
Toronto University Library, 130 St. George St, Toronto, Ont. M53 1A5
Trades Union Congress Library, Congress House, Great Russell Street, WC1B 3LS
Trinity House, Tower Hill, London, EC1N 4DH
University of South Florida, Tampa Campus Library, 4202 Fowler Avenue, Tampa, FL 33620–4500
University of Texas at Austin, Library, Austin, TX 78713
Victoria & Albert Museum (Department of Prints and Drawings), Cromwell Road, South Kensington, London, SW7 2RL
Waddesdon Manor (National Trust), near Aylesbury, Buckinghamshire, HP18 0JH
The Wellcome Institute for the History of Medicine, The Wellcome Building, 183 Euston Road, London, NW1 2BE
Western Reserve Historical Society, History Library, 10825 East Bd, Cleveland, OH 44106
Western Union Telegraph Company International Inc., 34 Southwark Bridge Road, London, SE1
Wilberforce Museum and Georgian House, 25 High Street, Hull, E. Yorkshire, HU1 1NE
Wimbledon Lawn Tennis Museum, All England Club, Church Road, Wimbledon, London, SW19 5AE

Bibliography

The publications listed below provide a lead-in to different aspects of ephemera and their contexts. They include general works of reference and books on topics that are not specifically covered by entries in the encyclopedia or the specialist publications listed after some of them. Many books have been included (particularly under costume) for their usefulness when dating ephemera. Items are arranged under the following headings:

Ephemera: general
Reference: general
Dictionaries of engravers, illustrators, and printers

Design
Illustration and prints
Letterforms
Printing

American history
British history
Costume
Country life
Food and drink
Home life
Leisure and entertainment
Shops and shopping
Travel and transport

Shire publications

Ephemera: general

Advertisers' Pocketbook (London: International Correspondence Schools Ltd, 1913)

Barry, Kit, *Reflections: Ephemera from Trades, Products and Events*, 2 vol. (Brattleboro, VT, 1993, 1994)

Ephemera: Journal der Ephemera Gesellschaft Österreich (Ephemera Society of Austria, 1991–)

Ephemera Canada (Ephemera Society of Canada, 1991–)

Ephemera News (Ephemera Society of Australia Inc., 1987–)

Ephemera News (Ephemera Society of America Inc., 1981–)

The Ephemera Journal (Ephemera Society of America Inc., 1987–)

The Ephemerist (London: The Ephemera Society, 1975–)

James, Louis, *Print and the People 1819–1951* (London: Allen Lane, 1976)

The John Johnson Collection: Catalogue of an Exhibition (Oxford: Bodleian Library, 1971)

Lewis, John, *Collecting Printed Ephemera* (London: Studio Vista/Cassell & Collier Macmillan, 1976)

Lewis, John, *Printed Ephemera: The Changing Uses of Type and Letterforms in English and American Printing* (Ipswich: W.S. Cowell, 1962)

McCulloch, Lou W., *Paper Americana* (New York and London: A.S. Barnes, 1980)

Makepeace, Chris E., *Ephemera: A Book on its Collection, Conservation and Use* (Aldershot: Gower Publishing Co. Ltd, 1985)

Opie, Robert, *Remember When: A Nostalgic Trip through the Consumer Era* (London: Mitchell Beazley, 1999)

Pieske, Christa, *Das ABC des Luxuspapiers* (Berlin: Museum für Deutsche Volkskunde, 1983)

Presbrey, Frank, *The History and Development of Advertising* (Garden City, New York: Doubleday Doran & Co., 1929)

Rickards, Maurice, *Collecting Printed Ephemera* (Oxford: Phaidon/Christie's, 1988)

Roylance, Dale, *Graphic Americana: The Art and Technique of Printed Ephemera* (Princeton: Princeton University Library, 1992)

Sampson, Henry, *A History of Advertising from the Earliest Times* (London: Chatto & Windus, 1875)

The Saturday Book, edited by Leonard Russell (1941–53) and John Hadfield (1954–75) (London: Hutchinson, 1941–75). This series of volumes contains a range of articles on social life, some of which are illustrated with ephemera.

Smith, William, *Advertise. How? When? Where?* (London: Routledge, Warne, & Routledge, 1863)

Sullivan, Edmund B., *Collecting Political Americana* (New York: Crown Publishers Inc., 1980)

Twyman, Michael, *Printing 1770–1970: An Illustrated History of its Development and Uses in England* (London: Eyre & Spottiswoode, 1970; reprinted London: British Library and New Castle, DE: Oak Knoll Press, 1998)

Wood, Robert, *Victorian Delights* (London: Evans Brothers Ltd, 1967)

Reference: general

Adams, James Truslow (ed.), *Dictionary of American History*, 5 vol. (New York: Scribner's, 1951)

American National Biography (New York and Oxford: Oxford University Press, 1999)

Barber, Felix, and Jackson, Peter, *The History of London in Maps* (London: Barrie & Jenkins, 1990; reprinted 1991, 1992)

Baynton-Williams, Ashley, *Town and City Maps of the British Isles 1800–1855* (Salford: Dolphin Publications, 1993)

Bell, James, *A View of Universal History, Literature, and the Several Schools of Painting . . . Presented in Twenty-five Illuminated Chronological Tables, from the period of the Earliest Records to the Year 1842 . . .* 5th edn (London: Robert Baldwin, 1842)

Berry, W.T., and Poole, H.E., *Annals of Printing: A Chronological Encyclopaedia from the earliest Times to 1950* (London: Blandford Press, 1966)

British Standard 4000: 1968, *Specification for Sizes of Papers and Boards* (London: British Standards Institution, 1968)

Campbell-Kease, John, *A Companion to Local History Research* (London: A. & C. Black, 1989)

Churchill, W.A., *Watermarks in Paper in Holland, England, France, etc., in the XVII and XVIII Centuries* (Amsterdam: M. Hertzberger, 1935; reprinted Amsterdam, 1967)

Crockford's Clerical Directory, a Biographical and Statistical Book of Reference for Facts relating to the Clergy and the Church [*The Clerical Directory,* 1858–59] (London: 1858–)

Cowie, L.W., *The Wordsworth Dictionary of British Social History* (Ware: Wordsworth Reference, 1996)

Dictionary of National Biography from the Earliest Times to 1900, (London: 1885–1900, plus supplements updated to 1990). New edition, *New Dictionary of National Biography*, Oxford University Press, forthcoming

Dictionary of American Biography, 21 vol. and supplements (New York: Charles Scribner's Sons, 1928–74)

Directory of British Associations & Associations in Ireland, 14th edn, edited by S.P.A. Henderson and A.J.W. Henderson (Beckenham, Kent: CBD Research Ltd, 1998)

Eakins, Rosemary, *Picture Sources UK* (London and Sydney: Macdonald, 1985)

Everyman's Dictionary of Dates, 7th edn, revised by Audrey Butler (London and Melbourne: J. M. Dent, 1986), 8th edn published as *Collins Dictionary of Dates* (Glasgow: Harper Collins, 1996)

Garland, Ken, *Graphics, Design and Printing Terms: An International Dictionary* (New York: Design Press, 1990)

Gazetteer of the British Isles, 9th edn (Edinburgh: John Bartholomew & Son Ltd, 1966)

Goss, C.W.F., *The London Directories 1677–1855* (London: D. Archer, 1932)

Haydn's Dictionary of Dates and Universal Information Relating to All Ages and Nations, 25th edn (London: Ward, Lock, & Co., 1910). First published in 1841.

Hey, David, *The Oxford Companion to Local and Family History* (Oxford: Oxford University Press, 1991)

Huggett, Frank E., *A Dictionary of British History, 1815–1873* (Oxford: Blackwell, 1974)

Jacobi, Charles Thomas, *The Printers' Vocabulary* (London: Chiswick Press, 1888)

Johansens Museums & Galleries in Great Britain and Ireland (London: Johansens, 2000)

Kelly, P., *The Universal Cambist and Commercial Instructor; Being a Full and Accurate Treatise on the Exchanges, Monies, Weights, and Measures, of all Trading Nations and their Colonies. . .*, 2nd edn, 2 vol. (London: The Author, 1826)

Kendall, M.G. (ed.), *The Sources and Nature of the Statistics of the United Kingdom*, 2 vol. (London: Royal Statistical Society, 1952, 1957)

Loewenberg, Alfred, *The Theatre of the British Isles excluding London: A Bibliography* (London: Society for Theatre Research, 1971)

Morris, Richard B. (ed.), *Encyclopedia of American History enlarged and updated* (New York: Harper & Row, 1970)

Mulhall, Michael G., *The Dictionary of Statistics* (London: George Routledge & Sons, 1892)

Museums and Galleries 1999/2000: The Guide to over 1,800 Museums and Galleries in England, Northern Ireland, Scotland and Wales (Cambridge: Hobsons, 1999)

Museums of the World, 4th rev. edn (München, New York, London, Paris: K.G. Sauer, 1992)

Museums Yearbook, edited by Sheena Barbour (London: Museums Association)

Norton, Jane E., *Guide to the National and Provincial Directories of England and Wales, excluding London, published before 1856* (London: Royal Historical Society, 1950)

Ottley, George, *A Bibliography of British Railway History* (London: George Allen & Unwin, 1965; with a supp., London: HMSO, 1988); 2nd supp., ed. Grahame Boyes, Matthew Searle, and Donald Steggles, published as *Ottley's Bibliography of British Railway History* (York: National Railway Museum, 1998)

Palmer, A.W., *A Dictionary of Modern History, 1789–1945* (London: Cresset Press, 1962)

The Post Office London Directory (London: 1800–)

Register of Collections of Ephemera in the United Kingdom (Reading: Centre for Ephemera Studies, Department of Typography & Graphic Communication, The University of Reading, 2000). Available on disk; hard copy version forthcoming.

Robertson, Patrick, *The New Shell Book of Firsts* (London: Headline, 1995)

The Royal Blue Book or, Fashionable Directory . . . (London: T. Gardiner & Son, 1822–99)

The Royal Kalendar, or Correct Annual Register [afterwards: *and Court and City Register*] *for England, Scotland, Ireland . . . for 1767(–1850)* (London: 1767–1849)

World Guide to Libraries, 11th edn (München and London: K.G. Sauer, 1993)

World Guide to Special Libraries, edited by Helmut Opitz and Elisabeth Richter, 3rd edn (München and London: K.G. Sauer, 1995)

Dictionaries of engravers, illustrators, and printers

Baker, Charles, *Bibliography of British Book Illustrators 1860–1900* (Birmingham: Birmingham Bookshop, 1978)

Bryan, Michael, *Dictionary of Painters and Engravers, Biographical and Critical*, new edn, revised and enlarged by G.C. Williamson, 5 vol. (London: George Bell & Sons, 1903–05). First published in 1816.

Engen, Rodney K., *Dictionary of Victorian Engravers, Print Publishers and their Works* (Cambridge: Chadwyck Healey, 1979)

Engen, Rodney K., *Dictionary of Victorian Wood Engravers* (Cambridge: Chadwyck Healey, 1985)

Kelly's Directory of Stationers, Printers, Booksellers, Publishers, and Paper Makers of England, Scotland and Wales and the Principal Towns in Ireland (London: Kelly's Directories Ltd, 1872–1939)

[Hodson, W.H.], *Hodson's Booksellers, Publishers and Stationer's Directory 1855*, facsimile edn with introduction by Graham Pollard (Oxford: Oxford Bibliographical Society, 1972)

Houfe, Simon, *The Dictionary of British Book Illustrators and Caricaturists 1800–1914* (Woodbridge: Antique Collectors' Club, 1978)

Hunnisett, Basil, *A Dictionary of British Steel Engravers* (Aldershot: Scolar Press, 1989)

Glaister, G.A., *Encyclopedia of the Book*, 2nd edn with a new introduction by D.Farren [rev. edn of *Glossary of the Book*, 1979] (London: The British Library; New Castle, DE: Oak Knoll Press, 1996)

Mantle Fielding's Dictionary of American Painters, Sculptors, and Engravers, 2nd rev. edn, edited by Glenn B. Opitz (Poughkeepsie, NY: Apollo, 1986)

Schenck, David H.J., *Directory of the Lithographic Printers of Scotland 1820–1870* (Edinburgh: Edinburgh Bibliographical Society; New Castle, DE: Oak Knoll Press, 1999)

Thieme, Ulrich, and Becker, Felix., *Allgemeines Lexikon der bildenden Künstler*, 37 vol. (Leipzig: Wilhelm Engelmann, 1907–50; supp. vols 1953–62)

Todd, William B., *A Directory of Printers and Others in Allied Trades: London and Vicinity 1800–1840* (London: Printing Historical Society, 1972)

Twyman, Michael, *A Directory of London Lithographic Printers 1800–1850* (London: Printing Historical Society, 1976)

Wakeman, Geoffrey, and Bridson, G.D.R., *A Guide to Nineteenth Century Colour Printers* (Loughborough: Plough Press, 1975)

Young, William, *A Dictionary of American Artists, Sculptors and Engravers* (Cambridge, Mass.: William Young & Co., 1968)

Design

Crane, Walter, *The Bases of Design* (London: George Bell & Sons, 1898, and later edns)

Dresser, Christopher, *The Art of Decorative Design* (London: Day & Son, 1862)

Forty, Adrian, *Objects of Desire: Design and Society 1750–1980* (London: Thames & Hudson, 1986)

Gloag, John, *Georgian Taste: A Social History of Design from 1600 to 1830* (London: A. & C. Black, 1956; reprinted London: Spring Books, 1967)

Gloag, John, *Victorian Taste: Some Social Aspects of Architecture and Industrial Design, from 1820–1900* (London: A. & C. Black, 1962)

Hollis, Richard, *Graphic Design: A Concise History* (London: Thames & Hudson, 1994)

Jones, Barbara, *The Unsophisticated Arts* (London: The Architectural Press, 1951)

Jones, Owen, *The Grammar of Ornament* (London: Day & Son, 1856; later editions 1865, 1868, 1910; reprinted New York: Van Nostrand Reinhold, 1972; London: Studio Editions, 1986)

Lambert, Margaret, and Marx, Enid, *English Popular Art* (London: B.T. Batsford, 1951)

MacCarthy, Fiona, *A History of British Design, 1830–1870* (London: Allen & Unwin, 1979)

Meggs, Philip B., *A History of Graphic Design* (New York: Van Nostrand Reinhold; London: Allen Lane, 1983; 3rd edn, Chichester: John Wiley, 1998))

Olins, Wally, *Corporate Identity: Making Business Strategy Visible through Design* (London: Thames & Hudson, 1989)

Pevsner, Nikolaus, *Pioneers of Modern Design from William Morris to Walter Gropius*, 2nd edn (London: Penguin Books, 1975)

Racinet, A., *L'Ornement polychrome* (2 vol., Paris, 1869–87), published in England as *Polychromatic Ornament* (London: Sotheran and Co., 1877; reprinted London: Studio Editions, 1988)

Raffé, W.G., *Graphic Design* (London: Chapman and Hall, 1927)

Sparling, T.A., *The Great Exhibition: A Question of Taste* (New Haven, CT: Yale Center for British Art, 1982)

Thomson, Ellen Mazur, *The Origins of Graphic Design in America, 1870-1920* (New Haven and London: Yale University Press, 1997)

Illustration and prints

Anderson, Patricia, *The Printed Image and the Transformation of Popular Culture 1790–1860* (Oxford: Clarendon Press; New York: Oxford University Press, 1991)

Biggs, John R., *Illustration and Reproduction* (London: Blandford Press, 1950)

Bridson, Gavin, and Wakeman, Geoffrey, *Printmaking & Picture Printing: A Bibliographical Guide to Artistic and Industrial Techniques in Britain 1750–1900* (Oxford: Plough Press; Williamsburg: The Book Press Ltd, 1984)

Coe, Brian, and Hayworth-Booth, Mark, *A Guide to Early Photographic Processes* (London: Hurtwood Press in association with the Victoria & Albert Museum, 1983)

Dyson, Anthony, *Pictures to Print: The Nineteenth-century Engraving Trade* (London: Farrand Press; Williamsburg: The Book Press, 1984)

Fox, Celina A., *Graphic Journalism in England during the 1830s and 40s* (London and New York: Garland, 1988)

Gascoigne, Bamber, *How to Identify Prints* (London: Thames & Hudson, 1986; reprinted 1995)

Godfrey, Richard T., *Printmaking in Britain: A General History from its Beginnings to the Present Day* (Oxford: Phaidon, 1978)

Griffiths, Antony, *Prints and Printmaking: An Introduction to the History and Techniques*, 2nd edn (London: British Museum Press, 1996)

Hind, Arthur M., *An Introduction to a History of Woodcut*, 2 vol. (London: Constable & Co., 1935; reprinted New York: Dover Publications, 1963)

Ivins, William M. (jnr), *Prints and Visual Communication* (Cambridge, Mass.: Harvard University Press; London: Routledge & Kegan Paul Ltd, 1953; reprinted Cambridge, Mass.: Massachusetts Institute of Technology, 1978)

Lambert, Susan, *The Image Multiplied: Five Centuries of Printed Reproductions of Paintings and Drawings* (London: Trefoil Publications, 1987)

Mott, Frank Luther, *A History of American Magazines, 1865–1885* (Cambridge, Mass.: Harvard University Press, 1938)

Mott, Frank Luther, *A History of American Magazines, 1885–1905* (Cambridge, Mass.: Harvard University Press, 1957)

O'Connell, Sheila, *The Popular Print in England* (London: British Museum Press, 1999)

Pennell, Joseph, *Pen Drawing and Pen Draughtsmen* (London and New York: Macmillan, 1889; 2nd edn, 1894)

Peters, Harry T., *America on Stone* (New York: Doubleday, Doran & Co., 1931)

Twyman, Michael, *Lithography 1800–1850: The Techniques of Drawing on Stone in England and France and their Application in Works of Topography* (London: Oxford University Press, 1970)

Letterforms

Annenberg, Maurice, *Type Foundries of America and their Catalogs* (Baltimore: Maran Printing Services, 1975)

Bickham, George, *The Universal Penman*, facsimile of the 1743 edn with a foreword by Philip Hofer (New York: Paul A.Struck, 1941)

Brown, Michelle P., *The British Library Guide to Writing and Scripts: History and Techniques* (London: British Library; Toronto: Toronto University Press, 1998)

Carter, Sebastian, *Twentieth-century Type Designers*, 2nd rev. edn (London: Lund Humphries, 1995)

Denholm-Young, N., *Handwriting in England and Wales* (Cardiff: University of Wales Press, 1954)

Emmison, F. G., *How to Read Local Archives 1550–1700* (London: The Historical Association, 1967)

Gray, Nicolete, *Nineteenth Century Ornamented Typefaces, with a chapter on Ornamented Types in America by Ray Nash* (London: Faber & Faber, 1976)

Harris, Elizabeth, *The Fat and the Lean: American Wood Type in the 19th Cent.* (Washington, DC: Smithsonian Institution, 1983)

Heal, Ambrose, *The English Writing-masters and their Copy-books* (Cambridge: Cambridge University Press, 1931; reprinted Hildesheim: Georg Olms Verlagsbuchhandlung, 1962)

Ison, Alf, *A Secretary Hand ABC Book* (Reading, 1982)

Jackson, Donald, *The Story of Writing* (London: Cassell Ltd, 1981)

Jaspert, W.P., Berry, W.T., and Johnson, A.F., *The Encyclopedia of Type Faces*, 4th edn (London: Blandford Press, 1970; reprinted 1990)

Johnstone, Edward, *Writing & Illuminating & Lettering* (London: John Hogg, 1906, and later edns)

Kelly, Rob Roy, *American Wood Type 1828–1900* (New York: Van Nostrand Reinhold, 1969)

Lawson, Alexander, *Anatomy of a Typeface* (Boston: David R. Godine, 1990)

Nash, Ray, *American Penmanship 1800–1850* (Worcester: American Antiquarian Society, 1969)

Perfect, Christopher, and Rookledge, Gordon, *Rookledge's International Type Finder*, revised by Phil Baines (Carshalton Beeches: Sarema Press, 1990)

Updike, Daniel Berkeley, *Printing Types: Their History, Forms, and Use*, 3rd edn, 2 vol. (Cambridge, Mass.: Harvard University Press, 1962)

Vincent Figgins Type Specimens 1801 and 1815, facsimile with introduction by Berthold Wolpe (London: Printing Historical Society, 1967)

Wright, Andrew, *Court-hand Restored: or the Student's Assistant in Reading Old Deeds, Charters, Records, etc.*, 10th edn corrected and enlarged by Charles Trice Martin (London: Stevens & Sons, 1912). First published in 1776.

Printing

Bloy, C.H., *A History of Printing Inks, Balls and Rollers 1400–1850* (London: Wynkyn de Worde Society, 1967)

Burch, R.M., *Colour Printing and Colour Printers* (London: Sir Isaac Pitman; New York: Baker & Taylor, 1910; reprinted New York: Garland, 1981)

Coleman, D.C., *The British Paper Industry 1495–1860* (Oxford: Clarendon Press, 1958)

Gascoigne, Bamber, *Milestones in Colour Printing 1457–1859, with a Bibliography of Nelson Prints* (Cambridge: Cambridge University Press, 1997)

Gaskell, Philip, *A New Introduction to Bibliography* (Oxford: Clarendon Press, 1972, rev. edn 1974; reprinted New Castle, DE: Oak Knoll Press, 1995)

Hackleman, Charles W., *Commercial Engraving and Printing* (Indianapolis: Commercial Engraving Publishing Co., 1921; 2nd edn 1924)

Hansard, T.C., *Typographia* (London: Baldwin, Cradock, and Joy, 1825; facsimile edn London: Gregg Press Ltd, 1966)

Hills, Richard L., *Paper Making in Britain 1488–1988* (London and Atlantic Highlands, NJ: Athlone Press, 1988)

Hudson, Graham, *The Victorian Printer* (Princes Risborough: Shire Publications, 1996)

Journal of the Printing Historical Society (London, 1965–)

Knights, Charles C., *Printing: Reproductive Means and Materials* (London: Butterworth & Co., 1932)

Lewis, C.T. Courtney, *The Story of Picture Printing in England during the Nineteenth Century* (London: Sampson Low, Marston & Co. Ltd, [1928])

Lilien, Otto M., *History of Industrial Gravure Printing up to 1820* (London: Lund Humphries, 1972)

Marzio, Peter, *The Democratic Art. Pictures for a 19th-Century America* (Boston: David R. Godine, 1979; London: Scolar Press, 1980)

Moxon, Joseph, *Mechanick Exercises on the Whole Art of Printing (1683–4)*, edited by Herbert Davis and Harry Carter, 2nd edn (London: Oxford University Press, 1962; reprinted New York: Dover Publications, 1978)

Proudfoot, W.B., *The Origin of Stencil Duplicating* (London: Hutchinson & Co., 1972)

Rhodes, Barbara, and Streeter, William Wells, *Before Photocopying: the Art & History of Mechanical Copying 1780–1938* (New Castle, DE: Oak Knoll Press; Northampton, Mass.: Heraldry Bindery, 1999)

Rosner, Charles, *Printers Progress: A Comparative Survey of the Craft of Printing 1851–1951* (London: Sylvan Press, 1951)

Steinberg, S.H., *Five Hundred Years of Printing*, new edn, revised by John Trevitt (London: British Library; New Castle, DE: Oak Knoll Press, 1996)

Thomas, Isaiah, *The History of Printing in America* (Worcester, Mass.:1810; 2nd edn, Albany, NY, 1874: reprinted New York: Weathervane Books, 1970)

Twyman, Michael, *The British Library Guide to Printing: History and Techniques* (London: British Library; Toronto: Toronto University Press, 1998)

Twyman, Michael, *Early Lithographed Music* (London: Farrand Press, 1996)

Wakeman, Geoffrey, *Victorian Book Illustration: The Technical Revolution* (Newton Abbot: David & Charles, 1973)

Weber, Wilhelm, *A History of Lithography* (London: Thames & Hudson, 1966)

Weeks, L.H., *A History of Paper-manufacturing in the United States, 1690–1916* (New York: Lockwood Trade Journal Co., 1916)

American history

Adams, James Truslow, *The Album of American History*, 6 vol. (New York: Scribner's, 1944–60)

Beard, Charles A., and Beard, Mary R., *The Rise of American Civilization*, rev. edn (New York: Macmillan, 1937)

Boorstin, Daniel Joseph, *The Americans. The Colonial Experience* (New York: Random House, 1958)

Boorstin, Daniel Joseph, *The Americans. The National Experience* (New York: Random House, 1965)

Burns, Sarah, *Pastoral Inventions: Rural Life in Nineteenth-century American Art and Culture* (Philadelphia: Temple University Press, 1989)

Cooke, A., *Alistair Cooke's America* (Book Club Associates, 1977)

Fleming, Thomas, *Liberty! The American Revolution* (London and New York: Penguin Putnam Inc., 1997)

Good, Harry G., and Gehman, Harry, *A History of American Education* (New York: Macmillan, 1956)

Harris, Neil, *Cultural Excursions: Marketing Appetites and Cultural Tastes in Modern America* (Chicago: University of Chicago Press, 1990)

Hedrick, U.P., *A History of Horticulture in America to 1860*, with an addendum of books published from 1861–1920 by Elisabeth Woodburn (New York and London: Oxford University Press, 1950)

Horwitz, Elinor Lander (J. Roderick Moore, consultant), *The Bird, the Banner, and Uncle Sam: Images of America in Folk and Popular Art* (Philadelphia and New York: J. Lippincott Co., 1976)

Kull, Irving S., and Kull, Ness, M., *A Short Chronology of American History 1492–1950* (New Brunswick, NJ: Rutgers University Press, 1952)

McMurry, Sally, *Families & Farmhouses in 19th Century America, Vernacular Design and Social Change* (New York and Oxford: Oxford University Press, 1988)

Morison, Samuel Eliot, *The Oxford History of the American People* (London: Oxford University Press, 1965)

Noble, Stuart Grayson, *A History of American Education* (New York: Farrar & Rinehart, 1938; rev. edn New York: Rinehart & Co., 1956)

Nylander, Jane C., *Our Own Snug Fireside, Images of the New England Home, 1760–1860* (Yale: Yale University Press, 1994)

Partridge, Bellamy, and Bettmann, Otto, *As We Were: Family Life in America 1850–1900* (New York and London: Whittlesey House, 1946)

Peterson, Harold L., *American Interiors from Colonial Times to the Late Victorians: A Pictorial Source Book* (New York: Charles Scribner's Sons, 1971)

Slossom, Preston W., *Pictorial History of the American People* (Greenwich, CT: Bison Books, 1982)

Ward, G.C. *et al*, *The Civil War: An Illustrated History* (London: The Bodley Head, 1991; Pimlico edn, 1992)

British history

Adamson, J.W., *English Education 1789–1902* (Cambridge: Cambridge University Press, 1930)

Altick, Richard D., *The English Common Reader: A Social History of the Mass Reading Public 1800–1900* (Chicago: Chicago University Press, 1957; Cambridge: Cambridge University Press, 1957)

Ashton, T.S., *The Industrial Revolution 1760–1830* (London: Oxford University Press, 1948)

Barker, Ernest, *The Character of England* (Oxford: Clarendon Press, 1947)

Barker, Felix, and Jackson, Peter, *London. 2000 Years of a City and its People* (London: Cassell Ltd, 1974)

Barnard, H.C., *A Short History of English Education. From 1760 to 1944* (London: University of London Press, 1947; later edns with modified title)

Bayne-Powell, Rosamond, *The English Child in the Eighteenth Century* (London: John Murray, 1939)

Bott, Alan, *Our Fathers (1870–1900). Manners and Customs of the Ancient Victorians: A Survey in Pictures and Text of their History, Morals, Wars, Sports, Inventions & Politics* (London: Heinemann, 1931)

Bott, Alan, with text by Clephane, Irene, *Our Mothers: A Cavalcade in Pictures, Quotation and Description of Late Victorian Women 1870–1900* (London: Victor Gollancz, 1932)

Bowie, Archibald Granger, *The Romance of the British Post Office: Its Inception and Wondrous Development* (London: S.W. Partridge & Co., 1897)

Briggs, Asa, *Victorian Things* (London: B.T. Batsford, 1988)

Briggs, Asa, *Victorian Cities* (London: Odhams, 1963; London: Penguin Books, 1993)

Burke, Thomas, *The English Townsman as He Was and as He Is* (London: B.T. Batsford, 1946)

Clapham, J. H., *An Economic History of Modern Britain: The Early Railway Age, 1820–1850*, 2nd edn (Cambridge: Cambridge University Press, 1930)

Curtis, S. J., *History of Education in Great Britain* (London: University Tutorial Press, 1948; 4th edn, 1957)

Dodd, George, *Days at the Factories* (London: Charles Knight & Co., 1843; reprinted Augustus M. Keeley, 1967)

Dodds, John W., *The Age of Paradox: A Biography of England 1841–1851* (London: Victor Gollancz, 1953)

Gibbs-Smith, C.H., *The Great Exhibition of 1851* (London: HMSO for the Victoria & Albert Museum, 1950; rev. edn, 1964)

Hartley, Dorothy, *Water in England* (London: Macdonald and Jane's, 1964; rev. edn, 1978)

Hobhouse, Christopher, *1851 and the Crystal Palace* (London: John Murray, 1937)

Hobsbawm, Eric, *On History* (London: Weidenfeld & Nicolson, 1997)

Knight, Charles, *Passages of a Working Life during Half a Century*, 3 vol. (London: Charles Knight, 1864–5; reprinted Shannon: Irish University Press, 1971)

Lawson, J., and Silver, H., *A Social History of Education in England* (London: Methuen, 1973)

Luckhurst, Kenneth W., *The Story of Exhibitions* (London and New York: Studio Publications, 1951)

Mayhew, Henry, *London Labour and the London Poor*, 4 vol. (London 1851; enlarged edn 1861–2; reprinted 1967)

Roach, J.P.C., *A History of Secondary Education in England 1800–1870* (London: Longman, 1986)

Roach, J.P.C., *Secondary Education in England 1870–1902* (London: Routledge, 1991)

Thompson, E.P., *The Making of the English Working Class* (London: Victor Gollancz, 1963; London: Penguin Books, 1991)

Trevelyan, G.M., *Illustrated English Social History,* 4 vol. (London: Longmans Green & Co., 1949–52; reprinted Harmondsworth: Penguin Books, 1964)

Victoria County History of the Counties of England (London, 1899–; from 1933 published by the Institute of Historical Research of the University of London)

Vizetelly, Henry, *Glances Back through Seventy Years*, 2 vol. (London: Kegan Paul & Co., 1893)

Waller, Maureen, *1700 Scenes from London Life* (Sevenoaks: Hodder & Stoughton, 2000)

Watteville, Colonel H. de, *The British Soldier: His Daily Life from Tudor to Modern Times* (London: J.M. Dent & Sons Ltd, 1954)

Young, G.M., *Victorian England: Portrait of an Age* (London: Oxford University Press, 1936; Oxford Paperbacks, 1960)

Costume

Adburgham, Alison, *A Punch History of Manners and Modes, 1841–1940* (London: Hutchinson, 1961)

Buck, Anne M., *Victorian Costume and Costume Accessories* (London: Herbert Jenkins, 1961)

Cox, J. Stevens, *An Illustrated Dictionary of Hairdressing and Wigmaking* (London: The Hairdressers' Technical Council, 1966)

Cumming, Valerie, *Gloves* (London: B.T. Batsford, 1982)

Cunnington, C.W. and Cunnington, Phillis, *The History of Underclothes* (London: Michael Joseph, 1951; reprinted New York: Dover Publications, 1992)

Cunnington, C.W., Cunnington, Phillis, and Beard, Charles, *A Dictionary of English Costume* (London: A. & C. Black, 1960)

Cunnington, Phillis, *Costume of Household Servants from the Middle Ages to 1900* (London: A. & C. Black, 1974)

Cunnington, Phillis, and Lucas, Catherine, *Charity Costumes of Children, Scholars, Almsfolk, Pensioners* (London: A. & C. Black, 1978)

Cunnington, Phillis, and Buck, Anne, *Children's Costume in England from the Fourteenth to the end of the Nineteenth Century* (London: A. & C. Black, 1965)

Cunnington, Phillis, and Lucas, Catherine, *Costume for Births, Marriages and Deaths* (London: A. & C. Black, 1972)

Cunnington, Phillis, and Mansfield, Alan, *English Costume for Sports and Outdoor Recreation from the 16th to the 19th centuries* (London: A. & C. Black, 1969)

Cunnington, Phillis, and Lucas, Catherine, *Occupational Costume in England from the Eleventh Century to 1914* (London: A. & C. Black, 1967)

Davidson, Alexander, *Blazers Badges and Boaters* (Horndean, Hants: Scope Books, 1990)

Farrell, Jeremy, *Umbrellas & Parasols* (London: B.T. Batsford, 1985)

Gibbs-Smith, C.H., *The Fashionable Lady in the 19th Century* (London: HMSO for the Victoria & Albert Museum, 1960)

Swann, June, *Shoes* (London: B.T. Batsford, 1982)

Taylor, Lou, *Mourning Dress: A Costume and Social History* (London: George Allen & Unwin, 1983)

Country life

Davies, Maud, F., *Life in an English Village: An Economic and Historical Survey of the Parish of Corsley in Wiltshire* (London: Fisher Unwin, 1909)

Havinden, Michael Ashley, *Estate Villages: A Study of the Berkshire Villages of Ardington and Lockinge* (London: Lund Humphries for the University of Reading, 1966; 2nd rev. edn Reading: Rural History Centre of the University of Reading, 1999)

Horn, Pamela, *Labouring Life in the Victorian Countryside* (Dublin: Gill and Macmillan, 1976)

Horn, Pamela, *The Rural World 1780–1850: Social Change in the English Countryside* (London: Hutchinson, 1980)

Jenkins, Geraint J., *The English Farm Wagon* (Oakwood Press for the University of Reading, 1961)

Jusserand, J.J., *The English Wayfaring Life in the Middle Ages (XIVth Century)* (London: T. Fisher Unwin Ltd, 1889; 3rd edn, twelfth impression, 1925)

Lewis, June R., *The Village School* (London: Robert Hale, 1969)

Pulbrook, Ernest C., *English Country Life and Work* (London: B.T. Batsford, 1923)

Thompson, Flora, *Lark Rise to Candleford. A Trilogy* (London: Oxford University Press, 1945)

Trench, Charles Chevenix, *The Poacher and the Squire: A History of Poaching and Game Preservation in England* (London: Longmans, 1967)

Food and drink

Brett, Gerard, *Dinner is Served: A History of Dining in England 1400–1900* (London: Rupert Hart-Davis, 1969)

Hartley, Dorothy, *Food in England* (London: Macdonald, 1954)

Paston-Williams, Sara, *The Art of Dining: A History of Cooking and Eating* (London: The National Trust, 1993)

Pullar, Philippa, *Consuming Passions: A History of English Food and Appetite* (London: Hamish Hamilton Ltd, 1970)

Simon, André, *Bottlescrew Days: Wine Drinking in England during the Eighteenth Century* (London: Duckworth, 1926)

Simon, André, *A Concise Encyclopedia of Gastronomy* (London: Allen Lane, 1952)

Tannahill, Reay, *Food in History* (New York: Stein & Day, 1973)

Wilson, C. Anne, *Food and Drink in Britain from the Stone Age to Recent Times* (London: Constable, 1973; Harmondsworth: Penguin Books, 1984)

Home life

Beeton, Isabella Mary, *The Book of Household Management* (London: S.O. Beeton, 1861; many later edns with varying titles)

Gerard, Jessica, *Country House Life: Family and Servants 1815–1914* (Oxford: Blackwell, 1994)

Harling, Robert, *A Victorian Home: A Vignette* (London: Constable, 1938)

Palmer, Arnold, *Movable Feasts: A Reconnaissance of the Origins and Consequences of Fluctuations in Meal-Times* (London: Oxford University Press, 1952)

Visser, Margaret, *The Rituals of Dinner: The Origins, Evolution, Eccentricities, and Meaning of Table Manners* (London: Viking, 1991)

Wright, Lawrence, *Clean and Decent: The Fascinating History of the Bathroom & the Water Closet* (London: Routledge & Kegan Paul, 1960)

Wright, Lawrence, *Home Fires Burning: The History of Domestic Heating and Cooking* (London: Routledge & Kegan Paul, 1964)

Wright, Lawrence, *Warm and Snug: The History of the Bed* (London: Routledge & Kegan Paul, 1962)

Leisure and entertainment

Altick, Richard D., *The Shows of London. A Panoramic History of Exhibitions, 1600–1862* (Cambridge, Mass. and London: The Belknap Press of Harvard University Press, 1978)

Briggs, Susan, *Those Radio Times* (London: Weidenfeld and Nicolson, 1981)

Hartnell, Phyllis (ed.), *The Oxford Companion to the Theatre* (London: Oxford University Press, 1951)

Hole, Christina, *English Sports and Pastimes* (London: B.T. Batsford, 1949)

James, Louis, *Fiction for the Working Man 1830–50* (London: Oxford University Press, 1963)

Jay, Ricky, *Learned Pigs & Fireproof Women* (New York: Villard Books, 1987)

Mander, Raymond, and Mitchenson, Joe, *British Music Hall* (London: Studio Vista, 1965)

Mander, Raymond, and Mitchenson, Joe, *Musical Comedy* (London: Peter Davis, 1969)

Mander, Raymond, and Mitchenson, Joe, *Pantomime* (London: Peter Davis, 1973)

Mander, Raymond, and Mitchenson, Joe, *Revue* (New York: Tatlinger Publishing Co., 1971)

Melling, John Kennedy, *Discovering Theatre Ephemera* (Princes Risborough: Shire Publications, 1974)

Nicoll, Allardyce, *A History of English Drama 1660–1900*, 6 vol. (Cambridge: Cambridge University Press, 1952–9)

Opie, Iona & Robert, and Alderson, Brian, *The Treasures of Childhood* (London: Pavilion, 1989)

Pulling, Christopher, *They were Singing: and what they Sang about* (London: George Harrap & Co. Ltd, 1952)

Roth, Warwick, *Cremorne and the Later London Gardens* (London: Elliot Stock, 1907)

Roth, Warwick, *The London Pleasure Gardens of the Eighteenth Century* (London: Macmillan, 1896)

Shops and shopping

Adburgham, Alison, *Shops & Shopping* (London: George Allen & Unwin, 1964)

Alexander, David, *Retailing in England during the Industrial Revolution* (London: Athlone Press, 1970)

Briggs, Asa, *Marks and Spencers 1884–1989* (London: Octopus Books Ltd, 1989)

Brown, Jonathan, and Ward, Sadie, *The Village Shop* (Moffat, Dumfriesshire: Cameron & Hollis; Newton Abbot: David & Charles, on behalf of the Rural Development Commission, 1990)

Davis, Dorothy, *A History of Shopping* (London: Routledge & Kegan Paul, 1966)

Defoe, Daniel, *The Complete English Tradesman, in Familiar Letters, Directing him in all the Several Parts and Progressions of the Trade . . .* (London: Charles Rivington, 1726; 2nd edn with supp., 1727)

Evans, Bill, and Lawson, Andrew, *A Nation of Shopkeepers* (London: Plexus, 1981)

Heal, Ambrose, *The Signboards of Old London Shops: A Review of the Shop Signs Employed by the London Tradesmen during the XVIIth and XVIIIth Centuries* (London: B.T. Batsford, 1947)

Jefferys, James B., *Retail Trading in Britain 1850–1950* (Cambridge: Cambridge University Press, 1954)

Mass Observation, *Browns and Chester: Portrait of a Shop 1780–1946* ([London]: Lindsay Drummond Ltd, 1947)

Mui, Hoh-cheung, and Mui, Lorna H., *Shops and Shopkeeping in Eighteenth-Century England* (Kingston, Montreal, and London: McGill-Queen's University Press; London: Routledge, 1989)

Starr, Freda, *A Village Shop* (Woodbridge: Boydell Press, 1979)

Window Dressers' Pocketbook (London: International Correspondence Schools Ltd, 1912)

Williams, Bridget, *The Best Butter in the World: A History of Sainsbury's* (London: Ebury Press, 1994)

Winstanley, Michael J., *The Shopkeeper's World 1830–1914* (Manchester: Manchester University Press, 1983)

Travel and transport

Bird, Anthony, *The Motor Car, 1765–1914* (London: B.T. Batsford, 1960)

Bruno, Leonard C., *On the Move: A Chronology of Advances in Transportation* (Detroit: Gale Research Inc., 1990)

Burgess, Anthony, *Coaching Days of England. . . comprehending the Years 1750 until 1850* (London: Paul Elek, 1966)

Burke, Thomas, *Travel in England from Pilgrim and Pack-horse to Light Car and Plane* (London: B.T. Batsford, 1942)

Ellis, Cuthbert Hamilton, *British Railway History: An Outline from the Accession of William IV to the Nationalisation of Railways*, vol.1 1830–1876, vol.2 1877–1947 (London: George Allen & Unwin, 1954, 1959)

Ellis, Cuthbert Hamilton, *The Pictorial Encyclopedia of Railways* (Feltham: Hamlyn Publishing Group, 1968)

Faith, Nicholas, *The World the Railroads Made* (London: Bodley Head, 1990)

Fenton, William, *Railway Printed Ephemera* (Woodbridge: Antique Collector's Club, 1992)

Hissey, James John, *Across England in a Dog-cart from London to St Davids and back* (London: Richard Bentley & Son, 1891)

Mander, John, *Collecting Railwayana* (Ashbourne: Moorland Publishing Co. Ltd, 1988)

Margolies, John, and Baker, Eric, *See the USA: The Art of the American Travel Brochure* (San Francisco: Chronicle Books, 1999)

Ridley, Anthony, *An Illustrated History of Transport* (London: Heinemann, 1969)

Robbins, Michael, *The Railway Age* (London: Routledge & Kegan Paul, 1962)

Searle, Mark, *Turnpikes and Toll-Bars*, 2 vol. (London: Hutchinson, 1930)

Simmons, Jack, *The Railways of Britain: An Historical Introduction* (London: Routledge & Kegan Paul, 1961; several later edns)

Simmons, Jack, *The Victorian Railway* (London: Thames & Hudson, 1991)

Simmons, Jack, and Biddle, George (eds), *The Oxford Companion to British Railway History from 1603 to the 1990s* (Oxford: Oxford University Press, 1997)

Tristram, W. Outram, *Coaching Days and Coaching Ways* (London: Macmillan & Co., 1893)

Vale, Edmund, *The Mail-coach Men of the late Eighteenth Century* (London: Cassell, 1960)

Vaughan, John, *The English Guide Book c 1780–1870: An Illustrated History* (Newton Abbot: David & Charles, 1974)

Shire Publications

Many of the extensive series of introductory illustrated guides to selected topics published by Shire Publications Ltd (Princes Risborough) are relevant to ephemerists. The following are cited as examples, in addition to those referred to under other headings of this bibliography:

Bottomley, Ruth, *Rocking Horses* (1991)

Clarke, A.A., *Police Uniform and Equipment* (1991)

Clayton, Nick, *Early Bicycles* (1994)

Davidson, D.C., *Spectacles, Lorgnettes and Monocles* (1989)

Emmerson, Andrew, *Old Television* (1998)

Flick, Pauline, *Old Toys* (1985)

Green, Stephen, *Cricketing Bygones* (1982)

James, Duncan, *Old Typewriters* (1993)

May, Trevor, *The Victorian Schoolroom* (1994); *The Victorian Undertaker* (1996); *The Victorian Workhouse* (1997); *Victorian and Edwardian Horse Cabs* (1999)

Wright, Brian, *Firemen's Uniform* (1991)

Index

Black and white illustrations are shown in italic type, colour plates in bold type

ABC primer
academy/college broadside
account-book label
accounts, domestic
accounts, institutional
acquaintance card
admission ticket
advertisement
advertising booklet
advertising envelope
advertising fan
advertising novelty
advertising ring (embossed)
aerial leaflet
agency certificate
agricultural/horticultural show card
air-raid papers
air-sickness bag
air-transport label
album card
album frontispiece
almanac
amateur journal
ambrotype label
American Civil War papers
American seaman's certificate
amusement sheet
anamorphic image
anonymous letter
appointment card
AQ letter sheet
armed forces papers
army printing
arrangement of carriages diagram
artisan's bill/receipt
artwork for reproduction
assignat
'at home' card
attendance record, school
auditorium seating plan
badge
baggage sticker
ballad
ballot paper
band/banderole
bandbox
bando
banknote
'banknote', promotional
banknote, specimen
banknote-duty stamp
baptismal papers
bastardy papers
battledore
beer label
beer mat
bellman's verses
benefit ticket
bill of lading
bill of mortality
billhead
binder's ticket
birth certificate
biscuit/cracker label
blasphemy
blotting paper
boardgame
bond, personal
book label
book token
book-donor label
bookmark
bookmatch
bookplate
book-prize label
bookseller's label
braille
broadside/broadsheet
broom label
bumper sticker
burial club papers
burial in woollen affidavit
burial papers
burial-right deed
by-law/ordinance
cachet, postal
calendar
calendar of prisoners
call-back handbill
cameo card
campaign souvenir
can label
candle label
card of thanks
carmen figuratum
carrier bag
carrier's address
carte-de-visite
carte pneumatique
catalogue
cavallino
census papers
certificate
change of proprietor card
change packet
change pin-paper
changeable gentlemen/ladies card
chapbook
charity election card
charity petition
charity sermon hymn sheet
charity subscription list
charity ticket
charm/curse
charter party
cheese label
chemist's label
cheque/check
child lost/found form
children's advertising booklet
chimney-sweep certificate
chop paper
Christmas card
Christmas charity seal
chromo
church brief
cigar band/box label
cigarette card
cigarette pack
cigarette paper
'Cinderella' stamp
city ordinance broadside
classroom label
club flyer
coach ticket
coachmen's instructions
coal-seller's ticket
coin disc/sticker
colouring book/sheet
comic
commonplace book
compliments slip
compound-plate printing
compulsive note
copy-book
cotton bag
cover, postal
crate label
credit/cash card
crest/monogram
Cuban wrapper
Currier & Ives
cut-out toy
cutwork
cypher label
dance programme
dance token
dart flight
death certificate
deck plan
decorated paper
degree certificate/diploma
dental papers
deposit label
dice-duty wrapper
dietary tables
directions for use
directories
disinfected mail
display card
distraint, papers of
doctor's bill
donation list
donor card
draft
drawing book
driving licence
dust wrapper
eccentric advertising
election papers
electro-medical papers
electrotype
e-mail
embossing/lace paper
embroidery pattern
enclosure badge
engraved label
envelope
envelope, illustrated
envelope, stationer's
equivoque
erratum slip
evidence, notes of
execution broadside
facsimile
farthing novelette
fax
feather letter
fez label
film wallet
fire reward certificate
fireman's discharge certificate
fireman's membership certificate
firework/firecracker label
fish tally
flagday emblem
flap picture
Fleet marriage certificate
flicker book
fly-paper
fly-wagon bill
folk recipe
football programme
'foreign' English
forgery
form
form of prayer
Fraktur
free frank
frost-fair papers
fruit/vegetable sticker
fruit wrapper
funeralia
furniture label
game record
game-law papers
gaol papers
garment label
gift coupon
give-aways
gold-miners' papers, Australian
greetings card
greetings telegram
Gretna Green marriage certificate
guest list
hackney papers
hand-knitting pattern
handwritten ephemera
harlequinade ('turn-up')
hat-duty stamp
hidden-name card
hold-to-light
holiday card
hornbook
hospital recommendation document
hostel admission ticket
hotel/tour coupon
hotel papers
house journal
household regulations
housekeeping accounts
hymn number card
ice papers
illuminated address
imagerie populaire
imprint, printer's
imprint, publisher's
improvised currency
indenture
indulgence
inn tally
inset, magazine
inventory
invitation
iridescent printing
itinerary
jigsaw puzzle
joke ephemera
jumping jack
jury papers
keepsake
keepsake, novelty
king's evil certificate
kite bag
label
labour account
lavatory paper
leaflet
lecture ticket
letter seal
letterhead
licence
Liebig card
lighthouse-dues papers
linen-button card
linen-button label
lobby card
Lord's prayer
lottery papers
lunacy papers
magazine sample sheet
manual alphabet card
marriage certificate
marrowbone announcement
match-tax stamp
medicine-show papers
menu
milk-bottle closure
miniature newspaper
miniature text
mock money
moral-lesson picture
motto, shop window
Mulready caricature
Mulready envelope
myriorama
neck paper
needle packet
needle-box print
news bill
newspaper
notice to quit
nuisance papers
oath
opticians' papers
packaging
panorama, entertainment
panorama, newspaper give-aways
paper bag
paper clothing
paper doll
paper napkin
paper pattern
paper-cut
paper-duty label
papyrus
parking ticket
parliamentary envelope
pass/permit
passport
pastiche, printer's
peal card
peep-show
pen-box label
penman's flourish
pennant
perfume card
perfume label
perfume-duty label
petition
pew papers
pharmaceutical package
phenakistoscope disc
photographic ephemera
photo-lithographic view
phrenological chart
physician's directions
physiognomical chart
pillbox label
pin paper
pin synopsis card
pin-box label
place card
place mat
plague papers
plaster package
playing card
playing card, secondary uses
playing-card duty
playing-card wrapper
pledge card
pocket mirror, advertising
point-of-sale display
poison-gas papers
poor-law papers
postal diagnosis
postal history
postal label
postal stationery
postal swindle
postal-strike label
postcard
poster
poster slip
post-horse duty ticket
pratique, papers of
prescription
prescription paper/envelope
press book, film
pressed flowers
price list
price tag/ticket
printed handkerchief
printing, 'primitive'
procession programme
proclamation
prospectus, publisher's
public apology
public notice
punctuality card
puzzle
quack advertising
QSL card
race bill
rag book
rail ticket
railway carriage panel
railway luggage label
railway travelling chart
rainbow printing
ration papers
razor-blade wrapper
ream wrapper/label
rebus
receipt
recipe, folk
record, advertising
record cover
relief printing for the blind
religious card
removal card
reward of merit
reward papers
ribbon, lapel
riddle book
ring-gauge card
riot act
roll of honour
round robin
rules and regulations
sabbath papers
sailing notice/card
sale catalogue
sale notice
sales-tax token/receipt
satirical print
scholar's letter
school/college bill
school list
school prospectus
school report
school return
schoolboy's piece
scrap
scrapbook/album
seating plan, table
secondary uses of ephemera
security printing
seed packet
Seidlitz-powder label
sentiment card
servant's award
servant's 'character' reference
servant's registry papers
servant's timetable
Shaker papers
share certificate
sheet-music cover
shelf strip
shipping
ship's newspaper
shoe pattern
shoemaker's label
showcard
showcard, stock
signal code, navy
silhouette
silk
slave papers
society card
songster/song book
sports papers
squib
staffage
stage-play licence
stationer's label
stationery, decorative
stencil
stereotype
sticker
stock block
stock poster
street literature
street view
stud card/notice
sugar leaf
summons
tag label
tall-tale postcard
tax abstract
tax stamp
taxation papers
telegram/telegram form
telephone card
telephone directory
temperance papers
testimonial
textile label
thaumatrope
theatre programme
theatre ticket
thread paper
ticket
timetable
tinsel print
tithe papers
title-page
tobacco paper
toll/ferry rate-list
toll/turnpike ticket
touring map
toy book
toy theatre
trade advertiser
trade card
trade label
trade list
trade rhyme
trade union membership certificate
tramping card
transfer lithography
transparency
transportation papers (penal)
travellers' guide
trompe-l'oeil announcement
Tyburn ticket
typographica
unemployed appeal
union label
university mail
unstamped newspaper/periodical
vaccination papers
valentine
vice card
view card
violin label
visiting card
visiting craftsmen's papers
visitors' register
wafer
warrant
watchpaper
watermark
waybill
weight card
will
window bill, shop
window card, domestic
wine label
winkle bag
wood-engraving
writing paper, illustrated
writing tablet
xerography
'zine
zöetrope strip/disc